SMITH'S
PACIFIC NORTHWEST
AMERICANA

CHARLES W. SMITH'S

PACIFIC NORTHWEST
AMERICANA

A Check List of Books and Pamphlets
Relating to the History
of the
Pacific Northwest

Edition 3, Revised and Extended by

Isabel Mayhew

Oregon Historical Society

Binfords & Mort, *Publishers,*

PORTLAND, OREGON

1950

FOREWORD

IN April 1908, Charles W. Smith, Assistant Librarian of the University of Washington, was induced by fellow librarians to prepare a co-operative check list of books and pamphlets relating to the Pacific Northwest and available in libraries of the region. A plan was agreed upon whereby each library furnished a card list of its holdings to Mr. Smith, who as compiler codified the records and edited the resultant union list. The volume was published in 1909 by the Washington State Library under the title, *Check-List of Books and Pamphlets Relating to the History of the Pacific Northwest to be Found in Representative Libraries of That Region.* The title indicates clearly that the intention of the compiler and his collaborators was to prepare a list of actual holdings and not a comprehensive bibliography.

Twelve years later, most of the libraries had grown in stature and their holdings of Pacific Northwest Americana had more than trebled. It was time to prepare a second edition, revised and enlarged, and one might even say considerably improved for the librarians of the region had learned much about bibliography in more than a decade of growth and experience. This edition, bearing the short title, *Pacific Northwest Americana,* was published in 1921. Eighteen libraries co-operated in its preparation. The work became a popular and valued reference book and other libraries evinced an interest in being included in any future edition which might appear. Consequently, many libraries of the Pacific Northwest entered into an agreement to report regularly to the Bibliography Committee of the Pacific Northwest Library Association future additions to their holdings of Pacific Northwest Americana.

Since 1921 there has been a tremendous increase in the number of Pacific Northwest titles published and, as the libraries of the region have been better off financially, the resources of the region have grown geometrically. The desirability of an up-to-date check list has been indicated for the past ten years; edition two is out of print, and the thousands of new library acquisitions deserve recording in a union list.

Early in 1948 Isabel Mayhew of the Reference Division of the University of Washington was appointed editor of a third edition of the Check List. Her manuscript is a complete revision and the additions reflect not only new imprints dated 1948 and earlier, but also the resources of many new libraries. In all, thirty-eight institutions have now contributed lists of their holdings.

In such a compilation as this union Check List some errors are inevitable. This is due to the fact that it was prepared with the collaboration of many busy librarians and not by electronic robots. In spite of this, we have every right to believe that it will prove to be an invaluable guide to the location of more than 11,000 entries. Furthermore, it should prove a boon to book collectors and dealers as well as librarians.

This new edition of *Pacific Northwest Americana* is a project of the Bibliography Committee of the Pacific Northwest Library Association. The production of a co-operative reference tool such as a union check list entails much work on the part of many people. Acknowledgment is due all librarians who supplied the card entries from the thirty-eight participating libraries. Without their whole-hearted support, the union check list simply would not exist today. Isabel Mayhew devoted almost two years to the meticulous work of editing and preparing the manuscript. J. Ronald Todd, Curator of the Pacific Northwest Collection at the University of Washington, has been largely responsible for the maintenance of the expanding union catalog of Pacific Northwest resources from which the check list entries were drawn. He has also taken a lively part in fostering the work of the Editor. To the extent that the Check List is good, we are indebted to Charles W. Smith, compiler of the first two editions, who has guided the cumulation of manuscript entries for the third. What is more, he has examined the new manuscript searchingly. On the basis of his knowledge of Pacific Northwest Americana, it has been possible to winnow out many inappropriate entries that otherwise might have found their way into the final draft.

In the fall of 1949, the Executive Board of the Pacific Northwest Library Association endorsed the publication of the third edition, and agreed to sponsor its publication by the Oregon Historical Society. A debt of gratitude to this Society should be acknowledged. Its Superintendent, Lancaster Pollard, made an early publication possible. His enthusiastic willingness to publish the Check List and his skill in producing an attractive volume are much appreciated. Inez Haskell, Librarian of the Society, has also done much to augment the manuscript by supplying additional entries and bibliographical information essential to a well edited book.

Finally, a word of thanks to the authors of books about the Pacific Northwest. Their enterprise has made a new Check List of Pacific Northwest Americana essential and its contents of interest to everyone who appreciates the growth and development of Western United States and Canada.

HARRY C. BAUER

Chairman, Bibliography Committee
Pacific Northwest Library Association

3 July 1950

PREFACE TO THE THIRD EDITION

THE third edition of the Smith Check List, *Pacific Northwest Americana,* is based directly on the second edition (1921) which has been enlarged and extended to and including the year 1948. Both editions were sponsored by the Bibliography Committee of the Pacific Northwest Library Association.

The present edition shows in one volume the library regional resources of the area now served by the Pacific Northwest Bibliographic Center. Included within the area are the states of Idaho, Montana, Oregon, and Washington; together with British Columbia, Alaska, and the Yukon. To quote from the preface to the second edition, "The word history [as it appears in the subtitle] has been used in the broadest sense including a wide range of literature bearing upon the region." Furthermore, certain regional imprints have been arbitrarily included as have certain general works written by regional authors.

In order to keep the present edition within bounds, certain criteria have been established to govern content thus excluding whole classes of material, regardless of rarity or historical importance. For example, the second edition included "some few state and federal documents of rarity and importance" and "reprints and excerpts from magazines, when of historical importance." The third edition includes no documents, reprints, or excerpts because it is felt that these are covered by standard lists and indexes. Following is the list of material excluded: Broadsides, Chamber of Commerce publications, clippings, directories, documents (federal, state and local), excerpts from periodicals and books, manuscripts, maps, periodicals, reprints from periodicals, scrapbooks, and general works with only parts or sections pertaining to the Pacific Northwest. Books or pamphlets published as special numbers of periodicals have been included if they are devoted entirely to one Pacific Northwest subject. Imprints later than 1948 have not been included.

Pacific Northwest Americana is a union list of holdings of 38 representative libraries of the region, not a comprehensive bibliography of imprints. Consequently, no attempt has been made to check publishers' catalogues or other printed sources of information in order to assure coverage of all items relating to the region. If a title is not contained in one or more of the participating libraries, it is not included in the Check List, no matter how rare or important it may be.

The "Key to co-operating libraries" lists the symbols which are used to show the locations of each item unless seven or more libraries have a particular book, in which case the word "Many" is used. Obviously, the full strength of the co-operating libraries cannot be accurately guaged by the Check List because of excluded classes listed above, because most libraries have arrearages in cataloging, and because entries for the third edition were closed on July 1, 1949 when final editing began. It was the original intention of the Bibliography Committee to submit manuscript copies of the Check List to the contributing libraries in order that they might check their own holdings and thereby greatly increase the accuracy of the list. This proved inexpedient because of the time involved and the prohibitive cost of issuing the volume under such conditions.

ISABEL MAYHEW

July 3, 1950

KEY TO CO-OPERATING LIBRARIES

CV	Vancouver Public Library, Vancouver, B. C.
CVic	Victoria Public Library, Victoria, B. C.
CVicAr	Provincial Archives, Victoria, B. C.
CVicPr	Provincial Library, Victoria, B. C.
CVU	University of British Columbia Library, Vancouver, B. C.
IdB	Carnegie Public Library, Boise, Idaho
IdIf	Idaho Falls Public Library, Idaho Falls, Idaho
IdP	Pocatello Public Library, Pocatello, Idaho
IdTf	Twin Falls Public Library, Twin Falls, Idaho
IdU	University of Idaho Library, Moscow, Idaho
IdUSB	University of Idaho Southern Branch (now Idaho State College) Library, Pocatello, Idaho
MtBozC	Montana State College Library, Bozeman, Mont.
MtHi	Historical Society of Montana, Helena, Mont.
MtU	University of Montana Library, Missoula, Mont.
MtUM	Montana School of Mines, Butte, Mont.
Or	Oregon State Library, Salem, Or.
OrCS	Oregon State College Library, Corvallis, Or.
OrAshS	Southern Oregon College of Education, Ashland, Or.
OrHi	Oregon Historical Society, Portland, Or.
OrLgE	Eastern Oregon College of Education, La Grande, Or.
OrMonO	Oregon College of Education, Monmouth, Or.
OrP	Library Association of Portland, Portland, Or.
OrPR	Reed College Library, Portland, Or.
OrSa	Salem Public Library, Salem, Or.
OrSaW	Willamette University Library, Salem, Or.
OrU	University of Oregon Library, Eugene, Or.
OrUM	University of Oregon Medical School Library, Portland, Or.
Wa	Washington State Library, Olympia, Wash.
WaA	Aberdeen Public Library, Aberdeen, Wash.
WaE	Everett Public Library, Everett, Wash.
WaPS	State College of Washington Library, Pullman, Wash.
WaS	Seattle Public Library, Seattle, Wash.
WaSp	Spokane Public Library, Spokane, Wash.
WaT	Tacoma Public Library, Tacoma, Wash.
WaTC	College of Puget Sound Library, Tacoma, Wash.
WaU	University of Washington Library, Seattle, Wash.
WaW	Walla Walla Free Public Library, Walla Walla, Wash.
WaWW	Whitman College Library, Walla Walla, Wash.

EXPLANATIONS AND ABBREVIATIONS

The initials after each entry indicate the libraries in which the book or pamphlets may be found.   See "Key to co-operating libraries."

The following signs and abbreviations have been used:

[ ]	enclose material not on title page, supplied by cataloguer
assn.	association
b.	born
Bd.	Band (German)
c	copyright
ca	circa
col.	colored
comp.	compiled, compiler
d.	died
diagr.	diagram
ed.	edited, editor
enl.	enlarged
facsim.	facsimile
fl.	flourished
fold.	folded
front.	frontispiece
geneal.	genealogical
illus.	illustrated
introd.	introduction
l.	leaf, leaves
n.d.	no date of publication
n.p.	no place of publication
n.s.	new series
no.	number
p.	page, pages
photo.	photograph
port.	portrait
pseud.	pseudonym
pt.	part
pub.	publisher, publishing
rev.	revised
suppl.	supplement
tr.	traduit (French)
trans.	translated
univ.	university
v.	volume, volumes

Abbott, Edward Charles, 1860-1939.
We pointed them north; recollections of a cow-puncher, by E. C. Abbott ("Teddy Blue") and Helen Huntington Smith, illus. with drawings by Ross Santee and photographs. New York, Farrar [c1939.] xv, 281 p. front., illus., ports., map, facsim. Includes songs with music. Many **1**

Abbott, John Stevens Cabot, 1805-1877.
Christopher Carson, familiarly known as Kit Carson. New York, Dodd, 1873. 348 p.
MtU OrU WaSp **2**

Same. 1874. front., plates. OrHi WaU **3**

Same. 1898 [c1873] OrCS Wa **4**

Same. 1901. plate. Or OrP WaSp WaT **5**

Christopher Carson, known as Kit Carson, illus. by Eleanor Greatorex. New York, Dodd, 1877. 348 p. front., plates.
OrAshS WaPS **6**

Abbott, Newton Carl
Montana government; a study in state civics. Billings, Mont., Gazette Printing Co., c1937. 239 p. front., illus.
MtBozC MtHi MtU **7**

Montana in the making. Billings, Mont., Gazette Printing Co., c1931. 520 p. front., illus., 24 maps. MtHi MtU WaSp **8**
Same. 3d ed. 1934. MtBozC **9**
Same. 7th ed., complete rev. c1939. 544 p. front. (map) illus. MtBozC MtU WaU **10**

Abel, Annie Heloise, see no. 10062.

Aberdeen Plywood Company,
Aberdeen, Wash.
Facts about Douglas fir plywood. [Aberdeen, Wash., 193—] 11 p. illus., tables, diagr. WaPS **11**

Aborigines' Protection Society.
Canada west and the Hudson's Bay Company; a political and humane question of vital importance to the honour of Great Britain, to the prosperity of Canada, and to the existence of the native tribes. [London] Tweedie, 1856. 19 p. CVisAr **12**

Abraham, Mrs. Dorothy E.
Lone cone; a journal of life on the west coast of Vancouver Island [n.p., n.d.] 63 p. CVicAr **13**
Same. 2d ed. [Victoria, B. C.? 1945?.] 94 p. illus., maps. CV CVicAr WaS **14**
Romantic Vancouver Island; Vicortia, yesterday and today. [Victoria, B.C.? 1947?] 118 p. illus., map. CVicAr WaS **15**

Account and history of the Oregon territory; together with a journal of an emigrating party across the western prairies of America, and to the mouth of the Columbia River. 2d ed. London, William Lott, 1846. 160 p. CVicAr **16**

Achard, Eugene, 1884-
La grande decouverte de l'Ouest canadien. Montreal, Librairie generale canadienne [1942]. 123 p. illus. WaU **17**

Act of incorporation of the British Columbia and Victoria Steam Navigation Company, Limited, incorporated February 1860. Victoria, B.C., British Colonist, 1860. 11p. CVicAr **18**

Acton, John H.
Baccalaureate sermon preached before the faculty and graduating class of the Washington State University in the First Unitarian Church, Seattle, Washington, May 24, 1896. Seattle, West Coast Populist [1896]. 11 p. WaU **19**

Adair, Mrs. Bethenia Angelina (Owens) 1840-1926.
Dr. Owens-Adair; some of her life experiences. [Portland, Or., Mann & Beach, Printers, 1906]. 537 p. 7 ports.
Many **20**

The eugenic marriage law and human sterilization; the situation in Oregon; a statement, accompanied by text of two bills to be introduced into the Oregon Legislature, 1923. Salem, Or., 1922. 12 p.
Or OrU WaPS **21**

Human sterilization. [n.p., 1911?] 60 p.
Or OrHi **22**

Human sterilization, it's [!] social and legislative aspects. [Portland, Or., Metropolitan (Binfords & Mort) 1922. 442 p. front. (port.) facsim. Many **23**

A souvenir; Dr. Owens-Adair to her friends, Christmas 1922. [Salem, Or., Statesman Pub. Co., 1922] 63 p. illus., port.
Many **24**

Adair, James Barnett, 1853-
Adair history and genealogy. Los Angeles, 1924. 330 p. illus., plates, ports., map, coat of arms. WaU **25**

Adam, Graeme Mercer, 1839-1912.
Canadian North-west; its history and its troubles. Toronto, Rose, 1885, 390 p. front. (port.) 11 ports.
CV CVicAr WaPS WaU **26**

Same. 408 p. CVicAr MtU OrU WaSp WaU **27**

The Lewis & Clark exploring expedition, 1804-'06, by G. Mercer Adam; John Charles Fremont, by Charles Wentworth Upham. New York, Univ. Society, Inc., 1904. 189 p. (Makers of American history) WaW **28**
See also no. 10450.

Adam, Leonhard, 1891-
Nordwest-Amerikanische Indianerkunst. Berlin, Wasmuth [1923?] 44 p. 48 plates. (Orbis Pictus Westkunst-Bucherei, Bd. 17) CVic CVicAr WaS WaU **29**

Adams, Andy, 1859-1935.
Cattle brands, a collection of western campfire stories. Boston, Houghton [c1906] 316 p. Or OrP WaU **30**

The log of a cowboy; a narrative of the old trail days, illus. by E. Boyd Smith. Boston, Houghton [c1903] 387 p. front., 5 plates.   MtU Or OrP WaT WaU   31

Same. Pictures by R. Farrington Elwell. Boston, Houghton, 1927. 324 p. front. (Riverside bookshelf)   IdIf
MtHi MtU OrLgE OrMonO WaE 32

Same. Illus. by E. Boyd Smith. 1903 [c1931] 387 p. front., 5 plates. MtBozC OrLgE
WaTC   33

The outlet, illus. by E. Boyd Smith. Boston, Houghton [c1905] x [iv] 371 p. front., plates. Or OrP WaE WaS WaT WaU 34

Reed Anthony, cowman; an autobiography. Boston, Houghton, 1907. 384 p. front.   Or OrP WaS WaT WaU   35

A Texas matchmaker, illus. by E. Boyd Smith. Boston, Houghton [c1904]. 355 p. front., plates.
Or OrP WaE WaT WaU 36

Wells brothers, the young cattle kings. Boston, Houghton [c1911]. 356 p.
OrP WaE WaS WaU   37

Adams, Ansel Easton, 1902-
Born free and equal, photographs of the loyal Japanese-Americans at Manzanar Relocation Center, Inyo County, California. New York, U.S. Camera, 1944. 112 p. illus., ports.   Many 38

Adams, C. F., see no. 8688.

Adams, Emma Hildreth.
To and fro, up and down in Southern California, Oregon, and Washington Territory, with sketches in Arizona, New Mexico, and British Columbia. Chicago, Cranston [c1888]. 608 p. front., illus.
Many 39

Adams, Frederick H.
Poems. New Whatcom, Wash., Bellingham Bay Reveille, 1896. 45 p.   WaU 40

Adams, Glen Cameron.
Americana; a poem privately printed by hand press in the village of Fairfield, Spokane County, Washington. [Fairfield, Wash.] Ye Galleon Press [1940] 29 p. 1 illlus.   Wa 41

Adams, Harriet L.
A woman's journeyings in the new Northwest. Cleveland, B-P Printing Co., 1892. 180 p.   CVicAr WaU 42

Adams, Harrison, see no. 8498.

Adams, J. F. C.
Oregon Sol; or, Nick Whiffles's boy spy. 6th ed. New York, Beadle and Adams, c1878. 14 p. illus. (Beadle's half dime library. v. 2, no. 34).   WaU 43

Adams, James Orville, 1885-
The cruisers; a romance of the Idaho timber land frauds, illus. by Orrin C. Ross. Spokane, 1909. 283 p. front., 3 plates.
WaPS WaS WaSp WaU 44

Adams, Lester Forrest, 1895-
George W. Joseph; his life. [Portland, Or., Carlson Printing Co., c1931]. 88 p. port.
Or OrP 45

Adams, Leta Zoe.
Island of the red god, illus. by Armstrong

Sperry. New York, Rand McNally, c1939. 304 p. illus., map.   WaE WaSp   46
Adams, Ramon Frederick, 1889-
Charles M. Russell, the cowboy artist, a biography, by Ramon F. Adams and Homer E. Britzman, with bibliographical check list by Karl Yost. Pasadena, Calif., Trail's End Pub. Co. [1948] xii, 350 p. illus., col. plates, ports.
MtBozC Or   47

Western words; a dictionary of the range, cow camp and trail. Norman. Okla., Univ. of Okla. Press [1945]. xiv, 182 p.
IdU OrP OrPR WaU   48

Adams, William Lysander, 1821-1906.
Centennial address delivered by Dr. W. L. Adams of Portland, Oregon, at the Oregon State Fair. Portland, Or., G. H. Himes, 1876. 14 p.
Or OrHi OrP WaPS   49

Lecture on Oregon and the Pacific coast, delivered in Tremont Temple, Boston, Oct. 14, 1869. Boston, May, 1869. 39 p.
OrHi OrP WaU WaWW   50

Melodrame, entitled "Treason, strategems, and spoils." in five acts, by Breakspear. Portland, Or., Dryer, 1852. 32 p. illus.
OrHi   51

Brakespear. De lux. "Treason, strategems, and spoils." [Salem, 1899.] 38 p. Reprint, omitting illustrations of the originals.   Or Hi   51A

Oregon as it is; its present and future, by a resident for twenty-five years, being a reply to inquirers. Portland, Or., Bulletin, 1873. 61 p. tables.
OrHi OrP OrU WaSp WaU 52

Adamson, Thelma, ed.
Folk-tales of the coast Salish, collected and ed. by Thelma Adamson. New York, American Folk-lore Society, 1934. xv, 430 p. front. (map) songs with music. (Memoirs, v. 27)   Many 53

Additon, Mrs. Lucia H. Faxon.
Twenty eventful years of the Oregon Woman's Christian Temperance Union, 1880-1900, statistical, historical and biographical. Portland, Or., Gotshall, 1904. 112 p. illus., 29 ports., table. Many 54

Addresses and memorials, together with articles, reports, &c, &c, from the public journals upon the occasion of the retirement of Sir James Douglas from the governorship of the colonies of Vancouver's Island and British Columbia. Deal, E. Hayward, 1864. 74 p.
CVicAr CVU WaU   55

Addresses delivered at the inauguration of President Arnold Bennett Hall and the semi-centennial of the University of Oregon, Eugene, Oregon, Oct. 18-23, 1926. Eugene, Or., Univ. of Or. [1926]. 182 p.
WaU   56

Addresses presented to His Excellency, A. E. Kennedy, C. B., on assuming the governorship of Vancouver Island. [Victoria, B. C.?] 1864. 30 p.   CVicAr   57

Addresses upon the life and character of John J. McGilvra. [Seattle, Lowman & Hanford, 1904]. 78 p. illus., plate, port.
Wa WaPS WaS WaU 58

Adney, Tappan, 1868-
The Klondike stampede. New York, Harper, 1900. xii, 470 p. front., illus., plates (4 fold.) maps (1 double) facsims. Many **59**

An adopted citizen, see no. 11014.

Aflalo, Frederick George, 1870-1918.
Sunset playgrounds; fishing days and others in California and Canada, with many illus. London, Witherby & Co., 1909. xii, 251 p. front., plates.
CVU OrP Wa WaS WaU **60**

Agardh, Jacob Georg, 1813-1901.
Synopsis generis Lupini, auctore Jacobo Georgio Agardh. Lundae, typis excudit C. F. Bersing, 1835. xiv, 43 p. 2 plates.
WaU **61**

Aichel, Ordulf George, 1880-
The caisson as a new element in concrete dam construction; a proposal made in connection with the Columbia River power project. New York, Spon and Chamberlain, 1916. 32 p. diagrs. (part fold.)   OrP WaPS **62**

Aiken, George L.
The antelope boy; or, Smoholler, the medicine-man, a tale of Indian adventure and mystery. New York, Beadle and Adams [c1873]. 100 p. (Beadle's pocket novels. Pocket series no. 92.) Frontier adventures among the Nez Perce and Yakima Indians.   WaU **63**

Aikman, Duncan, 1889-
Calamity Jane and the lady wild cats. New York, Burt [c1927]. viii, 347 p. front. (port.) illus.   MtHi **64**

Same. New York, Blue Ribbon Books [c1927].   WaU **65**

The taming of the frontier, by ten authors. New York, Minton, Balch, 1925. 319 p. front., plates.   Many **66**

Ainslee, George, see nos. 805, 806.

Ajax, see nos. 7487, 7488.

Akademiia Nauk, Leningrad.
Prevoe morskoe pouteshevstvie Rossian predpriniatoe dlia reshenia geografisheskoi zadachi; Soediniaetsa li Azia s Amerikoi i sovershennoe v 1727, 28 i 29 godakh pod nachalstvom flota Kapitana I-go ranga Vitusa Beringa. S prisovokoupleniem kratkago biograficheskago svedenia o Kapitane Beringe i bivshikh s nim ofitserakh. S. Peterburg, pri Imperatorskoi Akademii Nauk, 1823. iv, 126 p. fold. map, tables (1 fold.)   WaU **67**

Pacific; Russian scientific investigations. Leningrad, Academy of Sciences, 1926. 190 p. illus., 11 ports., 6 maps, table.
MtU OrHi WaS WaU **68**

Akin, James
The journal of James Akin, Jr., ed. by Edward Everett Dale. Norman, Okla., Univ. of Okla., 1919. 32 p. map, facsims. (Bulletin, n.s. no. 172; Univ. studies, no. 9).   Many **69**

Akins, J. E.
History of steamboat navigation on Snake River. Lewiston, Idaho, Lewiston Tribune, 1927. 11 p.   WaPS **70**

Alaska Blacklock, see no. 5877.

Alaska Central Railroad Company.
Official prospectus. Seattle, Yerkes Printing Co. [1902]. [16] p. illus., map.
WaU **71**

Alaska Citizen.
Tanana special terminal edition. Tanana, Alaska, 1914. 12 p. illus. (Oct. 12, 1914).
WaU **72**

Alaska Commericial Company, San Francisco.
The school and family Russo-American primer, specially published for use in Alaska. San Francisco, 1871. 47 p. illus.
WaU **73**

To the Klondike gold fields and other points of interest in Alaska. San Francisco, c1898. 73 p. illus., fold. map.
WaPS WaS WaSp **74**

Alaska Copper Company, Seattle.
Alaska Copper Company office, Seattle, Washington; mines; Copper Mountain, Alaska. Seattle [1902?]. 35 p. illus., double map, diagrs.   WaU **75**

The Alaska Dispatch.
Golden spike edition. Seattle, E. C. Russell, 1922. 60 p. illus. (Fri., Dec. 22, 1922).   WaU **76**

Alaska facts; what Alaska is today; a word picture of America's last frontier and what it offers to those interested in this vast territory. [Seattle, 1945]. 62 p. illus., maps.
Or OrCS OrP OrSaW WaS WaU **77**

Alaska Historical Association.
Descriptive booklet on the Alaska Historical Museum, ed. by A. P. Kashevaroff. Juneau [n.d.]. 52 p. illus. CVicAr OrHi **78**

Same. 48 p.   CVicAr **79**
Same. 1922 61 p. CVicAr Or WaS WaU **80**
Same. [1929]. 52 p. illus., plates. WaU **81**
Same. Juneau, Daily Alaska Empire Print [1933?]. 52 p. illus., port.   WaU **82**

Alaska Life, the Territorial Magazine.
Pictorial edition, 1946. Seattle, 1946. 192 p. illus.   WaT **83**

Alaska Publicity and Trade Agency.
200 questions and answers on Alaska. Seattle, 1914. 31 p.   WaS **84**

The Alaska Railroad.
Alaska, the newest home land. Anchorage, 1930. 15 p. illus., maps.   WaU **85**
Same. 1931.   MtBozC **86**
Resources of Alaska. [n.p., 192-?] [54] p. tables.   WaPS **87**

Alaska Short Line Railway and Navigation Company.
The Alaska Short Line Railway and Navigation Company, incorporated under the laws of the state of Washington, December 1, 1903 [Seattle, Commonwealth, 1906?]. 36 p. front. (fold. map). WaU **88**

Alaska Sportsman.
Book of animals and birds, with Alaska oddities, by Weil. Juneau, Alaska Magazine Pub. Co., 1943, c40. 1 v. illus. WaS **89**

Alaska Steamship Company.
Alaska ahead. [Seattle, 1939] [31] p. illus., map.   WaPS **90**

An Alaska interlude. [Seattle, 1939?] [24] p. illus. WaPS 91

The Alaska line. Seattle [1920?] 40 p. illus. WaPS 92

My Alaska cruise. Seattle [19--?] 11 p. illus. WaPS 93

A trip to wonderful Alaska. Seattle, 1905. [24] p. illus. WaPS WaU 94

Same. 1906. 30 p. OrHi 95

Same. 1906. 32 p. WaU 96

Alaska, the Eldorado of the midnight sun. New York, Republic, 1897. 62 p. front., illus., fold. map. CVicAr 97

Alaska, the Richardson Road, Valdez to Fairbanks, an illustrated booklet descriptive of the road, the towns at either end and the surrounding country with beauties and possibilities of Alaska. [Valdez, Alaska, Valdez Miner] 1922. 40 p. illus., fold. map. WaU 98

Alaska tours to the national wonderland. [Chicago, Poole, c1898]. 59 p. illus., maps. CVicAr 99

The Alaska-Yukon gold book; a roster of the progressive men and women who were the Argonauts of the Klondike gold stampede and those who are identified with the pioneer days and subsequent development of Alaska and the Yukon Territory. [Seattle, Sourdough Stampede Assn., Inc., c1930]. 147 p. illus., plates, ports., map.
CVicAr WaPS WaS WaSp WaU 100

Albach, James R., comp.
Annals of the West; embracing a concise account of principal events which have occurred in the western states and territories from the discovery of the Mississippi Valley to the year eighteen hundred and fifty-six. [3d ed.] Pittsburgh, W. S. Haven, 1857. 1016 p. WaU 101

Albee, Bill, see no. 102.

Albee, Mrs. Ruth (Sutton).
Alaska challenge, by Ruth and Bill Albee with Lyman Anson. New York, Dodd, 1940. 366 p. illus., plates, ports., maps. Many 102

Alderson, Matt W.
Bozeman; a guide to the places of recreation and a synopsis of its superior natural advantages, industries and opportunities. Bozeman, Mont., 1883. 54 p. illus. map. MtHi 103

Alderson, Nannie (Tiffany) 1860-
A bride goes west, by Nannie T. Alderson and Helena Huntington Smith; drawings by J. O'H. Cosgrave II. New York, Farrar [1942] vii, 273 p. illus. Many 104

Aldrich, Clara Elizabeth.
The history of banking in Idaho. [Boise, Idaho, Syms-York Co., 1940?]. x, 101 p. ports., tables, diags. IdB IdUSB WaU 105

Aldrich, Herbert L.
Arctic Alaska and Siberia; or, Eight months with the Arctic whalemen. Chicago, Rand McNally, 1889. 234 p. illus., 24 plates. Many 106

Alexander, Charles, 1897-
Bobbie, a great collie, New York, Dodd, 1926. 114 p. front., 3 plates. Adventures of a dog in Oregon and Idaho. Many 107

The splendid summits. New York, Dodd, 1925. 289 p.
OrCS OrP OrSaW OrU WaE WaU 108

Alexander, Jesse H.
Indian horrors of the fifties; story and life of the only known living captive of the Indian horrors of sixty years ago. [Yakima, Wash., Yakima Bindery and Printing Co.] c1916. 170 p. front. (port.) WaU 109

Alla, Ogal, see nos. 6899, 6900.

Allan, Alexander.
Hunting the sea otter. London, H. Cox, 1910. iv, 188 p. front., plates.
CVicAr CVU MtU WaU 110

Allan, Allan Alexander, d. 1941.
Gold, men and dogs, by A. A. ("Scotty") Allan. New York, Putnam, 1931. vii, 337 p. front. (port.) 11 plates. Many 111

Allan, George W., see no. 9490.

Allan, Marjorie.
Christ Church Cathedral, 1889-1939. [Vancouver, B. C., Univ. Press] 1939. 30 p. illus., ports. CVicAr 112

Allan, Scotty, see no. 111.

Allee, Marjorie (Hill) 1890-
Smoke jumper, illus. by Manning de V. Lee. Boston, Houghton, 1945. 160 p. illus. Juvenile story of northwestern Mont. Many 113

Allen, A. J., comp.
Ten years in Oregon; travels and adventures of Doctor E. White and lady west of the Rocky Mountains; incidents of two sea voyages via. Sandwich Islands around Cape Horn; containing also a brief history of the missions and settlement of the country; origin of the Provisional Government; number and customs of the Indians; incidents witnessed in the territory; description of the soil, production and climate of the country. Ithaca, N. Y., Mack, 1848. 399 p. port. Many 114

Same. 430 p. CVicAr
OrHi OrP OrSaW WaSp WaU 115

Same. Ithaca, N. Y., Andrus Gauntlett & Co., 1850. 430 p. Many 116

Thrilling adventures, travel, and explorations of Dr. Elijah White, among the Rocky Mountains and in the far West. New York, Yale, 1859. 430 p.
WaWW 117

Allen, A. S., see no. 6998.

Allen, Albert Cooper, 1875-
Meeko, illus. by Helen Hughes Wilson. Caldwell, Idaho, Caxton, 1947. 232 p. illus. Juvenile story of southern Or.
Or OrP WaS WaSp WaU 118

Allen, Arthur H., see no. 10971.

Allen, Edward Tyson.
The ambitious tree; a story for western children. [Portland, Or., Glass & Prudhomme, n.d.] [8] p. Or 119

Forests, lumber and the consumer; an address delivered at the National Chautauqua, Chautauqua, N. Y., July 10, 1914, by E. T. Allen, forester, Western Forestry and Conservation Association. [St. Paul? 1914]. 12 p. OrCS WaU 120

Practical forestry in the Pacific Northwest; protecting existing forests and growing new ones, from the standpoint of the public and that of the lumberman, with an outline of technical methods. Portland, Or., Western Forestry & Conservation Assn., 1911. 130 p. Many 121

Allen, Edward Weber, 1885-
North Pacific: Japan, Siberia, Alaska, Canada, New York, Professional & Technical Press, 1936. xvi, 282 p. col. front., 24 plates (incl. maps). Many 122

Allen, Eleanor Waggoner, 1896-
Canvas caravans; based on the journal of Esther Bells McMillan Hanna, who, with her husband, Rev. Joseph A. Hanna, brought the Presbyterian colony to Oregon in 1852. Portland, Or., Binfords & Mort [c1946]. 125 p. Many 123

Seeds of earth. Portland, Or., Metropolitan, 1933. 66 p. Portland poet.
Or OrCS OrHi OrP OrSaW WaU 124

Allen, Eric W., see no. 8533.
Allen, Gardner W., see no. 2230.
Allen, Gina.
On the Oregon Trail, illus. by Sidney E. Fletcher. Evanston, Ill., Row Peterson, c1942. 34 p. col. illus.
Or OrP WaSp WaU 125

Allen, Harriet Day, see no. 10954.
[Allen, Lucius H.]
Judge O. C. Pratt of San Francisco, as a Pacific coast pioneer and as an early associate justice of the Supreme and District Courts of the United States, Territory of Oregon. [San Francisco, 1887] 14 p. Or 126

Allen, M. W., see no. 10280.
Allen, Mrs. Maryland (Riley)
The price of victory. Garden City, N. Y., Doubleday, Page, 1927. 356 p. Or. author. Western setting. Or OrP OrU 127

Allen, Merritt Parmelee, 1892-
The spirit of the eagle, decorations by Avery Johnson. New York, Longmans, 1947. vi, 234 p.
IdB IdIf Or OrP WaSp WaT 128

Western star, a story of Jim Bridger. New York, Longmans [1944, c1941]. 186 p. illus. WaU 129

Allen, Paul, 1775-1826.
Captains Lewis and Clarke and command States Army, daring and successful explorers of the American northwestern territory truthfully told in easy narrative style. Akron, Ohio, Superior Printing Co. [c1915]. ii, 176 p. WaU 130

"In camp on White Bear Island," conflict with Indians, singular adventures of the Captains Lewis and Clarke and command of the U. S. soldiers in the vast unexplored West. Akron, Ohio, Superior Printing Co. [c1915]. iv, 195 p. WaU 131

"In the Rocky Mountains." Akron, Ohio, Superior Pub. Co. [c1910]. ii, 186 p.
CVicAr 132

Same. [c1915]. OrP WaU 133

Lewis and Clarke, pioneers of the great American Northwest. New York, Mac-

Lellan Book Co. [c1910]. v, 381 p. front. (Everybody's books series). CVicAr 134

Same. 2 v. (v. 2 only) MtBozC 135

Stirring adventures "up the Missouri" with Lewis and Clarke, pioneers of the great Northwest. Akron, Ohio, Superior Printing Co. [1915]. ii, 190 p. (Superior library) Or WaU 136

See also no. 5894.

Allen, Thomas Newton, 1839-
Chronicles of Oldfields. Seattle, Harriman, 1909. 157 p. front. (port.)
OrSaW Wa WaS WaU 137

Allen, W. O., see no. 8824.
Allen, William Alonzo, 1848-
The Sheep Eaters. New York, Shakespeare Press, 1913. 78 p. front. (port.) 5 plates. Idaho Indian story. Many 138

See also no. 10644.

Allen, William N.
The climate of Washington; a careful and elaborate treatise on the climatic conditions, with reference to temperature, winds, rainfall and snowfall. Seattle, Brintnall [c1900] 44 p. maps. WaT 139

Washington [suppl. to Frye's Geography] New York, Ginn, c1912. 14 p. illus., map. WaT 140

Allen, Willis Boyd, 1855-
The gold hunters of Alaska. New York, H. M. Caldwell Co. [c1889] 348 p. illus., plates. WaU 141

Gulf and Glacier; or, The Percivals in Alaska. Boston, Lothrop [c1892] 243 p. 8 plates. WaU 142

The red mountain of Alaska. Boston, Estes & Lauriat [c1889]. 348 p. front., illus., 15 plates. Many 143

Aller, Curtis Cosmos.
Industrial survey of Seattle. Seattle, Univ. of Wash., 1918. 64 p. (Bureau of Industrial Research, bulletin no. 3) Many 144

Alley, B. F.
Description and resources of Lane County, Oregon, and its cities and towns. Portland, Or., D. Steel, 1890. 59 p. front. OrU 145

History of Clarke County. Washington Territory, comp. from the most authentic sources [by B. F. Alley and J. P. Munro-Fraser]. Also biographical sketches of its pioneers and prominent citizens. Pub. by the Washington Publishing Company. Portland, Or., A. G. Walling, 1885. 399 p. front., plates, ports. OrHi OrP OrSaW WaU 146

Linn County, Oregon, descriptive and resources, its cities and towns. Albany, Or., Royce [c1889] 111 p. OrHi 147

Washington Territory, descriptive and historical. Thurston County, by B. F. Alley and J. P. Munro-Fraser. Olympia, Wash., Cavanaugh, 1886. 142 p. table. OrP WaU 148

Alliance Francaise. Cercle de Seattle.
Statuts. [Seattle] 1910. 11 p. WaU 149

Alling, Horatio.
Why we vote; a discussion of the government of the state of Washington.

Olympia, Wash., Westland, 1900. 163 p.
map.   WaPS WaU WaWW **150**

Same. Tacoma, Westland, 1900. 196 p.
OrU WaE WaTC WaWW **151**

Same. Seattle, Westland, 1903.
Wa WaPS WaS WaSp **152**

Allison, Guy Selwin.
Poems of the Pacific. San Francisco, H. S.
Crocker Co., 1918. ix, 48 p. front. (port.)
Wa WaU **153**

Allison, William L., see no. 9060.

Almack, John Conrad, 1883-
The painted pony, illus. by Harold Sichel.
Santa Barbara, Calif., W. Hebberd,
c1944. 161 p. illus. Juvenile story of East-
ern Wash., Idaho, and Calif.
Or OrP OrU WaT **154**

Track of the sun, drawings by Bernard
Hinshaw. Portland, Or., Metropolitan
[c1937] 113 p. front., plates.   Many **155**

Almirall, Leon Vincent, 1884-
Canines and coyotes, with a preface by
R. L. Sutton and a foreword by Patrick
Chalmers. Caldwell, Idaho, Caxton, 1941.
150 p. front., illus., plates, ports.
MtHi Or WaSp WaU **156**

Alsop, Richard, see no. 5206-5211.

Alston, Edward Graham, d. 1873.
A handbook to British Columbia and
Vancouver Island, with map. [London]
F. Algar, 1870. 18 p. fold. map.
CVicAr CVU **157**

Same. 41 p.   CVicAr **158**

Alten, Carol.
Planning a new home, published by a
group of leading business firms and
distributed through the courtesy of The
Spokesman-Review. Spokane [c1937] 31
p. illus., port.   WaPS **159**

Same. Tacoma, Tacoma News Tribune,
c1937. Plates of Tacoma residences to
illustrate text.   WaT **160**

Alter, J. Cecil, 1879-
James Bridger, trapper, frontiersman,
scout and guide; a historical narrative,
with which is incorporated a verbatim
copy, annotated, of James Bridger, a
biographical sketch, by Maj. Gen. Grenville M. Dodge. Salt Lake City, Shepard
Book Co. [c1925] xvii, 546 p. front., plates.
ports., map.   Many **161**

Through the heart of the scenic West.
Salt Lake City, Shepard Book Co., c1927.
xiv, 220 p. front., plates, map.
IdTf MtU WaS WaU **162**

Altrocchi, Julia (Cooley) 1893-
The old California trail, illus. from photos.
by the author. Caldwell, Idaho, Caxton,
1945. 327 p. front., plates, ports.
Many **163**

Alward, Silas.
"Our western heritage", "Then and now",
or "Thirty years after"; lectures delivered. Saint John, N. B., Saint John
Globe, 1910. 58 p.   CVicAr **164**

America-Japan Student Conference, 2d,
Portland, Or., 1935.
The second America-Japan Student Conference, 1935. Portland, Or., Executive
Committee of Assn. of American Delegates, 1936. 66 p. illus., plates, ports.,
map.   OrCS OrP OrU WaU **165**

**American Association for the Advancement
of Science. Pacific Coast Committee.**
Nature and science on the Pacific coast;
a guide book for scientific travelers in
the West. San Francisco, Elder [c1915]
302 p. illus., 42 plates, 14 maps, table.
Many **166**

**American Association of Social Workers.
Oregon Chapter.**
Report of the Joint Committee on Juvenile
Deliquency and child welfare. [n.p.]
1946. 4 p.   OrP **167**

**American Association of University Women.
Spokane Branch.**
Highlights of the state of Washington;
written to accompany the historical
pictorial map of the state, published
and copyrighted by the Spokane Branch
of American Association of University
Women. Spokane, c1931. 18 p. Many **168**

American Bankers' Association.
American banker's guide to the forty-first
annual convention to be held at Seattle,
Wash., September 6th to 10th, 1915. New
York, Steurer [1915?] 96 p. illus.
WaS WaU **169**

Facts about Seattle and the state of Washington, advisable trips. [Seattle, 1915] 32
p. fold. map.   WaU **170**

American Book Company.
Geography of Oregon and a brief outline
of the history of the "Oregon country";
based on McMaster's school history of
the United States; handbook for the use
of Oregon teachers. New York, 1897.
17 p.   OrHi **171**

American Chemical Society.
Chemical resources and industrial opportunities of the state of Washington; an
authorative exposition of transportation,
power, mineral, climatic and other advantages, published expressly for the
1915 convention, Seattle, Aug. 31, Sept.
1-2. Seattle, 1915. 28 p.   WaPS **172**

American Council on Public Relations.
Summary of lectures and discussions of
the short course in public relations at
Reed College, July 31 to August 11, 1939.
[n.p.] 1939. 69 p.
OrCS OrP OrPR OrU **173**

The American Falls Press.
Commemorating the dedication of the
American Falls Dam, conservation giant
of the Snake River Valley. [American
Falls, Idaho, 1925] [44] p. illus., ports.,
maps. (Official souvenir ed., July 13,
1925)   IdB IdUSB **174**

**American Federation of Teachers. National
Academic Freedom Committee.**
The Keeney case; big business, higher
education, and organized labor; report
of an investigation made by the National Academic Freedom Committee of the
American Federation of Teachers into
the causes of the recent dismissal of
Professor Philip O. Keeney, librarian,

from Montana State University and the role played by certain business and political interests in the affairs of the university. Chicago [1939] 30 p.
Many 175

American Home Investment Company.
The story of Rochester; a new western city. [Seattle? 1912?] [12] p. illus.
WaPS 176

American Institute of Architects. Washington State Chapter.
Catalogue of the first annual exhibition of architecture and the allied arts, nineteen hundred seven and eight. Seattle [West Printing Co., 1908] 92 p. illus.
WaS WaU 177

American Institute of Mining and Metallurgical Engineers.
Ore deposits of the western states, ed. by the Committee on the Lindgren Volume, John Wellington Finch, chairman, with contributions by C. H. Behre, Jr., S. H. Ball, P. Billingsley and others. Lindgren volume. 1st ed. New York, 1933. xxxiv, 797 p. front. (port.) illus., maps, diagrs.
Many 178

American Journal of Progress.
Special extra number descriptive of and illustrating Spokane. New York [1904] 33 p. illus.
WaSp 179

Special extra number descriptive of and illustrating Tacoma, the manufacturing and shipping center of the Pacific Northwest. New York [1905] 33 p. front., illus.
WaT 180

American Legion. Idaho. John Regan Post No. 2
Pioneers, O pioneers! Old Oregon Trail centennial celebration; souvenir program, Boise Basin days, June 12, 13, 14, 1930. [Boise, Idaho, 1930] [24] p. illus.
IdB OrP WaU 181

American Legion. Montana
Condensed report of the proceedings of the Third Annual Convention of the American Legion of the Department of Montana, held at the Judith Theatre. Lewistown, Mont., State Pub. Co. [1921] 133 p. front., ports.
MtHi MtU 182

American Legion. Montana. Silver Bow Post No. 1.
Silver Bow County in the world war. [n.p., 1919] 108 p. illus.
MtUM 183

American Legion. Oregon. Portland Post.
The Pacific Northwest welcomes the American Legion. Portland, Or., 1932. 24 p. illus., ports.
WaS 184

American Legion. Washington (State) Child Welfare Committee.
American Legion questionnaire and information on Washington child welfare laws; questions and answers on ways and means of aiding dependent children of servicemen in Washington. [Seattle, 1933?] 26 p.
WaU 185

The A. L. A. in Alaska, July 1925. Itinerary and members of parties. [Seattle, 1925] 12 p.
WaU 186

American Library Association.
Seattle Conference, A. L. A. 1925. [Chicago, 1925] [490] p. plates.
WaU 187

American Mail Line.
A billion potential customers, ed. and printed under the auspices of American Mail Line. Seattle [c1928-c1930] 2 v. fronts., illus. Article on trade with the Orient.
OrCS
OrP (v. 2 only) WaS WaTC WaU 188

American Pioneer Trails Association.
The trails of Lewis and Clark, 1804-1806. [n.p.] Clarke Press, 1945. 53 p. map.
Or OrP 189

American Pioneer Trails Association. Oregon Council.
Lone Tree Valley, illus. by Colista Dowling. [n.p.] c1944. 7 p. illus. (Tales of the trail, no. 1)
Or OrP 190

American Public Health Association.
An appraisal of public health activities of Portland, including the activities of official and voluntary agencies for the years 1928-1929, by James Wallace. Portland, Or., Portland Public Health Survey Committee [1930?] 112 p. map, table, diagrs.
Or OrP OrPR OrU 191

[Ames, Edwin G.] comp.
Seattle and the Sound. [n.p., 1915?] [42] p. photos.
Wa 192

Ames, Merlin McMain, 1879-
Sparks from a thousand campfires; days and nights with the fur traders. St. Louis, Webster Pub. Co., c1937. 326 p. illus. maps.
Or OrAshS WaSp 193

Ameteur traveler, see no. 9911.

Amoretti, Charles, see no. 3045.

Amundsen, Roald Engelbregt Gravning, 1872-1923.
"The northwest passage"; being the record of a voyage of exploration of the ship "Gjoa", 1903-1907. New York, Dutton, 1908. 2 v. illus., port., 44 plates, 3 maps, table.
CVU MtHi OrP WaPS WaS WaT 194

Roald Amundsen, my life as an explorer. Garden City, N. Y., Doubleday, Page, 1927. 282 p. front., illus., maps, diagr., facsims.
Many 195

Roald Amundsen's "The North West passage"; being the record of a voyage of exploration of the ship "Gjoa" 1903-1907, with a supplement by First Lieutenant Hansen, vice-commander of the expedition; with about one hundred and thirty-nine illustrations and three maps. London, Constable, 1908. 2 v. front., illus., 3 maps.
CVicAr CVU WaS 196

Amundson, Carroll John, 1904-
History of the Willamette Valley and Cascade Mountain Wagon Road Company. Eugene, Or., Univ. of Or., 1930. 32 p. (Thesis series, no. 17) Reproduced through Work Projects Administration.
OrCS OrU WaS WaSp WaU 197

Anaconda Copper Mining Company.
The Anaconda Reduction works, Jan. 1919. Anaconda, Mont., c1919. 55 p. front., illus.
MtU 198

Same. [c1920] 60 p. illus., plates, diagr.
MtBozC MtHi WaS WaU 199

A brief description of the Anaconda reduction works. [Butte, Mont., Montana

Standard, 193-?] 44 p. illus.   MtU 200
A brief description of the Washoe smelter.
Anaconda, Mont., Standard Pub. Co.,
1916. 46 p.   MtBozC 201
Great Falls departments, Great Falls,
Montana: a brief description. 7th ed.,
Nov. 1930. [Great Falls, Mont., 1930]
61 p. illus.   MtBozC MtU 202
A monster monopoly; an exposition of the
methods of the Anaconda Mining Com-
pany, how it defrauded the taxpayers
of Montana. [n.p., 189-] 16 p. MtHi 203

Anaconda Standard Publishing Company.
A souvenir of Anaconda's silver jubilee, July
4, 1908. The city of Anaconda, its first
twenty-five years, 1883-1908. Anaconda,
Mont., 1908. 40 p. front. (port.) illus.
                              MtHi 204

Anacortes American.
Thanksgiving edition. Anacortes, Wash.,
J. M. Post, 1908. 36 p. illus., ports., maps.
(v. 19, no. 30, Nov. 26, 1908) WaU 205

Anacortes Packing Company, Ltd.
Memorandum and articles of association.
[Victoria, B. C., 1896] [5] p.   WaU 206

**Ancient Arabic Order of the Nobles of the
Mystic Shrine. Imperial Council.**
Journal of the Imperial Council 41st
annual session, comp. and pub. under
the personal direction of Mr. John B.
Gallagher, president of the John B.
Gallagher Co. of Joliet, Ill. Seattle, Low-
man & Hanford, 1915. [144] p. front.
(port.) plates, ports.   WaS WaU 207
Official program; 62d annual session of
the Imperial Council, A. A. O. N. M. S.,
July 13-16, 1936, Seattle, Washington.
Seattle, 1935. 19 p.   WaS 208

**Ancient Arabic Order of the Nobles of the
Mystic Shrine. Nile Temple.**
Official souvenir, 62d annual session
Imperial Council, A. A. O. N. M. S.
[Seattle, 1936] [98] p. illus., ports.
                          WaS WaU 209

**Ancient Arabic Order of the Nobles of the
Mystic Shrine. Zuhrah Temple.**
Zuhrah's pilgrimage to Seattle. [Minne-
apolis] 1936. [11] p. illus.   WaPS 210

Ancient Order of Hibernians. Oregon
The Oregon school fight, a true history
compiled from the arguments of pro-
ponents and opponents of bill and the
arguments on the constitutionality of
the measure as argued before the honorable federal judges, W. B. Gilbert,
C. E. Wolverton and R. S. Bean in
Portland, Oregon, Jan. 15th, 1924; and
the complete text of the decision handed
down by Judges William B. Gilbert,
Charles Wolverton and Robert S. Bean
of the U. S. District Court for Oregon,
Mar. 31, 1924, whereby the Oregon compulsory school law is declared uncon-
stitutional. Portland, Or. [1924?] 152 p.
                              OrP 211

**Ancient Order of United Workmen, British
Columbia.**
Constitution of the grand lodge of British
Columbia, together with constitution for
subordinate lodges. Victoria, B. C.,
Cohen, 1892. 88 p.   CVicAr 212

**Ancient Order of United Workmen. Grand
Lodge of Oregon.**
Revised constitution, general laws and
rules of order. Portland, Or., Beach,
1893. 129 p.   OrHi 213

Anderson, Abraham C., see no. 3644.

Anderson, Ada Woodruff.
The heart of the red firs; a story of the
Pacific Northwest, illus. by Charles
Grumwold. Boston, Little, 1908. 313 p.
front., 3 plates   Many 214
Same. 1909.   Wa WaU 215
Same. 1920. [c1908]
                  OrCS OrP OrU WaS 216
The rim of the desert, with front. by
Monte Crews. Boston, Little, 1915. 402 p.
front.   Many 217
Strain of white, illus. by Frances Rogers.
Boston, Little, 1909. 300 p. front., 3
plates   Many 218
Same. 1920 [c1909]   OrU 219
Same. 1921 [c1909]   WaSp WaT 220

Anderson, Alexander Caulfield, 1814-1884.
A brief account of the province of British
Columbia; its climate and resources; an
appendix to the British Columbia direc-
tory, 1882-83. Victoria, B. C., Williams,
1883. 33 p. fold. map. CVicAr CVU 221
The Dominion at the West; a brief description of the province of British Columbia, its climate and resources; the
government prize essay, 1872. Victoria,
B. C., Wolfenden, 1872. iv, 112, xlii p.
                  CVicAr CVU WaU 222
Hand-book and map to the gold region of
Fraser's and Thompson's Rivers, with
table of distances; to which is appended
Chinook jargon, language used, etc., etc.
San Francisco, LeCount, 1858. 31 p. fold.
map.   CV CVicAr CVU WAU 223
Notes on north-western America. Montreal, Mitchell & Wilson, 1876. 22 p.
                  CVicAr CVU WaU 224

Anderson, Andrew, 1840-1916?
Autobiography. Olympia, Wash. Recorder,
1916. 19 p. front. (port.) (Early Methodism in the Pacific Northwest. Pamphlets, v. 1, no. 3).   WaTC 225

Anderson, C. R.
Helena earthquakes; a story of earthquakes that rocked Helena, Mont. and
vicinity in the fall of 1935, together with
the attempts of science to explain it all,
and a short history of the city, by C. R.
Anderson and M. P. Martinson. [Helena,
Mont., Independent Pub. Co.] c1936. 129
p. illus., diagr. MtBozC MtHi MtUM 226

Anderson, Eva (Greenslit) 1889-
Chief Seattle, illus. by Fern Cousineau
Duncan. Caldwell, Idaho, Caxton, 1943.
390 p. front., illus., col. plates, col. ports.,
maps, geneal. table.   Many 227
A child's history of Washington, illus. by
Terry Townsend. Lincoln, Neb., Univ.
Pub. Co., c1938. 186 p. illus., maps.
                              Many 228
Dog-team doctor; the story of Dr. Romig.
Caldwell, Idaho, Caxton, 1940. 298 p.
front., plates, ports., facsims. Many 229

Indian boy on the Columbia River, by Eva Greenslit Anderson and Dean Collins, illus. by Paul Keller. Lincoln, Neb., Univ. Pub. Co. [c1943]. 80 p. illus.
                    Or OrP Wa WaS WaSp 230

Pioneer days in old Oregon, by Eva Greenslit Anderson and Dean Collins, illus. by Paul Keller. Lincoln, Neb., Univ. Pub. Co. [1943]. 64 p. illus., map.
                    Or WaS WaU 231

Stories of Oregon, by Eva Greenslit Anderson and Dean Collins. illus. by Paul Keller. Lincoln, Neb., Univ. Pub. Co. [1943]. 256 p. illus., maps.   Many 232

Anderson, Florence Mary (Bennett) 1883-
In memoriam, Ellen Garfield Smith, librarian of the Walla Walla Public Library, 1907-1938, written at the request of the Altrusa Club of Walla Walla, and read at a meeting of that club, January 21, 1939. [Walla Walla, Wash.? 1939?] [8] p. front. (port.)   Wa WaU 233

Anderson, Frank Marion, 1863-
Lower cretaceous deposits in California and Oregon. [New York] Geological Society of America, 1938. x, 339 p. plates, maps, tables. (Special papers, no. 16, Nov. 30, 1938)   MtUM Or OrP 234

Anderson, Hobson Dewey, 1897-
Alaska natives; a survey of their sociological and educational status, by H. Dewey Anderson and Walter Crosby Eells. Stanford Univ., Calif., Stanford Univ. Press, 1935. 472 p. front. (map) illus., tables, fold. diagrs.   Many 235

Anderson, James.
Sawney's letters and Cariboo rhymes. Toronto, Johnston, 1895. 49 p.
                    CVicAr CVU WaU 236

Anderson, Nancy Mae, 1910-
Swede homestead. Caldwell, Idaho, Caxton, 1942. 188 p. front., plates, ports.
                    Many 237

Anderson, Robert T.
The old timer and other poems. [Edmonton,, Alta., Edmonton Printing & Pub. Co., c1909]. 103 p. Poems of Canadian Northwest and Kootenai Hills. CV 238

Anderson, Rudolph M., see nos. 9856, 9857.

Anderson, Sherwood, see no. 9379.

Anderson, Thomas McArthur, 1836-1917.
Monograph of the Anderson, Clark, Marshall and McArthur connection. [n.p., n.d.] 36 p. charts.   OrHi OrP 239

Should republics have colonies? An address before the Oregon Commandery of the Loyal Legion, Nov. 14, 1906. Boston, Bliss, 1906. [8] p.   Or OrP 240

Andree, S. A., see no. 10039.

Andrew. F. William.
The story of Summerland. Penticton, B.C., Penticton Herald [1945]. 55 p. front. (map).   CV CVicAr CVU WaS 241

Andrews, Clarence Leroy, 1862-
The eskimo and his reindeer in Alaska, illus. by photos. taken by the author. Caldwell, Idaho, Caxton, 1939. 253 p. front. (map) plates, ports.   Many 242

Nuggets of northland verse, panned from the gravels of the past. Seattle, 1935. 46 p.   OrU WaS WaU 243

The pioneers and the nuggets of verse they panned from the gravels of the past. Seattle, c1937. 55 p. illus.
                    OrU Wa WaS WaU 244

Sitka, the chief factory of the Russian American Company. 3d ed. Caldwell, Idaho, Caxton, 1945. 144 p. front., plates, ports.   Many 245

The story of Alaska. Seattle, Lowman & Hanford, 1931. 258 p. front., 7 plates, 3 ports., map.   Many 246

Same. 1938. 303 p.   Many 247

Same. 5th rev. ed. 1942, c1938. 308 p.
                    WaT 248

The story of Sitka; the historic outpost of the northwest coast, the chief factory of the Russian American Company. Seattle, Lowman & Hanford [1922]. 108 p. front., plates, fold. diagr.   Many 249

Wrangell and the gold of the Cassiar; a tale of fur and gold in Alaska. Seattle, L. Tinker, c1937. 60 p. illus., map.
                    CVU OrU Wa WaS WaU 250

Angelo, C. Aubrey.
Idaho; a descriptive tour and review of its resources and route, by C. Aubrey Angelo (Chaos). San Francisco, H. H. Bancroft & Co., 1865. 52 p. Photostat copy.
                    WaU 251

Sketches of travel in Oregon and Idaho, with map of South Boise. New York, 1866. 181 p. map.   OrHi 252

Angle, Grant Colfax, 1868-
Lumbering in the Northwest and the logger at his work. Shelton, Wash., Journal Press, c1905. 30 p. illus.   WaWW 253

Angus, Henry Forbes, 1891-   ed.
British Columbia and the United States; the north Pacific slope from fur trade to aviation, by F. W. Howay, W. N. Sage, and H. F. Angus, ed. by H. F. Angus. Toronto, Ryerson, for the Carnegie Endowment for International Peace, Division of Economics and History, 1942. 408 p. illus., maps.   Many 254

Anise, see no. 9970.

Annabel, Russell.
Hunting and fishing in Alaska. New York, Knopf, 1948. xiv, 341, v p. plates.
                    Or OrCS WaE WaS WaT WaU 255

Anson, Lyman, see nos. 102, 1153, 1154.

Anstey, Arthur.
The romance of British Columbia. Toronto, Gage, 1927. 6, 216 p. front., illus., ports., maps.   Many 256

Anthony, Reed, see no. 35.

Anti-Monopoly Association of the Pacific Coast
A history of the wrongs of Alaska; an appeal to the people and press of America, printed by order of the association, February, 1875. San Francisco, 1875. 43 p. Photostat copy.   WaU 257

Anti-Prohibition Association.
The state-wide prohibition initiative measure no. 3; the official argument for and

against as filed with the Secretary of
State; a compilation of facts about pro-
hibition. Seattle, Sherman Printing &
Binding Co. [1914]. 79 p.
                    WaPS WaSp WaU 258

Anti-Saloon League of Oregon.
Campaign manual, compiled by R. P. Hutton. Portland, Anti-Saloon League of Oregon [1914]. 96 p.   Or OrHi 258A

Antonovich, Emile P.
Post-war program for Tacoma improvements; a report. Tacoma, 1944. 23 p.
map.   WaS WaT 259

Ap-i-kum-i, see nos. 9096, 9098, 9107.

Apperson, John Thomas, 1834-1917.
A brief history of the Apperson family in
Oregon, by Captain John T. Apperson,
assisted by A. King Wilson. [n.p., 1908]
32 p. front.   Or OrHi OrP WaU 260

Applegrowers Association, Hood River, Or.
Standard packing and grading rules. [Hood
River, Or.] 1917. 8 p.   OrP 261

Appleby, M., ed.
Told by the innkeeper. London, Old Roy-
alty Book Pub. [n.d.] 143 p. B. C. stories
taken from life.   CV CVicAr CVU 262

Applegate, Jesse, 1811-1888.
A day with the cow column in 1843; recollections of my boyhood, by Jesse A.
Applegate, Oregon pioneer of 1843, ed.
with introd. and notes by Joseph Schafer.
Chicago, Printed for the Caxton Club,
1934. 207 p.   Many 263
The Yangoler chief, the Kommema and his
religion; winter of deep snow in the
basin of the lakes; mystery of the Nop-
pol; the fall of man. Roseburg, Or. [Re-
view Pub. Co.] 1907. [67] p. port. Or 264

See also no. 8837.

Applegate, Jesse Applegate, 1835-1919.
Recollections of my boyhood; Oregon pioneer of 1843. Roseburg, Or., Review Pub.
Co., 1914. 99 p. Also included in his
father's book, entry 263.   Many 265

Appleton, Marian Brymner, see no. 10970.

The Aquinian.
Kamloops 125th Anniversary number. [n.
p.] 1937. 1 v. illus. (June, 1937).
                          CVicAr 266

Arboretum Foundation, Seattle, Wash.
Handbook of rhododendrons. Seattle, 1946.
vii, 198 p.
        CV IdU OrCS OrU WaS WaTC 267

Archer, S. A., see no. 836.

Arctander, John William, 1849-1920.
The apostle of Alaska; the story of William
Duncan of Metlakahtla. New York, Re-
vell [c1909]. 395 p. front. (port.) 27 plates,
4 ports., map.   Many 268
Same. 2d ed.   Wa WaU 269
The lady in blue; a Sitka romance, illus.
by courtesy of Mr. W. H. Case. Seattle,
Lowman & Hanford [c1911]. 63 p.
                      WaS WaU 270

Arctic Club, Seattle, Wash.
Officers, committees, members, by-laws
and rules. Seattle, 1910. 66 p. front., illus.
                          WaS 271
Same. 1913.   Wa 272

Arctic miscellanies; a souvenir of the late
polar search, by the officers and seamen
of the expedition. London, Colburn and
Co., 1852. xviii. 347 p. col. front., illus.
                    CVicAr WaS WaU 273

Argonaut, see no. 2901.

An argument upon the justice and expedi-
ency of the order issued by government
for the detaining all ships bound to the
ports of Spain, freighted with treasure
or warlike stores. London, Stockdale,
1805. 63 p. Treats of Nootka Sound controversy.   CVicAr WaS 274

The Argus.
Alaska-Yukon-Pacific edition. Seattle, 1909.
80 p. illus. (Feb. 20, 1909). WaS WaU 275
Men behind the Seattle spirit; the Argus
cartoons. [Seattle, H. A. Chadwick, 1906]
365 p. illus.   WaS WaU 276
Seattle and Puget Sound. [Seattle, Gra-
ham-Hickman Co., 1905] [2] p. 18 plates.
                          WaU 277
Washington golden jubilee number. Seattle,
1939. 64 p. illus. (Feb. 25, 1939).
                      WaS WaU 278

Ariss, E. Augusta.
Historical sketch of the Montana State
Association of Registered Nurses and
related organizations. [Great Falls,
Mont.? 1936?]. 54 p. illus., ports.
                    MtBozC MtU 279

Arlington Times.
Pioneer edition. Arlington, Wash., 1941. 8
p. illus., plans. (Aug. 21, 1941). WaU 280
Pioneer edition of 1942. Arlington, Wash.,
1942. 6 p. illus., ports., diagr. (Aug. 20,
1942)   WaU 281

Armin, Jule.
Animated Northwest stories, illus. by auth-
or, with copies of stick-pictures made
by her fourth grade pupils in one of
their handicraft expressions of facts
acquired from use of this text. Los
Angeles, Perry Eldredge Pub. Co., c1936.
194 p. illus.   Many 282
Same. Portland, Or., Metropolitan [c1936].
                    OrP WaU WaW 283

Armsmith, Catherine.
Fairy tales of Kootenay. London, A. H.
Stockwell [1929]. 80 p.   CVU 284

Armstrong, A. N.
Oregon; comprising a brief history and
full description of the territories of Oregon and Washington, the Indian tribes of
the Pacific slope, their manners, etc., interspersed with incidents of travel and
adventure. Chicago, Scott, 1857. 147 p.
                          Many 285

Armstrong, Sir Alexander, 1818-1899.
A personal narrative of the discovery of
the Northwest Passage; with numerous
incidents of travel and adventure during
nearly five years' continuous service in
the Arctic regions while in search of the
expedition under Sir John Franklin, by
late surgeon and naturalist of H. M. S.
"Investigator." London, Hurst and
Blackett, 1857. xxii, 616 p. col. front.,
fold. map.   CVicAr WaS 286

Armstrong, Benjamin G., 1820-
Early life among the Indians; reminiscences from the life of Benj. G. Armstrong; treaties of 1835, 1837, 1842, and 1845; habits and customs of the red men; incidents, biographical sketches, battles, etc., dictated to and written by Thos. P. Wentworth. Ashland, Wis., A. W. Bowron,1892. 266 p. front., illus., plates, port.
CVicAr **287**

Armstrong, Margaret Neilson, 1867-
Field book of western wild flowers, by Margaret Armstrong in collaboration with J. J. Thornber, with five hundred illus. in black and white and forty-eight plates in color drawn from nature by the author. New York, Putnam, 1915. xx, 596 p. col. front., illus., col. plates. Many **288**
Same. [1927]. OrPR WaU **289**
Same. [1935, c1915]. WaT **290**

Armstrong, Moses Kimball, 1832-1906.
History and resources of Dakota, Montana and Idaho. Yankton, Dakota Ter., G. W. Kingsbury, 1866. 72 p. front. (fold. map).
IdB **291**
Same. [Pierre, S. D., Hipple Printing Co., 1928]. 62 p. MtHi MtU WaSp WaU **292**

Armstrong, Nevill Alexander Drummond
After big game in the upper Yukon. London, Long [1937]. 287, 8 p. front., illus., 15 plates, maps. CVicAr WaS **293**
Yukon yesterdays; thirty years of adventure in the Klondike. London, Long, 1936. 287 p. front. (port.) illus., 15 plates, facsims. CVic CVicAr CVU WaS WaU **294**

Arney, C. E., see no. 2074.
Arnold, E. M., see no. 297.
Arnold, Oren.
Wonders of the West; a book for young people, and all others who would know western America, with front. by George Elbert Burr, seven full-color plates by Lillian Wilhelm Smith, thirty-two full page camera studies and numerous informal sketches by Reg Manning. Dallas, Texas, B. Upshaw and Co. [c1936]. xiii, 229 p. col. front., illus., plates (part col.) ports.
IdB WaE WaS WaU **295**

Arnold, Royal Ross, 1878-
Indian wars of Idaho, illustrated. Caldwell, Idaho, Caxton, 1932. 268 p. front., illus., ports., map, facsims. Many **296**
Outlines of the Constitution of the United States, of the state of Idaho, and of the history of Idaho, by R. R. Arnold and E. M. Arnold, approved by State Board of Education, Boise, Idaho. Caldwell, Idaho, Caxton [c1928]. 31 p. illus.
IdIf IdU WaSp **297**

Art, Carl William.
Seattle; world city that had to be! Seattle, Metropolitan, c1930. 63 p. front., illus.
CV WaS WaT WaU **298**

Art, Historical and Scientific Association, Vancouver, B. C.
Catalogue. [Vancouver, B. C., n.d.] 16 p.
WaU **299**
Guide and handbook to the museum. Vancouver, B. C., Evans & Hastings [c1908]. 68 p. illus., ports. CVicAr **300**

The Indians of B. C. [Vancouver, B. C. n. d.]. 16 p. CV **301**
The museum. Vancouver, B. C., 1915. 108 p. CV **302**
Retain the Court House Square; resolutions adopted by public organizations of Vancouver. Vancouver, B. C. [1908]. 14 p. CVicAr **303**

Art work in Montana, pub. in 12 parts. Chicago, W. H. Parish Pub. Co., 1896. 12 pts. MtBozC MtU **304**

Art work of Seattle and Alaska. Racine, Wis., W. D. Harney Photogravure Co., 1907. 8 pts. in 2 v. OrP WaS WaU **305**

Art work of Seattle and western Washington. Ed. de luxe of photogravures. Racine, Wis., W. D. Harney Photogravure Co., 1910. 78 plates. Text: History of a great country, by W. D. Bayles.
OrP Wa WaS **306**

Art work of Tacoma and vicinity, Washington. Racine, Wis., W. D. Harney Photogravure Co., 1907. 27 p. illus., plates. Text by Louis W. Pratt of Tacoma. WaS WaT WaTC WaU **307**

Art work of the Inland Empire; eastern Washington, northern Idaho. Racine, Wis., W. D. Harney Photogravure Co., 1906. 27 p. illus., 66 plates.
Or Wa WaSp **308**

Art work of the state of Oregon. Oshkosh, Wis., Art Photogravure Co., 1900. 12 v. plates. Text: Oregon in 1900, by William Reid.
OrHi OrP OrPR OrU WaPS WaS **309**
Same. Ed. de luxe of photogravures. Portland, Or. W. D. Harney Photogravure Co., 1909. 9 pts. in 1 v. plates. Text: Oregon a great state, by George H. Williams. IdU Or OrHi WaPS **310**

Art work of the state of Washington. Oshkosh, Wis., Art Photogravure Co.,1900. 10 pts. plates. Text by Edmund S. Meany.
Wa WaPS WaS WaTC WaU **311**

Art work on eastern Washington and western Idaho. Chicago, C. T. Daily, 1900. 12 pts. in 1 v. illus., plates.
IdU WaPS WaSp **312**

Arthur, John, 1849-
William Henry Upton, grand master of Masons, 1888-9; memorial address before M. W. Grand Lodge F. & A, M. of Washington. Tacoma, Allen & Lamborn, 1907. 19 p. front. WaU **313**

Arthur, William, 1860-
Well-ordered household; or, The ideal city, containing plan and specifications for a proposed model city [Dunshalt, Wash.] [Omaha?] 1905, 69 p. WaU **314**

Articles of Agreement for carrying on an expedition by Hudson's Streights for the discovery of a North West passage to the western and southern ocean of America, dated March 30, 1745. Dublin, 1746. 16 p. CVicAr **315**

Artigue, Jean d'.
Six years in the Canadian North-West, trans. from the French by L. C. Corbett and Rev. S. Smith, Toronto, Hunter, 1882. 206 p. CVicAr CVU WaU **316**

As one thief to another. [Salem, Or., Winning the World, 1945] 24 p.   OrU   **317**

"As we see 'em"; cartoons and caricatures of Portland citizens. [Portland, Or., E. A. Thomson, c1906] 150 plates.
    OrHi OrPR OrU WaPS   **318**

Ashburner, William.
Report on the Newport and Eastport coal mines of Coos Bay, Oregon, by William Ashburner, Isaac Shone, and F. T. Gilmore. New Bedford, Mass., Mercury Pub. Co., 1883. 15 p.   ·OrP   **319**

Ashcroft Print Company, Ltd.
Ashcroft the gateway to northern British Columbia. [n.p., n.d.] 1 v. illus., map.
    CVicAr   **320**

Ashland Tidings, Ashland, Or.
Rogue River Valley, southern Oregon. Ashland, Or., 1885. [15] p. tables.
    OrHi OrP   **321**

Ashley, Mildred, see no. 3008.

Ashley, William Henry, see no. 2224, 2225.

Ashton, James M.
Historical sketch of Troop B, "Tacoma City Troop" of Washington National Guard. [Tacoma, Bell Press, 1910] 1 v. illus., ports.   WaT   **322**

Ashton, John.
F 63, being an account of the events and wanderings of that unit during the great war, 1917-1919; comp. and ed. by John Ashton, Sandy Martin, F. J. English, R. K. Beymer, and H. V. Morgan; drawings by G. W. Coblenz and S. Martin, with photos. by men of Battery F. Tacoma, 1919. 102 p. illus.   WaT   **323**

Associated Industries of Seattle.
The industrial court of Kansas. [Seattle, 1920?] [38] p.   WaU   **324**

Association of Professional Enginers of the Province of British Columbia.
The engineering profession in British Columbia; the Engineering Act, the profession's student system. Vancouver, B. C., 1930. 120 p. ports., fold. form.
    CVU OrCS   **325**

Association of Provincial Land Surveyors, British Columbia.
Constitution and by-laws. [n.p.] 1891. 17 p.
    CVicAr   **326**

Asociation of Teachers of the State College of Washington.
Salaries and educational efficiency at the State College of Washington [a report to the president and Board of Regents] [Spokane, Shaw & Borden, 1920] 39 p.
    WaPS   **327**

Astor, John Jacob, see no. 7978.

Astoria, Or. First Evangelical Lutheran Church.
25th anniversary; souvenir album. [Rock Island, Ill., 1905] 1 v.   OrHi   **328**

Astoria, Or. The Regatta Committee.
Astoria [6th] annual regatta; souvenir, August 21, 22, and 23, 1899, containing the program, prizes, courses, and sailing rules; also a history of the organization of the regatta and other matters of interest. [Astoria, Or., J. S. Dellinger, 1899] [40] p. illus., ports.   WaU   **329**

Astoria and Columbia River Railroad Company.
The Oregon coast from Portland to a summer paradise in four hours. Portland, Or., Glass & Prudhomme [n.d.] [32] p. illus.   Or OrHi   **330**

Same. Astoria, J. S. Dellinger Co. [n.d.] [32] p. illus.   OrHi   **330A**

Portland to the seaside in four hours. Portland, Or., Lewis & Dryden, 1898. 7 p. illus., table.   WaPS   **331**

The Astoria Centennial, Aug. 10 to Sept. 9, 1911. [Astoria, Or.?] 1911. 31 p. illus., port.   OrHi OrU   **332**

Astoria. Fire Department.
Souvenir, Astoria Fire Department, 1870-1905, compiled by Allen M. Robinette, and published in the interest of the relief fund. Astoria, Daily News [1905]. [84] p. illus.   OrHi   **332A**

Astoria Homestead Association.
Prospectus, certificate of incorporation and constitution of the Astoria Homestead Association, Astoria, Oregon; also maps of the town plot and adjacent country, incorporated April 26, 1870. San Francisco, Spaulding & Barto, Printers, 1870, 12 p. map.   Or   **333**

Astorian-Budget, Astoria, Or.
Magazine section; "a story in words and pictures of the green land by the western sea, ships of the world on the mighty Columbia, commerce, industry, agriculture, logging, the famed Astoria Regatta, world renowned salmon canneries, sunny ocean beach resorts, scenery, highways, mountains and streams, all in a setting of rich historic interest", Feb. 22, 1937. Astoria, Or., 1937. 1 v. illus.   WaS   **334**

[**Atcheson, Nathaniel**] 1771-1825.
On the origin and progress of the North-West Company of Canada with a history of the fur trade as connected with that concern and observations on the political importance of the company's intercourse with, and influence over the Indians or savage nations of the interior. London, Cox, 1811. 38 p. fold. map.   CVicAr   **335**

Same. Photostat copy.   CVicAr CVU   **336**

The Athens Club, Pullman, Wash.
Constitution and by-laws. Pullman, Wash., 1929. 8 p.   WaPS   **337**

Atherton, Gertrude Franklin (Horn) 1857-
Perch of the devil. New York, Stokes [c1914] 373 p. Novel about Butte, Mont.
    Many   **338**

Rezanov, illus. in water-colors. New York, Authors and Newspapers Assn., 1906. 320 p. col. plates   Many   **339**

Same. With an introd. by William Marion Reedy. New York, Boni and Liveright, c1906. vii, 255 p.   WaU   **340**

Atkinson, George Henry, 1819-1889.
First day, Sabbath, its law. Portland, Or., D. H. Stearns, 1879. 15 p.
    OrU WaSp   **341**

Funeral services in memory of Mrs. M. F. Eells, one of the pioneer missionaries of the A. B. C. F. M., to the Spokane Indians of Oregon, in 1838; held at Skokomish and Seattle, W. T., August 11 and 13, 1878. Portland, Or., Himes, 1878. 9 p.
OrHi OrP Wa WaU WaWW **342**

History of the Congregational Church of Oregon City, Or. [n.p., 1876] 4 p.
OrHi **343**

Northwest coast, including Oregon, Washington and Idaho; a series of articles upon the N. P. R. R. in its relations to the basins of the Columbia and of Puget's Sound. Portland, Or., Walling, 1878. 56 p. map. CVicAr WaWW **344**

Same. 2d ed. Many **345**

Reminiscences of Rev. E. Walker, funeral discourse. Portland, Or., Himes [1877] 8 p. OrP WaSp WaWW **346**

Sermon, charge and address, on giving the right hand of fellowship, as delivered at the ordination of Mr. Thomas Condon, Portland, O. T., April 7, 1853. Portland, Or., Dryer, 1853. 15 p. OrHi **347**
See also no. 2757.

Atkinson, Mrs. Nancy (Bates)
Biography of Rev. G. H. Atkinson; journal of sea voyage to Oregon in 1848, and selected addresses and printed articles; and a particular account of his church work in the Pacific Northwest, prepared by Rev. Myron Eells. Portland, Or., Baltes, 1893. 508 p. illus., 3 ports.
Or OrHi OrP OrU WaU WaWW **348**

Atwater, Mary Meigs.
The shuttle-craft book of American handweaving. New York, Macmillan, 1941. 281 p. illus. Basin, Mont. author.
MtHi **349**

Atwater, Montgomery Meigs.
Flaming forest, illus. by R. Farrington Elwell. Boston, Little, 1941. vii, 211 p.
Or Wa WaE WaS **350**

Government hunter. New York, Macmillan, 1940. 158 p. illus. Mont. ranch story. CV MtHi Or WaS WaSp **351**
Same. With pictures by Fred C. Rodewald. 1943 [c1940] WaU **352**

Atwood, Albert, 1832-
Conquerors; historical sketches of the American settlement of the Oregon country, embracing facts in the life and work of Rev. Jason Lee. [Cincinnati] Jennings and Graham [c1907] 316 p. front. (port.) 8 plates, 12 ports., 2 maps, facsim. Many **353**

Glimpses in pioneer life on Puget Sound. Seattle, Denny-Coryell, 1903. 483 p. illus., port. A history of Methodism in the Pacific Northwest. Many **354**

The Oregon Trail souvenir. [Seattle?] Rainier Printing Co. [1907?] [37] p. illus., ports. Anon. WaPS **355**
See also no. 100.

Aubert, Frederic.
L'ouest canadien et le Jukon (Alaska). Chartres, Laffray, 1907. 87 p.
CV CVU **356**

Audouard, Mme. Olympe (de Jouval) 1830-1890.
Le far-west. Paris, E. Dentu, 1869. 370 p. front. (port.) WaU **357**

Audubon, John James, 1785-1851.
Birds of Washington and Oregon; fifty Audubon prints. [n.p., n.d.] 50 col. plates in box. Wa WaT **358**

Auer, Harry Anton.
Camp fires in the Yukon. Cincinnati, Stewart, 1916. vi, 204 p. front., illus., 15 plates. Many **359**
Same. 1917. WaTC WaU **360**
Same. London, 1926. CVU **361**
Same. New York, Appleton, 1926 [c1916] WaU **362**

Augur, Helen.
Passage to glory; John Ledyard's America. Garden City, N. Y., Doubleday, 1946. 310 p. plates, ports. Many **363**

Augur, Herbert Bassett, 1874-
Government in Oregon; a supplement to S. E. Forman's The American republic. New York, Century, 1919. 74 p.
Or OrP OrU WaU **364**
The Oregon system. [Portland, Or.] Jefferson High School Press, 1915. 18 p.
OrP **365**

Aumack, Thomas M., 1920-
Rivers of rain; being a fictional account-ing of the adventures and misadventures of John Rodgers Jewitt, captive of the Indians at Friendly Cove on Nootka Island in Northwest America. Portland, Or., Binfords & Mort [1948] 216 p.
Many **366**

Ausherman, B. N., see no. 4476.

Austin, Charles W.
The great Seattle fire of June 6, 1889, containing a succinct and complete account of the greatest conflagration on the Pacific coast, by Charles W. Austin and H. S. Scott. Tacoma, Puget Sound Printing Co., 1889. 44 p. illus., port. OrHi WaS WaU **367**

Austin, Mrs. Grace Bell (Jones) ed.
Annals of the S. W. R. Jones family, Oregon, 1853-1930. [Eugene, Or., Shelton-Turnbull-Fuller Co.] 1930. 108 p. illus., ports. Or OrHi **368**

Austin, Margaret Elizabeth, 1918-1944.
Arrowy time. [Bozeman, Mont., Published by a group of friends in cooperation with the Alumni Assn. of Mont. State College, c1947] 65 p. MtBozC **369**

Austin, Mrs. Margon.
Moxie and Hanty and Bunty; with illus. by the author. New York, Scribner, c1939. 1 v. Juvenile story of Or.
Or OrP WaS WaSp WaT **370**
Once upon a springtime, with illus. by the author. New York, Scribner, c1940. 1 v. illus. Or WaS WaSp WaT **371**
Willamette way. New York, Scribner, 1941. [44] p. col. illus. Many **372**

Austin, W. L.
Nickel deposits near Riddle's, Oregon. Denver, App Stott Printing Co. [1896?] 27 p. illus. OrP **373**

Automobile Club of Washington.
Lest we forget. [Seattle? 1935] 77 p.
WaU 374

Sportsmanlike driving, a teachers' outline
for a course in traffic safety and driving for high schools. Rev. Seattle
[ca1935] 51 p. illus. (High School series
no. 1)   WaPS 375

Automobile road book of western Washington; a road guide book, descriptive
and maps, showing the best automobile
routes, together with all related roads of
record and other valuable information
for the use of automobilists. 4th ed.
1913. Seattle, Lowman & Hanford Co.
[1913] 313 p. maps (part fold., 2 in pock-
ets)   WaU 376

Auzias de Turenne, Raymond, 1861-
Comment naquit le quarante-deuxieme etat
de la federation americaine; l'etat de
"Washington" et sa ville reine "Seattle".
[Paris,   Comite   "France-Amerique",
1929?] 16 p.   OrP WaS WaU 377
Le dernier mamouth. Paris, Calmann-Levy
[1904] 286 p. Alaska story.   WaU 378
Le roi du Klondike. Paris, Levy [18–?]
288 p.   WaU 379
Voyage au pays des mines d'or, le Klon-
dike. Paris, Levy, 1898, 318 p. illus.,
plates, port., fold. maps.   WaU 380
Same. 1899.   CV CVicAr CVU WaU 381
Same. 3d ed. 1899.   OrU WaU 382

Averill, H. C.
Yukon nights. London, Wright & Brown,
1946. 192 p.   WaS 383

Avery, Mary Williamson, 1907-
Government of the state of Washington,
based on part II of The history and
government of the state of Washington
(an outline) by Herman J. Deutsch.
Pullman, Wash., State College of Wash.,
1944. 131 p. diagrs., forms.
Wa WaPS WaS WaSp WaU 384
Guide to government of the state of
Washington, for use with Avery, Government of the state of Washington,
based on part II of The history and
government of the state of Washington
(an outline) by Herman J. Deutsch.
Pullman, Wash., State College of Wash.,
1946. 35 p.   WaS WaU 385

Avery & Potter.
Tacoma beautiful. Tacoma, Allen & Lam-
born [191?] 40 p. illus., plates, photos.
WaT 386

Axelrod, Daniel, see no. 1623.

Axling, Phil. L., see no. 3385.

Axtell, Mrs. Helen.
Lost valley. Portland, Or., Metropolitan
[c1939] 126 p. Poetry
Or OrU WaU WaW 387

Axtell, Juliet L., comp.
Gospel hymns in Nez Perce language.
[n.p., 1897] 30 p. front. (port.) port.
Second   title-page: Taaiskt   wanipt
nummiputimtki. Sapahautin wiwakamana
titwihinatuna uyitpa kamyah curchpa.
Rev. H. H. Spaulding, Rev. Robert
Williams, Rev. James Hayes, Imam
Askap Levi W. Jonas.   WaPS 388

Ayer, Fred Carleton, 1880-
A rural survey of Lane County, Oregon,
by Fred C. Ayer and Herman N. Morse.
[Eugene, Or.] Univ. of Or. [1916] 109 p.
illus., maps, tables, diagrs. (Bulletin,
n. s., v. 13, no. 14, Aug. 15, 1916)
OrCS OrP OrPR OrU WaU 389

Ayer, I. Winslow.
Life in the wilds of America and wonders
of the West in and beyond the bounds
of civilization. Grand Rapids, The
Central Pub. Co., 1880. 528 p. front.,
illus.   CVicAr OrCS OrP WaU 390

Ayer, W. B., see no. 3194.

B., R., see no. 1206.

Babcock, John Pease.
"Peace River Joe". Victoria, B. C., Litchfield's, 1924. 24 p. The prize winning
story of the Imperial Order Daughters
of the Empire 1924 competition.
CVicAr CVU WaU 391

Baber, D. F., see no. 10686.

Bacher, Albert P.
Souvenir book, early history of the state
of Washington, Tacoma, and the Swiss
societies, by Mr. and Mrs. Albert Bacher.
1889-1939. Dedicated to the Tacoma Swiss
Society for their fiftieth anniversary.
Tacoma? [1939?] 56 p. illus., ports.
WaPS 392

Back, Sir George.
Narrative of the Arctic land expedition to
the mouth of the Great Fish River, and
along the shores of the Arctic Ocean, in
the years 1833, 1834 and 1835. London,
Murray, 1836. 663 p. front., plate, map.
CV CVicAr CVU WaPS WaSp 393
Same. Philadelphia, Carey, 1836. 456 p.
CVicAr WaU 394
Same. 2d ed. 1837.   OrHi 395

Back, Capt. H. S.
Something about Alaska and the Arctic
region, especially the Yukon Plateau.
Caldwell, Idaho, Caxton, [c1927]. 32 p.
front. (port.)   WaPS WaSp 396

Backus, Manson Franklin, 1853-1935.
The development of the Northwest; address delivered at the sixteenth annual
convention of the Investment Bankers
Association of America. Seattle, 1927. 12
p.   CV WaS WaU 397

Bacon, Edwin Munroe.
Direct elections and law-making by popular vote; the initiative, the referendum, the recall, commission government
for cities, preferential voting, by E. M.
Bacon and Morrill Wyman. Boston,
Houghton, 1912. 167 p. 2 forms (sample
ballots from Seattle election of Mar. 5,
1912).   OrP OrU WaPS WaS 398

Bade, William Frederick, see nos. 7140, 7143.

Badlam, Alexander.
The wonders of Alaska. San Francisco,
Bancroft, 1890. vii, 152 p. front., illus., 28
plates, 8 maps.   Many 399
Same. 2d ed. rev. 148 p.
CVicAr WaPS WaU 400

Same. 3d ed. 1891. 154 p.
  CVicAr WaS WaT WaU 401

Badminton Club of Victoria, B. C.
Articles of constitution and by-laws; established May 15th, 1894. Victoria, Province Pub. Co. [n.d.]. 11 p.   CVicAr 402

Baer, K. E. v., see no. 10620.

Baets, Maurice de, 1863-1931.
The apostle of Alaska; life of the Most Rev. Charles John Seghers, a trans. of Maurice de Baets' "Vie de monseigneur Seghers," by Sister Mary Mildred, S. S. A., with a foreword by the Most Rev. John C. Cody. Paterson, N. J., St. Anthony Guild Press, 1943. xi, 292 p. front. (port.) illus., coat of arms, Many 403
Monseigneur Seghers, l'apotre de l'Alaska. Paris, H. Oudin, 1896. xcii, 237 p., 2 ports., 2 fold. maps, facsim.   CVicAr 404

Bagley, Clarence Booth, 1843-1932.
The acquisition and pioneering of old Oregon. Seattle, Argus Print, 1924. 41 p. front., 4 plates, 16 ports.   Many 405
Early Catholic missions in old Oregon. Seattle, Lowman & Hanford. 1932. 2 v. fold. plate.   Many 406
History of King County, Washington. Chicago, S. J. Clarke Pub. Co., 1929. 3 v. front., illus., ports. Volumes 2 and 3 biographical.
  Wa WaPS WaS WaT WaU 407
History of Seattle from the earliest settlement to the present time. Chicago, S. J. Clarke Pub. Co., 1916. 3 v. fronts., plates, ports. Volume 2, p. 701-822 and v. 3 biographical.   Many 408
In the beginning; a sketch of some early events in western Washington while it was still a part of "Old Oregon." Seattle, Lowman & Hanford, 1905. 90 p.
  Many 409
Indian myths of the Northwest. Seattle, Lowman & Hanford, 1930. 145 p. front. (port.)   Many 410
Pioneer Seattle and its founders. [Seattle? 1924?] 17 p. Anon.   WaS WaU 411
Same. 1925. 17 p. ports.
  Wa WaPS WaW 412
Same. Seattle, Argus Print, 1926. 17 p. front., ports.   WaS 413
Same. 1928.   OrHi WaSp WaU 414
Seattle; de luxe supplement to the History of Seattle. Chicago, S. J. Clarke Pub. Co., 1916. 623 p. illus., plates, ports.
  WaS WaSp WaU 415
See also no. 11045.

Baidukov, Georgii Filipovich.
Over the North Pole. New York, Harcourt [c1938] xiv, 99 p. plates, ports. Many 416

Bailey, Alfred Marshall, 1894-
Birds of arctic Alaska. [Denver] Colo. Museum of Natural History, 1948. 317 p. illus., ports., map. (Popular series no. 8).   WaS WaU 417

The birds of Cape Prince of Wales, Alaska. [Denver, Colo. Museum of Natural History, 1943] 113 p. illus., map. Proceedings, v. 18, no. 1, Feb. 1, 1943). WaU 418

Bailey, Mrs. Florence Augusta (Merriam) 1863-
Handbook of birds of the western United States, including the great plains, great basin, Pacific slope and lower Rio Grande Valley. Boston, Houghton, 1902. 512 p. front., illus., plate, map. Many 419
Same. 2d ed. 1903. 574 p.   Wa 420
Same. 2d ed. rev. 1904. 514 p.   Many 421
Same. 3d ed. rev. [c1902]. IdP MtBozC 422
Same. 4th ed. rev. 1914. 570 p.
  OrU WaU WaWW 423
Same. 1915.   MtHi OrP WaU 424
Same. 7th ed. rev. 1917. 574 p.
  CVU MtBozC OrSa OrU Wa WaPS 425
Same. [1902, 1917] 590 p.   WaPS 426
Same. Rev. ed. 1924, c1902-1917. 590 p.
  CVU 427
Same. 1927.   OrLgE
  OrP Wa WaS WaTC WaWW 428

Bailey, Frank.
The richest section of Yale District; Nicola, Similkameen and Tulameen Valleys. [Vancouver, B. C., Ward, n.d.] [128] p. illus., ports, 2 fold. maps.
  CVicAr CVU 429

Bailey, J. A., see no. 1484.

Bailey, Mrs. Margaret Jewett (Smith)
Grains; or passages in the life of Ruth Rover, with occasional pictures of Oregon, natural and moral. Portland, Or., Carter, 1854. 190 p.   Or OrU 430

Bailey, Robert Gresham, 1874-
Hell's Canyon, a story of the deepest canyon on the North American continent, together with historical sketches of Idaho, interesting information of the state, Indian wars and mythology, poetry and stories. Lewiston, Idaho, 1943. 575 p. illus., ports., maps.   Many 431

River of no return (the great Salmon River of Idaho) a century of central Idaho and eastern Washington history and development; together with the wars, customs, myths, and legends of the Nez Perce Indians. Lewiston, Idaho, Bailey-Blake Printing Co., 1935. xxiv, 515 p. front., illus.   Many 432

Same. Rev. ed. 1947. 754 p.
  IdB IdU MtBozC OrP WaU WaW 433

Baillie-Grohman, William Adolph, 1851-1921.
Camps in the Rockies; being a narrative of life on the frontier and sport in the Rocky Mountains, with an account of the cattle ranches of the West, with an original map based on the most recent U. S. government survey. New York, Scribner, 1882. viii, 438 p. fold. map. Many 434

Same. New ed. 1905 [c1882].   WaU 435

Fifteen years' sport and life in the hunting grounds of western America and British Columbia, with a chapter by Mrs. Baillie-Grohman, illus. by 77 photos., including the best trophies of North America big game killed by English and American sportsmen, with table of measurements and notes, with 3 specially prepared maps of the northwest coast of the United States, British Columbia and the Kootenay District. London, Cox, 1900. xii, 403 p. illus., port., 15 plates, fold. maps.   Many 436

Same. 2d ed. 1907.   WaPS 437

The Kootenay valleys. London, Witherby, 1886. 6 p. fold. map.   CVicAr 438

Baily, Joshua L., Jr. see nos. 5408, 5409.

Bain, James Arthur.
Life and adventures of Nansen, the great Arctic explorer; with numerous illustrations and map. London, Walter Scott Pub. Co., [1907] xix, 449 p. front., illus., 4 plates, 3 ports, map.   CVicAr 439

Bain, Joe Staten, 1912-
The economics of the Pacific coast petroleum industry. Berkeley, Calif., Univ. of Calif. Press, 1944-1947. 3 v. tables.
                                              Many 440

Baird, Irene.
Waste heritage. Toronto, Macmillan, 1939. 329 p. Story of sit-in strike of the unemployed in B. C.   CVicAr 441

Same. New York, Random House [c1939].
          CVU Or OrP WaS 442

Baiseley, Albert H., see no. 1206.

Bakeless, John Edwin, 1894-
Lewis and Clark, partners in discovery. New York, Morrow, 1947. xii, 498 p. illus., ports., maps (1 fold. col.)   Many 443

Baker, A. J., see no. 9444.

Baker, Charlotte, 1910-
The house on the river, story and pictures by Charlotte Baker. New York, Coward-McCann [1948]. 128 p. illus. Juvenile story of houseboat on Willamette.
          Or OrHi OrP WaS WaSp WaU 444

Baker, Edward Dickinson, 1811-1861.
Masterpieces of E. D. Baker, ed. (with glances at the orator and his time) by O. T. Shuck. San Francisco, 1899. 336 p. front. (port.) (Eloquence of the far West, no. 1). Oregon author.
          OrP OrU WaPS WaS WaU 445

See also no. 9438.

Baker, Ernest Everhart.
The heart of the last frontier and other verses. Oregon, booklover's ed. Salem, Or. [Statesman Pub. Co.] 1915. 143 p.
                                              Many 446

Baker, Frank Collins, see no. 2104.

Baker, Hugh Potter, 1878-
The pulp and paper industry in the Pacific coast states; and, The business of manufacturing paper in the United States. [New York] American Paper and Pulp Assn., 1927. [32] p. illus.
          Or OrCS WaS WaT WaU 447

Baker, James.
Report on the mining industries of Kootenay. Victoria, B. C., "The Colonist" Steam Presses, 1895. 8 p.   WaU 448

Baker, John Clapp.
Baptist history of the north Pacific coast. Philadelphia, American Baptist Pub. Society [1912]. 472 p. front. (port.) illus., ports.   Many 449

Baker, W. W.
Forty years a pioneer; business life of

Dorsey Syng Baker, 1848-1888. Seattle, Lowman & Hanford, 1934. 257 p. illus., plate, ports.   Many 450

Baker-Boyer National Bank, Walla Walla, Wash.
Fiftieth anniversary, 1869-1919. [Walla Walla, Wash., Bulletin Press] 1919. [32] p. illus., port., table.   OrHi 451

Baker Herald, Baker, Or.
The land of opportunity; Baker County, Oregon and adjacent territory. Coming west ed. Baker, Or., 1915. 1 v. illus.
          Or OrP 452

Balch, Edwin Swift, 1856-1927, ed.
Letters and papers relating to the Alaska frontier. Philadelphia, Allen, 1904. 134 p. maps.   CVicAr MtHi WaS WaU 453

Mount McKinley and mountain climbers' proofs. Philadelphia, Campion and Co., 1914. 142 p. illus.
          Or OrP OrU WaS WaU 454

Balch, Frederick Homer, 1861-1891.
Bridge of the gods; a romance of Indian Oregon. Chicago, McClurg, 1890. 280 p.
          Or OrU WaA WaW WaWW 455

Same. 4th ed. 1899.   WaU 456

Same. 5th ed. 1900.   WaU 457

Same. 7th ed. with eight full-page illus. by L. Maynard Dixon. 1902. 280 p. front., plates.   OrHi OrSa WaTC WaU 458

Same. 9th ed. 1904.   OrSaW 459

Same. 10th ed. 1904.   CVicAr 460

Same. 11th ed. 1907, c1890, 1902. 280 p. front., illus.   WaT 461

Same. 12th ed. 1909 [c1902].   IdU 462

Same. 1911.   CVU 463

Same. 1912.   IdB 464

Same. 27th ed. 1925 [c1902]   WaU 465

Same. Portland, Or., Binfords & Mort, [1938?] 286 p.   WaU 466

Genevieve; a tale of Oregon, with port. and biographical sketch. Portland, Or., Metropolitan, 1932. xxiii, 340 p. front. (port.)   Many 467

Memaloose; three poems and two prose sketches, introd. and notes by Alfred Powers. Portland, Or., Privately printed by Myron Ricketts & Thomas Binford, 1934. 35 p.   Many 468

Balch, Glenn, 1902-
Indian Paint; the story of an Indian pony, illus. by Nils Hogner. New York, Crowell [c1942]. 244 p. illus. Boise, Idaho, author. IdB Or OrP Wa WaS WaSp 469

Wild horse, illus. by Pers Crowell [c1947]. 338 p. illus.
          IdB OrCS WaE WaS WaT 470

Balch, Thomas Willing.
Alaska frontier. Philadelphia, Allen, 1903. 198 p. front., maps.   Many 471

Baldwin, George Partridge, comp.
Anacortes illustrated; containing a general description of the state of Washington and a review of resources, terminal advantages, general industries and climate of Anacortes and its tributary country. Anacortes, Wash., Allmond and Boynton, Printers [c18--?] [40] p. illus. WaU 472

Ball, John, 1794-1884.
  Autobiography, comp. by his daughters, Kate Ball Powers, Flora Ball Hopkins, Lucy Ball. Grand Rapids, Dean-Hicks Co., 1924. 230 p. front., plate, ports.
  OrU **473**
Same. 1925. Many **474**
  John Ball, member of the Wyeth expedition to the Pacific Northwest, 1832; and pioneer in the old Northwest; autobiograpy comp. by his daughters, Kate Ball Powers, Flora Ball Hopkins, and Lucy Ball. Glendale, Calif., A. H. Clark Co., 1925. xi, 230 p. plates, ports.
  CVU IdIf IdU WaWW **475**

Ball, Lucy, see nos. 473-475.

Ball, S. H. see no. 178.

Ballaine, John Edmund, 1868-
  Strangling of the Alaska railroad, government owned project built at cost of over $62,000,000, developments suppressed, millions wasted, victim of intrigue centering in New York, confidential contracts in evidence; the simple remedy, a constructive program of developments honestly applied. [Seattle? 1923?]. 42 p.
  WaS WaU **476**

Ballantyne, Robert Michael, 1825-1894.
  The golden dream; or, Adventures in the Far West. London, J. Nisbet & Co., 1860. viii, 358 p. plates. CVicAr **477**
Same. London, J. F. Shaw and Co., 1861.
  WaS WaU **478**
  Handbook to the new gold fields; a full account of the richness and extent of the Fraser and Thompson River gold mines, with a geographical and physical account of the country and its inhabitants, routes, etc., etc. Edinburgh, A. Strahan, 1858. iv, 116 p. front. (fold. map)
  CVicAr CVU OrHi WaS **479**
  Hudson's Bay; or, Every-day life in the wilds of North America during six years' residence in the territories of the honourable Hudson's Bay Company. Edinburgh, Blackwood, 1848. 328 p. front., illus., plates. CVU WaU **480**
Same. 2d ed.
  CVicAr CVU OrHi OrU Wa WaS **481**
Same. 3d ed. London, Nelson, 1857. 322 p. illus. CV WaWW **482**
Same. Boston, Phillips, 1859. 298 p. front., plates. CVicAr Wa WaSp WaU **483**
Same. 4th ed. London, Nelson, 1876. 367 p.
  CVicAr **484**
Same. 1886. 367 p. front., illus., plates.
  WaU **485**
Same. Boston, Phillips, 1890. Or **486**
Same. London, Nelson, 1897. 367 p. port.
  CVU MtU OrP WaPS WaT **487**
  The pioneers; a tale of the western wildnerness illustrative of the adventures and discoveries of Sir Alexander Mackenzie. London, Nisbet [1872?] 126 p. front., plates. CV CVU **488**
  The pioneers, a tale of the western wilderness, illustrative of the adventures and discoveries of Sir Alexander MacKenzie.

London, Nisbet, 1872. viii, 150 p. front.
  WaPS WaU **489**
Same. 1883. 128 p. WaU WaW **490**
  Snowflakes and sunbeams; or, the young fur traders, a tale of the far North. London, Nelson, 1856, vi, 429 p. front., plates. CVicAr CVU WaU **491**
Same. Boston, Phillips, Sampson, 1859. 432 p. front., 2 plates. CVicAr **492**
  Twice bought; a tale of the Oregon gold fields. London, Nisbet [n.d.] 268 p. illus.
  OrP OrU **493**
  Wild man of the West; a tale of the Rocky Mountains. Philadelphia, Lippincott, 1874. 419 p. illus. WaSp **494**
  See also no. 10384.

[Ballard, D. P.]
  Washington Territory and the far Northwest, Oregon, Idaho, and Montana; facts by an old settler, not in the interest of railroads or localities. Chicago [1889] 60 p. MtU WaU **495**

Ballard, Martha E.
  Poems of Washington state. Seattle, Lowman & Hanford, c1939. 31 p. port. In honor of first golden jubilee of state.
  WaS **496**

Ballard Plannery Co., Spokane, Wash.
  The modern bungalow, a treatise on the construction and arrangement of the modern bungalow, showing floor plans and exterior views as designed and arranged by Ballard's plannery. Spokane [1908] [39] p. illus., plans. WaPS **497**

Ballou, Bertha, see no. 9750.

Ballou, John.
  The lady of the West; or, The gold seekers. Cincinnati, Printed for the author by Moore, Wilstach, Keys & Overend, 1855, 544 p. CVicAr **498**

Ballou, Maturin Murray, 1820-1895.
  New Eldorado; a summer journey to Alaska. Boston, Houghton [c1889] 355 p.
  Many **499**
Same. 2d ed. 1890. 352 p. Differs from 1st ed. in ommission of index.
  CVU WaS **500**
Same. 3d ed. 1890. CVU **501**
Same. 1891. xxi, 355 p. front., maps.
  WaU **502**
Same. 6th ed. 1892. xi, 352 p. CVicAr **503**
Same. 1899. CVicAr **504**

Ballou, Robert.
  Early Klickitat Valley days. [Goldendale, Wash., Goldendale Sentinel, c1938] 496 p. illus., ports. Many **505**

Baltz, John D.
  Hon. Edward D. Baker, U. S. senator from Oregon; Colonel Baker's defense in the battle of Ball's Bluff, fought October 21, 1861, in Virginia, and slight biographical sketches of Colonel Baker and Generals Wistar and Stone. Lancaster, Pa., Inquirer Printing Co., 1888. 248 p. front., plates, ports., map. Many **506**

[Bancroft, A. L. and Co.]
  Historical works of Hubert Howe Bancroft in their relation to the progress

and destiny of the Pacific states. [San
Francisco, n.d.] [25] p. map.
                    OrP WaU **507**

Bancroft, Frederic.
The life of William H. Seward. New York,
Harper, 1900. 2 v. fronts., ports.
                    OrU WaPS WaS WaU **508**

Bancroft, Hubert Howe, 1832-1918.
History of Alaska, 1730-1885. San Fran-
cisco, 1886, 775 p. illus., map. Many **509**
Same. San Francisco, History Co., 1890.
                                WaU **510**
History of British Columbia, 1792-1887.
San Francisco, History Co., 1887. xxxi,
792 p. illus., map.   Many **511**
Same. 1890.
    CVicAr CVU MtU WaTC WaW **512**
History of Oregon. New York, Bancroft
Co. [n.d.] 2 v. illus.   WaSp **513**
Same. San Francisco, History Co., 1886.
2 v. illus., map.   Many **514**
Same. 1888 [c1886]   Many **515**
History of the northwest coast. New York,
Bancroft Co. [n.d.] 2 v. illus., maps (1
fold.)   CVicAr WaSp **516**
Same. San Francisco, 1884.   Many **517**
Same. San Francisco, History Co., 1886
[c1884]   Many **518**
History of Washington, Idaho and Mon-
tana, 1845-1889. San Francisco, Calif.,
History Co., 1890. 836 p. illus. Many **519**
Literary Industries. San Francisco, His-
tory Co. 1890. 808 p. 1 port. Many **520**
Literary industries; a memoir. New York,
Harper, 1891. 808 p. port.   CV **521**
Native races of the Pacific states of
North America. New York, Appleton,
1874. 5 v. illus., 10 maps, table.
        MtHi Or OrHi OrP OrU **522**
Same. 1875.   OrHi OrU **523**
Same. New York, Bancroft Co., 1882.
                              Many **524**
Same. San Francisco, History Co., 1886.
                              Many **525**
New Pacific. New York, Bancroft Co.,
1900. 738 p. front., map.
        OrCS OrHi OrP WaS WaU **526**
Same. Rev. ed. 1912. x, 549 p. front. (map)
    IdU Or OrP OrPR WaPS WaT **527**
Same. 1913.
    CVicAr MtU OrCS OrU Wa WaU **528**
Same. 3d ed. rev. 1915.
        OrCS WaSp WaU **529**
The works. San Francisco, A. L. Bancroft
& Co., 1882-90. 39 v. front. (port.) illus.,
maps.   Many **530**

Bandel, Eugene, 1835-1889.
Frontier life in the army, 1854-1861; trans.
by Olga Bandel and Richard Jente, ed.
by Ralph P. Bieber. Glendale, Calif.,
A. H. Clark Co., 1932. 330 p. front., illus.,
plates, port., map.
        MtHi MtU OrP WaS WaSp **531**

Bandel, Olga, see no. 532.

The banditti of the Rocky Mountains and
Vigilance Committee in Idaho; an
authentic record of startling adventures
in the gold mines of Idaho. 20th thou-

sand. Chicago, Post Office Box 3179,
1865. vi. [25]-143 (i. e. 133) p. illus.,
plates.   WaU **532**

Banks, Charles Eugene, 1852-1932.
A child of the sun, illus. by Louis Betts.
Chicago, L. W. Walter Co. [c1900] 166 p.
col. front., col. plates. Seattle poet.
        Wa WaS WaU **533**
The love trail; sonnets. Hilo, Hawaii, Hawaii Post-Herald [c1921]. 58 p. front.
(port.)   Wa WaU **534**
Sword and cross and other poems. Chicago, Rand McNally [c1899]. 269 p.
                    WaS WaU **535**

Banks, Louis Albert.
Censor echoes; or, Words that burned.
Portland, Or., Himes, 1882. 162 p. illus.,
ports., table. Articles on liquor problem
in Or. and Wash.   Many **536**
Live boys in Oregon; or, An Oregon boy-
hood. Boston, Lee, 1900. 173 p. 8 plates.
                              Many **537**
An Oregon boyhood. Boston, Lee and Shep-
ard, c1897. 173 p. front., 3 plates.
                              OrSa **538**
Same. 1898. [c1897].   Many **539**
Same. 1898.   CVicAr WaU **540**

Bankson, Russell Arden, 1889-
The Klondike nugget. Caldwell, Idaho,
Caxton, 1935. 349 p. front. (port.) plates.
Eugene C. Allen's experiences in the
Klondike and a history of his news-
paper,"The Klondike Nugget." Many **541**
Spokane House. [Spokane, Maag & Port-
er, 1936]. 32 p. illus., plans. A demonstra-
tion residence designed by Harold C.
Whitehouse.   WaPS **542**

Banwell, Selwyn, 1880-
A frontier judge; British justice in the
earliest days of farthest west. Toronto,
Rous & Mann, 1938. 30 p. front. (port.)
The judge was Sir Matthew Baillie Beg-
bie.   CVic CVicAr CVU **543**

Baptists. Oregon. General Association.
Proceedings of a convention to organize
the Oregon Baptist General Association,
held with the French Prairie Baptist
Church, Sept. 25, 26, and 27, 1857. [Oregon
City, Or., Argus, 1857?] [4] p.
                    OrP OrU **544**

Barbeau, Charles Marius, 1883-
Alaska beckons, illus. by Arthur Price.
Caldwell, Idaho, Caxton, 1947. 343 p.
front., illus.   Many **545**
The downfall of Temlaham. Toronto,
Macmillan, 1928. 253 p. front., plates.
B. C. legend.   Many **546**
Indian days in the Canadian Rockies, illus.
by W. Langdon Kihn. Toronto, Mac-
millan, 1923. 207 p. col. front., col. ports.
                              Many **547**
The Indian speaks, by Marius Barbeau
and Grace Melvin. Caldwell, Idaho, Cax-
ton, 1943. 117 p. illus.   Many **548**
Mountain cloud, illus. by Thoreau Mac-
Donald. Caldwell, Idaho, Caxton, 1944.
300 p. front., illus.   Many **549**
Three songs of the west coast recorded

from singers of Nass River tribes, Canada. London, Harris [n.d.] 14 p. CVicAr 550

Totem poles of the Gitksan, upper Skeena River, British Columbia. Ottawa, Acland, 1929. 275 p. illus., map. (National Museum of Canada. Bulletin no. 61. Anthropological series, no. 12) Many 551

Barber, Charles Fitch.
Our garden and glimpses through its secret gate; photographs by the author. Portland, Or., Binfords & Mort, c1939. 135 p. front. (port.) illus., ports.
Or OrP WaSp WaT WaU 552

Bard, Andreas, 1873-
Giafar, a tradgedy. Walla Walla, Wash., Evening Bulletin, c1907. 110 p. WaU 553

Scattered leaves; "Life, love, light". Kansas City, Mo., Brown-White, 1940, 128 p. Poems. WaWW 554

Bard of the Kuskokwim, see no. 1947.

Barker, B.
The Indian bucanier; or, The trapper's daughter; a romance of Oregon. Boston, F. Gleason, 1847. 50 p. WaU 555

Barker, Bertram.
North of '53; the adventures of a trapper and prospector in the Canadian far north. London, Methuen [1934] ix, 242 p. front., 11 plates. CVicAr CVU 556

Barker, Burt Brown, 1873-
A description of the memorial to Dr. Prince L. Campbell. [n.p., 1933?] 8 p.
OrP OrU 557

See also nos. 6434, 7707.

Barnand, Sir Frank Stillman.
Fifty years a member of the Union Club. [Victoria, B. C., British Colonist, 1931] [36] p. illus., ports. CVicAr 558

Barneby, William Henry, 1843-
Life and labour in the far, far West; being notes of a tour of the western states, British Columbia, Manitoba, and the North-west Territory. London, Cassell, 1884. xvi, 432 p. Many 559

Same. 2d ed. illus., fold map.
CVicAr WaSp 560

Barnes, Albert Henry, 1876-
From Tacoma to Paradise Park. This publication is direct from the original photographs, and not from hand made sketches. While some of the subjects were photographed under select conditions the majority of them were made, one after the other, as the tourist finds them. Tacoma [1905] [28] plates.
WaU 561

Our greatest mountain and Alpine regions of wonder. [n.p., c1911] 69 p. front., illus.
OrP Wa WaS 562

Same. [Chicago, Wells & Co., c1911] 69 p. illus. (part. col.) col. plates. WaU 563

Barnes, B. E., see no. 4827.

Barnes, J. C.
Jobs, currency, a minimum wage. Medford, Or., Mail Tribune, 1934. 190 p.
Or OrU 564

Barnes, Kathleen, see no. 3852.

Barnes, Lemuel Call, 1854-1938.
Intensive powers on the western slopes. Philadelphia, Judson Press [c1922] 53 p. front., plates, maps (1 fold.) tables, diagr. Or OrU WaU 565

Barnes, William Croft, 1858-
Western grazing grounds and forest ranges; a history of the live-stock industry as conducted on the open ranges of the arid West, with particular reference to the use now being made of the ranges in the national forests. Chicago, The Breeder's Gazette, 1913. 390 p. col. front., illus., col. plates. Many 566

See also no. 8469.

Barnett, Grace Treleven, 1899-
Beaded buckskin, by Grace and Olive Barnett; illus. by the authors. London, Oxford Univ. Press [c1940] 149 p. col. front., illus., col. plates. Mont. pioneer story. WaE WaU 567

Grasshopper gold, by Grace and Olive Barnett, illus. by the authors. London, Oxford Univ. Press [c1939] 89 p. col. front., illus. Juvenile story of pioneer days in Mont.
MtHi Or WaS WaSp WaU 568

The mystery in Mission Valley, by Grace and Olive Barnett. New York, Oxford Univ. Press, 1947. 171 p. illus. Juvenile mystery story of Mont. WaSp WaU 569

Barnett, James Duff, 1870-
Operation of the initiative, referendum and recall in Oregon. New York, Macmillan, 1915, xi, 295 p. plate. Many 570

Outline of the government of Oregon, by James D. Barnett, U. G. Dubach, F. G. Franklin, Ray R. Hewitt, F. A. Magruder, Richard C. Spender. [n.p., n.d.] 113 p. OrCS 571

Same. [Corvallis, Or., Oregon State College, 1922] 109 p. OrP 572

Same. 3d ed. [n.p.] 1925. 127 p.
OrCS OrP OrSa 573

Same. by James D. Barnett, U. G. Dubach, Roy R. Hewitt, Roy M. Lockenour, W. P. Riddlesbarger. 7th ed. [Corvallis, Or.] Or. State College, 1932. 131 p.
OrCS OrP 574

Same. Summary of constitution and statutes. 8th ed. [Corvallis, Or.] Or. State College, 1934. 132 p. OrP OrU 575

Same. 9th ed. 1936. 120 p. OrCS 576

Same. 10th ed. 1938. 3, 143 p.
OrCS OrP OrPR 577

Same. 11th ed. 1940. 4, 136 p.
OrCS OrP 578

Barnett, Joel.
A long trip in a prairie schooner. Glendale, Calif., A. H. Clark [1928] 134 p. Trip across plains to Walla Walla in 1859. OrP OrU WaSp WaU 579

Barnett, Olive, see nos. 567-569.

[Barnston, George]
The Oregon Treaty and the Hudson's Bay Company [by George Barnston and John Swanston] [n.p., n.d.] 15 p.
CVicAr 580

Barnum, Francis.
Grammatical fundamentals of the Innuit language as spoken by the Eskimo of the western coast of Alaska. Boston, Ginn, 1901. xxv, 384 p.　WaS WaU **581**

Barnwell, see no. 8765.

Barr, Hymen Max.
The geography of Oregon. Chicago, Rand McNally, c1929. 48 p. illus., map, diagr.
WaS **582**
See also no. 604.

Barrett, John, 1866-1938.
The trans-Pacific opportunity to the businessmen and people of Portland. Bangkok, Siam, 1896. 14 p.　OrP **583**

Barrett-Lennard, Charles Edward.
Travels in British Columbia with the narrative of a yacht voyage round Vancouver's Island. London, Hurst, 1862. 307 p. plate.　Many **584**

Barrette, Paul A., see no. 8203.

Barrington, Daines.
The possibility of approaching the North Pole asserted. New ed. London, Printed for Allman, 1818. xxiv, 258 p. front. (fold. map)　CVicAr **585**
Same, with an appendix containing papers on the same subject and on a northwest passage, by Col. Beaufoy. 2d ed. London, Allman, 1818. 258 p. map.
OrHi WaU **586**
The probability of reaching the North Pole discussed. London, Heydinger, 1775. 90 p.　CVicAr **587**

Barritt, Mrs. Frances Fuller, see no. 10549.

Barrows, Benjamin H.
The Columbia River, "briefest of the mighty streams of earth". Omaha, Union Pacific Railroad [c1910] 94 p. illus., maps.
IdIf OrHi OrP WaPS WaU **588**

Barrows, John Rumsey, 1864-
Ubet [record of experience on the Montana frontier] illus. by R. H. Hall. Caldwell, Idaho, Caxton, 1934. 278 p. illus.
Many **589**

Barrows, William, 1815-1891.
Oregon; the struggle for possession. Boston, Houghton, 1883. 363 p. maps.
Or OrCS WaWW **590**
Same. 1884 [1883]　Many **591**
Same. 2d ed.　CV **592**
Same. 3d ed. 1885.　OrP **593**
Same. 4th ed. 1886.　CVicAr OrSaW **594**
Same. 5th ed. 1888.　CVU IdU MtHi **595**
Same. 6th ed. 1890.　OrSa WaPS **596**
Same. 7th ed. 1892. [c1883]
CV MtBozC **597**
Same. 9th ed. 1896.　MtU WaW **598**
Same. 10th ed. 1898.
IdUSB OrCS WaS WaU **599**
Same. 1901.　OrSa OrU Wa WaS **600**

Barry, John Neilson.
Dedication of tablet commemorating the naming of Mount Hood on Oct. 30, 1792. by Lt. W. R. Broughton, R. N., Aug. 24, 1929, Crown Point, Oregon. [n.p.] 1929. 1 v.　CVicAr **601**

Fort William, 1835, established by Nathaniel G. Wyeth of Boston, Mass., the beginning of American occupancy of Oregon Territory. Portland, Or., Hill Military Academy [1927] [5] p.
CVicAr WaSp **602**
Same. [7] p. illus. Or OrHi OrP WaU **603**
Redskin and pioneer, brave tales of the great Northwest, by John Nielson Barry and Hy Max Barr, illus. with drawings by William Wallace Clarke. New York, Rand McNally [c1932] 244 p. front., illus.　Many **604**

Barstow, Charles Lester, 1867-　ed.
The westward movement. New York, Century, 1912. 231 p. front., illus. (Century readings in U. S. history.)
Or OrAshS OrLgE OrP WaT WaU **605**

Barstow, W. S. and Co., Inc., engineers.
Oregon Electric railway system. New York, 1909. 24 p. illus., maps (Bulletin no. 21)　OrP **606**

Bartlett, Lanier, see no. 729.

Bartlett, Mrs. Laura Belle (Downey) 1853-
Chinook-English songs. [Portland, Or., Kubli-Miller Co., 1914] 39 p.　Many **607**
Dictionary of the intertribal Indian language, commonly called Chinook. Tacoma, Smith-Digby, 1924. 91 p.
CV Or OrAshS OrHi OrP WaU **608**
Students' history of the Northwest and the state of Washington. Tacoma, Smith-Digby [c1922] 232 p. front., illus., ports., maps.　Many **609**

Bartlett, Robert Abram, 1875-
The last voyage of the Karluk, flagship of Vilhjalmar Stefansson's Canadian Arctic expedition of 1813-16. Boston, Small, Maynard [c1916] 329 p. front., plates, ports., maps, plans, facsims.
Many **610**
The log of Bob Bartlett; the true story of forty years of seafaring and exploration. 27 illus. New York, Putnam, 1928. xii, 352 p. front., plates, ports.　Many **611**
See also no. 4587.

Bartley, Deane C., ed.
Cachets of the U. S. frigate Constitution, Pacific coast cruise, 1933-34. [Seattle] c1934. [128] p. illus., ports., facsims.
WaU **612**

Bartley, George.
An outline history of Typographical Union No. 226, Vancouver, B. C., 1887-1938. [Vancouver, B. C., Vancouver Typographical Union] 1938. 64 p. 2 plates.
CVicAr **613**

Barto, Harold E., 1896-
History of the state of Washington, by Harold E. Barto and Catherine Bullard. Boston, Heath [1947] vi, 321 p. illus., ports., maps.　Many **614**
Washington; its history, government, industries, and resources; study guide with exercises, by Harold E. Barto and Catharine Bullard. Portland, Or., Binfords & Mort [1942?] 64 p. illus., maps.
WaU **615**
Same. [1943]　WaE WaS WaT **616**

Barzee, Clark Louis, 1864-
Oregon in the making; 60's to gay 90's, illus. by P. J. Rennings. Salem, Or., Statesman Pub. Co. [c1936] 140 p. front., illus. Many **617**

A song of the Columbia River Highway. [Portland, Or.] c1925. [35] p. illus. Poem.
IdU Or OrHi OrP WaU **618**

Bashford, Herbert, 1871-1928.
At the shrine of song; with introd. by George Wharton James. San Francisco, Whitaker & Ray, 1909. 128 p. front. Poems. Or OrU WaS WaT **619**

Beyond the gates of care. San Francisco, Whitaker & Ray, 1901. 100 p. Poems.
Wa WaS WaU **620**

A man unafraid; the story of John Charles Fremont, by Herbert Bashford and Harr Wagner. San Francisco, Harr Wagner [c1929] 406 p. front., 2 col. mounted illus., 10 plates, 5 ports. Many **621**

Nature stories of the Northwest. San Francisco, Whitaker & Ray, 1898. 149 p. col. front., illus. Many **622**

Songs from Puget Sea. San Francisco, Whitaker & Ray, 1898. 100 p. Poems. Many **623**

Stories of western pioneers. San Francisco, Harr Wagner, c1928. 192 p. front. (port.) ports. Many **624**

The tenting of the Tillicums; a story of boy-life on Puget Sound, illus. by Charles Copeland. New York, Crowell [c1906] 200 p. front., plates.
Wa WaS WaU **625**

The wolves of the sea and other poems. San Francisco, Whitaker & Ray, 1901. 63 p. Wa WaS WaT WaU **626**

Bashford, James Whitford.
The Oregon missions; the story of how the line was run between Canada and the United States. New York, Abingdon Press [c1918] 311 p. front. (map)
Many **627**

Baskine, Gertrude.
Hitch-hiking the Alaska highway. Toronto, Macmillan, 1944. x, 317 p.
CV CVicAr WaS WaU **628**

Bass, M. Florence.
Stories of early times in the great West for young readers. Indianapolis, Bobbs-Merrill, c1927. 203 p. illus.
WaS WaT WaU WaW **629**

Bass, Mrs. Sophie (Frye)
Pig-tail days in old Seattle, illus. by Florenz Clark. Portland, Or., Metropolitan [c1937] 178 p. col. front., illus., plates.
Many **630**

When Seattle was a village, illus. by Florenz Clark. [Seattle, Lowman & Hanford, c1947] 209 p. front., illus., plates.
Or WaE WaS WaT WaU **631**

Bassett, S. P.
Montana Publishing Co.'s statistical almanac for 1869, and year-book of facts showing the material resources of Montana, comp. by S. P. Bassett and Jos. Magee. Helena, Mont., Mont. Pub. Co., 1869. 40 p. MtHi **632**

[Bassett, William Burnet Kinney] 1908-
Dust from a grindstone, by Peter Darien [pseud.] Tacoma, Pacific Book Assn. [c1932] 61 p. front. Poems. Or WaS **633**

Bate, Mark.
History of the Bastion. [n.p., n.d.] [4] p.
CVicAr **634**

Same; issued by Post No. 3, Native Sons of B. C., Nanaimo, B. C. [Nanaimo, B.C., Beattie, n.d.] 11 p. illus. CVicAr **635**

Bates, Charles Francis, 1862-
Custer's Indian battles. Bronxville, N. Y. [c1936] 36 p. front. (map) illus.
MtBozC MtHi WaU **636**

Bates, Mrs. D. B.
Incidents on land and water, or, Four years on the Pacific coast; being a narrative of the burning of the ships Nonantum, Humayoon and Fanchon, together with many startling and interesting adventures on sea and land. Boston, J. French and Co., 1857. 336 p. front., plates. CVicAr **637**

Same. 2d ed. OrP **638**

Same. 5th ed. Boston, Libby, 1858.
CVicAr **639**

Same. 7th ed. CVicAr IdU Wa **640**

Same. 10th ed. 1860, c1857. WaS WaT **641**

Bates, Mrs. Josephine (White)
Bunch-grass stories. Philadelphia, Lippincott, 1895. 268 p. Stories of Or., Wash., Calif. MtHi Or WaU **642**

[Bates, Philip S.]
Residential Portland, 1911; Portland, Oregon, "The Rose City". Portland, Or., Newspaper Syndicate, 1911. [4] p. 93 plates. WaPS **643**

Bates, Russell S.
The man on the dump, his songs and adventures, a booklet of verse, with decorations by the author. A. Y. P. souvenir ed. Seattle, O. Patten & Co. [c1909] [67] p. OrU Wa WaPS WaU **644**

Battelle Memorial Institute, Columbus, Ohio.
Survey report on Washington fuel requirements and supplies to Washington State Department of Conservation and Development, comp. by R. J. Lund and John D. Sullivan. [Columbus, Ohio] 1947. 369 p. maps, tables, diagrs. Loose-leaf.
Wa WaTC **645**

Batterton, J. H.
Facts and acts, what has been done and what is going on in British Columbia; a letter to the people of British Columbia, by one of themselves. Victoria, B. C., British Colonist, 1860. 16 p.
CVicAr **646**

Baudot, Victor.
Au pays des peaux-rouges: six ans aux Montagnes Roucheuses; monographies indiennes. Lille, Societe Saint-Augustin [1911] 238 p. illus. CV **647**

Baumann, John.
Old man Crow's boy; adventures in early Idaho. New York, Morrow, 1948. 278 p. map. IdB WaS WaT WaU **648**

Baxter, Bruce Richard, see no. 3479.

Baxter, Dow Vawter, 1898-
Importance of fungi and defects in handling Alaskan airplane spruce, by Dow V. Baxter and Reed W. Varner. Ann Arbor, Mich., Univ. of Mich. Press, 1942. 34 p. plates. (School of Forestry and Conservation, Circular no. 6) WaU   **649**

Baxter, Mrs. Marion (Babcock)
Bits of verse and prose. Seattle. Lowman & Hanford [c1910] 54 p. front.
Wa WaU   **650**

Bay, Jens Christian, 1871-
A handful of western books, 1st-3d. Cedar Rapids, Iowa, Torch Press, 1935-1937. 3 v. fronts. (ports.)   CVicAr WaU   **651**

Bayles, W. D., see no. 306.

Bayley, Frank S.
Looking ahead after sixty years. Seattle [1936?] 1 v. illus. Sketch of the Y.M.C.A. in Seattle.   WaS   **652**

Bayly, William. see no. 1995.

Beach, Rex Ellingwood, 1877-
The barrier, New York, Burt [c1908] 309 p. front., plate. Klondike story.
Or OrU WaE   **653**
The barrier; a novel. New York, Harper, 1908. 309 p. 4 plates.   Many   **654**
Iron trail; an Alaska romance. New York, Burt [c1913] 390 p. front., 3 plates.
Wa WaE WaS WaT   **655**
Same. New York, Harper, 1913. Many   **656**
Pardners. New York, Burt [c1905] 278 p. front., plates. Alaska and western stories.   MtU Wa WaE WaU   **657**
Same. New York, McClure, 1905.
WaS WaSp WaU   **658**
The silver horde; a novel, illus. by Harvey T. Dunn. New York, Burt, 1909. 389 p. front. Alaskan salmon fisheries.
Or OrU WaE WaPS WaT   **659**
Same. New York, Harper [c1909]
Many   **660**
Same. Yukon ed.   WaU   **661**
The spoilers. New York, Burt [c1905] 313 p. front., 2 plates. Klondike region and Nome.   IdU Or WaE WaT   **662**
Same. New York, Harper, 1906. Many   **663**
Same. [c1907] Yukon ed.   MtU WaU   **664**
Winds of chance. New York, Harper, 1918. 521 p. front., 3 plates. Alaska story.
OrU WaA WaPS WaS WaU WaW   **665**
Same. Yukon ed.   WaU   **666**
The world in his arms. New York, Putnam [c1945] 214 p. Nome story.
Many   **667**

Beach, William Nicholas.
In the shadow of Mount McKinley; foreword by John Burnham; introd. by Robert Sterling Yard; illus. from paintings by Carl Rungius and from photographs by the author. New York, Derrydale Press, 1931. xiii, 289 p. col. front., 34 plates, ports., fold. map.
WaS WaSp WaU   **668**

Beadle, John Hanson, 1840-1897.
Undeveloped west; or, Five years in the territories, being a complete history of that vast region between the Mississippi and the Pacific. Philadelphia, National Pub. Co. [c1873] 823 p. illus., plates.
Many   **669**
Western wilds and the men who redeem them; an authentic narrative, embracing an account of seven years travel and adventure in the far West; wild life in Arizona; perils of the plains; life in the canon and death on the desert; adventures among the red and white savages of the West; the Mountain meadow massacre; the Custer defeat; life and death of Brigham Young, etc. Cincinnati, Jones Bros. & Co. 1878 [c1877] 624 p. front. (fold. map) illus.
IdB Or OrU WaPS WaS WaU   **670**

Beal, Merrill D., 1898-
A history of southeastern Idaho; an intimate narrative of peaceful conquest by empire builders. Caldwell, Idaho, Caxton, 1942. 443 p. front., illus., ports., map.
Many   **671**

Beal, Samuel M.
The Snake River fork country; a brief history of peaceful conquest in the upper Snake River basin. Rexburg, Idaho [Rexburg Journal] 1935. 64 p. front. (port.) illus., map.
IdB IdIf IdU IdUSB WaPS   **672**

Bealby, John Thomas, 1858-
Fruit ranching in British Columbia. London, A. and C. Black, 1909. xi, 196 p. front., plate, map.
CVU Or OrCS WaS WaU   **673**
How to make an orchard in British Columbia; a handbook for beginners. London, A. and C. Black, 1912. 86 p.
WaS WaU   **674**

Beall, Tom.
Legends of the Nez Perces; as told by Tom Beall to R. D. Leeper. [Lewiston, Idaho, Lewiston Tribune, 1931] 23 p.
IdB OrP WaPS   **675**

Beals, Frank Lee, 1881-
Kit Carson, illus. by Jack Merryweather. Chicago, Wheeler Pub. Co. [c1941] 187 p. illus.   Or WaS WaSp WaU   **676**

Beals, Walter Burgess, see no. 9666.

Bean, Harold L., see nos. 7470, 7472.

Bean, Ormand R.
Questions and answers concerning the proposed Portland sewage disposal system. [Portland, Or., 1936] 15 p. OrP   **677**

Bean, Robert S., see no. 211.

Beanlands, Arthur John, 1857-1917.
British Columbia; a problem of colonial development. London, Royal Colonial Institute [n.d.]. 12 p.   CVicAr   **678**

The "Bear," see no. 10215.

Bear River Mining Company, Seattle, Wash.
The '49ers set the pace for '39; an opportunity for you to participate in an exceptional gold mining speculation. Seattle, [1939]. [7] p. illus.   WaPS   **679**

Beaton, Welford.
City that made itself; a literary and pictorial record of the building of Seattle. Seattle, Terminal Pub. Co. [c1914]. 275 p. front. (port.) 21 plates, 8 ports.

CVicAr OrU WaPS WaS WaSp WaU **680**

Beattie, George A., comp.
Vancouver Island, British Columbia, the gem of the Pacific. [n.p.] 1908. [48] p. illus., ports. CVicAr **681**

Beattie, Kim.
Brother, here's a man! The saga of Klondike Boyle, with a foreword by Her late Majesty, Queen Marie of Roumania. New York, Macmillan, 1940. xiv, 309 p. front., plates, ports.
IdB Or OrP WaS WaSp WaU **682**

Beattie, R. Kent, see nos. 8167-8171.

Beattie, Ronald N., see no. 7089.

Beauchamp, Grace.
Beneath the millstone. New York, H. Harrison [c1937]. 63 p. Poems by Seattle author. Wa WaU **683**

Beaufoy, Colonel, see no. 586.

Beauties of Spokane, Wash. Spokane, John W. Graham, c1892. 1 v. WaWW **684**

Beautiful Bellingham; Whatcom and Fairhaven consolidated, December 28, 1903; typical views of this thriving Washington city, one of the chief milling centers of the Pacific coast; the beauties of its surroundings and its substantial streets and architecture. Published for Sherman & Gosswein, Bellingham. Buffalo, W. G. MacFarlane [1903]. [37] p. illus. 1 fold.).
WaPS **685**

Beautiful British Columbia. [Victoria, B. C., Banfield, n.d.]. 16 p. plates. (part col.)
CVicAr **686**

Bebb and Mendel.
The work of Bebb and Mendel, architects. [Seattle] 1906. [30] plates. WaU **687**

Bebenroth, Charlotta M.
Meriwether Lewis, boy explorer, illus, by Edward Caswell. Indianapolis, Bobbs-Merrill [1946]. 182 p. illus. (the childhood of famous Americans series).
Or OrP WaS WaSp WaU **688**

Bechdolt, Frederick Ritchie, 1874-
Giants of the old West. New York, Century [c1930] 245 p. front., illus., plates, ports., maps, plan. Many **689**

The hard rock man. New York, Moffat, 1910. 224 p. Western construction camp story. Wa WaU **690**

When the West was young. New York, Century, 1922. 309 p. front. Many **691**

Beck, Norman Edward.
A souvenir of the Duke of Connaught's Own, the 158th (overseas) Battalion. Vancouver, B. C., 1916. 20 p. illus., plates. History of early B.C. militia. CVicAr **692**

Becker, Mrs. May (Lamberton) 1873- ed.
Golden tales of the far West, selected with an introd. by May Lamberton Becker; decorations by Lois Lenski. New York, Dodd, 1935. 304 p. Many **693**

Beckwourth, James P., 1798-1867.
Life and adventures of James P. Beckwourth, mountaineer, scout, pioneer, and chief of the Crow Nation of Indians, written from his own dictation, by T. D.

Bonner. London, Unwin, 1856. 537 p. plates, ports. IdB **694**

Same. New York, Harper, 1856.
CVicAr MtBozC OrHi WaSp **695**

Same. 1858. 440 p. MtU **696**

Same. New ed., ed. with preface by Charles G. Leland ("Hans Breitman") London, Unwin, 1892. 440 p. front., plates, ports. (The adventure series)
CVicAr IdU MtHi WaPS WaS **697**

Same. New York, Knopf, 1931. xl, 405 p. front. (port.) (Americana deserta)
OrP OrPR OrU WaS WaSp WaU **698**

Same. Preface by Harry Carr. Los Angeles, U. S. Library Assn., c1932. 87 p. port. MtU Or WaS **699**

Beebe, Mrs. Iola.
True life story of Swiftwater Bill Gates, by his mother-in-law. [n.p., c1908]. 139 p. illus., ports. CVicAr CVU Or Wa WaS **700**

Same. [Seattle, Lumberman's Printing Co., c1915]. WaSp WaU **701**

Beebe, Lucius, see no. 4507.

Beecham, R. K.
Sacajawea and other poems; souvenir ed., Lewis and Clark Centennial Fair, Portland, Oregon, 1905. [Everett, Wash., Ray, 1905?] 24 p. plates.
OrHi WaPS WaU **702**

Beechey, Frederick William, 1796-1856.
Narrative of a voyage to the Pacific and Beering's Strait, to co-operate with the polar expeditions; performed in His Majesty's ship Blossom in the years 1825, 26, 27, 28. London, Colburn, 1831. 2 v. ports., plate, maps. Many **703**

Same. Octavo ed. WaU **704**

Same. Philadelphia, Carey, 1832. 493 p.
OrP **705**

Reise nach dem Stillen Ocean und der Beeringstrasze zur Mitwirkung bei den Polarexpeditionen, ausgefuhrt in Konigl Engl. Schiffe Blossom unter dem Commando des Capitain F. W. Beechey in den Jahren 1825, 26, 27, und 28; hrsg. im Auftrage der Lords-Commissare der Admiralitat, aus dem Englischen ubersetzt. Weimar, Verlage des Landes-industrie, 1832, 2 v. fold. plate, map, table. (Neue Bibliothek der wichtigsten Reisebeschreibunger der Erd- und Volkerkunde, Bd. 59, 61) WaU **706**

A voyage of discovery towards the North Pole performed in His Majesty's ships Dorothea and Trent, under the command of Captain David Buchan, R. N., 1818; to which is added a summary of all the early attempts to reach the Pacific by way of the Pole. London, Bentley, 1843. 351 p. front., plate, chart (in pocket). CVicAr WaU **707**

The zoology of Captain Beechey's voyage, comp. from the collections and notes made by Captain Beechey, the officers and naturalist of the expedition during a voyage to the Pacific and Behring's Straits, performed in His Majesty's ship Blossom in the years 1825, 26, 27, and 28, **illus. with plates by Sowerby.** London, Bohn, 1839. xii, 180 p. 44 col. plates, 3 maps (part fold.) CVicAr **708**

Beer, Frank M., see no. 1888.

Beeson, John, b. 1803.

Plea for the Indians, with facts and features of the late war in Oregon. New York, 1857. 143 p.

OrHi OrP OrU WaWW **709**

Same. 3d ed. 1858.

CVicAr Or WaS WaSp WaU **710**

Begg, Alexander, 1825-1905.

The great Canadian North West; its past history, present condition and glorious prospects. Montreal, Lovell, 1881. 135 p.

CVicAr MtU WaU **711**

History of British Columbia from its earliest discovery to the present time. Toronto, Briggs, 1894. 568 p. illus., port., map. Many **712**

Same. London, Sampson, c1894. WaW **713**

A sketch of the successful missionary work of William Duncan amongst the Indian tribes in northern British Columbia from 1858 to 1901. Victoria, B. C., 1901. 32 p. front. CV CVicAr WaU **714**

Begg, Alexander, 1839-1897.

"Dot it down;" a story of life in the Northwest. Toronto, Hunter, 1871. 381 p.

CVicAr WaU WaWW **715**

History of the Northwest. Toronto, Hunter, 1894-1895. 3 v. 33 ports. Many **716**

Practical hand-book and guide to Manitoba and the Northwest. Toronto, Belford Bros., 1877. 110 p. CVicAr CVU **717**

Seventeen years in the Canadian Northwest. [London, Spottiswoode, 1884]. 35 p. CVicAr **718**

See also no. 6371.

Beginnings, progress and achievement in the medical work of King County, Washington. [Seattle, Peters Pub. Co., 1930?] 145 p. front., illus. WaT WaU **719**

Behre, C. H., Jr., see no. 178.

The Behring Sea arbitration; letters to the Times by its special correspondent; together with the award. London, Clowes, 1893. 87 p. CVicAr **720**

Beim, Jerrold, see no. 721.

Beim, Lorraine (Levey) 1909-

The little igloo, by Lorraine and Jerrold Beim, pictures by Howard Simon. New York, Harcourt [1941]. [72] p. col. illus.

Or OrP Wa WaS WaSp WaU **721**

Beistel, Matthew J.

Northwest Sanitarium; a health institution having all modern equipment for the treatment of acute and chronic medical and surgical cases, Pullman, Washington. [Pullman, Wash., 1919?] [8] p. illus.

WaPS **722**

Belding, Lyman, 1829-1917.

Land birds of the Pacific district. San Francisco, Academy of Sciences, 1890. 274 p. (Occasional papers 2)

OrCS OrP WaS **723**

Belding, Mary Ellen (Dowell) 1869-

Mollie Belding's memory book. Long Beach, Calif. [Ward Ritchie press] 1945. xi, 105 p. illlus., ports. OrP **724**

Belisle, David W.

The American family Robinson; or, The adventures of a family lost in the great desert of the West. Philadelphia, Porter & Coates [1853]. 360 p. front.

Or OrP WaU **725**

Same. 1869. plates. CVicAr **726**

Bell, Archie, 1877-

Sunset Canada, British Columbia and beyond; an account of its settlement, its progress from the early days to the present, including a review of the Hudson's Bay Company, its amazing variety of climate, its charm of landscape, its unique cities and attractive towns and their industries, a survey of the different peoples to be found there, including the Japanese and Doukobors, and analysis of what it offers in opportunity to the home seeker, the agriculturist, the business man, the sportsman and the traveller, with a map and fifty-six plates, of which eight are in colour. Boston, Page, 1918. xii, 320 p. col. front., plates (part col.) ports., fold. col. map. Many **727**

Same. [1925] ("See America first" series)

WaU **728**

Bell, Augustus V., see no. 9666.

Bell, Edward, see no. 6665.

Bell, Horace, 1830-1918.

On the old west coast; being further reminiscences of a ranger, ed. by Lanier Bartlett. New York, Morrow, 1930. xiv, 336 p. front., illus., plates, ports. facsims.

Many **729**

Bell, James C., see no. 11046.

Bell, Margaret Elizabeth, 1898-

Danger on Old Baldy, illus. by Hamilton Greene. New York, Morrow, 1944 [i.e. 1945]. 224 p. col. front., illus.

Or WaS WaSp WaU **730**

Enemies in Icy Strait, illus. by George M. Richards. New York, Morrow, 1945. 206 p. col front., illus., map.

Or OrP WaS WaU **731**

The pirates of Icy Strait, illus. by Harvey Kidder. New York, Morrow, 1943. 224 p. illus. Or OrP Wa WaS WaSp WaT **732**

Same. Victory ed. [1944]. WaU **733**

Watch for a tall white sail; a novel, front. by Louis Darling. New York, Morrow, 1948. 222 p. col. front.

Or OrP WaS WaT WaU **734**

Bell, Marjorie, see no. 7228.

Bell, Robert N., 1864-

Mine and ore resources of Lemhi County, Idaho, written by Robert N. Bell, with additional later information by the mining companies. Salmon, Idaho, Businessmen's Assn. [1917?]. 32 p. illus. IdB **735**

Bell, Salomon, see no. 9629.

Bell, William Hemphill, 1834-1906.

The quiddities of an Alaskan trip. Portland, Or., C. A. Steel & Co., 1873. [67] p. illus. OrP WaS WaSp WaU **736**

Bell, William S.

Old Fort Benton, what it was and how it came to be. Helena, Mont., 1909. 31 p.

CVicAr MtHi MtU OrHi WaSp WaU **737**

Bellamy, William, see no. 10349.

Bellemin, Frank James.
Beyond the furrow's end. [Amity, Or., Standard Press, c1925] [20] p. Oregon poet and author. Or **738**

Our present day poets, their lives and works. v. 1. [Amity, Or., Standard Press, c1926]. 136 p. illus., ports. Or WaU **739**

Same. v. 2. 1927. Or OrSaW **740**

Road dust and roses. [Amity, Or., Standard Press, c1925]. [20] p. front. Or **741**

Robert Burns, ploughboy-poet-gentleman. [Amity, Or., Standard Press, 1925?] [4] p. Or **742**

Tales by candlelight. [Amity, Or., Standard Press, c1925]. [15] p. Poems.
Or OrCS OrP **743**

Bellessort, Andre, 1866-1942.
La Perouse, avec un portrait et une carte. Paris, Plon-Nourrit et cie. [c1926]. 126 p. front. (port.) fold. map. (Nobles vies, grandes oeuvres 8). WaU **744**

Bellinger, C. B. see no. 6152.

Bellingham Bay Railway and Navigation Co.
Articles of incorporation; together with the by-laws, and so much of the acts of Congress as affects the same; names of trustees, officers, etc., printed for the use of the company, but not published. Olympia, Wash., Partisan Steam Printing House, 1886. 20 p. map. WaS **745**

Bellingham Herald.
An album with a thousand thrills; photo and word pictures of beautiful spots, resources and industries of northwestern Washington. [Bellingham, Wash.] 1922. 96 p. illus., ports., map.
WaS WaU **746**

Bellot, Joseph Rene, 1826-1853.
Journal d'un voyage aux polaires, execute a la recherche de Sir John Franklin, en 1851 et 1852, precede d'une notice sur la vie et les travaux de l'auteur, par M. Julien Lemer. Paris, Perrotin, 1854. lvi, 414 p. front. (port.) fold. map. CVicAr **747**

Memoirs; with his Journal of a voyage in the polar seas. London, Hurst, 1855. 2 v. front. (port.) CVicAr **748**

Bemis, Katharine Isabel, see no. 4594.

Bench and Bar of Oregon.
Program and proceedings in honor of the 75th birthday of Hon. Thomas A. McBride, Justice of the Supreme Court of Oregon on the 15th day of November, 1922. [Portland, Or., 1922.]. 24 p. OrU **749**

Resolutions and memorial addresses on the life and character of Cyrus A. Dolph, delivered at a meeting of the Bench and Bar, held at the County Court House in the city of Portland, Oregon, Saturday, July 11, 1914. [Portland, Or., Beach-Thomas Co., 1914?] 55 p. front. (port.).
OrHi OrP OrPR OrUL WaU **750**

Bend, Palmer, see no. 8444.

Bend Bulletin.
Deschutes County fair edition. Bend, Or., 1945. 1 v. illus. (v. 54, no. 90, Sept. 20, 1945). **751**

Benham, Daniel.
Sketches of the life of Jan August Miert, acting interpreter of the Esquimaux language to the Arctic expedition on board H.M.S. "Investigator," Captain M'Clure 1850, 1851, 1852, 1853. London, Mallalieu, 1854. 34 p. front. (port.) CVicAr **752**

Benjamin, Israel Joseph, 1818-1864.
Reise in den Nordwestgegenden Nord-Amerika's. Hanover, Benjamin II, 1862. 69 p. OrP WaU **753**

Same. viii, 132 p. CVU **754**

Benjaminoff, John, see no. 4934.

Bennett, Edward H.
Greater Portland plan, ed. by M. N. Dana. Portland, Or., 1912. 45 p.
OrHi OrP OrU WaS WaW **755**

Bennett, Emerson, 1822-1905.
Forest and prairie; or, Life on the frontier. Philadelphia, J. W. Bradley, 1860. 411 p. front., plates. WaU **756**

Lena Leoti; or, Adventures in the far West; a sequel to "Prairie flower." Cincinnati, James, c1850. 110 p.
Or OrHi OrU **757**

"Prairie flower" written by Sidney Walter Moss, no. 7107.
Same. Philadelphia, T. B. Peterson & Bros. c1889. 235 p. OrP **758**

Bennett, Jean Frances, see no. 2528.

Bennett, Richard, 1899-
Mick and Mack and Mary Jane. Garden City, N. Y., Doubleday [1948]. 42 p. illus. (Junior books). Northwest loggers and a mouse. WaU **759**

Mister Ole. New York, Doubleday, 1940. 60 p. col. front., illus. (part col.) col. plate. Juvenile story of Wash.
Or OrP Wa WaS WaSp WaU **760**

Puget Sound; twelve woodcuts, with a foreword by Edith H. Walton. Seattle, Univ. of Wash. Book Store, 1931. [20] p. plates. (Chapbooks, no. 47) Many **761**

Skookum and Sandy. New York, Junior Literary Guild and Doubleday, 1936. [71] p. illus. Juvenile story of Northwest.
IdIf WaT **762**

Same. New York, Doubleday, 1942 [c1935]. [67] p. front., illus. Wa **763**

Bennett, William.
Builders of British Columbia, with a foreword by Malcolm Bruce. [Vancouver, B. C., Broadway Printers, 1937] 159 p. illus., port. CV WaS WaT WaU **764**

Benoist, Charles.
Les Francais et la Nord-Ouest Canadien. Bar-le-Duc, Imprimerie de l'oeuvre de Saint Paul, 1895. 128 p. CVicAr **765**

Benson, Gilbert Thereon, d. 1928.
The trees and shrubs of Western Oregon. Stanford Univ., Calif., Stanford Univ. Press, 1930. 170 p. front. (map) (Contributions from the Dudley Herbarium, v. 2)
MtBozC Or OrP OrU WaS WaT **766**

Benson, Henry Kreitzer, 1877-
Post-war development possibilities in Clallam County, Olympic Peninsula, state of Washington [n.p., 1945?]. 16 p. WaS **767**

The pulp and paper industry of the Pacific Northwest; proceedings of the Pulp and Paper Conference held at the University of Washington, Oct. 26, 1928. Seattle, Univ. of Wash., 1929. 89 p. illus., diagrs. (Engineering Experiment Station series, report no. 1)
OrP WaE WaS WaT WaU WaW **768**

Benson, Mary Lou, see no. 9756.

Benteen, Frederick William, 1834-1898.
The Custer fight; Capt. Benteen's story of the battle of the Little Big Horn, June 25-26, 1876; with comments on the Rosebud fight of June 17, 1876, by Robert E. Strahorn, arranged by E. A. Brininstool. Hollywood, Calif., E. A. Brininstool, 1933. 36 p. front. (port.) port. MtHi MtU **769**
Same. 1940. 30 p. 2d printing.   CVU **770**

Bentley, William R.
Bentley's hand-book of the Pacific coast, containing a complete list of the prominent seaside and mountain resorts, mineral springs, lakes, mountains, valleys, forests, and other places and objects of interest on the Pacific coast. Oakland, Calif., Pacific Press Pub. House, 1884. 143 p. illus., plates.
WaU **771**

Benton, Thomas Hart, 1782-1858.
Selections of editorial articles from the St. Louis Enquirer, on the subject of Oregon and Texas, as originally published in that paper in the years 1818-1819; and written by the Hon. Thomas H. Benton, to which is annexed his speech in the Senate of the United States, in March, 1825, on the bill for the occupation of the Columbia River. St. Louis, Missourian Office, 1844. 45 p.
WaS **772**
Thrilling sketch of the life of Col. J. C. Fremont (U. S. Army) with an account of his expedition to Oregon and California, across the Rocky Mountains and discovery of the great gold mines. [London] Field [1850] 21 p.   **773**

Benton County Citizen's League.
Benton County, Oregon. Corvallis, Or. [n.d.] 58 p. illus.   OrCS OrHi **774**
Same. Comp. by C. E. Woodson. [1904?]
Or **775**
Same. [n.p.] 1904. 10 p.
OrCS OrP OrU WaU **776**

[Beresford, William] fl. 1788.
Voyage autour du monde et principalement a la cote nord-ouest de l'Amerique fait en 1785, 1786, 1787, et 1788 a bord du King-George et de la Queen-Charlotte, par les capitaines Portlock et Dixon, tr. de l'Anglois par M. Lebas. Paris, Maradan, 1789. 499, 46 p. 17 plates (part fold.) 5 fold. maps, tables, music.
CVicAr **777**
Same. 2 v.   OrP WaU **778**
A voyage round the world; but more particularly to the north-west coast of America; performed in 1785, 1786, 1787, and 1788, in the King George and Queen Charlotte, Captains Portlock and Dixon, by Captain George Dixon. London, G.

Goulding, 1789. xxix, 360 p. 17 plates (7 col., 2 fold.) 5 fold. maps, tables, music.   Many **779**
Same. 2d ed.
CVicAr MtHi OrHi WaU **780**

Berge, Wendell, 1903-
Economic freedom for the West. Lincoln, Neb., Univ. of Neb. Press, 1946. xiv, 168 p. illus., maps.   Many **781**

Bergen, Joseph Young, 1851-1917.
Bergen's botany, key and flora, Pacific coast ed., prepared by Alice Eastwood. Boston, Ginn [c1901] 199 p. illus.
CVicAr Or OrCS OrP WaPS **782**

Bergendahl, Erling.
Alaskadage, en tre tusen mils faerd gjennem "The top of the world". Oslo, Some & Co.'s Forlag, 1926. 211 p. illus., facsims.   WaU **783**

Bergman, Hans.
British Columbia och dess svenska innebyggare. Victoria, B. C., 1923. 314 p. illus., 5 col. plates, ports.
CVicAr Wa WaU **784**
History of Scandinavians in Tacoma and Pierce County, with brief history of Tacoma and early settlement. Tacoma, 1926. 200 p. illus., ports.   Many **785**

Bering Sea Commercial Company.
Alaska whaling as an investment under modern methods. [Chicago, n.d.] 23 p. front.   WaU **786**

Bering Sea Company.
Report of the Board of Directors to the stockholders of the Bering Sea Company, Oct. 16, 1913. [New York? 1913] 8 p.   WaU **787**

[Berkh, Vasilii Nikolaevich] 1781-1824.
Khronologicheskaia istoriia otkrytiia Aleutskikh ostrovov ili podvigi ross-iiakago kupechestva. S prisovokupleniem istorich veskago izviestiia o miekhovoi torgovlie. Sanktpeterburg, N. Grech, 1823. iii, 169 p. fold. map, fold. tables.
WaU **788**

Berlin. Staatliche Museen. Ethnologische Abteilung.
The north-west coast of America, being results of recent ethnological researches, from the collections of the Royal museums at Berlin, pub. by the directors of the Ethnological Dept., trans. from the German. New York, Dodd [1882?]. 12 p. 13 plates.
CVicAr OrHi WaSp WaU **789**

Bernhardt, Joshua, 1893-
The Alaskan Engineering Commission; its history, activities and organization. New York, Appleton, 1922. xii, 124 p. double map. (Institute for Government Research. Service monographs of the U. S. government, no. 4).   Many **790**

Berreman, Joel Van Meter, 1900-
Tribal distribution in Oregon. Menasha, Wis., American Anthropological Assn. [1937]. 67 p. maps (Memoirs, no. 47)
Many **791**

Berry, see nos. 5861, 5862.

Berry, James Berthold, 1880-
Western forest trees; a guide to the identification of trees and woods to accompany Farm Woodlands; a handbook
for students, teachers, farmers, and
woodsmen. Yonkers-on-Hudson, N. Y.,
World Book Co., 1924. xii, 212 p. front.,
illus. (New world agriculture series).
Many **792**

Same. 1926. WaT **793**

Berthold, Victor Maximilian, 1856-1932.
The pioneer steamer California, 1848-1849.
Boston, Houghton, 1932. 106 p. plates,
facsims. CVicAr WaS **794**

Betiero, Thomas Jasper.
Nedoure, priestess of the Magi. Rev. ed.
An historical romance of white and
black magic; a story that reveals wis-
dom of the ancient past. Seattle, W. F.
Wohlstein & Co. [c1916]. 247 p.
WaS WaU **795**

Beurhaus, George Henry, 1890-
Know your real estate. San Francisco,
c1946. 196 p. diagrs., forms. Many **796**

Who handles your real estate? Seattle,
[Metropolitan, 1944]. 113 p.
CV Wa WaS WaSp WaT **797**

Same. 3d ed. rev. [1945]. xiii, 154 p.
diagrs., forms. Wa WaS WaT WaU **798**

Same. 4th ed. rev. Seattle. [Mercury Press]
c1947. 182 p. illus., diagrs., forms.
WaE WaS WaSp **799**

Beymer, R. K., see no. 323.

Bibb, Thomas William.
History of early common school education
in Washington. Seattle, Univ. of Wash.
Press, 1929.vi, 154 p. (Publication in
social sciences, v. 6, no. 1) Many **800**

Bible. Old Testament. Genesis.
The lost book of Genesis, trans. by Joseph
Smith; ed. with an introd. and finale by
Linden Dalberg. [Kent, Wash.] J. Vic-
tor [c1945]. 100 p. WaU **801**

— — — — — — Selections. Haida.
Old Testament stories in the Haida lang-
age, by Rev. C. Harrison. London, Society for Promoting Christian Knowledge,
1893. 92 p. CVicAr WaU **802**

— — — New Testament. Acts. Haida.
The Acts of the Apostles, in Haida. London, British and Foreign Bible Society, 1898. 145 p. CVicAr **803**

— — — — — — John. Haida.
The Gospel according to Saint John, in
Haida. London, British and Foreign
Bible Society, 1899. 116 p. CVicAr **804**

— — — — — — — — Nez Perces.
Johnnim taaiskt; Gospel according to
John, trans. into the Nez Perces language by Rev. Geo. Ainslie. Philadelphia, Presbyterian Board of Pub., 1876.
116 p. WaPS WaU **805**

Uyitpa Johnnim timas; first epistle general of John, trans. into the Nez Perces
language by Rev. Geo. Ainslie. Philadelphia, Presbyterian Board of Pub.,
1876. 17 p. WaU **806**

— — — — — — — — Tsimshian.
Am da malshk ga na Damsh, St. John;

ligi the Gospel according to St. John,
trans. into Zimshian. London, Society
for Promoting Christian Knowledge,
1889. 47 p. WaU **807**

— — — — — — Luke. Haida.
The Gospel according to St. Luke, in
Haida. London, British and Foreign
Bible Society, 1899. 156 p. CVicAr **808**

— — — — — — — — Tsimshian.
Am da malshk ga na Damsh, St. Luke;
ligi the Gospel according to St. Luke,
trans. into Zimshian. London, Society
for Promoting Christian Knowledge
[1889?].63 p. CVicAr CVU WaU **809**

— — — — — — Mark. Chinook jargon.
St. Mark's kloosh yiem, kopa nesika
Saviour Jesus Christ. London, British
and Foreign Bible Society, 1912. 111 p.
CV CVicAr **810**

— — — — — — — — Tsimshian.
Am da malshk ga na Damsh, St. Mark;
ligi the Gospel according to St. Mark,
trans. into Zimshian. London, Society
for Promoting Christian Knowledge
[1889?]. 40 p. WaU **811**

— — — — — — Matthew. Aleut.
Gospoda nashego iisusa Khrista evangelie
napisannoe apostolom Matfeem. C
Russkago iazyka na Aleutsko - Lis'
evskii perevel cviashchennik doann
Veniaminov 1928 goda, i v 1836 godu
ispravil; a sviashchennik Iakov Nets-
vietov, razsmatrivaia ego okonchatel'no,
svoimi poiasneniiami sdielal poniatnym i
dlia Atkhintsev imieiushchikh svoe
nariechie. Sanktpeterburg, Sinodal'naia
tipografiia, 1896. xiv [261] p. Aleut and
Russian in parallel columns. WaU **812**

— — — — — — Haida.
Saint Matthew gie giatlan las St. Matthew, Haida, trans. by Charles Harrison.
London, British and Foreign Bible Society, 1891. 143 p. CVicAr **813**

— — — — — — — — Nez Perces.
Matthewnim taaiskt, trans, by Rev. H. H.
Spalding. Clear Water, Idaho, Spalding
Mission Press, 1845. 81 p. OrHi **814**

Same. Photostat. WaU **815**

Same. New York, American Bible Society.
1871. 130 p.
CVicAr OrHi OrP OrU WaPS WaU **816**

— — — — — — — — Quagutl.
The Gospel according to St. Matthew,
trans. into the Qa-gutl (or Quoquds language) by the Rev. A. J. Hall. London, British and Foreign Bible Society,
1882. 121 p. CVicAr **817**

— — — — — — — — — Tsimshian.
Am da malshk ga na Damsh. St. Mat-
thew; ligi the Gospel according to St.
Matthew, trans. into Tsimshian. Lon-
don, Society for Promoting Christian
Knowledge [1889?] 59 p. CVU WAU **818**

— — — Selections. Blackfoot.
Readings from the Holy Scriptures in the
language of the Blackfoot Indians,
trans. by the Rev. J. W. Tims. London,
Society for Promoting Christian Knowledge, 1890. 47 p. WaSp **819**

Biddle, Henry Jonathan, 1862-1928.
Beacon Rock on the Columbia; legends and traditions of a famous landmark. [n.p., n.d.] 11 p. illus.   OrP **820**
Wishram. Eugene, Or., Koke-Chapman [n. d.] 18 p. illus., maps.   OrHi OrP **821**
Bieber, Ralph P., see no. 531.
Bigelow, John, 1817-1911.
Memoir of the life and public services of John Charles Fremont. New York, Derby, 1856. 480 p. plates, port., table.
Many **822**
Bighead, Kate, see no. 6531.
Bilby, Julian W.
Nanook of the North. New York, Dodd, 1926. 261 p.   Or OrP Wa WaS **823**
Bilir, Kim, see nos. 9017-9019.
Bill, Buffalo, see no. 6488.
Bill, Platinum, see no. 9620.
Billecocq, J. B. L. J., see nos. 6074, 6075, 6688, 6689.
The Billings Gazette.
The land of shining mountains. Billings, Mont. [1936?] [36] p. illus., map, (v. 48, no. 83)   MtBozC **824**
The land of shining mountains, scenic grandeur supplement of the Billings Gazette, Jan. 28, 1936. Billings, Mont., 1936. [64] p. illus., map.   WaPS **825**
Billingsley, P., see no. 178.
Bindloss, Harold, 1866-
Alton of Somasco; a romance of the great Northwest. New York, Stokes, c1905. vii, 355 p. front., 5 plates.   WaT **826**
The boy ranchers of Puget Sound, with eight illus. by Edwin Megargee. New York, Stokes [1910]. 326 p. front., plates.
Or WaU **827**
Frontiersman. New York, Burt, c1929. 332 p.   WaW **828**
Northwest! New York, Stokes [1922]. 309 p.   Or OrCS OrP **829**
Valley gold. New York, Grosset, c1934. 355 p.   WaT **830**
Same. Stokes.   Or WaW **831**
A wide dominion. London, Unwin, 1899. 239 p. (Overseas library, 7)   CVU **832**
[Binford, Thomas P.] 1900-
Paul Bunyan in the army, by John Rogers Inkslinger [pseud.] as told to Bethene Miller) illus. by Tom O'Brien. Portland, Or., Binfords & Mort [1942]. [64] p. col. illus.   MtU WaSp WaU **833**
Bingham, Joseph Walter, 1878-
Report on the international law of Pacific coastal fisheries. Stanford Univ., Calif., Stanford Univ. Press. c1938. 75 p.   Many **834**
Binheim, Max, see no. 11155.
Binns, Archie, 1899-
Backwater voyage, drawings by Edward A. Wilson. New York, Reynal [c1936]. 67 p. col. front., illus., col. plates. Washington author.   Wa **835**
The land is bright. New York, Scribner, 1939. 349 p.   Many **836**
The laurels are cut down. New York, Literary Guild [c1937]. 332 p.
IdUSB OrCS OrHi WaE WaW **837**

Same. Reynal.   Many **838**
Lightship. New York, Reynal, c1934. 345 p.   Many **839**
Same. New York, Modern Age Books [1938, c1934]. 243 p.   WaU **840**
Mighty mountain. New York, Scribner, 1940. 440 p.   Many **841**
Northwest gateway; the story of the port of Seattle. Garden City, N. Y., Doubleday, 1941. ix, 313 p. plates, port.
Many **842**
Same. 1945 [c1941].   IdU WaPS **843**
The roaring land. New York, McBride [1942]. 284 p. front. plates.   Many **844**
The timber beast. New York, Scribner, 1944. 345 p.   Many **845**
You rolling river. New York, Scribner, 1947. 342 p.   Many **846**
See also no. 8022.
Bird, Annie Laurie.
Boise, the peace valley. Caldwell, Idaho, Caxton, 1934. 408 p. illus.   Many **847**
Bird, I. L., see no. 857.
Birkeland, Knut Bergesen, 1857- 1925.
The whalers of Akutan; an account of modern whaling in the Aleutian Islands. New Haven, Yale Univ. Press, 1926. 171 p. front., plates, ports.
OrP WaS WaTC WaU **848**
Birket-Smith, Kaj, 1893-
The Eyak Indians of the Copper River delta, Alaska, by Kaj Birket-Smith and Frederica De Laguna. Kobenhavn, Levin, 1938. 591 p. illus., ports., maps.   WaS **849**
Birney, Hoffman, 1891-
Vigilantes, a chronicle of the rise and fall of the Plummer gang of outlaws in and about Virginia City, Montana, in the early 60's; drawings by Charles Hargens. Philadelphia, Penn [c1929]. 346 p. front., illus., plates, ports., map. facsim.   Many **850**
Bisbee, William H., see no. 7745.
Bischoff, William Norbert.
The Jesuits in old Oregon, 1840-1940. Caldwell, Idaho, Caxton, 1945. xvii, 258 p. maps.   Many **851**
Bishop, Ernest Franklin.
The timber wolf of the Yukon. [Chicago, Digest Press, c1925] xiv, 278 p. col. front., port.   WaU **852**
Bishop, Mrs. Isabella (Bird) 1831-1904.
A lady's life in the Rocky Mountains. London, Murray, c1880. xii, 296 p. front., plates.   CVicAr CVU IdTf **853**
Same. 3d ed. New York, Putnam, 1881.
CVicAr MtU WaU WaW **854**
Same. 4th ed. London, Murray, 1881.
CVicAr OrP **855**
Same. 7th ed. 1910. CVicAr WaSp WaU **856**
Voyage d'une femme aux Montagnes Rocheuses, tr. de l'anglais de I. L. Bird par E. Martineau des Chesnez. Paris, E. Plon, 1888. 284 p.   WaU **857**
Bishop, Thomas G.
An appeal to the government to fulfill sacred promises made 61 years ago [review of treaty agreements with In-

dians of Washington] Tacoma [1915].
42 p. front.   WaT 858

[Bissett, Clark Prescott] 1875-1932.
John T. Condon. [Seattle, Montgomery
Printing Co., 1926] [9] p. port. Or 859
Same. [13] p.   WaU 860

Bjarke, Nils.
The Naches Pass highway to be built
over the ancient Klickitat trail, the
Naches Pass Military Road of 1853.
Fern Hill, Tacoma, 1945. [22?] p. 2 fold.
maps.   WaS WaSp WaT 861
Naches Pass trail, 1853. Tacoma, Fern
Hill Historical Society, 1942. 21 p. illus.
                    WaS WaT WaU 862

Black, Jesse R.
History of Custer County, Idaho. [Challis,
Idaho, Challis Messenger, n.d.] 21 p.
Essay in Idaho history, written by
High School boy from files of Challis
Messenger verified by Thomas Jose, pio-
neer of Challis, Idaho.   IdIf 863

Black, Martha Louise (Munger) Purdy, 1886-
My seventy years as told to Elizabeth
Bailey Price. London, Nelson [1938]
317 p. front., 10 plates, 5 ports., facsim.
Yukon life.   CV CVic CVicAr WaS 864
Same. [1939].   CVU 865
Yukon wild flowers, with 100 illus. from
original photographs by Hon. George
Black. Vancouver, B. C., Price, Tem-
pleton Syndicate [1940?] 95 p. illus.
                                CVU 866

Black Carbon Coal Company, Seattle, Wash.
Coal is king. Seattle, c1925. 49 p. front.,
illus.   WaTC 867

Blacklock Alaska, see no. 5877.

Blackmore, E. H.
Check-list of the macrolepidoptera of
British Columbia (butterflies and moths).
Victoria, B. C., Banfield, 1927. 46 p.
(Provincial Museum of Natural History)
                                 CV 868

Blaikie, William Garden, 1820-1899.
Summer suns in the far West; a holiday
trip to the Pacific slope. London, Nelson, 1890. 160 p. front.
            CVicAr CVU WaPS WaU 869

Blaine Journal.
Conquering the wilderness. Blaine, Wash.,
1906. [36] p. illus., ports. (v. 21, no. 46,
Mar. 9, 1906)   WaU 870

Blair, Walter, 1900-
Horse sense in American humor from
Benjamin Franklin to Ogden Nash.
Chicago, Univ. of Chicago Press [1942]
xv, 341 p. front., illus., ports. Spokane
author.   Many 871
Tall tale America, a legendary history of
our humorous heroes, illus. by Sgt.
Glen Rounds. New York, Coward-
McCann, Inc. [1944] ix, 262 p. illus.
                               Many 872

Blake, Clinton Frederick.
Poems of old Champoeg. Philadelphia,
Dorrance [c1925] 76 p.   Many 873

Blake, E. Vale, see no. 10383.

Blanchard, John.
Caravans to the Northwest, under the direction of the Northwest Regional Coun-

cil, Portland, Oregon. Boston, Houghton
[c1940]. 123 p. illus., maps, diagrs., facsims.   Many 874

Blanchet, Francis Norbert, 1795-1883.
A comprehensive, explanatory, correct pro-
nouncing dictionary and jargon vocabu-
lary; to which is added numerous con-
versations enabling any person to speak
the Chinook jargon. 2d ed. Portland, O.
T., S. J. McCormick, 1853, 39 p. Anon.
Authority for author's name: Pilling,
J. C. Bibliography of Chinookan lang-
uages.   OrHi 875
Same. 7th ed. Portland, Or., F. L. Mc-
cormick, 1879. 26 p.   IdU 876
See also no. 2394.
Historical notes and reminiscences of early
times in Oregon. [n.p.,] 1883. 32 p.
                          OrHi WaU 877
Historical sketches of the Catholic Church
in Oregon for the past forty years.
Portland, Or. [Catholic Sentinel Press]
1878. 186 p.
      OrHi OrP WaT WaU WaW WaWW 878
OrP copy has added title page with im-
print: Washington, 1884.
Same. 2d ed. Ferndale, Wash., 1910. 72 p.
                     OrHi WaU WaWW 879
Jubilee of the fiftieth anniversary of the
ordinance to the priesthood celebrated
on the 18th of July, 1869 in Portland,
Oregon. Portland, Or., Walling, 1869. 15
p.   OrHi 880
The key to the Catholic Ladder; containing a sketch of the Christian religion
and universal history. Useful to all. New
York, T. W. Strong, 1859. 32 p.
                          OrHi WaU 880A

[Blanchet, Francois Xavier] 1835-1906.
Dix ans sur la cote du Pacifique, par un
missionaire canadien. Quebec, Brousseau,
1873. 100 p.   Many 881

Bland, Thomas Augustus.
Life of Alfred B. Meacham, together with
his lecture: The tragedy of the lava
beds. Washington, D. C., T. A. & M. C.
Bland, 1883. 30, 48 p. front., illus., ports.
Or OrP OrU OrSaW WaU WaWW 882

Blaney, Warren W.
Our Pacific coast. Bellingham, Wash.,
c1926. 96 p. front., illus. WaPS WaS 883

[Blankenship, George Edward] 1858-
Lights and shades of pioneer life on Puget
Sound, by a native son. Olympia, Wash.,
1923. 90 p.   Many 884

Blankenship, Georgina (Mitchell) 1860- comp.
Early history of Thurston County, Washington, together with biographies and
reminiscences of those identified with
pioneer days. Olympia, Wash., 1914. 392
p. front., plates, ports.   Many 885
Same. 1916. Or OrHi Wa WaSp WaU 886

Blankenship, Russell.
And there were men. New York, Knopf,
1942. xi, 300, iii p. plates, ports. Many 887

Blanpied, Charles W.
A humanitarian study of the coming immigration problem on the Pacific coast;

being a digest of the Pacific Coast Immigration Congress held in San Francisco, California, April 14-15, 1913, and showing its relation to the Tacoma Immigration Conference held in Tacoma, Washington, February 21-22, 1912. San Francisco [1913] 63 p. OrP WaS WaU **888**

Block, Rudolph.
Smile with Nile! Having to do with the 1936 National Shrine Convention. Seattle, 1936. 59 p. illus.   WaS **889**

Blomfield, James.
Rod, gun, and palette in the high Rockies; being a record of an artist's impressions in the land of the Red gods. Chicago, W. E. Wroe, 1914. 116 p. illus., 4 col. plates. Gallatin County, Mont. WaSp **890**

Blossom, Robert H.
First things pertaining to Presbyterianism on the Pacific coast. Portland, Or. [Wells and Co., Printers] 1913. 18 p. illus. (Pulpit of the First Presbyterian Church, Rev. John H. Boyd, pastor, v. 1, no.6)
Or WaU **891**

Blue, George Verne, see nos. 1785-1787.
Blue, Teddy, see no. 1.
Blumenthal, Albert, 1902-
Small-town stuff. Chicago, Univ. of Chicago Press [c1932] 416 p. illus. Sociological survey of typical mining town in Mont.   Many **892**

Blythe, S. F.
Hood River, Wasco County, Oregon, August, 1900; a pen picture of Hood River and Hood River Valley, by S. F. Blythe and E. R. Bradley. Hood River, Or., 1900. 17 p. illus.   OrP **893**

Board of Trade Company, Olympia, Wash.
Articles of incorporation and by-laws. Olympia, Wash., Partisan Book and Job Rooms, 1887. 29 p.   WaU **894**

Boaz, Franz, 1858-1942, ed.
Bella Bella tales. New York, American Folklore Society, 1932. 178 p. (Memoirs, v. 25).   CV CVicAr **895**

Bella Bella texts. New York, Columbia Univ. Press, 1928. ix, 291 p. (Contributions to anthropology, v. 5).
CVU Wa WaS WaSp **896**

Contributions to the ethnology of the Kwakiutl. New York, Columbia Univ. Press, 1925. vi, 357 p. (Contributions to anthropology, v. 3)   Many **897**

Facial paintings of the Indians of northern British Columbia. [New York] American Museum of Natural History, 1898. 23 p. 5 plates, map. (Memoirs, v. 11) (Jesup North Pacific Expedition. Anthropology, v. 1, pt. 1)   Many **898**

Folk-tales of the Salishan and Sahaptin tribes, collected by J. A. Teit, Livingston Farrand, M. K. Gould, H. J. Spinden; ed. by Franz Boas. Lancaster, Pa., American Folklore Society, 1917. 205 p. (Memoirs, v. 11).   Many **899**

Geographical names of the Kwakiutl Indians. New York, Columbia Univ. Press, 1934. 83 p. 22 maps. (Contributions to Anthropology, v. 20)
CVicAr WaS WaU **900**

Grammatical notes on the language of the Tlingit Indians. Philadelphia, Univ. Museum, 1917. 179 p. fold. plate. (Anthropological publications, v. 8, no. 1)
CVicAr MtU WaS **901**

Indianische Sagen von der Nord-Pacifischen Kuste Amerikas. Berlin, Asher, 1895 363 p. map.   CVicAr WaU **902**

Kwakiutl culture as reflected in mythology. New York, Stechert, 1935. xii, 190 p. (American Folklore Society. Memoirs, v. 28) CVic CVicAr OrU WaS WaU **903**

Kwakiutl tales. Leyden, Brill, 1910. viii, 495 p. (Columbia Univ. Contributions to anthropology, v. 2)   Many **904**

Same. New series. Translations. New York, Columbia Univ. Press, 1935. 230 p. (Contributions to anthropology, v. 26, pt. 1).
CV CVicAr CVU OrU WaS WaU **905**

Same. Texts. 1943.   228 p. (Contributions to anthropology, v. 26, pt. 2)
CV CVU WaSp WaU **906**

Kwakiutl texts, by Franz Boas and George Hunt. Leyden, Brill, 1906. 2 v. (Jesup North Pacific Expedition. Publications, v. 3, pt. 1; v. 10, pt. 1)
CV CVicAr WaS WaSp **907**

The religion of the Kwakiutl Indians. New York, Columbia Univ. Press, 1930. 2 v. illus. (Contributions to anthropology, v. 10).
CV CVicAr OrU WaS WaSp **908**

The use of masks and head-ornaments on the northwest coast of America. [n.p.] 1890. 9 p. 2 plates.   CVicAr **909**

Uber seine Reisen in Britisch Columbien. Berlin, Erdkunde, 1889. 12 p. CVicAr **910**
See also nos. 10051, 10162.

Boddam-Whetham, John Whetham, 1843-
Western wanderings; a record of travel in the evening land. London, Bentley, 1874. xii, 364 p. front., plates. Many **911**

Bodilly, Ralph Burland.
The voyage of Captain Thomas James for the discovery of the Northwest passage, 1631. London, Dent, 1928. 215 p. front. (map).   CV CVicAr CVU Wa **912**

Boeing Aircraft Company, Seattle, Wash.
Boeing's role in the war, 1943; a report for the year 1943. [n.p., 1943] 16 p. charts.
WaS WaT **913**

Case history of one company's contribution to the winning of World War II. [Seattle, 1946?] [32] p. illus.   WaS **914**

Philosophy of fighter design. [Seattle, 1943] 17 p. illus., diagrs. Was WaU **915**
Quarter-century plant, 1916-1941. [n.p., 1941] [8] p. illus.   WaS WaT **916**

Agreement, 1941-1942. [With Seattle and International Assn. of Machinists, Aeronautical Industrial District, Lodge 751] Seattle, Craftsman Press [1940?] 23 p.
WaS **917**

Bogle, D. B., see no. 1107.
Bogue, John Lyman.
The order of the Red Triangle; Y. M. C. A.; historical, America's largest can-

tonment, Camp Lewis. [n.p., 1919?] 46 p.
WaU **918**

Bohdanowicz, Karol, 1865-
Ocherki Nome. Sankt-Peterburg, A. S.
Suvorin, 1901. viii, 116 p. plates, fold.
map. WaU **919**

Boillot, Leon.
Aux mines d'or du Klondike du Lac Bennett a Dawson City. Paris, Hachette, 1899.
256 p. front., illus., fold. map.
CVicAr **920**

Same. 1909. CVicAr **921**

Boise Capital News.
Anniversary edition. Boise, Idaho, 1917.
[84] p. illus., ports., map. (v. 38, no. 22,
Feb. 4, 1917) WaU **922**

Golden anniversary book. [Boise, Idaho]
1940. 48 p. illus. IdB **923**

Boise Junior College, Boise, Idaho.
Lallah Rookh Rockwell memorial library
presented by Irvin E. Rockwell to Boise
Junior College, 1944. [Boise, Idaho] 1944.
[19] p. IdB **924**

Bolduc, Jean Baptiste Zacharie, 1818-1889.
Mission de la Colombie; deuxieme lettre
et journal. Quebec, Frechette, 1845. 28
p. CVicAr MtU **925**

Same. Photostat. WaU **926**
Mission de la Colombie; lettre et journal
de Mr. J.-B. Z. Bolduc, missionaire de la
Colombia. Quebec, J.-B Frechette, pere
[1844]. 95 p. CVicAr WaU **927**

Boller, Henry A.
Among the Indians; eight years in the far
West: 1858-1866, embracing sketches of
Montana and Salt Lake. Philadelphia,
T. E. Zell, 1868. 428 p. front. (fold. map)
MtHi WaSp WaU **928**

Bolles, Henry Jason, 1899 or 1900-1942.
Magpies' nest. Bozeman, Mont., Martha
Bolles, 1943. xv, 147 p. Poems.
MtBozC MtHi MtU Or WaS **929**

Bolster, Evelyn.
Come gentle spring. New York, Vanguard
[c1942] 378 p. Idaho farm setting.
IdU Or WaS WaSp WaU **930**

Morning shows the day. New York, Vanguard [c1940]. 301 p. Puget Sound setting. Many **931**

Bolton, Charles Edward.
Notes from letter written while lecturing
in the Northwest. Cambridge, Mass., 1892.
15 p. port. OrP **932**

Bolton, Frederick Elmer, 1866-
A selected bibliography of books and
monographs on education. Olympia,
Wash., Published by Mrs. Josephine
Corliss Preston, 1921. 103 p.
OrU WaS WaU **933**

Bolton, Herbert Eugene, 1870-
Fray Juan Crespi, missionary explorer on
the Pacific coast, 1769-1774. Berkeley,
Calif., Univ. of Calif. Press, 1927. lxiv,
402 p. front., 3 plates, 6 maps, facsim.
CVicAr CVU WaS **934**

Rim of Christendom; a biography of Eusebio Francisco Kino, Pacific coast pioneer. New York, Macmillan, 1936. xiv,
644 p. 12 plates, 8 fold. maps, 3 facsims.
Many **935**

See also nos. 7285, 11211.

Bompass, Mrs. Charlotte Selina (Cox) 1830-1917.
A heroine of the North; memoirs of Charlotte Selina Bompas, wife of the first
Bishop of Selkirk (Yukon) with extracts
from her journal and letters, comp. by
S. A. Archer. Toronto, Macmillan [1929].
187 p. front., map.
CV CVic CVicAr CVU WaS WaU **936**

Bompas, William Carpenter, bp., 1834-1906.
Diocese of Mackenzie River. London, Society for Promoting Christian Knowledge, 1888. 108 p. front. (map) (Colonial church histories)
CVicAr CVU WaU **937**

Lessons and prayers in the Tenni of Slavi
language of the Indians of Mackenzie
River in the North-West Territory of
Canada. London, Society for Promoting
Christian Knowledge, 1892. 126 p. front.,
illus. WaU **938**

Northern lights on the Bible, drawn from
a bishop's experience during twenty-five
years in the great North-west. London,
Nisbet [18—?] vi, 211 p. front. (fold.
map). CV WaPS **939**

See also nos. 1844-1848.

Bon Marche, Seattle, Wash.
The Bon Marche, 1890-1929. [Seattle, 1929]
[28] p. illus. (part col.) plates.
WaS WaU **940**

Bond, Fred G., 1852-
Flatboating on the Yellowstone, 1877.
New York [Printed at the New York
Public Library] 1925. 22 p. front. (port.)
Many **941**

Bond, James H., 1906-
From out of the Yukon, with foreword
by J. Hammond Brown. Portland, Or.,
Binfords & Mort [1948] x, 220 p. illus.,
ports, maps. OrCS OrHi WaS WaU **942**

Bond, William.
The early history of Mormonism; and,
the true source where the aborigines of
this continent came from. Portland, Or.,
Schwab Bros., 1890. 24 p. OrP **943**

Bone, Scott Cardelle, 1860-
Chechahco and sourdough; a story of
Alaska. [Atascadero, Calif., Western
Pub. Inc., c1926]. 281 p. plates, map.
Or Wa WaS WaT WaU **944**

Bonechek, Herman S.
Borah and his American ideals. 5th ed.
[Youngstown, Ohio]. Hagbon Press,
c1936. 79 p. IdB **945**

Bonggen, Jacob, see no. 9502.

Bonner, T. D., see nos. 695-699.

Bonneville, Benjamin Louis Eulalie de, see
nos. 4960-4991, 5041, 5043, 5046, 5047.

Bonneville Dam Chronicle, Cascade Locks,
Oregon.
Bonneville dam in pictures. [Cascade
Locks, Or., 1934?] 32 p. illus.
OrHi OrP WaPS **946**

Bonney, Benjamin Franklin, 1838-
Across the plains by prairie schooner;
personal narrative of B. F. Bonney of
his trip to Sutter's fort, California in

1846, and of his pioneer experiences in Oregon, during the days of Oregon's Provisional Government, by Fred Lockley. Eugene, Or., Koke-Tiffany Co. [192-?] 19 p.
IdB OrAshS OrCS WaPS WaSp WaU 947

Recollection of Benjamin Franklin Bonney, by Fred Lockley. [n.p., n.d.] 19 p.
WaS 948

Also pub. article title: Across the plains by prairie schooner.

Bonney, William Pierce, 1856-
History of Pierce County, Washington. Chicago, Pioneer Historical Pub. Co., 1927. 3 v. plates, ports. Volume 3 biographical.
Wa WaPS WaS WaT WaTC WaU 949

Old Fort Nisqually lives again. Tacoma, Published for Young Men's Business Club of Tacoma by Lee P. Merrill & Co., c1934. 1 v. illus. Anon. Or WaT 950

Boone, Henry L.
Trail dog; or, The wild voyageurs of the Columbia River; a romance of the western wilderness. New York, R. M. DeWitt, c1874. 99 p. front. (DeWitt's ten cent romances, no. 116)   WaU 951

Boone, Lalla Rookh.
Captain George Vancouver and his work on the Northwest coast. [n.p.], 1934. 114 p.
OrHi 951A

Booster.
[Alaska-Yukon-Pacific Exposition number] Kelso, Wash., Prompt Printing Co., 1908. [20] p. front., illus. (v. 1, no. 7, Jan. 1908.   WaU 952

Booth, Ernest Sheldon.
Birds of the West, illus. by Harry Baerg and Carl Petterson. [College Place, Wash.] 1948. 397 p. illus. WaT WaTC 953

Field key to the amphibians and reptiles of the Northwest. [College Place, Wash.?] c1941. 22 p. WaS WaSp WaT 954
Same. 1942.   WaU 955

Booth, John Martin, 1895-
A critical analysis of educational administration in Idaho, with emphasis on administration at the state level and with recommendations for reorganization. [n. p.] 1946. xv, 429 p. tables, map.
IdU IdUSB 956

[Booth, M. S.]
The Governor's committee; what they have done and what they have left undone; an episode in the history of the insane asylum of Washington Territory. Seattle, Hanford & McClaire, 1880. 20 p.
WaSp WaU 957

Boots, John Mercer, see no. 6744.

Borden, Courtney Louise (Letts)
The cruise of the Northern Light; explorations and hunting in the Alaskan and Siberian Arctic, in which the sea-scouts have a great adventure. New York, Macmillan, 1928. xi, 317 p. front., illus., ports.   Many 958

Borland, Harold G., 1900-
Rocky Mountain tipi tales. New York, Doubleday, 1926. 245 p. front. Montana Indian folklore.   IdIf 959

Borup, George, 1884-1912.
A tenderfoot with Peary, with a preface by G. W. Melville, with 46 illus. from photos. and a map. New York, Stokes [1911]. xvi, 317 p. front., plates, ports., fold. map. Or OrP WaE WaS WaSp 960

Same. Souvenir ed. for 11th annual dinner of American Booksellers' Assn.
Wa WaT 961

Bostwick, Prudence, see no. 2290.

Boswell, Harry James, 1874-
American blue book; western Washington, not compiled as a biographical history, but intended as one means of giving brief insight into the wonderful advancement of the best state of the Northwest, and in recognition of the activities of some of the men who have done and are doing their part to make future progress certain. [n.p.] c1922. 213 p.   Wa WaS WaT 962

The blue book of Portland and adjacent cities; not compiled as a biographical history, but intended to give a brief insight into the wonderful progress of the best state in the Northwest, and some of those who have, and are doing their part to make it so. [Portland, Or., Boyer Pub. Co.] 1921. 184 p.
OrP OrU WaS WaT 963

Bothwell, James Latimer, 1910-
The Alexander Bothwell senior (Scotland-Ireland-America, b. 1762? d. 1811) and allied families; genealogical data. [n.p.] 1947. 33 p. Idaho residents.   IdU 964

Botting, Roland B.
James M. Comstock, pioneer citizen. [Pullman, Wash.] State College of Wash., 1938. 18 p. plates. Spokane biographee.
Wa 965

Boughton, Jennie.
Forty years of library service. [Spokane, 1943]. 7 p.   WaSp 966

Spokane from memory. [Spokane, State Printing & Pub. Co., c1941]. 9 p.
WaSp 967

Bouis, Amedee Theodore.
Le Whip-poor-will, ou les Pionniers de l'oregon. Paris, Conon et Cie., 1847. 427 p.   CVicAr OrHi WaU 968

Boultbee, Sweet & Company, Ltd., Vancouver, B. C.
Pictorial greater Vancouver; the gateway to British Columbia's scenic wonderland. [Vancouver, B. C., Keystone Press, 1935?] 27 p. illus.   WaPS 969

Bourke, John Gregory, 1843-1896.
On the border with Crook. New York, Scribner, 1891. 491 p. front. (port.) illus., 3 plates, ports.   MtHi WaS 970
Same. 2d ed. 1892. IdB MtHi OrCS WaSp 971
Same. 1902.   MtBozC WaW 972

Bourlez, M., see no. 9549.

Bourne, Edward Gaylord, see nos. 2766, 7908, 7909.

Bovet, Louis A., Jr.
Moose hunting in Alaska, Wyoming, and Yukon Territory. Philadelphia, Dorrance, c1933. 143 p. illus., plates, maps. WaS 973

Bowden, Angie (Burt)
Early schools of Washington Territory. Seattle, Lowman & Hanford, 1935. 631 p. front., illus., 19 plates. **Many 974**

Bowen, Alfred D., ed.
Oregon and the Orient; a work designed to show the great natural and industrial advantages of Oregon. Portland, Or., 1901. 159 p. illus., ports., table.
CVicAr Or OrHi OrP OrU WaU **975**

Seattle and the Orient. Seattle, Seattle Times, 1900. 183 p. illus.
Wa WaS WaU WaWW **976**

Bowen, Robert Sidney, 1900-
Red Randall in the Aleutians. New York, Grosset [1945]. v. 214 p., front. Juvenile.
WaU **977**

Bowen, William H. C., see no. 6842.

Bower, B. M., see nos. 9473-9480.

Bowers, Floyd Kenneth.
Budget manual for Oregon cities, for the Bureau of Municipal Research and Service, University of Oregon, in cooperation with the League of Oregon Cities and the Oregon Finance Officers Association. [Eugene, Or., 1947] ii, 53 p. (Finance bulletin no. 6, May 1947) OrU **978**

Bowers, Nathan Abbott, 1886-
Cone-bearing trees of the Pacific coast. New York, London, Whittlesey House, McGraw-Hill Book Co. [c1942]. ix, 169 p. col. front., illus., tables. **Many 979**

Bowles, E. comp.
School district taxation in Washington; its inequalities illustrated by a series of tables. [n.p., 1909?] 23 p. tables. WaU **980**

Bowles, John Hooper, see no. 2340.

Bowles, Samuel, 1826-1878.
Across the continent. a stage ride over the plains, to the Rocky mountains, the Mormons, and the Pacific states, in the summer of 1865, with Speaker Colfax. New ed. Springfield, Mass., S. Bowles & Co., 1869. xx, 390 p. illus.
OrCS WaPS **981**

Across the continent: a summer's journey to the Rocky Mountains, the Mormons, and the Pacific states with Speaker Colfax. Springfield, Mass., S. Bowles, 1865. xx, 452 p. front. (fold. map)
Many 982

Same. 1866. **Many 983**

Our new West; records of travel between the Mississippi River and the Pacific Ocean; Colorado, Wyoming, Utah, Idaho, Montana, Nevada, California, Oregon, Washington, and British Columbia. Hartford, Hartford Pub. Co., 1869. 524 p. illus., plate. **Many 984**

Same. 1870. 524 p. front. (ports.) 12 plates, map. CVicAr IdB WaTC **985**

Pacific railroad open; how to go; what to see; guide for travel to and through western America. Boston, Fields, 1869. 122 p. **Many 986**

Bowman, Anne.
The bear hunters of the Rocky Mountains. Boston, Crosby & Nichols, 1864. iv, 474 p. front., 7 plates. CVicAr **987**

Bowman, Earl Wayland.
Arrowrock; songs and stories of a prodigal with front. by the author. Caldwell, Idaho, Caxton [c1931] 340 p. front.
IdB ItTf IdU MtU WaSp **988**

See also nos. 7188, 7189.

Bowman, Isaiah, 1878-
The pioneer fringe. New York, American Geographical Society, 1931. ix, 361 p. front., illus., maps, diagrs. (Special publications no. 13) **Many 989**

Bowman, James Cloyd, 1880-
The adventures of Paul Bunyan. New York, Century [c1927] xiii, 286 p. front., illus., plates.
MtU Or OrU WaS WaTC WaU **990**

See also no. 7938.

A Boy, pseud., see no. 9573.

Boy Scouts of America. Spokane Area Council.
Starting the troop right. [Spokane, n.d.] 19 p. WaPS **991**

Boyce, John Shaw, 1889-
Decay in Pacific Northwest conifers. New Haven, Yale Univ., 1930. 51 p. 10 plates. (Osborn Botanical Laboratory bulletin no. 1)
IdU OrCS OrP WaS WaSp WaU **992**

Boyd, Eunice (Mays)
Murderer wears mukluks. New York, Farrar [1945] 248 p. CV WaU **993**

Boyd, James Penny, 1836-1910.
Recent Indian wars under the lead of Sitting Bull and other chiefs; with a full account of the Messiah craze and ghost dances. [Philadelphia] Publishers Union, 1891. 320 p. front., plates, port.
MtU Or OrU **994**

Boyd, L. F., comp.
Manual, 1900-1901; city of Spokane, Washington. Spokane, Union Printing Co. [c1900?] 31 p. WaU **995**

Boyd, Robert, see no. 8352.

Boyd, T. J.
Kelso and Cowlitz County; a picture by pen and camera of the best town and best county in south-western Washington. [Kelso, Wash.] Prompt Printing Co. [191-?] [30] p. illus., ports. WaPS **996**

Boys' and Girls' Aid Society of Oregon.
Answering your questions. [n.p., 1941] 13 p. illus., diagrs. OrP **997**

Protected adoptions. [n.p., c1947] 23 p. illus. OrP **998**

Bozarth, R. Malcolm, ed.
"A poet's dozen"; an anthology of Thurston County verse; first anniversary ed. [Olympia, Wash.] "Of words and verse" Pub. Co., c1942. 23 p. Wa **999**

Bozeman, Mont. First Presbyterian Church.
Quarter centennial, 1872-1897. [Bozeman, Mont.] Hamilton-Springhill [1897?] 92 p. photos. MtHi MtU **1000**

75th anniversary, June 1872-1947. [Bozeman, Mont., 1947] 80 p. illus. MtHi **1001**

Brabant, Augustin J., 1845-1912.
Vancouver Island and its missions, 1874-1900; reminiscences. [n.p., 1899] 89 p. illus., port. CVicAr **1002**

Same. [New York, Messenger of the Sacred Heart Press, 1900]
CVic CVU MtU WaU **1003**
See also no. 4397.

Bracken, Claire Boyle.
A child's Idaho, illus. by Pearl Anderson Bracken. [Boise, Idaho, Syms-York Co., 1942] 179 p. illus. (1 col.) map. IdU **1004**

Brackett, Albert Gallatin, 1829-1896.
General Lane's brigade in central Mexico. Cincinnati, Derby, 1854. 336 p. port. Military career of 1st Territorial Governor of Oregon. OrHi OrP OrU **1005**

Braddy, Emmanell Backus, see no. 5581.

Bradford, A. H.
The voice from the Northwest; a paper prepared for the national anniversary of the American Home Missionary Society, in Chicago, June 7-10, 1881. [n.p., n.d.] 8 p.   OrU WaWW **1006**

Bradley, E. R., see no. 893.

Bradley, Henry Crum.
Flying chips. Caldwell, Idaho, Caxton, 1929. 80 p.   IdIf IdU WaSp **1007**
Splinters. Nampa, Idaho, Leader-Herald office, c1915. 71 p.   IdB **1008**

Bradley, Lawson G.
Official guide to the Lewis and Clark Centennial Exposition, Portland, Oregon, June 1 to October 15, 1905. [Portland, Or.] c1905. 62 p. front. (fold. map) illus., map.   Or OrHi OrP OrU **1009**

Bradley, Thomas Henry, b. 1838.
O'Toole's mallet; or, The resurrection of the second national city of the U. S. A. 2d ed. Seattle [Calvert Co.] 1894. 65 p. Pertains to Port Angeles, Wash.
WaU **1010**

Brady, Cyrus Townsend, 1861-1920, comp.
Northwestern fights and fighters, illus. with original drawings, maps and photos. New York, McClure, 1907. 373 p. front., illus., plates, ports., maps.
Many **1011**
Same. Garden City, N. Y., Doubleday, Page [c1907] xxv, 373 p.
IdB Or OrSa WaPS **1012**
Same. 1909 [c1907] [xx] 373 p.
IdB IdU WaTC **1013**
Same. 1910, c1907.   WaT **1014**
Same. 1913 [c1907]
MtU OrU Wa WaU **1015**
Same. 1919.   WaU **1016**
Same. 1923.   IdIf **1017**

Brady, Fred J., comp.
Souvenir book of the Portland police and fire departments. Portland, Or., Press Printing and Advertising Co., 1915. [126] p. illus., ports.   OrP **1018**

Brain, Belle Marvel.
True story of Marcus Whitman. New York, Willet [n.d.] 15 p.   Or WaWW **1019**

Brainerd, Erastus, comp.
Bibliography of the name Brainerd. Seattle, 1904. 18 p.   WaS WaU **1020**
[Lake Washington Canal. n.p., 1902] 57 p. plate, table.   WaS WaU **1021**

Braithwaite, John, see no. 8791.

Braley, Berton, 1882-
Pegasus pulls a hack; memoirs of a modern minstrel. New York, Minton, Balch [c1934] 329 p. Author resided in Butte, Mont. 1905-1908.
IdB MtHi Or WaS **1022**

Bramble, Charles A.
Klondike; a manual for goldseekers. New York, Fenno [c1897] 313 p. 11 plates, port., map.
CV CVicAr CVU WaS WaU **1023**

Branch, Edward Douglas, 1905-
Westward; the romance of the American frontier, woodcuts by Lucina Smith Wakefield. New York, Appleton, 1930. 626 p. illus., maps (1 double) Many **1024**

Brand, Charles Alvan, 1872-
Horse-and-buggy essays. Portland, Or., Binfords & Mort [c1940] 79 p. illus.
Many **1025**

Brandstrom, Axel John Felix, 1898-
Analysis of logging costs and operating methods in the Douglas fir region, by Axel J. F. Brandstrom, senior forest economist, Pacific Northwest Forest Experimental Station, Forest Service, United States Department of Agriculture, pub. by the Charles Lathrop Pack Forestry Foundation under the auspices of the West Coast Lumbermen's Association, June, 1933. [Seattle] 1933. 117 p. illus., diagrs., plans.   Many **1026**

Brandt, Herbert.
Alaska bird trails; adventures of an expedition by dog sled to the delta of the Yukon River at Hooper Bay, illus. with paintings by Major Allan Brooks and Edward R. Kalmbach, with photographs by Frank Dufresne, Olaus J. Murie, and the author, and with pen sketches by C. G. Mitchell, J. R. Moodey, and L. B. Towle. Cleveland, Bird Research Foundation, 1943. xviii, 464 p. col. front., illus., plates (part col.)
CVU OrP WaPS WaS WaT WaU **1027**

[Brandt, Inez Denney]
History of the First Baptist Church, Tacoma, Washington, 1883-1941. [Tacoma. 1941?] 165 [60] p. plate, ports.
WaT WaTC WaU **1028**

Branson, B. B.
Dayton and Sheridan narrow gauge railroad; the true history of the road; the Branson case for the collection of freight receipts claims; the effort of Henry Villard to destroy the road; the history of the extension of the road by Wm. Reid; Villard's lease of the road. Portland, Or., Ireland, 1884. 20 p.
OrHi **1029**

Branson, Helen (Kitchen) 1919-
Let there be life; the contemporary account of Edna L. Griffin. Pasadena, Calif., M. S. Sen [1947] 135 p. front. (port.) Idaho author.   IdB **1030**

Brant, Irving.
The Olympic forests for a national park. New York [Emergency Conservation Committee] 1938. 20 p. illus., maps. (Publication no. 68)   WaS WaU **1031**

Brattin, Mertie W., see no. 7600.

A brave man and his belongings; being some passages in the life of Sir John Franklin, first discoverer of the North-West Passage. London, Taylor, 1874. 61 p. CVicAr **1032**

Brazier, Samuel, see no. 10349.

Breakspear, see no. 51.

Breckenridge, Sophonisba B., see no. 10528.

Breitman, Hans, see nos. 697-699.

Bremerton Central Trades and Labor Council.
Bremerton, "home of the Pacific Fleet"; labor's year book 1932. Bremerton, Wash., c1932. 64 p. ports. WaE **1033**

Bremerton Sun and the Daily News-Searchlight.
Navy Day edition, Friday, October 24, 1947. Bremerton, Wash., 1947. [60] p. illus. (v. 47, no. 172; Oct. 24, 1947) WaU **1034**

Brenna, Paulo.
Interessi dell' emigrazione Italiana negli stati di Washington, Oregon, Idaho e Montana. Rome, Tipografia Cartiere Centrali, 1916. 40 p. OrP WaS WaU **1035**

Brent, John.
The empire of the West; a compilation. Omaha, Union Pacific Railway Co. [c1910] 303 p. illus., 3 maps. IdU **1036**

Brereton, Bernard John Stephen, 1868-1942.
Lumber and log exporter's guide. 2d ed. Contains the Brereton log scale; gives actual contents in board feet of poles, piling and logs, formula or construction of Pacific coast log scales in general use, grading rules for cedar poles, piling and logs. Seattle, c1924. 52 p. front., illus. OrCS OrP WaS WaU **1037**

Same. 3d ed. Operation of vessels in the foreign export lumber and log trade; the mathematically correct "Brereton log scale"; formula or construction of log scales used in the Douglas fir and California redwood regions, valuable information for buyers, sellers, and carriers of lumber or logs. Seattle, c1929. 111 p. front. (port.) illus., tables. Many **1038**

Lumberman's and logger's guide; merits and uses of Douglas fir, California redwood and the leading commercial woods of the Pacific coast; rapid methods of computing specifications, contents and weight of squared and tapering lumber, octagon spars and logs; log tables, log conversion tables and information relative to foreign export cargo shipments; table of distances from Pacific coast ports to foreign ports, also inland waters of Puget Sound, Columbia River, and British Columbia. Tacoma [c1919] 136 p. illus., tables, diagrs. Or WaT WaU **1039**

The practical lumberman. Short methods of figuring lumber, octagon spars, logs, specifications and lumber carrying cap-

acity of vessels. [n.p.] 1908. 119 p. diagrs. WaE **1040**

Same. 2d ed. [Tacoma, c1911] 247 p. WaT **1041**

Same. 3d ed. [Tacoma, Commercial Bindery and Printing Co., c1915] 255 p. illus. Or OrHi **1042**

Same. 4th ed. [c1921] 144 p. CVU OrP WaT **1043**

Brereton, Robert Maitland, 1834-1911.
Question: Did Sir Francis Drake land on any part of the Oregon coast? Portland, Or., J. K. Gill [1907] 24 p. maps. CVicAr CVU OrHi OrP WaU **1044**

Reminiscences of an old English civil engineer, 1858-1908. Portland, Or., Irwin-Hodson Co., 1908. 111 p. illus., port., maps, facsim., table. OrHi OrP OrU WaPS **1045**

A thought for year 1903; the brotherhood of man. Woodstock, Or. [1903] 14 p. plates. OrHi WaU **1046**

Bretherton, Vivien R.
The rock and the wind. New York, Dutton, 1942. 618 p. Oregon setting. Many **1047**

Breton, J. B. J., see no. 2000.

Bretz, J. Harlen, 1882-
The Grand Coulee. New York, American Geographical Society, 1932. x, 89 p. illus., maps (1 fold.) (Special publication no. 15). Many **1048**

Brevig, Tollef Larson, 1857-1935.
Apaurak in Alaska; social pioneering among the Eskimos, trans. and comp. from the records of the Rev. T. L. Brevig, pioneer missionary to the Eskimos of Alaska from 1894 to 1917, by Dr. Walter Johnshoy. Philadelphia, Dorrance [1944] 325 p. front., 71 plates. CVicPr Or WaS WaT WaU **1049**

Brewer, Charles.
Reminiscences. [n.p., 1884] 67 p. Pertains to Alaska. CVicAr **1050**

Brewer, William Fisk, 1870-
Higher education in Montana; an address delivered before the faculty of Montana State College, Apr. 9, 1946. Bozeman, Mont., 1946. 20 p. MtBozC MtHi **1051**

Brewerton, G. Douglas, see no. 4181.

Brewster, William Lewis.
William Mead Ladd of Portland, Oregon; a biographical sketch. [Portland, Or., Metropolitan] 1933. xi, 102 p. front. (port.) 4 ports. Many **1052**

Bridges, Robert, 1862-
Merchant marine and kindred subjects [an address delivered before the King County Democratic Club on March 25, 1916. Seattle, 1916] 16 p. WaS WaU **1053**

"Patriotism and war"; an address delivered at Renton and Issaquah, Wash., on July Fourth, 1917. [Seattle, Pigott Printing Concern] 1917. [13] p. WaU **1054**

Public ownership and operation of water and rail terminal facilities produce the greatest dispatch and economy. Seattle, Pigott Printing Concern, 1915. 15 p. OrU WaS WaU **1055**

Public ownership of docks and railway

terminal facilities means the industrial and commercial supremacy of the city of Seattle. [Seattle, 1912?] 15 p.

WaS WaU 1056

Rail and water terminal facilities. [Seattle, Port Commission] 1916. 16 p.

OrU WaS WaU 1057

Seattle's public terminals and their relation to northwest wheat. [Seattle] Piggot Printing Concern [1916] 23 p.

OrU WaS WaU 1058

Bridges, Woodrow, see no. 11185.

Brief and concise information on salmon fishing and the industry. [n.p., 1896?] 20 p. WaU 1059

A brief notice of the recent outrages committee by Isaac I. Stevens, governor of Washington Territory; the suspension of the writ of habeas corpus, the breaking up of courts, and the kidnapping of judges and clerks. Olympia, Wash., 1856. 32 p. WaU 1060

Brier, Howard Maxwell, 1903-
Det hemmelige flyet, oversatt av Einar Diesen. [Oslo] Gyldendal Norsk Forlag, 1947. 224 p. WaU 1061

Panthom backfield; illus. by Jay Hyde Barnum. New York, Random House [1948] 246 p. illus. WaU 1062

Sky freighter, a story of bush pilots who fly freight to the radium mines of arctic Canada, illus. by Willard Rosenquist. New York, Random House [1942] 277 p. front., illus., double map. Many 1063

Sky blazer, illus. by Dwight Logan. New York, Random House [1946] vii, 265 p. front. (map) illus., plates. Many 1064

Skycruiser, pen and ink drawings by Hans Kreis. New York, Random House, c1939. 238 p. illus. Many 1065

Smoke eater, illus. by Louis Cunette. New York, Random House [c1941] 251 p. illus.

Or OrP Wa WaS WaSp WaU 1066

Swing shift, illus. by S. Levenson. New York, Random House [1943] 265 p. illus.

Many 1067

Waterfront beat. New York, Random House [c1937] 237 p. front.

Or Wa WaS WaSp WaT WaU 1068

Brier, Warren Judson, 1850-
Twenty-five lessons in citizenship, by Warren J. Brier and D. L. Hennessey, ed. for state of Washington. [Seattle] 1934. 66 p.

WaPS 1069

Same. 9th ed. 1935. 63 p.

OrPR WaWW 1070

Briggs, Harold Edward, 1896-
Frontiers of the Northwest; a history of the upper Missouri valley. New York, Appelton-Century, c1940, xiv, 629 p. front., illus., plates, ports., maps.

Many 1071

Briggs, Lloyd Vernon, 1863-1941.
California and the West, 1881, and later. [Boston, Wright and Potter Printing Co.] 1931. xiv, 214 p. front., illus., 43 plates. CVicAr OrHi 1072

Briggs, William M., 1896-
Taxation of municipal or publicly-owned

utilities. Ashland, Or. [Ashland Daily Tidings, n.d.] v, 29 p.

Or OrCS OrHi OrP 1073

Brigham, Harold Frederick, 1897-
Report of a survey of the Tacoma Public Library for the Board of trustees of the Tacoma, Washington, Public Library, conducted for the American Library Association by Harold F. Brigham and Andre S. Nielsen with the collaboration, as building consultant, of Carl Vitz. Chicago, American Library Assn., 1946. 80 p. Wa WaS WaT WaU 1074

Bright, Verne, 1893-
Mountain man. Limited ed. Caldwell, Idaho, Caxton, 1948. 190 p. Portland author. Many 1075

Brimlow, George Francis.
The Bannock Indian War of 1878. Caldwell, Idaho, Caxton, 1938. 241 p.

Many 1076

Cavalryman out of the West; life of Gen. William Carey Brown. Caldwell, Idaho, Caxton, 1944. 442 p. front., plates, ports.

Many 1077

Brining, Myron, 1900-
Singerman. New York, Farrar, 1929. 446 p. Montana author.

MtBozC MtHi MtU Or WaS WaT 1078

The sisters. New York, Farrar [c1937] 570 p. Many 1079

The sun sets in the west. New York, Farrar, c1935. 360 p.

MtHi MtU Wa WaE 1080

This man is my brother. New York, Farrar [c1932] vii, 342 p.

MtHi MtU WaS WaSp WaU 1081

Wide open town. New York, Farrar, c1931. 306 p.

MtHi MtU WaS WaSp WaU 1082

Brininstool, Earl Alonzo, 1870-
Fighting Red Cloud's warriors; true tales of Indian days when the West was young. Columbus, Ohio, The Hunter-Trader-Trapper Co., 1926. 241 p. front., illus., ports. (Frontier series, v. 2)

MtHi Or OrHi WaSp 1083

A trooper with Custer and other historic incidents of the battle of the Little Big Horn. Columbus, Ohio, The Hunter-Trader-Trapper Co., 1925. 214 p. front., illus., ports. (Frontier series, v. 1)

IdU MtHi MtU OrHi WaSp 1084

Same. 2d ed. 1926 [c1925] IdU Or 1085

See also nos. 769, 770, 3723, 4288, 9785.

Brink, Mrs. Carol (Ryrie) 1895-
Anything can happen on the river! illus. by W. W. Berger. New York, Macmillan, 1936 [c1934] 224 p. Idaho author.

IdU 1086

Buffalo coat. New York, Macmillan [c1944] 421 p. CV IdB Or 1087

Same. 1945. Many 1088

Caddie Woodlawn, illus. by Kate Seredy. New York, Macmillan, 1936 [c1935] 270 p. illus. IdU 1039

Brinley, Mrs. Gordon.
Away to the Canadian Rockies and British

Columbia, illus. by D. Putnam Brinley. New York, Dodd, 1938. x, 301 p. col. front., illus., plates (part col.)
Many **1090**

Same. Toronto, McClelland & Stewart [c1938] CV CVicAr **1091**

Brisbin, James Sanks, 1837-1892.
The beef bonanza; or, How to get rich on the plains, being a description of cattle-growing, sheep-farming, horse-raising, and dairying in the West. Philadelphia, Lippincott, 1881. 222 p. front., 7 plates.
MtBozC MtHi MtU WaU **1092**

Personal record. [n.p., n.d.] 8 p.
MtHi **1093**

Brissenden, Paul Frederick, 1885-
Butte miners and the rustling card. [n.p., n.d.] 21 p. MtHi **1094**

[British Columbia. University]
The University of British Columbia; twenty-first anniversary, 1915-1936. [Vancouver, B. C.] 1936. 38 p. plates, ports.
CV CVU WaU **1095**

The **British Columbia almanac** specially compiled for this province with other information, 1895-98. Victoria, B. C., British Colonist, 1895-98. 4 v.
CVicAr **1096**

British Columbia and the Canadian Pacific Railway; complimentary dinner to Hon. Mr. Trutch, 10th April, 1871. Montreal, Gazette Printing House, 1871. 12 p.
CVicAr **1097**

British Columbia and Vancouver Island; a complete handbook replete with the latest information concerning the newly discovered gold-fields. [London, W. Penny, 1858] 67 p. map. CVicAr **1098**

British Columbia Automobile Club.
Official motorist's guide of British Columbia. [n.p.,n.d.] 71 p. maps. WaT **1099**

British Columbia District Telegraph & Delivery Co.
1891-1941; fifty years of service. Vancouver, B. C., 1941. [16] p. illus., 2 plates.
CVicAr **1100**

British Columbia Electric Railway Co. Ltd.
The Stave Falls Power Development, completed Sept. 1925. Vancouver, B. C., 1925. 15 p. illus. CV **1101**

Twenty-nine years of public service. [Vancouver, B.C., 1925] 47 p. illus.
CV CVU **1102**

British Columbia Horticultural Estates, Ltd.
Walhachin, British Columbia [n.p, n.d.] 40 p. illus., fold. plate. CVicAr **1103**

British Columbia Indian Arts and Welfare Society.
Native designs of British Columbia. Victoria, 1948. 5 p. 12 plates.
CVicAr CVU Or OrCS OrHi WaS **1103A**

British Columbia Land Surveyors.
Roll of honour; British Columbia land surveyors, the great war, 1914-1918. [Victoria, B. C., British Colonist, n.d.] 1 v. 24 ports. CV **1104**

The **British Columbia Mercantile Agency.**
Vancouver.
Victoria, B. C., British Colonist, 1892. 68 p. CVirAr **1105**

British Columbia Mining Journal.
Overland to Klondike through Cariboo, Omineca, Cassiar and Lake Teslin; the poor man's route. Peoria, Ill., Franks, 1898. 34 [30] p. illus., map.
CVirAr **1106**

British Columbia mining record, Christmas 1899. Victoria, B. C., 1899. 101 p. front., illus. Contents: Alaska question, by Sir C. H. Tupper.—Prehistoric races of B. C., by C. Hill-Tout.—B. C. before confederation, by E. O. S. Scholefield.—Indians of B. C., by J. W. MacKay.—Last Indian battle, by G. Sheldon-Williams.—Victoria; its natural advantages, by C. H. Gibbons.—Introduction of capital in new countries, by D. B. Bogle.
Was WaU **1107**

British Columbia Mining Stock Board, Victoria, B. C.
Constitution and by-laws, organized Dec. 6, 1877. Victoria, B. C., Colonist Steam Presses, 1878. 24 p. WaU **1108**

British Columbia Monthly.
University number. Vancouver, B. C. [1926] 16 p. illus. (v. 25, no. 3)
WaU **1109**

British Columbia Mountaineering Club.
Northern Cordilleran. Vancouver, B. C., 1913. 50 p. front., illus., plates, maps.
CV CVU WaS WaU **1110**

British Columbia Orphans' Friend.
Historical number, pub. under the direction of the Rt. Rev. Alexander MacDonald. Victoria, B. C. [Press Pub. Co.] 1913. 208 p. illus., ports., map.
CVicAr CVU WaSp **1111**

British Columbia, pictorial and biographical. Winnipeg, Clarke, 1914. 2 v. 298 ports.
CVic CVicAr CVU **1112**

British Columbia Pioneer Society.
Constitution, by-laws and rules of order of the British Columbia Pioneer Society, organized April 28, 1871, pub. by order of the Board of Directors, Victoria, B.C., 1874-9. Victoria, B. C., Rose & Pottinger, 1874-1879. 2 v. CVicAr **1113**

British Columbia Political Equality League.
Points in the laws of British Columbia regarding legal status of women. [Vancouver, B. C., J. F. Morris, Printer, n.d.] 20 p. CV **1114**

— — — Vancouver Branch.
Constitution and by-laws. [n.p., n.d.] 8 p.
CVicAr **1115**

British Columbia Power Corporation.
Ruskin power development complete November 1930. [Vancouver, B. C., Rose, 1930]. 34 p. illus., port. CV **1116**

The British Columbian.
The Fraser Valley centennial edition, Nov. 27, 1912. New Westminster, B. C., 1912. 94 p. illus. CV **1117**

A British North American, pseud.
Reply to letter of "Old Settler", published in the "Times" newspaper, on the selection of a terminus on the Pacific coast for the proposed Canadian Pacific Railway. London, Sulman [n.d.] 34 p.
CVicAr **1118**

Brittain, Horace Leslie, 1874-
An investigation and survey into the municipal organization of Burnaby, B. C., in November 1932. Vancouver, B. C., Burnaby Broadcast, 1933. 54 p. VC **1119**

Britzman, Homer E., see no. 47.

Broadus, Eleanor Hammond.
John Jewitt, the captive of Nootka. Toronto, Ryerson [c1928] 32 p. illus. (Ryerson Canadian history readers)
CVirAr Or WaE WaS WaU **1120**

Brock, Reginald Walter, see nos. 9856, 9857.

Brock, Stuart, see no. 10316.

Brockett, Linus Pierpont, 1820-1893.
Our western empire; or, The new West beyond the Mississippi; the latest and most comprehensive work on the states and territories west of the Mississippi, containing description of the geography, geology, the climate, soil, agriculture, the mineral and mining products; to which is added the various routes, and prices of passage and transportation, with full information concerning Manitoba, British Columbia, and those regions in the Atlantic adapted to settlement. Philadelphia, Bradley, Garretson, 1881 [c1880]. 1312 p. front., plates, maps (part double). Many **1121**
Same. 1882.
IdU OrCS OrHi Wa WaPS WaWW **1122**

Brockett, Norwood Waite.
Lumberman's review and guide of western Washington; a complete gazetteer of the lumber and shingle industry in the entire western portion of this state. Seattle, Lumberman's Review Co. [n.d.] 98 p. illus. WaU **1123**

Brockman, Christian Frank, 1902-
The story of Mount Rainier National Park. [Longmire, Wash., Mt. Rainier National Park Natural History Assn., c1940] 63 p. illus.
OrU Wa WaS WaT **1124**

Broderick, Henry, 1880-
The commandment breakers of Walla Walla. Seattle, F. McCaffrey, 1934. 95 p. front., illus. WaS WaU **1125**
First person singular. Seattle, F. McCaffrey, 1943. 55 p. Wa WaS WaU **1126**

Broderick, Therese.
The brand, a tale of the Flathead reservation, by Therese Broderick (Tin Schreiner). Seattle, Harriman, 1909. 271 p. front. Many **1127**

Broke, Horatio George.
With sack and stock in Alaska. London, Longmans, 1891. 158 p. map. Many **1128**

Brondel, John Baptist.
The Right Reverend John B. Brondel, Bishop of Helena; a memorial. Helena, Mont., State Pub. Co., 1904. 54 p. front. (port.) plates, ports. MtHi WaU **1129**
See also no. 7852.

Bronson, Edgar Beecher, 1856-1917.
Cowboy life on the western plains; the reminiscences of a ranchman New York, Grosset [c1910]. 369 p. front.
MtBozC MtU WaS **1130**

Reminiscences of a ranchman. New York, McClure, 1908. 314 p. MtHi MtU **1131**
Same. New rev. ed., with new matter and numerous illus. Chicago, McClurg, 1910. 369 p. front., plates, port.
WaU WaW **1132**

Brontman, Lazar Konstantinovich.
On the top of the world, the Soviet expedition to the North Pole, 1937. London, Gollancz, 1938. 287 p. illus., 24 plates, fold. map. CVicAr **1133**

Brook-Nook Stock Ranche.
Catalogue of trotting stock at Brook-Nook Stock Ranche, Home Park, Madison County, Mont.; the property of C. K. Larrabee. Cleveland, Winn & Judson, 1894. 120 p. MtHi **1134**

Brooks, Alfred Hulse, 1871-1924.
Mountain exploration in Alaska. [Philadelphia, American Alpine Club, 1914] 22 p. illus. (Alpina Americana, no. 3)
Or OrP **1135**

Brooks, Allan, 1869-
A distributional list of the birds of British Columbia by Allan Brooks and H. S. Swarth. Berkeley, Calif., Cooper Ornithological Club, 1925. 158 p. col. front., illus., fold. map. (Pacific coast avifauna, no. 17) Many **1136**

Brooks, Charles Wolcott.
Japanese wrecks stranded and picked up adrift in the North Pacific Ocean, ethnologically considered as furnishing evidence of a constant infusion of Japanese blood among the coast tribes of northwestern Indians. San Francisco, Academy of Sciences. 1876. 23 p. map.
CVicAr OrHi **1137**

Brooks, Noah, 1830-1903.
First across the continent; the story of the exploring expedition of Lewis and Clark in 1803-4-5. New York, Scribner, 1901. xii, 365 p. front., 23 plates, ports., fold. map, tables. Many **1138**
Same. 1902. IdIf MtU OrSa WaS **1139**
Same. 1904. Many **1140**
Same. 1908 [c1901] IdP WaS WaT **1141**
Same. 1917 [c1901] OrU **1142**
Same. 1930. WaW **1143**

[Brooks & Schreiber, North Yakima, Wash.]
Pictorial souvenir, Yakima Valley, Washington. [North Yakima, Wash., 1909] 72 p. illus. Wa **1144**

Brosnan, Cornelius James, 1882-
History of the state of Idaho. New York, Scribner, c1918. xiii, 237 p. front., illus., 11 maps. Many **1145**
Same. New ed. [c1926] 260 p. front., illus., ports., maps. Many **1146**
Same. Rev. ed. [c1935] 423 p. col. front., illus., plates (part col.) ports., maps.
IdB IdIf IdP IdU OrHi OrP **1147**
Same. New ed. 1948. Many **1147A**
Jason Lee, prophet of the new Oregon. New York, Macmillan, 1932. 348 p. front. (port.) Many **1148**

Brother Jonathan's bed; or, Wait until your legs grow longer; a fairy tale for politicians who are too young to have learned anything, or who are so old that they have forgotten everything. New York, Graham, 1846. 23 p. illus. Oregon boundary dispute. OrHi **1149**

Brothers of the Christian Schools.
Christian brothers' silver jubilee celebration. Portland, Or., 1911. 120 p. illus., ports. OrP **1150**

Broughton, Lieutenant, see no. 10460.

Brouillet, Jean Baptiste Abraham, 1813-1884.
Authentic account of the murder of Dr. Whitman and other missionaries by the Cayuse Indians of Oregon in 1847, and the causes which led to that horrible catastrophe. 2d ed. Portland, Or., McCormick, 1869. 108 p. Many **1151**

Protestantism in Oregon; account of the murder of Dr. Whitman and the ungrateful calumnies of H. H. Spalding, Protestant missionary. New York, Cozans, 1853. 107 p.
CVicAr OrHi WaU WaWW **1152**

Brower, Charles D., 1863-
Fifty years below zero; a lifetime of adventure in the far North, in collaboration with Philip J. Farrelly and Lyman Anson. New York, Dodd, 1942. x, 310 p. front., plates, ports. Many **1153**

Same. 1944 [c1942] WaPS **1154**

Brower, Jacob Vradenberg, 1844-1905.
The Missouri River and its utmost source, curtailed narration of geologic, primitive and geographic distinctions descriptive of the evolution and discovery of the river and its headwaters. St. Paul [Pioneer Press] 1896. lxiii, 150 p. front., illus. MtBozC MtHi **1155**

Same. 2d ed. Containing an archaeological [!] addendum. 1897. 206 p. front. (map) illus., plates, ports., maps.
MtHi MtU OrU WaU **1156**

Brown, Alec, see no. 1652.

Brown, Arthur Judson, 1856-
Higher education in the Pacific Northwest; a sermon preached Sunday morning, Feb. 8, 1891. Portland, Or. [First Presbyterian Church] 1891. 12 p.
OrHi OrP **1157**

Brown, Audrey Alexandra, 1904-
The log of a lame duck [experiences in the House of Good Hope on Vancouver Island, a hospital for crippled children] with a foreword by Lady Tweedsmuir. [New York] Macmillan, 1939. 292 p.
IdB Or WaE WaS WaSp WaT **1158**

Brown, Benjamin Harrison, 1866-
A little astronomy. Walla Walla, Wash. [Walla Walla Union Press] 1927. 22 p.
WaPS **1159**

Brown, Clara Spalding.
Life at Shut-in Valley, and other Pacific coast tales. [Franklin, Ohio, Editor Pub. Co., c1895] 188 p. WaU **1160**

Brown, Mrs. Dazie M. (Stromstadt)
Metlakahtla. Seattle, H. M. Hill Pub. Co., 1907. 19 p. WaU **1161**

Brown, Dee, see no. 9053.

Brown, Henry.
Taxation of church property; an appeal

to the citizens of Washington. Spokane, Spokane Printing Co., 1892. 81 p. illus.
WaSp WaTC **1162**

Brown, Horatia Jones, 1879-
Timber estimating in the Pacific Northwest; a digest of the various methods practised on the Pacific slope. 2d ed. Portland, Or., Brown & Brown, Inc. [c1916] 31 p. front., illus., map, fold. tables. OrP **1163**

Brown, J. Hammond, see no. 942.

Brown, Mrs. Jennie Broughton.
Fort Hall on the Oregon Trail; a historical study; with Ferry Butte, by Susie Boice Trego. Caldwell, Idaho, Caxton, 1932. 466 p. front. (port.) illus.
Many **1164**

Same. 1934 [c1932]
CVicAr CVU IdIf IdP OrSaW **1165**

Brown, John, 1797-1861.
The North-West Passage, and the plans for the search for Sir John Franklin; a review. London, E. Stanford, 1858. 463 p. front., 2 fold. maps.
CV CVicAr WaU **1166**

Same. 2d ed., with a sequel, including the voyage of the "Fox". 1860. xiii, 463, 64 p. front., 3 maps (2 fold.) fold. facsim.
WaS WaU **1167**

Brown, John W.
An Abridged history of Alaska. Seattle, Gateway Printing Co., 1909. 96 p. illus.
Many **1168**

Brown, Joseph Henry.
Brown's political history of Oregon, v. 1. Portland, Or., Allen, 1892. 462 p. 2 ports., map, 2 facsims., table. Many **1169**

Pocket book and table manual; comp. from standard works. Salem, Or., 1872. 16 p.
OrHi **1170**

[Brown, Robert] 1842-1895.
Vancouver Island; exploration, 1864. Victoria, B. C., Harries and Co. [1865?] ii, 27 p. CV CVicAr CVU WaS **1171**

See also no. 5207.

Brown, Robert Christopher Lundin, d. 1876.
British Columbia; an essay. New Westminster, B. C., Royal Engineer Press, 1863. 64, 33 p.
CV CVicAr CVU WaU **1172**

Klatsassan, and other reminiscences of missionary life in British Columbia. London, Society for Promoting Christian Knowledge, 1873. viii, 199 p. front. (port.) 2 plates, fold. map.
CV CVicAr CVU WaS WaU **1173**

Brown, Robert Neal Rudmose, 1879-
The polar regions, a physical and economic geography of the Arctic and Antarctic, with 23 maps. London, Methuen [1927] ix, 245 p. maps (part fold.)
CVU IdU OrU Wa WaT **1174**

Brown, Stewardson.
Alpine flora of the Canadian Rocky Mountains; illus. with water-colour drawings and photographs by Mrs. Charles Schaffer. New York, Putnam, c1907. xxxix, 353 p. front., 79 plates (part col.) Many **1175**

Brown, T. B., comp.
Victoria Country Club, Ltd., Victoria, B. C. Victoria, B. C., British Colonist, 1909. 1 v. illus., ports.   CVicAr **1176**

Brown, Valentine.
Armageddon. Portland, Or., 1902. 151 p.
OrHi OrP OrU WaWW **1177**
The chieftain and satires. Portland, Or., 1903. 190 p.
OrHi OrP OrU WaPS WaU **1178**
Poems. Portland, [n.p.] 1900. 336 p. port.
Or OrHi OrP OrU **1178A**
Tales and other verse. Portland, Or., 1904. 173 p.   OrHi OrP OrU **1179**

Brown, W. C., see no. 7745.

Brown, W. R.
St. Andrew's Presbyterian Church, Merritt, B. C.; souvenir book marking the thirteenth anniversary of the opening of the church; a short history of the church in the Nicola Valley and sketch of the valley and the city of Merritt, 1923. [n.p., 1923?] 36 p.
CV CVicAr **1180**

Brown, William.
The adventures of an American doughboy, comp. and arranged from his notes by Birdeena Tuttle. Tacoma, Smith-Kinney [c1919]. 77 p. front. (port.) plates.
WaS WaT WaU **1181**

Brown William Compton, 1869-
Early Okanogan history. Gives an account of the first coming of the white men to this section and briefly narrates the events leading up to and attending the establishment of the first settlement in the state of Washington under the American flag, an event which occurred at the mouth of the Okanogan River, September 1, 1811. Okanogan, Wash., Okanogan Independent [1911]. 27 p. illus., port.   Many **1182**

Brown, William G.
Report on report and survey of Port of Portland of North Portland harbor, and resolutions of industries affected. [Portland, Or.] North Portland Industries [1920]. 16 p. map.   OrCS OrP **1183**

Browne, Mrs. Alice (Harriman) 1861-1925.
Chaperoning Adrienne; a tale of the Yellowstone National Park, with illus. by Charles M. Russell and photos. [Seattle, Metropolitan, n.d.] 92 p. front, illus. Washington author.
Or Wa WaU WaWW **1184**
A man of two countries; chapter headings by C. M. Dowling, New York, Harriman, 1910. 301 p.   WaS **1185**
Pacific history stories. Montana ed., v. 1. San Francisco, Whitaker & Ray, 1903. 198 p. col. front, illus. (Western series of readers)
MtBozC MtHi MtU WaU **1186**
Songs o' the Olympics, illus. by B. C. Bubb. Seattle, Harriman, 1909. 70 p. front., illus., 13 plates.   Many **1187**
Songs o' the Sound; illus. by Frank Calvert. Seattle, Stuff Printing Concern, 1906. [27] p. front., illus., plates.
MtHi Or WaS WaU WaWW **1188**

Wilt thou not sing? a book of verses. New York, Harriman, c1912. 94 p.
Wa WaT **1189**

Browne, Belmore, 1880-
Camp Lewis; history of the development of the largest permanent military cantonment in the United States, Tacoma, Commercial Bindery & Printing Co., c1918. [41] p. illus., ports., maps.
OrP WaU **1190**
Conquest of Mount McKinley; the story of three expeditions through the Alaskan wilderness to Mount McKinley, North America's highest and most inaccessible mountain; appendix by Herschel C. Parker with 100 illus. from original drawings by the author and from photographs and maps. New York, Putnam, 1913. 381 p. front., plates, map.
Many **1191**
The frozen barrier; a story of adventure on the coast of Behring Sea, with illus. from original drawings by the author. New York, Putnam, 1921. 267 p. front., 4 plates.   Or WaS WaT **1192**
The quest of the Golden Valley; a story of adventure on the Yukon. New York, Putnam, 1916. 279 p. front., 7 plates.
IdIf WaS WaT WaU **1193**
The white blanket; the story of an Alaskan winter, with illus. from original drawings by the author. New York, Putnam, 1917. 317 p. front., 4 plates.
WaS WaT **1194**
Same. [1925, c1917]   WaT **1195**

Browne, George Waldo, see no. 10815.

Browne, John Ross, 1821-1875.
Resources of the Pacific slope; a statistical and descriptive summary of the mines and minerals, climate, topography, agriculture, commerce, manufactures, and miscellaneous productions, of the states and territories west of the Rocky Mountains, with a sketch of the settlement and exploration of Lower California. San Francisco, H. H. Bancroft and Co., 1869. 674, 200 p.   Many **1196**

Browne, Peter Arrell, 1782-1860.
Lecture on the Oregon Territory: I. Title of the United States to its sovereignty; II. Its capabilities and value to our country; III. And the necessity of an immediate settlement of it from the states. Philadelphia, U. S. Book and Job Printing Office, 1843. 20 p.
CVicAr OrP WaWW **1197**
Same. Photostat.   WaU **1198**

Browne, William Henry James.
Ten coloured views taken during the Arctic expedition of Her Majesty's ships "Enterprise" and "Investigator" under the command of Captain James C. Ross, drawn by W. H. Browne, with a summary of the expeditions in search of Captain Sir John Franklin. London, Ackermann and Co., 1850. 8 p. 10 col. plates.   CVicAr **1199**

Brownlee, Mrs. L. A. G.
Helois. Victoria, B. C., Cusack Pub. Co., 1917. x, 68 p. front. (port.) 8 plates.
CVicAr **1200**

Brownson, T. G.
An educational policy for the Baptists of the Pacific coast. [n.p., n.d.] 23 p.
OrU 1201

Trials and triumphs of fifty years of Baptist work in Oregon. Portland, Ore., Chronicle Pub. Co., 1894. 18 p.
OrHi OrP OrU WaU 1202

Brownsville, Or., First Presbyterian Church
Historical souvenir of the semi-centennial jubilee, Apr. 11, 1907. Brownsville, Or., 1907. 31 p. illus., ports.
Or OrHi OrP OrU WaPS WaU 1203

Bruce, John P., see no. 6645.

Bruce, Malcolm, see no. 764.

Bruce, Miner Wait.
Alaska; its history and resources, gold fields, routes and scenery. Seattle, Lowman & Hanford, 1895. 128 p. front., illus., plates, ports.
Many 1204

Same. 2d ed. rev. & enl. New York, Putnam, 1899. x, 237 p. front., illus., 36 plates, 7 fold. maps (1 in pocket).
Many 1205

Bruce, R. Randolph, see no. 9490.

Bruce, Robert, 1873-
Three old plainsmen; by Robert Bruce. Initiation of a bullwhacker, by Albert H. Baiseley. Echoes of the old West, by Col. George W. Stokes. A frontier episode; a conversation between William Francis Hooker and A. H. Oleson, reported by "R. B." New York [c1923]. 24 p. ilus.
MtHi Or OrHi OrP WaS WaU 1206

Bruce, William Speirs, 1867-1921.
Polar exploration. London, Williams and Norgate [c1911]. 256 p. charts.
CVU OrPR Wa WaS 1207

Same. New York, Holt [c1911]. (Home Univ. library of modern knowledge, no. 8)
Many 1208

Bruhl, Gustav, 1826-1903.
Zwischen Alaska und Feuerland, Bilder aus der neuen Welt. Berlin, Verlag von A. Asher & Co., 1896. 722 p.
WaU 1209

Bruet, Edmond.
L'Alaska; geographie, exploration, geologie, mineralogie, faune, peuplement, flore, ressources naturelles. Paris, Payot, 1945. 451 p. illus., maps.
WaS 1210

Bruffey, George A., 1842-
Eighty-one years in the West. Butte, Mont., Butte Miner Co., 1925. 152 p. front.
Many 1211

Brummitt, Mrs. Stella (Wyatt)
Brother Van. New York, Missionary Education Movement of the U. S. and Canada [c1919]. ix, 171 p. front. (port.) plates, ports., facsim. William Wesley Van Orsdel.
MtHi OrP WaTC WaU 1212

Bruneau, Lyda Hoffman.
Stories of Idaho, with illus. depicting life in the state of Idaho from pioneer days to the present time. Lewiston, Idaho, R. G. Bailey Printing Co. [c1940]. 95 p. illus., ports.
IdIf IdU IdUSB WaSp WaU 1213

Brunner, Edmund de Schweinitz, 1889-
A church and community survey of Pend Oreille County, Washington. New York, Doran, c1922. 51 p. front., illus., map, diagrs. (Committee on Social and Religious Surveys. Unique studies of rural America, Town and country series, no. 2)
OrCS OrP Wa WaPS WaSp WaT 1214

Bruseth, Nels.
Indian stories and legends of the Stillaguamish and allied tribes. [Arlington, Wash., c1926]. 21 p.
Many 1215

Bryan, Enoch Albert, 1855-1941.
An address concerning higher agricultural education; delivered before the Educational Congress of the Lewis and Clarke Exposition at Portland, Or. [Pullman, Wash., State College of Wash., 1905]. 16 p.
WaPS 1216

Historical sketch of the State College of Washington, 1890-1925. [Pullman, Wash., Inland-American Printing Co., c1928]. 556 p. front., illus., ports.
Many 1217

Legal status of the functions of the State College of Washington and the University of Washington; a brief. Pullman, Wash., State College of Wash., 1915. 25 p.
WaPS 1218

Same. [c1916?] 37 p.
OrCS WaPS WaU 1219

Memorial address on Samuel G. Cosgrove. [n.p., n.d.] [7] p.
OrU WaPS 1220

Orient meets occident; the advent of the railways to the Pacific Northwest. Pullman, Wash., The Students Book Corp. [c1936]. vii, 269 p. illus., ports., maps.
Many 1221

Bryant, William Cullen, 1794-1878.
Thanatopsis. Seattle [John Julius Johnck and Frank Montana West] 1908. [14] p.
WaU 1222

Bryant Souvenir Co., Seattle, Wash.
Souvenir of the centennial celebration in honor of the discovery of Puget Sound by Capt. Geo. Vancouver, May 8, 1792, at Port Townsend, Wash., May 6 and 7, 1892. Seattle [1892?]. 1 l. fold to [11] p. plates. Consists of photos. mounted on fold. leaf contained in wooden case. Verso has article on Capt. Vancouver. "This cabinet of native woods of Washington: myrtle, ash, oak, maple, pine and Douglas fir."
WaU 1223

Bryce, George, 1844-1931.
Holiday rambles between Winnipeg and Victoria. Winnipeg, 1888. 87 p.
CVicAr 1224

Mackenzie, Selkirk, Simpson, Ed. de luxe. Toronto, Morang, 1905. 305 p. front. (port.) 2 ports., facsims. (Makers of Canada)
CVicAr 1225

Same. 1906. (Makers of Canada. Parkman ed.)
WaU 1226

Same. New ed. Toronto, Morang, 1910. 369 p. front. (port.) 6 plates, 3 ports. (Makers of Canada. Univ. ed., v. 5).
CVicAr CVU OrHi Wa WaTC 1226A

Same. 1912. (Makers of Canada, ed. by D. C. Scott & others. Univ. ed., v. 5, pt. 1)   CV CVU WaS **1227**

Same. Illus. under the direction of A. H. Doughty. New York, Oxford Univ. Press, 1926. 351 p. front., 8 plates, 3 ports. (Makers of Canada. Anniversary ed., v. 9)   CVU IdU MtU **1228**

Remarkable history of the Hudson's Bay Company including that of the French traders of northwestern Canada and of the North-West, X Y, and Astor fur companies. London, Low, 1900. 501 p. front., plates, ports., 5 maps, facsim., coat of arms.   Many **1229**

Same. Toronto, Briggs, 1900.
          CV CVicAr CVU WaU **1230**

Same. New York, Scribner, 1900.
          WaT WaU **1231**

Same. 2d ed. London, Low, 1902.
          OrU WaE WaSP **1232**

Same. Toronto, Briggs, 1904.   WaA **1233**

Same. 3d ed. London, Low [1910]
          CVU IdB WaS WaSP **1234**

Same. New York, Scribner [1910]
          Many **1235**

Sketch of the life and discoveries of Robert Campbell. Winnipeg, Manitoba Free Press, 1898. 18 p. front. (port.) illus.
          CVicAr **1236**

Buache, Jean Nicolas, 1741-1825.
Memoire sur les pays de l'Asie et de l'Amerique situes au nord de la mer du Sud. Paris, 1775. 22 p. fold. map.
          CVicAr **1237**

Buaken, Manuel, 1911-
I have lived with the American people. Caldwell, Idaho, Caxton, 1948. 358 p.
          WaT **1238**

Buchanan, C. M., see nos. 1968, 1969.
Buchanan, James, pres. U. S., 1791-1868.
Last letter of Mr. Buchanan to Mr. Pakenham on the American title to Oregon. Baltimore, Constitution Office, 1845. 16 p.   OrHi **1239**

See also no. 1383.

Buchanan, John A.
Indian legends and other poems; souvenir ed. of the Lewis and Clark fair. San Francisco, Whitaker & Ray, 1905. 140 p. front., 5 plates.   OrHi WaU **1240**

Buchanan, Laura D.
Souvenir of Chief Seattle and Princess Angeline, gleaned from Indian traditions and historic sources of Puget Sound. [n.p., c1909]. [11] p. front. (port.) 6 plates, port.   WaS **1241**

[Buckham, Sidney H.]
A triumphant life [Margaret Meany Younger]. [San Mateo, Calif.? 1945?] [4] p.   WaU **1242**

Buckingham, Nash, see no. 8453.
Buckingham, William, 1832-1915.
The Hon. Alexander Mackenzie, his life and times, by William Buckingham and Hon. Geo. W. Ross. Toronto, Rose Pub. Co., Ltd., 1892. 678 p. front., illus., plates, ports.   CVU **1243**

Same. 5th ed.   CVicAr CVU WaU **1244**

Bucklin, Carrie (Hawley) 1873-1925.
Essays, addresses and poems. Seattle, Lowman & Hanford, 1927. 114 p. Seattle author.   WaU **1245**

[Buckskin] pseud.
The passing of the buffalo. Vancouver, B. C., Selkirk Press, 1916. 47 p. Verse.
          CV CVU WaU **1246**

Buckskin, Mose, see no. 8057.

Budd, Ralph, 1879-
The Pacific Northwest and the engineer; address before the American Society of Civil Engineers, Tacoma, Washington, July 8, 1931. [St. Paul, 1931]. 16 p.
          Many **1247**

Significance of the Rocky Mountains to transcontinental railways; address before the National Association of Railroad and Utilities Commissioners at their 41st annual convention, Glacier Park, Montana, Aug. 28, 1929. [n.p.] 1929. 12 p.   MtHi WaS **1248**

Buell, Bradley, see no. 1371.
Buffalo Bill, see no. 6488.
Buffalo Child Long Lance, Blood Indian Chief, 1896?-1932.
Long Lance; the autobiography of a Blackfoot Indian chief, with a foreword by Irvin S. Cobb. London, Faber & Gwyer, Ltd. [1928]. 304 p. front., plates, ports.   MtU **1249**

Same. New York, Cosmopolitan Book Corp., 1928. 278 p. front., 10 plates.
          Many **1250**

Same. 1929.   CVicAr **1251**

See also no. 6733.

Bulfinch, Thomas, 1796-1867.
Oregon and Eldorado; or, Romance of the rivers [Columbia and Amazon]. Boston, Tilton, 1866, 464 p.   Many **1252**

Bulhak, A. G.
U. B. C. panorama. [Vancouver, B. C., 1945]. 87 p.   CVicAr CVU **1253**

Bull, Sitting, see nos. 2190-2192.
Bull, William K.
A lecture on the subject of "current events" at the Mechanics' Literary Institute of Victoria, December 11, 1883. Victoria, B. C., McMillan, 1884. 19 p.   CVicAr **1254**

Bullard, Catharine, see nos. 614-616.
Bulosan, Carlos.
America is in the heart; a personal history. New York, Harcourt [1946]. 326 p. Author was labor leader among the Filipinos on the Pacific coast.   Many **1255**

Bunnell, Clarence Orvel.
Legends of the Klickitats; a Klickitat version of the story of the bridge of the gods. Portland, Or., Metropolitan, 1933. 64 p. front., illus.   Many **1256**

Same. 1935. 66 p.   IdIf Or OrU **1257**

Buntline, Ned, see nos. 5355, 5356.
Burall, W. F.
A trip to the far West of British Columbia; a 13,000 miles tour. Wisbech, W. Earl [n.d.] 26 p. illus.   WaU **1258**

Same. [1891]. CVicAr **1259**

Burbank, Elbridge Ayer, 1858-
Burbank among the Indians as told by
Ernest Royce, ed. by Frank J. Taylor,
illus. by E. A. Burbank. Caldwell, Idaho,
Caxton, 1944. 232 p. col. front., plates,
ports. Many **1260**

Burbank Company, Burbank, Wash.
Burbank. Seattle, 1913?]. 30 p. illus.
WaPS **1261**

Burd, Harry A., see no. 1953.

Burdett, Charles, 1815-
Kit Carson; life and adventures of Christopher Carson; also his services ren-
dered the United States government as
guide to the various expeditions under
Col. J. C. Fremont and others. Philadelphia, Evans, 1860. 374 p. front. (port.)
5 plates. WaSp **1262**

Life of Kit Carson, the great western
hunter and guide; comprising wild and
romantic exploits as a hunter and trapper in the Rocky Mountains; thrilling
adventures and hairbreadth escapes
among the Indians and Mexicans; his
daring and invaluable services as a
guide to scouting and other parties, etc.,
etc., with an account of various government expeditions to the far West. New
York, Lovell, Coryell & Co. [n.d.] 382 p.
illus. WaPS **1263**

Same. Philadelphia, John E. Potter [c1865]
WaSp **1264**

Same. [c1869]. MtHi Or OrP Wa WaS **1265**
Same. New York, Perkins Book Co. [1869].
x, 376 p. (Heroes of history). WaU **1266**

Burdick, Usher L., see no. 10236.

Bureau of Municipal Research, New York.
Organization and business methods of the
city government of Portland, Or. New
York, 1913. 118 p.
Or OrP WaS WaU **1267**

[Burges, Sir James Bland] 1752-1824.
A narrative of the negotiations occasioned
by the dispute between England and
Spain in the year 1790. [n.p., 1791?].
vii, 307 p. CVicAr **1268**

Burglon, Nora, 1896-
Lost island, illus. by James Reid. Chicago,
J. C. Winston Co. [c1949]. vii, 261 p. col.
front., illus. Alaska story. WaU **1269**

Burk, Mrs. Martha Jane (Cannary) 1850-1903.
Life and adventures of Calamity Jane, by
herself. [n.p.,n.d.] 7 p. MtHi **1270**

Burke, Thomas, 1849-1925.
Address delivered on the occasion of a
patriotic mass meeting presided over by
the consul of France under the auspices
of the France-Amerique Society of Seattle, Sunday, July 14, 1918. [n.p., 1918?].
11 p. WaU **1271**

"The basis of all sound trade is sound
money." Address delivered in Seattle
Opera House, Friday evening, Sept. 18,
1896 under the auspices of Business
Men's Sound Money Club of Seattle.
[Seattle, Lowman & Hanford, 1896?]
15 p. WaU **1272**

Transportation; speech delivered before

Seattle Chapter, American Institute of
Bank Clerks, Elk's Hall, Alaska Building, March 9, 1906. [Seattle, 1906?].
15 p. WaS WaU **1273**

Burkholder, Mabel, 1881-
Captain Cook. Toronto, Ryerson [c1928].
32 p. (Canadian history readers)
CVicAr WaE WaS **1274**

Burks, Arthur J., 1898-
Here are my people. New York, Funk &
Wagnalls, 1934. vi, 314 p. Early setlers of
Big Bend country in Wash. Many **1275**

Rivers into wilderness, by Burke MacArthur [pseud.] New York, Mohawk Press.
1932. 295 p. Homestead farm in Moses
Coulee of eastern Wash. Wa WaU **1276**

[Burleigh, George Shepard] 1821-1903.
Signal fires on the trail of the Pathfinder.
New York, Dayton and Burdick, 1856.
162 p. Poems about John C. Fremont.
CVicAr OrP **1277**

Burlingame, Merrill Gildea, 1901-
The Montana frontier, end plates and
maps drawn by Thomas A. Balzhiser.
Helena, Mont., State Pub. Co. [1942] xiii,
418 p. illus., maps. Many **1278**

Burn, Mrs. June.
Living high, an unconventional autobiography. New York, Duell, Sloan and
Pearce [c1941] x, 292 p. Homesteading
on a Puget Sound island. Many **1279**

Burnett, Peter Hardeman, 1807-1895.
An old California pioneer, by first governor of the state, foreword by Joseph A.
Sullivan. Oakland, Calif., Biobooks
[c1946]. iv, 287 p. 3 fold. maps, fold.
facsim. (The Calif. centennials 5). Reprint ed. of Recollections and opinions
of an old pioneer.
Wa WaS WaT WaU **1280**

The path which led a Protestant lawyer
to the Catholic Church. 5th ed. New
York, [Benzigen? Brothers, 1859]. 741 p.
OrHi **1280A**

Same. New York, Appelton, 1860. xiv,
741 p. Oregon pioneer and author.
WaU **1281**

Recollections of an old pioneer. New
York, Appleton, 1880. xiii, 448 p.
Many **1282**

Burney, James, 1750-1821.
A chronological history of northeastern
voyages of discovery; and of early eastern navigations of the Russians. London, Payne and Foss, 1819. viii, 310 p.
fold. maps.
CV CVicAr CVU WaS WaU **1283**

Burney, W. T., see no. 9467.

Burnham, Howard J.
Government grants and patents in Vancouver, Washington. Vancouver, Wash.,
Clark County Abstract & Title Co., 1947.
38 p. OrP **1284**

Burnham, John, see no. 668.

Burnie, Donald, see no. 5808.

Burpee, Lawrence Johnstone, 1873-
Among the Canadian Alps, with four illus.
in colour, 45 reproductions from photographs and 5 maps. New York, John

Lane Co., 1914. 239 p. col. front., illus.,
plates (part col.) maps.

CV OrP WaS WaSP WaU **1285**

Same. 1915. CVU OrU **1286**

Influence of the war of 1812 upon the settlement of the Canadian West. Ottawa
[n.d.] 9 p. WaS **1287**

Jungling in Jasper. Ottawa, Graphic Pub.,
Ltd. [c1929] 200 p. front., 15 plates.

CVic CVicAr CVU WaS WaSP **1288**

On the old Athabasca trail. New York,
Stokes [1926]. 259 p. front., 16 plates.

IdIf OrP OrSa WaS **1289**

Same. Toronto, Ryerson [1926].

CVic CVicAr CVU **1290**

Same. London, Hurst & Blackett [1927]

CVicAr OrP WaSP **1291**

Same. New York, Stokes [1927?]

Or OhHi **1292**

Sandford Fleming, empire builder. [To-
ronto] Oxford Univ. Press, 1915. 288 p.
front., 11 plates, 4 ports., facsim.

CV CVic CVicAr CVU OrP WaU **1293**

Scouts of empire; the story of the discovery of the great North-West. Toronto,
Musson [1912] v, 104 p.

CVicAr WaS **1294**

The search for the Western sea; the story
of the exploration of northwestern
America. London, A. Rivers, 1908. lx,
651 p. front., plates, ports., maps.

WaU **1295**

Same. New York, Appleton, 1908.

Many **1296**

Same. Toronto, Musson [1908] Many **1297**
Same. New and rev. ed. Toronto, Macmillan, 1935. 2 v. front., plates, ports., fold.
maps. Many **1298**

Same. New York, Macmillan, 1936.

Wa WaSP **1299**

Two western adventurers; Alexander
Henry and Peter Pond. Toronto, Ryerson [c1928]. 28 p. port. (Canadian history readers)

CVicAr Or OrHi OrP **1300**

See also no. 5768.

Burr, Agnes Rush.
Alaska, our beautiful northland of opportunity. Boston, Page, 1919. xii, 428 p.
front., 53 plates, map. (See America first
series) Many **1301**

Same. [1920] OrU **1302**

Same. [1929, c1919] WaU **1303**

Burrell, Orin Kay, 1899-
A study of the operating costs of master
plumbers in Oregon, 1928. [Eugene, Or.]
Univ. of Or., 1929. 31 p. tables, diagrs.

OrCS OrU WaPS **1304**

Burrell, Percy Jewett, see nos. 8045-8047.
Burris, Martin, 1856-
True sketches of the life and travels of
Martin Burris on the western plains, the
Rocky Mountains and the Pacific coast,
U. S. A. [Salina, Kan., Padgett] 1910.
67 p. front. (port.) WaS **1305**

Burrows, C. L., see no. 4906.
Burrows, Elizabeth.
Irene of Tundra Towers, illus. by James

Daugherty. New York, Doubleday. 1928.
311 p. col. front., illus. Alaska story.

Or OrP OrSa WaU **1306**

Judy of the Whale Gates; the strange
happenings that followed the stranding
of the yacht Aphoon among the volcanic islands of Alaska, illus. by James
Daugherty. Garden City, N. Y., Doubleday, 1930. 296 p. col. front., illus.

Or OrP OrU WaSP WaW **1307**

Burson, Henry Clay.
By the wayside; a medley of ballads,
songs and verse. Seattle, Pigott-Washington Printing Co., 1930. 102 p.

Many **1308**

[Burton, Harold Hitz] 1888- ed.
600 days' service; a history of the 361st
Infantry Regiment of the United States
Army. [Portland, Or., James, Kerns &
Abbott Co., 1921]. 276 p. ports., maps,
tables. Wa WaS WaT WaU **1309**

Burwash, Edward Moore Jackson.
The geology of Vancouver and vicinity.
Chicago, Univ. of Chicago Press, 1918.
106 p. illus., plates, fold. maps.

CVU MtU WaU **1310**

Burwell, C. E.
The Vancouver water supply. [n.p.] 1913.
28 p. illus. CV **1311**

[Buschlen, John Preston] 1888- ed.
Big Horn County (Mont.) in the world
war, 1917-1918-1919. [Hardin, Mont., Hardin Tribune, 1919] [112] xxxii [9] p.
illus, ports. WaU **1312**

[Bush, Asahel Nesmith]
Pioneer Trust Co., Salem, Oregon. [Salem,
Or.? 1943?] [37] p. illus, ports. Or. **1313**

Business Men's Cotterill Committee,
Seattle, Wash.
Our great restricted district under Mayor
Gill, report of grand jury, Nov. 1911.
Seattle, 1911. 13 p. WaU **1314**

Business Service Association, Spokane, Wash.
The Coeur d'Alene of Spokane, Washington, "The hotel with a personality".
[Spokane, Shaw and Borden, 190-?] 32
p., illus., ports. IdU WaPS **1315**

Buskett, Nancy.
Fingers that see. Seattle, Stuff Printing
Concern, 1914. 138 p. front.

Wa WaPS WaS WaU **1316**

Bussell, Charles B.
Tide lands, their story. Seattle [n.d.] [16]
p. illus. WaU **1317**

Butler, Gurdon Montague, 1881-
Preliminary survey of the geology and
mineral resources of Curry County, Oregon, by G. M. Butler and G. J. Mitchell.
[Corvallis, Or.] 1916. 132 p. illus., fold.
map, diagrs. (Mineral resources of Or.,
v. 2, no. 2)

MtUM OrP OrSa WaS WaTC **1318**

Butler, Jonathan A.
General report of athletic conditions within the Pacific Coast Intercollegiate Athletic Conference with comments and
recommendations. [Los Angeles, Pacific
Coast Intercollegiate Athletic Conference, 1932] 48 p. tables.

IdU Or OrCS WaPS **1319**

Butler, Julia.
Singing paddles, illus. by Dorothea Cooke. Los Angeles, Suttonhouse, c1935. 255 p. illus., map. Story of Fort Vancouver and the Oregon country. Many **1320**

Same. New York, Holt, c1937. 274 p.
Or OrAshS OrP WaS **1321**

[Butler, Nora B.]
Playgrounds and pastimes of Seattle children. [Seattle? 19—?]. 39 p. illus.
Wa WaS WaU **1322**

Butler, Sir William Francis, 1838-1910.
Far out; rovings retold. London, Isbister, 1880. xx, 329 p. CVicAr **1323**

Same. xxiv, 386 p.
CV CVicAr CVU WaS **1324**

Same. 1881. xx, 329, iii p. WaU **1325**

Great lone land; a narrative of travel and adventure in the Northwest of America. London, Low, 1872. x, 388 p. 6 plates, fold. map.
CV CVicAr MtU Or Wa **1326**

Same. 2d ed. 1872. CVicAr **1327**

Same. 3d ed. 1872. CVicAr CVU Wa **1328**

Same. 4th ed. 1873. 386 p.
CVicAr WaU **1329**

Same. 5th ed. 1873. CVicAr **1330**

Same. 6th ed. 1874. CVicAr WaPS **1331**

Same. 7th ed. 1875. CVicAr **1332**

Same. 9th ed. 1879. WaU **1333**

Same. 1883. CVU **1334**

Same. 12th ed. 1886. CVicAr **1335**

Same. 15th ed. [n.d.] CVicAr **1336**

Same. [1891] CVU **1337**

Red Cloud, the solitary Sioux; a story of the great prairie; new and cheaper ed. London, Low, 1887. 327 p. front., 7 plates.
CVicAr CVU **1338**

Wild northland; being the story of a winter journey with dogs across northern North America. London, Low, 1873. x, 358 p. front. (port.) 15 plates, map.
Wa WaT **1339**

Same. 2d ed. 1874. CVU **1340**

Same. 3d ed. 1874. CVU **1341**

Same. 4th ed. 1874. CVU **1342**

Same. Montreal, Dawson, 1874.
CVicAr **1343**

Same. 4th ed. Philadelphia, Porter & Coates, 1874. MtHi OrHi WaU **1344**

Same. 10th ed. London, Low, 1896.
CVicAr **1345**

Same. New York, Amsterdam Book Co., 1903. 360 p. front. (map). OrU WaU **1346**

Same. New York, A. S. Barnes and Co., 1904. xxii, 360 p. front.(fold. map) (Trail makers) CVU MtU Wa WaPS **1347**

Same. Toronto, Musson, 1910. xiii, 364 p. front., 14 plates, map. CVic **1348**

Same. With introd. by W. L. Grant. Toronto, Courier Press, Ltd., 1911. 360 p. front. (Trail makers of Canada)
CVU MtU OrHi WaU **1349**

Same. New York, Allerton Book Co., 1922 [c1904] xxi, 360 p. front. (fold map).
IdU WaS **1350**

Same. Toronto, Musson, 1924. VCU **1351**

Butte Business Men's Association.
Butte, Montana [contains statistics of mineral production, depths or mines, photographs of buildings and plants. Butte, Mont., McKee Printing Co., 1904?] 31 p. illus., tables. MtUM **1352**

Butte Miner.
Semi-centennial ed. Butte, Mont., 1926. [92] p. illus., ports. (v. 63, no. 282, July 5, 1926) WaU **1353**

Butte Newswriters' Association.
A newspaper reference work; men of affairs and representative institutions of the state of Montana, comp. for the newspaper editors of Montana. [Butte, Mont.] 1914. [94] p. ports. MtU **1354**

Butterbaugh, Grant Illion, 1893-
The measurement of business activity in the Puget Sound area. Chicago, Univ. of Chicago Press[1943]. v, 72 p. map, tables, diagrs. (Studies in business administration, v. 13, no. 2) Many **1355**

Butterfield, Consul Willshire, 1824-1899.
History of the discovery of the Northwest by John Nicolet in 1634 with a sketch of his life. Cincinnati, R. Clarke & Co., 1881. 113 p. OrP WaTC WaU **1356**

Butterworth, Hezekiah, 1839-1905.
Log school-house on the Columbia; a tale of the pioneers of the great Northwest. New York, Appleton, 1890. 250 p. illus., 12 plates. Many **1357**

Same. 1893. WaSp **1358**

Same. 1897. CVicAr **1359**

Same. 3d ed. 1898. IdU WaU **1360**

Same. 1901. WaS **1361**

Same. 1903. OrHi OrSa **1362**

Same. 1911, c1890. WaT **1363**

Same. 1913. IdB **1364**

Zigzag journeys in the great Northwest; or, A trip to the American Switzerland. Boston, Dana [c1890]. 319 p. illus., plate, 2 ports. WaS WaT **1365**

Same. Boston, Estes and Lauriat [c1890] (Zigzag series, v. 12)
OrP Wa WaPS WaS WaU **1366**

By the west to the east; memorandum on some imperial aspects of the completion of the Canadian Pacific Railway. [n.p.] 1885. 11 p. CVicAr **1367**

Bynner, Witter, see no. 10714.

Byrne, Charles David, 1895-
Coordinated control of higher education in Oregon. Stanford Univ., Calif., Stanford Univ. Press, c1940. 150 p. tables, diagrs., charts (1 fold) Many **1368**

Bynum, Lindley, see no. 9358.

Byrne, Patrick Edward, 1869-
Soldiers of the plains. New York, Minton Balch, 1926. 260 p. Indian wars, 1866-1895.
Many **1369**

C. P. R. vs. the people of British Columbia; the Coast-Kootenay Railway; the history of the struggle to obtain a competitive railway from the coast to the interior, and how the enterprise has been blocked by the Dunsmuir government; the policy of a "Business men's government." Victoria, B. C., T. R. Cusack, 1901. 25 p.   CVicAr CVU **1370**

Cadbury, Mrs. Olive Clinton (McCabe)
Social work in Seattle; an inventory and appraisal, by Olive C. Cadbury and research staff; recommendations as to Community Fund future policy, by Bradley Buell; directed by the Graduate Division of Social Work, University of Washington. [Seattle?] 1935. 137 p. front. (map) tables, charts.
                Or OrP WaPS WaS WaU **1371**

Cadzow, Donald A.
Native copper objects of the Copper Eskimo. New York, Museum of the American Indian, Heye Foundation, 1920. 22 p. 11 plates. (Indian notes and monograhps)
                Many **1372**

Cagni, U., see no. 6136.

Cahail, Alice Kellogg.
Sea captains of Whidby Island. [n.p., n.d.] [12] p.   WaS **1373**

Calamity Jane, see no. 1270.

[Calasanz, Marie Joseph, soeur] 1860.
The voice of Alaska; a missioner's memories. Lachine, Quebec, Sisters of St. Ann Press, 1935. 340 [8] p. plates, ports., fold. map.   CVic CVicAr CVU WaU **1374**

Voix d'Alaska; fondation de la mission Sainte Croix (Koserefsky) [Memoires de Soeur Marie Joseph Calasanz, religieuse missionaire de la Congregation des soeurs de Sainte Anne] Lachine, Quebec, Procure des missions des soeurs de Sainte Anne, 1930. 209 p. illus., ports.
                CVic WaU **1375**

Caldwell, Elsie (Noble) 1882-
Alaska trail dogs. New York, R. R. Smith, 1945. 150 p. front. (map) plates, ports., facsim.   Many **1376**

Caldwell, Erskine, see no. 11052.

Caldwell, Frank, 1867-
Wolf, the storm leader. New York, Dodd, 1930. 183 p. front., illus., plates. IdIf **1377**

Caldwell, J. B.
Introducing Alaska. New York, Putnam [1947] xii, 202 p. plates.   Many **1378**

Calgary route to the Klondike gold fields; description of routes; miners' and prospectors' outfitting guide. [n.p., n.d.] 10 p.   CVicAr **1379**

[Calhoun, Anne Hornsby.]
Points on Puget Sound. [Seattle, 1936] [26] p. illus.   WaS WaU **1380**

Puget Sound calendar, 1935. [n.p.] 1934. [12?] p.   WaS **1381**

A Seattle heritage; the Fine Arts Society. Seattle, Lowman & Hanford, 1942. 121 p. front., illus.   Many **1382**

Calhoun, John Caldwell, 1782-1850.
Oregon; the claim of the United States to Oregon, as stated in the letters of the Hon. J. C. Calhoun and the Hon. J. Buchanan to the Right Hon. R. Pakenham, with an appendix containing the counter statement of Mr. Pakenham to the American secretaries of state. London, Wiley, 1846. 55, 16 p. fold. map.
                CVicAr OrHi OrP WaS WaU **1383**

Calhoun, Scott.
[Proposal of the receivers of the Seattle, Renton & Southern Railroad] to the citizens and taxpayers of the city of Seattle, and especially the taxpayers and residents of Rainier Valley, by Scott Calhoun and Joseph Parkin. Seattle [1913] 12 p.   WaS **1384**

California Oregon Power Company.
Klamath County survey. [n.p., 1924?] 12 p. maps, diagr.   OrCS OrP **1385**

[Calkins, John U.?]
History of the 347th Machine Gun Battalion, comp. from official records and the personal notes of various members of the battalion. Oakland, Calif., Horwinski Company [1919?] 140 p. front., plates, ports. Trained at Camp Lewis, Washington.   Wa WaU **1386**

Call, Hughie (Florence) 1890-
Golden fleece, with illus, by Paul Brown. Boston, Houghton, 1942. 250 p. illus. Life as wife of Montana sheep rancher.
                Many **1387**

The Call of the Coast, British Columbia, Canada. Vancouver, B. C., B. C. Advertisers [n.d.] 94 p. illus. CV CVU **1388**

Callahan, James Morton, 1864-
The Alaska purchase and Americo-Canadian relations. Morgantown, W. Va., W. Va. Univ., 1908. 44 p. (Studies in American history. Series 1, Diplomatic history, nos. 2 and 3)   WaTC WaU **1389**

Callicotte, Mrs. Alma Francis (Brown) 1863-
Seeds of truth. Seattle, Bull Bros., 1905. 79 p. illus., port. Rev. and enl. ed. Poems.
                Wa WaU **1390**

Calvert, Elizabeth Henderson (McRobie)
The boat-man god and other poems. Seattle, Calvert Co. [c1898] 69 p.
                Wa WaS WaU **1391**

Sealth, the city by the inland sea. [n.p., c1897] [22] p. front., 13 plates, port.
                WaS WaU **1392**

Calvert, Frank, ed.
The cartoon; a reference book of Seattle's successful men, with decorations by the Seattle Cartoonists' Club. [Seattle, Metropolitan] c1911. [245] p. illus., ports.
                WaS WaU **1393**

See also no. 4603.

Calvin, Jack.
Fisherman 28, with illus. by Mahlon Blaine. Boston, Little, 1930. 325 p. col. front., 4 plates. Alaska story.
                IdIf OrP WaS WaT **1394**

See also nos. 8661, 8662.

Camas Valley High School.
Pioneer history of Camas Valley, by the student body. Roseburg, Or. [Sun Printing Co., 1923] 20 p.   Or OrHi **1395**

Cambern, Muriel.
Ten thousand years ago and now; pen drawings and historical data. Tacoma, Pioneer, Inc., c1925. 48 p. illus.
WaT **1396**

Cameron, Agnes Deans, 1863-1912.
The new North; being some account of a woman's journey through Canada to the Arctic. New York, Appleton, 1910. xix, 398 p. front. (port.) illus., map.
Many **1397**

Same. 1912. CVicAr **1398**

Cameron, Charlotte (Wales-Almy)
A cheechako in Alaska and Yukon. London, Stokes [1920] 291 p. front. (port.) plates.
Many **1399**

Same. Unwin. map.
CV CVU WaS WaU **1400**

Cameron, D. R., see no. 10067.

Cameron, William Bleasdell, 1862-
The war trail of Big Bear, being the story of the connection of Big Bear and other Cree Indian chiefs and their followers with the Canadian North-west rebellion of 1885, the Frog Lake massacre and events leading up to and following it, and of two months imprisonment in the camp of the hostiles. Boston, Small, Maynard, 1927. 256 p. front., plates, ports., map, facsim.
CVicAr CVU MtHi OrCS OrP WaSp **1401**

See also nos. 2411, 6893.

Camp, Charles L., see nos. 1826, 10657.

Camp, Frank Bernard, 1882-
Alaska nuggets. Anchorage, Alaska Pub. Co., 1921. 45 p. Poems. OrP WaS **1402**

Same. 1922. 66 p. illus. CVicAr **1403**

Songs of the North West. Bonners Ferry, Idaho, Kootenai Valley Pub. Co., 1929. 114 p. IdB IdU **1404**

War and peace. Caldwell, Idaho, Caxton, 1932. 160 p. Poems. WaSp **1405**

Camp, James McIntyre, 1858-1927.
Official history of the operations of the first Idaho infantry, U. S. V. in the campaign in the Philippine Islands, written by Private James Camp, who was with the regiment throughout the campaign, through the courtesy of Major Daniel W. Figgins. [n. p., 1899] 60 p. illus.
Wa WaPS WaS WaU **1406**

Camp Lewis. Seattle, Clark Co., 1917.
75 p. illus., fold. plate, ports. On cover: 91st Division. National Army, Camp Lewis.
WaSp WaU **1407**

Campaign Songs of the Multorpor Quartette. Portland, Or., Geo. H. Foss [1896?] [12] p. illus. WaPS **1408**

Campbell Mrs. A. C.
Memorial of Mrs. Caroline A. Ladd, April 20, 1910. [n.p.] 1910. [18] p. Or **1409**

Campbell, Sir Alexander, 1822-1892.
In the case of Louis Riel, convicted of treason and executed therefor. Ottawa, MacLean, Roger, 1885. 10 p.
CVicAr **1410**

Campbell, Alice V.
Short history of Rosalia, Whitman County, Washington. [n.p., 1930] 10 p. illus.
Wa WaSp **1411**

Campbell, Archibald, bp. of London.
A sermon preached in Westminster Abbey on St. Matthias Day, 1859, at the consecration of the first bishop of British Columbia. London, Rivingtons, 1859, 20 p.
CVU **1412**

Campbell, Colin, comp.
The White Pass and Yukon route to the golden North. Seattle, Press of the Trade Register, 1901. 104 p. illus.
WaU **1413**

Campbell, Mrs. Helen (Stuart) 1839-1918.
White and red; a narrative of life among the northwest Indians, by Helen C. Weeks. New York, Hurd & Houghton, c1869. 266 p. front., plates. WaPS **1414**

Campbell, Jess G.
What we do at the beach. [Portland, Or., Kilham Stationery & Printing Co., c1939] 17 p. col. illus. OrU **1415**

Campbell, John Lyle, 1818-1886.
The great agricultural and mineral West; a hand-book and guide for the emigrant to the most inviting agricultural fields of the western states, and to the richest gold and silver regions of the Rocky Mountains and Pacific slope; itinery [!] of the routes, features of the country and journal of residence in Idaho and Montana. 3d annual ed. Chicago, Church, Goodman & Donnelley, 1866. 79 p. illus., map. OrP **1416**

Idaho and Montana gold regions; the emigrant's guide overland, 1864. [n.p.] c1865. 52, 16 p.. illus. OrP **1417**

Idaho; six months in the new gold diggings; the emigrant's guide overland, itinerary of the routes, features of the country, journal of residence, etc. New York, 1864. 62 p. front. (map) illus.
OrU **1418**

Same. Microfilm copy. WaU **1419**

Campbell, Patricia, 1901-
Eliza. Seattle, Superior Pub. Co. [1947] 349 p. Washington author. Many **1420**

Lush valley. Seattle, Superior Pub. Co. [1948] 367 p.
OrP WaE WaS WaT WaU **1421**

Campbell, Richard Posey.
A daughter of the Rogues, a tale of the Rogue River Valley. Ashland, Or. [Ashland Tidings Press] c1919. [63] p. Verse.
Or OrCS OrP OrU WaSp WaU **1422**

Campbell, Robert, 1808-1894.
The discovery and exploration of the Youcon (Pelley) River. Winnipeg, Manitoba Free Press, 1885. 18 p.
CVicAr **1423**

Campbell, Walter S., see no. 7941.

Campbell, William, 1880-
Arctic Patrols; stories of the Royal Canadian Mounted Police. Milwaukee, Wis., Bruce Pub. Co. [c1936] 335 p. front. (port.)
Many **1424**

Campbell-Johnston, Ronald Campbell.
The story of the totem. [Vancouver, B. C.,
Citizen Printing & Pub. Co., n.d.] 62 p.
illus.   CVicAr **1425**
Same. [Vancouver, B. C. Pyott, 1924]
CV CVU WaS WaT WaU **1426**

Canada Steamship Lines, Ltd., Montreal.
Catalogue of a selection of early views,
maps, charts and plans of the Great
Lakes, the Far West, the Arctic and
Pacific Oceans from the William H.
Cloverdale Collection of historical Can-
adiana at the Manoir Richelieu, Murray
Bay, P. Q., exhibited by the Thunder
Bay Historical Society, Fort William,
Ontario, Port Arthur, Ontario; March
13 to April 30, 1943. Montreal [1943]
22 p. illus. maps. Cover-title: The Far
West.   WaU **1427**

Canada's Alaskan dismemberment; an
analytical examination of the fallacies
underlying the tribunal award. Niagara-
on-the-Lake, Ont., C. Thonger, 1904. 76 p.
CV CVicAr CVU OrSaW WaSp WaU **1428**

Canadian Club of Victoria.
Constitution. [Victoria, B. C.] Sweeney-
McConnell press, 1907. 9 p. CVicAr **1429**

Canadian Library Association.
Canadian biographies: artists and authors.
[Vancouver, B. C.] 1948. 1 v. (loose-leaf)
WaU **1430**

Canadian Memorial Chapel, dedicated in
1928 at Vancouver, B. C. in memory of
those who made the supreme sacrifice
for Canada, 1914-1918. [Vancouver, B. C.,
Sun Pub. Co., Ltd., n.d.] 16 p. illus.,
port.   CVicAr **1431**

Canadian National Railways.
The Canadian Rockies. [n.p.] 1935. 23 p.
illus., fold. map.   WaPS **1432**

The Canadian Rockies and the Pacific
Coast; the triangle tour. [Montreal,
1935] 22 p. illus., fold. map. WaPS **1433**

The Canadian Rockies, Jasper and the
triangle tour. [Montreal?] 1931. 23 p.
illus.   WaPS **1434**

Canadian Rockies, Jasper, Mount Robson
and the fiords of the North Pacific.
[Montreal, 1934] 23 p. illus., fold. map.
WaPS **1435**

Jasper National Park. [Montreal, 1937]
36 p. illus. (part col.) maps (1 fold.)
WaPS **1436**

Jasper Park Lodge in the Canadian Rockies. [Montreal?] 1936. 23 p. illus., maps.
WaPS **1437**

Jasper Park Lodge, Jasper National Park,
Alberta, in the heart of the Canadian
Rockies. [Montreal? 1931] 31 p. illus.
WaPS **1438**

Same. 1932. 32 p. front. (plan) illus. (part
col.)   WaPS **1439**

What to do at Jasper National Park and
Mount Robson. [Montreal? 1936] 19 p.
illus.   WaPS **1440**

Canadian Pacific Railway Company.
British Columbia, Canada's Pacific province; its advantages, resources and

climate. [n.p., 1908?] 63 p. illus., maps
(1 fold.)   WaU **1441**

British Columbia, Canada's Pacific province; its natural resources, advantages
and climate. [n.p.] 1910. 80 p. illus., fold.
map.   WaU **1442**
Same. 1911. 77 p.   CVicAr WaU **1443**

British Columbia, Canada's Pacific province; its position, advantages, resources
and climate. [n.d., 1906] 64 p. illus., maps
(1 fold.)   WaU **1444**
Same. [1907] 63 p. illus., map. WaU **1445**

British Columbia, the most westerly
province of Canada, its position, advantages, resources and climate; new fields
for mining, farming, fruit growing and
ranching along the lines of the Canadian
Pacific Railway; information for prospectors, miners, and intending settlers.
[n.p., 1900] 64 p. illus., maps (1 fold)
WaU **1446**
Same. [1902]   WaU **1447**
Same. [1905]   WaU **1448**

Business and industrial opportunities in
western Canada. Winnipeg, 1926. 85 p.
fold. map.   WaPS **1449**

By-laws. Ottawa, MacLean, Roger, 1881.
13 p.   CVicAr **1450**

The Canadian Northwest; dairy farming,
ranching, mining. Rev. ed. [n.p., 1891]
64 p. illus., fold. map.   CVicAr **1451**

Canada's evergreen playground. [Victoria,
B.C.?] 1936. [6] p. illus.   WaPS **1452**

Canadian Pacific Rockies. [n.p.] 1923. 32 p.
illus., maps (1 fold. col.)   WaPS **1453**

Canadian Rockies. [n.p., 1936] 16 p. illus.,
maps.   WaPS **1454**

Chalet-bungalow camps in the Canadian
Rockies. [n.p., 1936] 12 p. illus., tables.
WaPS **1455**

The challenge of the mountains; the
Candaian Rockies, the playground of
America. [Montreal? 19—?] 48 p. illus.,
map.   CV CVU **1456**

1000 miles of cruising through the fiords
of British Columbia via Canadian Pacific "Princess Line". [Vancouver, B. C.]
1936. [6] p. illus., map.   WaPS **1457**

Pacific coast tours through the Canadian
Pacific Rockies. [n.p., 191—?] [16] p.
illus., fold. map.   WaPS **1458**

The province of British Columbia, Canada; its resources, commercial position
and climate and description of the new
field opened up by the Canadian Pacific Railway. [n.p., n.d.] 48 p. front.
(map) illus., fold. map.   CVicAr **1459**
Same. [Montreal, 1886] CVicAr MtU **1460**

Reports and documents in reference to
the location of the line and a western
terminal harbour, 1878. Ottawa, Mac-
Lean, Roger, 1878. 104 p. fold. maps.
CV CVicAr CVU WaU **1461**

Roads of adventure through the Canadian
Rockies, Alaska and the evergreen playground. [n.p.] 1932. 32 p. illus., fold.
map.   WaPS **1462**

Southern British Columbia, the garden of Canada; Kootenay, Boundary and Okanagan districts and Vancouver Island; brief description of their wonderful natural resources and scenic beauties, presented by the Canadian Pacific Railway Company to the homeseeker, investor, sportsman and tourist, 1906. [Montreal?] 1906. 77 p. illus.
CVicAr CVU **1463**

Southern British Columbia, the garden of Canada; Kootenay, Boundary, Okanagan and Columbia River districts; brief description of their wonderful natural resources and scenic beauties. [Calgary? 1909] 78 p. illus. CV OrHi WaU **1464**

Victoria and Vancouver Island. [n.p.] 1924. 16 p. illus., fold. map. WaPS **1465**

Western provinces of Canada; Manitoba, Saskatchewan, Alberta, British Columbia. Calgary [n.d.] 128 p. illus., map, tables. OrHi **1466**

Women's work in western Canada. [n.p.] 1906. 68 p. illus. CVicAr **1467**

Canadian Standard Guides.
Opportunities in British Columbia, 1924, containing extracts from Heaton's Annual. Toronto, Ernest Heaton, c1924. 96 p. illus. WaT **1468**

Canary, Martha Jane, see no. 1270.

Cane, Claude Richard John.
Summer and fall in western Alaska; the record of a trip to Cook's Inlet after big game. London, H. Cox, 1903. 191 p. front., plates.
CVicAr CVU WaS WaU **1469**

Canestrelli, Philippo.
Catechism of Christian doctrine prepared and enjoined by the order of the third plenary council of Baltimore, trans. into Flathead by a father of the Society of Jesus. Woodstock College, Md., 1891. 102 p. Anon.
OrP WaPS WaSp WaU **1470**

Linguae Ksanka (Kootenai); elementa grammaticae. Auctore Philippo Canestrelli e Societate Jesu. Santa Clara, Calif., 1894. 144 p. CV CVU WaU **1471**

Canfield, Dorothy, see nos. 5460-5463.

Canfield, Thomas Hawley, 1822-
Life of Thomas Hawley Canfield, his early efforts to open a route for the transportation of the products of the West to New England by way of the Great Lakes and his connection with the early history of the Northern Pacific Railroad. Burlington, Vt., 1889. 48 p. front. (port.)
MtHi **1472**

Northern Pacific Railroad; partial report to the Board of Directors, or a portion of a reconnoissance made in the summer of 1869 between Lake Superior and the Pacific Ocean accompanied with notes on Puget Sound, by Samuel Wilkeson, May, 1870. [New York? 1870] 96, 44 p. fold. maps. WaU **1473**

Cannary, Martha Jane, see no. 1270.

Cannon, Carl L., see no. 5281.

Cannon, Miles.
Waiilatpu, its rise and fall, 1836-1847; a story of pioneer days in the Pacific Northwest based entirely upon historical research, featuring the journey of Narcissa Prentiss Whitman, the first American woman to cross the continent and look upon the Columbia River. Boise, Idaho, Capital News Job Rooms, 1915. ix, 171 p. front., plates, ports. Many **1474**

Canse, John Martin, 1869-
Captain Robert Gray and the northwest coast. Montesano, Wash., Robert Gray Memorial Assn. [n.d.] 14 p. (Bulletin no. 1). CVicAr **1475**

Pilgrim and pioneer; dawn in the Northwest. New York, Abingdon Press [c1930] 306 p. front. (port.) 6 plates, map.
Many **1476**

See also no. 7983

Canton, Frank M., 1849-1927.
Frontier trails; the autobiography of Frank M. Canton, ed. by Edward Everett Dale. Boston, Houghton, 1930. xvii, 236 p. front., plates, ports. Alaska and Oklahoma.
MtHi MtU Or OrP WaS WaSp **1477**

Cantwell, Robert.
The land of plenty. New York, Farrar [c1934] 369 p. Washington mill city story.
Many **1478**

Laugh and lie down. New York, Farrar [c1931] lxxv, 269 p. Washington mill city story. Many **1479**

Capek, Karel, see no. 10837.

The Capital.
Holiday trade number. Boise, Idaho, 1899. 1 v. (v. 3, no. 15, Dec. 23, 1899) IdB **1480**

Capilano, Chief Joe, see no. 5247.

Capital Journal.
Golden anniversary and capitol occupation edition. Salem, Or., 1938. [112] p. illus., ports. (50th year, no. 157, July 2, 1938) OrP WaU **1481**

Capital Typographical Union No. 210.
Constitution, by-laws and scale of prices. Salem, Or., 1899. 1 v. OrHi **1482**

— — — **Textbook Committee.**
Why the state should print your textbooks. Salem, Or. [1916?] 8 p. Pr OrP **1483**

Capitol's who's who for Oregon, 1936-1937, comp. under the direction of R. O. Norman; J. A. Bailey, ed. Portland, Or., Capitol Pub. Co. [c1936] 608 p.
Many **1484**

Capitol's who's who for Oregon, 1948-1949. Portland, Capitol Pub. Co. [1948]. 624 p. ports. Many **1484A**

Captain Cook, bi-centenary, 1928; souvenir of the bicentenary celebrations arranged in the Cleveland district. Middlesbrough, Hood, 1928. 24 p. front., plates, ports., facsims. CVicAr CVU **1485**

Cardwell, James Robert, 1830-1916.
Brief history of early horticulture in Oregon. [Portland, Or.?] 1906. 37 p.
Or OrCS OrHi OrP WaU **1486**

Early horticultural days in Oregon; address at the recent meeting of the State Horticultural Society, held in Portland Dec. 7, 1909. [Salem, Or.? 1909?] 8 p. port. OrP OrU WaPS WaSp WaU **1487**

Cardwell, Mrs. Mae Harrington Whitney, d. 1920.
In memoriam, Dr. James Robert Cardwell. Portland, Or., Western Printing Assn. [n.d.] 3 p. front. (port.)
OrHi OrP **1488**

Carey, Charles Henry, 1857-
A general history of Oregon prior to 1861. Portland, Or., Metropolitan, 1935-36. 2 v. front., 8 plates, 7 ports., 10 maps, facsim.
Many **1489**

History of Oregon. Chicago, Pioneer Historical Pub. Co. [c1922] 3 v. fronts., plates, ports., maps (1 fold.) facsim. Volumes 2, 3 biographical, for which author does not claim responsibility.
Many **1490**

Same. Author's ed. 1016 p. front., plates, ports., maps (1 fold.) facsims.
Many **1491**

See also nos. 4150, 10112.

Carey and Harlan Company.
Final traction plan and redraft of service at cost franchise, city of Portland. [Portland, Or.] 1930. 49 p. OrP **1492**

[Report on valuations and rates of the Portland Electric Power Co.; an investigation for the purpose of procuring a reduction in electrical rates. Portland, Or.] 1930. 1 v. maps, plans. OrP **1493**

Traction plan [report pertaining to a suggested plan for the revision of the present street railway system in the city of Portland] Portland, Or., 1930. 31 p.
OrP **1494**

Carhart, Edith Beebe.
The Angora wool rabbit, a manual for the beginner. Bellingham, Washington, c1930. 64 p. illus. Many **1495**

A history of Bellingham, Washington, comp. from newspaper articles, city directories and books of local history. Bellingham, Wash., 1925. [40] p.
WaE **1496**

Same. [50] p. CV CVU Wa **1497**
Same. Bellingham, Wash., Argonaut Press, 1926. 99 p. Many **1498**

Cariboo Automobile Association.
The historic Cariboo road, British Columbia, describing the most interesting auto tour in British Columbia. [Vancouver, B. C., Wrigley Printing Co., 1922] 48 p. illus. fold. map. CVicAr CVU **1499**

Cariboo; the newly discovered gold fields of British Columbia, fully described by a returned digger. London, Darton, 1862. iv. 76 p. tables. CVicAr **1500**
Same. iv, 78 p. CVicAr **1501**

Carlow, Philip.
Seattle spirit, illus. by E. R. Claybourne. [Seattle, c1909] [12] p. illus. Verses.
WaS **1502**

Carlson, Frank.
Chief Sealth. [Seattle, 1903?] 35 p. illus. (plan) geneal. table. (Univ. of Wash. Bulletin. Series 3, no. 2, Dec. 1903)
CVicAr OrHi OrP WaS WaSp WaU **1503**

Carlton, Mabel Mason.
John C. Fremont, pathfinder of the West. Providence, Livermore & Knight Co., c1927. 16 p. illus., map. WaPS **1504**
Lewis and Clark, pathfinders of the great Northwest. [Boston?] John Hancock Mutual Life Insurance Company [c1925] 16 p. illus. (Issue no. 106)
WaPS WaU **1505**

Carmack, George Washington
My experiences in the Yukon. [Seattle, Trade Printery, c1933] 16 p. illus., port.
CV CVicAr CVU WaS WaU **1506**

Carmichael, Alfred.
Indian legends of Vancouver Island, illus. by J. Semeyn. Toronto, Musson [c1922] 97 p. front., illus. Many **1507**

Carmichael, William M.
These sixty years, 1887-1947; being the story of First Baptist Church, Vancouver. [Vancouver, B. C., Capitol Printers, 1947] 55 p. 11 plates (incl. ports.)
CVicAr **1508**

Carnarvon Club.
Constitution. [n.p., 1876?] [4] p.
CVicAr **1509**

Carnegie Institution of Washington.
Eocene flora of western America, by Ethel I. Sanborn, Susan S. Potbury, and Harry D. MacGinitie. Washington, D. C., 1937. 156 p. illus. plates, maps, diagr. (Contribution to palaeontology)
OrCS WaS **1510**

Middle Cenozoic floras of western North America. [Washington, D. C.] 1936. 152 p. illus. plates, maps, diagr. (Contributions to palaeontology)
OrCS WaS WAWW **1511**

A carnival of water, Portland, Oregon, June, 1894. Portland, Or., Lewis & Dryden [1894] 13 p. illus. OrP **1512**

Carpenter, Frank George, 1855-1924.
Alaska, our northern wonderland, with 123 illus. from original photographs and two maps in colour. Garden City, N. Y., Doubleday, Page, 1923. xv, 319 p. front., plates, ports., fold. maps. (Carpenter's world travels) Many **1513**
Same. 1925 [c1923]
IdP OrP OrU Wa WaS WaT **1514**
Same. 1928. WaA WaPS WaTC **1515**

Carpenter, Herman M.
Three years in Alaska. Philadelphia, Howard [1901] 105 p. plates, port.
CVicAr **1516**

Carpenters and Joiners Union No. 1 of Rossland.
Constitution and by-laws adopted January 26th, 1900. Rossland, B. C., Stunden Printing Co. [n.d.] 20 p. CVirAr **1517**

Carr, Emily, 1871-1945.
The book of Small. Toronto, Oxford Univ. Press, 1942. viii, 245 p. front. (port.) Reminiscences of author's childhood in Victoria, B. C. Many **1518**

Emily Carr; her painting and sketches, pub. for the National Gallery of Canada and the Art Gallery of Toronto. Toronto, Oxford Univ. Press [1945] 64 p.
CVicAr OrHi WaU **1519**

Growing pains, the autobiography, with a foreword by Ira Dillworth. Toronto, Oxford Univ. Press, 1946. xvi, 381 p. col. front., plates (part col.) ports. (1 col.) Many **1520**

The house of All Sorts. Toronto, Oxford Univ. Press, 1944. vii, 222 p. col. front., 1 illus. CV CVicAr CVU WaS WaU **1521**

Klee Wyck, with a foreword by Ira Dilworth. Toronto, Oxford Univ. Press, 1941. xi, 155 p. col. front. (port.) col. plates. CV CVicAr CVU **1522**

Same. New York, Farrar, c1942. 174 p. col. front., col. illus. Many **1523**

Carr, Harry, 1877-
The West is still wild, romance of the present and the past. Boston, Houghton, 1932. iv, 257 p. front., illus. Many **1524**

See also no. 699.

Carr, Mary Jane.
Children of the covered wagon; a story of the Old Oregon Trail. New York, Crowell, c1934. 318 p. front., illus. Many **1525**

Young Mac of Fort Vancouver, illus. by Richard Holberg. New York, Crowell, 1940. vi, 238 p. front., illus., plates (part col. and double) Many **1526**

Same. Junior Literary Guild, c1940. WaT WaW **1527**

Carr, Robert Van, 1877-
Cowboy lyrics. Chicago, W. B. Conkey Company [c1908] 182 p. WaU **1528**

Carr, Sarah (Pratt) 1850-
The cost of empire in four acts; libretto for the opera Narcissa by Mary Carr Moore. Seattle, Stuff Printing Concern [c1912] 22 p. WaE WaS **1529**

The iron way; a tale of the builders of the West, with four illus. by John W. Norton. Chicago, McClurg, 1907. 367 p. front., 3 plates. Or Wa WaU **1530**

Carre, William H., pub.
Art work on British Columbia, Canada. [n.p.] 1900. 21 p. plates. Text by R. E. Gosnell. CV CVicAr CVU **1531**

Carrel, Frank, 1870-
Canada's West and farther west; latest book on the land of golden opportunities. Toronto, Musson, 1911. xiv, 258 p. front., 59 plates. CV CVic CVicAr CVU OrU **1532**

Same. Quebec, Telegraph Printing Co., 1911. CVU WaU **1533**

Carreno, Alberto M., see no. 7129.

Carrico, James L.
Our westermost point, Bandon-by-the-sea. Portland, Or., Columban Press, 1922. 22p. Or **1534**

Carrigan, John Beardslee.
The city of Havaheart; Tiny's travelogue; a key to the Community Chest, Portland, Or. [1921] 28 p. illus. OrP **1535**

Carrington, Henry B., see no. 1538.

[Carrington, Mrs. Margaret Irvin (Sullivant)] 1831-1870.
Ab-sa-ra-ka, home of the Crows; being the experience of an officer's wife on the plains, with outlines of the natural features and resources of the land, tables of distances, maps, and other aids, to the traveler; gathered from observation and other reliable sources. Philadelphia, Lippincott, 1868. 284 p. front. (fold. map) illus., plans, MtU WaU **1536**

Same. 1869. MtU Or WaS WaU **1537**

Ab-sa-ra-ka, land of massacre; being the experience of an officer's wife on the plains, with an outline of Indian operations and conferences from 1865 to 1878, by Col. Henry B. Carrington. (3d ed. of Mrs. Carrington's narrative) Rev., enl. and illus. with maps, cuts, Indian portraits, etc. Philadelphia, Lippincott, 1878. xx, 13-383 p. front., illus., plates, ports., 2 fold. maps. WaU **1538**

Carrington, Thomas Spees, see no. 9631.

Carroll, H.
History of Nanaimo pioneers. Nanaimo, B. C., Herald, 1935. 71 p. ports. CVicAr **1539**

Carrothers, William Alexander, 1889-
The British Columbia fisheries, with a foreword by H. A. Innes. Toronto, Univ. of Toronto Press, 1941. 136 p. tables. Many **1540**

Carruth, J. H., see no. 8136.

Carson, Christopher, 1809-1868.
Kit Carson's autobiography, ed. by Milo Milton Quaife. Chicago, Donnelley, 1935. xxxviii, 192 p. front. (port.) facsim. (Lakeside classics) OrP WaS WaSp WaU **1541**

Kit Carson's own story of his life, as dictated to Col. and Mrs. D. C. Peters about 1856-57, and never before published; ed. by Blanche C. Grant. Taos, N. M., 1926. 138 p. front., illus., plates, ports., facsim. MtU OrP WaSp **1542**

See also nos. 8064-8069.

Carson, Mildred.
A history of the Idaho County free press, Grangeville, Idaho, for fifty years, 1886-1936. [Grangeville, Idaho? E. M. Olmstead? 1936?] 27 p. WaPS **1543**

Carter, John Wesley.
From the heights [tribute to grandeur of Mt. Rainier] Chicago, McClurg, 1911. 41 p. front. WaT WaU **1544**

Carter, Nicholas, see no. 2060.

Carter, W. N.
Harry Tracy, the desperate western outlaw; a fascinating account of the famous bandit's stupendous adventures and daring deeds, the most thrilling man-hunt on record. Chicago, Laird & Lee [c1902] 296 p. front., illus., 2 plates, port. OrP WaS WaSp WaT **1545**

Cartoons and caricatures of Seattle citizens. [Seattle, Associated Cartoon Service, c1906] 199 p. illus. Wa WaS WaU **1546**

Carvalho, S. N.
Incidents of travel and adventure in the far West; with Col. Fremont's last expedition across the Rocky mountains,

including three months' residence in Utah and a perilous trip across the great American desert to the Pacific. New York, Derby & Jackson, 1857. 380 p. front.   Many **1547**

Same. 1859. 250, 130 p.   WaSp **1548**

Same. 1860.   CVicAr WaU **1549**

Caryl, John.
Our new heraldry; a drama. Seattle, Lowman & Hanford [1902] 208 p. WaU **1550**

Cascade County Coal Operators Association.
The coal strike, by Fred H. Sturm. Secretary. [Great Falls, Mont.? 1922] [8] p.
                                           MtU **1551**

Cascade Tunnel Association.
Smash the granite line! [Seattle, 1926?] [4] p.   WaS WaU **1552**

Case, Robert Ormond, 1895-
Big timber; a novel. Philadelphia, Macrae, Smith, 1937. 271 p. Lumbering in Oregon.
                                          Many **1553**

Same. 2d printing.   Many **1554**

Empire builders. New York, Doubleday, 1947. x, 333 p.   Many **1555**

Last Mountains; the story of the Cascades, by Robert Ormond Case and Victoria Case. Garden City, N. Y., Doubleday, 1945. 236 p. plates.
                                          Many **1556**

Riders of the Grande Ronde. Garden City, N. Y., Doubleday, 1928. 373 p.
                    MtU Or OrP OrSa OrU Wa **1557**

River of the West; a story of opportunity in the Columbia empire; research by William Price Gray. Portland, Or., Northwestern Electric Co.; Pacific Power and Light Co., c1940. 47 p. illus., port., map, diagrs.   Many **1558**

Same. 2d ed.   WaU **1559**

Whispering Valley. New York, Burt [c1932] vi, 311 p. Condon, Or. and vicinity.
                             Or OrP WaU **1560**

The Yukon drive. Garden City, N. Y., Doubleday, 1930. vi, 359 p.
                 CVicAr CVU OrSa WaW **1561**

Same. 1st ed. Garden City, N. Y. Doubleday, Doran & Company Co. [!] inc.
              CVU MtU Or WaPS WaU **1562**

Case, Victoria, see no. 1556.

Case of Baptiste Cadien, for murder; tried at Three Rivers in the March session 1838 [first record of a crime trial west of the Rocky Mountains] Three Rivers, G. Stobbs, 1838. 24 p.   CVicAr **1563**

The case of the Hudson's Bay Company.
[n.p., n.d.] 3 p.   CVicAr **1564**

Cash, Gwen.
I like British Columbia, illus. by J. M. Donald. New York, Macmillan, 1938. xiii, 192 p. illus., plates (part col.)
                                          Many **1565**

Same. Toronto.   CVic **1566**

Same. 1939.   CVU WaTC **1567**

A million miles from Ottawa [Diary of a Canadian journalist on Vancouver Island, Feb.-Apr., 1942] Toronto, Macmillan, 1942. x, 152 p.
              CV CVic CVicAr WaS WaU **1568**

Cashmere Valley Record.
Special clam feed edition. Cashmere, Wash. 1941. 8, 12 p. illus., ports. (Mar. 20, 1941)   WaU **1569**

Cass Frank Hadley, ed.
Looking northwest, illus. by Lewis Crutcher. Portland, Or., Binfords & Mort [c1938] 201 p. front., plates. Many **1570**

Castera, J., see nos. 6380, 6381, 8991.

Castera, M., see no. 5542.

Cataldo, Joseph Mary, 1837-1928.
Jesus-Christ-nim kinne uetas-pa kut kakala time-nin i-ues pilep-eza-pa taz-pa tamtai-pa numipu-timt-ki. 1914. The life of Jesus Christ from the four gospels in the Nez Perces language. [Portland, Or., Schwab Printing Co., c1915] xix, 386 p.
                  OrP WaPS WaSp **1571**

"Kuailks Metacopum" (Black robe three-times-broken) [being a series of interviews with Father Joseph Cataldo, by Laurence E. Crosby] Wallace, Idaho, Wallace Press Times [1925] 16 p. illus., ports.   Many **1572**

A Numipu or Nez-Perce grammar, by a missionary of The Society of Jesus in the Rocky Mountains. Desmet, Idaho, Idaho Indian Boys' Press, 1891. 255 p. Anon. Included by error. Same as no. 7101.   WaU **1573**

Prayers, catechism, hymns in the Nuimpu language (Nez Perce) for the use of the St. Joseph's Missions, S. J., in Oregon and Idaho. Pendleton, Or., Pendleton Printery, J. Huston, 1909. 48 p.
                               WaPS **1574**

Catalogue of British Columbia minerals as exhibited in specimen case at Kurtz & Co.'s cigar store. 2d ed. [Victoria. B. C., British Colonist, n. d.] 22 p.
                             CVicAr **1575**

Cathlamet, Washington. Centennial Celebration.
Souvenir program, August 23-25, 1946. [Cathlamet, Washington?] 1946. 29 p.
                                OrP **1576**

Catholic Church. Catechisms. Kootenai.
[Kootenai catechism. Desmet, Idaho? Desmet Mission Printer, 1892] 16 p.
                         WaPS WaU **1577**

Catholic Church. Liturgy and ritual. Nez Perces.
A catechism of Christian doctrine in the Nez Perce language, composed by the missionaries of the Society of Jesus. [Desmet, Idaho?] Desmit Mission Printer [n.d.] 24 p.   WaU **1578**

Catholic Church in the U. S. Archdiocese of Portland, Or.
Synodus diocesana Portlandensis in Oregon, tertia. [Portland, Or., Sentinel Printery, 1935?] 1 v.   OrU **1579**

Catholic Church; its condition on the Pacific coast forty years after its establishment. [n.p., 1879] 11 p.   OrHi **1580**

Catholic clergy of the province of Oregon.
Address to the Catholics of the United States on President Grant's Indian policy in its bearings upon Catholic

interests at large. Portland, Or., Catholic Sentinel, 1874. 16 p.   OrP **1581**

Catholic Northwest Progress.
Diamond Jubilee number, 1838-1912. Seattle, 1912. 120 p. illus., ports. (v. 15, no. 35, June 7, 1912)   WaS WaU **1582**

Issue complementary to the Supreme Convention of the knights of Columbus, Seattle, August, 1915. Seattle, 1915. 76 p. illus.   WaS **1583**

Catholic Sentinel.
The centenary; 100 years of the Catholic Church in the Oregon country. Portland, Or., 1939. 90 p. illus. (May 4, 1939. Supplement)   Or OrHi **1584**

St. Vincent's Hospital golden jubilee, 1875-1925. Portland, Or., 1925. 40 p. illus. (Aug. 20, 1925. Supplement)   Or **1585**

Official paper, 39th anniversary number. Portland, Or., 1909. 64 p. illus., ports. (June 17, 1909)   WaU **1586**

Catto, William.
The Yukon administration. Dawson, Yukon, King St. Job Office, 1902. 43 p.   CVicAr **1587**

Caughey, John Walton.
History of the Pacific coast. Los Angeles, 1933. xiii, 429 p. front., illus., 5 plates, ports., maps.   Many **1588**

History of the Pacific coast of North America. New York, Prentice-Hall, 1938. xiii, 429 p. front., illus., plates, ports., maps.   IdU OrLgE OrU WaT **1589**

Hubert Howe Bancroft, historian of the West. Berkeley, Calif., Univ. of Calif. Press, 1946. ix, 422 p. front., plates, ports., facsims.   Many **1590**
See also no. 8022.

Cavana, Violet Virginia.
Alaska basketry. Portland, Or., Beaver Club of Oregon, 1917. 49 p. mounted col. front., mounted illus. (part col.)   Many **1591**

Cave, Will.
Nez Perce Indian war of 1877 and Battle of the Big Hole. Missoula, Mont. [n.d.] 24 p. illus., port. MtHi WaSp WaU **1592**

Cayton, Horace Roscoe, comp.
Cayton's campaign compendium of Washington, 1908. Seattle [1908] 95 p. illus., ports.   WaPS WaS WaU **1593**

Cayton's legislative manual, the ninth legislature of Washington, 1905. Seattle, The Seattle Republican, 1905. 56 p. illus., ports., tables. (Washington[State] Legislature. Legislature [souvenir] manual. 1905b)   Wa WaU **1594**

Cee, Jay, see no. 9600.

Centennial of Catholicity in Montana.
St. Mary's and Montana's hundred years, 1841-1941; a memorial souvenir booklet. [n.p., 1941] 36 p. illus., ports. MtU **1595**

Central Municipal League, Portland, Or.
Declaration of principles and by-laws. Portland, Or., Glass & Prudhomme, 1895. 12 p.   OrP **1596**

Central Okanagan Land and Orchard Company, Ltd.
Fruit lands of the celebrated Okanagan Valley at Kelowa, B. C. [Kelowna, B. C., n.d.] 32 p. illus.   CVicAr **1597**

Central Oregon Irrigation Company.
Estimated cost of proposed reclamation of the 26,700 irrigable acres, the north canal unit, in Central Oregon, land between Prineville, Redmond and Bend; report of C. M. Redifeld; report of O. Laurgaard. [n.p., 1914] 19 p. illus., map.   OrP **1598**

Central Oregon Press, Bend, Or.
Industrial edition, January, 1925. Bend, Or., 1925. 64 p. illus.   Or **1599**

Centralia, the hub city, Lewis County, Washington.
[Centralia, Washington, 1909?] [43] p. illus.   WaU **1600**

Chadwick, Frederick Austin Pakenham.
1928 souvenir of St. John's Church, Victoria. [Victoria, B. C., Acme Press] 1928. 35 p. illus. port.   CVicAr **1601**

Chadwick, S. F., see no. 7682.

Chadwick, Stephen J., see nos. 9638-9640.

Chaffee, Allen.
Brownie, the engineer of Beaver Brook. Springfield, Mass., Milton [c1925] 99 p. front., illus. Idaho juvenile story.   IdIf **1602**

Western wild life. Caldwell, Idaho, Caxton, 1944. 205 p. front., illus., plate.   Or OrHi Wa WaS WaSp WaWW **1603**
Same. 1945.   WaT WaU **1603A**

Chaffin, Mrs. Lorah B.
Sons of the West; biographical account of early-day Wyoming. Caldwell, Idaho, Caxton, 1941. 284 p. plates, ports.   Many **1604**

Chaldecott, Francis Millar, 1863-
Jericho and golf in the early days in Vancouver, 1892-1905. [n.p., 1935] 16 p. illus.   CVicAr CVU **1605**

[The Challis Messenger, Challis, Idaho]
Central Idaho, the Switzerland of America. [Challis, Idaho, 192-] [16] p. illus.   IdUSB **1606**

Chalmers, Patrick, see no. 156.

Chamberlain, S. Belle.
Early history of Idaho. [n.p., 1909] 18 p.   IdB **1607**

Special days' programs for the schools of Idaho. Boise, Idaho, Syms-York [n.d.] 46 p.   IdB **1608**

Chamberlain, Ellen, J., ed.
In the beginning, a souvenir of old Willamette days, in memory of Lucy Anna Maria Lee, 1905. [n.p., 1905?] 38 p. illus.   CVicAr Or OrHi OrP WaPS WaS **1609**

Chambers, Andrew Jackson, d. 1908.
Recollections. [n.p., 1947] 40 p. Contents: Pt. 1. Crossing the plains in 1845.- Pt. 2. First flat-bottomed boat to cross over the Cascade Falls, 1846-1847.- Pt. 3. Settlement on Puget Sound.- Pt. 4. Indian War, 1855-1856.- Pt. 5. Customs of doctoring and burial and religious beliefs of the Indians on Chambers Prairie in 1848.   WaU **1610**

Chambers, Edith Lois (Kerns)
Genealogical narrative; a history of the Claggett-Irvine clans. Ltd. ed. Eugene, Or., 1940. 150 p. front. (port.) plates, ports.   MtHi OrP OrU WaS **1611**

Genealogical narrative; a history of three pioneer families: the Kerns, Popes, and Gibsons. Ltd. ed. [Portland, Or., Binfords & Mort] 1943. 93 p.
        Or OrHi OrP OrU WaS **1612**

I remember a Christmas in pioneer days, with pictures by Maude I. Kerns. [n.p., 1944] [22] p. illus.   OrP OrU **1613**

Chambers, Mrs. Elizabeth Harrison.
Incidents in the life of Elizabeth Harrison Chambers, collected from memory's pages. [n.p.] 1910. [13] p.   OrHi **1614**

Chambers, Ernest John, 1862-1925.
The Royal North-West Mounted Police, a corps history. Montreal-Ottawa, Mortimer Press, c1906. 160 p. front., illus., ports.
CV CVicAr CVU WaS WaSp WaU **1615**

Chambers, Mrs. Margaret (White) 1833-1911.
Reminisences [!] written 1894. [n.p., 1903] 48 p.   OrHi WaU **1616**

[Chambers, William] 1800-1883.
Excursion to the Oregon. [London, W. & R. Chambers, 1869?] 32 p.
        CVicAr CVU WaU **1617**

Chandler, George.
Text book of civics for the state of Washington. New York, American Book Co. [c1910] 418 p. front., illus.   Many **1618**

Chandler, Katherine.
Bird-woman of the Lewis and Clark expedition. New York, Silver, c1905. 109 p. front. (port.) illus.   Many **1619**

In the reign of Coyote; folklore from the Pacific coast, drawings by J.W. Ferguson Kennedy. Boston, Ginn [c1905] xii, 161 p. front., illus.   WaS WaSp WaU **1620**

Chaney, Ralph Works, 1890-
The ancient forests of Oregon. Eugene, Or., Or. State System of Higher Education, 1948. xiv, 56 p. front., plates. (Condon lectureship series no. 3) OrCS **1621**

The Goshen flora of west central Oregon, by Ralph W. Chaney and Ethel I. Sanborn. [Washington, D. C.] Carnegie Institution of Washington, 1933. 103 p. 40 plates. (Contributions to paleontology)
        Many **1622**

Pliocene floras of California and Oregon, ed. by Ralph W. Chaney; contributors: Ralph W. Chaney, Carlton Condit and Daniel Axelrod. Washington, D. C. [Carnegie Institution of Washington] 1944. vii, 407 p. front. (map) illus., 64 plates, tables (2 fold.) (Contributions to paleontology)   Many **1623**

See also no. 5439.

Chanwos Chats.
Bremerton number. Norfolk, Va., Chanwos Club, 1929. 60 p. illus., ports. (v. 9, no. 3, July 1, 1929)   WaS **1624**

Chaos, see no. 251.

Chapel, Beatrice Shaw.
Peggy the nomad, decorations by Agnes

Randall Moore. Caldwell, Idaho, Caxton, 1935. 159 p. front., illus. Idaho in 1897.
        Many **1625**

Chaplin, Ralph, 1887-
The Centralia conspiracy. [Seattle? 1920] 80 p. illus., ports.
        Or WaPS WaSp WaU **1626**

Same. The truth about the Armistice Day tragedy. 3d ed. rev. Chicago, General Defense Committee [c1924] 143 p. illus., ports.   WaTC **1627**

Somewhat barbaric, a selection of poems, lyrics and sonnets. Seattle, F. McCaffrey, 1944. 95 p. front. (port.) WAT WaU **1628**

Wobbly, the rough-and-tumble story of an American radical [an autobiography]. Chicago, Univ. of Chicago Press [1948] vi, 435 p. ports.   OrHi WaU **1629**

Chapman, Charles Hiram, 1859-1934.
Introdctory letter, additional explanation, bill for a law and suggested amendments to the Constitution of Oregon. Portland, Or., Allied Printing Trades Council, 1909. 40 p.   Or OrP Was **1630**

The story of Oregon and its people. Chicago, Barnes [c1909] 176 p. plates, ports., maps.   Many **1631**
Same. [1912] 192 p.   OrU WaS **1632**

Chapman, John Wight, 1858-1939.
Alaska's great highway. Hartford, Church Missions Pub. Co. [1909] 15 p. front., plates. (A round robin to the older juniors. Publication no. 71)   CVU **1633**

A camp on the Yukon. Cornwall-on-Hudson, N. Y., Idlewild Press, 1948. 214 p. illus., map.   WaS **1634**

Ten'a texts and tales from Anvik, Alaska, with vocabulary by Pliny Earle Goddard. Leyden, E. J. Brill, Ltd., 1914. vi, 230 p. (Publications of the American Ethnological Society, v. 6)   Many **1635**

Chapman, Katharine Hopkins, 1874-
Fusing force; an Idaho idyl, illus. by W. Herbert Dunton. Chicago, McClurg, 1911. 416 p. col. front.   IdB **1636**

Chapman, R. H., see no. 5471.

Chappe, Eli Albert, 1912-
Guns of the Oregon trail. New York, Phoenix Press [1945] 256 p.
        CV OrU WaS WaU **1637**

Chapple, Ann Grace.
Good fellows all, a simple chronicle of the White Ensign Club, Nov. 1942 to July 1945. Portland, Or., Metropolitan [1946?] 108 p. plates, ports.   OrHi OrP **1638**

Charges against Victor Smith and the evidence upon which they are based [removal of custom house of Puget Sound District from Port Townsend to Port Angeles. N.p., 1864?] 24 p.   WaU **1639**

Charles, Bishop of Columbia, see no. 3209.

Charlton, E. P., & Co.
In and about Portland, Oregon. Portland, Or., c1904. [32] p. illus.   Or **1640**

Chase, Salmon Portland, 1808-1873.
Specific contract law; opinions; also, Address to the people of Oregon, by J. Quinn Thornton. [Salem, Or., Statesman Book and Job Office, 1865] 24 p.
        OrHi OrP **1641**

Chase, William Henry, 1874-
Alaska's mammoth brown bears. Kansas City, Mo., Burton Pub. Co. [1947] 129 p. illus., ports. WaS WaU **1642**

Reminiscences of Captain Billie Moore. Kansas City, Mo., Burton Pub. Co. [1947] 236 p. port. WaS WaU **1643**

The sourdough pot. Kansas City, Mo., Burton Pub. Co. [1943] 206 p. front. WaS WaT WaU **1644**

Cheadle, W. B., see nos. 6844-6854.

Cheap railway transportation; narrow gauge railroads, their success in Oregon and Washington Territory. [n.p., 1879] 7 p. OrHi **1645**

Chehalis Advocate.
[Golden jubilee edition] Chehalis, Wash., 1939. 12 p. illus., ports. (v. 47, no. 7, Aug. 22, 1939) WaU **1646**

Chehalis Bee-Nugget.
Historical souvenir edition. Chehalis, Wash., 1915. 48 p. illus. ports. (May 15, 1915 magazine section) WaPS WaS WaSp WaU **1647**

Chehalis High School. Class of 1904.
Brief history of Lewis County, state of Washington. [n.p., n.d.] [20] p. WaU **1648**

The Chelan Leader.
Special edition. Chelan, Wash., 1904. 1 v. illus., ports. (v. 13, no. 32, Mar. 4, 1904) WaS **1649**

Chelan Valley Mirror.
Booster edition. Chelan, Wash, 1937. [14] p. illus., map. (v. 47, no. 6, Jan. 28, 1937) WaU **1650**

Chelan valley fair edition. Chelan, Wash., 1939. 24 p. illus., ports. (v. 49, no. 51, Nov. 30, 1939) WaU **1651**

Cheliuskin Expedition, 1933-1934.
The voyage of the Chelyuskin by members of the expediton, trans. by Alec Brown. New York, Macmillan, 1935. 325 p. front., illus., plates, ports., maps. Russian Arctic flights. Many **1652**

Cheney, W. D.
Central Oregon. [Portland, Or.?] Ivy Press 1918. 149 p. front. (map) Or OrP OrU WaS WaU **1653**

Cheney, Warren, 1858-
The way of the North; a romance of the days of Baranof. New York, Doubleday, 1905. 320 p. WaU **1654**

Same. Alaska-Baranof. 1906. (Historical series) WaS WaU **1655**

Chenoweth, Maurene.
Faraway song. New York, Wm. Penn, c1942. 301 p. front. Idaho ranch story. WaT **1656**

Chesnez, E. Martineau, see no. 858.

Chestnut, Robert Henry.
Rambling rhymes of the British Columbia coast. [Vancouver, B. C., Clarke & Stuart,, 1933] 76 p. CV CVicAr CVU **1657**

Chevigny, Hector, 1904-
Lord of Alaska; Baranov and Russian adventure. New York, Viking, 1942. 320 p. Many **1658**

Same. London, Hale [1946] 255 p. WaU **1659**

Lost empire; the life and adventures of Nikolai Patrovich Rezanov. New York, Macmillan, 1937. 356 p. front. (port.) Many **1660**

Same. 1939 [c1937] MtU **1661**

Chicago & Northwestern Railway Company.
The Indian, the Northwest, 1600-1900; the red man, the war man, the white man, and the North-western line. [Chicago, 1901]. 114 p. front., illus., ports, maps (1 fold.) IdU MtHi OrHi WaS WaU WaW **1662**

Pacific Northwest; a description of the natural resources, scenic features and commercial advantages of Oregon, Washington and Idaho. Chicago, 1905. 51 p. illus., map. OrHi OrP WaU **1663**

Same. 3rd ed. 1906. OrHi **1664**

Same. 4th ed. 1907. 46 p. front., illus., maps. WaPS **1665**

Same. 1915. 56 p. OrHi OrP **1666**

The Pacific Northwest and Alaska. [Chicago, n.d.] 47 p. front., illus., maps. WaT **1667**

Seattle, Alaska-Yukon-Pacific exposition, June 1-Oct. 16, 1909. [n.p., 1909?] 20 p. illus. WaU **1668**

Chicago, Burlington & Quincy Railroad Company.
A business of your own in Poultryland, the Pacific Northwest. [Chicago] c1923. 31 p. illus. Published jointly by C. B. & Q., N. P., and G. N. Or OrCS OrP WaT **1669**

Glacier National Park and the new Logan Pass detour. [Chicago, 193-?] [29] p. illus., map. WaPS **1670**

The land of better farms, the Pacific Northwest. [Chicago] 1923. 95 p. illus., map. Published jointly by C. B. & Q., N. P., and G. N. IdUSB Or OrP WaPS WaT **1671**

The land of opportunity now, the great Pacific Northwest. [Chicago] 1923. 39 p. illus. Published jointly by C. B. & Q., N. P., and G. N. IdUSB Or OrP WaPS WaT **1672**

Same. 1924. WaT WaU **1673**

Same. 1925. OrP **1674**

The Pacific Northwest. Chicago [1925?] 8 fold. p. illus. Published jointly by C. B. & Q., N. P., and G. N. WaPS **1675**

Power for supremacy; the Pacific Northwest. [Chicago] 1923. 31 p. illus., maps. Published jointly by C. B. & Q., N. P., and G. N. Many **1676**

There is a happy land, the Pacific Northwest. [Chicago] 1923. 38 p. illus., maps. Published jointly by C. B. & Q., N. P., and G. N. IdUSB Or OrP OrU WaT WaU **1677**

Through the American wonderland, the Pacific Northwest. [Chicago] c1923. [31] p. illus. Published jointly by C. B. & Q., N. P., and G. N. Or OrP WaPS WaT **1678**

Timber billions of the Pacific Northwest. [Chicago] 1923. 31 p. illus., maps. Published jointly by C. B. & Q., N. P., and G. N.   Or OrCS WaPS WaT WaU **1679**

Treasure lands of the Pacific Northwest. [Chicago] 1924. 31 p. illus., maps. Published jointly by C. B. & Q., N. P., and G. N. Or OrP WaPS WaT WaU **1680**

Washington for the farmer. [Chicago] 1923. 77 p. illus., map., table. Published jointly by C. B. & Q., N. P., and G. N.   OrP WaTC **1681**

Same. 1924.   WaPS **1682**

The western gateway to world trade; the Pacific Northwest. [Chicago?] 1924. 31 p. illus., map. Published jointly by C. B. & Q., N. P., and G. N.   Many **1683**

Same. 1925.   IdU **1684**

Chicago Illustrated Review.
Seattle-Alaska-Yukon exposition number. [Chicago, Saturday Pub. co., 1909]. 23 p. illus. (v. 4, no. 27, Mar. 13, 1909)   WaU **1685**

Chicago, Milwaukee, & Puget Sound Railway Company.
The mountain of the great snow; issued by the Passenger Departments of the Chicago, Milwaukee & Puget Sound Railway and Tacoma Eastern Railroad. [Seattle? 19—?]. 16 p. front., illus.   WaPS **1686**

Chicago, Milwaukee & St. Paul Railway Company.
Deer Lodge Valley. [Chicago, Poole Bros., 1913]. 30 p. illus., maps.   MtU **1687**

The Judith Basin, Fergus County, Montana. [Chicago, Poole Bros., 1913] 18 p. illus, map.   MtU **1688**

The Judith Basin, central Montana. [Chicago, 1927?] 15 p. illus., map.   WaPS **1689**

The Musselshell country, Montana. [Chicago, Poole Bros., 1913] 22 p. illus., map.   MtU **1690**

Rainier National Park, by Chicago, Milwaukee & St. Paul Railway and Tacoma Eastern Railroad. [Seattle, Lowman & Hanford, 191—?] 23 p. illus., fold. map.   WaPS **1691**

Same. [Omaha, 1923] 31 p. illus., map.   WaPS **1692**

Chicago, Milwaukee, St. Paul and Pacific Railroad Company.
Montana dude ranches. [Chicago, 1937?] 19 p. illus.   WaPS **1693**

Montana, the treasure state. [Chicago, Poole Bros., 1916] 60 p. illus., fold. map.   WaPS **1694**

Mt. Rainier National Park, Washington; the throne room of the monarch mountain. [Chicago, Rand McNally, 1915?] [16] p. plates, map.   WaU **1695**

North Pacific coast country. [n.p., c1909] 63 p. front., illus., maps.   OrP **1696**

Notes along the Olympian Trail. [Chicago, 1934?] 43 p. illus., map.   WaPS **1697**

The Pacific Northwest and Alaska, an empire of matchless pleasurelands. [Chicago, Poole Bros., 1915?] 48 p. illus., maps.   WaPS WaU **1698**

Rainier National Park, Washington. [n.p.] c1916. 38 p. illus., fold. map.   WaT WaTC **1699**

Reconnaissance of the golden Northwest. [Buffalo, Matthews, c1883.] 104 p. illus.   OrHi **1699A**

The trail of the Olympian; 2000 miles of scenic splendor; Chicago to Puget Sound. [Chicago, Rogers & Co., c1914] [40] p. plates, map.   WaPS WaU **1700**

Same. [c1916] [38] p.   OrHi WaPS **1701**

Same. [Poole Bros., c1924] [40] p.   WaPS **1702**

Vacation suggestions; Pacific Northwest. [Chicago, 1935] 36 p. illus., maps.   WaPS **1703**

Washington. [Chicago, 1915] 34 p. illus., fold. map.   OrP **1704**

Washington, the evergreen state. Chicago [1932?] 14 p. illus., map.   WaPS **1705**

Chicago Record.
Klondike; a book for gold seekers. Philadelphia, Globe Bible Pub Co., 1897. 555 p. front., plates, maps. diagrs.   Or OrSa **1706**

Klondike; the Chicago Record's book for gold seekers. Chicago, 1897. 413 p. front., illus. (Souvenir ed.)   CVicAr CVU WaSP WaU **1707**

Same. 555 p. front., plates, maps.   Wa WaU **1708**

Same. Boston, Desmond Pub Co., 1897.   CVicAr **1709**

Same. Chicago, Monroe Book Co. [1897]   CVic OrHi OrU WaPS WaS WaSp **1710**

Same. Toronto, Briggs [c1897]   CVic **1711**

[Chicago, Rock Island & Pacific Railway Company]
How the Oregon pioneers were dictated to and imposed upon when journeying east to St. Paul, Chicago and New York in the fall of 1883. Chicago, Knight, 1883. 23 p. map.   OrP **1712**

Chicanot, Eugene Louis, ed.
Rhymes of the miner; an anthology of Canadian mining verse, illus. by Geo. A. Cuthbertson. Gardenvale, Quebec, Federal Publications Ltd. [1938?] 222 p. illus.   CVicAr **1713**

Chikamin, Nika Tikegh, see no. 9376.

Chilberg, A., Steamship Agency.
The globe trotter, full of useful information to travelers. Seattle, 1902. 80 p. illus.   WaU **1714**

Child Welfare League of America.
Brief study of the program for children's work in Seattle and King County, Washington, and its evaluation, together with recommendations for a future program. [n.p.] 1937. 18 p.   WaU **1715**

Childe, Rheta Louise, see no. 5577.

Childers, Sarah, see no. 8206.

Childs, Charles.
The Oregon legislature; a pamphlet describing legislative procedure and com-

menting on the legislative branch of state government; with House and Senate rules, and sections of the state constitution affecting legislative organization and procedure. Portland, Or., Metropolitan [c1937] 74 p.
Or OrCS OrMonO OrP OrPR OrU **1716**

Chillman, James, see no. 6256.

Chinard, Gilbert, see no. 5695.

Chinook short grammar. [n.p.] 1923. 16 p.
CVicAr **1717**

Chisam, Mignon Maynard, see no. 8966.

Chisholm, Arthur Murray, 1872-
The land of big rivers; a story of the Northwest. London, Hodder & Stoughton [c1924] 305 p. CVU **1718**

Same. New York, Burt, 1924. OrSa **1719**

Same. New York, Chelsea House [c1924]
WaS WaT **1720**

Chittenden, Hiram Martin, 1858-1917.
The American fur trade of the far West; a history of the pioneer trading posts and early fur companies of the Missouri Valley and the Rocky Mountains and of the overland commerce with Santa Fe. New York, Harper, 1902. 3 v. front., 4 plates, map, plan, 3 facsims. Many **1721**

Same. With introd. and notes by Stallo Vinton and sketch of the author by Dr. Edmond S. Meany. New York, Press of the Pioneers, Inc., 1935. 2 v. front. (port.) plates, map. Many **1722**

Same. New York, R. R. Wilson, 1936.
IdIf IdP MtU **1723**

The Puget Sound and Inland Empire Railway; "Cascade Tunnel route", by Itothe Phucher [pseud.] Seattle, Harriman [c1909] 31 p. plate, maps (1 fold.) plan, fold. diagr. WaS WaU **1724**

Report of an investigation by a board of engineers of the means of controlling floods in the Duwamish-Puyallup valleys and their tributaries in the state of Washington. Seattle, Lowman & Hanford, 1907. 32 p. plates, fold. map.
WaS WaTC WaU **1725**

Verse. Seattle, Holly Press [1916] 83 p.
WaS WaU **1726**

See also nos. 9544, 9545.

Chittenden, Newton H.
Health seekers', tourists' and sportsmen's guide to the sea-side, lake-side, foothill, mountain and mineral spring, health and pleasure resorts of the Pacific coast. 2d ed. San Francisco, C. A. Murdock & Co., 1884. 311 p. illus., plates (part fold.) ports., maps.
CVicAr CVU IdP OrP WaS WaU **1727**

Settlers, prospectors, and tourists guide; or, Travels through British Columbia; Circular 10 of "The worlds guide for home, health and pleasure seekers." Victoria, B. C., 1882. 84 p.
CV CVU WaSP WaU **1728**

Travels in British Columbia and Alaska; circular 10 of the World's guide for home, health and pleasure- seekers, containing new and valuable information concerning this comparatively unknown

region, its physical features, climate, resources and inhabitants. Victoria, B. C., 1882. 84 p. CVicAr WaT **1729**

Travels in Oregon, Washington and northern Idaho. [n.p., 1882] 80 p. WaSP **1730**

Chittick, Victor Lovitt Oakes, 1822- ed.
Northwest harvest, a regional stocktaking. Contributions by Peter H. Odegard [and others] New York, Macmillan, 1948. xvi, 226 p. Many **1731**

Ring-tailed roarers; tall tales of the American frontier, 1830-60, ed. with an introd. by V. L. O. Chittick, wood engravings by Lloyd J. Reynolds. Caldwell, Idaho, Caxton, 1941. 316 p. front., illus.
Many **1732**

Same. 1943. MtHi **1733**

Choir, Melody.
Choir's pioneer directory of the city of Seattle and King County; history, business directory and immigrant's guide to and throughout Washington Territory and vicinity. Pottsville, Pa., Miners' Journal Book and Job Rooms, 1878 [c1876] 124 p. CVicAr WaS WaU **1734**

Same. Seattle, 1882. WaWW **1735**

Christian Science Monitor.
State of Washington supplement. [Boston, 1926] [44] p. illus., ports. (v. 18, May 3, 1926 suppl.) WaU **1736**

Christoe, Alice Henson.
Treadwell, an Alaskan fulfillment; the text by Alice Henson Christoe; the drawings by Adelaide Hanscom Leeson. [n.p., 1909?] [29] p. illus. WaU **1737**

Chronological history of the 364th Field Hospital Company. Portland, Or. [Portland Printing House Co.] 1921. 126 p. plates, ports. WaU **1738**

Chuck, Skookum, see no. 2146.

[Church, Campbell]
Westward. [Seattle. 1931?] 11 p. front., illus., map. WaU **1739**

Same. [1932?] 11 p. front., illus., plates, map. WaU **1740**

Church, Herbert E.
An emigrant in the Canadian Northwest. London, Methuen [1928] 132 p. front., 7 plates. CV CVU **1741**

Same. [1929] ix, 134, 8 p. front., 7 plates.
CVicAr CVU **1742**

Church Missionary Society.
Historical notice of the formation of the Church Missionary Society's Northwest America Mission and its progress to August 1848. London, Seeleys, 1849. 87 p. Rupert's Land. WaS **1743**

— — — **Deputation of Metlakatla.**
Report. [n.p., n.d.] 44 p. CVicAr **1744**

Church of England. Book of Common Prayer.
Sh'atjinkujin, parts of the communion service for the use of the Lower Fraser Indians in the All Hallows' Mission Chapel, Yale. [London, Darling] 1894. 8 p. CVicAr **1745**

— — — — — **Haida.**
Portions of the Book of Common Prayer

in Haida, trans. by J. H. Keen. London, Society for Promoting Christian Knowledge, 1899. 39 p.　　CVicAr **1746**

— — — — — — **Kwagutl.**
A Kwagutl version of portions of the Book of Common Prayer. London, Society for Promoting Christian Knowledge [n.d.] 62 p.　　CVicAr **1747**

— — — — — — **Nishg'a.**
A Nishg'a version of portions of the Book of common prayer, trans. by J. B. McCullagh. London, Society for Promoting Christian Knowledge [1890] 79 [14] p.
　　CVicAr **1748**

— — — — — — **Tsimshian.**
Selections. Tsimshian. Wila Yelth. [Morning prayer in Tsimshian] [n.p., n.d.] 21 p.　　CVicAr **1749**

Churchill, Mrs. Claire Frances (Warner)
Mt. Hood Timberline Lodge; the realization of a community vision made possible by the Works Progress Administration. Portland, Or., Metropolitan [1936] [28] p. col. front., plates (part col.)　　OrP **1750**

Slave wives of Nehalem. Portland, Or., Metropolitan, 1933. 104 p.　Many **1751**

South of the sunset; an interpretation of Sacajawea, the Indian girl that accompanied Lewis and Clark, illus. by Agnes C. Lehman. New York, R. R. Wilson, 1936. vii, 287 p. front., illus.　Many **1752**

Same. Junior Library Guild, c1936.
　　IdIf Or OrU OrUM **1753**

See also nos. 2681, 2682.

Churchill, J. D.
British Columbia and Vancouver Island considered as a field for commercial enterprise and emigration, by J. D. Churchill and James Cooper. London, Rees & Collins, 1866. 15 p. CVicAr **1754**

Churchill, William, 1859-1920.
Beach-la-mar; the jargon or trade speech of the western Pacific. [Washington, D. C., Carnegie Institution of Washington, 1911] 54 p. (Publications, 154)
　　Many **1755**

City and County Medical Society of Portland.
Constitution and by-laws [as adopted Mar. 2, 1892] including amendments adopted to 1903. Portland, Or., Rogers, 1903. 16 p.　　OrHi **1756**

City Bank Farmers Trust Company, New York.
Everett Railway and Electric Company to the Farmers' Loan and Trust Company; first mortgage or deed of trust, dated April 1st, A.D. 1893. New York, The Evening Post Job Printing House [1893] 36 p.　　WaU **1757**

The city beautiful, Spokane, Wash. [Spokane, John W. Graham, 191—?]
26 mounted photos.　　Wa **1758**

City Club of Portland, Or.
"Portland improvement", a report to the people on the Moses plan. Portland, Or. [1944] 98 p.　　WaT **1759**

— — — **City Planning Bureau.**
City plan of the west side flat of Portland; its street system structure and traffic facilities; a preliminary study, October, 1921. Portland, Or., 1921. 27 p. illus., map, diagrs.　Or OrCS OrP **1760**

— — — **Education and Recreation Section.**
The platoon plan in the Portland schools; an appraisal of the platoon plan as it operates in the schools of Portland. [Portland, Or., 1928] 23 p. fold. tables. (Bulletin, v. 9, no. 19, Sept. 14, 1928)
　　Or WaU **1761**

— — — **Public Health Bureau.**
Public health methods and their application in Portland; a preliminary study, February, 1922. [Portland, Or., 1922] 40 p.　　Or OrP **1762**

The city of Albany, state of Oregon. Portland, Or., Lewis & Dryden [1891?] 48 p. illus., ports., map.　　Or **1763**

City of Everett and Snohomish County.
[Everett? 1931?] 46 p.　　WaU **1764**

The city of Seattle illustrated. [Seattle, E. P. Charlton & Co., c1909] 40 p. illus.
　　WaU **1765**

"The city of Smokestacks"; Everett, the new manufacturing and commercial city at the end of the Great Northern Railway on Puget Sound. [Everett, Wash., Everett Land Co., 1893?] 46 p. illus., map.　　CVicAr WaU **1766**

City Trust Co., Boston, Mass.
Whatcom County Railway and Light Company and the City Trust Company; first mortgage, securing $750,000 five per cent gold bonds, dated December 1, 1902. [n.p., 1903] 48 p.　　WaU **1767**

Claim of the missionary station of St. James at Vancouver, W. T., to 640 acres of land. [n.p., n.d.] 6 pts. in 1 v.
　　CVicAr OrHi **1768**

Clallam County Immigration Association.
Port Angeles, the gate city of the Pacific coast. 2d ed. [Port Angeles, Wash.] c1896. 40 p. illus., ports.　　WaU **1769**

Clampitt, John Wesley, 1839-
Echoes from the Rocky Mountains; reminiscences and thrilling incidents of the romantic and golden age of the great West, with a graphic account of its discovery, settlement, and grand development. Chicago, Belford, Clarke, c1888. 671 p. front., illus., plates, ports., facsim.　　IdB MtUM **1770**

Same. 1889.　　Many **1771**

Clapham, Sir John, see nos. 4760-4762.

Clapp, Cephas F.
Mrs. Abbie Walker Staver. [n.p., n.d.] 45 p. port.　　OrHi OrP **1772**

Clapp, H. F.
Members of clubdom, 1902, [comp. by H. F and A. W. Clapp] Portland, c1901. [109] p.　　OrHi OrP WaS WaU **1772A**

Clark, Barzilla Worth, 1881-
Bonneville County in the making. Idaho Falls, Idaho, 1941. 140 p. front. (map) illus., ports.　　Many **1773**

Clark, Charles Badger, 1883-
Sun and saddle leather, illus. from photos.

by L. A. Huffman. New ed. Boston, R. G. Badger [c1917] 60 p. front., plates. Poems of Montana.
MtBozC MtU OrU WaU **1774**

Clark, Dan Elbert, 1884-
The West in American history. New York, Crowell [c1937] xi, 682 p. Many **1775**
See also nos. 7707, 7880.

Clark, Ernest Dunbar, 1886-
The salmon canning industry, by Ernest D. Clark and Ray W. Clough. [Seattle, Blyth & Co., 1927?] 26 p. illus.
WaPS **1776**

Clark, Florence Matilda.
Roadhouse tales; or, Nome in 1900. Girard, Kan., Appeal Pub Co., 1902. 263 p. front., plates. Wa WaTC WaU **1777**

Clark, Harold Ballard, 1893-
Washington business law and forms, with articles on property and family rights. Seattle, Law Book Company, 1928. 125 p.
Wa WaS WaT **1778**

Clark, Henry W.
Alaska; the last frontier. New York, Grosset [c1939] xi, 246 p. fold. front., illus., plates, maps, diagr. CVicAr
WaS WaSp WaT WaU WaWW **1779**
History of Alaska. New York, Macmillan, 1930. x, 208 p. front. (double map) illus., 14 plates, 6 maps. Many **1780**

Clark, Horace Fletcher, d. 1928.
Miners' manual; United States, Alaska, the Klondike. Containing annotated manual of procedure; statutes and regulations of the Northwest Territory, British Columbia and Yukon district; glossary on mining terms, and information regarding Alaska and the Klondike, by Horace P. Clark, Charles C. Heltman, and Charles F. Consul. Chicago, Callaghan & Co., 1898. 404 p. illus., fold. map. CVU WaU **1781**

Clark, James E.
Appeal for teachers' institutes and proceedings of the Washington Teachers' Institute and Educational Association. Olympia, Washington, Courier Book Printing Office, 1880. 67 p.
OrU WaS WaSp WaU **1782**
Proceedings of the Washington Teachers' Institute at the fifth annual meeting; and Washington school law. Olympia, Washington, Courier Printing Office, 1881. 94, 24 p. OrU WaS WaU **1783**

Clark, R. D.
Camp Lewis. Seattle, Clark Co., 1917. 75 p. illus., fold. plate, ports.
Wa WaT **1784**

Clark, Robert Carlton, 1877-
A history of Oregon, by Robert Carlton Clark, Robert Horace Down, and George Verne Blue. Chicago, Row, Peterson [c1925] xii, 356 p. front., illus., maps.
Many **1785**
Same. c1926. Many **1786**
Same. Rev. ed. Evanston, Ill., Row, Peterson, c1931. 356 p.
OrCS OrLgE WaWW **1787**
History of the Willamette Valley, Oregon. Chicago, S. J. Clarke Pub Co., 1927. 3 v.

front., illus., plates, ports., maps. Volumes 2 and 3 biographical and without author's name. Many **1788**

Clark, William, see nos. 130-135, 3116, 3117, 3465-3471, 4939, 5887-5916.

Clarke, Albert Gallatin, Jr.
The Arickaree treasure and other brief tales of adventurous Montanians. New York, Abbey Press [c1901]
MtHi WaU **1789**

Clarke, Clinton C., comp.
Natural history of the Pacific Crest Trail System; a descriptive list of the typical species of the trees, animals, birds and flowers living in the high mountains of Washington, Oregon, and California; identified to location on the P. C. T. S. route as described in the "log" of daily itinerary. Pasadena, Calif. [1936] 75 p. map. (Pacific Crest Trail System Conference. Bulletin no. 4) Many **1790**
Same. 1945. [29] p. (Bulletin no. 21)
OrCS **1791**
The Pacific Crest Trail, Canada to Mexico. Pasadena, Calif. [1935] [48] p.
OrP OrU WaT WaU **1792**
The Pacific Crest Trailway. Pasadena, Calif., Pacific Crest Trail System Conference, 1945. 126 p. 12 plates, 8 fold. maps. Many **1793**

Clarke, J. M., see no. 6738.

Clarke, R. Milton, see no. 9403.

Clarke, Samuel Asahel, 1827-1909.
Pioneer days of Oregon history. Portland, Or., J. K. Gill Co., c1905. 2 v. front., 10 plates, 2 ports., map. Many **1794**
Same. Cleveland, 1905. MtU WaT **1795**
Sounds by the western sea and other poems, specimens by Clarke. [Salem, Or., Willamette Farmer Office, 1872] 38 p. Or OrHi OrP OrU WaSp **1796**

Clarke, Sidney A.
The prune industry in the Pacific Northwest. Portland, Or., Posson's Seed Store [1893?] 97 p. illus.
Or OrHi OrU WaS **1797**

Clarke, William, see nos. 130-135, 3116, 3117, 3465-3471, 4939, 5887-5916.

Clason Map Company.
Clason's Oregon green guide; state and city maps, auto road logs, railroads; commercial index of towns giving hotels, industries, altitudes, population, etc. Chicago [1920?] 39 p. illus., maps, (2 fold.) OrP WaPS **1798**
Clason's Washington green guide. New census ed., Denver [192—?] 40 p. photos., tables, diagrs. WaPS **1799**
Index to map of Oregon; Clason's commercial index of Oregon towns, gives railroads, population, elevations, banks, hotels and industries. Denver [c1911] 32 p. fold. map. OrHi OrP WaPS **1800**

Claudet, Francis George.
"Gold". New Westminster, B. C., "Mainland Guardian," 1871. 32 p.
CVicAr CVU **1801**

Clausen, Elmer E.
A history of early printing in the Pacific

Northwest. Vancouver, Wash., Western
Washington College of Education Exten-
sion, 1948. 15 p. illus.
OrCS OrHi OrP OrU WaS **1801A**

Clayson, Edward.
Historical narratives of Puget Sound;
Hoods Canal, 1865-1885; the patriarch,
the experiences of an only free man in
a penal colony. [Seattle, R. L. Davis
Printing Co.] c1911. 106 p. front. (port.)
Wa WaS WaU **1802**

The muck rake. Cumtux? Seattle, White
& Davis Printing Co., 1908. 106 p. front.
(port.) Cumtux (or Comtox or Kumtux)
is a Chinook word meaning understand.
WaS WaU **1803**

Samson and Delilah; American effemi-
nately vanquished; loss of national character. [Seattle, 1899] 146 p. WaS **1804**

Clearing House Association of Seattle.
Articles of association and rules and regulations. Seattle [1917?] 37 p. WaU **1805**

Cleland, Alexander M., 1862-
Through wonderland. [St. Paul? 1910] 69
p. illus. (part col.) map.   WaU **1806**

Cleland, Mabel Goodwin, 1876-
Early days in the fir tree country. Seattle,
Washington Printing Co. [c1923] 212 p.
illus.   Many **1807**

Little pioneers of the fir-tree country. Boston, Houghton, c1924. 124 p. col. front., 3
plates.   Many **1808**

Cleland, Robert Glass, 1885-
Pathfinders [illus. by Howard Simon] Los
Angeles, Powell [c1929] 452 p. plates,
maps.   Or WaSp WaU **1809**

Clements, Mrs. Edith Gertrude (Schwartz)
Flowers of coast and sierra, with 32 plates
in color. New York, H. W. Wilson, 1928.
226 p. col. front., 31 col. plates. Colored
plates through courtesy of National Geographic Society.   Many **1810**

Flowers of mountain and plain. 3d ed.
New York, H. W. Wilson, 1926. 79 p.
col. front., 24 col. plates.
MtBozC MtU WaS **1811**

Clements, Frederick Edward, 1874-
Rocky Mountain flowers; an illustrated
guide for plant-lovers and plant-users.
White Plains, N. Y., H. W. Wilson, 1914.
xxxi, 392 p. col. front., illus., 46 plates (24
col.) chart.   Many **1812**

Clements, J. H., pub.
Kamloops, B. C. Kamloops, B. C. [n.d.] 1
v. illus.   CVicAr **1813**

Clements, James I.
The Klondyke; how the brakeman gained
his thousands in four months; a complete guide to the gold fields, ed. by G.
Wharton James. Los Angeles, B. R.
Baumgardt & Co., 1897. 98 p. plates,
port., map.   WaU **1814**

Cleverdon, W. T., Company.
Pacific coast coastwise lumber fleet. San
Francisco, [n.d.] 79 p. illus., tables.
OrP **1815**

Clifford, Henry B., 1859-
Masterly address of Hon. Henry B. Clifford on the resources and future of the

state of Washington, delivered at the
Boston Music Hall, January 14, 1890.
[n.p.] Published by the Northern Syndicate for circulation in New England.
[1890?] 80 p.   WaU WaWW **1816**

The climate of Puget Sound and custom
house statistics. Seattle, Clarence Hanford, Printer, 1883. 8 p.   WaU **1817**

Cline, Walter, see no. 9740.

Clinton, Riley Jenkins, 1894-
Oregon school system and law. Corvallis,
Or., Coop Book Store, c1939. 191 p.
charts.   Many **1818**

Clise, James William, 1855-
Personal memoirs, 1855-1935. [n.p., n.d.]
[56] p. Seattle pioneer and author.
WaS WaU **1819**

Same. [c1935] 60 p.   Wa **1820**

Cloman, Mrs. Flora (Smith) Clement, 1869-
I'd live it over. New York, Farrar [c1941]
iv, 380 p. front., plates, ports. Autobiography of life on western frontiers.
Many **1821**

Clothier, George Lemon.
Report on the re-cruise of about 14,000
acres of timber land belonging to the
agricultural college & scientific school
grants, made under the act approved
Feb. 11, 1899, for rendering available
the endowment of the agricultural college, experiment station and school of
science of the state of Washington.
Pullman, Wash., 1912. 20 p.   WaPS **1822**

Clothier, Marshall M., 1842-
Sixtieth birthday souvenir. Prairie, Wash.,
1902. [21] p. front. (port.) Poem.
WaU **1823**

Cloud, Archibald Jeter.
Our constitutions, national and state; an
elementary text in government and citizenship for use in the state of Washington, by A. J. Cloud and Edmond S.
Meany. Chicago, Scott, Foresman [c1925]
350 p. front., illus.
Or Wa WaE WaS WaT WaU **1824**

Cloud, D. Gerald, see no. 7750.

Clough, Ray W., see no. 1776.

Club and Society Blue Book Company,
Portland, Or.
Portland clubs and clubdom, 1910-1911.
Portland, Or. [1010?] 82 p.   OrP **1825**

Clutterbuck, W. J., see nos. 5809-5811.

Clyman, James, 1792-1881.
James Clyman, American frontiersman,
1792-1881; the adventures of a trapper
and covered wagon emigrant as told in
his own reminiscences and diaries, edited by Charles L. Camp. San Francisco,
California historical society, 1928. 297
[4] p. front., port., maps (1 fold.) facsim.
(Special publication no. 3)
MtHi OrHi WaSp **1826**

Coast Committee for the Shipowners.
A. B. C.'s of the maritime strike; a primer
of basic facts; hiring halls, ship subsidy,
arbitration awards enforcement. San
Francisco, 1936. 18 p.   OrP **1827**

The Pacific maritime labor crisis. San
Francisco [1936] [14] p.   OrP **1828**

Coates, Grace Stone.
Black cherries. New York, Knopf, 1931.
213 p. Montana author. IdIf
MtHi MtU OrCS OrP WaSp **1829**

Mead & mangel-wurzel. Caldwell, Idaho,
Caxton [c1931] 151 p. Poems.
MtU WaSp **1830**

Portulacas in the wheat. Caldwell, Idaho,
Caxton, 1932. 71 p. Poems.
MtHi MtU Or WaSp **1831**

See also nos. 10332, 10333.

Coats, Robert Hamilton, 1874-
Sir James Douglas, by Robert Hamilton
Coats and R. E. Gosnell. Ed de luxe.
Toronto, Morang, 1908. 369 p. front.
(port.) plate. (Makers of Canada, ed. by
D. C. Scott, P. Edgar and W. D. Le-
sueur) CVicAr CVU OrU WaU **1832**

Same. 1910. CVU OrHi **1832A**
Same. 1912. (Parkman ed. v. 20)
CVic CVU OrHi WaS WaU **1833**

Same. Illus. under the direction of A. H.
Doughty. London, Oxford Univ. Press,
1926. vii, 386 p. front., 2 plates, port.
(Anniversary ed. v. 9)
CVU IdU MtU **1834**

Cobb, Irving S., see nos. 1249-1251.
Coburn, Wallace David, 1872-
The battle of the Little Big Horn. [n.p.]
Overland-Outwest Pub. [c1936] [31] p.
mounted photos, mounted ports.
MtHi **1835**

Rhymes from the round-up camp. Great
Falls, Mont., Ridgley Press, c1899. 138
p. plates by C. M. Russell.
MtHi Wa WaS **1836**

Cochran, John Eakin, 1857-
Pioneer days in eastern Washington and
northern Idaho. Spokane, Knapp Book
Store, 1942. 2 v. in 1. illus., maps, mounted
ports., mounted photos.
IdU WaS WaW **1837**

Cochran, William H.
Washington's state institutions. [n.p.,
1915?] 87 p. mounted port.
WaS WaU **1838**

Cochrane, Ben H.
Disillusion, a story of the labor struggle
in the western wood-working mills, by
Ben H. Cochrane and William Dean
Coldiron. Portland, Or., Binfords &
Mort [c1939] 279 p. Many **1839**

Cochrane, Charles Norris, 1889-
David Thompson, the explorer. Toronto,
Macmillan, 1924. 173 p. col. front. (Cana-
dian men of action, no. 2) Many **1840**

Coddington, Anne Bartlett, see no. 2642.
Codman, John, 1814-1900.
The round trip by way of Panama
through California, Oregon, Nevada,
Utah, Idaho, and Colorado; with notes
on railroads, commerce, agriculture,
mining, scenery, and people. New York,
Putnam, 1879. xii, 331 p. Many **1841**
Same. 1881. WaU **1842**

Cody, Edmund R.
History of the Coeur d'Alene mission of
the Sacred Heart; old mission, Cataldo,
Idaho; on the Union Pacific between
Spokane and Wallace and on the Yellowstone Trail between Coeur d'Alene
and Kellogg. [Caldwell, Idaho, Caxton,
c1930] 45 p. illus., ports. Many **1843**

Cody, Hiram Alfred, 1872-
An apostle of the North; memoirs of the
Right Reverend William Carpenter
Bompas, D.D., first bishop of Athabas-
ka, 1874-1884, first bishop of Mackenzie
River, 1884-1891, first bishop of Selkirk
(Yukon) 1891-1906, with an introd. by
the Most Rev. S. P. Matheson. London,
Seeley, 1908. 385 p. front. (port.) 35
plates, 4 ports. CVU WaU **1844**

Same. New York, Dutton, 1908.
CVU WaS **1845**

Same. Toronto, Musson [1908]
CVic CVicAr CVU WaU **1846**

Same. 2d ed. London, Seeley, 1910.
CVicAr **1847**

Same. 3d ed. New York, Dutton, 1913.
CVicAr **1848**

Cody, John C., see no. 403.

Cody, William Frederick, 1846-1917.
The life of Hon. William F. Cody, known
as Buffalo Bill, the famous hunter,
scout and guide; an autobiography.
Hartford, Bliss [c1879] 365 p. front.
(port.) illus. IdU **1849**

Story of the wild West and camp-fire
chats, by Buffalo Bill; a full and complete history of the renowned pioneer
quartette; Boone, Crockett, Carson and
Buffalo Bill; including a description of
Buffalo Bill's conquests in England with
his Wild West Exhibition. San Francisco, History Co. [c1888] 766 p. col.
front., illus., port. WaPS **1850**

See also nos. 4924-4926, 6488.

Coe, Alice Rollit.
Lyrics of fir and foam; etchings by L.
Ross Carpenter. Seattle, Harriman, 1908.
51 p. front., illus., plates. Washington
poet. Wa WaPS WaS WaT WaU **1851**
Same. 88 p. front., 14 plates.
CVic OrP WaS WaU **1852**

Coe, Douglas, pseud.
Road to Alaska; the story of the Alaska
Highway, story by Douglas Coe [pseud.
for Samuel and Beryl (Williams) Ep-
stein] pictures by Winfield Scott Hoskins. [New York] Messner [1943] 175 p.
double front. (map) illus., maps.
Many **1853**

Coe, George Albert, see no. 11138.
Coe, Urling Campbell, 1881-
Frontier doctor. New York, Macmillan,
1939. ix, 264 p. illus. Many **1854**
Same. 1940. IdB IdU Or WaE **1855**

Coe, William Robertson, see no. 11244.

Coeur d'Alene Mine Makers Association.
Facts about the Coeur d'Alene; truth and
publicity. Wallace, Idaho [1909?] 56 p.
illus, tables. MtUM **1856**

Coeur d'Alene Press.
Golden anniversary edition. 1887-1937.
[Coeur d'Alene, Idaho] 1937. [82] p. illus.,
ports. WaSp WaU **1857**

Coffin, Charles Carleton, 1823-1896.
Great commercial prize; addressed to every American who values the prosperity of his country. Boston, A. Williams. 1858. 23 p. An account of the Puget Sound region, Frazer River and Oregon; exposing the attempt of Great Britain to gain control of the Northwest and an impassioned appeal to all Americans to "wake up".   WaSp **1858**

The seat of empire. Boston, Fields, 1870. viii, 232 p. 5 plates, fold. map.
          Or WaS WaSp WaU **1859**

Same. [n.p.] Edgewood Pub. Co. [c1870] viii, 232 p. front., 4 plates.
          OrU WaPS WaU **1860**

Same. Boston, Osgood, 1871.   WaU **1861**

Coffin, Geraldine, see no. 10769.

Coffman, Noah Berry, 1857-1940.
Old Lewis County, Oregon Territory; an address delivered before the Southwest Washington Pioneers, Rochester, Thurston Co., Washington, August 12, 1926. [Chehalis, Wash., 1926] [26] p. illus.
          Or OrHi Wa WaPS WaS WaU **1862**

Some unwise tendencies in banking as viewed from the standpoint of a country banker [an address delivered before the tenth annual convention of the Washington State Bankers Association held in Portland, Or., July 20-22, 1905] [n.p., 1905?] 27 p.   WaU **1863**

Visions and tasks; the new Americanism: "when you see a good thing go get it". Land settlement possibilities — western Washington valleys—what they are and what they can be made [address at Yakima Dec. 19, 1918. Chehalis, Wash.] Bee-Nugget [1918] 15 p. fold. table.
          WaU **1864**

Washington landmarks located in Lewis County; the Jackson Prairie court house, Washington's oldest judicial and administrative building and the O. B. McFadden home in Chehalis, commemorating the seventy-fifth anniversary of its construction. [Chehalis, Wash., Chehalis Pub. Co.] 1934. 9 p.
          WaS WaT WaU **1865**

Coffman-Dobson Bank & Trust Co.,
Chehalis, Wash.
Forty-five years of banking in southwest Washington, 1884-1929. Chehalis, Wash. [n.d.] [17] p. illus.   WaPS **1866**

Same. [1929] [20] p. front., illus., ports.
          CVicAr WaU **1867**

Cogswell, O. H.
History of British Columbia. Victoria, B. C., British Colonist, 1893. 101 p.
          CV CVic CVicAr CVU **1868**

Same. Adapted for the use of schools. 1894.   CVicAr CVU OrHi WaU **1869**

Cohan, Charles Cleveland.
Born of the crucible. Boston, Cornhill Co. [c1919] 321 p. Novel about Butte, Mont.
          WaU **1870**

Cohen, Arthur G.
Resume of legislative action on appropriations for higher educational institutions. [Seattle, 1925] 14 p.   WaU **1871**

Coker, Tracy.
Ee-dah-how. Caldwell, Idaho, Caxton, 1933. 290 p.
          IdB IdIf IdP IdTf Or WaPS **1872**

Same. 1935.   IdU WaU **1873**

Colbert, Mildred.
Kutkos, Chinook tyee, illus. by Keith Shaw Williams. Boston, Heath [c1942] xi, 228 p. illus., col. plates (1 double).
          Or OrP OrU WaS WaU WaW **1874**

Same. London, Heath [c1947] 187 p. illus.
          CVicAr **1875**

[Colby, Mary Ellen (Richardson)] 1858-
The Richardson family, pioneers of Oregon and Utah; an account of the lives of the descendants of Shadrach and Betsy Richardson of Kentucky, comp. from the family traditions and records covering the migration of its members from Kentucky to Illinois, Iowa, Oregon and Utah. [Dallas, Or., Itemizer-Observer, 1940] 39 p. front., illus., ports.
          Or OrP WaU **1876**

The story of the Richardson family. Dallas, Or., Itemizer-Observer, 1929. 22 p. ports.
          Or OrP OrU Wa WaPS WaU **1877**

Colby, Merle Estes, 1902-
Alaska, a profile, with pictures; with an invitation from the Governor Ernest Gruening. [New York, Duell, Sloane & Pearce, c1940] [58] p. front., illus.
          Many **1878**

Coldiron, William Dean, see no. 1839.

Cole, George E.
Early Oregon; jottings of personal recollections of a pioneer of 1850. [Spokane, Shaw & Borden, c1905] 95 p. front. (port.)   Many **1879**

[Cole, Robert B.]
The history of the 39th Infantry during the World War. [New York, J. D. McGuire, c1919] 160 p. illus., ports. First infantry trained at Camp Lewis.
          WaU **1880**

Coleman, Arthur Philemon, 1852-1939.
Canadian Rockies; new and old trails. London, Unwin, 1911. 383 p. front., 32 plates, map.   OrCS WaPS WaSp **1881**

Same. New York, Scribner, 1911.
          WaS **1882**

Same. Toronto, Frowde, 1911.
          CVicAr CVU **1883**

Same. 1912.   CVic CVU OrP WaU **1884**

Coleman, Christopher B., see no. 6992.

Coleman, Edmund T.
Prize essay and poem of the Literary Institute, V. I., on the beauties of the scenery as surveyed from Beacon Hill. Victoria, B. C., McMillan, 1868. 15 p.
          CVicAr WaU **1885**

Coleman, Rufus Arthur, ed.
The golden west in story and verse. New York, Harper, c1932. 442 p.   MtHi **1886**

Western prose and poetry, selected and ed. by Rufus A. Coleman. New York, Harper, 1932. xxi, 502 p. 10 plates.
          Many **1887**

The Coleoptera of Washington. Carabidoe: Agonini, by Barbara Gray and Melville H. Hatch; Sphaeritidae and Histeridae, by Rita Margaret McGrath and Melville H. Hatch; Buprestidae, by Frank M. Beer and Melville H. Hatch. Seattle, Univ. of Wash., 1941. 144 p. 25 plates. (Publications in biology, v. 10, no. 1-3, Aug. 1941) **Wa WaTC WaU 1888**

Collie, J. Norman, see no. 10002.

Collier, Donald.
Archaeology of the upper Columbia region, by Donald Collier, Alfred E. Hudson, and Arlo Ford. Seattle, Univ. of Wash. Press [1942] 176 p. illus., 22 plates, maps, plans, tables, profiles. (Publications in anthropology, v. 9, no. 1, Sept. 1942)
Wa WaS WaSp WaT WaTC WaU 1889

Collier, William Ross.
The reign of Soapy Smith, monarch of misrule in the last days of the old West and the Klondike gold rush, by William Ross Collier and Edwin Victor Westrate; illus. from photographs. Garden City, N. Y., Doubleday, 1935. vi, 299 p. front. (port.) plates. **Many 1890**

Colliery Engineer Company.
Placer mining; a hand-book for Klondike and other miners and prospectors with introductory chapters regarding the recent gold discoveries in the Yukon Valley, the routes to the gold fields, outfit required, and mining regulations, of Alaska and the Canadian Yukon; also a map of the Yukon Valley, embracing all the information obtainable from reliable sources up to December 1, 1897. Scranton, 1897. 146 p. illus., fold. map.
CVicAr CVU WaU 1891

Collins, Dean, 1887-
The cheddar box. Portland, Or., 1933. 293 p. front. (facsim.) plates, ports.
Many 1892

Stars of Oregon, illus. by Paul Keller. Portland, Or., Binfords & Mort, 1943. 117 p. front. (port.) illus. **Many 1893**

White crown singing. Portland, Or., Binfords & Mort, c1946. 94 p. Poetry.
Many 1894

See also nos. 66, 230-232.

Collins, Elizabeth M. (Smith) 1844-
The cattle queen of Montana; a story of the personal experience of Mrs. Nat. Collins. narratives of thrilling adventures and descriptions of the plains, the mines, cattle raising industry, and other features of western life, gleaned from a fifty years' residence in the far West, illus. from special photographs taken in the early days. Rev. and ed. by Alvin E. Dyer. Spokane, Dyer Printing Co., 1894. 260 p. illus., plates, ports. Related by Mrs. Collins and written by Charles Wallace. **IdU 1895**

Same. [1914] **WaU 1896**
Same. [n.d.] **MtHi MtU WaSp 1897**

Collins, Isaac Sidwell, 1872-
Conjecture and speculation. Spokane, Success Printing Co., c1939. 26 p.
WaPS 1898

Collis, Septima M. (Levy)
A woman's trip to Alaska; being an account of a voyage through the inland seas of the Sitkan Archipelago in 1890, by Mrs. General C. H. T. Collis, illus. by American Bank Note Co., New York. New York, Cassell Pub. Co. [c1890] 194 p. illus. (part col.) fold. plate, port., map.
Many 1899

Collison, Thomas.
Flying fortress; the story of the Boeing bomber. New York, Scribner, 1943. 168 p. illus. ports. **Many 1900**

The superfortress is born; the story of the Boeing B-29. New York, Duell, Sloan & Pearce [1945] 218 p. illus., plates, ports.
CV Or OrP WaS WaT WaU 1901

Collison, William Henry, 1847-
In the wake of the war canoe; a stirring record of forty years' successful labour, peril and adventure amongst the savage Indian tribes of the Pacific coast and the piratical head-hunting Haidas of the Queen Charlotte Islands, B. C., with an introd. by the Lord Bishop of Derry. Toronto, Musson [n.d.] 351 p. front., 15 plates, map. **CVicAr CVU 1902**

Same. London, Seeley, 1915.
CVic WaU 1903

Same. New York, Dutton [1916] **Many 1904**

Colmer, J. G., see nos. 9842-9844.

Colnett, James, 1755-1806.
Journal aboard the Argonaut from April 26, 1789 to Nov. 3, 1791, ed. with introd. and notes by F. W. Howay. Toronto, Champlain Society, 1940. xxxi, 328 p. plates, maps (Publications no. 26)
Many 1905

The Colonial Church Chronicle and Missionary Journal.
Mission of the Russian Church to the Aleoutine Islands. [n.p.] 1849, 1851. 2 pts.
CVicAr 1906

Colonization of Vancouver Island.
London, Burrup & Son, 1849. 28 p. map.
CVicAr 1907

Columbia Basin Fisheries Development Association, Astoria, Oregon.
Wealth of the river; a presentation of fact concerning the Columbia River salmon industry and a petition for the conservation of this industry, submitted with reference to proposals to construct various high dams on the Columbia River and its tributaries. Ed. 2 rev. [Astoria, Or.?] 1946. 18 p. **Or OrP 1908**

Columbia Basin Irrigation League.
Columbia Basin Irrigation Project. Spokane [192—?] [7] p. illus., maps, table.
WaPS 1909

Same. 1928. 17 p. fold. map. **Or WaPS 1910**

Columbia County, Oregon; information in regard to its resources, development and possibilities. St. Helens, Or., Beegle & Davis, 1897. 31 p. **Or 1911**

Columbia Merchants Association.
Constitution and by-laws of the Columbia Merchants Association, organized Oct. 23, 1901. [Brewster, Wash.? 1901?] [7] p.
WaU 1912

Columbia Mission special fund obtained during a ten months' appeal by the Bishop of Columbia, with a statement of the urgent need which exists for sympathy and support in aid of the Columbia Mission. London, R. Clay, 1860. xiv, 33 p.
CVicAr **1913**

Columbia River and Pacific Steam Navigation Company. White Collar Line.
[Up the Columbia] Portland, Or., C. H. Crocker Co. [1902] [40] p. illus., port., map.   OrU WaU **1914**

Columbia River Fishermen's Protective Union.
Columbia River fisheries. Astoria, Or., Snyder, 1890. 30 p.   WaU **1915**

Columbia River Log Scaling and Grading Bureau, Portland, Or.
Official log scaling and grading rules for the Pacific Northwest, west coast logs. Portland, Or. [1946?] 20 p.   OrCS **1916**

Columbia River Shipbuilding Corporation.
Review of Columbia River Shipbuilding Corporation's accomplishments. [n.p., n. d.] 77 p. illus., ports.   OrP **1917**

[Columbia Southern Irrigation Company]
Government irrigated land, Oregon. [Portland, Or., n.d.] 6 p. illus., map.
OrHi OrP **1918**

Columbia Southern Railway Company.
Homeseekers guide; 10,000 free farms, April 1902. [Portland, Or., C. H. Crocker Co.] 1902. 22 p.   Or OrHi **1919**

The Columbian, Vancouver, Washington.
Golden jubilee edition, Nov. 9, 1939. Vancouver, Wash., 1939. 1 v. illus., ports.
OrP **1920**

Columbus, Ohio. Citizens' Committee.
Report on the territory of Oregon, by a committee appointed at a meeting of the citizens of Columbus to collect information in relation thereto [report of Mr. Medary from the committee] Columbus. Ohio Statesman, 1843. 21 p. map.
OrU WaU **1921**

Colyer, Vincent, 1825-1888.
Bombardment of Wrangel, Alaska. Washington, D. C., 1870. [33] p. illus.
CVicAr **1922**

Coman, Katharine, 1857-1915.
Economic beginnings of the far West; how we won the land beyond the Mississippi. New York, Macmillan, 1912. 2 v. fronts. illus., 40 plates, 4 maps. Many **1923**
Same. 1921 [c1912]   IdU **1924**
Same. 1925. 2 v. in 1.   Many **1925**
Same. 1930.   MtU WaU **1926**

Commander, Kingsmill.
Vikings of the stars, illus. by J. Augustus Knapp. New York, H. Vinal, 1928. xxv, 97 p. front., plates, maps. Tacoma author.   Wa WaS WaT WaU **1927**

Comments on the convention with Spain [relating largely to the Pacific Ocean, northwest coast of America, and especially to Nootka Sound] London, Axtell, 1790. 28 p.   CVicAr OrP **1928**

The Commercial, Winnipeg.
Special supplement relating to Vancouver

Island, the adjacent coast and northern interior of British Columbia. Winnipeg, 1893. [32] p. 5 plates.   CVicAr **1929**

Committee of Business and Professional Men, Spokane, Washington.
The needs of the State College of Washington. [Spokane, 1925] 16 p. diagrs.
WaPS **1930**
A summary of the needs of the State College of Washington, Spokane, 1925. 1 v.
WaPS **1931**

Commons, Rachel S., see no. 9740.

Commonwealth Builders, Inc.
Crusade to end poverty in Washington. [n. p., n.d.] 1 v.   WaE WaTC **1932**

Commonwealth Conference, Eugene, Oregon.
The rural-urban fringe; proceedings, University of Oregon, April 16-17, 1942. [Eugene, Or.?] Univ. of Or. [1942] 80 p. illus.
CVicAr OrP **1933**

Commonwealth Fund. Child Health Demonstration Committee.
Child health in Marion County, Oregon. New York, 1927. 19 p. map. (Bulletin no. 2)   Or OrP WaWW **1934**
Children of the covered wagon; report of the demonstration in Marion County, Oregon, 1925-1929 by Estella Ford Warner, M. D. and Geddes Smith. New York, 1930. 123 p. front., illus., plates, diagrs.   Many **1935**

The Commonwealth Review of the University of Oregon.
The life and work of Frederick G. Young. Eugene, Or., 1929. 120 p. front., port. (Frederick G. Young memorial number)
OrHi OrP WaU **1936**

Community Chest and Council, Seattle and King County.
South district recreational study. Seattle, 1946. 41 p. table, map.   WaS **1937**

Community Concert Association, Boise, Idaho.
Souvenir booklet; ten years of great artists. Boise, Idaho, 1940. [11] p. illus., ports.   IdB **1938**

Community Hotel Corporation of Seattle.
Amended plan of reorganization and report to the bondholders and stockholders of Community Hotel Corporation of Seattle and to the stockholders of Olympic Hotel Company, Seattle, May 15, 1933. [Seattle, 1933] [16] p.   WaU **1939**

Company I, 361st Infantry; over here and over there. [Portland, Or., Kilham Stationery and Printing Co., 191—?] 84 p. illus.   OrP WaU **1940**

Comparative chronological statement of the events connected with the rights of Great Britain and the claims of the United States to the Oregon Territory. [London, W. S. Johnson, 1945?] 15 p.
CVicAr WaS **1941**

Concatenated Order of Hoo-Hoo.
Souvenir programme, Fourteenth annual Concatenated Order of Hoo-Hoo, September 8-14, '05, Portland, Oregon; comp. by Edna P. Jones. Portland, Or., Union Printing Co., 1905. 272 p. illus., ports.
OrP WaSp **1942**

Concrete Enterprise, Concrete, Washington.
Fourth annual number [containing The
story of Skagit County, by Otto Klem-
ent] Concrete, Wash., 1913. 20 p. illus.,
ports. (v. 4, no. 15, Dec. 13, 1913)
                                   WaU **1943**
Looking forward; the story of Concrete
and the upper Skagit Valley. [Concrete,
Wash., 1913?] 84 p. illus.   WaU **1944**

Condit, Carlton, see no. 1623.

Condliffe, J. B., see no. 4936.

Condon, Thomas, 1822-1907.
Oregon geology: a revision of "The two
islands", with a few tributes to the life
and work of the author, ed. by Ellen
Condon McCornack. Portland, Or., J. K.
Gill Co., 1910. 187 p. front (port.) 30
plates.   Many **1945**
Two islands and what came of them. Portland, Or., J. K. Gill Co., 1902. 211 p. 30
plates, port.   Many **1946**

Cone, Edward.
Beyond the skyline; short poems pertaining to the northland, by "bard of the
Kuskokwim". New York, Boullion-Biggs,
1923. 90 p.   WaU **1947**

Confederation Celebration Committee, British Columbia.
Canada's diamond jubilee of confederation. Greater Vancouver, B. C., 1927. 64
p. illus.   WaT **1948**

**Conference of Northwest Cities on Standards
of Care for Homeless and Transient Men.**
Summary of Conference of Northwest
Cities held June 26, 1931 on standards of
care for homeless and transient men.
[Seattle] 1931. [19] p.   WaU **1949**

Conference of Western Governors.
Proceedings of the Conference of Western
Governors held at Salt Lake City, Utah,
June 5, 6, and 7, 1913. Denver, Smith-
Brooks Printing Co. [c1914] 119 p.
                              OrU WaU **1950**
Same. Held April 7, 8, 9, 10, and 11, 1914.
116 p.   Or WaU **1951**
Same. Held at Seattle, Washington, May
18, 19, and 20, 1915 and at Portland, Or.
September 22, 1915; reported by Earl E.
Richards. Olympia, Wash., Lamborn
[1915?] 97 p.
           MtU OrP OrU WaPS WaS WaU **1952**

Conference on Consumer Credit, University
of Washington, 1940.
Proceedings of the Conference on Consumer Credit, held at the University of
Washington, November 13, 14, 1940,
sponsored by the College of Economics
and Business, the School of Law, the
Graduate School of Social Work, the
School of Home Economics, the Department of Political Science, ed. by Henry
A. Burd. [Seattle? 1941?] 92 p.
                       OrU Wa WaTC WaU **1953**

**Conference on the History of the Trans-
Mississippi West,** University of Colorado,
1929.
The trans-Mississippi West; papers read
at a conference held at the University
of Colorado, June 18-June 21, 1929, ed. by

James F. Willard and Colin B. Goodykoontz. Boulder, Colo., Univ. of Colo.,
1930. xi, 366 p.   Many **1954**

Congdon, Mary Alice.
Mt. Hood, our Indians' Pah'-to. Portland,
Or. [Gibson Pub. Co., c1911] [47] p.
illus.   Many **1955**

Conger, Paul Sydney, see no. 2104.

Congregational Home Missionary Society.
Testimony of the workers, given at the
fifty-eighth anniversary of the American
Home Missionary Society at Saratoga
Springs, New York, June 3-5, 1884. New
York, 1884. 30 p.   WaU **1956**

Conkey Company.
Official guide to the Klondyke country
and the gold fields of Alaska, with the
official maps, vivid descriptions and
thrilling experiences; the most complete
and thoroughly exhaustive collection of
every known information necessary to
a full realization of the immense resources of the gold fields of Alaska.
Chicago, 1897. 296 p. illus., plates, maps.
             CVicAr CVU WaSp WaU **1957**

Conkle, Ellsworth Prouty, 1899-
200 were chosen; a play in three acts.
New York, French, 1937. 49 p. front.
Reclamation colony in Matanuska Valley, Alaska.
             IdU Or OrCS WaE WaS **1958**

Connelley, William Elsey, 1855-1930.
Wild Bill and his era; the life and adventures of James Butler Hickok, with
introd. by Charles Moreau Harger. New
York, Press of the Pioneers, 1933. xii,
229 p. front. (port.) plates, port.
                       MtU Or OrP **1959**

Connelly, Kenneth A.
Chaplain's assistant; from the correspondence of Corporal Kenneth A. Connelly,
jr., illus. by Marjorie Holroyd. Seattle,
Craftsman Press, 1945. 1 v. illus.
                              WaS **1960**

Conner, Sabra.
Captain Redlegs. Chicago, Reilly & Lee
[c1930] 313 p. Portland author.
                              Many **1961**
The fighting Starrs of Oregon. Chicago,
Reilly & Lee [c1932] 286 p.   Many **1962**
On Sweetwater trail, decorations by Edgar
Miller. Chicago, Reilly & Lee [c1928] 326
p. maps.
       Or OrMonO OrP OrU WaSp WaU **1963**
The quest of the Sea Otter. Chicago,
Reilly & Lee [c1927] 263 p. front. (map)
                              Many **1964**

Conners, Maria (Wheeler) 1832-1890?
A wreath of maple leaves; or, A collection
of household poems. Seattle, Wm. H.
Hughes Co., 1888. 95 p.   WaU **1965**

Connolly, Christopher Powell, 1863-1933.
The devil learns to vote, the story of
Montana. New York, Covici [c1938] 310
p. front., plate, ports.   Many **1966**

Connor, Ralph, see nos. 3660-3666, 3672-3677.

Connor, Thomas, see no. 3477.

Conover, Charles Tallmadge, 1862-
In the matter of the proposal to change
the name of Mount Rainier: statement
of C. T. Conover, representing numerous
citizens of the state of Washington in
favor of retaining the present name,
and oral presentation by C. T. Conover
and V. J. Farrar. The decision [n.p.,
n.d.] 58 p. illus.   Many **1967**
Same. Addenda: Statements by John Muir,
C. M. Buchanan, Edwin Eells, H. B.
McElroy, W. G. Steel, Elwood Evans.
[Seattle, Lowman & Hanford, n.d.] 76 p.
WaSp **1968**
Same. [Tacoma, Thurston County Pioneer
& Historical Society, 1924?]   Or **1969**
Mirrors of Seattle, reflecting some aged
men of fifty; with an introd. by Hon.
George Donworth. Seattle, Lowman &
Hanford, 1923. 277 p.
Or OrU Wa WaSp WaT WaU **1970**
Thomas Burke, 1849-1925. Seattle [Acme
Pub. Co] 1926. 173 p. front (port.)
Many **1971**

**Consecration of the Right Rev. Dr. D'Herbo-
mez, O. M. I.,** which has taken place in
the Cathedral of St. Andrews, Victoria,
V. I., Oct. 9, 1864. [n.p., n.d.] 10 p.
CVicAr **1972**

Consolidated Lumber Company, Elk, Wash-
ington.
Choice lands at low prices on easy terms.
[Contains Facts regarding worth of cut-
over lands in eastern Wash., by C. E.
Flagg] [Spokane? 1914?] 12 p. illus.
WaPS **1973**

[Constable, Guy]
Kootenay Flats reclamation in the Creston
Valley. [Calgary, Western Printing &
Lithograph Co., n.d.] 15 [1] p. illus.
CVicAr **1974**

Consul, Charles F., see no. 1781.

Consumers' League of Oregon. Social Survey
Committee.
Report on wages, hours and conditions of
work and cost and standard of living of
women wage earners in Oregon. Portland, Or., 1913. 71 p.
Or OrCS OrP OrU WaS WaU **1975**

Cook, Frederick Albert, 1865-1940.
My attainment of the Pole; being the
record of the expedition that first
reached the Boreal center, 1907-1909,
with the final summary of the polar
controversy. New York, Polar Pub. Co.,
1911. xx, 604 p. front., illus., plates,
ports., facsims., diagrs.
CVicAr OrCS OrHi WaPS WaS **1976**
Same. New York, M. Kennerley, 1912.
WaT WaTC WaU **1977**
To the top of the continent; discovery,
exploration and adventure in sub-arctic
Alaska; the first ascent of Mt. McKinley, 1903-1906, illus. from photographs
by the author, a frontispiece in color,
drawings, and maps. London, Hodder &
Stoughton, 1908. xxi, 321 p. col. front.,
illus., 23 plates, port., maps.
CVicAr WaU **1978**
Same. New York, Doubleday, 1908.
Many **1979**

Cook, Harl J., 1857-
Our fathers of the West, an epic of the
old-new world, an historical pageant, by
Harl J. Cook and William S. Lewis.
Spokane [n.d.] [12] p.   WaU **1980**

Cook, James, 1728-1779.
An abridgment of Captain Cook's last
voyage, performed in the years 1776,
1777, 1778, 1779, and 1780, for making
discoveries in the northern hemisphere,
by order of His Majesty. Extracted from
the 4th ed. in 3 volumes, containing a
relation of all interesting transactions,
particularly those relative to the unfortunate death of Captain Cook; with
his life, by Captain King. 2d ed. London,
Kearsley, 1784. xxvi, 441 p. front., fold.
map.   WaU **1981**
Auf unbekannten Meeren; James Cooks
Tagebuch seiner dritten Entdeckungs-
fahrt in die Sudsee und das Nordliche
Eismeer, ausgewahlt von Paul Schneider. Hrsg. von der freien Lehrer Ver-
einigung fur Kunstpfege zu Berlin. Leipzig, R. Voigtlanders Verlag [n.d.] 235 p.
front., plates.   WaU **1982**
An authentic narrative of a voyage performed by Captain Cook and Captain
Clerke in His Majesty's ships Resolution and Discovery during the years
1776, 1777, 1778, 1779, and 1780 in search
of a north-west passage between the
continents of Asia and America; including a faithful account of all their
discoveries, and the unfortunate death
of Captain Cook. Altenburg, G. E. Rich-
ter, 1788. 2 v. fold. maps.   WaU **1983**
Same. Illus. with a chart and a varitey of
cuts. By W. Ellis, assistant surgeon to
both vessels. London, Robinson, 1782.
2 v. 21 plates, map.
CVicAr CVU WaS WaU **1984**
Same. 2d ed. 1783.   OrHi OrP WaU **1985**
Same. 3d ed. 1784.   CVicAr OrP **1986**
An authentic narrative of a voyage to the
Pacific Ocean, performed by Captain
Cook and Captain Clerke in His Britan-
nic Majesty's ships the Resolution and
Discovery, in the years 1776, 1777, 1778,
1779, and 1780, by an officer on board
the Discovery. Philadelphia, Robert Bell,
1783. 2 v. in 1.   WaU **1987**
Captain Cook's third and last voyage to
the Pacific Ocean in the years 1776,
1777, 1778, 1779 and 1780, faithfully
abridged from the quarto edition published by order of His Majesty. London,
Fielding and Stockdale (1785?] xii, 372 p.
front. (port.) plates. CVicAr WaU **1988**
A compendious history of Captain Cook's
last voyage performed in the years 1776,
1777, 1778, 1779 and 1780; in which all the
interesting transactions are recorded,
particularly those relative to his unfortunate death, with a map of the new
discoveries and the track of the ships.
A new ed. London, Kearsley, 1784. 1 v.
maps. Anon.   CVU **1989**
Dritte Entdeckungs-Reise nach dem Nordpol hinauf unternommen und mit den

Schiffen Resolution und Discovery wahrend der Jahre 1776 bis 1780 ausgefuhrt; aus dem Englischen ubersetzt von Georg Forster. Berlin, Haude, 1787. 2 v. plates, port., table, maps.   OrP **1990**

Dritte und letzte Reise oder Geschichte einer Entdeckungsreise nach dem Stillen Ocean unter der Anfuhrung der Captaine Cook, Clerke, und Gore in Sr. Majestat Schiffen, der Resolution und der Discovery, wahrend den Jahren 1776, 1777, 1778, 1779 und 1780, aus den Tagbuchern der Capitaine James Cook und James King, eine Uebersetzung nach der zwoten grossen Englischen Ausgabe, von Johann Ludwig Wetzel. Anspach, Kosten des Uebersetzers gedruckt mit Messererischen Schriften, 1787. 4 v. front. (port.) plates, maps.   WaU **1991**

Journal of Captain Cook's last voyage to the Pacific Ocean on Discovery, performed in the years 1776, 1777, 1778, 1779; illus. with cuts and a chart showing the tracts of the ships employed in this expedition, faithfully narrated from the original ms. Dublin, Price, Whitestone, Chamberlaine, 1781. xlvii, 396 p. front., plates, fold. map.   WaU **1992**

Same. London, Newbery, 1781. xlvii, 388 p. front., plates (part fold.) fold. map.
CVicAr CVU WaU **1993**

Same. New ed. 1785. 376 p. 10 plates, fold. map.   CVicAr OrHi **1994**

The original astronomical observations made in the course of a voyage to the northern Pacific Ocean for the discovery of a north east or north west passage, wherein the north west coast of America and north east coast of Asia were explored in H. M. ships, the Resolution and Discovery in the years 1776, 1777, 1778, 1779 and 1780, by Capt. James Cooke and Lt. James King and Mr. William Bayly, published by order of the Commissioners of Longitude at the expence of whom the observations were made. London, Richardson, 1782. 351 p. diagr. This edition published anonymously is attributed to John Rickman.
CV CVicAr **1995**

Troisieme voyage de Cook, ou journal d'une expedition faite dans la mere Pacifique du sud & du nord, en 1776, 1777, 1778, 1779 & 1780, tr. l'anglois. Paris, Pissot, 1782. x, 508 p. front., map.
CVicAr CVU WaU **1996**

Same. 2. ed. Paris, Belin, 1782.
CVicAr WaU **1997**

Same. 3. ed. 1783. x. 454 p.
CVU OrP WaU **1998**

Troisieme voyage de Cook; ou, Voyage a l'Ocean Pacifique, ordonne par le roi d'Angleterre, execute sous la direction des Capitaines Cook, Clerke & Gore, sur les vaisseaux la Resolution & la Decouverte, en 1776, 1777, 1778, 1779 & 1780. Tr. de l'anglois par M. D. Paris, Hotel de Thou, 1785. 4 v. and atlas.
CVU WaPS WaU **1999**

Troisieme voyage de James Cook, autour du monde, sur la cote nord-ouest d' Amerique, la cote nord-est d'Asie, et dans les regions du pole boreal; fait en 1776, 1777, 1778, 1779 et 1780, tr. nouv. par J. B. J. Breton. Paris, Lepetit, 1804. 4 v. in 2. (Bibliotheque portative des voyages, t. 26-29)   WaU **2000**

A voyage to the Pacific Ocean for making discoveries in the Northern Hemisphere; performed under the direction of Captains Cook, Clerke, and Gore in the years 1776, 1777, 1778, 1779, 1780, by Captain James Cook, F. R. S. and Captain James King, LL.D and F. R. S., illus. with elegant plates and a large chart. New York, Printed by Tiebout and O'Brien for Benjamin Gomez, 1796. 4 v. 56 plates.   CVU **2001**

A voyage to the Pacific Ocean for making discoveries in the Northern Hemisphere under the direction of Captains Cook, Clerke, and Gore in the years 1776, 7, 8, 9, and 80, with an introductory review of maritime discovery down to the time of Captain Cook; with 28 copperplate engravings. Leith. Printed by and for William Reid & Son and Henry Constable, Edinburgh, 1831. 1 v. 28 plates.   CVU **2002**

A voyage to the Pacific Ocean; undertaken, by the command of His Majesty, for making discoveries in the Northern Hemisphere to determine the position and extent of the west side of North America; its distance from Asia; and the practicability of a northern passage to Europe; performed under the direction of Captains Cook, Clerke, and Gore, in his Majesty's ships the Resolution and Discovery, in the years 1776, 1777, 1778, 1779, and 1780. Vol. I and II written by Captain James Cook, Vol. III by Captain James King. Illustrated with maps and charts, from the original drawings made by Lieut. Henry Roberts . . . and . . . Mr. Webber . . . Published by order of the Lords Commissioners of the Admiralty. London, Printed by W. and A. Strahan for G. Nicol and T. Cadell, 1784. 3 v. & atlas. plates (part fold.) maps (part fold.)
CVU OrHi OrP OrSaW WaS WaU **2002A**

A voyage to the Pacific Ocean; undertaken by the command of His Majesty for making discoveries in the Northern Hemisphere; performed under the direction of Captains Cook, Clerke, and Gore in the years 1776, 1777, 1778, 1779, and 1780; being a copious, comprehensive, and satisfactory abridgement of the Voyage, written by Captain James Cook and Captain James King, illus. with cuts. In four volumes. London, Printed for J. Stockdale, Scatcherd and Whitaker, J. Fielding, and J. Hardy, 1784. 4 v. plates (part fold.) maps (part fold.)
WaU **2003**

Same. London, Printed for C. Stalker, 1788.   WaU **2004**

Same. Volumes I and II written by Captain James Cook, F. R. S. Volume III by

Captain James King, LL. D. and F. R. S. Published by order of the Lords Commissioners of the Admiralty. 3d ed. London, Printed by H. Hughs for G. Nicol and T. Cadell, 1785. 3 v. plates (part fold.) maps (part fold.) CVU **2005**

Same. Compiled from the various accounts of that voyage hitherto published. Perth, Printed by R. Morison for R. Morison and Son, 1785. 4 v. front., plates, maps. WaU **2006**

Zuverlassige Nachricht von der dritten und letzen Reise der Capitans Cook und Clerke in den koniglichen Schiffen, die Resolution und Discovery, in den Jahren von 1776 bis 1780, besonders in der Absicht, eine Nordwestliche Durchfahrt zwischen Asia und Amerika ausfindig zu machen. Aus dem Englischen ubersetzt. Frankfurt, Kosten der Verlags Kasse, 1783. 324 p. map. CVU WaU **2007**

See also no. 5797.

Cook, James Henry, 1857-
Fifty years on the old frontier, as cowboy, hunter, guide, scout, and ranchman, with an introd. by Brigadier General Charles King. New Haven, Yale Univ. Press, 1923. xix, 291 p. front., plates (1 col., 2 fold.) ports. Many **2008**

Cook, James M., 1858-
The Canadian Northwest as it is today. Los Angeles, c1912. 47 p. front. (port.) illus., plates. CVicAr WaU **2009**

Cooke, Mrs. Belle (Walker) 1834-1919.
Tears and victory and other poems. Salem, Or., Waite, 1871. 253 p.
IdU OrHi OrP OrSaW WaU **2010**

Cooke, Clarence M., 1878-
Our daily life, Oregon civil government, 1946. Portland, Or., Binfords & Mort [c1947] iv, 416 p. maps, diagrs. Many **2011**

Cooley, Fred Smith, 1869-1933.
A history of the Montana extension service, ed. by Charles E. Potter. [Bozeman, Mont., Alpha of Epsilon Sigma Phi, 1924] 26 p. MtBozC **2012**

Cooley, Thomas McIntyre, 1824-1898.
Oregon mortgage tax law; opinion. [Ann Arbor, Mich.? 1885] 30 p. Or OrP **2013**

Coolidge, Louis Arthur, 1861-1925.
Klondike and the Yukon country a description of our Alaska land of gold from the latest official and scientific sources and personal observations, with a chapter by John F. Pratt; new maps and photographic illus. Philadelphia, H. Altemus, 1897. 213 p. 18 plates, 2 maps. CVicAr CVU WaS WaU **2014**
Same. 251 p. front., 46 plates, fold. map. CVicAr **2015**

[Coombs, Samuel F.]
Dictionary of the Chinook jargon as spoken on Puget Sound and the Northwest, with original Indian names for prominent places and localities with their meanings; historical sketch, etc. Seattle, Lowman & Hanford [1891] 38 p. OrP WaU **2016**

Coontz, Robert Edward, 1864-
From the Mississippi to the sea. Philadelphia, Dorrance [c1930] 483 p. front., plates, ports. Western author. WaS WaU **2017**

Cooper, C. E.
Washington state supplement [to McMurry's Advanced Geography] [New York] Macmillan, c1921. 32 p. col. front., illus., maps. Wa WaPS **2018**
Same. Rev. by T. F. Hunt, 1929. WaT **2019**

Cooper, Courtney Riley, see no. 5803.

Cooper, Dorothy, 1888-
Mother, sweet mother; words by George W. Cooper, music by Dorothy Cooper. Orofino, Idaho, George W. Cooper [1936] [8] p. music. WaPS **2020**
Sweet Orofino; words by George W. Cooper, music by Dorothy Cooper. Orofino, Idaho, George W. Cooper [1936] [4] p. music. WaPS **2021**

Cooper, George W., see nos. 2020, 2021.

Cooper, Jacob Calvin, 1845-1937.
Military history of Yamhill County [Souvenir G. A. R. encampment, 1899, McMinnville, Oregon] [McMinnville, Or? 1899] [124] p. front., illus., plates, ports.
Or OrHi OrP OrU WaS WaU **2022**
Old Fire Tongue and Hoop Snake dance, a playlet, Indian legend dramatized for schools and societies. McMinnville [Telephone Register Print] 1932. 13 p.
OrHi **2022A**
Red pioneers; romance of early Indian life in the West. Author's ed. McMinnville, Or., 1928. 251 p. col. front. Many **2023**
The red pioneers, from the novel of the same name; dramatized by Frances Osborne Stallings. [n.p.] c1928. 20 p. WaPS **2024**
Seven Cooper brothers and three sisters, Oregon; children and descendants of Elder E. E. and Nancy Cooper, by J. C. and M. P. Cooper. [McMinnville, Or., 1913] 45 p. front. (port.) ports.
OrP WaU **2025**
Walnut growing in Oregon. [n.p.] Southern Pacific Co. [n.d.] 64 p. illus., map. OrHi **2026**
Same. Portland, Or., Passenger Departments, Oregon Railroad and Navigation Co., Southern Pacific Co., c1910.
Or OrP WaPS **2027**
Same. [1912?] OrP WaU **2028**
Yamhills, an Indian romance. McMinnville, Or., 1904. 187 p. illus. Many **2029**

Cooper, James, see no. 1754.

Cooper, James Graham, 1830-1902.
The natural history of Washington Territory, with much relating to Minnesota, Nebraska, Kansas, Oregon and California, between the thirty-sixth and forty-ninth parallels of latitude, being those parts of the final reports on the survey of the Northern Pacific Railroad route, containing the climate and

physical geography, with full catalogues and descriptions of the plants and animals collected from 1853 to 1857, by J. G. Cooper, M. D., and Dr. G. Suckley; this ed. contains a new preface giving a sketch of the explorations, a classified table of contents, and the latest additions by the authors, with fifty-five new plates of scenery, botany, and zoology, and an isothermal chart of the route. New York, Balliere Bros., 1859. 3 pt. in 1 v. 66 plates (part col.) fold. map.

    CVicAr OrCS OrP WaSp WaU **2030**

Same. 2d ed.   CVicAr **2031**

See also no. 10004.

Cooper, M. P., see no. 2025.

Coos Bay Bridge Committee.
    Official souvenir program; Coos Bay Bridge celebration, a complete schedule of events, North Bend, Oregon on Coos Bay, June 5-6-7, 1936. [North Bend, Or., Coos Bay Harbor Printers, 1936] [12] p. illus.   OrU **2032**

Coos Bay Times.
    Celebrating the dawn of a "new era" for southwestern Oregon, 1937. [Marshfield, Or., 1937] 80 p. illus., ports, maps. (v. 54, no. 52, Dec. 29, 1937)   Or OrU **2033**

Coos County Agricultural Conference.
    Report of the Coos County Agricultural Conference conducted in Coquille, Oregon, Mar. 10 and 11, 1936. [Bandon, Or., Western World Print, 1936] 34 p. illus.   OrU **2034**

Coppens, Charles, see no. 5764.

Copper River & Northwestern Railway.
    The finding of an empire. [Seattle, White Advertising Bureau, 1909?] 19 p. front., illus., photos.   WaU **2035**

Copper River Joe, see no. 8601

Coquina, see no. 9420.

Corbett, Edward Annand.
    Blackfoot trails. Toronto, Macmillan, 1934. 139 p. col. front (port.) col. plates.   CVU WaU **2036**

Corbett, L. C., see no. 316.

Corbett, Vivian Miller.
    In Portland we do! [Portland, Beattie & Hofmann for the Author, 1946.] 29 p. illus., port.   Or OrHi **2036A**

Cornelison, J. M.
    Weyekin stories; titwatit Weyekishnim. San Francisco, E. L. Mackey & Co. [c1911] 20 p. front., illus., ports. Umatilla Indian legends.
    Or OrHi OrP OrSa WaS WaU **2037**

Corning, Howard McKinley, 1896-
    Deerfoot prints; an Oregon portrait. Portland, Or., Metropolitan, 1935, c1931. 36 p. Portland author.   Or **2038**

    The mountain in the sky, a book of Oregon poems. Portland, Or., Metropolitan, 1930. 112 p.   Many **2039**

    Willamette landings; ghost towns of the river. [Portland, Or.] Binfords & Mort [c1947] 201 p. illus., map. "Research for this book was begun by the W.P.A. Oregon Writers' Project in 1936."
    Many **2040**

See also no. 10536.

Cornish, George Augustus, 1872-
    Canadian geography for juniors. British Columbia ed. Toronto, Dent [1934] 388 p. front., illus., maps, diagrs. CVU **2041**

Cornish, Reynelle George Edward, 1890-
    Dry facts; the Oregon prohibition law. Portland, Or., Woodard, Clarke & Co. [c1915] 14 p.   OrP **2042**

Cornwallis, Kinahan, 1839-1917.
    The new El Dorado; or, British Columbia. London, T. C. Newby, 1858. xxviii, 405 p. front., fold. map.
    CVicAr CVU IdU WaS WaU **2043**

Same. 2d ed.
    CVicAr CVU IdU WaS WaSp **2044**

Correspondence respecting the Canadian Pacific Railway Act so far as regards British Columbia. April, 1875. London, Harrison and Sons [1875] 1 v.
    CVU **2045**

Corry, Trevor.
    The White Pass & Yukon route; the scenic railway of the world. Seattle [Century Printing Co., n.d.] 1 v.
    CVU **2046**

Corser, Harry Prosper, 1864-1936.
    Legendary lore of the Alaska totems. Juneau, Purity Pharmacy, c1910. 1 v. illus., 9 plates.   WaS WaT **2047**

    Seventy-six page history of Alaska. [n.p.] 1927. 76 p. front (port.) illus, ports.
    WaPS WaS WaSp WaU **2048**

    Through the thousand islands of Alaska. Juneau, Nugget Shop [n.d.] 46 p. illus.
    WaSp **2049**

    Totem lore and the land of the Totem; including Totem lore, 6th ed. and Through the ten thousand islands of Alaska, 2d ed. Juneau, Nugget Shop [n.d.] 97 p. illus. OrP OrU WaU **2050**

    Same. Including Totem lore, 7th ed. and Through the ten thousand islands of Alaska, 3d ed. 102 p. illus.
    CVicAr OrSaW Wa WaU **2051**

    Same. Including Totem lore, 8th ed. and Through the ten thousand islands of Alaska, 4th ed. 110 p. illus.   OrU **2052**

    Totem lore of the Alaska Indians. 3d ed. Ketchikan, Alaska, Ryus Drug Co. [n.d.] 66 p. illus., music. CV Wa WAU **2053**

    Same. 5th ed. Juneau, Nugget Shop [n.d.] 59 p. illus.   WaS WaSp **2054**

    Totem lore of the Alaska Indian and the land of the totem. New ed. rev. Wrangell, Alaska, Bear Totem Store [c1932] 83 p. illus., ports.   Many **2055**

Corson, Fred P., see no. 2518.

Corvallis, Or. First Methodist Church.
    Centennial Observance, 1848-1948. November 7, 1948. Corvallis, Or. [1948] 32 p. illus., ports.   OrCS **2056**

Corvallis Water Company.
    Water rates, rules and regulations. Corvallis, Or., Craig, 1890. 17 p. OrHi **2057**

[Cory, Vivian]
A girl of the Klondike, by Vivian Cross [pseud.] New York, Mitchell Kennerley [n.d.] 317 p.   WaU 2058

Coryell, Hubert Vansant, 1889-
Klondike gold; illus. by Armstrong Sperry. New York, Macmillan [c1938] vi, 319 p. illus.   Many 2059

[Coryell, John Russell] 1851-1924.
A Klondike claim; or, Won by sheer nerve, by Nicholas Carter [pseud.] New York, Street & Smith [c1897] 218 p.
                                       WaU 2060

Cosgriff, Robert James.
Wastelands. Los Angeles, Wetzel Pub Co. [c1928] 316 p. Seaside, Oregon, and lumbering on Tillamook Head.
                                   Or WaU 2061

Costello, Joseph A.
The Siwash, their life legends, and tales; Puget Sound and Pacific Northwest. Seattle, The Calvert Co., 1895. vii, 169 p. front., illus., plates, ports.   Many 2062
Same. 1896.   Wa 2063

Cotsworth, Moses Bruine, 1859-
British Columbia's supreme advantages in climate, resources, beauty and life. [Victoria, B.C., Wolfenden, 1909] 77 p. front., illus., plate.   CV CVicAr WaS 2064

[Cotter, Frank J.]
Rhymes of a roughneck, by Pat O'Cotter [pseud.] Seward, Alaska, 1918. 92 p.
                           CVU WaTC WaU 2065

Cotterill, George Fletcher, 1865-
The climax of a world quest; the story of Puget Sound, the modern Mediterranean of the Pacific. Seattle, Olympic Pub Co. [1928?] 226 p. ports., maps.   Many 2066
Municipal ownership of street railways in Seattle; an address delivered by Hon. George F. Cotterill at Christensen's Hall, Seattle, Saturday, November 25, 1905, published by order of the Seattle Municipal Ownership League. [Seattle, 1905?] 24 p.   WaU 2067

Cotton, Sam J.
Stories of Nehalem. Chicago, Donohue [1915] 147 p. front., 4 plates, port.
                                       Many 2068

Cotton, W. W.
Alfalfa in the Willamette Valley. Portland, Or., Southern Pacific Railroad, 1906. 21 p.   OrHi 2069

Coues, Elliott, see nos. 4350, 5700, 5902, 8148.

Council for Economic and Social Research of Portland, Oregon.
One year's study of the economic and social problems of our time. [n.p.] 1933. 47 p.   OrP 2070

Courier-Herald, Oregon City, Oregon.
Souvenir Clackamas Co., Oregon. New Year number. [Oregon City, Or.] 1901. 28 p. illus.   OrP 2071

Covey, Roland, see no. 8410.

Cowan, George Henry.
British Columbia's claim upon the Dominion government for better terms. Vancouver, B. C., Independent Printing Co., 1904. 31 p. port.
                         CV CVicAr CVU WaU 2072

Cowan, I. M., see no. 7169.

Cowan, William T.
Senator Wm. T. Cowan's address at the meeting of the M. S. L. A., October 8-10, 1928, Havre, Montana. [early history of northern Montana] [n.p., n.d.] [13] p.
                                       MtU 2073

Cowboy Evangelist, see no. 5438.

Cowen, Edward David, 1857-
Newspaper career of E. D. Cowen, with biographic sketches by Charles A. Murray, Slason Thompson, R. E. M. Strickland, C. E. Arney, Hugh Hume, Frank M. Dallam, Jr. [Seattle, Western Co., c1930] 151 p. mounted port., facsim.
                           IdU MtU WaU 2074

Cowles, B. K.
Alaska; interesting and reliable information relating thereto; containing also the organic act of the Territory. Madison, Wis., Democrat Co., 1885. 16 p.
                                       WaU 2075

Cox, Harold Robert Wakeford, 1907-
Greenhorns in blue pastures, illus. by Lucinda Smith Wakefield. New York, Smith and Durrell [1945] vii, 162 p. illus. British Columbia fishing.   Many 2076
Same. New York, A. S. Barnes, 1945.
                                     OrLgE 2077

Cox, Ross, 1793-1853.
Adventures on the Columbia River, including the narrative of a residence of six years on the western side of the Rocky Mountains. London, Colburn, 1831. 2 v.   Many 2078
Same. New York, Harper, 1832. 335 p.
                                       Many 2079
The Columbia River; or, Scenes and adventures during a residence of six years on the western side of the Rocky Mountains. 2d ed. London, Colburn, 1832. 2 v. table.   Many 2080
Same. 2 v. in 1.   CVicAr 2081
Same. 3d ed. 2 v. table.   Many 2082

Cox, William Thomas, 1878-
Fearsome creatures of the lumberwoods, with a few desert and mountain beasts, illus. by Coert Du Bois. Washington, D. C., Judd & Detweiler 1910, 47 p. illus.
                                   Wa WaU 2083

[Coxe, Richard Smith] 1792-1865.
Extent and value of the possessory rights of the Hudson's Bay Company in Oregon, south of forty-ninth degree. [n.p.] 1848-49. 51 p.   OrHi 2084

Coxe, William, 1737-1828.
A comparative view of the Russian discoveries with those made by Captains Cook and Clerke, and a sketch of what remains to be ascertained by future navigators. London, J. Nichols, 1787. 31 p.   CVicAr OrP WaS 2085

Cradlebaugh, J. H.
Nyeena Kloshe illahee (Songs of the good country). Salem, Or., 1913. 67 p. front. (port.) 8 plates.   Many 2086

Craig, Lulu Alice.
Glimpses of sunshine and shade in the far North; or, My travels in the land of the

midnight sun. Cincinnati, Editor Pub. Co., 1900. 123 p. front., 12 plates, port., map.

CVICAr CVU WaPS WaS WaU **2087**

Craig, Morte H.
In the shadow of the Pole. 2d ed. [Seattle, Acme Pub. Co., c1909] [34] p. illus.

CVicAr **2088**

Craighead, James Geddes, 1823-1895.
Story of Marcus Whitman; early Protestant missions in the Northwest. Philadelphia, Presbyterian Board of Pub., 1895. 211 p. Many **2089**

Same. 1900, c1895. WaS WaT **2090**

Same. 1908 [c1895] IdU **2091**

Craine, Edith Janice, 1881-
Evermay ranch, illus. by Marjorie Lee Ullberg. Philadelphia, David McKay Co. [c1940] 269 p. illus. Montana ranch story.

WaSp WaU **2092**

Crandall, Julie V.
The story of Pacific salmon. Portland, Or., Binfords & Mort [1946] 59 p. plates.

Many **2093**

Crandall, Lathan Augustus, 1850-
Days in the open, decorations by Louis Rhead. New York, H. Revell [c1914] 270 p. front., illus., plates. OrP WaU **2094**

Crandall, Lulu D., see no. 8771.

Crane, Alice Rollins, comp.
Smiles and tears from the Klondyke, a collection of stories and sketches. New York, Doxey's [1901] 203 p. front. (port.) plates, ports. CVicAr OrU WaU **2095**

Crane, Florence R.
Faithful Indians of St. Ignatius, by Redfeather, daughter of White Buffalo. [n.p.] 1907. 114 p. front. (port.) plate, ports. Wa WaS WaU **2096**

Crane, Warren Eugene.
Totem tales. New York, H. Revell [c1932] 95 p. front., plates. Many **2097**

Cranston, Earl, see no. 4501.

Crawford, Charles Howard.
Scenes of earlier days in crossing the plains to Oregon, and experiences of western life. Petaluma, Calif., J. T. Studdert, Book and Job Printer, 1898. 186 p. front. (port.) illus. WaSp WaU **2098**

Crawford, Harriet Ann (Pettijohn)
The Washington State Grange, 1889-1924; a romance of democracy. Portland, Or., Binfords & Mort [c1940] 334 p. front., illus., plate. Many **2099**

Crawford, Lewis Ferandus, 1870-1936.
Rekindling camp fires, the exploits of Ben Arnold (Connor) (Wa-si-cu Tam-a-he-ca) an authentic narrative of sixty years in the old West as Indian fighter, gold miner, cowboy, hunter and army scout. Bismarck, N. D., Capital Book Co. [c1926] 324 p. front (port.) 10 plates, map.

IdU MtHi MtU WaE WaSp WaU **2100**

Crawford, Mary Mazeppa, 1898-
The Nez Perces since Spalding; experiences of forty-one years at Lapwai, Idaho, with introd. by Miss Julia Fraser.

[Berkeley, Calif., The Professional Press] 1936. 64 p. front., ports.

Many **2101**

Crawford, Medorem, d. 1891.
Journal; an account of his trip across the plains with the Oregon pioneers of 1842. Eugene, Or., Star Job Office, 1897. 26 p. (Sources of the history of Or., v. 1, no. 1) Many **2102**

Crawford, Samuel L., see no. 7537.

Crawford, W. J., see no. 6608.

Cremer, Henry, 1895-
History of teacher training in the public higher institutions of Washington. Indiana, Pa., R. S. Grosse Print Shop, 1929. 11 p. WaS WaU **2103**

Cressman, Luther Sheeleigh, 1897-
Archaeological researches in the northern Great Basin [by] L. S. Cressman with the collaboration of F. C. Baker, P. S. Conger, H. P. Hansen, and R. F. Heizer. Washington, D. C., Carnegie Institution of Washington, 1942. 158 p. front., 45 plates (1 col.) (Publication 538) Many **2104**

Archaeological survey of the Guano Valley region in southeastern Oregon. Eugene, Or., Univ. of Or. [1936] 48 p. illus., maps, tables, diagrs. (Studies in anthropology no. 1) Many **2105**

Contributions to the archaeology of Oregon; final report on the Gold Hill burial site. Eugene, Or., Univ. of Or. [1933] 24 p. illus., tables, diagr. (Studies in anthropology v. 1.) Many **2106**

Early man in Oregon, archaeological studies in the northern Great Basin, by Luther Sheeleigh Cressman, Howel Williams and A. D. Krieger. Eugene, Or., Univ. of Or., 1940. viii, 78 p. 5 plates. (Studies in anthropology no. 3)

Many **2107**

Petroglyphs of Oregon. Eugene, Or., Univ. of Or. [1937] 78 p. illus., diagrs., maps (Studies in anthropology no. 1 (i.e. 2) June, 1937) Many **2108**

Crewe, E. O.
Gold fields of the Yukon and how to get there. Chicago, Cole [c1897] 61 p. illus., 2 maps. CVicAr **2109**

Crewe, Fred.
Poems of Klondyke's early days and Alaska's long white trail; photographs of the Klondyke Stampede taken in 1897-98. Milwaukee, Wis., North American Press, c1921. [60] p. front. illus., plates (1 col.) CVU **2110**

The Cricket, see no. 3755.

Cridge, A. D., see no. 2780.

Cridge, Edward, 1817-1913.
Diocesan synod; address of the Dean of Christ Church to the congregation. [n.p., n.d.] [6] p. CVicAr **2111**

Pastoral address on the occasion of the consecration of Christ Church, Victoria, Dec. 7, 1865, with statement of facts respecting the church reserve. Victoria, B. C., Daily Chronicle [1865] 7 p.

CVicAr **2112**

"Spiritualism" or Modern necromancy; a sermon with preface and notes. Victoria, B. C., Higgins, 1870. 12 p.   CVicAr **2113**

Trial of the Very Reverend Edward Cridge, rector and dean of Christ Church Cathedral, Victoria; documents, evidence given in the Bishop's court and in the Supreme Court of the province. Victoria, B. C., Victoria Standard, 1875. 61 p.   CVicAr CVU **2114**

See also no. 3018.

Crimont, Joseph Raphael.
Sketch of the martyrdom of Archbishop Charles John Seghers. [Victoria, B. C., Diggon-Hibben, 1944] 30 p. illus., ports.
   CVicAr **2115**

Crisler, Lois, see no. 8222.

Criswell, Elijah Harry.
Lewis and Clark; linguistic pioneers. Columbia, Mo., Univ. of Mo., 1940. ccxi, 102 p. (Studies, V. 15, no. 2)   Many **2116**

Crocker, A. B., see no. 4874.

Crocker, F. G., see no. 4874.

Crofutt, George A.
Crofutt's new overland tourist and Pacific coast guide over the Union, Central and Southern Pacific railroads, their branches and connections by rail, water and stage. v. 1, 1878-9. Chicago, Overland Pub. Co., 1878. 322 p. front., illus., double plates.   Many **2117**

Same. v. 2, 1879-80. c1879. 272 p.
   MtHi OrU WaU **2118**

Same. Omaha, Overland Pub Co., 1880. 281 p. illus.   Or WaPS **2119**

Same. 1883. 275 p. front., illus., double plates.   WaU **2120**

Crofutt's overland tours; consisting of nearly five thousand miles of main tours and three thousand miles of side tours; also two thousand miles by stage and water. Chicago, Ill., A. H. Day, 1888. 254 p. front., illus., 6 double plates, ports., maps.   OrU WaPS WaSp **2121**

Same. Chicago, H. J. Smith, 1889. 252 p. illus., plates, fold. map.   WaU **2122**

Crofutt's overland tours consisting of over six thousand miles of main tours and three thousand miles of side tours, also six thousand miles by stage and water. Chicago, H. J. Smith, 1889. 264 p. front., illus., 6 plates, ports., fold. map.
   IdU WaT **2123**

Crofutt's trans-continental tourist's guide, containing a full and authentic description of over five hundred cities, towns, villages; how to go and whom to stop with while passing over the Union Pacific Railroad, Central Pacific Railroad of Cal., their branches and connections by stage and water. 3d v., 2d annual revise. New York, 1871. 215 p. front., illus., fold. map.   WaSp WaWW **2124**

Same. 4th v. 3d annual revise. c1872. 224 p. front., illus., fold. map.
   OrHi WaSp **2125**

Same. 5th v., 4th annual revise. c1873.
   CVicAr IdB WaSp **2126**

Same. 6th v., 5th annual revise.
   OrHi **2126A**

Same. 7th v., 6th annual revise. New York, G. W. Carleton, 1875. 160 p. front., illus., 2 fold. maps, fold table.   WaSp **2127**

Cronies' Club, Tacoma, Washington.
Cronies o' mine. Tacoma, 1919. 72 p. front., plates, ports.   WaU **2128**

Crook, George, 1828-1890.
General George Crook; his autobiography, ed. and annotated by M. F. Schmitt. Norman, Okla., Univ. of Okla. Press, 1946. 326 p. illus. Hero of Oregon Indian wars.   Many **2129**

Crook County, Oregon.
Crook County, Oregon, schools and resources. [n.p.] 1915. 141 p. illus.
   OrHhi OrP OrU **2130**

Crosby, Edward John.
The story of the Washington Water Power Company and its part in the history of electric service in the Inland Empire, 1889-1930 inclusive. [Spokane? 1930?] 33 p. illus., ports., map.
   IdU WaPS WaSp WaU WaWW **2131**

Crosby, Mrs. Elizabeth.
Our work; how the Gospel came to Fort Simpson. [Toronto, Woman's Missionary Society of the Methodist Church, n.d.] 8 p.   CVicAr **2132**

Crosby, Katharine.
Blue-water men and other Cape Codders. New York, Macmillan, 1946. 288 p. front., plates. Seattle author.   Many **2133**

Crosby, Laurence E., see no. 1572.

Crosby, Thomas, 1840-1914.
Among the An-ko-me-nums or Flathead tribes of Indians of the Pacific coast, by Rev. Thomas Crosby, missionary to the Indians of British Columbia. Toronto, Briggs, 1907. 243 p. front., illus., 13 plates, ports.   Many **2134**

Up and down the north Pacific coast by canoe and mission ship. Toronto, Missionary Society of the Methodist Church, Young People's Forward Movement Dept. [c1914] 403 p. front. (port.) 19 plates, 12 ports.
   CV CVicAr CVU WaS WaU **2135**

Cross, Osborne, 1803-1876.
The march of the mounted riflemen, first United States military expedition to travel the full length of the Oregon Trail from Fort Leavenworth to Fort Vancouver, May to October, 1849, as recorded in the journals of Major Osborne Cross and George Gibbs and the official report of Colonel Loring; ed. by Raymond W. Settle. Glendale, Calif., A. H. Clark Co., 1940. 380 p. front. (port.) plates, fold. map. (Northwest historical series, 3)   Many **2136**

Cross, Vivian, see no. 2058.

Crouse, Nellis Maynard, 1884-
In quest of the western ocean. London, Dent [c1928] ix, 480 p. maps (part fold.)
   CVU **2137**

Same. New York, Morrow [c1928]
   Many **2138**

The search for the Northwest Passage. New York, Columbia Univ. Press, 1934. 533 p. front., 3 plates, map. Many **2139**

Crowther, James Edwin, 1877-
The wayfarer, a pageant of the kingdom. [n.p.] c1921. 123 p. Vocal score with piano accompaniment.
Wa WaS WaT WaU **2140**

[Croy, Paul] 1905-
Old blazes; dedicated to the white tail deer and mountain trout of America. Spokane, Sterling Press, c1937. 32 p. illus., mounted port. IdU **2141**

Cruzan, J. A., see no. 3728.

Cubberley, Ellwood Patterson, 1868-
Portland survey; a textbook on city school administration based on a concrete study. Yonkers-on-Hudson, N. Y., World Book Co., 1915. 441 p. Many **2142**

Same. 1916 [c1915] 441 p. illus. (School efficiency series) IdU **2143**

Cubery, William M.
Cubery's visitors guide to Victoria. [n.p.] 1875. 8 p. CVicAr **2144**

Cullen, Mary, see no. 5715.

Cumming, Robert Dalziel, 1871-
Paul Pero. [Toronto, Ryerson, c1928] 30 p. British Columbia author. CVU **2145**

Skookum Chuck fables; bits of history through the microscope (some of which appeared in the Ashcroft Journal) by Skookum Chuch [pseud.] [Ashcroft, B.C., c1915] 167 p. front.
CV CVicAr CVU WaU **2146**

Cummings, Charles H.
Western trips in 1887 and 1890. [n.p., 1890?] 32 p. WaU **2147**

Cummins, Mrs. Sarah J. Walden (Lemmon) 1828-
Autobiography and reminiscences. [n.p., c1914] 61 p. ports. OrCS WaSp **2148**

Same. Cleveland, A. H. Clark Co., c1914. 63 p. WaWW **2149**

Same. [Freewater, Or., Mrs. J. J. Allen, c1914] 61 p., illus. WaPS **2150**

Same. La Grande, Or., La Grande Printing Co. [c1914] 63 p. front. (port.)
Many **2151**

Same. Touchet, Wash., c1914. OrSa **2152**

Same. [Walla Walla, Wash., Walla Walla Bulletin, c1914] IdU OrP WaW **2153**

Same. [Freewater, Or., Mrs. J. J. Allen, 1927, c1914] Or **2154**

Cunningham, Eugene, 1896-
Triggernometry; a gallery of gunfighters; with technical notes on leather slapping as a fine art, gathered from many a loose holstered expert over the years; foreword by Eugene Manlove Rhodes; illus., from the Rose collection, San Antonio. Caldwell, Idaho, Caxton, 1941. xvii, 441 p. illus., plates, ports.
Many **2155**

See also no. 8198.

Cuppage, Mrs. Edith M. (Reade)
"Here and there" on Vancouver Island,

British Columbia. [Victoria, B. C., Buckle, n.d.] 28 p. illus.
CVicAr WaS **2156**

Island trails, highways and byways on Vancouver Island. Victoria, B. C., Buckle, 1945. 36 p. illus., map.
CVicAr CVU **2157**

Same. Cover design and decorations by Maude Paget. Victoria, B. C., Buckle, 1946. 42 p. illus., map.
CVicAr WaS WaT **2158**

Curl, Grace Voris.
Young Shannon, scout with Lewis and Clark, illus. by Paul Lantz. New York, Harper [c1941] vii, 236 p. front., illus., plates. Or OrP WaSp WaU **2159**

Currey, Jesse A.
Portland roses; history, planting, cultivation. Portland, Or., Portland Rose Society, c1923. 24 p. illus.
Or OrP WaPS WaS **2160**

Currie, Sir Arthur, see no. 8143.

Currie, George Graham, 1867-
How I once felt; songs of love and travel. Montreal, John Lovell & Son, 1893. 142 p. plates. Dedicated to Burrard Literary Society of Vancouver, B. C.
CVU WaU **2161**

Curry County Reporter.
Progress number, August, 1926. Gold Beach, Or., 1926. [57] p. illus., ports.
Or OrHi OpP **2162**

Curtin, Jeremiah, 1840-1906.
Myths of the Modocs. Boston, Little, 1912. xii, 389 p. Many **2163**

Same. London, Low [c1912] OrU **2164**
See also no. 8986.

Curtin, Walter Russell.
Yukon voyage; unofficial log of the steamer Yukoner. Caldwell, Idaho, Caxton, 1938. 299 p. front. (map) plates, map, plan, facsims. Many **2165**

Curtis, Edward S., 1868-
In the land of the head-hunters, illus. with photographs by the author. Yonkers-on-Hudson, N. Y., World Book Co., 1915. xi, 112 p. front., plates. (Indian life and Indian lore) Many **2166**

Indian days of the long ago, illus. with photographs by the author and drawings by F. N. Wilson. Yonkers-on-Hudson, N. Y., World Book Co., 1915. x, 221 p. front., illus., plate. (Indian life and Indian lore). Salish Indians.
Many **2167**

The North American Indian; being a series of volumes picturing and describing the Indians of the United States and Alaska, written, illus. and pub. by Edward S. Curtis; ed. by Frederick Webb Hodge, foreword by Theodore Roosevelt; field research conducted under the patronage of J. Pierpont Morgan. [Seattle, Wash.] 1907-1930. 20 v. fronts., plates and 20 v. of plates. Many **2168**

Curwood, James Oliver, 1878-1927.
The Alaskan; a novel of the North, with illus. by Walt Lauderback. New York, Cosmopolitan Book Corp. [c1922] 326 p. front., 3 plates. WaE **2169**

Same. **1923.**
IdB Or Wa WaPS WaS WaU 2170
Same. Toronto, Copp [1923] CV 2171
Same. New York, Grosset, c1923. c1922.
WaE WaT WaU 2172
Danger Trail. Indianapolis, Bobbs-Merrill, 1910. 305 p. front., illus., plate.
WaA WaS WaW 2173
The flaming forest; a novel of the Canadian Northwest, with illus. by Walt Louderback. Toronto, C. Clark Co. [c1921]. 296 p. front., plates. WaU 2174
Honor of the big snows, with illus. by Charles Livingston Bull. Indianapolis, Bobbs-Merrill, 1911. 317 p. col. front., col. plates.
Or OrP WaA WaS WaSp WaW 2175
Same. New York, Burt [c1911]
WaPS WaU 2176
Philip Steele of the Royal Northwest Mounted Police, illus. by Gayle Hoskins. Indianapolis, Bobbs-Merrill, 1911. 307 p. front., illus.
CV Or WaA WaS WaSp 2177
Same. New York, Burt, 1911. WaU 2178
Steele of the Royal Mounted; (Philip Steele) a story of the great Canadian Northwest. New York, Burt [c1911] 306 p. front. WaE WaPS WaU 2179
The valley of silent men; a story of the Three River country. New York, Triangle Books [c1920] 298 p. Wa 2180

Cushing, Caleb. 1800-1879.
Treaty of Washington; its negotiation, execution and the discussions relating thereto. New York, Harper, 1873. 280 p.
Many 2181

Cusick, William Conklin, 1842-1922.
Check list of the plants of the portion of eastern Oregon lying east and south of the Blue Mountains. Union, Or., 1901. [11] p. OrP 2182

Custer, Mrs. Elizabeth (Bacon) 1842-1933.
"Boots and saddles"; or, Life in Dakota with General Custer. London, Low, 1885. 312 p. WaU 2183
Same. New York, Harper, 1885.
CVicAr MtU OrHi WaTC 2184
Following the guidon. New York, Harper, 1890. xx, 341 p. front., illus., 11 plates, ports. Many 2185
Tenting on the plains; or, General Custer in Kansas and Texas. New York, L. Webster, 1887. 702 p. front. (port.) illus., maps. Or OrP WaSp 2186
Same. 1893. x [17] 403 p.
MtBozC WaS 2187
See also no. 2669.

Custer, George, see no. 4305.

Custer, George A., see no. 3337.

Custer, George Armstrong, 1839-1876.
My life on the plains; or, Personal experiences with Indians. New York, Sheldon & Co., 1874. 256 p. front., 3 plates, 4 ports. CVicAr
MtHi OrU WaS WaSp WaU 2188
Same. 1876. WaSp 2189

Wild life on the plains and horrors of Indian warfare, with a graphic account of his last fight on the Little Big Horn, as told by his wily foe Sitting Bull; also sketches and anecdotes of the most renowned guides, scouts and plainsmen of the West; General Crook and the Apaches. Battle Creek, Mich., Walker and Daigneau, 1883. 528 p. front., plates, ports. WaU 2190
Same. St Louis, Sun Pub. Co., 1885. 528 p. plate. MtU WaS 2191
Same. St. Louis, Excelsior Pub Co., [c1891] 592 p. front., illus., port. MtHi 2192

Custis, Vanderveer, 1878-
Address on the income tax delivered before County Assessors' Convention at Olympia, Wash., Jan. 19-21, 1914. [Olympia, Wash., 1914] 14 p. WaU 2193
The state tax system of Washington. Seattle, Univ. of Wash., 1916. 142 p.
Many 2194

[Cuthbert, Herbert]
Impressions of Victoria, British Columbia, Canada, the "empress" city of the golden West. [Victoria, B. C., Cusack, 1907?] [12] p. illus. CVicAr 2195
An outpost of empire, Victoria, British Columbia. [Victoria, B. C., British Colonist, 1907] 48 p. illus.
CVicAr WaPS WaU 2196
Picturesque Victoria, B. C. Victoria, B. C., Tourist Assn., 1902. 32 p. illus., fold. map.
CVicAr WaPS WaU 2197

Cuthrell, Mrs. Faith (Baldwin) 1893-
White magic. New York, Farrar, 1939. 305 p. Sun Valley, Idaho.
IdB Or OrP WaE WaS 2198

Cutter, Charles.
Unsurpassed natural resources and advantages and incomparable scenic beauty of the Paradise Valley route. Tacoma, Tacoma Eastern Railroad [1905?] 24 p. illus. WaU 2199

D., M., see no. 1999.

Dabney, Owen P.
True story of the lost shackle; or, Seven years with the Indians. [n.p., c1897] 98 p. illus. Indian captivity in Northwest.
MtHi OrP Wa 2200
Same. [Salem, Or., Capital Printing Co., c1897] 98 p. front., illus.
IdU Or OrHi OrP WaS WaU 2201

Daggett & Macrae, comp.
Portland clubdom, 1905. Portland, Or., Mann & Beach, 1905. 128 p.
Or OrHi 2202

Dahlquist, Frederick C.
The land of beginning, copyright by F. C. Dahlquist, Theodore E. Faulk, the authors. Portland, Or., Commonwealth Pub. Co., c1922. 96 p. front., col. plates, fold. map. Many 2203

Daily Alaska Empire, Junean, Alaska.
Progress and development edition, March 22, 1936. Juneau, 1936. [48] p. illus., ports. (v. 47, no. 7228) WaS **2204**

Same. 1939. [44] p. (v. 53, no. 8061, Mar. 26, 1939) WaU **2205**

Progress ed. Juneau, 1935. [40] p. illus., ports. (v. 45, no. 6905, Mar. 10, 1935) WaU **2206**

Same. 1941. [52] p. (Mar. 23, 1941) WaU **2207**

Daily Colonist, Victoria, B. C.
The church and the Indians; the trouble at Metlakahtla, July 26, 1882. [Victoria, B. C., 1882?] 8 p. CV **2208**

Jubilee edition, marking 75 years of growth in trade and industry; Victoria and Vancouver Island. Victoria, B. C., 1937. 84 p. illus., ports. (Aug. 1, 1937) WaU **2209**

Vancouver Island. Victoria, B. C., 1901. [40] p. illus., ports., maps. (v. 85, no. 34, Jan. 20, 1901) WaU **2210**

Tre Daily Gazette-Times, Corvallis, Or.
Progress edition telling of Benton County and Corvallis, Oregon. Corvallis, Or., 1911. [52] p. illus., ports. (Oct. 16, 1911) OrU **2211**

Daily Independent, Everett, Washington.
The city of Everett; a souvenir ed. Everett, Wash., 1900. 63 p. illus., ports. WaU **2212**

Daily Journal of Commerce, Seattle, Wash.
50th anniversary, 1893-1943. Seattle, 1943. 44 p. illus., ports. (v. 50, no. 187, Aug. 6, 1943) WaU **2213**

Daily Missoulian, Missoula, Mont.
Souvenir edition. 2d ed. Missoula, Mont., 1922. 64 p. illus. (July 20, 1922) MtU **2214**

The Daily Olympian, Olympia, Washington.
Louisiana purchase edition, 1904. Olympia, Wash., 1904. [24] p. illus., photos., ports. (June 2, 1904) Wa **2215**

Olympia, Washington golden jubilee, 1889-1939. Olympia, Wash., 1939. [44] p. illus., ports. (v. 48, no. 205, Nov. 8, 1939) WaU **2216**

Daily World, Vancouver, B. C.
A. Y. P. book of Vancouver, B. C. Vancouver. B. C., World Press & Pub. Co., 1909. 99 p. illus. CV WaS **2217**

British Columbia development number. Vancouver, B. C., 1922. 82 p. illus. CV CVU **2218**

The British Columbia review, being a series of articles, descriptive of the Pacific province, its magnificent resources, and its present and probable development, contributed by writers, authorities and experts, collated and arranged by J. Edward Norcross and Harry Hume. Vancouver, B. C., 1906. 112 p. illus., ports. WaU **2219**

Progress and building edition, Jan. 6, 1912. Vancouver, B.C., 1912. 96 p. illus. (Jan. 6, 1912) CV **2220**

Vancouver city; its wonderful history and future prospects, a historical and statistical review of the Pacific terminus of the C. P. R. [Vancouver, B. C., 1891?] 1 v. illus., 11 plates, 51 ports. (The Vancouver Daily World illustrated souvenir publication) CV **2221**

Dake, Henry Carl, 1896-
Mineral Club history. 1st ed. Portland, Or., Durham, Ryan & Downey Co., 1943. 64 p. illus., ports.
Or OrP OrU WaS WaSp WaT **2222**

Dalberg, Linden, see no. 802.

Dalby, Milton Arthur, 1904-
Milton A. Dalby has here set forth the sea saga of Dynamite Johnny O'Brien, American master mariner for fifty-three years; a seaman for sixty-five years; whose shipmates and friends called him the "Nestor of the Pacific"; who feared God but defied His storms; who fought the good fight; whose fists were as hard as his spirit was stout. Seattle, Lowman & Hanford, 1933. 249 p. front., illus., plate, 3 ports.
WaE WaS WaSp WaT WaU **2223**

Dale, Edward Everett, see nos. 69, 1477.

Dale, Harrison Clifford, 1885-
The Ashley-Smith explorations and the discovery of a central route to the Pacific, 1822-1829, with the original journals. Rev. ed. Glendale, Calif., A. H. Clark Co., 1918. 352 p. front., 3 plates, map. Many **2224**

Same. 1941. 360 p. Many **2225**

Dalgliesh, Alice, see no. 5175.

Dall, William Healey, 1845-1927.
Alaska and its resources. Boston, Lee, 1870. 627 p. front., illus., 14 plates, map. Many **2226**

Same. London, Low, 1870. 628 p. OrU WaU **2227**

Same. Boston, Lee, 1897. 627 p. WaU **2228**

See also no. 11292.

Dallam, Frank M., Jr., see no. 2074.

Dallas, Alexander Grant, 1828?-1882.
San Juan, Alaska, and the north-west boundary. London, Henry S. King & Co., 1873. 11 p. CVicAr CVU **2229**

Dallas, Francis Gregory, 1824-1890.
The papers of Francis Gregory Dallas, United States Navy; correspondence and journal, 1837-1859, ed. by Gardner W. Allen. New York, Printed for the Naval History Society by the De Vinne Press, 1917. li, 303 p. front., facsims. (Publications of the Naval History Society, v. 8) OrP WaU **2230**

The Dalles Business Men's Association.
The Dalles and Dufur, Oregon. The Dalles, Or. [n.d.] 48 p. illus., map. Or OrHi **2231**

The Dalles Optimist, The Dalles, Or.
Annual harvest-industrial edition. The Dalles, Or., 1922. 1 v. illus., ports. (July 28, 1922) Or **2232**

Dalrymple, Alexander, 1737-1808.
Memoir of a map of the lands around the North Pole, 1789; scale 1/10 of an inch to 1° of latitude. London, Bigg, 1789, 20 p. port., map. CVicAr **2233**

Plan for promoting the fur-trade and securing it to this country by uniting the operations of the East-India and Hudson's Bay Company. London, Bigg, 1789. 32 p.   CVicAr 2234

The Spanish memorial of 4th June considered. London, Bigg, 1790. 21 p.
                          CVicAr 2235

Same. London, Elmsly, 1790. CVicAr 2236

The Spanish pretensions fairly discussed. London, Bigg, 1790. 19 p.
                      CVicAr WaU 2237

Same. London, Elmsley, 1790. 19 p. port., maps, facsim.   CVicAr 2238

Dalton, Mrs. Annie Charlotte (Armitage) 1865-
The silent zone. [Vancouver, B. C., Cowan & Brookhouse, c1926) 111 p.
                          CVicAr 2239

Daly, Mrs. Emma Ring.
Flowering agates. Caldwell, Idaho, Caxton, 1938. 77 p. Poems. WaS WaU 2240

Daly, George Thomas.
Catholic problems in western Canada, with a preface by the Most Reverend O. E. Mathieu, archbishop of Regina, Toronto, Macmillan [c1921] 352 p.
                          WaU 2241

Daly, Hugh.
Biography of Marcus Daly of Montana. Butte, Mont. [1935] 30 p. front. (port.)
                          MtHi 2242

Damacaulie, see no. 6184.

Damon, Samuel Chenery, 1815-1885.
A journey to lower Oregon & upper California, 1848-49. San Francisco, J. J. Newbegin, 1927. 86 p. front. (port.)
          CVicAr OrU WaS WaSp WaU 2243

[Dana, C. W.]
The garden of the world; or, The great west: its history, its wealth, its natural advantages, and its future; also comprising a complete guide to emigrants with a full description of the different routes westward, by an old settler; with statistics and facts from Hon. Thomas H. Benton, Hon. Sam Houston, Col. John C. Fremont and other "old settlers." Boston, Wentworth and Co., 1856. 396 p. illus.   Many 2244

The great West; or The garden of the world: its history, its wealth, its natural advantages, and its future; also comprising a complete guide to emigrants with a full description of the different routes westward; with statistics and facts from Hon. Thomas H. Benton, Gen. Sam Houston, and Col. John C. Fremont. Boston, Wentworth and Co., 1857. 396 p. illus.   Many 2245

Same. 1858.   CVicAr 2246

Same. 1861.   MtU 2247

Same. Boston, Thayer & Eldridge, 1861.
                          OrU 2248

Dana, Edmund.
Geographical sketches on the western country; designed for emigrants and settlers. Cincinnati, Looker, 1819. 312 p. table.   CVicAr OrHi OrP OrU 2249

Dana, Francis.
Leonora of the Yawmish; a novel. New York, Harper, 1897. 310 p. Olympic Peninsula setting.   WaTC WaU 2250

Dana, Marshall Newport, see nos. 755, 4532, 5993.

Danenhower, John Wilson, 1849-1887.
Lieutenant Danenhower's narrative of the "Jeannette". Boston, Osgood, 1882. x, 102 p. front. (port.) illus., plate, double map.
                      WaTC WaU 2251

Daniel, Hawthorne, 1890-
Bare hands; being the story of the extraordinary steamboat that was built on Devil's Island off the coast of Alaska by four shipwrecked men, illus. by Arthur A. Jansson. New York, Coward-McCann, 1929. 244 p. col. front., plates.
                      IdIf WaS 2252

See also no. 5618.

Daniels, Bradford Kempton.
The outer edge. Caldwell, Idaho, Caxton, 1943. 326 p. front. (port.) plates, ports. Account of establishing a farm home in Puget Sound Region.   Many 2253

Daniels, Joseph, 1884-
Coal in Washington; distribution, geology, mining, preparation, uses, and economic value of coal resources of Washington. Seattle, Univ. of Wash., 1934. 17 p. fold. map, fold. diagr. (Engineering experiment station series. Report no. 3)
                          WaU 2254

Iron and steel manufacture in Washington, Oregon, California and Utah. Seattle, Univ. of Wash., 1929. 69 p. illus., tables (Engineering Experiment Station series. Report no. 2)   Many 2255

[Dankoler, Harry Edward] 1863-
James Griffin's adventures in Alaska, by Harry Dee [pseud.] with sixteen full-page halftone illustrations. Milwaukee, Wis., J. H. Yewdale, 1903. 276 p. front., illus., 17 plates. (Adventure series).
                          WaU 2256

Darien, Peter, see no. 633.

Daring adventures of Carson and Fremont. New York, Hurst [n.d.] 493 p.
                          WaSp 2257

Darling, Esther Birdsall.
Baldy of Nome, an immortal of the trail. San Francisco, A. M. Robertson, 1913. 75 p. front., illus., plate.
                      WaSp WaU 2258

Same. Philadelphia, Penn, 1917. 301 p. col. front., illus., plates, ports. CVicAr 2259
Same. Decorations by Hattie Longstreet. Philadelphia, Penn [c1918]
              IdB Or OrP WaS WaW 2260

Same. 1929.   IdIf Wa 2261

Luck of the trail, illus. by Morgan Dennis. Garden City, N. Y., Doubleday, 1933. 309 p. col. front.
          IdIf OrMonO WaS WaSp WaU 2262

Navarre of the North, illus. by Charles Livingston Bull. Garden City, N. Y., Doubleday, 1930. 268 p. front.
                          Many 2263

Up in Alaska, illus. by Mary Crete Crouch. Sacramento, Calif., Jo Anderson Press [c1912] 59 p. illus. Poems.
WaPS WaU **2264**

Dart, Ada Carter.
Mystery of Silver Spring ranch. Caldwell, Idaho, Caxton, 1932. 301 p. WaPS **2265**

Dart, John, see nos. 6748-6751.

d'Artigue, Jean, see no. 316.

The Dashaway Association of Victoria.
Constitution and by-laws. Victoria, B. C., Printed by Amor de Cosmos at the Colonist Office [1860?] 8 p. CVicAr **2266**

Dassow, Ethel, see no. 4746.

Daughters of the American Revolution. Idaho.
History and register, Idaho state society. Caldwell, Idaho, Caxton, 1936. 124 p. front., illus., ports. IdP IdU WaU **2267**

—— —— Oregon. Multnomah Chapter.
Dedication of tablets honoring the founders of the Provisional Government, Dayton, Oregon, April 15, 1931. [n.p., 1931] [19] p. Or **2268**

Same. With life sketches by Mrs. John F. Dobbs. 46 p. Or OrHi WaPS **2269**

History and by-laws. Portland, Or. [Irwin-Hodson] 1903. xxxii p. illus. WaU **2270**

History of Multnomah Chapter number 228. Portland, Or., 1915. 45 p. OrP **2271**

To honor one of those patriots who on May 2, 1843, at Champoeg, saved the Oregon country to this nation; dedication of tablets honoring the founders of the Provisional Government, October 29 and November 5, 1930, Pacific University, Forest Grove, Ore. [n.p., 1930] [15] p.
Or OrHi **2272**

—— —— Susannah Lee Barlow Chapter, Clackamas County, Oregon.
Historic houses of Clackamas County. [n.p., 1947] 64 p. OrHi OrP **2273**

—— —— Washington.
History and register, Washington state society, Daughters of the American Revolution. Seattle, Lowman & Hanford. [1924] 213 p. illus., ports.
Wa WaE WaPS WaS WaSp WaU **2274**

History of the National society, Daughters of the American Revolution. [n.p., 1939] 1 v. Wa WaT **2275**

—— —— Elizabeth Forey Chapter.
[Pierce County casualty list in World War II; record of the names of the men and women of Pierce County who gave their lives in the service of their country. n.p., n.d.] 1 v. WaT **2276**

—— —— Rainer Chapter, Seattle, Washington.
By-laws of Rainier Chapter of the National society of the Daughters of the American Revolution. Seattle, 1903. 10 p.
WaS WaU **2277**

—— —— Robert Gray Chapter.
Captain Robert Gray; an account of the unveiling by Robert Gray Chapter, Daughters of the American Revolution,

of a tablet at "Lone Tree", Damon's Point, May 7, 1911, in memory of the discoverer of Gray's Harbor. [Gray's Harbor, Wash. 1911?] 15 p. front. (port.) mounted plate. WaU **2278**

Davenport, Homer Calvin, 1867-1912.
The country boy; the story of his own early life, embellished with sixty-two illus. made from his original drawings. Chicago, Donohue, c1910. 191 p. illus. Silverton, Or.
OrCS OrHi OrU WaS **2279**

Same. New York, Dillingham [1910] 191 p. front. (port.) illus. Many **2280**

Davenport, Noah C., see no. 3156.

Davenport, Timothy W., 1826-1911.
Swamp lands; examination of the subject; methods by which lands have been acquired by speculators; frauds both upon the state and general government. Albany, Or., Burkhart, 1856. [48] p.
OrHi **2281**

Davenport, Warren G.
Butte and Montana beneath the X-ray; being a collection of editorials from the files of the Butte X-ray during the years 1907-8. London, C. F. Cazenove, 1909. 381 p. MtHi **2282**

Davidson, A. F.
Little cabin in the prairie; a story of a woman's love. Salem, Or., Craig, 1878. 21 p. Or OrHi WaU **2283**

Davidson, George, 1825-1911.
The Alaska boundary. San Francisco, Alaska Packers' Assn., 1903. 235 p. port., map. Many **2284**

Francis Drake on the northwest coast of America in the year 1579; the Golden Hinde did not anchor in the Bay of San Francisco. [San Francisco, 1908] iv, 114 p. (Geographical Society of the Pacific. Transactions and proceedings, series 2, v. 5) Many **2285**

Tracks and landfalls of Bering and Chirikof on the northwest coast of America, 1741. [San Francisco, Partridge] 1901. 44 p. CVicAr **2286**

Davidson, Gordon Charles, 1884-
The North West Company. Berkley, Calif., Univ. of Calif. Press, 1918. 349 p. front. (fold. map) 4 fold. maps. (Publications in history, v. 7) Many **2287**

Davidson, Innes N.
The Arctic Brotherhood; a souvenir history of the order, setting forth its aims, its ambitions and the good it has accomplished from its incipiency, its relations to Alaska and the great northland, supplemented by individual histories of its various subordinate camps; richly illuminated with graphic scenes of the northland, embellished with portraits and interspersed with business announcements, etc., pub. under the auspicies of the Executive Building Board. Seattle, Acme Pub. Co., 1909. 104 p. illus., ports.
WaSp WaU **2288**

Davidson, John, 1878-
Conifers, junipers and yew; gymnosperms of British Columbia, pictures specially drawn by Miss Ivy Abercrombie. London, Unwin, 1927. xvii, 72 p. front., 38 plates (part col.) diagr. (Illustrated botany of British Columbia, 1)
CVU IdU OrP **2289**

Davidson, Levette Jay, 1894- ed.
The literature of the Rocky Mountain West, 1803-1903, selected and ed. by Levette Jay Davidson and Prudence Bostwick. Caldwell, Idaho, Caxton, 1939. 449 p. Many **2290**

Davies, Arthur.
Exclusia; a dream containing phantasy, with an epilogue containing fact. Victoria, B. C., Hibben, 1907. 15 p.
CVicAr **2291**

Davies, Carolyn, see no. 4545.

Davies, Griffith, d. 1924?
The complete Chinook jargon or Indian trade language of Oregon, Washington, British Columbia, Alaska, Idaho and other parts of the North Pacific coast. Seattle, 1888. 40 p. WaU **2292**

Davies, John F., librarian.
Civics of Montana. Butte, Mont., Sold by B. E. Calkins, Inter Mountain Print, 1896 [c1895] 128 p. front. (port.) illus.
MtBozC MtHi MtU WaU **2293**

Davies, John Francis.
The great dynamite explosions at Butte, Montana, January 15, 1895. Butte, Mont., Butte Bystander, 1895. 43 p. illus.
MtHi MtU WaU **2294**

Davies, Mary Carolyn.
The skyline trail; a book of western verse. Indianapolis, Bobbs-Merrill [c1924] 159 p.
Many **2295**

Davies, Raymond Arthur, 1908-
Arctic Eldorado; a dramatic report on Canada's northland, the greatest unexploited region in the world, with a workable four year plan. Toronto, Ryerson [1944] xiii, 97 p.
CV CVic CVicAr Or WaS WaU **2296**

The great Mackenzie in word and photograph; photos. by George Zuckerman. Toronto, Ryerson [1947] x, 139 p. illus., ports. CV CVicAr **2297**

Davis, Carol Beery, comp.
Songs of the totem. Juneau, Empire Printing Co., c1939. 48 p. front., illus., music. Words in Tlingit and English.
CV MtU Or OrP WaS WaSp **2298**

Davis, Clay C.
Organization and operation of a cooperative dairymen's association. Bellingham, Wash.. Whatcom County Dairymen's Assn. [n.d.] 1 v. diagr. WaT **2299**

Davis, Deborah.
Idaho civics. Boise, Idaho, Syms-York Co. [c1941] 195 p. plates, diagrs.
IdB IdIf IdUSB **2300**

Davis, Duke, 1878-
Flashlights from mountain and plain. Bound Brook, N. J., Pentecostal Union, 1911. 266 p. plates, port. MtHi MtU **2301**

Davis, E. A.
Commemorative review of the Methodist, Presbyterian and Congregational churches in British Columbia; a retrospect of the work and personalities of the churches in British Columbia up to the time of their union into the United Church, together with a prophetic forecast for the future. Vancouver, B. C., Joseph Lee, 1925. xxxii, 380 p. plates, ports.
CV CVicAr CVU WaTC WaU **2302**

Davis, Ellis A.
Davis' new commercial encyclopedia; Washington, Oregon and Idaho; the Pacific Northwest. Berkeley, Calif., 1909. 190 p. ports., maps.
OrHi Wa WaPS WaSp WaU **2303**

Davis' standard encyclopedia. Montana, Idaho, Alaska, Washington and Oregon; the Pacific Northwest. Berkeley, Calif., c1910. 216 [10] p. illus., 3 fold. maps.
WaSp **2304**

Davis, Eva May.
Rhymes of reminiscence. [Stanwood, Wash., Stanwood News, 1921?] 32 p.
WaU **2305**

Davis, Frank Edison, 1871-
Shall Oregon have an old age pension law? Portland, Or., Old Age Pension League, c1927. 54 p. port. OrP **2306**

Davis, George Thompson Brown, 1873-
Metlakahtla; a true narrative of the red men. Chicago, Ram's Horn Co., 1904. 128 p. illus., ports.
CV CVU OrU WaS WaU **2307**

Davis, George Wesley, 1861-1929.
Sketches of Butte (from Vigilante days to prohibition). Boston, Cornhill Co. [c1921] 179 p. front., plates. Many **2308**

Davis, Harold Lenoir, 1896-
Harp of a thousand strings. New York, Morrow, 1947. 438 p. Oregon author.
Many **2309**

Honey in the horn. New York, Harper, 1935. 380 p. Many **2310**

Same. 2d ed. OrP WaT WaU **2311**

Proud riders, and other poems. New York, Harper [1942] viii, 86 p.
MtU Or OrP WaS WaU **2312**

See also no. 9898.

Davis, Henry D., Lumber Co., Portland, Or.
Some information and observations about Pacific Coast woods, methods of production and so forth for wholesale distributors, salesmen and users of fir, cedar, spruce, hemlock (gray fir) lumber. Portland, Or. [1919] 24 p.
OrP **2313**

Davis, Horace, 1831-1916.
Record of Japanese vessels driven upon the northwest coast of North America and its outlying islands; read before the American Antiquarian Society at their April meeting 1872. Worcester, Mass., Hamilton, 1872. 22 p. plates.
CVicAr **2314**

Davis, J. B., see nos. 9386-9388.

Davis, J. Charles.
Fishing in Pacific waters, illus. by Abraham Richman. New York, Sentinel Books [c1946] 127 p. illus.   OrP WaT **2315**

Davis, John, & Co.
[Puget Sound life. Seattle, Seattle Engraving Co., 19—?] [36] plates.   WaU **2316**

Seattle. Seattle, Gateway Printing Co. [1915?] 1 v. illus.   WaS **2317**

Seattle, the gateway; New Year's souvenir, 1901. Seattle, 1901. [18] p. front., illus.   WaU **2318**

Davis, Joseph Stancliffe, 1885-
International trade in its bearing on agricultural exports from the Pacific northwest [address delivered at the annual Extension conference and all agricultural staff conference, Oregon State Agricultural College, Corvallis, Oregon, January 9, 1932] [n.p., 1932?] 7 p.
OrCS **2319**

Davis, Julia.
No other white men. Chicago, E. M. Hale & Co. [n.d.] 242 p. illus., ports., maps.
IdIf **2320**

Same. 1st ed. New York, Dutton, c1937.
Many **2321**

Same. With maps by Caroline Gray. [1941, c1937]   WaU **2322**

Davis, Kenneth C.
Strictly legal, a novelette. Seattle, 1934. 64 p.   WaU **2323**

Davis, Lewis Jay, 1865-
Our kinsmen; a family history. Portland, Or., Metropolitan, 1936. 131 p. front., illus., ports.
Or OrHi OrP OrU WaS WaU **2324**

Davis, Mrs. Mary Lee (Cadwell)
Alaska, the Great Bear's cub, illus. by pen and ink illus. by Olaus Johan Murie and author's photographs. Boston, W. A. Wilde Co. [c1930] 314 p. front. (port.) illus., plates.   Many **2325**

Sourdough gold, the log of a Yukon adventure. Boston, W. A. Wilde Co. [c1933] 351 p. front., plates, ports., maps (1 fold.)
Many **2326**

Uncle Sam's attic, the intimate story of Alaska, illus. by author's photographs. Boston, W. A. Wilde Co. [c1930] xvi, 402 p. front., plates, ports., maps.
Many **2327**

We are Alaskans, illus. by author's photographs and sketches by Olaus J. Murie. Boston, W. A. Wilde Co. [c1931] xi, 335 p. front., plates, ports.   Many **2328**

Davis, Nelle Portrey.
Stump ranch pioneer. New York, Dodd, 1942. 245 p. Idaho pioneer story.
Many **2329**

Same. 1943 [c1942]   WaPS **2330**

Davis, William B., 1902-
The recent mammals of Idaho; contribution from the Museum of Vertebrate Zoology, University of California, Berkeley. Caldwell, Idaho, Caxton, 1939. 400 p. front., illus., maps, diagrs.   Many **2331**

Davis, William J., see no. 8684.

Davydov, Gavriil Ivanovich, 1784-1809.
Dvukratnoe puteshestvie v Ameriku morskikh ofitserov Khvostova i Davydova, pisannoe sim posliednim. S. Peterburg, Morskaia tipografiia, 1810-1812. 2 v. in 1.
WaU **2332**

Dawson, Aeneas MacDonell, 1810-1894.
The North-West Territories and British Columbia. Ottawa, C. W. Mitchell, 1881. iv, 223 p.   CV CVicAr CVU WaU **2333**

Dawson, Carl Addington, ed.
The new North-West. Toronto, Univ. of Toronto Press [c1947] x, 341 p. illus., maps.   CV CVicAr OrCS WaU **2334**

Settlement of the Peace River country; a study of a pioneer area, by C. A. Dawson assisted by R. W. Murchie, Toronto, Macmillan, 1934. xii, 284 p. illus., maps, tables. (Canadian frontiers of settlement, v. 6)   Many **2335**

Dawson, Charles.
Pioneer tales of the Oregon Trail and of Jefferson County. Topeka, Kan., Crane & Co., 1912. 488 p. front., illus., ports., maps. Jefferson County, Neb.
OrP OrU WaSp WaU **2336**

Dawson, George Mercer, 1849-1901.
Dominion of Canada, Province of British Columbia, evidence of Dr. Dawson. Ottawa, MacLean, Roger, 1883. 21 p.
CVicAr **2337**

Notes and observations on the Kwakiool people of Vancouver Island. Montreal, 1888. 36 p. plate. (Royal Society of Canada. Transactions, v. 5, sec. II, 1887)
Many **2338**

Notes on the Shuswap people of British Columbia. Montreal, 1891. 44 p. illus., map. (Royal Society of Canada. Transactions, v. 9, Sec. II, 1891)   Many **2339**

See also no. 11292.

Dawson, William Leon, 1873-
The birds of Washington; a complete, scientific and popular account of the 372 species of birds found in the state, by W. L. Dawson assisted by John Hooper Bowles, illus. by more than 300 original half-tones of birds in life, nests, eggs, and favorite haunts, from photographs by the author and others; together with 40 drawings in the text and a series of full-page color plates by Allan Brooks. Author's ed. Seattle, Occidental Pub. Co., 1909. 2 v. fronts., illus., plates (part col.)
Many **2340**

Dawson Daily News.
The Klondike. [n.p., n.d.] 1 v. illus., fold. plate.   CVicAr **2341**

The Klondike, Dawson News' souvenir, July 1905. [n.p., 1905] 32 p. plate, fold. panorama of Dawson.   MtUM **2342**

Sourdough edition, midsummer number. [Dawson, Yukon Ter.] 1913. 74 p. illus., ports., maps.   WaU **2343**

Yukon silver and gold fields edition, Nov. 27, 1922 [and] The all-Yukon annual review, Dec. 3, 1923. Dawson, Yukon Ter., 1922-1923. 2 nos. in 1 v. illus.
WaU **2344**

Day, Holman Francis.
The eagle badge; or, The Skokums of the Allagash. New York, Harper, 1908. 289 p. illus.   WaS **2345**

Day, John Mills, see no. 4725.

Day, Luella.
The tragedy of the Klondike; this book of travels gives the true facts of what took place in the gold fields under British rule. New York, c1906. 181 p. front. (port.) illus., 4 plates.
          CV CVicAr CVU WaS WaU **2346**

[**Day, Mrs. Patience**]
Pioneer days, Provincial Royal Jubilee Hospital. Victoria, B.C. [British Colonist, 1924] 20 p. illus., ports.   CVicAr **2347**

Deady, Matthew Paul, 1824-1893.
An address to the graduating class of the University of Oregon, Eugene. Portland, Or., G. H. Himes, 1878. 15 p.
          Or OrHi OrP WaU **2348**

Addresses: Centennial celebration Washington's inauguration, Portland, Oregon, April 30, 1889; and Fourth of July, Vancouver, Washington, 1889. Portland, Or., Himes Printing Co., 1890. 36 p.
          OrP WaU **2349**

Commencement address delivered at St. Helen's Hall, Portland, Oregon, June 9, 1880. Portland, Or., Himes the Printer, 1880. 16 p.   Or OrUL **2350**

Law and lawyers; a lecture delivered before the Portland Law Association, Dec. 6, 1866. Portland, Or., McCormick [n.d.] 27 p.   OrP OrUL **2351**

Oration delivered at Portland, July 4, 1885, published by the Committee of Arrangements. Portland, Or., A. G. Walling, 1885. 33 p.   OrP OrUL **2352**

Oration delivered at Roseburg, July 4, 1877, published by the Committee of Arrangements. Portland, Or., G. H. Himes,, 1877. 28 p.
          OrHi OrP OrU OrUL WaU **2353**

"To be or to have" 1879; an address to the graduating class of the University of Oregon. Portland, Or., Himes the Printer, 1879. 19 p.
          Or OrHi OrP WaPS **2354**

Dean, Christopher C.
Hugh Clifford; or, Prospective missions on the Northwest coast and at the Washington Islands. Boston, Mass. Sabbath School Union, 1832. 102 p.
          CVicAr WaU **2355**

Dean, John Marvin, 1875-
Rainier of the last frontier. New York, Crowell [c1911] 373 p. front. WaU **2356**

Deane, Richard Burton, 1848-
Mounted police life in Canada; a record of thirty-one years' service. London, Cassell and Co. [1916] 311 p. front., plates, fold. map.   CVicAr CVU MtHi WaU **2357**

Same. New York, Funk & Wagnalls, 1916.
          CVU OrP WaT **2358**

Deans, James, 1827-
Tales from the totems of the Hidery; collected by James Deans, ed. by Oscar Lovell Triggs. Chicago, 1899. 96 p. front.,

5 plates. (Archives of the International Folk-lore Association, v. 2) Many **2359**

DeBusk memorial essays, ed. by Henry Davidson Sheldon. Eugene, Or., Univ. of Or. [1937?] 68 p. front. (port.)
          Or OrP OrSaW WaPS WaTC **2360**

Decalves, Alonso, pseud.
New travels to the westward; or, Unknown parts of America, being a tour of almost fourteen months, containing an account of the country, upwards of two thousand miles, west of the Christian parts of North America; with an account of white Indians, their manners, habits, and many other particulars. Boston [n.d.] 43 p.   WaS **2361**

Dechmann, Louis.
Postal souvenirs of "Qui Si Sana". [Seattle, 1913] [80] p. 20 photos.   WaPS **2362**

Dedication of tablet commemorating the naming of Mount Hood on October 30, 1792 by Lieutenant W. R. Broughton, R. N. August 24, 1929, Crown Point, Oregon. [Portland, Or.? 1929] [8] p. illus. maps.   Or OrP WaU **2363**

Dee, Harry, see no. 2256.

Dee, Mrs. Minnie (Roof) 1866-
From oxcart to airplane; a biography of George H. Himes. Portland, Or., Binfords & Mort [c1939] 148 p. front., ports.
          Many **2364**

Historical rhymograms; verses of pioneer days in the Northwest from 1725 to 1851. [Portland, Or., Gotshall Printing Co., c1924] 40 p.   Many **2365**

Deegan, Harry W.
History of Mason County, Washington. [n.p., 1943] 24 p.   Wa **2366**

Defenbach, Byron, 1870-
Idaho; the place and its people; a history of the gem state from prehistoric to present days. Chicago, American Historical Society, 1933. 3 v. front., illus., ports.
          IdB IdIf IdP IdTf IdU WaPS **2367**

Red heroines of the Northwest, illus. by original drawings and photographs. Caldwell, Idaho, Caxton, 1929. 299 p. front., 11 plates, 2 ports., map, facsim.
          Many **2368**

Same. 2d printing. 1930. 303 p. 17 plates, 3 ports., map.   MtHi **2369**

Same. 1935. 299 p.   Many **2370**

The state we live in, Idaho. Caldwell, Idaho, Caxton, 1933. 355 p. col. front., illus.   Many **2371**

de Fonte, Bartholomew, see no. 2483.

DeGroot, Henry.
British Columbia; its condition and prospects, soil, climate, and mineral resources, considered. San Francisco, Alta Calif. Job Office, 1859. 24 p.
          CVicAr CVU WaS **2372**

De Koven, Reginald, see nos. 6660, 6675.

De Laguna, Frederica, 1906-
The archaeology of Cook Inlet, Alaska, with a chapter on skeletal material by Brune Oetteking. Philadelphia, Pub. for

the Univ. Museum by the Univ. of Pa. Press, 1934. 263 p. plates, maps, diagrs. OrU WaS WaU **2373**

Fog on the mountain. Garden City, N. Y., Doubleday, 1938. 275 p. front., map. Alaska story. IdB WaE WaT **2374**

The prehistory of northern North America as seen from the Yukon. Menasha, Wis., 1947. x, 360 p. illus., plates, maps. (Memoirs of the Society for American Archaeology, no. 3) WaT WaU **2375**
See also no. 849.

[Delaney, Arthur K.]
Alaska Bar Association and sketch of judiciary, anno domini 1901. San Francisco, Sanborn, Vail & Co., 1901. 79 p. 8 ports. WaE **2376**

Delaney, Mrs. Matilda J. (Sager) 1839-
A survivor's recollections of the Whitman massacre. [Spokane? Esther Reed Chapter, D. A. R.? c1920] 46 p. port. Many **2377**

Delano, Alonzo, 1806-1874.
Across the plains and among the diggings; a reprint of the original edition with reproductions of numerous photographs taken by Louis Palenske and foreword and epilogue by Rufus Rockwell Wilson. New York, Wilson-Erickson, 1936. xviii, 192 p. front., illus. Many **2378**

Life on the plains and among the diggings; being scenes and adventures of an overland journey to California, with particular incidents of the route, mistakes and sufferings of the emigrants, the Indian tribes, the present and future of the great West. 2d thousand. Auburn, N. Y., Milner, Orton & Mulligan, 1854. 384 p. front., 3 plates. CVicAr IdB IdU WaS **2379**

Same. 4th thousand. New York, Miller, Orton & Co. 1857. CVicAr WaSp WaU **2380**

Same. New York, Saxton, 1861. WaU **2381**

Delanty, Hugh M.
Along the waterfront; covering a period of fifty years on Gray's Harbor and the Pacific Northwest. [Aberdeen, Wash., Quick Printing Co., c1943] 109 p. illus. WaS WaT **2382**

DeLape, George W.
DeLape's tourist guide of the Pacific Northwest. [Tacoma, Commercial Bindery and Printing Co.] 1910. 27 p. illus. CVicAr **2383**

De Launay, J. Belin, see nos. 6853, 6854.

Delessert, Edouard.
Les Indiens de la Baie d'Hudson; promenades d'un artiste parmi les Indiens de l'Amerique du Nord, depuis le Canada jusqu'a l'ile de Vancouver et l'Oregon a travers le territorie de la Compagnie de la Baie d' Hudson. Paris, Amyot, 1861. 273 p. WaU **2384**

De l'Isle, see no. 5868.

Dell, Sidney.
Astoria and Flavel, the chief seaport of the Columbia River watershed. [n.p., c1893] 32 p. illus. Or OrP **2385**

Book of Clatsop County; its farms and timber lands in detail. Astoria, Or., Anderson, 1899. 49 p. Anon. OrHi OrP **2386**

Same. Souvenir ed. for National Editorial Association. Astoria, Or., Committee of Astoria Citizens, 1899. WaPS **2387**

Dellenbaugh, Frederick S., see nos. 9149, 10906.

De Loach, Daniel Barton, 1904-
The salmon canning industry. Corvallis, Or., Or. State College [1939] 118 p. tables, diagrs. (Monographs. Economic studies, no. 1) OrUM
WaS WaSp WaT WaTC WaU **2388**

DeLong, Emma, see no. 2389.

De Long, George Washington, 1844-1881.
Voyage of the Jeannette; the ship and ice journals of G. W. De Long, Lieutenant-commander U. S. N. and commander of the polar expedition of 1879-1881, ed. by his wife, Emma De Long. Boston, Houghton, 1883. 2 v. fronts., illus., plates, ports., maps (part fold.) WaS WaSp **2389**

Same. London, K. Paul, 1883. CVicAr **2390**

Same. Boston, Houghton, 1884. WaU **2391**

Delong, Willard W.
Seattle home builder and home keeper, by W .W. Delong and Mrs. W. W. Delong. Seattle, Commercial Pub. Co., 1915. 160 p. illus., plans. Wa **2392**

Deluge [Engine] Company no. 1, Victoria, B. C.
Constitution and by-laws. Victoria, B. C., British Colonist, 1863. 18 p. CVicAr **2393**

Demers, Modeste.
Chinook dictionary, catechism; prayers and hymns composed in 1838 and 1839; revised, corrected and completed in 1867 by F. N. Blanchet; with modifications and additions by L. N. St. Onge. Montreal, 1871. 68 p. illus. OrP WaWW **2394**

[Democratic Review]
Oregon war. [n.p., 1856] 8 p. OrP **2395**

De Mofras, Eugene Duflot, see nos. 2596-2600.

De Moss, Mrs. Catherine (Cornwall)
Blue bucket nuggets; a tale of Oregon's lost immigration. Portland, Or., Binfords & Mort [c1939] 139 p. Many **2396**

Denis, Ferdinand Jean, 1798-1890.
Les Californies, l'Oregon et l'Amerique russe. [Paris, Didot, 1849] 108 p. CVU OrP WaS **2397**

Denison, E. S.
Pacific coast souvenir. Oakland, Calif. [c1888] 11 p. 15 plates. OrU WaU **2398**

Denison, Merrill, 1893-
Klondike Mike, an Alaskan odyssey. New York, Morrow, 1943. xiv, 393 p. plates, ports., facsims. Many **2399**

Same. Cleveland, World Pub. Co. [1945, c1943] WaU **2400**

Denison, Muriel (Goggin)
Susannah of the Yukon, illus. by Marguerite Bryan. New York, Dodd, 1937. 343 p. front., illus., plates. Or WaT **2401**

Denman, Asahel Holmes, 1859-
Mount Tacoma; its true name. 5th ed.
[Tacoma, Mt. Tacoma Club, 192—?] [12]
p.   WaU **2402**

The name [Mt. Tacoma] 4th ed. [Tacoma]
Mt. Tacoma Club [n.d.] [8] p. illus.
                             Or WaU **2403**

Same. [192—?]   WaU **2404**

The name of Mount Tacoma, urging the
official removal from America's most
sublime mountain of the name Rainier
and perpetuation by official adoption of
the original Indian name therefor.
Tacoma, Smith-Kinney Co., 1924. 93 p.
                                 OrHi **2405**

Same. Published by the Rotary Club.
                                 Many **2406**

Dennis, James Teackle, 1865-1918.
On the shores of an inland sea. Philadel-
phia, Lippincott, 1895. 79 p. front., illus.
Alaska travel. CVicAr WaS WaU **2407**

Denny, Arthur Armstrong.
Pioneer days on Puget Sound. Seattle,
Bagley, 1888. 83 p.   Many **2408**

Same. Ed. by Alice Harriman. Seattle,
Harriman, 1908. 103 [13] p. front., illus.,
36 plates, fold. map, facsims. Many **2409**

[**Denny, Cecil Edward**] bart., 1859-1928.
The law marches west; ed. and arranged
by W. B. Cameron with a foreword by
Hon A. C. Rutherford. Toronto, Dent
[1939] 319 p. front. (port.) 9 plates, 8
ports., fold. map.
           CV CVicAr CVU MtHi **2410**

The riders of the plains, a reminiscence of
the early and exciting days in the
Northwest. Calgary, Herald Co.[c1905] 223
p. illus., ports.   CVU WaU **2411**

Denny, Emily Inez.
Blazing the way; or, True stories, songs,
and sketches of Puget Sound and other
pioneers. Seattle, Rainier Printing Co.,
1909. 504 p. front., 12 plates, 7 ports.
                                 Many **2412**

Denton, Vernon Llewellyn, 1881-1944.
The far West coast, with 12 illus. and 7
maps. Toronto, Dent, 1924. ix, 297 p.
illus., ports., maps.   Many **2413**

Simon Fraser. Toronto, Ryerson [c1928]
32 p. illus. (Canadian history readers:
Explorers and colonists)
           CV CVicAr WaE WaS **2414**

Desjardins, Joseph-Alphonse.
En Alaska; deux mois sous la tente. Montreal, Imprimerie du Messager, 1930.
293 [1] p. illus., ports.   CVicAr **2415**

Desmond, Alice (Curtis) 1897-
The sea cats, illus. by Wilfred Bronson.
New York, Macmillan, 1946 [c1944] 216
p. illus. Alaska sealing story. WaU **2416**

Desmond, Edward., ed.
Seattle leaders. Seattle, Pioneer Printing
Co. [1923?] [143] p. ports.
                    WaPS WaT WaU **2417**

Same. 1924.   OrP WaS **2418**

De Tremaudan, Auguste Henri, 1874-1931.
The Hudson Bay road (1498-1915) with 30
illus. and 2 maps. London, Dent, 1915.

xvi, 264 p. front. (port.) 29 plates, 2 fold.
maps.   CV CVic CVU OrP WaU **2419**

Same. New York, Dutton, 1916.
                         MtU WaS **2420**

Deutsch, Herman Julius.
History and government of the state of
Washington; an outline with supple-
mentary readings. Pullman, Wash., State
College of Wash., 1941. [274] p. loose-
leaf.   Many **2421**

Same. 1943. [286] p. Rev.   OrU Wa **2422**

Same. Abridged ed. [1944?] [153] p.
                         Or WaU **2423**

See also nos. 384, 385.

DeVeny, William, 1852-
The establishment of law and order on
western plains. Portland, Or., 1915. 120
p. front., illus., plates, port.   OrP **2424**

DeVere, William, 1844-1904.
Tramp poems of the West, illus. by G.
LaFayette from original designs by the
author. Tacoma, Cromwell Printing Co.,
1891. 102 p. front. (port.) illus.
                  CVU WaTC WaU **2425**

DeVighne, Harry Carlos, 1876-
The time of my life, a frontier doctor in
Alaska. Philadelphia, Lippincott [c1942]
236 p.   Many **2426**

See also no. 10925.

Devine, Edward James, 1860-
A travers l'Amerique de Terre-Neuve a
l'Alaska (Impressions de deux ans de
sejour sur la cote de Bering) premiere
tr. francaise. Abbeville, F. Paillart
[1905?] 267 p. plates, double map.
                              WaU **2427**

Across wildest America, Newfoundland to
Alaska, with the impressions of two
years' sojourn on the Bering coast.
Montreal, Canadian Messenger, 1905. 307
p. front. (port.) 24 plates, fold. map.
           CVU WaPS WaS WaU **2428**

Same. New York, Benziger Bros., 1906.
           CVicAr CVU MtU WaU **2429**

De Voto, Bernard Augustine, 1897-
Across the wide Missouri; illus. with paintings by Alfred Jacob Miller, Charles
Bodmer and George Catlin, with an
account of the discovery of the Miller
collection by Mae Reed Porter. Boston,
Houghton, 1947. xxviii, 483 p. plates
(part col.) maps.   Many **2430**

DeWindt, Harry, 1856-1933.
Through the gold fields of Alaska to
Bering Straits. New York, Harper, 1898.
314 p. 31 plates, port., map. Many **2431**

Same. London, Chatto, 1898. viii, 312 p. 29
plates, 2 ports., 2 maps.   Many **2432**

Same. New ed. 1899.   CVicAr CVU **2433**

The Dexter Horton Building. Seattle [Grett-
ner-Diers Printing Co., 1924] [33] p.
illus., plan.   WaU **2434**

Dexter Horton National Bank, Seattle, Wash.
A bit of history; the Dexter Horton
National Bank and Washington Trust
and Savings Bank, Seattle. Seattle
[1911?] [18] p. illus.   WaU **2435**

Fifty years of progress; the golden anniversary of the establishment of credit

in Seattle (1870-1920) Seattle [Lumberman's Printing Co., 1920?] [32] p. illus., ports. WaS WaU **2436**

Deynoodt, Francois.
P. J. de Smet, de la Compagnie de Jesus, missionnaire belge aux Etats-Unis; esquisse biographique. Bruxelles, Vromant, 1878. 50 p. WaU **2437**

[D'Herbomez, Louis J.]
Secular schools versus denominational schools. [n.p.] St. Mary's Mission, 1881, 28 p. CVicAr **2438**

Dhu, Oscar, see no. 6361.

Dice, Lee Raymond, 1887-
Distribution of the land vertebrates of southeastern Washington. Berkeley, Univ. of Calif. Press, 1916. [55] p. (Publications in Zoology. v. 16, no. 17)
WaU WaWW **2439**

Notes on Pacific coast rabbits and pikas. Ann Arbor, Mich., Univ. of Mich. Press, 1926. 28 p. (Museum of Zoology. Occasional papers no. 166)
OrP WaU **2440**

Dick, Everett Newfon, 1898-
The story of the frontier; a social history of the northern plains and Rocky Mountains from the earliest white contacts to the coming of the homemaker. New York, Tudor [1947, c1941] 574 p. illus. MtBozC WaSp WaWW **2441**

Vanguards of the frontier, a social history of the northern plains and Rocky Mountains from the earliest white contacts to the coming of the homemaker. New York, Appleton-Century, 1941. 574 p. front. (port.) plates. Many **2442**

Dickie, Donalda James.
The Canadian West. Toronto, Dent, [n.d.] 319 p. front., illus., 12 col. plates, ports. CVicAr **2443**

Same. 2d ed. [1927] 323 p. col. front., illus., col. plates. CVU **2444**

Dickson, Albert Jerome.
Covered wagon days; a journey across the plains in the sixties, and pioneer days in the Northwest; from the private journals of Albert Jerome Dickson, ed. by Arthur Jerome Dickson. Cleveland, A.H. Clark Co., 1929. 287 p. front., plates, ports., fold. map. Many **2445**

Dickson, Arthur Jerome, see no. 2445.

Dickson, Helen, see no. 8623.

Dickson, Howard Knox, 1890-
Practical horticulture for the Pacific slope; a text for high school students and practical orchardists, by H. K. Dickson and Henry L. Holmes. San Francisco, Harr Wagner [c1927] vii, 343 p. front., illus. Or OrCS OrP Wa WaS WaU **2446**

Dickson, Margaret Ball.
One man and a dream. Minneapolis, Argus Pub. Co. [n.d.] 72 p. illus. "Compliments of Poetry section of Spokane."
WaSp **2447**

Dictionary of the Chinook or Indian trade language of the North Pacific coast. Victoria, B. C., Hibben [n.d.] 29 p.
CVicAr CVU OrP WaU **2448**

Same. [1877] 32 p. OrHi Wa WaU **2449**
Same. 1883. CVicAr WaU WaWW **2450**
Same. 1899. 35 p.
OrP WaS WaSp WaTC **2451**

Dictionary of the Numipu or Nez Perce Language, by a missionary of the Society of Jesus in the Rocky Mountains: Pt.1; English-Nez Perce (all that is published) Mont., St. Ignatius' Mission Print., 1895. 242 p. WaSp WaU **2452**

Diesen, Einar, see no. 1061.

Dietz, Arthur Arnold.
Mad rush for gold in frozen North, illus. from photographs by W. A. Sharp. Los Angeles, Times-Mirror Printing and Binding House, 1914. 281 p. front. (ports.) plates, ports. CVU WaS WaU **2453**

Dill, Clarence Cleveland, 1884-
The state of Washington, history, government, resources. Spokane, c1942. 164 p. illus., map. Many **2454**

Dill, W. S.
The long day, reminiscences of the Yukon. Ottawa, Graphic Pub., 1926. iii, 232 p.
CVicAr CVU WaU **2455**

Dillon, Tom.
Over the trails of Glacier National Park. St. Paul, 1911. 1 v. illus. MtHi **2456**

Dilworth, Ira, see nos. 1520, 1522, 1523, 7748.

Dimsdale, Thomas Josiah, d. 1866.
The vigilantes of Montana; or, Popular justice in the Rocky Mountains, being a correct and impartial narrative of the chase, trial, capture and execution of Henry Plummer's road agent band, together with accounts of the lives and crimes of many of the robbers and desperadoes, the whole being interspersed with sketches of life in the mining camps of the far West. Virginia City, Mont., Mont. Post Press, 1866. 228 p.
MtHi Or WaSP WaU WaWW **2457**

Same. 2d ed. Virginia City, Mont., D. W. Tilton, 1882. 241 p.
MtBozC MtHi WaU **2458**

Same. 3d ed. Helena, Mont., State Pub. Co. [c1915] 290 p. front., plates, ports., facsims. Many **2459**

Same. 3d printing. Butte, Mont., W. F. Bartlett, 1915. 276 p.
CVicAr IdB IdU WaU **2460**

Same. 4th printing. Virginia City., Mont., T. E. Castle and C. W. Bank, 1921. 276 p. illus. MtBozC Or WaPS WaU **2461**

Same. 5th printing. Butte, Mont., McKee Printing Co., 1924. 268 p. plates.
WaSp WaU **2462**

Same. 7th printing. 1929. 269 p. plates.
Wa WaSp WaTC WaU **2463**

Same. 8th printing. 1937. IdIf MtBozC **2464**

Same. 4th ed. Helena, Mont., State Pub. Co. [n.d.] 290 p. front., 11 plates, 17 ports.
IdP MtBozC MtHi OrP WaSp **2465**

Dingee, Mrs. Ruby Lusher, comp.
Historical sketches of Pend Oreille County. Newport, Wash., Miner Print, 1930. 35 p.
OrHi WaPS WaS WaSp WaT WaU **2466**

Diomedi, Alexander, 1843-
Sketches of modern Indian life. [Woodstock, Md.? 1894?] 79 p. WaS WaU **2467**

Dionne, Emil.
Men of destiny. Spokane, 1945. 224 p. 6 plates, 5 ports.   Wa WaS WaSp WaT **2468**

Direct Legislation League of the State of Washington.
Direct legislation; or, The initiative, referendum and recall. Seattle [1910?] 16 p.
WaS WaU **2469**

A Disciple of the Washington School, pseud.
Oregon; the cost and the consequences. Philadelphia, 1846. 14 p.
CVicAr Or OrP WaS WaSp WaU **2470**

Disciples of Christ. Mont.
Historical report of the secretary. St. Paul, Pioneer Press, 1885. 27 p.   MtHi **2471**

Diven, Mrs. Lou Gertrude.
A Rocky Mountain sketch, by Mrs. C. L. Diven. Boston, Usher, 1898. 27 p. Wa **2472**

Diven, Robert Joseph.
A daughter of the hills; a sketch. [Albany, Or., Albany Printing Co., 1916] 45 p.
WaPS **2473**

Rowdy, illus. by Charles Livingston Bull. New York, Century [c1927] vii, 220 p. front., plates. Alaska dog story.
Or WaS WaU **2474**

Dixon, Dorothy Elizabeth.
Bibliography of the geology of Oregon. Eugene, Or., Univ. of Or. [1926] 125 p. (Geology series, v. 1, no. 1. June, 1926)
Many **2475**

Dixon, George, d. 1800?
Further remarks on the voyages of John Meares, Esq., in which several important facts misrepresented in the said Voyages relative to geography and commerce are fully substantiated, to which is added a letter from Captain Duncan containing a decisive refutation of several unfounded assertions of Mr. Meares and a final reply to his answer. London, Stockdale, 1791. 80 p.   CVicAr **2476**

Remarks on the voyages of John Meares, Esq. in a letter to that gentleman. London, Stockdale, 1790. 37 p.
CVicAr CVU WaU **2477**

See also nos. 777-780, 4708, 8299, 8301, 8302, 8304, 8305.

Dixon, Joseph Kossuth.
The vanishing race, the last great Indian council; a record in picture and story of the last great Indian council, participated in by eminent Indian chiefs from nearly every Indian reservation in the United States, together with the story of their lives as told by themselves; their speeches and folklore tales, their solemn farewell and the Indians' story of the Custer fight, written and illus. by Dr. Joseph K. Dixon, leader of the expeditions to the North American Indian to perpetuate the life story of these first Americans; the concept of Rodman Wannamaker. This volume is illus. with 80 photogravures of Indian chiefs and Indian life. Garden City, N. Y., Doubleday, 1913. xviii, 231 p. front., plates, ports.,

map. Council held in Little Big Horn Valley in Mont.   WaPS WaS **2478**

Same. 1914.   CVicAr **2479**

Same. Philadelphia, National American Indian Memorial Assn. Press, 1925. 239 p. front., plates, ports., map.
MtHi WaU **2480**

Dixon, Margaret Collins (Denny) 1882-
Denny genealogy, by Margaret Collins Denny Dixon and Elizabeth Chapman Denny Vann. New York, National Historical Society [c1944-c1947] 2 v. plate, ports., facsims, coats of arms. WaU **2481**

Dixon, Winifred Hawkridge.
Westward hoboes; ups and downs of frontier motoring, photographs by Katherine Thaxter and Rollin Lester Dixon. New York, Scribner, 1921. ix, 377 p. front., plates.   Many **2482**

Dobbs, Arthur, 1689-1765.
An account of the countries adjoining to Hudson's Bay, in the north-west part of America; containing a description of their lakes and rivers, the nature of the soil and climates, and their methods of commerce, &c. shewing the benefit to be made by settling colonies, and opening a trade in these parts; whereby the French will be deprived in a great measure of their traffick in furs, and the communication between Canada and Mississippi be cut off. With an abstract of Captain Middleton's journal, and observations upon his behaviour during his voyage, and since his return. To which are added, I. A letter from Bartholomew de Fonte, giving an account of his voyage from Lima to Peru, to prevent, or seize upon any ships that should attempt to find a north-west passage to the South sea. II. An abstract of all the discoveries which have been publish'd of the islands and countries in and adjoining to the great western ocean between America, India, and China. &c. III. The Hudson's bay company's charter. IV. The standard of trade in those parts of America; with an account of the exports and profits made annually by the Hudson's bay company. V. Vocabularies of the languages of several Indian nations adjoining to Hudson's bay. The whole intended to show the great probability of a northwest passage. London, Printed for J. Robinson, 1744. ii, 211 p. front. (fold. map)   CVicAr OrP WaU **2483**

Remarks upon Capt. Middleton's defence: wherein his conduct during his late voyage for discovering a passage from Hudson's Bay to the South-Sea is impartially examin'd whereby it will appear, with the highest probability, that there is such a passage as he went in search of. With an appendix of original papers. London, Printed by the author's appointment, and sold by J. Robinson, 1744. 171 p. map.   CVicAr WaU **2484**

Reply to Capt. Middleton's answer to the remarks on his vindication of his conduct to which is added, a full answer to a late pamphlet published by Capt. Mid-

dleton, called Forgery detected. London, Robinson, 1745. 128 p.   OrP **2485**
See also nos. 5868, 6783-6785.

Dobbs, Mrs. Caroline (Conselyea)
Men of Champoeg; a record of the lives of the pioneers who founded the Oregon government. Portland, Or., Metropolitan, 1932. 218 p. front., 4 plates. Many **2486**

Dobbs, Mrs. John F., see nos. 2269, 2272.

Dobie, Alexander, see no. 10230.

Docking, Anna Mynott.
The bank lady (Harriet E. Moorehouse) written of a woman, by a woman, for a woman. [Portland, Or., n.d.] 12 p. front. (port.)   OrHi OrP **2487**

Documentary history of the Oregon Central and Oregon and California Railroad Company. [n.p. n.d] 121 p.
          OrHi OrP **2488**

Dodds, James.
Hudson's Bay Company, its position and prospects; the substance of an address at a meeting of the shareholders, in the London Tavern, on the 24th January, 1866. London, Stanford 1866. 77 p. front. (fold map.)   CVicAr OrP WaS **2489**

Dodge, Mrs. Angie M.
History of the Washington State Branch of the National Congress of Mothers and Parent-Teacher Associations. [n.p., 1923] 12 p.   WaT **2490**

Dodge, Grenville Mellen, 1831-1916.
Biographical sketch of James Bridger; mountaineer, trapper and guide. [Kansas City, Mo., R. M. Rigby Printing Co. 1904?] [20] p. plate, port.
          MtHi WaSp WaW **2491**
Same. New York, Unz & Co., 1905. 27 p.
          Many **2492**
See also no. 161.

Dodge, Howard Lewis, 1869-
Attraction of the compass; or, The blonde Eskimo; a romance of the North based upon facts of a personal experience. 2d ed. Long Beach, Calif., Seaside Printing Co., 1916. 243 p. front. (port.) plates.
          CVU **2493**

Dodge, John W.
A wonderful city, leading all others in Washington, Oregon, Montana, Idaho and British Columbia; Seattle, its past history, recent progress and present advanced position. Seattle, Lowman & Hanford, 1890. 48 p. front., illus., maps.
          WaS WaU **2494**

Dodge, Norman L., see no. 5214.

Dodge, Orvil.
Pioneer history of Coos and Curry Counties, Or.; heroic deeds and thrilling adventures of the early settlers, pub. under the auspicies of the Pioneer and Historical Association of Coos County, Orvil Dodge, historian. Salem, Or., Capital Printing Co., 1898. 468, 103 p. front., illus., ports.   Many **2495**
See also no. 5551.

Dodge, Richard Irving, 1827-1895.
Our wild Indians; thirty-three years' personal experience among the red men of the great West; a popular account of

their social life, religion, habits, traits, customs, exploits, etc., with thrilling adventures and experiences on the great plains and in the mountains of our wide frontier, with an introd. by General Sherman. Hartford, A. D. Worthington, 1882. 650 p. front. (port.) illus., 16 plates.
          CVicAr MtU Or Wa WaS WaSp **2496**
Same. 1883.
          CVU IdB MtBozC MtHi OrHi WaU **2497**
Same. St. Louis, H. M. Brockstedt, 1885.
          WaSp **2498**

The plains of the great West and their inhabitants, being a description of the plains, game, Indians, etc. of the great North American desert. New York, Putnam, 1877. 488 p. plates, ports., map.
          Or OrHi OrU WaS WaSp WaU **2499**

Dodge, William Sumner.
Oration by Hon. Wm. Sumner Dodge, delivered at Sitka, Alaska, Saturday, July 4th, 1868; "Liberty: her struggles, perils and triumphs". San Francisco, Alta California Printing House, 1868. 30 p.   WaU **2500**

Dodson, W. D. B.
Official history of the operations of the second Oregon Infantry, U. S. V. in the campaign in the Philippine Islands. [San Francisco] Hicks-Judd Co., 1899. 119 p. illus.
          Or Wa WaPS WaS WaU **2501**

Doe, Ernest, comp.
History of Salmon Arm, 1885-1912. [Salmon Arm, B. C., Printed by the Salmon Arm Observer, 1947] 83 p. illus., ports.   CVU WaU **2502**

"Dok", see nos. 3947, 3948.

[Dole, Nathan Haskell] 1852-1935.
Our northern domain: Alaska, picturesque, historic and commercial. Boston, D. Estes & Co. [c1910] 237 p. front., plates.
          CV IdP OrU WaS WaT WaU **2503**

Dolge, Ernest.
Industrial Douglas fir; a discussion of the problems concerning the better utilization of the physical and mechanical properties of this splendid wood. Tacoma [Allstrum Printing Co.] 1927. 235 p. illus., 20 plates, charts, diagrs. (1 fold.)
          WaT WaTC **2504**

Dollar, Robert, 1844-1932.
Memoirs. San Francisco, W. S. Van Cott and Co. [c1917-1925] 3 v. fronts., plates, ports. Northwest shipping and lumber interests.
          CV CVU Or OrP WaSp WaWW **2505**

Dominion Illustrating Company.
Greater Vancouver, illustrated, Canada's most progressive Twentieth Century metropolis; a glance at her history, a review of her commerce, a description of her business enterprises, with illus. of her public and commercial buildings, her beautiful residences, hotels, residence and business streets, parks and points of interest in and about the city. Vancouver, B. C. [1908?] 216 p. illus., 65 ports.   CV CVU **2506**

Dominion of Canada, Pacific Railway, and Northwest Territories. [Manitoba?1855?] 32 p. front. (fold. map) Contents: Pacific Railway and the Northwest, by A. W. Ross. — Manitoba soils, by G. K. Gilbert.—Northwest prairies, by W. Fream.—Notes on the Canadian Northwest, by J. P. Sheldon.—Advantages of Canadian Northwest, by H. Tanner. WaU **2507**

Donaldson, Jessie Louise, see no. 9113.

Donaldson, Thomas B., see no. 2508.

Donaldson, Thomas Corwin, 1843-1898.
Idaho of yesterday; introd. by Thomas B. Donaldson. Caldwell, Idaho, Caxton, 1941. 406 p. front., plates, ports., facsims. Many **2508**

Donan, Patrick.
Alaska; the marvellous land of gold and glacier. San Francisco, Pacific Coast Steamship Co., 1899. 37 p. illus. WaS **2509**

Astoria; the peerless maritime metropolis of the golden Northwest. [n.p., n.d.] [36] p. illus. Or OrHi WaU **2510**

The Columbia River empire; some hurried glimpses of a region where all glories of scene, all charms of climate and all riches of resource meet and shake hands. Portland, Or., Or. Railroad and Navigation Co. [n.d.] 64 p. illus., map. OrU **2511**

Same. Portland, Or., Baltes & Co., 1898. 70 p. WaPS **2512**

Same. Portland, Or., Or. Railroad and Navigation Co. [1898] [72] p. illus., map. Or OrHI OrP OrU WaS WaU **2513**

Same. [1899] 68 p. OrCS WaS WaU WaW WaWW **2514**

Same. 1902. 72 p. IdU WaW **2515**

Gold fields of Baker County, Eastern Oregon. Portland, Or., Or. Railroad and Navigation Co. [n.d.] 35 p. illus., fold, map. OrHi OrU Wa WaWW **2516**

The new bonanzaland; with a brief dissertation on booms. Portland, Or., Or. Railroad and Navigation Co., 1897. 63 p. illus., fold. map. WaWW **2517**

Doney, Carl Gregg, 1867-
The broken circle; the life of Paul Herbert Doney, with foreword by Fred. P. Corson. New York, H. Revell Co. [1943] 187 p. front. (port.) Willamette Univ. President, 1913-1934. Or OrP OrSaW WaS WaU **2518**

Cheerful yesterdays and confident tomorrows. Portland, Or., Binfords & Mort [1942] 190 p. front. (port.) Many **2519**

Donkin, John G.
Trooper and Redskin in the far Northwest; recollections of life in the Northwest Mounted Police, Canada, 1884-1888. London, Low, 1889. xi, 289 p. front. (port.) fold. map. CVicAr CVU WaU **2520**

Donnell, Mrs. Camilla T., see no. 10206.

Donnelly, Charles, 1869-
The facts about the Northern Pacific land grant, by Charles Donnelly, president, Northern Pacific Railway Company. [St. Paul, 1924] 24 p. Many **2521**

Donnelly, Eleanor Cecilia, 1838-1917.
A Klondike picnic; the story of a day, with genuine letters from two gold-seekers in Alaska. New York, Benziger Bros., 1898. 160 p. CVU **2522**

Donworth, George, see no. 1970.

Dorcy, Ben Holladay, 1860-
Ancestors of Eliza S. Dorcy (nee Downe); notes extracted and comp. by Ben Holladay Dorcy. [n.p., 1921] [57] p. 2 double geneal. tables. Portland family. OrHi OrP **2523**

Dorcy, Mary Jean, Sister, 1914-
An army in battle array; Dominican saints and blessed. Milwaukee, Bruce Pub. Co. [1947] 112 p. illus. Everett, Wash. author. Wa WaU **2524**

A crown for Joanna. New York, Sheed and Ward, 1946. 95 p. illus., plates. WaU **2525**

Mary, my mother; a Mary-book for little boys and girls, illus. by the author. New York, Sheed & Ward, 1944. 65 p. front., illus. WaU **2526**

Our Lady's feasts; considerations on the feasts of the Queen of Heaven for those who are young—in heart or in actuality, illus. by the author. New York, Sheed and Ward, 1945. 101 p. front., illus. Wa WaU **2527**

A shady hobby, by Jean Frances Bennett [pseud.] Milwaukee, Bruce Pub. Co. [c1944] 71 p. front., illus., plates. Wa WaU **2528**

Truth was their star. Milwaukee, Bruce Pub. Co. [1947] 124 p. Wa WaU **2529**

Dorr, Joseph W., 1855-
Babylon, a historical romance in rhyme of the time of Nimrod, the mighty hunter-king; "The evergreen shore", The "homesick prospector," "The ride of '42," and other poems. Tacoma, Commercial Printing Co., 1897. 221 p. front. (port.) plates. Many **2530**

On the sunset shore; a book of poems and rhymes. Seattle, Souvenir Pub. Co., 1908. 211 p. front. (port.) illus., plates. Or OrHi Wa WaS WaSp WaU **2531**

Dorrance, James French, 1879-
The golden Alaskan. New York, Macaulay Co. [c1931] 311 p. WaU WaW **2532**

Dorsey, Edward.
Sunny old Spokane; words by Frank Finney; music by Edward Dorsey. Chicago [n.d.] 5 p. music. WaPS **2533**

Dosch, Henry Ernst, 1841-
Horticulture in Oregon. [Portland, Or.] Lewis and Clark Centennial Exposition Commission for the State of Or., 1904. 32 p. front., illus., tables. OrHi OrP **2534**

Vigilante days at Virginia City; personal narrative of Col. Henry B. Dosch, member of Fremont's body guard and one-time pony express rider. Portland, Or., F. Lockley [1924] 19 p. Many **2535**

Douglas, Charles H. J., see nos. 7930, 7936.

Douglas, Dick.
Boy Scout in the grizzly country. New

York, Putnam, 1929. 181 p. front., plates. Alaska story. **IdIf 2536**

Douglas, George Mellis.
Lands forlorn; a story of an expedition to Hearne's Coppermine River, introd. by James Douglas, LLD. New York, Putnam, 1914. 285 p. front. (port.) illus., 2 fold maps.
CV CVicAr WaS WaSp **2537**

Douglas, James, see no. 2537.

Douglas, Robert W.
How books may help you; an address, by Robert W. Douglas, Librarian, Carnegie Library, Vancouver, B.C. Vancouver, B. C., Burrard Pub. Co., 1914. 22 p.
CVicAr **2538**

Douglas, Walter B., see no. 5107.

Douglas Fir Plywood Association, Tacoma.
Catalog of plywood boat plans. Tacoma, 1948. 28 p. OrP **2539**

Douglass, Harlan Paul, 1871-
The Portland church survey, a study of the church in the metropolitan area of Portland, Oregon, 1945, by H. P. Douglass, C. H. Richardson, and Frederick Shippey. Portland, Or., Portland Council of Churches, 1945. 67 p. tables.
OrP **2540**

Douthit, Mary Osborn, ed.
Souvenir of western women. Portland, Or., Anderson, 1905. 200 p. front., illus., plate.
Many **2541**

Dovell, William Thomas.
"A scrap of paper". [Seattle, 1924] 19 p. Treaty of 1855 with Nez Perces Indians and its abrogation by the government.
·Or OrP Wa WaS WaU **2542**

Dow, Peter.
Alaska, America's northern wonderland. [Hot Springs, Ark., c1927] 128 p. 57 plates (1 col.) port. WaS **2543**

Dowell, Benjamin Franklin.
Petition asking pay for two companies of Oregon volunteers and their expenses, called into service in 1854. Jacksonville, Or., Oregon Sentinel, 1869. 14 p.
OrHi OrP OrU **2544**

Dowling, C. M., see no. 1185.

Down, Robert Horace.
A history of the Silverton country. Portland, Or., Berncliff Press, 1926. 258 p. front., illus., map. Many **2545**
See also nos. 1785-1787.

Downen, Mrs. Lula.
Covered wagon days in the Palouse country. [Pullman, Wash.] Pullman Herald, 1937. 32 p. front., illus. Wa **2546**

Downey, Fairfax Davis, 1893-
Indian-fighting army, illus. from drawings by Frederick Remington, Charles Schreyvogel and R. F. Zogbaum. New York, Scribner, 1941. xii, 329 p. front., illus., plates. Many **2547**

Same. 1944 [c1941] WaU **2548**

Downie, Ralph Ernest.
A pictorial history of the state of Washington. Seattle, Lowman & Hanford [c1937] 157 p. col. front., illus., plates, ports., fold. map. Many **2549**

Same. 2d ed. 163 p.
CVicAr OrCS OrP OrU WaS WaT **2550**
See also no. 4304.

Downing, A.
Region of the upper Columbia and how I saw it. Vancouver, B. C., Beeson, 1881. 33 p. tables. OrHi **2551**

Downing & Clarke, pub.
Pocket dictionary of the Chinook jargon, the Indian trading language of Alaska, the Northwest Territory, and the northern Pacific coast. San Francisco, 1898. 32 p. CVicAr **2552**

Downs, Winfield Scott, see nos. 2858, 2859.

Dowse, Thomas.
The new Northwest; Montana. Helena; its past, present and future. Chicago, Commercial Advertising Co., 1880. 24 p. illus., map. MtBozC MtHi **2553**

[Doyle, John T.]
Oregon election; effect of a majority of votes cast for a candidate constitutionally disqualified. San Francisco, Winterburn, 1876. 28 p. OrHi **2554**

[Drage, Theodorus Swaine) supposed author, see nos. 10040, 10041.

Drago, Harry Sinclair, 1888-
Montana road. New York, Morrow, 1935. vi, 306 p. WaU **2555**

Drake, Frank V.
"Oregon", a jubilee hymn, 1846-1896; half century anniversary of the treaty with England whereby Oregon came under the jurisdiction of the United States. [Portland, Or., Oregon Pioneer Assn., 1896] 8 p. Also published in Transactions 1896. OrHi **2556**

Drake, Marie.
Alaskana; our last frontier: glimpses of its colorful yesterdays and high lights of today. Juneau, Daily Alaska Empire, c1938. 48 p. illus., map. WaS WaU **2557**

Drake, Samuel Adams, 1833-1905.
The making of the great West, 1512-1883. London, Unwin, 1887. xii, 339 p. front., illus., ports., maps. CVicAr CVU **2558**

Same. New York, Scribner, 1887.
CVicAr MtU Or WaTC WaU WaW **2559**

Same. [n.p.] Young People's Missionary movement of U. S. and Canada, 1887. (Mission study reference library no. 117) OrSa **2560**

Same. New York, Scribner, 1891.
CVicAr IdU **2561**

Same. 1899. WaT **2562**

Same. 1901. Wa **2563**

Same. 1905, c1887. OrP WaT **2564**

Same. 1908. IdB **2565**

Drannan, William F., 1832-
Capt. W. F. Drannan, chief of scouts, as pilot to emigrant and government trains, across the plains of the wild West of fifty years ago, copiously illus. by E. Bert Smith. Chicago, T. W. Jackson [c1910] 407 p. front., illus., plates, ports.
WaPS WaU **2566**

Same. Chicago, Rhodes [c1910]
Or OrP WaS **2567**

Thirty-one years on the plains and in the mountains; or, The last voice from the plains; an authentic record of a life time of hunting, trapping, scouting and Indian fighting in the far West. Chicago, Rhodes, 1899. 586 p. illus., ports.
MtHi OrHi **2568**

Same. 1900. Many **2569**

Same. Chicago, Jackson [c1900] 654 p. illus., ports. Many **2570**

Same. Chicago, Rhodes, 1904. 586 p. front., illus. Wa **2571**

Same. 1906. CVicAr IdB **2572**

Same. 1908. 572 p. front., illus., plates, ports. OrU WaPS **2573**

Same. 1910. 586 p. front., illus., 58 plates, 13 ports. IdU WaS **2574**

Draycot, Walter M. L.
Lynn Valley, from the wilds of nature to civilization; a short history of its resources, natural beauty and development, also its part in the Great War. [North Vancouver, B. C., North Shore Press, 1919] 41 p. illus. CV CVicAr **2575**

Same. [1920?] CVU **2576**

Driggers, G. H.
The true situation in Washington with regard to the state managed workmen's compensation fund. New York, Market World and Chronicle [1913] 31 p. illus. Address before the Committee on labor and capital of the Montana State Legislature at Helena, Feb. 6, 1913.
Or WaS WaU **2577**

Driggs, Benjamin Woodbury, 1858-
History of Teton Valley, Idaho. Caldwell, Idaho, Caxton, 1926. 227 p. front., plates.
Many **2578**

Driggs, Howard Roscoe, 1873-
Westward America, with reproductions of 40 water color paintings by William H. Jackson. Trails ed. New York, Putnam [c1942] 312 p. col. front., col. plates.
Many **2579**

See also nos. 4610, 6243, 6244, 6701, 6702, 7712, 7942, 7944, 8874-8876, 11091, 11092.

Driggs, John Beach, 1854-
Short sketches from oldest America. Philadelphia, W. Jacobs & Co. [c1905] 163 p. front., 4 plates. Arctic Alaskan traditions and legends. OrP Wa WaU **2580**

Driscoll, Joseph, 1902-
War discovers Alaska. Philadelphia, Lippincott, 1943. 351 p. front., plates, port.
Many **2581**

Droonberg, Emil, 1864-
Die Goldwascher am Klondike; Roman aus der Zeit der grossen Goldfunde in Kanada und Alaska. 13.-15. Aufl. Leipzig, Wilhelm Goldmann Verlag, c1925. 284 p. WaU **2582**

Das Siwash-madchen; Erzahlungen aus dem Kanadischen Felsengebirge und vom der Kuste des Stillen Ozeans. 4. Aufl. Leipzig, Wilhelm Goldmann Verlag, c1925. 119 p. WaU **2583**

Drucker, Arthur Eilert, 1877-
Cheap power and new industries in Washington; possible applications of large amounts of cheap hydro-electric power to mineral and metal production in the Pacific Northwest, by A. E. Drucker and Carl F. Floe. [Pullman, Wash.] Printed for the Wash. Natural Resources Assn. [1933]. [14] p. (Mines Information Bureau. Information circular no. 3)
OrU WaE **2584**

Drumheller, Daniel Montgomery, 1840-1925.
"Uncle Dan" Drumheller tells thrills of western trails in 1854. Spokane, Inland American Printing Co., 1925. 131 p. front. (port.) port. Many **2585**

[Drumheller, Ehrlichman & White, Seattle, Wash.]
A review of the salmon industry with particular reference to Pacific American Industries, Inc., Seattle, c1935. 27 p. illus., tables, diagrs. WaS WaU **2586**

Statistical and analytical review of the Puget Sound Power & Light Company. [Seattle, 1935] 23 p. map.
WaS WaU **2587**

Drumm, Stella M., see no 6150.

Drury, Clifford Merrill, 1897-
Elkanah and Mary Walker, pioneers among the Spokanes. Caldwell, Idaho, Caxton, 1940. 283 p. front., plates, ports., maps, facsims. Many **2588**

Henry Harmon Spalding. Caldwell, Idaho, Caxton, 1936. 438 p. front., plates, ports. (1 col.) facsims. Many **2589**

Marcus Whitman, M. D., pioneer and martyr. Caldwell, Idaho, Caxton, 1937. 473 p. front., illus., ports., facsims.
Many **2590**

The Spalding - Lowrie correspondence. [Philadelphia, 1942] 114 p. (Presbyterian Historical Society. Journal of the Department of History, v. 20, no. 1, 2, 3. Mar., June, Sept., 1942) Many **2591**

Dryden, Cecil, see no. 11192.

Dubach, Ulysses Grant.
The government of Oregon; supplement to Our America, the elements of civics, by John A. Lapp. Indianapolis, Bobbs-Merrill, c1919. [55] p. Or OrCS **2592**

See also nos. 571-578.

Dubbe, Marvin C.
Grains of wheat. Caldwell, Idaho, Caxton, 1934. 190 p. front., illus., diagrs. Wheat farming in Idaho. Many **2593**

Du Bois, Cora Alice, 1903-
The feather cult of the middle Columbia. Menasha, Wis., Geo. Banta Pub. Co., 1938. 45 p. illus., map. (General series in anthropology, no. 7) Many **2594**

Duffy, Joseph H.
Butte was like that, a novel, cover design by Charles W. Pearson, jacket design by James W. Masterson. 1st ed. Butte, Mont. [c1941] 379 p.
MtHi MtU WaSp WaU **2595**

Duflot de Mofras, Eugene, 1810-1884.
Duflot de Mofras' travels on the Pacific coast, trans., ed. and annotated by Marguerite Eyer Wilbur; foreword by Dr. Frederick Webb Hodge. Santa Ana, Calif., Fine Arts Press, 1937. 2 v. illus., plates, maps (1 fold.) facsim. Many **2596**

Exploration du territoire de l'Oregon, des Californies et de la Mer Vermeille, executee pendant des annees 1840, 1841, et 1842. Paris, Bertrand, 1844. 3 v. plates, maps, table. Volume 3 is an atlas. Many **2597**

Same. 2 v. in 4, without atlas. OrHi **2598**

Same. Ouvrage publie par ordre du roi, sous les auspices de M. le Marechal Soult, duc de Dalmatie et de M. le ministre des affaires etrangeres. Paris, Librairie de la societe de geographie, 1844. 3 v. fronts. (v. 1 and 2 only.) Wa **2599**

L'Oregon. Paris. Plon Freres, 1846. 44 p. CVicAr MtU **2600**

Dufresne, Frank, 1896-
Alaska's animals & fishes, illus. by Bob Hines. New York, A. S. Barnes and Co. [1946] xvi, 297 p. col. front., illus., col. plates. Many **2601**

Dufur, A. J., comp.
Statistics of the state of Oregon; containing a description of its agricultural development and natural and industrial resources, together with the physical, geographical, geological and mineral statistics of the state. Salem, Or., "Willamette Farmer" Office, 1869. 128 p. table. Many **2602**

Dugas, George, 1833-1928.
The Canadian West; its discovery by the Sieur de la Verendrye; its development by the fur trading companies down to the year 1822, trans. from the French. Montreal, Beauchemin, 1905. 320 p. Many **2603**

Histoire de l'Ouest canadien de 1822 a 1869; epoque des troubles. Montreal, Librairie Beauchemin [c1906] 514 p. CVicAr CVU WaU **2604**

Legendes du Nord-Ouest. Montreal, Cadieux & Derome [c1883] 141 p. CVicAr CVU **2605**

Same. Par M. Dugast [!] Montreal, Librairie Saint-Joseph, 1883. 141 p. front. CVicAr WaU **2606**

Same. Montreal, Librairie Beauchemin, 1912. 140 p. front. CVU WaU **2607**

L'Ouest Canadien; sa decouverte par se sieur de la Verendrye son exploitation par les compagnies de traiteurs jusqu'a l'annee 1822. Montreal, Cadieux & Derome, 1896. 413 p. maps. WaU **2608**

La premiere Canadienne du Nord-Ouest; ou, Biographie de Marie-Anne Gaboury, arrivee au Nord-Ouest en 1806, et decedee a Saint-Boniface, a l'age de 96 ans, par M. l'abbe G. Dugast [!] Montreal, Cadieux & Derome, 1883. 108 p. front. (Bibliotheque religieuse et nationale 1. ser.) CVicAr WaU **2609**

Dugast, G., see nos. 2606, 2609.

Dugmore, Arthur Radclyffe, 1870-
The romance of the beaver, being the history of the beaver in the western hemisphere. Philadelphia, Lippincott [19—?] xiv, 225 p. front., illus., plates, diagrs. CVicAr WaU **2610**

Dumbell, Kate Ethel Mary, 1868-
California and the far West; suggestions for the west bound traveler. New York, J. Pott & Co. [c1914] 198 p. map. OrP WaPS WaU **2611**

Seeing the West; suggestions for the westbound traveller. Garden City, N. Y., Doubleday, 1920. 206 p. front., illus., map. CVU Or OrP WaS WaT WaU **2612**

Dun, R. G., & Co.
Facts and figures regarding Montana, comp. by Philip S. Rush, District Manager. Butte, Mont., 1918. 16 p. illus., maps. MtU **2613**

The mercantile agency reference book (and key) containing ratings of the merchants, manufacturers, and traders generally, throughout the Pacific states and territories. Sept. 1894. San Francisco, 1894. 1 v. OrP **2614**

Oregon statistics. Portland, Or., 1926. [20] p. OrSaW **2615**

Washington statistics. New York, 1926. 18 p. WaT **2616**

Dunbar, Elizabeth.
Three Forks, the gateway. [n.p.] c1926. 15 p. MtHi **2617**

Dunbar, Ruth.
The story of a state museum. Olympia, Wash., State Capitol Historical Assn. [1947?] 20 p. illus., ports. CVicAr Or Wa WaS WaT **2618**

Dunbar, Seymour, see nos. 7761, 7762.

Duncan, Capt., see no. 2476.

Duncan, Donald D.
Duncan's Tacoma guide and city map. Tacoma, South Tacoma Star, c1946. 52 p. illus., map. WaT **2619**

Duncan, Edith M., see no. 4650.

Duncan Eric, 1858-1944.
Fifty-seven years in the Comox Valley. Courtenay, B. C., Comox Argus Co., 1934. 61 p. front. (port.) illus. CVicAr CVU **2620**

From Shetland to Vancouver Island; recollections of seventy-five years. Edinburgh, Oliver and Boyd, 1937. 277 p. front. (port.) CV CVicAr CVU WaU **2621**

Same. 3d ed. enl. 1939. 304 p. CVic **2622**

Rural rhymes and The sheep thief. Toronto, Briggs, 1896. 64 p. CVicAr **2623**

Duncan, Kunigunde.
Blue star, told from the life of Corabelle Fellows. Caldwell, Idaho, Caxton, 1938. 211 p. front., plates, ports., facsims., music. IdB Wa WaS **2624**

Duncan, Lee, 1904-
Over the wall, by Lee Duncan, ex-convict no. 9256, Oregon State Prison. New York, Dutton [c1936] 368 p. front. Or OrCS OrP WaS WaU **2625**

Duncan, Nora M.
The heroine of Moodyville. [n.p., n.d.] [4] p. port. Poem. CVicAr **2626**

Duncan, Robert Gordon.
Ghosts and Vandals of the Wemme cases, by Gordon Duncan (the Oregon Wildcat). Portland, Or., Wemme [c1932] 374 p. plates. OrP **2627**

Duncan, Sinclair Thomson, 1828-1928.
From Shetland to British Columbia, Alaska and the United States, being a journal of travels, with narrative of return journey after three years' exploration. Lerwick, Scotland, Charles J. Duncan, 1911. 282 p. front. (port.)
     CVicAr CVU WaU **2628**

[**Duncan, William**] 1832-1915?
Appendix a shimalgiagum liami, hymns in Zimshian for the use of the church at Metlakatla. Metlakahtla, B. C. [n.d.] [9] p.   CVicAr **2629**

Metlakahtla and the Church Missionary Society. Victoria, B. C., Munroe Miller, 1887. 44 p. Defense of the position taken by the native Christians and their teachers and an answer to the charges brought against them, most of which are written by Wm. Duncan and Robert Tomlinson. CVicAr WaU **2630**

Metlahkatlah; ten years' work among the Tsimsheean Indians. Salisbury Square, London, Church Missionary House, 1869. 135 p. map.   CVicAr CVU **2631**

Same. 4th ed. 1871. viii, 119 p. fold. map. (The missions of the Church Missionary Society, no. 2) CVicAr **2632**

Dunham, Samuel Clarke, 1855-1920.
The goldsmith of Nome and other verse. Washington, D. C., Neale Pub. Co., 1901. 80 p.   Many **2633**

The men who blaze the trail and other poems, with an introd. by Joaquin Miller. New York, Barse & Hopkins [c1913] 126 p. Or WaU **2634**

Dunham, Wayland A., 1898-
Blue enchantment, the story of Crater Lake. Caldwell, Idaho, Caxton, 1942. 109 p. col. front., illus., col. plates.
     Many **2635**

Duniway, Mrs. Abigail (Scott) 1834-1915.
Captain Gray's company; or, Crossing the plains and living in Oregon. Portland, Or., S. J. McCormick, 1859. [342] p.
     Many **2636**

David and Anna Matson. New York, S. R. Wells & Co., 1878. 194 p. front. (port.) plates. Poetry. OrP WaU **2637**

Same. Portland, Or., Duniway Pub. Co., 1881. OrHi Wa WaS WaU **2638**

From the West to the West; across the plains to Oregon. Chicago, McClurg, 1905. 311 p. plate. Many **2639**

My musings; or, A few fancies in verse. Portland, Or., Walling, 1875. 32 p.
     OrHi **2640**

Oregon, land of promise. Portland, Or., Rhodes, 1907 [c1876] 12 p.
     OrHi OrP OrU **2641**

Path breaking; an autobiographical history of the equal suffrage movement in Pacific coast states. [Portland, Or., James, c1914] 291 p. front. (port.) illus.
     Many **2642**

Same. 2d ed. 297 p.
   IdU Or OrP WaPS WaU **2643**

Dunlap, Edward N., comp.
Key to the ancestry of Anne (Marbury) Hutchinson and Katherine (Marbury) Scott, who landed at Boston, Massachusetts, September 18, 1634, comp. from the manuscripts of Anne Bartlett Coddington; foreword by Geoffrey Wardle Stafford. [Seattle, 1934] 16 p. (Pacific Northwest Foundation for Genealogical Research. Publication no. 1)
    MtHi WaS WaU **2644**

Dunn, A. W., see nos. 3152-3155.

Dunn, Alexander.
Experiences in Langley and memoirs of prominent pioneers. New Westminster, B. C., Jackson Printing Co., 1913. 100 p. Contains his: Presbyterianism in B. C.
     CVicAr CVU **2645**

Sermon and missionary journeys. [New Westminster, B. C., Jackson Printing Co.] 1925. 16 p. CVU **2646**

Dunn, Jacob Piatt, 1855-1924.
Massacres of the mountains; a history of the Indian wars of the far West. London, Low, 1886. 784 p. front., illus., plates, ports., maps, plans.
     CVicAr WaU **2647**

Same. New York, Harpers, 1886.
     Many **2648**

Dunn, John.
History of the Oregon Territory and British North-American fur trade; with an account of the habits and customs of the principal native tribes on the northern continent. London, Edwards, 1844. 359 p. map. Many **2649**

Same. 2d ed. 1846. Many **2650**

Same. Philadelphia, Zieber, 1845.
  CV IdB OrHi OrP WaS WaU **2651**

The Oregon Territory and the British North American fur trade. Philadelphia, Zieber, 1845. 236 p. (The home and travellers library, semimonthly. No. 8)
     CVicAr CVU **2652**

Dunn, Mrs. Mary M. (Hill)
Undaunted pioneers ever moving onward-westward and homeward, etchings by Ina Collins Pruitt. [Eugene, Or., Valley Printing Co., 1929] 54 p. illus., port.
     Or **2653**

Dunn, Michael.
The Cascade metre; or, Poems pertaining to Oregon, copyright by Bro. Michael Dunn. [Huntington, Ind., Printed at office of Our Sunday Visitor] c1921. 60 p. illus. OrHi WaPS WaU **2654**

Dunn, Robert Steed, 1877-
The shameless diary of an explorer, with illus. from photographs by the author. New York, Outing Pub. Co., 1907. viii, 297 p. front., 10 plates, 2 fold. maps. "Our aim was to reach the top of Mt. McKinley". Author was member of Cook expedition. WaS WaU **2655**

Dunne, Peter Masten, 1889-
Pioneer black robes on the west coast. Berkeley, Calif., Univ. of Calif. Press, 1940. xiii, 286 p. front., illus., plates, maps, facsims. Many **2656**

Dunraven, Windham Thomas Wyndham-Quin, 4th earl of, 1841-1926.
Canadian nights, being sketches and remi-

niscences of life and sport in the Rockies, the prairies, and the Canadian woods. London, Smith, Elder, 1914. 296 p.
CVicAr CVU **2657**

The great divide; travels in the upper Yellowstone in the summer of 1874, with illus. by Valentine W. Bromley. London, Chatto & Windus, 1876. xvi, 377 p. front., illus., plates, maps.
CVicAr CVU MtBozC MtHi WaS **2658**

Same. New York, Scribner, Welford & Armstrong, 1876. MtU **2659**

Du Pont de Nemours, E. I., & Company.
Dupont explosives in the Pacific Northwest; instructions for farmers, contractors and loggers in the selection and use of explosives. Wilmington, Del. [c1934] 48 p. illus., diagrs. Or WaPS **2660**

Durham, Kathleen MacNeal.
Thoughts from Oregon to greet a friend, decorations by Estelle Wallace Paris. Portland, Or. [Baltes & Co.] 1916. 59 p. Poems. IdU Or OrHi OrP **2661**

Durham, Nelson Wayne, 1859-1938.
History of the city of Spokane and Spokane County, Washington, from its earliest settlement to the present time. Spokane, Clarke, 1912. 3 v. front., illus., plates, ports. Volues 2 and 3 biographical. Many **2662**

Durien, Paul, see no. 2663.
Durieu, Paul, 1830-1899.
Chinook Bible history, by the Rt. Rev. Paul Durien [!] Kamloops, B. C., 1899. 112 p. front. (port.) illus. Written in Chinook shorthand by J. N. Le Jeune.
CVicAr CVU WaU **2663**

See also nos. 5828, 5835, 5840.

Durkee, Elton S.
On the shores of Baker's Bay, a song written in memory of Captain Robert Gray who discovered the Columbia River, May eleventh, 1792. Chinook, Wash., Fenn [c1922] [5] p. Or WaU **2664**

Durlach, Mrs. Theresa (Mayer) 1891-
The relationship system of the Tlingit, Haida and Tsimshian. New York, American Ethnological Society, G. E. Stechert and Co., 1928. 177 p. fold. table. (Publications, v. 11)
CVicAr Wa WaS WaU **2665**

Duro, D. Cesareo Fernandez, see nos. 7484, 7485.

Durtain, Luc, 1881-
Decouverte de Longview, nouvelle inedite, avec des gravures de Franz Masereel. Paris, R. Kieffer, 1927. 48 p. illus.
WaPS WaU **2666**

Quarantieme etage. Paris, Gallimard, Editions de la Nouvelle Revue Francaise [c1927] 247 p. (Conquetes du monde: Amerique, no. 1) Contents: Crime a San Francisco.—La cite que batit la vision.—Smith Building.
CVU IdU WaS WaT WaU **2667**

Duryea, M. J.
Willamette Valley, Oregon; for distribution at Panama-Pacific International Exposition, San Francisco, California.

[n.p.] Willamette Valley Exposition Assn., 1915. 32 p. Or **2668**

Dustin, Fred, 1866-
The Custer fight; some criticisms of Gen. E. S. Godfrey's "Custer's last battle" in the Century Magazine for Jan. 1892; and of Mrs. Elizabeth Custer's pamphlet of 1921. Hollywood, Calif., 1936. 33 p.
MtHi **2669**

The Custer tragedy; events leading up to and following the Little Big Horn Campaign of 1876. Ann Arbor, Mich., Edwards, 1939. xxii, 251 p. illus., ports., 3 fold. maps. MtHi MtU **2670**

Duthie, David Wallace, see nos. 9321, 9322.
Dutton, Capt., see nos. 9386-9388.
Duvall, D. C., see no. 11143.
Dvorak, August, 1894-
Clark County school consolidation. [Seattle, 1930?] 16 p. map, tables.
WaU **2671**

Lewis County school consolidation. [Seattle, 1931?] 19 p. tables, fold. diagr.
WaU **2672**

Dwight, Mary E.
Word songs, illus. by Marjorie Grace. New York, House of Field [c1939] 52 p. Spokane author. Wa WaSp **2673**

Dye, Mrs. Eva (Emery) 1855-
Conquest; the true story of Lewis and Clark. Chicago, McClurg, 1902. 443 p. plate. Many **2674**

Same. New York, Grosset, 1902.
CVU **2675**

Same. Chicago, McClurg, 1903.
MtU Wa **2676**

Same. 4th ed. 1909. OrSaW **2677**

Same. 7th ed. 1914. Wa **2678**

Same. Garden City, N. Y., Doubleday, 1922.
IdB **2679**

Same. 1924 [c1902] Wa WaPS **2680**
Same. 10th ed. Introd. by Claire Warner Churchill; illus. by Howard Simon. New York, Wilson-Erickson, 1936. xiii, 448 p. front., plates, ports.
OrP OrSaW WaSp WaU **2681**

Same. [Portland, Or., Binfords & Mort, c1936] CVicAr OrCS WaSp **2682**

McDonald of Oregon; a tale of two shores. Chicago, McClurg, 1906. 395 p. plates.
Many **2683**

Same. Illus. by Walter F. Enright. 2d ed. 395 p. front., illus. CVU Wa **2684**

Same. 2d ed. 1907. 395 p. front., 5 plates.
IdB IdU OrCS WaSp WaT WaTC **2685**

McLoughlin and old Oregon, a chronicle. Chicago, McClurg, 1900. 381 p. front. (port.) Many **2686**

Same. 2d ed. 1900. CVicAr **2687**
Same. 3d ed. 1901.
CVicAr IdU WaPS **2688**

Same. 4th ed. 1902.
OrSaW OrU WaU **2689**

Same. 5th ed. 1903.
MtU OrSaW WaSp **2690**

Same. 6th ed. 1906.
CVicAr IdB MtU **2691**

Same. 7th ed. 1910 [c1900]
CVU OrCS Wa **2692**

Same. 8th ed. 1913.   IdB IdU OrU **2693**
Same. Garden City, N. Y., Doubleday, Page, 1921.
OrHi OrSaW WaSp WaTC **2694**

Same. 14th ed. Introd. by Sydney Greenbie; illus. by Howard Simon. New York, Wilson-Erickson, 1936. 386 p. front. (port.) 5 plates.
OrP OrSaW WaSp WaU **2695**

Same. 15th ed. Portland, Or., Binfords & Mort [c1936]   CVicAr **2696**
Same. 16th ed. 1936.
CVicAr OrCS OrU **2697**

The soul of America; an Oregon Iliad. New York, Press of the Pioneers, 1934. 366 p. front.   Many **2698**

Stories of Oregon. San Francisco, Whitaker & Ray, 1900. 203 p. illus., plate.
Many **2699**

Same. 1904 [c1900] 203 p. col. front., illus., ports. (Western series of readers, v. 7)
OrP OrPR WaS WaT **2700**

See also no. 11272.

Dyer, E. Jerome.
The gold fields of Canada and how to reach them; being an account of the routes and mineral resources of North-Western Canada. London, Philip, 1898. 268 p. front., maps (1 fold.)
CVicAr CVU WaS **2701**

The routes and mineral resources of North Western Canada, pub. under the auspices of the Incorporated London Chamber of Mines. London, Philip, 1898. xx, 268 p. front., 2 maps.
CV CVic CVicAr CVU WaU **2702**

Dyker, Bob.
Get your man; an autobiography of the North-West Mounted. London, Low [1934] ix, 244 p.   CVU **2703**

Dynes, W. M., comp.
Dynes' tours of Alaska. Juneau, Dynes' Alaska Directory Co. [n.d.] 84 p. illus., fold. map.   OrSa WaS WaT **2704**

Same. [1920?] 140 p.   Wa **2705**

Same. [1921?] 143 p.   WaE WaU **2706**

[Dyott, Luther R.]
Memorial church in memory of Rev. Dr. George H. Atkinson. Portland, Or. [n.d.] 12 p. port.   OrP **2707**

Eagle, Cathlamet, Wash.
Cathlamet centennial [1846-1946] August 23-25. Cathlamet, Wash., 1946. [24] p. (v. 56, no. 20, Aug. 22, 1946 and Special Centennial ed.)   WaS WaU **2708**

East, Allan W.
A history of community interest in a juvenile court; positive and negative manifestations during the period 1885-1942 in Multnomah County, Oregon. Portland, Or., Or. Probation Assn., c1943. 30 p.   Many **2709**

Problems of school attendance regulation

in Portland, Oregon, and in the state at large; attempted control of truancy and non-attendance during the period 1843-1939. Portland, Or., 1940. 33 p. tables.
Or OrCS OrP OrUM **2710**

East Washingtonian, Pomeroy, Wash.
First Garfield County pioneer edition, June 6, 1914. Pomeroy, Wash., 1914. [40] p. illus., ports.   WaU **2711**

East Waterway Dock & Warehouse Co., Seattle, Wash.
Harbor island terminal. [Seattle, 1918?] 62 p. illus., tables, map.
Or WaS WaU **2712**

Eastern Oregon Land Company.
Statement concerning The Dalles Military Road land grant; also abstract of title to the Eastern Oregon Land Co. San Francisco, Bosqui, 1886. 52 p.
CVicAr OhHi **2713**

Eastern Washington State Historical Society
Artists' ball. [Spokane, 1925?] 16 p.
WaU **2714**

History, constitution and annual report, 1918. Spokane [Shaw & Borden, 1918?] **16 p.**
OrU WaPS WaSP WaU WaWW **2715**

Eastham, John William, 1879-
Supplement to 'Flora of southern British Columbia' (J. K. Henry) comprising descriptions of additional species and varieties, significant extensions of range and corrections. Victoria, B. C., Provincial Museum, 1947. 119 p. (Special publication, no. 1)   OrCS **2716**

Easton, Charles Finley.
Mount Baker cartogram; a pictorial brochure of the great Koma Kulshan of the Lummis. [Bellingham, Wash.] Engberg Pharmacy [1912?] 20 p. illus., maps (1 fold.)   OrCS WaU **2717**

Easton, Theodore Sydney.
The secret of the Wallowa cave. Portland, Or., Metropolitan, 1934. 127 p. col. front., illus.   Many **2718**

Eastwood, Alice, see no. 783.

Eastwood, Carlin.
The master road. Seattle, Harriman, 1910. 251 p. front.   WaU **2719**

Eaton, Allen Hendershott, 1878-
The Oregon system, the story of direct legislation in Oregon: a presentation of the methods and results of the initiative and referendum, and recall in Oregon, with studies of the measures accepted or rejected, and special chapters on the direct primary, popular election of senators, advantages, defects and dangers of the system. Chicago, McClurg, 1912. 195 p.   Many **2720**

Eaton, Howard, see no. 8680.

Eaton, Jeanette.
Narcissa Whitman, pioneer of Oregon, illus. by Woodi Ishmael. New York, Harcourt [c1941] 318 p. front., illus., plates, map.   Many **2721**

Eaton, Walter Prichard, 1878-
Boy Scouts at Crater Lake; a story of Crater Lake National Park and high Cascades, illus. with photographs by

Fred H. Kiser. Boston, W. A. Wilde Co. [c1922] 292 p. front., plates.

Or OrP Wa WaS WaSp WaU **2722**

Boy Scouts in Glacier Park; the adventures of two young easterners in the heart of the high Rockies, illus. with photographs by Fred H. Kiser. Boston, W. A. Wilde Co. [c1918] 336 p. front., plates.

IdIf OrP WaE WaS WaSp WaW **2723**

Skyline camps; a note book of a wanderer over our northwestern Rockies, Cascade Mountains and Crater Lake, illus. by Fred H. Kiser. [Boston] W. A. Wilde Co. [c1922] 245 p. front., 17 plates.

Many **2724**

[Eavenson, Howard Nicholas] 1873-
Two early works on Arctic exploration by an anonymous author. [Pittsburgh] 1946. 14 p. WaS **2725**

Eberhard, Elias Eugene, 1851-
Champoeg, and other poems. Chicago, Authors' and Writers' Union, c1903. 216 p. WaWW **2726**
Same. 1904.

OrHi OrP WaPS WaU WaW **2727**

Eberstadt, Edward.
William Robertson Coe collection of Western Americana. New Haven, privately printed, 1948. 110 p. front. (port.) illus. Also published in Yale University Library Gazette, v. 23, no. 2, Oct. 1948.

WaU **2728**

Eberstadt, Edward & Sons, Booksellers, New York.
The northwest coast; a century of personal narratives of discovery, conquest & exploration from Bering's landfall to Wilkes' surveys, 1741-1841; books, maps & manuscripts offered for sale. New York [1941] 127 p. front., illus., plates, facsims. (Catalogue no. 119)

Many **2729**

Eckerson, Theodore John.
When my ship comes in, and other poems of camp and hearth. Portland, Or., F. W. Baltes and Co. [c1881] 113 p. Portland poet. Or WaU **2730**
Same. 1891, c1881. OrHi OrP **2731**

Eddy, John Whittemore, 1872-
Hunting on Kenai Peninsula and observations on the increase of big game in North America. [Seattle] Lowman & Hanford, 1924. 90 p. front., illus., 21 plates. Many **2732**

Hunting the Alaska brown bear; the story of a sportsman's adventures in an unknown valley after the largest carnivorous animal in the world. New York, Putnam, 1930. 253 p. front., illus., plates, ports., 2 fold. maps.

CVicAr OrP Wa WaS WaSp WaU **2733**

Edelstein, Julius C.
Alaska comes of age. New York, American Council, Institute of Pacific Relations, 1942. 62 p. illus., maps. (Far Eastern pamphlets, no. 8)

Or OrP WaU **2734**

Eden, Charles Henry, 1839-1900.
The home of the wolverene and beaver; or, Fur-hunting in the wilds of Canada. London, Society for Promoting Christian Knowledge [n.d.] 254 p. front., illus.

CVicAr MtU **2735**

Edgren, Adolph.
Jubel kantat for solo, kvartett och kor utford pa Svenska dagen den 31 juli 1909 a Alaska-Yukon-Pacific exposition; libretto af Emanuel Schmidt och musik af Adolph Edgren. Seattle, Edgren School of Music [c1909] [60] p. illus., ports. WaU **2736**

Edington, Arlo Channing, 1890-
Tundra, romance and adventure on Alaskan trails, as told by former Deputy United States Marshal Hansen to the Edingtons. New York, Century [c1930] 334 p. Many **2737**

Educational Publishing Company, Boston, Mass.
John Charles Fremont and Kit Carson. Boston [n.d.] 29 p. front. (port.)

OrU **2738**

Educational statistical survey; comparing higher education in Montana with that in eleven other Northwest and Rocky Mountain states. [n.p., 1928] 90 p. tables (part fold.) OrCS **2739**

Edward, H. P., see no. 9579.

Edwards, Deltus Malin, 1874-
The toll of the Arctic seas, illus. by G. A. Coffin and from photographs. London, Chapman & Hall, 1910. x, 449 p. front., plates, ports., fold. map. CVicAr **2740**
Same. New York, Holt, 1910.

CVicAr MtU Or OrP WaS **2741**

Edwards, George, 1858-
Montana the treasure state. [n.p., n.d.] 12 p. MtHi **2742**

Edwards, Jonathan, 1847-1929.
Illustrated history of Spokane County, state of Washington. [Spokane] Lever, 1900. 726 p. front. (map) plates, ports.

Many **2743**

Marcus Whitman, M.D., the pathfinder of the Pacific Northwest and martyred missionary of Oregon; a sketch of his life, character, work, massacre, and monument. Spokane, Union Printing Co., 1892. 48 p. ports. OrHi OrP

WaPS WaU WaW WaWW **2744**

Edwards, Philip Leget, 1812-1869.
Sketch of the Oregon Territory; or, Emigrants' guide. Liberty, Mo., Printed at the "Herald" Office, 1842. 20 p. Photostat copy. WaU **2745**

[Edwards, T. A.]
Daring Donald McKay; or, The last wartrail of the Modocs; the romance of the life of Donald McKay, government scout, and chief of the Warm Springs Indians. 3d ed. Erie, Pa., Herald Printing and Pub. Co., 1884. viii, 110 p. illus.

WaSp **2746**

The last war-trail of the Modocs; the romance of the life of Donald McKay, government scout and chief of the Warm Springs Indians. Erie, Pa., Herald Printing & Pub. Co., 1884. 110 p. illus.

CVicAr **2747**

Edwards, William Seymour, 1856-1915.
In to the Yukon. Cincinnati, R. Clarke & Co., 1904. [320] p. front., plates, maps.

CVicAr OrP WaS WaU **2748**

Same. New York, Clarke, 1904. 319 p. plates, maps. OrP WaSp **2749**

Same. 2d ed. Cincinnati, 1905. [335] p. front., plates, maps.
CVicAr CVU WaSp WaU **2750**

Eells, Edwin, see nos. 1968, 1969.

Eells, Myron, 1843-1907.
The Congregational Church of Forest Grove, Oregon, 1859-1901. Shelton, Wash., Journal Printer, 1901. 1 v.
OrHi WaWW **2751**

The duties of parents to baptized children. Boston, Beacon Press, 1885. 20 p.
WaU **2752**

Father Eells; a sketch, 1810-1893. Walla Walla, Wash., Whitman College [n.d.] 9 p. WaWW **2753**

Same. 14 p. OrP **2754**

Father Eells; or, The results of fifty-five years of missionary labors in Washington and Oregon; a biography of Rev. Cushing Eells, with an introd. by Rev. L. H. Hallock. Boston, Congregational Sunday-School and Pub. Society [c1894] 342 p. front. (port.) 7 plates, port.
Many **2755**

Hand of God in the history of the Pacific coast; annual address delivered before the trustees, faculty, students and friends of Whitman College at the 6th Commencement, June 1, 1888. [n.p., 1888?] 15 p. OrP WaS WaU **2756**

History of Indian missions on the Pacific coast; Oregon, Washington, and Idaho, with an introd. by G. H. Atkinson. Philadelphia, American Sunday-School Union [c1882] 270 p. front., plates, port.
Many **2757**

History of the Congregational Association of Oregon and Washington Territory; the Home Missionary Society of Oregon and adjoining territories; and the Northwestern Association of Congregational Ministers. Portland, Or., Himes, 1881. 124 p. table. Many **2758**

Hymns in the Chinook jargon language. Portland, Or., Himes, 1878. 30 p.
OrHi WaPS WaWW **2759**

Same. 2d ed. Portland, Or., Steel, 1889. 40 p. Many **2760**

In memoriam, Rev. S. H. Marsh, D. D., first president of Pacific University, born August 29, 1825, died Feb. 2, 1879. Portland, Or., Himes, 1881. 58 p.
Many **2761**

Marcus Whitman, M.D.; proofs of his work in saving Oregon to the United States, and in promoting the immigration of 1843. Portland, Or., Himes, 1883. 34 p. Many **2762**

Marcus Whitman, pathfinder and patriot. Seattle, Harriman, 1909. 349 p. front., 20 plates, ports., fold. map. Many **2763**

Memorial of Mrs. Mary R. Walker [the discourse preached at Forest Grove, Or., at the funeral of Mrs. Mary Richardson Walker, Dec. 7, 1897] [n.p., Hatchet Printery, n.d.] 12 p.
OrHi OrP OrU WaU **2764**

The relations of the Congregational colleges to the Congregational churches read before the Congregational Council of the Pacific Coast, at Portland, Or., June 27, 1888. New York, Tobitt, 1889. 16 p. OrHi OrP WaS WaU **2765**

A reply to Professor Bourne's "The Whitman legend". Walla Walla, Wash., Statesman Printing Co., 1902. 122 p. (Whitman College Quarterly, v. 4, no. 3)
Many **2766**

Rev. Samuel Parker. Walla Walla, Wash., Whitman College, 1898. 34 p. (Quarterly, v. 2, no. 3, Oct. 1898) IdU WaU **2767**

Ten years of missionary work among the Indians at Skokomish, Washington Territory, 1874-1884. Boston, Congregational Sunday-School and Pub. Society [c1886] 271 p. front., illus., plate, 2 ports.
Many **2768**

Worship and traditions of the aborigines of America; or, Their testimony to the religion of the Bible. [n.p., n.d.] 40 p.
OrP **2769**

Same. [1884?] CVicAr OrP WaS **2770**
See also nos. 348, 8788.

Eells, Walter Crosby, see no. 235.

Egan, Howard, 1815-1878.
Pioneering the West, 1846 to 1878; Major Howard Egan's diary, also thrilling experiences of pre-frontier life among Indians, their traits, civil and savage, and part of autobiography, inter-related to his father's comp. and connected in nearly chronological order, by Wm. M. Egan. Richmond, Utah, 1917. 302 p. illus., plates, ports.
MtHi OrU WaS WaSp WaU **2771**

Egan, William M., see no. 2771.

Egan Dramatic and Operatic School, Seattle, Wash.
Egan Dramatic and Operatic School. [Seattle, White Advertising Bureau, 1904?] [16] p. plates, ports., facsim.
WaU **2772**

Egelston, Edna L., ed.
An account of the early settlement and development of Woodland and vicinity, Idaho County, Idaho, 1895-1944, based upon data secured by personal interviews and various other reliable sources of information concerning local history. [Newberg, Or.] Mimeographed by Bertha L. Cressman [1944] 145 p. double diagr.
WaU **2773**

Egerton, Mrs. Fred.
Admiral of the fleet, Sir Geoffrey Phipps Hornby, a biography. Edinburgh, Blackwood, 1896. xi, 404 p. front., ports. Admiral Hornby was one of the English captains in the San Juans during the joint occupation. CVU WaU **2774**

Eggert, Mrs. Elizabeth Avery.
Review of the work and activities of the ladies' aid organization of the First Congregational Church. Portland, Oregon, 1851-1923. Portland, Or., Ivy Press, 1923. 16 p. OrHi **2775**

[Eggleston, Charles H.]
Helena's social supremacy; Helena, Mont.,

1894. [Anaconda, Mont., Anaconda Capital Committee, 1894] 48 p. illus.
MtHi MtU **2776**

When Bryan came to Butte. Anaconda, Mont., Anaconda Standard, 1897. 6 p.
MtHi **2777**

Same. Butte, Mont., J. F. Davies, 1912. [8] p. Poem. WaU **2778**

Eggleston, William G.
Clackamas County assessments and taxes in 1910; showing the difference between assessments and taxes under the general property tax system and the land value or single tax and exemption system proposed in the Clackamas County tax and exemption bill to be voted on at the Nov. 1912 election. Portland, Or., Multnomah Printing Co. [1912] 159 p. table. OrHi OrP **2779**

People's power and public taxation, by William G. Eggleston, A. D. Cridge, and W. S. U'Ren. 2d ed. Portland, Or., Multnomah Printing Co., 1910. 128 p. illus.
OrP OrU WaS **2780**

Eide, Arthur Hansin, see no. 3601.

1845-1945 Washington centennial commemorative booklet. [n.p., 1945?] 56 p. illus.
MtHi OrHi **2781**

Einarson, Arthur Skogman, 1897-
The pronghorn antelope and its management. Washington, D. C., Wildlife Management. Institute, 1948. 238 p. illus., maps, tables. Oregon author.
MtBozC WaS **2782**

Eisenlohr, Louis Henry, 1859-
Memories from Philadelphia to Charlestown, Maryland, via Nome, Alaska, by Louis H. Eisenlohr and Riley Wilson. [Philadelphia, Keystone Pub. Co., c1918] 96 p. illus., ports., facsims.
CVicAr **2783**

El Commando, see no. 8105.

Electric Journal, Seattle, Wash.
Souvenir edition, showing some views of Seattle and of the power plants [of the Puget Sound Traction, Light & Power Co.] Seattle, 1912. 90 p. illus. (v. 2, no. 5, June 1912) WaS **2784**

Eliel, Frank, d. 1936.
Our little old home town, Dillon, Montana. Dillon, Mont., Eliel Bros., 1925. 35 p.
MtHi **2785**

Eliot, Samuel A., see no. 8780.

Eliot, Thomas Lamb.
In memoriam: Mary E. Frazar. [Portland, Or., 1886] 28 p. OrP **2786**

Eliot, W. G., see no. 4874.

Eliot, Willard Ayres.
Birds of the Pacific coast, including a brief account of the distribution and habitat of one hundred and eighteen birds that are more or less common to the Pacific coast states and British Columbia, many of which are found eastward to the Rocky Mountains and beyond, with fifty-six color plates by R. Bruce Horsfall. New York, Putnam, 1923. xvii, 211 p. col. front., col. plates.
Many **2787**

Forest trees of the Pacific coast; including a brief account of the outstanding characters, distribution and habitat of the trees native to Alaska, British Columbia, Washington, and Oregon; most of which are also found in Idaho and northern California and eastward to the western slopes of the Rocky Mountains, by Willard Ayres Eliot assisted by G. B. McLean, illus. principally from original photographs by George C. Stephenson. New York, Putnam, 1938. 565 p. front., illus., plates. Many **2788**
Same. Rev. ed. [1948, c1938] CV OrP **2789**
Pacific coast birds; lectures. [n.p., n.d.] 29 p. WaPS **2790**

Elkington, Joseph, 1859-
The Doukhobors, their history in Russia, their migration to Canada, illus. with numerous photographs of the Doukhobors and their surroundings, with portraits and maps. Philadelphia, Ferris & Leach, 1903. viii, 336 p. front., plates, ports., 2 maps (1 fold.) fold. plan.
CVU OrP WaSp WaT **2791**

Elko, British Columbia, the key to the great Columbia Kootenay Valley. [n.p., n.d.] 1 v. illus. CVicAr **2792**

Elks, Benevolent and Protective Order of.
Elks of Washington, with a short account of the growth of the Benevolent and Protective Order of Elks of the United States of America. Madison, Wis., 1903. 184 p. front., 2 plates, 151 ports.
WaSp **2793**

— — — Seattle Lodge No. 92.
A history of Seattle Lodge No. 92, B. P. O. Elks, published as a souvenir on the dedication of the new building nineteen fourteen. [Seattle, Pioneer Printing Co., 1914] [156] p. illus., ports. WaU **2794**

Ellensburg Dawn.
Historical and descriptive history of the city of Ellensburg, Kittitas County; souvenir edition. [Ellensburg, Wash., 1900] [54] p. illus., plan. (Dec. 28, 1900)
WaU **2795**

Ellice, Edward, see no. 10998.

Elliot, John F., 1840-
Driftwood. 2d ed. Bellingham, Wash., Irish Printing Co., 1924. 80 p. port.
WaU **2796**

Elliott, Edward Charles, 1874-
Expert survey of public school system, Boise, Idaho, by Edward C. Elliott, Charles H. Judd, George D. Strayer. [Boise, Idaho? 1913?] 31 p.
OrPR WaPS **2797**

Elliott, Eugene Clinton, 1912-
A history of variety-vaudeville in Seattle from the beginning to 1914. Seattle, Univ. of Wash., 1944. 83 p. front., plates (Publications in drama, no. 1)
CVicAr WaS WaSp WaT WaTC WaU **2798**

Elliott, Harry S., see no. 10230.

Elliott, Henry Wood, 1846-1930.
An Arctic province, Alaska and the Seal Islands, illus. by many drawings from nature and maps. London, Low, 1886. xv, 473 p. front., illus., 45 plates, ports., 2 maps. CVU WaS WaSp WaU **2799**

Same. New York, Scribner, 1886.
CVU **2800**

Our Arctic province: Alaska and the Seal Islands. New York, Scribner, 1886. xv, 473 p. front., illus., 48 plates, 3 maps. (1 fold.) OrP WaPS WaU **2801**

Same. 1887. CVicAr WaU **2802**

Same. 1897. (Library of contemporary exploration and adventure) CVicAr **2803**

See also nos. 4897-4899.

Elliott, Howard, 1860-1928.

Address delivered at the third National Apple Show, Spokane, Washington, November 14, 1910. [Spokane? 1910?[17 p.
WaU **2804**

Four "ifs"; a talk before the Commercial Club of Lewiston, Idaho, at a dinner given at the Lewis-Clark Hotel, Lewiston, Idaho, Friday, October 19, 1923. [n.p., Northern Pacific Railway, 1923] 18 p. port. WaPS **2805**

The land of fortune; address at National Irrigation Congress, Spokane, Wash., Aug. 11, 1909. St. Paul, McGill-Warner Co. [1909?] 18 p.
OrCS OrU WaPS **2806**

Montana; an address delivered at the Interstate Fair, Bozeman, Mont., September 1, 1910. [St. Paul? 1910] [14] p.
MtU OrU WaPS **2807**

The people and the railroads; official facts concerning the transportation situation in the country in general and in the Northwest in particular. [n.p.] 1907. 28 p. Or OrP **2808**

The relation of the railway to community and statewide advertising; address before the Oregon Development League in annual convention, Salem, Oregon, November 29, 1910. [St. Paul? 1910?] 14 p.
Or OrCS OrP OrU WaPS WaU **2809**

Elliott, Simon G.

Anti-monopoly speech delivered at Knox Butte, Linn County, Oregon; March 11, 1882. Albany, Or., Watts & Godfrey [n.d.] 32 p. OrP **2810**

Report on the preliminary survey of the California and Oregon Railroad by the chief engineer. Boston, Rand [n.d.] 41 p. map. OrHi OrP **2811**

Elliott, Thompson Coit, 1862-1943.

David Thompson, pathfinder, and the Columbia River. Kettle Falls., Wash., Scimitar Press, 1911. 9 p. Many **2812**

Same. Eugene, Or., Koke-Tiffany, 1925. 12 p. front. Wa **2813**

The earliest travellers on the Oregon trail. Portland, Or., Ivy Press, 1912. 16 p. port.
CVU OrHi WaU **2814**

The fur trade in the Columbia River Basin prior to 1811. Portland, Or., Ivy Press, 1915. 16 p. front. Many **2815**

Spokane House. [Spokane, Old National Bank and Union Trust Co., 1930] 14 p. illus. OrHi
OrP WaPS WaSp WaU **2816**

Spokane House as it probably appeared in 1810. [Spokane, 1934] 14 p. illus.
WaU **2817**

See also nos. 9490, 10953.

Ellis, Overton Gentry, 1860-

The court's work; address delivered before the Washington State Bar Association at the 26th annual convention at Wenatchee, Wash., Aug. 5 and 6, 1914. Olympia, Wash., Recorder Press, 1915. 8 p.
Wa **2818**

Ellis, Mrs. Salone.

The last wilderness. Boston, Small, Maynard [c1925] 356 p. Novel about Olympic National Forest.
Or WaWaS WaT WaU **2819**

The logger. Boston, Small, Maynard [c1924] 377 p. Or Wa WaA WaS WaT WaTC **2820**

Ellis, T. Mullett.

Tales of the Klondyke. London, Bliss, 1898. 164 p. CVU WaU **2821**

Same. Toronto, Copp Clark Co., 1898.
CVicAr WaS **2822**

Ellis, W., see nos. 1984-1986.

Ellison, Orlo L., see no. 8962.

Ellison, Robert S., see no. 7745.

Ellison, William George Hollingsworth.

The settlers of Vancouver Island; a story for emigrants. [London, Chilver, n.d.] 154 p. front., plate.
CV CVic CVicAr WaU **2823**

Same. [1908?] WaS **2824**

Ells, Sydney ●Clarke, 1879-

Northland trails, illus. by the author. [n.p., 1938?] 189 p. illus. CVicAr CVU **2825**

Ellsberg, Edward, 1891-

Hell on ice; the saga of the "Jeannette." New York, Dodd, 1938. x, 421 p. 1 illus., map., Personal narrative of G. W. Melville, chief engineer of expedition.
Many **2826**

Elmendorf, Mrs. Mary (Johnson).

Two wives and other narrative poems. Caldwell, Idaho, Caxton, 1935. 153 p.
Many **2827**

See also no. 10748.

Elmore, C. D.

The gravel pirate; historical, instructive, humorous and pathetic, the only real book ever written and published exclusively by home talent in Tacoma. Tacoma, Western Blank Book Co., 1911. 123 p. front. (port.) illus. Wa WaTC **2828**

Elrod, Morton John, 1863-

The butterflies of Montana, with keys for determination of species, by Morton John Elrod assisted by Frances Inez Maley; a nature study bulletin for the use of teachers, students and others who wish to study the butterflies; with one col. plate, twelve plates in black and white, and one hundred and twenty five figures. Missoula, Mont., Univ. of Mont., 1906. xvi, 174 p. illus., 12 plates, map, (Bulletin no. 30. Biological series no. 10)
Many **2829**

Elrod's guide and book of information of Glacier National Park, approved by the National Park Service. over 100 illus. and maps. Missoula, Mont. [c1924] 208 p. illus., maps (1fold.) MtHi MtU Or **2830**

Same. 2d ed. [c1930] 258 p. illus., maps.
MtBozC **2831**

Pictured rocks; Indian writings on the rock cliffs of Flathead Lake, Montana. Missoula, Mont., Univ. of Mont., 1908. 10 p. illus., plates, maps. (Bulletin no. 46. Biological series no. 14) Many **2832**

Vacation in Montana. Bloomington, Ill., Univ. Press, 1899. 12 p. illus. OrU **2833**
See also no. 9448.

Elsensohn, Alfreda, Sister, 1897-
Pioneer days in Idaho County. Caldwell, Idaho, Caxton, 1947. 512 p. plates, ports., map. Many **2834**

Elvin, Charles A., see no. 11155.

Elwell, E. H.
Proceedings of the railroad convention at Portland, Oct. 14, 1852. Portland, Or., Harmon & Williams, 1852. 16 p.
CVicAr **2835**

Ely, H. Ashley.
Bear Gap cranberries. Portland, Or., Bear Gap Cranberry Co., 1917. 86 p. illus., map, tables. OrP **2836**

Emberson, Alfred.
All about Victoria, British Columbia, pen and ink sketches by M. Emberson. [Victoria, B. C.] Victoria Printing and Pub. Co., 1916. 104 p. plates.
CV CVicAr CVU WaU **2837**

Emblem Club, Bend, Or.
Seattle contrasts; dedicated to the Seattle Ad Club. Bend, Or. [191-?] [24] p. of views. Each page contains 2 pictures of same section of city taken at intervals of from 2 to 28 years.
WaPS WaS WaU **2838**

[Emergency Conservation Committee, New York]
The proposed Olympic National Park. New York, 1934. 16 p. illus., map.
MtBozC Or WaS WaU **2839**

Protect the Roosevelt elk. New York, 1938. 8 p. illus., map. (Publication no. 69)
WaPS WaU **2840**

Emerson, Charles Leon, 1901-
This is Oregon. Portland, Or., Geographers, Inc. 1936. 207 p. illus. Many **2841**

Emerson, George H.
Building a modern city. [Seattle, 1907] [6] p. Read before the stockholders of the Metropolitan Building Co. in Seattle, Oct. 14, 1907. WaU **2842**

Emerson, Willis George, 1856-
The builders. Chicago, Forbes & Co., 1906. 361 p. Novel of mining in northern Idaho. IdIf **2843**

The Emerson Co., New York.
City of Seattle; report on library department. New York [1912] 24 p. WaT **2844**

Efficiency reports on the city of Seattle. Seattle [1913?] 2 v. WaS **2845**

Emery, George Davis, 1856-
The miners manual; a hand-book of the law of mines and mining. Everett, Wash. [Herald Pub. Co., c1905] 284 p.
WaU **2846**

Emery, James Augustin, 1876-
Mutual interests of employer and employee; the value and need of organization and cooperation; an address delivered before the business men of Seattle, August 12, 1915. [Seattle, Mechanics Pub. Co., 1915?] [13] p. WaU **2847**

Emery, Russell Guy, 1908-
Adventure north, illus. by Manning de V. Lee. Philadelphia, Macrae, Smith Co. [1947] 246 p. illus.
Or Orp Wa WaS WaSp WaU **2848**

The emigrant soldiers' gazette and Cape Horn chronicle, published originally on manuscript forms kindly furnished by Captain W. D. Marsh, R. E., during the voyage from Gravesend to Vancouver Island of the detachment of Royal Engineers selected for service in British Columbia between the 10th October, 1858 and 12th April, 1859, ed. by C. Sinnett, R. E., assisted by Lieut. H. S. Palmer, R. E., with addenda by Lieut.-Colonel R. Wolfenden, 1907. [Victoria, B. C.] Printed by Howard Wolfenden, 1907. [83] p. col.front., plates, ports., fold. map. (No. 1-17, Nov. 6, 1858 — Apr. 2, 1859)
CVU WaU **2849**

Emmerson, John.
British Columbia and Vancouver Island; voyages, travels & adventures. Durham, Printed and pub. for the author by W. Ainsley, 1865. 154 p. CVicAr CVU **2850**

Emmons, Della Florence (Gould)
Old Fort Nisqually lives again; Point Defiance Park, Tacoma. [Tacoma, Fort Nisqually Restoration Council, c1946] [12] p. illus. Wa WaS WaT **2851**

Sacajawea of the Shoshones. Portland, Or., Binfords & Mort [c1943] 316 p.
Many **2852**

Emmons, George Thornton.
The Emmons journal. Eugene, Or., Koke-Tiffany Co. [n.d.] 11 p. illus., diagr.
WaU **2853**

Jade in British Columbia and Alaska and its use by the natives. New York, Museum of the American Indian, Heye Foundation, 1923. 53 p. illus., 35 plates (part col.) (Indian notes and monographs, Miscellaneous no. 35) Many **2854**

Slate mirrors of the Tsimshien. New York, Museum of the American Indian, Heye Foundation, 1921. 21 p. front., illus., 4 plates. (Indian notes and monographs)
Many **2855**

The Tahlton Indians, illus. by specimens in the George G. Heye collection. Philadelphina, Pa. Univ. Museum, 1911. 120 p. illus., 19 plates, map. (Anthropological publications, v. 4, no. 1)
CVicAr CVU WaS WaU **2856**

The whale house of the Chilkat. New York, American Museum of Natural History, 1916. 33 p. illus., plates, (4 col.) (Anthropological papers, v. 19, pt. 1)
CVicAr OrU WaU **2857**

The Empress Hotel, Victoria, British Columbia. [n.p., n.d.] 40 p. illus.
CVicAr **2858**

Encyclopedia of northwest biography, Winfield Scott Downs, editor, assisted by a notable advisory board. New York, American Historical Co., 1941. 515 p. front., plate, ports. **Many 2859**

Same. 1942. 475 p. **OrHi 2859A**

Same. 1943. 299 p.
Or OrCS OrHi OrP Wa WaT **2860**

Enders-Schichanowsky, Augusta.
Im Wunderland Alaska; Erlebnisse und Eindrucke einer deutschen Frau in der Arktis. Leipzig, Dieterich, 1926. 208 p. front. (port.) 7 plates, 2 maps.
WaS WaU **2861**

Endicott, Wendell, 1880-
Adventures in Alaska and along the trail, with one hundred fifty-eight illus. from photographs. New York, Stokes, 1928. xvi, 344 p. front., illus., plates.
CV CVicAr CVU OrSa WaS WaU **2862**

Engelhardt, Lisa von, see no. 10615.

Engle, Nathanael Howard, 1893- ed.
Marketing in the West, sponsored by Pacific Advertising Association. New York, Ronald Press Co. [1946] xii, 263 p. illus., map, diagrs. **Many 2863**

Englebert, Renny.
This is Vancouver Island. Victoria, B. C., Diggon-Hibben [c1948] 88 p. illus., map.
CVicAr CVU OrCS **2864**

English, F. J., see no. 323.

Enock, Charles Reginald, 1868-
Farthest west; life and travel in the United States. London, Longmans, 1910. 332 p. front., 31 plates, fold map.
OrU **2865**

Same. New York, Appleton, 1910.
MtU Or OrP WaPS WaS WaU **2866**
Great Pacific coast; twelve thousand miles in the golden West; being an account of life and travel in the western states of North and South America, from California, British Columbia, and Alaska to Mexico, Panama, Peru and Chile; and a study of their physical and political conditions. London, Richards, 1909. xi, 356 p. front., 63 plates. **Many 2867**

Same. New York, Scribner, 1910.
CVicAr CVU WaS WaSp WaU **2868**

Same. 1913. OrCS WaPS **2869**

The Enumclaw Courier-Herald.
Golden anniversary, White River Lumber Co., 1896-1946. Enumclaw, Wash., 1946. [34] p. illus. (no. 46, Aug. 8, 1946)
WaS **2870**

Epitome of parliamentary documents in connection with the North-West Rebellion. 1885. Ottawa, MacLean Roger, 1886. 389 p. **MtHi 2871**

Epler, Franklin, 1888?-1938.
Impatient seas and other poems. [Seattle, Ivy Press, c1937] 176 p. front. (mounted port.) illus. **Many 2872**

Epstein, Beryl (Williams) see no. 1853.

Epstein, Samuel, see no. 1853.

Erdmann, Hugo, 1862-1910.
Alaska; ein Beitrag zur Geschichte nordischer Kolonisation; bericht, dem Herrn Minister der geistlichen, uterrichts—und medizinal-angelegenheiten Erstattet, mit 68 Abbildungen und Kartenskizzen im Text und einer Karte von Alaska. Berlin, D. Reimer (Ernst Vohsen) 1909. xv, 223 p. front., illus., plates, ports., maps (1 fold.) WaPS **2873**

Erickson, Oliver Theodore, 1858-
A campaign story dealing with our water supply and power plant investments. [Seattle, c1931] [19] p. illus.
WaS WaU **2874**

Ernest, Brother, 1897-
Boys of the covered wagons; illus. and jacket by Herbert Heywood. Portland, Or., Binfords & Mort [c1939] 203 p. illus. plates.
OrMonO OrP OrU Wa WaU WaW **2875**

Ernst, Mrs. Alice (Henson)
Backstage in Xanadu, a book of plays, with illus. by Constance Cole. Portland, Or., Binfords & Mort [c1938] 129 p. front., plates.
MtU OrCS OrP OrU Wa **2876**
High country; four plays from the Pacific Northwest, with foreword by Edith J. R. Isaacs, illus. by Constance Cole. Portland, Or., Metropolitan, 1935. xv, 208 p. front., illus. **Many 2877**

Erskine, Mrs. Gladys (Shaw) 1895-
Broncho Charlie; a saga of the saddle; the life story of Broncho Charlie Miller, the last of the pony express riders. New York, Crowell [c1934] xiv, 316 p. front., illus., plates, ports., maps (1 fold.) facsim.
IdB Or Wa WaS WaSp WaU **2878**

Escobosa, Hector.
Seattle story. Seattle, F. McCaffrey, c1918. 135 p. illus. (part col.) **Many 2879**

Eshelman, Albert Daniel.
Picturesque Seattle. Seattle [c1901] 62 p. illus. Poems. WaU **2880**
Seattle. [Seattle, 1900?] 16 p. illus. Views of Seattle. Anon. WaU **2881**

Eshelman, Llewellyn and Co., Seattle, Wash.
Pamphlet descriptive of King County, Washington Territory, showing its wonderful natural resources and commercial advantages, with a short sketch of Seattle, the largest and most flourishing city in the territory: its present and future prospects. Seattle, 1884. 10 p.
WaU **2882**

The Puget Sound catechism; a convenient compendium of useful information respecting Washington Territory and its chief city, Seattle, the commercial metropolis of Washington and future great city of the Northwest; for intending immigrants and investors. Seattle [1888] 32 p. OrU **2883**

Same. Seattle [1891?] 27 p. WaU **2884**
Seattle, Washington, U. S. A. Seattle, 1891. 48 p. illus., maps. WaS **2885**

What Uncle Sam and Aunt Columbia think of their no. 42 state of Washington. Seattle [189-?] 30 p. illus., map.
WaU **2886**

[Espinosa y Tello, Jose] 1763-1815.
Relacion del viage hecho por las goletas

Sutil y Mexicana en el ano de 1792, para reconocer el estrecho de Fuca; con una introduccion en que se da noticia de las expediciones executadas anterior mente por los espanoles en busca del paso del noroeste de la America. De orden del rey. Madrid, Imprenta real, 1802. 2 v. and atlas, 8 plates, 9 maps.
Many **2887**

A Spanish voyage to Vancouver and the north-west coast of America; being the narrative of the voyage made in the year 1792 by the schooners Sutil and Mexicana to explore the Strait of Fuca, trans. from the Spanish with an introd. by Cecil Jane, illus. with a folding map and six illus. London, Argonaut Press, 1930. xiv, 142 p. fold. front., illus., ports., fold. map.
Many **2888**

[**Esquimalt and Nanaimo Railway**]
Rules and regulations for the guidance of employees. [n.p.] 1886. 48 p.
CVicAr **2889**

The timber, agricultural and industrial resources of Vancouver Island. Manchester, McGeoch [n.d.] 47 p. illus.
CVicAr **2890**

Vancouver Island. [n.p., 1896?] 24 p. illus., maps (2 fold.) tables. CVicAr **2891**

Esquimalt Naval Club, Esquimalt, B. C.
Rules of the Naval Club, Esquimalt, V. I. Victoria, B. C., Higgins, 1867. 10 p.
CVicAr **2892**

Essig, Edward Oliver, 1884-
Insects of western North America; a manual and textbook for students in colleges and universities and a handbook for county, state and federal entomologists and agriculturists as well as for foresters, farmers, gardeners, travelers, and lovers of nature. New York, Macmillan, c1926. xi, 1035 p. illus. Many **2893**

Estes, George.
The old cedar school. Portland, Or., Luther I. Powell [1922] 44 p. illus.
OrHi OrP WaU **2894**

The rawhide railroad. Canby, Or., Clackamas County News, c1916. 53 p. illus., **port.** Many **2895**

Same. 2d ed. Troutdale, Or. [c1924]
Or WaSp WaWW **2896**

The Roman Katholic Kingdom and the Ku Klux Klan. Troutdale, Or., [1922?] 32 p. OrP **2897**

Same [c1923] WaU **2898**

The stagecoach. Troutdale, Or. [c1925] xvi, 409 p. front. (port.) illus. (1 col.) plates (1 fold., 1 col.) Envelope containing seeds mounted between p. 400 and 401.
Or OrHi OrP WaPS WaSp WaU **2899**

Estes, L. E., see no. 4827.

[**Etches, John Cadman**]
An authentic statement of all the facts relative to Nootka Sound; its discovery, history, settlement, trade and the probable advantages to be derived from it; in an address to the King. London, Debrett, 1790. 26 p.
CVicAr OrP OrU WaU **2900**

Continuation of an authentic statement of all the facts relative to Nootka Sound, its discovery, history, settlement, commerce, and the public advantages to be derived from it, with observations on a libel, which has been traced to a foreign ambassador; in a second letter, by Argonaut. London, W. S. Fores, 1790. 34 p.
CVicAr **2901**

Eugene Daily News, Eugene, Or.
Oregon Trail Pageant edition, Eugene, Or., 1941. 6 sections in 1. illus., ports. (v. 20, no. 84, July 20, 1941) CVicAr Or **2902**

Eugene Library Association, Eugene, Or.
Constitution and by-laws of the Eugene Library Association, organized Feb. 18, 1874. Eugene City, Or., 1874. 18 p.
OrU **2903**

The Eugene News, Eugene, Or.
Oregon Trail edition, Eugene, Or., 1937. [36] p. illus., ports., map. (v. 13, no. 63, July 18, 1937) WaU **2904**

[**Eugene Register**] Eugene, Or.
Lane County, the head of Willamette Valley, the most beautiful spot in all Oregon. [Eugene, Or., 1902?] 30 p. illus.
OrP OrU **2905**

Eugene Register-Guard, Eugene, Or.
Oregon Trail edition. Eugene, Or., 1937. [30] p. illus. (part col.) (v. 93, no. 18, July 18, 1937] OrP OrU **2906**

Oregon Trail Pageant edition, Eugene, Or., 1941. 3 sections in 1. illus., ports. (v. 98, no. 200, July 20, 1941) CVicAr **2907**

European and Oregon Land Company, San Francisco, Calif.
Eisenbahn-landereien im westlichen Oregon werden zu billigen Preisen und liberalen Bedingungen verkauft; ausserordentliche vortheile fur Emigranten. San Franscico, Bosqui, 1872. 34 p. fold. map.
Or **2908**

Railroad lands in western Oregon for sale at low rates and liberal terms; extraordinary inducements to emigrants. San Francisco, Bosqui, 1872. 32 p. fold. map.
Or WaSp WaU **2909**

Euwer, Anthony Henderson, 1877-
By scarlet torch and blade. Rhymes of our valley and other poems, with illus. by the author. Portland, Or., Metropolitan, 1935 [c1923] 194 p. col. front., plates. Hood River author.
Or OrP WaPS WaU **2910**

The friendly firs, illus. by the author. Portland, Or., Metropolitan, 1931. 136 p. front., plates. Poems. Many **2911**

The limeratomy; a compendium of universal knowledge for the more perfect understanding of the human machine, done in the limerick tongue and copiously visualized with illustragraphs by the perpetrator. New York, J. B. Pond, 1917. 96 p. front., illus.
Or OrCS OrP OrU WaPS **2912**

Rhymes of our valley. New York, J. B. Pond, 1916. 95 p. front. Hood River Valley. Or OrCS OrU **2913**

Same. 1917 [c1916].
IdP IdU OrSaW WaT WaTC WaU **2914**

Evalenko, Alexander M.
The message of the Doukhobors; a statement of true facts by "Christians of the Universal Brotherhood" and by prominent champions of their cause. New York, International Library Pub. Co., 1913. 146 p. illus.
CV CVicAr CVU WaPS 2915

Evans, Allen Roy.
Meat; a tale of the reindeer trek, 1929-1935. London, Hurst [n.d.] 288 p. front., plates, map.   CVU 2916
Reindeer trek. New York, Coward-McCann, Inc. [1935] 269 p.
IdB Or OrCS OrP WaS WaSp 2917

[Evans, C. H.]
Chilliwack pioneer ladies, by One of the Old Boys. [Chilliwack, B. C., Chilliwack Progress, n.d.] 27 p.   CVicAr 2918

Evans, Sir Edward Ratcliffe Garth Russell, 1881-
British polar explorers, with 8 plates in colour and 19 illus. in black and white. London, Collins, 1943. 47 p. illus., ports. (part col.) col. plates. (Britain in pictures)   CVicPr WaSp 2919

Evans, Elwood, 1828-1898.
Annual address before the Western Washington Industrial Association, and its fourth annual exhibition, held in Olympia, Washington Territory, Friday, October 9, 1874. Olympia, W. T., R. H. Hewitt, Printer, 1875. 32 p.   WaU 2920
History of the Pacific Northwest: Oregon and Washington, embracing an account of the original discoveries on the Pacific coast of North America, and a description of the conquest, settlement and subjugation of the vast country included in the original Territory of Oregon, also interesting biographies of the earliest settlers and more prominent men and women of the Pacific Northwest, including a statistical and graphic description of the soil, climate, productions, industries, improvements and occupations, as well as the natural advantages and resources and artificial acquirements of the great states of Oregon and Washington. Portland, Or., North Pacific History Co. [c1889] 2 v. plates (part fold.) ports., facsims. Anon.   Many 2921
Memoir of Tyrus Himes, born at Troy, Bradford County, Pennsylvania, April 14, 1818, died on his farm, five miles east of Olympia, Washington Territory, April 24, 1879. [n.p., 1879?] 15 p. Anon.
Or 2922
Oration, Portland, Or., July 4, 1865. [Portland, Or., 1865?] 16 p.
OrHi WaS WaU 2923
Puget Sound, its past, present and future. [n.p., n.d.] 16 p. Anon.
CVicAr Wa WaU WaWW 2924
Puget Sound; its past, present and future; an address delivered at Port Townsend, Washington Territory, January 5, 1869 for the benefit of the hall fund for the Good Templars. Olympia, W. T., 1869. 16 p.
CVicAr OrHi Wa WaU WaWW 2925

Puyallup Indian Reservation; address delivered before the Tacoma Chamber of Commerce, May 17, 1892. [Tacoma, 1892] 14 p.   OrHi WaS WaU 2926
The re-annexation of British Columbia to the United States, right, proper and desirable; an address delivered before the Tacoma Library Association, Olympia, W. T., January 18, 1870. [n.p., 1870] 24 p.
CVicAr OrHi WaU 2927
Same. [Victoria, B. C., 1932] 61 p.
CVU 2928
State of Washington; a brief history of the discovery, settlement and organization of Washington, the evergreen state. [Tacoma, World's Fair Commission of the State of Wash., 1893] 224 p. illus. Anon.   Many 2929
Washington Territory; her past, her present, and the elements of wealth which ensure her future; address delivered at the Centennial Exposition, Philadelphia, Sept. 2, 1876, and in joint convention of the Legislature of Washington Territory, Oct. 13, 1877. Olympia, Wash., Bagley, 1877. 51 p.   Many 2930
See also nos. 1968, 1969.

Evans, Evan, pseud.
Montana rides. New York, Penguin Books [1946, c1933] 220 p.   WaU 2931

Evans, Lewis O., 1871-
Address of L. O. Evans, chief counsel of the Anaconda Copper Mining Company, before the Chamber of Commerce at Missoula, Montana, Wednesday, August 29, 1917. [n.p., n.d.] 31 p. plate.
MtU 2932

Evarts, Hal George, 1887-
Fur brigade, a story of the trappers of the early West. Boston, Little, 1928. 279 p.
Many 2933
Same. New York, Burt [c1928] WaSp 2934
The moccasin telegraph. Boston, Little, 1928. 275 p.   WaU 2935

Evening Capital News, Boise, Idaho.
The marvelous Snake River Valley. [Boise, Idaho, 1906] 62 p. illus., ports. (Annual mid-winter no., Feb. 6, 1906. WaU 2936

Everett, T. Thomson, ed.
Victoria illustrated; a brief history of Victoria from 1842. Toronto, Victoria Pub. Co, 1892. 32 p. illus.   CVicAr 2937

Everett, Wash. First National Bank.
The first fifty years. [Everett, Wash., 1942] [16] p. illus.   WaE 2938
Thirty-three years of progress, 1892-1925. Everett, Wash., 1925. 20 p. illus.
WaE 2939

The Everett Daily Herald, Everett, Wash.
Diamond jubilee edition. Everett, Wash., 1936. 56 p. illus. (Jan. 14, 1936). Seventy-fifth anniversary of founding of Snohomish County.   WaE WaS 2940
Everett's 21st anniversary, 1892-1913; progress edition. [Everett, Wash., 1913] [36] p. illus., ports. (Mar. 20, 1913)
WaU 2941
Snohomish, "the garden city of Puget Sound", her resources, industries, home

attractions, climate and scenery. Everett, Wash., 1901. 16 p. illus., map. (Supplement to July 27, 1901 ed.) WaU **2942**
Special pictorial ed. for investors and homeseekers. [Everett, Wash., 1906] 32 p. illus., ports. (June 30, 1906)
WaU **2943**

The evergreen playground of Oregon, Washington, and British Columbia. [n.p., 193—?] [22] p. illus., map.
WaPS WaT **2944**

Evergreen playground of Oregon, Washington, and British Columbia; a glimpse and guide into the freshest spot on earth. [n.p., 193—?] [14] p. illus., map.
WaPS **2945**

Everitt, Nicholas.
Round the world in strange company: America, British Columbia and the West. London, T. W. Laurie [1915] 283 p. front., plates. CVU **2946**

Everts, Henry H.
The Oregon almanac for the year of our Lord and Savior Jesus Christ, 1848; being bisextile leap year and until July 4th the 72nd year of the independence of the United States, calculated for Oregon City in equal or clock time. Oregon City, Or., Printed at the Spectator Office by W. P. Hudson [1848] 24 p. table. OrHi OrP **2947**
Same. Photostat copy. Or **2948**

Ewan, Joseph, see no. 417.

Ewart, Jessie.
The geology of the Princeton dstrict; a paper read to the Similkameen Historical Association 28 April, 1933. [n.p.] Similkameen Historical Assn., 1933. [4] p. CVicAr **2949**

The Excalibur, diamond jubilee number, 1864-1939, St. Ann's School for Boys, Duncan, B. C. [n.p.] 1939. 1 v. illus.
CVicAr **2950**

Extent and value of the possessory rights of the Hudson's Bay Company in Oregon, south of forty-ninth degree. Montreal, Lovell [n.d.] 51 p. CVicAr **2951**

Eyre, Alice.
The famous Fremonts and their America. [Santa Ana, Calif.] Fine Arts Press, 1948. 374 p. front. (port.) 9 plates, 12 ports., 6 maps (part double) 2 facsims.
CVicAr OrHi **2952**

F., V. W.
Vancouver through the eyes of a hobo. Vancouver, B. C., 1934. 63 p. illus. (port.)
CV CVicAr **2953**

Facsimile of the Chinook jargon as used by the Hudson's Bay Company and all the Indian tribes and early settlers of the Pacific Northwest, comp. by an old employee formerly of the Hudson's Bay Company. [n.p., n.d.] 6 p. OrHi WaWW **2954**

Facts and figures about Lane County, Oregon; the new railroad center of the Northwest. [Eugene, Or., n.d.] 31 p.
OrP **2955**

Facts for the people of Portland relating to the levee case. Portland, Or., 1860. 15 p.
OrHi **2956**

Fadden, H. D., ed.
Port of Seattle victory book 1944. Seattle [n.d.] 95 p. illus., 2 maps, tables.
WaE **2957**

Fagan, David D.
History of Benton County, Oregon. Portland, Or., Walling, 1885. 532 p. plates.
Many **2958**

Fair Hesperides, Wenatchee, Wash.
Premium list of the first Fair Hesperides to be held at Wenatchee, October 21, 22, 23, 24 and 25, 1913. [Wenatchee?] Republic Printing, 1913. 36 p. WaU **2959**

Fair Tariff League.
Farmers' tariff studies; what the tariff does to Washington, Oregon, and Idaho. New York, 1924. 31 p. tables. OrP **2960**

Fairbairn, Archibald Macdonald Duff.
Plays of the Pacific coast: Ebb-tide, The tragedy of Tanoo, A Pacific coast tragedy, The war drums of Skedans. New York, French, c1935. 111 p. diagrs.
CVicAr Wa WaW **2961**

Fairbanks, Harold Wellman, 1860-
The western United States; a geographical reader. Boston, Heath, 1904. 302 p. front., illus., maps. Many **2962**

Fairbanks Daily News Miner, Fairbanks, Alaska.
Goldfields edition. [Fairbanks, Alaska, Tanana Pub. Co., 1937] [64] p. illus., ports., tables. (Nov. 29, 1937)
WaU **2963**
The low-down truth of Alaska; constituting the 1923 annual of the Fairbanks Daily News-Miner. Fairbanks, Alaska [Tanana Pub. Co.] 1923. 48 p. illus., port., map. WaS WaU **2964**

Fairbanks Times.
Industrial edition. Fairbanks, Alaska, 1910. 28 p. illus. (Supplement to Sunday Times, Apr. 3, 1910) WaS **2965**

Fairford, Ford.
British Columbia, with an introd. by the Hon. J. H. Turner. London, Sir I. Pitman & Sons, 1914. xiii, 137 p. front., illus., fold. map.
CV CVicAr CVU WaU **2966**

Fairhaven illustrated; containing a general review of the state of Washington and a compilation of the resources, terminal advantages, general industries and climate of the "Focal city" and the country tributary to it. Chicago, Baldwin, c1890. [60] p. front., illus. WaU **2967**

Les faits relatifs a l'administration des affaires des sauvages du Nord-Ouest. [n.p., n.d.] 77 p. CVicAr **2968**

Falconer, Thomas, 1805-1882.
The Oregon Question; or. A statement of the British claims to the Oregon Territory, in opposition to the pretensions of the government of the United States of America. 1st ed. London, Clarke, 1845. 46 p. CVicAr OrHi OrP WaS WaU **2969**
Same. 2d ed. 50 p. Many **2970**

Same. 47, 7, 12 p. "Postcript to the 2d ed., May 28, 1845." 4 p. "Second postcript to a pamphlet, Aug. 7, 1845." 12 p.
Or WaWW **2971**

Same. New York, Taylor, 1845. 40 p.
OrHi **2972**

See also no. 3839.

Family Society of Seattle.
A guide to personal counsel. [Seattle, n.d.] 15 p.   WaS **2973**

Far North-West; being the record, with pictures, of a journey over the Canadian Pacific to Alaska, to California, to the Yellowstone, and home by the Northern Pacific. Newark, N. J., 1906. 40 p. 63 plates, map. Record of a librarian's trip to the A. L. A. meeting at Portland, Or., 1905.
CVicAr OrHi OrP WaS WaU **2974**

Fargo, Idaruth (Scofield) 1870-
Brown leaves burning. Dallas, Tex., Mathis, Van Nort & Co. [c1942] 101 p. Poems by an Or. author.   Many **2975**

Fargo, Lucile Foster, 1880-
Come, colors, come. [New York] Dodd [c1940] xvi, 283 p. front., illus., plates. Couer d'Alene mines story.
Or OrP WaS WaT WaU **2976**

Faries, Hugh, see no. 3477.

Faris, John Thomson, 1871-
The Alaskan pathfinder; the story of Sheldon Jackson for boys. New York, H. Revell Co. [c1913] 221 p. front. (port.) plates.   Or WaSp WaU **2977**

Same. With introd. by John A. Marquis. [c1926]   WaS WaU **2978**

On the trail of the pioneers; romance, tragedy and triumph of the path of empire, New York, Doran [c1920] 319 p. col. front., plates, port., maps.
Many **2979**

Seeing the far West. Philadelphia, Lippincott. 1920. 303 p. front., 112 plates, 2 maps.   Many **2980**

Winning the Oregon country. New York, Eaton & Mains [c1911] x, 241 p. front., 15 plates, 7 ports., map, facsim.
OrHi OrSa WaSp WaU **2981**

Same. New York, Literature Dept., Presbyterian Home Missions [c1911]
Many **2982**

Same. New York, Missionary Education Movement of the U. S. and Canada, 1911.   CVicAr Wa WaT **2983**

Same. Philadelphia, Westminster Press. 1922.   IdUSB **2984**

Faris, Paul Patton, ed.
The Whitmans and Spaldings; four pioneers of 1836; their lives and achievements; why America in 1936 celebrates their fame. Philadelphia, General Assembly's Publicity Dept., Presbyterian Church in the U. S. A., 1936. 8 p.
WaPS **2985**

Farley, Andrew George, 1875-
The advocate. [Pomeroy, Wash., East Washingtonian, c1938] 90 p. ports.
WaU **2986**

Farm Journal.
Idaho county basic data. Philadelphia [1945] 44 p.   OrHi **2986a**

Montana county basic data. Philadelphia [1945] 56 p.   OrHi **2986b**

Oregon county basic data, comp. and pub. by Market Research Department. Philadelphia [1945] [38] p.
OrCS OrHi OrU **2987**

Washington county basic data. Philadelphia [1946?] 39 p.   OrHi WaS **2988**

Farmers' Union. Washington-Idaho Division.
The Farmers' Union, Washington-Idaho Division: history, aims and purposes; what it is and what it is doing. [n.p., n.d.] 16 p.   WaU **2989**

Farming and ranching in the Canadian North-West. [n.p., 1888] 56 p. illus., 2 fold. maps.   CVicAr **2990**

Farnham, Mary Frances.
Catalogue of rare books from the library of Pacific University, exhibited at the Lewis and Clark fair, 1905. [n.p., n.d.] 23 p. illus., port.   Many **2991**

Farnham, Thomas Jefferson, 1804-1848.
History of Oregon Territory; it being a demonstration of the title of these United States of North America to the same. New York, Winchester, 1844. 80 p. front. (map)   Many **2992**

Same. 2d ed. New York, Taylor [c1844]
OrU **2993**

Same. 1845. 83 p.   OrP **2994**

Life, adventures, and travels in California, to which are added the conquest of California, travels in Oregon, and history of the gold regions. New York, Nafis, 1849. 468 p. 44 plates, 7 ports.   CVicAr
Wa WaSp WaU WaW WaWW **2995**

Same. Pictorial ed. 1850. 514 p.
CVicAr OrSaW OrU WaT **2996**

Same. 2d ed. New York, Cornish, Lamport & Co., 1852.   Or OrHi **2997**

Same. New York, Sheldon, Lamport, and Blakeman, 1855. 468 p.
OrP WaT WaU **2998**

Travels in the great western prairies, the Anahuac and Rocky Mountains, and in the Oregon Territory. Poughkeepsie, N. Y., Killey, 1841, 197 p. MtBozC Wa **2999**

Same. 1843. 199 p.   CVicAr **3000**

Same. New York, Greeley, 1843.
Many **3001**

Same. New York, Wiley, 1843.
CVicAr OrHi OrP WaT **3002**

Same. London, Bentley, 1843. 2 v.
CVicAr WaS WaSp WaU **3003**

Same. [And] Oregon missions and travels over the Rocky Mountains in 1845-46, by P. J. de Smet, ed. with notes, introd., index, by R. G. Thwaites. Cleveland, Clark, 1906. 2 v. illus. WaSp WaU **3004**

Wanderungen uber die Felsengebirge in das Oregon-Gebiet, aus dem Englischen von Fr. Gerstacker. Leipzig, Mayer, 1846. viii, 310 p.   CVicAr OrP OrU WaU **3005**

Farnsworth, E. L.
The development of financial institutions;

address delivered at the 6th annual Pacific States Savings and Loan Conference held at Portland, Or., Aug. 29, 30, and 31, 1927. [Portland, Or.? 1927] 11 p.
WaU 3006

Farquhar, Francis Peloubet, 1887-
A brief chronology of discovery in the Pacific Ocean from Balboa to Capt. Cook's first voyage, 1513-1770. San Francisco [Grabhorn Press] 1943. 14 p. illus.
OrHi WaU 3007

A list of publications relating to the mountains of Alaska, by Francis P. Farquhar and Mildred P. Ashley. New York, American Alpine Club, 1934. 37 p. CVU 3008

Farrand, Livingston, see no. 899.

Farrar, Frederic W.
The Arctic regions and the hopes of discovering the lost adventurers; a poem which obtained the Chancellor's medal at the Cambridge commencement, 1852. [n.p., n.d.] 12 p. CVicAr 3009

Farrar, Victor John, 1886-
The annexation of Russian America to the United States. Washington, D. C., W. F. Roberts, 1937. [viii] 142 p.
Many 3010

An elementary syllabus of Alaskan history. [Seattle? 1924] 19 p.
Wa WaS WaU 3011

The purchase of Alaska. Washington, D. C., 1934. 50 p. OrCS WaS 3012

Same. Washington, D. C., W. F. Roberts, 1935. 118 p. MtU WaU 3013

See also nos. 1967-1969.

Farrell, John D.
Is the Lake Washington canal a general necessity at this time; what will be the cost to the taxpayers of King County? What is their ability to bear the burden which will be imposed? [n.p., 1909?] [16] p. fold. map. WaS WaT 3014

Farrelly, Philip J., see nos. 1153, 1154.

Father Herman. [n.p., n.d.]
12 p. port. Russian missionary to Alaska.
WaU 3015

Faubion, Nina (Lane)
Some edible mushrooms and how to know them, illus. by the author. Portland, Or., Binfords & Mort [c1938] 127 p. illus.
Many 3016

Faulk, Theodore E., see no. 2203.

Faville, David E., see no. 7769.

Favour, Alpheus Hoyt, 1880-
Old Bill Williams, mountain man. Chapel Hill, N. C., Univ. of N. C. [c1936] 229 p. col. front., plates, ports., fold. map, facsims, geneal. tables.
OrHi OrP WaS WaU 3017

Fawcett, Edgar, 1847-1904.
Reminiscences of Bishop Cridge. [n.p., n.d.] 46 p. CVicAr 3018

Some reminiscences of old Victoria. Toronto, Briggs, 1912. 294 p. front., 19 plates. Many 3019

Feary, Amelia Ann.
Origin and development of family social work in Portland, Oregon. [n.p.] 1936. iii, 217 p. (Univ. of Or. thesis)
OrP OrU 3020

Federal Council of the Churches of Christ in America. Research and Education Department.
The Centralia case; a joint report on the Armistice Day tragedy at Centralia, Washington, November 11, 1919; issued by the Department of Research and Education of the Federal Council of the Churches of Christ in America, the Social Action Department of the National Catholic Welfare Conference, and the Social Justice Commission of the Central Conference of American Rabbis. [Brooklyn, Brooklyn Eagle] 1930. 48 p.
Or OrU WaS WaSp WaTC WaU 3021

Federal Reserve Bank of Minneapolis. Helena Branch.
Your banks; historical sketches of Montana banks and bankers. Helena, Mont., 1946. 157 p. illus., ports.
MtHi WaS 3022

Federated East Side Clubs, Mercer Island, Washington.
A modern marvel; the world's largest floating concrete bridge, gateway to the east Lake Washington District. [Seattle?] 1939. [16] p. illus., ports.
WaS WaU 3023

Fedix, P. A.
Notice sur l'Oregon. [n.p., n.d.] [22] p.
CVicAr 3024

L'Oregon et les cotes de l'ocean Pacifique du nord, apercu geographique, statistique, et politique. Paris, Amyot, 1846. 258 p. map. CVicAr
OrHi OrP WaS WaSp WaU 3025

Fee, Chester Anders.
Chief Joseph; the biography of a great Indian; with a foreword by Colonel Charles Erskine Scott Wood. New York, Wilson-Erickson, c1936. xiii, 346 p. front., plates, port., maps. Many 3026

Rimes o' Round-up. Portland, Or., Metropolitan, 1935. 78 p.
Or OrLge OrP OrU Wa WaU 3027

Fell, Sarah.
Threads of Alaskan gold. [n.p., n.d.] 35 p. illus., plates, port. Photostat copy.
WaU 3028

Felton, Harold W., 1902- ed.
Legends of Paul Bunyan, illus. by Richard Bennett. New York, Knopf, 1947. xxi, 418 p. illus. (part col.) Many 3029

Fenneman, Nevin Melancthon, 1865-
Physiography of western United States. New York, McGraw, 1931. 534 p. illus., maps (1 fold. in pocket) diagrs.
Many 3030

Fenton, Carroll Lane, see no. 7984.

Fenton, Mary M.
The state of Washington; supplement to "New geography, book two," of the Frye-Atwood geographical series. Boston, Ginn [c1921] 20 p. illus., double map.
Wa WaU 3031

Fenton, William David, 1853-1925.
"A tale that is told"—"A twice told tale";
a "public service commission." [n.p.,
1916?] 100 p.   OrP **3032**

Same. 2d ed. [Portland, Or., Glass & Prudhomme 1917]   Or OrP **3033**
See also no. 11245.

Ferber, Edna, 1887-
Great son. Garden City, N. Y., Doubleday,
1945. 281 p. Seattle novel.   Many **3034**

Same. 254 p.   IdU MtBozC
                    MtU OrU WaPS WaWW **3055**

Ferbrache, James G.
A legend of the Kootenai trail. Spokane,
Art Printing Co., 1921. 115 p. illus. Poem.
                    WaSp **3036**

Trapper's tales. Spokane, Art Printing Co.,
1921. 96 p.   WaSp **3037**

Ferguson, C. F., see no. 8782.

[Ferguson, John H.] comp.
Wealth and opportunity on the Pacific
coast. Reading, England, Nicholas' Foreign Estates [1913] 72 p. plates, 2 fold.
maps.   WaU **3038**

Fern Hill Historical Society, Tacoma, Wash.
Fern Hill, the village where memories
linger. Tacoma, 1941. 21 p. illus.
                    Wa WaT WaU **3039**

Pierce County census 1854 and 1860. Tacoma, 1941. [19] p.
                    WaS WaSp WaT WaU **3040**

The story of a road; Byrd's Mill Road.
[Tacoma, 1939] 6 p. map.
                    WaS WaT WaU **3041**

Fernie Free Press, Fernie, B. C.
Fernie, B. C., from 1897 to 1903. Fernie,
B. C., 1902. 1 v. illus., ports.
                    CVicAr **3042**

Ferrer Maldonado, Lorenzo, d. 1625.
Viaggio dal mare Atlantico al Pacifico
per la via del Nordouest fatto dal capitano Lorenzo Ferrer Maldonado l'anno
MDLXXXVIII; tradotto da un mano-
scritto Spagnuolo inedito della Biblio-
teca Ambrosiana di Milano da Carlo
Amoretti, 1810. [n.p.] 1810. 72 p. maps.
                    CVicAr **3043**

Same. Milano, Silvestri, 1811. 98 p.
                    CVicAr **3044**

Voyage de la mer Atlantique a l'ocean
Pacifique par le Nordouest dans la mer
Glaciale, par le capitaine Laurent Ferrer
Maldonado l'an MDLXXXVIII; traduit
d'un manuscrit espagnol et suivi d'un
discours qui en demontre l'authenticite
et la veracite, par Charles Amoretti.
Plaisance, De l'imprimerie del Majno,
1812. 84 p. 3 fold. plates (2 maps)
                    CVicAr CVU WaU **3045**

Ferry, Elisha P., see no. 5867.

Fetherstonhaugh, Robert Collier, 1892-
The Royal Canadian Mounted Police. New
York, Carrick & Evans [c1938] xii, 322 p.
front., plates, maps (part fold.)
                    Many **3046**

Same. New York, Garden City Pub. Co.
[1940] xii, 294 p. plates, maps (part double)   CVU Wa **3047**

**A few words on the Hudsons's Bay Com-
pany.** [London? Montgomery, Printer,
1846?] 24 p. Contains petition of natives
of Rupert's Land to Her Majesty for
redress of grievances.   CVicAr **3048**

Field, Henry Martyn, 1822-1907.
Our western archipelago. New York,
Scribner, 1895. 250 p. 12 plates.
                    Many **3049**

Same. 1896.   OrHi WaS **3050**

Fielde, Adele Marion, 1839-1916, comp.
Parliamentary procedure, a compendium
of its rules, comp. from the latest and
highest authorities, for the use of students and for the guidance of officers
and members of clubs, societies, boards,
committees, and all deliberative bodies.
Seattle, Helen N. Stevens [1914, c1899]
213 p. Seattle author.
                    IdU OrPR WaU **3051**

That billion dollars. Seattle, 1910. 7 p. illus.
                    WaS **3052**

Fielding, Loraine Hornaday.
French heels to spurs, with introd. by
Will James, illus. by Eve Ganson. New
York, Century, c1930. 203 p. illus. Au-
thor's experience on TZ Ranch in Mont.
                    WaS WaT **3053**

Fifth (B. C.) Coast Brigade, R. C. A.
(N. P. A. M.) history and tradition, a
spur to esprit de corps. Victoria, B. C.
[British Colonist] 1940. 22 p.
                    CVicAr **3054**

Filippi, Filippo de, 1869-1938.
The ascent of Mount St Elias [Alaska]
by H. R. H. Prince Luigi Amedeo di
Savoia, duke of the Abruzzi, narrated by
Filippo de Filippi, illus. by Vittorio
Sella and trans. by Signora Linda Villare with the author's supervision. Westminster, Constable, 1900. xiv, 240 p.
front., illus., plate, port., maps.
                    CV CVicAr WaU **3055**

Same. London, Stokes [1899?] 240 p. front.,
illus., 33 plates, ports, 2 fold. maps.,
4 fold. diagrs.
                    CVicAr OrP WaS WaT **3056**

Financial News & Mercantile Review.
Silver supplement, the story of a reviving
British Columbia industry. [Vancouver,
B. C., 1935] 14 p. illus., diagr.
                    WaPS **3057**

Financial Reform Association, Liverpool.
The Hudson's Bay Company versus Magna
Charta and the British people. Liverpool [1857] 36 p. fold. map. (Financial
reform tracts. New series, no. 21)
                    CVicAr OrP WaU **3058**

The Hudson's Bay monopoly. Liverpool
[1858] 32 p. (Financial reform tracts.
New series, no. 24.)   CVicAr **3059**

Finch, John Willington, see no. 178.

Finck, Henry Theophilus, 1854-1926.
Pacific coast scenic tour; from southern
California to Alaska, the Canadian Pa-
cific Railway, Yellowstone Park and the
Grand Canyon. New York, Scribner,
1890. xiv, 309 p. 20 plates, map.
                    Many **3060**

Same. 1891.   WaPS **3061**

Same. London, Low, 1891.
CVicAr CVU WaSp **3062**
Same. New York, Scribner, 1907.
IdB OrCS WaS WaSp **3063**
Finerty, John Frederick, 1846-1908.
War-path and bivouac; or, The conquest of the Sioux; a narrative of stirring personal experiences and adventures in the Big Horn and Yellowstone Expedition of 1876 and in the campaign on the British border in 1879. Chicago, Donohue [c1890] 460 p. CVicAr
MtBozC MtHi WaPS WaSp **3064**
Finke, George, 1869-
Winning the Pacific Northwest. Columbus, Ohio, Book Concern [c1936] 128 p. illus., ports. Many **3065**
Finlay, A. H., see no. 6325.
Finlayson, Roderick, 1818-1892.
Biography of Roderick Finlayson. [Victoria, B. C.? 1891?] 27 p.
CVicAr CVU **3066**
Finley, Irene, see nos. 3069, 3070.
Finley, J. M.
Picturesque Washington [typography and arrangement, Bert L. Swezea; art sketches and research, Byron MacPherson] Seattle, Pioneer Pub. Co., c1945. 44 p. illus., maps. WaS WaT **3067**
Finley, William Lovell, 1876-
Game and fish protection and propagation in Oregon, 1911-1912. Portland, Or., Boyer Pub. Co. [1912] 23 p. illus. OrHi **3068**
Little Bird Blue, by William L. and Irene Finley; with illus. by R. Bruce Horsfall and from photographs. Boston, Houghton, 1915. 60 p. front., illus., plates.
Or OrAshS OrMonO OrP WaS **3069**
Wild animal pets, by William L. and Irene Finley. New York, Scribner, 1928. 311 p. front., plates. Many **3070**
Finney, Frank, see no. 2533.
Finnie, Richard, 1906-
Canada moves north. New York, Macmillan, 1942. 227 p. illus., plates, ports., map. Many **3071**
Same. Rev. ed. 1948. 239 p. WaT **3072**
Canol, the sub-Arctic pipeline and refinery project constructed by Bechtel-Price-Callahan for the Corps of Engineers, United States Army, 1942-1944; text and documentary photographs. San Francisco, Ryder & Ingram, 1945. 210 p. col. front., illus. (part col.) maps.
CVU IdU MtBozC OrCS WaS **3073**
Lure of the North. Philadelphia, David McKay [c1940] 227 p. front., illus., ports.
CVicAr CVU WaS WaSp WaT **3074**
Fireman's Fund Insurance Co.
County atlas of Oregon and Washington, showing all towns, post offices, railroads, county roads, stage lines carrying passengers, mail and express, and distances between points, drawn by Edward E. Eitel. San Francisco, Stanley, c1894. 19 p. maps. Or OrHi **3075**
Firland Sanatorium, Richmond Highlands, Wash.
Firland; a story of Firland Sanitarium.

[Richmond Highlands, Wash., 1933?] 94 p. front., illus. WaU **3076**
Same. [Seattle, 1936?] WaS **3077**
Firman, Sidney G., see no. 6810.
Fischer, Mrs. Augusta Catherine, 1891-1938.
Searchlight; an autobiography. Seattle, 1937. 233 p. plates, ports.
Wa WaS WaU **3078**
Fish, Herbert Clay.
Our state of Washington. New York, Scribner [c1927] 102 p. front., illus., map.
Many **3079**
See also no. 8815.
Fisher, Amy Woodward, 1879-
Colored leaves; a book of ninety sonnets. Caldwell, Idaho, Caxton, 1933. 102 p. Idaho author. IdU WaSp WaU **3080**
The seventh hill; an historical novel in blank verse. illus. by Doris Stenger Roberts. [Caldwell, Idaho, Caxton, c1942] 258 p. illus., plates.
IdB IdU WaSp WaU **3081**
Two stars in a window. Caldwell, Idaho, Caxton, 1946. 79 p. Poems.
IdB WaSp WaU **3082**
[Fisher, Mary] 1888-
The journal of a recluse; trans. from the original French. New York, Crowell, [c1909] xi, 334 p. front. Bellingham author. OrP Wa WaSp **3083**
Same. 7th ed. WaU **3084**
Fisher, Vardis, 1895-
Adam and the serpent. New York, Vanguard [1947] 335 p. Idaho author.
Many **3085**
Same. DeLuxe ed. WaU **3086**
April; a fable of love. Garden City, N. Y., Doubleday, 1937. 206 p. Many **3087**
The Caxton printers in Idaho, a short history. Cincinnati, Society of Bibliographers, 1944. viii, 32 p. front. (port.)
Many **3088**
Children of God; an American epic. New York, Harper, 1939. 769 p. Many **3089**
Same. [c1939] IdIf IdTf WaU **3090**
Same. 13th ed. IdU **3091**
City of illusion, a novel. New York, Harper [c1941] 382 p. Many **3092**
Dark Bridwell. Boston, Houghton, 1931. 376 p. Many **3093**
Darkness and the deep. Caldwell, Idaho, Caxton, 1943. 296 p. DeLuxe ed.
WaU **3094**
Same. New York, Vanguard [1943]
Many **3095**
The divine passion. New York, Vanguard [1948] xi, 373 p. WaU **3096**
Same. DeLuxe ed. WaU **3097**
Forgive us our virtues; a comedy of evasions. Caldwell, Idaho, Caxton, 1938. 347 p. Many **3098**
The golden rooms. New York, Vanguard [c1944] 324 p. Many **3099**
Same. DeLuxe ed. WaU **3100**
In tragic life. Caldwell, Idaho, Caxton, 1932. 464 p. Many **3101**
Same. Garden City, N. Y., Doubleday, 1933. IdUSB WaU **3102**

Intimations of Eve. New York, Vanguard [1946] 331 p. Many **3103**

Same. DeLuxe ed. Caldwell, Idaho, Caxton [c1946] WaU **3104**

The mothers. Caldwell, Idaho, Caxton, 1943. viii, 334 p. DeLuxe ed. WaU **3105**

Same. An American saga of courage. New York, Vanguard [c1943] Many **3106**

The neurotic nightingale. Milwaukee, Wis., Casanova Press [c1935] 71 p.
IdB IdIf MtU WaU **3107**

No villian need be. Caldwell, Idaho, Caxton and Garden City, N. Y., Doubleday, 1936. .387 p. IdB IdU MtU WaTC **3108**

Same. Garden City, N. Y., Doubleday, 1936.
IdIf IdP OrCS WaU **3109**

Odyssey of a hero. Philadelphia, Ritten House, c1937. 21 p. IdB **3110**

Passions spin the plot. Garden City, N. Y., Doubleday, 1934. 428 p. Many **3111**

Sonnets to an imaginary madonna. New York, Vinal, 1927. 47 p. IdB IdIf **3112**

Toilers of the hills. Boston, Houghton, 1928. 361 p.
IdB IdIf IdP IdU MtU WaS **3113**

Same. Caldwell, Idaho, Caxton, 1933 [c1928] 361 p. IdU WaPS WaS WaU **3114**

We are betrayed. Garden City, N. Y., Doubleday, 1935. 369 p. Many **3115**

See also no. 8597.

Fisher, William.
New travels among the Indians of North America; being a compilation, taken partly from the communications already published, of Captains Lewis and Clark to the President of the United States; and partly from other authors who travelled among the various tribes of Indians; containing a variety of very pleasant anecdotes, remarkably calculated to amuse and inform the mind of every curious reader; with a dictionary of the Indian tongue. Philadelphia, Sharan, 1812. 300 p. front., port. Counterfeit pub. WaS WaU **3116**

See also no. 4939.

Fisher's Comic Almanac.
54-40; the whole of Oregon or none. [Philadelphia, Turner & Fisher, 1847] [36] p.
WaU **3117**

Fishing Vessel Owners Association, Seattle, Wash.
A protest against the ratification of the report of the American-Canadian fisheries of the state of Washington. Seattle, 1919. 6 p. fold. map. WaU **3118**

Fisk, James Henry, 1833-
The mineral resources of Oregon, by J. H. Fisk; and Oregon, the sportsman's paradise, by A. E. Gebhardt. [Portland, Or.] Lewis and Clark Centennial Exposition Commission for the State of Or., 1904. 40 p. illus. OrHi WaS **3119**

Fisk & Hatch, New York.
To the bondholders of the Central Pacific Railroad Company, January 1, 1872. [New York, 1872] 25 p. WaU **3120**

Fiske, John, 1842-1901.
Unpublished orations: "The discovery of the Columbia River, and the Whitman controversy"; "The Crispus Attucks memorial"; and "Columbia memorial". Boston, Bibliophile Society, 1909. 118 p. front. (port.) Many **3121**

Fitch, Thomas, 1838-1923.
Address on the life and character of Col. Edward D. Baker. Placerville, Calif., Placerville Republican Office, 1862. 7 p.
OrU **3122**

Fitchett, Carlton, 1886-1946.
Rimes of a reporter, a collection of the best verse of the Northwest's beloved humorist. Seattle, Superior Pub. Co., 1946. 157 p. WaU **3123**

Fitz, Frances Ella.
Lady Sourdough, as told to Jerome Odlum. New York, Macmillan, 1941. 319 p. front., illus., plates, ports., facsim. Many **3124**

Fitzgerald, James Edward.
An examination of the charter and proceedings of the Hudson's Bay Company with reference to the grant of Vancouver's Island. London, Trelawney Saunders, 1849. xv, 293 p. fold. map.
Many **3125**

Vancouver's Island, the Hudson's Bay Company, and the government. London, Simonds, 1848. 30 p. OhHi **3126**

Fitzgerald, La Verne Harriet.
Black Feather, Trapper Jim's fables of Sheepeater Indians in the Yellowstone. Caldwell, Idaho, Caxton, 1933. 193 p. front., illus.
IdIf MtHi Or WaSp WaU **3127**

Same. 1938. IdIf **3128**

Flack, Marjorie, see nos. 6029, 6030.

Flagg, C. E., see no. 1973.

Flagg, Edmund, see nos. 10228, 10229.

[Flahaut, Mrs. Martha (Reekie)]
The wild flowers of Washington. Seattle [1932] 30 p. CVU WaU **3129**

Flaherty, Frances Hubbard,
see nos. 3130, 3131.

Flaherty, Robert Joseph, 1844-
My Eskimo friends; "Nanook of the North", in collaboration with Frances Hubbard Flaherty. Garden City, N. Y., Doubleday, 1924. 170 p. col. front., illus., plates (part col.) ports. (part col.) fold. map. OrHi WaE WaS **3130**

Same. London, Heinemann, 1924.
WaSp **3131**

Flanagan, John T., see no. 9630.

Flandrau, Mrs. Grace C. (Hodgson) 1889-
Astor and the Oregon country. [St. Paul? Great Northern Railroad? n.d.] 48 p. front., illus., ports., map.
IdU MtHi MtU WaPS WaT WaU **3132**

Same. [1926] OhHi **3133**

Same. [1929] Or **3134**

The Columbia River Historical Expedition, 1926. [n.p., Great Northern Railroad, 1926] 23 p. illus. IdU MtU WaU **3135**

Frontier days along the upper Missouri. [St. Paul? n.d.] 40 p. front., illus., ports., map.
IdU MtHi OrP WaPS WaT WaU **3136**

A glance at the Lewis and Clark exposition. [St. Paul? Great Northern Railway, 1925?] 29 p. illus., port., map.
Many **3137**

Historic adventure land of the Northwest. [n.p.] Great Northern Railway [n.d.] 40 p. illus., ports., fold. map.
IdB MtBozC MtU OrP OrSa WaSp **3138**

Same. [1927] IdB WaE **3139**

Same. [1929] Many **3140**

Historic northwest adventure land. [St. Paul? Great Northern Railway, n.d.] 32 p. front., illus., map.
IdU MtU WaPS WaT **3141**

Koo-koo-sint, the star man; a chronicle of David Thompson. [St. Paul? Great Northern Railway, n.d] 36 p. illus., ports., map. IdU MtU WaPS WaU **3142**

The Lewis and Clark expedition. [n.p.] Great Northern Railway [1927] 55 p. illus., fold. map.
MtU OrP OrSa WaSp **3143**

The Oriental and Captain Palmer. [St. Paul? 1924] 8 p. illus., map. WaU **3144**

Seven sunsets. [St. Paul, Gill-Warner Co., n.d] 48 p. front., illus., double col. map.
OrHi WaPS WaU **3145**

The story of Marias Pass. [n.p.] Great Northern Railway [n.d.] 22 p. front., illus., ports., map. Many **3146**

Same. [1925] Many **3147**

Flathead facts descriptive of the resources of Missoula County. Missoula, Mont., Missoula Pub. Co., 1890. 28 p. illus., ports.
MtHi MtU Or **3148**

Flathead scenery; views of the Mission Mountains, Flathead Lake and Valley, Mont. Brooklyn, Albertype Co. [n.d.] 21 plates. OrU **3149**

Fleetwood, Frank, see no. 7331.

Fleming, Archibald Lang, 1883-
Fort George. [n.p.] Ace Publications [n.d.] 15 p. illus., ports., map. CVicAr **3150**

Fleming, R. Harvey, ed.
Minutes of Council, Northern Department of Rupert Land, 1821-31; with an introd. by H. A. Innis; general ed. E. E. Rich. Toronto, Champlain Society, 1940. lxxvii, 480 p. front. (Publications. Hudson's Bay Company series, 3) Many **3151**
See also no. 8700.

Fleming, Samuel Edgar, 1885-
Civics. Seattle; King County [Supplement to A. W. Dunn's The community and the citizen] Seattle, Seattle Public Schools, 1918. 76 p. WaS WaU **3152**

Same. 1919. 80 p. plates, plan.
WaS WaU **3153**

Same. 1922. 98 p. illus. WaU **3154**

Same. 1927. 142 p. WaS WaU **3155**

Government in Seattle; city, county, state, national, by Samuel E. Fleming and Noah C. Davenport. Seattle, Seattle Public Schools, 1935. vi, 201 p. front., illus., plates, maps, diagr.
Or OrHi Wa WaA WaS WaU **3156**

Government of the state of Washington.

Boston, Ginn [c1928] 78 p. maps., tables.
WaU **3157**

Supplement to Hughes' Community civics, for the state of Washington. [Seattle? 1918?] 48 p. illus. WaPS **3158**

Fleming, Sir Sandford, 1827-1915.
England and Canada; a summer tour between old and new Westminster, with historical notes. London, Low, 1884. xi, 449 p. front. (fold. map)
CVicAr CVU Wa WaSp WaU **3159**

Flenner, J. D., 1851-1915?
Syringa blossoms. [Caldwell, Idaho, Caxton, 1912-1915?] 2 v. fronts., ports.
IdB IdIf IdP IdU (v. 2 only)
WaPS WaU **3160**

Fletcher, Robert H.
American adventure; story of the Lewis and Clark expedition, illus. by Irvin Shope. New York, American Pioneer Trails Association [1945] 54 p. illus., map. MtHi OrP **3161**

Fletcher, Robert Henry.
Coral dust. Helena, Mont., State Pub. Co., c1934. 87 p. illus. MtHi **3162**

Montana highway historical markers. [Helena, Mont., Naegle Printing Co., c1938] [64] p. illus., double map.
MtBozC MtHi MtUM WaU **3163**

Fletcher, Sidney E., see no. 11100.

Flick, C. L.
A short history of the 31st British Columbia Horse. Victoria, B. C., Buckle, 1922. [50] p. front., plates, ports.
CVicAr **3164**

Flint, Elizabeth Canfield.
The pine tree shield; a novel based on the life of a forester. Garden City, N. Y., Doubleday, 1943. 251 p. plates.
Many **3165**

Flint, Stamford Raffles, 1847-
Mudge memoirs; being a record of Zachariah Mudge and some members of his family. Truro, England, Netherton, 1883. 258 p. ports. Mudge was at Nootka Sound on the Discovery. CVicAr **3166**

[Flint, Timothy] 1780-1840.
The Shoshonee Valley; a romance, by the author of Francis Berrian. Cincinnati, E. H. Flint, 1830. 2 v. OrHi WaU **3167**

Floe, Carl F., see no. 2584.

Floren, Lee.
Hangman's range. New York, Phoenix [c1947] 256 p. Montana cowboy story.
WaE WaU **3168**

Floyd, Charles, see no. 5910.

Fogarty, Kate Hammond.
The story of Montana. New York, A. S. Barnes [c1916] 302 p. front., illus., maps.
Many **3169**

Fogler, Doris.
Rusty Pete of the Lazy AB, by Doris Fogler and Nina Nicol, illus. by Doris Fogler. New York, Macmillan, 1929. 106 p. front., plates. Montana ranch story.
IdIf Or OrP WaS WaSP **3170**

Foisie, Frank Patrick.
Decasualizing longshore labor and the

Seattle experience. For the waterfront employers of Seattle. [Seattle] 1934. 23 p. tables (part fold.)
                                   WaS WaT WaU **3171**

Folsom, David E.
Folsom - Cook exploration of the Upper Yellowstone in the year 1869, with a preface by Nathaniel P. Langford. St. Paul, Collins, 1894. 22 p.
                                   MtHi MtU WaU **3172**

Fonte, Bartholomew de, see no. 2483.

Foote, Arthur deWint.
The Idaho Mining and Irrigation Company report. New York, De Vinne, 1884. 38 p. illus., diagrs., 4 fold. maps.
                                   IdB **3173**

Foote, George B., see no. 3855.

Foote, Mrs. Mary (Hallock) 1847-1938.
The chosen valley. Boston, Houghton [c1892] 314 p. Idaho author. Many **3174**
Same. 1893.   IdU **3175**
Coeur d'Alene. Boston, Houghton [c1894] 240 p. Idaho mining story. Many **3176**
Same. 1899.   IdP **3177**
Same. 1908 [c1894]   Many **3178**
The cup of trembling, and other stories. Boston, Houghton, 1895. 273 p. Tales of Coeur d'Alene country.
                                   IdB Or WaT **3179**
The desert and the sown. Boston, Houghton, 1902. 313 p.
                                   IdB Or WaPS WaU **3180**
Edith Bonham. Boston, Houghton, 1917. 342 p.   IdP OrP **3181**
The ground-swell. Boston, Houghton, 1919. 283 p.   IdB Or OrP **3182**
In exile, and other stories. Boston, Houghton, 1894. 253 p. IdB WaPS WaSp **3183**
John Bodewin's testimony. Boston, Houghton [c1885] 344 p.   IdB **3184**
Last assembly ball, and The fate of a voice. Boston, Houghton, 1889. 275 p.
                                   IdB Or **3185**
The Led-Horse claim, a romance of a mining camp, illus. by the author. Boston, Houghton, 1882. 279 p. front., plates.
                                   IdB **3186**
Same. c1911.   IdIf MtU Or OrP **3187**
Little fig-tree stories, with illus. by the author. Boston, Houghton, 1899. 183 p. plates.   IdB **3188**
A picked company; a novel. Boston, Houghton, 1912. 416 p. Oregon immigration of 1842.   Many **3189**
The prodigal, with illus. by the author. Boston, Houghton, 1900. 99 p. front., 3 plates.   IdB Or WaS **3190**
The royal Americans. Boston, Houghton, 1910. 386 p. IdB OrP WaE WaS **3191**
A touch of sun, and other stories. Boston, Houghton, 1903. 273 p.
                                   IdB IdU Or Wa WaPS **3192**
The valley road. Boston, Houghton, 1915. 359 p.   IdB Or Was WaSp **3193**

Foothills Farm, Carlton, Or.
Foothills Farm herd of milking short-

horns, Hampshire sheep, Carlton, Oregon; W. B. Ayer, owner; R. G. Fowler, superintendent. [Portland, Or.? 1919] 14 p. illus.   OrHi OrP **3194**

Footner, Hulbert, 1879-
New rivers of the North; the yarn of two amateur explorers of the headwaters of the Fraser, the Peace River, the Hay River, Alexandra Falls, with photographs by Auville Eager and the author. New York, Outing Pub. Co., 1912. 281 p. front., plates, map.
                                   CVic CVicAr WaS WaW **3195**
Same. London, Unwin, 1913.
                                   CVicAr CVU **3196**
Same. Toronto, McClelland & Stewart [c1912]   CVU **3197**

Forbes, Bertie Charles, 1880-
Men who are making the West. New York [c1923] 343 p. front., ports. Many **3198**

Forbes, Edward, see no. 8649.

Forbes, Mary D.
Report of a survey of public health nursing, Multnomah County, Oregon, 1942. [n.p., n.d.] 1 v.   OrUM OrP **3199**

Ford, Arlo, see no. 1889.

Ford, Clellan Stearns, 1909-
Smoke from their fires; the life of a Kwakiutl chief. New Haven, Pub. for the Institute of Human Relations by Yale Univ. Press, 1941. 248 p. front. (port.) illus., col. plates, map.   Many **3200**

Ford, Corey, 1902-
Short cut to Tokyo; the battle for the Aleutians. New York, Scribner, 1943. 141 p.   Many **3201**

Ford, John Thorp.
Pioneering in the Oregon country; brief biographical sketches of Colonel Nathaniel Ford, Marcus Aurelius Ford, Dr. James W. Boyle. [n.p., n.d.] 13 p.
                                   OrCS OrP **3202**
Sparkling Rickreall and the Frost King's pencilling. [Dallas, Or., Itemizer-Observer, 1927] 7 p.   OrHi **3203**

Fording, Addison H., see no. 10609.

Foreman, A. E.
A basic cause of British Columbia's financial troubles; address delivered before the Vancouver School Principals' Association, April 4, 1933. [Vancouver, B. C.? 1933?] 32 p. maps, charts.
                                   CVU WaT **3204**

Forester, Harry.
Ocean jottings from England to British Columbia; being a record of a voyage from Liverpool to Vancouver's Island via the Straits of Magellan, the steamship "West Indian" and embracing scenes and incidents of the Chilian revolution (1891). Vancouver, B. C., Telegram, 1891. 108 p.   CVicAr **3205**
Same. 111 p.   CVU **3206**

Foresters of America. Court Nanaimo.
Constitution and by-laws of Court Nanaimo Foresters' Home No. 5886. Nanaimo, B. C., Nanaimo Free Press Steam Print, 1885. 43 p.   CVicAr **3207**

Forgo, William.
Washington, Oregon, Idaho. Brooklyn
[n.d.] 80 p. illus. OrP **3208**

The form and order of the consecration
in the Cathedral Church of Christ in the
diocese of British Columbia in the city
of Victoria, by the Right Rev. Father in
God Charles, Bishop of Columbia. [Vic-
toria, B. C., British Colonist] 1929. 47 p.
CVicAr **3209**

Forrest, Earl R., see no. 6842.

Forrest, Mrs. Elizabeth Chabot.
Daylight moon, with thirty-eight reproductions from photographs taken by the
author. New York, Stokes, 1937. x, 340 p.
front., illus., plates, ports. Educational
work among Eskimos of Alaska.
Many **3210**

Forster, Georg, 1754-1794.
Cook, der Entdecker. [Leipzig, P. G. Kummer, 1789] 232 p. WaU **3211**

Geschichte der Reisen die Seit Cook an
der Nordwest-und Nordost-kuste von
Amerika. Berlin, In der Vossischen
Buchhandlung, 1791. 380 p. illus., map,
tables. OrHi **3212**

Same. Und in dem nordlichsten Amerika
selbst von Meares, Dixon, Portlock,
Coxe, Long u. a. m. unternommen wor-
den sind; aus dem Englischen ausgear-
beitet von Georg Forster. Berlin, Vossischen Buchhandlung, 1792. 3 v. front.,
plates, maps. WaU **3213**

See also nos. 1990, 6681, 8300.

Forster, Johann Reinhold, 1729-1798.
History of the voyages and discoveries
made in the North, translated from the
German and elucidated by a new and
original map of the countries situated
about the North Pole. Dublin, Printed
for White and Byrne, 1786. xvi, 489 p.
front. (fold. map) CVicAr CVU **3214**

Same. London, Printed for G. G. J. and
J. Robinson, 1786. xvi, 489 p.
OrHi **3214A**

[Forsyth, John] comp.
Views of Victoria, British Columbia, the
most picturesque city of Canada. Victoria, B. C., Hibben [n.d.] 32 p. col. illus.,
map. WaSp **3215**

Fort Hall Centennial Association.
Idaho yesterday and today, souvenir hand-
book, 1834-1934. Pocatello [Graves &
Potter, 1934] 117 p. illus., photos., ports.
OrHi **3215A**

Fort Langlie centennial, May 2, 1925; sou-
venir programme. [Langley Prairie,
B. C., Times Printer] 1925. 31 p. illus.
CV **3216**

Fort Missoula, Mont.
Corso motori a combustione interna. [Fort
Missoula, Mont.] Scuole Fort-Missoula
[1943] 318 p. diagrs. WaU **3217**

Most used English words. [Fort Missoula,
Mont.] Scuole Fort-Missoula [1943?] 23
p. WaU **3218**

Fortier, Malcolm Vaughn, 1890-
The life of a P. O. W. under the Japanese;

in caricature. [Spokane, C. W. Hill
Printing Co., 1946] 150 p. illus., port.
WaS WaT WaU **3219**

The Forum.
Historical number, December 31, 1910.
Tacoma [E. E. Ryan, 1910] [16] p. illus.,
ports. (v. 13, no. 12, Dec. 31, 1910)
WaS WaT WaU **3220**

Souvenir ed., featuring the State Historical Society. [Tacoma, 1915] 32 p. illus.,
ports. WaSp WaU **3221**

Tacoma; past, present and future. Tacoma,
1907. 48 p. front., illus., ports. (v. 8, no.
12, Dec. 21, 1907] WaT WaU **3222**

Foster, Mrs. Anne Harvie (Ross) 1875-
The Mohawk princess, being some account
of the life of Tekahion-wake (E. Pauline
Johnson). Vancouver, B. C., Lions' Gate
Pub. Co., 1931. 216 p. front., ports.,
facsims.
CV CVic CVicAr CVU WaU **3223**

Foster, Michael G., 1904-
American dream. New York, Morrow,
1937. 506 p. Seattle author. Many **3224**

Forgive Adam. New York, Morrow, 1935.
276 p.
MtU OrCS Wa WaS WaSp WaU **3225**

To remember at midnight. New York,
Morrow, 1938. 281 p. Many **3226**

Foster, Walter Bertram, 1869-
In Alaskan waters, illus. by Winfield S.
Lukens. Philadelphia, Penn., 1903. 363 p.
illus. WaS **3227**

[Foster, William Trufant] 1879-
Comrades of the quest; the story of Reed
College. [n.p., 1917?] 15 p. OrP **3228**

Foster and Kleiser Company.
Facts on the basic economy of the Pacific
Coast. [San Francisco, c1943] 20 p. maps
(4 fold.) tables.
Or WaS WaT WaU **3229**

Forty years of advertising, 1901-1941. [n.p.,
1941] 29 p. OrP **3230**

Outdoor advertising. [n.p.] 1945. 11 p. illus.
OrP **3231**

The Pacific Coast as a market for com-
modities and the outdoor advertising
facilities available in this territory;
facts and figures for the producer, manufacturer or distributor in planning merchandising and advertising activities in
the states of California, Oregon, Washington, and Arizona. San Francisco
[c1926] 145 p. illus., col. plates, maps,
diagrs. Or OrP WaS **3232**

Same. 2d ed. c1928. 190 p. Many **3233**

Foulkes, David.
The typography of Oregon newspapers as
it appears to an old timer. Chicago,
Ludlow Typograph Co., 1928. 16 p.
Or OrP **3234**

Fountain, Paul.
Eleven eaglets of the West. London, Mur-
ray, 1905. 362 p. Many **3235**
Same. 1906. Many **3236**
Same. New York, Dutton, 1906.
IdB IdU OrP **3237**

Fouty, Constance Bennett.
Sea bride. Whatcom, Wash., I. C. Parker
[n.d.] 144 p. front. (port.) plate.
Wa **3238**

Fowler, Constance E.
The old days in and near Salem, Oregon, written and illus. by Constance E. Fowler. Seattle, F. McCaffrey, 1940. 20 plates. Many **3239**

Fowler, R. G., see no. 3194.

Frachtenberg, Leo Joachim.
Coos texts. New York, Columbia Univ. Press, 1913. 6, 216 p. (Contributions to Anthropology, v. 1) Many **3240**

Lower Umpqua texts and notes on the Kusan dialects. New York, Columbia Univ. Press, 1914. 6, 156 p. (Contributions to Anthropology, v. 4) CVicAr OrP OrU WaS WaSp WaU **3241**

See also no. 5090.

Fraenkel, K. see no. 10037.

Frame, John W.
Frame's Alaska pocket pilot; one thousand questions on the most wonderfully misunderstood country in the world asked and answered. Ketchikan, Alaska, 1929. [49] p. WaPS **3242**

France, George W.
Struggles for life and home in the Northwest, by a pioneer homebuilder; Life, 1865-1889. New York, Goldman, 1890. 607 p. illus., port., facsim. Many **3243**

Franchere, Gabriel, 1786-1863.
Narrative of a voyage to the Northwest coast of America in the years 1811, 1812, 1813 and 1814; or, The first American settlement on the Pacific, trans. and ed. by J. V. Huntington. New York, Redfield, 1854. 376 p. 3 plates. Many **3244**

Relation d'un voyage a la cote du Nordouest de l'Amerique Septentrionale, dans les annees 1810, 11, 12, 13, et 14. Montreal, C. B. Pasteur, 1820. 284 p. CVicAr CVU OrHi WaSp WaU **3245**

Franck, Harry Alverson, 1881-
The lure of Alaska, with 100 reproductions of photographs, most of them taken by the author. New York, Stokes, 1939. xiv, 306 p. front., plates, ports. Many **3246**

Same. With 80 reproductions of photographs, most of them taken by the author. Garden City, N. Y., Blue Ribbon Books [1943, c1939] xiii, 306 p. plates, ports. CVU WaU **3247**

Frank, Herman Washington, 1860-
Scrapbook of a western pioneer. Los Angeles, Times-Mirror [c1934] 256 p. front., plates, ports., facsims. IdU Or WaS WaWW **3248**

Frank, Mary, see no. 6586.

Franklin, Earl Raymond, comp.
Digest of Oregon Land Use Committee reports, 1938. [n.p., n.d.] 70 p. OrCS **3249**

Franklin, F. G., see nos. 571-573.

Franklin, Sir John, 1786-1847.
Journey to the shores of the Polar Sea in 1819-20-21-22; with a brief account of the second journey in 1825-26-27. London, J. Murray, 1829. 4 v. fronts., plates, ports., fold. map. CVicAr **3250**

Narrative of a journey to the shores of the Polar Sea in the years 1819, 20, 21, and 22, with an appendix on various subjects relating to science and history. London, J. Murray, 1823. xiv, 768 p. col. front., plates (part col.) 4 fold. maps. CVicAr MtU **3251**

Same. 2d ed. 1824. 2 v. front. (fold. map) fold. maps. CVicAr **3252**

Same. 3d ed. CVicAr CVU MtU OrP WaS WaSp **3253**

Same. London, Dent [1910] x, 434 p. double map. (Everyman's library. Travel and topography, no. 447) CVicAr CVU **3254**

Narrative of a second expedition to the shores of the Polar Sea in the years 1825, 1826, and 1827, including an account of the progress of a detachment to the eastward by John Richardson. London, J. Murray, 1828. xxiv, 320, clvii p. front., plates, 6 fold. maps. CVicAr CVU MtU **3255**

Thirty years in the Arctic regions; a narrative of the explorations and adventures of Sir John Franklin. New York, Dayton, 1859. 743 p. CVicAr **3256**

Same. Philadelphia, J. E. Potter [c1859] 480 p. front. (port.) OrHi **3257**

Franklin, Viola (Price) 1855-
Stevenson in Monterey; or, An afternoon with Jules Simoneau. Salem, Or., Statesman Pub. Co., 1925. 18 p. Or OrP OrSaW **3258**

A tribute to Hazel Hall. Caldwell, Idaho, Caxton, 1939. 87 p. front. (port.) Or OrP OrSaW WaS WaU **3259**

Franzen, Andrew.
Poems of Oregon and other verse. Portland, Or., Chausse-Prudhomme Co., 1914. 78 p. Or OrHi OrP WaPS WaU **3260**

Story of a toiler. [n.p., n.d.] 24 p. OrHi OrP **3261**

Fraser, Agnes, 1859-
British Columbia for settlers; its mines, trade and agriculture, by Frances Macnab [pseud.] London, Chapman, 1898. 369 p. front. (fold. map) 2 fold maps. Many **3262**

Fraser, Charles McLean, 1872-
Hydroids of the Pacific coast of Canada and the United States. Toronto, Univ. of Toronto Press, 1937. 207 p. 44 plates. Many **3263**

See also no. 7295.

Fraser, Donald A., 1875-1948.
Centenary; a collection of verses arranged in celebration of the one-hundredth birthday of the city of Victoria, B. C., 1843-1943. [Victoria, B. C., Diggon-Hibben, 1943] 38 p. CVicAr **3264**

Same. [1945] 39 p. CVicAr **3265**

My nugget-poke. Victoria, B. C. [n.d.] 108 p. port. CVicAr **3266**

The three kings and other verses for children. Victoria, B. C., Cusack, 1922. 64 p. illus. CVicAr **3267**

Fraser, Hugh C., see nos. 3269, 3270.

Fraser, James Duncan.
The gold fever; or Two years in Alaska,

a true narrative of actual events as ex-
perienced by the author. [Honolulu,
Hawaii, c1923] 100 p.
WaPS WaS WaU **3268**

Fraser, Julia, see no. 2101.

Fraser, Mrs. Mary (Crawford)
Seven years on the Pacific slope, by Mrs.
Hugh Fraser and Hugh C. Fraser. New
York, Dodd, 1914. 391 p. front., 15 plates.
Many **3269**

Same. London, Laurie [1915] CVicAr **3270**

Fraser, Simon, see nos. 6596, 6597.

Fraternal Order of Eagles.
Official souvenir program, tenth annual
session, Grand Aerie, Fraternal Order
of Eagles, Seattle, Aug. 11 to 15, 1908.
[Seattle, General Lithography & Printing Co., 1908] [40] p. illus., ports.
WaU **3271**

The royal Eagle, Mother Aerie, Seattle,
No. 1, F. O. E.; program and history
[Seattle, Pioneer Printing Co. n.d.] [20]
p. illus. WaU **3272**

— — — Youth Guidance Institute.
Report on Spokane; survey of recreational
and cultural resources. [n.p., 1946?] 1 v.
WaSp **3273**

[**Frazier, Raymond Robert**] 1873-
Brief presented on behalf of the mutual
savings banks to the Advisory Tax Commission of the state of Washington.
[Seattle] 1929. 16 p. WaU **3274**

Fream, W., see no. 2507.

Frede, Pierre.
Aventures lointaines; voyages, chasses et
peches aux iles Sitka; voyage en cara-
vane a travers la Perse; un jambon d'
hyene; Yegor de pisteur d'ours. Paris,
Firmin-Didot, 1882. 356 p. CVU **3275**

Aventures lointaines; voyage aux iles
Sitka. Paris, Firmin-Didot, 1887. 128 p.
illus. CVicAr **3276**

Aventures lointaines; voyage aux iles
Sitka, ancienne Amerique Russe. Paris,
Firmin-Didot, 1890. 142 p. front., plates.
CVicAr WaU **3277**

Fredenholm, Axel.
Purpur och hemspunnet; dikter och
sanger. Seattle, Svea Pub. Co., 1909. 118
p. WaU **3278**

Frederick, James Vincent, 1896-
Ben Holladay, the stagecoach king; a
chapter in the development of transcontinental transportation. Glendale,
Calif., 1940. 334 p. front., plates, port.,
fold map. Many **3279**

Frederick & Nelson, Seattle, Wash.
Frederick & Nelson and you. Seattle, 1944.
64 p. illus., ports. WaS **3280**

Frederickson, Earle M., comp. and ed.
State of Washington, "The Evergreen
Empire", produced by the convention
committee, 61st annual convention, the
American Federation of Labor. [Seattle,
1941] 143 p. illus., ports.
WaE WaS WaSp WaT **3281**

**Free Citizens Union of Montana. Grand
Lodge.**
Constitution. [n.p.] 1888. 8 p. MtHi **3282**

Free homes in Manitoba and the Canadian
North-West. [n.p., 1886?] [52] p. fold.
map. CVicAr **3283**

Freed, V. H.
2,4-D as a weed killer in Oregon, by V. H.
Freed and Rex Warren. Corvallis, Or.,
Or. State College, 1948. 16 p. illus., tables.
(Extension bulletin, no. 687) OrP **3284**

Freeman, Harry Campbell.
A brief history of Butte, Montana; the
world's greatest mining camp; including
a story of the extraction and treatment
of ores from its gigantic copper properties. Chicago, Shepard, 1900. 123 p. col.
front., illus., ports. Many **3285**

Freeman, Lewis Ransome, 1878-
Down the Columbia. New York, Dodd,
1921. xx, 383 p. front., 23 plates, ports.,
map. Many **3286**

Same. London, 1922. CVU **3287**

Down the Yellowstone. New York, Dodd,
1922. 282 p. front., plates, ports.
MtHi Or OrP Wa WaT **3288**

Same. London, Heinemann, 1923.
CVic **3289**

The nearing North. New York, Dodd
[c1928] xii, 385 p. front., 15 plates, ports.
Many **3290**

On the roof of the Rockies, the great
Columbia icefield of the Canadian
Rockies. New York, Dodd, 1925. xiii,
270 p. front., plates. Many **3291**

Freeman, Otis Willard, 1889-
Geography and geology of Fergus County.
Lewistown, Mont., 1919. 71 p. illus.
(Fergus County High School. Bulletin
no. 2) MtBozC **3292**

Grand Coulee and neighboring geological
wonders. [Cheney, Wash., c1937] 20 p.
illus., plates. WaSp WaU **3293**

Same. Spokane, c1937.
OrCS OrP WaTC **3294**

Same. Rev. ed. Cheney, Wash., 1938. 40 p.
illus., maps. Or WaS WaT **3295**

Living geography, by Huntington, Benson,
McMurry; Washington supplement. New
York, Macmillan, 1932. 56 p. front. (map)
WaSp **3296**

The Pacific Northwest, a regional, human,
and economic survey of resources and
development; editorial committee, Otis
W. Freeman and Howard H. Martin.
New York, Wiley, 1942. xvi, 542 p. front.,
illus., maps (1 fold. in pocket) tables,
diagrs. Many **3297**

Washington geography source material.
Cheney, Wash., Eastern Wash. College
of Education, Extension Division, 1936.
6 p. WaPS WaU **3298**

Freemasons. British Columbia.
Proceedings of the convention to organize
the M. W. Grand Lodge of Free
and Accepted Masons of British Columbia. Victoria, B. C.; Daily Standard,
1872. 45 p. CVicAr **3299**

Proceedings of the 2d annual communication of the Most Worshipful Grand
Lodge of Ancient Free and Accepted

Masons of British Columbia, by Henry Frederick Heisterman. Victoria, B. C., Higgins, 1873. 40 p. CVicAr **3300**

22d annual communication of the M. W. Grand Lodge of British Columbia, Ancient Free and Accepted Masons; laying cornerstone of the British Columbia Protestant Orphans' Home. June 24, 1893. Victoria, B. C., British Colonist, 1893. 11 p. CVicAr **3301**

— — — Montana. Grand Lodge.
Constitution and code of statutes. Helena, Mont., State Pub. Co., 1912. 127 p.
MtU **3302**

— — — Oregon.
By-laws of Harmony Lodge No. 12, held at the city of Portland. Portland, Or., Walling, 1866. [32] p. OrHi **3303**

By-laws of Jennings Lodge No. 9, Dallas, Oregon, adopted March 4, 1871. Dallas, Or., Oregon Republican, 1872. 8 p.
OrHi **3304**

By-laws of Salem Lodge No. 4, A. F. & A. M., to which is annexed the constitution of the R. W. Grand Lodge. Portland, Or., Dryer, 1852. 1 v. OrHi **3305**

By-laws of the Eugene City Lodge No. 11, Free and Accepted Masons, held in Eugene City, Oregon. Eugene, Or., People's Press, 1859. 11 p. OrU **3306**

By-laws of Thurston Lodge No. 28, held at Harrisburg, Or. Portland, Or., Farmer Job Office, 1866. 12, 20 p. OrHi **3307**

By-laws [of Warren Lodge No. 10] [Jacksonville, O. T.?] 1855. 7 p. OrU **3308**

By-laws of Washington Lodge No. 46 adopted March 13, 1869. Portland, Or., Himes, 1871. 27 p. OrHi **3309**

Multnomah Lodge No. 1, Oregon City, Oregon, 1846-1920. [n.p., n.d.] [4] p.
OrHi **3310**

Willamette Lodge No. 2, A. F. & A. M., 1850-1900, Portland, Oregon. [Portland, Or., Rogers, 1900?] [82] p. front., ports.
OrHi OrP WaU **3311**

— — — — — — Grand Commandery of Knights Templar.
Organization of the Grand Commandery Knights Templar of Oregon, 1887. Salem, Or., F. J. Babcock, 1887. 22 p.
OrHi OrP **3312**

— — — — — — Grand Lodge.
Act of incorporation, constitution and by-laws, decisions and resolutions of the M. W. Grand Lodge, 1900. Portland, Or., Baltes, 1900. 84 p. OrP **3313**

Same. 1908. Eugene, Or., Yoran's Printery, 1908. 84 p. OrP WaPS **3314**

Constitution, by-laws, manual of the lodge, forms of documents. 1st ed. [Portland, Or., Rogers] 1911. 297 p. illus.
OrU WaPS **3315**

Same. 7th ed. Eugene, Or., Koke-Tiffany, 1919. 352 p. illus. OrP **3316**

Same. 8th ed. [n.p.] 1920. WaU **3317**

Same. 11th ed. [Portland, Or.] 1923. 330 p. illus. WaPS **3318**

Constitution, penal code, standing resolutions, uniform by-laws and funeral service adopted by the M. W. Grand Lodge of Oregon. Portland, Or., Walling, 1875. 40 p. OrP **3319**

Constitution, standing orders, and resolutions of the Grand Lodge of Oregon, A. F. & A. M. New York, Milnor, 1857. 15 p. OrHi **3320**

Digest of decisions, resolutions, edicts and authoritative reports of the Grand Lodge of Oregon. [n.p., 188—?] 56 p.
WaPS **3321**

Organization of the Most Worshipful Grand Lodge of Ancient Free and Accepted Masons for years 1878-'79. [n.p., 1878] [3] p. OrHi **3322**

Proceedings of the special communication held in the city of Salem, Oct. 8, A. D. 1873, for the purpose of laying the cornerstone of the state capitol. Portland, Or., 1873. 47 p.
Or OrHi OrP **3323**

— — — — — — Grand Royal Arch Chapter.
Book of constitutions and laws in force. Portland, Or., Himes, 1878. 47 p.
OrHi **3324**

By-laws [of Oregon Chapter No. 4] Jacksonville, Or., T. S. Pomeroy, 1862. 8 p.
OrU **3325**

Constitution of the Grand Chapter, Royal Arch Masons of the state of Oregon. [Portland, Or., Irwin-Hodson, 1898?] 39 p. WaPS **3326**

Oregon code of capitual Masonry, Grand Chapter R. A. M., state of Oregon. 2d ed. [Portland, Or., Rogers] 1916. 222 p. illus.
WaPS **3327**

— — — Washington Territory.
Installation ceremonial, M. W. Grand Lodge, Free and Accepted Masons, W. T. Olympia, W. T., Bagley, 1880. 29 p.
WaU **3328**

— — — — — — Franklin Lodge.
By-laws of Franklin Lodge No. 5, Free and Accepted Masons, held at Teekalet, Washington Territory. Olympia, W. T., Pioneer and Democrat Office. 1860. [16] p. WaU **3329**

— — — Washington (State) Grand Lodge.
Constitution and Masonic code of the M. W. Grand Lodge of Washington, F. & A. Masons, as revised and amended June 1882. Olympia, Wash., Bagley, 1882. xvi, 66 p. WaU **3330**

Semi-centennial celebration of the foundation of the Grand Lodge of Free and Accepted Masons of Washington, Olympia, Dec. 7-8, 1908. Tacoma, Allen & Lamborn, 1909. 124 p. front., plates, ports., facsims. Wa WaU **3331**

Washington Grand Lodge bulletin; a quarterly publication devoted to the interests and ideals of Freemasonry. Seattle, 1925. 47 p. port., fold. plate. (v. 1, no. 1, June 1925) No more published.
WaU **3332**

Washington Masonic code, 1913; adopted by Grand Lodge, June 11, 1913, rev. to

June 15, 1921; containing copies of manuscript old charges, etc.; also forms for the use of lodges, and a synopsis of decisions and approved reports of the Committee on Jurisprudence, now in force. Tacoma, Allen & Lamborn, 1921. 184 p. WaPS WaU 3333

The Washington monitor and Freemason's guide to the symbolic degrees. comp. originally by Thomas Milburne Reed. 7th ed. [Seattle] 1917. 171 p. illus.
WaU 3334

———— ———— ———— Committee on Masonic Research and Education.
Report to the Grand Lodge of Washington, 1924-1925. Seattle, 1925. 29 p. (Bulletin no. 2, series no. 3) WaU 3335

———— ———— ———— Special Committee on Grand Lodge Library.
Plan for Masonic Grand Lodge Library: report of special committee on Grand Lodge Library, adopted by the Most Worshipful Grand Lodge, F. & A. M., of Washington, 19 June 1945. [Tacoma, 1945?] 22 p. WaS 3336

———— ———— ———— Knights Templars. Grand Commandery.
A history of the activities of the thirty-sixth triennial committee, Knights Templar, for the conclave of the Grand Encampment of the United States of America held at Seattle July 27, 28, 29, 30, 31, 1925, by the Historical Committee, George A. Custer, chairman, David W. Hughes, vice-chairman, assisted by William C. Lyon. [Seattle, Lowman & Hanford, 1925?] 203 p. plates, ports.
Wa WaU 3337

Program and souvenir booklet; a dedication to the resources and attractions of the Pacific Northwest, together with the complete program of events as a part of the entertainment of the thirty-sixth Triennial Conclave of Knights Templar of the United States of America, held at Seattle, Wash., July 1925. [Seattle, Sherman Printing and Binding Co., 1925] [119] p. illus., ports.
WaS WaU 3338

Freeport, Andrew, pseud.
The case of the Hudson's Bay Company in a letter to Lord Palmerson. London, Stanford, 1857. 18 p.
CVicAr CVU WaU 3339

Frelinghuysen, Mrs. Carl, see nos. 8092, 8093.

Fremont, Elizabeth Benton.
Recollections of Elizabeth Benton Fremont, daughter of the pathfinder General John C. Fremont and Jessie Benton Fremont, his wife, comp. by I. T. Martin. New York, Hitchcock, 1912. 184 p. front., 4 plates, 3 ports. OrP OrU WaU 3340

Fremont, Mrs. Jessie (Benton) 1824-1902.
Far-West sketches. Boston, Lothrop [c1890] 206 p. WaS WaU 3341

Souvenirs of my time. Boston, Lothrop [1887] 393 p. front., plates, ports.
OrP OrU WaTC WaU 3342

See also nos. 3340, 3350.

Fremont, John Charles, 1813-1890.
The exploring expedition to the Rocky Mountains, Oregon and California, with recent notices of the gold region from the latest and most authentic sources. Buffalo, Derby, 1850. 456 p. front. (port.) illus. IdIf 3343

Same. 15th thousand. 1852. Or WaSp 3344

Same. New York, Miller, 1855.
MtBozC 3345

Die Felsengebirge, Oregon und Nordcalifornien: aus dem Englischen ubersetzt von Dr. Kottenkamp. Stuttgart, Franckh, 1847. viii, 324 p.
CVicAr OrP WaS 3346

Same, 2te Ausg. 1851. CVicAr 3347

Geographical memoir upon Upper California, addressed to the Senate of the United States; to which are now added extracts from Hakluyt's collection of voyages, La Peyrouse's voyage; letter from Com. Jones to the Secretary of the Navy, Oct. 25, 1848, ed. of the Oregon Spectator, his account of Oregon, by William McCarthy. Philadelphia, McCarthy, 1849. 80 p. CVicAr 3348

The life of Col. John Charles Fremont and his narrative of explorations and adventures in Kansas, Nebraska, Oregon, and California, the memoir by Samuel M. Schmucker. New York, Miller, 1856. 493 p. front. (port.) 8 plates, table.
Many 3349

Memoirs of my life, including in the narrative five journeys of western exploration, during the years 1842, 1843-4, 1845-6-7, 1848-9, 1853-4; together with a sketch of the life of Senator Benton, in connection with western expansion, by Jessie Benton Fremont. Chicago, Belford, 1887. 655 p. front. (port.) 72 plates, 9 ports., 7 maps. Many 3350

Narrative of the exploring expedition to the Rocky Mountains in the year 1842 and to Oregon and California in the years 1843-44. 2d ed. Washington, D. C., Taylor [1845] 278 p. 2 maps.
Or WaSp WaU 3351

Same. 2d ed. Washington, D. C., Polkinhorn, 1845. CVU OrHi 3352

Same. Cooperstown, N. Y., H. & E. Phinney, 1846. 186 p. WaSp 3353

Same. London, Wiley & Putnam, 1846. 324 p. front., plates, fold. map. Many 3354

Same. New York, Appleton, 1846. 186 p.
Many 3355

Same. New York, A. S. Barnes, 1848. 427 p. plates. CVU OrCS WaPS WaSp 3356

Same. New York, Appleton, 1849. 186 p.
CVicAr OrP WaU 3357

Oregon and California; the exploring expedition to the Rocky Mountains, Oregon and California; to which is added a description of the physical geography of California, with recent notices of the gold region from the latest and most authentic sources. Buffalo, Derby, 1849. 456 p. front. (port.) port.
CV Or OrCS WaU 3358

Same. 1850.   IdB WaWW 3359
Same. 1851.
    CVicAr OrP WaS WaU WaWW 3360
Same. 1852.   OrP WaT 3361
Same. Auburn, N. Y., Miller, 1854.
                    OrSaW WaU 3362
Reisen durch die Vereinigten Staaten von
    Nordamerika nebst einem Ausfluge nach
    Canada nach F. v. Raumer, F. Ger-
    stacker, E. V. Gerstner sowie nach dem
    Felsengebirge im Jahre 1842 und nach
    dem Oregongebiet und Nord-Californien
    in den Jahren 1843 und 1844. Leipzig,
    Fleischer, 1848. x, 747 p. front., fold.
    map.   WaU 3363
Fremont's explorations of the Rocky Moun-
    tains and California. [n.p., n.d.] [27] p.
                            OrP 3364

French, Chauncey Del, 1890-
Railroadman. New York, Macmillan, 1938.
    vi, 292 p. plates, ports., facsim.
                          Many 3365
French, Hiram Taylor, 1861-
History of Idaho; a narrative account of
    its historical progress, its people and its
    principal interests. Chicago, Lewis Pub.
    Co., 1914. 3 v. fronts., illus., plates, ports.
                          Many 3366
French, Jane E. L.
Poems and lyrics. Victoria, B. C., Victoria
    Printing & Pub. Co. [n.d.] 96 p.
                        CVicAr 3367
French, Joseph Lewis, 1858-1936, ed.
The pioneer West; narratives of the west-
    ward march of empire, selected and ed.
    by Joseph Lewis French, with a fore-
    word by Hamlin Garland, illus. in col. by
    Remington Schuyler. Boston, Little, 1923.
    386 p. front., 3 plates. Many 3368
Same. 1924. IdIf MtHi OrSaW WaU 3369
French, Leigh Hill, 1863-
Nome nuggets; some of the experiences of
    a party of gold seekers in northwestern
    Alaska in 1900. New York, Montross,
    Clarke & Emmons, 1901. 102 p. front.,
    illus., 13 plates.
                CVicAr OrU WaU 3370
Seward's land of gold; five seasons ex-
    perience with the gold seekers in north-
    western Alaska. New York, Montross,
    Clarke & Emmons [1905?] xii, 101 p.
    front., plates, ports.
              CVicAr Wa WaS WaU 3371
Frewen, T. A.
Fifty years of plumbing in Portland. [Port-
    land, Or.] Portland Master Plumbers
    Assn., 1934. 18 p. illus.   OrP 3372
Freyd, Bernard.
Repeal of the direct primary. Seattle, Mc-
    Kay Printing Co. [c1925] 65 p.
                Or WaS WaT WaU 3373
Friedline, Mrs. Apal Alpha (Burns) 1893-
Generations, illus. by Marie Haasch White-
    sel. [Caldwell, Idaho, Privately printed,
    Caxton, c1941] 267 p. front., illus.
                            IdB 3374
A friend of the Anglo-Saxons, see no. 7644.
**Friends of the Indians of British Columbia,
The Conference of.**
The British Columbia Indian land question

from a Canadian point of view; an ap-
    peal to the people of Canada, recom-
    mended by the Indian Affairs Commit-
    tee of the Social Service Council of
    Canada. [Victoria, B. C.] Witness Press
    [1914] 16 p. front.   CVicAr WaU 3375
The Nishga petition to His Majesty's
    Privy Council. [n.p.] 1915. 107 p. ports.
                        CVicAr 3376

Froelich, Adele, see no. 8579.

Frost, J. H., see no. 5800.

Frothingham, Robert, 1865-
Trails through the golden West. New
    York, McBride, 1932. 272 p. front., 30
    plates.   Many 3377

**Fruit lands in the beautiful Windemer Val-
    ley** of the Columbia River, B. C. [n.p.]
    1911. 24 p. illus.   CVicAr 3378

Fry, Charles Luther, 1894-1938.
A census analysis of far western villages;
    being a study of the 1920 census data for
    34 villages in 6 far western states:
    Montana, Colorado, Idaho, Washington,
    Oregon, and California. [New York]
    Institute of Social & Religious Research,
    c1924. 152 p. illus., map. (American
    village studies, pt. 4)
              Or OrU WaS WaU 3379

Fry, F.
Fry's traveler's guide and descriptive
    journal of the great north-western terri-
    tories of the United States of America;
    comprising the territories of Idaho,
    Washington, Montana, and the state of
    Oregon, with sketches of Colorado, Utah,
    Nebraska, and British America. The
    grain, pastural [!] and gold regions
    defined, with some new views of their
    future greatness. Cincinnati, Applegate,
    1865. 264 p.   Many 3380

Frye, Theodore Christian, 1869-
Elementary flora of the Northwest, by
    Theodore C. Frye and George B. Rigg.
    New York, American Book Co. [c1914]
    256 p.   Many 3381

Ferns of the Northwest, covering Wash-
    ington, Oregon, Idaho, British Columbia,
    Montana, Wyoming, central and north-
    ern California. Portland, Or., Metropoli-
    tan, 1934. 177 p. illus.   Many 3382

Northwest flora, by Theodore C. Frye and
    George B. Rigg. Seattle, Univ. Book-
    store [1912?] 453 p.   Many 3383

Fuhrmann, Ernst, 1886-
Tlinkit u. Haida, Indianerstamme der
    Westkuste von Nordamerika kultische
    Kunst und Mythen des Kulturkreises.
    Hagen, Foldwant-verlag, 1922. 46 p. 61
    plates (Schriftenreihe Kulturen der
    Erde, Material zur Kultur—und Kunst-
    geschichte aller Volker, Bd. 22)
    CV CVic CVicAr WaS WaSp WaU 3384

Fullenwider, Elmir D., see no. 5499.

Fuller, Archimedes Edward, comp.
Handbook of Washington, 1901, comp. by
    A. E. Fuller, ed. by Phil. L. Axling.
    [Seattle] Daily Bulletin [c1901] 191 p.
    illus.   OrU WaS WaU 3385

Fuller, Emeline L., 1847-
Left by the Indians; story of my life. [Mt. Vernon, Iowa, Hawk-eye Steam Print, 1892] 40 p. ports.
CVicAr IdB WaSp **3386**
Same. [New York, E. Eberstadt, 1936]
IdB IdU OrP OrSaW WaU **3387**

Fuller, Mrs. Ethel (Romig) 1883-
Kitchen sonnets (and lyrics of domesticity). Portland, Or., Binfords & Mort [c1931] 108 p.
MtU WaE **3388**
Same. [1938, c1931]
OrU **3389**
Same. Portland, Or., Metropolitan, 1931.
Or OrP OrSaW Wa WaS **3390**
White peaks and green. Chicago, Willett, Clark and Colby, 1928. 91 p. Poems.
Many **3391**
Same. Portland, Or., Metropolitan, 1928.
WaE **3392**
Same. 1933.
OrHi WaU **3393**
See also no. 7684.

Fuller, George Washington, 1876-
A bibliography of bookplate literature, ed., with a foreword, by George W. Fuller, bibliographical work by Verna B. Grimm. Some random thoughts on bookplate literature, by Winward Prescott. Spokane, Spokane Public Library, 1926. 151 p.
Many **3394**
A history of the Pacific Northwest. New York, Knopf, 1931. xvi, 383 p. front., plates, ports., maps (1 fold.)
Many **3395**
Same. 2d ed. rev. 1938. xvi, 383 p. front., 6 plates, 19 ports., 10 maps (1 fold.)
Many **3396**
Same. 1941.
WaT **3397**
Same. With special emphasis on the Inland Empire. 2d ed. rev. New York, Knopf, 1946. xvi, 383 [16] p. front., plates, ports., maps.
OrU **3398**
The Inland Empire of the Pacific Northwest, a history. Spokane, H. G. Lindermann, 1928. 4 v. plates, ports., maps (2 fold.) Fourth vol. biographical.
Many **3399**

Fuller, Richard Eugene, 1897-
The geomorphology and volcanic sequence of Steens Mountain in southeastern Oregon. Seattle, Univ. of Wash., 1931. 130 p. illus., table (Publications in geology, v. 3, no. 1)
Many **3400**
A sketch of the historical background of Japanese art. Seattle [Seattle Art Museum] 1935. 24 p.
WaS WaU **3401**

Fullerton, James, 1853-
Autobiography of Roosevelt's adversary. Boston, Roxburgh Pub. Co. [1912] 162 p. front., plates. Frontier life in Northwest.
Or Wa WaS WaU **3402**

Fulton, Reed.
Davy Jones's locker; an adventure story of the Astorian expedition, illus. by Manning De V. Lee. Garden City, N. Y., Doubleday, 1928. 330 p. col. front., illus. Seattle author.
Or WaPS WaS WaSp **3403**
Same. 1936. (Young Moderns Bookshelf)
WaU **3404**

The Grand Coulee mystery, a story of the engineers. Garden City, N. Y., Doubleday, 1941. x, 284 p. front.
Or Wa WaS WaSp WaU **3405**
Lardy the Great. Garden City, N. Y., Doubleday, 1932. viii, 268 p. col. front.
WaS WaU **3406**
Moccasin trail, the story of a boy who took the trail with Kit Carson, illus. by Ernest Walker. Garden City, N. Y., Doubleday, 1929. x, 308 p. col. front.
OrU WaS WaSp WaU **3407**
The powder dock mystery (a story for girls and boys) illus. by Starr Gephart. Garden City, N. Y., Doubleday, Page, 1927. 325 p. col. front.
Wa WaS WaSp WaU **3408**
Stevedore, a story of the water front. Garden City, N. Y., Doubleday [c1948] 216 p.
WaU **3409**
The tide's secret, a mystery story, illus. by Frank Dobias and Robert Haberstock. Garden City, N. Y., Doubleday, 1930. x, 281 p. col. front. Wa WaU **3410**
The fur-trade and the Hudson's Bay Company. [Edinburgh, W. and R. Chambers, n.d.] 31 p. illus. (Chamber's repository of instructive and amusing tracts, no. 65)
WaU **3411**

Furlong, Charles Wellington, 1874-
Let 'er buck, a story of the passing of the old West, with fifty illus. taken from life by the author and others. New York, Putnam, 1921. xxxviii, 242 p. illus., 35 plates.
Many **3412**
Same. 1927 [c1921]
IdIf OrCS **3413**

Furrer, Edward, comp.
General statistics and other information regarding the suitability of Kamloops as a health resort. Kamloops, B. C., Inland Sentinel [n.d.] [8] p.
CVicAr **3414**

Futcher, Winnifred M., ed.
The great north road to the Cariboo, illus. from early photographs. [Vancouver, B. C.] Wrigley Printing Co., c1938. 113 p. illus., plates, map.
CV CVic CVicAr CVU MtHi WaS **3415**

Fyfe, Alexander.
Christ and MacGregor, in the plan that changed the world. Nampa, Idaho, 1939. 201 p.
IdB WaSp **3416**

Gabriel, Gilbert Wolf, 1890-
I got a country, a novel of Alaska. Garden City, N. Y., Doubleday, 1944. 432 p.
Many **3417**
I, James Lewis. New York, Doubleday, 1932. 334 p. Novel about Astor party.
Many **3418**

Gabriel, Ralph Henry, 1890-
The lure of the frontier; a story of race conflict. New Haven, Yale Univ. Press, 1929. 327 p. col. front., illus., ports., maps, facsims. (Pageant of America, v. 2)
Many **3419**
Same. "Liberty Bell ed."
WaTC **3420**

Gabrielson, Ira Noel, 1889-
Western American alpines. New York,
Macmillan, 1932. 271 p. plates, map.
Many **3421**
See also no. 5205.

Gage, Mrs. Eli, see nos. 4092-4097.

Gail, William W.
Yellowstone County, Montana, in the
world war, 1917-1918-1919. [Billings,
Mont., War Book Pub. Co., c1919] 226
p. illus., ports. (part col.) MtHi **3422**

[Gaines, Franklin Wilks] 1856-
Faults of the Oregon politician and how
to cure them; how our Tax Commission
and our Railroad Commission are selling
us into slavery to the corporations.
[Portland, Or., Clarke-Kundret Printing Co., c1914] 22 p. Or OrP WaPS **3423**

Is the Railway Commission and the Tax
Commission of the state of Oregon in a
mutual conspiracy to sell the people of
Oregon into slavery to the railroads?
[n.p., 1908?] 14 p. Or OrP OrU **3424**

Gaines, Mrs. Nettie Viola (Stewart) 1864-
comp.
Pathway to western literature, cover design by W. S. Rice. Stockton, Calif.
[c1910] xii, 245 p. CVicAr WaU **3425**

Gairdner, George W.
The Gairdner & Harrison prospectors'
guide map and pamphlet to the Omenica,
Cassier, Liard, Klondyke and Yukon
gold fields via the Edmonton Route.
Edmonton, Alta. [Bulletin Print, 1897]
1 v. CVU **3426**

Gale, Samuel.
Notices on the claims of the Hudson's
Bay Company and the conduct of its
adversaries. Montreal, Gray, 1817. 161 p.
CVicAr **3427**

Notices on the claims of the Hudson's Bay
Company, to which is added a copy of
their royal charter. London, Murray,
1819. 69 p. CVicAr **3428**

Gallagher, John B., see no. 207.

Gallagher, John S.
The government of Washington. New
York, Macmillan, 1922. 72 p.
Wa WaE WaU **3429**

Gallatin, Albert, 1761-1849.
The Oregon question. [n.p., n.d.] 75 p.
OrU **3430**

Same. New York, Bartlett & Welford,
1846. Many **3431**

Galloway, C. F. J.
Call of the West; letters from British
Columbia. London, Unwin [1916] 328 p.
front., 55 plates, map.
CV OrP WaPS **3432**

Same. New York, Stokes, 1916.
CVU OrP WaS WaU **3433**

Same. 2d ed. London, Unwin, 1917.
CVicAr CVU WaSp WaU **3434**

Galloway, Charles V.
Fair and honest taxation in Oregon.
[Salem, Or., 1942] [14] p. (Radio address
over KGW, May 2, 1942)
Or OrHi OrU **3435**

Galvin, J. J., see no. 4540.

Gambrill, J. Montgomery, see no. 11145.

Gannett, Henry, see no. 8224.

Ganssle, Mrs. Margaret P., see no. 6935.

Gapanovich, Ivan Ivanovich, 1891-
Rossiia v severo-vostochnoi Azii. Pekin
[Pekinskaia Russkaia Missiia] 1933-1934.
2 pt. in 1 v. 2 maps (1 fold.) WaU **3436**

Garber, Clark McKinley, 1891-
Stories and legends of the Bering Strait
Eskimos. Boston, Christopher Pub.
House [c1940] 260 p. front., plates, ports.,
maps. WaU **3437**

Gard, Robert Edward.
Johnny Chinook; tall tales and true from
the Canadian West. London, Longmans,
1945. 360 p. front., illus. Many **3438**

Gardiner, A. Paul.
The house of Cariboo and other tales from
Arcadia, illus. by Robert A. Graef. New
York, 1900. 218 p. front., illus., 5 plates.
CVicAr CVU **3439**

Gardiner, Dorothy.
West of the river. New York, Crowell, 1941.
vi, 347 p. col. front., illus., col. plates, col.
ports., map. Many **3440**

Gardner, Mac.
Mom counted six. New York, Harper [1944]
267 p. Puget Sound novel. Many **3441**

Garfielde, Selucius, 1822-1883.
Climates of the Northwest; being con-
densed notes of a lecture. Philadelphia,
Ringwalt and Brown, 1871. 18 p.
CVicAr OrU WaU **3442**

Same. 1872. 20 p.
OrHi OrP WaS WaSp **3443**

Same. 25 p. CVicAr Or OrP **3444**

The Northwest coast, a lecture delivered
in Lincoln Hall, Washington city on
Monday, November 15, 1869. Washington,
D. C., Pearson, 1869. 26 p.
CVicAr WaU WaW **3445**

Garland, Hamlin, 1860-1940.
Long trail; a story of the northwest wilderness. New York, Harper, 1907. 262 p.
front. 7 plates. Klondike trail. Many **3446**

Same. "Border ed." WaU **3447**

The trail of the goldseekers; a record of
travel in prose and verse. New York,
Macmillan, 1899. viii, 264 p.
CVicAr OrP WaPS WaSp WaU **3448**

Same. 1906. MtU WaU **3449**

See also nos. 3368, 3369.

Garnett, Porter, 1871-
A pageant of May: I. The masque Proser-
pine; II. The revels of May; produced
by the author in City Park, Walla Walla,
Washington, Friday and Saturday, May
22 and 23, 1914, under the auspices of
the Woman's Park Club. Walla Walla,
Wash., 1914. 32 p. WaWW **3450**

Garrett, Charles Walter, 1873-
Aurilly, the virgin isle. Boston, Christopher
Pub. House [c1923] 152 p. front. Alaska
novel. WaU **3451**

Garrett, I. W., comp.
Official manual of the state of Idaho, 1895-
96. [n.p., n.d.] 110 p. OrU **3452**

Garrett, Robert Max, 1881-
A word list from the Northwest. New Haven, American Dialect Society, 1919. 6 p. WaU **3453**

Garrioch, Alfred Campbell, 1848-1934.
The far and furry North; a story of life and love in the days of the Hudson's Bay Company. [Winnipeg, Douglass-McIntyre] 1925. 238 p.
CV CVicAr CVU **3454**
A hatchet mark in duplicate. Toronto, Ryerson [c1929] 282 p. CVicAr **3455**

Garrison, Abraham Elison, 1810-1890.
Life and labour of Rev. A. E. Garrison, forty years in Oregon: seven months on the plains, historical sketches of Oregon, January 1, 1887. [n.p., 1943] 130 p. ports. Many **3456**

Garrison, George Pierce, 1853-1910.
Westward extension, 1841-1850. New York, Harper, 1906. 366 p. port., 9 maps. (American nation, v. 17) Many **3457**

Garrison, Mrs. L. A.
Some birds of the Boise Valley. [n.p., n.d.] 1 v. IdB **3458**

Garst, Doris Shannon, 1899-
Scotty Allen, king of the dog-team drivers, illus. by Dan Sweeney. New York, Messner [1946] 238 p. front. (port.) illus. Many **3459**
Wish on an apple, illus. by Jon Nielsen. New York, Abingdon-Cokesbury [1948] 191 p. illus. Hood River apple orchard story. WaU **3460**

Garver, Frank Harmon.
Lewis and Clark in Beaverhead County. Dillon, Mont., Examiner, 1913. 1 v.
MtHi **3461**
Marking historical sites in Montana. Dillon, Mont. [Examiner, 1915?] 36 p. illus.
MtHi MtU WaU **3462**
Significance of county names of Montana. Dillon, Mont. [n.d.] 16 p. MtHi **3463**

Garvin, Jno. C., see no. 7133.

Gass, Patrick, 1771-1870.
Gass's journal of the Lewis and Clark expedition, by Seargeant Patrick Gass, one of the persons employed in the expedition, introd. by James Kendall Hosmer. Chicago, McClurg, 1904. liii, 298 p. port., 6 plates. Many **3464**
Journal of the voyages and travels of a corps of discovery under the command of Capt. Lewis and Capt. Clarke of the Army of the United States, from the mouth of the River Missouri through the interior parts of North America to the Pacific Ocean, during the years 1804, 1805, and 1806. Pittsburgh, M'Keehan, 1807. 262 p. table.
CVicAr MtHi OnP Wa WaU **3465**
Same. 1808. iv, 381 p.
CVicAr OrHi WaS WaU **3466**
Same. 2d ed. Philadelphia, Carey, 1810. 262 p. front., 5 plates. CVicAr OrP **3467**
Same. 3d ed. 1811. MtU WaU WaWW **3468**
Lewis and Clarke's journal to the Rocky Mountains in the years 1804-5-6. New ed. Dayton, Ohio, Ellis, 1847. 238 p. illus., 2 ports.
CVicAr CVU Or OrHi OrP WaU **3469**

Voyage des capitaines Lewis et Clarke, depuis l'embouchure du Missouri, jusqu'a l'entree de la Colombia dans l'Ocean Pacifique; fait dans les annees 1804, 1805, et 1806, par ordre du gouvernement des Etats-Unis; contenant le journal authentique des evenements les plus remarquables du voyage, ainsi que le description des habitants, du sol, du climat, et des productions animales et vegetales des pays situes a l'ouest de l'Amerique Septentrionale, redige en anglais par Patrice Gass, employe dans l'expedition, et traduit en francais par A. J. N. Lallemant, avec des notes, deux lettres du capitaine Clarke, et une carte gravee par J. B. Tardieu. Paris, Arthus-Bertrade, 1810. xviii, 443 p. map.
VCicAr OrHi OrP WaU **3470**
See also no. 5081.

Gaston, Joseph, 1838-1913.
The centennial history of Oregon, 1811-1912, with notice of antecedent explorations. Chicago, S. J. Clarke Pub. Co., 1912. 4 v. front. (port.) 63 plates, 644 ports., 13 maps, 12 facsims. Volumes 2-4 biographical. Many **3471**
Nehalem coal and timber road. [n.p., n.d.] [10] p. map, table. Anon. OrHi **3472**
Oregon, pictorial and biographical. DeLuxe supplement. Chicago, S. P. Clarke Pub. Co., 1912. 515 p. ports. A selection of biographies and ports. from v. 2-4 of Centennial history of Or. Anon.
OrSaW OrU WaU **3473**
Portland, Oregon, its history and builders in connection with the antecedent explorations, discoveries and movements of the pioneers that selected the site for the great city of the Pacific. Chicago, S. J. Clarke Pub. Co., 1911. 3 v. illus., maps. Many **3474**
Portland, the rose city; pictorial and biographical. DeLuxe supplement. Chicago, S. J. Clarke Pub. Co., 1911. 2 v. ports. Reprinted from v. 2-3 of Portland, Or.; its history, and builders. Anon.
Many **3475**

Gates, Charles Marvin, ed.
Five fur traders of the Northwest; being the narrative of Peter Pond and the diaries of John Macdonnell, Archibald N. McLeod, Hugh Faries, and Thomas Connor; with an introd. by Grace Lee Nute. [Minneapolis] Pub. for the Minn. Society of the Colonial Dames of America, Univ. of Minn. Press, 1933. v, 298 p. illus. maps. Many **3476**
Messages of the governors of the Territory of Washington to the Legislative Assembly, 1854-1889. Seattle, Univ. of Wash. Press, 1940. xx, 297 p. front., ports., maps (part fold.) (Publications in the social sciences, v. 12) Many **3477**
Readings in Pacific Northwest history. Washington, 1790-1895. Seattle, Univ. of Wash. Bookstore, 1941. 345 p. Many **3478**

Gatke, Robert Moulton, 1896-
Chronicles of Willamette, the pioneer university of the West, introd. by Bruce

Richard Baxter. Portland, Or., Binfords & Mort [c1943] 702 p. plates, ports.
Many **3479**

Gatlin, George Oury, 1888-
Some must wander; introd. by Arthur Sullivant Hoffman, illus. by W. F. McIlwraith. Portland, Or., Metropolitan, 1934. 133 p. front. (port.) illus. Portland poet.
Or OrCS OrHi WaSp WaU **3480**

Gatschet, Albert S., see no. 5090.

Gay, Theressa.
Life and letters of Mrs. Jason Lee, first wife of Rev. Jason Lee of the Oregon mission. Portland, Or., Metropolitan [c1936] 224 p. front., plates, ports., facsims.
Many **3481**

Gearhart, Dick, see no. 7607.

Geary, Edward R.
1876 centennial history of the Presbytery of Oregon. [n.p.] 1876. 12 p.   OrP **3482**

Gebhard, Elizabeth Louisa, 1859-1924.
The life and ventures of the original John Jacob Astor. Hudson, N. Y., Bryan Printing Co., 1915. 321 p. front. (port.) illus., 20 plates.
IdB MtU OrP OrU WaU **3483**

Gebhardt, A. E., see no. 3120.

Gee, George Edward.
Survivors [poems] [Poulsbo, Wash.? 194—?] 94 p. Poulsbo, Wash. author.
WaU **3484**

Geer, Theodore Thurston, 1851-1924.
Fifty years in Oregon: experiences, observations, and commentaries upon men, measures, and customs in pioneer days and later times. New York, Neale, 1912. 536 p. front. (port.) 12 plates.
Many **3485**
Same. 1916 [c1912]
IdP IdU OrLgE Wa WaPS WaU **3486**
Same. 1916. 540 p.   WaTC **3487**

Gellatly, Dorothy Hewlett.
A bit of Okanagan history; pen sketches by E. H. Emmens. Kelowna, B. C., Kelowna Printing Co., 1932. 80 p. front., illus.   CV CVic CVicAr CVU **3488**

Gellman, Paul, illus.
Tacoma and surroundings, introd. by Burke W. Ormsby, Tacoma. Nandoral Service Bureau [194—?] 1 v. illus.
WaT **3489**

General Defense Committee.
Eight men buried alive; the Centralia case calls to every decent man and woman in the state of Washington to act quickly. Chicago, 1924. 31 p.   WaU **3490**
These are the facts! The truth about the attempted mob outrage in Centralia on Armistace Day in 1919. Chicago [19—?] 15 p.   WaT **3491**

A general historical and descriptive review of the city of Seattle, Washington: her resources and advantages, her unexcelled transportation facilities by rail and water; her unrivalled industrial advantages and facilities for distribution as a wholesale jobbing center; a graphic description of her many enterprises and select representation of her banking,

shipping, professional and manufacturing interests. San Francisco, San Francisco Journal of Commerce Pub. Co., 1890. 32 p. plates, ports. WaS WaU **3492**

General history, Alaska Yukon Pacific Exposition, fully illustrated, compliments of Hotel Butler Annex, Seattle, Washington. [Seattle] 1909. 1 v. illus., ports.
CVicAr WaSp **3493**

General Steamship Corporation, Ltd.
Pacific coast shipping handbook, a desk manual for all those interested in maritime shipping and travel to and from the Pacific coast. [San Francisco] c1935. 63 p. illus., maps.
CV OrP WaS WaU **3494**
Same. c1938. 84 p.   OrCS OrU WaS **3495**

Gentry, L. W., Book and Job Printer, Corvallis, Or.
Corvallis, 1892; the metropolis and county seat of Benton County, Oregon. Corvallis, Or., 1892. 16 p. illus.
OrP OrU **3496**

Geographical description of the state of Texas: also of that part of the west coast of North America which includes Oregon and upper California. Philadelphia, Cowperthwait & Co., 1846. 62 p. illus., fold. map, tables.   OrP **3497**

Geography of Oregon, with page references to the natural geographies and a brief outline of the history of the Oregon country, based on McMaster's school history of the United States; handbook for the use of Oregon teachers. New York, American Book Co., 1897. 17 p.
OrHi WaU **3498**

George, Marian M., see nos. 5465, 5981-5983.

George, Melvin Clarke, 1849-
The Columbia Highway booklet; through the gorge of the Columbia River with geologic interpretations, former Indian tribes, topographic, historic, climatic and other interesting features; a guide with descriptions, maps and views from Portland to The Dalles, Oregon. [Portland, Or., n.d.] 72 p. illus., map.
CV OrP **3499**
Same. [Portland, Or., Printed by James, Kerns & Abbott, 192-?]   WaU **3500**
Same. [1923].   Or OrCS WaSp **3501**

George, W. G., see no. 6932.

George, William.
A sealer's journal; or, A cruise of the schooner "Umbrina". Victoria, B. C., Waterson, 1895. 136 p.   CVicAr **3502**

George, firm, pub., Bristol, England.
Rare old English and French classics and early books on Pacific coast explorations at your own prices. [1902-03, 1905, 1908. Bristol, 1902-08] 4 v. in 1. Sale in Seattle sponsored by Edmond S. Meany.
WaU **3503**

Georgetown Gazette-News, Seattle, Wash.
Duwamish edition. Seattle (Georgetown Station) 1911. 112 p. (Sept. 29-Oct. 6, 1911)   WaS **3504**

Gerlinger, Irene (Hazard)
A brief history of the Republican Party,

comp. for the Council of Oregon Republican Women and all Republicans. [Portland, Or.] 1946. 17 p. Or OrP OrU **3505**

A history of the Doernbecher Memorial Hospital for children and a history of the Doernbecher Hospital Guild. Portland, Or., 1931. 20 p. illus. Anon.

Or OrP **3506**

Money raising, how to do it. Los Angeles, Suttonhouse [c1938] 311 p. Many **3507**

Gerould, Mrs. Katharine (Fullerton) 1879-
The aristocratic West. New York, Harper, 1925. 220 p. front., plates. Many **3508**

Gerrish, Theodore, 1846-
Life in the world's wonderland; a graphic description of the Northwest, from the Mississippi River to the Land of the Midnight Sun; beauties of the Oregon and Columbia Rivers, and the famous inland passage from Tacoma, Washington Territory, to Sitka, Alaska; descriptions of the old Indian battle fields; stories of old trappers, freighters, miners and Indian fighters. [n.p.,n.d.] 421 p. front., illus. CVicAr **3509**

Same. [1886]
MtU Or OrP WaPS WaS **3510**

Same. Biddeford, Me., Biddeford Journal [1886] CVicAr OrU WaSp **3511**

Same. (From St. Paul, Minnesota instead of "from the Mississippi River") 1887.
CVicAr WaSp WaU **3512**

Gerstacker, Friedrich Wilhelm Christian, 1816-1872.
Les pionniers du far-west, tr. de l'anglais par B.-H. Revoil. Paris, Levy, 1874. 265 p.
WaU **3513**

The wanderings and fortunes of some German emigrants. New ed. London, Bogue, 1850. viii, 310 p. CVicAr **3514**

Western lands & western waters, with illus. from designs by eminent artists. London, S. O. Beeton, 1864. xii, 388 p. illus. CVicAr WaU **3515**

Wild sports in the Far West, with tinted illus. by Harrison Weir. London, G. Routledge, 1854. xi, 396 p. front., 7 plates.
CVicAr **3516**

Same. Boston, Crosby, Nichols, 1859.
CVicAr **3517**

The young gold-digger; or, A boy's adventures in the gold regions. London, Routledge, Warne, & Routledge, 1860. vii, 339 p. front. plates. CVicAr **3518**

See also nos. 3005, 3363.

Gerstner, E. V., see no. 3363.

Gertsmon, Simon, 1875-
Poems of the West. [n.p., n.d.] 33 p. plates.
WaU **3519**

Same. Boston, R. G. Badger [c1912] 67 p. front., plates. OrP **3520**

Gervais, Isaac Wilkinson.
The production and marketing of Douglas-fir Christmas trees on western Oregon farms. [Corvallis, Or., 1945] 1 v.
OrCS **3521**

Getchell, Mrs. Alice McClure.
Bibliography of Oregon Indian myths,

reprinted with additions from the Oregon Sunday Journal, July 27, 1924. [Salem, Or., State Library, 1924] 3 p. (Booklist 24, Dec. 1924.
Or OrHi OrU **3522**

Getty, Agnes K.
Blue gold; a romance of the Rockies. Caldwell, Idaho, Caxton, 1934. 358 p. Montana story.
IdIf MtU WaE WaPS WaS **3523**

Getty, Jennie Violet, 1861-1913.
Bird life in Washington; treating of the birds of the state of Washington, their songs and nesting habits; with 20 drawings by the author and 42 photographs. [Seattle] Lowman & Hanford [c1916] 134 p. front. (port.) illus.
Wa WaS WaU **3524**

Little friends of the snow; treating of the mountain flowers of the state of Washington, illus. from drawings by the author, and photographs. [Seattle] Lowman & Hanford [c1914] [90] p. illus.
OrP Wa WaU **3525**

Ghent, William James, 1866-1942.
The early Far West; a narrative outline, 1540-1850. New York, Longmans, 1931. xi, 411 p. front., plates, ports., maps.
Many **3526**

Same. New York, Tudor Pub. Co., 1936 [c1931] Many **3527**

The road to Oregon, a chronicle of the great emigrant trail, with 32 illus. and a map. London, Longmans, 1929. xvi, 274 p. front., plates, ports., map. Many **3528**

Same. New York, Tudor Pub. Co., 1934.
CVU MtBozC WaWW **3529**

See also no. 3941.

Gianetti, Michelangiolo.
Elogy of Captain James Cook, composed and publickly recited before the Royal Academy of Florence, trans. into English by a member of the Royal Academy of Florence. Florence, Printed for G. Cambiagi [1785] 87 p. WaU **3530**

Gibbon, John Murray, 1875-
Canadian Pacific history; four addresses. [n.p.] 1936. 36 p. ports. CVicAr **3531**

The romantic history of the Canadian Pacific; the Northwest Passage of to-day. New York, Tudor Pub. Co., 1937. 423 p. front., illus., plates (part col.) ports., maps (2 fold.) facsims.
WaU **3532**

Steel of empire; the romantic history of the Canadian Pacific, the Northwest Passage of today. Indianapolis, Bobbs-Merrill [c1935] 423 p. col. front., illus., 43 plates (9 col.) 7 col. ports., 3 fold. maps, facsims. Many **3533**

Gibbons, Cardinal, see no. 5352.

Gibbons, Charles Harrison.
A sourdough Samaritan. London, Hodder [1923] 320 p. CVicAr CVU **3534**
See also no. 1107.

Gibbs, George, 1815-1873.
Alphabetical vocabularies of the Clallam and Lummi. New York, Cramoisy Press, 1863. 40 p. (Shea's library of American linguistics. 11) CVicAr WaU **3535**

Alphabetical vocabulary of the Chinook language. New York, Cramoisy Press, 1863. 23 p. (Shea's library of American linguistics, 13)
CVicAr OrP WaS WaU 3536

Dictionary of the Chinook jargon, or trade language of Oregon. New York, Cramoisy, 1863. xiv, 43 p.
CVicAr MtU Or WaSp WaU 3537
See also nos. 2136, 7871.

Gibson, Dan Ward.
Rainier, the epic of the mountain, illus. by Eustace Paul Ziegler, decorations by Roy H. Terry. [Seattle, Craftsman Press] 1947. 1 v. illus. WaS 3538

Gibson, J. Watt, b. 1829.
Recollections of a pioneer. [St. Joseph, Mo., Nelson-Hanne Printing Co., 1912] 216 p. front. (port.) IdB WaU 3539

Gibson, Paris, 1830-1920.
The founding of Great Falls and some of its early records. [n.p., 19—] 27 p.
MtHi 3540

Gibson Will E.
The why of governmental costs of Multnomah County. [n.p., 1933?] 18 p.
OrP 3541

Giffen, Naomi Musmaker.
The roles of men and women in Eskimo culture. Chicago, Univ. of Chicago Press [1930] xiii, 113 p. (Publications in anthropology. Ethnological series) CVicAr CVU MtU OrPR OrSaW WaWW 3542

Gilbert, Alfred B.
The way of the Indian, original drawings by Carrie M. Gilbert. Portland, Or., Frances E. Gotshall [n.d.] [55] p. front., illus. OrHi Wa 3543
Same. [1908?] 37 p. front., illus., 4 plates, 3 ports. OrHi WaPS WaSp 3544

Gilbert, DeWitt, see no. 8056.

Gilbert, Edmund William.
The exploration of western America, 1800-1850; an historical geography. Cambridge [Eng.] Univ. Press, 1933. xiii, 233 p. illus., plates, ports., 3 fold. maps. Many 3545

Gilbert, Frank T.
Historic sketches of Walla Walla, Whitman, Columbia and Garfield Counties, Washington Territory. Portland Or., Walling, 1882. 447 [12] 66 p. illus., plates, ports. Biographical supplement, 66 p. at end. Many 3546
Same. 488 [12] 66 p. Many 3547
Resources, business, and business men of Montana, 1888. [Walla Walla, W. T.] Historic Pub. Co. [1888] 112 p. illus.
MtHi MtU OrU 3548

Gilbert, G. K., see no. 2507.

Gilbert, James Henry, 1878-
The development of banking in Oregon. [Eugene, Or.] Univ. of Or. [1911] 30 p. (Bulletin. New series, v. 9, no. 1)
IdU Or OrCS OrP OrU WaU 3549
Fugitive works. Eugene, Or., Univ. Press, 1947. 10 p. OrP 3550
Trade and currency in early Oregon; a study in the commercial and monetary history of the Pacific Northwest. New York, Columbia Univ. Press, Macmillan Co., agents, 1907. 126 p. diagr. (Studies in history, economics, and public law, v. 26, no. 1) Many 3551

Gilbert, John Failing.
Greater Spokane's builders; containing cartoons of one hundred business and professional men of Spokane, Washington. Spokane, Walton-Gilbert Pub. Co. [1906] 205 p. illus. WaSp 3552

Gilbert, Kenneth.
Bird dog bargain; drawings by Ernest Norling. New York, Holt [1947] 200 p. illus. Or OrP Wa WaS WaSp WaU 3553

Gilbert, W. S.
Oregon in the Philippines. [n.p.] 1899. 33 p. OrHi OrP 3554

Gilbert, Walter Edwin.
Arctic pilot; life and work on North Canadian air routes as told to Kathleen Shackleton. London, Nelson [1940] 256 p. front., plates, ports.
CVicAr CVU WaS 3555

Gilbert, William A.
An old church in a new land, being an historical sketch of the Episcopal Church in the upper Kittitas Valley, Episcopal Church in this field held at Calvary Church, Roslyn, on Decoration Day, 1941. [n.p., 1941?] 5 p. Wa 3556

Gilbert, William Allen.
The orthographic keyboard. [Spokane, Shaw & Borden, 1930] 94 p. illus.
WaS WaSp 3557

Gilbert, William B., see no. 211.

Gilder, William Henry, 1838-1900.
Schwatka's search; sledging in the Arctic in quest of the Franklin records. New York, Scribner, 1881. xvi, 316 p. front. (port.) illus., plates, 3 maps.
CVicAr OrHi OrP WaS WaU 3558

Gilfry, Henry H.
An address delivered at the Pacific Coast Building, Philadelphia, Friday, August 4th, 1876, at 11 o'clock a. m. on the growth, history, etc., of Oregon. Salem, Or., Carter, 1878. 62 p.
OrP WaWW 3559

Gilkey, Gordon W., 1912-
A series of etchings showing construction progress of the University of Oregon Library, including: Advent of the library, by Frederick M. Hunter; A symbol of human progress, by C. Valentine Boyer; New University of Oregon Library Building, by M. H. Douglass; A few words from one of the architects, by Ellis F. Lawrence. [n.p., 1936] 6 p. 30 plates. Or OrP OrU 3560

Gilkey, Helen Margaret, 1886-
Handbook of northwest flowering plants, by Helen M. Gilkey assisted by Garland M. Powell. Portland, Or., Metropolitan [c1936] vi, 407 p. illus., 3 plates.
Many 3561

Same. [Corvallis, Or., 1942] vi, 413 p. 2d ed., 2d printing. CVU OrCS OrP WaU 3562

Same. [c1946] OrCS OrU WaE 3563

A spring flora of northwestern Oregon. [Corvallis, Or., c1929] xxxii, 153 p. illus.
Many **3564**

Gill, Frances.
Chloe dusts her mantel; a pioneer woman's idyl. New York, Press of the Pioneers, 1935. 88 p. Oregon story.
Many **3565**

Gill, Mrs. Harriet (Markham)
Highways of Oregon, with scenes of the Oregon country. Portland, Or., Metropolitan, 1932. 65 p. front., 4 plates. Poems.
Many **3566**

[Gill, J. K., Co.]
Picturesque Oregon. [Portland, Or., 1916?] [24] p. illus.
Or **3567**

Gill, John Kaye, 1851-1929.
Gill's dictionary of the Chinook jargon, with examples of use in conversation, comp. from all existing vocabularies and greatly improved by the addition of necessary words never before published. 9th ed. Portland, Or., [18—?] 62 p.
WaPS **3568**

Same. 10th ed. 1884. 60 p.
OrU **3569**

Same. 11th ed. 1887. Anon.
Or OrHi OrP Wa WaU **3570**

Same. 12th ed. 1889. 63 p. Anon.
OrCS OrMonO OrU WaPS WaU **3571**

Same. 13th ed. 1891. Anon.
OrP WaS WaU WaWW **3572**

Same. 14th ed. 1902.
CVU OrHi OrP WaWW **3573**

Same. 15th ed. 1909. 84 p. Contains notes upon tribes and tongues.
Many **3574**

Some. 17th ed. 80 p.
Many **3575**

Gillett, E. J., see no. 4686.

Gillham, Charles Edward.
Beyond the Clapping Mountains; Eskimo stories from Alaska, illus. by Chanimun. New York, Macmillan, 1943. 134 p. illus.
Or WaS WaSp WaT WaU **3576**

Raw North; illus. by Bob Hines. New York, A. S. Barnes, c1947. 275 p. illus.
Or OrP WaS **3577**

Gillilan, James David.
Thomas Corwin Iliff; apostle of home missions in the Rocky Mountains. New York, Methodist Book Concern [c1919] 193 p. front. (port.) 2 plates, 2 ports.
IdB MtHi **3578**

Trail tales. New York, Abington Press [c1915] 182 p. front. (port.) 2 plates, port.
IdB IdP IdU OrP WaSp WaU **3579**

Gillis, Charles J.
Another summer; the Yellowstone Park and Alaska. [New York, 1893] 76 p.
CVicAr MtHi WaU **3580**

Gillis, W. D.
The Idaho Legislature; a survey of Idaho legislative procedure together with a compilation with indexes, of the rules of its Senate and House of Representatives and of those constitutional provisions, statutory enactments in reference to the Legislature. [Arco, Idaho, Arco Advertiser] 1928. 119 p. IdIf **3581**

Gillmore, Parker.
A hunter's adventures in the great West. London, Hurst, 1871. x, 336 p. front.
MtHi WaU **3582**

Gilman, Daniel Coit, 1831-1908.
The life of James Dwight Dana, scientific explorer, mineralogist, geologist, zoologist, professor in Yale University. New York, Harper, 1899. xii, 409 p. front., plates, ports., map.
Many **3583**

Gilman, Isabel Ambler.
Alaska, the American Northland, illus. with maps and with engravings from photographs. Yonkers-on-Hudson, N. Y., World Book Co., 1923. viii, 343 p. front., illus. (Interamerican geographical readers)
CV Or WaPS WaS WaSp WaU **3584**

Same. 1924 [c1922]
WaU **3585**

Same. 1926 [c1922]
Wa **3586**

Alaskaland; a curious contradiction. New York, Harriman [c1914] 110 p. front., plates.
WaS WaU **3587**

Great Northwest. [Olympia, Wash., Recorder Press, c1909] [12] p. illus.
OrHi WaU **3588**

Gilman, William.
Our hidden front. New York, Reynal [c1944] 266 p. plates.
Many **3589**

Gilmore, Charles Whitney, 1874-1945.
Papers concerning the palaeontology of the Cretaceous and later Tertiary of Oregon, of the Pliocene of northwestern Nevada, and of the late Miocene and Pleistocene of California, by Charles W. Gilmore, John H. Maxson, John C. Merriam, and Chester Stock. Washington, D. C., Carnegie Institution of Washington, 1928. v, 58 p. illus., plates. (Contributions to palaeontology. Pub. no. 393)
Many **3590**

See also no. 6759.

Gilmore, F. T., see no. 319.

Gilmore. W. A., comp.
Souvenir, Portland Fire Department, Portland, Oregon, pub. in the interests of the Firemen's Relief Fund. Portland, Or., Irwin-Hodson Co., 1905. 304 p. illus., ports.
OrHi WaPS **3591**

Souvenir, Tacoma Fire Department. illus.; pub. in the interest of the Firemen's Relief Fund, September, 1902. Tacoma, Vaughan & Morrill Printing Co., 1902. 150 p. illus.
WaT **3592**

Souvenir. Walla Walla Police Department and Fire Department. [Walla Walla, Wash.] Union Printing & Pub. Co., 1903. 80 p. illus., ports.
WaPS **3593**

Gilpin, William, 1822-1894.
The central gold region; the grain and gold regions of North America, with some new views of its physical geography; and observations on the Pacific railroad. Philadelphia, Sower, Barnes & Co., 1860. 194 p. front. (fold. map) 5 fold. maps.
OrU WaU **3594**

Gilstrap, W. H., see no. 10762.

[Giorda, Joseph] 1823-1882.
A dictionary of the Kalispel or Flathead Indian language, comp. by the missionaries of the Society of Jesus. [St. Ignatius] Mont., St. Ignatius Printery, 1877-79. 2 v.
Many **3595**

Lu tel kaimintis kolinzuten kuitlt smiimii: Some narratives from the Holy Bible in Kalispel, comp. by the missionaries of the Society of Jesus. [n.p.] St. Ignatius Printery, Mont., 1879. 140, 14 p.
CV MtHi WaPS WaSp WaU **3596**

Smimii lu tel kaimintis kolinzuten: Narratives from the Holy Scripture in Kalispel. [St. Ignatius] Mont., St. Ignatius Printery, 1876. 140, 14 p.
WaPS WaU **3597**

Szmimeies-s Jesus Christ; catechism of the Christian doctrine in the Flathead or Kalispel language, comp. by the missionaries of the Society of Jesus. [St. Ignatius] Mont., St. Ignatius Printery, 1880. 45 p.
MtU WaU **3598**

Gipson, Alice Edna.
Silence. Caldwell, Idaho, Caxton, 1930. 214 p. front.
Many **3599**

Giraud, Marcel.
Le metis canadien; son role dans l'histoire de provinces de l'Ouest. Paris, Institut d'Ethnologie, 1945. lvi, 1296 p. illus., 8 plates, 4 fold. maps. (Universite de Paris. Travaux et memoires de l'Institut d'Ethnologie, v. 44)
CVicAr **3600**

Gischler, Pearl Clements, see nos. 4236-4238.

Gist, Arthur Stanley, 1883-
New stories from Eskimo land, by Arthur S. Gist and Arthur Hansin Eide and Ruth Palmer Gist. San Francisco, Harr Wagner [c1930] viii, 214 p. illus., plates, map. Seattle authors.
Or WaS **3601**

The teaching and supervision of reading, by Arthur S. Gist and William A. King. New York, Scribner [c1927] xi, 337 p. illus., diagrs.
Many **3602**

Gist, Ruth Palmer, see no. 3601.

Gladfelter, Katharine Eleanor.
Under the North Star; a course on Alaska for junior boys and girls. New York, Friendship Press [c1928] viii, 135 p. fold. plates.
Wa **3603**

Gladston, W. S., see no. 5692.

The Glasgow Courier, Glasgow, Mont.
Fort Peck ed. Glasgow, Valley County, Mont., 1914. 128 p. (v. 10, no. 45, Mar. 20, 1914)
MtU **3604**

Golden anniversary, Fort Peck progress edition. Glasgow, Mont., 1937. [72] p. illus. (Nov. 30, 1937)
WaSp **3605**

Glasscock, Carl Burgess, 1884-
The war of the copper kings; builders of Butte and wolves of Wall Street. Indianapolis, Bobbs-Merrill [c1935] 314 p. front., plates, ports., facsims.
Many **3606**

Same. New York, Grosset [c1935]
CVicAr WaE WaTC WaU **3607**

Glassley, Ray Hoard, 1887-
Visit the Pacific Northwest. Portland, Or., Binfords & Mort [c1948] 182 p. front., illus.
Many **3608**

Glazebrook, G. P., see no. 4059.

Glazebrook, T., see no. 4059.

Glimpses of the Alaska-Yukon-Pacific Exposition, Seattle, Washington, and the great Northwest; realistic views illustrating the wonderful growth and resources of the great western America. Chicago, Laird & Lee, c1909. [112] p. of illus.
OrP WaS **3609**

Glimpses of the Lewis and Clark Exposition, Portland, Oregon, and the golden West, illustrating the nation's wonderful progress and development. Chicago, Laird & Lee, c1905. [180] p. front., illus.
Or OrP WaT WaU **3610**

Glisan, Rodney, 1827-1890.
Journal of army life. San Francisco, A. L. Bancroft and Co., 1874. xi, 511 p. front., 20 plates, fold table. Oregon and Wash. Indian wars.
Many **3611**

Glody, Robert, see no. 6576.

Glorious Kottenay, [n.p., n.d.] 30 p. illus., map, table.
CVicAr **3612**

Glover, Eli Sheldon, 1845-1919.
The diary of Eli Sheldon Glover, October-December, 1875; transcribed from the original by the Oregon Historical Records Survey project, Division of Professional and Service Projects, Work Projects Administration, sponsored by the University of Oregon. Portland, Or., Historical Records Survey Project, 1940. 41 p.
IdB Or OrHi WaS WaU **3613**

Glynn-Ward, H., see nos. 4689-4693.

Goddard, Frederick Bartlett, 1834-
Where to emigrate and why; describes the climate, soil, productions, minerals and general resources, amount of public lands, the quality and price of farm lands in nearly all sections of the United States; and contains a description of the Pacific railroad, the homestead and other land laws, rates of wages throughout the country, etc. New York, 1869. 591 p. plates, maps (part. fold. and col.)
IdB OrU WaS WaSp WaU **3614**

Where to emigrate and why, homes and fortunes in the boundless West and the sunny South, with a complete history and description of the Pacific railroad. Philadelphia, Peoples Pub. Co., 1869. 591 p. 15 plates, 19 maps (part fold.)
CVicAr MtU Or OrP WaPS WaU **3615**

Goddard, John. W.
Washington, the Evergreen state, yesterday, today, tomorrow. New York, Scribner [1942] 311 p. front., illus.
Many **3616**

Goddard, Pliny Earle, 1869-1928.
Indians of the Northwest coast. New York [American Museum of Natural History Press] 1924. 176 p. front., illus., plates, fold. map. (Handbook series no. 10)
Many **3617**

Same. 2d ed. 1934.
Many **3618**

Same. 2d ed. 1945.
CVU OrHi OrU WaT WaU **3619**

See also no. 1635.

Godenrath, Percy F.
Mother Earth's treasure vaults and other true tales of achievement, development and opportunity in the Boundary, southern Okanagan, Similkameen, Nicola districts of B. C. Victoria, B. C., British Colonist [1905] 56 p. illus., plates.
CVicAr **3620**

Godfrey, E. S., see nos. 2669, 7222.

Godsell, Philip Henry, 1889-
Arctic trader; the account of twenty years with the Hudson's Bay Company. New York, Putnam [c1934] 329 p. front. (port.) 11 plates. Many **3621**

Red hunters of the snows; an account of thirty years' experience with the primitive Indian and Eskimo tribes of the Canadian North-west and Arctic coast, with a brief history of the early contact between white fur traders and the aborigines. Toronto, Ryerson [c1938] 324 p. front., 16 plates, fold. map.
CVic CVicAr CVU **3622**

The romance of the Alaska Highway. Toronto, Ryerson [c1944] xv, 235 p. front., plates, ports., map. Many **3623**
Same. [1945, c1944]
CV CVicAr OrCS OrU **3624**

They got their man; or, Patrol with the North West Mounted. Toronto, Ryerson, [c1939] 287 p. front. (port.) 7 plates.
CVicAr **3625**

The vanishing frontier; a saga of traders, mounties and men of the last North West. Toronto, Ryerson [c1939] 285 p. front., 15 plates, fold. map.
CVicAr CVU **3626**

Godwin, George Stanley, 1889-
The eternal forest. London, Philip Allan [c1929] 318 p. British Columbia novel.
CVicAr CVU **3627**

Vancouver, a life, 1757-1798. [London] Philip Allan, 1930. xi, 308 p. front. (port.) illus., 5 plates (1 fold.) ports., maps (2 fold.) facsims. Many **3628**
Same. New York, Appleton, 1931.
Many **3629**

Goetze, O. D.
Souvenir of north western Alaska, illus. San Francisco, Wm. Brown Engraving Co. [n.d.] 48 plates. WaPS WaSp **3630**

Goffin, Mrs. Marie Miller, 1877-
The trail of the plow, an historical novel. Portland, Or., Binfords & Mort [c1940] 272 p. Many **3631**

Gold Flotation Development Company, Mullan, Idaho.
Gold Flotation Development Company, Incorporated under the laws of Idaho. Everett, Wash., Kane & Harcus [1921?] 20 p. illus., maps, facsims. Property located near Salmon, Lemhi County, Idaho. WaPS **3632**

Goldenstein, Pauline (Garrison)
Home songs, drawings by Laura Edith Darrow. Caldwell, Idaho, Caxton, 1926. 19 p. col. illus., plate. IdIf IdU **3633**

Golder, Frank Alfred, 1877-1929.
Bering's voyages; an account of the efforts of the Russians to determine the relation of Asia to America. New York, American Geographical Society, 1922-25. 2 v. plates, maps (1 fold.) facsims, fold. chart. (Research series, no. 1, 2)
Many **3634**

Father Herman, Alaska's saint. Pullman, Wash. [191—?] 29 p. front. (port.)
WaU **3635**

Russian expansion on the Pacific, 1641-1850; an account of the earliest and later expeditions made by the Russians along the Pacific Coast of Asia and North America, including some related expeditions to the Arctic regions. Cleveland, A. H. Clark Co., 1914. 368 p. front., maps, facsim. Many **3636**

Goldfrank, Esther Schiff.
Changing configurations in the social organization of a Blackfoot tribe during the reserve period (The Blood of Alberta, Canada). New York, J. J. Augustin [1945] vii, 73 p. front., 4 plates. (Monographs of the American Ethnological Society, 8) CVicAr WaS WaU **3637**

Goldschmidt, Levin, see no. 3879.

Goldson, William.
Observations on the passage between the Atlantic and Pacific Oceans in two memoirs on the Straits of Anian and the discoveries of DeFonte elucidated by a new and original map to which is prefixed an historical abridgement of discoveries in the North of America. Portsmouth, Mobray, 1793. xii, 162 p. front. (fold. map). CVicAr OrP **3638**

Golombek, Bedrich, see no. 10836.

Golovnin, Vasilii Mikhailovich, 1776-1831.
Puteshestvie vokrug svieta po povelieniiu gosudaria imperatora sovershennoe na voennom shliupie Kamchatkie v 1817, 1818 i 1819 godakh, flota kapitanom Golovninym. Sankpeterburg, Moraskaia tipografiia, 1822. 2 v. fold. maps, tables (part fold.) WaU **3639**

Good, John Booth, 1833-1916.
Offices for the solemnization of matrimony, the visitation of the sick and the burial of the dead, trans. into the Nitlakapamuk or Thompson Indian tongue. Victoria, B. C., St. Paul's Mission Press, 1880. 15 p. CVicAr **3640**

A vocabulary and outlines of grammar of the Nitlakapamuk or Thompson tongue (the Indian language spoken between Yale, Lillooet, Cache Creek and Nicola Lake); together with a phonetic Chinook dictionary adapted for use in the province of British Columbia. Victoria, B. C., St. Paul's Mission Press, 1880. 46 p. CVicAr OrHi WaU WaWW **3641**

Good, Rachel Applegate, see no. 9493.

Goodfellow, Florence (Agassiz) 1854-1940.
Memories of pioneer life in British Columbia. Wenatchee, Wash., 1945. 43 p. ports.
CVicAr CVU WaS WaT WaU **3642**

Goodfellow, John C.
The totem poles in Stanley Park. [Vancouver, B. C., Art, Historical and Scientific Assn., 1928?] 44 p. plates.
CV CVicAr CVU OrU WaS WaU **3643**

Goodhart, George Walter, 1842-1927.
The pioneer life of George W. Goodhart and his association with the Hudson's Bay and American Fur Company's traders and trappers; trails of early Idaho, as told to Abraham C. Anderson; illus.: photos by Abraham C. Anderson, draw-

ings by Jo G. Martin. Caldwell, Idaho, Caxton, 1940. 368 p. col. front., illus., plates. Many **3644**

Goodhue, Cornelia.
Journey into the fog; the story of Vitus Bering and the Bering Sea. Garden City, N. Y., Doubleday, 1944. x, 179 p.
Many **3645**

Goodloe, Abbie Carter, 1867-
At the foot of the Rockies. New York, Scribner, 1905. 290 p. front., 3 plates.
CVicAr CVU Or **3646**

Goodman, A. E.
Klondyke gold fields, Yukon District; map of routes, mining regulations. [n.p., n.d.] 32 p. front. (fold. map) CVicAr **3647**

Goodrich, Frederick W., ed.
Oregon Catholic hymnal. Portland, Or., Catholic Book and Church Supply Co., c1912. 162 p. OrHi **3648**

[Goodrich, Samuel Griswold] 1793-1860.
The manners, customs, and antiquities of the Indians of North and South America, by the author of Peter Parley's tales. Boston, Bradbury, Soden and Co., 1844. 336 p. front., illus. WaS WaU **3649**

Same. Boston, Rand, 1849. WaWW **3650**

Goodsir, Robert Anstruther.
An Arctic voyage to Baffin's Bay and Lancaster Sound in search of friends with Sir John Franklin. London, J. Van Voorst, 1850. viii, 152 p. front., fold. map.
CVicAr CVU **3651**

Goodspeed, George Edward, see no. 11095.

Goodwin, Arthur Eliot.
Markets: public and private, their establishment and administration. Seattle, Montgomery Printing Co. [c1929] xxiii, 315 p. illus., diagrs.
Or OrP Wa WaS **3652**

Goodwin, Cardinal Leonidas, 1880-
John Charles Fremont, an explanation of his career. Stanford, Univ., Calif., Stanford Univ. Press, 1930. xi, 285 p. fold. map. Many **3653**

The trans-Mississippi West (1803-1853) a history of its acquisition and settlement. New York, Appleton, 1922. x, 528 p. maps (part fold.) Many **3654**

Same. 1930. IdIf WaTC **3655**

[Goodwin, Joseph]
The Northwest America Mission of the Church Missionary Society. [London, Johns, 1856?] 20, 24 p. 2 maps.
CVicAr **3656**

Goodyear, Watson Andrews, 1838-1891.
The coal mines of the western coast of the United States. San Francisco, A. L. Bancroft & Co., 1877. 153 p.
CVicAr Or OrP WaPS WaT WaU **3657**

Same. New York, Wiley, 1879. 153 p. illus.
IdU OrCS OrU WaS WaU **3658**

Goodykoontz, Colin Brummitt, 1885-
Home missions on the American frontier, with particular reference to the American Home Missionary Society. Caldwell, Idaho, Caxton, 1939. 460 p. Many **3659**
See also no. 1954.

Gordon, Charles William, 1860-1937.
Corporal Cameron of the North West Mounted Police; a tale of the Macleod Trail, by Ralph Connor [pseud.] New York, Doran [c1912] 454 p. Many **3660**

Same. New York, Grosset, c1912.
CV Wa WaE WaSp WaT WaW **3661**

Same. Toronto, Westminster Co. [1906]
CVU WaU **3662**

Doctor; a tale of the Rockies, by Ralph Connor [pseud.] New York, Revell [c1906] 399 p. OrP Wa WaE WaWW **3663**

Same. Toronto, Westminster Co. [c1906]
CVU WaSp **3664**

The doctor of Crows Nest, by Ralph Connor [pseud.] London, Hodder & Stoughton, 1906. viii, 399 p. CVU **3665**

Same. 1907. CVicAr **3666**

The Gaspards of Pine Croft; a romance of the Windermere. New York, Burt [c1923] 318 p. WaSp WaT **3667**

Same. New York, Doran [1923]
Or Wa WaE **3668**

Same. Toronto, McClelland [c1923]
CV CVicAr CVU **3669**

Life of James Robertson; missionary superintendent in the Northwest Territories. New York, Revell [c1908] 403 p. front. (port.) 6 ports.
OrP Wa WaT **3670**

Same. Toronto, Westminster Co. [c1908]
CVU **3671**

The patrol of the Sun Dance Trail, by Ralph Connor [pseud.] New York, Burt, c1914. 363 p. WaT **3672**

Same. New York, Hodder & Stoughton, Doran [c1914] Many **3673**

Same. Toronto, Westminster Co. [c1914]
CVU WaU **3674**

Prospector; a tale of the Crow's Nest Pass, by Ralph Connor [pseud.] New York, Revell [1904] 401 p.
OrSaW WaE WaWW **3675**

Same. Toronto, Westminster Co. [c1904]
CVU WaSp **3676**

Same. Special ltd. ed. New York, Grosset [c1904] Or OrP **3677**

Gordon, Daniel Miner.
Mountain and prairie; a journey from Victoria to Winnipeg, via Peace River Pass. London, Low, 1880. x, 310 p. front., plates, fold. maps.
CV CVic CVicAr CVU MtHi WaU **3678**

Same. Montreal, Dawson Bros., 1880.
CVicAr CVU IdU WaU **3679**

Gordon, George Byron, 1870-1927.
In the Alaskan wilderness. Philadelphia, Winston, 1917. 247 p. front. (port.) plates, maps (part fold.)
CVicAr CVU Or WaS WaU **3680**

Gordon, Lord Granville Armyne, 1856-
Nootka; a tale of Vancouver Island. London, Sands, 1899. 245 p. front., 11 plates, map.
CV CVicAr CVU OrP WaT WaU **3681**

Gordon, John.
In memoriam, Douglas Wright Williams. [n.p., 1891] 45 p. port.   Or OrP **3682**

Gordon, Kenneth Llewellyn, 1899-
The Amphibia and Reptilia of Oregon. Corvallis, Or., Or. State College [1929] 82 p. illus. (Monographs. Studies in zoology, no. 1)   OrAshS
    OrP OrSaW WaS WaT WaTC **3683**

The natural history and behavior of the western chipmunk and the mantled ground squirrel. Corvallis, Or., Or. State College, 1943. 104 p. illus., tables (Monographs. Studies in zoology, no. 5, Feb. 1943)
    OrSaW WaPS WaS WaSp WaTC **3684**

Gordon, Ralph Semmes.
Allez oop! a far from depressing book on the depression, illus. by the author. Seattle, Seattle Daily Times, 1931. 47 p. illus.   Wa **3685**

"Hello, Bill!" An historical compendium of the world's greatest gang of good fellows, illus. by the author. Seattle, F. McCaffrey, 1931. [59] p. illus.
    Wa WaU **3686**

Pioneer daze, a history a la carte and a la cartoon, wherein may be found an absent treatment of historical facts concerning the early days of Seattle and the Puget Sound country, which should settle for all time the question that the name of the mountain is Rainier. The tome is supported by art work from the studio of the author, co-adjutated by Stoddard King. Seattle, Lowman & Hanford, 1930. [25] p. front., illus.
    IdU Wa WaS WaU **3687**

Gordon, Samuel.
Recollection of old Milestown, Montana. Miles City, Mont., Yellowstone Journal, 1918. 42 p. front. (port.) illus., 16 plates, 2 ports.   MtHi **3688**

Gordon, William John.
Round about the North Pole, with woodcuts and other illus. by Edward Whymper. London, Murray, 1907. 294 p. front., plates, ports, maps.
    CVicAr IdB OrP **3689**

Gordon, William Steward.
The western spirit; a bunch of breezy poems. New York, Methodist Book Concern [c1914] 157 p. front. (port.) illus.
    Or OrHi OrP OrSaW WaU **3690**

Gorham, William H., 1816-1891.
An address upon the occasion of the dedication of a monument to the memory of Brother John Webster, first Worshipful Master of St. John's Lodge No. 9, F. & A. M., at Seattle, Washington. Seattle, St. John's Lodge No. 9 [c1905] [15] p.
    WaU **3691**

Gorham Manufacturing Co.
The soul of Alaska; a comment and a description, to which is added a catalogue raisonne of a series of bronze statuettes illustrative of Alaska Indian characteristics and social habitudes, modelled by Louis Potter and cast in bronze by the Gorham Company. New York, 1905. 96 p. front., plates.
    WaU **3692**

Gorrell, Joseph R.
A trip to Alaska, with compliments of the author. Newton, Iowa, 1905. [40] p.
    CVicAr WaS **3693**

Gose, J. Gordon, see no. 5332.

Gosnell, R. Edward, 1860-1931.
British Columbia; a digest of reliable information regarding its natural resources and industrial possibilities. Vancouver, B. C., News-Advertiser, 1890. 47 p.   CVic CVicAr WaU **3694**

Compiled from the Year book of British Columbia and manual of provincial information, to which is added a chapter containing much special information respecting the Canadian Yukon and Northern Territory generally. Victoria, B. C., 1897. 284 p. front., illus., fold. plate, ports., maps.   Many **3695**

Same. 1897 [1901]   CVU **3696**

A history; British Columbia, comp. by the Lewis Pub. Co. [Victoria, B. C.?] Hill Binding Co., 1906. x, 783 p. front., plates, ports. CV CVicAr CVU WaSp WaU **3697**

The story of confederation, with postscript on Quebec situation. [Victoria, B. C.? c1918] 156 p. illus., ports.
    CV CVic CVicAr CVU WaPS WaU **3698**

The story of Hatley Park, residence of the late Hon. James Dunsmuir of pioneer Vancouver Island family. [Victoria, B. C., Diggon-Hibben, n.d.] [8] p. Abridged from author's "Sixty years of progress."
    CVicAr **3699**

See also nos. 1832-1834, 9066.

Goss, Oliver Perry Morton, 1878-
Structural timber hand book on Pacific Coast woods, written and comp. by O. P. M. Goss assisted by Carl Heinmiller. [Seattle, West Coast Lumbermen's Assn., c1916] 289 p. illus., map, diagrs.
    Many **3700**

Gosset, William Driscoll.
Industrial exhibition; circular respectfully addressed to the inhabitants of British Columbia, by W. Driscoll Gosset and J. Vernon Seddall. New Westminster, B. C., Printed at the R. E. Camp, 1861. 20 p.   CVicAr **3701**

Goudey, Edward E.
Portland mortgages. [Portland, Or., 1914?] 16 p.   OrP **3702**

Gould, Dorothy Wheaton (Fay).
Beyond the shining mountains. Portland, Or., Binfords & Mort [c1938] 206 p. front., illus.   Many **3703**

Gould, L. McLeod.
From B. C. to Baisieux; being the narrative history of the 102d Canadian Infantry Battalion. Victoria, B. C., Cusack, 1919. 134 [96] p. front. (port.) illus., ports., plan.   CV CVU **3704**

Gould, Mrs. Lauretta Bernard, d. 1936.
History of the Aged and Infirm Women's Home, Victoria, 1897-1928. [Victoria, B. C., Banfield, 1928] 16 p. plates, ports.
    CVicAr **3705**

Gould, M. K., see no. 899.

Gould, Rupert Thomas, 1890-
Captain Cook. London, Duckworth [1935] 144 p. illus., maps. (Great lives, 49)
                                   CVicAr CVU **3706**

Goulder, William Armistead, 1821-
Reminiscences; incidents in the life of a pioneer in Oregon and Idaho. Boise, Idaho, T. Regan, 1909. 376 p. front. (port.)   Many **3707**

Gove, George.
Seattle, historical, civic and architectural data comp. for the Women's Univ. Club. [Tacoma] 1938. 18 p. maps (blueprints)
                                   WaS WaT **3708**

Gowen, Herbert Henry, 1864-
Church work in British Columbia, being a memoir of the episcopate of Acton Windeyer Sillitoe, first bishop of New Westminster. London, Longmans, 1899. xxv, 232 p. front., plates, ports.
                                   Many **3709**
First twenty years of the Monday Club of Seattle, 1906-1926. [Seattle, 1926?] 14 p.
                                   WaU **3710**
Pioneer church work in British Columbia; being a memoir of the episcopate of Acton Windeyer Sillitoe, first bishop of New Westminster. London, Mobray [1899] 232 p. front. (port.) 9 plates, port.
                                   CVU WaS **3711**
Some early missionaries in our Northwest. [n.p., n.d.] 14 p. port.   CVicAr **3712**
Same. Olympia, Wash., Historiographer [1945?]   WaS **3713**

Graefenberg Co.
Almanac; Story, Redington & Co.'s edition for California and Oregon. New York, 1856. 1 v.   OrHi **3714**

Graham, Angus.
The golden grindstone; the adventures of George M. Mitchell, recorded by Angus Graham. London, Chatto & Windus, 1935. viii, 304 p. front. (port.) illus., maps.   CVicAr CVU **3715**
Same. Philadelphia, Lippincott [1935]
                    Wa WaE WaPS WaS WaU **3716**

Graham, Clara.
Fur and gold in the Kootenays. [Vancouver, B. C., Wrigley Printing Co., 1945] xiii, 206 p. front. (map) illus., ports.
            CV CVicAr CVU MtHi WaS WaU **3717**

Graham, Evelyn.
Ornamental shrubs and woody vines of the Pacific Coast with a chapter on the structure and functions of flowering plant organs, by Evelyn Graham and H. E. McMinn. Berkeley, Calif., Gillick Press, 1941. 259 p. col. front., illus., 22 col. plates.   Many **3718**
Same. Oakland, Calif., Mills College, 1941.
                                   WaT **3719**

Graham, Stephen, 1884-
Tramping with a poet in the Rockies, with 38 emblems by Vernon Hill. New York, Appleton, c1922. 279 p. illus. "Vachel Lindsay is the poet."   Many **3720**
Same. 1926.   WaW **3721**
Same. 1932.   WaT **3722**

Graham, William Alexander, 1875-
Major Reno vindicated; an interesting analysis justifying his conduct of the fight in the river bottom and timber, during the Battle of the Little Big Horn, June 25-26, 1876, commonly referred to as "Custer's last fight", from a letter written in 1925, by Col. W. A. Graham, with comments by E. A. Brininstool. Hollywood, Calif., E. A. Brininstool, 1935. 30 p. front., illus., port.
                            MtU WaS WaU **3723**
The story of the Little Big Horn; Custer's last fight. New York, Century [c1926] 174 p. front. (port.) 11 plates, 14 ports., maps.   Many **3724**

Grahame, Nigel B. M.
Bishop Bompas of the frozen North; the adventurous life story of a brave and self-denying missionary amongst the red Indians and Eskimos of the great Northwest. London, Seeley, 1925. 60 p. front., illus. (Seeley's missionary lives for children, v. 6)   CVicAr WaU **3725**

Grainger, M. Allerdale.
Woodsmen of the West. London, Arnold, 1908. ix, 206 p. front., 7 plates.
                                   Many **3726**
Same. Toronto, Musson, 1908.
                                   WaS WaU **3727**

Grames, Sarah Katherine, see no. 7934.

Grand Army of the Republic, Dept. of Oregon. George Wright Post, No. 1.
Decoration ceremonies at Lone Fir Cemetery and New Market Theater, Portland, Oregon, Monday May 30, 1881. Decoration sermon by Comrade J. A. Cruzan, May 29, 1881. Portland, Or., Schwab & Anderson, 1881. 20 p.   Or **3728**

Grand Coulee Dam, Columbia River, state of Washington. [Spokane] Shaw & Borden, c1935. [18] p. illus., map.
                                   WaU **3729**
Same. Souvenir booklet, presidential edition. [1938]   WaT **3730**

Grand Coulee Dam; the biggest man-made structure of all time, with the cooperation and assistance of the U. S. Bureau of Reclamation. Tacoma, Pioneer, c1940. 1 v. illus., map.   WaT **3731**

Grand Trunk Pacific Railway Company.
Plateau and valley lands in central British Columbia; general information for the intending settler. Winnipeg, 1919. 32 p. illus., fold. map.   CVicAr **3732**
Prince Rupert, B. C., the Pacific coast terminus of the Grand Trunk Pacific Railway. Montreal, 1911. 24 p. illus., maps.   CVicAr **3733**
Same. 31 p.   CVicAr **3734**
Statutes. [n.p., n.d.] 80 p.   CVicAr **3735**

Grange News.
Golden Jubilee edition, 50th anniversary, Washington State Grange. Seattle, 1913. [40] p. illus., ports, maps.   WaU **3736**

Grant, Blanche C., see no. 1542.

Grant, Carol L., see no. 3741.

Grant, Delbert A. Stewart, 1915-
Blazing a gospel trail to Alaska; an Alcan

adventure; seven thousand miracle miles by army plane and jeep through Canada and Alaska. Springfield, Mo. [c1944] 55 p. illus., ports. WaS WaU **3737**

Grant, Ethel Austin, see no. 3740.

Grant, Frederick James, 1862-1894.
History of Seattle, Washington, with illus. and biographical sketches of some of its prominent men and pioneers. New York, American Pub. and Engraving Co., 1891. 526 p. 53 ports. CVicAr OrU Wa WaPS WaSp WaU **3738**

Washington, the evergreen state and Seattle, its metropolis. [Seattle, Crawford & Conover, 1890] 59 p. illus. Anon.
WaS WaU **3739**

Grant, George M., see no. 6471.

Grant, Howard Franklin, comp.
The story of Seattle's early theatres, comp. by Howard F. Grant, assisted in research by Ethel Austin Grant, with a foreword by Glenn Hughes. Seattle, Univ. of Wash. Book Store, 1934. 47 p. front. (maps) illus.
OrP Wa WaS WaSp WaU **3740**

Grant, John A.
Trees and shrubs for Pacific Northwest gardens, by John A. Grant and Carol L. Grant. What to grow and how to grow them. Pen drawings by Phyllis Heady. Seattle, F. McCaffrey, 1943. 335 p. front., illus. Many **3741**

Grant, Roland Dwight.
Vancouver, the mecca of the tourist. [Vancouver, B. C.] Vancouver Tourist Assn. [1905?] 12 p. illus., fold. plate.
CVicAr **3742**

Grant, W. L., see nos. 1349, 6392-6394.

Grants Pass Bulletin.
Special mining section featuring the early history and development of mining in southern Oregon. Grants Pass, Or., 1937. 1 v. (Jan. 29, 1937) WaPS **3743**

Grants Pass Courier.
First annual mining display edition. Grants Pass, Or., 1937. 1 v. (Jan. 27, 1937) Includes stories of early days in Josephine County. WaPS **3744**

Golden anniversary edition. Grants Pass, Or., 1935. [105] p. illus., ports. (April 3, 1935) Or OrP WaU **3745**

The Graphic.
The State of Washington extra. Chicago [1891] 64 p. illus., ports., maps. (Suppl. to v. 5, no. 14, Oct. 3, 1891)
WaS WaU **3746**

Grasserie, Raoul de la, see no. 5640.

[Graupner, Adolphus E.] ed.
War book of "E" Company, 364th Infantry, "Ever ready" 91st Division. [Tacoma? 192—?] 130 p. WaU **3747**

Graves, Charles Sumner.
Lore and legends of the Klamath River Indians. Yreka, Calif., Press of the Times, 1929. 157 p. front., illus., ports.
Or OrP WaS WaU **3748**

Graves, Frank H.
In memoriam, Judge George Turner; an address delivered before the Spokane Bar, February 20, 1932. [Spokane, Spokane County Bar Assn., 1932] [8] p.
WaU **3749**

Graves, Jackson Alpheus, 1852-
Out of doors, California and Oregon. Los Angeles, Grafton Pub. Co., 1912. viii, 122 p. front. (port.) plates.
OrP OrU Wa WaPS WaS WaU **3750**

[Graves, S. H.]
On the "White Pass" pay-roll, by the president of the White Pass & Yukon route. Chicago [Lakeside Press] 1908. 258 p. front., 14 plates.
CVicAr CVU WaS WaU **3751**

Graves, Walter H., comp.
Some facts and near facts relative to the logged-off lands of western Oregon. Portland, Or. [n.d.] 4 p. OrP **3752**

Gray, Arthur Amos, 1885-
Men who built the West. Caldwell, Idaho, Caxton, 1945. 220 p. front., plates, ports., maps, facsim. Many **3753**

Gray, Barbara, see no. 1888.

Gray, Carl Raymond, 1867-
The significance of the Pacific railroads; the Cyrus Fogg lectureship, Princeton Univ., April 9, 1935. [Princeton, N. J.? 1935] 25 p.
OrCS OrP WaPS WaSp **3754**

[Gray, Clarence F.]
Ancilla DeMontes; or, One summer, with key, by The cricket [pseud.] [San Francisco] 1885. 135 p. B. C. novel.
CVU **3755**

Gray, Muriel, see no. 3905.

Gray, William Henry, 1810-1889.
A history of Oregon, 1792-1849, drawn from personal observation and authentic information, pub. by the author for subscribers. Portland, Or., Harris & Holman, 1870. 624 p. front. Many **3756**

Same. [Washington, D. C., American Historical Society, 1923] OrP **3757**

Same. Portland, Or., Harris & Holman, 1870 [1925?] 706 p. illus., ports., col. coats of arms. Or OrHi WaU **3758**

The moral and religious aspect of the Indian question; a letter addressed to Gen. John Eaton, Dept. of the Interior, Bureau of Education, Washington, D. C. Astoria, Or., Astorian Book and Job Print, 1879. [67] p. Two parts: Pt. 1, First letter, Dec. 1, 1878. 35 p.—Pt. 2, Second letter, May 1, 1879. 32 p.
OrHi OrP OrU Wa WaWW **3759**

See also no. 8788.

Gray, William Price, see no. 1558.

Gray Wolf, Peter, see no. 9350.

Grays Harbor Forestry Conference.
Proceedings, Morck Hotel, Aberdeen, January 20, 1939; called by the Grays Harbor County Planning Commission. [n.p.] 1939. 17 p. WaS WaT **3760**

Grays Harbor Railway and Light Co.
Wood pulp on Grays Harbor; a survey of Grays Harbor resources and advantages with regard to the location of pulp and paper mills. [Aberdeen, Wash.] 1927. 27 p. illus. Or **3761**

Grays Harbor Washingtonian,
Hoquiam, Wash.
Annual edition. Supplement to the Daily Washingtonian, Jan. 25, 1913. Hoquiam, Wash., 1913. 1 v. illus. (35th year, no. 25, Jan. 25, 1913)   WaS 3762

Paul Bunyan jubilee edition. Hoquiam, Wash., 1939. [60] p. illus., ports. (51st year, no. 84, Aug. 6, 1939)
                              WaT WaU 3763

Great Falls, Montana; Great Falls and the midland empire, midway between the Great Lakes and Pacific. [Great Falls, Mont., W. T. Ridgley Calendar Co., 1908] [16] p. illus., map.   MtU 3764

Great Northern Daily News, Seattle, Wash. New Year greetings from the Great Northern Daily News. [Seattle] 1921. 112 p. illus.   Or WaS WaU 3765

Great Northern Railway Co.
Alaska tours to the national wonderland. [Chicago, Poole, c1898] 59 p. illus., maps.
                              WaU 3766

An atlas of the Northwest, with maps of the United States and the world. Chicago, Rand, McNally [1890] [20] p. illus., maps, plans.   WaU 3767

Same. Buffalo, N. Y., c1894.   MtHi 3768

Bright, busy, beautiful Spokane, the capital of the "Inland Empire"; the wonderful Northwest mining center; a brief description of the beautiful city that is the center of an empire of minerals and fruit unequaled on earth. [n.p., 1900] 54 p. illus. (Great Northern Pocketbooks no. 9)   OrP 3769

The call of the mountains: vacations in Glacier National Park. [St. Paul, n.d.] 32 p. illus. (prt col.) maps. Anon.
                              OrU WaU 3770

The call of the mountains; Glacier National Park, Waterton Lakes National Park. [St. Paul, 19—?] 48 p. illus. (part col.) map. Anon.
                        Or WaPS WaU 3771

Dedication and opening of the new Cascade Tunnel, a monument to James J. Hill: addresses delivered during the coast to coast radio broadcasting program and at the banquet in the construction camp, Scenic, Washington, January 12, 1929. [n.p., 1929) 23 p. illus.
                MtUM OrP WaS WaT WaU 3772

The Empire Builder; and some of the men who participated in the development of the Great Northwestern Empire. [St. Paul? 1929?] 31 p. illus.
                    Or OrP WaPS WaS 3773

The fertile Flathead Valley, Montana. [St. Paul, 1909] 22 p. illus., maps (1 fold.)
                              MtHi 3774

From the car window. St. Paul [1926?] 56 p. illus.   OrP WaPS 3775

Glacier National Park and Waterton Lakes National Park. [St. Paul, 1935?] [32] p. illus., maps.   WaPS 3776

Same. 36 p.   WaPS 3777

Glacier National Park; Waterton Lakes Park, "America's most sublime wilder-

ness, lying partly in the United States in northwest Montana, and partly in the lower Canadian Rockies." [St. Paul? 1937?] 32 p. illus., map.   WaPS 3778

Glacier Park in pictures. [St. Paul, 1938] [22] p. illus., map.   WaPS 3779

Great Northern Railway long tunnel through Cascade Range. [Seattle?] 1926. 15 p.   WaU 3780

Great Northern vacations; route of the Empire Builder. [St. Paul, 192—?] [22] p. front., illus., maps.   WaPS 3781

An important visit; Zebulun Montgomery Pike, 1805. [St. Paul? 1925?] [10] p. illus., port., map.
            MtHi MtU OrHi OrP WaT 3782

Same. 14 p.   IdU 3783

Irrigation projects in Montana along the Great Northern Railway. [St. Paul, 1922?] 20 p. illus., tables. Anon.
                              MtU 3784

Last year of the "Switch-back." 2d ed. [St. Paul, 1900?] 19 p. illus., maps. (Great Northern Pocketbook no. 7)
                              WaU 3785

Montana. St. Paul [n.d.] 36 p. plates, illus., maps, tables.   OrSa 3786

Same. [1924]   WaPS 3787

Montana mountain resorts. [St. Paul? 1925?] 40 p. illus., maps.   WaPS 3788

Montana, the land of independence. [St. Paul, 1918?] 36 p. illus., maps (part col.)
                              WaPS 3789

Montana, the treasure state. [St. Paul, 1916] 36 p. illus., maps.   WaPS 3790

New Cascade Tunnel. [St. Paul? 1929] [16] p. illus., map.
            Or OrP OrU WaT WaU 3791

Opportunities for the home builder in a real pioneer empire; treasure lands of the Pacific Northwest. [n.p., n.d.] 28 p. illus., maps. Glacier County, Mont.
                              OrU 3792

Oregon. [St. Paul, 1911?] 32 p. illus., maps.   OrP 3793

Same. [1912?]   OrP 3794

Same. [1914]   Or WaPS 3795

Same. [1915?]   OrP 3796

Oregon, the Twentieth Century state. [St. Paul, 1912?] 32 p. illus., map.
                OrU WaPS WaWW 3797

Over mountain trails in Glacier National Park and Waterton Lakes National Park. [St. Paul, 193—?] [29] p. front., illus., map. Anon.   WaPS 3798

Program of Upper Missouri Historical Expedition; itinerary of Upper Missouri Special. [n.p.] 1925. 11 p. map.
                        OrHi WaU 3799

The scenic Northwest. [n.p., n.d.] [48] p. illus., fold. map.   Or OrP 3800

Same. [40] p.   OrP 3801

Same. [St. Paul, 192—?] 50 p. front., illus., fold. map.   OrSa WaPS 3802

Seeing Glacier Park. [St. Paul, 1937?] 15 p. illus., map.   WaPS 3803

Special all expense fare for the Columbia River Historical Expedition of 1926. [n.p., 1926] [5] p. WaU **3804**

Taxation of railroad property in the state of Washington. [n.p., 1913?] 30 p. Published jointly with N. P., O. W. R. & N., and C. M. & St. P. railway companies. Or WaPS WaS WaU **3805**

To the evergreen Pacific Northwest and California through the Great Northern adventure land. [St. Paul, 193—?] 23 p. illus., map. WaPS **3806**

Trail riding in Glacier National Park. [St. Paul] 1935. 31 p. illus., map. WaPS **3807**

Trail riding in the Rockies: Glacier National Park. [St. Paul, 192—?] [28] p. front., illus. WaPS **3808**

The Upper Missouri Historical Expedition. [n.p., 1925] [8] p. illus. Anon. MtU WaU **3809**

Washington. St. Paul [n.d.] 36 p. front., illus., plates, maps, tables. OrSa **3810**

Same. [1915?] 35 p. WaPS **3811**

Same. [1927?] 36 p. WaT **3812**

Washington land agents. St. Paul [191—?] 30 p. WaPS **3813**

Washington, northern Idaho, British Columbia. [St. Paul? 1911?] 35 p., illus. WaPS **3814**

Wenatchee north country. [St. Paul, Randall Co., 1914?] 36 p. illus., maps. WaPS **3815**

Zone of plenty; Minnesota, North Dakota, Montana, Washington, Oregon, Idaho. [n.p., n.d.] 36 p. illus., maps. OrP OrSa OrU **3816**

Same. [1914?] WaPS **3817**

Same. [1926?] WaPS **3818**

Same. [1929?] Or **3819**

The Great Northwest. Cleveland, 1916. 1 v. CVicAr **3820**

Great Western Malting Co.
Growing barley for malting in Oregon, Washington, and northwestern Idaho and Montana. Vancouver, Wash. [n.d.] 21 p. WaPS **3821**

[Greeley, Horace] 1811-1872.
Life of Col. Fremont. [New York, Greeley and M'Elrath, Tribune Office] c1856. 32 p. illus. WaU **3822**

Greeley, William B., see nos. 4554-4556.

Greely, Adolphus Washington, 1844-1935.
Handbook of Alaska; its resources, products, and attractions. London, Unwin, 1909. xiii, 280 p. front., plates, maps, tables. CVU **3823**

Same. New York, Scribner, 1909. Many **3824**

Same. New ed., with prefatory chapter on Alaska in 1914 and a map showing proposed railroad routes. New York, Scribner, 1914. xxxii, 280 p. front., plates, maps (part fold.) tables. CVicAr CVU Or WaS **3825**

Same. 3d ed., with new chapters on fisheries, fur-farming, fur seals, game, gold-

mining, petroleum and coal, railroads, reindeer, and volcanoes. New York, Scribner, 1925. x, 330 p. front., plates, maps (1 fold.) Many **3826**

True tales of Arctic heroism in the New World. New York, Scribner, 1912. 385 p. front., 15 plates, ports., maps. Or OrP WaSp WaT **3827**

Green, Alfred John, 1851-1926.
Jottings from a cruise; Capt. Green's experiences as recorded by him on the ill-fated voyage of the barque "Metrola"; also his further adventures aboard the barques "Grassendale" and "Wilhelm Tell." [Seattle, Kelly Printing Co., 1944] xv, 257 p. front., illus., ports., facsims., coat of arms. Vashon Island author. Many **3828**

Same. 2d ed. 1947, c1944. 451 p. illus., ports. Or OrCS OrPR WaSp **3829**

Green, Elmer, see no. 8899.

Green, Fletcher Melvin, 1895-
Romance of the western frontier; an outline for individual and group study. Chapel Hill, N. C., Univ. of N. C. Press [1932] 75 p. (Extension bulletin, v. 11, no. 8) Or OrP WaS WaSp **3830**

Green, George.
History of Burnaby and vicinity. [Vancouver, B. C., Shoemaker, McLean & Veitch, 1947] 233 p. front., illus., ports., plan. CV CVicAr CVU **3831**

Green, John L., 1868-
Pioneer Evangelists of the Church of God in the Pacific Northwest. Portland, Or., Loomis Printing Co. [1939] 204 p. front. (port.) OrHi OrP **3832**

Green, William Spotswood, 1847-
Among the Selkirk glaciers; being the account of a rough survey in the Rocky Mountain regions of British Columbia. New York, Macmillan, 1890. xv, 251 p. front., 8 plates, fold map. Many **3833**

Green Lake News, Seattle, Wash.
Anniversary number. [Seattle, 1903] 16 p. illus., ports. (v. 3, no. 1, Nov. 26, 1903) WaU **3834**

Greenbie, Sydney, 1889-
Frontiers and the fur trade. New York, John Day Co. [1929] xii, 235 p. front., plates. Many **3835**

Furs to furrows; an epic of rugged individualism. Caldwell, Idaho, Caxton, 1939. 413 p. front., plates, ports., map. Many **3836**

See also nos. 2695-2697.

Greenburg, Dan W., see no. 7745.

Greene, Roger Sherman, 1840-
A primer trilogy, as is pointed out by Roger S. Greene. London, Regor Pub. Co., 1914. 343 p. 25 plates, fold. diagr. WaU **3837**

Greenfield Advertising Agency, Butte, Mont.
Montana in rotogravure. [San Francisco, Pacific Gravure Co., c1930] [68] p. illus. MtU MtUM **3838**

Greenhow, Robert, 1800-1854.
Answer to the strictures of Mr. Thomas

Falconer of Lincoln's Inn on the history of Oregon and California. Washington, D. C., 1845. 7 p.   OrHi OrP **3839**

Geography of Oregon and California and the other territories on the north-west coast of North America, illus. by a new and beautiful map of those countries. Boston, Freeman, 1845. 120 p. map.
OrHi **3840**

Same. New York, M. H. Newman, 1845. 42 p. front. (fold. map)   OrP WaU **3841**

The history of Oregon and California, and the other territories on the Northwest coast of North America: accompanied by a geographical view and map of those countries, and a number of documents as proofs and illustrations of the history. Boston, Little, 1844. xviii, 482 p. front. (fold. map) illus.   Many **3842**

Same. London, Murray, 1844. Many **3843**

Same. 2d ed., rev., corrected and enlarged. Boston, Little, 1845. xviii, 492 p. fold. map.   Many **3844**

Same. 3d ed., rev., corrected and enlarged. New York, Appleton, 1845. Many **3845**

Same. 4th ed., rev., corrected and enlarged. Boston, Freeman and Bolles, 1847.
Or WaU WaWW **3846**

Same. 4th ed. Boston, Little, 1847.
WaWW **3847**

Memoir, historical and political, on the Northwest coast of North America, and the adjacent territories; illus. by a map and a geographical view of those countries. New York, Putnam, 1840. xi, 228 p. front. (fold. map)   Many **3848**

Greenough, W. Earl.
First 100 years, Coeur d'Alene mining region, 1846-1946; address before the Montana Section of the American Institute of Mining & Metallurgical Engineers, Helena, Montana, November 16, 1946. Rev. and enlarged. Mullan, Idaho, c1947. 40 p. illus., map.
MtHi MtUM WaSp **3849**

Greenwood, Mrs. Annie (Pike)
We sagebrush folks. New York, Appleton-Century, 1934. xi, 483 p. front., illus., plates, ports., facsim. Idaho author.
Many **3850**

Greenwood, William Hamar, see no. 7295.

[Greeters Association, Vancouver, B. C.]
The Greeter's tourist and shopping guide; where to go and what to see in and around Vancouver, Victoria, and the triangle cities of the Northwest. [Vancouver, B. C.] c1922. 72 p. illus. CV **3851**

Gregg, Herbert C., see no. 4843.

Gregory, Homer Ewart, 1886-
North Pacific fisheries, with special reference to Alaska salmon, by Homer E. Gregory and Kathleen Barnes. San Francisco, American Council, Institute of Pacific Relations, 1939. xviii, 322 p. tables, diagrs. (Studies of the Pacific, no. 3)   Many **3852**

Greiner, Frank W.
A souvenir of mountain poems to commemorate the crossing of the Olympics

by the Mountaineers, 1913. [Seattle, 1913] [12] p.   WaU **3853**

A souvenir of mountain poems to commemorate the 1915 outing party of the Mountaineers. [Seattle? c1915] [12] p.
WaU **3854**

Greiner, Ruth, see no. 10767.

Grenier, Ernest.
Reports on the Alta Montana Co.'s mines and silver reduction works at Wickes, Montana, by Ernest Grenier and George B. Foote. New York, Wilbur & Hastings, 1879. 23 p. 4 maps.   MtHi **3855**

Greve, Alice Wheeler.
From out this house. Portland, Or., Binfords & Mort [1945] 299 p. Many **3856**

Shadow on the plains. Portland, Or., Binfords & Mort [1944] 272 p. Many **3857**

Grew, David.
The sorrel stallion, illus. by Paul Brown. New York, Scribner, 1932. xi, 321 p. illus., 25 plates. Clearwater, Idaho story.
WaE WaSp **3858**

Grewingk, Constantin Caspar Andreas, 1819-1887.
Beitrag zur Kenntniss der orographischen und geognostischen Beschaffenheit der Nord-West Kuste Amerikas, mit den anliegenden Inseln. St. Petersburg, K. Kray, 1850. 351 p. plates, maps.
CVicAr **3859**

Grey, Viscount of Falloden, see no. 10944.

Grey, Zane, 1872-1939.
Rogue River feud. New York, Harper, [c1930] 218 p.   Many **3860**

Same. [1948, c1930]   WaU **3861**

Grey Owl, 1888-1938.
Tales of an empty cabin, by Wa-sha-quon-asin (Gray Owl). New York, Dodd, 1936. 323 p. front. (port.) plates. Many **3862**

Grier, Albert C.
Message of the truth; three sermons by pastor of the Church of the Truth, Spokane, Washington. [n.p.] No rights reserved [n.d.] 45 p.   WaSp **3863**

Grierson, John, 1909-
High failure; solo along the Arctic air route. London, Hodge, 1936. 305 p. front., plates, map, facsim.   CVicAr **3864**

Griffin, D. F.
First steps to Tokyo; the Royal Canadian Air Force in the Aleutians. Toronto, Dent [1944] vi, 50 p. plates, ports.
CV CVicAr **3865**

Griffin, Eldon, 1895-
China's railways as a market for Pacific Northwest products; a study of a phase of the external relations of a region. Seattle, Univ. of Wash., 1946. xii, 78 p. front., plates (part fold.) maps (1 fold.)
OrCS WaT WaU **3866**

Clinching the victory. Seattle, Wilberlilla Pub., 1943. 365 p. front., 1 col. illus.
Many **3867**

Oysters have eyes; or, The travels of a Pacific oyster. Seattle, Wilberlilla Pub., 1941. 53 p. illus.   Many **3868**

Griffin, George H.
Legends of the Evergreen Coast. Van-

couver, B. C., Clarke & Stuart [c1934]
141 p. front., illus., plates.
CV CVic CVicAr CVU WaS WaU **3869**

Griffin, Harold.
Alaska and the Canadian Northwest, our
new frontier. New York, Norton [1944]
221 p. plates, double map. Many **3870**

Griffin, John Smith.
A historic sketch descriptive of Jesuit
warfare, together with a defensive appeal addressed to the younger ministers
and intelligent laymen of the Congregational laymen of the churches of Oregon and Washington. Hillsboro, Or., 1881.
49 p. OrP WaWW **3871**

Griffith, Franklin T.
Industrial and hydro-electric development
in Oregon; an address delivered before
the annual Oregon Business and Industrial Conference. Portland, Oregon, January 8, 1925. Portland, Or., Oregon Public Utility Information Bureau, 1925.
16 p. Or OrP **3872**

Griffiths, Austin Edwards, 1863-
Address on playgrounds and legislation in
relation thereto, with special reference
to the Washington playground bill
vetoed. Seattle [Seattle Playgrounds
Assn. 1908] 19 p. Anon. WaS WaU **3873**

The blight; labor excesses and consequences. [Seattle, Peacock Printing Co.,
1939] 28 p. (Griffgram on. 24)
Or WaPS **3874**

The Cascade Tunnel; an imperative necessity of the state of Washington; letters
and observations thereon in the light of
Columbia River competition. Seattle
[1925] 27 p. (Griffgram no. 11)
WaPS WaT WaTC WaU **3875**

An intimate view of our relations with the
Orient, in general; Japan, China, Philippines, Pacific Coast; an address by the
late judge of Superior Court of the state
of Washington before Municipal League
of Seattle, Feb. 25, 1930. Seattle [1930]
[20] p. WaU **3876**

The lawyer's responsibility for business
ability in public office; address before
the American Bar Association, Judicial
Section, Seattle, July 24, 1928. [Seattle,
Allied Printing, 1928] 27 p. front.
WaU **3877**

Griggs, Robert Fiske, 1881-
The Valley of Ten Thousand Smokes, with
9 maps and 233 illustrations. Washington, D. C., National Geographic Society,
1922. xv, 341 p. fold. front., illus., col.
plates, maps (part fold.) diagrs.
Many **3878**

[Grimm, Ferdinand] 1806-1895.
Northwest water boundary; report of the
experts summoned by the German
emperor as arbitrator under articles
34-42 or the Treaty of Washington of
May 8, 1871, preliminary to his award
dated October 21, 1872, ed. with a trans.
by Hunter Miller. Seattle, Univ. of
Wash., 1942. vii, 75 p. map. (Publications
in the social sciences, v. 13, no. 1, Jan.
1942) The experts who made the report

were Ferdinand Grimm, Levin Goldschmidt and Heinrich Kiepert.
CVicAr CVU Wa WaTC WaS WaU **3879**

Grimm, Verna B., see no. 3394.

Grinnell, Elizabeth, see no. 3904.

Grinnell, George Bird, 1849-1938.
Beyond the old frontier; adventures of
Indian fighters, hunters, and fur traders.
New York, Scribner, 1913. xii, 374 p.
front., 11 plates, 4 ports., map, plan.
Many **3880**

Blackfeet Indian stories. New York, Scribner, 1913. viii, 214 p. col. front.
IdIf Or OrP WaS WaSP WaT **3881**

Same. 1917. MtHi **3882**

Same. 1920. WaU **3883**

Blackfoot lodge tales; the story of a
prairie people. New York, Scribner,
1892. xv, 310 p. Many **3884**

Same. 1912. WaSp **3885**

Same. 1921. WaSp **3886**

By Cheyenne campfires, with photographs
by Elizabeth C. Grinnell. New Haven,
Yale Univ. Press, 1926. xvii, 305 p. front.,
plates. Many **3887**

The fighting Cheyennes. New York, Scribner, 1915. viii, 431 p. maps (part fold.)
MtHi MtU WaS WaSp WaTC **3888**

Hunting at high altitudes; the book of the
Boone and Crockett Club. New York,
Harpers, 1913. 511 p. front. (port.) illus.,
17 plates. MtHi OrP WaS **3889**

Jack among the Indians; or, A boy's sum-
mer on the Buffalo Plains, illus. by
Edwin Willard Deming. New York,
Stokes [c1900] 301 p. front., plates.
IdIf Or OrP WaS **3890**

Jack in the Rockies; or, A Boy's adven-
tures with a pack train, illus. by Edwin
Willard Deming and by half-tone en-
gravings of photographs. New York,
Stokes [c1904] 272 p. front., 7 plates.
IdIf Or OrP **3891**

Jack, the young canoeman; an eastern
boy's voyage in a Chinook canoe; illus.
by Edwin Willard Deming and by half-
tone engravings of photographs. New
York, Stokes [c1906] 286 p. illus.
IdIf Or OrP WaS WaSp WaU **3892**

Jack, the young cowboy; an eastern boy's
experience on a western round-up, with
8 illus. from photographs. New York,
Stokes [c1899] 278 p. front., 7 plates.
IdIf **3893**

Same. [1913] Or OrP WaS **3894**

Jack, the young explorer; a boy's experiences in the unknown Northwest,
illus. by William H. Cary and by half-
tone engravings of photographs. New
York, Stokes [c1908] 308 p. front., plates.
IdIf Or OrP WaSp WaW **3895**

Jack, the young ranchman; or, A boy's
adventures in the Rockies. New York,
Stokes [c1899] 304 p. IdIf Or OrP **3896**

Jack, the young trapper; an eastern boy's
fur hunting in the Rocky Mountains,
illus. by Walter King Stone. New York,
Stokes [c1907] 278 p. front., 3 plates.
IdIf Or OrP WaSp **3897**

Trails of the pathfinders. New York, Scribner, 1911. x, 460 p. front., illus., 14 plates, port., map.   Many 3898

Same. 1913.   MtHi 3899

Same. 1926 [c1911]   WaU 3900

Two great scouts and their Pawnee battalion; the experiences of Frank J. North and Luther H. North, pioneers in the great West, 1856-1882, and their defence of the building of the Union Pacific Railroad. Cleveland, A. H. Clark Co., 1928. 299 p. front. (double map)
        Many 3901

When buffalo ran. New Haven, Yale Univ. Press, 1920. 114 p. front., plates.
        Many 3902

Same. [1940, c1920]   OrU 3903

Grinnell, Joseph, 1877-1939.
Gold hunting in Alaska as told by Joseph Grinnell, ed. by Elizabeth Grinnell. Elgin, Ill., David C. Cook Pub. Co. [c1901] 96 p. illus. Kotzebue Sound and Nome.
        Many 3904

Grissen, Charles.
Birth of Oregon; a poem commemorative of the discovery, settlement and progress of the great Oregon country, by Muriel Gray [pseud.] special drawings by F. G. Cooper; Indian photos. by Lee Moorehouse; cover design by Frank Wortman. McMinnville, Or., Telephone Register [n.d.] [16] p. illus.   OrHi 3905

Ideala; a romance of idealism. Portland, Or., J. K. Gill Co. [c1893] 167 p. plates. Poems.   Or OrHi OrU WaU 3906

Grissom, Irene (Welch) 1873-
A daughter of the Northwest. Boston, Cornhill Co. [c1918] 225 p. port. Idaho poet laureate since June 1923.
        Many 3907

Same. 1923 [c1918]   Wa WaU 3908

The passing of the desert. Garden City, N. Y., Country Life Press, 1924. xi, 69 p. front., port. IdB IdIf IdP IdTf IdU 3909

Passing of the sagebrush, and other verse. Idaho Falls, Idaho, Scotts, 1916. 42 p.
        IdIf OrP 3910

The superintendent. New York, Harriman, 1910. 228 p.
        IdB IdIf Or Wa WaS WaU 3911

Under desert skies. Caldwell, Idaho, Caxton, 1935. 54 p. illus. poems.
        IdP IdTf OrCS 3912

Verses of the new West, with illus. by Glen H. Spurgeon. Caldwell, Idaho, Caxton, 1931. viii, 102 p. front., illus., plates.
        Many 3913

We harness a river. Caldwell, Idaho, Caxton, 1946. 155 p. front., plates.
        IdB IdIf IdU Or WaU 3914

Whirling saws. Boston, B. Humphries [c1941] 160 p.   IdIf Wa WaU 3915

Gromer, Mrs. Belle Burns.
Young Navy man. New York, H. C. Kinsey & Co., 1934. 305 p. Puget Sound Navy Yard.   WaS WaU 3916

Grondal, Bror Leonard, 1889-
Durable Douglas fir, America's permanent lumber supply. [Seattle, West Coast

Lumber Trade Extension Bureau, c1926] 32 p. illus., diagrs.   Or WaU 3917

Same. [c1928]   OrP 3918

Group of Twelve, Seattle, Wash.
Some work of the Group of Twelve, Seattle, Washington. Seattle [F. McCaffrey, 1937] [14] p. col. illus.   WaU 3919

Grover, Isabel M.
A soul victorious; a little story of McMinnville College. [McMinnville, Or., n.d.] 7 p.
        WaU 3920

Grover, L. F., see no. 7682.

Grover, L. H.
Vivette. [Victoria, B. C., Diggon-Hibben, c1920] 43 p.   CVicAr 3921

Groves, Hubert Beckwith.
Portland (east side) 1930. Portland, Or., Portland Bulletin, 1930. 64 p. illus., ports., tables.   OrHi OrP 3922

[Grubbs, Francis Herron] ed.
Memorial services at the re-interment of remains of Rev. Jason Lee, Salem, Oregon, Friday, June 15, 1906. [Salem, Or.? 1906?] 73 p. plates, ports.   Many 3923

Grubstakes Publishing Co.
Klondike grubstakes; where to get them; what to take, practical information for Yukoners and others. Seattle, c1898. 40 p.
        OrHi 3924

Gruening, Ernest, see no. 1878.

The Guard, Eugene Or.
Souvenir year book of Eugene and Lane County, Oregon. Eugene, Or., 1909. 62 p. illus.   OrU 3925

Guberlet, Mrs. Muriel Lewin.
Animals of the seashore. Portland, Or., Metropolitan [c1936] xii, 412 p. illus. Washington author.   Many 3926

Hermie's trailer house, illus. by Marjorie Kincaid Illman. Lancaster, Pa., J. Cattell Press [1946?] 32 p. col. illus.
        WaSp WaU 3927

Guide to the cities of Vancouver Island. Victoria, B. C., Hibben, 1912. 1 v. maps.
        CVicAr 3928

Guide to the Klondike and the Yukon gold fields in Alaska and Northwest Territories. Seattle, Lowman & Hanford, 1897. 115 p. illus.   CVicAr 3929

Guide to the province of British Columbia for 1877-8; comp. from the latest and most authentic sources of information. Victoria, B. C., Hibben, 1877. 410 p. illus. Contains dictionary of Chinook jargon.
        Many 3930

Guie, Heister Dean.
Tribal days of the Yakimas. [Yakima, Wash.] Republic Pub. Co., 1937. 54 p. illus. (part col.) col. plate.   Many 3931

See also nos. 6476, 7126.

Gunn, W. Chalmers, see no. 8352.

Gunsaulus, Frank W., see nos. 7327-7329.

Gunther, Erna, see no. 4954.

Gustin, see no. 10137.

Guthrie, Alfred Bertram, Jr., 1901-
The big sky. New York, Wm. Sloane Associates [1947] 386 p. front. (map)
        Many 3932

Guthrie, John Dennett, 1878- ed.
Forest fire and other verse, collected and ed. by John D. Guthrie. [Portland, Or., Dunham Printing Co.] 1929. ix, 321, xiii p. col front.

        CVU OrP Wa WaPS **3933**

The forest ranger, and other verse, collected and ed. by John D. Guthrie. Boston, R. G. Badger [c1919] 174 p. front.   IdU MtU Or OrP WAU **3934**

Gwinn, Gardner J., Inc., Seattle, Wash.
The real estate investment of today. Seattle [193-?] 32 p. illus., ports.

        WaPS WaS **3935**

Hackett, John A.
Rhymes of the North, and other rhymes. Victoria, B. C., Diggon [c1924] 66 p.

        CV **3936**

Hagerman, Augusta.
Berattelser fran har och dar, fran nu och da. Seattle, 1945. 316 p.   WaS **3937**

Gokens och larkans land; en reseskildring fran ett besok i Sverige och Finland sommaren 1936. Seattle, Consolidated Press, 1944. 255 p. illus. WaS **3938**

Mormors stuga, barndosminnen och folklivsbilder. Seattle, Post Printers, 1945. 255 p.   WaS **3939**

Haehlen, Gottlieb V.
Historical sketch of the Pine Street Coffee House; also, early history of the city of Portland. [Portland, Or., Kerns & Abbott] 1914. [24] p. illus. Or WaU **3940**

Hafen, Le Roy R., 1893-
Broken Hand, the life story of Thomas Fitzpatrick, chief of the mountain men, by Le Roy R. Hafen and W. J. Ghent. Denver, Old West Pub. Co., 1931. 316 p. front., 3 plates, ports., double map.

        Many **3941**

Fort Laramie and the pageant of the West, 1834-1890, by Le Roy R. Hafen and Francis Marion Young. Glendale, Calif., A. H. Clark Co., 1938. 429 p. front., plates, ports., fold map, plans.

        Many **3942**

The overland mail 1849-1869; promoter of settlement, precursor of railroads. Cleveland, A. H. Clark Co., 1926. 361 p. front., plates, ports., fold. map, facsims.

        Many **3943**

Trans-Mississippi West; hand cart migration across the plains. Glendale, Calif., A. H. Clark Co. [n.d.] 19 p.   OrP **3944**

Western America; the exploration, settlement, and development of the region beyond the Mississippi, by Le Roy R. Hafen and Carl Coke Rister. New York, Prentice-Hall, 1941. xxiv, 698 p. front., illus., maps.   Many **3945**

Hagedorn, Herman, 1882-
The magnate; William Boyce Thompson and his time, 1869-1930. New York, John Day [1935] 343 p. front. (port.) 8 plates. Montana biographee.   Many **3946**

Hager, John Ross.
Sport and the kid, by "Dok" [pseud.] of J. R. Hager, cartoonist Seattle Daily Times. Seattle, Lowman & Hanford [c1913] 48 p. illus. WaS WaU **3947**

The umbrella man, by "Dok". Seattle, Lowman & Hanford, 1911. [52] p.

        WaS WaU **3948**

Haggen, R. W.
Historical sketch of Cariboo Lodge No. 4, F. & A. M., New Westminster, B. C., Jackson Printing Co. [n.d.] 7 p. plate.

        CVicAr **3949**

Haig-Brown, Roderick Langmere Haig, 1908-
Ki-Yu, a story of panthers, with illus, by Kurt Wiese. Boston, Houghton, 1934. 213 p. illus. Vancouver Island hunting.

        Many **3950**

Panther, with illus. by Theyre Lee-Elliott. New ed. London, Collins [1946] 191 p. illus. (part col.) WaS WaU **3951**

Pool and rapid, the story of a river. London, Black, 1932. 239 p. front. (map) Tashish River. CVicAr IdB Wa **3952**

Same. London, J. Cape, 1932. CV **3953**

Same. With illus. by C. F. Tunnicliffe. London, J. Cape [1936] 239 p. front., illus.   CV CVicAr WaU **3954**

Return to the river; a story of the Chinook run, with illus. by Charles DeFeo. New York, Morrow, 1941. 248 p. plates, map.

        Many **3955**

A river never sleeps, illus. by Louis Darling. New York, Morrow, 1946. vii, 352 p. illus., plates.   Many **3956**

Saltwater summer. New York, Morrow, 1948. 256 p. col. front. Salmon fishing on B. C. coast. WaS WaT WaU **3957**

Starbuck Valley winter, illus. by Charles DeFeo. New York, Morrow, 1943. 310 p. illus.   Many **3958**

Timber, a novel of Pacific coast loggers. New York, Morrow, 1942. vi, 410 p.

        Many **3959**

Same. Toronto, Collins [1946] 256 p.

        CVU **3960**

The western angler; an account of Pacific salmon and western trout. New York, Derrydale Press [c1939] 2 v. col. fronts., illus., plates (part col.) maps (1 fold.) fold. table.   Many **3961**

The western angler; an account of Pacific salmon and western trout in B. C. 2d ed., illus., by T. Brayshaw. New York, Morrow, 1947. xii, 356 p. col. front., col. plate, maps (1 double). Many **3962**

Hailey, John, 1835-1921.
The history of Idaho. Boise, Idaho, Syms-York, 1910. 395 p. front. (port.)

        Many **3963**

Haines, Francis.
Red eagles of the Northwest; the story of Chief Joseph and his people. Portland, Or., Scholastic Press, 1939. xi, 361 p. mounted front., illus., maps. Many **3964**

The story of Idaho, illus. by Conan E. Mathews. Boise, Idaho, Syms-York [1942] 169 p. illus.

   CVicAr MtU Or WaSp WaU **3965**

Hakluyt, see no. 3348.

Halcombe, John Joseph.
The emigrant and the heathen; or, Sketches of missionary life. London, Society for Promoting Christian Knowledge [18—?] 330 p. front., plates. CVicAr WaU **3966**

Stranger than fiction, pub. under direction of the Tract Committee. London, Society for Promoting Christian Knowledge [1872] 256 p. front., plates, ports. William Duncan at Metlakahtla. WaU **3967**

Same. 3d ed. 1873. 275 p. WaSp **3968**

Same. 4th ed. 1874. CV CVicAr CVU **3969**

Same. 1877. WaU **3970**

Same. 1878. CVicAr **3971**

Same. 1880. OrU **3972**

Hale, Edward B., Jr., see no. 7932.

Hale, Horatio Emmons, 1817-1896.
An international idiom; a manual of the Oregon trade language, or Chinook jargon. London, Whittaker, 1890. 63, 32 p. Many **3973**

Half hours in the far North; life amid snow and ice. London, Daldy, 1878. 308 p. illus., plate. (The half hour library of travel, nature and science for young readers). CVicAr **3974**

Half hours in the wide West, over mountains, rivers and prairies. London, Isbister, 1877. 345 p. front., illus. (The half hour library of travel, nature and science for young readers). CVicAr **3975**

Hall, A. J., see no. 818.

Hall, Arnold Bennett, 1881-1936.
Outline of studies for Oregon mothers with the problems and policies of the University of Oregon. [n.p., n.d.] 173 p. OrP **3976**

Hall, Charles, 1880-
Address of Senator Charles Hall of Coos and Curry Counties on the occasion of the Convention of the Federated Womens' Clubs of Oregon, June 2, 1925. [n.p.] 1925. [8] p. WaPS **3977**

Hall, Charles Francis, 1821-1871.
Life with the Esquimaux; the narrative of Capt. Charles Francis Hall of the whaling barque "George Henry" from the 29th May, 1860 to the 13th Sept., 1862, with the results of a long intercourse with the Innuits and full description of their mode of life, the discovery of actual relics of the expedition of Martin Frobisher of three centuries ago, and deductions in favor of yet discovering some of the survivors of Sir John Franklin's expedition. London, Low, 1864. 2 v. front., illus., plates.
CVicAr Wa WaSp WaU **3978**

Hall, Charles Gilbert, 1866-
The greatest adventure. New York, Nelson, 1935. 80 p. front., illus. (Our changing world). Lewis and Clark expedition.
Or OrMonO WaT **3979**

Hall, Daniel Weston, 1841-
Arctic rovings; or, The adventures of a New Bedford boy on sea and land. Boston, A. Tompkins, 1861. 171 p. front. (port.) CVicAr **3980**

[Hall, Edward Hagaman] 1858-1936.
Alaska, the eldorado of the midnight sun; marvels of the Yukon, The Klondike discovery, Fortunes made in a day; How to go, what to take and what it costs; Routes, rates and distances; Attractions and dangers; Land laws; Practical counsel for prospectors, tourists and stay-at-homes. New York, Republic Press, 1897. 62 p. front., fold. map. WaSp **3981**

Hall, Edward Hepple.
Appleton's hand-book of American travel; The northern tour. 9th annual ed. New York, Appleton, 1867. xvi, 456, viii p. front. (fold. map) WaSp **3982**

The great West: emigrants', settlers' & travellers' guide and hand-book to the states of California and Oregon, and the territories of Nebraska, Utah, Colorado, Idaho, Montana, Nevada, and Washington, with a full and accurate account of their climate, soil, resources, and products. New York, Tribune Office, 1864. 89 p. front. (fold. map)
CVicAr MtHi OrU WaU **3983**

The great West: railroads, steamboat, and stage guide and hand-book for travellers, miners, and emigrants to the western, northwestern, and Pacific states and territories, with a map of the best routes to the gold and silver mines. New York, Appleton [c1866] 181 p. fold. map. IdB OrP WaU **3984**

The great West: travellers', miners', and emigrants' guide and hand-book to the western, north-western, and Pacific states and territories, with a map of the best routes to the gold and silver mines, and complete tables of distances; also the United States homestead law, mining laws of the respective states. New York, Appleton, 1865. 198 p. fold. map, tables.
CV MtU OrHi WaS WaSp WaU **3985**

Lands of plenty in the new Northwest; a book for all travellers, settlers and investors in Manitoba and North-west Territory. Toronto, Hunter, Rose & Co. [1880] xiv, 152 p. front., fold. map, plates. MtU **3986**

Hall, Ernest Fenwick.
Under the Northern Lights; an intimate disclosure of Alaska, its people and tradition of the "Land of the midnight sun". [Denver, c1932] 70 p. illus., port., fold. map. WaS **3987**

Hall, George E.
Our church and its architecture, with sketches by Colista Dowling. Portland, Or., 1st Presbyterian Church [c1946?] 20 p. illus. OrP **3988**

Hall, George Lyman, 1913-
Sometime again (E'lot neg-oo-soo-li). Seattle, Superior Pub. Co., 1945. 217 p. illus. Many **3989**

Hall, Harold, see no. 8410.

Hall, James, 1793-1868.
Legends of the West. Cincinnati, Applegate & Co., 1857. 435 p. WaU **3990**

Notes on the western states; containing descriptive sketches of their soil, climate,

resources and scenery. Philadelphia, Harrison Hall, 1838. 304 p. tables.
OrP OrU WaU **3991**

Hall, Mrs. Mabel (Kinney)
Echoes from M. A. C. Bozeman, Mont. [Republican-Courier, c1909] 31 p. State College of Agriculture and Mechanical Arts, Mont. Poems. MtBozC MtHi **3992**

Hall, Rinaldo M.
Oregon outings, where new life awaits; a brief description of the summering places in the western part of the state; where they are and how to reach them. Portland, Or., Southern Pacific Co., 1906. 31 p. illus., fold. map. OrHi WaPS **3993**

Oregon, Washington, Idaho and their resources. [Portland, Or.] Passenger Depts. of the Or. Railroad & Navigation Co. and Southern Pacific Co., 1903. 88 p. illus., fold. map.
OrHi OrP WaS WaU WaWW **3994**
Same. 1904. Or OrSaW WaS **3995**
Same. 1905. Many **3996**
Same. 1906. OrHi WaPS WaS WaU **3997**

Restful recreation resorts of the Pacific Northwest. Portland, Or., Or. Railroad & Navigation Co., 1903. 48 p. illus., fold. map. Anon. OrHi OrP **3998**
Same. 1904. OrP **3999**
Same. 1905. OrP **4000**
Same. 1906. OrP **4001**

Hall, Warner.
Even Jericho, a novel. Philadelphia, Macrae-Smith Co., 1944. 288 p. Alaska World War II story. CV Or OrP WaU **4002**

Hallahan, Daniel Francis, 1852-
Tourists in the Northwest, where they went, what they saw and those whom they met on the way. [Philadelphia, F. McManus, c1914] 151 p. front., plates.
WaU **4003**

Haller, Granville Owen, 1820-1897.
The dismissal of Major Granville O. Haller of the Regular Army of the United States by order of the Secretary of War, in Special Orders no. 331 of July 25, 1863; also, a brief memoir of his military services and a few observations. Paterson, N. J., Daily Guardian Office, 1863. 84 p.
OrHi **4004**

Halliday, William May, 1866-
Potlatch and totem, and the recollections of an Indian agent, illus. from 30 original photographs by the author. London, Dent [1935] xvi, 240 p. front., plates.
CV CVic CVicAr CVU WaS WaU **4005**

Hallock, Charles, 1834-1917.
Our new Alaska; or, The Seward purchase vindicated, illus. from sketches by T. J. Richardson. New York, Forest & Stream Pub. Co., 1886. 209 p. front., illus., plate, fold. map. Many **4006**
Same. 1894. CVicAr WaS WaTC **4007**

Peerless Alaska, our cache near the Pole, illus. from sketches by George G. Cantwell. New York, Broadway Pub. Co., 1908. 224 p. front., illus., 6 plates, port.
OrP Wa WaS WaU **4008**

Hallock, Leavitt Homan, 1842-1921.
Why our flag floats over Oregon; or, The conquest of our great Northwest. Portland, Me., Smith & Sale, 1911. vii, 76 p. front., plates, ports. Many **4009**
See also no. 2755.

Halminen, Matti.
Sointula, Kalevan Kansan ja Kanadan suomalaisten historiaa. [Helsingiaal] Mikko, 1936, 143 p. illus., ports. Malcolm Island, B. C. Finnish community.
CVicAr **4010**

Hamilton, Alexander.
British Columbia; the work of a pioneer. [London, Vacher, 1939?] 7 p. Story of John Cunningham Brown. CVicAr **4011**

Hamilton, Basil G.
The legend of Windermere. 2d ed. [Invermere, B. C., 1921] 12 p. WaU **4012**

Naming of Columbia River and the province of British Columbia. [Cranbrook, B. C., Cranbrook Courier, n.d.] 16 p.
CVicAr WaU **4013**

Hamilton, Bill, see nos. 4019, 4020.

Hamilton, Eloise, see no. 10536.

Hamilton, Franklin Robert.
Pictorial poems of the scenic West, illus. with photographic studies from the best artists. Denver, Miles and Dryer [c1929] 122 p. front. (port.) plates. WaU **4014**

Hamilton, James H., 1879-
Western shores; narratives of the Pacific Coast, by Capt. Kettle (James H. Hamilton) illus. with photographic reproductions. Vancouver, B. C., Progress Pub. Co., 1932. 218 p. illus. CV CVicAr **4015**
Same. 1933. CVU WaS **4016**
See also no. 6504.

Hamilton, James McClellan, 1861-1940.
Supplement to Hughes' Community civics for the state of Montana. Boston, Allyn [1921] 96 p. illus. MtBozC WaU **4017**

Hamilton, Mrs. S. Watson.
A pioneer of thirty-three. Albany, Or., Herald Press, 1905. 139 p. front. (port.)
OrHi OrU **4018**

Hamilton, William Thomas, 1822-
My sixty years on the plains trapping, trading, and Indian fighting, by W. T. Hamilton ("Bill Hamilton") ed. by E. T. Sieber; with a full-page illus. by Charles M. Russell. New York, Forest and Stream Pub. Co., 1905. 244 p. front. (port.) 7 plates.
IdB BtBozC MtHi MtU WaS WaU **4019**
Same. 1909. IdIf WaSp WaU **4020**

Hamilton, Wilson.
The new empire and her representative men; or, The Pacific Coast, its farms, mines, vines, wines, orchards, and interests; its productions, industries and commerce, with interesting biographies and modes of travel. Oakland, Calif., Pacific Press Pub. House, 1886. 189 p. illus. CVicAr MtHi WaU **4021**

Hamlin, Charles Simeon, 1868-
Old timers on the Yukon; decline of Circle City, romances of the Klondike.

Los Angeles, Wetzel Pub. Co. [c1928]
172 p. front., plates, ports., facsim.
CVicAr WaS WaU **4022**

Hammond, C. S., & Co.
Hammond's atlas of the state of Washington, pub. for D. A. Hollowell. New York,
1909. 104, 16, 7 p. illus., maps. WaS **4023**

Hammond, Isaac B.
Reminiscences of frontier life. [Portland,
Or?] 1904. 134 p. illus., port.
IdU OrHi OrP OrU WaS WaU **4024**

Hamot, Mrs. Alice (Turnidge) 1871-
The trail blazers; historical and genealogical record of early pioneer families
of Oregon, Missouri, and the South.
Portland, Or., 1935. 459 p. front. (port.)
illus. Turnidge, Crowley and Pigge
families. Or OrP WaT WaU **4025**

Hancock, Samuel.
The narrative of Samuel Hancock, 1845-
1860; with an introd. by Arthur D.
Howden Smith and a map of the Oregon
Trail. London, Harrap [1927] xxii, 217 p.
double map. (The Argonaut series, 1)
CVU OrSaW **4026**

Same. New York, McBride, 1927.
Many **4027**

Same. "On large paper".
CVU IdIf WaU **4028**

The handbook of British Columbia, and
emigrant's guide to the gold fields, with
map and two illus. from photographs by
M. Claudet. London, W. Oliver [1862?]
82 p. front. (fold. map) 2 plates (1
double) CVicAr OrHi **4029**

A handbook of information regarding Umatilla County, the richest agricultural
county in the state of Oregon and the
opportunities offered you by the Teel
Irrigation District in irrigated lands.
[Pendleton, Or., East Oregonian, 1921]
18 p. col. illus., map. WaPS **4030**

Handleman, Howard.
Bridge to victory; the story of the reconquest of the Aleutians. New York,
Random House [1943] 275 p. front.
(port.) plates. Many **4031**

Handly, James.
The resources of Madison County, Montana. San Francisco, Francis & Valentine, 1872. 60 p. MtHi **4032**

Handsaker, Samuel.
Pioneer life. Eugene, Or., 1908. 104 p. illus.,
col. plate, port., facsim.
OrHi OrP OrU WaSp WaU **4033**

Handy, F. M.
Investigation of the mineral deposits of
northern Okanogan County. Pullman,
Wash., State College of Wash. [1915?]
27 p. diagrs. (Dept. of Geology, bulletin
no. 100) WaS WaSp **4034**

Handy, Ray DeWitt, 1879-
Paul Bunyan and his big blue ox; stories
and pictures of the lumberjack hero of
American folklore. Chicago, Rand McNally, c1937. 64 p. illus.
OrU WaS WaU **4035**

Hanford, Cornelius Holgate, 1849-1926.
Boundary disputes with our northern
neighbors, settled and unsettled; annual
address before the Washington Pioneers,
June 7, 1899. Seattle, Lowman & Hanford [1899] 20 p. WaU **4036**

Build the Cascade Tunnel. Seattle, Stewart
Maling List Co., 1925. [8] p. (Wash.
Forum, v. 1., no. 1, July 1925)
WaS WaU **4037**

General Claxton; a novel. New York,
Neale Pub. Co., 1917. 263 p. front. (port.)
Pacific Northwest story.
Wa WaPS WaS WaU WaWW **4038**

Halcyon days in Port Townsend; historical
novel. Seattle, Apex Printing Co., c1925.
118 p. plates, map. Many **4039**

San Juan dispute [eminent men connected
with the international controversy respecting the right of possession of the
Haro Archipelago] Seattle, Dilettante
Pub. Co., 1900. 15 p. port. (Dilettante
booklet series, no. 1) WaU **4040**

Seattle and environs, 1852-1924. Chicago,
Pioneer Historical Pub. Co., 1924. 3 v.
illus., ports. Volumes 2 and 3 biographical. Many **4041**

Statement of his case. [n.p., 19—?] 17 p.
WaS WaU **4042**

See also nos. 5500, 9638-9640.

Hanigsman, Ethel.
Charming Alaska in verse and picture.
Ketchikan, Alaska, 1938. 1 v. illus.
WaS **4043**

Hanks, Lucien Mason, 1910-
Observations on northern Blackfoot kinship. New York, J. J. Augustin [1945]
iv, 31 p. diagrs. (Monographs of the
American Ethnological Society, 9)
CVicAr WaS **4044**

Hanley, Bill, see no. 6920.

Hanly, James Frank, 1863-1920.
A day in the Siskiyous; an Oregon extravaganza. [Indianapolis, Art Press,
c1916] 154 p. plates (part col.)
Many **4045**

Hanna, Esther Bells McMillan, see no. 23.

Hanna, Joseph A.
Dr. Whitman and his ride to save Oregon.
[Los Angeles? 1903] 8 p. front. (port.)
OrHi OrU WaSp WaT WaWW **4046**

Hannibal, Harold, see nos. 5410, 5411.

Hansell, J. E., see no. 8370.

Hansen, A. H., see no. 2737.

Hansen, 1st Lt., see no. 197.

Hansen, Carl, 1860-
Nisqually : biografier — skitser — fortaellinger og oversaettelser. Kobenhavn
Nationale Forfatteres Forlag, 1912. 177 p.
WaU **4047**

Hansen, Henry Paul, see no. 2104.

Hansen, Sofus E., comp.
Tacoma to Anchorage and Kodiak via
inside passage. 2d ed., rev. and enl.
Seattle, Lowman & Hanford [c1919] 327
p. illus., map. WaU **4048**

Hanson, Earl Parker, 1899-
Stefansson, prophet of the North. New
York, Harper [c1941] xiv, 241 p. illus.,
plates, ports., map, photos. Many **4049**

Hanson, Howard A., see no. 7476.

Hanson, Joseph Mills, 1876-
The conquest of the Missouri; being the story of the life and exploits of Captain Grant Marsh, with map and 36 illus. Chicago, McClurg, 1909. xiv, 485 p. front. (port.) 21 plates, 6 ports., fold. map, facsim.   Many **4050**

Same. 3d ed. 1916.   MtBozC Wa **4051**

Same. New York, Murray Hill Books, Inc, [c1946] xviii, 458 p. plates, ports., fold. map, facsim.
CVicPr IdU MtBozC WaT **4052**

Frontier ballads, with pictures in color and other drawings by Maynard Dixon. Chicago, McClurg, 1910. 92 p. col. front., illus., col. plates.   MtHi **4053**

With Carrington on the Bozeman road. Chicago, McClurg, 1912. 411 p. front., plates. ("Among the Sioux" series).
IdB MtHi WaU **4054**

Hanzlik, Edward John, 1886-
Trees and forests of western United States. Portland, Or. [Dunham Printing Co.] 1928. 128 p. front. (map) illus.
Many **4055**

Harber, Nora E., pub.
Our Fort Benton, "the birthplace of Montana"; a collection of stories and pictures of early day and modern Fort Benton. Fort Benton, Mont. [193-] [48] p. illus., ports.
MtBozC MtHi MtU WaU WaW **4056**

Hardy, Martha.
Tatoosh, illus. by Glen Rounds. New York, Macmillan, 1946, 239 p. illus. Forest fire lookout in Columbia National Forest.
Many **4057**

Same. 1947.   OrCS **4058**

Harger, Charles Moreau, see no. 1959.

Hargrave, James, 1798-1865.
The Hargrave correspondence, 1821-1843; ed. with introd. and notes by G. P. de T. Glazebrook. Toronto, Champlain Society, 1938. xxvi, 472 xii p. front., 2 plates, fold. map. (Publications, 24).   Many **4059**

Hargrave, Letitia (Mactavish) 1813-1854.
The letters of Letitia Hargrave, ed. with introd. and notes by Margaret Arnett Macleod. Toronto, Champlain Society, 1947. cliv, 310, xv p. plates, ports., map. (Publications, 28). Hudson's Bay Company and Canadian Northwest history.
Many **4060**

Hargreaves, Sheba May, 1882-
The cabin at the trail's end, a story of Oregon. New York, Burt, c1928. 341 pp.
OrSa WaW **4061**

Same. New York, Harper, 1928. front.
Many **4062**

City planning. [Portland, Or.] c1926. 8 p. illus.   Or WaU **4063**

The Columbarium Hall of Peace. [Portland, Or.] c1926. 8 p. illus.
OrP WaU **4064**

Heroine of the prairies, a romance of the Oregon Trail. New York, Burt [c1930] vi, 288 p.   IdB WaPS WaW **4065**

Same. New York, Grosset, c1930.
OrSa **4066**

Same. New York, Harper, 1930.
Many **4067**

Modern nomads. [Portland, Or.] c1926. 8 p.
OrP WaU **4068**

Ward of the redskins. New York, Burt, 1929. viii, 299 p. illus.   OrSa **4069**

Same. New York, Harper, 1929.
Many **4070**

Harlow, Alvin Fay, 1875-
Old waybills; the romance of the express companies. New York, Appleton-Century, 1934. xii, 503 p. front., illus., plates, ports., facsims.   Many **4071**

Harman, Mrs. Dolly Stearns.
Beach fires. Boston, Christopher Pub. House [c1935] 132 p. Bellingham poet.
WaU **4072**

Sea-wind and mountain trail; Olympic Peninsula verses. Dallas, Texas, Kaleidoscope Pub., 1931. 38 p.
MtU OrAshS WaS **4073**

Harmon, Orrin E., b. 1854.
Voices from the Cascades. Chehalis, W. T., Lewis County Bee Print, 1886. 63 p.
OrP WaU **4074**

Harmon, William E.
Supplement to Reinsch's Civil government for the state of Montana. Boston, Sanborn [c1912] 73 p. illus.   MtBozC **4075**

Harness, Aldon.
Lewis and Clark; a souvenir book. Portland, Or., 1905. 12 p. Oregon poet.
CVicAr Or **4076**

Oregon and other poems. Roseburg, Or., Plaindealer, 1902. [12] p.   OrHi **4077**

Poems for mental workers. [Roseburg, Or., Bellemin Press, c1927] [12] p.
Or OrU **4078**

Harnett, Leigh.
Two lectures on British Columbia. Victoria, B. C., Higgins, 1868. 50 p.
CVicAr CVU WaU **4079**

Harnisch, Wilhelm, 1787-1864.
Hearne's, Mackenzie's, Lewis and Pike's Entdeckungsreisen im innern Nord-Amerika's nebst einer Beschreibung der Nordwestkuste und Neu-Spaniens. Wien, Mausberger's Druck und Verlag, 1826. 285 p, fold. front., fold. plates, 2 fold. maps.
CVicAr **4080**

Harper, Frank B.
Fort Union and its neighbors on the upper Missouri; a chronological record of events. [St Paul? Great Northern Railway, 1925] 36 p. illus., plate.   Many **4081**

Harper, Franklin, see no. 10973.

Harper, Guy R.
Digest of the Oregon state income tax act and regulations. [Portland, Or., Miles Standish Co., c1924] 55 p.
Or OrHi OrP OrPR **4082**

Harper, Theodore Acland, 1871-
Allison's girl. New York, Viking Press, 1936. 279 p. front., illus. Willamette Valley story.   Many **4083**

The janitor's cat, by Theodore Acland in collaboration with Winifred Harper,

drawings by J. Erwin Porter. New York, Appleton, 1927. 207 p. front., illus. Story of J. K. Gill Co. of Portland.
Or OrP WaSp **4084**

Harper, William P., & Son, Seattle, Wash.
The Columbia River Inter-state Bridge. Seattle, 1923. 12 p. illus.   WaPS **4085**
First mortgage bonds of the Pacific Northwest; the safest form of mortgage investment. Seattle [n.d.] 12 p. illus., diagr., table.   WaPS **4086**

Harper, Winifred, see no. 4084.

Harper's Weekly.
Pacific Northwest number. New York, 1909. 34 p. illus. (v. 53, no. 2728, Apr. 3, 1909).   WaU **4087**

Harriman, Alice, see nos. 2409, 10653.

Harriman Alaska Expedition, 1899.
Alaska. New York, Doubleday, Page, 1901-1909. 12 v. illus., plates (part col.) maps.
Many **4088**
Alaska; giving the results of the Harriman Alaska Expedition carried out with the cooperation of the Washington Academy of Sciences. London, Murray, 1902. 2 v. illus., plates (part col.) maps.
CVicAr WaU **4089**

Harrington, John Lyle, 1868-
Final report; the Columbia River interstate bridge, Vancouver, Washington to Portland, Oregon, for Multnomah County, Oregon, Clark County, Washington, by John Lyle Harrington and Ernest Emmanuel Howard. [Kansas City, Mo., Printed by A. W. Hirsch Printing Co., c1918] 61 p. front., illus., fold. map, fold. plan.
Or OrP WaSp WaU **4090**

Harrington, M. R., see no. 5805.

Harrington, Mrs. Rebie.
Cinderella takes a holiday in the Northland; journeys in Alaska and Yukon Territory. New York, H. Revell [c1937] 269 p. front., plates, ports., fold map.
WaS WaU **4091**

Harris, A. C.
Alaska and the Klondike gold fields, containing a full account of the discovery of gold; enormous deposits of the precious metal; routes traversed by miners; how to find gold; camp life at Klondike; practical instructions for fortune seekers, etc., etc., including a graphic description of the gold regions; land of wonders; immense mountains, rivers and plains; native inhabitants, etc.; including Mrs. Eli Gage's experiences of a year among the Yukon mining camps; Mrs. Schwatka's recollections of her husband as the Alaskan pathfinder; prosaic side of gold hunting, as seen by Joaquin Miller, the poet of the Sierras; embellished with many engravings. [n.p., J. R. Jones, c1897] 528 p. front., illus., plates, maps.
CVicAr OrP Wa WaT **4092**
Same. Chicago, J. S. Ziegler & Co. [c1897] 556 p.   WaPS **4093**
Same. Chicago, Monroe Book Co. [c1897]
CVicAr Or WaU **4094**

Same. Chicago, Smith and Simon [1897] 528 p.   WaS **4095**
Same. Cincinnati, W. H. Ferguson Co. [1897] 556 p.
CVU OrP OrU WaSp WaT **4096**
Same. Philadelphia, National Pub. Co. [c1897] 528 p.   Many **4097**

Harris, Aurand.
Once upon a clothesline, a play for children. Evanston, Ill., Row, Peterson & Co. [c1945] 72 p. front., plates. "One of the prize-winning plays in the second playwriting contest conducted by Seattle Junior Programs, Inc."   WaS WaU **4098**

Harris, Charles Edward Smith, ed., see no. 9580.

Harris, Elizabeth, see no. 10726.

Harris, Frank, 1854-1930.
History of Washington County and Adams County [Idaho] [Weiser, Idaho, Weiser American, 192—?] 74 p. front. (port.)
IdB IdU WaU **4099**

Harris, Josiah.
Direct route through the North-west territories of Canada to the Pacific Ocean; the chartered Hudson's Bay & Pacific Railway route. London, Spottiswoode, 1897. 66 p. fold. map.
CVU WaS **4100**

Harris, Lawrence Thomas, 1873-
A history of the judiciary of Oregon; a paper read before the Oregon Bar Association, on November 19, 1917. San Francisco, Bender-Moss Co., 1918. 16 p.
Or OrP OrU **4101**

[Harris, Martha Douglas]
History and folklore of the Cowichan Indians, cover and illus. by Margaret C. Maclure. Victoria, B. C., British Colonist, 1901. 89 p. front., illus.   Many **4102**

[Harris, Morris Charles]
Walla Walla Valley, Washington Territory; its resources, climate, river and railroad systems, cities and towns, land and land-laws, and general advantages as a place of residence, together with pen-sketches of prominent business houses. Walla Walla, Wash., Statesman Book and Job Press, 1879. 36 p. illus.
WaW WaWW **4103**

Harrison, Charles.
Ancient warriors of the north Pacific: the Haidas; their laws, customs and legends, with some historical account of the Queen Charlotte Islands. London, Witherby, 1925. 222 p. front., 10 plates, map.
Many **4104**
The Hydah Mission, Queen Charlotte's Islands, an account of the mission and people. London, C. M. House [1884?] 23 p. illus.   CVicAr **4105**
See also nos. 803, 814.

Harrison, Edward Sanford.
Alaska: geography, physiography, climate, history, and government. [Seattle, Gateway Printing Co., 1909] 8 p map.
WaU **4106**
Alaska, the sportsman's paradise. [Seattle, Gateway Printing Co., 1909] 12 p. illus.
WaU **4107**

Industrial progress in Alaska. [Seattle, Gateway Printing Co., 1909] 32 p.

OrHi WaS WaU **4108**

Nome and Seward Peninsula; a book of information about northwestern Alaska. [Seattle, 1905] 112 p. illus., fold. map.

OrSaW WaPS WaS WaU **4109**

Nome and Seward Peninsula; history, description, biographies and stories. Seattle [Metropolitan, c1905] 392 p. illus., plates, ports. (Souvenir ed.)

CVicAr Wa WaS WaU **4110**

Resources of Alaska. [Seattle, Gateway Printing Co., 1909] 32 p. illus. WaU **4111**

Scenic Alaska. [Seattle, Gateway Printing Co.? 1909] 8 p. illus. WaU **4112**

Harrison, J. M.
Guide and resources of the Pacific slope. Pt. 1 embracing Washington Territory, giving a minute description of its lands and facilities for settlement, land laws, climate, resources, etc. San Francisco, M. D. Carr & Co., 1872. 35 p. WaU **4113**

Same. 2d ed. San Francisco, C. A. Murdock & Co., 1876. WaU **4114**

Harrison and Eaton, consulting petroleum geologists.
Report on investigation of oil and gas possibilities of western Oregon. [Portland, Or.] 1920. 40 p. illus. (Mineral resources of Or., v. 3, no. 1)

MtUM OrP OrSa WaS WaTC **4115**

Harry Bridges Defense Committee.
Harry Bridges, who he is, what he has been doing in the labor movement, why he is on trial for deportation! [n.p., 1939?] 12 p. port. OrP **4116**

Hart, Alan, 1890-
Dr. Finlay sees it through. New York, Harper [c1942] 370 p. Seattle author.

Many **4117**

Doctor Mallory. New York, Norton [c1935] 320 p. Oregon small town story.

Many **4118**

In the lives of men. New York, Norton [c1937] 451 p. Pacific Coast town doctor story. Many **4119**

The undaunted. New York, Norton, 1936. 310 p. Many **4120**

Hart, Albert Bushnell, 1854-1943.
Extracts from official papers relating to the Bering Sea controversy, 1790-1892. New York, A. Lovell & Co., 1892. 26 p. (American history leaflets no. 6, Nov. 1892). OrU WaS **4121**

Same. c1893. WaU **4122**
See also no. 10347.

[Hart, F. J., & Co., Ltd.]
For twenty years, 1891-1911. [Vancouver, B. C., Metropolitan, 1911] 28 p. plates, ports. CVU **4123**

The Fraser Valley and Chilliwack. New Westminster, B. C. [n.d.] 96 p. illus., facsims. CVicAr **4124**

Hart, Louis Folwell, 1862-
Efficiency and economy under the administrative code, reviewed by Governor of Washington before the Republican State Central Committee, Seattle, April 22,

1922. [Olympia, Wash.] Printed and distributed by the Republican State Central Committee [1922] 15 p. WaU **4125**

Hartley, Roland Hill, 1864-
The educational question; speech delivered by Governor Roland H. Hartley in Seattle, May 5, 1926. [n.p. 1926?] 12 p.

WaPS WaU **4126**

Review of state administrative and legislative problems; an address delivered at Spokane on February 25, 1926. [Olympia, Wash.? 1926?] 23 p. WaPS **4127**

The truth about state timber sales; address at Aberdeen, Wash., August 9, 1926, together with the preliminary report of examiners of the State Department of Efficiency on timber sales as shown by the records in the office of Commissioner of Public Lands. [Olympia, Wash.? 1926?] 15 p. WaPS **4128**

Hartley Recall Organization, Seattle, Wash.
$4,183,158 state tax increase under Governor Hartley. Seattle [1926?] [12] p.

WaPS **4129**

Hartman, Mrs. Etta (Venen) see no. 10530.

Hartman, Henry, 1889-
Studies relating to the harvesting and storing of Bosc pears from the Rogue River Valley, by Henry Hartman and F. C. Reimer. [Corvallis, Or.? State Horticultural Society? 1925?] 14 p. tables.

WaPS **4130**

Hartman, John Peter, 1857-
Address at Spokane, Washington, January, 1907. [Spokane?] Ivy Press [1907?] [15] p. WaU **4131**

Address of President of the Board of Regents of the University of Washington delivered at the ground breaking ceremony of the Alaska-Yukon-Pacific Exposition, June 1907. [Seattle, Ivy Press, 1907] [6] p. WaU **4132**

Brief history of the Washington State Good Roads Association, prepared pursuant to a resolution of the 1938 convention at Seattle and particularly emphasizing the work of Honorable Samuel Hill, the founder. [Seattle, 1939] 32 p. ports. Anon.

CVicAr WaE WaS WaT WaU **4133**

Creation of Mount Rainier National Park; an address upon the creation of Mount Rainier National Park, delivered at the 37th annual convention of Washington Good Roads Association, at Olympia, Washington, on September 27 and 28, 1935. [Seattle, Drew & Tomlinson, 1935?] 11 p. maps. WaPS WaS WaU **4134**

Hartwich, Mrs. Ethelyn (Miller) comp.
In valiant quest; poems selected from Washington verse, 1937-1941 and arranged by Evelyn Miller Hartwich. Tacoma, Johnson-Cox Co., 1941. 136 p.

Wa WaS WaSp WaT WaTC **4135**

Harvey, Arthur, 1834- comp.
A statistical account of British Columbia. Ottawa, Printed by G. E. Desbarats, 1867. 41 p. map.

CVicAr CVU WaS WaU **4136**

Same. 1870. CVicAr **4137**

Harvey, Athelstan George, 1884-
Douglas of the fir, a biography of David Douglas, botanist. Cambridge, Mass., Harvard Univ. Press, 1947. x, 290 p. illus., ports., maps. **Many 4138**

Harvey, Peggy.
A whimsical Vancouverite. [n.p., n.d.] [31] p. illus. **CVicAr 4139**

Harvey, William Earl, 1898-
Ballads of the West. Vancouver, B. C., Pacific Printers, 1920. 94 p.
CV CVicAr 4140

Songs of the West. [St. Paul, c1927] 68 p. illus. **CV 4141**

[Haselhurst, Mrs. May A.]
Days forever flown. New York, Privately printed [by Gilliss Bros.] 1892. 401 p. front. (port.) 25 plates. Journal of travel through Northwest and Alaska.
WaSp 4142

Hasell, F. H. Eva.
Canyons, cans and caravans, illus. from photographs by the author. London, Society for Promoting Christian Knowledge, 1930. 320 p. front., plates. Sunday School caravan through Canadian Northwest. **WaU 4143**

Haskell, Daniel Carl, 1883- comp.
The United States Exploring Expedition, 1838-1842, and its publications, 1844-1874; a bibliography, with an introductory note by Harry Miller Lydenberg. New York, New York Public Library, 1942. xii, 188 p. front. (port.) plates, ports., facsim.
Many 4144

Haskell, William B.
Two years in the Klondike and Alaskan gold fields; a thrilling narrative of personal experiences and adventures in the wonderful gold regions of Alaska and the Klondike, with observations of travel and exploration along the Yukon, including full and authentic information of the countries described. Hartford, Hartford Pub. Co., 1898. 558 p. front., illus. 25 plates, fold. map. **Many 4145**

Haskin, Leslie Loren, 1882-1949.
Wild flowers of the Pacific Coast, in which is described 332 flowers and shrubs of Washington, Oregon, Idaho, central and northern California and Alaska; 182 full-page illus. by Leslie L. Haskin, photographs by Leslie L. and Lilian G. Haskin. Portland, Or., Metropolitan, 1934. x, 407 p. col. front., illus. **Many 4146**

[Hassell, Mrs. Susan (Whitcomb)] comp.
A hundred and sixty books by Washington authors; some other writers who are contributors to periodical literature, lines worth knowing by heart. [Seattle, Lowman & Hanford, c1916] 40 p. **Many 4147**

Hastings, Lansford Warren, 1819-ca.1870.
The emigrants' guide to Oregon and California, containing scenes and incidents of a party of Oregon emigrants; a description of Oregon; scenes and incidents of a party of California emigrants; and a description of California; with a description of the different routes to those countries; and all necessary information

relative to the equipment, supplies, and the method of traveling, by Lansford W. Hastings, leader of the Oregon and California emigrants of 1842. Cincinnati, G. Conclin, 1845. 152 p. **OrHi 4148**

Same. Photostat copy. **WaU 4149**

Same. Reproduction in facsimile from the original edition of 1845, with historical note and bibliography by Charles Henry Carey. Princeton, N. J., Princeton Univ. Press, 1932. xxix, 157 p. front. (port.)
Many 4150

A new description of Oregon and California; together with the Oregon treaty and correspondence, and a vast amount of information relating to the soil, climate, productions. rivers and lakes, and the various routes over the Rocky Mountains; also an account, by Col. R. B. Mason, of the gold region and new route to California. Cincinnati, H. M. Rulison, 1857. 160 p. front.
OrHi OrP WaS WaU WaWW 4151

Hatch, Alden, see nos. 7569-7571.

Hatch, Melville H., see no. 1888.

Hatch, Rufus. 1832-1893.
"Uncle Rufus" and "Ma"; the story of a summer jaunt with their friends in the new Northwest. [n.p.] 1882. 67 p.
CVicAr MtHi 4152

Hathaway, Ella C.
Battle of the Big Hole in August 1877 as told by T. C. Sherrill, a volunteer member of Gen. Gibbon's command which was so nearly wiped out on that occasion. [n.p., 1919] [14] p. illus., ports.
Many 4153

Hathway, Marion, 1895-
The cost and volume of social work and public health in Seattle, 1929. [Seattle, 1930] 114 p. table, 36 charts. **WaS 4154**

The migratory worker and family life. Chicago. 1934. xiv, 240 p. illus., maps, plans. (Univ. of Chicago. Social service monographs, no. 21). **Many 4155**

Hatt, Daniel E.
Okanagan. [n.p.. 1917] 20 p. **Wa 4156**
Outdoor verse. Seattle, Judson Press Book Store [1938] 64 p. **Wa 4157**

Sitka spruce; songs of Queen Charlotte Islands. Vancouver. B. C.. R. P. Latta [c1919] 51 p. **CV CVicAr CVU Wa 4158**

Hauthal, Luise (Velthusen) see no. 5394.

Haverly, Charles E.
Klondyke and fortune. London, Southwood, Smith [n.d.] iv, 135 p. **CVicAr 4159**

Havighurst, Walter, 1901-
Pier 17: a novel. New York, Macmillan, 1935. 260 p. Pacific Coast longshoremen's strike story. **Many 4160**

Haweis, Lionel.
Tsoqalem, a weird Indian tale of the Cowichan monster; a ballad, foreword by Charles Hill-Tout. Vancouver, B. C., Citizen Printing & Pub. Co., 1918. 65 p.
CVicAr CVU WaS 4161

Hawes, Ed. M., see no. 4162.

Hawes, Ferdinand B.
Miscellaneous writings, collected and pub-

lished by his family, ed. by Ed. M. Hawes. Everett, Wash., Hawes, 1915. 53 p. front. (port.) WaU 4162

Hawk, M. E.
Workbook in Idaho history. Caldwell, Idaho, Caxton [c1931] 118 p. illus., maps. WaSp 4163

Hawkes, Clarence, 1869-
Silversheene, king of sled dogs, illus. by Charles Livingston Bull. Springfield, Mass., Milton [c1924] xvii, 234 p. front., plates. OrP WaU 4164

Hawkes, Ernest William, 1883-
The dance festivals of the Alaskan Eskimo. Philadelphia, Univ. Museum, 1914. 41 p. 6 plates. (Anthropological publications, v 6, no. 2)
MtU OrP OrU WaS WaSp WaU 4165

Hawkins, D. H.
Poems; Hail Portland! Rose carnival souvenir, 1908. [Portland, Or., 1908?] [7] p. OrU 4166
Where lie the Oregons, Portland's rose-carnival souvenir; an address descriptive of Oregon's resources and marvelous granduer [!] Medford, Or., Hull Printing Co. [1908] 17 p. Poem.
Or OrP OrU WaU 4167

Hawkins, John.
Broken river, by John and Ward Hawkins. New York, Books, Inc., distributed by Dutton [c1943] 212 p. Wartime logging in the Pacific Northwest. IdB Or 4168
Same 1944..
CV OrP WaPS WaS WaT WaU 4169
Pilebuck, by John and Ward Hawkins. New York, Dutton, 1943. 319 p. Seaboard shipyard novel.
CV Or OrP WaS WaSp WaU 4170

Hawkins, Ward, see nos. 4168-4170.

Hawley, James E., 1847-1929, ed.
History of Idaho, the gem of the mountains. Chicago, S. J. Clarke Pub. Co., 1920. 4 v. front., plates, ports., map. Volumes 2-4 biographical. Many 4171

Hawley, Robert Emmett.
Skquee mus; or, Pioneer days on the Nooksack, being a series of personal memoirs, ed. by a friend, P. R. J. Bellingham, Wash. [Miller & Sutherlen Printing Co.] 1945. 189 p. illus., ports. Or Wa WaS 4172

Haworth, Paul Leland, 1876-
On the headwaters of Peace River; a narrative of a thousand-mile canoe trip to a little-known range of the Canadian Rockies. New York, Scribner, 1917. xvii, 295 p. front., plates, maps.
CVicAr Or WaTC WaU 4173
Trailmakers of the Northwest. New York, Harcourt [c1921] viii, 277 p. front., 23 plates, fold. map. Many 4174
Same. Toronto, F. D. Goodchild [c1921] CVic CVU 4175
See also no. 11208.

Hawthorne, Hildegarde.
Born to adventure; the story of John Charles Fremont, pictures by Bruce Adams. New York, Appleton - Century [1947] ix, 230 p. illus. Or WaSp WaU 4176

Enos Mills of the Rockies, by Hildegarde Hawthorne and Esther Burnell Mills. Boston, Houghton, 1935. 260 p. front., plates, ports. Many 4177
No road too long, illus. by James MacDonald. New York, Longmans, 1940. 261 p. illus. Fremont and overland journeys.
Or OrP WaS WaSp WaT 4178
Ox-team miracle; the story of Alexander Majors, decorations by James MacDonald. New York, Longmans, 1942. ix, 236 p. illus. Or OrP WaSp 4179
Westward the course, a story of the Lewis and Clark expedition. New York, Longmans, 1946. vi, 280 p.
Or OrP Wa WaS WaSp WaU 4180

Hawthorne, Julian, 1846-1934.
History of Washington, the Evergreen state, from early dawn to daylight, with ports. and biographies; Julian Hawthorne, ed., assisted by Col. G. Douglas Brewerton. New York, American Historical Pub. Co., 1893. 2 v. fronts. (ports.) ports. Many 4181
The story of Oregon; a history, with ports. and biographies. New York, American Historical Pub. Co., 1892. 2 v. front., plates, ports. Many 4182

Hawthorne, Mont, 1865-
The trail led north, Mont Hawthorne's story, related by Martha Ferguson McKeown. New York, Macmillan, 1948. 222 p. maps. Many 4183

Hay, Marion E., 1865-
Real progress in state government; constructive achievements of the four years past; the record of a business man's administration. [n.p., 1912?] 16 p. tables. WaPS 4184

Hay, Oliver Perry, 1846-1930.
The Pleistocene of the western region of North America and its vertebrated animals. [Washington, D. C.] Carnegie Institution of Washington, 1927. 346 p. illus., 12 plates, maps. (Publication no. 322B). Many 4185

Haycox, Ernest, 1899-
Action by night. New York, Grosset [c1942] 286 p. Portland author.
Wa WaE WaT 4186
Same. [c1943].
CV Or OrP OrU WaS WaU 4187
Alder Gulch. Boston, Little, 1942. 302 p. Many 4188
Same. New York, Grosset [c1942].
Wa WaE WaT 4189
The border trumpet. Boston, Little, 1939. 306 p. Or OrP WaE WaS WaSp 4190
Same. New York, Grosset [c1939]
CV WaT WaU 4191
Same. New York, Sun Dial [c1939]
IdB 4192
Same. Los Angeles, Braille Institute of America, 1940. 3 v. OrP 4193
Bugles in the afternoon. Boston, Little, 1944. 306 p. Many 4194
Same. Garden City, N. Y., Sun Dial [1945].
WaU 4195

Canyon passage. Boston, Little, 1945. 264 p.
Many **4196**

Same. New York, Grosset [c1945] 264 p.
front., plates.   Or OrCS Wa **4197**

Chaffee of Roaring Horse. New York, Burt
[c1930] 291 p.   MtU **4198**

Same. New York, Doubleday, 1930.
Or **4199**

Deep West. Boston, Little, 1937. 301 p.
Or OrU WaSp **4200**

Same. New York, Triangle Books [c1937]
CV OrP WaT **4201**

Free grass. Garden City, N. Y., Doubleday, 1929. 274 p.   Or **4202**

"Hi-yukloshe muck-a-muck, hi-yu wa-wa,
hi-yu hee-hee!" Portland, Or. [n.d.] 22 p.
illus., maps.   OrP **4203**

Long storm. Boston, Little, 1946. 296 p.
Portland, Or. Civil War story.
Many **4204**

Man in the saddle. Boston, Little, 1938. 307
p.   Or WaS **4205**

Same. New York, Grosset, 1938. WaT **4206**

Same. New York, Triangle Books [c1938].
OrP **4207**

Same. Los Angeles, Braille Institute of
America, 1939. 2 v.   OrP **4208**

Riders west. Garden City, N. Y., Doubleday, 1934. 296 p.   Or OrU **4209**

Rim of the desert. Boston, Little, 1941. [i.e.,
1940] 305 p.   IdB Or OrP WaSp **4210**

Same. Garden City, N. Y., Sun Dial [1942]
CV **4211**

Same. New York, Grosset [c1941]
WaU **4212**

Same. Philadelphia, Blakiston. c1941.
WaE WaT **4213**

Rough air. Garden City., N. Y. Doubleday, 1934. 310 p.   Or OrP WaS **4214**

Saddle and ride. Boston, Little, 1940. 291
p. Or OrP Wa WaS WaU **4215**

Same. Garden City, N. Y., Sun Dial [c1940]
WaE **4216**

Same. New York, Grosset [c1940]
WaT **4217**

The silver desert. Garden City, N. Y.,
Doubleday, 1935. 310 p. OrP OrU WaSp **4218**

Starlight rider. Garden City, N. Y., Doubleday, 1933. 309 p.   Or **4219**

Sundown Jim. Boston, Little [c1937] 292 p.
Or OrP WaSp **4220**

Same. New York, Grosset [c1938] WaU **4221**

Same. New York, Pocket Books [c1938]
WaU **4222**

Same. New York, Triangle Books [c1938]
WaE WaT **4223**

Trail smoke. Garden City, N. Y., Doubleday, 1936. 293 p. front.
IdB Or OrP OrU **4224**

Trail town. Boston, Little, 1941. 298 p.
IdB Or OrP OrU WaSp **4225**

Same. New York, Grosset [c1941]
OrHi Wa WaE WaT **4226**

Trouble shooter. Garden City, N. Y., Doubleday, 1937. 291 p.   Or OrP WaSp **4227**

Same. Garden City, N. Y., Sun Dial [1938].
WaS **4228**

Whispering range. Garden City, N. Y.,
Doubleday [c1930] 320 p.
MtU Or OrP WaS **4229**

The wild bunch. Boston, Little, 1943. 245 p.
Or OrP OrU WaS **4230**

Same. New York, Grosset, c1942.
WaT **4231**

Same. Philadelphia, Blakiston, c1943.
CV WaE **4232**

Hayden, Ferdinand Vandeveer, 1829-1887.
The great West, its attractions and resources; containing a popular description
of the marvellous scenery, physical geography, fossils, and glaciers of this wonderful region; and the recent explorations in the Yellowstone Park; also,
valuable information to travellers and
settlers concerning climate, health, mining, husbandry, education, the Indians,
Mormonism, the Chinese; with the homestead, pre-emption, land, and mining
laws, by a corps of able contributors.
Bloomington, Ill., C. R. Brodix, 1880. 528
p. front. (7 ports.) plates, maps.
MtU WaPS WaSp **4233**

Same. Philadelphia, Franklin Pub. Co.,
1880.   CVicAr MtU WaU **4234**

Sun pictures of Rocky Mountain scenery,
with a description of the geographical
and geological features, and some account of the great West. New York, J.
Bien, 1870. 150 p. front., 29 plates.
CVicAr IdU OrHi **4235**

See also nos. 9386-9388.

Hayden, Gwendolen Lampshire, 1904-
Muslin town; a story about gold rush
days in Oregon, by Gwendolen Lampshire Hayden and Pearl Clements Gischler. Portland, Or., Binfords & Mort [1946]
70 p. illus.   Many **4236**

Thunder Hill, by Gwendolen Lampshire
Hayden and Pearl Clements Gischler.
Portland, Or., Binfords & Mort [1947] 74
p. front., illus., plates.   Many **4237**

Same. [1948, c1947].   WaU **4238**

Hayden, Mrs. Mary Jane (Bean)
Pioneer days. San Jose, Calif., Murgotten
Press, 1915. 49 p. port. Vancouver, Wash.
author and pioneer.   OrHi WaS **4239**

Haydon, Arthur Lincoln, 1872-
The riders of the plains, a record of the
Royal Northwest Mounted Police of
Canada, 1873-1910. London, A. Melrose,
1910. xvi, 385 p. front., illus., 24 plates, 2
ports., fold. map, fold. diagr. Many **4240**

Same. 1914.   CVU **4241**

Same. 7th impression. 1918, xx, 417 p.
CVU **4242**

Same. 1919.   WaU **4243**

Same. 1926.   WaPS **4244**

Hayes, Mrs. Florence (Sooy) 1895-
Arctic gateway. New York, Friendship
Press [c1940] 132 p. plates, ports.
Or OrP **4245**

The Eskimo hunter, illus. by Kurt Wiese.
New York, Random House [1945] 275 p.
col. front., illus. (1 col.) plates.
Or OrP WaS WaSp WaU **4246**

Hayes, Isaac Israel, 1832-1881.
An Arctic boat-journey in the autumn of 1854, ed. with an introd. and notes by Dr. Norton Shaw. London, R. Bentley, 1860. 379 p. fold. map. CVicAr **4247**

The open Polar Sea; a narrative of a voyage of discovery toward the North Pole, in the schooner "United States." New York, Hurd and Houghton, 1867. 454 p. front. (port.) illus., plates, maps.
CVicAr **4248**

Hayes, James Gordon, 1877-
Robert Edwin Peary; a record of his explorations, 1886-1909. London, Richards [1929] xv, 299 p. front., illus., 7 plates, port., 4 maps. CVicAr WaS **4249**

Hayes, Jeff W., 1853-1917.
Looking backward at Portland; devoted to the old timer of the early '80's, with humorous and interesting stories and historical data, illus. by Fred A. Routledge. Portland, Or., Kilham Stationery & Printing Co., 1911. 97 p. illus., ports.
Many **4250**

Paradise on earth. Portland, Or., Baltes & Co., 1913. 112 p. front. (port.)
OrP OrSaW **4251**

Portland, Or., A. D. 1999, and other sketches. Portland, Or., Baltes & Co., 1913. 112 p. front. (port.)
Or OrHi OrP OrU WaPS **4252**

Tales of the Sierras, with illus. by John L. Cassidy. Portland, Or., Baltes & Co., 1900. 136 p. front. (port.) illus., plates.
Many **4253**

Same. 1905. OrHi **4253A**

Hayes, Mrs. Kate Simpson (Markwell)
The legend of the West; souvenir ed., illus. by Lilian J. Clarke. [Victoria, B. C., 1908] [17] p. illus. Poem. CVicAr **4254**

Hayhurst, Mrs. Elizabeth.
Twenty years with the Oregon Parent Teachers, 1907-1927. [n.p., 1927?] 20 p.
Or OrP **4255**

Hayman, Herbert Harry, 1910-
That man Boone, frontiersman of Idaho. Caldwell, Idaho, College of Idaho. [c1948] 228 p. front. (port.) WaU **4256**

Hayne, Coe Smith, 1875-
Red men on the Bighorn; contains the story of Swift Eagle, based on Crow legends as told by Plenty Crows (Red Neck) to his son Alvin; ed. by the Department of Missionary Education, Board of Education of the Northern Baptist Convention. Philadelphia, Judson Press [c1929] 123 p. front., plates, ports.
MtHi WaPS WaS **4257**

Hayne, M. H. E.
The pioneers of the Klondyke; being an account of two years police service on the Yukon, narrated by M. H. E. Hayne and recorded by H. West Taylor, illus. by photographs taken on the spot by the narrator. London, Low, 1897. xii, 184 p. front. (port.) 15 plates, map. Many **4258**

Hays, Creighton E.
The settlement of the Boise Basin. [n.p., n. d.] 1 v. OrU **4259**

Haystead, Ladd, 1903-
If the prospect pleases; the West the guidebooks never mention. Norman, Okla., Univ. of Okla. Press, 1945. xiii, 208 p. Many **4260**

Preacher's kid, drawings by John Gincano. New York, Putnam [1942] xiii, 217 p. front., illus.
Or Wa WaPS WaS WASp WaU **4261**

Hayward, J. Abram.
The city of Spokane. [n.p.] c1936. 4 p.
WaPS **4262**

Hazard, Joseph Taylor, 1879-
The glacier playfields of the Mt. Rainier National Park. [Seattle] Western Printing Co., 1920. 96 p. illus.
Or OrP Wa WaPS WaS WaU **4263**

Our living forests, the story of their preservation and multiple use. Seattle, Superior Pub. Co [1948] xii, 302 p. illus.
Many **4264**

Pacific crest trails from Alaska to Cape Horn. Seattle, Superior Pub. Co. [1946] 317 p. front., plates. Many **4265**

Same. Enlarged rev. ed. [c1948] 352 p.
Many **4266**

Snow sentinels of the Pacific Northwest. Seattle, Lowman & Hanford, 1932. 249 p. front., 27 plates. Many **4267**

Hazard, Lucy Lockwood, 1890-
The frontier in American literature. New York, Crowell [c1927] 308 p. WaSp **4268**

Same. New York, Barnes & Noble, 1941.
IdUSB OrSaW WaTC WaU **4269**

Hazelton, Elizabeth C.
Alaskan forget-me-nots. [Seattle, Lowman & Hanford, c1923] [28] p. illus.
WaPS WaU **4270**

Same. 2d ed. [c1925] WaU **4271**

Hazlitt, William Carew, 1834-1913.
British Columbia and Vancouver Island; comprising a historical sketch of the British settlements in the Northwest coast of America; and a survey of the physical character of that region, comp. from official and other authentic sources. London, G. Routledge, 1858. viii, 247 p. fold. map. Many **4272**

The great gold fields of Cariboo; with an authentic description, brought down to the latest period, of British Columbia and Vancouver Island. London, Routledge, 1862. viii, 184 p. front. (fold. map)
CV CVicAr CVU OrP WaS WaU **4273**

Hazzard, George, 1845-
Hand-book of democratic politics of the state of Washington for the year 1890, comp. by authority of the Central Democratic Club of Pierce County. Tacoma, 1890. 58 p. CVicAr WaPS **4274**

The proposed soldiers' home; some facts for the voters of Washington to consider. Tacoma, 1890. 14 p. WaU **4275**

He-mene Ka-wan "Old Wolf", see no. 6475.

Head, Lewis M.
Neah-kah-nie Mountain; the most beautiful spot on the Pacific Coast. Portland, Or., S. G. Reed, c1910. [26] p. illus., map.
Or OrP WaPS **4276**

The Oregon Coast. [n.p.] Astoria & Columbia River Railroad Co., 1909-1910. [20] p. illus.   Or **4277**

Heald-Mennerey Co., Inc., Portland, Or.
New authentic commercial, geographical and recreational survey index of the state of Oregon, containing list of all towns, keyed and indexed, O. & C. homestead lands, Coos Bay Wagon Road grant lands, list of streams stocked by Fish Commission, complete detailed information of all counties in state, issued in conjunction with Geographical, commercial and recreational survey map of Oregon. Portland, Or. [c1926] 95 p.
                            Or OrP **4278**

New authentic geographical and industrial survey of the state of Washington issued in connection with our new and complete classified road survey. Portland, Or., Portland Printing House, c1918. 88 p.   OrP WaS WaU **4279**

Same. c1920. 80 p.   OrSa WaPS **4280**

Heald-Walkup Pub. Co., San Francisco, Calif.
Survey index of the state of Washington containing list of all towns, double keyed and indexed with 1920-1930 census populations, railroad connections, post offices, express telegraph offices, etc. San Francisco, [1934?] 28 p.   WaU **4281**

Hearne, Samuel, 1745-1792.
Journals of Samuel Hearne and Philip Turnor, ed. with introd. and notes by J. B. Tyrell. Toronto, Champlain Society, 1934. xviii, 611 p. maps (part fold.) fold. plan, fold. facsim. (Publications 21)
        CVU MtU WaS WaSp WaU **4282**

A journey from Prince of Wales's fort in Hudson's Bay to the Northern Ocean, undertaken by order of the Hudson's Bay Company, for the discovery of copper mines, a northern passage, etc., in the years 1769, 1770, 1771, & 1772. London, Strahan, 1795. 458 p. front. (fold. map) plates (part fold.) fold. maps.
CVU MtHi OrHi WaS WaSp WaU **4283**

Same. Dublin, Printed for P. Byrne and J. Rice, 1796.   OrP **4284**

Same. New ed. with introd., notes, and illus. by J. B. Tyrell. Toronto, Champlain Society, 1911. xv, 437 p. plates, ports., maps (part fold.) (Publications 6)
                        CVU WaU **4285**

Heaton's guide to western Canada; descriptions of towns and farming districts. Toronto, Heaton's Agency, 1913. 288 p. illus., maps.   CV **4286**

Heawood, Edward, 1863-
A history of geographical discovery in the seventeenth and eighteenth centuries. Cambridge, Cambridge Univ. Press, 1912. xii, 475 p. illus., ports., maps (3 fold.) (Cambridge geographical series)
                    CVicAr IdU OrP **4287**

Hebard, Grace Raymond, 1861-1936.
The Bozeman Trail; historical accounts of the blazing of the overland routes into the Northwest, and the fights with Red Cloud's warriors, by Grace Raymond Hebard and E. A. Brininstool, with in-

trod. by General Charles King. Cleveland, A. H. Clark Co., 1922. 2 v. front., plates, ports., maps (1 fold.) plans.
                            Many **4288**

The pathbreakers from river to ocean; the story of the great West from the time of Coronado to the present. Chicago, Lakeside Press, 1911 [c1911] x, 263 p. front., illus., 4 maps.   Many **4289**

Same. 2d ed. 1912 [c1911]
        IdU OrHi OrP WaE WaU **4290**

Same. 3d ed. 1913.   IdIf MtU **4291**

Same. Chicago, Univ. Pub. Co., 1917 [c1911] x, 261 p. front. IdU Wa WaPS WaU **4292**

Same. 6th ed., rev. and enlarged, with four maps and ninety-three illus., many by William H. Jackson. Glendale, Calif., A. H. Clark Co., 1932. 312 p. front., illus., ports., 4 maps (1 double).   Many **4293**

Same. 7th ed. 1940 [c1932]   MtU **4294**

Sacajawea, a guide and interpreter of the Lewis and Clark expedition, with an account of the travels of Toussaint Charbonneau, and Jean Baptiste, the expedition papoose. Glendale, Calif., A. H. Clark Co., 1933. 340 p. front., plates, ports., maps (1 fold.) facsims.   Many **4295**

Washakie; an account of Indian resistance of the covered wagon and Union Pacific Railroad invasions of their territory. Cleveland, A. H. Clark Co., 1930. 337 p. front., plates, ports., maps (part fold.)
                            Many **4296**

Heclawa, see no. 4484.

Hedges, Mrs. Ada Hastings.
Desert poems. Portland, Or., Metropolitan, 1930. 65 p. Portland poet.   Many **4297**

[**Hedges, Cornelius**].
Art work of Montana. Chicago, W. H. Parish Co., 1896. 88 p. plates. (Part 12 of 12 parts).   MtBozC MtHi **4298**

Hedges, Gilbert Lawrence, 1874-1929.
Where the people rule; or, The initiative and referendum, direct primary law and the recall in use in the state of Oregon. San Francisco, Bender-Moss Co., 1914. vii, 214 p.   Or OrP OrU WaPS **4299**

Hedges, James Blaine.
Building the Canadian West; the land and colonization policies of the Canadian Pacific Railway. New York, Macmillan, c1939. 422 p. illus., maps (1 fold).
                            Many **4300**

Henry Villard and the railways of the Northwest. New Haven, Yale Univ. Press, 1930. 224 p. 2 maps.   Many **4301**

Hedley, John.
The labor trouble in Nanaimo District; an address given before the Brotherhood of Haliburton Street, Methodist Church. [n.p., n.d.] 19 p.   CVicAr **4302**

Hedrick, Helen, 1902-
The blood remembers. New York, Knopf, 1941. 288 p. Klamath River., Or. setting.
                            Many **4303**

Heffelfinger, Charles Hook.
Directed studies in Washington history and government, by C. H. Heffelfinger

and Ralph Ernest Downie. Seattle, Frayn Printing Co. [1943?] iv, 90 p. illus., maps.
WaS WaT WaU **4304**

The Evergreen citizen; a textbook on the government of the state of Washington, by C. H. Heffelfinger in collaboration with George Custer. Caldwell, Idaho, Caxton, 1941. 343 p. front., illus., diagrs.
Many **4305**

Heflin, Alma.
Adventure was the compass, illus. by Martha Powell Setchell. Boston, Little, 1942. 285 p. illus. Airplane trip to Alaska.
Or Wa WaS WaSp WaT WaU **4306**

Hegardt, Gustave B.
Portland, Oregon; its channel approach, harbor railroad facilities, navigable waterways and tributary territory. [n.p., 1913?] 45 p. fold. map. WaPS **4307**

Hegg, Eric A.
Souvenir of Alaska and Yukon Territory. [Skaguay, Alaska? 1900] 104 p. illus.
CVicAr WaPS **4308**

Heidergott, Hazel.
The heart to find. Philadelphia, Macrae-Smith Co., 1945. 242 p. Seattle novel.
WaU **4309**

Heileman, William H.
The Klamath Irrigation Project. [n.p., 1908] 23 p. illus. WaPS WaT **4310**

Heilprin, Angelo, 1853-1907.
Alaska and the Klondike; a journey to the new Eldorado, with hints to the traveller. London, G. Arthur Pearson, 1899. x, 315 p. front., 34 plates, 3 maps, diagrs.
CVicAr CVU **4311**

Same. New York, Appleton, 1899.
Many **4312**

Heinmiller, Carl, see no. 3700.

[**Heinze, Frederick Augustus**] 1869-1914.
The political situation in Montana, 1900-1902. [Butte, Mont.? 1902] 63 p.
MtBozC MtHi MtU **4313**

Heise, Irvin F.
Early Legion days in Washington. Seattle, American Legion, Dept. of Wash., 1937. 5 p. WaS WaU **4314**

Heistand, Henry Olcot Sheldon, 1856-
The Territory of Alaska; a brief account ·of its history and purchase; its inhabitants, geographical features and resources, with especial reference to the goldfields and methods of reaching them, comp. from official government records and the latest and most reliable sources. Kansas City, Mo., Hudson-Kimberly Pub. Co., 1898. 195 p. 16 plates, 3 fold. maps.
CVicAr WaU **4315**

Heisterman, Henry Frederick, see no. 3300.

Heizer, Robert Fleming, see no. 2104.

Held, Albert.
Souvenir, Spokane, Washington. [Spokane, Cole Printing Co., 1904?] [60] p. illus.
WaSp **4316**

Helena Citizens' Alliance, Helena, Mont.
An address setting forth the objects of the Citizens' Alliance of Helena, Montana, Wm. Muth, secretary. Helena, Mont., 1903. 8 p. MtHi **4317**

Helena's social supremacy. Helena, Mont., 1894. 48 p. illus. MtHi MtU **4318**

Hellaby, H. A., see no. 10719.

Hellenthal, John Albertus.
The Alaskan melodrama. London, Allen and Unwin, c1936. xvi, 312 p. front., 11 plates, map. CVic **4319**

Same. New York, Liveright [c1936]
CVicAr OrP WaS WaSp WaU **4320**

Helm, McKinley, see no. 7846.

Helm, Richard Izer, 1873-
Blue waters, an Indian romance. Portland, Or., Binfords & Mort [c1938] 251 p. front.
Many **4321**

[**Helmcken, John Sebastian**]
Fac-similes and a history of specimen gold coins made in British Columbia in 1862. [n.p., n.d.] [4] p. illus. CVicAr **4322**

Helmericks, Constance, 1918-
Our summer with the Eskimos, by Constance and Harmon Helmericks. Boston, Little, 1948. xiv, 239 p. illus., ports., col. map. WaU **4323**

We live in Alaska. Boston, Little, 1944. 266 p. plates, ports. Many **4324**

Same. Engravings by Gwenda Morgan. London, Hodder & Stoughton [1945] 304 p. illus. CVicAr **4325**

We live in the Arctic, by Constance and Harmon Helmericks. Boston, Little, 1947. xvi, 329 p. illus., ports., map. Many **4326**

Helmericks, Harmon, see nos. 4323-4326.

Heltman, Charles C., see no. 1781.

Heming, Arthur Henry Howard, 1870-
The drama of the forests, romance and adventure, illus. by the author with reproductions from a series of his paintings owned by the Royal Ontario Museum. Garden City, N. Y., Doubleday, 1921. xiii, 324 p. col. front., col. plates, col. ports. Canadian Northwest.
Or OrCS **4327**

Henderson, Alice Palmer.
The Ninety-first, the first at Camp Lewis. Tacoma, J. C. Barr [c1918] 510 p. front. (port.) illus., ports., forms. Many **4338**

The rainbow's end; Alaska. Chicago, H. S. Stone & Co., 1898. 296 p. front., plates, ports. Many **4329**

Henderson, Daniel, see no. 6568.

Henderson, Daniel MacIntyre, 1880-
From the Volga to the Yukon; the story of the Russian march to Alaska and California, paralleling our own westward trek to the Pacific. New York, Hastings House [c1944] x, 256 p.
IdIf Or OrP WaS WaSp **4330**

Same. [1945]
CV CVicAr Or OrU WaS WaU **4331**

Henderson, Frank Downey.
Looking into the sunset. Chicago, Howard A. Burk & Co. [c1940] 108 p. Poems.
WaS WaU **4332**

Henderson, Lester Dale, 1886-
Alaska; its scenic features, geography, history and government. Juneau, Daily Alaska Empire, c1928. 112 p. illus., maps, diagr. CVicAr WaU **4333**

Same. 2d printing, 1929 rev. 114 p.
WaPS WaS WaU **4334**

Same. c1936. 143 p. WaT **4335**

Hendricks, George David.
The bad man of the West, drawings by Frank Anthony Stanush. San Antonia, Naylor Co., 1942. xv, 310 p. front., illus., plates, ports., facsim. WaE WaU **4336**

Hendricks, Robert J.
Bethel and Aurora; an experiment in communism as practical Christianity, with some account of past and present ventures in collective living. New York, Press of the Pioneers, 1933. 324 p. front., plates, ports. Many **4337**

Innnnnnng haaaaaaa! Savage warfare, southern chivalry, facts stranger'n fiction; The war to end the white race; Soul of Philip knit with soul of Davis. Salem, Or., 1937. 52 p. front., plates, music. Or OrHi OaSaW WaT WaU **4338**

Pageant of the pioneers. 1st rev. ed. [Salem, Or., Printed on Statesman Pub. Co. Press, c1931] 46 p. illus.
OrCS OrP WaU **4339**

The West saved America and democracy; Innnnnnng haaaaaaa!!! number two; continuation of the trilogy in the anabasis of the westernmost West; men who learned in the free air of the early pioneer settlements lessons which brought victory to the banners of Liberty in the time of her desperate need. Salem, Or., 1939. 134 p. WaU **4340**

Hendrix, E. R., see no. 9807, 9808.

Hendryx, James Beardsley, 1880-
Blood on the Yukon Trail, a novel of Corporal Downey of the Mounted. Garden City, N. Y., Doubleday, 1930. 305 p.
WaU **4341**

Connie Morgan hits the trail, illus. by Ernest Walker. Garden City, N. Y. Doubleday, 1929. vi, 221 p. front. (Windmill books) WaU **4342**

Connie Morgan in Alaska. New York. Putnam [c1916] vi, 341 p. front., illus.
Or WaS WaU **4343**

Connie Morgan in the Arctic. New York, Putnam [c1936] 239 p. front. Wa **4344**

North. New York, Burt [c1923] 334 p.
WaU **4345**

On the rim of the Arctic. Garden City, N. Y. Doubleday, 1948. 224 p. IdB **4346**

Outlaws of Halfaday Creek. New York, Burt [c1935] viii, 299 p. WaU **4347**

Henley, G. F.
Guide to the Yukon-Klondike mines: full information of outfit, climate, Dawson City, with notes on alluvial and metalliferous prospecting; routes described in detail; report of Wm. Ogilvie, F. R. G. S. and diary of the late Archbishop Seghers. [Victoria, B. C., Province Pub. Co., 1897] 63 p. illus. CVU **4348**

Hennessey, D. L., see no. 1069.

Hennessy, W. B.
Tracy the bandit; or, the romantic life and crimes of a Twentieth Century desperado, twenty-five full page pictures by C. D. Rhodes. Chicago, Donohue [1902] 336 p. plates. WaU **4349**

Henry, Alexander, 1739-1824.

New light on the early history of the greater Northwest; the manuscript journals of Alexander Henry and of David Thompson, 1799-1814; exploration and adventure among the Indians on the Red, Saskatchewan, Missouri and Columbia Rivers, ed. with copious critical commentary by Elliott Coues. New York, Harper, 1897. 3 v. front. (port.) maps. Many **4350**

Henry, Anson G.
Rogue River war; speech delivered before the citizens of Corvallis on Dec. 3, 1855, on the subject of the pending Rogue River war. Oregon City, Or., Argus, 1855. 14 p. OrHi OrP **4351**

Henry, Charles K.
Expose of the methods and doings of the Provident Trust Company of Portland, Oregon. Portland, Or. [n.d.] 23 p.
OrHi OrP **4352**

Henry, Francis.
The old settler, illus. by Maj. W. A. Bell. [Olympia, Wash.? c1892] [11] p. illus., plate, port., music. OrHi **4353**
Same. [1902] Wa WaU **4354**

Henry, Horace Chapin.
The art collection of H. C. Henry. Seattle [192—?] [62] p. plates. WaU **4355**

Henry, Joseph Kaye.
Flora of southern British Columbia and Vancouver Island, with many references to Alaska and northern species. Toronto, Gage [c1915] xiii, 363 p.
CV CVU IdU OrPR WaSp WaU **4356**
See also no. 2716.

Henry, Marguerite.
Alaska in story and pictures; pictures by Kurt Wiese, Chicago, A. Whitman & Co., c1941. [28] p. illus. (part col.) (Pictured geography)
Or OrP WaS WaSp WaU **4357**

Henry, P. F., see nos. 10466-10468.

[Henry, Ralph Chester] 1912-
High border country, by Eric Thane [pseud.] New York, Duell, Sloan & Pearce [1942] ix, 335 p. (American folkways) Idaho and Mont. included in High Border country. Many **4358**

Henry, William Elmer, 1857-1936.
Why the University of Washington Library brought forth the University Library School, 1906-1911; the direction of the school's activity through its first administration; William E. Henry, librarian 1906-1929, director of the Library School 1911-1931, Librarian Emeritus 1929. [n.p.] 1935. [7] p. WaS WaU **4359**

Henry & Geiger, Pub.
Tri-county atlas; Meagher, Sweet Grass and Carbon. [Big Timber, Mont., 1902?] 112 p. illus., ports. MtBozC **4360**

Henson, Matthew Alexander, 1866-
A negro explorer at the North pole, with a foreword by Robert E. Peary and an introd. by Booker T. Washington, with illus. from photographs. New York, Stokes [1912] 200 p. front., plates, ports.
CVicAr OrP WaS WaSp **4361**

Henty, George Alfred, 1832-1902.
Redskin and cow-boy; a tale of the western plains, with twelve illus. by Alfred Pearse. New York, Scribner [c1919] 384 p. col. front., plates. WaE WaU **4362**

Herbert, Agnes.
Two Dianas in Alaska, by Agnes Herbert and a shikari. London, Lane Co., 1909 [1908] xii, 316 p. front. (port.) 28 plates.
CV CVU WaS WaSp WaU **4363**
Same. 2d ed. WaSp WaU **4364**
Same. London, Nelson [1909] 256 p.
CVic **4365**

Herkenrath, August, 1881-
Canada und die Hudson's Bay Company. Bonn, Seb. Foppen, 1904. 136 p.
WaU **4366**

Hermiston Herald, Hermiston, Or.
Anniversary edition, 1906-1936. Hermiston, Or., 1936. [26] p. illus., ports. (v. 30, no. 6, Sept. 17, 1936) WaU **4367**

Herndon, Carrie P.
Lewis and Clark expedition. Dansville, N. Y., F. A. Owen Co. [c1912] 20 p. illus., map. (Instructor literature series)
OrP **4368**

Herndon, James A.
To him that endureth, a romance of the Salmon River country. Caldwell, Idaho, Caxton, c1929. 326 p. front., plates.
Many **4369**
Same. 1930 [c1929] IdU MtHi **4370**

Herndon, Mrs. Sarah (Raymond)
Days on the road; crossing the plains in 1865. New York, Burr Printing House, 1902. xvi, 270 p. front. (port.)
Many **4371**

Herrick, Elisabeth Webb.
Native Northwest novelties; or, What to look for besides scenery; this is a new kind of guidebook, designed to turn trippers into old settlers, and old settlers into tourists. Seattle, C. W. Art [c1937] 109 p. illus. Many **4372**

Herrick, Mrs. Una (Brasfield)
Twenty years at Montana State College. [n.p., n.d.] 118 p. MtBozC **4373**

Herring, Frances Elizabeth, 1851-
Among the people of British Columbia, red, white, yellow, and brown. London, Unwin, 1903. xvi, 299 p. front. (port.) 19 plates. Many **4374**
Canadian camp life. London, 1900. 247 p. front., plates, port.
CVicAr CVU WaSp WaU **4375**
Same. 2d ed. London, Griffiths, 1913. 188 p. front., 7 plates. CV **4376**
The gold miners; a sequel to The pathless West; with a pref. by Judge F. W. Howay. London, Griffiths, 1914. 120 p. front. (port.) 7 plates.
CV CVicAr CVU WaU **4377**
In the pathless West with soldiers, pioneers, miners and savages. London, Unwin, 1904. xiii, 240 p. front., 11 plates, 2 ports.
CV CVicAr CVU WaPS WaT WaU **4378**
Nan and other pioneer women of the West.

London, Griffiths, 1913. 171 p. front. (port.) plates.
CV CVU Or WaSp WaU **4379**

Herron, Edward Albert, 1912-
Alaska, land of tomorrow. New York, McGraw [1947] 232 p. plates, map.
Many **4380**

Hershey, Oscar H., 1874-
Origin and distribution of ore in the Coeur d'Alene. [n.p., 1916?] 32 p. map.
WaPS **4381**

Hessem, Louis de, see no. 7851.

Hestwood, James O.
The Evergreen state souvenir, containing a review of the resources, wealth, varied industries and commercial advantages of the state of Washington, pub. for distribution at the World's Columbian Exposition. Chicago, W. B. Conkey Co., c1893. 72 p. illus., ports., maps.
WaS WaU **4382**

Heuston, Benjamin Franklin, 1859-1907.
The law of the state of Washington relating to real estate transfer. [Tacoma, Commonwealth Title and Trust Co., c1894] 42 p. WaPS **4383**
Same. [1898, c1894] 58 p. Wa WaU **4384**
The rice mills of Port Mystery. Chicago, C. H. Kerr & Co., 1891. 206 p. (Library of progress, no. 3) Pacific Northwest novel. WaU **4385**
Same. (Unit library, no. 8) WaPS **4386**
Same. 2d ed. 1892. Many **4387**
Same. 3d ed.
Or WaPS WaS WaSp WaT **4388**

Hewes, Agnes (Danforth)
The golden sleeve, illus. by Herbert Morton Stoops. New York, Junior Guild, 1937. 280 p. front. Wash. and Or. adventure. IdIf Or OrP WaS WaT WaU **4389**
Same. Garden City, N. Y., Doubleday, 1943 [c1937] WaU **4390**
Jackhammer; drill runners of the mountain highways. New York, Knopf, c1942. 268 p. Cascade Mountains.
Or OrP Wa WaS WaSp WaT **4391**
Same. 1944 [c1942] WaU **4392**

Hewitt, Randall Henry, 1840-
Across the plains and over the divide; a mule train journey from East to West in 1862, and incidents connected therewith, with map and illus. New York, Broadway Pub. Co [c1906] iii, 521 p. front., illus., plates, ports., fold. map.
Many **4393**
Notes by the way; memoranda of a journey across the plains from Dundee, Ill., to Olympia, W. T., May 7 to Nov. 3, 1862. Olympia, Wash., Wash. Standard, 1863. 58 p. OrHi WaU **4394**
Same. Photostat copy. Wa WaU **4395**

Hewitt, Roy R.
Our government in Oregon. [Chicago, Laidlaw, 1925] 48 p. OrP **4396**
See also nos. 571-578.

Heyden, Joseph van der.
Life and letters of Father Brabant, a Flemish missionary hero. Louvain, J.

Wouters-Ickx [1920?] 249 p. front., plates, ports. B. C. missions.
CVicAr MtU WaS WaU **4397**

Heydinger, C., see no. 9801.

Hiatt, Isaac.
Thirty-one years in Baker County; a history of the county from 1861 to 1893. Baker City, Or., Abbott & Foster, Printers, 1893. 208 p. Or OrHi WaU **4398**

Hibben, Tertius Napier.
Chinook jargon as spoken by the Indians of the Pacific Coast; for the use of missionaries, traders, tourists and others who have business intercourse with the Indians: Chinook-English, English-Chinook. [Victoria, B. C., 1931] 30 p. illus.
CV CVicAr CVU WaS WaU **4399**

Dictionary of Indian tongues, containing most of the words and terms used in the Tsimpsean, Hydah, & Chinook with their meaning or equivalent in the English language. Victoria, B. C., 1862. 15 p.
OrP **4400**

Same. 1865. 14 p. WaU **4401**

A dictionary of the Chinook jargon; or, Indian trade language of the North Pacific Coast. Victoria, B. C. [187—?] 29 p. CVicAr **4402**

Same. [1875] WaU **4403**

Same. [c1877] 33 p. CVicAr Wa **4404**

Same. [c1878] 26 p. CVicAr **4405**

Same. New ed. Victoria, B. C., B. C. Stationery Co., 1887. 33 p.
CVicAr WaU **4406**

Same. Hibben, 1899. 32 p.
CV WaT WaU **4407**

Same. 1906. 42 p. CVicAr **4408**

Same. [Diggon, 1931] 30 p. illus.
CVicAr **4409**

Hibbs, Frank W.
"Comparative tests of yellow pine and Puget Sound fir". Seattle, Pacific Northwest Society of Engineers, c1902. 44 p. illus., tables. (Proceedings, v. 1, no. 5, Nov. 1902) Wa **4410**

Hickey, Thomas A.
The story of a bull pen at Wardner, Idaho. New York, National Executive Committee, Socialist Labor Party, 1900. 31 p. (People library) IdU **4411**

Hicks, Arthur C., see no. 9403.

Hicks, Granville, 1901-
John Reed; the making of a revolutionary, by Granville Hicks, with the assistance of John Stuart. New York, Macmillan Co., 1936. viii, 445 p. front. (port.) Portland biographee. Many **4412**

One of us; the story of John Reed in lithographs by Lynd Ward, narrative by Granville Hicks. [New York] Equinox Cooperative Press [1935] [64] p. illus., plates. MtU OrP **4413**

Hicks, J. P., see no. 8138.

Hicks, John Donald, 1890-
The constitution [!] of the northwest states. Lincoln, Neb. [Univ. of Neb., 1923] 162 p. (Univ. studies, v. 23, no. 1, 2, Jan.-Apr., 1923).
MtBozC Or OrU WaU **4414**

Hicks, Urban East, 1828-
Yakima and Clickitat Indian wars, 1855 and 1856; personal recollections of Capt. U. E. Hicks. Portland, Or., Himes [n.d.] 20 p. IdU OrHi OrP **4415**

Hidden, Maria L. T.
Oregon pioneers, illus. by Colista Murray Dowling. Portland, Or., Chapman [c1910] 10 p. illus. Many **4416**

Higday, Hamilton.
Port of Port Townsend and Jefferson County, Washington. Port Townsend, Wash. [1926?] 35 p. illus.
WaPS WaT **4417**

State insurance and first aid; an address before the twenty-fifth annual convention of the Washington State Bar Association, Seattle, August 7, 8, 1913. Olympia, Wash., Wash. Standard [1913?] [15] p.
Or WaU **4418**

Higgins, Beth Bell.
Memory pictures of Puget Sound region. New York, Dodge Pub. Co. [c1900] 53 p.
Wa WaPS WaS WaT WaU **4419**

Higgins, David Williams, 1834-
The mystic spring, and other tales of western life. Toronto, Briggs, 1904. 407 p. front., plates. Many **4420**

Same. New & rev. ed. New York, Broadway Pub. Co. [c1908] 312 p. front. (port.) 6 plates. CV CVicAr CVU WaU **4421**

The passing of a race and more tales of western life. Toronto, Briggs, 1905. 304 p. front., 6 plates. Many **4422**

Higgins, Mrs. Mary A.
A few of the wild flowers of British Columbia. [n.p., n.d.] 8 p. illus., plates.
CVicAr **4423**

Higgins, Ruth, see no. 4684.

Higginson, Mrs. Ella (Rhoads) 1862-1940.
Alaska, the great country. New York, Macmillan, 1908. x, 537 p. front. (port.) plates, double map. Bellingham, Wash. author and poet. Many **4424**

Same. 1909 [c1908] CVicAr CVU Wa **4425**

Same. 1910. WaS WaU **4426**

Same. 1912. OrP Wa WaU **4427**

Same. New ed., with new matter. 1917. xii, 583 p.
MtU OrCS Wa WaA WaPS WaS **4428**

Same. 1919, c1917. OrP **4429**

Same. 1923. CVicAr WaU **4430**

A bunch of western clover. New Whatcom, Wash., Edson & Irish, 1894. [26] p. Poems. Or WaS **4431**

Ella Higginson. a tribute, ed. by the Washington State Federation of Women's Clubs. [Bellingham, Wash., Union Printing Co., 1941] 88 p. illus., port.
Wa WaU **4432**

The flower that grew in the sand, and other stories. Seattle, Calvert Co., 1896. 256 p. plates.
OrU Wa WaPS WaS WaU **4433**

A forest orchid, and other stories. New York, Macmillan, 1927. 242 p.
Or OrHi WaPS WaU **4434**

Same. 1902.
OrHi OrU Wa WaS WaU WaWW **4435**

Four-leaf clover. Whatcom, Wash., Edson & Irish, 1901. 27 p. Wa **4436**

From the land of the snow-pearls; tales from Puget Sound. New York, Macmillan, 1897. 268 p. Many **4437**

Same. 1902. Many **4438**

Mariella; of out-west. New York, Macmillan, 1902. viii, 435 p. Many **4439**

Same. Tacoma, P. K. Pirret & Co., 1924. OrHi Wa WaU **4440**

The snow pearls, a poem, illus. by Maud Miner Biglow. [Seattle] Lowman & Hanford, 1897. 10 p. illus., 4 plates. WaS WaU **4441**

The vanishing race and other poems. Bellingham, Wash., C. M. Sherman, 1911. 28 p. Or OrU Wa WaS WaSp WaU **4442**

The voice of April-land and other poems. New York, Macmillan, 1903. x, 121 p. Many **4443**

When the birds go north again. New York, Macmillan, c1898. xii, 175 p. Or WaPS WaS **4444**

Same. 1902. OrCS OrP OrU Wa WaT WaU **4445**

Same. 1907. Wa WaSp WaWW **4446**

Same. 1911, c1898. WaT **4447**

Same. 1912. WaU **4448**

High handed proceedings on Vancouver's Island; or, How settlers were evicted in 1895. [n.p., n.d.] 40, vi p. CV CVicAr **4449**

The highlands. [Seattle, Lowman & Hanford, 1925?] 41 p. plates, ports. WaU **4450**

Hilborn, Burton E., see no. 4694.

Hildebrand, August.
A primer of Pacific Northwest history, up-to-date. 3d ed. [n.p., 1926?] [3] p. Or OrP OrU WaU **4451**

The promised land; and Indian story, as narrated by A. B. Wattson. [n.p., n.d.] [8] p. Or OrP WaPS WaU **4452**

Roll call, sixty-seven years after; or The American Civil War, 1861-1865, in retrospect. [Astoria, Or., 1928] 20 p. illus., ports. Or WaU **4453**

A trip to Nea-Kah-Nie, the treasure mountain. [Astoria, Or.? 1926?] [8] p. illus., port. Or OrP WaPS WaU **4454**

Hilger, David, 1858-1937.
An open letter to the Tax Reform Committee of the State Association of County Officials, by David Hilger, William Lindsay, Charles R. Leonard. [Helena, Mont., 1920] 20 p. MtU **4455**

Hill, Alexander Staveley, 1825-1905.
From home to home; autumn wanderings in the Northwest in the years 1881, 1882, 1883, 1884, illus. from sketches by Mrs. Staveley Hill and photographs by A. S. Hill. New York, O. Judd Co., 1885. vii, 432 p. front., illus., plates, 2 fold. maps. Many **4456**

Same. 2d ed. London, Low, 1885. MtHi WaS WaU **4457**

Hill, C. L., see no. 8972.

Hill, Edgar Preston, 1861-1938.
Desdemona sands. Portland, Or. [Irwin-Hodson Co.] 1906. 118 p. front. (port.) Many **4458**

[**Hill, Mrs. Edith Marian** (Knight)]
Happy endings, by Marian Miller [pseud.] Portland, Or. [Metropolitan, 1934] 80 p. front. (port.) illus. Or OrP **4459**

Hill, Frank Ernest, 1888-
The westward star. New York, John Day Co. [c1934] 275 p. Novel in verse. WaU **4460**

Hill, George W.
Vocabulary of the Shoshone language. Salt Lake City, Desert News, 1877. 36 p. CVicAr WaU WaWW **4461**

Hill, Mrs. Grace (Livingston) 1865-1947.
Miranda. [New York] Grosset, c1915. 344 p. "Early occupation of Oregon when threatened by English rule." WaE WaT **4462**

[**Hill, Howard**]
Facts and fancies of 363rd Field Hospital Company, 316th Sanitary Train, 91st Division, U. S. A., 1917-1919. [Portland, Or., Kleist, 1919] 60 p. illus., ports. Or OrP **4463**

Hill, J. L.
Passing of the Indian and buffalo. Long Beach, Calif., G. W. Moyle Pub. Co. [n.d.] 47 p. illus., plate. OrU WaSp **4464**

Hill, James Jerome, 1838-1916.
Address at the opening of the Alaska-Yukon-Pacific exposition, Seattle, Wash., June 1, 1909. [n.p., 1909] 26 p. OrU WaU **4465**

Great Northern and the Northwest; James J. Hill's letter to the stockholders on retiring from the chairmanship of the Board of Directors, July 1, 1912. [n.p., n.d.] 23 p. WaSp **4466**

What is the Northwest Development League? St. Paul [n.d.] 15 p. OrP **4467**

Hill, John A., see no. 4805.

Hill, Samuel, see no. 10760.

Hill Military Academy, Portland, Or.
Honoring General U. S. Grant, stationed at Columbia Barracks, Vancouver, Washington, 1853. Portland, Or. [1927] [12] p. illus. Or OrU WaU **4468**

Hill-Tout, Charles, 1858-1944.
British North America: I. The far West, the home of the Salish and Dene. London, Constable, 1907. xiv, 263 p. front., 32 plates, fold. map. (The native races of the British Empire) Many **4469**

The great Fraser midden. [Vancouver, B. C.] Art, Historical & Scientific Assn. [1938] [16] p. illus. CVicAr CVU OrU **4470**

Same. 1948. 29 p. CVicAr **4471**

Monuments of the past in British Columbia; Vancouver city museum; to commemorate the meeting of the Fifth Pacific Science Congress at Vancouver, B. C., June 1933. [Vancouver, B. C., 1933] [4] p. illus. CVicAr WaU **4472**

See also nos. 1107, 4161.

Hills, Agnes Conner.
Pioneer trails and romances of Oregon. New York, Henry Harrison [1948]. 64 p.
OrHi   **4472A**

Hills, George, 1816-1895.
The "Occasional paper"; two letters from the Bishop of Columbia to the Rev. E. Cridge and Bishop Demers. Victoria, B. C., British Colonist, 1860. 8 p.
CVicAr   **4473**

Pastoral address to the clergy and laity of the diocese of Columbia, Mar. 26, 1863. Victoria, B. C., British Colonist, 1863. 10 p.
CVicAr   **4474**

A sermon preached at the farewell service celebrated in St. James Church the day previous to his departure or his diocese, with an account of the meeting in aid of the Columbia Mission. London, Rivingtons, 1859. 55 p.   CVicAr   **4475**

A tour in British Columbia, etc, by the Right Rev. the Lord Bishop of Columbia. London [Clay, Printers] 1861. 74 p.
CVicAr   **4476**

Hills, W. James, comp.
Klondike; mining laws, rules and regulations of the United States and Canada applicable to Alaska and Northwest Territory, comp. by W. J. Hills and B. M. Ausherman. [Seattle, Lowman & Hanford] c1897. 143 p.   CV   **4477**

Hilscher, Herbert H.
Alaska now. Boston, Little, [c1948] x, 299 p. illus.
IdB OrCS OrP WaS WaT WaU   **4478**

Himes, George Henry, 1844-1940.
Holcombs; some account of their origin, settlement, and scatterment, as elicited at their 1st and 2d family reunions held at LeRoy, Pa. Oct. 1879 and Mount Airy, N. J. Aug 1886. Portland, Or., 1887. 33 p.
OrHi   **4479**

Souvenir of the second annual reunion of the Ruddell-Himes families, pioneers of Oregon, 1850-1853, and Thurston County, Washington, 1852-1853, held July 18, 1926. [n.p., n.d.] [4] p. illus.
Or WaSp   **4480**

Souvenir of the 72d anniversary of the organization of the first American government west of the Rocky Mountains and the fifteenth celebration of the same, at old Champoeg, thirty-three miles south of Portland on the east bank of the Willamette River, Saturday, May 1, 1915. Portland, Or. Historical Society, 1915. [8] p. port.   IdIf   **4481**

Same. 75th anniversary; 17th celebration; 1918.   IdIf   **4482**

Wallamet or Willamette. [Portland, Or., 1875] 66 p. Anon.   Many   **4483**

[Himmelwright, Abraham Lincoln Artman] 1865-
In the heart of the Bitter-Root Mountains; the story of "the Carlin hunting party", September-December, 1893, by Heclawa [pseud.] New York, Putnam, 1895. xx, 259 p. front., illus., 12 plates, fold. map.
Many   **4484**

Hind, Henry Youle, 1823-1908.
A sketch of an overland route to British Columbia. Toronto, W. C. Chewett & Co., 1862. 129 p. front. (fold. map). CVU   **4485**

Hines, Edward, Lumber Co.
50 years, Edward Hines Lumber Co.; commemorating a pioneer in the nation's oldest industry, the company which bears his name and their first-half-century of accomplishment. Chicago, c1942. 47 p. illus. (part. col.) ports., fold. map.
Or OrU   **4486**

Hines, Gustavus, 1809-1873.
Life on the plains of the Pacific: Oregon; its history, condition and prospects; containing a description of the geography, climate and productions, with personal adventures among the Indians during a residence of the author on the plains bordering the Pacific while connected with the Oregon Mission; embracing extended notes of a voyage around the world. Buffalo, N. Y., Derby & Co., 1850. 437 p. front. (port.)   Or   **4487**

Same. Auburn, N. Y., Derby & Miller, 1851.
Many   **4488**

Same. Buffalo, N. Y., Derby & Co., 1851.
Many   **4489**

Same. 1852.
CVicAr OrHi OrP WaSp WaT   **4490**

Same. New York, Miller, 1857.
CVicAr OrHi OrSa WaWW   **4491**

Same. New York, Saxton, 1859.
CVicAr IdU OrHi WaSp WaW   **4492**

Same. New York, Hurst [c1881]
CVicAr OrP OrSaW WaU WaWW   **4493**

Oregon and its institutions; comprising a full history of the Willamette University, the first established on the Pacific Coast. New York, Carlton & Porter [c1868] 326 p. front. (port.) plates.   Many   **4494**

A voyage round the world; with a history of the Oregon Mission, to which is appended a full description of Oregon Territory, its geography, history and religion; designed for the benefit of emigrants to that rising country. Buffalo, N. Y., Derby, 1850. 437 p.   Many   **4495**

Wild life in Oregon; being a stirring recital of actual scenes of daring and peril among the gigantic and terrific rapids of the Columbia River (the Mississippi of the Pacific slope). New York, Hurst [18—] 437 p. front. (Arlington ed.)
Or OrSaW   **4496**

Same. New York, Butler [n.d.]
CVicAr   **4497**

Same. New York, Hurst [c1881] Many **4498**

Same. New York, Worthington [c1881]
IdU MtU OrHi OrP   **4499**

Same. 1889.   OrSaW WaU   **4500**

Hines, Harvey Kimball, 1828-1902, comp.
At sea and in port; or, Life and experience of William S. Fletcher, for thirty years seaman's missionary in Portland, Or., comp. from his journal and other authentic sources, with an introd. by

Bishop Earl Cranston. Portland, Or., J. K. Gill Co., 1898. 251 p. front. (port.)
Many **4501**

An illustrated history of the state of Oregon from the earliest period of its discovery to the present time, together with glimpses of its auspicious future; illus. and full-page portraits of some of its eminent men and biographical mention of many of its pioneers and prominent citizens of to-day. Chicago, Lewis, 1893. 1300 p. front. (port.) 8 plates, 20 ports.
Many **4502**

An illustrated history of the state of Washington, containing biographical mention of its pioneers and prominent citizens. Chicago, Lewis, 1893. 933 p. illus., plates, ports.
Many **4503**

Same. 1894. 771 p. OrHi WaPS **4504**

Jason Lee the pioneer of Methodism and civilization on the Pacific Coast. San Francisco, Hammond, 1896. 43 p.
Or OrU WaTC WaWW **4505**

Missionary history of the Pacific Northwest, containing the wonderful story of Jason Lee, with sketches of many of his co-laborers, all illustrating life on the plains and in the mountains in pioneer days. Portland, Or. [c1899] 510 p. front. (port.) 2 plates, 16 ports. Many **4506**

Hines, John Chesterfield, 1877-
Minstrel of the Yukon, an Alaskan adventure, with a foreword by Lucius Beebe. New York, Greenberg [1948] v, 231 p.
Many **4507**

[Hines, Joseph Wilkinson].
Touching incidents in the life and labors of a pioneer on the Pacific Coast since 1853. San Jose, Calif., Eaton & Co., Printers, 1911. 198 p. front. (port.) Many **4508**

Hinz, John.
Grammar and vocabulary of the Eskimo language, as spoken by the Kuskokwim and southwest coast Eskimos of Alaska. Bethlehem, Pa., Society for Propagating the Gospel, Moravian Church [1944] xiii, 194 p. CV CVU WaS WaU **4509**

Hipkoe, George.
Koma Kulshan s-whee-ame (Lummi Indian for Mount Baker stories) Kulshan; his wives and his children; two versions of the one legend of Mount Baker. Bellingham, Wash., 1934. 4 p. WaU **4510**

Hippard, George Rollin.
A philosophical aspect of masonry. Seattle, Committee on Masonic Research and Education, 1925. 25 p. WaU **4511**

His next best friends, see no. 5818.

Historical and descriptive review of the industries of Walla Walla, 1891; commerce, trade and manufactures, with pen sketches of the principal business houses and manufacturing advantages. [Walla Walla, Wash.?] Trade and Commerce Pub. Co., 1891. 111 p. WaWW **4512**

Historical review of the Tacoma guardsmen. Tacoma, Bell Press [1909?] 1 v. illus.
WaS **4513**

Historical sketch and essay on the resources of Montana; including a business directory of the metropolis. Helena, Mont., Herald Book and Job Printing Office, 1868. 168 p. CVicAr MtHi **4514**

An historical sketch of Richmond Presbyterian Church in Marpole, B. C., 1861-1925. [Vancouver, B. C., Ward] 1925. 37 p. front., illus., ports. CVicAr **4515**

History of activities of Seattle labor movement and conspiracy of employers to destroy it and attempted suppression of labor's daily newspaper, the Seattle Union Record. [Seattle, 1919] 69 p. WaU **4516**

History of Headquarters Company. 361st Infantry, 91st Division. [n.p., 19—] 77 p. front., facsim. Wash. state personnel trained at Camp Lewis. WaU **4517**

History of Idaho Territory, showing its resources and advantages; with illus. from original drawings. San Francisco, W. W. Elliott & Co., 1884. 304 p. front., illus., plates (part fold.) ports., maps.
IdB IdIf IdP IdU WaS WaU **4518**

History of the adventurous voyage and terrible shipwreck of the U. S. steamer "Jeannette" in the Polar Seas, together with a full and particular account of the death of Lt. DeLong and his brave shipmates in the Siberian deserts; and the rescue of Danenhower, Melville, and their heroic companions; carefully comp. from authentic records. New York, DeWitt, 1882. 95 p. illus. CVicAr **4519**

History of the Bench and Bar in Oregon. Portland, Or., Historical Pub. Co., 1910. 286 p. illus., ports. Many **4520**

A history of the 361st Ambulance Company, 316th Sanitary Train, 91 "Wild West Division" during its training at Camp Lewis, Washington, and its activities as part of the American Expeditionary Forces, by members of the organizations. [Tacoma? 1918?] 53 p. illus.
OrU WaU **4521**

History of the wrongs of Alaska; an appeal to the people and press of America printed by order of the Anti-Monopoly Association of the Pacific Coast, Feb. 1875. San Francisco, 1875. 43 p.
CVicAr WaSp **4522**

Hitchcock, Grace Willhoite.
Fathers' Day silver anniversary, 1935. Spokane, Lighthouse Pub. Co., 1935. [40] p. illus., ports. WaPS **4523**

Hitchcock, Mary E.
Two women in the Klondike; the story of a journey to the gold-fields of Alaska, with 105 illus. and map. New York, Putnam, 1899. xiv, 495 p. front., illus., fold. map. Many **4524**

Hitchcock, Ripley, 1857-1918.
The Lewis and Clark expedition. Boston, Ginn & Co., 1905. viii, 117 p. front., illus., plates, ports., maps. Many **4525**

See also no. 4669.

Hitchler, Theresa, see no. 2251.

Hittell, John Shertzer, 1825-1901.
Bancroft's Pacific Coast guide book. San Francisco, A. L. Bancroft & Co., 1882. 270 p. illus., fold. maps.　　WaU **4526**

Mining in the Pacific states of North America. San Francisco, H. H. Bancroft & Co., 1861. 224 p.
CVicAr OrCS OrHi OrU Wa WaU **4527**

Same. New York, Wiley, 1862. CVicAr **4528**

Hixon, Arthur T., 1916-
Canol. Philadelphia, Dorrance & Co. [1946] 284 p.　　WaSp WaU **4529**

Hoad, Louise (Green) 1872-
Kickapoo Indian Trails. Caldwell, Idaho, Caxton, 1944. 129 p. col. front., plates.
Or Wa WaU **4530**

[Hobbs, James] b. 1819.
Wild life in the far West; personal adventures of a border mountain man; comprising hunting and trapping adventure; captivity and life among the Comanches; services under Doniphan in the war with Mexico; desperate combats with Apaches, grizzly bears, etc. Hartford, 1873. 483 p. illus., plates.　WaU **4531**

Hobson, Dorothy Anne, 1928-
The Valsetz Star; issues of the community newspaper of the same name, arranged comp. and annotated by Sammy Sampson; with a preface by Marshall Dana and an introd. by Herbert A. Templeton. Portland, Or., Creation House [1942] a-k, 165 p. front. (mounted port.) 1 illus.
Or OrP OrU **4532**

Hobson, George C., ed.
Gems of thought and history of Shoshone County, sponsored by the Allied Fraternities Council, Shoshone County. [Kellogg, Idaho] Kellogg Evening News, 1940, 84 p. 2 illus., 4 ports.
IdB WaU **4533**

Hodge, Edwin Thomas, 1887-
Geology of north central Oregon. Corvallis, Or., Or. State College [1942] 76 p. illus., diagrs., tables. (Monographs, Studies in geology, no. 3).
OrHi OrP WaS WaSp WaT WaTC **4534**

Mount Multnomah, ancient ancestor of the Three Sisters. Eugene, Or., Univ. of Or., 1925. v, 158 p. illus., fold. map. (Publication, v. 3, no. 2 (i. e. v. 2, no. 10) Apr. 1926).　　Many **4535**

Hodge, Frederick Webb, see nos. 2168, 2596, 6107.

Hodges, A. C.
Memorial sketches of Rev. Asa B. Smith, Sarah G. Smith and Harriett E. Smith. Boston, Beacon Press, 1889. 27 p. The Smiths came West in same party with Marcus Whitman.　　WaWW **4536**

Hodges, Lawrence Kaye, 1857-1938, ed.
Mining in the Pacific Northwest; a complete review of the mining resources of Washington and British Columbia. Seattle, Post-Intelligencer, 1897. 192 p. front., illus., 28 maps (part fold.)
Many **4537**

Twenty eventful years, introd. by Paul

Kelty. New York, Wilson-Erickson, 1937. xiv, 523 p. front. (port.)　　Many **4538**

Hodgins, Thomas, 1828-1910.
The Alaska boundary tribunal and international law; a review of the decisions. Toronto, Carswell, 1904. 24 p. 2 maps.
CV CVicAr CVU WaS **4539**

Hodgkin, Frank E.
Pen pictures of representative men of Oregon, by Frank E. Hodgkin and J. J. Galvin. Portland, Or., Farmer and Dairyman Pub. House, 1882. xxv, 199 p. 2 photos.　　Many **4540**

Hodgson, Allen H.
Logging waste in the Douglas fir region, with a supplementary article, Unutilized trees left after logging in the Douglas fir region. [Portland, Or., 1930] xl p. illus., tables.　　Many **4541**

See also no. 9374.

Hodson, John Milton, 1839-1910.
Address of J. M. Hodson, Grand Master of the M. W. Grand Lodge of Masons of Oregon. [n.p.] 1900. 20 p.　WaPS **4542**

Masonic history of the Northwest [with] brief biographies of many of the founders and builders of Masonry in the Northwest. San Francisco, History Pub. Co. [1902] 574, 51 p. illus. plates, ports.
Many **4543**

Hofer, Ernest.
The strawberry industry on the northwest Pacific Coast. Salem, Or., Hofer Bros., 1902. 44 p. illus., port.　Or OrCS **4544**

Hofer, Ernst, 1855-1934.
Circuit rider, by E. Hofer, Winifred Watson, and Carolyn Davies. Salem, Or., Lariat Press [1927] [8] p.　　OrHi **4545**

Jack Norton. Boston, R. G. Badger [c1912] 292 p.　　Or OrP WaU **4546**

Hoffine, Lyla.
White buffalo; a story of the Northwest fur trade, illus. by E. A. Furman. New York, Longmans, c1939. 284 p. illus.
MtHi Or OrP WaS WaSp WaT **4547**

Hoffland, Laura Hildreth, see no. 9051.

Hoffman, Al, composer.
It's a hundred to one you're from Washington. [n.p.] 1938. 5 p. music.
WaE WaT **4548**

Hoffman, Arthur Sullivant, see no. 3480.

Hoffman, Bruce E.
Management possibilities in Douglas fir forests. Washington, D. C., Charles Lathrop Pack Forestry Foundation, 1941. 45 p. col. plates, diagrs. (1 fold.) forms, tables. Or OrCS WaT WaTC WaU **4549**

Hoffman, J. Wesley, see nos. 8608, 8609.

Hoffman, Ralph, 1870-
Birds of the Pacific states, containing brief biographies and descriptions of about four hundred species, with especial reference to their appearance in the field, with ten plates in color and over two hundred illus. in black and white by Major Allan Brooks. Boston, Houghton, 1927. xix, 353 p. col. front., illus., col. plates.　　Many **4550**

Hogeboom, Amy, 1891-　comp.
The boys' book of the West, illus. by Richard Bennett. New York, Lothrop,

Lee and Shepard Co. [1946] vii, 419 p. illus. CV Or WaSp WaU **4551**

Holbrook, Henry.
British Columbia gold mines. Liverpool, Haram [1884] 24 p. CVicAr **4552**

Holbrook, Mary H.
Souvenir commemorating the exodus of the Couch and Holbrook pilgrims from Boston to Portland, Oregon in 1852. Portland, Or., Baltes, 1899. 27 p. OrHi **4553**

Holbrook, Stewart Hall, 1893-
Burning an empire, the story of American forest fires, with a foreword by Colonel William B. Greeley. New York, Macmillan, 1943. xiv, 229 p. front., illus., plates, maps. Portland author. Many **4554**
Same. Armed services ed. 317 p. WaS **4555**
Same. 1944 [c1943] xiv, 229 p. IdU IdUSB MtHi MtU OrHi **4556**

Ethan Allen. New York, Macmillan, 1940. 283 p. illus., map. Many **4557**

Green commonwealth; a narrative of the past and a look at the future of one forest products community, pub. for their friends by Simpson Lumber Company, Shelton, Washington 1895-1945; illus. by Phyllis Heady. Seattle, F. McCaffrey [1945] 163 p. col. front., col. illus., plates, ports. Many **4558**

Holy old mackinaw; a natural history of the American lumberjack. New York, Macmillan, 1938. viii, 278 p. Many **4559**

Iron brew; a century of American ore and steel. New York, Macmillan, 1939. 352 p. Many **4560**

Let them live. New York, Macmillan, 1938. 178 p. Many **4561**
Same. 1939. OrU **4562**

Little Annie Oakley & other rugged people. New York, Macmillan, 1948. x, 238 p. OrHi WaU **4563**

Lost men of American history. New York, Macmillan, 1946. xiv, 370 p. plates., ports., facsims. Many **4564**

Murder out yonder; an informal study of certain classic crimes in back-country America. New York, Macmillan, 1941. 255 p. Many **4565**

A narrative of Schafer Bros. Logging Co.'s half century in the timber, illus. by Phyllis Heady. Seattle, F. McCaffrey, 1945. 110 p. illus. (part col.) ports., maps. Many **4566**

None more courageous; American war heroes of today. New York, Macmillan, 1942. 245 p. plates, ports. Many **4567**

Promised land; a collection of Northwest writing. New York, Whittlesey House [1945] xviii, 408 p. Many **4568**

The story of American railroads. New York, Crown [1947] 468 p. illus., ports., maps. Many **4569**

Tall timber, with illus. by Armstrong Sperry. New York, Macmillan, 1941. ix, 179 p. front., illus. Many **4570**
See also no. 9400.

Holden, Edward Singleton, 1846-1914.
List of recorded earthquakes in California, Lower California, Oregon, and Washington Territory, comp. from published works and from private information, printed by direction of the regents of the University of California. Sacramento, Calif., State Printing Office, 1887. 78 p. CVU MtHi Or WaPS WaSp WaU **4571**

Holden, Horace, b. 1810.
A narrative of the shipwreck, captivity, and sufferings of Horace Holden and Benj. H. Nute, who were cast away in the American ship Mentor on the Pelew Islands in the year 1832, and for two years afterwards were subjected to unheard of sufferings among the barbarous inhabitants of Lord North's Island. Boston, Russell, Shattuck and Co., 1835. 133 p. front., plates. Oregon author, immigrant of 1844. Or OrHi WaS WaSp WaU **4572**

Holden, Charles Frederick, 1851-1915.
The fishes of the Pacific Coast; a handbook for sportsmen and tourists. New York, Dodge Pub. Co. [c1912] 122 p. front., plates. Many **4573**
Recreations of a sportsman on the Pacific Coast. New York, Putnam, 1910. ix, 399 p. front., 55 plates, ports. Many **4574**

Holiday.
State of Washington. Sept. 1947. [Philadelphia, Curtis Pub. Co.] 1947. 138 p. illus. (part col.) (v. 2, no. 9) WaS WaSp WaU **4575**

Holland, Edward.
To the Yukon and the Klondike gold fields. San Francisco, 1897. 56 p. illus., fold. map, facsims. CVicAr **4576**

Holland, Ernest Otto, 1874-
Memorial to Adam Duncan Dunn, delivered by President E. O. Holland at the dedication of the tablet at Pacific International Livestock Exposition, Portland, Oregon, November 4, 1928. [Pullman, Wash.] 1928. 11 p. front. (port.) WaPS **4577**

Holland, Melvin Ned, 1898-
The haunted island. Philadelphia, Dorrance [1947] 218 p. front., plates. San Juan Islands story. WaU **4578**

[Holland, Richard Rowe] 1891-
· 150th anniversary of arrival of Captain George Vancouver, R. N., at Burrard Inlet, 1792 [n.p., 1942] [8] p. map. CVicAr **4579**

Holland, Charles William, 1870-
The valley of youth. Caldwell, Idaho, Caxton [c1948] 357 p. col. front., plates, ports., map. Autobiographical account of pioneer life in the Okanagan Valley of B. C. CVU WaU **4580**

Hollingsworth, Charles Mahlon, 1848-
The "Oregon plan"; is it a political panacea? Washington, D. C., 1911. 21 p. Or WaU **4581**

Holman, Albert M.
Pioneering in the Northwest: Niobrara-Virginia City Wagon Road; Pioneers, short sketches of Charles Floyd, War Eagle, Theophile Bruguier, and others, by Constant R. Marks. Sioux City, Iowa, Deitch & Lamar Co., 1924. 150 p. ports. IdIf IdU MtU OrHi WaSp **4582**

Holman, Frederick Van Voorhies, 1852-1927.
Dr. John McLoughlin, the father of Oregon. Cleveland, A. H. Clark Co., 1907. 301 p. front. (port.) port.   Many **4583**

Roses at Portland, Oregon and how to grow them; papers and an address, by F. V. Holman and W. S. Sibson. Portland, Or., Portland Rose Society, 1902. 90 p.   OrHi OrP WaS **4584**

Some instances of unsatisfactory results under initiative amendments of the Oregon Constitution. Portland, Or., Bar Assn., 1910. 46 p.
OrCS OrHi OrP OrU WaU **4585**

Holman, Glen O.
Uncle Sam's own story; Colum and me. Portland, Or., c1898. 21 p. illus. OrHi **4586**
Same. 4th ed. 27 p.   Or **4586A**

Holman, John Paulison, 1881-
Sheep and bear trails; a hunter's wanderings in Alaska and British Columbia, introd. by Robert A. Bartlett. New York, Walters, 1933. xvi, 211 p. front., 23 plates, ports.
CV CVic IdB OrSa WaS **4587**

Holman, Woodford C.
Twenty-four years' residence in California and Oregon. St. Louis. Mo., 1870. 25 p.
OrP **4588**

Holmes, Elizabeth Nowland, see no. 7973.

Holmes, Ernest E.
The geography of Idaho. [New York] Macmillan [c1925] 34 p. illus., maps (1 col.)
IdUSB **4589**

Holmes, Harry L., see no. 2446.

Holmes, Henry Elliott, 1849-
Pioneer links; a narrative of the establishment of the Independent Order of Odd Fellows on the Pacific Coast and a history of Odd Fellowship in Washington to 1880; souvenir of thirty-two years in the Grand Lodge of Washington, I. O. O. F. Seattle, Wash. Odd Fellow [c1913] 232 p. front., illus., plates, ports.
CVicAr Wa WaTC WaU **4590**
See also no. 7525.

Holmes, J. J.
Silent songs of the North. Eureka, Mont., 1926. 52 p. front. (port.)   WaTC **4591**

Holmes, Mabel Dodge, see nos. 7942, 7944.

Holmes, Maurice.
An introduction to the bibliography of Captain James Cook, R. N. London, F. Edwards, 1936. 59 p.
CV CVU WaS WaU **4592**

Holmstrom, Frances.
Western windows. Portland, Or., Metropolitan [c1937] 92 p. Poems.
IdIf MtU Or OrP OrU WaU **4593**

Holtz, Mathilde Edith.
Glacier National Park; its trails and treasures, by Mathilde Edith Holtz and Katharine Isabel Bemis, illus. from photographs. New York, Doran [c1917] 263 p. front., plates.   Many **4594**

Holzworth, John Michael, 1888-
The twin grizzlies of Admiralty Island.

Philadelphia, Lippincott [c1932] 250 p. front., illus.
Or OrLgE OrP WaS WaT **4595**

The wild grizzlies of Alaska; a story of the grizzly and big brown bears of Alaska, their habits, manners and characteristics, together with notes on mountain sheep and caribou, collected by the author for the United States Biological Survey, with 84 illus. from photographs and a map. New York, Putnam, 1930. xxi, 417 p. col. front., plates, ports.
Many **4596**

[Home Book Publishers, San Francisco, Calif.]
Pacific Northwest book of homes, over 100 pictures and 65 plans; new ideas by famous architects, outdoor living kitchens, interiors, prize winning homes. [San Francisco, 1947] 82 p. illus., plans.
OrP **4597**

Home Building Plan Service, Portland, Or.
Home building plan service. [Portland, Or., 1947] [18] p. illus.   OrP **4598**

Homes. Portland, Or. [c1948] 1 v. illus., plans.   OrP **4599**

The home decorator. [Spokane, John W. Graham & Co., n.d.] 34 p. col. illus.
WaPS **4600**

Home Missions Council.
Oriental mission work on the Pacific Coast of the United States of America; addresses and findings of conferences of Home Missions Council and Council of Women for Home Missions in Los Angeles and San Francisco, Calif., Oct. 13, 14, 15, 1920. New York, 1920. 48 p.
OrP **4601**

Homes, Henry Augustus, 1812-1887.
Our knowledge of California and the Northwest Coast one hundred years since, read before the Albany Institute, February 15, 1870. Albany, N. Y., Munsell, 1870. 20 p.   OrP **4602**

Homes and gardens of the Pacific Coast: Beaux Arts Village, Lake Washington. [Seattle] Beaux Arts Society, c1913. [153] p. illus. Frank Calvert, ed.
Wa WaU **4603**

Hood, Margaret Graham.
Tales of discovery on the Pacific slope. San Francisco, Whitaker & Ray, 1900 [c1898] 172 p. col. front., illus., plates. (Western series of readers, ed. by H. Wagner, v. 4)
Wa WaPS WaS WaU **4604**

Hood, Robert Allison.
Ballads of the Pacific Northwest, its discovery and settlement. Toronto, Ryerson [c1946] xii, 170 p. col. front., plates. Poems.   Many **4605**

By shore and trail in Stanley Park; legends and reminiscences of Vancouver's beauty-spot and region of romance with historical and natural history details. Toronto, McClelland, c1929. 156 p. front., illus., 31 plates.
CV CVicAr CVU WaS WaU **4606**

The chivalry of Keith Leicester; a romance of British Columbia. Toronto,

McClelland, Goodchild & Stewart [c1918]
339 p.   CVU Or WaU 4607

Hood's Canal Land and Improvement Co.
Union City, its resources and prospects.
Port Townsend, Wash., Morning Leader
Printing House, 1890. 19 p. WaWW 4608

Hook, Harry H.
Spokane Falls illustrated the metropolis
of eastern Washington; a history of the
early settlement and the Spokane Falls
of to-day, by H. H. Hook and F. J. Mc-
Guire. Minneapolis, F. L. Thresher, 1889.
59 p. illus., maps.   WaPS WaSp 4609

Hooker, William Francis, 1856-1938.
The bullwhacker; adventures of a frontier
freighter, ed. by Howard R. Driggs, illus.
with drawings by Herman Palmer and
with photographs. Yonkers-on-Hudson,
N. Y., World Book Co., 1924. 167 p. front.,
illus., ports. (Pioneer life series)
                          Or WaS 4610
The prairie schooner. Chicago, Saul Bros.,
1918. 156 p. col. front., illus., plates.
                          Many 4611
See also no. 1206.

Hooker, Sir William Jackson, 1785-1865.
The botany of Captain Beechey's voyage;
comprising an account of the plants col-
lected by Messrs. Lay and Collie during
the voyage to the Pacific and Bering's
Strait, performed in His Majesty's ship
Blossom in the years 1825, 26, 27, and 28.
London, Bohn, 1841. 485 p. 99 plates.
                          CVicAr 4612

Flora Boreali-Americana; or, The botany
of the northern parts of British America; the plants collected by Dr. Richardson and Mr. Drummond on the late
northern expeditions to which are added
those of Mr. Douglas from North-west
America, and other naturalists. London,
Bohn, 1840. 2 v. 238 plates, fold. map.
Volume 1 text; v. 2 plates.
                          CVicAr Wa WaU 4613

[Hooker Electrochemical Co., Tacoma,
Wash.]
Elon Huntington Hooker. [n.p., 1938] 1 v.
front., illus., port.   WaT 4614

Hooper, C. E., see nos. 11179-11181.

Hooper, William Hulme, 1827-1854.
Ten months among the tents of the Tuski,
with incidents of an Arctic boat expedition in search of Sir John Franklin, as
far as the Mackenzie River and Cape
Bathurst. London, Murray, 1853. xv, 417
p. col. front., illus., plates (part col.)
fold. map.   CVicAr WaSp WaU 4615

Hoopes, Alban W.
Indian affairs and their administration,
with special reference to the far West,
1849-1860. Philadelphia, Univ. of Pa.
Press, 1932. ix, 264 p.   Many 4616

Same. (Thesis).   OrHi WaU 4617

Hopkins, Flora (Ball) see nos. 473-475.

Hopkins, Mrs. Sarah Winnemucca.
Life among the Piutes; their wrongs and
claims, ed. by Mrs. Horace Mann. Boston, Cupples, 1883. 268 p.   Many 4618

Hopson, William L.
Cowpoke justice. New York, Phoenix Press
[c1941] 254 p. Montana cowboy story.
                          WaSp WaU 4619

Hoquiam Sawyer, Hoquiam, Wash.
Hoquiam, Wash., Grays Harbor; gateway
to the world of commerce. Hoquiam,
Wash., 1910. [54] p. illus., ports. (Industrial ed.)   WaPS 4620

Hoquiam Washingtonian, Hoquiam, Wash.
New Year edition. Hoquiam, Wash., Dean
and Tilly, 1900. [20] p. illus., ports.
                          WaU 4621

Horan, Jack.
"Poems of the West", illus. by Leo Beau-
leaurie. Great Falls, Mont., Call Printing Co.[1929?] 53 p. front. (port.) illus.
                          MtHi 4622

Horetzky, Charles.
Canada on the Pacific; being an account
of a journey from Edmonton to the Pacific by the Peace River Valley; and of
a winter voyage along the western coast
of the Dominion; with remarks on the
physical features of the Pacific railway
route and notices of the Indian tribes of
British Columbia. Montreal, Dawson
Bros., 1874. x, 244 p. fold. plan, fold. map.
                          Many 4623

The North-west of Canada; being a brief
sketch of the north-western regions and
a treatise on the future resources of the
country. Ottawa, A. S. Woodburn, 1873.
30 p.   CVicAr 4624
Some startling facts relating to the Canadian Pacific Railway and the Northwest lands; also a brief discussion regarding the route, the western terminus
and the lands available for settlement.
Ottawa, Printed at the office of the
"Free Press", 1880. 76 p.
                          CV CVicAr WaU 4625

Horn, Paul Whitfield, 1870-
Report of supplementary survey of Portland Public Schools. [Portland, Or.] Jefferson High School Press, 1917. 64 p.
                      MtU OrCS OrP OrU 4626

Hornaday, William Temple, 1854-1937.
Camp-fires in the Canadian Rockies. Lon-
don, T. W. Laurie, 1906. 374 p. illus.
                      CVicAr CVU OrP 4627
Same. Illus. by John M. Phillips. New
York, Scribner, 1906. xvii, 353 p. front.,
illus., 53 plates, 2 maps.
                      CVU Or WaTC WaU 4628
Same. 1907.
            Wa WaS WaSp WaT WaTC WaU 4629
Same. 1909 [c1906]   Wa 4630
Same. 1912.   OrP WaPS 4631
Same. 1919 [c1906]   IdP 4632
Same. 1927.   WaT 4633
See also no. 6345.

Horner, John Baptiste, 1856-1933.
Days and deeds in the Oregon country;
ten-minute stories offered as side lights
on Pacific Northwest history. Portland,
Or., J. K. Gill, 1928. 201 p. illus., ports.
                          Many 4634
Same. Rev. illus. ed. 1929. 211 p. illus.,
ports., maps.   Many 4635

Life of Elias Ruark Horner, pioneer circuit rider in the Pacific Northwest, published by the family of the deceased for gratuitous distribution among friends and relatives. [n.p.] 1915. 11 p. ports. Anon.　　　　　　　　　　　　Or **4636**

Same. 19 p. illus., 4 plates (ports.)
　　　OrHi OrP OrU WaPS WaS **4637**

Oregon: her history, her great men, her literature. Corvallis, Or., Gazette-Times, c1919. 408 p. front. illus., ports. Many **4638**

Same. Portland, Or., J. K. Gill, 1919. "War ed."　　　　　　　　MtU OrSaW **4639**

Same. Rev. and enlarged ed. [c1921] 366 p.　　　　　　　　　　　　Many **4640**

Oregon history and early literature; a pictorial narrative of the Pacific Northwest. Rev. and enlarged ed. Portland, Or., J. K. Gill [c1931] 442 p. front., illus., maps (1 fold.)　　　　Many **4641**

Oregon literature. Corvallis, Or., 1899. 104 p. front., plates, ports.　　Many **4642**

Same. 2d ed. 1902. 253 p.　　Many **4643**

A short history of Oregon. Portland, Or., J. K. Gill [c1924] 201 p. front., illus.
　　　　　　　　　　　　　　Many **4644**

See also no. 6984.

[Horton, Edward W.]
1890-1940, Sharon United Church, golden jubilee anniversary, Sunday, February 25, 1940. Murrayville, B. C. [Langley Advance] 1940. 15 p. illus.　CVicAr **4645**

Horton, Mrs. Emily (McCowen) 1841-
My scrapbook. Seattle, 1927. 63 p. illus., ports.　　　　　　　　　　WaU **4646**

Hosford, Hester Eloise, 1892-
A warning to wives. Boston, Stratford Co., 1924. 461 p. front.　　WaU **4647**

Hosie, John, see no. 9381.

Hosmer, Hezekiah L.
Montana; an address before the Travellers Club, New York City, January 1866. New York, New York Printing Co., 1866. 23 p.　　　　　　　　MtHi MtU **4648**

Hosmer, James Kendall, see nos. 3464, 5887-5891, 8916, 8917.

Hosmer, John Allen, 1850-1907.
A trip to the states by the way of the Yellowstone and Missouri, with a table of distances. Virginia City, Mont. Ter., Beaver Head News Print, 1867. 82, 12 p.
　　　　　　　　　　　　　　MtU **4649**

A trip to the states in 1865, written and printed at Virginia City, Mont., in 1867, ed. by Edith M. Duncan. Missoula, Mont., Univ. of Mont. [1932] 27 p. (Historical reprints. Sources of Northwest history no. 17)　　　　　　　　　　Many **4650**

Hosmer, Paul.
Now we're loggin'. Portland, Or., Metropolitan, 1930. 210 p.　　Many **4651**

Hotchkiss, Clarence R., comp.
Third Infantry, Oregon National Guard. Portland, Or., 1914. 97 p. illus.
　　　　　　　　　　　Or OrP **4652**

Hotel Greeters of America.
Spokane greeters tourist guide to Spokane, northern Idaho, and Montana.

[Spokane, 1937?] 52 p. illus., maps (part fold.)　　　　　　　　　WaPS **4653**

Hotel Portland, Portland, Or.
Guide book; descriptive sketch of the Hotel Portland; also sketches of objects and places of interest, and condensed guide to all places in and around the city and vicinity. Portland, Or., Ellis & Sons, 1890. 96 p. illus., maps.
　　　　　　　OrP WaPS WaU **4654**

Hotson, John William, 1870-
Key to the rusts of the Pacific Northwest. Seattle, Univ. of Wash. Press, 1934. 193 p. illus. (Publications in biology, v. 3, Nov. 1934)　　　　Many **4655**

Hough, Emerson, 1857-1923.
The covered wagon. New York, Appleton, 1922. 378 p. front.　　Many **4656**

Same. New York, Grosset [c1922] 379 p. front., plates.　　　　　Many **4657**

54-40 or fight, with illus. by Arthur I. Keller. Indianapolis, Bobbs-Merrill, 1909. 402 p. front., plates.　　Many **4658**

Same. New York, Burt, c1909. 402 p. front.
　　　　　　　　　　　　　　Many **4659**

Same. New York, Grosset, 1909.
　　　　　　　　　　IdB WaT **4660**

The frontier omnibus, containing three complete novels: The way to the West, The story of the outlaw, The way of a man. New York, Grosset [1936] [1199], p.
　　　　　　　WaS WaU **4661**

The magnificent adventure; this being the story of the world's greatest exploration, and the romance of a very gallant gentleman; a novel, illus. by Arthur I. Keller. New York, Appleton, 1916. 355 p. front., 3 plates.　　　Many **4662**

Same. New York, Grosset [c1916] OrU **4663**

Same. New York, Appleton, 1923 [c1916]
　　　　　　　　　　　　　IdU **4664**

Same. 1931, c1916.　　　WaT **4665**

The passing of the frontier; a chronicle of the old West. New Haven, Yale Univ. Press, 1918. x, 181 p. front., 9 plates, ports., fold. map. (Chronicles of America series, Allen Johnson, ed. v. 26)
　　　　　　　　　　　　　　Many **4666**

Same. 1921. "Textbook ed."　IdUSB
MtBozC OrSaW WaS WaTC WaW **4667**

Same. Roosevelt ed.　OrHi WaSp **4668**

The story of the cowboy, illus. by William L. Wells and C. M. Russell. New York, Appleton, 1897. xii, 349 p. front., 9 plates. (Story of the West series, ed. by R. Hitchcock).
IdU MtHi Or OrLgE WaE WaTC **4669**

Same. 1902.　　　　　MtU OrP **4670**

The story of the outlaw; a study of the western desperado, with historical narratives of famous outlaws; the stories of noted border wars; vigilante movements and armed conflicts on the border. New York, Grosset, c1905. xii, 401 p. front., 16 plates, ports.　WaSp **4671**

Same. New York, Outing Pub. Co., 1907.
　　　　　　　CVicAr Or WaSp **4672**

The way to the West, and the lives of three

early Americans; Boone, Crockett, Carson, with illus. by Frederick Remington. New York, Grosset [c1903] 446 p. front., plates. Or OrP WaS WaSp WaU **4673**

The young Alaskans. New York, Harper [c1908] 291 p. front., 3 plates.
IdIf Or OrP WaS **4674**

Young Alaskans in the far North. New York, Harper, c1918. 250 p. front., plates.
IdIf Or WaPS WaS WaSp WaT **4675**

The young Alaskans in the Rockies. New York, Harper, c1913. 325 p. front., plates.
WaS WaT **4676**

The young Alaskans on the Missouri. New York, Harper [c1922] 377 p. front., plates.
WaU **4677**

The young Alaskans on the trail. New York, Harper, 1911. 321 p. front., plates.
WaS WaT **4678**

Houghland, Laura.
The kindling of a flame; an historical comedy in two acts for the junior actor. Evanston, Ill., Row, Peterson & Co. [c1945] 56 p. "One of the prize-winning plays in the second play-writing contest conducted by Seattle Junior Programs, Inc." WaS WaU **4679**

Houghton, F. L., comp.
H. M. C. S. Skeena, 1931-1932. Victoria, B. C., Buckle, 1932. 92 p. front., illus., ports., map. CVicAr **4680**

House, Julius T., see no. 7250.

Houston, Mrs. Elizabeth Lina, 1860-1933.
Early history of Gallatin County. Bozeman, Mont., Bozeman Chronicle, c1933. 58 p. illus., ports. MtBozC MtHi **4681**

Hovious, Lynette.
The spirit of Mt. Tahoma, a pageant-masque. [Tacoma, 1921] [14] p.
WaT WaU **4682**

Howard, Addison.
Capt. John Mullan. [n.p. n.d.] 17 p.
MtHi **4683**

Howard, Bonnie C.
On the trail with Lewis and Clark, by Bonnie C. Howard, assisted by Ruth Higgins, illus. by Paul Laune. New York, Silver Burdett [c1939] 154 p. illus.
Many **4684**

Howard, Daniel Franklin.
Oregon's first white men. Rainier, Or., Rainier Review, 1927. 72 p. front. (port.)
Many **4685**

Howard, E. C., see nos. 8111, 8112.

Howard, Ernest Emmanuel, see no. 4090.

Howard, George Franklin, 1858-
Outlines in civil government for Washington and the United States, by Geo. F. Howard and E. J. Gillett. [Rochester, Wash., Hack & Wegner Printing Co.] 1916. 48 p. WaPS **4686**

Howard, Harry Winsmore, 1899-
Salmon fishing on Puget Sound; salmon fishing contribution from the practical side; how, when and where to troll for salmon, spinning, mooching, etc. [Portland, Or., Binfords & Mort, c1947] viii, 122 p. front. (port.) illus., plates.
Many **4687**

Howard, Helen Addison.
War chief Joseph, by Helen Addison Howard, assisted in the research by Dan L. McGrath; maps and illus. by George D. McGrath. Caldwell, Idaho, Caxton, 1941. 362 p. col. front., illus., plates, ports., maps. Many **4688**

[Howard, Mrs. Hilda (Glynn)] 1887-
The glamour of British Columbia, by H. Glynn-Ward [pseud.] illus. with photographs by the author. London, Hutchinson & Co. [1926] xiv, 238 p. front., 31 plates, fold. map. CVU **4689**

Same. New York, Century [c1926]
Many **4690**

Same. Toronto, Macmillan, 1926.
CV CVicAr CVU **4691**

Same. Toronto, Doubleday, 1932.
CVicAr **4692**

The writing on the wall, by H. Glynn-Ward [pseud.] [n.p., c1921] 326 p.
CV CVicAr **4693**

Howard, Joseph E.
My Washington, words by Burton E. Hilborn, music by Joseph E. Howard. [n.p., c1911] 5 p. "The official state song adopted by Gov. M. E. Hay." WaU **4694**

Howard, Joseph Kinsey.
Montana; high, wide, and handsome. New Haven, Yale Univ. Press, 1943. vi, 347 p.
Many **4695**

Same. [1944] WaU **4696**

Montana margins, a state anthology. New Haven, Yale Univ. Press, 1946. xviii, 527 p. Many **4697**

Howard, Minnie Frances, 1872-
Early life and times of the First Congregational Church of Pocatello. [Pocatello, Idaho, Tribune Pub. Co., 1928] 65 p. illus., ports. IdP IdU IdUSB **4698**

Howard, Oliver Otis, 1830-1909.
My life and experiences among our hostile Indians; a record of personal observations, adventures, and campaigns among the Indians of the great West, with some account of their life, habits, traits, religion, ceremonies, dress, savage instincts, and customs in peace and war; beautifully illustrated with full page engravings, chiefly from photographs supplied by the Bureau of Ethnology, Washington, and a series of colored plates showing Indian objects of interest and curiosity in facsimile. Hartford, A. D. Worthington & Co. [c1907] 570 p. front. (port.) illus., 29 plates (10 col.)
Many **4699**

Nez Perce Joseph; an account of his ancestors, his lands, his confederates, his enemies, his murders, his war, his pursuit and capture. Boston, Lee and Shepard, 1881. xii, 274 p. front., port., maps (part fold.) Many **4700**

Same. New York, C. T. Dillingham, 1881.
IdU **4701**

Howard, Tilghman Ashurst, 1797-1844.
Remarks on the settlement of Oregon, delivered before Monroe County Lyceum, May 24, 1841. Bloomington, Iowa, A. E. Drapier, 1841. 14 p. Or **4702**

Howay, Frederick William, 1867-1943.

British Columbia from the earliest times to the present, by His Honour, F. W. Howay and E. O. S. Scholefield. Vancouver, B. C., S. J. Clarke Pub. Co. [1913?] [39] p. front., illus., ports., facsims.   CVU **4703**

Same. [1914?] [40] p.   WaU **4704**

British Columbia, the making of a province. Toronto, Ryerson [c1928] ix, 289 p. front., illus., plates, map.   Many **4705**

Builders of the West, a book of heroes. Toronto, Ryerson [1929] v, 251 p. illus. CV CVic CVicAr CVU WaSp WaU **4706**

Captain George Vancouver. Toronto, Ryerson [c1932] 32 p. illus. (Ryerson Canadian history readers).

CVU Or OrHi OrP OrU WaS **4707**

The Dixon-Meares controversy, containing Remarks on the voyages of John Meares, by George Dixon; An answer to Mr. George Dixon, by John Meares; and Further remarks on the voyages of John Meares, by George Dixon; ed. by F. W. Howay. Toronto, Ryerson [c1929] xii, 156 p. front., illus., maps, facsims.

Many **4708**

Presidential address; the early literature of the Northwest coast. Ottawa, Royal Society of Canada, 1924. 31 p. CVU **4709**

Voyages of the "Columbia" to the Northwest coast, 1787-1790 and 1790-1793. [Boston] Mass. Historical Society, 1941. xxvii, 518 p. front., ports., maps, facsims., tables. (Collections, v. 79).   Many **4710**

The work of the Royal Engineers in British Columbia, 1858-1863; being an address delivered before the Art, Historical, and Scientific Association of Vancouver on 9th February, 1909. Victoria, B. C., Wolfenden, 1910. 17 p. plates (1 col.)   Many **4711**

See also nos. 254, 1905, 4377, 9490.

Howe, Henry, 1816-1893.

The great West; containing narratives of the most important and interesting events in western history; remarkable individual adventures; sketches of frontier life; descriptions of natural curiosities; to which is appended historical and descriptive sketches of Oregon, New Mexico, Texas, Minnesota, Utah, California, Washington, Nebraska, Kansas. Enlarged ed. New York, Geo. F. Tuttle, 1857. 576 p. col. front., col. plates, map.

WaU WaWW **4712**

Historical collections of the great West; containing narratives of the most important and interesting events in western history; remarkable individual adventures; sketches of frontier life; descriptions of natural curiosities; to which is appended historical and descriptive sketches of Oregon, New Mexico, Texas, Minnesota, Utah, and California; illus. with numerous engravings. Cincinnati, 1851. 2 v. in 1. front., 32 plates, maps.

Or OrCS OrSaw OrU WaPS WaT **4713**

Same. 1852.   Or OrP WaU **4714**

Same. 1853.	CV WaSp WaU	**4715**
Same. 1854.	OrHi WaS WaU	**4716**
Same. 1855.	Wa	**4717**
Same. 1856. 448 p.	Wa	**4718**
Same. 1857. 2 v. in 1.		
	IdU MtU OrU WaWW	**4719**
Same 1872. 565 p.	IdB WaU	**4720**
Same. 1873. 464 p.	Or	**4721**

Howe, James Hamilton, 1856-1934.

The Olympic suite; Opus 50, composed for pianoforte, voice and orchestra, illus. with half-tones of Washington scenery. Seattle, Dragon Pub. Co., c1922. 1 v. front., illus.   WaS **4722**

Howe, R. S., ed.

The Great Northern country, illustrating and describing the country, opportunities, and scenery along the lines of the Great Northern Railway and Northern Steamship Co.; Alaska, its resources, scenery and how to get there; the Oriental trade, its beginning, development and possibilities, especially for the Pacific Northwest. December ed., 1902, ed. and illus. by R. S. Howe. St Paul, Great Northern Railway [1902] 115 p. illus., map.

WaU **4723**

Same. 1903. [160] p.   WaU **4724**

Howell, Edgar W.

The new mining laws of the state of Washington; how to locate claims (with forms) by E. W. Howell and John Mills Day. Seattle, W. O. Peterson, 1915. 11 p. illus.   Wa **4725**

Howell, Edward Beach, 1857-

Howell's miners' code for the use of miners in Montana and Idaho, with forms. Butte, Mont., Miner Pub. Co., 1899. 96 p.   MtHi **4726**

Howell, Thomas, 1842-1912.

Catalogue of the flora of Oregon, Washington, and Idaho. [n.p., n.d.] 22 p. Anon.

OrP WaU **4727**

A catalogue of the known plants (Phaenogamia and pteridophta) of Oregon, Washington, and Idaho. Arthur, Or., 1887. 28 p.

OrCS OrHi OrP OrU WaU **4728**

A flora of northwest America; containing brief descriptions of all the known indigenous and naturalized plants growing without cultivation north of California, west of Utah, and south of British Columbia. V. I. Phanerogamae, Portland, Or., 1897. 792 [24] p.   Many **4729**

Same. 1903.   Many **4730**

Howse, Joseph.

A grammar of the Cree language; with which is combined an analysis of the Chippeway dialect. London, Rivington, 1844. 324 p.   MtHi WaS **4731**

Hoy, Calvin I.

John Jacob Astor, an unwritten chapter. Boston, Meador Pub. Co., 1936. 86 p. front. (port.)   OrP WaSp **4732**

Hoyman, Howard S.

Health-guide units for Oregon teachers (grades 7-12) prepared for Oregon State Department of Education, Salem,

Oregon: [Portland, Or.] E. C. Brown Trust, Univ. of Or. Medical School [1946, c1945] xv, 429 p. forms. Many **4733**

Hrdlicka, Ales, 1869-1943.
Alaska diary, 1926-1931, pub. with the permission of the secretary of the Smithsonian Institution. Lancaster, Pa., Jaques Cattell, 1943. xv, 414 p. front., illus., ports., maps. (Humanizing science series). Many **4734**

The Aleutian and Commander Islands and their inhabitants. Philadelphia, Wistar Institute of Anatomy and Biology, 1945. xx, 630 p. front., illus., maps. Many **4735**

The anthropology of Kodiak Island. Philadelphia, Wistar Institute of Anatomy and Biology, 1944. xix, 486 p. front. (port.) illus., maps.
CVicPr OrU WaS WaTC **4736**

Hubback, Theodore Rathbone.
To far western Alaska for big game; being an account of two journeys to Alaska in seach of adventure. London, Ward, 1929. 232 p. front., 39 plates, 3 maps (1 fold.) IdB WaS **4737**

Hubbard, Bernard Rosecrans, 1888-
Cradle of the storms, illus. from photographs taken by the author. New York, Dodd, 1935. xv, 285 p. front., plates, ports., maps. Many **4738**

Mush, you malemutes! New York, America Press, 1932. xiv, 179 p. front., plates, ports., maps. Many **4739**

Same. 1943 [c1932] vi, 179 p. WaU **4740**

One hundred pictures of little known Alaska. [New York?] c1935. [72] p. illus., map. WaS WaU **4741**

Hubbard, LaFayette Ronald, 1911-
Buckskin brigades. New York, Macaulay Co. [c1937] 316 p. Northwest fur trade story. WaS WaU **4742**

Hubbard, Ralph.
Queer person, illus. by Harold von Schmidt. Garden City, N. Y., Doubleday, 1930. 336 p. front., plates. Montana Indian story. Or OrP WaSp **4743**

Same. 1932. IdIf **4744**

Hubbs, Carl Leavitt, 1894-
The scientific name of the Columbia River chub, by Carl Leavitt and L. P. Schultz. Ann Arbor, Mich., Univ. of Mich., 1931, 6 p. illus. (Museum of zoology. Occasional papers). OrP **4745**

Huber, Louis R., comp.
The Alaska sportsman book of 100 events that built Alaska, ed. by Ethel Dassow. Ketchikan, Alaska, Alaska Magazine Pub. Co., 1944. 1 v. illus. WaS **4746**

[**Hubler, H. J.**]
Pacific County and its resources. South Bend, Wash., South Bend Journal [1909?] [72] p. illus., ports., map. WaU **4747**

Hudelson, Vernon L., see no. 3461.

Hudson, Alfred E., see no. 1889.

Hudson, Will E.
Icy hell; experiences of a news reel cameraman in the Aleutian Islands, eastern Siberia and the Arctic fringe of Alaska, with a map and 32 illus. from photographs by the author. London, Constable [1937] xii, 307 p. front., plates, ports., fold. map.
CVicAr Or Wa WaS WaT WaU **4748**

Same. New York, Stokes [1938]
CVic OrCS **4749**

Hudson's Bay Company.
Charters, statutes, orders in council, &c. relating to the Hudson's Bay Company. London, 1931. 284 p.
CV CVivAr CVU **4750**

Deed poll, by the governor and company of Hudson's Bay with respect to their chief factors and chief traders for conducting their trade in Ruperts Land and North America. London, Causton, 1834. 17 p. CVicAr **4751**

Same. 1871. 11 p. CVicAr **4752**

Exhibition of ancient maps and charts. [n.p., n.d.] 20 p. col. map.
CVicAr WaU **4753**

Hudson's Bay Company, incorporated 2d May 1670; a brief history. London, 1934. x, 68 p. front., illus., plates, ports., facsim., mounted col. coat of arms.
Many **4754**

Same. 2d rev. ed. Winnipeg, Hudson's Bay House, 1936. 48 p. CVicAr Or **4755**

Same. 3rd rev. ed. [1938] 44 p.
CV WaS **4756**

Hudson's Bay Company's historical exhibit at Winnipeg. 4th ed., Aug. 1924. [Winnipeg, 1924?] 76 p. illus. Anon.
WaSp **4757**

List of Books relating to Hudson's Bay Company, inc. 2d May 1670. [London] 1935. 13 p.
CVicAr IdP Or WaSp WaU **4758**

Milestones in the progress of the Hudson's Bay Co., 275th anniversary. [n.p., 1945?] 31 p. illus. WaS **4759**

Minutes of the Hudson's Bay Company, 1671-1674, ed. by E. E. Rich, with an introd. by Sir John Clapham. lxviii, 276, xi p. (Publications of the Hudson's Bay Record Society, no. 5). Many **4760**

Same. 1679-1682. 1945. 378 p. (Publications no. 8) Many **4761**

Same. 1682-1684. 1946. 368 p. (Publications no. 9) MtHi OrHi WaSp WaU **4762**

The royal charter for incorporating the Hudson's Bay Company, granted by His Majesty King Charles II, in the 22d year of his reign, A. D. 1670. London, J. Brettell, 1810. 21 p. WaU **4763**

Same. London, Causton, 1865. 24 p.
CVicAr **4764**

Rules and regulations; subject to the provisions of the deed poll. Winnipeg, Call, 1887. 18 p. CVicAr **4765**

Victoria's centenary, 1843-1943. [Victoria, B. C., British Colonist] 1943. 12 p.
CVicAr **4766**

The Hudson's Bay Company; "a million" shall we take it? addressed to the shareholders of the company, by one of themselves. London, Baily, 1866. 38 p.
CVicAr **4767**

The Hudson's Bay Company; Canada, west; and the Indian tribes. [n.p., n.d.] 12 p.   CVicAr **4768**

The Hudson's Bay Company; what is it? London, Baily, 1864. v, 81 p.
     CVicAr WaS WaU **4769**

Hudspeth, Charles Ernest, 1876-
Oregon chief; illus. by Lee Townsend. New York, Ginn [c1927] 166 p. illus.
     Many **4770**

Hulswitt, Ignatz.
Tagebuch einer Reise nach den Vereinigten Staaten und der Nordwestkuste von Amerika. Munster, Coppenrath, 1828. iv, 379 p.   WaU **4771**

Hueston, Mrs. Ethel (Powelson) 1887-
Calamity Jane of Deadwood Gulch. Indianapolis, Bobbs-Merrill [c1937] 306 p.
     IdB MtHi Or OrP WaS WaSp **4772**

The man of the storm; a romance of Colter who discovered Yellowstone. Indianapolis, Bobbs-Merrill [c1936] 312 p.   Many **4773**

Star of the West; the romance of the Lewis and Clark expedition. Indianapolis, Bobbs-Merrill [c1935] 372 p.
     Many **4774**

Same. Special autographed ed.
     WaPS **4775**

Same. New York, Burt [c1935] IdIf **4776**

Huffman, Adrian.
Atonement's offerings. [Walla Walla, Wash., Agenda Press, c1934. 63 p. illus. Poems.   WaU **4777**

Huffman, Bert, 1870-
Echoes of the Grande Ronde, collected and published by Eldridge Huffman. La Grande, Or., La Grande Printing Co., c1934. 87 p. illus., port. Prose and verse.
     Or OrLgE OrU **4778**

Song of the Oregon pine and other poems. Pendleton, Or., East Oregonian, 1907. [36] p. plates, port.
     OrHi OrP WaU **4779**

See also no. 8915.

Huffman, Eldridge, see no. 4778.

Huggins, Roy, 1914-
The double take. New York, Morrow, 1946. 240 p. Portland setting.
     CV OrP WaS WaSp WaU **4780**

Hughes, Babette (Plechner) 1906-
Last night when we were young. New York, Rinehart [c1947] 251 p. Seattle author; autobiographical. Many **4781**

Hughes, David W., see no. 3337.

Hughes, Glenn Arthur, 1894-
The Penthouse theatre; its history and technique. New York, S. French, 1942. xii, 125 p. front., plates, plan.
     Many **4782**

Same. 1945 [c1942]   WaPS **4783**
University of Washington poems, first series; selected and ed. with an introd. Seattle, Univ. of Wash. Press [c1924] 117 p. IdU Wa WaS WaU WaWW **4784**

Same. 2d series. Seattle, Univ. of Wash. Book Store [c1926] 108 p.
     IdU Wa WaS WaU **4785**

Same. 3d series, illus. by Wesley Kilworth. 1927. 98 p. illus.   Wa WaS **4786**
See also no. 3740.

Hughes, Katherine.
Father Lacombe, the black-robe voyageur. New York, Moffat, 1911. xxi, 467 p. front., plates, ports., map.   Many **4787**

Hughes, Lora (Wood) 187—?—
No time for tears, decorations by Edwin Earle. Boston, Houghton [1946] 305 p. illus. (Life in America series).
     Many **4788**

Hughes, R. O., see no. 8634.

Hughey, Mrs. Bertha Ellen (Robinson) 1869-
Stover genealogy, biography and history; a genealogical record of the descendents of William Stover, pioneer, and other Stovers. Portland, Or. [c1936] 246 p. front. (port.) plates.   WaU **4789**

Huish, Robert, 1777-1850, comp.
The last expedition of Capt. John Ross, R. N., for the discovery of a North-west passage; with an abridgement of the former voyages of Captains Ross, Parry, and other celebrated navigators to the northern latitudes, comp. from authentic information and original documents transmitted by William Light. London, George Virtue [1835] ii, 716, 44 p. front. (port.) plates, fold. tables.   Wa **4790**

The last voyage of Capt. Sir John Ross, to the Arctic regions; for the discovery of a North west passage; performed in the years 1829-30-31-32-33, to which is prefixed an abridgement of the former voyages of Capts. Ross, Parry, & other celebrated navigators to the northern latitudes; comp. from authentic information and original documents, transmitted by William Light, purser's steward to the expedition; illus. by engravings taken on the spot. London, Saunders, 1835. 716 p. front. (port.) 6 plates, map.   CVicAr CVU **4791**

Same. 1836.   CV **4792**

A narrative of the voyages and travels of Captain Beechey to the Pacific and Behring's Straits; performed in the years 1825, 26, 27, and 28, for the purpose of co-operating with the expeditions under Captains Parry and Franklin, and of Captain Back, R. N., to the Thlew-ee-choh River and the Arctic Sea, in search of the expedition under Capt. J. Ross, R. N., being the conclusion of the series of voyages instituted for the discovery of the North west pasage, comp. from original and authenticated documents. London, W. Wright [1836?] vi, 704 p. front., plates, ports.   OrU WaSp **4793**

The North-West Passage; a history of the most remarkable voyages made in search of the North-West Passage form the earliest periods. London, Printed for the booksellers, by M'Gowan & Co., 1851. iv, 418 p. front., plates, ports. WaU **4794**

Hulbert, Archer Butler, 1873-1933, ed.
The call of the Columbia; iron men and saints take the Oregon Trail, ed., with bibliographical resume. 1830-1835. [Colo-

rado Springs] Stewart Commission of Colo. College [1934] xvii, 317 p. front., port., maps. (Overland to the Pacific, v. 4) **Many 4795**

Marcus Whitman, crusader, ed. by Archer Butler Hulbert and Dorothy Printup Hulbert; with maps and illus. [Colorado Springs] Stewart Commission of Colo. College [c1936-c1941] 3 v. front., plates, fold. maps. (Overland to the Pacific, v. 6-8). **Many 4796**

The Oregon crusade; across land and sea to Oregon, ed. with bibliographical resume, 1830-1840, by Archer Butler Hulbert and Dorothy Printup Hulbert. [Colorado Springs] Stewart Commission of Colo. College [1935] xvi, 301 p. front., plate, port., 2 maps (1 fold.) (Overland to the Pacific, v. 5.) **Many 4797**

Where rolls the Oregon; prophet and pessimist look Northwest; ed with bibliographical resume 1825-1830, with maps and illus. [Colorado Springs] Stewart Commission of Colo. College [1933] xv, 244 p. front., plates, maps. (Overland to the Pacific, v. 3) **Many 4798**

Hulbert, Dorothy Printup, see nos. 4796, 4797.

Hulbert, Robert William, 1879- comp.
Illustrated historical souvenir of 13th Field Artillery Brigade, Camp Lewis, Wash. Tacoma, c1918. [50] p. illus.
Or WaS **4799**

Official illustrated souvenir and program commemorating visit of Pacific Fleet to Tacoma, Washington, September 15, 16, 17, 1919. Tacoma, 1919. 1 v. illus., ports.
WaT **4800**

Hull, Alexander, 1887-
Shep of the Painted Hills. New York, Burt [c1930] 302 p. Western setting.
Or OrCS OrP WaE **4801**

Hull, Lindley M., comp.
A history of central Washington, including the famous Wenatchee, Entiat, Chelan and Columbia Valleys, with an index and eighty scenic-historical illus. [Spokane, Shaw & Borden] 1929. 624 p. front., illus., ports.
OrHi Wa WaPS WaS WaSp WaU **4802**

Hultin, C. A.
Open the Cascade Mountain Range barrier.. [n.p., n.d.] 1 v. WaS **4803**

Hultz, Fredric Samuel, 1893-
Range beef production in the seventeen western states. New York, Wiley [1930] xv, 208 p. front., illus., diagrs.
Many 4804

Range sheep and wool in the seventeen western states. Pt. 1. Range sheep, by Fred S. Hultz. Pt. 2. Wool, by John A. Hill. New York, Wiley, 1931. 374 p. front., illus., diagrs. **Many 4805**

Hum-ishu-ma, see nos. 7125, 7126.

Humboldt, Alexander von, see nos. 6908, 6910.

Hume, Harry, comp.
Prosperous Washington; a series of articles descriptive of the Evergreen State, its magnificent resources, and its present and probable development. [Seattle] Seattle Post-Intelligencer, 1906. 160 p. illus., ports., map. WaS WaT WaU **4806**
See also no. 2219.

Hume, Hugh, see no. 2074.

Hume, M.
Seattle architecturally, 1902, published by Bebb and Mendel, Saunders & Lawton, and deNeuf & Heide. Seattle [Dearborn Printing Co., 1902] [3] p. 41 plates.
WaU **4807**

Hume, R. D.
Salmon of the Pacific Coast, with engravings, showing the apparatus used for their artificial propagation, and the operations of salmon fishing and canning as conducted at Gold Beach, Curry County, Oregon, U. S. A. [San Francisco, Schmidt Label and Lithographic Co.] 1893. 64 p. illus., port. **Many 4808**

Hume-Douglas, Sallie, see no. 7846.

Humfreville, James Lee.
Twenty years among the hostile Indians; describing the characteristics, customs, habits, religion, marriages, dances and battles of the wild Indians in their natural state, together with the entrance of civilization through their hunting grounds, fully illus. from original photographs. New York, Hunter [1899] 479 p. front., port., illus. IdB MtU WaT **4809**

Same. 2d ed., rev., enlarged and improved with many new and rare illus. selected by the author. [c1903] MtU WaU **4810**

Twenty years among our savage Indians; a record of personal experiences; observations and adventures among the Indians of the wild West, fully illus. with upwards of 250 engravings, chiefly from photographs supplied by the Bureau of Ethnology. Hartford, Hartford Pub. Co., 1897. 674 p. illus., ports. MtHi **4811**

Humphry, Seth King, 1864-1932.
Following the prairie frontier. [Minneapolis] Univ. of Minn. [c1931] 264 p. front.
MtU OrP WaE WaU **4812**

Hunt, Frazier, 1885-
Custer, the last of the cavaliers, illus. by Capt. John W. Thomason. New York, Cosmopolitan Book Corp., 1928. 209 p. front. (port.) 6 plates, 4 ports.
IdU MtHi WaS **4813**
See also no. 11107.

Hunt, George, see no. 907.

Hunt, George Washington, 1831-
A history of the Hunt family from the Norman conquest, 1066 A. D. to the year 1890; early settlement in America and different states in the Union, settlement in Oregon, mining experiences in California in 1849, incidents of pioneer life and adventures among the Indian tribes of the Northwest. Boston, McDonald, Gill & Co., 1890. 79 p. Or OrP WaU **4814**

Hunt, Harold, see no. 6984.

Hunt, Herbert, 1869-
Tacoma, its history and its builders; a half century of activity. Chicago, S. J. Clarke Pub. Co., 1916. 3 v. fronts., plates, ports., maps. Volumes 2 and 3 biograph-

ical. Wa WaS WaT WaTC WaU 4815

Washington, west of the Cascades; historical and descriptive; the explorers, the Indians, the pioneers, the modern; by Herbert Hunt and Floyd C. Kaylor. Chicago, S. J. Clarke Pub. Co., 1917. 3 v. front., plates, ports. Volumes 2 and 3 biographical. Many 4816

Hunt, Mary Agnes.
Oregon's Middletown, Klamath Falls; thesis submitted to the Honors Council, University of Oregon, June, 1931. [Eugene, Or., Univ. of Or.] 1931. 56 p. illus.
Or OrCS OrHi OrP 4817

Hunt, Robert, see no. 11107.

Hunt, T. F., see no. 2019.

Hunt, Wilson Price, see no. 9977.

[Hunter, Fenley]
Frances Lake, Yukon. Dawson, 1887; Hunter, 1923. Flushing, N. Y., 1924. 103 p. front., plates, ports., maps (1 fold.)
CVU 4818

Hunter, George, 1835-
Reminiscences of an old timer; a recital of the actual events, incidents, trials of a pioneer, hunter, miner and scout of the Pacific Northwest; the several Indian wars. San Francisco, H. S. Crocker Co., 1887. xxv, 454 p. front. (port.) 15 plates. Many 4819

Same. 3d ed. Battle Creek, Mich. Review and Herald, 1888. xxv, 508 p.
IdB IdU MtU Wa WaT 4820

Same. 4th ed. 1889.
CVicAr CVU OrU WaSp 4821

Hunter, John Dunn, 1798-1827.
Memoirs of a captivity among the Indians of North America from childhood to the age of nineteen; with anecdotes descriptive of their manners and customs; to which is added some account of the soil, climate and vegetable productions of the territory westward of the Mississippi. London, Longman, 1823. 447 p. front. (port.) MtHi MtU OrU WaU 4822

Same. 3d ed. 1824. 468 p. OrHi 4823

Hunter, Martin.
Canadian wilds; tells about the Hudson's Bay Company northern Indians and their modes of hunting, trapping, etc. Columbus, Ohio, A. R. Harding Pub. Co. [c1907] 277 p. port.
CVicAr CVU MtU Or OrP 4824

Hunter, William Crosbie, 1866-
Frozen Dog tales, and other things. Boston, Everett Press, 1905. 188 p. illus. (part col.) Frozen Dog, Idaho stories.
WaSp WaU 4825

Hunting, Nathaniel S., see no. 10349.

Huntington, J. V., see no. 3244.

Hunt's Point, Wash. Property Owners.
Some features of the proposed Lake Washington Canal which will interest you; read, think, and then act. [Seattle, 1908] [9] p. WaS 4826

Hurd, Mrs. Catharine Terry.
Stairways to stars, by C. T. Hurd, L. E. Estes, B. E. Barnes. [Roanoke, Va.,

Russell L. Paxton, 1945] 24 p. Poems selected from western newspapers.
WaSp 4827

Hurd, P. A., see no. 9525.

Hussey, Ernest Bertrand.
Introduction of Freemasonry into the United States. [Seattle] Committee on Masonic Research and Education, Grand Lodge, F. & A. M. of Wash. [n.d.] 9 p. (American Masonic historical series. Bulletin no. 1). WaU 4828

Hutchins, Charles Bowman.
Whiff o' the West; new notes and rustic rimes of the great West; its birds, trees, flowers, and natural charms, by Charles Bowman Hutchins and Helen Owen Hutchins. 7th ed. Portland, Or., Binfords & Mort 193—?] 96 p. WaPS 4829

Hutchins, George L.
Portland, Oregon "The city of roses". [Portland, Or., Walker & Weinstein Bros., 190—] 47 p. illus. WaU 4830

Hutchins, Helen Owen, see no. 4829.

Hutchinson, Arthur Howard, 1876-
Little saints annoy the Lord. Seattle, Greenwood Press, 1938. 227 p. front., illus., 2 fold. maps. Story of Marcus Whitman. Many 4831

Hutchinson, C. J.
How to go; a guide to Seattle. Seattle, 1941. 32 p. maps. WaS 4832

Hutchinson, Calvin G., see no. 10349.

Hutchinson, Isobel Wylie, 1889-
The Aleutian Islands; America's back door. London, Blackie, 1942. 182 p. col. front., plates, ports. CVic 4833

North to the rime-ringed sun; being the record of an Alaska-Canadian journey made in 1933-34. London, Blackie [c1934] viii, 262 p. col. front., plates (part col.) ports., fold. map.
CVic WaS WaSp WaU 4834

Stepping stones from Alaska to Asia. London, Blackie [1937] x, 246 p. col. front., plates (part col.) fold. map.
CVic CVicAr Or WaS WaU 4835

See also nos. 6582, 8496.

Hutton, May Arkwright.
The Coeur d'Alenes; or, A tale of the modern inquisition in Idaho. [Wallace, Idaho] 1900. 246 p. front., plates, ports.
Many 4836

The Hutton settlement, Spokane, Wash.
The Hutton settlement. [Spokane, Shaw & Borden, 1929] 16 p. illus., plans.
WaPS 4837

Hyack Engine Company No. 1, New Westminster, B. C.
Constitution, bye-laws and rules of order. New Westminster, B. C., British Columbian, 1864. 12 p. CVicAr 4838

Hyde, George E., 1882-
The early Blackfeet and their neighbors. Denver, John VanMale, 1933. 45 p. (The Old West series, no. 2). MtHi 4839

Hyde, John, 1848-1929.
Northern Pacific tour; the Pacific Northwest and Alaska, with a description of the country traversed by the Northern Pacific Railroad. St. Paul, W. C. Riley, 1889. 94 p. front., illus.   WaU **4840**

Idaho. University.
The Idaho pageant "The light on the Mountains"; a community drama done at the University of Idaho commencement, 1923. [Moscow, Idaho, 1923] 40 p. (The Blue Bucket, v. 1, no. 3, June 1923)
IdB IdU IdUSB OrHi WaPS WaU **4841**
— — —   — — —   Associated students.
Songs of the Vandals, comp. and arranged by J. Morris O'Donnell, '33; pub. by authority of the Associated Students, Univ. of Idaho. Caldwell, Idaho, Caxton, 1933. 42 p.   IdIf IdU WaU **4842**
— — —   World's Fair Commission.
Idaho, gem of the mountains, by Herbert C. Gregg; official souvenir, illus. under direction of T. McWhorter. St. Paul, Pioneer Press, 1893. [70] p. illus., plates (1 fold.) ports.   IdB WaPS **4843**
Idaho Chain Stores Association, Inc.
Idaho's $25,000,000 industry. [Boise, Idaho, 1939] 45 p. illus., table.   IdB **4844**
Idaho Cooperative Loan Corporation.
Self-help cooperatives in Idaho, 1935-1939. [Boise, Idaho? 1939] 28 p. tables.
IdB OrCS OrU **4845**
Idaho Mining Association.
Mining salutes Idaho's 50 years of statehood, 1890-1940. [Boise, Idaho, 1940] 36 p. illus.   IdB Or OrCS WaSp **4846**
[Idaho Power Co.]
Boise's power terminal. Boise, Idaho, Syms-York Co. [1924?] 1 v. illus.   IdB **4847**
Idaho Statesman.
The chosen valley; impressions of Boise Valley, a typical part of the great Idaho homeland and of the many valleys that compose it, reflecting the aims, ambitions and accomplishments of the people who live there. Boise, Idaho, c1923. 16 p. (Suppl. Sunday, Dec. 30, 1923)
IdB **4848**
[Golden anniversary number, state of Idaho] Boise, Idaho, 1940. 63 p. illus.
WaSp **4849**
Idaho, the gem of the mountains. [n.p., 1899] 726 p. plates, ports.   IdU **4850**
Idaho yesterday and today; souvenir handbook, Fort Hall Centennial, 1834-1934, Pocatello, Idaho, August 5, 6, 7, 8, 1934. [Pocatello, Idaho, Graves & Potter, c1934] 117 p. col. front., illus. Contents: Idaho yesterday.—Fort Hall centennial.—Idaho today. — Builders of Idaho.
IdIf OrHi **4851**
Ide, Arthur W.
Helena, Montana; its past, present and future, by Arthur W. Ide and W. D. Rumsey. New York, South Pub. Co. [n.d.] 125 p. map.   MtHi MtU **4852**

Igo, Sophia Edith.
Sharon Valley. Marcola, Or., C. & S. Pub. Co., c1947. 206 p.   IdB Or OrCS **4853**
A visitor's impression of Victoria, B. C. Portland, Or., Oregon Pub. Co., c1936. [8] p.   CVicAr **4854**
An illustrated history of Baker, Grant, Malheur and Harney Counties, with a brief outline of the early history of the state of Oregon. [Chicago] Western Historical Pub. Co., 1902. xxiii, 788 p. 14 plates, ports.   Or OrHi OrP OrU WaSp **4855**
An illustrated history of central Oregon embracing Wasco, Sherman, Gilliam, Wheeler, Crook. Lake and Klamath Counties, **state of Oregon.** Spokane, Western Historical Pub. Co., 1905. xxx, 1097 p. front., plates, ports.   Many **4856**
An illustrated history of Klickitat, Yakima and Kittitas Counties; with an outline of the early history of the state of Washington. [Chicago] Interstate Pub. Co., 1904. xxiii, 941 p. front., plates, ports.
Many **4857**
An illustrated history of north Idaho, embracing Nez Perces, Idaho, Latah, Kootenai and Shoshone Counties, state of **Idaho.** [n.p.] Western Historical Pub. Co., 1903. xxviii, 1238 p. front., 12 plates, 255 ports.   Many **4858**
An illustrated history of Skagit and Snohomish Counties; their people, their commerce and their resources, with an outline of the history of the state of Washington, endorsed as authentic by local committees of pioneers. Chicago, Interstate Pub. Co., 1906. xxvii, 1117 p. plates, ports.   Many **4859**
An illustrated history of southeastern Washington, including Walla Walla, Columbia, Garfield, and Asotin Counties, Washington [comp. by F. A. Shaver, R. F. Steele, and A. P. Rose] [Spokane] Western Historical Pub. Co., 1906. xxii, 874 p. illus., 19 plates, 40 ports.
WaPS WaS WaSp WaU WaW **4860**
An illustrated history of the state of Idaho, containing a history of the state of Idaho from the earliest period of its discovery to the present time, together with glimpses of its auspicious future; illus. and biographical mention of many pioneers and prominent citizens of to-day. Chicago, Lewis Pub. Co., 1899. xv, 726 p. front., illus., plates, ports.
CVicAr IdB IdU WaS WaSp WaU **4861**
An illustrated history of the Yellowstone Valley, embracing the counties of Park, Sweet Grass, Carbon, Yellowstone, Rosebud, Custer and Dawson, state of Montana. Spokane, Western Historical Pub. Co. [1907?] xxi, 669 p. front., plates, ports.
MtBozC WaU **4862**
An illustrated history of Union and Wallowa Counties, with a brief outline of the early history of the state of Oregon. [Chicago?] Western Historical Pub. Co., 1902. xvi, 677 p. ports.
Or OrU Wa WaSp **4863**

An illustated history of Whitman County, state of Washington. [n.p.] W. H. Lever, 1901. xiii, 469 p. front., plates, ports. Biographical, p. 245-469.
IdU Wa WaPS WaU 4864

Ilo, William O., 1861-
Hazel Pierce. New York, Hograve, 1902. 318 p. front. OrP 4865

Imhaus, Nicholas Edward, 1856-
Handbook on some minerals and rocks. Baker, Or., Ryder Bros. [1908] 24 [[11] p. OrHi OrP 4866

Immigration Aid Society of North-western Washington.
North-western Washington; its soil, climate, productions and general resources. Port Townsend, Wash., 1880. 52 p. front. (map). WaU 4867

Imperial Order Daughters of the Empire, Canada. Sir James and Lady Douglas Chapter.
1843-1943 [history and description of Victoria, B. C., pub. in collaboration with Victoria section of the B. C. Historical Association] Victoria, B. C., 1943. 32 p. illus., ports. CVicPr WaS 4868

Improved Order of Red Men. Oregon. Great Council.
By-laws. [n.p., n.d.] 29 p. OrHi 4869
Constitution und Nebengesetze des Willamette Stammes No. 6 Portland, Or., Himes, 1890. [48] p. OrHi 4870

In memorial. Robert Washington Donnell. New York, 1892. 63 p. front. (port.)
MtHi 4871

In memoriam: Donald Milton Erb, 1900-1943, president, University of Oregon, 1938-1943. [Eugene, Or., 1944] 17 p. Port.
OrP OrSaW OrU 4872

In memoriam: Frantz Hunt Coe; addresses delivered at the memorial services held under the auspices of King County Medical Society, July 22, 1904 at the First Presbyterian Church, Seattle, Washington. [Seattle? 1904?] 45 p. front. (port.)
WaU 4873

In memoriam: John Harte McGraw; a tribute to his memory embodying addresses delivered at various ceremonies. Seattle, Chamber of Commerce. 1911. 84 p. front., plate, port. CVicAr WaSp 4874

In memoriam, Julia E. Hoffman, 1856-1934. [n.p., 1945] [17] p. illus. Contents: A personal tribute, by W. G. Eliot. — The tree of life, by R. M. Steiner.— The design, by A. B. Crocker and F. G. Crocker.
Or OrP 4875

In memoriam; memorial services under the auspices of the Seattle Chapter, American Red Cross, in honor of those citizens of King and Kitsap Counties who made the supreme sacrifice for their country in the Great World's War. [Seattle, 1919] [8] p. WaU 4876

In memoriam, Mrs. Anna Pentland Brooks. [n.p., 1912?] 15 p. port. WaU 4877

In memoriam, Mrs. Daniel K. Pearsons (Mrs. Marietta Chapin Pearsons). Hindsdale, Ill., Merrill Printing Co. [1906?] [20] p.
WaWW 4878

In memoriam; Mrs. E. R. Phelps. [n.p., n.d.] 25, 4 p. OrHi OrP 4879

In memoriam; Ralph Woods, May 17, 1878-January 17, 1944. [Tacoma?] 1944. 16 p. illus., ports. WaS WaT 4880

In memoriam; Rev. George Atkinson, born May 10, 1819, died Feb. 25, 1889. [n.p.] Atkinson, 1889. 51 p. Many 4881

In memoriam [Stephen J. McCormick] [n.p., 1891] 27 p. port. OrHi 4882

In memoriam; the story of the Second Regiment, Oregon Volunteers in the Philippine wars. Portland, Or., In Memoriam Pub. Co., 1899. 1 v. illus., ports.
OrP WaPS 4883

In memory of Harry Anson Fairchild. [n.p., 1911] 15 p. front. (port.)
WaS WaSp WaU 4884

In memory of John Franklin Boyer, 1824-1897. Walla Walla, Wash., 1897. 18 p.
WaWW 4885

In the service; the great World War honor roll, southwest Washington [Centralia, Wash., F. H. Cole Printing Co., 19—] 216 p. illus., ports. Wa WaU 4886

Indian bazaar. Victoria, B. C., J. J. Hart & Co. [189—] 44 p. Haida Indian legends.
CVicAr 4887

Indian Sentinel.
Chirouse number. Washington, D. C., Bureau of Catholic Indian Missions, 1918. 48 p. illus. (v. 1, no. 7, Jan. 1918).
WaS WaU 4888

Indian War Veterans of the North Pacific Coast.
Memorial to Congress, by the Indian War Veterans of the North Pacific Coast. Salem, Or., Moores Bros., 1886. 15 p.
OrU 4889
Memorial to Congress in reference to the payment of claims and expenses of the Indian wars in Oregon and Washington Territory in 1855-56. Salem, Or., 1895. 18 p. Or 4890
— — — Multnomah Camp No. 2.
Roster, Nov. 15, 1892. Portland, Or., A. A. Anderson Co., 1892. [7] p.
OrHi OrP OrU 4891

Industrial Army news. v. 1, April 20, 1894. Seattle, 1894. [4] p. Pub. by Coxey's Army in Seattle. WaU 4892

Industrial British Columbia; featuring B. C.'s resources. Vancouver, B. C., Canadian Printing and Pub. Co. [1920] 58 p. illus.
CV 4893

Ingersoll, Ernest, 1852-1946, ed.
Alaskan bird-life as depicted by many writers. New York, National Assn. of Audubon Societies, 1914. 72 p. col. front., illus., 6 col. plates.
OrP Wa WaPS WaS WaSp WaU 4894
The crest of the continent; a record of a summer's ramble in the Rocky Mountains and beyond. Chicago, Donnelley, 1885. 344 p. front., illus., fold. map.
Many 4895
Same. 1889 [c1885] 36th ed.
WaSp WaU 4896
Gold fields of the Klondike and the won-

ders of Alaska; a masterly and fascinating description of the newly-discovered gold mines; how they were found; how worked; what fortunes have been made; the extent and richness of the gold fields; how to get there; outfit required; climate; the natives; other vast riches of Alaska; other great gold mines of the world; the great seal fisheries, etc., with an introd. by Hon. Henry W. Elliott. [n.p.] Edgewood Pub. Co. [c1897] 512 p. front., plates.
CVicAr CVU WaS WaSp WaU **4897**

Same. 487 p. Or **4898**

Same. Philadelphia, World Bible House [c1897] 512 p. WaU **4899**

Golden Alaska; a complete account to date of the Yukon Valley; its history, geography, mineral and other resources, opportunities and means of access. [Chicago] Rand McNally, c1897. 149 p. illus., plates, maps. Or WaSp **4900**

Same. 278 p. CV CVicAr CVU **4901**

Same. 160 p. front., illus., plates, maps (1 fold.) WaS WaU **4902**

In richest Alaska and the gold fields of the Klondike; how they were found, together with a history of this wonderful land from its discovery to the present day and practical information for gold seekers. Chicago, Dominion Co. [1897] 512 p. front., plates, fold. map.
WaPS WaU **4903**

Knocking around the Rockies. New York, Harper, 1883. viii, 220 p. front., illus., plates. WaS WaU **4904**

Ingham, Clara Cogswell.
Girl of the Oregon wood. [Portland, Or., Dunham's, c1946] 159 p. illus. Or OrCS **4905**

Ingham, Ernest Graham.
Sketches in western Canada, by Bishop Ingham & Rev. C. L. Burrows. London, Hodder [1913] 151 p. front., 14 plates.
CV CVU **4906**

Ingham, George Thomas, 1851-
Digging gold among the Rockies; or, Exciting adventures of wild camp life in Leadville, Black Hills and the Gunnison country; giving a graphic history of the various discoveries of gold and silver in the United States, the development and extent of our mining industries. Philadelphia, Hubbard Bros. [1880] 508 p. front., plates. OrP Wa **4907**

Same. [1882] MtU **4908**

Ingraham, Prentiss, see no. 6488.

Ingstad, Helge Marcus, 1899-
Land of feast and famine. London, Gollancz, 1933. 352 p. front., illus., plates, ports., music. Hunting in Northwestern Canada. WaSp **4909**

Same. New York, Knopf, 1933. Many **4910**

Inkslinger, John Rogers, see no. 834.

Inkyo, pseud.
The reflections of Inkyo on the great company. London, London General Press, 1931. 207 p. Hudson's Bay Company financial history. CVU OrP **4911**

Inland Automobile Association.
Inland automobile road guide. Spokane, Northwest Guide Book Co. [n.d.] 60 p. illus., maps. WaPS **4912**

Inland Catholic.
Centenary and silver jubilee souvenir book for Spokane and the Inland Empire; 1838-1913-1938. [Spokane] 1938. 61 p. (Dec. 1938) WaSp **4913**

Inland Empire Council of Teachers of English.
Northwest books; report of the Committee on Books of the Inland Empire Council of Teachers of English, August, 1933. Missoula, Mont., H. G. Merriam [1933?] viii, 69 p. Many **4914**

Same. 1942; review of over 1100 books, selected magazine bibliography. Portland, Or., Binfords & Mort [1942] 356 p.
Many **4915**

Recommended course in literature for the four years of high school, prepared by the Secondary School Committee of the Inland Empire Council of the Teachers of English, April 1, 1921. [n.p., 1921] [19] p. WaPS **4916**

Inland Empire Development League, Spokane, Wash.
A farm for you. [Spokane? 191—?] 38 p. photos., map. WaPS **4917**

Inland Empire Education Association.
Student mortality in a secondary and higher schools of the Inland Empire; report of a committee appointed by the Inland Empire Education Association and the Northwest Association of Secondary and Higher Schools. [n.p.] Apr. 1, 1925. 15 p. tables, diagrs. WaPS **4918**

Inland Empire Hotel Association.
Old Oregon trail; Omaha, Cheyenne, Pocatello, Boise, Portland information. [n.p., n.d.] 13 p. illus., map, mileage table.
OrP WaT **4919**

Inland Empire Industrial Research, Inc.
Power utilization as an aid to full employment in the Pacific Northwest; a research study. [n.p.,] 1945. 7 p. fold. map, tables, diagrs. WaS **4920**

[Inland Empire Waterways Association]
Brief, containing fundamental facts pertinent to the welfare of the Inland Empire of the Pacific Northwest, May 15, 1935. [n.p., n.d.] 1 v. illus. WaSp **4921**

The Inland Sentinel, Kamloops, B. C.
1880-1905, the land of heart's desire, the Inland Sentinel, quarter century commemorative number. Kamloops, B. C., 1905. 71 [10] p. illus., ports.
CV CVicAr **4922**

Inman, Clifton L.
Whisperings from ancient Oregana. Boston, Chapman & Grimes [c1944] 174 p. Epic poem. Or OrP OrU **4923**

Inman, Henry, 1837-1899.
The Great Salt Lake Trail, by Colonel Henry Inman and Colonel William F. Cody. New York, Macmillan, 1898. xiii, 529 p. front. (2 ports.) illus., 7 plates, fold. map. Many **4924**

Same. Topeka, Kan., Crane & Co., 1899.
Many **4925**

Same. 1914. MtHi Or Wa WaSp WaU   **4926**

Inner Harbour Association of Victoria.
The harbour and city of Victoria. [Victoria, B. C., Victoria Printing & Pub. Co., 1917] 54 p. illus.   CVicAr   **4927**

Innes, H.A., see no. 1540.

Innes, John.
"The epic of Western Canada". [Vancouver, B. C., Gehrke's] 1928. 15 p.
CVicAr   **4928**

"From trail to rail", the epic of transportation told in twenty-one oil paintings. [Vancouver, B. C.? Gehrke's, 1930] 19 p.
CVicAr   **4929**

Innis, Harold Adams, 1894-
The fur trade in Canada; an introduction to Canadian economic history, with a preface by R. M. MacIver. New Haven, Yale Univ. Press, 1930. 444 p. plates, map.
Many   **4930**

The fur-trade of Canada. Toronto, Univ. of Toronto Library, 1927. 172 p. plates. (Univ. of Toronto studies; history and economics, v. 1, no. 1).   Many   **4931**

A history of the Canadian Pacific Railway. London, P. S. King & Son, 1923. viii, 365 p.
CVicAr CVU MtU OrP WaSp WaU   **4932**

Peter Pond, fur trader and adventurer. Toronto, Irwin & Gordon, 1930. xi, 153 p. fold. map.   Many   **4933**

See also no. 3151.

Innokentii, Metopolitan of Moscow, 1797-1879.
Zamiechaniia o koloshenskom i kad'iakskom iazykakh i otchasti o prochikh Rossiisko-Amerikanskikh s prisovokupleniem Rosiiskokoloshenskago slovaria, soderzhashchago boliee 1000 slov, iz koikh na niekotoryia sdielany poiasneniia, Sostavil Ivan Venieminov. Sanktpeterburg, Tipografiia Imperatorskaia akademiia nauk, 1846. 81 p. fold. table.
WaU   **4934**

Zapisko ob ostrovakh unalashkinskago otdiela, sostavlennyia I. Veniaminovym, izdano izhdiveniem Rossiisko-Ameriknaskoi kompanii.   Sankt - Peterburg [Rossiiskaia Akademiia] 1840, 3 v. tables (part fold.)   WaU   **4935**

Institute of Pacific Relations. 2d Conference, Honolulu, 1927.
Problems of the Pacific; proceedings of the 2d Conference of the Institute of Pacific Relations, Honolulu, Hawaii, July 15 to 29, 1927, ed. by J. B. Condliffe. Chicago, Univ. of Chicago Press [1928] xiii, 630 p. fold. front., fold. maps. diagrs. (part fold.)   Many   **4936**

Institute of World Affairs. Summer session, Seattle, 1928.
The Pacific area; addresses, conference papers and round table reports of the Northwest session of the Institute of International Relations, University of Washington, Seattle, July 22-27, 1928, ed. by Charles E. Martin and K. C. Leebrick. Seattle, Univ. of Wash. Press, 1929. xiii, 405 p. front. (port.) (Proceedings, v. 3)
WaSp WaT WaU   **4937**

Intelligence, pub.
Oregon, Idaho, Washington, Montana di-rectory of the superintendents and principals of public schools, 1900-1901. Oak Park (Chicago) [1901] 47 p. WaU   **4938**

An interesting account of the voyages and travels of Captains Lewis and Clark, in the years 1804, 1805, and 1806; giving a faithful description of the River Missouri and its source, of the various tribes of Indians through which they passed, manners and customs, soil, climate, commerce, gold and silver mines, animal and vegetable productions; to which is added a complete dictionary of the Indian tongue, by William Fisher, esq. Baltimore. Printed by Anthony Miltenberger for the purchasers, 1812. 326 p. double front. (2 ports.) A spurious ed.
MtU OrP OrSaW WaSp WaU   **4939**

Interesting particulars of the loss of the Admiral Gardner & Brittannia outward bound Indiamen and of the Apollo, wrecked on the Goodwins, January 24, 1809; also the loss of the Russian ship St. Peter. London, Printed for Tegg [n. d.] 28 p. front.   CVicAr   **4940**

Intermountain Institute, Weiser, Idaho.
Account of its founding, its progress and prospects. [n.p., n.d.] 15 p. illus., port.
OrHi   **4941**

Intermountain Playground, Inc.
Tourists & homeseekers guide. 2d ed. [Spokane? 192—?] [35] p. illus.   WAP   **4942**

International Apple Shippers' Association.
27th annual convention; souvenir program, held in the city of Seattle, Washington, July 24 to 28, 1922. [Seattle, 1922] 64 p.
WaU   **4943**

International Association of Chiefs of Police. Traffic Division.
Report of a follow-up study of the Portland, Oregon, Police Department Traffic Division, submitted by Franklin M. Kreml. [n.p., 1947] 147 p.   OrP   **4944**

International Coast Seamen and Sealers' Union of British Columbia.
Constitution and by-laws. Victoria, B. C., Waterson, 1892. 48 p.   CVicAr   **4945**

International Harvester Company of New Jersey. Agricultural Extension Department.
Getting a start with alfalfa in the Inland Empire. Chicago [1913?] 17 p. illus.
WaPS   **4946**

International Irrigation Congress, 8th. Missoula, Mont., 1899.
Historic and scenic Missouri and Ravalli Counties, Montana; the Missoulian souvenir of the National Irrigation Congress, comp. by Wagner and Sevigne. [Missoula, Mont., Missoulian, 1900?] 97 p.   MtU   **4947**

International Longshoremen's Association. Local 38-79.
The maritime crisis; what it is and what it isn't. 2d ed. San Francisco [1936?] [22] p. illus.   WaU   **4948**

International Order of Good Templars. Oregon and Washington (Ter.) Grand Lodge.
Proceedings of the 4th annual session of the Grand Lodge, I. O. G. T., of Oregon and Washington Territory, held in Al-

bany, Oregon, Sept. 1st, 2d, 3d, and 4th, 1868. Corvallis, Or., Bro. W. B. Carter, 1868. 40, 28 p. OrU **4949**

— — — Washington (State) Grand Lodge. Constitutions of the Grand Lodge, District Lodge, and Subordinate Lodge of the International Order of Good Templars; and by-laws of the Grand and Subordinate lodges, with amendments to July 1, 1905. Seattle, 1904-1905. 86 p. WaPS **4950**

International Typographical Union.
Official souvenir, 85th convention, Vancouver, August 16th to 23d, 1941. [Vancouver, B. C., Sun Pub. Co.] 1941. 1 v. illus., ports. CVicAr **4951**

Interstate Committee on High School-College Relations. (Or.-Wash.)
Mapping your education; a guide to planned education; a cooperative project, prepared under the editorial direction of the co-chairmen: Merle S. Kuder and Douglas V. McClane. Portland, Or., James, Kerns & Abbott Co. [1947] ix, 210 p. illus.
Or OrCS OrP OrSaW WaS **4952**

Interstate Fair Association.
Prospectus; 1894 Northwest Inter-State Fair opens Aug. 15, closes Nov. 1, Tacoma, Wash. Tacoma [1893] 14 p. illus. WaT **4953**

Inverarity, Robert Bruce, 1909-
Movable masks and figures of the North Pacific Coast Indians, with an introd. by Erna Gunther. [Bloomfield Hills, Mich.] Cranbrook Institute of Science, 1941. [4] p. 18 col. plates.
CV CVicAr OrCS OrP WaS WaU **4954**

Northwest Coast Indian art, a brief survey. [Seattle] Wash. State Museum, Univ. of Wash., 1946. [36] p. illus. (Museum series no. 1) Many **4955**

Ireland, DeWitt Clinton, 1836-
Astorian; pamphlet containing information for the public concerning the resources of Oregon. Astoria, Or., 1877. 16 p. illus., tables. OrHi **4956**

Oregon's sea-port Astoria. Astoria, Or., 1875. 24 p. OrHi **4957**

Iron Mountain Tunnel Company.
Prospectus of the Iron Mountain Tunnel Company, Missoula, Montana. Butte, Mont., McKee Printing Co., 1905. 46 p. illus. MtHi **4958**

Irvine, Albert.
How the Makah obtained possession of Cape Flattery, told to Albert Irvine, trans. by Luke Markistun. New York, Museum of the American Indian, Heye Foundation, 1921. 11 p. (Indian notes and monographs) Many **4959**

Irving, Washington, 1783-1859.
The adventures of Captain Bonneville. Chicago, Belford, Clarke & Co. [n.d.] 300 p.
Or Wa **4960**

Same. Chicago, Donohue Bros. [n.d.] 297 p. IdP **4961**

Same. New York, Co-op Pub. Society [n.d.] 358 p. IdIf **4962**

Same. New York, Crowell [n.d.] 292 p.
OrSa OrSaW WaPS **4963**

Same. [New York, Putnam, n.d.] 2 v. fronts, plates, ports. (Pocantico ed.)
OrCS **4964**

Same. Paris, Baudry, 1837. (Collection of ancient and modern British authors, v. 193). OrP **4965**

Same. New York, Crowell [1843] 291 p. IdU **4966**

Same. New York, Putnam [1843] (Handy volume ed.) OrP **4967**

Same. 1860. 428 p.
CVU MtHi OrU WaSp WaWW **4968**

Same. c1865. 459 p. Many **4969**
Same. c1868. 524 p. Many **4970**

Same. 1881. 428 p.
CVU MtHi OrU WaSp WaWW **4971**

Same. 1883.
CVU MtHi OrU WaSp WaWW **4972**

Same. New York, Millar, 1884. 300 p.
CVicAr **4973**

Same. New York, Alden, 1887.
WaA WaWW **4974**

Same. Philadelphia, Univ. Library Assn. [189-?] 524 p. front. (Connoisseur ed.)
CVU **4975**

Same. [New York, Putnam, 1895] 2 v. fronts., ports., plates, maps (Holly ed.)
OrCS OrPR **4976**

Same. New York, Collier, 1897. 358 p.
Wa **4977**

Adventures of Captain Bonneville; or, Scenes beyond the Rocky Mountains of the far West. London, R. Bentley, 1837. 3 v. in 1. CVicAr CVU OrCS **4978**

Same. Paris, A. and W. Galignani, 1837. 303 p. WaU **4979**

Same, New York, Putnam [c1865] 3 v.
WaTC **4980**

Same. [c1868] 698 p. (Author's rev. ed.)
WaTC **4981**

The adventures of Captain Bonneville, U. S. A., in the Rocky Mountains and the far West, digested from his journal and illus. from various other sources. The author's rev. ed. New York, Putnam [n. d.] 524 p. (Student's ed.)
IdIf IdU IdUSB **4982**

Same. 1849. 428 p. front. (fold. map) (New ed. rev., v. 10)
IdIf WaPS WaSp WaU **4983**

Same. 1851.
MtHi **4984**

Same. London, Bohn, 1859. 280 p.
CVicAr **4985**

Same. New York, Putnam, 1864. 428 p. 2 plates. (Author's rev. ed. New ed., rev., v. 10). WaE **4986**

Same. [1865] 524 p. front. (Kinderhook ed., v. 6) WaU WaW **4987**

Same. 1868. 503 p. WaWW **4988**

Same. People's ed.
IdB MtU WaU WaWW **4989**

Same. 524 p.
Or OrP WaS WaT **4990**

Same. 1898. 2 v. front., plates, fold. map. (Pawnee ed.) WaSp WaU **4991**

Astoria; oder Die Unternehmung jenseit

des Felsengebirges, aus den Englischen von A. von Treskow. Quedlinburg, G. Basse, 1837. 2 v. in 1.   WaU 4992

Astoria; oder, Geschichte einer Handelsexpedition jenseits der Rocky Mountains, aus dem Englischen. Stuttgart, Verlag der J. G. Cotta'schen Buchhandlung, 1838. xviii, 390 p. (Reisen und Landerbeschreigungen der alteren und nuesten Zeit hrsg. von Dr. Eduard Widenmann und Dr. Hermann Hauff 14. Lieferung)   WaU 4993

Astoria of avontuurlyke reise naar en over het klipgebergte van Noord-Amerika, ondernomen in het belang der door den Heer J. J. Astor opgerigte peltery compagnie naar het Engelsch. Haarlem, W. A. Loosjes, 1837. 2 v.   WaU 4994

Astoria. London, Chesterfield Society [n.d.] 376 p. (Ed. de luxe). WaSp 4995

Same. New York, Burt [n.d.] 387 p   MtBozC 4996

Same. New York, Collier [n.d.] 2 v.   WaSp 4997

Same. New York, Crowell [n.d] 488 p.   OrWaSp 4998

Same. New York, Kelmscott Society [n.d.] 376 p. front. (port.)   CVic IdP 4999

Same. New York, Putnam [n.d.] xix, 389 p. front. (Handy volume ed.)   CVic IdU OrCS OrPR Wa WaT 5000

Same. 2 v. in 1.   OrPR Wa WaT 5001

Same. 698 p. (Hudson ed.)   Or Wa WaS 5002

Same. (Kinderhook ed., v. 7).   OrSaw WaSp 5003

Same. 2 v. (Pocantico ed.)   OrCS 5004

Same. (Student's ed.)   Or 5005

Same. New York, Putnam, c1849. (Stuyvesant ed.)   OrU 5006

Same. (Spuyten Duyvil ed.)   IdB 5007

Same. London, Routledge, 1851.   WaSp 5008

Same. Philadelphia, Univ. Library Assn. [1851] 698 p. front. (Connoisseur ed.)   CVU WaS WaSp WaU 5009

Same. New ed. rev. New York, Putnam, 1855. 519 p. (Works, v. 8)   CVicAr Or 5010

Same. London, Bohn, 1861. 340 p. front. (Works, v. 8)   CVicAr 5011

Same. New York, Alden, 1887. 649 p.   WaA WaPS WaSp WaWW 5012

Same. Philadelphia, Univ. Library Assn. [189?] 698 p. front. (Connoisseur ed.)   CVU 5013

Same. [New York, Putnam, 1895] 2 v. fronts., ports., plates, maps. (Holly ed.)   OrCS OrPR WaSp 5014

Same. New York, Collier, 1897. 464 p.   Wa 5015

Same. 545 p. illus. (Works, v. 8)   WaT 5016

Same. [n.d.] Sproul, 1899.   IdB 5017

Same. New York, Collier, 1904.   IdUSB 5018

Same. London, Bell, 1906. (Bohn's standard library).   WaSp 5019

Astoria; or, Anecdotes of an enterprise beyond the Rocky Mountains. Chicago, Belford, Clarke & Co. [n.d.] 2 v. in 1.   Or 5020

Same. Chicago, Donohue Bros. [n.d.] 387 p.   IdP WaW 5021

Same. New York, Crowell [n.d.] 376 p.   OrSaW WaPS WaSp WaT WaU 5022

Same. Philadelphia, Carey, Lea & Blanchard, 1836. 2 v. front. (fold. map).   Many 5023

Same. 1841.   WaSp 5024

Same. New York, Putnam, 1849. viii, 519 p.   WaSp WaU 5025

Same. Author's rev. ed. London, Bohn, 1850. xii, 340 p. front. (port.)   CVicAr 5026

Same. New York, Putnam, 1863. 519 p. front. (Works, new ed., rev., v. 8)   WaE 5027

Same. [c1868] (Hudson ed.)   IdB 5028

Same. [1868?] Author's rev. ed. 698 p. (Standard library ed.)   Many 5029

Same. 1881, 649 p.   WaWW 5030

Same. New York, Millar, 1884. 387 p.   CVicAr 5031

Same. New York, Putnam, 1893. Rev ed. (Hudson ed.)   OrSa 5032

Same. 1897, 2 v. front., plates. (Tacoma ed.)   CV OrU WaSp WaT WaU 5033

Astoria; or, Enterprise beyond the Rocky Mountains. London, Bentley, 1836. 3 v.   WaSp 5034

Same. 3 v. in 1.   CVicAr CVU WaU 5035

Paris, Baudry, 1836. 336 p. (Collection of ancient and modern British authors. v. 146).   CVU MtHi WaSp WaU 5036

Same. Paris, A. and W. Galignani, 1836. 336 p.   WaU 5037

Same. London, Bentley, 1839. viii, 440 p. front. (port.)   CVicAr 5038

Captain Bonneville. New York, Putnam [n.d.] [xxix] 389 p. (Handy volume ed.)   IdU OrPR WaT WaTC 5039

Same. [n.p.] Sproul, 1899.   IdB 5040

Captain Bonneville, or Enterprise beyond the Rocky Mountains; a sequel to "Astoria". 2d ed. London, Bentley, 1837. 3 v.   WaSp 5041

The Crayon miscellany. Author's rev. ed. [New York, Putnam, 1865] 459 p.   WaU 5042

The fur traders of the Columbia River and the Rocky Mountains, as described by Washington Irving in his account of "Astoria" and the record of "The adventures of Captain Bonneville". with some additions by the editor [Frank Lincoln Olmstead] New York, Putnam, c1903. xvii, 222 p. front., 8 plates. (Knickerbocker literature series, 3) Many 5043

Same. 1908. [c1903]   WaU 5044

Eine Reise auf den Prairien, aus dem Englischen. Frankfurt, D. Sauerlander, 1835. 256 p. front. (port.) (Washington

Irving's sammtliche Werke 48. bis 50. Bd.) WaU **5045**

The Rocky Mountains; or, Scenes, incidents and adventures in the far West; digested from the journal of Capt. B. L. E. Bonneville, and illus. from various other sources. Philadelphia, Carey, Lea & Blanchard, 1837. 2 v. illus. Many **5046**

Same. 1843. WaSp **5047**

Un tour dans les prairies a l'Ouest des Etats-Unis, tr. de l'anglais de Washington Irving par Ernest W. Nouv. ed. Tours, A. Mame et fils, 1872. 239 p. front., plates. (Bibliotheque de la jeunesse chretienne, 3. ser.). WaU **5048**

Tour on the prairies, by the author of "The sketchbook". London, Murray, 1835. xiii, 335 p. CVicAr WaSp **5049**

Same. London, Bohn, 1850. v, 137 p. CVicAr **5050**

Same. 1862. CVicAr **5051**

Same. New York, Millar, 1884. CVicAr **5052**

Voyages dans les contrees desertes de l' Amerique du Nord, entrepris pour la fondation du comptoir d' Astoria sur la cote nord-ouest. Paris, P. Dufart, 1839. 2 v. WaU **5053**

Voyages et aventures du captaine Bonneville a l'ouest des Etats-Unis d'Amerique, au dela des Montagnes Roucheuses, tr. de l'anglais par Benjamine Laroche. Paris, Charpentier, 1837. 2 v. WaU **5054**

The western journals of Washington Irving, ed. and annotated by John Francis McDermott. Norman, Okla., Univ. of Okla. Press, 1944. xiii, 201 p. illus., plates, port., fold. map. (American exploration and travel, no. 8). Many **5055**

Irwin, David, see no. 7501.

Irwin, Frederick.
The potlatch bug; a ragtime song of the golden potlatch, Seattle golden potlatch, July 15-20, 1912. Seattle, Empire Music Pub. Co. [c1912] [5] p. illus. WaPS **5056**

Irwin, Leonard Bertram, 1904-
Pacific railways and nationalism in the Canadian-American Northwest, 1845-1873. Philadelphia, [Univ. of Pa. Press] 1939. xii, 246 p. Many **5057**

Irwin, Violet, see nos. 9853, 9854.

Is lese majeste a crime in America? Should men be jailed for free speech? For making these speeches advocating the impeachment of Federal Judge C. H. Hanford, the speakers were arrested. [Seattle] Metropolitan [1911?] 32 p. Or WaS WaU **5058**

Isaacs, Edith J. R., see no. 2877.

Isbell, F. A.
Mining & hunting in the Far West, 1852-1870, with an introd. by Nathan P. Wreden. Burlingame, Calif., 1948. 36 p. front. (port.) WaU **5059**

Isbister, Alexander Kennedy, 1822-1883.
A proposal for a new penal settlement in connexion with the colonization of the uninhabited districts of British North America. London, Saunders, 1850. 22 p. CVicAr WaSp **5060**

Isely, Bliss, 1881-
Blazing the way west. New York, Scribner, 1939. xiv, 286 p. front., illus., plates, ports., maps. Many **5061**

Island County; a world beater. Everett, Wash., F. B. Hawes Co. [n.d.] 46 p. illus. WaS **5062**

Island County Farm Bureau News.
Deception Pass Bridge. Oak Harbor, Wash., 1935. 8, 4, 8 p. illus., port., map (v. 24, no. 36, July 25, 1935) OrHi WaS WaU **5063**

The Island Lantern.
The prison without walls, which is the story of the United States penitentiary at McNeil Island in the state of Washington, 1871-1931. [McNeil Island, Wash.] 1931. 12 p. WaS **5064**

Island Wappato.
Island Wappato [special historical number] Sauvies Island, Or., 1938. 4 p. illus., ports. (v. 1, no. 4, Feb. 1938). WaU **5065**

Island Farmers' Institute of British Columbia.
Saltspring Island, British Columbia. [Victoria, B. C.] British Colonist, 1902. [16] p. illus., fold. map. CVicAr **5066**

Isle, Joseph Nicholas de l', see nos. 5868, 5976.

It's the water. [Soap Lake, Wash.? n.d.] [8] p. illus. WaU **5067**

Ivins, Edward Gordon.
This way out. New York, Avondale Press [c1927] ix, 114 p. front. (port.) Story and Poems of "the Old West". MtHi MtU WaU **5068**

J., P. R., see no. 4172.

J. W. of Bayswater.
Perils, pastimes, and pleasures of an emigrant in Australia, Vancouver's Island, and California. London, T. C. Newby, 1849. 404 p. CVicAr **5069**

Jackson, Charles H.
Digest of the sworn testimony in the Reed Smoot investigation before the United States Senate committee in March, April, and May, 1904; democratic state platform relating to polygamy and church domination; we appeal to the public spirited citizens of Idaho to read this evidence and to vote to save Idaho from such shame. [n.p., 1904?] 37 p. IdB **5070**

Jackson, Charles Ross, 1867-1915.
The sheriff of Wasco, illus. by Louis F. Grant. New York, G. W. Dillingham Co. [1907] 318 p. front., 3 plates. Or OrP WaU **5071**

Jackson, Clarence S., see no. 5079.

Jackson, J. A.
Bella Bella transformed. [Toronto, Woman's Missionary Society of the Methodist Church, n. d.] 12 p. (Our work, no. 1). CVicAr **5072**

[Jackson, James] comp.
Basketry of the coast and islands of the Pacific, etc., exhibited April 1896, at the Portland library. Portland, Or., J. K. Gill [n.d.] 31 p.　　OrHi OrP OrU **5073**

Jackson, Joseph Henry, see no. 6103.

[Jackson, Joseph Sylvester]
What to tell them; a booklet designed to be of special service to counselors, guidance workers and agencies with reference to negro girls and boys in Seattle; and for the use of students themselves. Seattle, Seattle Urban League, 1938. 34 p. (Publication no. 1).
　　WaU **5074**

Jackson, Sheldon, 1834-1909.
Alaska, and missions on the North Pacific Coast. New York, Dodd [c1880] 327 p. front. (port.) illus., plates, ports., fold. map.　　Many **5075**

Same. 400 p.　　Many **5076**

Facts about Alaska. New York, Woman's Executive Committee of Home Missions of the Presbyterian Church [1894] 22 p. illus.　　CVicAr MtHi **5077**

Same. [1902?] 29 p.　　WaU **5078**

Jackson, William Henry, 1843-1942.
Picture making of the old West, William H. Jackson; text by Clarence S. Jackson. New York, Scribner, 1947. x, 308 p. illus., ports., map.　　Many **5079**

Jackson County, Or. Immigration Board.
Jackson County, Oregon; being a brief description of its geography, topography, climate, soil and resources, its rivers, valleys, towns and public building, together with a succinct view of its varied industries and business opportunities in agriculture, horticulture, mining, manufacturing, stock raising, and the facilities for acquiring a pleasant home. [Ashland, Or., Ashland Tidings Press, 1885] 16 p.　　Or OrP WaU **5080**

Jacob, John G.
The life and times of Patrick Gass, now sole survivor of the overland expedition to the Pacific under Lewis and Clark, in 1804-5-6; also a soldier in the war with Great Britain from 1812 to 1815, and a participant in the battle of Lundy's Lane; together with Gass' journal of the expedition condensed; and sketches of some events occuring during the last century in the upper Ohio country, biographies, reminiscences, etc. Wellsburg, Va., Jacob & Smith, 1859. 280 p. front., illus., 3 plates. Many **5081**

Jacobin, Louis, 1889-
Lou Jacobin's tourists' & sportsmen's guide to Alaska and the Yukon. 2d ed. [Juneau, Alaska Tourist Guide Co., c1947] 210 p. illus. (part col.) maps. WaU **5082**

Lou Jacobin's tourists' & sportsmen's pictorial guide to Alaska; authentic information on where to go, how to go, what to expect. [Juneau, Alaska Tourist Guide Co., c1946] 208 p. illus. (part col.) ports., maps.　　WaE WaS WaT **5083**

With the colors, from Whatcom, Skagit and San Juan Counties; an honor roll containing a pictorial record of the gallant and courageous men from northwestern Washington, U. S. A., who served in the World War, 1917-1918-1919. Seattle, Peters Pub. Co., 1921. 302 p. illus., ports., maps.
　　WaPS WaS WaU **5084**

Jacobs, Emma Atkins, 1885-
Trailer trio, illus. by Pelagie Doane. Philadelphia, Winston [1942] 280 p. col. front., illus.　　Many **5085**

Vicki's mysterious friend, illus. by Jean MacLaughlin. Philadelphia, Winston [c1947] xi, 210 p. illus. Wash. State setting.　　OrP WaS WaSp WaU **5086**

Jacobs, George P.
Early history of St. Andrew's Episcopal Church, Tacoma, Washington, 1890-1922; written at the request of St. Andrew's vestry. [Tacoma, St. Andrew's Episcopal Church, 1922] 1 v.　　WaT **5087**

Jacobs, Joseph, 1854-1916.
Concerning state development. Seattle, Ivy Press, 1922. 13 p. tables. WaPS **5088**

Jacobs, Melville, 1902-
Coos narrative and ethnologic texts. Seattle, Univ. of Wash. Press, 1939. 125 p. (Publications in anthropology, v. 8, no. 1, Apr. 1939).
　　OrP WaE WaSp WaTC WaU **5089**

Kalapuya texts: Pt. 1. Santiam Kalapuya ethnologic texts, by M. Jacobs. Pt. 2. Santiam Kalapuya myth texts, by M. Jacobs. Pt. 3. Kalapuya texts, by Albert S. Gatschet, Leo J. Frachtenberg, and M. Jacobs. Seattle, Univ. of Wash. Press, 1945. 394 p. map. (Publications in anthropology, v. 11, June 1945).
　　OrU WaS WaSp WaTC WaU **5090**

Northwest Sahaptin texts. New York, Columbia Univ. Press, 1934-1937. 2 v. (Contributions to anthropology, v. 19, pt. 1 and 2).　　Many **5091**

Texts in Chinook jargon. Seattle, Univ. of Wash. Press, 1936. vii, 27 p. (Publications in anthropology, v. 7, no. 1).
　　Many **5092**

Jacobs, Melvin Clay, 1885-
Winning Oregon; a study of an expansionist movement. Caldwell, Idaho, Caxton, 1938. 261 p.　　Many **5093**

Jacobs, Orange, 1827-1914.
An argument made before the Committee on Territories in favor of an "Enabling act" for the admission of the territory of Washington into the Union as a State. Washington, D. C., National Republican Printing House, 1878. 15 p.　　WaU **5094**

Memoirs of Orange Jacobs, written by himself; containing many interesting, amusing, and instructive incidents of a life of eighty years or more, fifty-six years of which were spent in Oregon and Washington. Seattle, Lowman & Hanford, 1908. 234 p. front. (port.)
　　Many **5095**

Jacobs, Peter.
Journal of the Rev. Peter Jacobs, Indian Wesleyan missionary, from Rice Lake to Hudson's Bay territory and returning, commencing May 1852; with a brief

account of his life and a short history of the Wesleyan Mission in that country. 2d ed. Boston, Rand, 1853. 55 p. front. (ports.) CVicAr 5096

Same. New York, 1857. 96 p.
CVicAr 5097

Jacobsen, Johan Adrian, 1853-
Capitain Jacobsen's Reise an der Nordwestkuste Amerikas, 1881-1883, zum Zwecke ethnologischer Sammlungen und Erkundigungen, nebst beschreibung personlicher erlebnisse, fur den deutschen Lesekreis bearbeitet, von A. Woldt. Leipzig, M. Spohr, 1884. viii, 431 p. illus., 3 maps (1 fold.)
CV CVicAr OrU WaS WaU 5098

Unter den Alaska-Eskimos. Berlin, Ullstein [n.d.] 155 p. maps. CVicAr 5099

Unter Indianern und Eskimos. Berlin, Hillger [n.d.] 32 p. CVicAr 5100

James, Bushrod Washington, 1863-1903.
Alaska; its neglected past, its brilliant future. Philadelphia, Sunshine Pub. Co., 1897. 444 p. front., 32 plates, 16 maps, tables. Many 5101

Alaskana; or, Alaska in descriptive and legendary poems. Philadelphia, Porter, 1892. 368 p. front., 15 plates.
CV CVicAr CVU WaS WaSp WaU 5102

Same. 2d ed. 1893. 402 p. front., 17 plates.
Wa WaSp WaWW 5103

Same. 3d ed. 1894. iv, 410 p.
Wa WaS 5104

James, George Wharton, see nos. 619, 1814.

James, James Alton, 1864-
The first scientific exploration of Russian America and the purchase of Alaska. Evanston, Ill., Northwestern Univ., 1942. xii, 276 p. plates, ports., double map. (Studies in the social sciences, no. 4).
Many 5105

James, Sister Mary.
Providence; a sketch of the Sisters of Charity of Providence in the Northwest, 1856-1931. [Seattle, Sisters of Charity of Providence, c1931] ix, 88 p. front., plates, ports. WaE WaS WaU 5106

James, Thomas, 1782-1847.
Three years among the Indians and Mexicans, ed. with notes and biographical sketches, by Walter B. Douglas. St. Louis, Mo. Historical Society, 1916. 316 p. front. (port.) 11 ports., map.
Many 5107

James, Will, 1892-1942.
All in a day's riding, illus. by the author. New York, Scribner, 1933. xiv, 251 p. illus.
IdB MtHi Or WaE WaS WaTC 5108

Same. Yonkers-on-Hudson, N. Y., World Book Co. [c1933] OrP 5109

Same. New York, Scribner, 1943 [c1933]
WaU 5110

The American cowboy, illus. by the author. New York, Scribner, 1942. 273 p. illus., plates. CV IdB Or OrU WaS WaT 5111

Big-enough, illus. by the author. New York, Scribner, 1931. 314 p. front. (port.) illus., plates.
MtU Or OrCS OrU WaE WaS 5112

Same. 1932. OrU 5113

Same. 1944 [c1931] WaU 5114

Same. Yonkers-on-Hudson, N. Y., World Book Co., 1946. MtHi 5115

Cow country, illus. by the author. New York, Grosset, [c1927] xii, 242 p. front., illus., plates. WaSp 5116

Same. New York, Scribner, 1927.
Many 5117

Same. 1931. WaW 5118

Same. 1938. OrMonO 5119

Cowboy in the making, arranged from the first chapters of "Lone cowboy", illus. by the author. New York, Scribner, 1937. 91 p. col. front., illus., plates (part col.)
Or OrP WaS WaSp WaT WaU 5120

Cowboys north and south, illus. by the author. New York, Scribner, 1924. xvii, 217 p. front., illus., plates.
MtU Or OrP WaA WaS WaU 5121

Same. 1926. MtHi 5122

Same. [c1928] WaE 5123

Same. 1931. WaSp 5124

Same. 1936. WaW 5125

Same. 1944 [c1924] IdU 5126

The dark horse. New York, Grosset, c1939. 277 p. illus. MtHi 5127

Same. Los Angeles, Braille Institute of America, 1940. 2 v. OrP 5128

Same. New York, Scribner, 1945 [c1939] xii, 306 p. col. front., illus., plates.
Many 5129

The drifting cowboy, illus. by the author. New York, Scribner [1925] xii, 241 p. illus., plates.
MtU Or OrP WaE WaS 5130

Same. 1945 [c1925] WaU 5131

Flint Spears, cowboy rodeo contestant, illus. with drawings by the author and photographs. New York, Scribner, 1938. 269 p. col. front., illus., plates.
Many 5132

Same. Yonkers-on-Hudson, N. Y., World Book Co., 1938. Or 5133

Same. 1946. MtHi MtUM 5134

Same. Los Angeles, Braille Institute of America, 1939. 2 v. OrP 5135

Home ranch, illus. by the author. New York, Scribner, 1935. xvii, 346 p. front., illus. Many 5136

Same. 1944 [c1935] WaU 5137

Same. Yonkers-on-Hudson, N.Y., World Book Co., 1946. MtHi 5138

Same. Embossed by the American Brotherhood for the Blind. Washington, D. C., Library of Congress, c1935. 2 v.
OrP 5139

Horses I've known. New York, Scribner, 1940. 280 p. col. front., illus., plates.
IdB Or OrCS OrP WaE WaS 5140

Same. Cleveland, World Pub. Co., 1940.
WaT 5141

Same. [1945, c1940] (Forum Books ed.)
WaU 5142

Same. 1946. MtHi 5143

In the saddle with Uncle Bill, illus. by the author. New York, Scribner, 1935. xiii, 289 p. front., illus., plates.
Or OrLgE OrP WaS 5144

Same. 1944 [c1935] WaU 5145

Lone cowboy; my life story, illus. by the author. New York, Scribner, 1930. x, 431 p. front. (port.) illus., plates. Many 5146

Same. 1932. WaTC 5147

Same. 1935. WaW 5148

Same. 1936. OrU 5149

Look-see with Uncle Bill, illus. by the author. New York, Scribner, 1938. x, 253 p. col. front., illus.
IdB Or Wa WaS WaU 5150

My first horse, illus. by the author. New York, Scribner, 1940. [45] p. col. illus.
Or OrP WaS 5151

Sand. New York, Burt [c1929] x, 328 p. front., illus. WaW 5152

Same. New York, Scribner, 1929.
Many 5153

Same. New York, Blue Ribbon Books, 1929. OrCS 5154

Same. New York, Burt, 1931. OrU 5155

Same. 1932. WaT 5156

Same. New York, Scribner, 1944 [c1929]
WaU 5157

Scorpion; a good bad horse, illus. by the author. New York, Grosset, c1936. 247 p. illus. MtHi 5158

Same. New York, Scribner, 1936.viii, 312 p. col. front., illus., plates.
Or OrP WaE WaS WaT 5159

Same. 1937. Wa WaW 5160

Same. 1945 [c1936] WaU 5161

Smoky, the cowhorse. New York, Scribner, 1926. 310 p. Many 5162

Sun up; tales of the cow camps. New York, Grosset [c1923] 312 p. illus.
CV 5163

Same. c1930. MtHi 5164

Same. c1931. Or WaT 5165

Same. New York, Junior Literary Guild, 1931. OrP 5166

Same. New York, Scribner, 1931.
Or OrCS WaE WaSp 5167

Same. 1932. OrU 5168

Same. 1934 [c1931] 342 p. front., illus.
WaU 5169

The three mustangeers, illus. by the author. New York, Scribner, 1933. xii, 338 p. front., illus., plates.
IdUSB Or OrCS WaE WaSp WaU 5170

Same. 1934. IdU WaS 5171

Same. 1946. MtHi 5172

Uncle Bill; a tale of two kids and a cowboy, illus. by the author. New York, Scribner, 1932. xii, 240 p. front., illus.
MtHi Or WaS 5173

Same. 1936. [c1932] OrLgE Wa WaU 5174

The Will James cowboy book, ed. by Alice Dalgliesh. New York, Scribner [c1938] 158 p. col. front., illus. Or WaU 5175

Young cowboy; arranged from "Big

enough" and "Sun up"; illus. by the author. New York, Scribner, 1935. 72 p., col. front., illus., plates.
Or OrAshS OrLgE WaS WaSp WaW 5176

Same. 1936. OrP 5177

Same. 1944 [c1935] WaU 5178

See also no. 3053.

James Bay Athletic Association.
By-laws and rules. Victoria, B. C., Colonist, 1903. 46 p. CVicAr 5179

[Jamieson, Mrs. R. E.]
The first ten years; a brief history of Shaughnessy Heights United Church up to November 30, 1937 [by Mrs. R. E. Jamieson and W. H. Smith] [Vancouver, B. C.] 1937. 15 p. CVicAr 5180

Jane, Calamity, see no. 1270.

Jane, Cecil.
A spanish voyage to Vancouver and the north-west coast of America; being the narrative of the voyage made in the year 1792 by the schooners Sutil and Mexicana to explore the Strait of Fuca, trans. from the Spanish with an introd. London, Argonaut Press, 1930. xiv, 142 p. front., illus., ports., fold map.
CVic CVicAr OrHi 5181

See also no. 2888.

Jannsen, Newman Carl.
Development of underground sources of water supply. Seattle [1937?] 9 p. illus., diagrs. WaT 5182

Ground water conditions in the state of Washington; a report. Seattle, 1937. 76 p. front., fold map.
Wa WaS WaT WaU 5183

Janvrin, Alice J., see nos. 8667, 8668.

Japan Society of Seattle.
Japanese exclusion issue. [Seattle] 1924. 25 p. WaU 5184

Japanese Association of Tacoma.
Port of Tacoma. Tacoma, 1922. [190] p. illus. WaU 5185

Japanese Association of the Pacific Northwest.
Japanese immigration, an exposition of its real status. Seattle, 1907. 48 p.
WaS WaU 5186

Jarvis, William Henry Pope.
The great gold rush, a tale of the Klondike. Toronto, Macmillan, 1913. xi, 355 p.
CVicAr CVU 5187

Jay, Mrs. Mae (Foster) 1881-
The shell, illus. by Harold Cue. Boston, W. A. Wilde, c1933. 314 p. illus. Seattle setting. WaS 5188

Jay Cee, see no. 9600.

Jeancon, Edwin M.
Souvenir of the Fifth Legislature of the state of Washington, designed and pub. by E. M. Jeancon and F. X. Sauvageot. Tacoma, c1897. [32] p. ports.
Wa WaPS WaS WaT WaU 5189

Jefferson, Thomas, Pres. U. S., 1743-1826.
Captain Meriwether Lewis. [Boston, Old South Assn., 1896] 16 p. (Leaflets. General series, v. 2, no. 4). Many 5190

Jellum, S. P.
Some central Idaho gold districts. Spokane,

Northwest Mining News, 1909. 84 p. illus., maps. WaSp WaU **5191**

Jenkins, Thomas, bp., 1871-
The man of Alaska, Peter Trimble Rowe. New York, Morehouse-Gorham Co., 1943. xvi, 340 p. col. front., plates, ports.
Many **5192**

Jenness, Diamond, 1886-
The people of the twilight, drawings by Claude Johnson. New York, Macmillan, 1928. xii, 247 p. front. (port.) illus., plates, map. Eskimos of Coronation Gulf region of Canada. Many **5193**

Jennings, D.
Manners and customs of the Indians of Simpson District, B. C. [Toronto, Women's Missionary Society of the Methodist Church, n.d.] 15 p. (Our work).
CVicAr **5194**

Jennings, Jack H.
Dregs, illus., Wm. W. Blood. Portland, Or., Binfords & Mort [c1939] 63 p. front., illus. Portland poet.
OrHi OrU WaU **5195**

Jennings, John Edward, 1906-
River of the West; a novel of the Astor adventure. New York, Doubleday, 1948. x, 368 p. Many **5196**

Jennings, Linda Deziah, comp.
Washington women's cook book, pub. by the Washington Equal Suffrage Association. Seattle, Trade Register Print, 1909. 256 p. Wa WaT WaU **5197**

Jenns, Eustace Alvanley.
Evening to morning; and other poems. Victoria, B. C., Hibben, 1880. [33] p.
CVicAr CVU **5198**
Orpheus and Eurydice and other poems. Vancouver, B. C., 1910. 110 p.
CVicAr CVU **5199**

[Jenson, Andrew] 1850-1941.
The Bannock stake. [Salt Lake City, 1890] [127] -162 p. maps. Prepared for Historical Record, v. 9, but never added. Hence page numbering. Bingham County, Idaho. WaU **5200**

Jente, Richard, see no. 531.

Jepson, Willis Linn, 1867-
School flora of the Pacific Coast. New York, Appleton, c1902. vi, 96 p. (Twentieth Century text books)
OrP OrSa OrSaW WaE WaU **5201**
Same. 1906 [c1902] CV IdU **5202**
Same. 1912. OrP OrPR **5203**

Jessett, Thomas Edwin.
St. Johns Church of Olympia (1853-1941) a brief history comp. upon the occasion of the Parochial Diamond Jubilee. [Olympia, Wash.? 1941?] 55 p. front., illus., ports. CVicAr Wa WaS WaU **5204**

Jewett, John Rodgers, see nos. 5206-5221.

Jewett, Stanley Gordon, 1885-
Birds of the Portland area, Oregon, by Stanley G. Jewett and Ira N. Gabrielson. Berkeley, Calif., Cooper Ornithological Club, 1929. 54 p. illus. (Pacific coast avifauna, no. 19) Or OrCS OrP OrPR **5205**

Jewitt, John Rodgers, 1783-1821.
The adventures and sufferings of John R.

Jewitt, only survivor of the ship Boston, during a captivity of nearly three years among the savages of Nootka Sound; with an account of the manners, mode of living, and religious opinions of the natives. America printed, Edinburgh, Reprinted for A. Constable & Co., 1824. iv, 237 p. Written by Richard Alsop.
Many **5206**

Same. Ed. with an introd. and notes by Robert Brown. London, C. Wilson, 1896. 256 p. front. (port.) illus., plates.
Many **5207**

The captive of Nootka; or, The adventures of John R. Jewett. New York, Peaslee, 1835. 259 p. front., illus. CVicAr **5208**

Same. Philadelphia, H. F. Anners, 1841. (Peter Parleys Little Library, v. 2)
CV CVU WaSp WaU **5209**

Same. Philadelphia, Lippincott, 1854.
CVicAr CVU WaS **5210**

Same. 1861. CVU WaSp **5211**

A journal kept at Nootka Sound, by John R. Jewitt, one of the surviving crew of the ship Boston, of Boston, John Salter, commander, who was massacred on 22d of March, 1803; interspersed with some account of the natives, their manners and customs. Boston, 1807. 48 p.
CVicAr **5212**

Same. Photostat copy. CVU WaU **5213**

A journal kept at Nootka Sound by John R. Jewitt, one of the survivors of the crew of the ship Boston, during a captivity among the Indians from March 1803 to July 1805, reprinted from the original ed., Boston, 1807, with an introd. and a check list of later accounts of Jewitt's captivity, by Norman L. Dodge. Boston, Goodspeed, 1931. xxiv, 91 p. front. Many **5214**

Narrative of the adventures and sufferings of John R. Jewitt, only survivor of the crew of the ship Boston, during a captivity of nearly three years among the savages of Nootka Sound, with an account of the manners, mode of living, and religious opinions of the natives. New York [1815?] 166 p. front., illus. Written by Richard Alsop. Many **5215**

Same. Embellished with a plate representing the ship in possession of the savages. Middletown, Conn., Loomis & Richards, 1815. 204 p. front., plate.
CVic Ar CVU OrHi OrP WaSp WaU **5216**

Same. Middletown, Conn., Loomis, Wakefield, Hurst, 1816. 208 p. front. (port.) plate. CVicAr CVU **5217**

Same. New York, Printed by Daniel Fanshaw, 1816. 208 p. front. (port.) plates. 3d ed. CVU WaU **5218**

Same. Middletown,, Conn., Loomis & Richards, 1820. 280 p. front. (port.) plate.
CVicAr CVU OrHi **5219**

Same. Ithaca, N. Y., Mack, Andrus & Co., 1849. 166 p. front., illus.
CVicAr CVU OrU WaPS **5220**

Same. Andrus, Gauntlett & Co., 1851.
CVicAr CVU OrHi WaU **5221**

Jillson, Willard Rouse, 1890-
A bibliography of the geology and paleontology of the John Day region, Oregon;
102 titles. Frankfort, Ky. [State Journal
Co.] 1923. 13 p. Or OrCS OrP WaS 5222

Jobson, Anthony.
Sketches of pionering in the Rocky Mountains, B. C. West Hartlepool, Ord, 1905.
38 p. front., 3 plates. CVicAr 5223

Jochelson, Vladimir Il'ich, 1856-
Archaeological investigations in the Aleutian Islands. Washington, D. C., Carnegie Institution of Washington, 1925. ix,
145 p. illus., 28 plates, maps (1 fold.)
(Publication no. 367). Many 5224
History, ethnology and anthropology of
the Aleut. Washington, D. C., Carnegie
Institution of Washington, 1933. 91 p.
illus. (Publication no. 432). Many 5225

Joe, Copper River, see no. 8601.

Johann, A. E., see no. 11149.

Johansen, Lieutenant, see nos. 7207-7209.

Johansen, Dorothy O.
Simeon G. Reed, pioneer. Boston, Business
Historical Society, 1936. [7] p. port. (Bul-
letin, v. 10, no. 3) OrP 5226

John Fritz Medal. Board of Award.
Presentation of the John Fritz gold medal
to John Frank Stevens by the John
Fritz Medal Board of Award representing
the American Society of Civil Engineers,
American Institute of Mining and Metallurgical Engineers, American Society
of Mechanical Engineers, and the American Institute of Electrical Engineers,
Monday evening, March 23, 1925. New
York, Engineering societies building,
[1925] 61 p. front. (port.) illus., 3 plates,
map, facsim. Award for work at Panama
and for Great Northern Railroad in
Mont. Many 5227

Johnshoy, Walter, see no. 1049.

Johnson, Albert Garfield.
Keeping green the memory of Dr. Walter
Benwell Hinson, the Spurgeon of the
Pacific. [Portland, Or., Durham, Ryan
& Downey, 1935] 54 p. port. OrP 5228

Johnson, Charles, see no. 8410.

Johnson, Claudius Osborne, 1894-
Borah of Idaho. New York, Longmans.
1936. xi, 511 p. front., illus., plates, ports.
Many 5229
George Douglas Minnick. [Pullman,
Wash.] State College of Wash., 1939.
23 p. (Contributions to the history of
the Pacific Northwest, no. 2).
Or OrU WaS WaSp 5230

Johnson, Clifton, 1865-1940.
Highways and byways of California, with
excursions into Arizona, Oregon, Washington, Nevada and Idaho; written and
illus. by Clifton Johnson. New York,
Macmillan, 1915. xi, 323 p. front., 62
plates. (American highways and byways
series) Or OrU WaS WaSp WaT 5231
Same. 1926 [c1908] WaPS WaSp 5232
Highways and byways of the Pacific Coast,
written and illus. by Clifton Johnson.
New York, Macmillan, 1908. xi, 323 p.

front., 62 plates. (American highways
and byways, no. 1). Many 5233
Same. [1913] Many 5234

Johnson, Ebenezer.
A short account of a northwest voyage
performed in the years 1796, 1797 & 1798.
Massachusetts, 1798. 15 p. CVU 5235
Same. Photostat copy. WaU 5236

Johnson, Edwin Ferry, 1803-1872.
Railroads to the Pacific, northern route;
its general character, relative merits,
etc. 2d ed. New York, Railroad Journal
Printing Office, 1854. 166 p. front. (fold.
diagr.) 8 plates, 3 maps (2 fold.)
MtU OrP WaS WaSp WaU 5237

Johnson, Emily Pauline, 1861-1913.
Canadian born. Toronto, Morang, 1903. 1
v. Indian poetess, Tekahionwake, of Vancouver, B. C. CVU 5238
Flint and feather, with short biographical
sketch of the author. Toronto, Musson,
[1912] xx, 156 p. front., 5 plates, port.
CVic CVicAr 5239
Flint and feather (collected verse) with
introd. by Theodore Watts-Dunton, illus.
by J. R. Seavey. 2d ed. rev. and enl. Toronto, Musson [1913[xxx, 165 p. front.,
5 plates. CVic CVicAr CVU 5240
Same. 3d ed. rev. and enl. 1914. WaS 5241
Flint and feather (collected verse) rev.
and enl. ed., including poem written during her final illness, with introd. by J.
R. Seavey. Toronto, Musson [1914] xxx,
166 p. front. (port.) illus.
CVicAr CVU 5242
Flint and feather; the complete poems of
E. Pauline Johnson ("Tekahionwake")
with introd. by Theodore Watts-Dunton
and a biographical sketch of the author.
5th ed. rev. and enl. Toronto, Musson
[c1917] 176 p. front., 5 plates, port.
CV WaS WaTC WaU 5243
Same. 6th ed. 1920. c1917. WaS 5244
Same. 9th ed. [c1917] WaU 5245
Same. 12th ed. [1928, c1917] WaU 5246
The legend of the salt Chuk Oluk; abbre-
viated from "Legends of Vancouver" as
related by Chief Joe Capilano and set
down by "Tekahionwake", decorations
by L. Haweis. [Vancouver, B. C., n.d.]
[8] p. CVU 5247
Legends of Vancouver. Vancouver. B. C.,
1911. x, 89 p. CVU 5248
Same. New ed. Toronto, McClelland
[c1911] 165 p. front. (port.) 5 plates.
Many 5249
Same. 2d ed. Vancouver, B. C., Forsyth, 1912 [c1911] 89 p.
CV CVU IdU 5250
Same. 3d ed. Vancouver, B. C., Thompson Stationery Co., 1912. 167 p. front.
(port.) illus., plates. CVU 5251
Same. 4th ed. Vancouver, B. C., Forsyth,
1912 [c1911] xiv, 138 p. illus.
CVicAr CVU IdU WaPS 5252
Same. 6th ed. Vancouver, B. C., Thompson Stationery Co., 1913. xiii, 138 p.
front., illus., plates. WaPS WaS 5253

Same. Vancouver, B. C., Forsyth, 1913 [c1911] xiii, 138 p. front. (port.) illus.
CVU WaU 5254

Same. 8th ed. Vancouver, B. C., Saturday Sunset Press, 1913 [c1911] xvii, 138 p. front. (port.) illus., plates.
Many 5255

Same. New ed. Toronto, McClelland & Stewart [c1920] xvi, 165 p. front. (port.) 6 plates.
CVicAr CVU Or OrCS OrHi Wa 5256

Same. New ed., illus. with decorations by J. E. H. MacDonald. Toronto, McClelland & Stewart [c1922] xvi, 165 p. front. (port.)
WaU 5257

Same. 1924, c1922. WaS 5258

Same. [c1926] WaSp 5259

Same. 1928 [c1925] WaU 5260

Same. [1931] CVU 5261

The moccasin maker. Toronto, Ryerson [c1913] 221 p. front., plates, ports.
CVicAr 5262

Same. With introd. by Sir Gilbert Parker. Toronto, Briggs, 1913. 248 p. front., plates.
CVU WaU 5263

The shagganappi. Toronto, Briggs, 1913. 257 p. front., 3 plates.
CVicAr CVU 5264

Same. Toronto, Ryerson [c1913] 316 p. front., 3 plates. CVicAr CVU 5265

"When George was king" and other poems. Brockville, Ont., Brockville Times, 1908. 11 p. port. CVicAr 5266

The white wampum. London, J. Lane, 1895. 87 p. Poems. CVicAr 5267

Same. Toronto, Copp Clark, 1895.
CVU 5268

Johnson, H. F.
Poems of Idaho, with notes by the publisher. Weiser, Idaho, Signal Job Printing House, 1896. 128 p. IdU 5269

Johnson, James William, 1885-
The Bitterroot trail, illus. by L. D. Cram. Caldwell, Idaho, Caxton, 1935. 342 p. front., 6 plates. Many 5270

Johnson, Jesse G., see no. 5599.

Johnson, John, 1860-
Childhood, travel, and British Columbia. [Abertillery, Eng., P. Wilson Raffan & Co., 1907?] 349 p. front. (port.) plates, ports.
CV CVicAr CVU WaS WaU 5271

Johnson Levi.
Hillockburn, past, present, future. [Portland, Or., n.d.] 19 p. illus., map.
OrP 5272

The homeless unemployed man; a practical and suggestive solution of the problem. [n.p., c1915] 11 p. Man's resort in Portland, Or. OrP 5273

Johnson, Lionel A., 1872?-
Oregon at Malabon, and other poems, Portland, Or. [F. W. Baltes & Co.] 1905. 19 p. illus. OrHi OrP WaU 5274

Johnson, M. E.
Dayspring in the far West. London, See-

ley, 1875. xi, 215 p. 19 plates, 5 ports., fold. map.
CVicAr CVU WaS WaU WaWW 5275

Johnson, Myrtle Elizabeth, 1881-
Seashore animals of the Pacific coast, by Myrtle Elizabeth Johnson and Harry James Snook. New York, Macmillan, 1927. xiv, 659 p. col. front., illus., 11 col plates. Many 5276

Same. 1935 [c1927] IdU Wa 5277

Johnson, Neil William, 1901-
Preliminary report of farm business analysis of 175 irrigated farms in Yakima County, Washington, 1921, by N. W. Johnson and S. B. Nuckols. [Pullman, Wash.] 1922. 16 p. WaPS 5278

Johnson, Overton.
Route across the Rocky Mountains, with a description of Oregon and California; their geographical features, their resources, soil, climate, productions, etc., by Overton Johnson and Wm. H. Winter of the emigration of 1843. Lafayette, Ind., J. B. Semans, 1846. 152 p
OrP WaU 5279

Same. Photostat copy. WaU 5280

Same. Reprinted with preface and notes by Carl L. Cannon, from the ed. of 1846. Princeton, N. J., Princeton Univ. Press, 1932. xix, 199 p. plate, 2 facsims. (Narratives of the trans-Mississippi frontier). Many 5281

Johnson, Reginald A.
The West coast and the negro. [n.p., 1944] 24 p. OrP 5282

Johnson, Richard Byron.
Avonturen in British-Columbia. Arnhem, Voltelen [n.d.] 243 p. CVicAr 5283

Dans l'extreme far West; aventures d'un emigrant dans la Colombie anglaise. 2. ed. Paris, Hachette & Ciel, 1874. 244 p. plates. CVicAr CVU 5284

Very far west indeed; a few rough experiences on the North-west Pacific Coast. London, Low, 1872. 280 p.
Many 5285

Same. 2d ed. CVU WaS WaT 5286

Same. 4th ed. OrP WaSp 5287

Same. 5th ed. 1873. CVicAr WaT 5288

Johnson, Robert Cummings, 1864-
John McLoughlin; patriarch of the Northwest, jacket and chapter heading illus. by Constance Cole. Portland, Or., Metropolitan, 1935. 302 p. front., illus., plates, ports., maps. Many 5289

Johnson, Sidona Viola, 1785- comp.
A short history of Oregon; early discoveries, the Lewis and Clark exploration, settlement, government, Indian wars, progress. Chicago, McClurg, c1904. 329 p. front., plates, ports., fold. facsims., fold. map. Many 5290

Johnson, Theodore Taylor, b. 1818.
California and Oregon; or, Sights in the gold region and scenes by the way. 3d ed., with an appendix containing full instructions to emigrants by the overland route to Oregon, by Hon. Samuel R. Thurston; also particulars

of the march of the regiment of U. S. riflemen in 1849; together with the Oregon land-bill. Philadelphia, Lippincott, 1851. xii, 348 p. front., 5 plates.
                                    WaU 5291
Same. 4th ed.   WaU 5292
Same. 4th ed. 1853 [c1851]   IdU 5293
Same. 4th ed. 1857, c1851.
                        Or OrHi OrP 5294
Same. 1865.   OrP WaT 5295

Sights in the gold region and scenes by the way. New York, Baker, 1849. xii, 278 p.   OrU WaPS WaU 5296
Same. Dublin, M'Glachan, 1850. 308 p.
                                    WaSp 5297

Johnson, W. Carey, see no. 6608.

Johnson, William E., see no. 6474.

Johnsone, Delphene.
Glimpses; a book of verse. Seattle, Sherman Printing & Binding Co. [1921] 89 p.   Wa WaS WaU 5298

Johnston, G. Chalmers.
The 2d Canadian Mounted Rifles (British Columbia Horse) in France and Flanders, from the records of Lt.-Col. G. C. Johnston. [Vernon, B. C., Vernon News, 1931?] 174 p. 13 plates, 3 ports.
                                    CV 5299

Johnston, Lukin.
Beyond the Rockies, three thousand miles by trail and canoe through little-known British Columbia, with fifty-two illus. and a map. London, Dent [1929] xii, 212 p. front., plates, ports., double map.
                                    Many 5300

Johnston, Samuel Perry, 1865-
Alaska Commercial Company, 1868-1940; a more or less "documented" history, evidenced by papers from governmental files and books; by old letters from company files; by newspaper articles; by memories of officials and employes of long standing. [San Francisco, E. E. Wachter, Printer, 1940] 65 p. illus., ports.   WaU 5301

Johnston, William Alfred, 1874-
Gold-dredging possibilities in the Barkerville area, B. C. [n.p.] Canadian Institute of Mining & Metallurgy, 1922. 17 p.
                                    CVicAr 5302

Johnstone, Catherine Laura, 1838-1923.
Winter and summer excursions in Canada. London, Digby, Long & Co. [1894] xv, 213 p. illus., plates.
Northwestern Canada.   CVU 5303
Same. [19—?]   WaU 5304

[Joint Alumni Association for Higher Education in Oregon]
The welfare of Oregon demands the speedy relief of the Oregon Agricultural College, the University of Oregon, and the Oregon State Normal School. [Portland, Or., 1924?] 15 p.   OrHi OrP 5305

Joint Committee of the Mazama Club and the Sierra Club.
Report of the Joint Committee of the Mazama Club and the Sierra Club on the Mt. Rainier National Park. [n.p., 1905?] 15 p. plates.   WaU 5306

Joint Organization through Employee Representation of Longshoremen and Truckers, and Waterfront Employers of Seattle.
Plan of joint organization through employee representation of longshoremen and truckers and the Seattle waterfront employers, effective March 15, 1921, Seattle. [Seattle, 1921] 19 p.
                                    WaU 5307
Standard practice handbook, rev. June 1927. [Seattle] 1927. 18 p.   WaS 5308

Jolly, William.
Christian progress. Salem, Or., E. M. Waite, 1870. 151 p. Independent Church of Or.   Or OrHi OrP WaPS 5309

Jonas, Imman Askap Levi W. see no. 388.

Jonasson, Jonas Adalsteinn.
Bricks without straw, the story of Linfield College. Caldwell, Idaho, Caxton, 1938. 215 p. front., plates, ports.
                                    Many 5310

Jones, B. F.
Pen pictures of Oregon. Newport, Or. [n.d.] 5 p.   OrP 5311

Jones, Charles H., see no. 9967.

Jones, Com., see no. 3348.

Jones, Edna P., see no. 1942.

Jones, Edward Richard, 1882-
Bunyan's progress, a volume of verse on Paul Bunyan up to date, illus. by Bob Amundson. Madison, Wis. [c1929] 76 p. illus.   WaS WaU 5312

Jones, Fred O., 1912-
Grand Coulee from "hell to breakfast"; a story of the Columbia River from molten lavas and ice to the Grand Coulee Dam; drawings by Charles W. Zack. Portland, Or., Binfords & Mort, c1947. 64 p. illus., maps (part col.) diagrs.   Many 5313

Jones, George Neville, 1904-
A botanical survey of the Olympic peninsula, Washington. Seattle, Univ. of Wash. Press, 1936. 286 p. front., 8 plates, map, table. (Publications in biology, v. 5, June 1936)   Many 5314
The flowering plants and ferns of Mount Rainier. Seattle, Univ. of Wash. Press, 1938. 192 p. front., 8 plates. (Publications in biology, v. 7, Dec. 1938)
        OrP WaE WaS WaSp WaTC WaU 5315

Jones, John
British Naval Station, Esquimalt, B. C. Victoria, B. C., British Colonist [n.d.] 15 plates.   CVicAr 5316

Jones, John Paul.
The history of the development of the present campus plan for the University of Washington. [Seattle, 1940] [39] p. illus., plans, table. (Bulletin)Many 5317

Jones, Livingston French, 1865-1928.
Indian vengeance. Boston, Stratford Co., 1920. 68 p. front. (port.) 3 plates. Alaskan Indian story.   Many 5318
A study of the Thlingets of Alaska. New York, F. H. Revell [c1914] 261 p. front., 15 plates, double map.   Many 5319

Jones, N. W.
Indian bulletin for [1868, containing a

brief account of Chinese voyages to the North-west coast of America, and the interpretation of 200 Indian names] New York, C. A. Alvord, 1869. 26 p. (Indian bulletin, v. 2)
CVicAr OrP WaS WaU 5320

Jones, Nard, 1904-
All six were lovers, a novel. New York, Dodd, 1934. 253 p. Seattle author.
Many 5321

The case of the hanging lady. New York, Dodd, 1938. 271 p.
OrU Wa WaS WaSp 5322

Evergreen land, a portrait of the state of Washington. New York, Dodd, 1947. x, 276 p. plates. (Sovereign states)
Many 5323

The island, a novel. New York, W. Sloane [1948] 339 p.
Many 5324

Oregon detour. New York, Payson & Clarke, 1930. 283 p.
Many 5325

The Petlands. [New York] Brewer, Warren & Putnam [c1931] 341 p. Many 5326

Scarlet petticoat. New York, Dodd, 1941. 303 p.
Many 5327

Still to the West. New York, Dodd, 1946. 268 p.
Many 5328

Swift flows the river. London, Hamilton [1940] 449 p.
CVicAr 5329

Same. New York, Dodd, 1940. Many 5330

Same. Los Angeles, Braille Institute of America, 1940. 5 v.
OrP 5331

Same. Portland, Binfords & Mort [1948]. 449 p.
OrHi 5331a

West, young man! By Nard Jones and J. Gordon Gose; illus. by Howard Edwards. Portland, Or., Metropolitan [1937] 204 p. plates.
Many 5332

Wheat woman. New York, Duffield and Green [c1933] 334 p.
Many 5333

Jones, Reuben W.
Memories of my Mallie May. Seattle [Lowman & Hanford] 1933. 44 p. Poems.
WaU 5334

Jones, Thomas Lewis, 1841-
From the gold mine to the pulpit, the story of the Rev. T. L. Jones, backwoods Methodist preacher in the Pacific Northwest, during the closing years of the Nineteenth Century. Cincinnati, Jennings and Pye [c1904] 169 p. front., 8 plates, 16 ports.
Many 5335

Jones, William P., see no. 8224.

Jonveaux, Emile, see no. 10981.

Jordan, David Starr, 1851-1931.
Matka and Katik; a tale of the Mist Islands. San Francisco, Whitaker & Ray, 1897. 68 p. front., illus., plates, map. Seals in Bering Sea.
OrP 5336

Same. 1900. 79 p.
WaU 5337

The story of Matka; a tale of the Mist Islands. San Francisco, Whitaker & Ray, c1897-1909. 80 p. front., illus., plates, map. (School ed.)
Or 5338

Same. 1910.
WaU 5339

Same. Illus. with engravings from photographs and with original drawings by

Chloe Lesley Starks. Yonkers-on-Hudson, N. Y., World Book Co., 1921. 78 p. front., illus. (Animal life series)
OrP 5340

Same. 1921-1923.
WaS 5341

See also no. 6814.

Joscelyn, Archie Lynn, 1899-
Trail to Montana, by Lynn Westland [pseud.] New York, Phoenix [1943] 253 p.
WaU 5342

Jose, Thomas, see no. 863.

Joseph, George W.
Radio address against Chief Justice John L. Rand, candidate for re-election to the Oregon Supreme Court, delivered over station KXL Sept. 13, 1928. Portland, Or., Houghton-Carson Co. [1928] 16 p.
Or 5343

The truth about Rand; a few reasons why John L. Rand is unfit to be Justice of the Oregon Supreme Court. [Portland, Or., Houghton-Carson Co., 1928] 15 p.
Or 5344

Josephine County, Or.
Josephine County as it is! Climate and resources; facts and information for those intending to make homes in the glowing West! [Portland, Or., Lewis & Dryden, 1892?] 16 p. illus., maps.
Or 5345

Josephine County Agricultural Program Conference, 1946.
Report of the 1946 Agricultural Program Planning Conference for Josephine County, Josephine County courthouse, February 6, 1946. [Grants Pass, Or., The Bulletin, 1946] 23 p.
OrU 5346

Joslin, Falcon.
The needs of Alaska; an address delivered at the annual meeting of the American Mining Congress, Chicago, Oct. 17-22, 1921. [n.p. 1921] 13 p. WaU 5347

Journal of Geography.
Washington number; under the editorial direction of Prof. E. J. Saunders, University of Washington. Madison, Wis., 1916. 309-372 p. map, tables. (v. 14, no. 9, May 1916)
OrU WaS WaSp WaT WaU 5348

[Journal Printing Co., Ketchikan, Alaska]
Facts about Alaska; a series of questions and answers covering the population, government, history, commerce, resources, industries, and climate of America's last frontier. [Ketchikan, Alaska] 1932. 82 p. illus.
CV WaPS WaS WaT WaU 5349

Same. Rev. 1935.
WaE WaU 5350

Same. Rev. 1938 [c1938]
OrCS WaS WaT WaU 5351

Joyce, Alice V., see no. 8915.

Judd, Charles H., see no. 2797.

Judge, Charles Joseph.
An American missionary; a record of the work of Rev. William H. Judge, S. J., by a priest of St. Sulpice, introd. by His Eminence, Cardinal Gibbons. Baltimore, J. Murphy Co. [1904] 293 p. front., plates, ports., fold. map.
WaS 5352

Same. 2d ed. rev. Boston, Catholic Foreign Mission Bureau, 1904. xix, 308 p. facsim.
CVU WaU **5353**

Same. 4th ed. Ossining, N. Y., Catholic Foreign Missionary Society [c1907] xix,. 304 p. WaS WaU **5354**

Judson, Edward Zane Carroll, 1823-1886.
Buffalo Bill and his adventures in the West, by Ned Buntline [pseud.] New York, Ogilvie, c1886. 314 p. illus.
WaSp **5355**

Same. Chicago, Ogilvie, c1886. Wa **5356**

Judson, Katharine Berry.
Early days in old Oregon. Chicago, McClurg, 1916. 263 p. front., illus., 12 plates, maps. Many **5357**

Same. 3d ed. Portland, Or., Metropolitan, 1935. 275 p. Many **5358**

Same. 4th ed. [1936] Many **5359**

Same. 5th ed. Portland, Or., Binfords & Mort [1944] c1916-1919. WaT **5360**

Montana, "the land of shining mountains". Chicago, McClurg, 1909. 244 p. front., illus., 24 plates, ports., fold. map.
Many **5361**

Same. 6th ed. 1913. WaU **5362**

Same. 14th ed. 1918 [c1909]
MtBozC OrU **5363**

Same. 16th ed. 1928. WaW **5364**

Myths and legends of Alaska, selected and ed. by Katharine Berry Judson. Chicago, McClurg, 1911. 148 p. front., 31 plates. Many **5365**

Myths and legends of British North America. Chicago, McClurg, 1917. 211 p. front., 17 plates. Many **5366**

Myths and legends of the Pacific Northwest especially of Washington and Oregon, with 50 illus. from photographs. Chicago, McClurg, 1910. 144 p. front., 24 plates, ports. Many **5367**

Same. 2d ed. 1912.
MtU MtUM WaPS WaU **5368**

Old crow stories. Boston, Little, 1917. 163 p. front., plates. Northwest Indian folklore. IdIf Or **5369**

Pacific Northwest; a brief descriptive list of books with suggested outline of study. [Seattle] 1910. 12 p. (Seattle Public Library. Reference list no. 3) Many **5370**

When the forests are ablaze. Chicago, McClurg, 1912. 380 p. col. front., 5 plates (2 col.) OrP Wa WaPS WaS **5371**

Same. 2d ed. WaU **5372**

See also no. 6432.

Judson, Mrs. Phoebe Newton (Goodell) 1832-1926.
A pioneers search for an ideal home, by Phoebe Goodell Judson, who crossed the plains in 1853 and became a resident on Puget Sound before the organization of Washington Territory. Bellingham, Wash. [Union Printing, Binding and Stationery Co.] 1925. 309 p. front. (ports.)
Many **5373**

Jukes, A.
Paper prepared to be read at the annual meeting of the Canadian Medical Association held at Banff, Tuesday and Wednesday, August 13 & 14, 1889, but not read on that occasion. Winnipeg, Northern Lancet [n.d.] 16 p. (Suppl. Jan. 1890) "The endemic fever of the Northwest Territories" CVicAr **5374**

Jung, Aloysius M.
Jesuit missions among the American tribes of the Rocky Mountain Indians. Spokane, Gonzaga Univ., 1925. 30 p. illus., ports. Many **5375**

Ka-wan, He-mene, see no. 6475.

Kafka, John.
The apple orchard. New York, Coward-McCann [c1947] 264 p. Idaho pioneer story. Or WaS WaU **5376**

Kahlo, Dorothy Miller, comp.
History of the police and fire departments of the city of Seattle. Seattle, Lumbermen's Printing Co., 1907. 291 p. front., illus., ports. WaS WaU **5377**

Kaiser, Lawrence S.
The municipal water system of Portland, Oregon; historical, descriptive, statistical. [n.p., 1922] 151 p. OrP **5378**

Kaiser Company, Inc., Portland, Or. Child Service Dept.
Child service centers. Portland, Or. [1945] [21] p. illus., diagrs. Or OrP **5379**

160,874 children! Portland, Or., 1944. [25] p. OrP **5380**

Kaler, James Otis, 1842-1912.
Antoine of Oregon; a story of the Oregon Trail, by James Otis [pseud.] New York, American Book Co. [c1912] 149 p. front. (map) illus. Many **5381**

Kamloops centenary celebration; 1812-1912; held in commemoration of the establishment of the first white settlement at the junction of the North and South Thompson Rivers in 1812. [n.p.] 1912. [8] p. CVicAr **5382**

Kamloops mining camp. Kamloops, B. C., Baillie & Bennet, 1897. 64 p. front., illus., ports., 2 fold. maps.
CVicAr **5383**

Kamloops Provincial Industrial Exposition, 1902.
Kamloops Agricultural Association; prize list, programme, constitution and by-laws. Kamloops, B. C., Inland Sentinel, 1902. 80 p. plates, ports. CVicAr **5384**

Kamloops Sentinel.
Celista pioneers. [Kamloops, B. C., 1943] 16 p. illus., ports. CVicAr **5385**

Fiftieth anniversary edition, 1884-1934. Kamloops, B. C., 1934. [72] p. illus., ports. (Dec. 14, 1934) WaU **5386**

Kamloops Standard.
"Sunnyside", a magnificent estate in the Kamloops District of British Columbia. [Kamloops, B. C., n.d.] 1 v. illus.
CVicAr **5387**

Kane, Elisha Kent, 1820-1857.
Adrift in the Arctic ice pack, from the

history of the first U. S. Grinnell expedition in search of Sir John Franklin. New York, Outing Pub. Co., 1915. 402 p. front. (double map) illus. (Outing adventure library, no. 5)

CVicAr OrP WaSp WaT 5388

Arctic explorations; the second and last United States Grinnell expedition in search of Sir John Franklin, with a biographical sketch of the author by Prof. Charles W. Shields. Hartford, R. W. Bliss and Co., 1869. 766 p. front. (port.) illus., plates. Wa 5389

Kane, Paul, 1810-1871.
Catalogue; pictures of Indians and Indian life. [n.p., n.d.] 20 p. CVicAr 5390

En'kunstners vandringer blandt Indianerne i Nordamerika fra Canada til Vancouvers o og Oregon gjennem Hudsonsbai-Kompagniets territorium og tilbage igjen, oversat fra engelsk ved F. K. Kjobenhavn, F. H. Eibes, 1863. 344 p.

CVU WaU 5391

Wanderings of an artist among the Indians of North America from Canada to Vancouver's Island and Oregon, through the Hudson's Bay Company's territory and back again. London, Longmans, 1859. 455 p. col. front., illus., col. plates, col. ports., fold map. Many 5392

Same. Toronto, Radisson Society of Canada, 1925. liv, 329 p. front. (port.) illus., port. (Masterworks of Canadian authors, v. 7) Many 5393

Wanderungen eines Kunstlers unter den Indianern Nordamerika's von Canada nach der Vancouver's-Insel und nach Oregon durch das Gebiet der Hudsons-Bay-Gesellschaft und zuruck, autorisirte Deutsche ausg. ubersetzt von Luise Hauthal, geb. Velthusen. Leipzig, H. Mattes, 1862. 224 p. front., illus., plate, tables. CV CVicAr CVU WaS WaU 5394

Kashevaroff, Andrew P.
St. Michael's Cathedral, Sitka, Alaska. Juneau, Empire Printing Co. [n.d.] 1 v. illus. WaS 5395

See also nos. 78-82.

Kastner, George Charles, 1895-
Riders from the West. Portland, Or., Metropolitan, 1932. 137 p. front., plates, ports. Many 5396

Kate Bighead, see no. 6531.

"Katharine", see nos. 9870, 9871.

Kay, John M., see no. 6954.

Kaylor, Floyd C., see no. 4816.

[Kearley, Mark H.]
Canadian premiere of "Klee Wyck", the Emily Carr film. [n.p., n.d.] [7] p. illus., port. CVicAr 5397

Keasey, Humason & Jeffery, Portland, Or.
Moore's Valley orchard tracts. [Portland, Or., Portland Printing House, n.d.] [12] p. illus. Or 5398

Keator, Frederic William, bp., 1855-1924.
The democracy of Masonry; address at the 66th annual communication of the Grand Lodge at Tacoma, Wash., June

13, 1923. [Tacoma?] Grand Lodge of Wash. [1923?] 13 p. WaU 5399

The influence of Masonry in the colonies. [Seattle] Committee on Masonic Research and Education, Grand Lodge F. & A. M. of Wash. [n.d.] 10 p. (Historical series, bulletin no. 2) WaU 5400

Some ideals of democracy; commencement address, University of Washington, 1913. [Tacoma, Smith-Kinney Co., 1913] 23 p.

WaU 5401

Keefe, Aurelia Cor.
Under northwestern skies. Tacoma [Pioneer, Inc., c1938] [75] p. illus. Tacoma poet. WaT 5402

Verses and visions of our mountain. [n.p., c1930] [21] p. illus. Anon. Wa WaT 5403

Keeler, Nicholas Edwin, 1851-
A trip to Alaska and the Klondike in the summer of 1905. Cincinnati, Ebbert & Richardson Co., 1906. 115 p. front., plates, port. CVicAr CVU WaU 5404

Keen, Angelina Myra, comp.
An abridged check list and bibliography of west North American marine Mollusca. Stanford Univ., Calif., Stanford Univ. Press, c1937. 84 p. map, diagrs.

CVU Or OrP OrU WaTC WaU 5405

Keen, J. H., see no. 1746.

Keen, J. M., and Co.
Tacoma; its interest to the tourist, investor and manufacturer. [n.p., 1894] 14 p. WaS 5406

Keep, Josiah, 1849-1911.
West American shells; a description in familiar terms of the principal marine, fresh water and land mollusks of the United States, found west of the Rocky Mountains, including those of British Columbia and Alaska; also a classified reference list of the species and varieties known to exist within the above limits. San Francisco, Whitaker & Ray, 1904. 300 p. front., illus. OrU 5407

West coast shells; a description in familiar terms of principal marine, fresh-water, and land mollusks of the United States, British Columbia, and Alaska, found west of the Sierra, rev. by Joshua L. Baily, Jr. Stanford Univ., Calif., Stanford Univ. Press, 1935. xi, 350 p. illus.

Many 5408

Same. c1947. OrHi WaE 5409

West coast shells; a description of the principal marine mollusks living on the West coast of the United States and of the land shells of the adjacent region; also a chapter on the fresh water mollusks of the Pacific slope by Harold Hannibal. Rev. ed. San Francisco, Whitaker & Ray, c1910. 346 p. col. front., illus. Or 5410

Same. 1911. Many 5411

West coast shells; a familiar description of the marine, fresh water, and land mollusks of the United States found west of the Rocky Mountains, with numerous illus. by Laura M. Mellen.

San Francisco, Bancroft Bros. & Co., 1887. 230 p. col. front., illus.

OrP WaS **5412**

Same. San Francisco, Carson, 1888.

CVicAr OrHi **5413**

Same. San Francisco, H. S. Crocker Co., 1893.

Wa WaSp **5414**

Keep Oregon Green Association.
Oregon Green Guard; service record and manual. Salem, Or. [n.d.] 59 p. illus.

Or OrCS **5415**

Keesing, Louise Edna Dearborn, 1865-
Before the war; or, The return of Hugh Crawford, illus. by Robert J. Davidson. Seattle, 1915. vii, 297 p. plates.

WaU **5416**

Keeton, Delpha B., see nos. 10324, 10325.

Kegley, C. B.
Good roads for Washington; summary of address before the Civic Forum of Seattle on the Grange plan for good roads, August 29, 1911. Olympia, Wash., Blakenship-Lee [1911?] 8 p. WaPS WaS **5417**

The mission of the Grange, delivered at Whidby Island Chautauqua, Grange Day, July 26, 1910. [n.p.] 1910. 27 p. port.

WaU **5418**

Kehrli, Herman.
Portland pension problems; a survey of pension provisions and retirement problems of the municipal service, submitted to the City Council of Portland. [Portland, Or?] 1934. ix, 97 p. diagrs.

Or OrP OrPR OrU **5419**

Keim, DeBenneville Randolph, 1841-1914.
Our Alaskan wonderland and Klondike neighbor; personal reminiscence and thirty years after. Washington, D. C., Harrisburg Pub. Co. [1898] 352 p. front., plates, port., map. (American destiny series) CVicAr CVU WaU **5420**

Sheridan's troopers on the borders; a winter campaign on the plains, with numerous engravings. London, Routledge, c1885. 308 p. front., (port.) 7 plates. MtHi WaS **5421**

Keith, Marshall Clark, 1874-
The story of Chief Washakie, the upright aborigine, an Indian odyssey. Caldwell, Idaho, Caxton, 1935. 218 p. front. (port.) Verse. MtU WaS WaU **5422**

Keithahn, Edward Linnaeus, 1900-
Igloo tales, illus. by George Aden Ahgupuk [Lawrense, Kan., Haskell Institute, 1945] 122 p. illus.

CVicPr WaS WaSp WaU **5423**

Monuments in cedar. Ketchikan, Alaska, R. Anderson, 1945. 160 p. illus., ports.

Many **5424**

Kellar, John L.
Free gold, how to get it. [La Grande, Or., Eastern Or. Review, n.d.] 24 p. illus.

WaSp **5425**

Kelley, Cornelius Francis, 1875-
The richest hill on earth [speech made in Butte, Mont., Sept. 10, 1947] [n.p., n.d.] 1 v. MtHi **5426**

Kelley, Hall Jackson, 1790-1874.
Discoveries, purchases of land, &c. on the north west coast, being a part of an in-

vestigation of the American title to the Oregon Territory. [Boston, 1838] 16 p.

CVicAr **5427**

A general circular to all persons of good character, who wish to emigrate to the Oregon Territory, embracing some account of the character and advantages of the country; the right and the means and operations by which it is to be settled; and all necessary directions for becoming an emigrant, by order of the American Society for Encouraging the Settlement of the Oregon Territory, instituted in Boston, A. D. 1829. Charleston, Mass., W. W. Wheildon, 1831. 27 p.

CVicAr Or OrHi OrP WaU **5428**

Same. Tarrytown, N. Y., Abbatt, 1918. 25 p. plan. (Magazine of history with notes and queries, extra no. 63, pt. 1)

WaS WaU **5429**

A geographical sketch of the part of North America called Oregon; containing an account of the Indian title; the nature of a right of sovereignty; the first discoveries; climate and seasons; face of the country and mountains— natural divisions, physical appearance and soil of each; forests and vegetable productions; rivers, bays, &c.; islands &c.; animals; the disposition of the Indians and the number and situation of their tribes; together with an essay on the advantages resulting from a settlement of the territory, to which is added a new map of the country. Boston, 1830. 80 p. front. (fold. map)

OrHi OrP WaU **5430**

Same. 2d ed. enl. with an appendix embracing an account of the expedition and directions for becoming an emigrant. Boston, J. Howe. 1831. [Tarrytown, N. Y., Abbatt, 1919] 104 p. fold. map. (Magazine of history with notes and querries, extra no. 67) Many **5431**

Hall J. Kelley on Oregon; a collection of five of his published works and a number of hitherto unpublished letters. ed. by Fred Wilbur Powell. Princeton, N. J., Princeton Univ. Press, 1932. xxi, 411 p. maps. (Narratives of the trans-Mississippi frontier) Many **5432**

A history of the settlement of Oregon and the interior of upper California; and of the persecutions and afflictions of forty years' continuance endured by the author. Springfield, Mass., Union Printing Co., 1868. xv, 128 p.

CVicAr WaU WaWW **5433**

A narrative of events and differences in the colonization of Oregon and the settlement of California; and also, a history of the claim of American citizens to lands on Quadra's Island; together with an account of the troubles and tribulations endured between the years 1824 and 1852 by the writer. Boston, Thurston, Torry and Emerson, 1852. 92 p. CVicAr OrHi **5434**

Kelley, Joseph.
Thirteen years in the Oregon Penitentiary, by Joseph (Bunko) Kelley. Portland,

Or., 1908. 142 p. front. (port.) 2 plates, 6 ports. Many **5435**

Kelley, William Darrah, 1814-1890.
The new Northwest; an address on the Northern Pacific Railway in its relations to the development of the northwestern section of the United States and to the industrial and commercial interests of the nation. [Philadelphia? 1871?] 32 p. Many **5436**

Kellogg, George Albert.
A history of Whidbey's Island (Whidby Island) state of Washington. [n.p.] c1934. 108 p. port. Many **5437**

Kellogg, Jay C.
The broncho buster busted and other messages, by the cowboy evangelist. 4th ed. [Tacoma, The Whole Gospel Crusaders of America, c1932] 61 p. illus., ports. WaU **5438**

Kellogg, Remington, 1893-
Additions to the palaeontology of the Pacific coast and Great Basin regions of North America, by Remington Kellogg, John C. Merriam, Chester Stock, Ralph W. Chaney and H. L. Mason. [Washington, D. C.] Carnegie Institution of Washington, 1927. 158 p. illus., plates, maps. (Publication 346) Many **5439**

Additions to the Tertiary history of the pelagic mammals on the Pacific coast of North America. Washington, D. C., Carnegie Institution of Washington, 1925. iii, 120 p. illus., 14 plates (1 fold.) (Publication 348) Many **5440**

The Kellogg Evening News.
[Fiftieth anniversary Bunker Hill & Sullivan M. & C. Co. and miners' picnic editions] Kellogg, Idaho [1935] 1 v. WaPS **5441**

Kelly, Luther Sage, 1849-1928.
"Yellowstone Kelly"; the memoirs of Luther S. Kelly, ed. by M. M. Quaife, with a foreword by Lieutenant-General Nelson A. Miles, U. S. A. New Haven, Yale Univ. Press, 1926. xiii, 268 p. front., plates, ports., fold map. Many **5442**

Kelly, Margaret Jean, Sister.
The career of Joseph Lane, frontier politician. Washington, D. C., Catholic Univ. of America Press, 1942. ix, 207 p. Many **5443**

Kelly, Raymond Ransome, 1882-
O-go the beaver. Chicago, Whitman, 1934. 148 p. front., illus., plates. Montana beaver story. IdIf Or WaSp **5444**

Kelly, Richmond.
The Kelly clan, Portland, Or., 1901. 78 p. front., coat of arms. Or OrHi OrP OrU **5445**

Kelsey, Vera.
Fear came first. Garden city, N. Y., Pub. for Crime Club by Doubleday, 1945. 188 p. illus. (plan) Lake Washington setting. Wa WaS WaSp WaU **5446**

Kelsonian-Tribune.
The resources and opportunities of Cowlitz County; being the Progress edition. Kelso, Wash., Kelso Pub. Co., 1925. 1 v. illus. OrHi WaS **5447**

Kelty, Paul, see no. 4538.

Kemp, Randall Harold, 1852-
A half-breed dance, and other far western stories; mining camp, Indian and Hudson's Bay tales based on experiences by the author. Spokane, Inland Printing Co., c1909. 135 p. illus. CVicAr **5448**

Kendall, A. C., see no. 10349.

Kendall, Isabelle Carpenter.
Across the continent. Seattle, Chicago, Milwaukee & Puget Sound Railway, c1911. [64] p. illus. (part col.) IdB WaU **5449**

Kendall, Nancy Noon.
The new house. Caldwell, Idaho, Caxton, 1934. 388 p. Pacific coast novel. Many **5450**

Kendall, Reese P.
Pacific trail camp-fires; containing The Missouri column, The Applegate battalion, The "Pathfinder" detachment, The Barneburg contingent. Chicago, Scroll Pub. Co., 1901. 437 p. OrHi WaU WaWW **5451**

Kendrick, Sylvester J.
Chilkoot Pass, and songs of Alaska. [Los Angeles, Coast Printing Co., c1926] 61 p. port. CVicAr WaPS **5452**

Kennedy, Elijah Robinson, 1844-1926.
The contest for California in 1861; how Colonel E. D. Baker saved the Pacific states to the Union. Boston, Houghton, 1912. xiv, 361 p. front., ports. Many **5453**

Kennedy, George W., 1847-
The pioneer campfire, in four parts: With the emigrants on the great plains. With the settlers in the log cabin homes. With the hunters and miners. With the preachers on the trails, at camp meetings and in the log cabins. Anecdotes, adventures and reminiscences. Portland, Or., Marsh Printing Co., 1913. 252 p. front. (port.) 6 plates. Many **5454**

Same. Portland, Or., Clarke-Kundret Printing Co., 1914. 240 p. Many **5455**

Kennedy, Howard Angus, 1861-1938.
The book of the West; the story of western Canada, its birth and early adventures, its youthful combats, its peaceful settlements, its great transformation, and its present ways. Toronto, Ryerson [c1925] xviii, 205 p. front., illus., plates, ports. CVicAr CVU MtU WaU **5456**

North-west Rebellion. Toronto, Ryerson [c1929] 1 v. illus. (Canadian history readers) CVicPr WaSp **5457**

Origin of the Canadian Pacific Railway. Toronto, Ryerson [c1928] 30 p. illus. (Canadian history readers—Master builders) CVicAr **5458**

Kennedy, Sir William Robert, 1838-1916.
Sporting adventures in the Pacific whilst in command of the "Reindeer". London, Low, 1876. 303 p. front., illus., 4 plates. CVicAr CVU WaS WaU **5459**

Kent, May E., see no. 10058.

Kent, Rockwell, 1882-
Wilderness; a journal of quiet adventure in Alaska, with drawings by the author and an introd. by Dorothy Canfield. New York, Putnam, 1920. xvii, 217 p. front., illus., plates. Many **5460**

Same. [1924, c1920] WaU **5461**

Same. New York, Blue Ribbon Books [1936, c1920] IdP **5462**

Same. With a new preface by the author. New York, B. A. Cerf & D. S. Klopfer, the Modern Library, 1930: xiii, 243 p. front., illus., plates.
Or WaS WaSp WaTC **5463**

Kephart, Horace, see nos. 8887-8889, 8894, 8895.

Kerby, George W.
The broken trail; pages from a pastor's experience in western Canada. Toronto, Briggs, 1909. 189 p. 6 plates.
CVicAr CVU **5464**

Kern, Mrs. Edith (Kingman) 1866?-1941.
A little journey to Alaska, for intermediate and upper grades, ed. by Marian M. George. Chicago, Flanagan, c1901. 95 p. illus., ports., map. WaS **5465**

See also nos. **5981-5983.**

Kerns, Gerald H.
The pleasure's all mine. [Seattle?] c1945. 57 p. Seattle poet. WaU **5466**

Kerr, Duncan John, 1883-
The story of the Great Northern Railway Company and James J. Hill; a Newcomen address. [Prinecton, N. J., Princeton Univ. Press] 1939. 43 p. front. (port.) illus., maps, 2 diagrs.
OrU WaSp WaU **5467**

Kerr, Harry J
History of Okanogan, published in June 1931 on the twenty-fifth anniversary of the establishment of the Okanogan Valley Bank, later converted into the First National Bank of Okanogan. [Okanogan, Wash., Independent Print, 1931] 112 p. illus. WaS WaSp **5468**

Kerr, J. B.
Biographical dictionary of well-known British Columbians; with a historical sketch. Vancouver, B. C., Kerr & Begg, 1890. xxx, 326 p. front., 42 ports.
Many **5469**

Kerr, John Leeds.
The story of a western pioneer; the Missouri Pacific; an outline history. New York, Railway Research Society, 1928. 50 p. plates, ports.
Or OrHi WaU **5470**

Kerr, Mark Birckell, 1860-
Table of elevations within the Pacific slope, comp. for the Sierra Club, by Mark B. Kerr and R. H. Chapman. San Francisco, 1895. 32 p. (Publications of the Sierra Club no. 8).
CVicPr OrU **5471**

Kerr, William Jasper, 1863-
Recent experiences in centralized control of higher education in Oregon. [n.p., 1933?] 24 p. charts. Or OrCS **5472**

Ketchikan Alaska Chronicle.
Alaska statehood and international development edition. Saturday, March 29, 1947. Ketchikan, Alaska, 1947. [80] p. illus., maps. (v. 89, no. 75, Mar. 29, 1947)
IdB OrP OrU WaU **5473**

American Legion special edition. Ketchikan, Alaska, Journal Printing Co., 1934. 24 p. illus., ports. (v. 55, no. 5001, Sept. 22, 1934). WaU **5474**

Annual fisheries edition, 1935. Ketchikan, Alaska, 1935. 32 p. illus. (Sept. 1, 1935).
WaS **5475**

Fisheries edition, 1939, by Ketchikan Alaska Chronicle with Ketchikan Tribune, Ketchikan Times, and Daily Progressive Miner. Ketchikan, Alaska, 1939, 44 p. illus., ports. (v. 68, no. 6340, Sept. 9, 1939). WaU **5476**

Kettle, Capt., see nos. 4015, 4016.

[Khelebnikov, Kiril Timofeevich] 1776-1838.
Zhizneopisanie Aleksandra Andreevicha Baranova glavnago pravitelia rossiiskikh kolonii v Amerikie. Sanktpeterburg, Morskaia tipografiia, 1835. 209 p.
WaU **5477**

Kibbe, P. Carlisle.
Damon and Pythias, a story of old Syracuse. Tenino, Wash., Independent Pub. Co., 1930. 228 p.
Wa WaE WaS WaSp WaT WaU **5478**

Random verse. Tenino, Wash., 1937. 29 p.
Wa **5479**

Kid, Klondike, see no. 10992.

Kidd, George E.
Report on collection of B. C. Indian skulls in the Vancouver museum. [n.p., n.d.] 8 p. WaU **5480**

Kidd, Thomas.
History of Lulu Island and occasional poems. [Vancouver, B. C.] Wrigley Printing Co., 1927. 247 p. port., facsim.
CV CVicAr CVU WaU **5481**

Kiepert, Heinrich, see no. 3879.

Killingsworth, William M., ed.
Oregon's pocket book; a graphic, statistical presentation of the wealth of Oregon. 3d ed. Portland, Or. [Metropolitan, 1899?] 64 p. illus. OrHi WaU **5482**

Kim Bilir, see nos. 9017-9019.

[Kimball, George W.]
The school patrol of Seattle, Washington. Seattle, Northwestern Mutual Fire Assn. and Northwest Casualty Co. [1930?] 7 p. illus., port., diagrs. WaU **5483**

Kimball, Henry Dox, 1841-1915.
Records of a journey, from sunrise to evening glow; an autobiography. Cincinnati, Jennings and Graham [c1911] 280 p. front., plates, ports. Willamette University founder.
OrSaW WaSP WaTC WaU **5484**

Kimball School of Theology, Salem, Or.
Inaugurating John Martin Canse as president of the Kimball School of Theology. [Salem, Or., 1927] 15 p. illus., port. (Bulletin, v. 6, no. 1, Jan. 1927).
OrP WaU **5485**

Kincaid, Harrison Rittenhouse, 1836-
The money question as discussed in editorials in the Oregon state journals at different times during a period of twenty years, 1877-1898. Salem, Or., 1898. 46 p. front. (port.) Or OrHi OrP **5486**

Kindersley, Sir Robert Molesworth, see no. 9069.

King, Charles, 1844-1933.
Campaigning with Crook and stories of army life. New York, Harper, 1890. 295 p. front., 9 plates.
MtBozC MtHi OrHi WaSp **5487**
See also nos. 2008, 4288.

King, Charles Francis, 1843-
Rocky Mountains and Pacific slope, supplementary and regular reading in the lower classes in grammar schools, public libraries and the home. Boston, Lee and Shepard, 1894. xi, 259 p. front., illus., map. (Picturesque geographical readers, 5th book: The land we live in, pt. 3).
WaU **5488**

King, Clarence, see nos. 9386-9388.

King, E. Alonzo.
Congregationalists in Washington; some things they have done and more they might do. Seattle, Congregational Conference, 1915. [8] p. map. WaU **5489**

King, Edward J., see no. 10774.

King, Ervin E.
Washington State Grange, master's address, delivered at forty-eight annual session, Aberdeen, Washington, June 2-5, 1936. [n.p., 1936?] 43 p. Wa **5490**

King, Frank Marion, 1863-
Pioneer western empire builders, a true story of the men and women of pioneer days, profusely illus., including an original illus. by Charles M. Russell. [Pasadena, Calif., Trail's End Pub. Co., 1946] 383 p. front., illus., plates, ports., map, facsim.
CVicPr IdU MtHi WaS WaU **5491**
Wranglin' the past; reminiscences, illus., including drawing of Charles M. Russell. 1st rev. ed. [Pasadena, Calif., Trail's End Pub. Co., 1946] 284 p. illus., plates, ports. MtBozC Or OrP OrU WaS **5492**

King, James, see nos. 1981, 1995, 2001, 2003-2005.

King, Richard, 1811?-1876.
The Franklin expedition from first to last. London, Churchill, 1855. 224 p. front., plates, maps. CVicAr CVU MtU **5493**
Narrative of a journey to the shores of the Arctic Ocean in 1833, 1834, and 1835, under the command of Capt. Back. London, R. Bentley, 1836. 2 v. in 1. fronts., plates, map.
CV CVicAr WaS WaU **5494**

King, Stoddard, 1889-1933.
Grand right and left. New York, Doran [1927] 132 p. Spokane author. Many **5495**
Listen to the mocking-bird. Garden City, N. Y., Doubleday, 1928. xii, 111 p.
Many **5496**
Raspberry tree and other poems of sentiment and reflection. Garden City, N. Y., Doubleday, 1930. xi, 144 p.
MtU OrP Wa WaS WaSp WaTC **5497**
What the queen said and further facetious fragments. New York, Doran [c1926] 149 p. Many **5498**

King, T. Starr, see no. 9438.

King, William Arthur, 1884-
The Pacific Northwest, its resources and industries, by William A. King and

Elmer D. Fullenwider, Cincinnati, South-western Pub. Co. [c1938] 390 p. illus., maps, diagrs. Many **5499**
See also no. 3602.

King County Bar Association, King County, Washington.
Celebration of John Marshall Day, February 4, 1901 at Seattle, Washington; report of the proceedings including orations by Hon. C. H. Hanford and Mr. Charles E. Shepard. Seattle, Lowman & Hanford, 1901. 60 p. front. (port.)
CVicAr WaS **5500**

King County Central Blood Bank, Inc.
King County Central Blood Bank, Inc., Seattle, Washington. Seattle [Seattle Printing and Pub. Co., 1947?] 16 p. illus.
WaS WaU **5501**

King County Industrial Association.
Premium list of the King County Industrial Association for 1879; fair from September 22 to 27, inclusive. [Seattle, Hanford & McClaire, Printers, Intelligencer Office, 1879] [32] p. WaU **5502**
Same. [16] p. WaU **5503**

King County Veterans Association.
Constitution and by laws. [Seattle, 1905?] [8] p. WaU **5504**

Kingcombe, John.
Station regulations and port orders for the squadron in the Pacific, 1863. Victoria, B. C., 1863. [83] p. CVicAr **5505**

Kingsley, Nellie F.
Four American explorers: Captain Meriwether Lewis, Captain William Clark, General John C. Fremont, Dr. Elisha K. Kane; a book for young Americans. New York, American Book Co. [c1902] 271 p. illus. (Four great American series.) WaW **5506**
Same. New York, Werner School Book Co. [c1902] Or OrP Wa WaS WaW **5507**
The story of Captain Meriwether Lewis and Captain William Clark for young readers, with an introd. by the ed. New York, Werner School Book Co. [c1900] 128 p. illus., ports. (Baldwin's biographical booklets) OrHi OrP WaS WaU **5508**
Same. New York, American Book Co., c1902. 132 p.
MtBozC Or Wa WaPS WaS WaW **5509**

Kingston, Ceylon Samuel.
An outline of the history of the Pacific Northwest, with special reference to Washington, by Ceylon S. Kingston and J. Orin Oliphant. Cheney, Wash., Eastern Washington College of Education, 1926. ix, 101 p. Many **5510**

Kingston, William Henry Giles, 1814-1880.
Adventures among the Indians. Chicago, Belford, Clarke & Co., 1888. 252 p. illus.
Wa WaS WaSp **5511**
Adventures in the far West. London, Routledge [c1889?] 192 p. illus.
WaSp **5512**
Captain Cook: his life, voyages, and discoveries. London, Religious Tract Society [1871] 352 p. front., illus., plates, map. WaU **5513**

The frontier fort; or, Stirring times in the Northwest Territory of British America. London, Society for Promoting Christian Knowledge [n.d.] 160 p. front., 2 plates.　　　CVicAr WaWW 5514

In the Rockies; a tale of adventure. Chicago, Homewood Pub. Co. [n.d.] 224 p. front.　　　WaU 5515

Kinnear, William Emera.
Inland emperors; a book of cartoons in the form of a personal directory of principal business and professional men of this section. Spokane, E. D. Van Dersal [c1908] 251 p. front., plates, ports.　　　IdU WaSp 5516

Kinney, Edwin Enoch.
Westward and other poems. Vancouver, B. C., Chalmers [1923] 75 p. front. (port.)　　　CVicAr CVU 5517

Kinscella, Hazel Gertrude.
Flag over Sitka, a story of the Alaska "transfer," illus. by Jacob Elshin. Lincoln, Neb., Univ. Pub. Co. [1947] 83 p. illus., map.　　　Wa WaS WaU 5518

Kip, Lawrence, 1836-1899.
Army life on the Pacific; a journal of the expedition against the northern Indians, the tribes of the Coeur d'Alenes, Spokans, and Pelouzes, in the summer of 1858. New York, Redfield, 1859. 144 p.　　　Many 5519

The Indian Council at Walla Walla, May and June 1855; a journal. Eugene, Or., Star Job Office, 1897. 28 p. (Sources of the history of Or., v. 1. pt. 2) Many 5520

The Indian Council in the valley of the Walla Walla, 1855. San Francisco, Whitton, 1855. 32 p.　　　OrHi 5521

Kipp, Joseph, see no. 5692.

Kippis, Andrew, 1725-1795.
Captain Cook's voyages with an account of his life, during the previous and intervening periods. New York, Knopf, 1925. xiii, 410 p. front., plates. (Blue jade library.)　　　Many 5522

The life of Captain James Cook. Basil, J. J. Tourneisen, 1788. 2 v.　　　CVU WaU 5523

Same. Dublin, H. Chamberlaine, 1788. xvi, 527 p. front. (port.)　　　WaU 5524

Narrative of Captain James Cook's voyages round the world, with an account of his life during the previous and intervening periods; also, an appendix, detailing the progress of the voyage after the death of Captain Cook. London, Jones and Co., 1839. 384 p. front., plates. Anon.　　　WaU 5525

Same. Halifax, Milner and Sowerby, 1852. xvi, 368 p. Anon.　　　WaU 5526

A narrative of the voyages round the world performed by Captain James Cook; with an account of his life during the previous and intervening periods. New York, American News Co. [n.d.] vi, 424 p. front. IdU WaPS 5527

Same. Philadelphia, Henry T. Coates & Co. [n.d.]　　　OrSaW Wa WaU 5528

Same. Chiswick, C. and C. Whittingham, 1826.　　　CVU 5529

Same. Boston, 1830. 2 v. illus.　　WaS 5530

Same. Philadelphia, Haswell, Barrington & Haswell, 1838. 2 v. in 1.　　WaU 5531

Same. Cooperstown, N. Y., H. & E. Phinney, 1841. 2 v. fronts., plates. WaU 5532

Same. Manchester, S. Johnson and Son, 1845. ix, 445 p. front.　　WaU 5533

Same. Philadelphia, J. Ball, 1851. 2 v. in 1.　　　WaU 5534

Same. Hartford, S. Andrus and Son, 1852.　　　WaU 5535

Same. Philadelphia, Daniels & Getz, 1853. 2 v. in 1. illus.　　WaS 5536

Same. New York, Derby & Jackson, 1858. vi, 424 p. front. (port.) plates. WaU 5537

Same. Philadelphia, Lippincott, 1863.　　　OrP 5538

Same. New York, Harper [188-?] ix, 445 p.　　　OrSaW 5539

Same. With twelve illus. reproduced in exact facsimile from drawings made during the voyages. London, Bickers and Son, 1883. x, 404 p. mounted front., mounted plates.　　　WaU 5540

Same. 1889.　　　CVic 5541

Vie du Captaine Cook, tr. de l'anglois du docteur Kippis, par M. Castera. Paris, 1789. 546 p.　　　WaU 5542

Voyages round the world from the death of Captain Cook to the present time, including remarks on the social condition of the inhabitants in the recently discovered countries, their progress in the arts; and more especially their advancement in religious knowledge. New York, Harper, 1844. 401 p. (The family library no. 172)　　CVicAr OrHi 5543

Same. 6th ed. London, Nelson, 1854. 517 p. front., 3 plates.　　　CVicAr 5544

Same. 1857.　　　WaPS 5545

Voyages round the world performed by Capt. James Cook, with an account of his life during the previous and intervening periods. London, Cowie, Low & Co., 1826. 2 v. front. (port.)　WaU 5546

Kirchof, N. A. J.
Auszug aus Cook und Kings Reise in den Jahren 1776 bis 80 nebst einem Verzeichnisse ihrer Beobachteten breiten und langen; ingleichen Bemerkungen uber die Abweichung der Magnetnadel, zum Beweise, dass die Lange der Oerter dadurch mit Gewissheit nicht bestimmet werden konne. Berlin, F. Nikolai, 1794. 62 p.　　　WaU 5547

Kirchoff, Theodor, 1828-1899.
Reisebilder und Skizzen aus Amerika. Altofa, C. T. Schluter, 1875-1876. 2 v.　　　OrHi 5548

Kirk, Robert C.
Twelve months in Klondike. London, Heinemann, 1899. xii, 273 p. front., illus., 23 plates, map.
　　CVicAr CVU OrU WaS WaU 5549

Kirkland, Burt Persons, 1881-
Forest resources of the Douglas fir region, with foreword from the Joint Committee on Forest Conservation.

[Portland, Or., Joint Committee on Forest Conservation] 1946. 74 p. maps, tables. CVicPr OrCS OrP WaU **5550**

[Kirkpatrick, J. M.]
The heroes of Battle Rock, or The miner's reward; a short story of thrilling interest. How a small canon done its work. Port Orford, Oregon, the scene of the great tragedy. A desperate encounter of nine white men with three hundred Indians. Miraculous escape after untold hardships. Historically true. Savages subdued and rich gold mines discovered, ed. by Orvil Dodge. [n.p.] 1904. 21 p.
Many **5551**

Kirkpatrick, Orion Ephraim, 1863-
History of Leesburg pioneers. [Salt Lake City, Pyramid Press, c1934] 172 p. illus., plates, port., diagr. Leesburg, Idaho.
IdB IdIf MtHi MtUM WaPS **5552**

Kirkwood, Joseph Edward, 1872-1928.
Northern Rocky Mountain trees and shrubs. Stanford Univ., Calif., Stanford Univ. Press, 1930. xvii, 350 p. front., illus., 35 plates. Many **5553**

Kiser Bros., Portland, Or.
Pacific Coast pictures, a representative collection of pictures of grand scenery in Oregon and Washington from Kiser Bros. famous collection of photographs. Portland, Or., Wonderland Souvenir Co. [1904?] [159] p. illus. Or OrHi OrP **5554**

Kitchakahalch, see no. 10215.

Kitchin, Edward A.
A distributional checklist of the birds of Mount Rainier National Park. [n.p.] 1939. 11 p. WaTC **5555**

Distributional checklist of the birds of the state of Washington. Seattle, Pacific Northwest Bird and Mammal Society, 1934. 28 p. (Northwest fauna series, no. 1, Feb. 1934) Many **5556**

Kitsap County Herald.
[40th anniversary. Progress edition, 1900-1940] Poulsbo, Wash., 1940. [28] p. illus., ports., maps. (Aug. 2, 1940) WaU **5557**

Kitson, Arthur.
Captain James Cook, "the circumnavigator". New York, Dutton, 1907. xvi, 525 p. front. (port.) illus., 6 plates, 2 ports., fold. map, 4 facsims.
CVU IdU OrP WaU **5558**

The life of Captain James Cook, the circumnavigator. 2d ed. London, Murray, 1911. 334 p. front. (port.) fold. map.
WaU **5559**

Same. 1912. CVU **5560**

Kittinger, Charles H.
Seattle. Seattle [1889?] [50] p. illus.
CVicAr Or WaPS WaS WaU **5561**

Kittlitz, Friedrich Heinrich, Freiherr von, 1799-1874.
Denkwurdigkeiten einer Reise nach dem russischen Amerika, nach Mikronesien und durch Kamtschatka. Gotha, Perthes, 1858. 2 v. fronts., illus., 2 plates.
CVicAr WaU **5562**

Twenty-four views of the vegetation of the coasts and islands of the Pacific, with explanatory descriptions, taken during the exploring voyage of the Russian Corvette "Senjawin" under the command of Capt. Lutke in the years 1827, 1828 & 1829; trans. from the German and ed. by Berthold Seamann. London, Longman, 1861. x, 68 p. 24 photos. CVicAr **5563**

Kiwanis Club of Spokane.
History of the Kiwanis Club of Spokane, 1920-1945, comp. by A. H. Syverson and Leon Starmont. [Spokane?] 1945, 39 p. illus. WaSp **5564**

The Kiwanis Magazine.
On to Seattle number. Chicago, Kiwanis International, 1928. 117-168 p. illus., ports., (v. 13, no. 3, Mar. 1928) WaU **5565**

Kizer, Benjamin Hamilton, 1878-
The U.S.-Canadian Northwest, a demonstration area for international postwar planning and development. Princeton, N. J., Princeton Univ. Press, 1943. xvi, 71 p. maps (part fold.) Many **5566**

Klahhane Club, Port Angeles, Wash.
The Klahhane Club annual, 1918. Port Angeles, Wash. [1918] [100] p. illus.
WaU **5567**

Klamath Basin Centennial.
Official souvenir program: pageant, August 22, 23, 24, 1946; Klamath County fair grounds, Klamath Falls, Oregon celebrating the 100th anniversary of the opening of the southern emigrant route to Oregon. [Klamath Falls, Or., 1945] [30] p. illus. Or **5568**

Kleiser, Elizabeth Margaret (Thompson)
Randon rhymes, by Elizabeth and Grenville Kleiser. [Paris, H. Clarke, 1926?] 23 p. IdU WaU **5569**

Same. New York, Funk & Wagnalls [c1926] 31 p. OrP **5570**

Kleiser, Grenville, see nos. 5569, 5570.

Klement, Otto, see no. 1943.

Klengenberg, Christian, 1869-
Klengenberg of the Arctic, an autobiography, ed. by Tom MacInnes. London, J. Cape [1932] 360 p. front. (port.) 7 plates.
CVU WaSp **5571**

Klickitat Academy, Goldendale, Wash.
Timblin memorial, Goldendale, Wash., June 15, 1922. [Goldendale, Wash., 1922] 18 p. ports. WaPS **5572**

Klickitat County Fair. Indian Conclave Committee.
Indian conclave (tribal gathering): a conclave of Northwest Indian tribes will be held in connection with the 18th Annual Klickitat County Fair, Goldendale, Washington, September 5, 6, 7, and 8, 1928. [Goldendale, Wash.? 1928?] [4] p. ports. WaPS **5573**

Klondike and all about it, by a practical mining engineer. New York, Excelsior, 1896. 143 p. fold. map, diagr. (Excelsior library of popular handbooks, no. 48.)
CVicAr WaS **5574**

Same. [c1897] CVU WaS **5575**

Klondike Kid, see no. 10992.

Klondyke mining laws; the Canadian gold fields, how to get there, where to purchase supplies. Victoria, B. C., Graphic [1897] 30 p. CVicAr 5576

Knapp, Frances.
The Thlinkets of southeastern Alaska, by Frances Knapp and Theta Louise Childe. Chicago, Stone and Kimball, 1896. 197 p. front., plates, ports.
CVicAr OrP OrU WaS WaU 5577

Knapp, Fred Church.
Ships, lumber and unemployment; an address delivered before the State Reconstruction Congress, January 9, 1919, at the public auditorium, Portland, Oregon. Portland, Or., 1919. 16 p. OrP 5578

Kneen, Orville Hayter, 1889-
Young pioneers on western trails; young explorer's own stories of adventure in the unknown West. New York, Stokes, 1929. vii, 311 p. front. Many 5579

Knight, Emerson B., Inc., Indianapolis, Ind.
An analysis of the Seattle market, prepared especially for Public Library from the 1930 Consumer research. Seattle, Post-Intelligencer Blue Room, 1930. 1 v.
WaS 5580

Knight, John Irvine, see no. 9848.

Knight, Neil Roy.
Gold horizon; the life story of Manson F. Backus, forty-five years a banker in the Pacific Northwest, with an introd. by Emmannell Backus Brady. Seattle, McCaffrey, 1937. 222 p. front., ports. Many 5581

Knight, William Henry, 1835-1925, ed.
Hand-book almanac for the Pacific states; an official register and year-book of facts for the year 1862. San Francisco, H. H. Bancroft & Co., 1862. 191 p. tables.
Many 5582

Same. An official register and business directory of the states of California and Oregon; the territories of Washington, Nevada and Utah; and the colonies of British Columbia and Vancouver Island, for the year 1863. San Francisco, H. H. Bancroft & Co. [1863] 420 p. tables.
CVicAr OrP Wa WaSp WaU 5583

Same. An official register and business directory of the states and territories of California, Nevada, Oregon, Idaho, and Arizona; and the colonies of British Columbia and Vancouver Island, for the year 1864. San Francisco, H. H. Bancroft & Co., 1864. 440 p. tables.
Orp WaU 5584

Same. 1865. OrP 5585

Knights of Columbus. Oregon.
History of Knights of Columbus in Oregon. [n.p., n.d.] 72 p. illus. ports.
OrP 5586

Knights of Pythias. Oregon. Mystic Lodge No. 2.
Constitution and by-laws of Mystic Lodge no. 2. Portland, Or., Himes, 1873. 32 p.
OrHi OrP 5587

[Knipe, C.]
Some account of the Tahkaht language as spoken by several tribes on the western coast of Vancouver Island. London, Hatchard & Co., 1868. 80 p. CVU 5588

Knippenberg, Henry, 1843.
History of the Society of the Framers of the Constitution of the State of Montana, July 4, 1889; August 17, 1889. [Indianapolis, Baker-Randolph Lithograph and Engraving Co., 1890] 154 p.
MtHi MtU WaSp WaU 5589

Knott, Joseph Carlton, 1893-
An analysis of the State College of Washington Holstein herd. [Pullman, Wash., 1936?] 49 p. tables, diagrs. WaPS 5590

Knowles, Robert Edward, 1868-
The singer of the Kootenay; a tale of today. New York, F. H. Revell Co. [c1911] 368 p. CVU Or WaU 5591

Knox, Olive Elsie.
By paddle and saddle. Toronto, Macmillan, 1943. ix, 270 p. Sir George Simpson story. CVicAr WaU 5592

Knox College, Galesburg, Ill. Library.
A catalogue of books and maps belonging to the Finley collection on the history and romance of the Northwest, arranged alphabetically by authors, collected and presented to the library of Knox College by Edward Caldwell of New York city and other donors. 2d ed. Galesburg, Ill., 1928. xv, 61 p. front., illus.
WaU 5593

Knudson, Gus L.
For your information; history of Woodland Park Zoological Gardens. [Seattle, n.d.] 6 p. WaS 5594

Koehler, R.
Bericht des Finanz-agenten, R. Kohler, uber die Nothwendigkeit des Erwerbs und des Ausbaues der Oregon Central Bahn durch die Besitzer der I. Mortgage-bonds der Oregon und California Bahn, nebst einer Orientirungs-karte. Frankfurt am Main, C. Naumann, 1878. 20 p. fold. map. OrHi WaU 5595

Report on the acquisition and extension by the Oregon and California Railroad of the Oregon Central Railroad. Frankfurt am Main, C. Naumann, 1878. 19 p. map. OrHi 5596

Koelsch, Charles F.
An exposition of the constitution of the state of Idaho. Boise, Idaho., G. J. Lewis, 1899. 128 p. IdB WaPS 5597

Same. 2d ed. [Boise, Idaho, Statesman Print, 1901. c1899] IdIf 5598

Koestler, August E.
Sourdough flights; 2d ed. of the Koestler Alaska flight cover catalogue. Rev. and pub. by Jesse G. Johnson. [Norfolk, Va., c1941] 60 p. illus., maps. First ed. was serial in Western stamp collector.
WaU 5599

Kofoid, C. A., see no. 8972.

Kootenay guide; guide to the mining camps of British Columbia and Klondike. Rossland, B. C., Young, 1898. 78 p. fold. map.
CVicAr 5600

The Kootenay Moning Protective Association.
Constitution and by-laws. Kaslo, B. C., Kootenaian Power Printing House, 1897. 6 p. CVicAr 5601

The **Kootenay valleys** and the Kootenay District in British Columbia. London, Kootenay Valleys Co. [18—?] 31 p. map.
CV **5602**

Koppert, Vincent Aloysius, 1898-
Contributions to Clayoquot ethnology. Washington, D. C., Catholic Univ. of America, 1930. viii, 124 p. illus., ports., maps. (Anthropological series, no. 1)
MtU OrU WaE WaU **5603**

Kottenkamp, Dr., see nos. 3346, 3347.

Koven, Reginald de, see nos. 6660, 6675.

Kramer, Arthur.
Chronological history of the Puget Sound Power & Light Company and predecessor companies, 1885-1938. Rev. [Seattle] 1939. 23 p.
WaU **5604**

Kramer, Harold Morton, 1873-1930.
The chrysalis, illus. by H. C. Edwards. Boston, Lothrop, Lee & Shepard Co. [1909] vii, 419 p. front., 5 plates. Spokane and Palouse country story.
IdB WaU **5605**

Same. New York, Grosset [1909]
WaU **5606**

Krause, Aurel, 1848-1908.
Die Tlingit-Indianer; Ergebnisse einer Reise nach der Nordwestkuste von Amerika und der Beringstrasse ausgefuhrt im Auftrage der Bremer Geographischen Gesellschaft in den Jahren 1880-1881, durch die Doctoren Arthur und Aurel Krause, geschildert von Dr. Aurel Krause. Jena, H. Costenoble, 1885. xvi, 420 p. illus., 4 plates, fold. map, tables.
CV CVicAr OrU WaS WaU **5607**

Kreider, Claude M.
Steelhead. New York, Putnam [1948] x, 182 p. illus.
Many **5608**

Kreml, Franklin M., see no. 4944.

Kress, Samuel Henry, 1863-
An exhibition of Italian paintings lent by Mr. Samuel H. Kress of New York to the Horace C. Henry Art Gallery of the University of Washington on view Thursday, September 28, 1933 to Sunday, October 29, 1933. [New York, Burland Printing Co., 1933] 55 p. illus.
WaS WaU **5609**

Krieger, A. D., see no. 2107.

Kruzenshtern, Ivan Fedorovich, 1770-1846.
Worter-sammlugen aus den Sprachen einiger Volker des ostlichen Asiens und der Nordwestkuste von Amerika, bekannt gemacht von A. J. v. Krusenstern. St. Petersburg, Druckerey der Admiralitat, 1813. xi, 68 p.
CVicAr OrP WaS WaU **5610**

Kuder, Merle S., see no. 4952.

Kuhlman, Charles.
Gen. George A. Custer; a lost trail and the Gall saga; some interesting deductions regarding the Battle of the Little Big Horn, June 25-26, 1876, with map of operations of battle, troops, and Indians. Billings, Mont., 1940. 46 p. map.
MtHi **5611**

Kummer, Frederic Arnold, 1873-
The Perilous Island; a story of mystery in the Aleutians. Philadelphia, Winston, c1942. 212 p. illus.
Wa WaT **5612**

Kurth, Godefroid, see no. 5766.

Kuskokwim, Bard of the, see no. 1947.

Kuykendall, George Benson, 1843-
History of the Kuykendall family since its settlement in Dutch New York in 1646, with genealogy as found in early Dutch church records, state and government documents, together with sketches of colonial times, old log cabin days, Indian wars, pioneer hardships, social customs, dress and mode of living of the early forefathers. Portland, Or., Kilham Stationery & Printing Co., 1919. [iii] 645 [20] p. front., illus., ports., fold. geneal. table. OrHi Wa WaU **5613**

A **Kwagutl** translation of hymns as sung in the C. M. S. missions on the north of Vancouver Island. London, Society for Promoting Christian Knowledge, 1899. iv, 30 p.
WaU **5614**

Kyne, Peter Bernard, 1880-
Cappy Ricks; or, The subjugation of Matt Peasley, illus. by Harvey Dunn and Anton Otto Fischer. New York, H. K. Fly Co. [c1916] 349 p. front., plates. Pacific Coast shipping industry novel.
Many **5615**

Same. New York, Grosset, c1916.
IdU WaT **5616**

Cappy Ricks retires, illus. by T. D. Skidmore. New York, Cosmopolitan Book Corp., 1922. 442 p. front., plates.
WaS WaT WaU **5617**

Kyner, James Henry, 1846-
End of track, as told to Hawthorne Daniel. Caldwell, Idaho, Caxton, 1937. 227 p. front., 23 plates, 5 ports.
Many **5618**

LaBarre, Mrs. Julia C.
The story of Wannetta. Portland, Or., Mann & Beach [n.d.] [14] p.
OrP **5619**

Labillardiere, Jacques Julien Houton de, 1755-1834.
An account of a voyage in search of LaPerouse undertaken by order of the Constituent Assembly of France and performed in the years 1791, 1792, and 1793 in the Recherche and Esperance ships of war under the command of Bruni D'Entrecasteaux; tr. from the French. London, J. Debrett, 1800. 2 v. 43 plates, fold. map. (v. 2 only)
CVicAr **5620**

Relation du voyage a la recherche de LaPerouse, fait par ordre de l'Assemblee constituante, pendant les annees 1791, 1792, et pendant la lere et la 2de annee de la Republique Francoise. Paris, H. J. Jansen, an VIII [1799] 2 v. tables.
CVU WaU **5621**

Same. 1800.
CVicAr **5622**

Voyage in search of LaPerouse; performed by order of the Constituent Assembly, during the years 1791, 1792, 1793, and 1794, and drawn up by M. Labillardiere, one of the naturalists at-

tached to the expedition, trans. from
the French, illus. with forty-six plates.
London, Stockdale, 1800. 2 v. fronts., 43
plates, fold. map, tables.
OrHi WaU 5623

Labor Exchange Association of Portland.
Communication [to Gov. Grover of Oregon offering suggestions on the subject
of immigration] Portland, Or., 1870. 11 p.
OrU 5624

Labor Journal, Everett, Wash.
Annual industrial edition. [50th anniver-
sary] Everett, Wash., 1941. 64 p. illus.,
map.   WaS 5625

[Lacombe, Albert] 1827?-1916.
La Pere Lacombe "l'homme au bon coeur"
d'apres ses memoires et souvenirs re-
cueillis par une soeur de la Providence.
Montreal, Imprime au devoir, 1916. 527
p. front., plates, maps.
CVicAr WaU 5626

Ladd, William J., see no. 10349.

Ladd and Bush Bank, Salem, Or.
70 years, March 29, 1869-March 29, 1939.
Salem, Or., 1939. [36] p. illus., ports.
Or OrCS OrU 5627

[Sixty-two milestones of progress, 1868-
1930] [n.p.] 1930. 33 p. illus., ports.
Or OrU WaU 5628

Ladd & Tilton Bank, Portland, Or.
An open door to banking. [Portland, Or.,
c1920] 34 p.   OrP 5629

Sixty milestones of progress, 1859-1919.
[Portland, Or., James, Kerns & Abbott Co., c1919] xi, 64 p. front., illus.,
ports.   Many 5630

"Then and now" (1859-1921) series of adver-
tisements. [Portland, Or.] 1921. [32] p.
illus.   OrHi OrP WaPS 5631

Ladies' Relief Society of Portland, Or.
Articles of incorporation and by-laws of
the Home, incorporated July 12, 1871.
Portland, Or., Himes & Bachelder, 1871.
11 p.   OrP 5632

Organization and by-laws of the Ladies'
Relief Society and articles of incorpora-
tion "The Home". Portland, Or., West
Shore Press, 1887. 18 p.   OrP 5633

La Du, Crumline.
Circular for spring, 1880; appendix to
catalogue of 1879. [Mt. Coffin, W. T?
1880] 7 p. Anon.   WaU 5634

Descriptive catalogue of small fruits in
cultivation at Columbia River Fruit
Gardens, Mount Coffin, W. T., La Du,
proprietor. Astoria, Or., Astorian Book
and Job Office, 1879. 7 p.   WaU 5635

Ladue, Joseph.
Klondyke facts; being a complete guide
book to the great gold regions of the
Yukon and Klondyke and the North-
west Territories and Alaska. Montreal,
J. Lovell [1897] 205 p. plates, maps.
CVicAr WaU 5636

Same. New York, American Technical
Book Co. [c1897] 205 p. front. (port.)
16 plates, fold. map.
CVicAr CVU OrU WaPS WaS WAU 5637

Klondyke nuggets; being a brief descrip-

tion of the famous gold regions of the
great Canadian Northwest and Alaska.
New York, American Technical Book
Co. [1897] 92 p. (American technical
series, no. 5)   CVicAr CVU 5638

See also nos. 5861, 5862.

LaGrande Evening Observer.
Northeastern Oregon edition. LaGrande,
Or., 1945. 1 v. illus. (Oct. 1, 1945)
WaU 5639

LaGrasserie, Raoul de, 1839-1914.
Cinq langues de la Colombie brittanique;
haida, tshimshian kwagiutl, nootka et
tlinkit; grammaires, vocabulaires, textes traduits et analyses. Paris, J. Maisonneuve, 1902. 530 p. (Bibliotheque
linguistique americaine, t. 24)
CVicAr CVU WaU 5640

Laguna, Frederica de, see nos. 850, 2373-2375.

Laing, F. W.
Colonial farm settlers on the mainland of
British Columbia, 1858-1871; with an
historical sketch. Victoria, B. C., 1939.
24, 517, 13, p.   CVU 5641

Laist, Alexander.
Official history of the operations of the
First Montana Infantry, U.S.V. in the
campaign of the Philippine Islands.
[San Francisco, Hicks-Judd Co.? 1899?]
94 p. illus., ports.   Many 5642

Lake, Mary.
Tsolo. New York, Hobson Book Press.
c1946. 140 p. illus. Mining story of Washington mountains.   WaS WaWW 5643

Lake, Stuart N.
Wyatt Earp, frontier marshal. Boston,
Houghton [1931] xiv, 392 p. front., 7
plates, 7 ports., facsim.   Many 5644

Lake County, Oregon. Lakeview, Or. [n.d.]
19 p. illus., maps.   OrP 5645

Lake Washington Belt Line Co.
Lake Washington, resources of the region
tributary to its eastern shores and the
Belt Line Railroad; Kirkland, the manufacturing city of the Puget Sound
region. Seattle, Lowman & Hanford,
1891. 47 p. illus., map.   WaU 5646

Lallemant, A. J. N., see no. 3470.

Lamb, Frank Haines.
The pioneers; an address before Peddie
Alumni Association, McAlpin Hotel, New
York city, Feb. 3, 1922 and other occas-
ions. Hoquiam, Wash., 1923. 18 p.
WaU 5647

Two neglected subjects; an address before the Grays Harbor Teachers Institute, Hoquiam, Wash., Sept. 5, 1923.
Hoquiam, Wash., 1923. 14 p. WaU 5648

Lamb, George, see no. 7985.

Lamb, Peter O.
The sign of the buffalo skull, the story
of Jim Bridger, frontier scout, with
fourteen illus. in black-and-white by
James Daugherty. New York, Stokes,
1932. xi, 288 p. front., illus., plates.
Or OrP WaS WaU WaW 5649

Lamb, W. Kaye, see no. 6433.

Lambert, Mrs. Alice Elinor.
Women are like that. New York, Van-

guard Press [c1934] 302 p. Pacific Coast
setting.   Or Wa WaE WaS WaU **5650**

Lambert, Mrs. Clara (Breakey) 1898-
The story of Alaska, with pictures by
C. H. DeWitt. New York, Harper [c1940]
[40] p. illus. (part. col.)
            Or OrP WaS WaSp WaT **5651**

Same. [1941]   WaT WAU **5652**

Lambert, Frederick, 1887-
Bygone days of the Old West, illus. by
the author. Kansas City, Mo., Burton
Pub. Co. [1948] 487 p. illus. Poems.
                           WaU **5653**

Lambert, Joseph Hamilton, see no. 6721.

Lambert, Thomas Wilson.
Fishing in British Columbia, with a chap-
ter on tuna fishing at Santa Catalina.
London, H. Cox, 1907. xv, 136 p.
                       CVU WaU **5654**

Lampman, Ben Hur, 1886-
At the end of the car line; editorial
sketches, essays and verse selected
from the Oregonian files of several
years. Portland, Or., Binfords & Mort
[1942] 191 p. front.   Many **5655**

The book of Oregon; a compilation of information and statistics for the benefit
of those who wish to know more about
the state, comp. and written by Ben
Hur Lampman and Ernest C. Potts.
[Portland, Or.] Portland Press Club,
1921. 70 p. illus.   WaU **5656**

Centralia tragedy and trial; joint publication of Grant Hodge Post no. 17,
Centralia, Wash. and Edward B. Rhodes
Post no. 2, Tacoma, Wash., The American Legion. [Tacoma, Wash.?] c1920.
79 p. illus., ports.
            Or OrP Wa WaS WaSp WaU **5657**

The coming of the pond fishes; an account of the introduction of certain
spiny-rayed fishes, and other exotic
species, into the waters of the lower
Columbia River region and the Pacific
Coast states, illus. by Ralph Penrose
Lee. Portland, Or., Binfords & Mort
[c1946] xii, 177 p. front., illus.
                             Many **5658**

Here comes somebody, illus. with drawings by Mahlon Blaine. Portland, Or.,
Metropolitan, 1935. 275 p. front., illus.,
plates.   Or OrP OrU WaSp WaW **5659**

How could I be forgetting? Being a compilation of some of his editorial writings and poems, heretofore pub. principally in the Morning Oregonian, illus.
by Howard L. Stroupe. Portland, Or.,
W. W. R. May, 1926. 196 p. front., illus.
    MtU Or OrCS OrP OrSaW **5660**

Same. New ed. Portland, Or., Metropolitan [c1926]   OrHi OrP WaSp **5661**

Same. 3d printing. 1933. 139 p.
            OrAshS OrU WaS WaU **5662**

The tramp printer, sometime journeyman
of the little home-town papers in days
that come no more. Portland, Or., Metropolitan, 1934. 58 p. illus., plates.
            Or OrU WaSp WaU **5663**

The wild swan and other sketches, illus.
by Quincy Scott. New York, Crowell
[1947] 205 p. illus.   Many **5664**

Lampman, Clinton Parks, 1862-
The great western trail. [New York] Putnam, 1939. 280 p. front., plates, ports.
            MtHi MtU WaE WaT **5665**

Lampman, Herbert Sheldon, 1907-
Northwest nature trails, a natural history of Oregon and Washington, illus.
by Quincy Scott, sponsored by Oregon
State Game Commission. Portland, Or.,
Metropolitan, 1933. 288 p. front., illus., 6
plates.   Many **5666**

Lancaster, G. B., see no. 6170.

Lancaster, Samuel Christopher.
The Columbia; America's great highway
through the Cascade Mountains to the
sea. Portland, Or., 1915. 140 p. col. front.,
illus. (part col.) ports., fold. col. plate.
            CVicAr Or OrP WaS **5667**

Same. 2d ed. 1916. 144 p.   Many **5668**

Same. 3d ed. Portland, Or., J. K. Gill Co.,
1926. 146 p.   Many **5669**

Romance of the gateway through the
Cascade Range. Portland, Or., J. K. Gill
Co. [c1929] 32 p. illus.   Many **5670**

Land of the Okanagan, British Columbia.
[Vancouver, B. C.] Daily Telegram
[1889?] 48 p. illus.   CVicAr WaSp **5671**

Landes, Henry, 1867-1936.
The geography of Washington. Chicago,
Rand McNally, 1910. 32 p. (Suppl. to
Dodge, Richard Elwood. Dodge's ad-
vanced geography)   WaS WaT **5672**

Washington. Chicago, Rand McNally
[c1899] 13 p. illus. (Suppl. to Bowen,
James A. Grammar school geography)
                             WaU **5673**

Landis, Paul Henry, 1901-
Fifty years of population growth in Washington; a study of the trends in numbers, composition, vital traits and migration of Washington population. Pullman, Wash., Wash. State College, 1942.
47 p. illus. (Agricultural Experiment
Station, Bulletin no. 419, Sept. 1942)
                             WaS **5674**

Rural population trends in Washington.
Pullman, Wash., Wash. State College,
1936. 64 p. (Agricultural Experiment
Station, Bulletin no. 333, July 1936)
                             WaS **5675**

Selected population problems of the west-
ern states in relation to agricultural ad-
justment; a paper presented at the
Ninth annual meeting of the Western
Farm Economics Association, Laramie,
Wyoming, July 30 and 31 and August 1,
1936. Pullman, Wash., Rural Sociology
Research Laboratory, 1936. 15 p. diagrs.
                         OrP WaPS **5676**

Lane, Joseph, 1801-1881.
Circular of Hon. Joseph Lane, delegate
from Oregon in reference to the settlement, soil and climate of Oregon Territory. Washington, D. C., J. T. Townes,
1852. 8 p.   OrU **5677**

Letter to the people of Oregon. Washington, D. C., 1859. 8 p. (Jan. 12, 1859)
OrCS OrHi OrU **5678**

Lang, Herbert O., ed.
History of the Willamette Valley, being a description of the valley and its resources, with an account of its discovery and settlement by white men, and its subsequent history; together with personal reminiscences of its early pioneers. Portland, Or., Himes & Lang, 1885. 902 p. front. (port.) 5 plates, facsim.
Many **5679**

Lange, Dietrich, 1863-
The Shawnee's warning; a story of the Oregon Trail. Boston, Lothrop, Lee & Shepard [c1919] 324 p. front., plates.
Or OrP WaS **5680**

Langford, Nathaniel Pitt, 1832-1911.
Address delivered before the Grand Lodge of Montana at its third annual communication, in the city of Virginia, Oct. 8, A.D. 1867. Helena, Mont., "Herald" Book Establishment, 1868. 16 p.
IdU MtHi **5681**

Vigilante days and ways; the pioneers of the Rockies; the makers and making of Montana, Idaho, Oregon, Washington and Wyoming. Boston, J. G. Cupples, 1890. 2 v. fronts., ports.   Many **5682**

Same. New York, D. D. Merrill Co. [c1890] 2 v. fronts., ports.   WaPS **5683**

Same. 1893 [c1890] MtU OrSaW WaU **5684**

Same. 2 v. in 1.   Many **5685**

Same. The makers and making of Montana and Idaho. Chicago, McClurg, 1912. 554 p. front., plates, ports.   Many **5686**

Same. New York, Burt [c1912] (Crescent library)   IdB WaW **5687**

Same. Chicago, McClurg, 1927 [c1912]
MtU OrU **5688**

Same. 1931 [c1912]   IdP WaTC **5689**
See also no. 3172.

Langsdorff, Georg Heinrich, Freiherr von, 1774-1852.
Langsdorff's narrative of the Rezanov voyage to Nueva California in 1806, being that division of Doctor Georg H. von Langsdorff's **Bemerkungen auf einer Reise um die Welt,** when, as personal physician, he accompanied Rezanov to Nueva California from Sitka, Alaska, and back; an English trans. rev., with the Teutonisms of the original Hispaniolized, Russianized, or Anglicized, by Thomas C. Russell; illus. with ports. and map. San Francisco, T. C. Russell, 1927. xiv, 158 p. front., plates (1 double) ports., fold. map, facsims. (Russell Calif. reprints)
OrU WaS WaU **5690**

Lanks, Herbert Charles, 1899-
Highway to Alaska; photographs by the author. New York, Appleton-Century [1944] 200 p. front., plates, ports.
Many **5691**

Lanning, C. M.
A grammar and vocabulary of the Blackfoot language, comp. by C. M. Lanning from original trans. by Joseph Kipp

and W. S. Gladston, Jr. Fort Benton, Mont. Ter., c1882. 143 p.   MtHi **5692**

Lansdowne, William Petty, 1st Marquis of, 1737-1805.
The substance of the speech of the Marquis of Lansdown in the House of Lords on the 14th of December, 1790; on the subject of the convention with Spain, which was signed on the 28th of October 1790, by one present. London, J. Debrett [1790?] 23 p.
CVicAr WaS WaU **5693**

Lantis, Margaret, 1909-
Alaskan Eskimo ceremonialism. New York, J. J. Augustin, c1947. 127 p. maps. (American Ethnological Society. Monographs, v. 11)   WaS **5694**

Laperouse, Jean Francois de Galaup, comte de, 1741-1788.
Le voyage de Laperouse sur les cotes de l'Alaska et de la Californie (1796) avec une introduction et des notes par Gilbert Chinard. Baltimore, Johns Hopkins Press, 1937. xlix, 144 p. front. (port.) plates, maps, plans, facsim. (Historical documents. Institut francais de Washington. Cahier 10)
CVicAr WaSp WaU **5695**
See also no. 3348.

Lapham, Stanton C.
The enchanted lake; Mount Mazama and Crater Lake in story, history and legend. Portland, Or., J. K. Gill Co. [c1931] 138 p. front., plates.   Many **5696**

Lapp, John A., see no. 2592.

Large, Thomas.
The challenge of inland waters. [Spokane? 1935] [4] p. illus. (Northwest science, v. 10, no. 2, May 1936 suppl.) WaPS **5697**

Laroche, Benjamine, see no. 5054.

LaRoche, Frank, illus.
En route to the Klondike; a series of photographic views of the picturesque land of gold and glaciers, picturing the actual places traveled over by gold seekers en route to the land of treasure, presenting to the eye its beauties, its grandeurs and its dangers; also showing many camps and parties of Argonauts going to the gold fields. Chicago, W. B. Conkey [1898] 6 pt. in 1 v. plates, maps.
CVU WaS WaU **5698**

Larowe, Mrs. Nina (Churchman).
An account of my life's journey so far: its prosperity, its adversity, its sunshine and its clouds; this book is dedicated lovingly to the Third Oregon Infantry. [Portland, Or., Kilham Stationery and Printing Co., 1917?] 68 p. port.
Or OrHi OrP WaPS **5699**

Larpenteur, Charles, 1803?-1872.
Forty years a fur trader on the upper Missouri; the personal narrative of Charles Larpenteur, 1833-1872; ed. with many critical notes by Elliott Coues. New York, F. P. Harper, 1898. 2 v. fronts., 5 plates, 7 ports., 6 maps (part fold.) (American explorers series, 2)
Many **5700**

Same. Historical introd. by Milo Milton Quaife. Chicago, Lakeside Press, 1933. xxiii, 388 p. front. (port.) fold. map. (Lakeside classics).
CVU WaS WaSp WaU **5701**

Larrabee, C. K., see no. 1134.

Larrison, Earl Junior.
A field guide to the birds of King County, Washington, with illus. by Elizabeth L. Curtis. Seattle [Seattle Audubon Society, c1947] 66 p. illus., maps (1 double). (Trailside series, no. 1, Nov. 1947).
WaE WaS WaT WaU **5702**

Larsell, Olof, 1886-
The development of medical education in the Pacific Northwest. Eugene, Or., Koke-Chapman Co. [1924] 47 p. plates, ports.
Or OrHi OrP OrU WaU WaWW **5703**

The doctor in Oregon; a medical history. Portland, Or., Binfords & Mort [1947] x, 671 p. illus., ports.   Many **5704**

The last of the buffalo comprising a history of the buffalo herd of the Flathead Reservation and an account of the Great Round Up. Cincinnati, Tom Jones, Engraver, 1909. 1 v. 23 illus. MtHi **5705**

"The last spike"; 1850-1883; a historical and descriptive review of the industries and resources of Oregon and Washington, their trade, commerce and manufactures; together with the principal business houses and manufacturing establishments. Portland, Or., von Otterstedt, 1883. 12 p. front. (ports.) illus., 4 plates, map.   WaU **5706**

Lathrop, George, 1830-1915.
Some pioneer recollections, being the autobiography of George Lathrop, one of the first to help in the opening of the West, and a statement made by John Sinclair relative to the rescue of the Donner party, also an extract from a letter written by Geo. McKinstry with reference to the rescue of the Donner party. Philadelphia, G. W. Jacobs, 1927. 32 p. port.
IdU **5707**

Same. Together with personal recollections of pioneer life, by Luke Vorhees. 32, 75 p.   WaS WaSp **5708**

Lathrop, West.
Juneau, the sleigh dog, illus. by Kurt Wiese. New York, Random House [1942] 279 p. illus.
Or OrPR Wa WaS WaSp WaT **5709**

Same. London, Museum Press, 1946, 1944. 224 p. illus.   WaS **5710**

Laughead, W. B.
The marvelous exploits of Paul Bunyan as told in the camps of the white pine lumbermen for generations, during which time the loggers have pioneered the way through the north woods from Maine to California, collected and embellished for publication; text and illus. by W. B. Laughead, pub. for the amusement of our friends. Minneapolis, Red River Lumber Co., 1922. 35 p. illus.
CVU MtU **5711**

Same. 3d ed. 1924.   WaSp WaT WaU **5712**

Same. 7th ed. [1935] 37 p.   WaU **5713**

Laughon, Albert J.
Spirit of the wild rosebush; a novel of the pioneer period of the Inland Empire. [Seattle] 1938. 362 p.
Wa WaS WaSp WaU WaWW **5714**

Laughton, Cathrine Carter, 1901-   ed.
Mary Cullens Northwest cook book. Portland, Or., Binfords & Mort [c1946] 340 p. illus.   Many **5715**

Launay, J. Belin de, see nos. 6853, 6854.

Laurelhurst. [Seattle, Lumbermen's Printing Co., 1906] [24] p. col. illus., col. plates, col. plan.   WaU **5716**

Laurgaard, O., see no. 1598.

Lauridsen, Gregers Marius, 1861-
The story of Port Angeles, Clallam County, Washington; an historical symposium, sponsored and written in part by G. M. Lauridsen; ed. and written in part by A. A. Smith. [Seattle, Lowman & Hanford, 1937] 276 p. front., illus., plates, ports., maps, facsim.   Many **5717**

Lauridsen, Peter, 1846-1923.
Vitus Bering; the discoverer of Bering Strait, rev. by the author, and trans. from the Danish by Julius C. Olson, with an introd. to the American edition by Frederick Schwatka. Chicago, C. S. Griggs & Co., 1889. xvi, 223 p. fold. maps.
Many **5718**

Vitus J. Bering og de Russiske opdagelsesrejser fra 1725-1743. Kjobenhavn, F. Hegel & Son, 1885. iii. 210 p. illus., plates, 4 fold. maps, table.   CVicAr **5719**

Laut, Agnes Christian, 1871-1936.
The 'Adventurers of England' on Hudson's Bay; a chronicle of the fur trade in the North. Toronto, Glasgow, Brook & Co., 1914. 133 p. front. (port.) 4 plates, port., 4 maps (2 fold.) (Chronicles of Canada, v. 18).   CVU **5720**

Same. 1920.   OrP WaS WaU **5721**

Same. 1922.   MtU WaE **5722**

The blazed trail of the old frontier, being the log of the Upper Missouri Historical Expedition under the auspices of the governors & historical associations of Minnesota, North and South Dakota and Montana for 1925, with many illus. from drawings by Charles M. Russell. New York, McBride, 1926. xii, 271 p. front., illus., plates, ports, maps (1 fold.) facsims.   Many **5723**

The Cariboo trail; a chronicle of the goldfields of British Columbia. Toronto, Glasgow, Brook & Co., 1916. viii, 115 p. col. front. (port.) 9 plates, 2 ports., fold. map. (Chronicles of Canada, v. 23)   Many **5724**

Same. 1920.   WaS WaU **5725**

Same. 1922.   MtU **5726**

The conquest of our western empire. New York, McBride, 1927. 363 p. front., plates, ports., maps.   Many **5727**

The conquest of the great Northwest; being the story of the Adventurers of England, known as the Hudson's Bay Company. Toronto, Musson [n.d.] 2 v.

fronts., 18 plates, 10 ports., 9 maps, facsims. CVicAr WaU **5728**

Same. [1908] CVU **5729**

Same. New pages in the history of the Canadian Northwest and western states. New York, Outing Pub. Co., 1908. 2 v. 2 fronts., 12 plates, 11 ports., 9 maps (part fold.) 6 facsims. Many **5730**

Same. New York, Moffat, 1911. 2 v. in 1. front., map. CVU IdU Or **5731**

Same. 1914. OrHi OrSaW WaS **5732**

Same. New York, Doran, c1918. 2 v. in 1. front., 3 fold. maps. Many **5733**

Same. 6th ed. Toronto, Musson [c1918] CVic **5734**

Enchanted trails of Glacier Park. New York, McBride, 1926. viii, 251 p. front., plates. Many **5735**

The freebooters of the wilderness. New York, Moffat, 1910. xiii, 443 p. Timber thefts in Washington, Oregon, Idaho and Montana. IdB Or WaPS WaS **5736**

Same. Toronto, Musson, 1910. CVicAr CVU WaU **5737**

The fur trade of America. New York, Macmillan, 1921. xv, 341 p. front., plates. Many **5738**

Heralds of empire; being the story of one Ramsay Stanhope, lieutenant to Pierre Radisson in the northern fur trade. New York, Appleton, 1902. viii, 372 p. CVU IdU WaU **5739**

Same. Toronto, Briggs, 1902. CVU WaU **5740**

John Tanner, captive boy wanderer of the border lands. Toronto, Ryerson [c1930] 32 p. illus. CVicAr **5741**

Lords of the North. New York, J. F. Taylor Co., 1900. 442 p. CVU IdU MtU WaPS WaTC **5742**

Same. Toronto, Ryerson [c1900] CV **5743**

Same. London, Heinemann, 1901. CVU **5744**

Same. New York, Doubleday, Page, 1906 [c1900] (Historical series). MtHi Wa **5745**

Same. Toronto, Briggs, 1909. WaU **5746**

The overland trail; the epic path of the pioneers to Oregon, with forty-nine illus. from photographs, two maps and two diagrs. New York, Stokes, 1929. xx, 358 p. front., illus., plates, maps. Many **5747**

Pathfinders of the West; being the thrilling story of the men who discovered the great Northwest: Radisson, LaVerendrye, Lewis and Clark, illus. by Remington, Goodwin, Marchand and others. New York, Grosset [c1904] xxv, 380 p. front., illus., plates, maps. CVU IdB OrHi WaT WaU **5748**

Same. New York, Macmillan, 1904. Many **5749**

Same. Toronto, 1904. CVU **5750**

Same. New York, Macmillan, 1914 [c1904] IdU OrP **5751**

Same. 1918 [c1904] CVicAr CVU IdIf OrU Wa **5752**

Same. 1922 [c1904] IdIf WA **5753**

Same. 1923 [c1904] Wa **5754**

Same. 1925 [c1904] IdP WaT **5755**

Pioneers of the Pacific Coast; a chronicle of sea robbers and fur hunters. Toronto, Glasgow, Brook & Co., 1915. viii, 139 p. col. front., 4 plates, 4 ports., fold. map. (Chronicles of Canada series). Many **5756**

Same. 1920. CVicAr WaS WaU **5757**

Same. 1922. MtU OrP WaE **5758**

The romance of the rails. New York, McBride, 1929. 2 v. fronts., illus., plates, ports., maps., facsims, music. OrHi WaS WaSp WaT **5759**

The story of the trapper. New York, Appleton, 1902. xv, 284 p. front., 7 plates. (The story of the West series). Many **5760**

Same. 1919. CVicAr IdIf **5761**

Vikings of the Pacific; the adventures of the explorers who came from the West eastward: Bering, the Dane; the outlaw hunters of Russia; Benyowsky, the Polish pirate; Cook and Vancouver, the English navigators; Gray of Boston, the discoverer of the Columbia; Drake, Ledyard, and other soldiers of fortune on the west coast of America. New York, Macmillan, 1905. xviii, 349 p. front., illus., 8 plates, 7 ports., maps. Many **5762**

Same. 1914 [c1905] IdU MtU WaTC **5763**

Laveille, E.

The life of Father DeSmet, S.J. (1801-1873) authorized trans. by Marian Lindsay, introd. by Charles Coppens. New York, Kenedy, 1915. xxii, 400 p. front., 4 plates, port., facsim. Many **5764**

Le P. DeSmet (1801-1873) 2me ed. Liege, Dessein, 1913. xiii, 560 p. front. (port.) fold map, facsim. CVicAr **5765**

Le P. DeSmet, apotre des Peux-Rouges (1801-1873) introd. par Godefroid Kurth. 4 ed. Louvain, Desbarax, 1928. xiv, 480 p. front. (port.) fold. map. (Museum lessianum. Section missiologique. Publications no. 9) WaU **5766**

Same. 4 ed. 12e mille. CVU **5767**

LaVerendrye, Pierre Gaultier de Varennes, sieur de, 1665-1749.

Journals and letters of Pierre Gaultier de Varennes de la Verendrye and his sons, with correspondence between the governors of Canada and the French court, touching the search for the western sea; ed. with introd. and notes by Lawrence J. Burpee. Toronto, Champlain Society, 1927. 548 p. 7 fold. maps. (Publications, no. 16) Many **5768**

LaVerne's Klondike songster. [n.p., 1898?] 16 p. WaU **5769**

Law Society of British Columbia.

Rules. [Victoria, B. C.] British Colonist [1869] 8 p. CVicAr **5770**

Lawing, Mrs. Nellie (Trosper) Neal.

Alaska Nellie. Seattle, Seattle Printing &

Pub Co. [c1940] 201 p. front., plates, ports. WaS WaSp WaU **5771**

Lawrence, Ellis F., see no. 3560.

Lawrence, John Craig, 1861-1928.
The story of my life. [n.p., 1925] 66 [16] p. fronts. (ports.) Wa **5772**

Lawrence, W. A., see no. 6699.

Lawson, Maria.
A history of British Columbia for use in public schools: History, by Maria Lawson; geography, by Rosalind Watson Young. Toronto, W. J. Gage & Co. [1906] 148 p. front., illus., map. (Gage's 20th Century series) CV CVU **5773**

Same. Toronto, Educational Book Co. [c1913] 156 p. front., illus., maps. (Dominion series) CVicAr CVU **5774**

Lawson, Will, 1876-
Pacific steamers. Glasgow, Brown, Son & Ferguson, 1927. xx, 244 p. front., plates. Many **5775**

Lawton, George, 1900-
Women go to work at any age. Portland, Or., Altrusa Club [c1947] 47 p. illus. Or OrCS OrP **5776**

Laycock, Edward Penard.
Canada's most western cathedral; the official handbook. London, Society for Promoting Christian Knowledge [n.d.] 44 p. illus. Christ Church Cathedral, Victoria, B. C. CVicAr **5777**

Laytha, Edgar, 1910-
North again for gold; birth of Canada's Arctic empire. New York, Stokes, 1939. xii, 360 p. front., 15 plates, maps. Many **5778**

Layton, Mark, see no. 8849.

Leach, Adoniram J.
Early day stories; the overland trail; animals and birds that lived here; hunting stories; looking backward. 2d ed. [Norfolk, Neb., Huse Pub. Co., 1916] 244 p. front., (port.) plates. IdU MtU WaU **5779**

Leacock, Stephen Butler, 1869-1944.
Adventures of the far North; a chronicle of the frozen seas. Toronto, Glasgow, Brook & Co., 1914. 152 p. col. front., plates., ports., fold map. (Chronicles of Canada series, 20) CVU MtU WaU **5780**

Same. 1920. CVicAr WaS **5781**

My discovery of the West; a discussion of East and West in Canada. Boston, Cushman & Flint [c1937] 272 p. Many **5782**

Leader, John.
Oregon through alien eyes. Portland, Or., J. K. Gill Co., 1922. 147 p. OrHi OrP WaU **5783**

Same. Portland, Or., Irwin-Hodson, 1922. Or OrCS OrP OrU WaPS **5784**

League of Oregon Cities.
Highway revenues and city streets, December 1938. Eugene, Or., 1938. 35 p. charts, tables. Or OrP OrU **5785**

Memorandum on the proposed constitutional amendment to the 6 per cent limitation, prepared by the League of Oregon Cities in cooperation with the Bureau of Municipal Research and Service,

University of Oregon. Eugene, Or., 1940. 22, vii p. WaU **5786**

The property taxpayer and Oregon's public revenue system; memorandum submitted to the Industrial Development Commission. Eugene, Or., 1942. 38 p. map, tables, diagrs. Or OrCS OrU WaU **5787**

Survey of the financial situation of the city Enterprise, Oregon, by Charles McKinley; tables and maps prepared by Arthur M. Cannon, Eugene, Or., 1934. vii, 115 p. tables, diagrs. OrCS OrU **5788**

League of Pacific Northwest Municipalities.
Constitution and by-laws, together with an account of the purpose and work of the League and the advantages to be derived from membership therein. Walla Walla, Wash., 1912. 16 p. OrP WaU **5789**

Third annual congress, November 10 to 12, 1914, under the auspices of the Seattle Rotary Club. Seattle, 1914. 48 p. Program and guide book to Seattle. WaS WaWW **5790**

League of Women Voters. Oregon.
Modernizing county government. [n.p.] 1942. 19 p. diagr. OrP **5791**

Leather, Fitzherbert.
Qui Si Sana, sanatorium and biological institution, Lake Crescent, Olympic Mountains, Piedmont P. O., Washington, U. S. A. [Seattle, Stuff Printing Concern, 19—?] [18] p. illus., plates (part col.) WaPS **5792**

Leavell, W. F.
Woods wren, summer storm and other verse. [n.p.] 1937. [5] p. Poems by Sultan, Washington, author. WaE **5793**

LeBourdais, Donat Marc, 1887-
Northward on the new frontier. Ottawa, Graphic Pub. [c1931] 311 p. plates, ports. CVicAr CVU WaS **5794**

Leckenby, Josephine.
Bright thicket of the stars. Boston, B. Humphries [1946] 111 p. Poems by Tacoma author. WaT WaU **5795**

Poems more or less. [Tacoma, Andrews Letter Shop, 1941] [76] p. illus. Wa WaT **5796**

Ledyard, John, 1751-1789.
A journal of Captain Cook's last voyage to the Pacific Ocean and in quest of a North-west passage between Asia and America, performed in the years 1776, 1777, 1778, and 1779, illus. with a chart showing the tracts of the ships employed in this expedition, faithfully narrated from the original ms. Hartford, N. Patten, 1783. 208 p. front. (fold. map). CVicAr CVU OrHi WaPS WaU **5797**

See also nos. 9720-9726.

Lee, Aaron, 1832-
From the Atlantic to the Pacific; reminiscenses of pioneer life and travels across the continent from New England to the Pacific Ocean, by an old soldier; also a graphic account of his army experiences in the Civil War. Seattle, Metro-

politan [c1915] 190 p. front. (port.) illus., plates.

CV Wa WaPS WaS WaSp WaU **5798**

Lee, Charles A.
Aleutian Indian and English dictionary; common words in the dialects of the Aleutian Indian language as spoken by the Oogashik, Egashik, Egegik, Ananga-shuk and Misremie tribes around Sulima River and neighboring parts of the Alaska Peninsula. Seattle, Lowman & Hanford, 1896. 23 p. Many **5799**

Lee, Daniel, 1806-1895.
Ten years in Oregon, by D. Lee and J. H. Frost. New York, J. Collord, 1844. 344 p. front. (fold. map). Many **5800**

Lee, Herbert Patrick.
Policing the top of the world; experiences of a private in the Royal Canadian Mounted Police in the most northerly police post in Canada, Ellesmere Land. London, John Land [1928] 250 p. front., plates, ports., 2 maps.

CVicAr CVU WaS **5801**

Lee, Jack H.
Powder River Jack and Kitty Lee's songs of the range. Chicago, Chart Music Pub., 1937. 50 p. illus. MtHi **5802**

West of Powder River, tales of the far West told in narrative verse, with a foreword by Courtney Riley Cooper, and with illus. by Paul Honore. New York, Huntington Press [c1933] 204 p. illus.

IdU MtHi WaE **5803**

Lee, Jason, see no. 7983.

Lee, Mrs. Jason, see no. 3481.

Lee, Kitty, see no. 5802.

Lee, William H., 1854-
Glimpses of the Lewis and Clark Exposition, Portland, Oregon, and the golden West, startling realistic scenes on the trail, official views illus the nation's wonderful progress and development. [Portland, Or.?] Official Photographic Co., c1905. 1 v. illus. WaPS **5804**

Leebrick, K. C., see no. 4937.

Leech, William H., see no. 6763.

Leechman, John Douglas, 1890-
String records of the Northwest, by J. D. Leechman and M. R. Harrington. New York, Museum of the American Indian, Heye Foundation, 1921. 64 p. front., illus., 6 plates. (Indian notes and monographs, Miscellaneous, no. 16). Many **5805**

Leehey, Maurice Daniel.
Mining code for the use of miners and prospectors in Washington and Alaska, with notes and annotations and forms for general use. [Seattle, c1900] 103 p.

CVicAr WaS WaU **5806**

The public land policy of the United States in Alaska; an address before the Northwest Mining Convention, Spokane, Feb. 16, 1912. Spokane, Franklin Press [c1912?] 16 p. WaS WaSp **5807**

Leeper, Robert Dwight, 1891-
Tsceminicum, Snake River people; poems by Donald Burnie [pseud.] Missoula, Mont., H. G. Merriam, 1930. 64 p.

Many **5808**

See also no. 675.

Lees, James Arthur.
B. C. 1887; a ramble in British Columbia, by J. A. Lees and W. J. Clutterbuck, with map and 75 illus. from sketches and photographs by the authors. London, Longmans, 1888. viii, 387 p. front., illus., 17 plates, map. Many **5809**

Same. New ed. 1889. WaU **5810**
Same. 1892.

CV CVic CVicAr CVU WaSp WaU **5811**

Leeson, Michael A. ed.
History of Montana, 1739-1885; a history of its discovery and settlement, social and commercial progress, mines and miners, agriculture and stock-growing, churches, schools and societies, Indians and Indian wars, vigilantes, courts of justice, newspaper press navigation, railroads and statistics, with histories of counties, cities, villages and mining camps. Chicago, Warner, Beers & Co., 1885. 1367 p. plates, ports., fold. map.

Many **5812**

LeFevre, Mrs. Lily Alice (Cooke)
The Lion's gate and other verses. Victoria, B. C., Province Pub. Co., 1895. 95 p.

CV CVU **5813**

Lefevre, Paul, see no. 6164.

Leforge, Thomas H., 1850-
Memoirs of a white Crow Indian, as told by Thomas B. Marquis. New York, Century [1928] 356 p. front., plates, ports.

IdP MtBozC MtHi MtU WaS **5814**

Lehmer, Derrick Norman, see no. 6613.

Leighton, Alexander Hamilton, 1908-
The governing of men; general principles and recommendations based on experience at a Japanese relocation camp. Princeton, N. J., Princeton Univ. Press, 1945. xvi, 404 p. illus., plates, maps, diagrs., plans. Many **5815**

Leighton, Ben Villeneuve, 1918-
The butterflies of Washington. Seattle, Univ. of Wash. Press, 1946. 49-63 p. (Publications in biology, v. 9, no. 2, Nov. 1946) WaS WaTC WaU **5816**

Leighton, Mrs. Caroline C.
Life at Puget Sound, with sketches of travel in Washington Territory, British Columbia, Oregon and California. Boston, Lee, 1884. ix, 258 p. Many **5817**

[Leisher, J. J.]
The decline and fall of Samuel Sawbones, M.D., on the Klondike, by his next best friend. Chicago, Neely Co. [c1900] 197 p. front., plates. CVicAr

CVU OrP WaPS WaU WaWW **5818**

LeJacq, J. M. J.
Our Lady of Lourdes. Kamloops, B. C., St. Louis Mission, 1893. 64 p. WaU **5819**

LeJeune, John Mary, 1855-
Benediction of a church [in Chinook Wawa shorthand] [Kamloops, B. C. n.d.] [16] p. music. WaU **5820**

Chinook and shorthand rudiments, with which the Chinook jargon and the Wawa shorthand can be mastered without a teacher in a few hours, by the editor of the "Kamloops Wawa". Kamloops, B. C., 1898. 15 p. CV CVicAr WaU **5821**

Chinook book of devotions throughout the year. Kamloops, B. C., 1902. 188 p.
CVU WaU 5822

Chinook first reading book including Chinook hymns, syllabary and vocabulary [in Wawa shorthand] Kamloops, B. C., 1893. 16 p.
WaU 5823

Chinook hymns [in Wawa shorthand] 4th ed. Kamloops, B. C., 1893. 16 p. Anon.
WaU 5824

Same. 6th ed. 1895. [18] p.
CV WaU 5825

Chinook primer. Kamloops, B. C., St. Louis Mission, 1892. 10 p.
WaU 5826

Chinook rudiments. [Kamloops, B. C.,] 1924. 36 p. (Kamloops Wawa, no. 1739, 3 May 1924) Anon.
CVicAr WaS WaSp WaU 5827

Chinook vocabulary; Chinook-English, from the original of Rt. Rev. Bishop Durieu, with the Chinook words in phonography, by J. M. R. LeJeune. 2d ed. Kamloops, B. C., 1892. 18 p.
WaU 5828

[Communion in Chinook shorthand. Kamloops, B. C., n.d.] 32 p. Anon.
WaU 5829

Elements of shorthand; or a phonetic syllabary after the Duployan system of phonography. 2d ed. Kamloops, B. C. [Kamloops Wawa] 1894. 16 p. Anon.
WaU 5830

Elements of shorthand, pt. 1, Kamloops, B. C. [Kamloops Wawa] 1891. 36 p. Anon.
WaU 5831

First catechism in Thompson language [in Wawa shorthand] [Kamloops, B. C., n.d.] 32 p. Anon.
WaU 5832

[Joseph sold by his brethren; an act played by the Shushwap Indians in 1892. Kamloops, B. C., Kamloops Wawa, 1892] 20 p. Anon.
WaU 5833

Latin manual; Mass (in Wawa shorthand). [Kamloops, B. C., n.d.] 16 p. Anon.
WaU 5834

Manual; or, Prayers and catechism, with the approbation of the Rt. Rev. P. Durien [!] bishop of New Westminster. Kamloops, B. C., 1896. 183 p. English, Chinook and Latin sections. Parts 1-4 of Polyglot manual. Anon. WaSp 5835

Messe royale [music with words in Wawa shorthand] [Kamloops, B. C., n.d.] 8 p. Anon.
WaU 5836

Missa de requiem [music with words in Wawa shorthand] [Kamloops, B. C., n.d.] 16 p. Anon.
WaU 5837

Night prayers in Ntla Kapmah or Thompson language. [Kamloops, B. C., n.d.] 17-32 p. Anon.
WaU 5838

Okanagan. [Kamloops, B. C., Kamloops Wawa] 1913. 64 p. Anon.
WaU 5839

Okanagan manual; or, Prayers and hymns and catechism in the Okanagan language, with the approbation of Rt. Rev. P. Durieu. Kamloops, B. C., 1897. 50 p. Anon.
WaU 5840

Polyglot manual. [Kamloops, B. C., 1896-1897.] 183, 30, 33, 31, 32, 63, 158 p. Each part has special title-page. Text, except pt. 1, in Duployan shorthand. Contents: [Pt. 1] English manual; or, Prayers and catechism in English typography. 1896. 19 p. [Pt. 2] Prayers and catechism in English phonography. 1896. 23-40 p. [Pt. 3] Chinook manual; or, Prayers, hymns and catechism in Chinook. 1896. 43-100 p. [Pt. 4] Latin manual; or, Hymns and chants in use by the Indians of B. C. 1896. 163-183 p. music. [Pt. 5] Stalo manual; or, Prayers, hymns and the catechism in the Stalo of lower Fraser language. 1897. 30 p. [Pt. 6] Thompson manual; or, Prayers, hymns and catechism in the Thompson or Ntla Kapmah language, 1897, 33 p. [Pt. 7] Lillooet manual; or, Prayers, hymns and catechism in the Lillooet or Statliemoh language. 1897. 31 p. [Pt. 8] Okanagan manual; or, Prayers and hymns in the Okanagan language. 1897. 32 p. [Pt. 9] Shushwap manual; or, Prayers, hymns and catechism in Shushwap. 1896. 63 p. [Pt. 10] Skwamish manual; or, Prayers, hymns and catechism in Skwamish. 1896. 56 p. [Pt. 11] Sheshel manual; or, Prayers, hymns and catechism in the Sechel [!] language. 1896. 57-109 p. [Pt. 12] Slayamen manual; or, Prayers, hymns and catechism in the Slayamen language. 1896, 111-158 p. Anon. CVicAr WaU 5841

Practical Chinook vocabulary. Kamloops, B. C., St. Louis Mission, 1886. 16 p. Anon.
WaWW 5842

Prayers before and after Holy Communion in several languages of the natives of British Columbia, extracted from the various books of the various tribes. Kamloops, B. C., 1925. 22 p. Anon.
CVicAr WaU 5843

Prayers for Communion in Ntla Kapmah or Thompson. [Kamloops, B. C., n.d.] 33-48 p. Anon.
WaU 5844

Prayers in Okanagan language [in Wawa shorthand] [Kamloops, B. C., 1893] 80 p. Anon.
WaU 5845

Prayers in Thompson language [in Wawa shorthand] 3d ed. Kamlopos, B. C., St. Louis Mission, 1894. 18 p. Anon.
WaU 5846

Prayers in Thompson or Ntla Kapmah [in Wawa shorthand] [Kamloops, B. C., n.d.] 32 p. Anon.
WaU 5847

Preces ante et post sacram communionem, in variis linguis sylvicolarum Columbiae Brittannicae in dioeceso Vancouveriense, excerptae ex eucologis variarum tribuum, approbatis ab ordinario. Kamloops, B. C., anno jubilaei, 1925. [Liege, H. Dessain, 1925?] 22 p. Anon.
WaSp 5848

[Shushwap manual in Wawa shorthand. Kamloops, B. C., n.d.] [107] p. Anon.
WaU 5849

Studies on Shuswap. [Kamloops, B. C.] 1925. 32 p. Anon.
CVicAr WaSp WaU 5850

The Wawa shorthand first reading book, by the editor of Kamloops "Wawa"

Kamloops, B.C., 1896. 16 p. CVicAr **5851**

The Wawa shorthand instructor; or, The Duployan stenography adapted to English, by the editor of the Kamloops "Wawa". Kamloops, B. C., 1896, 24 p. Anon.   CVicAr WaSp WaU **5852**

See also no. 2663.

Leland, Charles G.
Fusang; or, The discovery of America by Chinese Buddhist priests in the Fifth Century. London, Trubner & Co., 1875. xix, 212 p. CV CVicAr CVU WaU **5853**

See also nos. 697-699.

Lemer, Julien, see no. 747.

Lemmon, John Gill, 1832-1908.
Hand-book of west-American cone-bearers; approved English names with brief popular descriptions of the cone-bearing trees of the Pacific slope north of Mexico and west of Rocky Mountains. Oakland, Calif. [Pacific Press] 1892. 24 p. plates.   OrCS OrHi **5854**

Same. 2d ed.   OrCS WaU **5855**

Same. 3d ed. 1895. 104 p. front., 16 plates.
MtBozC OrU WaU **5856**

Same. 4th ed. 1900. 116 p.
Or OrP OrU **5857**

How to tell the trees and forest endowment of the Pacific slope; also some elements of forestry with suggestions by Mrs. Lemmon; 1st ser. The cone-bearers. Oakland, Calif., 1902. 66 p. front., illus., 2 plates.   OrP OrU **5858**

Le Moqueur, see no. 6901.

Lenox, Edward Henry, 1827-
Overland to Oregon in the tracks of Lewis and Clarke; history of the first emigration to Oregon in 1843, ed. by Robert Whitaker; illus. and introd. by R. Morgenier. Ltd. ed. Autograph copy. Oakland, Calif. [Dowdle Press] 1904. ix, 69 p. plates, ports., map.   Many **5859**

Leonard, Charles R., see no. 4455.

Leonard, Frances Sweet.
When evening shadows fall; poems. Caldwell, Idaho, Caxton, 1930. 287 p.
IdP IdTf **5860**

Leonard, John William, 1849-
The gold fields of the Klondike; fortune seekers guide to the Yukon region of Alaska and British America; the story as told by Ladue, Berry, Phiscator and other gold finders. Chicago, Marquis, 1897. 216 p. front., illus., plates, ports., fold. map.   CVicAr **5861**

Same. London, Unwin [1897]
CVic CVicAr WaS WaU **5862**

Leonard, Vivian Anderson.
Survey of the Seattle Police Department, Seattle, Washington, V. A. Leonard, consultant, June 1, 1945. [Seattle, 1945] 301 p. maps, tables, diagrs. WaS **5863**

Leonard, William Ellery, see no. 7928.

Leonard, Zenas, 1809-1858.
Leonard's narrative; adventures of Zenas Leonard, fur trader and trapper, 1831-1836; reprinted from the rare original of 1839, ed. by W. F. Wagner. Cleve-

land, Burrows Bros. Co., 1904. 317 p. front. (fold. map) illus., 2 ports.
Many **5864**

Le Rebeller, A., see no. 8824.

LeSourd, Gilbert Q.
Missionary to Oregon, Jason Lee. New York, Friendship Press, c1946. 23 p. (Frontier books, no. 3)
Or OrU WaT **5865**

Lessons and prayers in the Tenni or Slavi language of the Indians of Mackenzie River in the North-West Territory of Canada. London, Society for Promoting Christian Knowledge [1901] 81 p.
CVicAr **5866**

"Lest we forget"; notable addresses on Washington State Admission Day [by Miles C. Moore, the territorial governor and Elisha P. Ferry first state governor] [n.p., 1917?] 8 p. WaPS WaT **5867**

A letter from a Russian sea-officer to a person of distinction at the court of St. Petersburgh, containing his remarks upon Mr. de l'Isle's chart and memoir, relative to the new discoveries northward and eastward from Kamtschatka [by N. N.] Together with some observations on that letter by Arthur Dobbs. To which is added Mr. de l'Isle's explanatory memoir on his chart published at Paris and now trans. from the original French. London, Printed for A. Linde, 1754. 83 p.   WaU **5868**

Letters written during the late voyage of discovery in the western Arctic Sea, by an officer of the expedition. London, Printed for Sir R. Phillips and Co., 1821. iv, 124 p. front. (map) plates.
CVicAr WaSp **5869**

Levine, Louis, see no. 6121.

Levis, Gaston Gustave Marie Victurnien de Levis-Mirepoix, Marquis de, 1844-
Visite au Canada, suivie d'une course aux Montagnes-Rocheuses et a l'Ocean Pacifique en 1895. Chateaudun, Impr. de la Societe typographique, 1896. ii, 194 p.   CVicAr **5870**

Levy, Melvin P., 1902-
The last pioneers. New York, A. H. King [c1934] 368 p. Chronicles of a Washington waterfront town.   Many **5871**

Matrix. New York, T. Seltzer, 1925. 209 p. Seattle novel. Wa WaS WaTC WaU **5872**

Lewis, Alfred Henry, 1869-
South Vancouver past and present, an historical sketch of the municipality from the earliest days and its incorporation to the present, 1920; together with short biographical sketches of some of its leading business and public men. Vancouver, B. C., Western Pub. Bureau, 1920. 51 p. illus., ports.
WaSp **5873**

Lewis, C. J., ed.
Walnut culture in western and southern Oregon. Portland, Or., Southern Pacific Railroad [1916?] 46 p. illus.   OrP **5874**

Lewis, Clancey Montana, ed.
Fuller's yearbook of the greater Northwest; a record of the active concerns

and individuals who have been identified with the progress of the year 1910;
comp. and ed. by Clancey Montana
Lewis. Seattle, Fuller Pub. Co. [c1910]
112 p.   OrP WaS **5875**

Lewis, Edward Chester, see no. 5876.

Lewis, Frank Pardee, 1851-
Randall Lewis of Hopkinton, Rhode
Island, and Delaware County, New
York and some of his descendants; a
biographical and genealogical record,
by Frank Pardee Lewis and Edward
Chester Lewis. Seattle, Argus Press,
1929. 200 p. illus., ports.
                    Wa WaS WaU WaWW **5876**

Lewis, George Edward, 1870-
Nick of the woods, by Alaska Blacklock
[pseud.] Portland, Or. [Jensen Pub.
Co.] 1916. 222 p. illus., port.
                    CVicAr OrHi OrP **5877**

Yukon lyrics. Portland, Or., 1925. 69 p.
illus.   OrP WaU **5878**

Lewis, Howard Thompson, 1888-
The basic industries of the Pacific Northwest. [Seattle, Lowman & Hanford,
c1923] 174 p. fold. front., illus., plates.
                              Many **5879**

Same. With study questions prepared under the direction of Mrs. Corliss Preston. [Seattle, Lowman & Hanford,
c1925] 186, vi p. fold. front. (map) illus.,
plates.   Many **5880**

The economic resources of the Pacific
Northwest, ed. by Howard T. Lewis and
Stephen I. Miller. Seattle, Lowman &
Hanford [c1923] 523 p. fold. front., illus.,
plates, maps, fold. table, diagrs.
                              Many **5881**

Lewis, James, comp.
Snohomish County, Washington; a record
of remarkable achievement and a
prophecy of assured development, comp.
in conjunction with the commercial
organizations of its principal cities.
Everett, Wash., c1914. 64 p. illus., maps.
                          WaE WaU **5882**

Lewis, James, 1902- ed.
Doorway to good living; selected places:
where to eat, where to stay, where to
fish, where to play along the western
wonderland. Beverly Hills, Calif., Lewis
Publicity Service [1948] 334 p. illus.
                              Many **5883**

Lewis, John Gordon, 1862-
History of the Grand Ronde military
block house. Dayton, Or., Tribune Pub.
Co., 1911. [32] p. illus.
Or OrHi OrP WaS WaSp WaU **5884**

Lewis, John Howard, 1878-
Electric house heating with dissenting
opinion; Electric House Heating Committee, Pacific Northwest Regional
Planning Committee. Portland, Or.
[1934] [10] p.   OrP **5885**

Navigation and power development of
the Columbia River. [n.p.] 1935. 10 p.
                                OrP **5886**

Lewis, Margaret, see no. 5918.

Lewis, Meriwether, 1774-1809.
History of the expedition of Captains

Lewis and Clark, 1804-5-6; reprinted
from the ed. of 1814, with introd. and
index by James K. Hosmer. Chicago,
McClurg, 1902. 2 v. fronts. (ports.)
maps, plan.   Many **5887**

Same. 1903. 2d ed.   Many **5888**

Same. 3d ed. 1905.
                    IdB IdIf OrP WaSp **5889**

Same. 4th ed. 1917 [c1902] IdU OrSaW **5890**

Same. 5th ed. 1924 [c1902]   WaU **5891**

Same. [Louisville, Ky.] American Printing House for the Blind, 1937. 11 v.
Rev. Braille.   OrP **5892**

History of the expedition under the command of Captains Lewis and Clark to
the sources of the Missouri, across the
Rocky Mountains, down the Columbia
River to the Pacific, in 1804-6; a reprint of the ed. of 1814, to which all
the members of the expedition contributed. Toronto, Morang [n. d.] 3 v.
ports., facsim., maps.   CVicAr **5893**

History of the expedition under the command of Captains Lewis and Clark, to
the sources of the Missouri, thence
across the Rocky Mountains and down
the River Columbia to the Pacific
Ocean, performed during the years
1804-5-6, by order of the government
of the United States; prepared for the
press by Paul Allen. Philadelphia,
Bradford and Inskeep, 1814. 2 v. maps.
                              Many **5894**

Same. Rev. and abridged by the omission
of unimportant details, with an introd.
and notes by Archibald M'Vicker. New
York, Harper [c1842] 2 v. front. (fold.
map) plates, plans. (Harper's family
library, v. 154-155)   Many **5895**

Same. 1842-1843.   WaU **5896**

Same. 1868. v. 2 only.   WaU **5897**

Same. 1876. 2 v.   MtHi **5898**

Same. New York, Fowle, 1900.
                    CVic OrCS OrP OrSaW **5899**

Same. New York, Harper, 1901.
                          WaS WaU **5900**

Same. 1904.   WaTC **5901**

Same. A new ed. Original manuscript
journals and field notes of the explorers
together with a new biographical and
bibliographical introd., new maps and
other illus., and a complete index by
Elliott Coues. New York, F. P. Harper,
1893. 4 v. fronts., facsims., 3 maps.
                              Many **5902**

Same. A reprint of the ed. of 1814 to
which all the members of the expedition contributed. New York, New Amsterdam Book Co., 1902. 3 v. front., maps.
            IdP MtBozC OrP WaPS WaU **5903**

Same. With an account of the Louisiana
Purchase by Prof. John Bach Mc-
Master and notes upon the route. 3 v.
fronts., maps.   Many **5904**

Same. London, Nutt, 1905.   CVicAr **5905**

Same. New York, Allerton Book Co., 1922
[c1906]   Many **5906**

The journal of Lewis and Clarke, to the

mouth of the Columbia River beyond the Rocky Mountains, in the years 1804-5 & 6, giving a faithful description of the River Missouri and its source; of the various tribes of Indians through which they passed, manners and customs, soil, climate, commerce, gold and silver mines, animal and vegetable productions, etc. New ed. with notes, rev. and corrected; to which is added a complete dictionary of the Indian tongue. Dayton, Ohio, B. F. Ells, 1840. 240 p. fronts. (ports.) illus. "Counterfeit" pub.

OrHi WaPS WaU **5907**

The journals of Captain Meriwether Lewis and Sergeant John Ordway, kept on the expedition of western exploration, 1803-1806, ed. with introd. and notes by Milo M. Quaife. Madison, Wis., State Historical Society of Wis., 1916. 444 p. front., plates, port., maps (part fold.) facsims. (Collections, v. 22)

Many **5908**

Original journals of the Lewis and Clark expedition, 1804-1806; printed from the original manuscripts in the library of the American Philosophical Society and by direction of its Committee on Historical Documents, together with manuscript material of Lewis and Clark from other sources, including notebooks, letters, maps, etc., and the journals of Charles Floyd and Joseph Whitehouse, now for the first time published in full and exactly as written; ed. with introd., notes and index, by Reuben Gold Thwaites. New York, Dodd, 1904-1905, 8 v. fronts., illus. (part fold.) ports., facsims. Volume 8, atlas.

Many **5909**

Same. 8 v. in 15. fronts., illus., plates., ports., maps (part fold.) facsims. (part fold.) Printed on Van Gelder hand-made paper. Many **5910**

Travels in the interior parts of America; communicating discoveries made in exploring the Missouri, Red River and Washita, by Captains Lewis and Clark, Dr. Sibley, and Mr. Dunbar; with a statistical account of the countries adjacent, as laid before the Senate by the President of the United States in February 1806, and never before published in Great Britain. London, Printed for R. Phillips by J. C. Barnard, 1807. 116 p. CVicAr

MtHi OrP OrSaW WaPS WaS **5911**

The travels of Capts. Lewis and Clarke from St. Louis, by way of the Missouri and Columbia Rivers to the Pacific Ocean, performed in the years 1804, 1805, & 1806 by order of the government of the United States; containing delineations of the manners, customs, religion, &c. of the Indians, comp. from various authentic sources and original documents, and a summary of the Statistical view of the Indian nations from the official communication of Meriwether Lewis, illus. with a map of the country inhabited by the western tribes of Indians. London, Longman, 1809. ix, 309 p. front. (fold. map) "Counterfeit" pub.

CVicAr MtHi OrHi OrP WaS WAU **5912**

Travels to the source of the Missouri River and across the American Continent to the Pacific Ocean, performed by order of the government of the United States in the years 1804, 1805, and 1806 by Captains Lewis and Clarke; pub. from the Official report and illus. by a map of the route and other maps. London, Longman, 1814. xxiv, 663 p. fold. front., 3 maps.

CVicAr MtHi OrCS OrHi **5913**

Same. A new ed. in 3 v. 1815. 3 v. front. (fold. map) 5 maps.

CV CVicAr MtHi OrP OrSaW **5914**

Same. 1817. OrP WaU **5915**

See also nos. 130-135, 3116, 3465-3471, 4939.

Lewis, Oscar, 1914-
The effects of white contact upon Blackfoot culture, with special reference to the role of fur trade. New York, J. J. Augustin [c1942] vi, 73 p. il]us., maps. (Monographs of the American Ethnological Society, 6)

MtHi MtU OrU WaS **5916**

Lewis, Ralph Charles, 1903-
Surface catches of marine diatoms and dinoflagellates off the coast of Oregon by U. S. S. "Guide" in 1924. Berkeley, Univ. of Calif. Press, 1927. [16] p. (Scripps Institution of Oceanography, LaJolla. Bulletin, technical series v. 1, no. 11) Or OrP OrPR OrU WaU **5917**

Lewis, Thomas B.
What I have saved from the writings of my husband [by Margaret Lewis] San Francisco, Bonnard & Daly, 1874. 64, 59 p. Montana pioneer and poet. Contains chapter of facts on the history of Montana. WaSp WaU **5918**

Lewis, William Stanley, 1876-
The case of Spokane Garry. [Spokane, Cole Printing Co., n.d.] 68 p. front., 10 plates. CVicAr **5919**

Same. Being a brief statement of the principal facts connected with his career; and review of the charges made against him. [Spokane, 1917] 68 p. plates, ports. (Bulletin of the Spokane Historical Society, v. 1, no. 1) Many **5920**

The story of early days in the Big Bend country; breaking trails, rush of miners, coming of cattlemen, making homes, pioneer hardships in the Big Bend country. Autograph ed. Spokane, W. .D. Allen, 1926. 35 p. front., plates.

Many **5921**

See also nos. 1980, 6300, 11212.

Lewis and Clark Educational Congress, Portland, Or., 1905.
Program, organization and addresses; Lewis and Clark Educational Congress, Aug. 28 to Sept. 2, 1905. Portland, Or. [Anderson & Duniway Co., 1905] 121 p.

Many **5922**

Lewis County Agricultural Association.
Premium list, rules and regulations of the Lewis County Agricultural Association; fair to be held on their grounds at Chehalis, Wash., 1892. [Chehalis, Wash.] Chehalis Nugget, 1892. 20 p. WaU 5923

Lewiston, Idaho. 1st Methodist Episcopal Church.
Souvenir of the 31st anniversary. [n.p.] 1912. 44 p. illus. WaTC 5924

Lewiston, Idaho-Clarkston, Wash., the gateway cities; a picturesque and descriptive account of their mercantile and industrial interests and advantages. [Lewiston, Idaho, Lewiston Printing & Binding Co., n.d.] 24 p. illus.
IdU WaS 5925

Lewiston Morning Tribune.
Spalding centennial edition (1836-1936). Lewiston, Idaho, 1936. [94] p. illus., maps, ports. (May 3, 1936)
OrHi WaPS WaU 5926

Lewistown Democrat-News.
Christmas number. Lewistown, Mont., 1927. 12 p. illus., ports. (Dec. 18, 1927, sec. 5) Contains: Worthen, C. B. Fergus County, a miniature of the West.
WaU 5927

[Leyden James Alexander] 1826-1897.
A historical sketch of the Fourth Infantry from 1796 to 1861. Fort Sherman, Idaho, Press of the 4th U. S. Infantry, 1891. 20 p. Stationed on West Coast 1852-1861.
WaU 5928

The Liberal-Conservative Union of British Columbia.
Constitution and platform adopted September 13, 1902. [n.p., n.d.] 11 p.
CVicAr 5929

Life and labors of Francis Norbert Blanchet; together with funeral sermons by Charles J. Seghers. [Portland, Or., Catholic Sentinel, 1883] 16 p. port.
OrHi 5930

The life and work of Innocent, the archbishop of Kamchatka, the Kuriles and the Aleutian Islands. San Francisco [Cabery] 1897. 23 p. CVicAr WaU 5931

Life, explorations, and public services of John Charles Fremont. Boston, Ticknor, 1856. 356 p. illus., port. OrHi 5932

Life of Captain Cook. [n.p., n.d.] 32 p.
CVicAr 5933

The life of Captain James Cook; a new ed. London, C. F. Cook, 1831. 170 p. front., 3 plates. CVicAr 5934

Life of Colonel Fremont. [New York, Greeley & M'Elrath, 1856] 32 p. illus., port.
CVicAr WaU 5935

Life of Gen. Lewis Cass; comprising an account of his military service in the North-west during the war with Great Britain, his diplomatic career and civil history; to which is appended a sketch of the public and private history of Major-General W. O. Butler of the volunteer service of the United States. Philadelphia, Zieber & Co., 1848. 210 p. front. (port.) port. (Campaign biographies of the candidates for president and vice president on the Democratic ticket)
CVicAr MtU 5936

Life of the Rev. Mother Amadeus of the Heart of Jesus; foundress of the Ursuline Missions of Montana and Alaska; sketch comp. from convent annals by an Ursuline of Alaska. New York, Paulist Press, 1923. 233 p. front. (port.)
MtHi 5937

Life on beautiful Bellingham Bay. [n.p., n.d.] [24] p. illus. WaU 5938

The life, voyages and discoveries of Captain James Cook. 6th ed. London, J. W. Parker, 1859. 220 p. front., plates, ports.
WaU 5939

Liggett, Walter William, 1886-1935.
Pioneers of justice, the story of the Royal Canadian Mounted Police. New York, Macaulay [c1930] 249 p. Many 5940

Light, William, see nos. 4790-4792.

Lighton, William Rheem, 1866-
Lewis and Clark; Meriwether Lewis and William Clark. Boston, Houghton, 1901. 159 p. front. (2 ports.) (Riverside biographical series, no. 8) Many 5941
Same. 1905. OrSaW WaU 5942
Same. [c1929] IdU 5943

Lillie, William.
Oregon, my home where the wild grape blossoms grow; words and music composed and sung by William Lillie. [Portland, Or., Conger Printing Co., c1934] [8] p. ports. OrCS OrU 5944

Linck, James G.
Paulina preferred. Portland, Or., Binfords & Mort [c1945] 220 p. illus., plates, ports. Cascade Mountains and Paulina Lake, Or. Many 5945

Lincoln, Elliott Curtis, 1884-
The ranch; poems of the West. Boston, Houghton, 1924. ix, 105 p. Many 5946

Linderman, Frank Bird, 1868-1938.
American; the life story of a great Indian, Plentycoups, chief of the Crows, illus. by H. M. Stoops. New York, John Day Co. [c1930] xi, 313 p. front., illus. Montana author. Many 5947
Beyond law. New York, John Day Co., [c1933] 250 p. Adventure in the old West.
IdB MtU WaU 5948
Blackfeet Indians; pictures by Winold Reiss; story by Frank Linderman. [St. Paul, Brown & Bigelow, 1935] 65 p. col. illus., col. plates. Printed for Great Northern Railroad. Many 5949
Bunch grass and blue-joint. New York, Scribner, 1921. ix, 115 p. front. Poems.
IdU MtU OrPR Wa WaU 5950
How it came about stories, illus. by Carle Michel Boog. New York, Schibner, 1921. 221 p. col. front., illus., col. plates.
MtU OrP WaS 5951
Indian lodge-fire stories, illus. by Charles M. Russell. New York, Scribner [c1918] 117 p. front., illus. Or OrP 5952
Indian old-man stories; more sparks from War Eagle's lodge-fire; illus. by Charles M. Russell, the cowboy artist. New

York, Scribner, 1920. 169 p. col. front.,
7 col. plates. Blackfoot Indian legends.
MtHi MtU OrP WaS WaT   5953

Indian why stories; sparks from War
Eagle's lodgefire, illus. by Charles M.
Russell. New York, Scribner, 1915. xvi,
236 p. col. front., illus., col. plates.
MtU Or WaS WaT WaU   5954

Kootenai why stories, illus. by Charles
Livingston Bull. New York, Scribner,
1926. xx, 166 p. col. front., col. plates.
Many   5955

Lige Mounts; free trapper, illus. by Joe
DeYong. New York, Scribner, 1922.
330 p. front., illus.   MtHi   5956

Morning light (Lige Mounts; free trapper)
with decorations by Joe DeYong. New
York, John Day Co., c1930, c1922. 330 p.
MtU WaS WaSp WaT WaU   5957

Old man coyote (Crow) illus. by Herbert
Morton Stoops. New York, John Day
Co. [c1931] 254 p. front., illus.
Many   5958

On a passing frontier; sketches from the
Northwest. New York, Scribner, 1920.
214 p.   MtHi WaU   5959

Red mother, illus. by Herbert Morton
Stoops. New York, John Day Co. [c1932]
256 p. illus. Life story of Pretty-shield,
Crow medicine-woman.   Many   5960

Lindgren, Waldemar, see no. 178.

Lindgren volume, see no. 178.

Lindsay, Batterman.
Derelicts of destiny; being a few short
annals of a vanishing people. New York,
Neely Co., c1900. 76 p. Pacific Coast Indian stories.   WaS WaT WaU   5961

Same. Ltd. ed. re-arranged by Harry S.
Stuff. Seattle, Ivy Press, 1901.
WaU   5962

Lindsay, Charles, 1895-1931.
The Big Horn Basin. Lincoln, Neb., Univ.
of Neb. [1932] 274 p. illus., maps (part
fold.) (Univ. studies, v. 28, 29)
IdU MtBozC MtHi MtU OrPR OrU   5963

Lindsay, David Moore, 1862-
Camp fire reminiscences; or, Tales of
hunting and fishing in Canada and the
West. Boston, D. Estes & Co. [c1912]
233 p. front., plates.
OrP WaS WaU   5964

A voyage to the Arctic in the whaler
Aurora. Boston, D. Estes & Co. [c1911]
223 p. front., illus., plates, ports.
Many   5965

Lindsay, John, 1864-
Amazing experiences of a judge; with an
autobiography and tribute to Marcus
Daly. Philadelphia, Dorrance [c1939]
117 p.   McBozC MtHi MtU   5966

Lindsay, Marian, see no. 5764.

Lindsay, Nicholas Vachel, 1879-1931.
Going to the stars. New York, Appleton,
1926. 102 p. illus. Souvenir of a tramping tour through Glacier National Park.
IdIf   5967

Lindsay, William, see no. 4455.

Lindsey, Douglas.
Alaska; a complete book of reference and
guide to Alaska with three maps, the
latest mining laws and all necessary
information in regard to outfits, distances, rates of fare, etc. Stockton,
Calif., T. W. Hummel, 1897. 24 p. front.
(fold. map) illus.   WaU   5968

Lindsley, Aaron Ladner, 1817-1891.
Farewell sermon delivered upon closing
his ministry in the First Presbyterian
Church, Portland, Or. Portland, Or.,
1886. 43 p.   OrP OrU   5969

Sketches of an excursion to southern Alaska. [n.p., 1879?] 73 p.
OrHi OrP OrU   5970

Lindsley, John, see no. 10349.

Lines, Elizabeth Geisendorfer, comp.
Brief biography of Knox Butte pioneers,
1923-1939. Albany, Or. [1939] [25] p. illus.
OrP   5971

Linfield College, McMinnville, Or.
The Linfield Bulletin explaining the new
plan adopted by the faculty and Board
of Trustees, 1933. McMinnville, Or., 1933.
48 p. illus., ports. (Bulletin, v. 3, no. 3,
Apr. 1933)   WaPS   5972

Linton, C. E.
The earthomotor and other stories, illus.
by Murray Wade. Salem, Or., Statesman
Pub. Co. [192—?] 231 p. illus., plate
(port.)   OrHi OrP Wa WaU   5973

The storm's gift. Vancouver, Wash., Interstate Bindery [1920] 210 p. front.,
plates.   OrP OrU Wa WaU   5974

Lipps, Oscar Hiram, 1872-   comp.
Laws and regulations relating to Indians
and their lands. [Lewiston, Idaho, Lewiston Printing & Binding Co., 1913] 91 p.
IdU   5975

L'Isle, Joseph Nicolas de, 1688-1768.
Explication de la carte des nouvelles
decouvertes au Nord de la Mer du Sud.
Paris, Desaint et Saillant, 1752. 18 p.
CVicAr   5976

See also no. 5868.

Litchfield, Sarah.
Hello, Alaska, illus. by Kurt Wiese. Chicago, A. Whitman & Co., 1945. 31 p.
illus. (part col.)
Or OrAshS OrP WaS WaSp WaU   5977

Lister, John.
A vagabond's testament. Medford, Or.,
Klocker Printery, c1939. 36 p.
Or   5978

Litster, Mildred.
The Oregon vortex. Gold Hill, Or., c1944.
16 p. illus., diagrs.   Or WaU   5979

Little, Paul, comp.
The Pacific Northwest pulpit, foreword
by Charles Macaulay Stuart. New York,
Methodist Book Concern [c1915] 278 p.
Sermons preceded by short biographical
sketches.   Many   5980

Little journeys to Alaska and Canada:
Alaska, by Edith Kingman Kern; Canada, by Marian M. George. Chicago, A.
Flanagan Co., 1923. 80, 93 p. illus. (Library of travel)   WaU   5981

Same. 1926.   WaU   5982

Little journeys to Alaska and Canada; for intermediate and upper grades, ed. by Marian M. George. Chicago, A. Flanagan Co. [c1901] 80, 93 p. col. front., illus., col. plate, map.

Or WaPS WaS WaSp WaU **5983**

Livingston, Douglas Clermont, 1877-
Tungsten, cinnabar, manganese, molybdenum, and tin deposits of Idaho, with notes on the antimony deposits. Moscow, Idaho, Univ. of Idaho, 1919. 72 p. plates, maps (part fold.) (School of Mines. Bulletin, v. 14, no. 2)

MtUM OrCS WaS WaTC **5984**

Lloyd, Trevor, 1906-
Canada's last frontier. [Toronto, Canadian Institute of International Affairs and the Canadian Association for Adult Education, 1943] 32 p. illus., map. (Behind the headlines, v. 3, no. 4)   WaU **5985**

Lloyd-Owen, Frances.
Gold Nugget Charlie; a narrative comp. from the notes of Charles E. Masson. London, Harrap [1939] 259 p. front., plates, ports. "Saga of the West and the great white Northland."

CVicAr CVU WaU **5986**

Llwyd, John Plummer Derwent, 1861-
The message of an Indian relic. Seattle, Lowman & Hanford, 1909. 21 p. illus., 2 plates.

CVicAr Wa WaS WaT WaU **5987**

Lockenour, Roy M., see nos. 574-578.

Lockhart, Caroline.
The man from the Bitter Roots, with illus. in color by Gayle Hoskins. Philadelphia, Lippincott, 1915. 327 p. col. front., col. plates.   IdB **5988**

Lockley, Fred, 1871-
Captain Sol. Tetherow, wagon train master; personal narrative of his son, Sam Tetherow, who crossed the plains to Oregon in 1845; and personal narrative of Jack McNemee, who was born in Portland, Oregon, in 1848 and whose father built the fourth house in Portland. Portland, Or. [n.d.] 27 p.

Many **5989**

History of the Columbia River Valley from The Dalles to the sea. Chicago, S. J. Clarke Pub. Co., 1928. 3 v. front., illus., plates, ports. Volumes 2 and 3 biographical.   Many **5990**

Same. 1105 p.   CVicAr **5991**

Same. De luxe suppl. 1 v. OrHi OrP **5992**

"More power to you", by Fred Lockley and Marshall N. Dana. Portland, Or., Or. Journal, 1934. 112 p. illus.

Many **5993**

Oregon folks. "Or. Journal" ed. New York, Knickerbocker Press, 1927. vii, 220 p.

Many **5994**

Oregon trail blazers. New York, Knickerbocker Press, 1929. v, 369 p. Many **5995**

Oregon's yesterdays. New York, Knickerbocker Press, 1928. v, 350 p. Many **5996**

Same. 1929.   Wa **5997**

A picture story of how a great newspaper is made, and a bit of its history. Port-

land, Or., Or. Journal [1930?] 48 p. illus., ports.   Many **5998**

A talk with Edwin Markham. [n.p., 192—] [12] p. port.   OrP WaPS WaU **5999**

To Oregon by ox-team in '47; the story of the coming of the Hunt family to the Oregon country and the experiences of G. W. Hunt in the gold diggings of California in 1849. Portland, Or. [1924?] 15 p.   Many **6000**

See also nos. 947, 948, 2535.

Locklin, Harry D.
Berry cultivation in western Washington. Pullman, State College of Wash., 1930. 22 p. illus., tables (Western Wash. Experiment Station, Puyallup. Popular bulletin)   WaS **6001**

Lockwood, Alfred.
Rimes of the West, by a proletarian. Seattle, 1933. 53 p.   Wa **6002**

Loe, Kelley.
A tax report to industrial labor of Oregon. [n.p., 1947] 16 p.   Or OrP **6003**

Logan, George, 1852-
Histories of the North Montana Mission, Kalispell Mission, and Montana Deaconess Hospital, with some biographical and autobiographical sketches. [n.p., n.d.] 158 p. 158 p. front., illus., ports.

MtBozC MtHi MtU WaSp **6004**

Sagebrush philosophy on the problems of a tenderfoot. Helena, Mont., 1915. 41 p. illus.   MtHi **6005**

Lohn, Mrs. Agnette Midgarden.
The voice of the big firs. [Fosston, Minn., c1918] 428 p. front. Story of Hood River Valley.   Or WaPS **6006**

Same. [St. Paul, Pioneer Co., c1918]

Or WaU **6007**

Loisel, Regis, see no. 10062.

Lomax, Alan, see nos. 6022, 6023.

Lomax, Alfred Lewis, 1892-
Economic geography of Oregon; a work book for high schools, prepared for Oregon Committee of Economic Research and University of Oregon, by A. L. Lomax and C. E. Rothwell. [Eugene, Or., 1931] 155 p. maps.   OrP OrU **6008**

The facilities, commerce and resources of Oregon's coast ports. Eugene, Or., Univ. of Or. [1932] 53 p. (Studies in business no. 14)   Many **6009**

Marketing and manufacturing factors in Oregon's flax industry, by A. L. Lomax and Theodore VanGuilder. Eugene, Or. [1930] 43 p. (Studies in business no. 8)   Many **6010**

Pioneer woolen mills in Oregon; history of wool and the woolen textile industry in Oregon, 1811-1875. Portland, Or., Binfords & Mort [c1941] 312 p. front., plates, ports.   Many **6011**

Lomax, John Avery, 1872- comp.
Cowboy songs and other frontier ballads, with an introd. by Barrett Wendell. New York, Macmillan, 1910. 326 p. facsim.   CVicPr OrSaW **6012**

Same. New York, Sturgis & Walton, 1915. 326 p. facsim.   WaSp **6013**

Same. New York, Macmillan, 1916. 414 p. facsim.   MtBozC WaE WaS   6014

Same. 1918.   IdU OrP OrPR   6015

Same. 1919.   CVU Wa   6016

Same. 1922.   MtU   6017

Same. 1923.   WaU   6018

Same. 1925.   OrU   6019

Same. 1927.   WaS   6020

Same. 1931.   WaTC   6021

Same. Rev. and enl., collected by John A. Lomax and Alan Lomax. New York, Macmillan, 1938. 431 p. facsim.
                Many   6022

Same. 1944.   CVU   6023

Songs of the cattle trail and cow camp, with a foreword by William Lyon Phelps. New York, Macmillan, 1919. xi, 189 p.   Many   6024

Same. 1920.   IdU OrP   6025

Same. London, Unwin [1920] 111 p.
                MtBozC   6026

Same. New York, Macmillan, 1931. 189 p.
                OrPR   6027

Lombard, B.
Report on Oregon and Washington and Idaho Territories, by B. Lombard and W. A. Lombard. [New York?] Lombard Investment Co., 1888. 16 p.
                OrHi WaU   6028

Lombard, W. A., see no. 6028.

Lomen, Helen.
Taktuk; an Arctic boy, by Helen Lomen and Marjorie Flack; pictures by Marjorie Flack. New York, Doubleday, 1928. 139 p. col. front., illus., plates.
                Or OrP WaS WaSp   6029

Same. 1929.   IdIf WaS   6030

London, Jack, 1876-1916.
Burning daylight. New York, Macmillan [c1910] 361 p. Story of a Klondike millionaire.   Many   6031

Same. 1911. front., plates.   OrU   6032

Same. 1913.   OrSaW   6033

Same. 1915 [c1910]   IdU   6034

Same. New York, Review of Reviews, 1917. 361 p. front. (Works) OrSaW   6035

Same. New York, Grosset [1928?] 361 p. front., plates.   OrCS WaE   6036

The call of the wild. New York, Macmillan, 1903. 202 p.   OrP   6037

Same. New York, Review of Reviews, c1903. 198 p.   Wa   6038

Same, illus. by Philip R. Goodwin and Charles Livingston Bull, decorated by Chas. Edw. Hooper. New York, Grosset [c1903] 231 p. front., illus., plates.
                Many   6039

Same. New York, Macmillan, 1903. 231 p. col. front., col. illus., col. plates.
                OrMonO OrP WaE WaS   6040

Same, illus. by Paul Bransom. New York, Macmillan, 1912. 254 p. illus. (part col.) col. plates.   IdU MtU Wa   6041

Same, illus. by Philip R. Goodwin and Charles Livingston Bull, decorated by Chas. Edw. Hooper. New York, Grosset [1915] 211 p. front., illus., plates.
                OrCS OrLgE   6042

Same. (Every boy's library)
                OrPR OrU   6043

Same, illus. by Paul Bransom. New York, Macmillan, 1928 [c1912] 254 p. illus. (part col.)   IdU   6044

Same, ed. with introd. and notes by Theodor C. Mitchil. New York, Macmillan, 1917. 132 p. front. (Macmillan's pocket American and English classics)
                Or   6045

Same, and other stories, with an introd. by Frank Luther Mott. New York, Macmillan, 1926. xxxv, 268 p. front. (Modern readers' series)   WaTC   6046

Same. [c1927]   OrSaW   6047

Same. 1932.   CVU   6048

The faith of men, and other stories. New York, Macmillan, 1904. v, 286 p. Klondike tales.   OrP OrU WaA WaS   6049

Same. New York, Regent Press [c1904] 286 p.   WaU   6050

Same. New York, Macmillan, 1925, c1904.
                WaT   6051

Same. 1931. (Sonoma ed.)   WaS   6052

Love of life, and other stories. New York, Macmillan, 1906. v, 265 p.   CV   6053

Same. 1907.   Many   6054

Scorn of women, in three acts. New York, Macmillan, 1906. x, 265 p. Scene in Dawson in 1897.   IdB WaS WaSp   6055

Smoke Bellew, illus. by P. J. Monahan. New York, Century, 1912. 385 p. front., plates.   Many   6056

Same. New York, Grosset [c1912] 385 p. front., illus.
                IdIf OrP WaE WaS WaW   6057

The son of the wolf; tales of the far North. Boston, Houghton, 1900. 251 p. front.   IdU Or WaS   6058

Same. New York, Grosset [c1900]
                IdU OrP WaS WaU   6059

Same. Boston, Houghton, 1930, c1900.
                WaT   6060

Same. [c1928] 1930.   WaE   6061

White fang. New York, Grosset [c1905] 327 p. front., 3 plates. Klondike tales.
                Many   6062

Same. New York, Macmillan, 1905.
                WaS   6063

Same. 1906.   IdB Wa WaPS WaU   6064

Same. 1912.   OrP   6065

Same. 1922 [c1906] 329 p.   OrU   6066

London, International Exhibition, 1862.
Catalogue of the Vancouver contribution with a short account of Vancouver Island and British Columbia. London, 1862. 8, 8 p.   CVicAr   6067

Long, Elizabeth Emsley.
Flora, a Kitamaat waif. [Toronto, n.d.] [4] p.   CVicAr   6068

How the light came to Kitamaat. Toronto, Printed by the Woman's Missionary Society of the Methodist Church, 1917. 26 p.   CVicAr   6069

Long, Frederic J., comp.
Dictionary of the Chinook jargon: English-Chinook. Seattle, Lowman & Hanford, c1909. 41 p.   Many **6070**

Long, John [Indian trader]
See und Land Reisen unhaltend; eine Beschreibung der Sitten und Gewohnheiten der Nordamerikanischen Wilden, aus dem Englischen von C. A. W. Zimmermann. Hamburg, Hoffman, 1791. 334 p. fold. map.   CVicAr **6071**

Voyages and travels in the years 1768-1788, ed. with historical introd. and notes by M. M. Quaife. Chicago, Donnelley, 1922. xxx, 238 p. front. (fold. map) (Lakeside classics)   WaSp **6072**

Voyages and travels of an Indian interpreter and trader, describing the manners and cusoms of the North American Indians, with an account of the posts situated on the River St. Lawrence, Lake Ontario, &c.; to which is added a vocabulary of the Chippeway language, a list of words in the Iroquois, Mehegan, Shawanee and Esquimeaux tongues, and a table, showing the analogy between the Algonkin and Chippeway languages. London, Robson, 1791. 295 p. fold. map.   CVU **6073**

Voyages chez differentes nations sauvages de l'Amerique septentrionale, traduits de l'anglais par J. B. L. J. Billecocq. Paris, Preult, 1791. 320 p. fold. map.
CVicAr **6074**

Same. Paris, Lebel de Guitel, 1810.
CVU **6075**

See also no. 8300.

Long, Mrs. Mae Van Norman.
Rose of Sharon. Los Angeles, DeVorss [c1937] 280 p. Spokane author.
WaSp **6076**

The wonder woman, illus. by J. Marsey Clement. Philadelphia, Penn. 1917. 371 p. front., plates.   IdU WaSp **6077**

Long, Mrs. Mary Jane.
True story; crossing the plains in the year of 1852 with ox teams. McMinnville, Or. [n.d.] 17 p.   OrHi **6078**

Long, Morden Heaton, 1886-
Knights errant of the wilderness, tales of the explorers of the great North-west. Toronto, Macmillan, 1920. xi, 223 p. front., illus., 9 plates, ports., maps.
WaU **6079**

Long, Robert A.
An address on the occasion of the dedication of the Robert A. Long High School, Longview, Washington, July 15, 1928. [Longview, Wash., 1928] [18] p. illus.   WaPS **6080**

Long, William George.
Detention of juvenile delinquents in King County; a speech delivered at a luncheon meeting of the Council of Social Agencies, March 26, 1945. [Seattle] Seattle Council of Social Agencies, 1945. 20 p.   WaS **6081**

Final report concerning Juvenile Court construction project. [Seattle] 1946. 20 p.   WaS **6082**

Heading off crime at the source; the juvenile problem in King County, Washington, and its solution by community action; a handbook for Coordinating Council workers and all leaders of youth, prepared under the direction of Wm. G. Long, Superior Court judge in charge of the Juvenile Court and a Joint Committee of the Lions Clubs of Seattle. [Seattle, Argus] 1936. 19 p. tables, diagrs.
OrU WaE WaS WaT WaU **6083**

The Long-Bell Lumber Company.
Real Estate Dept.
Longview, Washington, a new industrial city. Kelso, Wash. [1922] 7 p. double plate.   WaPS **6084**

Long Lance, Buffalo Child,
see nos. 1249-1251, 6733.

Longstaff, Frederick Victor, 1879-
Esquimalt Naval Base; a history of its work and its defences. [Vancouver, B.C., Clarke & Stuart Co., c1942] 189 p. front., 12 plates.   CV CVic CVicAr WaU **6085**

History and topography of Okanagan for the active militia in camp, May 1914. [Vernon, B. C., Vernon News] 1914. [14] p.   CVicAr **6086**

Life on the west coast of Vancouver Island. [Victoria, B. C., British Colonist, 1925] [4] p.   CVicAr **6087**

Longstreth, Thomas Morris, 1886-
In scarlet and plain clothes; the history of the mounted police. New York, Macmillan, 1933. 365 p.   CVicAr
IdIf Or OrMonO WaE WaS **6088**

The silent force, scenes from the life of the mounted police of Canada. New York, Century [c1927] xiv, 383 p. front., illus., plates, ports., fold. maps.
CVicAr CVU WaE WaS WaT **6089**

Sons of the mounted police. New York, Century [1929] 257 p. front., ports., maps.
IdIf **6090**

Longsworth, Basil Nelson.
Diary of Basil Nelson Longsworth, March 15, 1853 to January 22, 1854, covering the period of his migration from Ohio to Oregon. Denver [Highland Chief, Printers] c1927. 43 p.   Many **6091**

Longview Company, Longview, Wash.
Longview, Washington, the city practical vision built. Longview, Wash. [n.d.] 40 p. illus., port., maps.   WaT **6092**

Same. [1924] 32 p.   WaPS **6093**

Longview, Washington, the new city of the Pacific Northwest. 2d ed. Longview, Wash. [1924] 32 p. illus., ports., maps (1 fold.)   WaU **6094**

Same. [1926] [48] p. illus., map.   Or **6095**

Longview, Washington, two years ago—pastures! Today—a city! Longview, Wash. [1925] [8] p. illus.   WaPS **6096**

What nationally known business men have to say about Longview, Wash. Longview, Wash., 1927. 1 v.   WaT **6097**

Where rail, water and highway meet; Longview, Washington. 3d ed. [Longview, Wash., 1925] 40 p. illus., ports., maps.   WaPS WaU **6098**

Longview Daily News.
Anniversary edition. Longview, Wash., Longview Pub. Co., 1926. 6 sections in 1 v. illus., ports., map. (Apr. 20, 1926) WaU **6099**

Longyear, Burton Orange, 1868-
Rocky Mountain wild flower studies; an account of the ways of some plants that live in the Rocky Mountain region, with illus. from nature by the author. [Denver, Merchants Pub. Co., c1909] 156 p. illus. IdU **6100**

Trees and shrubs of the Rocky Mountain region, with keys and descriptions for their identification, illus. with one hundred and twenty-eight pen drawings by the author and nine colored plates. New York, Putnam, 1927. xvii, 244 p. col. front., illus., col. plates. Many **6101**

Look.
The central Northwest, by the editors of Look in collaboration with Wallace Stegner; a handbook in pictures, maps and text for the vacationist, the traveler and the stay-at-home. Boston, Houghton [1947] 393 p. front., illus. (part col.) maps (1 fold.) (Look at America, no. 4). IdB OrCS OrU WaS WaT **6102**

The far West, by the editors of Look, with an introd. by Joseph Henry Jackson; a handbook in pictures, maps and text for the vacationist, the traveler and the stay-at-home. Boston, Houghton [c1948] 402 p. illus. (part col.) maps (1 fold.) (Look at America no. 7) Many **6103**

Looney, Mrs. M. A. (Gunsaulus)
Trip across the plains in 1853. Albany, Or., Albany Printing Co., 1912. [7] p. OrHi **6104**

The Loop (a tale of the Oregon country) by thirteen Oregon authors. Portland, Or., Metropolitan, 1931. 259 p. front. (map) Many **6105**

Loo-wit Lat-kla.
Gold hunting in the Cascade Mountains; a full and complete history of the gold discoveries in the Cascade Mountains; notes of travel, with incidents of the journey through that wild and unbroken region; together with an account of the red men who dwell in that lonely bode of nature, their habits and customs, religion, traditions, etc. Vancouver, W. T., L. E. V. Coon, 1861. 28 p. Photostat copy. WaU **6106**

Lopatin, Ivan Alexis, 1888-
Social life and religion of the Indians in Kitimat, British Columbia; foreword by Dr. Frederick W. Hodge. Los Angeles, Univ. of Southern Calif. Press, 1945. 118 p. plates, map. (Social science series, no. 26) Many **6107**

Lopp, William Thomas, 1864-
White Sox, the story of the reindeer in Alaska, illus. with drawings by H. Boylston Dummer. Yonkers-on-Hudson, N. Y., World Book Co., 1924. viii, 76 p. front., illus. (Animal life series) WaS WaU **6108**

Same. 1927. WaT **6109**

Lord, Mrs. Elizabeth (Laughlin)
Reminiscences of eastern Oregon. Portland, Or., Irwin-Hodson, 1903. 255 p. front., 10 plates, 3 ports. Many **6110**

Lord, John Keast, 1818-1872.
At home in the wilderness; being full of instructions how to get along and to surmount all difficulties by the way, by "The wanderer" [pseud.] London, R. Hardewicke, 1867. xvi, 323 p. front. (port.) illus. Pacific Northwest wilderness. OrHi **6110A**

Same. 2d ed.
CVicAr CVU Or WaSp WaU **6111**

At home in the wilderness; what to do there and how to do it; a handbook for travelers and emigrants. 3d ed. London, Hardwicke & Bogue, 1876. xvi, 323 p. front. (port.) illus. Many **6112**

The naturalist in Vancouver Island and British Columbia. London, R. Bentley, 1866. 2 v. fronts., 9 plates. Many **6113**

Lord, L. M., & Co.
Guide, map & history of the Klondyke Alaska gold fields. Chicago [n.d.] 46 p. illus., fold. map. CVicAr **6114**

Lord, William Rogers, 1847-1916.
A first book upon the birds of Oregon and Washington; a pocket guide and pupil's assistant in a study of most of the land birds and a few of the water birds of these states. Portland, Or., 1901. 195 p. front., plates. OrHi
OrP WaA WaPS WaTC WaU **6115**

Same. Rev. ed. 1902.
OrMonO OrP WaT WaU **6116**

Same. Rev. and enl. ed. 304 p. Many **6117**
Same. Portland, Or., J. K. Gill, 1902. 297 p. front., illus., 17 plates.
WaPS WaS **6118**

Same. 1913 [c1902] 308 [6] iv p.
OrU Wa WaS WaU **6119**

Loring, Colonel, see no. 2136.

Lorraine, Madison Johnson, 1853-
The Columbia unveiled; being the story of a trip, alone, in a rowboat from the source to the mouth of the Columbia River, together with a full description of the country traversed and the rapids battled, by an old voyager and whitewater man. Los Angeles, Times-Mirror Press, 1924. 446 p. front., illus., ports., fold. map. Many **6120**

Lorwin, Lewis Levitzki, 1883-
The taxation of mines in Montana, by Louis Levine. New York, B. W. Huebsch, 1919. 141 p. Many **6121**

Loutzenhiser, F. H., see no. 11044.

Love, Charles J.
Pacific Northwest garden guide for the Puget Sound country and northern Oregon. Seattle, Lowman & Hanford, 1933. 160 p. Many **6122**

Loveland, Lilly Ann Steel, see no. 9833.

Lovell, Josephine.
Watlala; an Indian of the Northwest. [New York] Platt & Munk, c1935. [12] p. illus. (part col.) WaT **6123**

Lowe, Martha Perry.
The story of Chief Joseph. Boston, Lothrop [1881]. 40 p. front., illus.
OrHi **6123A**

Lowe, Paul Emilius, 1850-
Tracy, the outlaw, king of bandits; a narrative of the thrilling adventures of the most daring and resourceful bandit ever recorded in the criminal annals of the world. Baltimore, I. & M. Ottenheimer, c1908. 184 p. illus.
OrP Wa WaS WaSp **6124**

Lowell, Daniel W., & Co.
Map of the Nez Perces and Salmon River gold mines in Washington Territory, comp. from the most recent surveys. San Francisco, Whitton, Waters & Co., 1862. 23 p. illus., map.
OrP WaSp WaU **6125**
Same. Photostat copy. WaPS **6126**

Lowman & Hanford Co., Seattle. Wash.
Scenic treasures of western Washington. Seattle, c1909. [36] plates. WaU **6127**
Seattle, the Queen city, illus. with descriptive text. Seattle, c1915. 1 v. illus.
WaS **6128**

Lowrie, John C., see no. 2591.

Lucas, Edwin P.
Bellingham Coal Mines, Inc., Bellingham, Washington; organization and operation of a modern coal mine, prepared under the direction of Clara Ketchum Tripp. [Seattle. Wash. Industries Education Bureau?] c1928. 7 p. diagr. (Monograph)
WaPS WaS **6129**

Luce, Edward S.
Keough, Comanche and Custer. [St. Louis, John S. Swift Co., c1939] xvii, 127 p. front., plates, ports. MtHi WaS **6130**

Ludington, Flora Belle.
The newspapers of Oregon, 1846-1870. Eugene, Or., Koke-Tiffany [c1926?] 33 p.
Many **6131**

Ludlow, Fitzhugh, 1836-1870.
The heart of the continent; a record of travel across the plains and in Oregon, with an examination of the Mormon principle. New York, Hurd and Houghton, 1870. vi, 568 p. front., 7 plates, 2 ports.
Many **6132**
Same. 1871. WaS WaSp **6133**

Lugrin, Charles Henry, 1846- comp.
Yukon gold fields; map showing routes from Victoria, B. C., to the various mining camps on the Yukon River and its branches; mining regulations of the Dominion government and forms of application, together with table of distances, extracts from Mr. Ogilvie's reports, and other information. Victoria, B. C., British Colonist, 1897. 32 p. fold. map.
CVicAr OrU WaU **6134**

Luhn, William Luke.
Official history of the operations of the First Washington Infantry, U.S.V., in the campaign in the Philippine Islands. [San Francisco, Hicks-Judd Co.? 1899?] 116 p. illus., ports.
Wa WaPS WaS WaU **6135**

Luigi, Duke of the Abruzzi, 1873-1933.
On the "Polar Star" in the Arctic Sea, by His Royal Highness Luigi Amedeo of Savoy, duke of the Abruzzi; with the statements of the Commander U. Cagni upon the sledge expedition to 86° 34' north, and of Dr. A. Cavalli Molinelli upon his return to the Bay of Teplitz; trans. by William le Queux. London, Hutchinson & Co., 1903. 2 v. fronts., illus., plates (part fold.) ports., maps (part fold.) diagrs. (part col.)
CVicAr OrP WaS WaT **6136**
See also nos. 3055, 3056.

Lukens, Fred Edward, 1888-
The Idaho citizen; a text book in Idaho civics. 2d ed. Caldwell, Idaho, Caxton, 1925. 163 p. map, fold. form.
IdB IdIf IdU IdUSB **6137**
Same. 3d ed. 1927. 168 p. IdIf **6138**
Same. 4th ed. [c1929] 179 p.
IdUSB OrSaW WaSp WaU **6139**
Same. 5th ed. 1933. 183 p. IdUSB **6140**
Same. 6th ed. 1935. 201 p.
IdUSB WaU **6141**
Same. 8th ed. 1939. 215 p. IdIf **6142**

Lukens, Matilda Barns.
The inland passage; a journal of a trip to Alaska. [n.p.] 1889. 84 p.
CVicAr **6143**

Lull, Herbert Galen, 1874-
Survey of the Port Townsend public schools, under the direction of Herbert G. Lull. Seattle, Univ. of Wash., 1915. 112 p. diagrs. (Extension ser. no. 17; general ser. no. 95) Many **6144**

Lull, Roderick.
Call to battle; a novel. Garden City, N. Y., Doubleday, 1943. 304 p. Novel of Japanese attack on Pacific coast.
MtU Or OrCS OrP WaSp **6145**

Lumberman Printing Co., Ltd.
Vancouver, the golden city of the West. [Vancouver, B. C., c1935] [36] plates.
CV WaU **6146**

Lund, R. G., see no. 645.

Lundberg, George Andrew.
Child life in Tacoma; a child welfare survey embracing the fields of health, delinquency, dependency, club work, sponsored and financed by the Rotary Club of Tacoma, directed, conducted, and report written by George A. Lundberg. [Tacoma, Rotary Club, 1926] 57 p. maps, tables. WaT WaTC WaU **6147**

Lundblad, S.
Verskronika om Svenska klubben, Seattle, Washington, 1892-1907; tillegnad alla klubbens medlemmar jemte damer afvensom de tusentals landsman och landsmaninnor, som under tidernas lopp ha besökt klubbens fester och utflykter. Seattle, Puget Sound Postens Boktryckeri, 1908. 199 p. ports. WaS **6148**

Lutheran Men's Association of Washington.
Constitution, by-laws and other valuable information. Seattle, 1937. 20 p.
WaT **6149**

Luttig, John C., d. 1815.
Journal of a fur-trading expedition on the upper Missouri 1812-1813, ed. by Stella M. Drumm. St. Louis, Mo. Historical

Society, 1920. 192 p. front., illus., ports., map, facsims.					Many	**6150**

Lydenberg, Harry Miller, see no. 4148.

Lyle, J. T. S., 1878-
State taxation and the lumber industry, prepared under the direction of a committee representing West Coast Lumbermen's Association, Logger's Information Association, Timber Products Manufacturers' Committee, Washington Forest Fire Association, Federated Industries of Washington. [Seattle? 1921] 19 p. 2 fold. tables.					WaU	**6151**

Lyman, Horace Sumner, 1855-
History of Oregon; the growth of an American state; associate board of editors: H. W. Scott, C. B. Bellinger and F. G. Young. New York, North Pacific Pub. Society, 1903. 4 v. fronts. (v. 1, 4) 45 plates, 63 ports., 15 maps, 2 facsims.					Many	**6152**

Mile posts in the development of Oregon and characteristics of Oregon as an American commonwealth, with a supplement. A world movement and a national movement that had important relations to the making of Oregon, by the editor of the Historical Series. Eugene, Or., Univ. of Or., 1898. 22 p. maps. (Semicentennial history of Or., 1; Historical series, v. 1, no. 1)					Many	**6153**

Lyman, William Denison, 1852-1920.
The Columbia River ; its history, its myths, its scenery, its commerce, with 80 illus. and a map. New York, Putnam, 1909. xx, 409 p. front., 74 plates, 3 ports., 2 fold. maps. (American waterways series)					Many	**6154**

Same. 3d ed., rev. and enl. 1911. xxi, 418 p.					CVicAr MtU Wa	**6155**

Same. 1917.					Or WaSp WaU	**6156**

Same. 1918.					Many	**6157**

Congregational home missionary associations of the Northwest; address, Pasco, Washington, Oct. 3, 1916. [n.p., 1916] 20 p.					OrU WaS WaSp	**6158**

County of Walla Walla, Washington. [Salem, Or., Statesman Pub. Co., 1905] [64] p. front., illus. Anon.					WaU WaWW	**6159**

History of the Yakima Valley, Washington, comprising Yakima, Kittitas and Benton Counties. [Chicago] S J. Clarke Pub. Co., 1919. 2 v. plates, ports.					Wa WaPS WaS	**6160**

An illustrated history of Walla Walla County, state of Washington. [San Francisco?] W. H. Lever, 1901. xiv, 510 p. front., 7 plates, 40 ports. Many	**6161**

Lyman's history of old Walla Walla County, embracing Walla Walla, Columbia, Garfield and Asotin Counties. Chicago, S. J. Clarke Pub. Co., 1918. 2 v. front., plates, ports. Volume 1, p. 477-716 and v. 2, biographical.					Many	**6162**

Lynch, Jeremiah, 1849-1917.
Three years in the Klondike. London, Arnold, 1904. 280 p. front., 23 plates, fold. map.					Many	**6163**

Trois ans au Klondike, traduit de l'anglais par Paul Lefevre. Paris, Librarie Ch. Delagrave [1905] 302 p. front., plates, fold. map.					CVU	**6164**

Lynch, Montgomery, see no. 6646.

Lyndon, John W., see no. 8216.

Lynn, Lyman Duval, see no. 8836.

Lyon, George Francis, 1795-1832.
The private journal of Captain G. F. Lyon of H. M. S. Hecla, during the recent voyage of discovery under Captain Parry. Boston, Wells and Lilly, 1824. 339 p.					CVU	**6165**

Same. London, J. Murray, 1824. xiii, 468 p. front., 6 plates, fold. map.					Wa WaU	**6166**

Lyon, William C., see no. 3337.

Lyons, Herbert H., comp.
6th Regiment, the Duke of Connaught's own rifles. Vancouver, B. C. [Evans & Hastings] 1907. 1 v. plates, port.					CV	**6167**

Lyons, Letitia Mary, sister, 1903-
Francis Norbert Blanchet and the founding of the Oregon missions (1838-1848). Washington, D. C., Catholic Univ. of America Press, 1940. xx, 200 p. (Studies in American church history, v. 30)					Many	**6168**

Lyons, W. F.
Brigadier-General Thomas Francis Meagher; his political and military career, with selection from his speeches and writings. New York, D. & J. Sadlier & Co., 1870. 357 p. front. (port.) Montana territorial secretary and temporary governor, 1865-1867.					MtHi MtU	**6169**

Lyttleton, Edith J.
The world is yours, by G. B. Lancaster [pseud.] New York, Appleton, 1934. 322 p. Yukon country in 1920's.					CV IdU Or WaE WaS WaSp	**6170**

M. D., see no. 1999.

Maack, Dorothy Howerton, see no. 3020.

McAbee, Mrs. Fannie Lawson.
Fifteen years; a monograph by Mrs. Staff Captain McAbee. [Seattle] Salvation Army, 1903. 16 p. illus.					WaU	**6171**

McArdle, L. D.
Some choice American selections; mostly Northwest items from the library of L. D. McArdle, Quilcene, Washington. [Quilcene, Wash.?] 1908. [7] p.					WaU	**6172**

Same. 38 p.					WaU	**6173**

Same. [1910?]					Wa	**6174**

MacArthur, Burke, see no. 1276.

McArthur, Clifton N.
The need of a constitutional convention; address delivered before the Oregon Bar Association at Portland, Oregon, May 17, 1910. Salem, Or., Statesman Pub. Co. [1910] 14 p.					OrU	**6175**

MacArthur, Dougall.
The legend whispered. Portland, Or., Binfords & Mort [1943] 308 p.   Many **6176**
McArthur, Mrs. Harriet (Nesmith)
Recollections of the Rickreall. Portland, Or., 1930. 24 p. front. (port.) 2 plates, port.   Or OrHi OrP **6177**
McArthur, Lewis Ankeny, 1883-
Oregon geographic names. Portland, Or., 1928. xii, 450 p. front., plates, fold. maps.
    Many **6178**
Same. 2d ed., rev. and enl. [Portland, Or.] Binfords & Mort, 1944. xii, 581 p.
    Many **6179**
[Oregon map list.] Portland, Or., 1934. 11 p.   OrP **6180**
Oregon place names; pen and ink illus. by Marilyn Campbell. Portland, Or., Binfords & Mort, 1944. 109 p. front., illus.   CVU Or OrHi **6181**
Results of spirit leveling in Clatsop County, Oregon, 1920-1929. Portland, Or., Pacific Power & Light Co., 1929. 16 p.
    Or OrP **6182**
Results of spirit leveling in Hood River County, Or., 1907-1928. Portland, Or., Pacific Power & Light Co., 1929. 16 p. map.   OrP WaU **6183**
MacAulay, D. A.
Thoughts and other poems of life, by Damacaulie. [Elma, Wash.] 1939. [20] p.
    Wa **6184**
McBain, J. Ford.
Geography of Montana. Boston, Ginn [c1931] 39 p. illus., maps (1 col.)
    MtBozC MtU **6185**
McBeth, Kate C., 1832-
The Nez Perces since Lewis and Clark. New York, F. H. Revell Co. [c1908] 272 p. front., plates, ports.   Many **6186**
MacBeth, Roderick George, 1858-1934.
Land in British Columbia. Covent Garden, London, William Stevens, 1920. 48 p.
    CVU **6187**
The making of the Canadian West; being the reminiscences of an eye witness. Toronto, Briggs, 1898. 230 p. front., illus., plates, ports.
    CV CVic CVicAr CVU WaS WaSp **6188**
Same. 2d ed. 1905. 279 p.
    CVU MtHi WaSp WaU **6189**
Peace River letters. [Vancouver, B. C., White & Bindon, 1915] 31 p. illus.
    CV CVicAr CVU **6190**
Policing the plains; being the real-life record of the famous Royal North-west Mounted Police. London, Hodder and Stoughton [1920] 320 p. front., plates, ports.   CVicAr **6191**
Same. New York, Doran [1921?]
    CVicAr **6192**
Same. London, Hodder and Stoughton, 1922.   CVU WaS WaSp WaU **6193**
Same. Rev. and enl. ed. Toronto, Musson [c1931] 252 p. front., plates, ports.
    CVU **6194**
The romance of the Canadian Pacific Railway. Toronto, Ryerson [c1924] 263 p. front., plates, ports.
    CV CVicAr CVU Wa WaU **6195**

The romance of western Canada. Toronto, Briggs [1918] xii, 309 p. front., plates, ports.
    CV CVicAr CVU WaPS WaU **6196**
Same. Toronto, Ryerson, 1920.
    CVicPr CVU MtHi WaU **6197**
The Selkirk settlers in real life, with introd. by Hon. Sir Donald A. Smith, K. C. M. G. Toronto, Briggs [1897] 119 p. front.   CVicAr WaU **6198**
See also no. 6535.
McBride, James Lloyd, 1882-
The Smoky Valley claim, illus. by E. Joseph Dreany. Caldwell, Idaho, Caxton, 1948. 260 p. illus. Alaska adventure story.   WaU **6199**
McBride, Richard, 1870-
British Columbia, her vast resources and great possibilities [address at annual banquet of the Canadian Manufacturers' Association at Vancouver, B. C., Sept. 22, 1910.] Vancouver, B. C., News-Advertiser, 1910. 12 p. front. (port.)
    CVic CVicAr WaS **6200**
McBride, Sister Mary Clotilde.
Ursulines of the West, 1535-1935; 1880-1935. [n.p.] 1935. 72 p. illus., plates, ports.
    MtHi **6201**
McBride, Thomas A.
Reminiscences of early judges and lawyers; address to the Pendleton Bar, May 2, 1922. Pendleton, Or., East Oregonian, 1922. 11 p. port.   OrHi **6202**
McCabe, Charles C., see no. 10789.
McCaffrey, Frank, 1894-
Campus memories; a sentimental stroll through the University of Washington campus with Professor Edmond S. Meany, photographs & sketches & printing by the author. Seattle, Dogwood Press, 1933. 96 p. front., plates.
    Wa WaS WaU **6203**
Concerning my Dodwood Press. [Seattle, 1931] [4] p. illus. Anon. WaS WaU **6204**
What the printer heard the books say. [Seattle, 1932] [21] p.   WaS WaU **6205**
McCain, Charles W.
History of the SS. "Beaver", being a graphic and vivid sketch of this noted pioneer steamer; also containing a description of the Hudson's Bay Company from its formation in 1670, down to the present time. Vancouver, B. C., [Evans & Hastings] 1894. 99 p. 5 plates, 2 ports., facsim.   Many **6206**
McCaleb, Walter Flavius, 1873-
The conquest of the West. New York, Prentice-Hall [1947] xiv, 336 p. maps.
    Many **6207**
McCalla, William Copeland.
Wild flowers of western Canada, with sixty plates from original photographs by the author. Toronto, Musson [c1920] 13? p. illus.   CV CVU **6208**
McCarthy, Joseph.
A one-house legislature and executive combined [paper read at meeting, Spokane County Bar Association, Spokane, Wash., Apr. 24, 1931] Spokane, 1931. [7] p.   WaS **6209**

A single house legislature and executive combined [paper read at meeting, Seattle Bar Association, Seattle, Wash., June 10, 1931] [Spokane] 1931. [11] p. WaS **6210**

The written real-estate commission contract; being paper read at meeting Spokane Realty Board, October 23, 1914. [n.p., 1914?] 8 p. WaPS **6211**

McCarthy, William, see no. 3348.

McCaustland, E. J.
Oregon roads; hints on their improvement and their construction and maintenance. Independence, Or., West Side Pub. Co., 1896. 22 p. OrHi **6212**

McClane, Douglas V., see no. 4952.

McClay, Max.
The liars club. Seattle, I. W. Emerson & Co. [c1905] 67 p. WaPS **6213**

McClellan, Rolander Guy.
The golden state; a history of the region west of the Rocky Mountains; embracing California, Oregon, Nevada, Utah, Arizona, Idaho, Washington Territory, British Columbia, and Alaska, from the earliest period to the present time, with a history of Mormonism and the Mormons. Philadelphia, W. Flint & Co. [c1872] 685 p. front., plates, ports., 4 maps. Many **6214**
Same. [1872] 711 p. WaPS **6215**
Same. 1874. CVU OrHi **6216**
Same. 1875. IdB IdU OrU WaU **6217**
Same. 1876. 820 p. WaU **6218**

McClernand, Edward J., see no. 8740.

McClintock, Mrs. Eva, see no. 11021.

M'Clintock, Sir Francis Leopold, 1819-1907.
In the Arctic seas; a narrative of the discovery of the fate of Sir John Franklin and his companions, with maps and illus. Philadelphia, Porter & Coates [n.d.] xxiii, 375 p. front., illus. CVicAr Wa **6219**
The voyage of the "Fox" in the Arctic seas. London, J. Murray, 1859. xxvii, 403 p. front., plates, 3 fold. maps, fold. facsim. CVicAr **6220**
Same. A narrative of the discovery of the fate of Sir John Franklin and his companions. Boston, Ticknor and Fields, 1860. xxiv, 375 p. front., illus., plates, maps (3 fold.) fold. facsim. CVicAr OrHi Wa WaU **6221**
Same. London, Murray, 1908. 78, 303 p. front. (port.) illus., 15 plates, 2 maps (1 fold.) facsim. CVicAr OrHi **6222**

McClintock, Walter, 1870-
The Blackfoot beaver bundle. Los Angeles, Southwest Museum, 1935. 2 v. illus. (Leaflet 2, 3) MtBozC **6223**
The Blackfoot tipi. Los Angeles, Southwest Museum, 1936. 11 p. illus. (Leaflet 5) MtBozC **6224**
Blackfoot warrior societies. Los Angeles, Southwest Museum, 1937. 30 p. illus. (Leaflet 8) MtBozC **6225**
Dances of the Blackfoot Indians. Los Angeles, Southwest Museum, 1937. 22 p.

illus. (Leaflet 7) MtBozC WaSp **6226**
Old Indian trails, with illus. from photographs by the author. Boston, Houghton, 1923. xii, 336 p. col. front., plates (part col.) ports., music. Many **6227**
The Old North Trail; or, Life, legends and religion of the Blackfeet Indians. London, Macmillan, 1910. xxvi, 539 p. col. front., illus., 8 plates, ports., fold. map. Many **6228**
Painted tipis and picture writing of the Blackfoot Indians. Los Angeles, Southwest Museum, 1936. 26 p. illus. (Leaflet 6) MtBozC WaSp **6229**
The tragedy of the Blackfoot. Los Angeles, Southwest Museum, 1930. 53 p. illus. (Papers 3) MtHi OrU **6230**

McClure, Alexander Kelly, 1828-1909.
Three thousand miles through the Rocky Mountains. Philadelphia, Lippincott, 1869. 456 p. front., 2 ports. Many **6231**

McClure, James G. K., see no. 7330.

McClure, Sir Robert John LeMesurier, 1807-1873.
The discovery of the North-west passage by H. M. S. "Investigator", Capt. R. M'Clure, 1850, 1851, 1852, 1853, 1854; ed. by Commander Sherard Osborn from the logs and journals of Capt. Robert LeM. M'Clure, illus. by Commander S. Gurney Cresswell. London, Longman, 1856. xix, 405 p. front., 3 plates, fold. map. CVicAr Wa WaS WaU **6232**
Same. 2d ed. 1857. xxxii, 463 p. CV CVU WaS **6233**
Same. 3d ed. 1859. CVicAr **6234**
Same. 4th ed. Edinburgh, Blackwood, 1865. xxvi, 358 p. fold. map. CVicAr **6235**

McCollum, Lee Charles.
History and rhymes of the lost battalion, by "Buck Private" McCollum; sketches by Franklin Sly and Tolman R. Reamer. [Seattle, Bucklee Pub. Co., c1937] 138 p. illus., ports. OrP OrPR WaU **6236**
Same. [c1939]. MtBozC Or Wa WaS WaU **6237**
Rhymes of a lost battalion doughboy, by "Buck Private" McCollum. [Seattle. 1921] [32] p. illus. WaU **6238**
Our sons at war, illus. by Arthur F. Niemeyer. Chicago, Bucklee Pub. Co. [c1940] 216 p. illus., plates, map. Wa WaE WaS WaSp WaTC **6239**

McConnell, John Ludlum, 1826-1862.
Western characters; or, Types of border life in the western states, with illus. by Darley. New York, Bedfield, 1853. 378 p. front., plates. Many **6240**

McConnell, Robert Ervie, 1896-
Publications of the faculty of the Central Washington College of Education, September 1891-November 1941 [prepared in commemoration of the 50th anniversary of the establishment of Central Wash. College of Education] Ellensburg, Wash., [1941] 16 p. (Quarterly, v. 34, no. 1, Oct. 1941) WaU **6241**

McConnell, William John, 1839-1925.
Early history of Idaho, by W. J. McConnell, ex-U. S. senator and -governor, who was present and cognizant of the events narrated, pub. by authority of the Idaho State Legislature. Caldwell, Idaho, Caxton, 1913. 420 p. front. (port.) port.
Many **6242**

Frontier law; a story of vigilante days, by William J. McConnell in collaboration with Howard R. Driggs, illus. with drawings by Herbert M. Stoops. Yonkers-on-Hudson, N. Y., World Book Co., 1924. xii, 233 p. front., illus. (Pioneer life series) Many **6243**

Same. 1926 [c1924] IdP MtHi WaT **6244**

McCord, Clarence Stewart, 1876-
Some items pertaining to the renovizing of a social order. Seattle, Geo. E. Minor Press [c1935] 184 p.
Wa WaS WaSp WaU **6245**

McCormick, Dell J.
Paul Bunyan swings his axe. Caldwell, Idaho, Caxton, 1936. 111 p. col. front., illus. Many **6246**

Same. 1937, c1936. OrP WaT **6247**

Tall timber tales; more Paul Bunyan stories, illus. by Lorna Livesley. Caldwell, Idaho, Caxton, 1939. 155 p. col. front., illus., plates. Many **6248**

Same. 1940. WaT **6249**

McCormick, Henry A.
An X-ray on the Naches Valley; a typical illustration of rural life in the valleys of the Yakima, with Naches Avenue of North Yakima, Washington, supplementary. [North Yakima, Wash., Republic Pub. Co., c1911] 90 p. illus., plates (1 col.) WaPS **6250**

McCormick, Robert Laird.
Address of greeting delivered on behalf of the State Historical Society of Wisconsin to the Washington University State Historical Society at the unveiling of monuments on San Juan Island, October 21, 1904, the anniversary of the date in 1870 when Emperor William I of Germany handed down his decision fixing the boundary line between the U. S. and the British provinces. [Seattle? Wash. University State Historical Society? 1904?] 7 p. WaT WaU **6251**

McCornack, Mrs. Ellen Condon.
A student's geological map of Oregon with notes. Eugene, Or., Univ. of Or. [1906] 24 p. fold. map. (Bulletin. n.s., v. 3, no. 5) WaSp **6252**

Thomas Condon, pioneer geologist of Oregon. Eugene, Or., Univ. of Or. Press, 1928. xv, 355 p. front., plates, ports., fold. map. Many **6253**

See also no. 1945.

McCoy, Sutherland, see no. 10206.

McCracken, Harold, 1894-
Alaska bear trails, illus. with photographs by the author. New York, Doubleday, 1931. 260 p. front., 15 plates.
CVU Or WaE WaS WaT WaTC **6254**

The biggest bear on earth, drawings by

Paul Bransom. Philadelphia, Lippincott [1943] x, 113 p. col. front., illus., plates. Alaska brown or Kodiak bear.
WaU **6255**

Frederic Remington, artist of the Old West; with a bibliographical check list of Remington pictures and books, introd. by James Chillman, Jr. Philadelphia, Lippincott [1947] 157 p. illus., plates (part col.) facsims.
MtHi WaT WaU **6256**

God's frozen children. New York, Doubleday, 1930. 291 p. front.
CVU Or OrP WaSp **6257**

The last of the sea otters, with drawings by Paul Bransom. Philadelphia, Stokes, 1942. 98 p. col. front., illus.
CVicAr Or WaS WaSp WaU **6258**

Sentinel of the snow peaks; a story of the Alaskan wild, illus. by Enos B. Comstock. Philadelphia, Lippincott [1945] 151 p. illus., plates. Many **6259**

Son of the walrus king, drawings by Lynn Bogue Hunt. Philadelphia, Lippincott [1944] x, 128 p. col. front., illus., plates.
WaU **6260**

McCrea, Walter Jackson, 1876-1946.
Pauline Johnson and her friends, by Walter McRaye [pseud.] Toronto, Ryerson [1947] 182 p. ports. B. C. Indian poetess biographee. CV CVicAr **6261**

McCreight, Major Israel, 1865-
Chief Flying Hawk's tales; the true story of Custer's last fight. New York, Alliance Press, c1936. 56 p. front. (port.) illus., 4 plates, 13 ports. Tehanta Tanka, Indian name of author. MtHi **6262**

McCullagh, James Benjamin, 1854-1921.
The Indian potlatch [substance of a paper read before C. M. S. annual conference at Metlakatla, B. C., 1899] [Toronto, Woman's Missionary Society of the Methodist Church, n.d.] 20 p.
CVicAr **6263**

Nisg'a primer: Part I. Spelling and reading, anspelsquon sim algiuk Rev. J. B. McCullagh; for use in the day school at Aiyansk Mission. Naas River, B. C. London, Society for Promoting Christian Knowledge, 1897. 32 p.
CVicAr **6264**

Red Indians I have known. London, Church Missionary Society [n.d.] 47 p. illus. CVicAr **6265**

Wila Yelth [morning prayer in Tsimshiam] [n.p., n.d.] 21 p. Anon.
CVicAr **6266**

See also no. 1748.

McCulloch, Henry Lawrence, 1865-
Life of John Robert Monaghan, the hero of Samoa. Spokane, Shaw & Borden, 1906. 415 p. front. (port.) 3 plates, 2 ports., fold. map. Spokane biographee.
WaPS WaSp WaU **6267**

McCulloch, John Herries.
The men of Kildonan; a romance of the Selkirk settlers. New York, Doran [c1926] 276 p. CVicAr **6268**

Same. Toronto, McClelland and Stewart [c1926] CVU **6269**

Same. Edinburgh, Moray Press [1935] 278 p. front. (fold. map)　　CVicAr **6270**

McCully, Mrs. Alice Woodruff (Anderson)
American alpines in the garden. New York, Macmillan, 1931. 251 p. front., 8 plates.　　Many **6271**

McCurdy, James G.
By Juan de Fuca's strait; pioneering along the northwestern edge of the continent. Portland, Or., Metropolitan [c1937] 312 p. front. (map) illus., parts., facsims.
　　Many **6272**

MacDermot, J. H.
J. S. Helmcken. [n.p.] 1946. 13 p. Vancouver Island biographee.　　CVicAr **6273**

McDermoth, Cora A.
Few fern fronds from Washington. [Aberdeen, Wash., Quick Print Co., n.d.] [20] p.　　OrHi **6274**

McDermott, John Francis, see no. 5055.

MacDonald, Adrian.
Sir Alexander Mackenzie. Toronto, Ryerson [c1928] 32 p. (Canadian history readers)　　CV CVicAr WaE WaS **6275**
Same. [1930?]　　CVU **6276**

MacDonald, Alexander, bp., 1858-1941.
A bit of autobiography. Victoria, B. C., Willows Press [1920] [61] p. front. (port.)
　　CVicAr **6277**
Stray leaves; or, Traces of travel. New York, Christian Press Assn. [c1914] 171 [11] p. front. (port.)　　CVicAr **6278**
See also no. 1111.

MacDonald, Alexander, 1878-
In search of El Dorado; a wanderer's experiences, with an introd. by Admiral Moresby. London, Unwin, 1905. xviii, 291 p. front., plates, ports.
　　CVicAr CVU WaU **6279**
Same. 2d impression. 1906.
　　CVicAr CVU **6280**
Same. 3d impression. 1910.
　　CVU OrP **6281**
The white trail; a story of the early days of Klondike, illus. by William Rainey. London, Blackie [c1908] 392 p. front., plates, map.　　WaPS **6282**
Same. Toronto, Musson [c1908].
　　WaU **6283**

McDonald, Alva L., see no. 7445.

McDonald, Archibald.
Peace River; a canoe voyage from Hudson's Bay to Pacific by the late Sir George Simpson (governor, Hon. Hudson's Bay Co.) in 1828; journal of the chief factor, Archibald McDonald (Hon. Hudson's Bay Company) who accompanied him, ed. with notes by Malcolm McLeod. Ottawa, J. Durie & Son, 1872. xix, 119 p. fold. map.　　Many **6284**

Macdonald, Augustin Sylvester, 1865-
A list of books. Californiana and the Pacific in the library of Augustin S. Macdonald. Oakland, Calif., Enquirer Pub. Co., 1903. 76p. CVicAr OrP OrU WaS WaU **6285**

MacDonald Betty (Bard)
The egg and I. Philadelphia, Lippincott [c1945] 277 p. Autobiographical of life on Olympic Peninsula.　　Many **6286**

Same. New York, Pocket Books [c1945] 278 p. (no. 566)　　WaU **6287**
Mrs. Piggle-Wiggle, illus. by Richard Bennett. Philadelphia, Lippincott [1947] 118 p. illus., col. plates.　　Many **6288**
The plague and I. Philadelphia, Lippincott [1948] 254 p.　　Many **6289**

Macdonald, Duncan George Forbes, 1823?-1884.
British Columbia and Vancouver's Island, comprising a description of these dependencies; also an account of the manners and customs of the native Indians. London, Longman, 1862. xiii, 524 p. fold. map. CV CVirAr CVU WaS WaU **6290**
Same. 2d ed.　　WaU **6291**
Same. 3d ed. 1863.　　CVU OrU **6292**
Lecture on British Columbia and Vancouver's Island delivered at the Royal United Service Institution on March 27, 1863. 59 p.　　CVicAr **6293**
See also no. 8666.

McDonald, Joseph Lane.
Hidden treasures; or, Fisheries around the Northwest Coast. Gloucester, Mass., Procter Bros., Printers, 1871. 110 p.
　　OrP **6294**
Same. Photostat copy.　　WaU **6295**

McDonald, Lucile Saunders, 1898-
Bering's potlatch, illus. by Nils Hogner. London, Oxford Univ. Press [1944] 232 p. front. (map) illus. Seattle author.
　　Many **6296**

MacDonald, Malcolm, 1901-
Down north, London, Oxford Univ. Press, 1943. xi, 274 p. front. (map)
　　CV CVicAr CVU **6297**
Down north, a view of northwest Canada. New York, Farrar [c1943] xiii, 274 p. front. (map) plates.
　　Or OrP WaE WaS WaSp WaU **6298**

MacDonald, P. M.
Letters from the Canadian West. Truro [1903] 55 p.　　CVicAr **6299**

MacDonald, Ranald, 1824-1894.
Ranald MacDonald, the narrative of his early life on the Columbia under the Hudson's Bay Company's regime; of his experiences in the Pacific whale fisheries; and of his great adventure to Japan; with a sketch of his later life on the western frontier, 1824-1894; ed. and annotated from the original manuscripts by William S. Lewis and Naojiro Murakami. Spokane, Pub. for the Eastern Wash. State Historical Society by the Inland-American Printing Co., 1923. 333 p. illus., plates, ports., maps, plan, facsim.　　Many **6300**

McDonald, Robert, archdeacon of Mackenzie River, 1829-1913.
A grammar of the Tukudh language. London, Society for Promoting Christian Knowledge, 1911. 201 p.　　WaU **6301**

McDonald, William, see no. 7933.

[Macdonald, William John] 1832-1916.
Pioneer, 1851. [n.p., 1914?] 30 p. British Columbia pioneer.　　CVicAr OrHi **6302**

MacDonnell, Allan.
The North-West Transportation Navigation and Railway Company; its objects. Toronto, Lovell & Gibson, 1858. 30 p.
CVicAr **6303**

Macdonnell, Amice.
The name on the rock; a play in three acts with prologue & epilogue. London, George Allen [c1933] 61 p. Deals with Sir Alexander Mackenzie. CVicAr **6304**

Macdonnell, John, see no. 3477.

McDougall, see no. 9438.

M'Dougall, George Frederick.
The eventful voyage of H. M. discovery ship "Resolute" to the Arctic regions in search of Sir John Franklin and the missing crews of H. M. discovery ships "Erebus" and "Terror", 1852, 1853, 1854. London, Longman, 1857. xi. 530 p. col. front., illus., col. plates, fold. map.
CVicAr **6305**

McDougall, John, 1842-1917.
Forest, lake and prairie; twenty years of frontier life in western Canada, 1842-62. Toronto, Briggs [c1895] 267 p. front., illus. CVicAr CVU **6306**

Same. Toronto, Ryerson [n.d.]
CVicAr **6307**

Same. 2d ed. Toronto, Briggs, 1910.
CVU **6308**

In the days of the Red River rebellion; life and adventures in the far West of Canada, 1868-1872. Toronto, Briggs, 1903. 303 p. illus., plates, ports.
CVU MtHi **6309**

Same. With illus. by J. E. Laughlin. 1911.
CVicAr CVU **6310**

On western trails in the early seventies; frontier life in the Canadian North-west. Toronto, Briggs, 1911. 279 p. front.
CVirAr CVU MtHi WaU **6311**

Pathfinding on plain and prairie; stirring scenes of life in the Canadian Northwest, with illus. by J. E. Laughlin. Toronto, Briggs, 1898. 277 p. front., 11 plates. CVicAr MtHi WaS WaU **6312**

"Wa-pee Moos-tooch" or "White Buffalo" hero of a hundred battles; a tale of life in Canada's great West during the early years of the last century. [Calgary, Herald, 1908] 336 p. plates. CVU MtHi **6313**

MacDowell, Lloyd W.
Alaska glaciers and ice fields. Seattle, Alaska Steamship Co., 1906. [16] p. illus.
OrHi WaU **6314**

Alaska Indian basketry. Seattle, Alaska Steamship Co., 1904. [14] p. illus. (part col.) WaT **6315**

Same. 1905. 16 p. OrHi WaS WaU **6316**

Same. 1906. [14] p. Wa WaS WaT **6317**

Totem poles of Alaska and Indian mythology. Seattle, Alaska Steamship Co., 1905. 16 p. illus.
OrHi WaT WaU WaWW **6318**
Same. 1906. WaT **6319**

McElrath, Thompson P.
The Yellowstone Valley; what it is, where it is, and how to get to it; a hand-book for tourists and settlers. St. Paul, Pio-

neer Press, 1880. 138 p. map. MtHi **6320**

McElroy, H. B., see nos. 1968, 1969.

McElroy, Robert McNutt, 1872-
The winning of the far west; a history of the regaining of Texas, of the Mexican War, and the Oregon question, and of the successive additions to the territory of the United States, 1829-1867. New York, Putnam, 1914. x, 384 p. col. front., 3 plates, 10 fold. maps. Many **6321**

McElwaine, Eugene.
The truth about Alaska, the golden land of the midnight sun. [Chicago] 1901. 445 p. front. (port.) illus., maps. WaU **6322**

McEvoy, Bernard, 1842-1932.
From the Great Lakes to the wide West; impressions of a tour between Toronto and the Pacific. London, Low, 1902. 288 p. front., plates. CVicAr CVU **6323**

Same. Toronto. W. Briggs, 1902.
CV CVic CVicAr CVU WaS WaU **6324**

History of the 72d Canadian Infantry Battalion Seaforth Highlanders of Canada, comp. from official records and various other sources by Bernard McEvoy & A. H. Finlay, with illus. from photographs and with tabular appendices. Vancouver, B. C., Cowan, 1920. 311 p. front., illus., 42 plates, 7 ports., 3 maps.
CV CVU **6325**

Verses for my friends. Vancouver, B. C., Cowan Brookhouse, 1923. 209 p.
CVicAr CVU **6326**

McEwen, Inez Puckett.
So this is ranching! Caldwell, Idaho, Caxton [c1948] 270 p. front., plates, ports. Southern Idaho.
IdB IdU OrP WaT WaU **6327**

MacFadden, Harry Alexander.
Rambles in the far West. Holidaysburg, Pa., Standard Printing House [c1906] 277 p. front. (port.) illus., plates.
WaU **6328**

McFarland, Cara Lee.
The United States National Bank of Portland, Oregon, a historical sketch. Portland, Binfords & Mort [1940] 147 p. front., plates (incl. ports.) tables, diagr. OrHi **6328A**

The United States National Bank of Portland, Oregon, a supplement to the historical sketch published in 1940, and made necessary by the subsequent purchase of the three banks chronicled herein. Portland, Binfords & Mort [1942]. 39 p. front., plates (ports.), tab.
OrHi **6328B**

MacFarlane, W. G.
Mountains and rivers of the great North West. Grand Rapids, Engraving Co. [n.d.] [61] p. illus. OrHi **6329**

Picturesque and scenic beauties of the Columbia River and the metropolis of the Pacific Northwest. Grand Rapids [n.d.] [30] p. illus. Or OrHi **6330**

Same. Toronto [n.d.] CVicAr **6331**

Picturesque British Columbia. Toronto. [n.d.] 1 v. CVU **6332**

Portland - Oregon and the Columbia River; being illustrations of the archi-

tecture and scenic surroundings of the growing metropolis of the North Pacific with magnificent views of the city and Mounts Hood, Adams and St. Helens in the distance; also pictures of the magnificent scenic features of the father of Pacific waters, the Columbia River. Buffalo [n.d.] [48] p. views.
WaU **6333**

Macfie, Matthew.
Vancouver Island and British Columbia; their history, resources and prospects. London, Longman, 1865. xxi, 574 p. front., illus., 2 fold. maps. Many **6334**

McGaffey, Ernest.
War lyrics from British Columbia. [n.p.] 1915. [12] p. CVicAr **6335**

McGee, L. R., comp.
Pacific Northwest swine husbandry. Rev. ed. North Portland, Or., Portland Union Stock Yards Co. [c1915] 63 p. illus., tables, diagrs.
OrHi OrP Wa WaPS **6336**

McGeer, Gerald Grattan.
Money and credit and its management; address delivered at annual meeting, B. C. Division, Canadian Credit Men's Trust Association, Vancouver, B. C., April 21, 1932. [Vancouver, B. C.] 1932. 23 p. CVU **6337**

McGeorge, Mrs. Alice Sutton.
Kamaiwea, the Coeur d'Alene (the heart of an awl). Kansas City, Mo., Burton Pub. Co. [c1939] 320 p. WaSp **6338**

MacGibbon, Mrs. Elma.
Leaves of knowledge. [Spokane, Shaw & Borden, c1904] 237 p. front. (port.) Western travel sketches. Many **6339**

MacGill, Mrs. Helen (Gregory)
Daughters, wives and mothers in British Columbia; some laws regarding them. Vancouver, B. C., Moore Printing Co., 1913. 66 p. CV **6340**

Laws for women and children in British Columbia. [Vancouver, B. C.] 1935. 61 p.
CVU **6341**

McGill, Thomas H., see no. 7537.

M'Gillivray, Duncan, d. 1808.
The journal of Duncan M'Gillivray of the North West Company at Fort George on the Saskatchewan, 1794-5, with introd., notes and appendix by Arthur S. Morton. Toronto, Macmillan, 1929. lxxviii, 79, 24, 6 p. maps (1 double).
Many **6342**

McGillivray, Simon, see no. 10998.

McGinitie, Harry D., see no. 1510.

McGinn, Henry E., 1850-1923.
Speech against the assembly plan. Portland, Or., Multnomah Printing Co., 1910. 30 p. OrP **6343**

McGrath, Dan L., see no. 4688.

McGrath, Rita Margaret, see no. 1888.

McGregor, J. Herrick.
The wisdom of Waloopi. For private circulation only. [Letchworth, Herts, Printed by Garden City Press, 1913?] 249 p. Vancouver Island poet. CVU **6344**

McGuire, F. J., see no. 4609.

McGuire, J. A.
In the Alaska-Yukon game-lands, introd. by William T. Hornaday (photographs by the author). Cincinnati, S. Kidd Co. [c1921] 215 p. plates, ports., map.
WaA WaU **6345**

Machell, Percy.
"What is my country? My country is the empire; Canada is my home"; impressions of Canada and the new Northwest. London, Sifton, 1912. [46] p.
CVicAr **6346**

Machetanz, Frederick.
On Arctic ice, with illus. by the author. New York, Scribner [c1940] 105 p. illus. (part col.)
Or OrP Wa WaS WaSp WaU **6347**

Panuck, Eskimo sled dog, illus. by the author. New York, Scribner [c1939] 94 p. illus. (part col.) Many **6348**

Machray, Robert, 1857-
Life of Robert Machray, archbishop of Rupert's Land, primate of all Canada, by his nephew. London, Macmillan, 1909. xix, 468 p. front., 9 plates (1 double) 2 ports., 5 groups of ports., map.
CVicAr CVU WaSp **6349**

Same. Toronto, Macmillan, 1909. CVU **6350**

McInnes, Alex P., 1868-
Dunlevy's discovery of gold on the Horsefly. Lillooet, B. C., Lillooet Pub. Co., c1938. iii, 27 p. illus., ports. (Chronicles of the Cariboo, no. 1).
CV CVicAr CVU **6351**

MacInnes, Charles Malcolm.
In the shadow of the Rockies. London, Rivington, 1930. viii, 347 p. plates, 5 ports., 2 fold. maps, 3 plans.
CVicAr CVU **6352**

MacInnes, Tom, 1867-
Chinook days; nine drawings by J. H. Smith, two by John Innes. [Vancouver, B. C., Sun Pub. Co., n.d.] 206 p. illus. Souvenir for opening of Grouse Mountain Highway and Scenic Resort, Sept. 1926. CV CVicAr CVU WaSp **6353**

Same. [193-?] WaU **6354**

How low along; a didactic poem. Vancouver, B. C., Clark and Stuart Co. [c1934] 68 p. CVicAr CVU **6355**

Oriental occupation of British Columbia. Vancouver, B. C., Sun Pub. Co., 1927. 170 p. CV CVicAr CVU WaS WaU **6356**

Rhymes of a rounder. Vancouver, B. C., Review Press [c1931] 79 p. CVU **6357**

See also no. 5571.

McIntosh, Walter H.
Allen and Rachel; an overland honeymoon in 1853. Caldwell, Idaho, Caxton, 1938. 156 p. front., illus., plates, ports.
Many **6358**

McIntyre, Alexander.
The Canadian west, a geography of Manitoba and the North-west Territories. Toronto, Morang, 1904. xv, 249 p. front., illus., double map, diagrs. (provincial geographies) CVU **6359**

MacIver, R. M., see no. 4930.

McKay, Allis.
They came to a river. New York, Mac-

millan, 1941. 651 p. Washington apple growing country. Many **6360**

Mackay, Angus, 1865-
By trench and trail in song and story, by Angus Mackay (Oscar Dhu) illus. by Lt. Wm. R. McKay. Seattle, Mackay Printing & Pub. Co., 1918. 144 p. front., illus., plates. CVU Wa WaS WaU **6361**

MacKay, Charles Angus, 1872-
Memoirs of the life of Charles Angus MacKay by himself. Victoria, B. C., Colonist Presses, 1930. 50 p. British Columbia prospector. CVicAr CVU **6362**

MacKay, Douglas.
The honourable company; a history of the Hudson's Bay Company, maps by R. H. H. Macaulay. Indianapolis, Bobbs-Merrill [c1936] 396 p. front. (port.) illus., plates, ports., maps, plans, 3 facsims. Many **6363**

Same. Toronto, McClelland and Stewart [c1936] CVic CVicAr **6364**

Same. London, Cassell and Co. [1937] CVU **6365**

Same. New York, Tudor Pub. Co., 1938. OrCS **6366**

MacKay, J. W., see no. 1107.

MacKay, Malcolm Sutherland.
Cow range and hunting trail, with 38 illus. New York, Putnam, 1925. xv, 243 p. front., plates, ports. Montana ranch story. MtHi MtU WaU **6367**

MacKaye, David Loring, 1890-
The far distant bugle; decorations by Avery Johnson. New York, Longmans, 1948. vi, 264 p. Western army outpost during Civil War.
Or OrP WaS WaSp WaU **6368**

McKee, Lanier.
The land of Nome; a narrative sketch of the rush to our Bering Sea gold-fields, the country, its mines and its people, and the history of a great conspiracy 1900-1901. New York, Grafton Press [1902] ix, 260 p.
CVicAr WaS WaSp WaU **6369**

McKee, Ruth (Karr) 1874-
Mary Richardson Walker; her book. Caldwell, Idaho, Caxton, 1945. 357 p. front., plates, ports., map, facsim. Many **6370**

McKelvie, Bruce Alastair, 1889-
The black canyon; a story of '58. London, Dent, 1927. ix, 173 p. front., plate. British Columbia author.
CVicAr WaU **6371**

Early history of the province of British Columbia. Toronto, Dent, 1926. ix, 118 p. illus., port.
CV CVicAr CVU WaS WaU **6372**

Fort Langley, outpost of empire, front. by George H. Southwell, decorations by C. P. Connorton. [Vancouver, B. C.] Vancouver Daily Province, 1947. ix, 98 p. front., illus.
CV CVicAr CVU WaS WaSp **6373**

Huldowget; a story of the North Pacific Coast. Toronto, Dent, 1926. ix, 221 p.
CV CVicAr CVU WaU **6374**

Maquinna the magnificent, illus. by Geo. H. Southwell. [Vancouver, B. C.] Van-

couver Daily Province [c1946] ix, 65 p. col. front., col. plates.
CV CVicPr OrHi WaS WaU **6375**

Pelts and powder; a story of the West coast in the making. London, Dent [1929] xiii, 238 p. front. (map) illus.
CVicAr CVU WaU **6376**

Mackenzie, Sir Alexander, 1763-1820.
Alexander Mackenzie's voyage to the Pacific Ocean in 1793; historical introd. and footnotes by Milo Milton Quaife. Chicago, Lakeside Press, 1931. xl, 384 p. front. (port.) fold. map. (Lakeside classics) Many **6377**

Reisen von Montreal durch Nordwestamerika nach dem Eismer und der Sudsee in den Jahren 1789 und 1793; nebst einer Geshichte des Pelzhandels in Canada, aus dem Englischen. Hamburg, B. G. Hoffman, 1802. x, 585 p. front. (port.) fold. map. CV CVicAr OrP WaU **6378**

Same. Berlin, 1802. 408 p. (Bibliothek der neuesten und interessantesten Reisebeschreibungen, Bd. 12) WaU **6379**

Tableau historique et politique du commerce des pelleteries dans le Canada, depuis 1608 jusqu'a nos jours; contenant beaucoup details sur les nations sauvages que l'habitent, et sur les vastes contrees qui y sont contigues; avec un vocabulaire de la langue de plusieurs peuple de ces vastes contrees, traduit de l'Anglais par J. Castera. Paris, Dentu, 1807. 310 p. front. (port.)
CVicAr **6380**

Voyages dans l'interieur de l'amerique septentrionale faits en 1789, 1792 et 1793; le 1.er de Montreal au fort Chipiouyan et a la mer Glaciale; le 2.me, du fort Chipiouyan jusqu'aux bords de l'Ocean pacifique, tr. de l'Anglais par J. Castera avec des notes et un itineraire, tires en partie des papiers du vice-amiral Bougainville. Paris, Dentu, 1802. 3 v. front., 3 fold. maps.
CVicAr CVU WaU **6381**

Voyages from Montreal on the River St. Lawrence through the continent of North America to the frozen and Pacific Oceans; in the years 1789 and 1793, with a preliminary account of the rise, progress, and present state of the fur trade of that country. London, T. Cadell, 1801. cxxxii, viii, 412 p. front. (port.) 3 fold. maps. Many **6382**

Same. 1802. 2 v.
CVicAr CVU (v. 2) WaSp **6383**

Same. 1st American ed. New York, G. F. Hopkins, 1802. ix, 94, 296 p. front. (fold. map) CVicAr WaU **6384**

Same. Philadelphia, John Morgan, 1802. viii, cxxvi, 392 p. fold. map. CVU **6385**

Same. 2 v. front. (port.) 3 maps.
CVicAr **6386**

Same. 3d American ed. New York, Evert Duyckinck, 1803. 437 p. front. (fold. map) CVicAr CVU **6387**

Same. New York, W. B. Gilley, 1814. 2 v. front. (port.) 3 fold. maps.
CVicAr CVU OrHi (v. 1) WaU **6388**

Same. New York, New Amsterdam Book Co., 1902. (Commonwealth library) Many **6389**

Same. New York, A. S. Barnes, 1903. (Trail makers) CVic OrHi WaPS **6390**

Same. Toronto, Morang [1911?] CVU **6393** CVicAr CVU **6391**

Same. With introd. by W. L. Grant. Toronto, Courier Press, 1911. 2 v. fronts., map. CVicAr WaSp **6392**

Same. Toronto, Morang, [1911?] CVU **6393**

Same. New York, Allerton Book Co., 1922. (American explorers) Many **6394**

Same. London, T. Cadell, 1801 [Toronto? 1927?] xxviii, 498 p. front. (port.) illus., plates, map. IdP WaU **6395**

Same. [Toronto, Radisson Society of Canada, 1927] Many **6396**

Mackenzie, Cecil Walter.
Donald Mackenzie, "King of the Northwest"; the story of an international hero of the Oregon country and the Red River settlement at Lower Fort Garry (Winnipeg). Los Angeles, I. Deach, Jr., 1937. 210 p. front. (port.) illus., plates, port. Many **6397**

Mackenzie, Henry.
Occupy till I come; a sermon preached at the first annual service of the Columbia Mission. London, Rivingtons, 1860. 24 p. CVicAr **6398**

McKenzie, N. M. W. J.
The men of the Hudson's Bay Company, 1670 A. D. - 1920 A. D. Fort William, Ont. [Times-Journal Presses, 1921] 214 p. front. (port.) CV CVicAr CVU WaS **6399**

McKenzie, Roderick Duncan, 1885-
Oriental exclusion, the effect of American immigration laws, regulations, and judicial decisions upon the Chinese and Japanese on the American Pacific Coast. Chicago, University of Chicago Press [1928] 200 p. diagrs. Many **6400**

McKeown, Martha Ferguson, see no. 4183.

McKinlay, Arthur Patch, 1871-
The passing show. [Los Angeles] Ward Ritchie Press, 1941. 68 p. Sonnets by Portland author. IdU **6401**

McKinley, Charles, see no. 5788.

McKinstry, George, see nos. 5707, 5708.

Mackintosh, Charles Herbert, 1843-
Potential riches of British Columbia, a province of marvellous resources. [n.p., n.d.] 55 p. CVicAr **6402**

Same. [Victoria, B. C., Victoria Printing & Pub. Co., 1907] 28 p. CVicAr **6403**

Mackintosh, William Archibald, 1895-
Agricultural cooperation in western Canada. Kingston, Ont., Queen's University [c1924] 173 p. diagrs. (Publications of the faculty of arts) CVU MtBozC **6404**

MacKnight, James Arthur.
The mines of Montana, their history and development to date; prepared for the National Mining Congress held at Helena, July 12, 1892. Helena, Mont.,

C. K. Wells Co., 1892. 138 p. front., illus., plates, ports., maps. CVicAr CVU MtBozC MtHi WaU **6405**

McKown, S. H.
The violence done by perpetuating the name Mount Rainier. 2d ed. Tacoma, Barrett-Redfield Press, 1924. 12 p. OrHi WaT **6406**

McLachlan, C., see no. 9362.

McLagan, J. C., see no. 6471.

McLain, John Scudder, 1853-
Alaska and the Klondike, illus. from photographs. New York, McClure, Phillips & Co., 1905. xiv, 330 p. front., illus., fold. map. CVU WaS WaSp WaU **6407**

Same. 1907. CVicAr WaU **6408**

MacLane, Mary, 1881-
I, Mary MacLane; a diary of human days. New York, Stokes, c1917. 317 p. front. (port.) Montana author. MtHi MtU MtUM **6409**

My friend Annabel Lee. Chicago, H. S. Stone and Co., 1903. 262 p. MtHi WaU **6410**

The story of Mary MacLane by herself. Chicago, H. S. Stone and Co., 1902. 322 p. front. (port.) CVicAr MtBozC MtHi MtU Wa WaU **6411**

Same. New ed. with a chapter on the present. New York, Duffield, 1911. 354 p. 2 plates. MtBozC **6412**

McLaughlin, Daniel, 1863-
Chronicles of a Northern Pacific veteran. [Spokane, c1930] 56 p. 2 ports. Wa **6413**

Maclauries.
Narrative or journal of voyages and travels through the northwest continent of America in the years 1789 and 1793. London, Lee, 1802. 91 p. plates. WaS **6414**

McLaurin, Colin Campbell, 1854-
Pioneering in western Canada, a story of the Baptists. Calgary, Alta., 1939. 401 p. front. (port.) 17 plates. CVicAr **6415**

McLean, G. B., see nos. 2788, 2789.

McLean, Henry Alberts.
An address delivered at the ground breaking ceremonies at Seattle, June 1, 1907. [Mt. Vernon, Wash., Argus Press, 1907] [8] p. Ground breaking for the Alaska-Yukon-Pacific Exposition. WaS WaU **6416**

McLean, John, 1799-1890.
John McLean's Notes of a twenty-five year's service in the Hudson's Bay territory, ed. by W. S. Wallace. Toronto, Champlain Society, 1932. xxxvi, 402 p. fold. map. (Publications 19) Many **6417**

Notes of a twenty-five year's service in the Hudson's Bay territory. London, R. Bentley, 1849. 2 v. Many **6418**

Same. 2 v. in 1. OrHi OrP OrU **6419**

MacLean, John, 1851-1928.
The warden of the plains and other stories of life in the Canadian Northwest, illus. by J. E. Laughlin. Toronto, Briggs, 1896. 301 p. front., plates. CVU MtHi **6420**

McLellan, Roy Davidson, 1892-
The geology of the San Juan Islands. Seattle, Univ. of Wash. Press, 1927. 185 p. front., illus., fold. map. (Publications in geology, v. 2, Nov. 1927)
Many **6421**

MacLennan, Catherine Mae.
Rambling round Stanley Park. Toronto, Ryerson [1935] 47 p. illus.
CV CVicAr CVU **6422**

McLeod, Archibald N., see no. 3477.

McLeod, George A.
History of Alturas and Blaine Counties, Idaho. Hailey, Idaho, Hailey Times, 1930. 119 p. IdB IdIf IdU WaSp **6423**
Same. Rev. ed. 1938. iv, 192, v-xx p. front. (port.) plates.
IdB IdIf IdTf IdU IdUSB MtHi **6424**

McLeod, John N., ed.
A pictorial record and original muster roll, 29th Battalion, Vancouver, Canada. Vancouver, B. C., Pub. for the 29th Battalion Assn. [1919?] 63 p. front., illus.
CV CVU **6425**

McLeod, Malcolm, 1821-1899.
Oregon indemnity; claim of chief factors and chief traders of the Hudson's Bay Company thereto as partners under the Treaty of 1846. [Ottawa] 1892. 57 p.
CVicAr Or OrHi OrU WaU **6426**

The Pacific Railroad; Britannicus' letters from the Ottawa Citizen. Ottawa "Citizen" Printing and Pub. Co., 1875. 42 p.
CVicAr **6427**

Pacific Railway, Canada; Britannicus letters, &c. thereon. Ottawa, Woodburn [1875] 36 p. CVicAr **6428**

The problem of Canada. Ottawa, Citizen, 1880. 72 p. Pacific Railroad problem.
CVicAr CVU **6429**
See also no. 6284.

Macleod, Margaret Arnett, see no. 4060.

Macleod, Norman, 1906-
The Bitter roots. New York, Smith & Durrell, 1941. 286 p.
MtBozC MtHi MtU WaSp WaU **6430**

McLernan, R. P., pub.
Some British Columbians, 1914-1918. Victoria, B. C., [1921] 121 plates. Caricatures and short biographies of B. C. World War veterans. CVicAr **6431**

McLoughlin, John, 1784-1857.
Documentary (letter) Dr. John McLoughlin to Sir George Simpson, March 20, 1844; (Introductory note) by Katharine B. Judson. Portland, Or., Ivy Press, 1916. 25 p. OrHi WaU **6432**

The letters of John McLoughlin from Fort Vancouver to the governor and committee, ed. by E. E. Rich, with an introd. by W. Kaye Lamb. [London] Champlain Society, 1941-1944. 3 v. fronts., fold maps. (Publications of the Hudson's Bay Record Society, no. 4, 6, 7) Many **6433**

Letters of Dr. John McLoughlin written at Fort Vancouver, 1829-1832, ed. by Burt Brown Barker. Portland, Or., Binfords & Mort, c1948. 376 p. Many **6434**

McMacken, Joseph G.
Geology of the Grand Coulee; Grand Coulee dam and Columbia Basin Irrigation Project. 2d ed. Spokane, c1936. 27 p. plates, map. WaS WaTC WaU **6435**
Same. 3d ed. 1937. 29 p. OrP Wa WaT **6436**
Same. 4th ed. c1938. OrCS **6437**

McMahon, Edward.
Supplement to Manley's The pursuit of happiness for the state of Washington. Chicago, B. H. Sanborn & Co., 1930. iii, 99 p. front., illus., tables..
WaT WaU **6438**

Supplement to Reinsch's Civil government for the state of Washington. Boston, B. H. Sanborn & Co. [c1910] 47 p. front.
WaPS WaU WaW **6439**
Same. Chicago, B. H. Sanborn & Co. [c1915] iii, 103 p. front., illus.
WaPs WaS **6440**

McManus, Robert.
The tourists' pictorial guide and hand book to British Columbia and the Northern Pacific waters. Victoria, B. C., "Tourists' Pictorial Guide" Pub. Co., 1890. 48 p. CVicAr **6441**

Macmaster, Sir Donald, bart., 1846-1922.
The seal arbitration, 1893. Montreal, Brown, 1894. 65 p. map.
CV CVicAr CVU **6442**

MacMaster, John Bach, see no. 5904.

McMillan, A. J.
The mineral resources of British Columbia and the Yukon; a lecture delivered at the Imperial Institute, London, on December 6. 1897. [London, Cassell. n.d.] 20 p. CVicAr **6443**

MacMillan, Miriam (Look)
Green seas and white ice. New York, Dodd, 1948. 287 p. illus., ports., maps.
CV CVicAr OrP WaE WaS WaT **6444**

McMillion, Ovid Miller.
New Alaska. Ann Arbor, Mich., Edwards Bros., 1939. xii, 216 p. illus., plates, maps (part fold.) Or WaU **6445**

McMinn, Howard Earnest, 1891-
An illustrated manual of Pacific Coast trees, by Howard E. McMinn and Evelyn Maino, with Lists of trees recommended for various uses on the Pacific Coast, by H. W. Shepherd. Berkeley, Calif., Univ. of Calif. Press, 1935. xii, 409 p. col. front., illus. Many **6446**
Same. c1937. IdUSB Wa WaE WaU **6447**
Same. 2d ed. 1946, c1937.
IdU Or OrHi OrP WaS **6448**
See also nos. 3718, 3719.

McMunn, Ella, 1875-
Seven miles out. [Salem, Or.] 1927. 35 p. front., illus.
Or OrP OrPR WaPS **6449**

McMurray, DeVon.
All aboard for Alaska! Boston, Heath [c1941] xii, 159 p. illus.
Or WaS WaSp WaT WaU **6450**

McMurry, Charles Alexander, 1857-1929.
Pioneers of the Rocky Mountains and the West. New York, Macmillan, 1904. x, 248 p. front., illus., maps. (Pioneer history stories, 3d book) Many **6451**

Same. 1906. CVicAr 6452
Same. 1924 [c1904] OrU 6453
Same. 1929 [c1904] OrCS 6454
Same. 1932. WaW 6455

MuMurtrie, Douglas Crawford, 1888-1944.
The first printing in British Columbia. Chicago, 1929. 22 p. fold. front., facsims. (1 double) Many 6456

The mining laws of the district of Idaho, ed. with an introd. by Douglas C. McMurtrie. Evanston, Ill., 1944. 14 p.
IdU WaS 6457

Montana imprints, 1864-1880; bibliography of books, pamphlets and broadsides printed within the area now constituting the state of Montana. Chicago, Black Cat Press, 1937. 82 p. fold. front., facsims.
WaS WaU 6458

Pioner printers of the far West. San Francisco, Red Tower Press, 1933. 11 p.
OrP 6459

McNab, Frances, see no. 3262.

McNamar, Mrs. Myrtle.
The vail of mist. Cottonwood, Calif., c1919. 31 p. Poem about Oregon. Or OrU 6460

McNaughton, Margaret.
Overland to Cariboo; an eventful journey of Canadian pioneers to the gold-fields of British Columbia in 1862. Toronto, Briggs, 1896. 176 p. front., illus., plates, ports. Many 6461

McNeal, Violet.
Four white horses and a brass band. New York, Doubleday, 1947. 267 p. Oregon author. Medicine show in West.
Or OrP Wa WaE WaU WaW 6462

McNeely, James.
Good roads; a lecture designed to help in the good roads movement. [Buckley, Wash? 1912?] 17 p. WaS 6463

McNeer, May Yonge, 1902-
The covered wagon, illus. by Florian. New York, Artists and Writers Gulid [1944] 28 p. col. front., illus. (part col.)
Or OrP WaS WaU 6464

McNeil, Fred H.
Wy'east, "The mountain"; a chronicle of Mount Hood, known to the Indians, who worshipped it, as Wy'east; to the white man, with equal eloquence, simply as "The mountain". Or. Journal ed. Portland, Or., Metropolitan [c1937] ix, 244 p. front., plates. Many 6465

McNeill, Kate.
Poems. [Vancouver, B. C., Evans & Hastings, 1918] 128 p. CVicAr CVU 6466

McNeilly, Mildred Masterson.
Heaven is too high. New York, Hampton Pub. Co., 1944. 432 p. A. A. Baranov fiction. Many 6467

Praise at morning. New York, Morrow, 1947. 409 p. Coming of Russian fleet to American waters. Many 6468

McNemee, Andrew J., 1848-
"Brother Mack" the frontier preacher; a brief record of the difficulties and hardships of a pioneer itinerant. Portland, Or., T. G. Robinson [1924] 79 p.
Many 6469

McNemee, Jack, see no. 5989.

Macoun, John, 1831-1920.
Autobiography of John Macoun, Canadian explorer and naturalist, 1831-1920; with introd. by Ernest Thompson Seton. Ottawa, Field-Naturalists' Club, 1922. x, 305 p. front. (port.) 5 plates, 2 ports.
CVic CVicAr CVU 6470

Manitoba and the great North-west; the field for investment, the home of the emigrant, being a full and complete history of the country, to which has been added the educational & religious history of Manitoba & the North-west, by George M. Grant; also Montana and the Bow River district compared for grazing purposes, by Alexander Begg; also sketch of the rise and progress of Winnipeg, by J. C. McLagan; to which has been added an appendix of statistics of the Dominion of Canada. Guelph, Ont., World Pub. Co., 1882. 687 p. fold. front., illus., plates, fold. maps, fold. plan, col. diagr. CVicAr CVU MtU WaU 6471

Same. London, T. C. Jack, 1883.
CVU OrP Wa 6472

MacRae Donald, 1907-
Dwight Craig. Boston, Houghton, 1947. 398 p. Portland author and western university setting. CV Or OrP WaS WaU 6473

MacRae, Katherine, see no. 8328.

McRaye, Walter, see no. 6261.

McTavish, P. D., see no. 10329.

McVicker, Archibald, see nos. 5895-5901.

McWhorter, Lucullus Virgil, 1860-
The crime against the Yakimas, with introd. by William E. Johnson. North Yakima, Wash., Republic Print [c1913] 56 p. illus., ports. Many 6474

The discards, by He-mene Ka-wan, "Old Wolf". [n.p., 1920] 22 p. illus., ports.
Many 6475

Tragedy of the Wahk-shum; prelude to the Yakima Indian war, 1855-56; the killing of Major Andrew J. Bolon; eyewitness account by Su-el-lil, locating the place of Bolon's death; and Indian legends; addendum: definition of "Yakima", introd. by H. D. Guie. Yakima, Wash. [c1937] 44 p. front., illus., plates, ports., fold. map. Many 6476
See also nos. 7125, 7126, 11252.

McWhorter, T., see no. 4843.

McWilliams, Carey, 1905-
Prejudice; Japanese-Americans; symbol of racial intolerance. Boston, Little, 1944. 337 p. Many 6477

What about our Japanese-Americans? [New York, Public Affairs Committee, 1944] 31 p. illus. (Pamphlets, 91)
MtU OrPR WaU 6478

Maddux, Percy, 1913-
The waters of Puget Sound. New York, Hobson Book Press, 1946. 38 p. front. (port.) Poems.
OrAshS Wa WaE WaS WaT WaU 6479

Magaret, Helene, 1906-
Father DeSmet, pioneer priest of the Rockies. New York, Farrar [c1940] 371 p. front. (port.) Many 6480

Magee, Mrs. Emma, see no. 8915.

Magee, Jos., see no.. 632.

[Magrini, Louis Arthur] 1915-
Meet the governors of the state of Washington. Seattle, 1946. 62 p. ports.
WaS WaT WaU **6481**

Magruder, F. A., see nos. 571-573.

Maguire, Amy Jane.
The Indian girl who led them, Sacajawea. Portland, Or., J. K. Gill, 1905. 87 p.
Many **6482**

Maguire, Horatio N.
The coming empire; a complete and reliable treatise on the Black Hills, Yellowstone and Big Horn regions. Sioux City, Iowa, Watkins, 1878. 177 p. illus., 7 plates. MtHi **6483**

Maguire, Jean Shepard.
Beside the point, illus. by Jay Warmuth. New York, G. W. Stewart [1944] 190 p. front., illus. Autobiographical of life at Three Tree Point on Vashon Island.
Many **6484**

Maguire, Thomas Miller, 1849-1920.
The gates of our empire: I. British Columbia. London, Anglo-British Columbian Agency, 1910. 76 p. 3 fold. maps.
CV CVicAr CVU **6485**

Maino, Evelyn, see nos. 6446-6448.

Mair, Charles, 1838-1927.
Through the Mackenzie Basin; a narrative of the Athabasca and Peace River treaty expedition of 1899, with a map of the country ceded and numerous photographs of native life and scenery; also notes on the mammals and birds of northern Canada by Roderick MacFarlane. Toronto, Briggs, 1908. 494 p. front., plates, ports., fold. map.
CVicAr CVU MtU WaS WaSp **6486**

Major, William Alexander.
Seattle, her opportunity, her duty, her destiny; a sermon at the Bethany Presbyterian Church, Seattle, Sunday morning, July 16, 1905. [Seattle, 1905] 14 p. front. (port.) WaS WaU **6487**

Majors, Alexander, 1814-
Seventy years on the frontier; Alexander Majors' memoirs of a lifetime on the Border, with a preface by "Buffalo Bill" (Gen. W. F. Cody) ed. by Prentiss Ingraham. Chicago, Rand McNally, 1893. 325 p. illus., plates. (Rialto series, no. 10)
MtHi OrHi WaSp WaU **6488**

Maley, Frances Inez, see no. 2829.

[Mallery, E. N.]
A brief history of Jacksonville, its churches and schools. [Jacksonville, Or., 1939] [16] p. illus., port. OrP **6489**

Mallet, Thierry.
Glimpses of the Barren Lands. New York, Revillon Freres, 1930. 142 p. illus. Mackenzie district tales. CVU **6490**

Plain tales of the North. New York, Revillon Freres, 1925. 136 p. illus.
CVU Wa **6491**

Same. New York, Putnam, 1926.
CVU WaS **6492**

Mallette, Gertrude Ethel, 1887-
Chee-cha-ko; illus. by Herbert Morton Stoops. New York, Doubleday, 1938. 299 p. front. Or Wa WaS WaT **6493**

Elsewhere land. [Seattle, Press of the Dept. of Journalism, Univ. of Wash.] 1909. 98 p. WaSP WaU **6494**

Mallinson, Mrs. Florence Lee.
My travels and adventures in Alaska, by Mrs. Florence Lee Mallinson, for nine years a resident in the Northland. Seattle, Seattle-Alaska Co., 1914. 200 p. front. (port.) 9 plates.
OrU WaS WaSp WaU **6495**

Maloney, Alice Bay, see no. 11211.

Mandelbaum, May, see no. 9740.

Mander, Linden A.
The Seattle Civic Unity Committee. Seattle, 1944. 19 p. WaS **6496**

Mangam, William Daniel.
The Clarks, an American phenomenon, with an introd. by Edward Alsworth Ross. New York, Silver Bow Press, 1941. ix, 257 p. front., ports., fold. facsim.
IdU MtHi MtU OrU WaSp WaU **6497**

The Clarks of Montana. [Washington, D. C., Service Printing Co.] c1939. iv, 221 p. front., ports., fold. facsim.
MtBozC MtHi MtU OrP **6498**

Manhart, George Born.
English search for a north-west passage in the time of Queen Elizabeth. Philadelphia, Univ. of Pa., 1924. 179 p.
OrHi WaS **6499**

Mann, Horace, see no. 4618.

Manring, Benjamin Franklin, 1866-
The conquest of the Coeur d'Alenes, Spokanes and Palouses; the expeditions of Colonels E. J. Steptoe and George Wright against the "Northern Indians" in 1858. [Spokane, Inland Printing Co., 1912] 280 p. front., port., plates, fold. map, facsims. Many **6500**

Mansfield, Mrs. Norma Bicknell.
Keeper of the wolves, front. by Joseph Stahley. New York, Farrar [c1934] 308 p. front. Alaska novel. WaU **6501**

Mantle, Mrs. Beatrice.
Gret; the story of a pagan. New York, Century, 1907. 403 p. front. Oregon novel.
OrP WaSp WaWW **6502**

Manual of liability insurance; rules and rates for states of Idaho, Washington and Oregon. [n.p., 1915?] 22, 131 p. OrP **6503**

Manufacturers' Association of British Columbia.
The industries of British Columbia, ed. by J. H. Hamilton. Vancouver, B. C., Progress Pub. Co. [c1918] 136 p. illus.
CV CVU **6504**

Who makes what in British Columbia, and where obtainable. Vancouver, B. C., Industrial Progress, 1914. 56 p.
CV CVU **6505**

Maples, Edward, ed.
American hotels and resorts and the men who run them. Pacific Coast ed. San Francisco [n.d.] [82] p. illus., port.
OrHi **6506**

Marchant, W. P.
An outline of Masonic law and jurisprudence of British Columbia. [n.p., n.d.] 27 p.   CVicAr **6507**

Marcy, Randolph Barnes, 1812-1887.
Border reminiscences. New York, Harper, 1872. 396 p. front., illus., 12 plates.
Many **6508**

The prairie traveler; a hand-book for overland expeditions, with maps, illus., and itineraries of the principal routes between the Mississippi and the Pacific. New York, Harper, 1859. 340 p. front., illus., plate, fold. map.   Many **6509**

Same. London, Truber, 1863, xvi, 251 p. front., illus., map.
CVicAr MtU OrHi WaU WaWW **6510**

Thirty years of army life on the border, comprising descriptions of the Indian nomads of the plains, explorations of new territory, a trip across the Rocky Mountains in the winter, descriptions of the habits of different animals found in the West and the methods of hunting them, with incidents in the life of different frontier men, &c., &c. New York, Harper, 1866. 442 p. front., illus., 13 plates.   Many **6511**

Margeson, Charles Anson.
Experiences of gold hunters in Alaska. [Hornellsville, N. Y.] 1899. 297 p. front. (port.) plates.   WaU **6512**

Marie, Queen of Rumania, see no. 682.

[Marietta College, Marietta, Ohio, Society of Alumni]
Addresses on the death of Hon. Joseph G. Wilson, representative in Congress from Oregon, July 22, 1873, including the resolution of the alumni and other memorial contributions, together with his own oration. Columbus, Ohio, Nevins & Myers, 1873. 64 p.   OrHi OrP **6513**

Marine Digest, Seattle, Wash.
Inernational maritime conference supplement of the Marine Digest, covering the proceedings of the 28th Conference of the International Labor Organization, Seattle, Wash., June 6-29 inclusive. Seattle, 1946. 43 p. illus. (v. 24, no. 44, suppl.)
WaS **6514**

National maritime day supplement. [Seattle, 1945] 34 p. illus., ports. (v. 23, no. 41, May 19, 1945 suppl.)   WaU **6515**

Port of Seattle. Seattle, 1947. 39 p. illus. (Suppl. to v. 25, no. 56, Aug. 16, 1947)
WaS **6516**

Marion, Elizabeth, 1916-
The day will come. New York, Crowell, 1939. 306 p. Eastern Washington novel.
Many **6517**

Ellen Spring. [New York] Crowell [c1941] 328 p. Eastern Wash. novel. Many **6518**

The keys to the house. New York, Crowell [1944] 247 p. Washington novel.
Many **6519**

Marion County annual for the year 1886 with tables calculated for this latitude, illus. by leading artists, mostly American. Salem, Or., L. R. Stinson & Co., 1886. 33 p. illus.   Or OrP WaSp **6520**

Marion County Community Federation.
Marion County, Oregon; plain facts without frills. [Salem, Or.] 1920. 48 p. map, table.   OrP **6521**

Maris, Paul Vestal, 1886-
An agricultural program for Oregon. Corvallis, Or., Or. Agricultural College Extension Service, 1923. 98 p. illus., maps, tables, diagrs. (Extension bulletin 367)
WaPS WaU **6522**

History of the Oregon Cooperative Council. [Corvallis, Or., 1928] 7 p.   Or **6523**

Maritime Federation of the Pacific Coast.
Conference for formation of maritime federation of the Pacific [and constitution] San Francisco, 1935. 5 p. OrP **6524**

Marketing and Distribution Conference, Corvallis, Or., 1946.
Dynamic factors affecting agricultural economy. [Corvallis, Or., 1946] 166 p. (Proceedings, Jan. 1946)
OrCS OrU **6525**

Markham, Sir Clements Robert, 1830-1916.
The threshold of the unknown region. 2d ed. London, Low, 1873. 357 p. front., illus., fold. maps.   CVicAr CVU **6526**

Same. 3d ed. 1875. xvi, 348 p.
CVicAr WaU **6527**

Markham, Mrs. Elizabeth (Winchell) 1805-1895.
Poems [by Mrs. Markham, an Oregon pioneer of 1847-1857] Portland, Or., J. K. Gill, 1921. 31 p.
IdU OrHi OrP WaU **6528**

Markistun, Luke, see no. 4959.

Markov, Al.
Russkie na vostochnom oceanie. Vostochnaia Sibir'-Rossiiskiia vladieniia v Amerikie - Byt   dikarei - Kaliforniia - Proekt Krugosvietnoi torgovoi ekspeditsii. Moskva, V. Universitetskaia tipografiia, 1849. 148 p.   WaU **6529**

Marks, Constant R., see no. 4582.

Marquis, A. S.
Dr. John McLoughlin (the great white eagle). Toronto, Ryerson [c1929] 31 p. illus. (Canadian history readers)
CV CVU Or OrHi OrP **6530**

Marquis, John A., see nos. 2978, 11278.

Marquis, Thomas Bailey, 1869-1935.
She watched Custer's last battle; her story interpreted in 1927. Hardin, Mont., Custer Museum, c1933. [8] p. Kate Bighead, Cheyenne Indian.   MtHi **6531**

A warrior who fought Custer, interpreted by Thomas B. Marquis. Minneapolis, Midwest Co., 1931. vii, 384 p. front., illus., plates, ports, maps.   Many **6532**
See also no. 5814.

Marquis, Thomas Guthrie, 1864-1936.
Hon. Alexander Mackenzie. Toronto, Ryerson [c1930] 31 p. port. (Canadian history readers)   Or OrHi OpP **6533**

Marriott, Mrs. Elsie (Frankland)
Bainbridge through bifocals. Seattle, Gateway Printing Co., 1941. 292 p. plates, ports. Bainbridge Island, Wash.
Wa WaS WaT WaU **6534**

Marsh, Edith L.
Where the buffalo roamed; the story of western Canada told for the young, with introd. by R. G. MacBeth, with illus. from paintings by Paul Kane and from photographs and drawings. Toronto, Briggs, 1908. 242 p. front., plates.
CVicAr WaU 6535

Marsh, James B.
Four years in the Rockies; or, The adventures of Isaac P. Rose of Shenango Township, Pennsylvania; giving his experience as a hunter and trapper in that remote region. New Castle, Pa., W. B. Thomas, 1884. 262 p. front. (port.)
OrSaW WaSp 6536

Marsh, Sidney Harper, 1825-1879.
An inaugural discourse by president of Pacific University, Oregon. Burlington, Vt., Free Press Office, 1856. 20 p.
Or WaU 6537

Marsh, W. D., see no. 2849.

[Marshall, D. Frank]
Langley; fifty years of progress, 1873-1923, Langley Fort. [n.p., n.d.] 11 p. illus., ports.
CV CVicAr CVU 6538
Same. Langley, B. C., 1923. [16] p.
CVicAr 6539

Marshall, Edison, 1894-
The deadfall; illus. by George W. Gage. New York, Cosmopolitan Book Corp., 1927. 290 p. illus. Alaska novel.
Or WaW 6540
The deputy at Snow Mountain. New York, Kinsey, 1932. 284 p. Alaska novel.
WaE WaW 6541
Doctor of Lonesome River. New York, Burt [c1931] 294 p. Alaska novel.
CV Or WaW 6542
The far call, illus. by Walt Louderback. New York, Cosmopolitan Book Corp., 1928. 284 p. front., illus., 4 plates. Pribilof Islands novel.
Or OrP WaT WaW 6543
The fish hawk. New York, Burt [c1929] 290 p. Alaska novel.
WaW 6544
The missionary, illus. by Jules Gotlieb. New York, Cosmopolitan Book Corp., 1930. 288 p. front., plates. Far North novel.
Or WaPS WaS 6545
Ocean gold; a novel for young people. New York, Harper [c1925] 383 p. front., 3 plates. Alaska novel.
Or OrP 6546
Seward's folly. Boston, Little, 1924. 312 p.
IdU Or WaE WaPS WaS WaT 6547
Same. New York, Burt [c1924]
CV WaU WaW 6548
Shepherds of the wild. Boston, Little, 1922. 300 p. front. Idaho novel.
IdU Or OrP WaSp 6549
The sleeper of the moonlit ranges; a new novel, illus. by Jes. W. Schlaikjer. New York, Cosmopolitan Book Corp., 1925. 311 p. front., plates (1 col. double) Aleutian Island novel.
Or OrP OrU WaS WaT WaU 6550
The voice of the pack, with front. by W. Herbert Dunton. Boston, Little, 1920. 305 p. front. Southern Or. novel.
IdIf Or OrP WaU 6551

Marshall, Robert, 1901-1939.
Arctic village. New York, Literary Guild [c1933] xii, 399 p. front., illus., plates, ports., music.
Many 6552
Same. New York, Smith and Haas, 1933.
Many 6553

Marshall, Thomas Maitland, 1876-
A history of the western boundary of the Louisiana Purchase, 1819-1841. Berkeley, Calif., Univ. of Calif. Press, 1914. xiii, 266 p. front. (map) 29 maps (part fold.) (Publications in history, v. 2)
Many 6554

Marshall, William Isaac, 1840-1906.
Acquisition of Oregon and the long suppressed evidence about Marcus Whitman. [Seattle, Lowman & Hanford, 1905] 2 v. front. (port.)
WaU 6555
Same. 1911.
Many 6556
The Hudson's Bay Company's archives furnish no support to the Whitman saved Oregon story. Chicago, Blakely, 1905. 36 p.
Many 6557
Same. [n.p.] 1905. Abridged ed. 8 p.
Many 6558

Marshfield Sun.
Illustrated special edition, Jan. 1901; a graphic description of the marvelous resources and magnificent attraction of Coos County, Oregon. Marshfield, Or., Sun Pub. Co. [1901] 30 p. illus., ports.
OrU 6559

Marston, Edward, 1825-1914.
Frank's ranche, or, My holiday in the Rockies. 2d ed. London, Low, 1886. xvi, 214 p. front., illus., map.
WaU 6560
Same. 4th ed.
WaU 6561
Same. [Boston] Riverside Press, 1886.
MtBozC MtHi 6562

Martig, Ralph Richard, 1905-
The Hudson's Bay Company claims, 1846-1869. Urbana, Ill. [Univ. of Ill.] 1934. [12] p. (Abstract of Ph. D. thesis)
OrHi OrP WaS WaU 6553

Martin, Archer Evans Stringer, 1865-
The Hudson's Bay Company's land tenures and the occupation of Assiniboia by Lord Selkirk's settlers, with a list of grantees under the Earl and the Company. London, Clowes, 1898. ix, 238 p. front. (port.) 2 fold. maps, 2 fold. plans.
CV CVic CVicAr CVU OrU WaU 6564

Martin, B. S.
Willamette musings; or, Legends and tales of our own beautiful river. Corvallis, Or., Gazette, 1893. 36 p. OrCS 6565

Martin, Boyd Archer, 1911-
The direct primary in Idaho. Stanford Univ., Calif., Stanford Univ. Press [1947] ix, 149 p.
IdB IdIf IdU MtHi WaS WaU 6566

Martin, Charles E., see no. 4937.
Martin, Charles H., see no. 6632.
Martin, Chester, see no. 9464.
Martin, Clinton S., ed.
Boy scouts and the Oregon Trail, 1830-1930; the story of the Scout pilgrimage to Independence Rock, Wyoming, to hold rendezvous in honor of the pioneers

who "won and held the West"; with a historical sketch of the Oregon Trail Memorial Association, under whose auspices, in cooperation with the Boy Scouts of America, the pilgrimage was undertaken, ed. by Eagle and veteran scout, Clinton S. Martin. New York, Putnam, 1930. xxii, 210 p. front., plates, ports., map.　　　OrP WaPS WaSp **6567**

Martin, Fredericka I.
The hunting of the silver fleece, epic of the fur seal. New York, Greenberg [1946] xxiii, 328 p. plates, port.
　　　　　　　　Many **6568**

Martin, George Washington, 1841-1914.
How the Oregon Trail became a road. Salt Lake City, Deseret News, 1906. 52 p. front. (port.) port. OrHi OrP **6569**

Martin, Howard H., see no. 3297.

Martin, I. T., see no. 3340.

Martin, Louise Anita.
North to Nome. Chicago, A. Whitman & Co., 1939. 316 p. front., plates.
　　　　　　WaS WaSp WaU **6570**

Martin, Robert Montgomery, 1803?-1868.
The Hudson's Bay territories and Vancouver's Island, with an exposition of the chartered rights, conduct, and policy of the hon'ble Hudson's Bay Corporation. London, Boone, 1849. vii, 175 p. front. (fold. map)　　　Many **6571**

Martin, Sandy, see no. 323.

Martindale, Thomas, 1845-1916.
Hunting in the upper Yukon. Philadelphia, Jacobs [c1913] 320 p. front., 23 plates, map.　　　　　　　Many **6572**

Martinson, M. P., see no. 226.

Martyr, Weston, see nos. 10613, 10614.

[Martz, Henry]
Alaska-Yukon-Pacific Exposition, 1909, an international fair, June 1 to October 15; showing the products, resources, advantages, and scenic beauty of the Alaska-Yukon country. Seattle, c1908. [110] p. illus.　　　　　　　WaU **6573**

Marvin, Frederick Rowland, 1847-1918.
Yukon overland; the gold-digger's handbook. Cincinnati, Ed. Pub. Co., 1898. 170 p. front., 18 plates, fold. map. Route overland from Spokane, Wash. Chinook vocabulary. p. 149-170.　　WaSp **6574**

Mary Dorothea, Sister.
The tenth decade; a dramatic pageant commemorating the one hundredth anniversary of the founding of the Diocese of Victoria. [Victoria, B. C., Jacobus, 1946] 1 v. illus., ports.　　CVicAr **6575**

[Mary Eustolia, Sister]
A shepherd of the far North; the story of William Francis Walsh (1900-1930) by Robert Glody [pseud.] San Francisco, Harr Wagner Pub Co. [c1934] xiv, 237 p. front., ports.　　　WaS WaU **6576**

Mary James, Sister, see no. 5106.

Mary Joseph Calasanctius, Sister, see nos. 1374, 1375.

Mary Leopoldine, Sister.
Fifty golden years; a short history of Sacred Heart Hospital, Spokane, Wash-

ington; years of jubilee, 1886-1936. [Spokane, Acme Stamp & Printing Co., 1936] 96 p. illus., ports.　　　WaSp **6577**

Mary Mildred, Sister, see no. 403.

Mary Theodore, Sister, 1856-
Heralds of Christ, the King; missionary record of the North Pacific, 1837-1878. New York, P. J. Kenedy & Sons, 1939. xiv, 273 p. front., plates, ports.
　　CV CVic CVicAr CVU WaS WaU **6578**

Pioneer nuns of British Columbia; Sisters of St. Ann. Victoria, B. C. [British Colonist] 1931. 146 p. front., plates, ports.
　　　　CV CVic CVicAr WaU **6579**

The seal of the cross: Mother Mary Anne, foundress of the Sisters of St. Ann, 1809-1890. Victoria, B. C., St. Ann's Convent, 1939. 129 p. front., illus., plates, ports., facsim.　　　　WaU **6580**

The Marysville Globe.
[Fiftieth anniversary edition, March 13, 1941] Marysville, Wash., 1941. 1 v. (v. 50, no. 11, Mar. 13, 1941)　　WaE **6581**

Masachele Opa Baruska, see no. 8357.

Masik, August, 1888-
Arctic nights' entertainments; being the narrative of an Alaskan-Estonian digger, August Masik, as told to Isobel Wylie Hutchison during the Arctic night of 1933-34 near Martin Point, Alaska. London, Blackie [1936] xiii, 234 p. col. front., plates, ports.　　　WaU **6582**

Masiker, Carson C., 1852-
Stories of early years; account of pioneer makers of history in old Wasco County. [The Dalles, Or., The Dalles Optimist, 1911] 22 p. (Suppl.)　　WaPS **6583**

Mason, Allen C.
Compendium of information concerning the city of Tacoma and Washington Territory. Portland, Or., A. Anderson & Co., Printers, 1888. 110 p. front.
　　Wa WaSp WaU WaWW **6584**

Tacoma and vicinity. Tacoma, c1888. [50] p. illus.　　　　CVicAr **6585**

Mason, Arthur, 1876-
The fossil fountain, by Arthur Mason and Mary Frank; illus. by Jay Van Everen. Garden City, N. Y., Doubleday, 1928. viii, 198 p. col. front., illus., plates. Western mountain setting.　　IdIf **6586**

Mason, David Townsend, 1883-
Timber ownership and lumber production in the Inland Empire. Portland, Or., Western Pine Manufacturers Assn., 1920. 111 p. illus.
　　　IdU Or OrCS WaSp **6587**

Mason, George.
In memory of Sir Jas. Douglas. [n.p., n.d.] 3 p.　　　　　CVicAr **6588**

Ode on the loss of the steamship "Pacific", November 4, 1875. Nanaimo, B. C., G. Norris, 1875. 4 p.
　　CVicAr OrHi OrU WaU **6589**

Prize poem; Lo! the poor Indian [read before the Mechanics' Literary Institute, Victoria, Thursday, Oct. 28, 1875] Victoria, B. C., A. Rose, 1875. 8 p.
　　CVicAr CVU OrHi WaU **6590**

Mason, H. L., see no. 5439.

Mason, James Tate.
Seattle's first physician, Dr. David Swinson Maynard. Seattle, Virginia Mason Hospital, 1933. 34 p. illus., ports. (Clinics, v. 12, special no., Dec. 1933) WaS **6591**

Mason, Michael Henry, 1900-
The Arctic forests. London, Hodder and Stoughton, 1924. xiii, 320 p. front., plates (1 col.) ports., 2 fold. maps. CVU **6592**

Mason, R. B., see no. 451.

Mason, William H.
Snohomish County in the war; the part played in the great war by the soldiers, sailors, marines and patriotic civilians of Snohomish County, Washington, U. S. A. Everett, Wash., Mason Pub. Co. [1926] 448 p. illus., ports., maps.
WaE WaPS WaS WaSp WaU **6593**

Mason County Journal, Shelton, Wash.
Special 1905 edition. Shelton, Wash., G. C. Angle, Pub., 1905. [16] p. illus., map, plan. WaU **6594**

Masonic log. [n.p., 1930]
99 p. ports. "Biographical sketches of Masons who are factors in the industrial financial and commercial progress of the Northwest." WaS **6595**

Masson, Charles E., see no. 5986.

Masson, Louis Francois Rodrique, 1833-1903.
Les bourgeois de la Compagnie du Nord-Ouest; recits de voyages, lettres et rapports inedits relatifs au Nord-Ouest canadien pub. avec une esquisse historique et des annotations par L. R. Masson. Quebec, A. Cote et Cie, 1889-90. 2 v. fold. map. Many **6596**

Catalogue of the late Hon. L. R. Masson's magnificent private library, to be sold by public auction on Saturday, Monday, Tuesday, 9, 11, 12 April 1904 at 2.30 and 7.45 P. M. [Montreal] La Patrie, 1904. 153 p. WaU **6597**

Masters, Joseph G., 1873-
Stories of the far West; heroic tales of the last frontier. Boston, Ginn [c1935] xii, 297 p. front., illus., maps.
IdB IdIf IdP MtHi OrHi **6598**

Masterson, Iver Williams.
A history of the consumer's co-operatives in Oregon prior to 1900. [Eugene, Or., Univ. of Or., 1939] 24, 26 p. (Thesis series, no. 8)
OrSaW WaS WaSp **6599**

Masterson, James W.
Montana's twenty-first Legislative Assembly Who's Who; a volume of personalities taken from the files of the Montana Standard. [Butte, Mont.] Mont. Standard, 1929. 94 p. illus. MtHi **6600**

It happened in Montana. [Miles City, Mont., c1940-1941] 2 v. illus. Cartoons about old Mont. MtU **6601**

Mathers, C. W.
A souvenir from the North. Edmonton, Alta., c1901. 23 p. CVicAr **6602**

Matheson, S. P., see nos. 1844-1848.

Mathews, Alfred E.
Pencil sketches of Montana. New York, 1888. 95 p. front., 31 plates (part fold.)
MtHi WaU **6603**

Mathieu, O. E., see no. 2241.

[Matthews, James Skitt] 1878-
Linking the Atlantic to the Pacific, ocean to ocean. [Vancouver, B. C., Wrigley, 1945] 34 p. illus., ports. CVicAr **6604**

The naming and opening of Stanley Park, 27 September 1888; a tribute to the sixty-seven park commissioners during the years 1888 to 1948. Vancouver, B. C., 1948. 11 p. CVicAr **6605**

Matthews, James Thomas, 1864-
Turn right to Paradise. Portland, Or., Binfords & Mort [1942] 196 p. front. (port.) Autobiography written for Willamette Univ. centennial.
OrP OrSaW OrU WaS **6606**

Mattoon, Charles Hiram, 1826-
Baptist annals of Oregon, 1844 to 1900, with an introd. by Hon. W. Carey Johnson. McMinnville, Or., Telephone Register Pub. Co. [c1905] 464 p. front. (port.) illus. Many **6607**

Baptist history of the North Pacific Coast; Baptist annals of Oregon from 1886 to 1910, introd. by Rev. W. J. Crawford. McMinnville, Or., Pacific Baptist Press, 1913. 485 p. front., illus., ports. (Baptist annals, v. 2)
OrHi OrP WaPS WaS WaU **6608**

Mattson, Esther M., see no. 6810.

Maty, Matthew, see no. 9801.

Mauermann, Bertha Merena.
Mosaic. Boston, Meador, 1935. 112 p. Poems. Wa WaS WaU **6609**

Maule, Francis I.
El Dorado "29", along with other weird Alaska tales, done into verse by Francis I. Maule. Philadelphia, Winston [c1910] 124 p. front., illus.
CVU Wa WaSp WaU **6610**

Maury, Henry Lowndes, 1875-
Maury's manual of Montana state government. [Butte, Mont., Butte Independent, 1930] 20 p. MtU **6611**

Maxey, Chester Collins, 1890-
Historical Walla Walla Valley. Walla Walla, Wash., Inland Printing Co. [193-?] 32 p. illus. WaPS WaS WaW **6612**

Maxey, Martha Harwood.
The masque of the Absaroka; music by Derrick Norman Lehmer, produced by Eurodelphian Fine Arts Society, Montana State College, Bozeman, June 4 and 6, 1927. [n.p., 1927] 36 p. front. (port.) illus. MtHi **6613**

Maxson, John H., see no. 3590.

Maxwell, Will J., comp.
Greek letter men of the Pacific Coast and Rocky Mountain states. New York, College Book Co., 1903. 696 p. illus., ports.
Or WaU **6614**

May, Cliff, see no. 10024.

May, Walter W. R.
The Pacific Northwest's industrial outlook from a power and rate point of view. [Portland, Or., Portland General Electric Co.? 1939] 34 p. Or OrU **6615**

Maynard, Harold Howard, 1889-
Marketing northwestern apples. New

York, Ronald Press, 1923. vii, 190 p. front., diagrs.   Many **6616**

Mayne, Richard Charles, 1836-1892.
Four years in British Columbia and Vancouver Island; an account of their forests, rivers, coasts, gold fields and resources for colonization. London, Murray, 1862. xi, 468 p. front., 17 plates, 2 maps (1 fold.)   Many **6617**

[Mayo, Edward S.]
Summer saunterings over the lines of the Oregon Railway and Navigation Co. and Northern Pacific Railroad, Pacific Division; routes of river and rail; neighborhoods of note; terms for tourists. Portland, Or., G. H. Himes, 1882. 35 p. front., plates.   Wa **6618**

Mayol, Mrs. Lurline (Bowles)
The big canoe, illus. by W. Langdon Kihn. New York, Appleton-Century [c1933] vi, 257 p. front., illus. Haida Indian stories.   Many **6619**

The talking totem pole; the tales it told to the Indian children of the Northwest; illus. by Edward Morgan. Akron, Ohio, Saalfield Pub Co., c1930. 142 p. col. front.
                    IdIf OrU WaS WaSp WaT **6620**

Same. Portland, Or., Binfords & Mort [1943]   Or OrHi OrP Wa WaU **6621**

Mazama Club and Sierra Club.
Joint Committee.
Report on the Mt. Rainier National Park. [n.p., 1905?] 15 p. plates.   OrU **6622**

Mazama history; being an account of the beginnings of the Mazamas, comp. from articles in their first annual, pub. 1896, reproduced by authority of the Mazamas. Portland, Or., 1932. 38 p.
                    Or OrHi OrP WaS WaU **6623**

Mazamas.
Constitution and list of members of the Mazamas. Portland, Or., 1896. 8 p.
                    OrHi **6624**

— — — **Outing Committee.**
Above the clouds on Rainier, king of mountains; mountaineers excursion July 19th to August 17th, 1897, under the management of the Mazamas. [n.p., 1897?] 30 p. illus.   WaSp **6625**

Meacham, Alfred Benjamin, 1826-1882.
The tragedy of the Lava-beds; a lecture, with an appendix containing an account of the rescue, the battles, the betrayal, the capture, trial and execution of the Modoc chief, and the exile of the survivors. [n.p.] c1877. 48 p. illus., ports. Photostat copy.   Or **6626**

Wi-ne-ma (the woman-chief) and her people. Hartford, American Pub. Co., 1876. 168 p. front., 8 plates, 5 ports. Modoc Indians.   Many **6627**

Wigwam and warpath; or, The royal chief in chains. Boston, J. P. Dale & Co., c1875. xxiii, 700 p. front., 11 plates, 8 ports.   Or OrHi **6628**

Same. 2d and rev. ed.   Many **6629**

See also no. 882.

Meacham, Walter E., 1879-
Applegate trail, illus. by Colista Dowling.

[Portland, Or., James, Kerns & Abbott, c1947] 26 p. illus., ports., map.
                    OrCS OrP **6630**

Barlow Road. [n.p., Or. Council, American Pioneer Trails Assn., c1947] 18 p. illus., ports., map. Anon.   OrP WaSp **6631**

Bonneville the bold, the story of his adventures and explorations in the old Oregon country, with a foreword by Charles M. Martin. Portland, Or., 1934. 47 p. front. (port.) fold. map.
                    Many **6632**

Let us travel the golden trails of memory to the land of yesterday. [n.p., Eugene Crosby, n.d.] [8] p. Anon.   OrP **6633**

Old Oregon Trail. Portland, Or., Oregon Tourist and Information Bureau, c1922. 24 p. maps.   OrHi **6634**

The old Oregon Trail; a narrative of the Wilson Price Hunt expedition from St. Louis to Astoria in 1811-12, etc. [Portland, Or.? Or. Tourist and Information Bureau?] c1922. 24 p. illus. WaPS **6635**

The old Oregon Trail, called by the Indians "The big medicine road". Baker, Or., Old Oregon Trail Assn. [c1926] 24 p. illus., map.   IdIf WaPS WaS **6636**

The old Oregon Trail, the road that won an empire. [Baker, Or., Old Oregon Trail Assn., c1924] 32 p. illus., maps. Anon.   Or OrHi WaT WaU **6637**

Same. [c1926] 24 p. Anon.
                    IdU MtU OrP OrSaW WaT WaU **6638**

The old Oregon Trail; the road which saved an empire. [Baker, Or., Old Oregon Trail Assn., c1923] 28 p. illus.
                    Or OrCS OrHi OrP OrSa WaT **6639**

Old Oregon Trail, roadway of American home builders; illus. by Irvin Shope; issued under sponsorship of American Pioneer Trails Association, Inc. Manchester, N. H., Clarke Press, c1948. 101 p. illus., double map.
                    OrCS OrHi WaS **6640**

Story of the old Oregon Trail, the world's most historic highway and the road to America's scenic wonderland. [Baker, Or., Old Oregon Trail Assn., c1922] 24 p. illus., maps. Anon.   Many **6641**

Territorial centennial, Old Oregon country, 1848-1948-49; the trail of destiny. [n.p., 1948?] 12 p. Anon.   OrP **6642**

See also no. 7710.

Meader, Stephen Warren, 1892-
Behind the ranges, illus. by Edward Shenton. New York, Harcourt [c1947] 222 p. front., illus. Olympic Mountain adventure.   Many **6643**

Meadows, Paul.
The people of Montana; a report to Montana Study, 1945. Missoula, Mont., Montana Study of Univ. of Mont. [1945] 36 p.
                    MtBozC WaS **6644**

Meagher, Thomas Francis, 1823-1867.
Lectures of Gov. Thomas Francis Meagher in Montana, together with his messages, speeches, etc., to which is added the eulogy of Richard O'Gorman, Esq., delivered at Cooper Institute, New York,

comp. by John P. Bruce. Virginia City, Mont., Bruce & Wright, 1867. 104 p.

MtHi **6645**

See also no. 6169.

Meany, Edmond Stephen, 1862-1935.

"Americanus", produced in the University of Washington stadium, Seattle, July 23-28, written and produced by Prof. Edmond S. Meany, Montgomery Lynch, under auspices of "Americanus" Pageant Society acting for the Associated Students, University of Washington. [Seattle, Pioneer Printing Co., 1923] [24] p. illus., ports. Or WaU **6646**

A block-print history of the Northwest; linoleum cut illus. by pupils under the direction of Helen Rhodes. Seattle, Univ. of Wash. Bookstore [n.d.] [24] p. front., illus. WaT **6647**

Same. 1923. CVicAr **6648**

Same. c1928. [30] p. Many **6649**

Governors of Washington, territorial and state. Seattle, Univ. of Wash. Dept. of Printing, 1915. vi, 114 p. illus., ports.

Many **6650**

History of the state of Washington. New York, Macmillan, 1909. xii, 406 p. front., 12 plates, 34 ports., 2 maps.

Many **6651**

Same. 1910. Many **6652**

Same. 1924. xv, 412 p. Many **6653**

Same. 1927. IdU OrP WaE WaT **6654**

Same. 1942 [c1937] WaU **6655**

Same. 1943. WaE **6656**

Indian geographic names of Washington. Seattle, Hyatt-Fowells School [c1908] [20] p. Or OrP WaS WaT WaU **6657**

Indian names of Washington. Seattle, Hyatt-Fowells School, 1911 [c1908] [24] p. illus. Wa WaU **6658**

Lincoln esteemed Washington. Seattle, F. McCaffrey, 1933. 57 p. front. (mounted port.) WaU **6659**

Loyal and true; university song; music by Reginald de Koven. [Philadelphia, Theodore Presser Co.] c1928. [8] p. music. Wa WaT **6660**

Marcus Whitman. [Seattle?] 1913. 7 p. front. (port.) Poem. WaU **6661**

Mount Rainier, a record of exploration. New York, Macmillan, 1916. xi, 325 p. front., 16 ports. Many **6662**

A mountain campfire. [Seattle, Gateway Printing Co., 1909] [16] p. illus. Poems. WaS WaU **6663**

Mountain camp fires. Seattle, Lowman & Hanford, 1911. viii, 90 p. front. Verses. Wa WaS WaSp WaTC WaU WaW **6664**

A new Vancouver journal on the discovery of Puget Sound by a member of the Chatham's crew, ed. by Edmond S. Meany. Seattle, 1915. 43 p. Anonymous journal ascribed to Edward Bell, clerk, and William Walker, Surgeon of the Chatham. Many **6665**

Origin of Washington geographic names. Seattle, Univ. of Wash. Press, 1923. ix, 357 p. Many **6666**

The Pacific Northwest, a syllabus. Seattle, 1927. [18] p. WaS WaU **6667**

A prophecy fulfilled; address before the Tulalip Indian School, Tulalip, Washington, 21 December 1920. [n.p., 1921?] [8] p. 300th anniversary of landing of Pilgrims. OrHi WaPS WaT WaU **6668**

Seattle's banking business. [Seattle, 1890] 8 p. Anon. WaU **6669**

United States history for schools. New York, Macmillan, 1913. xvii, 587 p. front., illus., maps. WaU **6670**

Vancouver's discovery of Puget Sound; portraits and biographies of the men honored in the naming of geographic features of northwestern America. New York, Macmillan, 1907. xvii, 344 p. front. (port.) 13 plates, 23 ports., 4 maps (1 double) Many **6671**

Same. 1915. IdU OrHi OrU Wa WaTC **6672**

Same. [Portland, Or.] Binfords & Mort [c1935] WaE WaSp **6673**

Same. 1942 [c1935] CVicAr IdIf WaU **6674**

Washington beloved; University song. [Cincinnati] Church, c1908. 7 p. Music by H. L. R. DeKoven. WaS WaU **6675**

"Washington beloved", the state anthem of Washington, with music by Reginald DeKoven. Seattle [F. McCaffrey] 1932. [4] p. Words only. WaU **6676**

Washington from life. Seattle, F. McCaffrey, 1931. ix, 15 p. 9 ports. George Washington's bicentennial, 1932.

Wa WaS WaU **6677**

See also nos. 311, 1722, 1723, 1824, 10663, 10718.

Meares, John, 1756?-1809.

An answer to Mr. George Dixon, late commander of the Queen Charlotte in the service of Messrs. Etches and Company, in which the remarks of Mr. Dixon on the Voyages to the north west coast of America, &c., lately published, are fully considered and refuted. London, Logographic Press, 1791. 32 p.

CVicAr CVU **6678**

Authentic copy of the memorial to the Right Honourable William Wyndham Grenville, one of His Majesty's principal secretaries of state dated 30th April 1790 and presented to the House of Commons May 13, 1790; containing every particular respecting the capture of the vessels in Nootka Sound. London, Debrett [1790] 65 p.

CV CVicAr OrHi WaS WaU **6679**

Histoire des voyages curieux et interessans en Chine en Amerique. Paris, Librairie Universelle [n.d.] 3 v. 3 fold. plans. Anon. Presumably a pirated ed. of "Voyages de la Chine". CVicAr **6680**

Des Kapitans John Meares und des Kapitans William Douglas Reisen nach der Nortwestkuste von America in den Jahren 1786 bis 1789; aus dem Englischen ubersetzt und mit Ammerkungen erlautert von George Forster, nebst einer

Abhandlung von eben demselben, uber die Nordwestkuste von America, und den dortigen Pelzhandel. Berlin, Voss, 1796. iv, 130, 302 p. 4 plates (2 fold.) 3 ports., 2 fold. maps. CVicAr **6681**

The memorial of John Mears to the House of Commons respecting the capture of vessels in Nootka Sound, with an introd. and notes by Nellie B. Pipes. Portland, Or., Metropolitan, 1933. 92 p. Many **6682**

Mr. Mears's memorial, dated 30th April 1790 (14 enclosures) to the Right Honourable William Wyndham Grenville, one of His Majesty's principal secretaries of state. [London? 1790?] 31 p. fold. table. CVicAr WaU **6683**

Tvanne resor fran Ostindien till Americas nordvastra kust, aren 1786, 1788 och 1789; sammandrag utur engelska originalet. Stockholm, I. Utter, 1797. 404 p. CVicAr WaU **6684**

Viaggi dalla China alla costa nord-ovest d'America, fatti negli anni 1788 e 1789 dal capitano G. Meares; prima traduzione Italiana, arricchita di note istoriche-scientifiche di vedute, marine, ritratti carta geografica etc. Firenze, G. Pagani, 1796. 4 v. front. (port.) illus., fold. map. charts. CVicAr CVU WaU **6685**

Same. 2. ed. Italiana corretta et accresciuta, coll' aggiunta di uno estratto de' Viaggi di Milord Mackartney. Napoli, Giuseppe Policarpo Merande, 1796. 4 v. in 2. front., plates, maps. WaU **6686**

Same. Prima versione Italiana. Torino, Soffietti, 1797-98. 4 v. front. (port.) plates, 3 ports., 3 maps. CVicAr **6687**

Voyages de la Chine a la cote nord-ouest d'Amerique, faits dans les annees 1788 et 1789; precedes de la relation d'un autre voyage execute en 1786 sur le vaisseau le Nootka, parti du Bangale; d'un recueil d'observations sur la probabilite d'un passage nord-ouest; et d'un traite abrege du commerce entre la cote nord-ouest et la Chine, etc., etc., tr. de l'anglois par J. B. L. J. Billecocq avec une collection de cartes geographiques, vues, marines, plans et portraits. Paris, F. Buisson [1793] 4 v. 28 maps in v. 4, atlas. CVU **6688**

Same. [1795?]
CVicAr CVU Or OrP WaS WaU **6689**

Voyages made in the years 1788 and 1789 from China to the north west coast of America, to which are prefixed an introductory narrative of a voyage performed in 1786 from Bengal in the ship Nootka, observations on the probable existence of a north west passage, and some account of the trade between the north west coast of America and China and the latter country and Great Britain. London, Logographic Press, 1790. viii [12] xcv, 372 [108] p. front., 15 plates, port., 10 maps (part fold.)
CVicAr OrHi OrP OrU Wa WaU **6690**

Same. 1791. 2 v. Many **6691**

Mears, Eliot Grinnell, 1889-
Maritime trade of western United States.

Stanford Univ., Calif., Stanford Univ. Press [c1935].
xvii, 538 p. front., maps, diagrs. (Business series). CV CVU WaPS **6692**

Resident Orientals on the American Pacific Coast; their legal and economic status. Chicago, Univ. of Chicago Press [c1928] xvi, 545 p. tables, diagrs.
CVU OrCS **6693**

Mecklenburg, George, 1881-
The last of the old West. Washington, D. C., Capital Book Co. [c1927] 149 p. plates, ports. Pioneer ministers in Mont.
Many **6694**

Medary, see no. 1921.

Medcraft, Mollie A.
The long, long miles (a narrative poem). Boston, Meador Pub. Co. [1945] 106 p. Covered wagon trip to Or. WaU **6695**

Medford Mail Tribune.
Oregon diamond jubilee edition. Medford, Or., 1934. [16] p. illus., ports. (June 4, 1934). WaU **6696**

Meeker, Ezra, 1830-1928.
Annual address of Ezra Meeker, president of the Washington State Historical Society, Tacoma, delivered January 22, 1904. [n.p., 1904?] [8] p. Medicine Creek treaty. WaU **6697**

The busy life or eighty-five years; ventures and adventures; sixty-three years of pioneer life in the old Oregon country; an account of the author's trip across the plains with an ox team, 1852; return trip, 1906-7; his cruise on Puget Sound, 1853; trip through the Natches Pass, 1854; over the Chilcoot Pass; flat-boating on the Yukon, 1898; the Oregon Trail: Seattle [1916] xii, 399 p. front. (port.) illus. Many **6698**

Hop culture in the United States; being a practical treatise on hop growing in Washington Territory from the cutting to the bale, with fifteen years experience of the author, to which is added an exhaustive article from the pen of W. A. Lawrence. Puyallup, Wash. [c1883] 170 p. front., illus., 3 plates, table.
Many **6699**

Kate Mulhall, a romance of the Oregon Trail, drawings by Margaret Landers Sanford, Rudolf A. Kausch and Oscar W. Lyons. New York [c1926] 287 p. front. (port.) illus., plates, map. Many **6700**

Ox-team days on the Oregon Trail, rev. and ed. by Howard R. Driggs, illus. with drawings by F. N. Wilson and with photos. Yonkers-on-Hudson, N. Y., World Book Co., 1922. vii, 225 p. front. (port.) illus. (Pioneer life series) Many **6701**

Same. 1927. IdIf **6702**

Ox team; or, The old Oregon Trail, 1852-1906. Indianapolis [1906] 248 p. illus.
IdB OrP **6703**

Same. Omaha [1906] Many **6704**

Same. New York [1907] 4th ed. Many **6705**

Personal experiences on the Oregon Trail sixty years ago. 5th reprint. Seattle, 1912. 150 p. illus. Many **6706**

Same. [St. Louis, McAdoo Printing Co.] 1912. IdIf WaPS WaU **6707**

Pioneer reminiscences of Puget Sound, the tragedy of Leschi; an account of the coming of the first Americans and the establishment of their institutions; their encounters with the native race; the first treaties with the Indians and the war that followed; seven years of the life of Isaac I. Stevens in Washington Territory; cruise of the author on Puget Sound 50 years ago; Nisqually House and the Hudson Bay Company. Seattle, Lowman & Hanford, 1905. xx, 554 p. illus., 10 plates, 15 ports., 2 facsims. (1 fold.) Many **6708**

Seventy years of progress in Washington. Seattle, 1921. 381, 52 p. front., illus., plates, ports. Many **6709**

Story of the lost trail to Oregon. [Seattle, 1915] 30 p. illus. Many **6710**

Uncle Ezra's pioneer short stories for children, to point a moral or teach a lesson. San Francisco [n.d.] 97 p. front., illus., port. WaT WaU **6711**

Uncle Ezra's short stories for children. Tacoma [n.d.] 100 p. illus. Many **6712**

Ventures and adventures of Ezra Meeker; or, Sixty years of frontier life, fifty-six years of pioneer life in the old Oregon country; the Oregon Trail. Seattle, Rainier Printing Co. [c1908] 384 p. illus. Many **6713**

Same. [1909] CVU WaPS WaS WaT WaU **6714**

Washington Territory west of the Cascade Mountains, containing a description of Puget Sound and rivers emptying into it, the Lower Columbia, Shoalwater Bay, Gray's Harbor, timber, lands, climate, fisheries, ship building, coal mines, market reports, trade, labor, population, wealth and resources. Olympia, W. T., Transcript Office, 1870. 52 p. tables. Many **6715**

Who named Tacoma? [Address to Wash. Historical Society at Tacoma, Jan. 22, 1904] Seattle, 1904. 8 p. Or OrHi OrP WaT WaU **6716** See also no. 7712.

"Meet Mr. Coyote"; a series of B. C. Indian legends (Thompson tribe); original illus. by "Wah-und", "Moo-mah", "Sis-malt", "Che-ma" and "Spup-aza" (pupils at the St. George's Indian school at Lytton, B. C.) [Victoria, B. C., Victoria Branch of the Society for the Furtherance of B. C. Tribal Arts and Crafts, 1941] 27 p. illus. CVicAr WaU **6717**

Meier, Walter Frederick, 1879- The heart of Elkdom. Seattle, Farwest Lithograph & Printing Co., 1925. 95 p. WaU **6718**

"The Mason's four-fold duty" and other selected Masonic addresses. [Seattle, c1922] 46 p. WaU **6719**

Meier & Frank Co., Portland, Or. Prospectus, 183,928 shares, capital stock par value $10.00 per share. [Portland, Or.] 1937. 43 p. OrP **6720**

Melville, G. W., see nos. 960, 2826.

Melvin, Grace, see no. 548.

A member of the congregation, see no. 9496.

Memoirs of an Oregon Pioneer [Joseph Hamilton Lambert] Portland, Or., E. L. E. White & Co., 1906. 8 p. front. (port.) OrCS OrHi OrP WaU **6721**

Memoranda concerning Sheldon Jackson and the moderatorship of the 109th General Assembly of the Presbyterian Church in the United States of America, Winona Assembly Grounds, Eagle Lake, Indiana, May 20-28, 1897, for private circulation. [n.p.] MacCalla & Co. [1897?] 126 p. front. (port.) OrU WaS **6722**

Memorandum on "a report of a committee of the Hon. Privy Council for Canada, 19th May 1881 and generally in support of the recent petition of the Legislative Assembly of British Columbia to H. M. the Queen". [n.p., n.d.] 44 p. Esquimalt and Nanaimo Railroad. CVicAr **6723**

Memorandum on the Royal Canadian Mounted Police. Ottawa, 1927. 6 p. CVicAr **6724**

Memorial against refunding the claim of the United States upon the Central Pacific Railroad Co. for $77,000,000. [n.p., n.d.] 13 p. WaPS **6725**

A memorial; an appreciation of the life work of Rev. W. G. M. Hays. [Pullman, Wash.? 1930?] 35 p. ports., illus. WaPS **6726**

Memorial celebration in honor of Sacajawea, the bird woman. Armstead, Montana, August 30, 1915. [n.p., 1915] 11 p. MtU **6727**

Memorial manual to the memory of Mrs. John Leary. Seattle, Lowman & Hanford, 1892. 65 p. front., port. WaU **6728**

Memorial of Edward R. Geary, D. D., late of Eugene City, Oregon, containing biographical sketches, memorial discourse and tributes of respect. Eugene, Or., Occident Printing House, 1887. 62 p. front. (port.) Many **6729**

Memorial of Joseph Scott, 1843-1906. [n.p., DeVinne Press] 1907. 65 p. front. (port.) plate, port. WaSp **6730**

Memorial services at re-interment of remains of Rev. Jason Lee, Salem, Oregon, Friday, June 15, 1906. [n.p., 1906?] 73 p. illus., 3 plates, port. IdU Or OrSaW WaT WaTC **6731**

Men of the Pacific Coast; containing portraits and biographies of the professional, financial and business men of California, Oregon and Washington, 1902-03. San Francisco, Pacific Art Co. [1903?] 634 p. ports. Many **6732**

Mentor. Indians of the Northwest, by Chief Buffalo Child Long Lance, and other articles. New York, Associated Newspaper School, 1924. 72 p. illus., ports. (v. 12, no. 2, serial no. 253, Mar. 1924) WaU **6733**

Menzies, Don. The Alaska Highway; a saga of the North. Rev. ed. Edmonton, Alta., Douglas, c1943. [48] p. illus. (part col.) map. CVicAr WaS **6734**

Mercer, Asa Shinn, 1839-1917.
The banditti of the plains; or, The cattlemen's invasion of Wyoming in 1892. [The crowning infamy of the ages] [Cheyenne, Wyo., c1894] 139 p. illus., ports. Washington author, pioneer, and educator.   WaU **6735**

Same. Sheridan, Wyo., I. G. McPherren, c1930. 166 p.   MtHi WaU **6736**

Same. [80] p.   WaU **6737**

Same. This ed. carries a new foreword by J. M. Clarke and illus. by Arvilla Parker. San Francisco, Grabhorn Press, 1935. xiv, 136 p. illus.
                      MtHi OrP WaS WaU **6738**

Big Horn County, Wyoming, the gem of the Rockies. Hyattville, Wyo. [c1906] 115 p. front., plates.   WaU **6739**

Indian Chief Washakie and the Big Horn Hot Springs. [Hyattville, Wyo.] 1916. 24 p. illus., port.   WaU **6740**

Material resources of Linn County, Oregon, embracing detailed descriptions and business directory. Albany, Or., Brown & Stuart, 1875. 72 p.   OrHi OrP **6741**

The material resources of Marion County, Oregon; with a complete business directory. Salem, Or., E. M. Waite, 1876. 80 p. fold. map.   OrP WaU **6742**

The pioneer. Chicago, Henneberry Co. [c1913] 47 p.   WaU **6743**

Powder river invasion; war on the rustlers in 1892, rewritten by John Mercer Boots. [Los Angeles, c1923] 146 p.
                      MtHi MtU WaU **6744**

Washington Territory; the great Northwest, her material resources and claims to emigration; a plain statement of things as they exist. Utica, N. Y., L. C. Childs, 1865. 38 p.   WaSp WaU **6745**

Same. Seattle, F. McCaffrey, 1939. 54 p. front., illus., tables. (Dogwood Press series of western Americana, no. 2] Contains historical note by Charles W. Smith: Regarding this special printing of Mercers "Washington Territory".
                                Many **6746**

Merchants National Bank of Seattle.
Telegraphic cypher. Seattle, W. H. Hughes Printing Co., 1888. 32 p.   WaU **6747**

Mercier, Mrs. Anne.
Father Pat, a hero of the far West, with a preface by the Right Rev. John Dart. Gloucester, Minchin & Gibbs, 1909. 109 p. front. (port.) 3 plates, B. C. missions.
                              CVicAr **6748**

Same. 2d ed.   CVU **6749**

Same. 4th ed. 1911.   CVU **6750**

Same. 5th ed. Westminster, Society for the Propagation of the Gospel in Foreign Parts, 1914. viii, 94 p. CVicAr CVU **6751**

Meredith, George, 1828-1909.
Exploring the last frontier. Portland, Or., Portland Club of Print House Craftsmen, 1940. 31 p.   OrP **6752**

Meredith, William John.
In the love of nature. Seattle, Metropolitan, 1900. xi, 54 p. Poetry of Puget Sound.   Wa WaPS WaU **6753**

Merk, Frederick, see nos. 9463, 10345, 10346.

Merrell, Wilma.
Winds that sing. Philadelphia, Dorrance [1944] 44 p. (Contemporary poets of Dorrance, 278). Clarkston Wash. poet.
                        IdB WaS WaU **6754**

Merriam, C. Hart, see no. 9393.

Merriam, Harold Guy, 1883-
Ethnic settlement of Montana; paper read at Western Folklore Conference, University of Denver, July 9, 1942. Missoula, Mont., 1942. 20 p.   MtBozC MtU **6755**

Northwest verse; an anthology ed. by Harold G. Merriam. Caldwell, Idaho, Caxton [c1931] 355 p.   Many **6756**

Merriam, Henry Clay, 1837-1912.
Report on miners' riots in the state of Idaho. [n.p.] 1899. 29 p. CVicAr IdB **6757**

Merriam, John Campbell, 1869-
Contribution to the geology of the John Day Basin. Berkeley, Calif., Univ. of Calif., 1901. [44] p. illus., map. (Publications in geology, v. 2, no. 9) OrP **6758**

Ichthyosaurian reptile from marine Cretaceous of Oregon, by J. C. Merriam and C. W. Gilmore, with one text-figure. [Washington, D. C., Carnegie Institution of Washington, 1928] v, 58 p. illus., 13 plates. (Publication, no. 393)
                              WaSp **6759**

See also nos. 3590, 5439.

Merrick, Rebecca.
Rain Harbor. Indianapolis, Bobbs-Merrill [1947] 275 p. Washington coast novel.
                    WaE WaS WaT WaU **6760**

Merrill, Lee P., and Company.
The Merrill almanac and handbook of the Pacific Northwest for the year 1934. Tacoma, 1934. 1 v.   CVicAr **6761**

Metcalf, Ralph, 1862?-
Direct primary legislation; a brief sketch of its progress in the various states, how the Washington law was passed, a comparison with the laws of other states; an address delivered before the University Club, Tacoma. Tacoma, Pioneer Bindery & Printing Co., 1907. 24 p.
                                  WaS **6762**

Methodist Alaska Yukon Pacific Commission.
1834-1909; Diamond Jubilee of Methodism of the Pacific, authorized by annual conferences of the Northwest, approved by the General Conference of the Methodist Episcopal Church, ed. by William H. Leech. Seattle [1909] 80 p. illus.
                    OrHi OrSa WaTC WaU **6763**

Methodist Episcopal Church. Conferences. Columbia River.
Handbook; forty-second session, September 1-6, 1915. [Spokane, Art Printing Co.] 1915. 25 p. port.   WaU **6764**

— — — — — — Puget Sound. Preachers' Aid and Permanent Fund Society.
Bylaws. [n.p., 1909?] 11 p.   WaU **6765**

— — — Home Mission and Church Extension Board.
Pastor's journal: Jason Lee centennial issue. [n.p., 1933] 1 v. (v. 5, no. 1, Jan. 1933)   Or OrHi OrP **6766**

— — — Joint High Commission on Merger of the Columbia River and Puget Sound Annual Conferences.
Pre-conference report. Seattle, 1929. 22 p.
WaTC WaU **6767**

— — — Portland District.
Anniversary exercises of the centennial of American Methodism and the semi-centennial of Oregon Methodism, held at Taylor Street M. E. Church, Portland, Oregon, May 4 and 5, 1885. Portland, Or., Swope and Taylor, 1885. 95 p.
OrP WaTC **6768**

The 100th anniversary of the first Independence Day address in Portland, Oregon, July 4, 1847. [n.p.] 1947. 1 v.
OrP **6769**

Methodist Missionary Society.
Letter from the Methodist Missionary Society to the Superintendent of Indian affairs respecting British Columbia troubles, with affidavits, declarations, etc. [n.p., n,d.] viii, 77 p. CVicAr **6770**

Metin, Albert, 1871-1918.
La Colombie britannique; etude sur la colonisation au Canada, avec vingt cartes et cartons et trente-trois phototypies hors texte. Paris, A. Colin, 1908. 431 p. 16 plates, maps (1 fold.)
CV CVicAr CVU WaU **6771**

La mise en valeur de la Colombie Britannique, etude de colonisation. Paris, A. Colin, 1907. 431 p. illus., 16 plates, fold. map, diagr. CVicAr CVU **6772**

Metlakahtla, Alaska; church manual. [n.p., n.d.] [34] p. CVicAr **6773**

Metropolitan Broadcasting Company.
Your police department. Portland, Or. [1932] 40 p. OrU **6774**

Metropolitan Building Co., Seattle, Wash.
The Cobb Building office tenancy restricted exclusively to physicians and dentists. Seatle, c1926. 19 p. illus., plans (1 double) WaPS **6775**

The Douglas Building, on the site where Seattle history was made. [Seattle, 192—?] [15] p. illus. WaPS WaU **6776**

Expanding metropolitan center service to meet Seattle's growing needs. Seattle [n.d.] [6] p. illus., ports. WaPS **6777**

The Skinner Building, Seattle. [Seattle, n. d.] 15 p. illus. WaPS **6778**

The Stimson Building office tenancy restricted exclusively to physicians and dentists, owned and managed by Metropolitan Building Company. Seattle, c1926. 18 p. illus., plans (1 double) WaPS **6779**

The White-Henry-Stuart Building. Seattle [1926?] [20] p. illus., 4 fold. plans.
WaPS **6780**

Metropolitan Press Printing Company, Seattle, Wash.
1896-1931 [dedication of new printing plant and celebration of 35th anniversary of business in Seattle] [Seattle, 1931] [20] p. illus., ports. WaU **6781**

Meyers, Alfred.
Murder ends the song. [New York] Reynal & Hitchcock [c1941] 304 p. illus., music. LaGrande, Or. setting.
IdU OrP WaE WaS WaSp WaT **6782**

Michaelis, D. E. F., see no. 9720.

Middleton, Christopher, d. 1770.
A rejoinder to Mr. Dobb's reply to Captain Middleton. London, Cooper, Brett, and Amey, 1745. 156 p. Northwest Passage controversy. CVicAr **6783**

A reply to the remarks of Arthur Dobbs, esq. on Capt. Middleton's vindication of his conduct when sent in search of a North-west Passage by Hudson's Bay. London, G. Brett, 1744. x, 192, 93 p.
CVicAr OrP WaU **6784**

A vindication of the conduct of Captain Christopher Middleton in a late voyage on board His Majesty's ship, the Furnace, for discovering a North-west Passage; in answer to certain objections and aspersions of Arthur Dobbs. London, J. Robinson, 1743. 206, 48 p.
CVicAr WaU **6785**

See also no. 2483.

Middleton, J. E., see no. 10382.

Midnight Sun Broadcasting Co., Fairbanks, Alaska.
KFAR keybook of interior Alaska. [Fairbanks, Alaska, Tanana Pub. Co., c1939] 63 p. illus. (part col.) maps (part col.) diagrs. (part col.) WaT WaU **6786**

Miers, Henry Alexander, 1858-
Yukon; a visit to the Yukon gold-fields. [n.p.] 1901. 32 p. CVicAr CVU **6787**

Mighels, Mrs. Earl Sterling (Clark) 1853-1934.
Wawona; an Indian story of the Northwest. San Francisco, Harr Wagner Pub. Co. [c1921] 117 p. illus., map.
CVU Or OrP **6788**

Mikkelsen, Ejnar, 1880-
Conquering the Arctic ice. London, Heinemann, 1909. 470 p. front., illus., ports., maps, diagr. WaS **6789**

Same. Philadelphia, Jacobs [1909?]
CVicAr WaT **6790**

Miles, Nelson Appleton, 1839-1925.
Personal recollections and observations of General Nelson A. Miles, embracing a brief view of the Civil War; or, From New England to the Golden Gate, and the story of his Indian campaigns, with comments on the exploration, development and progress of our great western empire; copiously illus. with graphic pictures by Frederic Remington and other eminent artists. Chicago, Werner, 1896. vii, 590 p. front., illus., plates, ports. MtU Or OrP WaWW **6791**

Same. 1897. vii, 591 p. Many **6792**

See also no. 5442.

Miles City Daily Star.
Golden jubilee edition. [Miles City, Mont., Star Printing Co., 1934] 1 v. illus., ports. (v. 25, no. 1, May 24, 1934)
MtBozC MtHi WaU **6793**

Milestones in the progress of the Hudson's Bay Company. [n.p., n.d.] 30 p. illus.
CVicAr **6794**

Miller, Alfred Lawrence, 1897-
A suggested basic building code for Washington cities, by Alfred L. Miller and Joshua H. Vogel, prepared for the Association of Washington Cities. [Seattle] 1941. [28] p. diagrs., form. (Univ. of Wash. Governmental Research Bureau. Report no. 47) WaS WaU **6795**
Same. 1943. 26 p. OrCS **6796**

Miller, Basil William, 1897-
Ken in Alaska. Grand Rapids, Zondervan Pub. House [1944] 71 p. WaU **6797**

Miller, Bethene, see no. 833.

Miller, Cincinnatus Hiner, see nos. 6803-6815.

Miller, David Hunter, 1875- ed.
San Juan archipelago; study of the joint occupation of San Juan Island. [Bellows Falls, Vt., Windham Press, 1943] 203 p. fold. map. Many **6798**
See also no. 3879.

Miller, G. W.
Battle of Walla Walla. [Walla Walla, Wash., Walla Walla Union, 1905] [8] p. OrHi WaSp **6799**

Miller, Horatio Hamilton.
Democracy in Idaho; a study of state governmental problems. Caldwell, Idaho, Caxton, 1935. 213 p. fold. diagr. IdB IdIF IdP IdU IdUSB **6800**
Same. 2d ed. rev. 1940. 215 p. IdB IdIf IdU WaU **6801**

Miller, Joaquin, 1841?-1913.
The complete poetical works of Joaquin Miller. San Francisco, Whitaker & Ray, 1897. 330 p. front., plates. Wa WaS WaWW **6802**
An illustrated history of the state of Montana, containing biographical mention of its pioneers and prominent citizens. Chicago, Lewis Pub. Co., 1894. 1 v. in 2. front., plates, ports. IdU
MtBozC MtHi MtU WaSp WaU **6803**
Joaquin et al. Portland, Or., S. L. McCormick, 1869. 112 p. OrHi OrP WaU **6804**
Same. London, J. C. Hotten, 1872. 124 p. WaU **6805**
Life amongst the Modocs; unwritten history. London, R. Bentley, 1873. viii, 400 p. Or OrHi WaS WaSp WaU **6806**
Memorie and rime. New York, Funk & Wagnalls, 1884. 237 p. IdU WaA WaSp WaU **6807**
My life among the Indians. Chicago, Morril, 1892. 253 p. illus. OrHi **6808**
My own story. Chicago, Belford-Clarke Co., 1890. 253 p. front. (port.) plates. OrHi OrP WaU **6809**
Overland in a covered wagon; an autobiography, ed. by Sidney G. Firman, illus. by Esther M. Mattson. New York, Appleton [c1930] 129 p. front., illus. Many **6810**
Paquita, the Indian heroine; a true story, presenting graphic pictures of Indian home life in peace and war as beheld by the author during his residence of four years among the red men. Hartford,

American Pub. Co., 1881. 445 p. front. (port.) 14 plates. OrP WaSp **6811**
A royal highway of the world. Portland, Or., Metropolitan, 1932. 23 p. front. (mounted port.) illus., plate, facsim. Joaquin Miller Trail, Burns to Canyon City in Oregon. OrHi OrP WaPS WaSp **6812**
Specimens. Portland, Or., Himes, 1868. 54 p. OrHi **6813**
True bear stories, with introductory notes by Dr. David Starr Jordan, together with a thrilling account of the capture of the celebrated grizzly "Monarch". Chicago, Rand, McNally [c1900] 259 p. front. (port.) plates (part col.) MtU WaS **6814**
Same. Portland, Or., Binfords & Mort, 1948. Many **6814A**
Unwritten history; life amongst the Modocs. Hartford, American Pub. Co., 1874. 445 p. front. (port.) 23 plates. CVU OrHi Wa WaSp WaU **6815**
See also nos. 2634, 4092-4097, 9386-9388.

Miller, Juanita.
My father, C. H. Joaquin Miller, poet. Oakland, Calif., Tooley-Towne [c1941] 218 p. front., illus., ports., facsims., music. Or OrP OrU **6816**

Miller, Marian, see no. 4459.

Miller, Max, 1901-
The beginning of a mortal; illus. by John Sloan. New York, Dutton, 1933. vii, 253 p. front. (port.) plates. Everett, Wash. author, autobiography. Many **6817**
C‡; a college commentary. Seattle, Sunset Pub. Co., c1922. 81 p. WaU **6818**
The far shore, with official U. S. Navy and Coast Guard photographs. New York, Whittlesey House [1945] 173 p. illus. Many **6819**
Fog and men on Bering Sea. [New York, Dutton, 1936] 271 p. illus., plates, maps. Many **6820**
The great trek; the story of the five-year drive of a reindeer herd through the icy waters of Alaska and northwestern Canada. [Garden City, N. Y.] Doubleday, 1935. 224 p. 8 plates. IdU OrCS OrMonO OrP WaE WaS **6821**
Same. 1936. CV CVic CVU OrCS WaU **6822**
He went away for a while. New York, Dutton, 1933. 248 p. CVU OrP Wa WaE WaS WaWW **6823**
I cover the water front. New York, Dutton [c1932] 204 p. Many **6824**
The man on the barge. New York, Dutton, 1935. 251 p. CVU IdU OrP Wa WaS **6825**

Miller, Milton Armington.
Plea for Champoeg momorial building. [Portland, Or. 1929] 8 p. Or OrP **6826**

Miller, Mrs. Nellie V.
Resources of the state of Washington. [Seattle? c1933] 30 p. WaS WaU **6827**

Miller, Queena Davison.
Singing down the dawn; a book of poems. [Tacoma, Tacoma Poetcrafters, c1942] 111 p. Wa WaT WaU **6828**

Miller, Stephen I., see no. 5881.

Miller, Wallace J., comp.
Southwestern Washington, its topography, climate, resources, productions, manufacturing advantages, wealth and growth, with illus. reviews of the principal cities and towns, and pen sketches of their representative business men; also biographical sketches of prominent state, county and municipal officials. Olympia, Wash., Pacific Printing Co., 1890. 224 p. illus., ports., map. OrU Wa WaS WaU **6829**

A trip along the Columbia River from British Columbia to the sea, with numerous illus. by the author and from photographs to which are appended brief sketches of several important cities and towns along the river in Oregon and Washington. [n.p.] 1890. 142 p. illus. WaPS WaS WaU **6830**

Millican, Ada Bradley.
The heart of Oregon; legend of the Wascos. Millican, Or. [n.d.] 15 p. illus. Or OrHi **6831**

Same. Colista M. Dowling, illus. Millican, Or. [Bend Bulletin, c1914] [16] p. illus. OrP WaPS WaS WaSp **6832**

Mills, Edward Laird, 1875-
Plains, peaks and pioneers; eighty years of Methodism in Montana. Portland, Or., Binfords & Mort [c1947] 244 p. plates, ports., 2 double maps, facsims. Many **6833**

Mills, Enos Abijah, 1870-1922.
The adventures of a nature guide. Boston, Houghton, c1920. xiv, 271 p. front., plates. IdTf OrP **6834**

Same. Garden City, N. Y., Doubleday, 1920. Wa WaA WaS **6835**

The Rocky Mountain wonderland. Boston, Houghton, c1915. xiii, 362 p. front., plates (1 double) map. Many **6836**

The spell of the Rockies, with illus. from photographs by the author. Boston, Houghton, 1911. xi, 355 p. front., plates. Many **6837**

Same. 1912. CVU WaU **6838**

Wild life on the Rockies, with illus. from photographs. Boston, Houghton, 1909. xi, 262 p. front., 23 plates. Many **6839**

Mills, Esther Burnell,, see no. 4177.

Mills, R. S.
Where Vancouver sleeps; a commemorative sketch; 1798-1948. [n.p., 1948] [4] p. CVicAr **6840**

Mills, Randall Vause, 1907-
Stern-wheelers up Columbia; a century of steamboating in the Oregon country. Palo Alto, Calif., Pacific Books [1947] 212 p. illus., maps. Many **6841**

Milner, Joe E., 1880-
California Joe, noted scout and Indian fighter, by Joe E. Milner, his grandson, and Earle R. Forrest, with an authentic account of Custer's last fight by Colonel William H. C. Bowen. Caldwell, Idaho, Caxton, 1935. 396 p. front., 9 plates, 12 ports. Many **6842**

Milton, William Fitzwilliam, viscount, 1839-1877.
A history of San Juan water boundary

question as affecting the division of territory between Great Britain and the United States, collected and comp. from official papers and documents, printed under the authority of the government respectively of Great Britain and Ireland and of the United States of America, and from other sources. London, Cassell, Petter, and Galpin, 1869. 422 p. front. (fold. map) fold. map. Many **6843**

The North-west Passage by land; being the narrative of an expedition from the Atlantic to the Pacific, undertaken with the view of exploring a route across the continent to B. C. through British territory by one of the northern passes in the Rocky Mountains, by Viscount Milton and W. B. Cheadle. London, Cassell, Petter, and Galpin [1865] xviii, 397 p. front., 21 plates, 2 fold maps. Many **6844**

Same. 2d ed., xxviii, 400 p.
CVicAr CVU Wa WaU **6845**

Same. 3d ed. CVU **6846**

Same. 4th ed. xxiv, 400 p. CVicAr **6847**

Same. 5th ed. [1866] CVicAr CVU **6848**

Same. 6th ed. CVicAr Or WaU **6849**

Same. 7th ed. [1867] xxiv, 394 p.
CVicAr OrHi Wa WaPS WaS WaU **6850**

Same. 8th ed. [1875] xviii, 396 p. front., 3 plates, fold. map. CVU **6851**

Same. New ed. (9th) with postscript. London, Cassell and Co., 1901. 396 p. front., 11 plates, fold. map.
CVic CVicAr CVU WaT **6852**

Voyage de l'Atlantique au Pacifique a travers le Canada, les Montagnes Rocheuses et la Colombie anglaise par le viscounte Milton et le dr. W. B. Cheadle, tr. de l'anglais avec l'autorisation des auteurs par J. Belinde Launay. Paris, L. Hachette, 1866. 387 p. front., plates.
CVicAr CVU WaSp WaU **6853**

Same. 2. ed. [1872] xxi, 315 p.
CVicAr CVU WaSp WaU **6854**

The miner; responsible organ of the British Columbia mining industry; historical and convention number. Vancouver, B. C., Black, 1936. 90 p. illus., ports., (v. 9, no. 10, Oct. 1936) CVicAr **6855**

Miners' News Publishing Company.
All about Klondike gold mines. New York [n.d.] 59 p. CVicAr **6856**

Minidoka Relocation Center, Idaho.
Minidoka interlude. Hunt, Idaho [1944?] 1 v. illus. WaS **6857**

Mining and Engineering Record.
Cariboo number. Vancouver, B. C., 1924. 80 p. illus. (v. 28, no. 1, Feb. 15, 1924) CVicAr CVU **6858**

Mining review of greater Helena region; discovery of "Last Chance Gulch", July 1935. [n.p.] 1935. 32 p. illus. MtHi **6859**

Mining salutes Idaho's 50 years of statehood, 1890-1940. [n.p., 1940] 36 p. illus., ports. IdIf **6860**

Minto, John, 1822-1915.
Rhymes of early life in Oregon and historical and biographical facts. Salem,

Or., Statesman Pub. Co. [191—?] 32 p. front. (port.)   Many   **6861**

Same. [1915?] 80 p.   Many   **6862**

Rhymes on life in Oregon. Salem, Or., R. E. Moores & Co., 1906. 26 p. front. (port.)   WaU   **6863**

Same. 1909. Or OrHi OrSa OrSaW WaU   **6864**

Speeches of presentation and acceptance of the oil painting of Dr. John McLoughlin, February 5, 1889. Salem, Or., State Printer, 1889. 20 p.   Or OrHi   **6865**

Minturn, William.
Travels west. London, S. Tinsley, 1877. x, 396 p.   CVU   **6866**

Minutes of a preliminary meeting of the delegates convened at Yale pursuant to the following call, Yale convention. [New Westminster, B. C., B. C. Printer, 1868] 12 p.   CVicAr   **6867**

Mirabeau, M. de, see no. 7536.

"Miriam", pseud.
Grey days and gold. Victoria, B. C. [Murphy & Chapman] 1933. 149 p. Religious poetry.   CVicAr   **6868**

Miriam Theresa, Sister, 1886-
Legislation for women in Oregon. [Washington, D. C., Catholic Univ. of America] 1924. ii, 153 p. (Ph. D. thesis) WaU   **6869**

Mirsky, Jeannette, 1903-
To the Arctic! The story of northern exploration from earliest times to the present, with an introd. by Vilhjalmur Stefansson. [Rev. and expanded ed. 1st Borzoi ed.] New York, Knopf, 1948. xxi, 334, xviii p. illus., maps (part fold.)   Many   **6870**

To the North! The story of Arctic exploration from earliest times to the present. New York, Viking, 1934. xx, 386 p. illus., plates, ports., maps (1 fold.) facsims.   CVicAr CVU OrCS   **6871**

The westward crossings; Balboa, Mackenzie, Lewis and Clark. New York, Knopf, 1946. xv, 365, xiii, p. plates, ports., maps (1 fold.) plan, facsims.   Many   **6872**

Mission City and Mission District. [n.p., n.d.] 35 p. illus., map.   CVicAr   **6873**

Missoula County Central Trades and Labor Council.
A graphic story of organized labor in Missoula County, 1896-1946. [n.p., 1946?] 52 p.   MtHi   **6874**

Missoulian Publishing Company.
Consolidated hand book. [Missoula, Mont., 1914] 30 p.   MtU   **6875**

Mitchell, Benjamin Wiestling, 1861-
Trail life in the Canadian Rockies. New York, Macmillan, 1924. xii, 269 p. plates.   CVU Wa WaS WaSp WaU   **6876**

Mitchell, Dwight Emerson.
Music week at Boise, Idaho; a historical sketch. [Boise, Idaho, Syms-York Co.] 1943. 30 p.   IdB   **6877**

Mitchell, E. B.
In western Canada before the war; a study of communities. London, J. Murray, 1915. xi, 205 p. map.   CVU OrP WaS WaU   **6878**

Mitchell, G. B., see no. 1318.

Mitchell, John Hipple, 1835-1905.
Letter to B. S. Huntington, esq., secretary Board of Trade, Dalles City, Oregon, on the interstate commerce bill. [n.p.] 1887. 13 p.   OrP   **6879**

The Northern Pacific Railroad; an open letter to Harvey W. Scott, ed. of the Oregonian, in answer to his editorial in the Daily Oregonian of Dec. 1, A. D. 1880. Washington, D. C., National Republican Printing House, 1880. 14 p.   OrHi OrP   **6880**

Oration delivered at Olympia, W. T., July 5, 1869 [importance of Washington and Oregon from a physical and commercial point of view] Olympia, W. T., Prosch, 1869. 19 p.   OrHi WaU   **6881**

Reply to the speech of Hon. Joseph Simon, United States Senator, made in the Senate of the United States, March 6, 1900, in which he, referring to the Legislative holdup in Oregon in 1897, asserted that "the failure of the House to organize is attributable to Mr. Mitchell and to him alone" and further that "whatever demoralization there was of the Legislature was caused by Mr. Mitchell and not Mr. Corbett". Portland, Or., 1900. 28 p.   Or   **6882**

Mitchell, Peter.
The West and North-west, notes of a holiday trip; reliable information for immigrants. Montreal, 1880. 64 p. front. (fold. map) illus., fold. map.   CVicAr   **6883**

Mitchell, R. H.
Resources of Columbia County, Oregon, gem of the Pacific. Rainier, Or., 1902. 19 p. illus.   OrHi   **6884**

Mitchell, Mrs. Rebecca.
Historical sketches; pioneer characters and conditions of eastern Idaho. [Idaho Falls, Bert P. Mill, 1906] 49 p. front., illus., ports.   IdIf IdU OrHi   **6885**

Mitchell, Samuel Augustus, 1792-1868.
Accompaniment to Mitchell's new map of Texas, Oregon, and California, with the regions adjoining. Philadelphia, 1846. 34 p. fold. map.   CVicAr WaU   **6886**

Same. 46 p.   IdU OrHi WaS WaU   **6887**

Same. [Tacoma] North Pacific Bank Note Co., 1925. 34 p. fold. map.   CVU Or OrCS OrU   **6888**

Description of Oregon and California, embracing an account of the gold regions; to which is added an appendix containing descriptions of various kinds of gold and methods of testing its genuineness, with a large and accurate map of Oregon and California comp. from the latest authorities. Philadelphia, Thomas, 1849. 76 p. illus., map.
CVicAr OrU WaS WaSp WaWW   **6889**

Texas, Oregon and California, foreword by Joseph A. Sullivan. Oakland, California, Biobooks, 1948. 46 p. fold. map. (Calif. centennial ed., 12]   WaS WaT   **6890**

Mitchelmore, Lawrence Hugh.
Jacksonville Church, her ministers and her ministry, 1857-1947, pub. on the occasion

of the ninetieth anniversary of the organization of the First Presbyterian Church of Jackson County, Jacksonville, Oregon, November 22, 1947. [Jacksonville, Or., 1947] [44] p. illus., plans. Anon.   OrU **6891**

A short history of the First Presbyterian Church, Moro, Oregon, 1887-1938. [Moro, Or., 1st Presbyterian Church] 1938. 40 p.   Or **6892**

Mitchil Theodor C., see no. 6045.

Moberly, Henry John, 1835-
When fur was king, by Henry John Moberly, retired factor of the Hudson's Bay Company, in collaboration with William Bleasdell Cameron, illus. by John Innes and from photographs. London, Dent, 1929. xvii, 237 p. front. (port.) plates, port., fold. map.   Many **6893**

Same. New York, Dutton [1929] 237 p. front. (port.) plates, port., fold. map.
    IdP MtHi WaPS WaS WaU **6849**

Moberly, Walter, 1832-1915.
Early history of C. P. R. road. [Vancouver, B. C., 1909?] 15 p. illus., port.
    CVicAr CVU WaPS WaS WaU **6895**

Rocks and rivers of British Columbia. London, Blacklock, 1885. 102 p.
    CVU OrHi WaS WaU **6896**

Same. 104 p. front. (fold. map) illus.
    CV CVic CVicAr Or OrP **6897**

Same. [Vienna, Kartographisches Institut, 1926] 102 p. illus.
    CVicAr MtU OrCS WaSp **6898**

See also no. 8721.

[Mock, F. G.]
Blue eye; a story of the people of the plains, by Ogal Alla [pseud.] Portland, Or., Irwin-Hodson, 1905. 245 p.
    IdIf MtHi Or OrP WaS WaU **6899**

A romance of the Sawtooth, by Ogal Alla [pseud.] Nampa, Idaho [c1917] 153 p.
    Many **6900**

Mock, Horace J., see no. 7767.

Mock, Lucy Byrd, 1880-
The maid of Pend d'Oreille, an Indian idyl, by Le Moqueur. Seattle, 1910. [12] p. illus. (Siwash ed.)   WaU **6901**

The Seattle spirit; overcoat pocket ed., a primer on Puget Sound; a bird's eye view of western Washington, past, present and future. Seattle, Sign of the Mocking Bird, c1911. 136 p. front., illus., 2 fold. maps.
    CVicAr OrU WaPS WaS WaU **6902**

Modjeski, Ralph, 1861-
A report of the mayor and City Council, with plans and estimates for the proposed bridge across the Willamette River at Portland, Oregon [Broadway Bridge] [n.p.] 1908. 16 p. maps.   OrP **6903**

A report and plans and estimates for the proposed bridge across the Columbia River between Portland, Oregon and Vancouver, Washington. Chicago, 1912. 10 p. front., plate, maps. OrP OrU **6904**

Supplemental report to a report dated September 15, 1912, with plans and estimates for the proposed bridge across the Columbia River between Portland, Oregon and Vancouver, Washington. Chicago [Sherman] 1913. 7 p. illus., tables.
    OrHi **6905**

Moe, George Gordon.
Wheat studies in British Columbia. [Vancouver, B. C., Univ. of B. C.] 1942. iii, 171 p. tables. diagr.   CVU **6906**

Moller, Joachim van.
Auf nach Alaska; ein Fuhrer fur Wagemutige. Charlottenburg, F. Thiel, 1897. 198 p. illus., fold. map.
    CVicAr CVU WaS WaU **6907**

Mollhausen, Balduin, 1825-1905.
Diary of a journey from the Mississippi to the coasts of the Pacific with a United States government expedition [Lt. Whipple's] with an introd. by Alexander von Humboldt, trans. by Mrs. Percy Sinnott London, Longman, 1858. 2 v. fronts., illus., plates (part col.) fold. map.
    CVicAr CVU OrHi OrP WaU WAW **6908**

Tagebuch einer Reise vom Mississippi nach den Kusten der Sudsee. Leipzig, Mendelssohn, 1858. 494 p. col. front., illus., col. plates., fold. map.   CVicAr **6909**

Wanderungen durch die Prairien und Wusten des westlichen Nordamerika vom Mississippi nach den Kusten der Sudsee, eingerfurst, von Alexander von Humboldt. 2d ed. Leipzig, Mendelssohn, 1860. 492 p. fold. map.   CVicAr **6910**

Mofras, Eugene Duflot de, see nos. 2596-2600.

Mohr, N.
Ein Streifzug durch den Nordwesten Amerikas; festfahrt zur Northern Pacific Bahn im Herbste 1883. Berlin, R. Oppenheim, 1884. vi, 394 p.   OrP WaU **6911**

[Mohun, Edward].
The sewarage system of Victoria, British Columbia [n.p., n.d.] 16 p. CVicAr **6912**

Molee, Elias, 1845-
Nu teutonish; an international union language. Tacoma, 1906. 128 p. port.
    IdU Wa WaS WaSp **6913**

Molinelli, A. Cavalli, see no. 6136.

Moll, Ernest George, 1900-
Blue interval; poems of Crater Lake, with illus. by Karl J. Belser. Portland, Or., Metropolitan, 1935. 41 p. illus.
    OrCS OrP **6914**

Campus sonnets. Portland, Or., Metropolitan 1934. 61 p.
    OrCS OrP OrSaw OrU WaU **6915**

Native moments and other poems. Portland, Or., Metropolitan 1931. 68 p.
    MtU OrP OrU WaU **6916**

Orlando John Hollis, acting president of the University of Oregon from January 6, 1944 to June 30, 1945; a tribute on behalf of the faculty delivered at a banquet in honor of Mr. Hollis on June 7, 1945. [Eugene, Or., Or. Univ. Press, 1945] 6 p.   OrCS OrU **6917**

Monaghan, James, 1891-
The Overland trail. Indianapolis., Bobbs-Merrill [1947] 431 p. plates, maps. (American trails series)   Many **6918**

Monroe, Anne Shannon, 1877-1942.

Behind the ranges. New York, Burt [c1925] 343 p. Oregon author. Central Oregon ranch story.

OrCS OrHi OrP WaT WaU **6919**

Feelin' fine! Bill Hanley's book, put together by Anne Shannon Monroe, photographic illus. by William L. Finley and others. Garden City, N. Y., Doubleday, 1930. xv, 304 p. plates, ports.   Many **6920**

Happy Valley; a story of Oregon, illus by. J. Allen St. John. Chicago, McClurg, 1916. 347 p. front., illus.   Many **6921**

Same. New York, Grosset [c1916]

OrSa WaU **6922**

The hearth of happiness. Garden City, N. Y., Doubleday, 1929. 307 p.

MtU OrCS OrP OrSaW OrU WaS **6923**

Making a business woman. New York, Holt, 1912. 311 p.   OrP WaS WaU **6924**

Mansions in the Cascades, by Anne Shannon Monroe and Elizabeth Lambert Wood. New York, Macmillan, 1936. vii, 325 p.   Many **6925**

Singing in the rain. Garden City, N. Y., Doubleday, 1926. viii, 340 p.   Many **6926**

Sparks from home fires. New York, Doubleday, 1940. viii, 267 p.   Many **6927**

Walk with me, lad. Garden City, N. Y., Doubleday [c1943] 291 p.   Many **6928**

The world I saw. Garden City, N. Y., Doubleday, 1928. vii, 331 p. front. Autobiography.   Many **6929**

Montague, Phil S.

Ready reference and hand book of the Klondyke and Alaskan gold fields. San Francisco, Hicks-Judd Co. [c1897] 58 p. plates, fold. map.   CVicAr **6930**

Montague, Sydney Robert.

North to adventure. New York, McBride [c1939] 284 p. plates.   Many **6931**

Montana. Citizens.

Proceedings of the mass convention held at Helena, December 7, 1903 [representing citizens of this state who are opposed to corporate domination in political affairs. Note "To the public" signed by W. G. George, state chairman, Antitrust Party] Butte, Mont. [1903] 32 p.

MtU **6932**

— — — National Guard.

Historical and pictorial review. Baton Rouge, La., Army and Navy Pub. Co., 1940. 69 p. photos.   MtHi **6933**

History of the Second Regiment Infantry, National Guard of Montana, comp. by W. M. Swaethout. [n.p.] 1916. 52 p. 69 ports.   MtHi **6934**

— — — University. English Department.

The Selish; a pageant-masque written by students of the State University of Montana and produced by the University and the community of Missoula under direction of Mrs. Margaret P. Ganssle, July 30, 1919. [Missoula, Mont., Univ. of Mont.? 1919] [63] p.

MtBozC MtHi WaT WaU **6935**

— — — — — — Montana study.

Life in Montana as seen in Lonepine, a small community, prepared by the Montana Study of the greater University of Montana, Montana State University. Missoula, Mont. [1945] 112 p. illus., maps, diagrs.   WaS WaTC WaU **6936**

Montana Agricultural, Mineral and Mechanical Association.

Premium list and racing programme with the rules and regulations of the seventeenth annual exhibition to be held at Helena, Montana, August 23, 24, 25, 26, 27, and 28, 1886. Helena, Mont., Independent Pub. Co., 1886. 48 p. WaU **6937**

Racing rules of the Montana Agricultural, Mineral and Mechanical Association. [Helena, Mont.] 1878. 64 p.   MtHi **6938**

Montana and the Northwest Territory; review of the mercantile, mining, milling, agriculture, stock raising and general pursuits of her citizens; historical sketch; the counties and towns arranged alphabetically. Chicago, Brown & Marsh, 1879. 85 p.   MtHi **6939**

Montana Federation Women's Clubs.

Local community history of Valley County, Montana, comp. by Mrs. Vesta O. Robbins, with illus. by H. Irvin Shope. Glasgow, Mont., Glasgow Courier, 1925. 78 p. illus.   MtBozC MtHi **6940**

Montana Historical Society. Library.

Catalogue of the library of the Historical Society of the State of Montana; also a report of the library for the years 1891-92, being the first biennial report and catalogue ever published by the state or society; in 2 parts: Part 1. The publications of this state and of other states and general history. Part 2. Publications of the United States which have been received at this library to November 1892, prepared by Wm. F. Wheeler, librarian. Helena, Mont., C. K. Wells Co., 1892. 128 p.   MtHi MtU **6941**

Montana Horticultural Society.

Papers read and discussed before the Montana Horticultural Society with constitution and by-laws, issued January 15, 1902. Kalispel, Mont., Bee Pub. Co., 1902. 69 p.   MtU **6942**

Montana; its climate, soil, scenery, resources and industries, New York, 1883. 32 p.

MtHi WaWW **6943**

Montana National Bituminous Conference.

Digest of proceedings of the 1935 Montana Conference on Modern Bituminous Practice held at Butte, Montana, November 12, 13, and 14, 1935. Helena, Mont., Naegele Printing Co., 1935. 139 p. illus.

MtBozC **6944**

Montana Power Co.

Public power means high taxes, socialism, and less money for irrigation. [n.p.] 1948. 1 v. map.   MtHi **6945**

Public power program wastes your taxes. [n.p.] 1948. 1 v. map.   MtHi **6946**

The story of Montana power. [Butte, Mont., Mont. Standard Press, 1941?] 80 p. illus., maps, diagrs. (part fold.) MtBozC **6947**

Montana Society of Engineers.

Constitution and by-laws adopted August

17, 1891. Helena, Mont., Williams & Thurber, 1891. 14 p. MtHi **6948**

Same. Helena, Mont., Independent [n.d.] 38 p. MtHi **6949**

Montana Society of Pioneers.
Constitution, members and officers, with portraits and maps. Akron, Ohio, 1899. 262 p. ports., maps.
MtBozC MtHi MtU MtUM OrU **6950**

Montana Society of the Framers of the Constitution.
First reunion, Helena, Montana, Saturday, November 8, 1890. [n.p., n.d.] 25 p.
MtHi MtU **6951**

Second reunion, 1891. Indianapolis, Baker-Randolph [n.d.] 202 p. MtHi MtU **6952**

Montana State Teachers' Association.
Annual address of John M. Kay before the Montana State Teachers' Association. Red Lodge, Mont., Picket Press, 1903. 32 p. MtHi **6953**

Montana World's Fair Commission, 1904.
Montana; its progress and prosperity, resources and industries, opportunities for homeseekers and capitalists; mining, stock raising, agriculture, horticulture, ed. by John B. Read. St. Louis, C. P. Curran Printing Co. [1904] 82 p. illus., fold. map. MtHi MtU **6954**

Montana Wildlife Federation.
Report of organization meeting. Helena, Mont., 1936. 54 p. map. MaBozC **6955**

Monteith, John B.
The status of young Joseph and his band of Nez Perce Indians under the treaties between the United States and Nez Perce tribe of Indians, and the Indian title to land. Portland, Or., Dept. of the Columbia, 1876. 49 p. Or OrP **6956**

The Montesano Vidette.
Golden anniversary edition, Oct. 12, 1933. Montesano, Wash. [1933] 8, 8 p. illus., ports. (v. 51, no. 41, Oct. 12, 1933)
WaU **6957**

Montgomery, Elizabeth Rider.
The story behind great stories, illus. by Elinore Blaisdell. New York, McBride [1947] 210 p. illus. Seattle author.
WaU **6958**

Montgomery, Ione.
Death won the prize. Garden City, N. Y., Doubleday, 1941. 272 p. Washington author; Seattle setting. WaU **6959**

[**Montgomery, Kathryn Bayard**]
Log of the good ship Potlatch, July 15th, 25th, 1914. Seattle, R. L. Davis, 1914. 27 p. WaU **6960**

Montgomery, Richard Gill, 1897-
Adventures in the Arctic, originally published under the title "Pechuck". New York [1932] xiv, 281 p. front. (port.) plates. WaU **6961**

Husky, co-pilot of the Pilgrim. New York, Holt, 1942. 271 p. illus. Alaska adventure story. WaT **6962**

"Pechuck"; Lorne Knight's adventures in the Arctic. New York, Dodd, 1932. xv, 291 p. front., plates, ports. CVU OrP **6963**

The White-Headed Eagle, John McLoughlin, builder of an empire. New York,

Macmillan, 1934. xiii, 358 p. front. (port.) plates, port. Many **6964**

Same. 1935.
CV CVic CVicAr CVU MtBozC MtHi **6965**

Young Northwest, illus. by Harold L. Price, New York, Random House [c1941] 309 p. illus., maps. Many **6966**

Same. 2d printing. IdU **6967**

Same. 2d ed., indexed and rev. Portland, Or., Binfords & Mort, c1941-48. 318 p. illus.
CVicAr OrHi OrU WaS **6968**

Montgomery, Robert, 1872-
After fifty years; a greeting to friends from one viewing the world from the serene tableland of middle life. [Puyallup, Wash.?] 1922. 11 p. WaS **6969**

Among the stars [abstract of an address delivered Nov. 25, 1930 at a banquet of the Caledonian and St. Andrew's Society, Tacoma, Wash.] [Puyallup, Wash., Puyallup Valley Tribune, 1930] [6] p.
WaU **6970**

Comments of a layman on lawyers and the law [an address delivered March 11, 1932 before the Pierce County Bar Association at the Tacoma Hotel, Tacoma, Wash.] [n.p., 1932] [7] p. WaU **6971**

Female suffrage from the viewpoint of a male democrat. Seattle, Equal Suffrage Assn. of Wash. [1909?] [28] p. WaU **6972**

Motherhood [an address delivered before a banquet of the Benevolent and Protective Order of Elks, at Tacoma, Wash.] [n.p., n.d.] [5] p. WaU **6973**

West of fifty-four; a greeting to friends from one who can now view the world from the serene tableland of middle life. [Puyallup, Wash., Puyallup Valley Tribune? 1926?] 12 p. WaU **6974**

Montgomery, Rutherford George, 1896-
Carcajou, illus. by L. D. Cram. Caldwell, Idaho, Caxton, 1936. xviii, 263 p. illus., plates. Canadian Northwest wolverine story. IdIf OrP WaS WaW **6975**

Iceblink, illus. by Rudolf Freund. New York, Holt [c1941] 288 p. illus., plates (1 double) double map.
Or OrP Wa WaS WaU **6976**

Yellow Eyes, illus. by L. D. Cram. Caldwell, Idaho, Caxton, 1937. 243 p. illus. Western mountain lion story.
IdIf OrP Wa WaE WaS **6977**

Moody, Dan W., 1853-
The life of a rover, 1865-1926, by D. W. Moody, author and pub., known in early western life as Dan Moody, the Indian scout. [Chicago, c1926] 116 p. illus., fold. map. WaSp **6978**

Mooney, O. P., Co.
Seattle, mistress of the North Pacific. New York, W. G. MacFarlane [1907?] [2] p. 47 plates (1 fold.) WaU **6979**

Moore, Bernard Nettleton, 1906-
Diatomite and pumice in eastern Oregon. [New York] American Institute of Mining and Metallurgical Enginers, c1934. 15 p. map. (Contribution, no. 73)
OrP **6980**

Moore, Bernice Starr.
Art in our community. Caldwell, Idaho, Caxton, 1947. 186 p. illus. Seattle author and community.   WaE WaT **6981**

Moore, Billie, see no. 1643.

Moore, Charles.
The Northwest under three flags, 1635-1796. New York, Harper, 1900. xxii, 401 p. front., plates, ports., maps (1 fold.)   CVicAr OrSa Wa **6982**

Moore, Charles Calvin.
The story of Idaho [radiologue broadcast from WMAG Dec. 4, 1926 for Chicago Daily News] [n.p., 1926?] 1 v.   IdB WaPS **6983**

Moore, Dallas, comp.
Sunset trails; an anthology of recent verse written by residents of Oregon, introd. by Dr. John B. Horner, preface by Harold Hunt. [Corvallis, Or.] New Univ. Press [c1933] 175 p.   Many **6984**

Moore, Fred S.
Map of Curry County, Oregon, showing location and holdings of the early tribes with early history of the county, prepared in the Office of County School Superintendent for use in the schools of Curry County, March 28, 1927. [Gold Beach, Or.] 1927. 13 p. illus., map.   Or **6985**

Moore, Helen Bispham.
The peaks watch on. Philadelphia, Dorrance [c1938] 110 p. Spokane author.   WaSp WaU **6986**

Moore, Irene.
Valiant LaVeranrye [!] Quebec, Ls-A. Proulx, 1927. 382 p.   Many **6987**

Moore, Mary Carr, see no. 1529.

Moore, Miles C., see nos. 5867, 9638-9640.

Moore, Nina, see nos. 8213, 8214.

Moore, Otis M., comp.
Washington illustrated, including views of the Puget Sound country and Seattle, gateway to the Orient, with glimpses of Alaska. Seattle, Puget Sound Bureau of Information [1901?] [116] p. illus., ports.   CVicAr Wa WaPS WaS WaU **6988**

Moore, Thomas Verner, 1856-1926.
History of the First Presbyterian Church of Helena, Montana. Helena, Mont., 1898. 29 p.   MtHi WaPS **6989**

Moore, William Cloud.
Eastern Oregon lumber survey. Moscow, Idaho, 1941. [142] p. tables, diagrs.   OrCS ORU WaU **6990**

Same. 1942 suppl. Moscow, Idaho, 1942. iii, 73 p. charts, tables.   IdU **6991**

Moorehead, Blanche Woods.
New world builders; thrilling days with Lewis and Clark, with an introd. by Christopher B. Coleman, illus. by Armstrong Sperry. Philadelphia, Winston [c1937] xii, 228 p. col. front., illus., double map.   IdIf OrCS WaSp WaU **6992**

Moores, Charles Bruce.
Oregon pioneer wa-wa; a compilation of addresses relating to Oregon pioneer history. [Portland, Or., Ivy Press, 1923] 141 p. front. (port.)   Many **6993**

Paper on "Jason Lee as the founder of Willamette University" on the occasion of the dedication of the Jason Lee Memorial Church at Salem, Oregon, June 15, 1912. Salem, Or., 1913. [6] p. (Willamette Univ. bulletin, n. s., v. 5, no. 9, Mar. 1913)   OrHi **6994**

Moorhouse, Lee, 1850-
Souvenir album of noted Indian photographs. Pendleton, Or., East Oregonian, c1905. 25 plates.   OrHi OrP WaPS WaU **6995**

Same. 2d ed. c1906.   Or OrCS WaU **6996**

Moqueur, le, see no. 6901.

Moran, Robert, 1867-
An address at the fiftieth jubilee meeting of the Pioneers Association of the State of Washington, June 6, 1939 in Seattle. [Seattle? Malcom E. Moran] c1939. 27 p.   Wa WaS **6997**

Moran Bros. Company, Seattle, Wash.
Souvenir of the great ship building plant of Moran Bros. Company, comp. by A. S. Allen. Seattle, Press Yerken Printing Co., 1902] [20] p. 27 plates.   WaU **6998**

Moreland, Julius C.
Governors of Oregon; address delivered at the reception of January 1, 1913 given by Governor and Mrs. West in honor of ex-governors and their wives. Salem, Or. [1913?] 21 p.   Or OrCS OrHi OrP OrSa OrU **6999**

Moresby, Admiral, see nos. 6279-6281.

[Morey, P. F.]
Facts and figures about water supply in Portland, Or. for the consideration of tax payers and consumers. Portland, Or., Anderson, 1885. 32 p. tables.   OrHi OrP **7000**

Morgan, Carrie Blake.
The path of gold. New Whatcom, Wash., Edson & Irish. c1900. 28 p.   IdU OrHi Wa WaU WaWW **7001**

Morgan, Edward E. P., d. 1939.
God's loaded dice; Alaska, 1897-1930, by Edward E. P. Morgan in collaboration with Henry Woods. Caldwell, Idaho, Caxton [c1948] 298 p. illus., ports. Many **7002**

Morgan, Grace Jones.
Salvage all. New York, Crowell [c1928] 337 p. Victoria seafaring story. CVicAr **7003**

Morgan, H. V., see no. 323.

[Morgan, Henry James] 1842-1913.
The tour of H. R. H., the prince of Wales, through British America and the United States, by a British Canadian. Montreal, J. Lovell, 1860. 271 p. front. (port.)   CVicAr WaU **7004**

Morgan, J. Pierpont, see no. 2168.

Morgan, Murray C., 1916-
Bridge to Russia; those amazing Aleutians. New York, Dutton, 1947. 222 p. Washington author.   WaS WaT WaU **7005**

Day of the dead, by Cromwell Murray [pseud.] Philadelphia, David McKay Co. [1946] 200 p.   Wa WaT WaU **7006**

[Morgan, S. P.]
Idaho; facts and statistics pertaining to its

early settlement and colonization with special reference to the Franklin colony, together with stories of the Indian troubles in the southeastern part of the state; information collected and comp. for the Idaho semi-centennial celebration held at Franklin, June 14 and 15, 1910. Salt Lake City, Skelton Pub. Co., 1910. 36 p.

IdB 7007

Morgenier, R., see no. 5859.

Morice, Adrian Gabriel, 1859-1938.

Au pays de l'ours noir; chez les sauvages de la Colombie britannique; recits d'un missionaire; ouvrage enrichi d'un carte, de 5 photogravures et de 26 gravures par l'auteur. Paris, Delhomme et Briguet, 1897. viii, 305 p. illus., map.

CV CVicAr CVU WaU 7008

The Carrier language (Dene family); a grammar and dictionary combined. St. Gabriel-Modling near Vienna, Austria, "Anthropos", 1932. 2 v. front. (port.) (Linguistische bibliothek, t. 9, 10)

CVic CVicAr CVU WaS WaSp WaU 7009

The Catholic Church in the Canadian Northwest. Winnipeg, 1936. 83 p. illus., ports.

CVicAr CVU WaS 7010

The Catholic Church in western Canada. Winnipeg, Canadian Pub., 1931. 26 p.

CVU 7011

Dictionnaire historique des Canadiens et des Metis francais de l'Ouest. Quebec, Garneau, 1908. xi, 329 p.

OrHi WaSp WaU 7012

Same. Quebec [Laflamme] 1908.

CVicAr 7013

Same. 2me. ed. augmentee d'un supplement. Quebec, Garneau, 1912. xl, 355 p.

CVicAr WaSp WaU 7014

Disparus et survivants; etudes ethnographiques sur les indiens de l'Amerique du nord. Winnipeg, 1928. 371 p. front. (port.)

CV CVicAr CVU 7015

Essai sur l'origine des Denes de l'Amerique du nord. Quebec, l'Evenement, 1915. 245 p. 12 plates, port.

CV CVicAr CVU 7016

Fifty years in western Canada; being the abridged memoirs of Rev. A. G. Morice, by D. L. S. Toronto, Ryerson, 1930. x, 267 p. front. (port.) 10 plates, 5 ports.

Many 7017

A first collection of minor essays, mostly anthropological. Quesnal, B. C., Stuart's Lake Mission, 1902. 74 p.

CVicAr WaU 7018

The great Dene race, with 23 photogravures and 66 figures in the text. St. Gabriel-Modling near Vienna, Austria, Mechitaristes [1928?] xvi, 256 p. illus., plates, ports., diagrs.

CV CVic CVicAr CVU 7019

Histoire abrege de l'Ouest Canadien: Manitoba, Saskatchewan, Alberta et Grand-Nord. St. Boniface [1914] 162 p. front. (map) illus.

CVicAr 7020

Histoire de l'eglise catholique dans l'Ouest canadien du Lac Superieur au Pacifique (1659-1905). Winnipeg, West Canada

Pub. Co., 1912. 3 v. front., 20 plates, 30 ports., fold. map, facsims. (1 fold.)

CVicAr 7021

Same. Nouvelle ed. St.-Boniface, 1915.

CVicAr 7022

Same. 1921-23. 4 v. CVicAr WaU 7023

History of the Catholic Church in western Canada from Lake Superior to the Pacific (1659-1895) with maps and illus. Toronto, Musson, 1910. 2 v. front., 15 plates, 22 ports., 2 fold. maps, facsims. (part fold.)

Many 7024

The history of the northern interior of British Columbia, formerly New Caledonia (1660-1880). Toronto, Briggs, 1904. xi, 349 p. front. (fold. map) 9 plates, 19 ports.

Many 7025

Same. 3d ed. 1905. xii, 368 p. Many 7026

Same. London, J. Lane, 1906.

CVicar CVU 7027

L'Ouest canadien; esquisse geographique, ethnographique, historique et demographique. Neuchatel, Paul Attinger, 1929. 98 p.

CVicAr 7028

Le petit catechisme a l'usage des sauvages porteurs; texte and traduction avec notes suivi des prieres du matin et du soir. [Quesnal, B. C.] Mission du Lac Stuart, 1891. 144 p.

CVicAr 7029

Precis de grammaire Nahanaise. [n.p., n.d.] 72 p.

CVicAr 7030

Souvenirs d'un missionnaire en Colombie Britannique. Winnipeg, 1933. 374 p. illus., facsims.

CVicAr CVU 7031

Vie de Mgr. Langevin, oblat de Marie Immaculee Archeveque de St.-Boniface. 3d ed. St.-Boniface, 1919. 398 p. front. (port.) plates.

CVicAr 7032

Voyages et aventures de Lebret a La Haye, Lisieux, Lourdes et Verdun. St.-Boniface, 1925. 310 p. plates. CVicAr 7033

Morning Astorian.

Astoria founders edition. Astoria, Or., 1926. [46] p. illus., ports. (no. 171, July 22, 1926)

OrHi WaU 7034

Astoria, Oregon, at the mouth of the great Columbna River; best harbor on the Pacific Coast. Astoria, Or., Dellinger, 1896. [28] p. illus. Or OrHi WaPS 7035

Centennial edition. Astoria, Or., 1911. 47 p. illus. (v. 38, no. 182, Aug. 1, 1911)

WaS 7036

Morning Enterprise, Oregon, City, Or.

Centennial edition. Oregon City, Or. [1929] 58 p. illus., ports. (v. 39, no. 108, Nov. 6, 1929. OrHi WaU 7037

Clackamas County, with its immense area of uncleared land offers wealth and health to home-seekers. Oregon City, Or., 1912. 64 p. illus. (Jan. 12, 1912)

OrP 7038

Progress and anniversary edition, Jan. 1913. Oregon City, Or., 1913. 64 p. illus.

WaWW 7039

Same. Suppl., July 15, 1915. Oregon City, Or., 1915. 48 p. illus., ports. Or 7040

Morning Express.

Klamath basin booster number. Klamath Falls, Or., 1909. [12] p. illus., ports, map.

OrU 7041

Morning Olympian.
Through 25 years with the Olympian. Olympia, Wash., Western Pub. Co., 1916. [22] p. illus., ports. (v. 26, no. 1, Mar. 15, 1916]   WaU **7042**

Morning Oregonian.
Fiftieth anniversary number. Portland, Or., 1911. [128] p. illus., ports. (v. 51, no. 15661, Feb. 4, 1911)   WaU **7043**

Fifty years, 1861-1911. [Portland, Or., 1911] [12] p. illus.   Or **7044**

Handbook of Portland and tributary country. Portland, Or., 1901. 64 p. illus., map.   OrHi OrU **7045**

The history of the Oregonian. [Portland, Or., 1947] [24] p. illus.   OrCS OrHi OrP **7046**

[Jubilee number. Portland, Or., 1925] [188] p. illus., ports. (v. 64, Dec. 4-6, 1925)   WaS WaU **7047**

KGW and the Pacific Northwest, what they offer the radio advertiser. Portland, Or. [n.d.] 12 p. illus.   OrP **7048**

Lewis and Clark centennial exposition number. Portland, Or., 1905. 52 p. illus. (v. 44, no. 13,749, Jan. 2, 1905)   WaS **7049**

New Year's edition, section 1, Jan. 1920. Portland, Or., 1920. 21 p. illus.   WaPS **7050**

New Year's edition. Portland, Or., 1922. [90] p. illus., ports. (v. 60, no. 19,069, Jan. 2, 1922)   WaU **7051**

The Oregon market in the land of opportunity and the great newspaper of the Pacific Northwest. Portland, Or., 1924. 47 p. illus., maps, tables, diagrs.   OrP OrU **7052**

The Oregonian; its history, its new building. Portland, Or., 1893. 32 p. illus.   WaU **7053**

The Oregonian souvenir, 1850-1892. Portland, Or., Lewis & Dryden, 1892. 200 p. front., illus., ports.   Many **7054**
The Oregonian's handbook of the Pacific Northwest. [Portland, Or., 1894] 631 p. illus.   Many **7055**

[Pacific Northwest progress and development edition] Portland, Or., 1938. [84] p. illus. (part col.) ports.   WaU **7056**

Progress edition. Portland, Or., 1939. [82] p. illus., ports. (v. 78, no. 24434, Feb. 22, 1939.   WaU **7057**

[Special number to record the completion of the Northern Pacific Railroad] Sept. 9, 1883. Portland, Or., 1883. 1 v.   WaSp **7058**

Morning Register, Eugene, Or.
Handbook edition, Jan. 1908. a concise resume of the resources and productions of Lane County, Oregon, at the head of the Willamette Valley. Eugene, Or., 1908. 48 p. illus.   OrU **7059**

Industrial edition, 1907: Eugene and Lane County, Oregon. Eugene, Or., 1907. 56 p. illus.   OrU **7060**

Morningstar, F. V.
Snapshots of Portland history, and the Pacific Northwest, 1792-1925. Portland, Or., c1925. 112 p.   Or OrHi OrP **7061**

Morrill, Helen G., see no. 8353.

Morris, Anna Van Rensselaer.
The apple woman of the Klickitat. New York, Duffield & Co., 1918. 271 p. front., plates.   Many **7062**

Morris, Benjamin Wistar, 1819-1906.
Address to the Board of Missions, Oct. 5, 1883. [n.p., n.d.] 8 p.   OrHi **7063**

Letter from the Bishop of Oregon and Washington Territory. [n.p.] 1874. 13-18 p. illus. (Mite Chest Pamphlet no. 2, July 1874) Anon.   WaU **7064**

The Oregon Mission. [New York, n.d.] 12 p. illus. (Protestant Episcopal Church in the U. S. A. Domestic Missions. Leaflet B)   Or OrHi OrP OrU WaPS **7065**

Primary address to the missionary convocation of Oregon and Washington. [n.p.] 1869. 19 p.   OrHi **7066**

[**Morris, C. A. F.**]
The northern route to Idaho and the Pacific Ocean. St. Paul, D. D. Merrill [n.d.] [6] p. fold. map.   Wa **7067**

Morris, Mrs. Ida Dorman.
A Pacific Coast vacation, illus. from photographs taken en route by James Edwin Morris. New York, Abbey Press [1901] 255 p. front. (port.) 67 plates, port.   CVicAr Or OrP WaU **7068**

Morris, Rhoda, see nos. 9872, 9873, 9875-9878.

Morris, Victor Pierpont, 1891-
Oregon's experience with minimum wage legislation. New York, Columbia Univ. Press, 1930. 236 p. 21 tables, 4 diagrs. (Studies in history, economics and public law, no. 320)   Many **7069**

[**Morris, W. J.**]
The new Northwest. [Perth, Ont.? Courier Office, 1887] 8 p.   CVicAr **7070**

The Winnipeg and North Pacific Railway, the great highway of the new Northwest, the route and its advantages, the country and its resources. Toronto, Mail [n.d.] 12 p. 2 maps (1 fold.) 2 plans (1 fold.   CVicAr **7071**

Morris, William Charles, 1874-
The Spokane book; a collection of personal cartoons. Chicago, Donnelly, 1914. [167] p. front., illus.   WaSp **7072**

Spokesman-Review cartoons. Spokane [Review Pub. Co.] 1908. [105] p. front. (port.) illus.   Wa WaSp **7073**

Same. 107 p.   WaPS WaSp **7074**

Morrison and Eshelman, Seattle, Wash.
Seattle. Seattle [1903?] [64] p. plates.   WaU **7075**

Seattle souvenir. [Seattle, 1902?] 13 plates on 1 fold. l.   WaU **7076**

Seattle souvenir calendar. [Seattle] 1901. [32] p. plates.   WaU **7077**

Morrow, Henry Andrew.
Address of General Henry A. Morrow at Tacoma, W. T., on Memorial Day, May 30, 1883. [n.p., 1883?] 12 p.   WaU **7078**

Morrow, Mrs. Honore (McCue) **Willsie,** 1880?-1940.

Argonaut. New York, Morrow, 1933. 316 p. Oregon author, Washington and Alaska setting.

CV IdU OrP WaE WaS WaT **7079**

Judith of the godless valley. New York, Stokes [c1922] 354 p. Western cattle ranch story. WaS **7080**

On to Oregon! the story of a pioneer boy. New York, Morrow, 1926. 247 p. front., plates. Many **7081**

Same. New ed., illus. by Edward Shenton. New York, Morrow, 1946, c1926. 239 p. front., illus. (part col.) (Morrow junior books) Or OrU WaS WaT **7082**

We must march; a novel of the winning of Oregon. New York, Burt, c1925. viii, 427 p. CV OrSa Wa WaT WaTC WaW **7083**

Same. New York, Grosset [c1925] IdIf **7084**

Same. New York, Stokes, 1925. Many **7085**

Morse, Herman N.

Rural survey of Lane County, Oregon, made by County Church Board of Home Missions, Presbyterian Church in the U. S. A. [n.p.] 1916. [72] p. illus., maps. OrHi **7086**

See also no. 389.

Morse, Mary Gay.

Lore of the Olympic-land. [Los Angeles, Biola Press, c1924] 157 p. illus., plates. Many **7087**

Wayside sketches. [n.p., 192—?] 30 p. Olympic peninsula stories. WaU **7088**

Morse, Wayne Lyman, 1900-

Final report on 1771 felony cases in Multnomah County, prepared by Wayne L. Morse and Ronald H. Beattie. [Eugene, Or., Univ. of Or., 1932] xi, 227 p. tables. (Survey of the administration of criminal justice in Oregon. Report no. 1) IdU OrPR WaU **7089**

Morskoi Sbornik.

Materialy dlia istorii russkikh zaselenii po beragam Vostochnago okeana. Sankt-peterburg, V tipografii Morskago ministerstva, 1861. 4 v. in 1. fold. tables.
Trans. Materials for the history of Russian settlements on the shores of the Eastern ocean. WaU **7090**

Morton, Arthur Silver, 1870-1945.

David Thompson. Toronto, Ryerson [1930] 32 p. illus. (Canadian history readers) Or OrHi OrP WaS **7091**

A history of the Canadian West to 1870-71; being a history of Rupert's land (The Hudson's Bay Company's territory) and of the North-west Territory (including the Pacific slope). London, T. Nelson & Sons [1939] xiv, 987 p. 12 maps (part fold.) Many **7092**

The Northwest Company. Toronto, Ryerson, 1930. 32 p. (Canadian history readers) WaS **7093**

Sir George Simpson, overseas governor of the Hudson's Bay Company; a pen picture of a man of action. [Portland, Or.] Binfords & Mort [c1944] xii, 310 p. front., plates, ports. Many **7094**

Same. Toronto, Dent [c1944]

CV CVicAr CVU OrSaW OrU WaSp **7095**

Under western skies, being a series of pen-pictures of the Canadian West in early fur trade times. Toronto, T. Nelson & Sons [1937] 232 p. front., plates, port., facsim. CVicAr CVU WaS WaU **7096**

See also no. 6342.

Morton, James.

The Churchill tree; songs of war and peace. [Victoria, B. C., Diggon-Hibben, n.d.] 43 p. CVicAr **7097**

Heresies and other poems. [n.p., n.d.] 64 p. illus. CVicAr **7098**

Honest John Oliver; the life story of the honorable John Oliver, premier of British Columbia 1918-1927. London, Dent [1933] xi, 272 p. front., plates, ports. CVicAr CVU WaU **7099**

[**Morvillo, Anthony**]

A dictionary of the Numipu or Nez Perce language, by a missionary of the Society of Jesus, in the Rocky Mountains. Pt. 1. English-Nez Perce. [n.p.] St. Ignatius' Mission, 1895. x, 242 p. WaPS WaU **7100**

Grammatica linguae numipu, auctore presbytero missionario e Soc. Jesu in Montibus Saxonis. Desmet, Idaho, typis Puerorum indorum, 1891. iv, 255 p. fold. tables. WaU **7101**

Mose, Buckskin, see no. 8057.

Moseley, Henry Nottidge, 1844-1891.

Oregon; its resources, climate, people, and productions. London, E. Stanford, 1878. 125 p. front. (fold. map) Many **7102**

Oregon; reports on land in Benton County, visited in July 1877. London, E. Stanford, 1877. 50 p. fold. map. OrP **7103**

Moser, Charles, comp.

Reminiscences of the west coast of Vancouver Island, by Rev. Chas. Moser, O. S. B., Kakawis, B. C. [Victoria, B. C., Acme Press, c1926] 192 p. illus., port., table. Many **7104**

Moses, William Schuyler.

Address delivered before the fraternity of Free and Accepted Masons of Jacksonville, Oregon, June 24, 1859, by past master of Golden Gate Lodge no. 30, San Francisco, California. [Jacksonville, Or.? 1859?] [7] p. Or OrHi OrU **7105**

Mosessohn, Moses, 1884-

A guide to American citizenship, especially adapted for use in the states of Oregon, Washington, Idaho, and California. Official ed. Portland, Oregon, J. K. Gill, 1917. 89 p. Or OrP WaU **7106**

[**Moss, Sidney Walter**]

Prairie flower; or, Adventures in the far West. New ed. Cincinnati, U. P. James [1850] 120 p. Usually attributed to Emerson Bennett who had it published and wrote a sequel "Leni Leoti". See Washington Historical Quarterly, v. 19, no. 2, Apr. 1928, p. 155. OrHi **7106A**

Same. New York, Carleton, 1881. 464 p. OrHi OrP WaS WaU **7107**

Matt, Frank Luther, see no. 6046.

Mt. Angel, Or. St. Mary's Church.
Souvenir of dedication, St. Mary's Church, Mt. Angel, Or., Sunday, June 30, 1912. Mt. Angel, Or., Benedictine Press [1912] 78 p. illus., ports.   Or **7108**

Mount Angel College and Seminary, St Benedict, Or.
Silver jubilee, 1887-1912. [Mt. Angel, Or., 1912] 44 p. illus., ports.   WaU **7109**

Mount Vernon Argus.
50th anniversary edition. Mt. Vernon, Wash., 1941. [56] p. illus., ports. (Feb. 20, 1941)   WaS WaU **7110**
Progress edition, December 1920. Mt. Vernon, Wash., 1920. 60 p. illus. WaPS **7111**

Mount Vernon Herald.
Community builders' edition, Oct. 10, 1931. Mt. Vernon, Wash. [1931] 16 p. illus., ports., map.   WaU **7112**
Skagit County, Washington; a magazine edition pub. by the Mount Vernon Herald, being a frank, fair and accurate exposition, pictorially and otherwise of the resources, industries, farming and dairying possibilities of this wonderful section of the great Evergreen state. Mt. Vernon, Wash., Herald Pub. Co. [1921] 96 p. illus. (Part of regular ed. of Sept. 1, 1921)   WaS WaU **7113**

[Mountain, George Jehoshaphat] bp. of Quebec, 1789-1863.
The journal of the Bishop of Montreal during a visit to the Church Missionary Society's North-west America Mission, to which is added by the secretaries an appendix giving an account of the foundation of the mission and its progress up to the present time. London, Seeley, 1845. 236 p. illus., map. CV CVicAr OrHi **7114**
Same. 2d ed. 1849. lxxix, 166 p. front., 3 plates, fold. map.
     CVicAr WaS WaU **7115**
Songs of the wilderness; being a collection of poems, written in some different parts of the territory of the Hudson's Bay Company and in the wilds of Canada on the route to that territory in the spring and summer of 1844, interspersed with some illustrative notes. London, Rivington, 1846. xxviii, 153 p. front., 3 plates.   Many **7116**

The Mountaineers, Inc., Seattle, Wash.
Climbers' notebook. Seattle, 1941. 57 p. diagrs.   Wa **7117**
Local walks, instructions and suggestions; lodge rules. Seattle, 1915. 9 p. WaU **7118**
Mountaineers handbook; the techniques of mountain climbing. Seattle, Superior Pub. Co. [c1948] 160 p. illus.
     WaS WaU **7119**
The Mountaineers [objects of the organization] [Seattle, n.d.] [4] p.   WaU **7120**
The Mountaineers; to all who love the out-of-doors, greetings. Seattle [n.d.] 8 p.
     WaU **7121**
The spirit of the mountaineer. [Seattle, n. d.] 3 p.   WaU **7122**

Mountin, Joseph Walter, 1891-
Study of public health service, Seattle, Washington. Washington, D. C., 1932. 66 p. Study started by Dr. Paul Preble in 1929.   WaS **7123**

[Mounts, Eli]
Islands in the ocean of memory. [Whatcom, Wash., Boyer-Culver Printing and Binding Co., 1901] 257 p. front. (port.)
     WaU **7124**

Mourning Dove, Okinagan Indian, 1888-
Co-ge-we-a, the half-blood; a depiction of the great Montana cattle range, by Humishu-ma "Mourning Dove", given through Sho-pow-tan, with notes and biographical sketch by Lucullus Virgil McWhorter. Boston, Four Seas Co. [c1927] 302 p. front. (port.)   Many **7125**
Coyote stories, by Mourning Dove (Humishuma) ed. and illus. by Heister Dean Guie, with notes by L. V. McWhorter (Old Wolf) and a foreword by Chief Standing Bear. Caldwell, Idaho, Caxton, 1933. 228 p. front. (port.) illus., plates.   Many **7126**

Mowery, William Byron, 1899-
Forbidden valley. New York, Burt, c1933. 294 p. Northwest Canadian story.
     WaW **7127**

Mowry, William Augustus, 1829-1917.
Marcus Whitman and the early days of Oregon. NewYork, Silver Burdett [c1901] xv, 341 p. front., 6 plates, 2 maps (1 fold.)
     Many **7128**

Mozino Suarez de Figueroa, Jose Mariono, 1757-1819.
Noticias de Nutka, diccionario de la lengua de los Nutkeses, y Descripcion del volcan de Tuxtla; precedidos de una noticia acerca del br. Mozino y de la expedicion cientifica del siglo xviii, por Alberto M. Carreno. Mexico, Impr. de la Secretaria de fomento, 1913. cix, 117 p. facsims.
     CVicAr CVU WaS WaU **7129**

Mudge, Zachariah Atwell, 1813-1888.
Fur-clad adventurers; or, Travels in skin-canoes, on dog-sledges, on reindeer, and on snow-shoes, through Alaska, Kamchatka, and eastern Siberia. New York, Phillips & Hunt, 1880. 342 p. front., illus., plates.   WaS WaU **7130**
Missionary teacher; a memoir of Cyrus Shepard, embracing a brief sketch of the early history of the Oregon Mission. New York, Carlton [c1848] 221 p. front., illus.   OrHi OrSaW WaS WaWW **7131**
Sketches of mission life among the Indians of Oregon. New York, Carlton & Phillips, 1854. 229 p. front., 3 plates.
     MtU OrSaW WaPS **7132**

Mueller, F., composer.
Miss Spokane the beautiful; words by Jno. C. Garvin. [n.p., n.d.] 5 p. music.
     WaPS **7133**

Muller, Gerhard Friedrich, 1705-1783.
Voyages from Asia to America for completing the discoveries of the north west coast of America, trans. from the High Dutch of S. Muller with the addition of three new maps by Thomas Jefferys. London, Jefferys, 1761. xliii, 76 p. maps (part fold.)   Many **7134**

Same. To which is prefixed a summary of voyages made by the Russians on the Frozen Sea in search of a north east passage. 2d ed. 1764. viii, 120 p. 4 fold. maps. CVicAr WaS WaU **7135**

Muller, Hermann Gerhard.

Oregon und seine Zukunft; ein Beitrag zur Entwicklungsgeschichte des fernen Westens. Coln, E. H. Mayer, 1872. 42 p. OrHi OrP OrU WaU **7136**

Muench, Joyce Rockwood, ed.

West coast portrait. New York, Hastings House [1946] 168 p. front., illus., 4 double col. plates. Many **7137**

Muenscher, Walter Conrad Leopold, 1891-

The flora of Whatcom County, state of Washington; vascular plants. Ithaca, N. Y., 1941. 134 p. plates. Many **7138**

Muir, Gladdys Esther.

Settlement of the Brethren on the Pacific slope; a study in colonization, drawings by Freeman G. Muir, authorized by the Church of the Brethren of the District of Southern California and Arizona. Elgin, Ill., Brethren Pub. House, 1939. 469 p. illus., plates, ports., maps. Or **7139**

Muir, John, 1838-1914.

The cruise of the Corwin; journal of the Arctic expedition of 1881 in search of DeLong and the Jeannette ed. by William Frederic Bade. Boston, Houghton, 1917. xxxi, 278 p. front., plates, map. Many **7140**

Picturesque California and the region west of the Rocky Mountains from Alaska to Mexico. New York, Dewing [c1887-1888] 2 v. fronts., illus., plates. IdIf IdU WaS WaU **7141**

Same. c1888. 3 v. OrU WaS **7142**

Steep trails, ed. by William Frederic Bade. Boston, Houghton [c1918] ix, 390 p. front., 11 plates. Many **7143**

Stickeen. Boston, Houghton, 1909. 73 p. Alaska story. OrSaW WaU **7144**

Same. 1917, c1909. OrCS OrU WaS WaT **7145**

Travels in Alaska [prepared for pub. by Mrs. Marion Randall Parsons] Boston, Houghton, 1915. ix, 326 p. front., 11 plates. Many **7146**

Same. [1917] CVU **7147**

Same. [1930, c1915] 317 p. CV **7148**

See also nos. 1968, 1969.

Mulford, Ami Frank.

Fighting Indians in the 7th United States Cavalry, Custer's favorite regiment. 2d ed. Corning, N. Y., Paul Lindsler Mulford [n.d.] 155 p. MtHi **7149**

Mulgrave, Constantine John Phipps, 2d barron, 1744-1792.

The journal of a voyage undertaken by order of His present Majesty for making discoveries toward the North Pole in His Majesty's sloops Racehorse and Carcase. London, Newbery, 1774. xxviii, 118 p. front. (fold. map) fold. map. CVicAr **7150**

Reise nach dem Nordpol. Bern, Gesell-

schaft, 1777. 304 p. 6 fold. plates, 5 fold. maps. CVicAr **7151**

A voyage towards the North Pole undertaken by His Majesty's command, 1773. London, J. Nourse, 1774. viii, 253 p. front., fold. plates, fold. maps, fold. plan. CV CVU **7152**

Mullan, John, 1830-1909.

Miners and travelers' guide to Oregon, Washington, Idaho, Montana, Wyoming, and Colorado via the Missouri and Columbia Rivers, accompanied by a general map of the mineral region of the northern sections of the Rocky Mountains. New York, Wm. M. Franklin, 1865. 153 p. Many **7153**

Mulloy, William Thomas, 1917-

The Hagen site, a prehistoric village on the lower Yellowstone, with articles by Everett Olson and Richard Snodgrass. Missoula, Mont., Univ. of Mont., 1942. ix, 106 p. illus. (Publications in the social sciences no. 1) MtHi WaSp **7154**

Mulrine, Bernard.

Portland, the rose city; liquor dealers directory and general information. Portland, Or., 1910. [15] p. OrHi **7155**

Multnomah Civic Club, Portland, Or. Power Committee.

The development of Portland and the entire Northwest through transmission and distribution of Bonneville power; a report. 2d ed. [Portland, Or.?] 1936. 40 p. map. OrCS OrP WaPS **7156**

Transmission and distribution of Bonneville power, a report. Portland, Or. [1936] 20 p. map, diagrs. OrP **7157**

Multnomah County Jockey Club.

Rules and regulations. Portland, Or., McCormick, 1860. 12 p. OrHi **7158**

Multnomah Hotel, Portland, Or.

Beauty spots of Oregon, "The summer playground of America". [Portland, Or., Bushong & Co., 192—?] [36] p. illus., map. WaU **7159**

Same. [1922] [32] p. Or OrU **7160**

Multnomah Typographical Union, no. 58.

Constitution and by-laws. Portland, Or., 1883. 26 p. OrHi **7161**

Constitution, by-laws and scale of prices. Portland, Or., 1885. 64 p. OrHi **7161A**

Munday, Mrs. Luta.

A mounty's wife, being the life story of one attached to the force, but not of it. London, Sheldon Press [1930] 217 p. front,. plates, ports. CVicAr CVU WaE **7162**

Munday, Walter Alfred Don, 1888-

The unknown mountain. London, Hodder & Stoughton [1948] xx, 268 p. front., plates, ports., maps (1 old.) Mt. Waddington, B. C. CVicAr CVU **7163**

Munford, Kenneth, 1912?-

John Ledyard; an American Marco Polo: jacket and end sheets by Harold Price. Portland, Or., Binfords & Mort [c1939] 308 p. front. (map) Many **7164**

Mungar, Thornton Taft, 1883-

Practical applications of silviculture to

overmature stands now existing on the Pacific [address delivered at the 5th Pacific Science Congress, Vancouver, B. C., June 13, 1933] [n.p.] 1933 [8] p. OrP **7165**

Municipal League of Seattle.
Seattle Municipal Light and Power system; report on past record and projected future growth. [Seattle, 1935] 48 p. tables (1 fold.) diagrs.			WaU **7166**

— — — Unemployment Relief Committee.
The report; the administration of unemployment relief in King County. [Seattle] 1933. 7 p.			WaS WaU **7167**

— — — Utilities and Service Committee.
Logging operations in the Seattle watershed; a report. [Seattle] 1943. 1 v. map.
			WaS **7168**

Munro, Jonathan Alexander.
A review of the bird fauna of British Columbia, by J. A. Munro and I. M. Cowan. Victoria, B. C., B. C. Provincial Museum. Dept. of Education, 1947. 285 p. illus., maps. (Special publications, no. 2, Dec. 1947]
CV CVic CVicPr CVU WaS WaTC **7169**

Munro-Fraser, J. P., see no. 146, 148.

Munro, Kirk, 1850-1930.
The fur-seal's tooth; a story of Alaskan adventure. New York, Harper, 1894. 267 p. front., plates, map.			WaS **7170**
Snow-shoes and sledges; a sequel to "The fur-seal's tooth". New York, Harper, 1985. 271 p. front., 3 plates.
			OrMonO WaS **7171**
Same. c1895, 1923.			WaS WaT **7172**

Munson, Lyman E.
Montana as it was and as it is. New Haven, Yale Review, 1899. 23 p.			MtHi **7173**

Murakami, Naojiro, see no. 6300.

Murchie, R. W., see no. 2335.

Murdock, William David Clark.
Our true title to Oregon. Georgetown, Md., 1845. 12 p.			OrP **7174**

Murphy, Clyde F., 1899-
The glittering hill. New York, Dutton, 1944. 478 p. Butte, Mont., novel, 1st Lewis and Clark Northwest contest winner.
			Many **7175**
Same. Cleveland, World Pub. Co. [1945]
			WaU **7176**

Murphy, Mrs. Emily (Ferguson) 1868-1933.
Bishop Bompas. Toronto, Ryerson [n.d.] 30 p. illus. (Canadian history readers) Church of England missionary in B. C. and Alaska.			CV **7177**

Murphy, Harry Daniel, 1880-
Harry Murphy's legislative sketches. Portland, Or., Tower Studio [1905] [52] p.
			Or OrHi **7178**
Leading business men of Portland in cartoon. [Portland, Or., Irwin-Hodson, c1912] 78 plates. OrP OrU WaPS **7179**

Murphy, I. I.
Spokane, Washington, the queen of the Inland Empire. Chicago, Western Progress, c1902. 84 p. illus. (no. 17, Aug. 1902)
			WaSp **7180**

Murphy, Jerre C.
The comical history of Montana, a serious story for free people; being an account of the conquest of America's treasure state by alien corporate combine, the confiscation of its resources, the subjugation of its people, and the corruption of free government to the uses of lawless enterprise and organized greed employed in "big business". San Diego, Calif., E. L. Scofield, 1912. 332 p.
			MtHi MtU MtUM WaU **7181**

Murphy, John C.
Facts concerning the government Palouse project; an appeal to the people and to Congress for rights, for fair play, for irrigation, for electric power. [Pasco, Wash.? Pasco Express, 1912] 34 p. 4 plates.			WaPS WaS **7182**
Same. [n.p. Sagemoor, 1912]
			WaS WaU **7183**

Murphy, John Mortimer.
The Oregon handbook and emigrant's guide. Portland, Or., S. J. McCormick, 1873. 136 p. front., plates, table. OrP **7184**
Rambles in north-western America from the Pacific Ocean to the Rocky Mountains. London, Chapman, 1879. xxii, 364 p. fold. map.			Many **7185**
Sporting adventures in the far West. London, Low, 1879. xi, 404 p.
CV CVicAr IdU OrHi OrP WaSp **7186**
Same. New York, Harper, 1880. 469 p. front., illus., plates.
			WaS WaSp WaU WaWW **7187**

Murphy, Patrick Charles, 1883-
Behind gray walls, by Patrick C. Murphy (life prisoner in the Idaho State Penitentiary); introd. by Earl Wayland Bowman. [Caldwell, Idaho, Caxton, c1920] 83 p. front. (2 ports.) plate. WaU **7188**
Same. Rev. ed. [c1927] 120 p.
			IdB IdIf IdU WaPS WaSp **7189**
Shadow of the gallows. [Caldwell, Idaho, Caxton, c1928] 192 p. front., illus., 2 plates. IdIf IdU MtHi WaPS WaSp **7190**

Murphy, Ralph, see no. 8706.

Murphy, Thomas Dowler, 1866-
Oregon, the picturesque; a book of rambles in the Oregon country and in the wilds of northern California; descriptive sketches and pictures of Crater and Klamath Lakes, the Deschutes River Canyon, the new Columbia Highway, the Willamette and Rogue River Valleys and the cities and towns of Oregon; also of the little-known lakes, rivers, mountains, and vast forests of northern California, to which is added a trip to the Yosemite and to the Roosevelt Dam and the petrified forest of Arizona by motor car, with a map covering the country described and showing the author's route. Boston, Page, 1917. 317 p. col. front., 39 plates (15 col.) fold. map.
			Many **7191**

Murphy, Ulysses Grant, 1869-
The anti-Japanese agitation. 2d ed. rev. Seattle [1928] 16 p.			WaU **7192**

Murray, Alexander Hunter, 1818-1874.
Journal of the Yukon, 1847-1848, by A. H. Murry [!] [n.p.] 1848. 93 [11] p. illus., plan, tables.			WaU **7193**

Murray, Charles A., see no. 2074.

Murray, Cromwell, see no. 7006.

Murray, Mrs. Genevieve (Allen)
The true story of Marias Pass. [n.p.] 1929. 39, iv p. MtU **7194**

Murray, Hazen T., see no. 8352.

Murray, Mrs. Margaret L.
St. Mary's of Lillooet. [Lillooet, B. C., Bridge River-Lillooet News, 1935] [8] p. illus. CVicAr **7195**

Murray, T. B.
Kalli, the Esquimaux Christian; a memoir. New ed. London, Society for Promoting Christian Knowledge [n.d.] 72 p. front. (port.) illus. CVicAr **7196**

Murray, William Henry Harrison, 1840-1904.
Daylight land; the experiences, incidents, and adventures, humorous and otherwise, which befel Judge John Doe, tourist, of San Francisco; Mr. Cephas Pepperrell, capitalist of Boston; Colonel Goffe, the man from New Hampshire, and divers others, in their parlor-car excursion over prairie and mountain, all of which I saw, and one of whom I was. Boston, Cupples and Hurd, 1888. 338 p. front., illus., plates. British Columbia travel. CVicAr CVU WaU **7197**
Same. London, Chatto, 1888. CVicAr **7198**

Murry, A. H., see no. 7193.

Muth, William, see no. 4317.

M'Vickar, Archibald, see nos. 5895-5901.

Myall, William.
The scenic West; a travelogue. Boston, Stratford Co. [c1929] iv, 231 p. front., plates, diagr. WaW **7199**

Myers, C. V.
Oil to Alaska. [Edmonton, Alta., Provincial News Co., 1944?] 40 p. illus., map. WaU **7200**

Myers, Charles Ellsworth, 1866-
Memoirs of a hunter; a story of fifty-eight years of hunting and fishing. Davenport, Wash. [1948] 309 p. illus., ports. WaU **7201**

Myers, Harriet Williams.
Western birds. New York, Macmillan, 1922. xii, 391 p. front., plates.
OrCS OrSa OrU WaPS WaT WaWW **7202**
Same. 1923. IdU MtU Wa WaU **7203**

Myrick, J. Buckner, see no. 8090.

Myrtle Creek Mail.
Progress edition, 1947. Myrtle Creek, Or., 1947. [16] p. illus. (v. 42, no. 20, Sept. 25, 1947) WaU **7204**

N. N., see no. 5868.

Nanaimo Free Press.
Diamond jubilee edition. Nanaimo, B. C., 1934. 30 p. illus., ports. (No. 1 of 61st year, Apr. 16, 1934) WaU **7205**
Fiftieth anniversary number, 1924. Nanaimo, B. C., 1924. 52 p. illus. CV **7206**

Nansen, Fridtjof, 1861-1930.
"Farthest north," being the record of a voyage of exploration of the ship Fram, 1893-96, and of a 15 months' sleigh journey by Dr. Nansen and Lieut. Johansen; with an appendix by Otto Sverdrup. Westminster, Constable, 1897. 2 v. illus., plates (16 col.) ports., maps. table. OrCS OrHi **7207**
Same. New York, Harper, 1897.
CVicAr **7208**
Same. Popular ed. 1898. 679 p. front., illus., plates, ports., map. CVicAr **7209**

Napier, Edna (Marwick)
Library levity. Seattle, F. McCaffrey, c1946. [36] p. CVU WaS **7210**

Nash, Wallis.
Farm, ranch and range in Oregon. Salem, Or., Lewis and Clark Centennial Exposition Commission for the State of Oregon, 1904. 32 p. illus.
Or OrHi OrP WaU **7211**
A lawyer's life on two continents. Boston, Badger [c1919] 212 p. front., plates., ports. Many **7212**
Oregon; there and back in 1877. London, Macmillan, 1878. xviii, 285 p. front., illus., 10 plates, map. Many **7213**
Selected chapters from "The settler's handbook to Oregon," "The six districts of Oregon" and "The farm and its industries". Portland, Or., J. K. Gill, 1905. 157 p. WaS **7214**
The settler's handbook to Oregon. Portland, Or., J. K. Gill, 1904. 190 p.
Many **7215**
Two years in Oregon. New York, Appleton, c1881. 311 p. front., illus., 7 plates.
OrSa **7216**
Same. 2d ed. 1882 [c1881] Many **7217**

National American Woman Suffrage Association.
41st annual convention of the National American Woman Suffrage Association, Plymouth Church, Seattle, Washington, July 1 to 6, 1909. "Woman suffrage day" at the AYP exposition, Wednesday, July 7. [Seattle, 1909] 16 p.
WaU **7218**

National Association of Letter Carriers, Seattle Branch no. 79.
Seattle letter carriers souvenir. Seattle, [1901] [78] p. ports. WaU **7219**

National Congress of Parents and Teachers. Washington State Branch.
Parent-teacher associations; how to organize them, uniform constitutions, aims and purposes, program outlines. [Yakima, Wash., 1920] 19 p. WaPS **7220**

National Council for Protection of Roadside Beauty.
The roadsides of Oregon, a survey. [Washington, D. C., American Nature Assn. of Washington, D. C., 1932] 34 p. illus. Many **7221**

National Custer Memorial Association.
The Custer semi-centennial commemoration 1876-June 25, 26, 1926; official report by E. S. Godfrey, and "The burial of the hatchet" at the crypt of the unknown soldier near Garryowen, Mon-

tana, June 26, 1876. Casper, Wyo., 1926. 19 p. illus., ports.   MtHi **7222**

National Education Association for Women.
Washington Alumnae Chapter.
Women of the Pacific Northwest; a study of their status today; their emotional adjustment and their thinking on the post-war period. Seattle, Pi Lambda Theta, 1945. 50 p. tables.
WaT **7223**

National Education Association of the United States.
Official program, sixty-fifth annual meeting, Seattle, Washington, July 3 to July 8, 1927. [Seattle, 1927] 63 p.   WaU **7224**

— — — **Washington State Council.**
From our singing sisters of the Sound. [Seattle?] 1927. [8] p.   WaPS **7225**

National Marine Engineers Beneficial Association. No. 38, Seattle, Wash.
Souvenir manual and directory of members, 1900. Seattle [1900?] 118 p.
WaU **7226**

National Probation Association.
The juvenile court and related agencies in Yakima, 1947; report of a survey by Milton G. Rector. New York [1947] 40 p.   WaU **7227**

The juvenile court of Multnomah County, Oregon; report of a survey by Marjorie Bell. [n.p.] 1930. 43 p.   OrP **7228**

Juvenile detention in Multnomah County (Portland) Oregon; report of a study [by] John Schapps. Portland, Or., 1946. 30 p. diagrs., table.   OrP **7229**

National Publishing Company, Seattle, Wash.
Greater Seattle illustrated; the most progressive metropolis of the twentieth Century. [Seattle, 1907?] 239 p. front., illus., ports.   CVicAr WaU **7230**

Seattle of today, illustrated; the metropolis of the Pacific Coast, the gateway to Alaska and the Orient, the most progressive city of the twentieth Century. [Seattle, 1907?] 231 p. front., illus., ports.
CVicAr WaU **7231**

National Safety Council.
Analysis of national traffic safety contest; report [on Portland, Or.] Chicago [1947] 34 p.   OrP **7232**

National Tuberculosis Association.
A study of the health of Indians on the Klamath Reservation in Oregon. New York [1929] 39 p.   Or WaU **7233**

Native Daughters of Oregon. Grand Cabin.
Constitution and laws of the Grand Cabin . . . and constitution for subordinate cabins. Portland, Or., W. A. Wheeler, 1899. [64] p.   OrHi **7233A**

Ritual, Portland, Or., Wheeler [n.d.] 42 p.   OrHi **7233B**

A native son, see no. 884.

Native Sons of British Columbia.
Romance of Vancouver, being a review of the development of Canada's western gateway from the first coming of the white man: destroyed by fire in 1886—Canada's third city in 1926. [Van-

couver, B. C., 1926] 60 p. illus., ports.
CV CVicAr WAS WaU **7234**

— — — **Post no. 2, Vancouver.**
Romance of Vancouver; jubilee number. [Vancouver, B. C.] 1936. 1 v.
CVicAr CVU **7235**

Native Sons of Oregon, Abernethy's Cabin no. 1.
Constitution and by-laws. [Portland, Or., Union Printing Co., n.d.] 56 p. Or **7236**

— — — Grand Cabin.
Constitution and laws of the Grand Cabin, and constitution for subordinate cabins. Portland, Or., Irwin-Hodson, 1898. 74 p.
OrHi OrP WaPS **7237**

Same. Portland, Or., W. A. Wheeler, 1899. 64 p.   Or OrHi **7238**

Native Sons of Oregon ritual. Portland, Or., W. A. Wheeler [n.d.] 62 p. Or **7239**

Native Sons of Washington.
Constitution, regulations, funeral ceremonies, memorial camp ceremonies, penal code, rules and duties of officers. Port Townsend, Wash., Call Printing Office, 1899. 32 p.   Wa WaPS **7240**

Natural History Society of British Columbia.
Revised constitution and list of members. Victoria, B. C., Colonist, 1900-1913. 2 v.
CVicAr **7241**

Nature's fury; the inside story of the disastrous British Columbia floods of 1948, comp. from the works of newspapermen. [Vancouver, B. C., South Hill] 1948. 62 p. illus., ports., map.   CVicAr **7242**

Navarette, Martin Fernandez de, 1765-1844.
Noticia historica de las expediciones hechas por los Espanoles en busca del paso del noroeste de la America, para serir de introduccion a la relacion del viage executado en 1792 por las goletas Sutil y Mexicana con el objeto de reconocer el estrecho de Fuca. Madrid, Imprenta Real, 1802. 168 p.   CVicAr **7243**

The Navy Family Magazine.
Seattle issue. Whittier, Calif., 1944. 31 p. illus. (v. 6, no. 10, Mar. 1944) WaS **7244**

Neale, John Dwight.
Credit and its influence on irrigation development; an address delivered before the annual convention of the Oregon Irrigation Congress. San Francisco, J. R. Mason & Co., 1925. 32 p. front., illus.
WaPS WaS **7245**

Necessity for the construction of the Lake Washington Canal. [Seattle, n.d.] 15 p.
WaU **7246**

Neff, Johnson Andrew.
A study of the economic status of the common woodpeckers in relation to Oregon horticulture. Rev. and pub. May 1, 1928. Marionville, Mo., Free Press, 1928. viii, 68 p. front., illus., diagrs.
Or OrCS **7247**

Neihardt, John Gneisenau, 1881-
The river and I. New York, Putnam, 1910. ix, 325 p. front., plates. Yellowstone and Missouri Rivers.
MtHi OrP OrU WaSp **7248**

The song of Hugh Glass. New York, Macmillan, 1915. ix, 126 p. Narrative poem of fur trade. Many 7249

Same. With notes by Julius T. House. 1919. xviii, 181 p. Wa WaPS WaT 7250

The song of Jed Smith. New York, Macmillan, 1941. 113 p.
Or OrP WaS WaSp WaT WaU 7251

Song of the Indian wars. New York, Macmillan, 1926. 231 p. illus.
CVU IdIf IdU 7252

Same. 1928 [c1926] 300 p. illus., maps. (Modern readers' series) WaTC WaU 7253

The song of the Messiah. New York, Macmillan, 1935. 110 p. Final narrative poem of "Cycle of the West".
MtU OrP WaSp WaT WaU 7254

The song of three friends. New York, Macmillan, 1925 [c1919] xv, 126 p.
WaU 7255

The splendid wayfaring; the story of the exploits and adventures of Jedediah Smith and his comrades, the Ashley-Henry men, discoverers and explorers of the great central route from the Missouri River to the Pacific Ocean, 1822-1831. New York, Macmillan, c1920. ix, 290 p. front., illus., plates, ports., maps (1 fold.) facsims. Many 7256

Same. 1924. WaE 7257

Neill, Judge Thomas.
Incidents in the early history of Pullman and the State College of Washington. Pullman, Wash., Pullman Herald, 1922. [15] p. illus. WaPS 7258

Nelson, Andres Winters. 1883-
Those who came first, being a varied collection of sketches dealing with historical facts and legendary fantasies relating to northeast Oregon, drawings by Lucile Stuart, block carvings by Don Poarch. LaGrande, Or., Nelson Press, 1934. 79 p. illus. Many 7259

Nelson, Charles F.
Slocan the beautiful. New Denver, B. C. [n.d.] 4 p. 20 plates. CVicAr IdU 7260

Nelson, Denys, 1876-1929.
Fort Langley, 1827-1927, a century of settlement in the valley of the lower Fraser River. [Vancouver, B. C., Evans & Hastings] 1927. 31 p. illus., ports. Many 7261

Nelson, Edward William, see no. 9858.

Nelson, Frederick, 1871-
Beyond the horizon. [Tacoma] c1930. 292 p.
WaPS WaTC 7262

Nelson, Ira Stephens, 1912-
On Sarpy Creek. Boston, Little, 1938. 298 p. Montana novel.
IdU Or OrP WaE WaS WaU 7263

Nelson, Joseph.
Direct route through the North-West Territories of Canada to the Pacific Ocean; proposed Hudson's Bay and Pacific Railway and new steamship route. London, H. Little & Son, 1894. 78 p. fold. map.
CVU 7264

The Hudson's Bay Company; what is it? London, Baily, 1864. 81 p. CVicAr 7265

Proposed Hudson's Bay and Pacific Railway and New Steamship Route. [London, Economic Printing and Pub. Co., 1893] 84 p. fold. map. CVicAr 7266

Nelson, Lucy M.
A brief history of Camas Prairie, Idaho. Caldwell, Idaho, Caxton, 1937. 1119 p. front., plates. IdB IdU WaU 7267

Nelson, Mrs. Rhoda Louise (Smith) 1891-
High timber, illus. by Mildred Boyle. New York, Crowell [1941] 280 p. illus., plates.
Or Wa WaS WaU 7268

Monday, Tuesday, Wednseday, of a time when the Northwest was young and of how people came to live there, illus. by the author. Portland, Or., Binfords & Mort [c1938] 256 p. front., illus., plates.
Many 7269

Wagon trail west, illus. by Elinore Blaisdell. New York, Crowell, 1939. 224 p. col. front., illus., plates (part col.)
WaS WaT WaU 7270

Nelson, B. C. merchants.
Poplar Creek goldfields (B. C.) the latest mining sensation. Nelson, B. C. [n.d.] 40 p. illus. CVicAr 7271

[Nesbitt, James Knight].
A message to the people of St. John's Church, Victoria, B. C. [Victoria, B. C., Diggon-Hibben, 1946] [9] p. illus.
CVicAr 7272

Nessly, J. E., pub.
Whitman County, Washington; greatest grain producing county in the world and its principal towns. Rosalia, Wash., 1893. 27 p. WaPS 7273

Netted gems of verse. [n.p.] Idaho Writer's League [1946] 64 p. IdB 7274

[Nettleton, Lulie].
With the "Mountaineers" in Glacier National Park; walking tours book. [St. Paul, Great Northern Railway Co., 1915] [56] p. illus. WaU 7275

Neuberger, Richard Lewis, 1912-
Our promised land. New York, Macmillan, 1938. xiv, 398 p. map. Many 7276

Neuman, Daniel S., see no. 8676.

Neville, Edith, pseud.
The smugglers; a story of Puget Sound. [n.p., n.d.] 265 p. Supposed author is Frank Stevens of Port Townsend, Wash.
WaS WaSp WaU 7277

Nevin, Evelyn C.
The lost children of the Shoshones, illus. by Manning De V. Lee. Philadelphia, Westminster Press [1946] 123 p. col. front., col. illus., col. plates. Many 7278

Nevin, Robert Peebles.
Black-robes, or sketches of missions and ministers in the wilderness and on the border. Philadelphia, Lippincott, 1872. 1 v. MtU OrP 7279

Nevins, Allan, 1890-
Fremont, pathmarker of the West. New York, Appleton, Century, 1939. xiv, 649 p. front., illus., plates, ports, maps.
Many 7280

Fremont, the West's greatest adventurer; being a biography from certain hither-

to unpublished sources of General John C. Fremont, together with his wife, Jessie Benton Fremont, and some account of the period of expansion which found a brilliant leader in the Pathfinder. New York, Harper, 1928. 2 v. fronts., plates, ports., maps (1 double) facsims.
Many 7281

The new Christ Church Cathedral, Victoria, B. C. [Victoria, B. C.? n.d] [8] p. illus.
CVicAr 7282

New Denver Elementary School, New Denver, B. C.
New Denver, eldorado of the past. [Rossland, B. C., The Miner, 1944?] 1 v. illus.
CVicAr 7283

New England and Oregon Mining Co.
The New England and Oregon Mining Company, incorporated March 22, 1880; six mines consolidated; location, Rye Valley, Baker County, Oregon; principal office: White's Opera House, Concord, N. H. [Concord, N. H.] Republican Press Assn., 1880. 23 p. illus.
Or 7284

A New Englander, see nos. 8923, 8924.

New Spain and the Anglo-American West; historical contributions presented to Herbert Eugene Bolton "a documentary collection". [Los Angeles, 1932] 2 v. front. (port.)
Many 7285

The new West extending from the Great Lakes across plains and mountains to the golden shores of the Pacific. Winnipeg, Canadian Historical Pub. Co., 1888. 205 p. front. (ports.) illus., 43 plates, 3 fold. maps.
CVicAr CVU 7286

[New Westminster, B. C.]
Souvenir, New Westminster Bridge, official opening July 23, 1904. [n.p., 1904] [9] p. 4 plates.
CVicAr WaU 7287

A souvenir of the visit of their majesties King George VI and Queen Elizabeth to New Westminster, British Columbia 1939. [New Westminster, B. C., 1939?] 12 p. ports., map, facsims., geneal. table.
WaU 7288

New York Evening Post.
Last blazes on the Oregon Trail; aged pioneer retraced his march of fifty-four years before; Ezra Meeker's journey from Puyallup to his Indiana home. [New York] 1907. 6 p. illus., ports.
OrP 7289

Newberg Enterprise, Newberg, Or.
Progress edition, October 11, 1912. Newberg, Or., 1912. 32 p. illus. WaWW 7290

Newberg Graphic, Newberg, Or.
Fiftieth anniversary progress edition, April 1939. Newberg, Or., Dimond & Cady, 1939. 1 v. illus., ports.
OrHi OrP 7291

Souvenir edition 1805-1905, centennial of old Oregon. [Newberg, Or.] 1905. 48 p. illus., ports.   Or OrHi OrP OrU 7292

Newcastle, Henry Fiennes Pelham Clinton, 5th Duke of.
Correspondence respecting certain officials in the colonies of British Columbia and Vancouver Island. London, West, 1863. 11 p.   CVicAr 7293

Newcombe, Charles Frederic, 1851-
Petroglyphs in British Columbia. Victoria, B. C. Margison Bros., 1907. [10] p. 5 plates.   Many 7294

The sea-lion question in British Columbia; report by Dr. Charles F. Newcombe, Wm. Hamar Greenwood, and Dr. C. McLean Fraser. Ottawa, J. de L. Tache, 1918. 39 p. plates, maps. (Contributions to Canadian biology)   CVU 7295

Newcomers Service, Seattle, Wash.
Helpful information for Seattle's new citizens. [Seattle c1936] 68 p. illus. WaS 7296
Same. c1939. 70 p.   WaS 7297
Same. Seattle, R. J. Cox & J. L. Arnold, 1948. 38 p.   WaS 7298

Newell, Bernice E.
The mountain, illus. by Dr. F. W. Southworth. Tacoma, Spike [n.d.] 1 v. 5 plates.
MtHi 7299

Newhem; an opportunity in land. [Portland, Or., Yamhill Orchard Land Co., n.d.] [16] p. illus., map.   OrP 7300

Newman, Mrs. Mary Wentworth, ed.
Poetry of the Pacific; selections and original poems from the poets of the Pacific states. San Francisco, Pacific Pub. Co., 1867. 415 p.
CVicAr OrCS OrHi OrU WaS WaU 7301

Newspaper Cartoonists' Association of British Columbia.
British Columbians as we see 'em, 1910 and 1911. [Vancouver, B. C., 1911?] 1 v.
CVU 7302

Newton, Harry L.
Hiram Birdseed at the Lewis and Clark Centennial Exposition; the funniest book of its kind ever written. New York, Rossiter [c1904] 130 p. illus.
Or OrP OrU WaU 7303

Niblett, Mollie Glen, see nos. 9842-9844.

Nichols, Jeannette (Paddock) 1890-
Alaska, a history of its administration, exploitation, and industrial development during its first half century under the rule of the United States. Cleveland, A. H. Clark Co. [c1923] 456 p. front., port., map.   CVic IdU WaE 7304
Same. 1924.   Many 7305

Nichols, Mrs. Marie Leona (Hobbs) 1880-
Joab Powell; homespun missionary. Portland, Or., Metropolitan, 1935. 116 p. front., port.   Many 7306

The mantle of Elias; the story of Fathers Blanchet and Demers in early Oregon. Portland, Or., Binfords & Mort [c1941] 337 p. front. (ports.)   Many 7307

Ranald MacDonald, adventurer, woodcuts by William J. C. Klamm and photostats from the Provincial Library collection of Victoria, B. C. Caldwell, Idaho, Caxton, 1940. 176 p. front., plates, ports., plans, facsims.   Many 7308

Nichols, Walter Hammond, 1866-
Cowboy Hugh; the oydssey [!] of a boy. New York, Macmillan, 1927. 284 p. front., plates. Idaho and Utah story.
IdIf IdU WaS WaU 7309

Nick, Uncle, see nos. 11088-11091.

Nickerson, Delmore E.
Report on the forty-second biennial legislative session of Oregon, 1943, with a brief review of restrictive legislation introduced or adopted in other states, submitted to the members of all A. F. of L. unions in Oregon. [n.p.] Oregon State Federation of Labor [1943] 32 p.
OrP **7310**

Nicol, Nina, see no. 3170.

Nicolay, Charles Grenfell.
The Oregon Territory; a geographical and physical account of the country and its inhabitants, with outlines of its history and discovery. London, Charles Knight and Co., 1846. 226 p. illus., fold. map.
Many **7311**

Same. 2d ed. London, Hodson and Son, 1860. 237 p. front., map. CVicAr CVU **7312**

Same. London, Renny, 1886. viii, 157 p. front., 2 maps. CVicAr **7313**

A proposal to establish a missionary college on the north-west coast of British America in a letter to William Ewart Gladstone. London, Saunders, 1853. 28 p.
CVicAr MtU WaS **7314**

Niederkorn, Mrs. Barbara.
Betty, a pioneer of Idaho. [Idaho Falls, Idaho, Scott, 1929] 35 p. Autobiographical. IdIf **7315**

Niedieck, Paul.
Cruises in the Bering Sea; being records of further sport and travel, trans. from the original German by R. A. Ploetz. London, Ward, 1909. xv, 252 p. front. (port.) 56 illus., 72 plates, fold. map. Many **7316**

Mes croisieres dans la mer de Behring; nouvelles chasses et nouveaux voyages, tr. de l'allemand par L. Roustan. Paris, Plon-Nourrit, 1908. ii, 296 p. front. (port.) illus., plates, fold. map.
CVicAr WaU **7317**

Nielsen, Andre S., see no. 1074.

[Niesz, Whittlesey & Co., Searchers of Titles, Seattle, Wash.]
Statement of title to Syndicate Addition, Terry's Fourth Addition and Terry's Fifth Addition to the city of Seattle. Seattle, B. B. Dearborn, 1888, 20 p.
WaU **7318**

Night in Seattle. New York, Newcomb Pub. Co., c1913. 15 plates. WaS **7319**

Nika Tikegh Chikamin, see no. 9376.

Nimmo, Edward.
Advantages of Oregon, giving information concerning the state and its resources. Portland, Or. [c1913?] 215 p. tables.
OrHi OrP **7320**

Oregon free government land for you; 320 or 160 acres; advantages of Oregon. Portland, Or. [c1911] 100 p.
WaSp WaWW **7321**

Niven, Frederick John, 1878-1944.
Canada west, illus. by John Innes. London, Dent [1930] xi, 188 p. front., illus., plates. (Outward bound library)
CV CVic CVicAr CVU WaSp **7322**

The lost cabin mine. New York, Lane, 1909 [1908] viii, 312 p. WaPS WaSp **7323**

The transplanted. Toronto, Collins [1944] 310 p. CV CVicAr **7324**

Wild honey. New York, Dodd, 1927. 251 p. B. C. setting. IdU OrCS WaS WaT **7325**

Same. Toronto, Macmillan, 1927.
CVicAr **7326**

See also no. 8104.

Nixon, Oliver Woodson, 1825-1905.
How Marcus Whitman saved Oregon; a true romance of patriotic heroism, Christian devotion and final martyrdom, with sketches of life on the plains and mountains in pioneer days, introd. by Rev. Frank W. Gunsaulus. Chicago, Star Pub. Co., 1895. 339 p. front., illus., 7 plates, 8 ports., fold. map. Many **7327**

Same. 5th ed. 1896 [c1895]
OrHi Wa WaSp **7328**

Same. 6th ed. OrSaW **7329**
Whitman's ride through savage lands, with sketches of Indian life, introd. by James G. K. McClure. [Chicago] Winona Pub. Co., 1905. 186 p. front., 12 plates, 4 ports.
Many **7330**

Nobile, Umberto, 1885-
With the "Italia" to the North Pole; English trans. by Frank Fleetwood. London, G. Allen & Unwin [1930] 358 p. front., plates, port., 2 fold. maps. CVicAr **7331**

Noel, Jacqueline, see no. 10755.

Noel, Norman P. R.
Blanket-stiff; or, A wanderer in Canada, 1911. London, St. Catherine Press, 1912. viii, 190 p. front. (port.) British Columbia setting. CVic **7332**

Nome Daily Gold Digger, Nome, Alaska.
Mining edition. Nome, Alaska, S. S. Stevens, pub., 1908. 28 p. WaS **7333**

Noonan, Dominic A.
Alaska, the land of now. Seattle [Sherman Printing Co.] 1921. 134 p. front. Poems. WaPS WaU **7334**

Norcross, J. Edward, see no. 2219.

Nord, Sverre.
A logger's odyssey. Caldwell, Idaho, Caxton, 1943. 255 p. front. (port.)
OrHi WaE WaPS WaT WaU **7335**

Le Nord-Ouest Canadien. [n.p., n.d.] 31 p.
CVicAr **7336**

Nordeen, John.
Genom Skrallboms glasogon. Seattle, Publications Press, c1946. 255 p. WaS **7337**

Svenska klubbens historia, 1892-1944. Seattle, Washington. Seattle, Consolidated Press, 1944. 176 p. illus. WaS **7338**

Nordenskiold, A. E., see no. 10615.

Nordhoff, Charles, 1830-1901.
Northern California, Oregon, and the Sandwich Islands. New York, Harper, 1874. 256 p. front., illus., ports., maps.
Many **7339**

Same. 1875. OrHi **7340**
Same. 1877. OrU WaU **7341**
Norling, Ernest, see nos. 7342-7348.

Norling, Josephine (Stearns) 1895-
Pogo's farm adventure, a story of soil, by Jo and Ernest Norling. New York, Holt [1948] 46 p. Seattle authors.
Or WaS WaU **7342**

Pogo's fishing trip, a story of salmon, by Jo and Ernest Norling. New York, Holt [1942] 40 p. illus.
OrPR Wa WaS WaU **7343**

Pogo's house, the story of lumber, by Jo and Ernest Norling. New York, Holt [1941] 42 p. illus.
Or Orp WaS WaSp WaU **7344**

Pogo's lamb, a story of wool, by Jo and Ernest Norling. New York, Holt [1947] 44 p. illus. OrP WaS WaU **7345**

Pogo's letter, a story of paper, by Jo and Ernest Norling. New York, Holt [1946] 42 p. illus. Many **7346**

Pogo's sky ride, a story of airplanes, by Jo and Ernest Norling. New York, Holt [1943] 44 p. illus.
Or OrP Wa WaS WaSp WaU **7347**

Pogo's train ride, a story of freight trains, by Jo and Ernest Norling. New York, Holt [1944] 40 p. illus.
Or OrP Wa WaS WaSp WaU **7348**

Norman, R. O., see no. 1484.

Norris, Frank, 1870-1902.
A deal in wheat and other stories of the new and old West, illus. by Remington, Leyendecker, Hitchcock and Hooper. New York, Doubleday, Page, 1903. 272 p. front., 3 plates. IdU WaS WaU **7349**

Norris, Luther ("Doc") see no. 10993.

Norris, Philetus W., 1821-1885.
The calumet of the Coteau and other poetical legends of the border; also, a glossary of Indian names, words and western provincialisms together with a guide-book of the Yellowstone National Park. Philadelphia, Lippincott, 1883. 275 p. front., 7 plates, 3 maps.
MtBozC MtHi **7350**
Same. 1884. WaSp WaU **7351**

North American Industrial Review, comp.
Montana, the most productive ore center of the intermountain region. Butte, Mont. [191—] 214 p. front., illus., 22 plates. MtHi **7352**

North American Transportation and Trading Company.
Alaska and the gold fields of Nome, Golovin Bay, Forty Mile, the Klondike, and other districts. Chicago [1900?] 136 p.
WaS WaSp WaU **7353**
Alaska and the gold fields of Nome, Port Clarence, Golovin Bay, Kougarok, the Klondike and other districts. [Seattle, 1900] 168 p. illus. WaU **7354**
Alaska and the gold fields of the Yukon, Koyukuk, Tanana, Klondike and their tributaries. [Seattle, 1900?] 117 p.
WaU **7355**

North Beach, Washington; a stretch of alluring seashore, the summer playground of the Northwest. [n.p.] 1923. 12 p. illus., map, tables. WaPS **7356**

North British & Mercantile Insurance Company.
The Golden West; an historical sketch of the states and territories of the Pacific slope. New York, 1911. 61 p.
IdB OrHi WaSp **7357**

The north Pacific, a true exhibit of Wash-ington Territory in 1880; the field for capital, the home for laborers. New Tacoma, Wash., Money & Co., 1880. 88 p. OrHi WaU **7358**

North Pacific Association of Amateur Oarsmen.
Souvenir programme of the 28th annual regatta; North Pacific Association of Amateur Oarsmen of Port Moody, B. C., Friday and Saturday, July 18, 19, 1924. [n.p., 1924?] 15 p. illus. CV **7359**

North Pacific Coast Indian War Veterans.
Constitution and by-laws. Portland, Or., Steel, 1890. [16] p. OrHi **7360**
Constitution and by-laws of Multnomah Camp no. 2. [n. p.] 1890. 10 p. OrHi **7361**
Memorial to Congress [review of the origin and cause of the Indian war in Oregon and Washington Territory, 1855-56] Salem, Or., Moores, 1886. 15 p.
OrHi **7362**
Same. 1895. 18 p. OrHi **7363**
Roster of Multnomah Camp no. 2, November 15, 1892. Portland, Or., Anderson, 1892. [6] p. OrHi **7364**

North Pacific Industrial Association.
Catalogue of the first annual exposition of the North Pacific Industrial Association of Portland, Sept. 26 to Oct. 26, 1889. Portland, Or., D. F. Riegle, 1889. 1 v. illus. OrP **7365**

North Pacific Publishing Company.
North Pacific almanac; information relating to Oregon, Washington, Idaho, Alaska and British Columbia. Portland, Or., 1890. 1 v. OrHi **7366**
North Pacific almanac and statistical handbook for 1890, containing valuable information about Oregon, Washington, Idaho, Alaska, and British Columbia. 2d ed. Portland, Or., Steel, 1890. 224 p. tables. Or OrP WaWW **7367**
Same. 3d ed. OrHi **7368**

Northern Baptist Convention, 2d. Portland, Or.
Annual, containing the proceedings of the second meeting held at Portland, Oregon, June 25 to July 2, 1909. Philadelphia, American Baptist Pub. Society, 1909. 204 [8] p. illus., tables.
OrHi OrP **7369**

Northern Life Insurance Company.
Silver anniversary, 1906-1931. [Seattle, 1931] 15 p, illus., ports. (Northern Light July 1931) WaU **7370**

Northern Pacific Railroad Company.
Across the continent via the Northern Pacific from the Lakes & Mississippi River to the Pacific, Columbia River, Puget Sound & Alaska. St. Paul, W. C. Riley [1890?] [30] p. Wa **7371**
Alaska. [St. Paul, 19—?] 31 p. illus.
WaPS **7372**
The Alaska-Yukon-Pacific exposition, Seattle, June 1-October 16, 1909. St. Paul [1909] 45 p. illus., map.
CVicAr IdB WaS WaT WaU **7373**
All about fruit and hop raising, dairying and general farming, lumbering, fishing

and mining in western Washington. [n. p., 1905?] 39 p. illus. WaSp 7374

All about the grain, fruit and stock lands of eastern Washington and northern Idaho. St. Paul [1899?] 31 p. illus. WaU 7375

Along the scenic highway. [n.p., n.d.] 131 p. illus., maps. MtHi OrP 7376

Same. 96 p. OrP 7377

A bit of northwestern history; early history of the territory traversed by the Northern Pacific Railway, route of Marechal Foch's special train. [n.p., n.d.] 1 v. MtHi WaT 7378

Central Oregon. [n.p., 1911?] 47 p. illus., maps. OrHi OrP WaPS 7379

The charter and amendments; the general mortgage on railroad and land grant and copy of first mortgage bond. [Philadelphia] Jay Cooke & Co. [1870?] 29 p. illus. MtHi WaT WaU 7380

The climate, soil and resources of the Yellowstone Valley, with accurate maps of the Yellowstone country and a plat and description of the town of Glendive. St. Paul, Pioneer Press, 1882. 100 p. 2 fold. maps. MtHi 7381

Communications in reply to a committee of citizens of the Northwest. [Hartford, Case, 1867] 16 p. WaU 7382

A concise description of the climate, soil, grazing lands, agricultural and mineral productions tributary to the Northern Pacific Railroad. Helena, Mont., Fisk Bros., 1882. 16 p. MtHi 7383

Dude ranch vacations. [St. Paul, 1938] 15 p. illus., map. WaPS 7384

Eastern Washington and northern Idaho. [n.p.] 1910. 54 p. illus., fold. map. WaSp 7385

Same. A description of the conditions and opportunities as they exist for the homeseeker and investor in this land of fortune. 3d ed. St. Paul [1911] 55 p. illus., map. WaPS 7386

The fertile and beautiful Palouse country in eastern Wash. St. Paul, Northwest Magazine, 1889. 32 p. WaWW 7387

The Flathead country, Montana, 1922. [n.p., n.d.] 31 p. illus. OrP 7388

General first mortgage, January 1, 1881. [n.p.] 1881. 46 p. MtHi 7389

Irrigation in Montana. [n.p., 1905?] 28 p. MtU 7390

[Kittitas County and Valley. n.p., n.d.] 31 p. illus., maps. OrP WaPS 7391

Last spike ceremonies; program of exercises. Portland, Or., Himes, 1883. [13] p. OrHi WaU 7392

National forest vacations in the American Rockies. [St. Paul, 1926?] 31 p. illus., maps (1 fold.) MtU 7393

North Pacific coast resorts. [St. Paul] 1909. 79 p. front., illus., fold. map. OrP WaPS 7394

Northern Pacific Coast vacation land in northern Idaho, Oregon, Washington.

[Chicago, n.d.] 31 p. front., illus., maps. OrP WaT 7395

Same [and] British Columbia. [St. Paul? 1930?] WaPS 7396

The Northern Pacific Railroad; its route, resources, progress and business; the new Northwest and its great thoroughfare. [Philadelphia] Jay Cooke & Co. [1871] 48 p. map. Many 7397

The Northern Pacific Railroad's land grant and the future business of the road. [Philadephia?] Jay Cooke and Co. [1870?] 28 p. CVicAr MtHi MtU WaU WaWW 7398

Official guide for the use of tourists and travelers over the lines of the Northern Pacific Railroad and its branches, embracing facts relating to the history, resources, population, industries, products and natural features of the great Northwest. St. Paul, Riley [c1897] 442 p. front., illus. WaS 7399

Same. c1891. 439 p. OrP WaPS 7400

The official Northern Pacific Railway guide for the use of tourists and travelers over the lines of the Northern Pacific Railway and its branches. St. Paul, Riley, c1899. 442 p. illus. WaT 7401

Opening excursion; list of guests. Portland, Or., Himes, 1883. 20 p. OrHi 7402

Opportunities; openings for business locations on the line of the Northern Pacific Railway. [n.p., n.d.] 78 p. WaS 7403

Same. St. Paul [1903] 78 p. illus. WaU 7404

Same. [1910] 109 p. WaPS 7405

Opportunities along the scenic highway through the land of fortune. [St. Paul] 1911. 149 p. illus. WaU 7406

Same. 1915. 112 p. WaU 7407

Oregon. [St. Paul, 1938?] 36 p. front. (map) illus., maps, diagrs. WaPS 7408

Oregon for the farmer. [St. Paul, 192—] 62 p. illus., maps. IdUSB 7409

Same. 1923. Or OrP 7410

Same. [1927?] OrP 7411

Oregon for the homeseeker. [St. Paul, n.d.] 31 p. illus., map, tables. OrP 7412

Same. Columbia Valley, Willamette Valley & western Oregon. [n.p., n.d.] 39 p. WaPS 7413

Over the scenic highway through the land of fortune. [St. Paul, 1912?] 72 p. illus., map. WaU 7414

The Pacific Northwest, a guide for settlers and travelers, Oregon and Washington Territory. New York, 1882. 81 p. map. WaU 7415

The Pacific Northwest; information for settlers and others, Oregon and Washington Territory. New York, 1883. 32 p. maps. Or 7416

Portland and the Columbia River. [St. Paul, 1918?] [24] p. illus., maps (1 double) Or WaPS 7417

President's report; abstract from report of the vice-president to the board of directors upon the condition of the Pacific

Coast division and the Puyallup coal fields; report made by the Purchasing Committee. September 29, 1875. [n.p., 1876] 44 p.   OrP **7418**

Puget Sound and Alaska. [St. Paul, 19—?] 32 p. illus., maps.   WaPS **7419**

Same. [1916]   WaPS **7420**

Rainier National Park; on the route of the air-conditioned North Coast Limited. [St. Paul, 1938] 15 p. illus.   WaPS **7421**

Ranches. St. Paul [1930] 64 p. illus., maps.   MtU **7422**

Report of the president to the stockholders at their annual meeting, September 21, 1882. New York, Sackett, 1882. 68 p. fold. map, tables.   OrP **7423**

Riding with the Indian chiefs on the new North Coast Limited. [n.p., 1930?] 28 p. illus., map.   WaT **7424**

Settlers' guide to Oregon and Washington Territory and to the lands of the North-ern Pacific Railroad on the Pacific slope. New York [1872] 32 p.
            CVicAr OrP OrU WaSp **7425**

The storied Northwest explored by Lewis and Clark in 1804-6 and developed by the Northern Pacific Railway. [n.p., n.d.] [16] p. illus.
        MtBozC Or OrP WaT WaU **7426**

Same. [St. Paul, 193—?]   WaPS **7427**

Tacoma the western terminus of the North-ern Pacific Railroad. Tacoma, 1885. 32 p. 3 plates (2 fold.) map.   OrP **7428**

Same. Tacoma, Ledger Printers, 1885. 32 p. 2 plates, maps.   OrP **7429**

Same. 43 p. 2 fold. maps.   WaT **7430**

Same. [Tacoma? 1887?] 31 p. 2 maps (1 fold.)   WaU **7431**

Same. Tacoma, News Pub. Co., 1889. 39 p. plates (1 fold.) tables.   WaPS **7432**

Through the fertile Northwest. St. Paul [n.d.] 23 p. illus., map.   WaT **7433**

2000 miles of scenic beauty. St. Paul [1935] 63 p. illus.   WaPS WaT **7434**

Uncle Sam will give you a home in the Flathead Indian Reservation, western Montana. [St. Paul, 1909] [13] p. front. (map) illus.   WaPS **7435**

Unification of Northern Pacific Railway Company and Great Northern Railway Company, plan and deposit agreement dated February 7, 1927. New York, Ballou Press [1927] 32 p.   WaU **7436**

Washington — northern Idaho. [St. Paul, McGill, Warner Co., 1921] 64 p. front. (map) illus., maps.
            WaPS WaS WAWW **7437**

Same. [St. Paul, 1929?]   IdUSB **7438**

Same. The lure of the North Pacific coast. [1931]   WaT **7439**

The western empire tributary to the North-ern Pacific Railroad. [n.p., 189?] 1 v.
                            WaU **7440**

Yakima Valley, Washington. [St. Paul? 1911?] [48] p. illus., maps, tables.
                            WaPS **7441**

Northern Pacific Terminal Company of Oregon.
Agreement between the Northern Pacific Terminal Company and the Oregon Short Line and Utah Northern Railway Compay, the Northern Pacific Railroad Company, the Southern Pacific Company. [n.p., 1890] 8 p.   OrP **7442**

Northern Permanente Foundation.
Northern Permanente Foundation, Vancouver, Washington; a manual for employees describing the Foundation's facilities, policies and special services. [n. p., n.d.] 16 p.   OrP **7443**

North-West-American mission. [London, T. C. Johns, n.d.] [43] p. map. CVicAr **7444**

Northwest Angora Goat Association.
Angora and mohair industry in the Northwest, also a full report and proceedings of the first annual convention held in Portland, Oregon, January 4-7, 1911, comp. by Alva L. McDonald, secretary-treasurer. Portland, Or., 1911. 69 p. illus., ports.   Or OrCS OrHi OrP OrU **7445**

Northwest American Japanese Association.
Outline history of Japanese people in the Northwest. [Tacoma] 1923. [7] 164 p. il-lus. Text in Japanese.   WaU **7446**

Northwest Association of Secondary and Higher Schools.
Aims, policies, standards, constitution. Spokane, 1940. 18 p. ,   Or OrP **7447**

— — — Commission on Higher Schools. Revised manual of accrediting higher schools, 1946. [n.p., n.d.] 32 p. OrCS **7448**

Northwest Aviation Planning Council.
Northwest Aviation Planning Council, Olympic Hotel, Seattle, Washington, March 25, 26, 27, 1940. [Seattle, Shingell Reporting-Pub. Service] 1940. 168 p.
                        MtHi Wa **7449**

Northwest Canada Company.
Manitoba and the new Northwest; land within reach of all. Edinburgh, Constable [n.d.] 38 p. plates, fold. maps.
                          CVicAr **7450**

Northwest Conference on Higher Education, Oregon State College, 1946.
Conference on the student as a factor in his education. Corvallis, Or., 1946. 71 p. illus.   OrCS **7451**

Northwest Development League.
Report containing annual address of the president, annual report of the secretary, resolutions of the Northwest Development Congress, articles of organization. St. Paul, McGill [1911-1912] 29 p.
                            WaS **7452**

Northwest Electric Light and Power Association.
Scholarship announcement and reference material for the benefit of students competing for scholarship offered. Seattle, Pliny L. Allen Co. [1923?] 47 p.
                            WaPS **7453**

Northwest Fruit Growers Commission.
How can Northwest fruit growers make their markets profitable; an organization program. [Yakima, Wash., 1924] 22 p.   WaPS **7454**

Northwest Homeseeker and Investor.
Inland empire and what it comprehends, together with a sketch of the principal cities and surrounding country. Spokane, 1905. 67 p.   WaSp **7455**

Northwest Irrigation and Development Congress, 1st. Seattle, Wash., 1920.
Proceedings of Northwest Irrigation and Development Congress held at Seattle, Washington, September 16-17, 1920, called by Joint Committee representing the principal cities of the Pacific Northwest. [Seattle? 1920?] 103 p.
    OrCS OrP WaSp WaT WaU **7456**

Northwest Magnesite Company.
Magnesite; a booklet containing information about its history, manufacture, use and properties; mines and plant at Chewelah, Washington, U. S. A. [San Francisco, 1919] 23 p. illus., 5 col. plates.
    WaU **7457**

Northwest Mapping Service, Seattle, Wash.
New Alaska highway packet; full color maps, travel guide, latest tourist information. [Seattle, 1948] 8 p. illus., fold. col. map.   OrCS **7458**

Northwest Mining Association.
Proceedings of the 1st annual convention, held at Spokane, Wash., October 2d and 3d, 1895. [Spokane, 1896] 76 p.
    OrP WaU **7459**

Northwest Nut Growers.
A report to the members. Newberg, Or., 1948. 12 p.   OrCS **7460**

Northwest Peace Jubilee, Tacoma, Wash.
[Souvenir and program. n.p., 1919] 72 p. illus., ports.   WaT **7461**

Northwest Public Power Association.
Minutes of meeting held to discuss power supply with Secretary of the Interior, J. A. Krug. Portland, Or., 1946. 1 v.
    OrU **7462**

Northwest Scientific Association, Spokane, Wash.
The Northwest Scientific Association; what it is, its aim, its method of work. [n.p., 1936] 8 p.   WaPS **7463**
Research needs of the immediate future in the Inland Empire. [n.p.] 1932. [14] p.
    WaPS **7464**

Northwest States Development Association.
Proposed program of development of Columbia drainage basin; emergency and immediate post-war projects; proposed development of land and water resources in Columbia River basin within the states of Wyoming. Idaho, Montana, Oregon, and Washington. [Spokane?] 1943. 55 p. maps.   WaS **7465**

Northwestern Business College, Spokane, Wash.
Northwestern Business College. Spokane [1919?] 16 p. illus.   WaPS **7466**

Northwestern Credit Association.
The northwestern credit book for Seattle and vicinity. 2d ed. Seattle, 1905 [c1903] 495 p.   WaU **7467**

Northwestern Electric Company.
Extension proposal and agreement for the first mortgage twenty-year sinking fund

gold bonds, Jan. 25, 1935. [Portland, Or.] 1935. 22 p. tables.   OrP **7468**

Northwestern Loan and Investment Co. of New Whatcom.
The city of New Whatcom, Wash. Fairhaven, Wash., Fairhaven Pub. Co., 1893. 72 p. front., illus., maps, plan.
    CVicAr **7469**

Northwestern Mutual Fire Association, Seattle, Wash.
Chelan County schools [a report to Superintendent of Schools, Chelan County, Prepared by Harold L. Bean; includes photos., description and plans of school buildings and property of all Chelan school districts except No. 121, Holden; also statistics of estimated valuation and insurance coverage and suggestions for improved fire protection] [Seattle, 1938] 1 v. mounted photos., plans, tables.
    WaU **7470**
Kitsap County schools [a report] [Seattle? 1937] [268] p. photos., plans (part fold.) tables.   WaU **7471**
[Lewis County schools; a report prepared by Harold L. Bean. Seattle? 1937] [27] p. mounted photos., plans (part fold.) tables.   WaU **7472**
Thurston County schools [a report] [Seattle?] 1937. 1 v. mounted photos., plans, tables.   WaU **7473**
— — — Inspection Department.
Burnt offerings; a visual presentation of fires and hazards for the use of those interested in fire prevention and protection. Seattle, 1928. 48 p. 44 photos.
    WaU **7474**

Northwestern Natural Gas Corporation.
Northwestern natural gas. [Seattle? 1935?] [14] p. illus., diagrs.   WaPS **7475**

Norwegian Singers' Association of the Pacific Coast. Souvenir program, Norwegian Sangerfest, July 30, 31, Aug. 1, 1904. comp. by Howard A. Hanson. [Seattle, 1904] [48] p. illus., ports.   WaU **7476**
Souvenir program; Twentieth Annual Sangerfest, Pacific Coast Norwegian Singers' Association, August 28th, 29th, 30th, and 31st, 1925. Portland, Or. [Hansen Printing Co., 1925?] [48] p.
    WaPS **7477**

Norwester.
Annual edition 1945; the story of the men and achievements of the Coast Guard Auxiliary and the temporary reservists from the auxiliary, in the Pacific Northwest during the second World War. Seattle, Coast Guard Auxiliary, 13th Naval District [1945] 139 p. illus., ports.
    WaS WaU **7478**

Notable men of Washington. Tacoma, Perkins Press, 1912. 65 p. illus., ports.
    OrP Wa WaS WaTC WaU **7479**

Notes and sketches collected from a voyage in the North-West, by a Sister of Charity [pseud.] of Montreal for the furtherance of a charitable object. Montreal, Callahan, 1875. 23 p.   CVicAr **7480**

Notes on our trip across British Columbia from Golden on the Canadian Pacific

Railway to Kootenai in Idaho on the Northern Pacific Railway, and of our visit to the American national park, "the Yellowstone" in Wyoming, thence home via St. Paul and the new Soo line. Hamilton, Spectator Printing Co., 1889. 34 p. fold. map. CV **7481**

Notice respecting the boundary between His Majesty's possessions in North America and the United States, with a map of America exhibiting the principal trading stations of the North-West Co. London, M'Millan, 1817. 12 p. fold. map.
CVicAr **7482**

Notice sur le territoire et sur la mission de l'Oregon, suivie de quelques lettres des soeurs de Notre-Dame etablie a St. Paul du Wallamette. Bruxelles, Bibliotheque d'education, 1847. 180 p. map.
CVicAr OrHi OrP WaU **7483**

Novo y Colson, Pedro de, 1846-1931.
Historia de las exploraciones articas hechas en busca del paso del nordeste con un prologo del Ilmo, Sr. D. Cesareo Fernandez Duro. Madrid, Fortanet, 1880. xiii, 260 p. port., fold. map. WaU **7484**

Same. 2d ed. 1882. CVicAr **7485**

Sobre los viajes apocrifos de Juan de Fuca y de Lorenzo Ferrer Maldonado recopilacion y estudio, contiene tambien este libro la disertacion del mismo autor titulada ultima teoria sobre la Atlantida. Madrid, Fortanet, 1881. 223 p.
CVicAr **7486**

Noyes, Alva Josiah, 1855-
In the land of Chinook; or, The story of Blain County, by Al J. Noyes (Ajax). Helena, Mont., State Pub. Co. [c1917] 152 p. plates, ports., facsims.
CVicAr MtHi MtU WaSp WaU **7487**

The story of Ajax; life in the Big Hole Basin. Helena, Mont., State Pub. Co., 1914. 158 p. front., 6 plates, 6 ports.
MtHi WaS **7488**

Nuckols, S. B., see no. 5278.

Nunn, George Emra, 1882-
Origin of the Strait of Anian concept. Philadelphia, 1929. 36 p. front., illus., maps.
Many **7489**

Nutchuk, see nos. 7569-7571.

Nute, Grace Lee, 1895-
Documents relating to Northwest missions, 1815-1827. St. Paul, pub. for the Clarence Walworth Alvord Memorial Commission by the Minn. Historical Society, 1942. xix, 469 p. (Publications, 1)
CVicAr MtHi MtU WaSp **7490**

See also no. 3476.

Nuttall, Reginald.
British Columbia; its present condition and future policy. Victoria, B. C., M'Millan, 1878. 13 p. CVicAr **7491**

Oak, Henry Lebbeus, 1844-1905.
"Literary industries" in a new light; a statement on the authorship of Bancroft's Native races and History of the

Pacific states. San Francisco, Bacon Printing Co., 1893. 89 p. OrHi OrP **7492**

Oakesdale Tribune, Oakesdale, Wash.
[Special edition on history of Oakesdale printed on silk] Oakesdale, Wash., 1924. 1 v. (v. 25, no. 28, Oct. 3, 1924)
WaPS **7493**

Oakland Real Estate Company, Oakland, Or.
All about Oakland and vicinity. Roseburg, Or., Strange & Ryan [1906] [23] p. illus.
Or **7494**

Oakleaf, Howard B.
Douglas fir ship building. [Portland, Or., Peninsula Shipbuilding Co., 1916] 9 p. illus., tables, diagrs. Or OrP **7495**

Lumber manufacture in the Douglas fir region. Chicago, Commercial Journal Co. [c1920] xii, 182 p. illus., diagrs.
Many **7496**

The wood-using industries of Oregon, with special reference to the properties and uses of Oregon woods. Portland, Or., 1911. 46 p. Many **7497**

Obadiah B. Hayden; editorial comment and news matter following his death January 10, 1916; also certain resolutions. [Tacoma? 1916?] [29] p. port. WaU **7498**

Oberholser, Harry Church, 1870-
Descriptions of new birds from Oregon, chiefly from the Warner Valley region. [Cleveland] 1932. 12 p. (Scientific publications of the Cleveland Museum of Natural History, v. 4, no. 1) OrP **7499**

Oberlander, Richard, 1832-1891.
Von Ozean zu Ozean; Kulturbilder und Naturschilderungen aus dem fernen Westen von Amerika. Leipzig, Otto Spamer [1884] viii, 256, iv p. front., illus.
WaU **7500**

O'Brien, John Sherman, 1898-1938.
Alone across the top of the world; the authorized story of the Arctic journey of David Irwin as told to Jack O'Brien; foreword by Russell Owen. Chicago, Winston [c1935] x, 254 p. front., plates, ports. OrCS WaS **7501**

Corporal Corey of the Royal Canadian Mounted. Chicago, Winston [c1936] 276 p. front., illus. CVicAr **7502**

Silver Chief, dog of the North, illus. by Kurt Wiese. New York, Winston [c1933] v, 218 p. front., illus., plates (part col.)
IdIf Or OrP WaS WaSp **7503**

Silver Chief to the rescue, illus. by Kurt Wiese. New York, Winston [c1937] vii, 235 p. col. front., illus., plates (part col.)
IdIf Or OrP OrU WaS WaSp **7504**

Valiant, dog of the timberline, illus. by Kurt Wiese. New York, Winston [c1935] x, 218 p. col. front., illus., plates (part col.) IdIf Or OrP WaS WaSp **7505**

An occasional paper on the Columbia Mission with letters from the Bishop, June 1860. London, Rivingtons [n.d.] 50 p. front., 2 fold. maps. CVicAr **7506**

O'Connor, Dominic, 1883-
Brief history of the diocese of Baker City. Baker, Or., Diocesan Chancery, 1930. xi, 203 p. front., illus., ports., map.
OrP WaSp **7507**

O'Connor, E. M.
Souvenir of Portland, Oregon, "The Rose City". Portland, Or., Gray Line Motor Tours [1934?] 36 p. illus.   WaPS **7508**
Same. [1937?]   WaPS **7509**

O'Connor, Harvey, 1897-
The Astors. New York, Knopf, 1941. viii, 488, xvi p. plates, ports.   Many **7510**

O'Connor, Mary Hamilton.
The "vanishing Swede"; a tale of adventure and pluck in the pine forests of Oregon. New York, R. G. Cooke, 1905. 209 p. front., illus.
Or OrP OrU WaPS WaU **7511**

O'Connor, Michael.
Souvenir of Olympia, Wash. New York, Albertype Co., c1898. [16] plates.
WaU **7512**

O'Connor, Paul, 1897-
Eskimo parish. Milwaukee, Wis., Bruce [1947] ix, 134 p. plates. WaS WaU **7513**

O'Cotter, Pat, see no. 2065.

Odd Fellows, Independent Order of. Idaho Encampment No. 1.
Constitution and by-laws of Idaho Encampment No. 1, I. O. O. F. Boise, Idaho, Idaho Statesman, 1878, 20 p. IdU **7514**

— — — Oregon. Grand Lodge.
Constitution of the Grand Lodge; constitution for subordinate lodges; Odd Fellowship, its aims and objects. Portland, Or., Ogilbee [n.d.] 44 p.   OrHi **7515**
Souvenir and official programme of the Sovereign Grand Lodge, Portland, Oregon, September 17th to 24th, 1892. Portland, Or., Peaslee, 1892. 64 p. OrHi **7516**

— — — — — — Lafayette.
Constitution and by-laws of Lafayette Lodge No. 29. Lafayette, Oregon. Portland, Or., Coburn, 1871. 62 p. OrHi **7517**

— — — — — — Odd Fellows Hall Association of Portland, Oregon.
Articles of incorporation, constitution and by-laws. Portland, Or., A. G. Walling, 1870. 16 [4] p.   WaU **7518**

— — — — — — Odd Fellows Library Association of Salem, Or.
By-laws of the Odd Fellows Library Association of the city of Salem, with regulations of the library adopted June 1, 1897. Salem, Or., E. M. Waite Printing Co. [1897?] 11 p.   WaPS WaU **7519**

— — — — — — Orient Lodge.
Constitution and by-laws of Orient Lodge, No. 17, Portland east side, Oregon; instituted May 18, 1867. Portland, Or., Ogilbee, 1896. 46 p.   OrHi **7520**

— — — — — — Overland Lodge.
Constitution and by-laws of Overland Lodge No. 23, Echo, Oregon. Portland, Or., Himes, 1887. 61 p.   OrHi **7521**

— — — — — — Samaritan Lodge.
Constitution, by-laws and rules of order of Samaritan Lodge No. 2. Portland, Or., Waterman, 1853. 48 p.   OrHi **7522**
Same. Portland, Or., Coburn, 1871. 62 p.
OrHi **7523**

— — — Washington (State) Grand Lodge.

Constitution of subordinate lodges of the Independent Order of Odd Fellows under the Grand Lodge of Washington. Olympia, Wash., C. B. Bagley, 1883. 47, 12 p.
WaU **7524**

Digest of the laws and decisions of the Grand Lodge of Washington, I. O. O. F., from its organization to and including the year 1906, with concordant notes from the decisions of the Sovereign Grand Lodge and an analytical index; also an appendix containing the constituition and rules of order of the Grand Lodge; the constitution of subordinate lodges, the constitution of the Rebekah Assembly; the constitution of Rebekah lodges; and forms, by H. E. Holmes. Seattle, Washington Odd Fellow, 1906. [256] p. front. (port.) forms.   WaU **7525**

— — — — — Seattle.
Lodge history of the Independent Order of Odd Fellows and the Knights of Pythias of Seattle, with a short history of their organization in the state of Washington; biographical sketches of members. Seattle, Calvert Press, 1895. 131 p.
WaU **7526**

O'Dea, Edward J., see no. 6576.

Odegard, Peter H., see no. 1731.

Odell, Margaretta (Grubbs) d. 1908.
A semi-centennial offering to the members and friends of the Methodist Episcopal Church, Salem, Oregon. [Salem, Or.] 1884. 109 p. front. (ports.) plates, ports.
IdU Or WaTC WaU WaWW **7527**
Same. Portland, Or., Swope [1885]
Many **7528**

Odell, W. H.
A legislative farce conceived in envy, prosecuted with malice, executed with criminal stupidity. Salem, Or., Statesman Job Office, 1903. 81 p. Anon.   OrP **7529**
Partial view of troubles among the breakers amid the busy rounds of human activities. [n.p., 1921?] 13 p.   OrP **7530**

Odeneal, T. B.
The Modoc war; statement of its origin and causes, containing an account of the treaty, copies of petitions, and official correspondence. Portland, Or., "Bulletin" Steam Book and Job Printing Office, 1873. 56 p.   OrP **7531**

Odlum, Jerome, see no. 3124.

[O'Donnell, A. M.]
A brief history and souvenir booklet of Knox Presbyterian Church, Trail, B. C., 1896-1921. [Trail, B. C., Trail News] 1921. 19 p. illus., ports.   CVicAr **7532**

O'Donnell, J. Morris, see no. 4842.

Oetteking, Bruce, see no. 2373.

The official guide to the Klondyke country and the gold fields of Alaska; with the official maps, vivid descriptions and thrilling experiences. Chicago, Conkey, 1897. 296 p. front., illus., plates, ports., 7 maps. CV CVicAr IdIf Or WaS WaU **7533**

Official history of the 13th Division. 1918-1919. [Tacoma, R. W. Hulbert, c1919] 40 p. illus., plates, ports. Or WaU **7534**

Official opening, Tacoma Narrows Bridge and McChord Field, June 30 — July 3, 1940, A. D. [Tacoma, 1940?] 37 p. illus., ports.
WaU 7535

Official papers relative to the dispute between the courts of Great Britain and Spain on the subject of the ships captured in Nootka Sound, with the proceedings in both houses of Parliament on the King's message; to which are added the report of M. de Mirabeau and the subsequent decrees of the National Assembly of France on the Family Compact. London, Debrett [1790] vii, 100 p.
CVicAr OrP WaS 7536

Official souvenir program; reception to First Washington U. S. Volunteer Regiment, Seattle, Nov. 5, 6, and 7, 1899 [ed. and comp. by Press Committee: Samuel L. Crawford, Thos. H. McGill, J. Howard Watson, chairman] Seattle, Metropolitan, 1899. 1 v. ports.
WaS 7537

Official souvenir, the opening of the Pattullo Bridge at New Westminster, Nov. 15, 1937. [n.p.] 1937. [12] p. illus., ports.
CVicAr 7538

Ogal Alla, see nos. 6899, 6900.

Ogden, Charles Burr, see no. 10910.

[Ogden, Peter Skene] 1794-1854.
Traits of American-Indian life and character, by a fur trader. London, Smith Elder, 1853. xiv, 218 p.
Many 7539

Same. San Francisco, Grabhorn Press, 1933. 107 p. front., 5 plates. (Rare Americana series, no. 9)
MtHi MtU OrHi Was WaU 7540

Ogilvie, David Shepherd, 1923-
A kandid view of Kiska. New York, William-Frederick Press, 1945. 31 p. (William-Frederick poets.)
WaS WaU 7541

Ogilvie, William, 1846-1912.
Early days on the Yukon and the story of its gold finds. New York, John Lane Co., 1913. xii, 306 p. front. (port.) 25 plates, 5 ports.
CV CVU WaS WaSp WaU 7542

Same. Ottawa, Thorburn & Abbott, 1913.
CVicAr WaT WaU 7543

The Klondike official guide; Canada's great gold field, the Yukon district, with regulations governing placer mining. Toronto, Hunter, Rose Co. [1898] 153 p. front., illus., maps (2 fold.)
CVic CVicAr CVU WaS WaU 7544

Lecture on the Yukon gold fields (Canada) delivered at Victoria, B. C., by Mr. William Ogilvie, explorer and surveyor of the government of Canada in the Canadian Yukon, rev., amplified and authorized by the lecturer. Victoria, B. C., Colonist Presses, 1897. 32 p. illus.
CVicAr WaSp 7545

See also nos. 4348, 6134, 11292.

O'Hagen, Thomas, 1855-1938?
Father Morice. Toronto, Ryerson [c1928] 31 p. port. (Ryerson Canadian readers)
CV CVicAr 7546

O'Hara, Edwin Vincent, 1881-
Catholic history of Oregon. 2d ed. Port-

land, Or., Catholic Book Co., 1916 [c1911] 165 p. front. (port.) 7 ports., maps. First ed. entitled Pioneer Catholic history of Oregon.
Many 7547

Same. 3d ed. 1925.
OrU WaU 7548

Pioneer Catholic history of Oregon. Portland, Or. [Glass & Prudhomme] 1911. xii, 236 p. illus., ports., map.
Many 7549

Same. Centennial ed. Paterson, N. J., St. Anthony Guild Press, 1939. xv, 234 p. front., illus., ports., map.
Many 7550

A program of Catholic rural action based on a religious survey of Lane County, Oregon. [Eugene, Or., National Catholic Welfare Council, 192-] 24 p. OrCS 7551

Welfare legislation for women and minors, by Rev. Edwin V. O'Hara, chairman, Social Survey Committee of the Consumers' League of Oregon [address delivered at annual meeting held at Portland, Hotel, Portland, Or., Tuesday, Nov. 19, 1912] [Portland, Or., Keystone Press, 1912?] [12] p.
Many 7552

O'Hara, Frank, 1876-
Unemployment in Oregon; its nature, extent and remedies, a report to the Oregon Committee on Seasonal Unemployment. Portland, Or., Keystone Press [1914] 39 p.
Or OrCS OrP OrPR OrU WaS 7553

Okanagan Gospel readings, [n.p., n.d.] [64] p.
CVicAr 7554

Okanagan Historical Society.
Songs of the Okanagan. Vernon, B. C., 1944. iv, 31 p. front. CVicAr CVU 7555

Okanagan Society for the Revival of Indian Arts and Crafts, Oliver, B. C.
Native Canadians, a plan for the rehabilitation of Indians. [n.p., Broadway Printers, n.d.] 20 p.
CVicAr 7556

Same. Ottawa [1945?]
WaU 7557

O'Kane, Walter Collins, see nos. 10673-10675.

Okanogan, Wash. High School. Junior Class.
Service record of the community war work. Okanogan, Wash. [1919] 65 p. illus.
WaU 7558

Old Fort Dalles Historical Society.
The Dalles, Oregon. [n.p., 1930?] [4] p. illus.
Or 7559

Old mission church of the Coeur d'Alene Indians. [n.p., n.d.] [15] p. illus., 2 plates, port.
WaSp 7560

Old Oregon Trail Association, Baker, Or.
Tourists' Old Oregon Trail and Columbia River Highway information and guide book. [Baker, Or.?] 1924, 1925. 1932. 3 v.
OrP 7561

An old Settler, see no. 2244.

Old Wolf, see nos. 6475, 7126.

Olden, Sarah Emilia.
Little slants at western life; a note book of travel and reflection. New York, H. Vinal, 1927. 245 p.
IdIf Or 7562

Shoshone folk lore, as discovered from the Rev. John Roberts, a hidden hero on the Wind River Indian Reservation in Wyoming. Milwaukee, Wis., Morehouse Pub. Co. [c1923] 97 p. plates, ports.
Or WaSp WaU 7563

Oldroyd, Mrs. Ida (Shepard) 1857-
Marine shells of Puget Sound and vicinity. Seattle, University of Washington Press, 1924. 271 p. plates (Publications, Puget Sound Biological Station, v. 4, Mar. 1924. WaS WaSp WaT WaU **7564**

The marine shells of the west coast of North America. Stanford University, Calif., 1924-1927. 2 v. in 4. plates. (Publications. University series. Geological sciences. v. 1, no. 1; v. 2, pt. 1-3)
Many **7565**

Oleson, A. H., see no. 1206.

Oliphant, James Orin, 1894-
The educational services of President N. D. Showalter. Spokane, Wash., printed for the Alumni Association of the State Normal School. Cheney, Wash., Inland-American Printing Co., 1926. 20 p. port.
Or WaPS WaS WaU **7566**

History of the State Normal School at Cheney, Washington. Spokane, Inland-American Printing Co., 1924. vi, 175 p.
Or OrHi Wa WaPS WaSp WaU **7567**

See also nos. 5510, 10843.

Oliver, Nola Nance, 1880-
Alaskan Indian legends, illus. by Frances Brandon. New York, Field-Doubleday, c1947. 67 p. illus. WaS **7568**

[**Oliver, Simeon**] 1903-
Back to the smoky sea, by Nutchuk, with Alden Hatch; illus., by Natchuk. New York, J. Messner [1946] 225 p. illus., plates, ports.
Or OrP WaS WaSp WaU **7569**

Son of the smoky sea, by Nutchuk with Alden Hatch; illus. by Nutchuk. New York, J. Messner [c1941] viii, 243 p. front. (port.) illus., plates, port.
Or OrP OrU Wa WaS WaSp **7570**

Same. [1943, c1941] WaU **7571**

Olmstead, Frank Lincoln, see nos. 5043, 5044.

Olson, Everett, see no. 7154.

Olson, Hattie V.
Cowlitz County, Washington, 1854-1947. [Kelso, Wash., Kelsonian-Tribune, 1947] 88 p. illus., map. OrHi WaS **7572**

Same. 2d ed. 96 p. WaT **7573**

Olson, Julius C., see no. 5718.

Olson, Ronald LeRoy, 1895-
Adze, canoe, and house types of the Northwest coast. Seattle, University of Washington Press, 1927. 38 p. illus., maps. (Publications in anthropology, v. 2, no.1)
Many **7574**

The Quinault Indians. Seattle, University of Washington Press, 1936. 194 p. illus., ports., maps. (Publications in anthropology, v. 6, no. 1) Many **7575**

Olson, Zenas A.
Following Fighting "F" being an intimate history of Company "F", 361st Infantry of the 91st Division. La Chapelle-Montligeon (Orne) Imprimerie de Montligeon. 1919. 86 p. Or OrP OrU WaU **7576**

Olympia, Wash. First Presbyterian Church.
History of the organization and directory of worship 1854-1904. [n.p., 1904?] [30] p. illus. WaU **7577**

Olympia Tribune.
Souvenir edition. Olympia, Wash., 1891. [20] p. illus., ports. WaU **7578**

The Olympic League, Olympia, Wash.
The Olympic peninsula; 2,000,000 acres of vacation land, western Washington. Olympia, Wash. [193—?] 12 p. illus.
WaPS **7579**

Same. [n.d.] [20] p. WaU **7580**

Olympic Review.
Seattle [summer number] Seattle, Farwest Lithograph & Printing Co., 1939. 24 p. illus., ports., map. (v. 3, no. 2) WaS **7581**

Olzendam, Roderic Marble.
After the war, wood! Lumber, fibres, chemicals, plastics; a talk given at the 39th Annual Convention of the Pacific Advertising Association, Rainier National Park, June 1942. [n.p., 1942] 15 p. illus. Or **7582**

Freedom through unity [remarks at the 33d annual banquet of the Canadian Society of Forest Engineers, Empress Hotel, Victoria, B. C.] [Tacoma, Weyerhaeuser Timber Co., 1943] [13] p. WaT **7583**

Timber is a crop; an address delivered at the Pacific Logging Congress. Seaside, Oregon. [n.p.] 1937. 22 p. Or OrU **7584**

Same. [n.p.] Weyerhaeuser Timber Co. [c1937?] [15] p. WaE WaU **7585**

Omak Chronicle.
Progress edition, 1928. Omak, Wash. [Emert Pub. Co.] 1928. [40] p. illus., map. Sept. 18, 1928) WaU **7586**

O'Meara, Arthur E.
The British Columbia Indian land situation, a great question to be settled. [Victoria, B. C., 1910] 12 p. CVicAr **7587**

Same. A lecture delivered in Aberdeen School, Vancouver, 22 April 1910. [n.p., 1910?] 16 p. CVicAr **7588**

Onderdonk, James Lawrence, 1854-1899.
Idaho; facts and statistics concerning the mining, farming, stock-raising, lumbering, and other resources and industries. San Francisco, Bancroft, 1885. 150 p.
IdB IdU MtU OrHi WaPS WaU **7589**

One of the Old Boys, see no. 2918.

Onraet, Anthony.
Sixty below, by Tony Onraet, Sergeant Anthony Onraet, Canadian army, with an introd. by Dr. Thomas Wood. Toronto, J. Cape [1944] 192 p. front., map.
WaU **7590**

Open River Association, Portland, Or.
Report of the Executive Committee. October 9, 1907. [Portland, Or., 1907?] 11 p.
Or **7591**

Opinions of the British Press on the British Columbian railway question. Victoria, B. C., Standard, 1877. 12 p.
CVicAr CVU **7592**

Oppenheimer, David, 1834-1897.
Mineral resources of British Columbia; practical hints for capitalists and intending settlers, with appendix containing the mineral laws of the Province and Dominion of Canada. Vancouver, B. C., News-Advertiser Manufacturing Station-

ers, Printers and Bookbinders, 1889. 50 p. CVicAr 7593

Oppenlander, John H.
The Columbia River guide and panorama, from Portland to the Dalles; myths, legends, history, geology, Lewis & Clark notations. [Portland, Or., c1924] 39 p. illus., map. (Penland guide series)
Or OrHi OrP 7594

Opportunities in British Columbia, 1921. [Toronto, Heaton, c1921] 88 p. illus. (Canadian provincial booklets) OrU 7595

The Optimist, Eugene, Or.
The city of Eugene and its tributary resources. Eugene, Or., C. L. Green, 1916. 24 p. illus. (v. 1, no. 1, Feb. 1916)
OrU 7596

The Optimist, Tacoma, Wash.
Tacoma, Washington; the city of opportunity. Tacoma, C. L. Green, 1915. 15 p. illus., map. (v. 1, no. 1, Oct. 1915)
WaT 7597

[Orchard, William C.]
A rare Salish blanket. New York [Vreeland Press] 1926. 15 p. col. front., illus., 3 plates. (Museum of the American Indian. Heye Foundation. Leaflets, no. 5)
CVicAr CVU MtU WaS 7598

Order of Railway Conductors of America.
The Order of Railway Conductors submits the following information for the use of the Legislative Assembly of the State of Washington. [n.p., 1892] 15 p. WaU 7599

Order of the Eastern Star. Montana. Grand Chapter.
Golden jubilee history; Grand Chapter, Order of Eastern Star of Montana, by Mertie W. Brattin, P. G. M., Grand Historian; and short history of the General Grand Chapter, by Anna Winston Smalley, P. M. W. G. M. Helena, Mont., State Pub. Co., 1941. 472 p. front., illus.
MtHi WaSp 7600

Order of Washington. Or.
Constitution and laws as made, rev. and amended, approved and adopted September 5, 1898. Portland, Or., 1898. 1 v.
OrHi 7601

Ordway, John, see no. 5909.

Oregon. Penitentiary. Prisoner 4382.
Prison tours and poems; a sketch of the Oregon State Penitentiary. Salem. Or., 1904. 88 p. OrSa WaPS 7602

Same. 1906. 87 p. 2 ports., plate.
OrHi OrP 7603

— — — — — — Prisoner 6435.
The Oregon Penitentiary. Salem, Or., 1917. 50 p. OrP WaU 7604

Sensational prison escapes from the Oregon State Penitentiary. [Salem, Or., 1922?] 44 p. Or OrP WaPS WaU 7605

— — — State Agricultural College, Corvallis.
The trail blazers. [Corvallis, Or., 1915] 76 p. illus. (Bulletin, no. 200)
OrCS OrU WaU 7606

— — — — — — Alumni Association.
The orange and black, ed. by Dick Gearhart; a record of the first seventy years in the life of Oregon State College, the illustrated story of her growth to the "major industry of the state", complete with the changing life and activity of her students and alumni. [Corvallis, Or.] 1938. 206 p. illus., ports. WaU 7607

— — — University.
Dedication of The Pioneer, an heroic statue in bronze erected on the campus of the University of Oregon by Joseph N. Teal of Portland, May 22, 1919. [Eugene, Or.] 1919. 31 p. front. (Bulletin, v. 17, no 1) OrCS OrP OrU 7608

In memory of Thomas Condon, born March 3, 1822, died February 11, 1907. Eugene, Or., 1907. 64 p. front. (port.) plates, port. (Bulletin, n.s., v. 4, no. 8) Many 7609

Mineral resources and mineral industry of Oregon for 1903, comp. by the Department of Chemistry. Eugene, Or., 1904. 113 p. 4 plates, map, tables. (Bulletin, n.s., v. 1, no. 4)
Or OrCS OrHi OrP OrU WaU 7610

Oregon Academy of Sciences.
Constitution. Portland, Or., 1905. 6 p.
OrHi 7611

Manual for 1892. Portland, Or., Baumgardt & Palmer, 1892. 1 v. OrU 7612

Oregon Alpine Club, Portland, Or.
Constitution, articles of incorporation and list of members, organized and incorporated at Portland, Or., Oct. 7, 1887. Portland, Or., Himes, 1887. [15] p. OrHi 7613

Oregon; American protection to American pioneers; or, Shall Oregon be surrendered to Great Britain? [n.p., n.d.] 7 p.
CVicAr 7614

Oregon and California Railroad Company.
Bericht des Delegirten des Comite zum Schutze der Besitzer der Bonds der Oregon und California Eisenbahn, 1876-78, 1880. Franfort, Osterrieth, 1874-89. 2 v.
OrHi 7615

Mittheilungen uber die gegenwartige Lage der Oregon und California Eisenbahn; veroffentlich von dem Comite zum Schutze der Besitzer 7 % Oregon and California mortgage bonds 1874-75. Frankfort, Adelmann, 1876, 1 v. OrHi 7616

Oregon and the Pacific Northwest; glimpses of pretty spots along the valley of the Columbia River from northern Montana to the Pacific Ocean, scenery along the line of the Northern Pacific Railroad showing the new transcontinental route in process of construction. Porland, Or., Himes [n.d.] 41 p. illus., photos. WaSp 7617

Oregon and Transcontinental Company.
Record of the recent injunction proceedings; facts for the stockholders. New York, 1889. 63 p. OrP 7618

Report to the stockholders with copies of resolutions passed at the special meeting held Nov. 5, 1889. New York, Searing, 1889. 14 p. OrP 7619

Second annual report of the Board of Directors to the stockholders for the year ending June 30, 1883. New York, Sackett & Rankin, 1883. 35 p. OrP 7620

Oregon and Washington Health Reform Association.
Constitution and the annual address. Salem, Or., American Unionist Job Office, 1868. 36 p.   WaU **7621**

Oregon and Washington Orphan Asylum Association, Vancouver, Wash.
Constitution and by-laws. Portland, Or., McCormick, 1860. 11 p.   OrHi **7622**

Oregon and Western Colonization Company.
Military road grant lands; 800,000 acres in central Oregon. St. Paul [n.d.] 31 p. illus.   OrP **7623**

Oregon Association for Highway Improvement.
Proposed convict labor laws prohibiting employment of convicts in competition with free labor, to be submitted at the general election Nov. 1912. Portland, Or., 1912. 4 p.   OrP **7624**

Oregon Association of Building and Construction.
Conference on apprentice education in the building trades. Portland, Or., 1924. 20 p.   OrP **7625**

Oregon Association of College, University and Normal School Appointment Bureaus.
A statement for school officials. [n.p., 1935] 8 p.   OrP **7626**

Oregon Association of Small Loan Companies.
Small loans in Oregon. [Portland, Or.] 1943. 23 p.   OrU **7627**

Oregon Automotive Conference, 1927.
Oregon bus and truck; regulation and taxation as proposed by the Oregon Automotive Conference, January 3, 1927. [Portland, Or.? 1927] 15 p.   WaU **7628**

Oregon Bankers' Association.
Gold; report of a conference held under the auspices of the Oregon Bankers' Association in Portland, Oregon, Sept. 5, 1918, to consider the gold problem. [Portland, Or., 1918] 29 p. tables, charts.
                                    OrP **7629**

Oregon Bar Association.
A complete list of both active and inactive members of the Oregon State Bar, prepared from records of and with the co-operation of Frederick M. Sercombe, secretary (corrected to October 1939). Portland, Or., Stevens-Ness [1939] 52 p.
                                    OrP **7630**

Oregon Building Congress. Committee on Low Cost Housing.
Report. Portland, Or. [1947] 13 p.
                                    OrP **7631**

Oregon Butter and Cheese Makers Convention.
Report, 1914. Portland, Or. [1914?] 91 p.
                                    OrP **7632**

Oregon Cascade Resorts Association.
Resorts of the Oregon Cascades. Bend, Or. [193—?] [10] p. illus., map. WaPS **7633**

Oregon Central Military Road Company.
Report of the recent surveys and progress of construction of the Oregon Central Military Road, made by B. J. Pengra, superintendent. Eugene, Or., 1865. 63 p.
                                    Or **7634**

Oregon Central Railroad Company.
The inside history of the Oregon Central Railroad Companies, with the reasons showing the Portland (or West Side Company) to be entitled to the U. S. land grant. Portland, Or., Walling, 1869. 39 p.   OrHi OrP **7635**

Statement of facts relative to the incorporation and organization of the Oregon Central Railroad Company of Salem, Oregon, incorporated April 22, 1867, and reasons why such company is entitled to the benefit of the land grant given by Congress in aid of a railroad and telegraph line from Portland, Oregon southerly through the Willamette, Umpqua and Rogue River valleys, to the Central Pacific road in California, passed July 25, 1866, and also why no other company has any legal or equitable right thereto. Portland, Or., Carter & Hines, 1868. 38 p.
                          Or OrP WaSp **7636**

Oregon Children's Aid Society.
Annual report, 3d, 1869-70. Salem, Or., Oregon Statesman, 1870. 16 p. OrP OrU **7637**

Oregon Citizens Educational League.
An appeal to good citizenship. Portland, Or. [1913?] 8 p.   Or OrP **7638**

Oregon City Courier-Herald.
Souvenir of Clackamas County, Oregon. [Oregon City, Or., 1901] 28 p. illus. (New Year no., Jan. 1901)   Or **7639**

Oregon City Enterprise.
"Territorial days" souvenir edition. Oregon City, Or. [1935?] 28 p. illus., ports. (Sept. 12)   WaU **7640**

Oregon Civic League.
Digest of survey of Portland public schools. [Portland, Or.] Schwab Printing Co., 1914. 32 p.   OrP **7641**

Oregon Congress of Mothers and Parent-Teacher Associations.
Junior exposition as part of a "back to the home" movement, Oct. 28 to Nov. 6, 1915. [Portland, Or., Boyer Printing Co.] 1915. 17 p.   OrP **7642**

Oregon Conservation Association.
Know your state. [Portland, Or.] Anderson & Duniway Co. [n.d.] 7 p.   OrP **7643**

Oregon controversy reviewed in 4 letters, by a friend of the Anglo-Saxons. New York, Leavitt, 1846. 54 p.
                          CVicAr OrHi **7644**

Oregon Editorial Association.
Souvenir of Portland and Oregon. Portland, Or. [1899] [96] p. illus., fold. plate.
                                    OrP **7645**

Oregon Emigration Society.
Articles of agreement. Boston, Ela [n.d.] 16 p.   OrHi **7646**

Oregon Federation of Garden Clubs.
Citations for distinguished achievement in horticulture, with biographies, 1944-45. [n.p.] 1944-45. 1 v.   OrP **7647**

Oregon Federation of Music Clubs.
Constitution and by-laws. [Portland, Or., Univ. of Portland, 1940] 6 p.   OrP **7648**

"Oregon first"; excursion to San Francisco to select site at Panama-Pacific International Exposition, 1915. [n.p.] 1912. [13] p.   OrHi **7649**

Oregon Forest Fire Association.
Articles of incorporation, by-laws, state forest fire bill. Portland, Or., Anderson & Duniway [1911?] 20 p.   OrP **7650**

Das Oregon-gebiet, "der Rechtstitel der Vereinigten Staaten klar und unbestreitbar"; offizielle Correspondenz des brittischen bevollmachtigten Ministers in Washington und des Staatssecretars der Vereinigten Staaten (ubersetzung). Bremen, Schunemann, 1846. 114 p.
OrP WaU **7651**

Oregon High School Activities Association.
Constitution and by-laws. [Portland, Or.?] 1942. 14 p.   OrU **7652**

A handbook for the Girl's Section of the Oregon High School Activities Association. 8th rev. ed. [n.p.] 1947. 73 p. illus., diagrs.   OrCS **7653**

Oregon, historical & descriptive, containing a full and accurate description of the country, a narrative of the discoveries and settlements connected with it, and also of the disputed claims of Great Britain and America. London, Gilbert [n.d.] 12 p. map.   OrHi **7654**

Oregon Historical Society, Portland, Or.
Articles of incorporation, by-laws, prospectus and officers. Portland, Or., Himes, 1899. 23 p.   OrHi OrP WaPS **7655**

Brief review of its work up to September 30, 1916, for presentation to the members of the twenty-ninth Legislative Assembly of Oregon. [n.p., n.d.] 11 p.
Or OrHi OrP OrU WaWW **7656**

Same. To September 30, 1918. 8 p.
OrHi **7656A**

The Oregon Historical Quarterly: Harvey W. Scott memorial number. [Salem, Or., 1913] 210 p. front. plates, ports. (v. 14, no. 2, June 1913.   Many **7657**

Oregon Humane Society.
Manual containing the state law for the prevention of cruelty to animals, the constitution, list of members, and report of anniversary meeting of 1885. Portland, Or., G. H. Himes, 1885. 7, 7 p.
OrHi WaU **7658**

Oregon Humane Society, containing an abstract of the state laws, the constitution and by-laws of the society. Portland, Or., G. H. Himes [n.d.] 16 p. OrHi **7659**

Oregon Improvement Company.
Anacortes, Skagit County, the metropolis of the Puget Sound basin; entrepot of the great mineral, timber and agricultural resources of Washington, the terminal point for railway and steamship transfer on the short and direct transcontinental and transoceanic line between all Atlantic and Pacific Ocean countries. Anacortes, Wash., 1890. 63 p. front., maps (2 fold.)   WaU **7660**

Eastern Washington territory and Oregon. [n.p. n.d.] 1 v.   WaPS **7661**

Oregon in color. [Portland, Or., Kilham Stationery & Printing Co., 1925] [31] p. illus.
WaPS **7662**

Oregon indemnity; claim of chief factors and

chief traders of the Hudson's Bay Company thereto. [n.p.] 1892. 1 v.
CVU OrHi **7663**

Oregon Industrial Exposition.
Official catalogue 1895. Portland, Or., 1895. 48 p. illus.   OrP **7664**

Oregon Iron and Steel Company.
Prospectus. [Portland, Or.? 1882?] 7 p.
OrP **7665**

Oregon; its resources, soil, climate and productions. Jacksonville, Or., Oregon Sentinel, 1871. 47 p.   WaWW **7666**

Oregon Journal, Portland, Or.
Fifth anniversary number, Sept. 8, 1907: coming of the white man; a symposium of facts, illustrative and representative of the agricultural, horticultural, irrigation, lumbering, manufacturing, wholesaling, financial, educational, real estate, mining and other vast interests of the Oregon country, including Portland, its metropolis. [Portland, Or.] 1907. [156] p. illus., map.   OrHi OrP WaS WaSp **7667**

Handbook for classified advertisers. [Portland, Or., c1930] 28 p.   OrP **7668**

Portland and the Oregon country; data on markets, resources and population of this great empire of the West; statistical data comp. by the Merchandising Service Bureau. Portland, Or. [1923?] [27] p. illus., tables, facsims.   OrU **7669**

Portland "the key city" and the Journal, 1929. [Portland, Or., 1929] [24] p. illus., map.   OrU **7670**

Portland, world seaport and the Journal. [Portland, Or.] 1930. 26 p. illus., map, tables.   Or OrP OrU **7671**

Standard market data issued for Portland, Or. Portland, Or., 1931. 5 p. maps, tables.
OrP **7672**

Oregon Land Company.
Compendium of information concerning the Willamette Valley and Salem, the capital city of Oregon. Salem, Or., Cronise & Wilson, 1888. 49 p. illus.
WaPS **7673**

Same. Salem, Or., 1889. 48 p. map. Or **7674**

Salem, Oregon's capital and manufacturing and agricultural centre. Salem, Or., [1891] [14] p. illus.   OrU **7675**

Oregon Mental Hygiene Society.
Study of commitment procedures in Oregon counties. [n.p.] 1947. 6 p. OrP **7676**

Oregon Methodist Historical Society.
Jason Lee, father of American Oregon. [Portland, Or., 1920?] 35 p. port.
Many **7677**

Oregon Mutual Fire Insurance Company.
Growth of the state of Oregon, 1930-1940; comp. from final figures released by the Bureau of Census, with compliments of Oregon Mutual Insurance Company. [McMinnville, Or., 1941?] 4 p.   OrU **7678**

Oregon Pacific Railroad Company.
Prospectus. New York, E. W. Sackett & Brother, 1880. 12 p. map.   OrU **7679**

Same. New York, Tyrrel [1882?] OrP **7680**

Oregon Pioneer Association.
Constitution and quotations from the register of the Oregon Pioneer Association, together with the annual address of Hon. S. F. Chadwick, remarks of Gov. L. F. Grover at reunion June 1874; other matters of interest. Salem, Or., E. M. Waite, 1875. 96 p. Many **7681**
Souvenir commemorative of the journey of the Oregon pioneer excursionists, October 1883. [n.p., n.d.] 6 p. illus.
OrHi **7682**

Oregon Poets; forword by Ethel Romig Fuller; ed. by the house of Henry Harrison, poetry publisher. New York [c1935] 160 p. Many **7683**

Oregon Police Training Schools.
Training Oregon's police; report, summary, and proceedings of the Oregon Police Training Schools conducted during March, April, and May 1937; sponsored by the University of Oregon Law School, Bureau of Municipal Research and Service, League of Oregon Cities. [Portland, Or.] League of Oregon Cities, 1937. 1 v. OrP **7684**

Oregon Press Association.
Constitution and by-laws; also announcements for 1890, together with list of officers and standing committees. Salem, Or., 1889. 18 p. Or OrHi **7685**

Oregon Railroad and Navigation Company.
Articles of incorporation, by-laws, mortgages, etc., Oregon Railway and Navigation Company. [Oregon Steam Navigation Company] Cascade Railroad Company, Willamette Transportation and Locks Company, Walla Walla & Columbia River Railroad Company, Washington & Dalles Railroad Company [Oregon Steamship Company] Portland, Or., Himes, 1880. 207 p. OrHi OrP **7686**

Eastern Washington Territory and Oregon; facts regarding the resources, productions, industries, soil, climate, healthfulness, commerce and means of communication, issued for general information with maps and appendix by the Land Department of the Oregon Railway and Navigation Company, particularly describing the prolific Palouse country and Powder River valley and principal towns in same. [Farmington, W. T., 1888] 48 p. fold. maps.
WaPS WaSp WaU **7687**

First mortgage to the Farmers Loan and Trust Company, trustee, dated July 1, 1879, and mortgages of further assurance, dated Sept. 1, 1880. [n.p., n.d.] 73 p. OrP **7688**

Indenture, Jan. 20, 1888 [with Oregon Shortline Railway Co., Union Pacific Railway Co., and Northern Pacific Railroad Co.] [n.p.] 1888. 39 p. OrP **7689**

Indenture [with Oregon Shortline Railway Co. and Union Pacific Co.] [n.p.] 1886. 24 p. OrP **7690**

Oregon; facts regarding its climate, soil, mineral and agricultural resources, means of communication, commerce and industry, laws, etc. for general information, with map and appendix. New York, 1880. 59 p. map, tables. Documents of same title and similar information without the appendix were issued by the Oregon Board of Immigration each year from 1875 to 1880. Or OrHi **7691**

Same. Chicago, 1881. OrHi OrP **7692**

Outings in Oregon. Portland, Or. [1911?] 64 p. map. OrHi **7693**

The Pacific Northwest; facts relating to the history, topography, climate, soil of Oregon and Washington Territory, issued for the information and guidance of settlers and others. New York, 1882. 88 p. front., 9 plates, map.
WaU **7694**

Summer saunterings over the lines of the Oregon Railway and Navigation Company and Northern Pacific Railroad, Pacific Division; routes of river and rail; neighborhoods of note; terms for tourists. Portland, Or., Himes, 1882. 35 p. 6 photos. OrHi WaU **7695**

To the stockholders, by Committee to Visit Oregon and Washington. [n.p., 1880] 8 p. OrP **7696**

Oregon Short Line Railroad Company.
Plan and agreement for the reorganization dated Feb. 20, 1896. [n.p.] 1896. 29 p. OrP **7697**

Oregon Spectator.
Territorial centennial bulletin for April-May, 1948. Oregon City, Or., 1948. 1 v. Modified reproductions of v. 1-3 pub. in Oregon City, O. T. in 1846.
OrHi OrP **7698**

Oregon State Agricultural Society.
List of premiums for the Oregon State Fair to be held at Salem, October 1870. Salem, Or., "Willamette Farmer" Job Press, 1870. 108 p. WaU **7699**

Oregon State Dental Association.
Constitution. Portland, Or., Madden, 1901. [13] p. OrHi **7700**

Oregon State Teachers' Association.
Report of Committee on State Printing of Public School Text Books, 1931. [Portland, Or? 1931] 20 p. ports.
OrP OrPR **7701**

Report of Oregon Education Plan Committee. [n.p.] 1930. 8 p. OrP **7702**

A summary of the reports of the investigating committees, Dec. 26, 1926. [n.p.] 1926. 37 p. OrP **7703**

Oregon Statesman, Salem, Or.
90th anniversary edition, 1851-1941. Salem, Or., 1941. [78] p. illus., ports. (Mar. 30, 1941) WaU **7704**

Oregon Territorial Centennial Commission
Old Oregon country, territorial centennial, 1848-1948-9. Portland, Or. [1948] [12] p. illus. Or OrHi **7705**

Oregon territorial centennial celebration, one hundred years of progress, 1848-1948. Portland, Or., 1948. [8] p. Contains historical sketch of Oregon printed on the Mission Press. OrHi **7706**

Oregon territory centennial, with maps showing states created from Oregon Territory, written by Dr. Burt Brown Barker, Dr. Dan E. Clark, and Lancaster Pollard. [n.p., 1948] 32 p. illus., ports. facsim. OrCS OrHi OrP **7707**

Territorial centennial, old Oregon country, 1848-1948-9; the trail of destiny. [Portland, Or., 1948] 12 p. Or OrHi **7708**

The Oregon Territory, consisting of a brief description of the country and its productions; and of the habits and manners of the native Indian tribes, with a map of the territory. London, M. A. Nattali, 1846. 78 p. front. (map) Many **7709**

Oregon Trail Centennial Commission.
Wagons west, 1843; Old Oregon Trail centennial, 1943. [Salem, Or., 1943] 30 p. illus., ports., map. Contributors: Philip H. Parrish, Walter Meacham. Many **7710**

Oregon Trail Memorial Association.
Articles of incorporation. [New York, n.d.] [4] p. Or. **7711**

Covered-wagon centennial and Ox-team days; Oregon Trail memorial ed., 29 December 1931. Yonkers-on-Hudson, N. Y., World Book Co. [c1932] viii, 156, 318 p. front. (port.) illus. "Ox-team days, by Ezra Meeker and Howard R. Driggs, illus. by William H. Jackson and F. N. Wilson and with photos." 318 p. Many **7712**

Oregon Trail, a plan to honor the pioneers, issued by the Oregon Trail Memorial Association. New York [1929?] 14 p. illus., ports., map. OrP WaS **7713**

Same. [1930?] Or **7714**

Oregon Trail Pageant, Eugene, Or.
Official souvenir program, Eugene, Oregon, July 22, 23, 24, 1937. [Eugene, Or., Koke-Chapman Co., 1937] 31 p. illus., ports. IdU **7715**

The Oregon Trail souvenir. [Seattle] Rainier Printing Co. [19—] [36] p. illus., ports. Many **7716**

Oregon Trunk Highway.
The Central Oregon empire. [Portland, Or., Bushong, n.d.] 1 v. map. OrP **7717**

Oregon Victory Liberty Loan Organization.
Who's who and what's what in the Oregon victory loan, April 21 to May 10, 1919. Portland, Or., 1919. 16 p. OrP **7718**

Oregon War Savings Committee.
Outline for county executive committee of the Oregon War Savings Committee in National War Savings Campaign, June 28, 1916. [n.p., n.d.] 19 p. OrP **7719**

Oregon-Washington Railroad and Navigation Company.
Astoria and its centennial, Aug. 10 to Sept. 9, 1911. Portland, Or., 1911. 31 p. illus. OrHi **7720**

The land that lures; summer in the Pacific Northwest. 4th ed. [Portland, Or., 1913?] 45 p. front., illus., plate, map. OrHi OrP WaS **7721**

The money makers; swine raising in the

Pacific Northwest. [Portland, Or., 19—?] 23 p. illus., map. WaU **7722**

Pointers for practical farmers. Portland, Or., C. L. Smith [192-?] 47 p. illus., port., map. WaPS **7723**

Portland, Or., the city of roses. Portland, Or., 1912. 48 p. illus., map. OrHi **7724**

Public lands in Oregon and Washington. Portland, Or. [1913?] 15 p. map. WaU **7725**

Seattle. [Portland, Or.? 191-?] [62] p. illus. WaPS **7726**

Seattle; manufactures and commerce. [Seattle, 1912?] 16 p. map. WaPS **7727**

Seattle; residential advantages and attractions for tourists. Portland, Or. [1913?] 15 p. illus., map. WaPS **7728**

Twenty-five reasons why you should come to western Washington. Portland, Or. [192-?] 8 p. illus., map. WaPS **7729**

— — — **War Auxiliary.**
Letters from O.-W. R.R. & N. boys at the front, overseas, and in camp, acknowledging Christmas greetings and relating some thrilling experiences. [n.p., 1919?] 69 p. OrU **7730**

Oregon Wildcat, see no. 2627.

Oregon's famous Columbia River Highway; a descriptive view book in colors, reproducing from actual photos. the most prominent views of America's most famous and featured highway. Portland, Or., Lipschuetz and Katz [1920] [61] p. col. illus. OrHi OrU WaU **7731**

Oregon's resources; Pan-American exposition, 1901. [n.p.] 1901. 48 p. illus., ports., maps. OrP **7732**

Oregon's White House Conference on Child Health and Protection.
Program, committee reports, etc. [n.p.] 1932. 1 v. OrP **7733**

O'Reilly, Harrington.
Life among the American Indians, fifty years on the trail; a true story of western life. London, Chatto & Windus, 1891. 381 p. front., illus. CVicAr **7734**

Ormond, Clyde, 1906-
Hunting in the Northwest. New York, Knopf, 1948. xiv, 274 p. illus. (Borzoi books for sportsmen) OrCS WaS WaT WaU **7735**

Ormonde, Czenzi, 1913-
Laughter from downstairs. New York, Farrar, 1948. 271 p. Puget Sound setting. OrP WaS WaT WaU **7736**

Ormsby, Burke W., see no. 3489.

Osborn, Edward Bolland, 1867-
Greater Canada; the past, present and future of the Canadian Northwest; together with a new map especially prepared for this volume from the latest governmental surveys. New York, Wessels, 1900. 243 p. WaS **7737**

Osborn, Henry Fairfield, see nos. 9856, 9857.

Osborn, Sherard, 1822-1875.
The polar regions; or, A search after Sir John Franklin's expedition. New York, Barnes, 1854. 216 p. CVicAr **7738**

Stray leaves from an Arctic journal; or, Eighteen months in the polar regions in search of Sir John Franklin's expedition in the years 1850-51, by Lieut. Sherard Osborn, commanding H. M. S. vessel "Pioneer". London, Longman, 1852. 320 p. front., illus., 3 plates, map.

CV WaS WaU **7739**

Same. New ed. Edinburgh, Blackwood, 1865. x, 334 p. illus., map.

CV CVicAr **7740**

See also nos. 6232-6235.

Oscar Dhu, see no. 6361.

Osgood, Cornelius, 1905-

The ethnography of the Tanaina. New Haven, Yale University Press, 1937. 229 p. illus., 14 plates, maps. (Publications in anthropology, no. 16)

CVU OrP WaU **7741**

Osgood, Ernest Staples.

The day of the cattleman. Minneapolis, University of Minnesota 1929. x, 283 p. front., plates, maps, facsims., diagrs. Many **7742**

Osgood, Harriett (Keeney) 1905-

Yukon River children, pictures by Lilian Neuner. New York, Oxford University Press, c1944. 80 p. illus., 4 col. plates.

Or OrLgE OrP WaS WaSp WaT **7743**

Ostenso, Martha, 1900-

The white reef. New York, Dodd, 1934. 288 p. Vancouver Island fishing village.

Many **7744**

Ostrander, Alson Bowles, 1849-

The Bozeman trail forts under Gen. Philip St. George Cooke in 1866, with letters from Brigadier Gen. William H. Bisbee and Brigadier Gen. W. C. Brown, also foreword by Robert S. Ellison, preface by Dan W. Greenburg. Casper, Wyo., Commercial Printing Co., 1932. 46 p. illus., ports.

MtHi Or OrHi OrP Wa WaS **7745**

The Custer semi-centennial ceremonies, 1876-June 25, 26, 1926. Casper, Wyo., Casper Printing and Stationery Co., 1926. 48 p. front. (port.) illus., ports.

MtHi Or **7746**

Oswego, Oregon. 1st Congregational Church.

Constitution and by-laws, adopted April 12, 1890. Portland, Or., Steel, 1890. 10 p.

OrHi **7747**

Otis, James, see no. 5381.

Ottawa, National Gallery of Canada.

Exhibition of Canadian west coast art, December 1927, arranged in cooperation with the National Museum, Ottawa, the Royal Ontario Museum, Toronto, McGill University and the Art Association, Montreal. Ottawa [1927] 16 p.

CVicAr WaU **7748**

Ottenheimer, Albert M.

The Washington State Theatre, theatre of youth; a handbook [designed by D. Gerald Cloud and written by Albert M. Ottenheimer, the photo. from "Peer Gynt" is by F. A. Kunishige, the others by Richard Erickson, seal design by Harry J. Bonaph] Seattle, Washington State Theatre, 1936. 32 p. illus. WaS **7749**

Our country: West. Boston, Perry Mason & Co., 1900, c1897. 256 p. illus. WaS **7750**

Same. 1902. (Companion series) WaSp **7751**

Our garden book, written by gardening and horticultural experts of the Pacific Northwest, the articles in this book have been selected from among those which have appeared in more extended form in "Garden; the home magazine" of the Sunday Journal. Portland, Or., Binfords & Mort [c1941] 190 p. front., illus., plates.

OrCS OrP Wa WaSp WaU **7752**

Our Pacific railroads; the Union and Central Pacific and northern routes; their character and relative merits. New York, 1868. 32 p. OrP **7753**

The Outing Magazine.

Special Pacific coast number. New York, 1906. 521-664 p. front., illus., plates, port. (v. 47, no. 5, Feb. 1906) WaU **7754**

Outram, Sir James, 1864-1925.

In the heart of the Canadian Rockies. New York, Macmillan, 1905. xii, 466 p. front., illus., plates, 3 maps (1 fold.) Many **7755**

Same. 1906. OrU WaS WaT **7756**

Same. 1923. CVU WaTC WaU **7757**

Overholser, Joel F.

Fort Benton centennial celebration program (1846-1946). [n.p.] 1946. 1 v. illus.

MtHi **7758**

Overholser, Wayne D., 1906-

Buckaroo's code. New York, Macmillan, 1947. 223 p. Many **7759**

Romantic history of central Oregon. [Bend, Or.? 194—?] 7 p. OrU **7760**

Owen, John, 1818-1889.

The journals and letters of Major John Owen, pioneer of the Northwest, 1850-1871, embracing his purchase of St. Mary's Mission; the building of Fort Owen; his travels; his relation with the Indians; his work for the government; and his activities as a western empire builder for twenty years, transcribed and ed. from the original manuscripts in the Montana Historical Society and the collection of W. R. Coe, Esq., by Seymour Dunbar, and with notes to Owen's text by Paul C. Phillips, with two maps and thirty plates. [Helena, Mont.] Montana Historical Society, 1927. 2 v. front., plates, ports., 2 maps, plan, facsims. MtBozC MtHi **7761**

Same. New York, E. Eberstadt, 1927.

Many **7762**

Owen, Robert Dale, see no. 10870.

Owen, Russell, see no. 7501.

Owens, H. K.

Some remarks on the water powers of the Puget Sound country and their utilization for manufacturing purposes. [Seattle, n.d.] 31 p. WaS **7763**

Owens-Adair, Mrs. Bethina Angelina, see nos. 20-24.

Owyhee Avalanche, Silver City, Idaho.

A historical, descriptive and commercial directory of Owyhee County, Idaho, January 1898. Silver City, Idaho, 1898. 140 [16] iv p. front., illus., plates, ports.

IdB WaU **7764**

Oxley, James Macdonald, 1855-
In the wilds of the west coast. New York, T. Nelson and Sons, 1895. 398 p. front., plates.
CV CVicAr CVU OrU WaS WaU **7765**
Same. 1905.   CVicAr WaSp **7766**

Pace, John W., comp.
The Montana blue book; a biographical, historical and statistical book of references, comp. by Jno. W. Pace and H. J. Mock, official biographers of the House, by resolution passed March 5, 1891. Helena, Mont., Journal Pub. co. [c1891] 184 p. front., ports. IdU MtHi MtU **7767**

Pacific Advertising Association.
How war is changing Pacific area markets, prepared for the Advancement of Business committees. [San Francisco?] 1943. 110 p. tables, diagrs.
Or WaS WaU **7768**
Products the West can produce and advertising's part in marketing them, prepared by the Market Study Committee, David E. Faville, chairman. [San Francisco] 1944. 140 p. illus., diagrs.
Many **7769**

Pacific American Shipowners and Waterfront Employers.
Hot cargo; the longshoremen's alibi for arbitration award violations, pub. by Pacific American Shipowners and Waterfront Employers of San Francisco, Seattle, Portland and San Pedro. San Francisco, Allied Printing, 1935. 16 p.   WaPS **7770**

Pacific Builder & Engineer.
Camp Lewis, Tacoma, construction number. Seattle, 1917. 84 p. illus., ports., fold. map. (v. 22, no. 51, Dec. 21, 1917)
IdU WaS WaU **7771**
Grand Coulee dam issue. [Seattle, 1934] 74 p. illus., ports. (v. 39, no. 15, Apr. 1934)
WaU **7772**

Pacific Clipper Line, Seattle, Wash.
Seattle to the Nome gold coast. [Seattle] Richardson, Feb. 1900. 44 p. illus.
WaU **7773**

Pacific Club, Victoria, B. C.
By-laws. Victoria, B. C., Colonist Steam Presses, 1905. 16 p.   CVicAr **7774**

Pacific Coast Blue Book Publishing Company.
The Pacific coast automobile blue book; California, Washington, Oregon, British Columbia. San Francisco, c1915. 1 v. maps.   OrU WaU **7775**

Pacific Coast Building Officials Conference.
Final preliminary draft of proposed uniform building code. [n.p.] 1926. 227 p.
OrP **7776**

Pacific Coast Coal Company.
Constitution of central and mine councils of Pacific Coast Coal Co., organized January 25, 1922; program for meetings, standard practice rules, constituting Mutual Benefit Association, all revised to

November 1, 1924. Seattle, 1924. 112 p.
WaU **7777**

Pacific Coast Conference of Delegates from American Federation of Labor Unions, Portland, Or., 1943.
Pacific Coast Conference of Delegates from American Federation of Labor unions in the states of Washington, Oregon and California, held April 21, 1943 at Portland, Oregon, reported by Merritt G. Dyer. Seattle [1943] 53 p.
WaS WaU **7778**

Pacific Coast Congregational Alliance for the Promotion of Education.
Christian education by Congregationalists in the seven Pacific coast states; theological seminary, colleges and academies associated with the churches in the Pacific Coast Congregational Alliance, September 1893. [San Francisco, Cubery & Co., 1893] 55 p. front., 14 plates, port. (Publication no. 1)
OrP OrU WaS WaWW **7779**

Pacific Coast Employing Printers' Congress.
Souvenir program, July 14, 15, 16, 17th, 1913, Seattle, U. S. A. [Seattle, Champion Coated Paper Co., 1913] 40 p. illus., ports.   WaU **7780**

Pacific Coast Fire Insurance Company.
Our fifty years, 1890-1940, the romantic story of Vancouver from pioneer days. Vancouver, B. C. [Rose, Cowan & Latta, c1940] 22 p. plates, port.
CVicAr CVU **7781**

Pacific Coast historical almanac, 1931. [Tacoma, Smith-Digby Co., c1931] 32 p.
WaS WaT **7782**

Pacific Coast Industries.
Lewis County, Wash. Tacoma, 1900. [40] p. illus., ports. (Suppl. to Chehalis Bee-Nugget, Oct. 19, 1900)   WaU **7783**
Olympia and Grays Harbor. Tacoma, 1900. [32] p. illus., ports. (July 1900) WaU **7784**

Pacific Coast Intercollegiate Athletic Conference.
Athletic code (with constitution) 1948. Los Angeles [1948] 117 p.   OrCS **7785**
Constitution and rules governing the conduct of athletics, as approved December 18, 1929. [n.p., 1930?] 42 p.
WaPS **7786**
See also no. 1319.

Pacific Coast League.
Baseball records from 1903-1940 inclusive. [n.p.] Helms Athletic Foundation [1940] 64 p.   WaT **7787**

Pacific Coast Mint Company, Klamath Falls, Or.
The Pacific Coast Mint Company, Incorporated, producers of peppermint oil, Klamath County's new industry. [Portland, Or., Glass & Prudhomme, 192—] 12 p.   Or **7788**

Pacific Coast Steamship Company, San Francisco, Calif.
Alaska excursions, season 1901. [San Francisco] 1901. 12 p. illus., map, plans.
WaU **7789**
All about Alaska. San Francisco, 1887. 32 p.   OrHi WaWW **7790**

Same. 1888. 62 p. illus. WaU 7791

Same. 1890. 63 p. illus. WaS 7792

Same. 1891. CVU WaU 7793

Same. 1894. WaPS WaU 7794

Four thousand miles north and south from San Francisco, covering coast travel from Mexico to Alaska. [San Francisco, 1896] 75 p. illus., map, plans.
WaPS WaU 7795

Pacific First Federal Savings & Loan Association.
Western living houses. [n.p., n.d.] 24 p. illus,. plans. WaT 7796

Pacific Great Eastern Railway.
British Columbia, the last great big game country. Vancouver, B. C. [193—?] [10] p. illus., map. WaPS 7797

The Pacific Great Eastern Railway belt; farm lands and natural resources. Victoria, B. C., Banfield, 1925. 45 p. illus., fold. map, tables. CVU 7798

Pacific Huts, Inc., Seattle, Wash.
The Pacific hut for fighters overseas. [Seattle, 1944] [148] p. illus., ports.
WaS WaU 7799

The story of the Pacific hut born to answer a war problem. Seattle, c1944. 1 v. front., illus., plates. WaT 7800

Pacific Lumber Trade Journal.
Washington, its lumber and wood working industries, special series no. 2. Seattle, 1899. 52 p. illus. WaU 7801

Pacific Lutheran College, Parkland, Wash.
Golden jubilee, 1894-1944. Parkland, Wash., 1944. 1 v. illus. (Bulletin, v. 24, no. 2, Nov. 1944) WaT 7802

Pacific Medical Service.
A "new deal" in medical care and costs. [Seattle, c1933] [14] p. illus. WaU 7803

Pacific Mills, Ltd., Vancouver, B. C.
A graphic history of Pacific Mills, Limited, manufacturers of pulp and paper and paper products. [Vancouver, B. C., 1946?] [106] p. illus.
CV CVicAr CVU 7804

Ocean Falls. [n.p., n.d.] [24] p. illus.
CVicAr 7805

Der Pacific Nordwest Einwanderungsgesellschaft. Portland, Or.
Der Pacific Nordwesten; sein Reichtum und seine Hilfsquellen; Oregon, Washington, Idaho. Portland, Or. [n.d.] 128 p. illus. OrP 7806

Pacific Northwest Boxed Apples, Inc.
Articles of incorporation and by-laws. Seattle [1926] 16 p. WaPS 7807

Pacific Northwest Cooperative Camps.
Spend your vacation in Mount Rainier National Park. [Seattle, 19—?] [4] p. illus.
WaPS 7808

The Pacific Northwest Hotel News.
Salutation of the Pacific Northwest to Longview, Washington, the new city and port of the mighty Columbia. [Portland, Or., 1923] 24 p. illus.
OrP WaPS WaS WaU 7809

Pacific Northwest Immigration Board, Portland, Or.
The Pacific Northwest, its wealth and resources; Oregon, Washington, Idaho. Portland, Or. [n.d.] 128 p. illus., plates.
OrHi OrP OrU WaU 7810

The Pacific Northwest; information for settlers and others; Oregon and Washington Territory. New York, Northwest, 1883. 32 p. map. MtU OrP WaSp 7811

Same. New York, Rankin, 1883.
MtU Wa 7812

Pacific Northwest Library Association.
Interlibrary loan policies of Pacific Northwest libraries, 1937, comp. by Reference Section of Pacific Northwest Library Association. Clara Van Sant, chairman. [n.p., 1937] 23 p. Many 7813

Report of the committee on pensions, June 1930. [Salem, Or.] 1930. 19 p.
OrP WaS WaT 7814

Report of the special committee on salaries. [n.p.] 1920. 23 p. tables.
OrHi OrP WaU 7815

Tentative draft of a revised public library act, for the state of Washington. [n.p., n.d.] 5 p. WaPS 7816

A union list of manuscripts in libraries of the Pacific Northwest, comp. by Charles W. Smith, chairman, Committee on Bibliography, Pacfic Northwest Library Association. Seattle, University of Washington Press, 1931. 57 p. Many 7817

Union catalogue of books in embossed type in the libraries of the Pacific Northwest. Seattle, 1932. 40 [16] p.
CVU IdU OrP WaS WaU 7818

See also no. 9583.

Pacific Northwest Loggers Association.
More timber; a forest program for the Pacific Northwest. [Portland, Or., Pacific Northwest Loggers Association and West Coast Lumbermen's Association, 1947] 36 p. illus., maps, tables, diagrs.
OrCS OrP WaT WaU 7819

See also no. 10865.

Pacific Northwest Product Survey.
Creating new jobs, new industries in the Pacific Northwest. Seattle, Gateway Printing Co., 1945. [14] p. WaS 7820

Pacific Northwest Tourist Association.
Automobiling in the Pacific Northwest. [Seattle, n.d.] [30] p. illus., fold. map.
OrP 7821

Fishing in the Pacific Northwest. [Seattle, n.d.] [22] p. illus. OrP WaE 7822

Golfing in the Pacific Northwest. [Seattle, n.d.] [22] p. illus. OrP WaE 7823

Mountaineering in the Pacific Northwest. [Seattle, n.d.] [22] p. illus.
OrP WaE 7824

The Pacific Northwest for your vacation. [Seattle, 192—?] 1 v. illus., maps.
WaE WaT 7825

The Pacific Northwest; the world's greatest out of doors. [Seattle, 1917?] [30] p. illus., map. OrP WaPS 7826

Yachting in the Pacific Northwest. Seattle [n.d.] [11] p. illus. OrP WaE **7827**

Pacific Northwest Wheat Improvement Conference.
Report of the Pacific Northwest Wheat Improvement Conference held at the State College of Washington, December 14, 1928. Pullman, Wash., 1928. 70 p. tables. WaU **7828**

Pacific Outlook.
Mining laws of Oregon; containing a synopsis of all the Oregon mining laws, including those of the last legislative assembly and also a digest of all the federal statutes pertaining to the mining industry; a compendium of useful information for the miner, prospector, rancher. Ed. 3. Grants Pass, Or., 1908. 60 p. OrP **7829**

Pacific Pathways Magazine.
Pacific Northwest in color. Los Angeles, c1947. [32] p. col. illus. WaS **7830**

Pacific Pine Lumber Co.
Tests of strength and other data of Douglas fir, commonly known as Puget Sound or Oregon pine, and comparisons with other woods used for structural purposes. San Francisco [1889] 36 p. front., plates. WaU **7831**

Pacific railway route, British Columbia. [n. p., n.d.] 8 p. CVicAr **7832**

Pacific Spruce Corporation.
"The last great stand." Portland, Or. [1924] 30 p. illus., maps, tables. OrP **7833**

Pacific states newspaper directory, containing a carefully prepared list of all the newspapers and periodicals published in California, Oregon, Washington, Idaho, Utah, Nevada, Arizona, New Mexico, Montana, Alaska, Wyoming, British Columbia, Texas, Colorado, Sandwich Islands, Mexico; arranged alphabetically by towns and also by counties, with a brief description of each state, territory and county. 3d ed. San Francisco, Palmer & Rey, 1888. 348 p. CVicAr **7834**
Same. 1890. 320 p. WaS **7835**

Pacific Steamship Company, San Francisco, Calif.
Alaska; top o' the world tours. [Seattle, c1924] 31 p. illus., maps. WaU **7836**
Cruising the world's smoothest waterway thru the Inside Passage and 10,000 islands of Alaska. [n.p.] 1929. 27 p. col. front., illus., fold. col. map, photos., tables. WaU **7837**
Same. [12] p. illus., map, photos., tables. WaU **7838**

Pacific Telephone and Telegraph Company.
History of the Pacific system. [San Francisco?] 1938. 40 p. WaPS **7839**
What interchange of telephone service would mean. Portland, Or. [1917] [8] p. OrP **7840**

Pacific University, Forest Grove, Or.
Diamond jubilee year, 75 years of service, 1849-1924. Forest Grove, Or. [1924] 48 p. illus., ports. OrU WaU **7841**
Fifty years of Pacific University, 1848-1898. [n.p., n.d.] 86 p.
OrHi OrP OrU WaU WaWW **7842**

The inauguration of the Rev. Thomas McClelland as president of Tualatin Academy and Pacific University, Forest Grove, Or., June 15, 1892. Forest Grove, Or., Times Steam Printing House [1892?] 32 p. OrHi WaU **7843**

Service in memory of Harvey Whitefield Scott under the auspices of Pacific University, Thursday, September twenty-nine, nineteen hundred and ten. [Portland, Or., Ivy Press, 1911] 37 p. port. Many **7844**

A souvenir bulletin of articles exhibited by Pacific University at the Alaska-Yukon-Pacific Exposition, 1909. [Forest Grove, Or., 1909] 24 p.
OrHi WaS WaU **7845**

Pack, Charles Lathrop, see nos. 10873, 11110.

Packenham, Bethel.
Here we have Idaho, by Bethel Packenham and McKinley Helm; music by Sallie Hume-Douglas. Caldwell, Idaho, Caxton, c1931. 1 v. IdB **7846**

Packenham, R., see no. 1383.

Padelford, Frederick Morgan, see no. 7995.

Paden, Irene (Dakin) 1888-
The wake of the prairie schooner, with pen and ink drawings by the author. New York, Macmillan, 1943. xix, 514 p. illus., maps. Many **7847**

Page, Elizabeth Merwin, 1889-
Wagons west; a story of the Oregon Trail. New York, Farrar [c1930] xiv, 361 p. front., plates, facsim. Many **7848**
Wild horses and gold; from Wyoming to the Yukon, illus. by Paul Brown. New York, Farrar [c1932] xiii, 362 p. front., illus., fold. map. Many **7849**

Painter, E. H.
History; what it is and how to teach it; address delivered before the Teachers' Institute of Lewis County, Wash., February 19, 1906. [n.p., 1906?] 10 p. WaU **7850**

Pajeken, Friedrich J., 1855-
Les trappeurs du Wyoming, tr. de Louis de Hessem. Tours, Alfred Mame et fils, 1892. 237 p. front., plates. Wyoming Territory including Montana. WaU **7851**

Palladino, Lawrence Benedict, 1837-1927.
Indian and white in the Northwest; or, A history of Catholicity in Montana, with an introd. by John B. Brondel. Baltimore, J. Murphy & Co., 1894. xxv, 411 p. front., 90 plates, 55 ports., fold. map, facsim. Many **7852**
Same. 2d ed., rev. and enl. Lancaster, Pa., Wickersham Pub. Co., 1922. xx, 512 p. front., illus., plates, ports. Many **7853**

Palliser, John, 1807-1887.
The solitary hunter; or, Sporting adventures in the prairies. 8th thousand, with illus. London, Routledge, 1856. xvi, 234 p. front., 6 plates. MtU WaSp **7854**
Same. New ed. 1857. CVicAr Or **7855**
Solitary rambles and adventures of a hunter in the prairies. London, Murray, 1853. xiv, 326 p. plates.
CVicAr MtBozC MtHi WaSp WaU **7856**

Palmer, Frederick, 1873-
In the Klondyke; including an account of a winter's journey to Dawson. New York, Scribner, 1899. x, 218 p. front., plates. Many **7857**

Palmer, Henry Spencer, 1838-1893.
British Columbia, Williams Lake and Cariboo; report on portions of the Williams Lake and Cariboo districts, and on the Fraser River from Fort Alexander to Fort George. New Westminster, B. C., Royal Engineer Press, 1863. 25 p. 3 maps (2 fold.) diagr. CVicAr CVU **7858**

Report of a journey of survey from Victoria to Fort Alexander via North Bentinck Arm. New Westminster, B. C., Royal Engineer Press, 1863. 30 p. tables. CVicAr **7859**

See also no. 2849.

Palmer, Howard, 1883-
A climber's guide to the Rocky Mountains of Canada, by Howard Palmer and J. Monroe Thorington. New York, American Alpine Club, 1921. xvii, 183 p. 183 p. front., maps (part fold.) WaS WaU **7860**

Same. New York, Knickerbocker Press, 1921. CV **7861**

Same. 2d ed. Philadelphia, American Alpine Club, 1930, c1921. xvii. 244 p. fold. map. MtU OrP WaT **7862**

Early explorations in British Columbia for the Canadian Pacific Railway. [n.p.] 1916. 17 p. CVU **7863**

Edward W. D. Holway, a pioneer of the Canadian Alps. Minneapolis, Minnesota University Press [c1931] xiii, 81 p. front. (port.) 5 plates, map.
CV CVic WaS WaT **7864**

Mountaineering and exploration in the Selkirks; a record of pioneer work among the Canadian Alps, 1908-1912, with 2 new maps and 219 illus. New York, Putnam, 1914. xxvii, 439 p. front., illus., plates (1 double) fold. maps, diagrs. (1 fold.) Many **7865**

Palmer, Joel, 1810-1881.
Journal of travels over the Rocky Mountains to the mouth of the Columbia River, 1845 and 1846; containing descriptions of the valleys of the Willamette, Umpqua, and Clamet; a general description of Oregon Territory, a list of necessary outfits for emigrants, and a table of distances from camp to camp on the route; also the organic laws of Oregon Territory; tables of about 300 words of the Chinook jargon, &c. Cincinnati, J. A. & U. P. James, 1847. 189 p. CVicAr OrHi OrP WaU **7866**

Palmer, Mrs. Katherine Evangeline Hilton (VanWinkle) 1895-
Honne, the spirit of the Chehalis; the Indian interpretation of the origin of the people and animals, as narrated by George Saunders, collected and arranged by Katherine VanWinkle Palmer. [Geneva, N. Y., W. F. Humphrey, c1925] 204 p. front., illus.
Or OrP Wa WaS WaSp WaU **7867**

Palmer, William Harry.
Pages from a seaman's log; being the first eighteen months of the cruise of H. M. S. Warspite in the Pacific. Victoria, B. C., 1891. 64 p. CVicAr CVU **7868**

Pan American Airways, Inc. Alaska Division.
Pan American airways system; the Panair way, handbook of information for personnel. [Seattle? 1943] 63 p. illus., port., map. WaU **7869**

Pan Pacific Progress.
Alaska edition. Los Angeles, 1930. 45 p. illus., port., map. (Mar. 1930)
OrU WaT **7870**

Pandosy, Marie Charles.
Grammar and dictionary of the Yakima language, trans. by George Gibbs and J. G. Shea. New York, Cramoisy Press, 1862. 59 p. Or WaS WaSp **7871**

Paneth, Philip.
Alaskan backdoor to Japan, with 2 maps and 16 pages illus. London, Alliance Press [1943] 108 p. illus., plates, maps.
WaS WaU **7872**

Panton, James Hoyes.
Rambles in the North-west across the prairies and in the passes of the Rocky Mountains. Guelph, Ont., Mercury Steam Printing House, 1885. 20 p. CV **7873**

Papanin, Ivan Dmitrievich, 1894-
Life on the ice floe, trans. from the Russian by Fanny Smitham. New York, Hutchinson [1940] 240 p. front. (map) plates. WaS **7874**

Papers on railway agreements between Dominion and provincial government of British Columbia. [Victoria, B. C., Wolfenden, 1877] 1 v. CVicAr **7875**

Paradigma verbi activi. Lingua numipu vulgo Nez Perce: studio PP missionariorum S. J. in montibus saxosis pro eorumdem privato uso. Desmit, I. T., Typis missionis S. S. Cordis, 1888. 50 p. CV **7876**

Paramore, Edward E., Jr.
The ballad of Yukon Jake, black and white illus. by Hogarth, Jr. New York, Coward-McCann, 1928. [42] p. front., illus. Hogarth, Jr. is pseudonym of Rockwell Kent. WaS WaU **7877**

Paramore, H. H., comp.
The practical guide to America's new El Dorado, Klondike gold fields. St. Louis, Myerson, 1897. 64 p. 12 plates, fold. map. CVicAr **7878**

Parham, Henry James, 1870-
A nature lover in British Columbia. London, Witherby [1937] 292 p. front., 20 plates, table. CV CVic CVicAr WaS **7879**

Parish, John Carl, 1881-1939.
The persistence of the westward movement and other essays, with an introd. by Dan Elbert Clark. Berkeley, Calif., University of California Press, 1943. xxii, 187 p. Many **7880**

Park, Joseph.
A practical view of the mining laws of British Columbia. Victoria, B. C., British Colonist, 1864. xii, 64, lxv-lxx p.
CVicAr **7881**

Park, William Zerbe.
Shamanism in western North America; a

study in cultural relationships. Evanston, Ill., Northwestern Univeristy, 1938. 166 p. (Studies in the social sciences, no. 2)   CVicAr CVU OrU WaWW   **7882**

Park, William Lee, 1859-
Pioneer pathways to the Pacific; drawings by P. H. F. Follett. Clare, Mich., Clara Aire [c1935] 284 p. front., plates, ports. OrP OrSaW OrU WaPS WaS   **7883**

Parker, Aaron F.
Forgotten tragedies of Indian warfare in Idaho; history of the "Sheepeater" campaigns of 1878-1879; vivid story of the last Indian wars in Idaho County. [Grangeville, Idaho, Idaho County Free Press, 1925] [12] p.   IdU WaS   **7884**

Parker, Adella M.
How Washington women lost the ballot. [Seattle? 18—?] [4] p.   WaU   **7885**

Parker, Frank J., ed.
Washington Territory; the present and prospective future of the upper Columbia country, embracing the counties of Walla Walla, Whitman, Spokane and Stevens, with a detailed description of northern Idaho. Walla Walla, Wash. [1881?] 17 p.   OrHi   **7886**
Same. Photostat copy.   WaU   **7887**

Parker, Frederick William.
The farmer's guest and other rhymes. Portland, Or., T. G. Robison [c1921] 23 p.   OrCS OrP OrU WaU   **7888**

Parker, Sir Gilbert, see no. 5263.

Parker, Henry Webster, 1822-1903.
Dr. Marcus Whitman, pioneer missionary to Oregon. [n.p., n.d.] 5 p. WaWW   **7889**
Rev. Samuel Parker, missionary to Oregon, 1835. [n.p.] 1895. 6 p. WaWW   **7890**

Parker, Herschel C., see no. 1191.

Parker, Hollon.
Lessons and incidents form the life of Hollon Parker of Walla Walla, Washington and other sketches. [n.p., n.d.] 86 p. port.   OrHi   **7891**

Parker, Samuel, 1779-1866.
An exploring tour beyond the Rocky Mountains in North America, under the direction of the American Board of Commissioners for Foreign Missions, performed in the years 1835, 1836, and 1837. Abridged. Dublin, William Porteus, 1840. 209 p.   WaU   **7892**
Journal of an exploring tour beyond the Rocky Mountains, under the direction of the American Board of Commissioners for Foreign Missions, in the years 1835, '36, and '37; containing a description of the geography, geology, climate, productions of the country, and the number, manners, and customs of the natives, with a map of Oregon Territory. Ithaca, N. Y., 1838. 371 p. front. (fold. map) plate, tables.   Many   **7893**
Same. 2d ed. 1840. 400 p.   Many   **7894**
Same. 3d ed. 1842. 408 p.   Many   **7895**
Same. 4th ed. 1844 [c1838] 416 p. Many   **7896**
Same. 5th ed. Auburn, N. Y., J. C. Derby, 1846. 422 p. front. (fold. map) plate.   Many   **7897**

A journey beyond the Rocky Mountains in 1835, 1836, and 1837, corrected and extended in the present edition. Edinburgh, W. & R. Chambers, 1841. 78 p.   CV CVicAr OrP WaSp WaT   **7898**
Tagebuch einer Reise uber das Felsengebirge nach dem Oregongebiet. Dresden, Waltersche Hofbuchhandlung, 1840. x, 241 p. (Magazin der neuesten Reisen und Landerbeschreibungen, hrsg. von Tr. Bromme. Bd. 1)   WaU   **7899**

Parkin, Joseph, see no. 1384.

Parkman, Francis, 1823-1893.
The California and Oregon trail; being sketches of prairie and Rocky Mountain life. New York, William L. Allison [n.d.] 320 p. Also published as The Oregon Trail.   OrSaW WaU   **7900**
Same. New York, Burt [n.d.] OrSaW   **7901**
Same. Chicago, Donohue [n.d.]   OrSaw   **7902**
Same. New York, Hurst [n.d.] 299 p.   IdP Wa   **7903**
Same. New York, Putnam, 1849. 448 p. front.   CVicAr OrHi WaSp WaU   **7904**
Same. 3d ed.   OrP   **7905**
Same. 4th ed. Boston, Little, 1872. 381 p.   OrCS OrHi OrP   **7906**
Same. New York, Hurst [1894] v, 299 p.   WaU   **7907**
Same. With an introd. by Edward G. Bourne. New York, Crowell [c1901] xix, 416 p.   IdIf WaU   **7908**
Same. Boston, Little [c1872-1914] 479 p.   IdIf   **7909**
The journals of Francis Parkman, ed. by Mason Wade. New York, Harper, 1947. 2 v. illus., ports., maps, facsims. Many   **7910**
The Oregon Trail; sketches of prairie and Rocky Mountain life. Cambridge, University Press, [n.d] 381 p. Also published as The California and Oregon Trail.   WaPS   **7911**
Same. New York, Burt [n.d.] 320 p. front.   IdP MtBozC OrCS WaA   **7912**
Same. New York, H. M. Caldwell [n.d.] 320 p. front. (port.) (Berkeley library)   WaU   **7913**
Same. 8th ed. rev. Boston, Little, 1872. xii, 381 p.   WaWW   **7914**
Same. 1885.   CVU   **7915**
Same. Illus. by Frederic Remington. 1892. xviii, 479 p. front., illus., plates.   WaPS   **7916**
Same. xvi, 411 p.   WaWW   **7917**
Same. London, Macmillan, 1892.   CVicAr WaU   **7918**
Same. Boston, Little, 1895. 381 p. WaU   **7919**
Same. xviii, 479 p. front., plates. (Works)   MtU   **7920**
Same. c1898. 381 p.   IdB   **7921**
Same. [c1900]   OrSaW WaU   **7922**
Same. 1901 c1872.   OrSa   **7923**
Same. 1904. xx, 411 p.   WaU   **7924**
Same. 1905. xiv, 381 p.   IdUSB   **7925**
Same. 1906. xx, 411 p.   OrSaW   **7926**

Same. 1910 [c1900] xviii, 479 p. (Works)
WaU **7927**

Same. Ed. by William Ellery Leonard. Boston, Ginn [c1910] xxxvi, 361 p. front. (map) (Standard English classics)
WaPS WaSp WaU **7928**

Same. Ed. with notes and an introd. by Ottis B. Sperlin. New York, Longmans, 1910. xix, 363 p. (Longmans' English classics)
CVicAr Or **7929**

Same. Ed. by Charles H. J. Douglas. New York, Macmillan, c1910. xxi, 362 p. front. (port.) map. (Macmillan's pocket American and English classics)
WaPS **7930**

Same. Ed. with an introd. and notes by C. W. Vail. New York, Merrill [c1910] 553 p. front. (port.) map. (Merrill's English texts)
IdB IdU OrP **7931**

Same. Ed. for use in schools with an introd. and explanatory notes by Edward E. Hale, Jr. New York, Newson and Co. [c1910] xxxi, 320 p. map. (Standard literature series, v. 70)
Or **7932**

Same. Ed. for school use by William MacDonald. Chicago, Scott [c1911] 406 p.
OrHi **7933**

Same. Retold and abridged by Sarah Katherine Grames. Danville, N. Y., F. A. Owen Co., c1912. 32 p. (Instructor literature series, no. 231)
Or WaU **7934**

Same. 8th ed. rev. Boston, Little, 1913. 381 p.
CVU **7935**

Same. Ed. by Charles H. J. Douglas. New York, Macmillan, 1917 [c1910] xxi, 362 p. front. (port.) map. (Macmillan's pocket American and English classics)
MtU **7936**

Same. Ed. by Harry G. Paul. New York, Holt, 1918. xvii, 397 p. front. (port.) illus., map. (English readings for schools, gen. ed., W. L. Gross)
WaU **7937**

Same. With an introd. by James Cloyd Bowman. New York, Scribner [c1924] xxv, 433 p. map. (Modern student's library, American division)
MtBozC OrCS **7938**

Same. With illus. in col. by N. C. Wyeth. Boston, Little, 1925. vii, 364 p. col. front. (port.) col. plates. (Beacon Hill bookshelf)
Many **7939**

Same. With an introd., notes, and questions by Russell A. Sharp. Boston, Houghton [c1925] xix, 350 p. front. (map). (Riverside literature series)
WaU **7940**

Same. Ed. for schools and libraries by Walter S. Campbell. Oklahoma City, Harlow Pub. Co., 1927. iii, 454 p. front. (port.) illus. (Western series of English and American classics)
WaU **7941**

Same. With an introd. by Hamlin Garland. New York, Macmillan, 1930. xv, 369 p. (Modern Readers' series)
OrP **7942**

Same. With an introd. by Mark VanDoren, illus. by James Daugherty. New York, Farrar [c1931] xvii, 385 p. illus. (part col.)
Many **7943**

Same. With notes by Mabel Dodge Holmes and an introd. by Howard D. Driggs,

with exclusive illus. drawn for the Oregon Trail Memorial Association by William H. Jackson. Philadelphia, Winston [c1931] xi, 388 p. col. front., plates (part col.)
CVic IdB IdU OrP WaU **7944**

Same. Ed. from his notebooks by Mason Wade and illus. by Maynard Dixon. [New York] Heritage Press [c1943] xxii, 297 p. illus., col. plates (part double) (Heritage illustrated bookshelf)
WaS WaU **7945**

Same. Illus. by Thomas Hart Benton. Garden City, N. Y., Doubleday, c1945. vi, 328 p. col. plates.
Or OrCS OrU **7946**

Same. 1946. [c1945]
WaU **7947**

Same. London, Oxford University Press [1946] viii, 279 p.
WaU **7948**

Prairie and Rocky Mountain life; or, The California and Oregon trail, 4th ed. New York, Riker, 1854. 448 p. front.
WaU **7949**

Same. Columbus, Ohio, Miller, 1856. 448 p. front., 13 plates.
CVicAr **7950**

Same. 1857.
WaPS **7951**

Same. St. Louis, Miller, 1858.
WaU **7952**

Parks, Henry Martin, 1872-
Handbook of the mining industry of Oregon; alphabetical list of properties; description of mining districts, by H. M. Parks and A. M. Swartley. [Corvallis, Or.] 1916. 306 p. fold. map, diagrs. (1 fold.) (Mineral resources of Oregon, v. 2, no. 4) MtUM OrP OrSa OrU WaTC **7953**

Parrish, Philip Hammon, 1896-
Before the covered wagon, with illus. by George A. Dowling. Portland, Or., Metropolitan, 1931, 292 p. illus.
Many **7954**

Same. 1934.
IdU **7955**

Historic Oregon. New York, Macmillan, 1937. viii, 254 p. col. front., illus., plates (part col.) ports.
Many **7956**

See also no. 7710.

Parrish, Randall, 1858-1923.
Bob Hampton of Placer. New York, Burt, c1906. 383 p. col. front.
WaT **7957**

Great plains; the romance of western American exploration, warfare, and settlement, 1527-1870. 2d ed. Chicago, McClurg, 1907. 399 p. front., 27 plates, 5 ports.
Many **7958**

Parrish, Rob Roy McGregor.
Echoes from the valley. Portland, Or., G. H. Himes, 1884. 156 p. front. (port.)
OrHi OrP OrU WaSp WaTC WaU **7959**

Parry, Edward, bp. of Dover, 1830-1890.
Memoirs of Rear-Admiral Sir W. Edward Parry, by his son. 7th ed. London, Longman, 1860. xvi, 365 p. front. (port.) map.
CvicAr **7960**

Same. New ed. 1872.
CVicAr **7961**

Memorials of Charles Parry, Commander, Royal Navy, by his brother. London, Strahan, 1870. 1 v.
CVicAr **7962**

Parry, Sir William Edward, 1790-1855.
Journal of a voyage for the discovery of a northwest passage from the Atlantic to the Pacific; performed in the years 1819-20 in His Majesty's ships Hecla and

Griper under the orders of William Edward Parry, with an appendix containing the scientific and other observations. London, Murray, 1821. xxix, 310, clxxix p. front., illus., plates, maps (part fold.)
CV CVicAr WaU 7963
Same. 2d ed. CVicAr 7964
Journal of a second voyage for the discovery of a north-west passage from the Atlantic to the Pacific, performed in the years 1821-22-23, in His Majesty's ships Fury and Hecla, under the orders of Captain William Edward Parry. London, Murray, 1824, xxx, 571 p. plates (4 fold.) maps (4 fold.) tables.
CV CVicAr WaU 7965
Same. 2 v. WaU 7966
Same. New York, E. Duyckinck, 1824. xx, 464 p. front., illus., tables. Wa 7967
Journal of a third voyage for the discovery of a northwest passage, from the Atlantic to the Pacific, performed in the years 1824-25 in His Majesty's ships Hecla and Fury. London, Murray, 1826. xxvii, 151 p. front., 5 plates (part fold.) 3 maps (part fold.) CVicAr CVU 7968
Journals of the first, second, and third voyages for the discovery of a northwest passage from the Atlantic to the Pacific in 1819-20-21-22-23-24-25, in His Majesty's ships Hecla, Griper, and Fury. London, Murray, 1828. 5 v. fronts. (1 port.) fold. map. CVicAr WaS 7969
Narrative of an attempt to reach the North Pole in boats fitted for the purpose and attached to His Majesty's ship Hecla in the year 1827 under the command of Captain William Edward Parry. London, Murray, 1828. xxii, 229 p. front., plates, fold. map. CVicAr CVU 7970
Three voyages for the discovery of a north-west passage from the Atlantic to the Pacific and narrative of an attempt to reach the North Pole. London, Murray, 1831. 5 v. fronts., 5 plates, map.
CVicAr 7971

[Parson, C. H.]
A short history of Mountain Lodge no. 11, A. F. & A. M., G, R. B. C., A. L. 5886-A. L. 5932. [Golden, B. C., Golden Star, n.d.] [12] p. CVicAr 7972

Parsons, Harriet Trumbull.
The garden; a manual of gardening for the Pacific Northwest, by Harriet Trumbull Parsons and Elizabeth Nowland Holmes. Seattle, Lowman & Hanford, 1933. 117 p. illus.
OrU WaS WaSp WaU 7973

Parsons, John, 1855-
Beside the Beautiful Willamette. Portland, Or., Metropolitan, 1924. 308 p. front., illus., ports. Many 7974

Parsons, Mable Holmes,
Listener's room. Portland, Or., Binfords & Mort [c1940] 72 p. Portland poet.
OrCS OrHi OrP OrU WaU WaW 7975
On the sun-dial road. Portland, Or., Kilham's [c1944] 52 p. OrP WaU 7976
Pastels and silhouettes; a book of verse, illus. by Phyllis Muirden. Boston, Stratford, 1921. 89 p. plates.
OrMonO OrP OrU 7977

Parsons, Mrs. Marian Randall, see nos. 7146-7148.

Parsons, William, 1844-
An illustrated history of Umatilla County, by William Parsons; and of Morrow County, by W. S. Schiach, with a brief outline of the early history of the state of Oregon. [Spokane] W. H. Lever, 1902. xv, 581 p. plates, ports. Many 7978

Parton, James, 1822-1891.
Life of John Jacob Astor, to which is appended a copy of his last will. New York, American News Co., 1865. 121 p.
CVU WaU 7979

Partridge, Welles Mortimer.
Some facts about Alaska and its missions. [Peabody, Mass., C. H. Shepard, 1900] 46 p. illus. CVicAr WaS 7980

The Pasco Express.
Souvenir illustrated edition, giving a brief description of the Pasco-Palouse Irrigation Project, Franklin County, and the Columbia River Basin. Pasco, Wash., 1906. 24 p. illus., ports., map. (v. 3, no. 52, July 19, 1906. WaPS 7981

Pasco Reclamation Co.
Pasco irrigated fruit lands, containing report of soil survey based on investigations made for United States Reclamation Service. [Pasco, Wash., 1910] [14] p.
Or 7982

Pask, Joseph A., see no. 11096.

The Pastor's Journal.
Material on Jason Lee: From Boston to Salem (the Jason Lee special). — Two thousand miles for a book, by Helen L. Willcox. — Associates of Jason Lee, by John M. Canse. — Diary of Jason Lee beginning April 20, 1834. Philadelphia, 1934. 24 p. illus. (v. 6, no. 2, Mar. 1934.
Or OrHi 7983

Patch, Edith Marion, 1876-
Mountain neighbors, by Edith M. Patch and Carroll Lane Fenton, drawings by Carroll Lane Fenton. New York, Macmillan, 1936. 156 p. front., illus. Rocky Mountain animal stories. Many 7984

Pate, Andrew J.
Confession of the murderer of George Lamb and two others, who was executed at Albany, Oregon, on Tuesday, the 27th day of May 1862. Albany, Or., Stinson, 1862. 21 p. OrHi 7985

Paterson, Arthur Henry, 1862-1928.
The daughter of the Nez Perces. American authorized ed. New York, G. G. Peck, 1894. 381 p. front. (port.) Many 7986

Paterson, James Venn, 1867-
Workmen's compulsory compensation system, state of Washington; a proved failure and a business menace; review by an employer of the First Annual Report of the Industrial Insurance Commission, by president Seattle Construction and Dry Dock Company, Seattle, Washington. [Seattle? 1912?] 24 p.
OrU WaS WaTC 7987
Same. [1913] 31 p. WaPS WaS 7988

Patrons of Husbandry. Oregon State Grange.
Argument regarding the proposed amend-

ments to the state constitution to be voted upon at the next general election, Nov. 1910, providing for the development of a new system of levying and classification of taxes. [Gresham, Or.] Beaver State Herald, 1910. 15 p.

OrP **7989**

Grange list of the state of Oregon, Washington and Idaho for the year 1876. Salem, Or., Waite, 1876. 12 p. OrHi **7990**

— — — Washington State Grange.

The grange; F. H. C. F.; being a concise statement of the aims, purposes and practical workings of the order of Patrons of Husbandry under the jurisdiction of Washington State Grange. Olympia, Wash. [1911] 22 p. WaU **7991**

Questions and answers on the power districts and the three constitutional amendments. [n.p.] 1936. 8 p. WaPS **7992**

— — — — — — **Legislative Committee.**

Facts and findings about Grange initiative measures numbers 84 to 86. [Seattle, Central Printing Co., 1934] 8 p.

WaPS **7993**

Patterson, Mrs. Sara K.

Out of the fog. Caldwell, Idaho, Caxton, 1934. 203 p.

Wa WaE WaS WaSp WaT WaU **7994**

Patterson, Mrs. Viola (Hansen)

Victoria, B. C.; twelve woodcuts, with a foreword by Frederick Morgan Padelford. Seattle, University of Washington Book Store, 1928. [22] p. illus. (Chapbooks, ed. by G. Hughes, no. 21)

CVicAr OrP WaE WaS WaTC WaU **7995**

Patton, Hal D., 1872-

Anniversary banquet given by Hal D. Patton celebrating the fiftieth anniversary of his birth, 1872-January 12, 1922. [Salem, Or., N. D. Elliott, 1922] 98 p. illus., port.

IdU Or OrHi OrP WaSp WaU **7996**

Reunion of old friends and schoolmates and commemorating the sixty years of my arrival in Salem. Salem, Or. [1932] [6] p. illus. Or **7997**

Pattullo, Thomas Dufferin, 1873-

British Columbia's claim for readjustment of terms of union. [n.p., 1934] 32 p.

CVicAr **7998**

Province of British Columbia's claim for readjustment of terms of union. [n.p., 1935] 33 p. CVicAr **7999**

Paul, Elliot Harold, 1891-

A ghost town on the Yellowstone. New York, Random House [1948] 341 p.

MtBozC **8000**

Paul, Harry G., see no. 7937.

Paul, Joshua Hughes, 1863-

Out of doors in the West; field notes on characteristic plants, on ways and usefulness of the native birds, and on life histories of certain notable insects of the Rocky Mountain region. Salt Lake City, Deseret News, 1914. 256 p. illus. (Pupil's ed.) IdU **8001**

Paxson, Frederic Logan, 1877-

History of the American frontier, 1763-

1893. Boston, Houghton, 1924. xvii, 598 p. illus., maps (2 double)

MtBozC MtHi OrHi OrP WaT WaU **8002**

Same. Students' ed. [c1924] IdIf WaU **8003**

The last American frontier. New York, Macmillan, 1910. xi, 402 p. front., illus., plates, maps. (Stories from American history) Many **8004**

Same. 1918. WaU **8005**

Same. 1922 [c1910]

IdIf MtBozC MtHi OrCS Wa **8006**

Same. 1924 [c1910] IdU WaW **8007**

Same. 1928 [c1910] IdP **8008**

When the West is gone. New York, Holt [c1930] 137 p. (Brown University, Colver lectures, 1929) Many **8009**

Same. New York, Peter Smith, 1941.

MtHi WaTC **8010**

Payer, Julius, Ritter von, 1842-1915.

New lands within the Arctic Circle; narrative of the discoveries of the Austrian ship "Tegetthoff" in the years 1872-1874, trans. from the German. London, Macmillan, 1876. 2 v. fronts. (1 col.) illus., plates, double map. WaU **8011**

Payette Valley Real Estate Agency.

The peerless Payette & Snake River valleys. Caldwell, Idaho, Caxton [n.d.] 23 p. illus., map. WaS **8012**

Payne, Mrs. Doris Palmer.

Captain Jack, Modoc renegade. Portland, Or., Binfords & Mort [c1938] 259 p. plates, ports. Many **8013**

Peacock, Alexander Hamilton, 1880-

Globe trotting with a surgeon, with photos. by the author. Seattle, Lowman & Hanford [c1936] 276 p. front., plates.

Wa WaS WaU **8014**

Peale, A. C., see nos. 9386-9388.

Pearce, John.

The agricultural depression at home and the resources, capabilities and prospects of the Canadian North-West. London, Sell, 1883. 32 p. CVicAr **8015**

Pearce, Richard, comp.

Marooned in the Arctic, August to December 1929. [n.p. n.d.] 71 p. 3 plates, 2 ports., map. CVicAr **8016**

Pearcy Bros.

Walnut, filbert and prune culture in western Oregon. Salem, Or. [1919?] 12 p.

Or OrCS **8017**

Pearse, Benjamin William, 1832-1902.

Vancouver's Island; survey of the districts of Nanaimo and Cowichan Valley. London, Eyre & Spottiswoode, 1859. 14 p.

CVicAr **8018**

Pearse, Mark Guy, see nos. 11260-11263.

Peary, Robert E., see no. 4361.

Pease, Raymond Burnette.

Realm and reign of Mt. Tah-Ho-Ma. [n.p., 1913] [18] p. WaU **8019**

Peaslee Bros.

Souvenir views of Portland's great flood, June 1894. [Portland, Or., 1894?] 20 plates. OrHi WaU **8020**

Peattie, Donald Culross, 1898-
Forward the nation. New York, Putnam [1942] 281 p. Lewis and Clark expedition story. Many **8021**

Peattie, Roderick, 1891- ed.
The Pacific coast ranges; the contributors; Archie Binns, John Walton Caughey, Lois Crisler, and others. New York, Vanguard Press [1946] xviii, 402 p. front., plates, maps. (The American mountain series) Many **8022**

Peck, John Mason, 1789-1858.
A new guide for emigrants to the West, containing sketches of Ohio, Indiana, Illinois, Missouri, Michigan, with the territories of Wisconsin and Arkansas and the adjacent parts. Boston, Gould, Kendall & Lincoln, 1836. 374 p.
OrP WaS WaSp **8023**

Same. 2d ed. 1837. 381 p. WaU **8024**

Peck, Morton Eaton, 1871-
A manual of the higher plants of Oregon. Portland, Or., Binfords & Mort [c1941] 866 p. front., map, diagrs. Many **8025**

[Peddicord, William J.]
Why we should care for the records and relics of our pioneers. [Portland, Or., Oregon Historical Society? 1913] 16 p. port. Or OrHi OrP OrU **8026**

The Pe Ell Tribune.
1936 progress edition. Pe Ell, Wash., 1936. [14] p. illus. (v. 22, no. 41, Mar. 12, 1936)
WaPS **8027**

Peery, Wilson Kimsey.
Silver sides, illus. by Marion Ackerman. Portland, Or., Metropolitan [c1936] 95 p. illus. Republished as Silver streams.
Wa **8028**

Silver streams, illus. by Marion Ackerman. Portland, Or., Metropolitan [c1936] 95 p. illus. Many **8029**

Peet, Creighton.
Dude ranch; the story of a modern cowboy. Chicago, A. Whitman & Co., 1939. [96] p. front., illus. Montana story.
Or OrP WaS WaSp WaU **8030**

Pelly, Thomas Minor, 1902-
Dr. Minor; a sketch of the background and life of Thos. T. Minor, M. D. (1844-1889). Seattle, Lowman & Hanford, 1933. 135 p. front. (ports.)
Wa WaS WaSp WaT WaU **8031**

Judgment and other poems. Seattle, Lowman & Hanford [c1925] 46 p.
Wa Was WaU **8032**

North-westward; signed woodblock frontispiece by W. C. Chase. Seattle, Lowman & Hanford, 1930. 30 p. col. front. Poems.
Wa WaS WaSp WaT WaU **8033**

The story of Restoration Point and the country club. Seattle, Lowman & Hanford, 1931. 71 p. front. (diagr.) plates.
WaS WaU **8034**

Peltret, Edouard, see no. 9003.

Pelz, Eduard, see no. 8508.

Pemberton, Joseph Despard, 1821-1893.
Facts and figures relating to Vancouver Island and British Columbia, showing what to expect and how to get there with illustrative maps. London, Longmans, 1860. ix, 171 p. fold. front., illus., fold. maps. Many **8035**

Pemberton, Holmes, Ltd.
The first sixty years. [n.p., n.d.] 24 p. illus.
CVicAr **8036**

[Pen pictures from the garden of the world; history of Oregon, n.p., n.d.] 1300 p. 8 plates, 20 ports. Or **8037**

Pendexter, Hugh, 1875-
Harry Idaho. Indianapolis, Bobbs-Merrill [c1926] 315 p. Idaho gold mining story. IdU IdUSB **8038**

Kings of the Missouri, illus. by Kenneth M. Ballantyne. Indianapolis, Bobbs-Merrill [c1921] 360 p. front., plates. Fur trade story. WaU **8039**

Pendleton Foundation.
The Pendleton Foundation; resolution and declaration of trust creating the Pendleton Foundation Trust. [Pendleton, Or., 1928?] 22 p. Or OrP **8040**

The Peninsula; a special publication giving a glimpse of greater Portland and St. Johns. [Portland, Or., Peninsula Publishing Co., 1909?] 128 p. illus., photos., maps. OrHi **8040A**

Pengra, B. J., see no. 7634.

Pennington, Levi Talbott, 1875-
All kinds of weather, with foreword by E. Merrill Root. Portland, Or., Binfords & Mort [1948] 95 p. Poems. OrHi OrP **8041**

Penrose, John, 1778-1859.
Lives of Vice-Admiral Sir Charles Vinicombe Penrose and Capt. James Trevenen, by their nephew. London, Murray, 1850. ix, 301 p. front. (port.)
CV WaS WaU **8042**

Penrose, Stephen Beasley Linnard, 1864-1947, ed.
At Waiilatpu; impressions and recollections of visitors to the Whitman Mission, 1836-1847, ed. by S. B. L. Penrose and S. B. L. Penrose, Jr. Walla Walla, Wash. Whitman Pub. Co. [1936?] 30 p. front., illus. (Whitman centennial souvenir)
Or OrHi WaS WaU **8043**

Great cities and their causes; excerpts from a speech before the Cascade Tunnel Association, June 4, 1926. [n.p., 1926?] [6] p. WaS WaU **8044**

How the West was won, by Stephen B. L. Penrose in collaboration with Percy Jewett Burrell, produced upon Pageant Field at Walla Walla, Washington, June 6-7, 1923. [Walla Walla, Wash., Bulletin Printing Co. c1923] [45] p. front. (port.)
IdU Or OrP WaPS WaU **8045**

Same. 2d ed. [1924?] 54 p. illus. Many **8046**

Same. 3d ed. [Walla Walla, Wash., Inland Printing and Pub. Co., 1927] 55 p.
OrP WaPS WaS WaU **8047**

Philosophy for lowbrows, by one of them. Walla Walla, Wash., Whitman Pub. Co. [c1941] 210 p. illus. Many **8048**

Three sermons, by three members of the Yale band in Washington. Seattle, F. McCaffrey, 1932. 35 p.
Wa WaS WaSp WaWW **8049**

Three Spokanes; address delivered at a banquet in the Davenport Hotel, Friday, September 4, 1931 at a celebration of the golden jubilee of the incorporation of the city of Spokane. [n.p., n.d.] 13 p.
WaSp **8050**

Whitman, an unfinished story, illus. by Ernest Ralph Norling. Walla Walla, Wash., Whitman Pub. co. [c1935] ix, 256 p. front. (port.) illus.   Many **8051**

People's Pacific Railroad Company.
Charter, organization, address of the president, Josiah Perham, with the by-laws of the Board of Commissioners. Boston, A. Mudge & Son, 1860. 24 p.
CVicAr OrP WaU **8052**

People's Power League of Oregon.
Introductory letter; draft of suggested amendment to the constitution of Oregon for people's representative government: The short ballot, proportional representation in the legislature of all the voters, majority election of governors and other chief officers by the first, second, and other choices method of voting. Portland, Or., 1911. 32 p.
OrP OrU WaS **8053**

Introductory letter with draft of proposed constitutional amendment for basing election of representatives on the voters' business occupations instead of partisan politics, abolition of state senate and subordinating executve department. 2d ed. rev. [Portland, Or., Multnomah Printing Co.] 1921. 16 p.   OrP **8054**

The People's Railway.
Circular letter to the people of British Columbia. [n.p., n.d.] [4] p. CVicAr **8055**

Perfect, Albert.
Mighty Oregon; march song, words by DeWitt Gilbert. 2d ed. Eugene, Or., Music Shop [1916] 5 p.   OrU **8056**

Perham, Josiah, see no. 8052.

[Perrie, George W.]
Buckskin Mose; or, Life from the lakes to the Pacific, as actor, circus-rider, detective, ranger, gold-digger, Indian scout, and guide, written by himself, ed., and with illus. by C. G. Rosenberg. New York, H. L. Hinton, 1873. 285 p. 12 plates.
CVicAr IdU WaSp **8057**

Perry Clifford A.
The golden heresy. Seattle, L. Hawkins, 1945. 94 p. front. (port.) Poems.
Wa WaE WaU **8058**

Perry, Grace.
Twelve block prints of Lake Chelan, by Grace Perry and Frances Wismer. Prosser, Wash., H. P. Hamcker, 1930, 1 v.
WaS **8059**

Perry, Harry G., see no. 8845.

Perry, Josephine.
Forestry and lumbering, by Josephine Perry and Celeste Slauson. New York, Longmans, 1939. 125 p. front., illus. Tacoma author.   Many **8060**

The plastics industry. New York, Longmans. 1947. 127 p. front., illus. (America at work)   Or WaS WaSp WaU **8061**

Perry, Martha Eugenie.
The girl in the silk dress and other stories. Ottawa, Overbrook Press, c1931. 144 p. B. C. fiction.   CV CVicAr WaS **8062**

Perry, Maude Caldwell.
Tide house, a novel. New York, Harcourt [c1929] 338 p. North Pacific coast story.
Many **8063**

Peter Gray Wolf, see no. 9350.

Peters, DeWitt Clinton, d. 1876.
Kit Carson's life and adventures, from facts narrated by himself, embracing events in the lifetime of America's greatest hunter, trapper, scout and guide, including vivid accounts of the every day life, inner character, and peculiar customs of all Indian tribes of the far West; a full and complete history of the Modoc Indians and the Modoc war. Hartford, Dustin, Gilman & Co., 1873. 604 p. front. (port.) 28 plates, 6 ports. First published as The life and adventures of Kit Carson. CVicAr **8064**

Same. 1874.   Many **8065**

Same. 1875.   OrHi **8065A**

The life and adventures of Kit Carson, the Nestor of the Rocky Mountains, from facts narrated by himself, with original illus. drawn by Lumley, engraved by N. Orr & Co. New York, W. R. C. Clark & Co., 1858. 534 p. front., 9 plates. WaU **8066**

Same. 1859.   CVicAr WaU **8067**

Pioneer life and frontier adventures, an authentic record of the romantic life and daring exploits of Kit Carson and his companions, from his own narrative. Boston, Estes and Lauriat [c1880] 567 p. front., plates. First published as The life and adventures of Kit Carson.
CVicAr **8068**

Same. 1881.   Or OrHi OrU **8069**

See also no. 1542.

Peters, H. C.
Clear Lake, Washington; the town with a pay roll. [Seattle? n.d.] 4 p. illus., map.
WaPS **8070**

Petersburg, Alaska. Parent Teachers' Association.
PTA cook book. Petersburg, Alaska [1941] 168 p. illus.   WaS WaT **8071**

Peterson, Arthur O., see no. 9199.

Peterson, Ethel M., 1900-
Oregon Indians and Indian policy, 1849-1871. [Eugene, Or., 1939] 82 p. (University of Oregon thesis series, no. 3)
Many **8072**

Peterson, Margaret, see no. 9199.

Peterson, Martin Severin, 1897-
Joaquin Miller, literary frontiersman. Stanford University, Calif., Stanford University Press [c1937] ix, 198 p. front. (port.)
Many **8073**

Peterson, Orval Douglas, 1902-
Washington-northern Idaho Disciples. St. Louis, Christian Board of Publication [1945] 223 p. front., plates, ports.
WaS WaTC WaU **8074**

Peterson, Roger Tory, 1908-
A field guide to western birds. Boston,

Houghton, 1941. xviii, 240 p. col. front., 25 plates (part col.) map, charts.
Many **8075**

Peterson, Stella Parker.
From honeymoon to massacre; the story of Marcus and Narcissa Whitman. Takoma Park, Md., Review and Herald Publishing Association [c1941] 192 p. front. (ports.) illus. IdP Or WaU **8076**

Petitot, Emile Fortune Stanislas Joseph, 1838-
Monographie des dene-dindjie. Paris, E. Leroux, 1876. 109 p. CVicAr CVU **8077**

Quinze ans sous le cercle polaire. Mackenzie, Anderson, Youkon; ouvrage accompagne de 18 gravures de H. Blanchard et d'une carte d'Erhard d'apres les dessins de l'auteur. Paris, E. Dentu, 1889. xxi, 332 p. front., illus., 10 plates, ports., fold. map. CVicAr **8078**

Traditions indiennes du Canada nordouest. Paris, Maisonneuve freres et C. Leclerc., 1886. xvii, 521 p. (Les litteratures populaires de toutes les nations, t. 23)
CVicAr WaU **8079**

Traditions indennes du Canada nordouest; textes originaux & traduction litterale. Alencon, E. Renaut de Broise, 1887. vi, 446 p. CVicAr WaU **8080**

Vocabulaire francais-Esquimau; dialect e des Tchiglit des bouches du Mackenzie et de l'Anderson, precede d'une monographie de cette tribu et de notes grammaticales. Paris, E. Leroux, 1876. lxiv, 76 p. (Pinart, A. L., ed. Biblioteque de linguistique et d'ethrographie americaines, v. 3., 1876. CVicAr **8081**

Pettibone, Anita.
The bitter country. Garden City, N. Y., Doubleday, 1925. 318 p. Northwest coast story. IdU Wa WaPS WaSp WaU **8082**

Johnny Painter. New York, Farrar [1944] 314 p. Washington Territory story.
Many **8083**

Same. New York, Grosset [c1944]
WaE WaS **8084**

Light down, stranger. New York, Farrar [1942] 310 p. Washington Territory story.
Many **8085**

Pettit, Edison, 1889-
Why is Crater Lake so blue? Washington, D. C., Carnegie Institution of Washington [n.d.] [8] p. illus. (News service bulletin, v. 4, no. 4) OrP **8086**

Pfaff, Emma.
A turbeculosis case-finding survey of Walla Walla County, Washington for the year 1928; conducted under the direction of the Walla Walla County Tuberculosis League, with the assistance of the Statistical Department, National Tuberculosis Association. [Walla Walla, Wash., 1929] 23 p. tables. WaU **8087**

Pfefferkorn, Richard.
Oregon flax for an American linen industry; a discussion of the Oregon fiber flax industry with special emphasis on processing methods here and abroad, and on the outlook for developing a permanent American linen industry. Corvallis, Or., Oregon State College Cooperative Assn., 1944. 46 p. illus., tables, diagrs. Or OrCs OrHi OrP **8088**

The Pharmaceutical Association of British Columbia.
Fifty years of progress in pharmacy, 1891-1941, golden jubilee souvenir. Vancouver, B. C., Western Druggist, 1941. 80 p. illus., ports. CVicAr CVU **8089**

Phelps, Frank Wesley.
Utilitarian economics; a series of fifty studies in utilitarian values, authors: F. Wesley Phelps, J. Buckner Myrick. Seattle, School of Utilitarian Economics, c1921. 261 p. MtU WaS WaU **8090**

Phelps, Mrs. Netta Sheldon, 1861-
The valiant seven, illus. by Helen Hughes Wilson. Caldwell, Idaho, Caxton, 1941. 221 p. col. front., illus., plates. Many **8091**

Phelps, Thomas Stowell, 1822-1901.
The Indian attack on Seattle, January 26, 1856, as described by the eye witness, Lieut. Thomas Stowell Phelps, who "took a prominent part in the sanguinary battle of Seattle", attached to the U. S. sloop-of-war "Decatur", reprinted from Reminiscences of Seattle, Washington Territory in the United Service magazine, v. 5, Dec. 1881, no. 6; with original notes, letters and first known picture, and a map of Seattle, collected by Mrs. Carl Frelinghuysen Gould, Seattle, Farwest Lithograph & Printing Co., 1932. 57 p. illus., port., map. CVicAr WaU **8092**

Same. 2d ed.
OrHi OrP WaPS WaS WaSp WaU **8093**

Phelps, William Lyon, see nos. 6024-6027.

Phi Beta Kappa. Washington Alpha, University of Washington.
The Phi Beta Kappa Society Alpha chapter in the state of Washington installation number, April 29, 1914; constitution, history and members. [Seattle, 1914] 39 p.
WaU **8094**

Phi Delta Kappa. Chi Chapter, University of Oregon.
The tax limitation amendment. Eugene, Or?] 1934 [34] p. table.
Or OrP **8095**

Philip, Alex.
The painted cliff. Ottawa, Graphic Pub. [c1927] 213 p. British Columbia story.
CVicAr CVU **8096**

Philips, Frederic.
Verse from a western isle. Victoria, B. C., T. R. Cusack [1909] 49 p. front., illus.
CVicAr CVU WaU **8097**

[Philips, George]
Travels in North America [purports to be an account of an Irishman who joined the Lewis and Clark expedition at St. Louis and remained with it until they reached Fort Mandan on the return] London, Rivington, 1831. 168 p. front., plates. OrP WaSp WaU **8098**

Phillipps-Wolley, Clive, 1854-1918.
Gold, gold, in Cariboo; a story of adventure in British Columbia, with six illus. by Godfrey C. Hindley. London, Blackie, 1894. 288 p. front., 5 plates.
CV CVicAr **8099**

Songs from a young man's land. Toronto, Thomas Allen [c1917] 160 p.
CV CVU WaU **8100**

A sportsman's Eden. London, R. Bentley and Son, 1888. xv, 261 p. 2 tables.
CV CVic CVicAr CVU WaS WaU **8101**

Trottings of a tenderfoot; or, A visit to the Columbian fiords. London, R. Bentley and Son, 1884. v, 252 p.
CV CVic CVicAr CVU **8102**

Same. and Spitzbergen, v. 350 p.
CV CVic CVicAr OrP WaU **8103**

Phillips, Paul Chrisler, see nos. 7761, 7762, 9974, 11212.

Phillips, Walter J.
Colour in the Canadian Rockies, by W. J. Phillips & Frederick Niven. Toronto, Nelson, 1937. 125 p. col. front., illus., 31 col. plates.
CV Or OrP **8104**

Phillips, Walter Shelley, 1867-
The Chinook book; a descriptive analysis of the Chinook jargon in plain words, giving instructions for pronunciation, construction, expression and proper speaking of Chinook with all the various shaded meanings of the words, by El Commancho. Seattle [R. L. Davis Printing Co.] 1913. 118 p. Many **8105**

Indian fairy tales; folklore-legends-myths; totem tales as told by the Indians; gathered in the Pacific Northwest, with a glossary of words, customs and history of the Indians; fully illus. by the author. Chicago, Star Pub. Co. [c1902] 326 p. front., illus., plates. Re-issue of Totem tales.
WaPS WaS WaT **8106**

Totem tales; Indian stories Indian told, gathered in the Pacific Northwest, with a glossary of words, customs and history of the Indians, fully illus. by the author. Chicago, Star Pub. Co. [c1896] 326 p. front., illus., plates. Many **8107**

Same. 1903. MtU **8108**

Same. 1904. OrP WaS WaSp WaWW **8109**

Phillips, William, 1827-
Crossing the plains in '46. Oregon City, Or., Courier-Herald, 1900. 32 p. Poem.
OrHi WaU WaWW **8110**

Phinney, Archie.
Nez Perce texts. New York, Columbia University Press. 1934. xii, 497 p. (Contributions to anthropology, v. 25)
Many **8111**

Phinney, Mary Allen.
Allen-Isham genealogy: Jirah Isham Allen, Montana pioneer, government scout, guide, interpreter and famous hunter, during four years of Indian warfare in Montana and Dakota, from 1839-1929, by his niece. Rutland, Vt., Tuttle Pub. Co. [1946] 162 p. front., plates, ports.
MtHi WaS WaU **8112**

Phiscator, see nos. 5861, 5862.

Phleger, Herman, 1890-
Pacific coast longshoremen's strike of 1934; arbitration before National Longshoremen's Board; oral argument of Herman Phleger in behalf of waterfront employers, September 25, 1934. [San Francisco? 1934?] 71 p. Many **8113**

Photographic view album of picturesque Victoria, Vancouver Island. Vancouver, B. C., Hibben [n.d.] 22 plates (1 fold.)
CVicAr **8114**

Photomobile Tourist Company.
The photomobile tourist; Oregon, Washington, Idaho. Seattle [c1919] 416 p. illus., maps. OrP Wa **8115**

Phucher, Itothe, see no. 1724.

Pi Lambda Theta. Washington Alumnae Chapter. Research Committee.
Women of the Pacific Northwest; a study of their status today, their emotional adjustment and their thinking on the postwar period. Seattle, 1945. 50 p. tables.
Many **8116**

Piatt, Guy X., ed.
The story of Butte. Butte, Mont., Standard Manufacturing and Printing Co., Apr. 15, 1897. 96 p. front., illus., 107 ports.
MtHi MtU **8117**

Pick, Harry.
Next year; a semi-historical account of the exploits and exploitations of the far-famed Barr colonists, who, led by an unscrupulous Church of England parson, adventured deep into the wilderness of Canada's great Northwest in the early days of the twentieth century. Toronto, Ryerson [c1928] xxii, 254 p.
CVU WaU **8118**

Picken, M., comp.
City of Vancouver, terminus of the Canadian Pacific Railway; British Columbia hand book. Vancouver, B. C., Daily News, 1887. 64 p. fold. map.
CV CVicAr **8119**

[Pickersgill, Richard]
A concise account of voyages for the discovery of a North-west Passage, undertaken for finding a new way to the East Indies, with reflections on the practicability of gaining such a passage, by a sea officer. London, Bew, 1782. xxviii, 69 p.
CVicAr **6120**

Pickett, Charles Edward, see no. 8322.

Pickwell, Gayle Benjamin, 1899-
Amphibians and reptiles of the Pacific states. Stanford University, Calif., Stanford University Press, c1947. 236 p. illus., plates, map. OrHi OrP WaE WaTC **8121**

A pictorial story of Grand Coulee Dam, the biggest man-made structure of all time. Tacoma, Pioneer Engraving Co. [1941?] 1 v. front., illus., map. WaT **8122**

Pictorial Vancouver Island. [Victoria, B. C., Buckle, n.d.] 28 p. illus. CVicAr **8123**

A picture journey through the Pacific Northwest; composed of sixty-five views of the scenic wonders in the territory adjacent to Puget Sound, showing how mountains, rivers and beautiful cities combine to make this country an ideal playground as well as a good place to live and work. [n.p.] Sunset press with the cooperation of "Puget Sounders and British Columbians, Associated" [1929?] 33 plates. WaS WaT WaTC **8124**

The picturesque land of gold, its magnificent mountain and water scenes. White

Horse, Yukon, Bennett News [n.d.] 4 p.
30 plates (1 fold.)   CVicAr 8125

Same. 58 illus. (1 fold.)   MtUM 8126

Picturesque Nanaimo, the coal city of British Columbia. Nanaimo, B. C., Pimbury
[n.d.] 19 plates (1 fold.)   CVicAr 8127

Picturesque Seattle. Seattle, Eshelman [c1901]
62 p. illus.   WaS 8128

Picturesque Victoria, British Columbia. Victoria, B. C., Hibben [n.d.] 23 plates (3
fold.)   CVicAr 8129

Pierce, Dixwell L.
What California has accomplished with its
sales tax; a paper read before the Oregon Tax Clinic at Portland, Oregon.
[n.p.] 1944. 17 p.   OrP 8130

Pierce, Frank Richardson.
Chuck Ryan, logger, front. by W. D.
White. Garden City, N. Y., Doubleday,
1928. 289 p. col. front. Puget Sound story.
                     WaS WaU 8131

Pierce, Mrs. Harry Paul, comp.
Roll of artists of the state of Washington.
[n.p.] 1926. 24 p.   WaS WaT 8132

Pierce, Henry Joshua.
Address before the Conference of Western
Governors at Seattle, Wash., May 18,
1915 [on federal legislation enabling development of power projects in western
states] [n.p., 1915?] 7 p.   WaPS 8133

Looking squarely at the water power
problem. Seattle [1915] 81 [86] p. plates.
                  OrP WaT WaU 8134

Pierce, W. E., and Co.
Boise City, Idaho, illustrated. [Boise,
Idaho, 1893] 27 p. illus.   WaU 8135

Pierce, W. H.
Thirteen years of travel and exploration
in Alaska, ed. by Prof. and Mrs. J. H.
Carruth. Lawrence, Kan., Journal Pub.
Co., 1890. 224 p. illus.   WaS WaU 8136

Pierce, Walter Marcus, 1861-
To Oregon voters. Salem, Or., 1926. 8 p.
                     OrP 8137

Pierce, William Henry, 1856-
From potlatch to pulpit; being the autobiography of the Rev. William Henry
Pierce, native missionary to the Indian
tribes of the Northwest coast of British
Columbia, ed. by J. P. Hichs. Vancouver,
B. C., Vancouver Bindery, 1933. 176 p.
front. (port.) illus.
               CV CVic CVicAr WaS 8138

Pierce County Pioneer Association, Tacoma,
Wash.
Commemorative celebration at Sequalitchew Lake, Pierce County, Washington,
July 5, 1906. [Tacoma, 1906] 101 p. 4
plates, 14 ports., map. (Publications, v.
1)   Many 8139

Same. 2d ed.   CVicAr OrU 8140

Pierrepont, Edward Willoughby.
Fifth Avenue to Alaska, with maps of
Leonard Forbes Beckwith. New York,
Putnam, 1884. vi, 329 p. fold. maps.
                    Many 8141

Same. 3d ed. 1885.   WaS 8142

Piers, Sir Charles Pigott, Bart., 1870-
Sport and life in British Columbia, with

a preface by General Sir Arthur Currie.
London, H. Cranton [1923] 159 p. front.,
plates.   Many 8143

[Piet, Josephus M.]
The land of the midnight sun; the missions of Alaska. [n.p., Schinner, 1925] 20
p. illus., ports.   CVicAr 8144

Pigott, Henry C., comp.
History and progress of King County,
Washington. [Seattle] C. J. Hutchinson,
1916. 53 p. illus., ports., map. Anon.
                    Many 8145

Legislation affecting the Port District;
mostly facts, and a few fancies, and the
recollections from his own and other
memories that are better. [Seattle, n.d.]
14 p.   WaS 8146

Pike, Warburton Mayer, 1861-1915.
Through the subarctic forest; a record of
a canoe journey from Fort Wrangel to
the Pelly Lakes and down the Yukon
River to the Behring Sea. London, Arnold, 1896. xiv, 295 p. front., plates, 2 fold.
maps.   Many 8147

Pike, Zebulon Montgomery, 1779-1813.
An account of expeditions to the sources
of the Mississippi, and through the
western parts of Louisiana, to the sources of the Arkansas, Kansas, La Platte,
and Pierre Jaun, rivers; performed by
order of the government of the United
States during the years 1805, 1806, and
1807; and a tour through the interior
parts of New Spain, when conducted
through these provinces, by order of the
captain-general, in the year 1807. Philadephia, C. & A. Conrad & Co., 1810.
5, 277, 66, 54, 87 p. front. (port.) tables.
                    OrHi 8147A

The expeditions of Zebulon Montgomery
Pike to headwaters of the Mississippi
River, through Louisiana Territory, and
in New Spain, during the years 1805-6-7.
New ed., now first reprinted in full
from the original of 1810, with copious
critical commentary, memoir of Pike
and complete index, by Elliott Coues.
New York, Harper, 1895. 3 v. front.
(port.) 7 maps (6 fold.) fold. facsim.
             MtHi OrHi WaS WaSp WaU 8148

Exploratory travels through the western
territories of North America; comprising
a voyage from St. Louis on the Mississippi to the sources of that river, and a
journey through the interior of Louisiana, and the north-eastern provinces of
New Spain, performed in the years
1805, 1806, 1807, by the order of the government of the United States. London,
1811. Denver, W. H. Lawrence & Co.,
1889. 394 p. front. (port.) 2 mounted
photos., 4 maps (2 double).
                 IdB WaSp WaU 8149

Zebulon Pike's Arkansaw journal: in search
of the southern Louisiana Purchase
boundary line (interpreted by his newly
recovered maps) ed. with bibliographical
resume, 1800-1810, by Stephen Harding
Hart and Archer Butler Hulbert. [Colorado Springs] Stewart Commission of
Colorado College [c1932] xcvi, 200 p.

front. (port.) 2 plates, 4 maps (Overland
to the Pacific. v. 1)   Many **8150**

Pilgrim, Mariette Shaw.
Alaska, its history, resources, geography,
and government. Caldwell, Idaho, Cax-
ton, 1939. 296 p. front. (fold. map) illus.
                                Many **8151**
Same. Rev. ed. 1945, c1939. 334 p.
                                WaT **8152**
Oogaruk, the Aleut, illus. by Helen Hughes
Wilson. Caldwell, Idaho, Caxton [c1947]
223 p. col. front., illus., plates.
                            WaS WaU **8153**

Pinart, Alphonse Louis, 1852-1911.
Catalogue des collections rapportees de
l'Amerique Russe (aujourd'hui territoire
d'Alaska). Paris, Imprimerie de J. Claye,
1872. 32 p.   WaU **8154**
La caverne d'aknanh, ile d'Ounga (Archipel Shumagin, Alaska). Paris, E. Leroux,
1875. 11 p. 7 plates, plan.
                          CVicAr WaU **8155**
A few words on the Alaska Dene in answer to Father Morice, accompanied by a
short vocabulary of the A'tana or Copper River Indian language. [n.p., n.d.] 7
p.   CVicAr **8156**
Voyages a la cote nord-ouest de l'Amerique executes durant les annees 1870-72
[v. 1, ptie. 1 Histoire naturelle] Paris, E.
Leroux, 1875. 51 p. 5 plates.
                   CVicAr WaPS WaU **8157**

Pine, George W.
Beyond the West; containing an account
of two years' travel in the other half of
our great continent far beyond the old
West, on the plains, in the Rocky Mountains, and picturesque parks of Colorado; also, characteristic features of
New Mexico, Arizona, Wyoming, Montana, Idaho, Oregon, Utah, Nevada, and
California, the end of the West; the
great continental railroad, together with
the most wonderful natural scenery in
the world. Utica, N. Y., T. J. Griffiths,
1870. 444 p. front., 5 plates.
                 CVicAr Or OrU WaS WaU **8158**
Same. 2d ed. 1871. 488 p.   OrHi **8158A**

Pinkerton, Mrs. Kathrene Sutherland (Ged-
ney) 1887-
Three's a crew. New York, Carrick &
Evans [c1940] 316 p. front., illus., plates.
British Columbia and Alaska. Many **8159**

Pinkerton, Robert Eugene, 1882-
The gentlemen adventurers, introd. by
Stewart Edward White. Toronto, Mc-
Clelland and Stewart [c1931] viii, 357 p.
front., 7 plates. CV CVic CVicAr **8160**
Hudson's Bay Company, introd. by Stewart
Edward White. New York, Holt, [c1931]
viii, 357 p. front. (ports.) plates.
                                Many **8161**
Same. London, T. Butterworth [1932] 320 p.
front. (ports.) 5 plates, double facsim.
                    CVU OrPR WaSp **8162**

**Pioneer Historical Society of the Stillagua-
mish Valley,** East Stanwood, Wash. Toftezen
Memorial Committee.
Dedication program: Toftezen Memorial,

Stanwood, Washington, May 27, 1939;
facts about the Toftezen pioneer family.
[East Stanwood, Wash., 1939] [13] p.
                                WaU **8163**

Pioneer, Inc., Tacoma, Wash.
Grand Coulee Dam; the biggest man-
made structure of all time. Tacoma,
c1940. [48] p. illus.   WaPS **8164**
[History of Pioneer, Inc., 1878-1928] Tacoma [1928] 1 v. front., illus., 5 ports.
                                WaT **8165**

Pioneer Ladies Club, Pendleton, Or.
Reminiscences of Oregon pioneers. Pendleton, Or., East Oregonian Pub. Co.,
c1937. 257 p.   Many **8166**

Pioneer Lumber Co., Seattle, Wash.
Salesman's hand book; Pacific coast lumber. Everett, Wash., Kane & Hareus Co.,
c1920. 96 p. fold. table.   CVU **8167**

Pioneer Seattle and its founders. [n.p., n.d.]
17 p. port.   CVicAr OrU **8168**

Piper, Charles Vancouver, 1867-1926.
Flora of southeastern Washington and ad-
jacent Idaho, by Charles V. Piper and R.
Kent Beattie. Lancaster, Pa., New Era
Printing Co., 1914. xi, 296 p. map.
                                Many **8169**
Flora of the northwest coast, including
the area west of the summit of the Cascade Mountains, from the forty-ninth
parallel south to the Calapooia Mountains on the south border of Lane County, Oregon, by Charles V. Piper and R.
Kent Beattie. Lancaster, Pa., New Era
Printing Co., 1915. xiii, 418 p. Many **8170**
Flora of the Palouse region; containing
description of all the spermatophytes
and puridophytes known to grow wild
in the area within thirty-five kilometers
of Pullman, Washington, by Charles V.
Piper and R. Kent Beattie. Pullman,
Wash., Washington State Agricultural
College, 1901. viii, 208 p.
                IdU WaPS WaSp WaU **8171**

Piper & Taft, Inc.
Taft's Sportsman's guide and handbook;
fishing edition, western Washington
state. Seattle, c1925. 184 p. illus. Wa **8172**

Pipes, Nellie B., see no. 6682.

Pittman, Mrs. Armena.
Pittmon's motor guide, with facts about
Oregon, maps and log of all state highways, short loop drives, fishing streams,
outing resorts, resources of Oregon,
maps of Pacific Highway from Canada
to Mexico, national park to park highways, transcontinental highways. Portland, Or., c1922. 136 p. illus., maps (part
fold.)   Or OrP WaPS **8173**
Pittmon's Portland guide with maps of
city and of Columbia scenic highway.
Portland, Or., c1920. 237 p. illus., maps.
                                OrHi **8174**
Same. c1921. 254 p.   WaU **8175**

Pittmon, E. T.
Portland street and street car directory
with map of city. Portland, Or. [n.d.] 126
p. map.   OrU **8176**

Placer mining; a handbook for Klondike and other miners and prospectors, with introductory chapters regarding the recent gold discoveries in the Yukon Valley. Scranton, Pa., Colliery Engineer Co., 1897. vi, 146 p. front. (fold. map) illus. CVicAr 8177

The plain American, Portland, Oregon, U. S. A. [I. W. W. and Armistice Day parade at Centralia] Portland, Or. [n.d.] 31 p. OrP 8178

Plant, Thomas G.
The Pacific coast longshoremen's strike of 1934; statement of president of the Waterfront Employers Union of San Francisco to the National Longshoremen's Board, July 11, 1934. [San Francisco? 1934] 43 p. WaE WaPS WaU 8179

Plaskett, Frank.
70th anniversary of St. Mary the Virgin, Sapperton. [New Westminster, B. C., Columbian] 1935. 32 p. illus., port. CVicAr 8180

"Platinum Bill", see no. 9620.

Platt, Ward.
The frontier. Cincinnati, Jennings & Graham [c1908] 292 p. front., plates, fold. maps. (Forward mission study courses, ed. under the direction of the Young People's Missionary Movement of the U. S. and Canada)
Or OrSa WaPS WaS WaU 8181

Plenty Crows, see no. 4257.

Ploetz, R. A., see no. 7316.

Plowhead, Ruth Gipson, 1877-
Lucretia Ann in the golden West, decorations by Agnes Randall Moore. Caldwell, Idaho, Caxton, 1935. 294 p. col. front., illus., col. plates. IdIf
OrMonO WaPS WaS WaSp WaT 8182
Same. 1946 [c1935] WaU 8163
Lucretia Ann on the Oregon Trail, illus. by Agnes Kay Randall. Caldwell, Idaho, Caxton, 1931. 244 p. col. front., illus., col. plates. Many 8184
Same. 1943 [c1931] WaU 8185
Lucretia Ann on the sagebrush plains; decorations by Agnes Randall Moore. Caldwell, Idaho, Caxton, 1936. 357 p. col. front., illus., col. plates.
IdIf WaS WaSp WaT 8186
Same. 1946 [c1936] WaU 8187
Mile high cabin, illus. by Johanna E. Lund. Caldwell, Idaho, Caxton, 1945. viii, 229 p. col. front., illus., plates. Idaho story.
Or OrLgE WaE WaS WaSp WaU 8188

Plummer, Fred Gordon, 1864-1913.
Illustrated guide book of Mount Tacoma, Pierce County, Washington, giving information regarding the roads and trails to the mountain; points of interest along the route; stopping places and supply points; tables of distances, etc. Tacoma [189—?] 12 p. plates, 2 maps. WaT 8189

Plummer, Mary Wright, see no. 2251.

Plummer, Sara A. C.
Falling leaves. [Seattle, I. N. Davidson, c1917] 32 p. front. (port.) WaU 8190

The whippoorwills. [Seattle, Clint W. Lee Co., c1938] 25 p. WaU 8191

Plywood and Door Manufacturers Industrial Committee, Tacoma, Wash.
[Survey of present day prices and wages as compared with early 1940] Tacoma, 1946. 37 p. diagrs. WaT 8192

Pochin, W. F.
Angling and hunting in British Columbia. Vancouver, B. C. [Sun Directories, Ltd.] 1946. 204 p. illus., plates (part col.) CVicAr OrP WaS WaSp 8193

Pocock, Roger S., 1865-1941.
A frontiersman. London, Methuen & Co., 1903. 307, 38 p. facsim. British Columbia and Alaska. CVicAr 8194
Same. Popular ed. London, Gay & Hancock [1911] v, 307 p. CVU 8195
The wolf trail. New York, Appleton, 1923. vii, 323 p. Oregon and British Columbia. CVicAr 8196

Poe, Edgar Allen, 1809-1849.
The journal of Julius Rodman. San Francisco, Colt Press, 1947. 76 p. col. illus. "Being an account of the first passage across the Rocky Mountains of North America ever achieved by civilized man". WaU 8197

Poe, Mrs. Sophie (Alberding)
Buckboard days, ed. by Eugene Cunningham, illus. with many photographs from the famous Rose collection of San Antonio and from private collections. Caldwell, Idaho, Caxton, 1936. 292 p. front., plates, ports.
IdB MtHi WaE WaS WaSp WaU 8198

The Poet; special pioneer number in recognition of the centennial anniversary of the Old Oregon Trail. San Francisco, Poets of the Pacific, 1944. 47 p. illus. (Spring-summer issue, 1944)
Or OrP WaS 8199

Pogue, Anna (Holm) 1889-
An Oregon interlude; a narrative poem. Boston, Bruce Humphries [1946] 58 p.
IdU Or OrHi OrP WaS WaT 8200
See also no. 10536.

[Pogue, Pollough].
Captivating Vancouver, "Canada's Pacific Port". Vancouver, B. C. [Sun Pub. Co.] 1924. 63 p. illus. CVU 8201

The Poindexter Presidential Club, Washington, D. C.
Miles Poindexter. Washington, D. C. [1920] 12 p. port. United States senator from Washington. WaU 8202

Point, Nicholas.
A journey in a barge on the Missouri from the Fort of the Blackfeet (Lewis) to that of the Assiniboine (Union) 1847, trans. from the French by Paul A. Barrette, Dept. of Language, St. Louis University. [n.p., 19—?] 19 p. MtHi 8203

Poling, Daniel Alfred, 1884-
John of Oregon. New York, Doran [c1926] 274 p. OrCS OrP OrSa WaPS WaT 8204

Polk County Centennial Committee.
Polk County centennial souvenir booklet and program. Dallas, Or., 1947. 96 p. illus., ports. Or OrU 8205

Polk County pioneer sketches. Dallas, Or., Polk County Observer, 1927-1929. 2 v. ports. Volume 1 comp. by Sarah Childress, Polk Chapter No. 6 D. A. R.
Or OrHi OrP OrU WaS WaU **8206**

Pollard, Lancaster, 1901-
From frontier village to world metropolis; Seattle. [illus. by Durwood Lapham] Seattle, Bonney-Watson Co. [c1939] 27 p. illus. Wa WaS WaT **8207**

A history of the state of Washington; Lloyd Spencer, editor-in-chief. New York, American Historical Society, 1937. 4 v. front., illus., ports. Volumes 3-4 biographical. Many **8208**

A history of the state of Washington. Portland, Or., Binfords & Mort [c1941] xxvi, 222 p. front., plates. Many **8209**

Oregon and the Pacific Northwest. Portland, Or., Binfords & Mort [1946] ix, 312 p. plates (part double) Many **8210**

Same [c1947] WaU **8211**

The state of Washington. [Tacoma, Wash. Historical Society, 1942] 60 p.
CVicAr Wa WaS WaSp WaT **8212**
See also nos. 7706A, 7707.

Pollen, A. Hungerford, see nos. 9656, 9657.

Pollock, Adelaide Lowry.
Excursions about birdland, from the Rockies to the Pacific; verse by Nina Moore. Seattle [c1925] 191 [38] p. front., illus.
Many **8213**

Wings over land and sea; verse by Nina D. Moore. Seattle, Lowman & Hanford, 1930. 139 p. front., illus., plates.
Wa WaS WaSp **8214**

Pollom, Noah Doc, 1868-
Epworth Methodist Church, golden jubilee. Tacoma, 1939. 96 p. front., illus., ports.
WaT **8215**

Pond, Peter, see no. 3477.

Poole, Francis.
Queen Charlotte Islands; a narrative of discovery and adventure in the north Pacific, ed. by John W. Lyndon [pseud.] London, Hurst and Blackett, 1872. xiv, 347 p. front., 2 plates, 2 maps. Many **8216**

Poor, Henry Varnum, 1888-
An artist sees Alaska, illus. by the author. New York, Viking, 1945. 279 p. illus., plates, ports., map. Many **8217**

Poor-man Gold and Silver Mining Co.
Poor-man Gold & Silver Mining Company of Idaho, incorporated under the laws of the state of New York, May 25, 1866. New York, C. O. Jones, 1867. 23 p. fold. col. map, diagrs. (1 fold.) WaU **8218**

Pope, Mary Knox, see no. 9756.

Poplar Creek gold fields (B.C.) the latest mining sensation. Nelson, B. C., Daily News [n.d.] 40 p. illus., map. CV **8219**

Port Angeles illustrated, containing a complete description of the location, attractions, resources, climate and advantages of the "Gate City" and its contributory country, comp. for the Citizens Association of Port Angeles, Washington. Seattle, Pacific Magazine, c1889. 30 p. illus.
WaWW **8220**

Port Orchard Independent, Port Orchard, Wash.
Supplement; Kitsap County business review, 1901. [Port Orchard, Wash.,? 1902?] 35 p. illus., ports. WaS **8221**

Porter, Gene Stratton, see no. 9798.

Porter, James.
The bonfire; a poem. [Victoria, B. C., 1908] [6] p. CVicAr **8222**

Porter, Kenneth Wiggins, 1905-
John Jacob Astor, business man. Cambridge, Mass., Harvard University Press, 1931. 2 v. fronts., plates, ports, facsim. (Harvard studies in business history 1)
Many **8223**

Porter, May Reed, see no. 2430.

Porter, Robert Percival, 1852-1917.
The West; from the census of 1880, a history of the industrial, commercial, social, and political development of the states and territories of the West from 1800 to 1880, by Robert P. Porter, assisted by Henry Gannett and Wm. P. Jones. Chicago, Rand McNally, 1882. 630 p. front. (fold. map) plates.
CVicAr OrP OrU WaPS WaS WaU **8224**

Portland, Or. [n.p., 1890?] 64 p. illus.
WaPS **8225**

Portland, Or. Atlantic - Pacific Highways and Electrical Exposition, 1925.
The 1925 Oregon exposition; what it will mean to Oregon and the Northwest. [Portland, Or.? n.d.] [28] p. OrP **8226**

— — — Calvary Presbyterian Church.
Manual. Portland, Or., Ellis Printing Co., 1904. 20 p. OrHi **8227**

— — — Citizens.
The great Northwest; proceedings of a meeting of the people of the city of Portland, Oregon, on the subject of the Pacific railroads; with the report and resolutions adopted December 18, 1867. Portland, Or., Walling, 1867. 17 p.
WaSp WaU **8228**

— — — Firemen's Association (exempt firemen)
Articles of association and by-laws. Portland, Or., Walling, 1874. 18 p. OrP **8229**

Same. Portland, Or., Swope, 1885.
OrHi **8230**

— — — Firemen's Relief and Pension Fund.
Laws and rules regulating the Firemen's Relief and Pension Fund. [Portland, Or., Kleist & Co., 1915?] 16 p. OrP **8231**

— — — First Baptist Church.
Catalogue of Sunday School library. Portland, Or., Himes, 1872. 19 p. OrHi **8232**

Directory of the First Baptist Church, the White Temple [with historical sketch of the church] [Portland, Or.] 1912. 60 p.
OrP **8233**

Historical sketch of the First Baptist Church of Portland, Oregon, [n.p., n.d.] 20 p. OrHi **8234**

Manual. Portland, Or., Himes, 1876. 34 p.
OrP **8235**

Manual and directory. [n.p.] 1906. 1 v.
OrHi **8236**

— — — First Congregational Church.
Proceedings of the business of the First
Congregational Church of Portland, Oregon, held pursuant to calls by the acting
pastor, Rev'd. Frederick R. Marvin, M.
D., to consider his resignation and questions arising incident thereto, other records connected therewith, and proceedings of the meeting of April 24, 1884.
[Portland, Or., Himes, 1884?] 23 p.
OrHi OrU 8237

— — — First National Bank.
The First National Bank of Portland, Oregon, established 1865. [n.p., 1932?] 19 p.
illus. OrP 8238

75 dramatic years in Oregon. [Portland,
Or., Irwin-Hodson, c1940] [46] p. illus.,
diagr. OrCS OrP 8239

Step by step for 65 years. [Portland, Or.,
1930?] 20 p. illus. OrP 8240

— — — First Presbyterian Church.
Dedication services; historical sketch and
list of members. [Portland, Or., Schwab
Bros.] 1899. 40 p. CVicAr OrHi 8241

Dr. Lindsley's letter of resignation. [Port-
land, Or., Himes, 1886] 43 p. OrHi 8242

History and directory of the First Presbyterian Church, corner of Alder and
Tenth Streets, Portland, Oregon, Rev.
Arthur J. Brown, pastor. Portland, Or.,
1889. 47 p. Many 8243

Manual of the First Presbyterian Church,
1891, 1892. [Portland, Or., 1891, 1892] 2 v.
OrHi 8244

A pioneer church; the first seventy-five
years of the First Presbyterian Church,
Portland, Oregon, 1854-1929, prepared
and printed for the Diamond Jubilee,
June 2-9, 1929. [Portland, Or., Bercliff
Printers] 1929. 142 p. front., plates, ports.,
tables. Many 8245

— — — First Unitarian Church.
Articles and covenants and roll of members. [n.p.] 1893. 1 v. OrHi 8246

— — — First Unitarian Society.
Constitution adopted June 26, 1866. Portland, Or., Carter, 1868. 12 p. OrHi 8247

— — — Grace Methodist Episcopal Church.
Souvenir program, twenty-fifth anniver-
sary, 1884-1909. Portland, Or., 1909. 12 p.
OrHi 8248

— — — — Lewis and Clark Centennial Expo-
sition, 1905.
By-laws. Portland, Or. [n.p.] 1903. 27 p.
OrHi 8248A

Catalogue of the fine arts exhibit of the
Lewis and Clark Centennial Exposition,
Portland, Oregon, June 1 to October 15,
1905. [Portland, Or.] Hess, 1905. 78 p.
OrHi 8248B

The exhibition of the district of Alaska
at the Lewis and Clark Centennial Exposition, Portland, Oregon, 1905, with a
foreword upon the Alaska exhibit and
Alaska. [Portland, Or., Irwin-Hodson,
1905] 65, ii p. illus., map. WaU 8249

Official catalogue for the department of
fine arts, Section A, including paintings
in oil, water colors, pastels, together

with miniatures, pictures in photography
and works in sculpture. Portland, Or.,
Hess, 1905. 128 p. OrHi 8249A

Official catalogue of exhibitors, Lewis and
Clark Centennial and American Pacific
Exposition and Oriental Fair, livestock
exhibit, September 19 to 29 inclusive.
Portland, Or., Hess, 1905. 113 p. illus.
OrHi 8249B

Official catalogue of the Lewis and Clark
Centennial and American-Pacific Exposition and Oriental Fair, Portland, Oregon, June 1 to October 15, 1905. Portland,
Or., Hess [1905] 160 p. fold. front., illus.,
ports., plans.
Or OrP Wa WaSp WaU 8250

Same. 143 p. OrHi 8250A

Official classification and rules of exhibit
department, Lewis & Clark Centennial
and American Pacific Exposition and
Oriental Fair, Portland, Or., U. S. A.,
June 1 to October 15, 1905. Portland, Or.
Glass, 1905. 62 p. WaU 8251

Same. Portland, Union Printing Co., 1905.
70 p. OrHi 8251A

— — — Oregon Industrial Exposition.
Official prospectus, 1899. Portland, Or.,
1899. 47 p. illus. OrP 8252

— — — St. David's Church.
Monograph; memorial; resolutions of
clergy; resolutions of vestry; resolutions
of Women's Guild; resolutions of Daughters of S. D. and Young Men's Guild;
resolutions of vestry of St. Paul's
Church, Oregon City; convention resolutions. Portland, Or., Lewis & Dryden,
1890. 24 p. front. (port.) In memoriam,
Rev. John W. Sellwood. OrP WaPS 8253

— — — Society of the New Church of
Christ, Scientist.
Articles of organization, adopted March
13, 1887. Portland, Or., Himes, 1887. 13 p.
OrHi 8254

— — — Taylor Street Methodist Episcopal
Church.
Catalogue of the Sunday School library.
Portland, Or., Himes, 1873. 16 p.
OrHi 8255

Portland, Art Association, Portland, Or.
Fiftieth anniversary exhibition, 1892-1942;
December 2, 1942-January 3, 1943. Port-
land, Or. [1942] [31] p. illus. OrU 8256

Paintings by Mark Tobey: Portland Art
Museum, San Francisco Museum of
Art, Detroit Institute of Arts, 1945-1946.
[Portland, Or., 1945?] [16] p. illus.
OrU 8257

Portland Art Museum; an exhibition of
contemporary paintings held on the
opening of the Solomon and Josephine
Hirsch Memorial Wing. Portland, Or.
[1939] [20] p. illus. WaPS 8258

Portland Automobile Club, Portland, Or.
Oregon's scenic highways. [Portland, Or.,
James Kerns & Abbott, 1915] 64 p. illus.,
fold. map. Or OrP OrU 8259

Portland block book, showing sizes of lots
and names of owners, comp. from latest

official records. Portland, Or., Portland Block Book Co., 1907. 2 v.

OrP WaPS WaS **8260**

Portland Chrysanthemum Society.
Chrysanthemums; how we grow them out of doors, by members of Portland Chrysanthemum Society and others. Rev. ed. [Portland, Or., Loomis Printing Co., c1946] 97 p. front., illus., plates.

Or OrCS OrP Wa WaS **8261**

Portland City and County Medical Society.
Constitution and by-laws as adopted March 2, 1892. Portland, Or., Rogers, 1903. 1 v.

OrHi **8262**

Portland Council of Churches, Portland, Or.
Weekly schools of religious education. Portland, Or., Portland Council of Churches and Portland Council of Re-religious Education [1927] [8] p.

OrP **8263**

Portland Council of Social Agencies.
Programs and services in Portland and Multnomah County, Oregon, for teen age and young adults. Portland, Or., 1945. 23 p.

OrP **8264**

The Shattuck neighborhood. Portland, Or. [1944] 8 p. map.

OrP **8265**

— — — Boys' and Girls' Council.
Something to do, places to go for summer fun in your own neighborhood. Portland, Or., 1944. 18 p.

OrP **8266**

Portland Electric Power Company.
Amended plan of corporate reorganization of Portland Electric Power Company. [Portland, Or.?] 1934. 15 p.

OrP **8267**

The might of the mountains is yours to command; the Oak Grove project. [n.p., n.d.] [14] p. illus.

OrP **8268**

Portland Federation of Women's Organizations.
Milk price study of the Portland market, Portland, Oregon, by Portland Federation of Women's Organizations, assisted by Portland League of Women Voters, February 14, 1942. [Portland, Or.] 1942. 25 [7] p. tables.

OrCS OrP OrPR **8269**

Portland Free Kindergarten Association.
Review of the kindergartens from their organization Nov. 10, 1884 to April 17, 1888 and of the Froebel Union, an organization of all the kindergartens of Oregon. Portland, Or., Baltes, 1888. 32 p.

OrP **8270**

Portland Gas & Coke Co.
Tariff no. 2, naming rates for gas, rental and maintenance service at Portland, Oregon, and containing rules, regulations and contract forms in effect on and after July 15, 1913. Portland, Or., 1913. 10 p.

OrP **8271**

Portland Housing Association.
A housing investigation in Portland, Oregon (1919) [Portland, Or., 1919] 15 p.

OrP **8272**

Portland Library Association, Portland, Or.
Catalogue. Portland, Or., 1878. 174 p.

OrP OrU **8273**

A classified catalogue of the Portland Library of Portland, Oregon; with an index of authors and subjects, consisting of about twenty-five hundred volumes. Portland, Or., 1868. vi, 49 p. OrHi OrP **8274**

In memoriam: Henry Failing, president of the Library Association of Portland. [Portland, Or., 1898] 6 p. OrHi OrP **8275**

List of books on agriculture. Portland, Or., 1909. 28 p. WaPS **8276**

Memorial number; Mary Frances Isom, librarian, 1902-1920. Portland, Or. [1920] 24 p. port. (Monthly bulletin, May 1920)

OrHi OrP WaU **8277**

Portland library system. Portland, Or. [1930] 9 p. illus. OrP **8278**

Retail stores; list of recent books for retail merchants in the Portland Public Library, comp. for Oregon Retail Merchants Association of Portland, Oregon, February 1928. [n.p.] 1928. [16] p.

OrCS **8279**

Portland Mechanics Fair, Portland, Or.
Third annual exhibition; rules, regulations and premium list, 1881. Portland, Or., Walling, 1881. 24 p. OrP **8280**

Web foot sketch book. Portland, Or., Walling, 1883. [18] p. OrHi **8281**

Portland, Oregon, and the Columbia River;
views of the city and Mounts Hood, Adams, and St. Helens in the distance. Buffalo, W. G. MacFarlane [n.d.] 48 p. illus. OrU **8282**

Portland Press Club, Portland, Or.
The Columbia River Highway; the world's most famous scenic thorofare. [Portland, Or., 1919] 20 p. illus. OrP **8283**

Same. [1920?] 23 p. WaPS **8284**

Oregon; a newspaper reference book. Portland, Or., 1920. 120 p. illus., ports., map.

OrHi OrP **8285**

Pictorial Oregon, the wonderland; an invitation to visit Oregon extended by the Portland Press Club. Portland, Or., 1915. 167 p. front., illus., ports., maps.

Many **8286**

Souvenir. [Portland, Or.] 1900. 78 p. illus., ports. OrHi **8287**

Portland Progressive Business Men's Club.
Roster, committees, constitution and by-laws, 1918. [Portland, Or., 1918] 1 v.

OrHi **8288**

Portland Railway, Light and Power Co., Portland, Or.
Earn, save and invest at home; a sound investment and what is back of it. [Portland, Or., 1922] 12 p. illus., maps, diagrs. OrP **8289**

Electric lighting, heating and power rates applying to Portland, Salem, Oregon City, Gladstone, Gresham, Milwaukie, Lents, Boring, Estacada, Troutdale, Fairview, Sandy, Oak Grove, Oswego, Woodburn, Silverton, Mt. Angel, Gervais, and the vicinity of above. Portland, Or., 1915. 4 p. OrP **8290**

Portland Relief Committee.
Relief of sufferers by the fire in Portland, Oregon, August 2, 1873; report of relief committee. Portland, Or., Himes, 1874. 62 p. OrHi OrP WaU **8291**

Portland School District. High School of Commerce. Silver Pencil Club.
Silver pencilings, by members of the Silver Pencil Club of the High School of Commerce of Portland, Oregon. [Portland, Or.] 1925. 48 p. Verse.   OrCS **8292**

Portland Stock Exchange and Mining Board.
Constitution and by-laws of the Portland Stock Exchange and Mining Board, organized March 29, 1887. Portland, Or., J. K. Gill, 1887. 44, iii, p.   OrU **8293**

Portland Taxpayers' League.
To the voters of the city. [Porland, Or., Irwin-Hodson Co.] 1909. [8] p. OrP **8294**

Portland, the queen city of the Northwest as I saw it; a descriptive viewbook in colors. Los Angeles, H. H. Tammen, c1913. 26 p. illus.   WaTC **8295**

Portland Union Stock Yards, Co., Portland, Or.
Book of the stock yards. North Portland [1914?] 16 p.   Or OrHi **8296**

Marketing live stock through the Portland Union Stock Yards, North Portland, Oregon. [North Portland, Or.] 1936. 24 p. illus., port., plan, form, tables.
OrCS OrP **8297**

Portland's problems. How to solve them; effect of deep sea traffic on business and industry. [n.p., n.d.] 65 p.   OrP **8298**

Portlock, Nathaniel, 1748?-1817.
An abridgment of Portlock and Dixon's voyage round the world, performed in 1785, 1786, 1787, and 1788. London, Stockdale and Goulding, 1789. 272 p. front. (port.)   CVU WaU **8299**

Nathaniel Portlock's und Georg Mortimer's Reisen an die Nortvestkuste von Amerika; nebst den Reisen eines Amerikanischen Dolmetschers und Pelzandlers, welch eine Beschreibung der Sitten und Gebrauche des Nord amerikanischen Wilden enthalten; hrsg. von John Long; aus dem Englischen ubersetzt und mit einer vorlaufigen Schilderung des Nordens von Amerika, begleitet von Georg Forster. Berlin, Bossischen Buchhandlung, 1796. viii, 384 p. front., plates, maps.   WaU **8300**

Reis naar de noord-west kust van Amerika, Gedaan in de jaren 1785, 1786, 1787 en 1788; door de kaptains Nathaniel Portlock en Georg Dixon, uit derzelyer oorspronklijke reisverhalen zamengesteld en vertaald. Amsterdam, Matthijs Schalekamp, 1795. xii [iv] 265 p. fold. plates, fold. port., fold. map.   WaU **8301**

Voyage of Captains Portlock and Dixon to King George's Sound and round the world. Philadelphia, Crukshank, 1803. 120 p.   CVicAr **8302**

A voyage round the world in the years 1785, 1786, 1787, and 1788 performed in the King George and the Queen Charlotte under the direction of the Incorporated Society for the Advancement of the Fur Trade. London, R. Randal, 1789. 151 p. front.   CV CVicAr **8303**

A voyage round the world; but more particularly to the north-west of America; performed in 1785, 1786, 1787, and 1788, in the King George and Queen Charlotte, Captains Portlock and Dixon, embellished with twenty copper-plates, dedicated by permission to His Majesty. London, Stockdale and Goulding, 1789. xii, 384, xl p. front. (port.) 12 plates (5 col.) port., 6 maps (5 fold.) tables. Another account published by Wm. Beresford.
Many **8304**

A voyage round the world in the years 1785, 1786, 1787, and 1788 performed in the King George commanded by Captain Portlock, and the Queen Charlotte commanded by Captain Dixon, under the direction of the Incorporated Society for the Advancement of the Fur Trade. Dublin, J. Whitworth, 1789. 144 p. Anon.
CVicAr WaU **8305**

See also nos. 777-780.

Portrait and biographical record of Portland and vicinity, Oregon, containing original sketches of many well known citizens of the past and present. Chicago, Chapman, 1903. 883 p. ports.   Many **8306**

Portrait and biographical record of the Willamette Valley, Oregon, containing original sketches of many well known citizens of the past and present. Chicago, Chapman, 1903. 1563 p. 194 ports.
Or OrCS OrHi OrU WaU **8307**

Same with 1571 p. reported by OrP OrSaw WaPS.

Portrait and biographical record of western Oregon, containing original sketches of many well known citizens of the past and present. Chicago, Chapman, 1904. 1033 p. ports.
CVicAr Or OrHi OrSaW OrU **8308**

Post, Frank Truman, 1862-
Proposed amendments to the state constitution; address at the forty-eighth annual meeting of the Washington State Bar Association, Sunrise Camp, Rainier National Park, July 31, 1936. [n.p., 1936] 12 p.   WaPS **8309**

Post, Mae Celeste.
Loitering in Oregon. [Portland, Or., Gotshall Printing Co.] c1914. 64 p. 2 plates.
OrHi OrP OrU WaU **8310**

Post, Mary (Brinker) 1906-
Annie Jordan; a novel of Seattle. Garden City, N. Y., Doubleday, 1948. 280 p.
Many **8311**

Postwar problems of the Pacific and world organization; a record of four institutes held on the Pacific coast: Los Angeles, San Francisco, Portland, Seattle, March 1 to 9, 1944. [n.p.] International Center, 1944. 68 p.   OrP **8312**

Potbury, Susan S., see no. 1510.

Potlatch, Idaho. Union Church.
Constitution of the Union Church, Potlatch, Idaho. [Palouse, Wash., Republic Printers] 1907. 24 p.   WaPS **8313**

Potter, Charles E., see no. 2012.

Potter, Jean Clark, 1914-
Alaska under arms; endpaper by Richard Edes Harrison. New York, Macmillan, 1942. x, 200 p. Many **8314**

The flying North. New York, Macmillan, 1947. xiv, 261 p. plates, ports. Pioneer bush pilots of Alaska. Many **8315**

Potts, Ernest C., see no. 5655.

Poussin, Guillaume Tell, 1794-1876.
Question de l'Oregon, 1846. Paris, W. Coquebert, 1846. 100 p. WaS WaU **8316**

Powell, Addison Monroe. 1856-
Trailing and camping in Alaska. New York, Wessels, 1909. 379 p. front., 26 plates, port. Many **8317**

Same. 1910. CVicAr CVU WaPS WaU **8318**

Powell, Edward Alexander, 1879-
The end of the trail; the far West from New Mexico to British Columbia. New York, Scribner, 1914. xiv, 462 p. front., 47 plates, fold. map. Many **8319**

Same. 1922, c1914. OrPR **8320**

Marches of the North, from Cape Breton to the Klondike, illus. with photographs. New York, Century [c1931] x, 311 p. front., plates, fold. map. Many **8321**

Powell, Fred Wilbur, see no. 5432.

Powell, Garland M., see no. 3561.

Powell, James Madison.
Powell history; an account of the lives of the Powell pioneers of 1851: John A. Noah, and Alfred; their ancestors, descendants and other relatives. [n.p.] 1922. 188 p. ports., facsim. Oregon pioneer family. Or OrHi **8322**

Powell, Lawrence Clark, 1906-
Philosopher Pickett, the life and writings of Charles Edward Pickett, esq., of Virginia, who came overland to the Pacific Coast in 1842-43 and for forty years waged war with pen and pamphlet against all manner of public abuses in Oregon and California; including also unpublished letters written by him from Yerba Buena at the time of the conquest of California by the United States in 1846-47. Berkeley, Calif., University of California Press, 1942. xv, 178 p. front., facsims. Many **8323**

Powell, Lyman Pierson, 1866-   ed.
Historic towns of the western states. New York, Putnam, 1901. xxxvi, 702 p. front., illus., ports. (American historic towns) Many **8324**

Powell, Major, see no. 10989.

Powell & Jacobs, Engineers, Seattle, Wash.
Report on bursting of city water main at intersection of Fourth Avenue and Marion Street, Seattle, on February 20, 1921. Seattle, 1921. 60 p. illus., diagrs. WaS **8325**

Power, Alice Rose, see no. 10648.

Powers, Alfred.
Alaska; America's last frontier. Cleveland, Travel League [192—?] 14 p. port. OrU **8326**

Buffalo adventures on the western plains, illus. from old prints. Portland, Or., Binfords & Mort, 1945. 66 p. illus. (part col.) Many **8327**

Dr. John McLoughlin. [Oregon City, Or., Oregon City Enterprise, n.d.] [8] p. illus., port. Anon. Introduction by Katherine McRae. Or OrU **8328**

Early printing in the Oregon country, pub. as a keepsake. [Portland, Or.] Portland Club of Printing House Craftsmen [1933] [16] p. illus. Many **8329**

History of Oregon literature, illus. with manuscripts, title pages, photographs of sculpture, and crayon drawings by Bernard Hinshaw. Portland, Or., Metropolitan, 1935. 809 p. front., plates, ports., facsims. Many **8330**

Legends of the four high mountains. Portland, Or., Junior Historical Journal. 1944. 92 p. Or OrU Wa WaSp WaW **8331**

Marooned in Crater Lake, stories of the Skyline Trail, the Umpqua Trail, and the Old Oregon Trail. Portland, Or., Metropolitan, 1930. 177 p. diagr. Many **8332**

Same. Myrtlewood ed. WaPS WaU **8333**

Poems of the covered wagons. Portland, Or., Pacific Publishing House, 1947. 142 p. illus. Many **8334**

See also no. 468.

Powers, Kate (Ball) see nos. 473-475.

Prather, J. B.
The land of the midnight sun; a beautiful collection of Alaska and Northwest Territory views, including totems, glaciers; also a trip to the gold fields of the Klondike. Douglas, Eng., c1899. 1 v. front. (port.) 43 plates. CVicAr **8335**

Pratt, Alice Day.
Animals of a sagebrush ranch, illus. by Kurt Wiese. New York, Rand McNally [c1931] 208 p. illus., col. plates. OrCS OrMonO Wa WaS **8336**

A homesteader's portfolio. New York, Macmillan, 1922. vi, 181 p. front., 7 plates. Many **8337**

Pratt, Daniel Lincoln.
Along the sunset shore. Seattle, Sherman Printing & Binding Co. [n.d.] 58 p. col. plates. Poems. Wa WaS **8338**

Pratt, John F., see nos. 2014, 2015.

Pratt, Laurence.
Rooms in Caliban's cave. Caldwell, Idaho, Caxton, 1942. 95 p. Poems. Or OrP WaS WaU **8339**

A saga of a paper mill. Caldwell, Idaho, Caxton, 1935. 77 p. Many **8340**

See also no. 10536.

Pratt, Louis W., see no. 307.

Pratt, Orville Clyde, 1873-
Brief history of Spokane and the Pacific Northwest. [n.p.] 1939. 27 p. Previously published as The story of Spokane. WaSp **8341**

Public school finance and taxation in Washington. [n.p.] 1930. 31 p. (Washington Education Assn. Service bulletin, v. 10, no. 2, series 1930) WaTC **8342**

Spokane and the Pacific Northwest. [n.p.] 1930. 28 p. WaPS **8343**

The story of Spokane. Spokane, 1935. 32 p.
WaS WaSp **8344**

Preble, Paul, see no. 7123.

Prentiss, Augustin Mitchell, 1890-
Spruce helped win the war; a portrayal of
the personnel, railroad construction,
timber cutting and shipping, camp life,
and kindred subjects necessary to the
production of airplane spruce in unlimited quantities for the United States and
her allies. Portland, Or., 1918. 32 p. illus.
Or OrHi OrP **8345**

Presbyterian Church in the U. S. A. Board
of National Missions.
The Whitman-Spalding centennial gavel,
presented to the moderator of the 148th
General Assembly of the Presbyterian
Church in the U. S. A., Syracuse, N. Y.,
by the Board of National Missions, May
29, 1936. [n.p.] 1936. 8 p. WaPS **8346**

— — — Presbytery of Alaska.
The Presbyterian Church in Alaska; an official sketch of its rise and progress,
1877-1884, with the minutes of the 1st
meeting of the Presbytery of Alaska.
Washington, D. C., T. McGill, 1886. 13 p.
WaPS **8347**

— — — Presbytery of Portland, Or.
The relation of this presbytery to the beginning of missionary work in Alaska.
Portland, Or., Ellis Printing Co., 1900.
12 p. Or OrP **8348**

— — — Presbytery of Willamette.
The king's business, our business. [n.p.,
1909?] 13 p. WaPS **8349**

Presbytery of Willamette; what our
churches are doing, the worthwhile business of presbytery. Albany, Or., F. K.
Churchill [1908] 11 p. Or **8350**

— — — Synod of the Columbia.
Souvenir of the fiftieth anniversary of
Willamette Church, Oakville, Oregon.
[Albany, Or., 1900] 32 p. illus., port.
Or OrHi **8351**

— — — Synod of Washington.
History of the Synod of Washington of the
Presbyterian Church in the United
States of America, 1875-1909, historian,
Rev. Robert Boyd, assistants, Rev. W.
Chalmers Gunn, Rev. Hazen T. Murray,
treasurer, E. S. Osborne. [n.p., 1910?]
287 p. front., illus., ports. Many **8352**

True copy of the records of the first Presbyterian Church in the territory of Oregon, organized in 1838 by Rev. H. H.
Spalding and Dr. Marcus Whitman, missionaries of the American Board of Commissioners for Foreign Missions; also a
copy of additional notes, or memoranda,
made by Rev. H. H. Spalding after the
massacre of Dr. Whitman. [Portland,
Or., Ellis Printing Co., 1903] [25] p.
Transcribed from manuscript and certi-
fied as to accuracy by George F. Whitworth and Helen G. Morrill.
Or OrHi WaPS WaS WaSp **8353**

Prescott, Anson Ward.
Oregon's educational system. [n.p.] printed
by direction of the Lewis and Clark Centennial Exposition Commission of the
State of Oregon, 1905. 16 p. WaSp **8354**

Prescott, Winward, see no. 3394.

Preston, Mrs. Corliss, see no. 5880.

Preston, Richard Joseph, 1905-
Rocky Mountain trees; a handbook of the
native species with plates and distribution maps. Ames, Iowa, Iowa State College Press, 1940. lix. 285, lxi-lxxxi p.
front. (map) illus. Many **8355**

Same. 2d ed. 1947. MtBozC **8356**

Price, Con, 1869-
Memories of old Montana, by Con Price
(Masachele Opa Barusha). Hollywood,
Calif., Highland Press [1945] 154 p.
plates, ports.
MtBozC MtHi MtU OrSaW WaS WaU **8357**

Trails I rode, illus, by Charles M. Russell.
Pasadena, Calif., Trail's End Publishing
Company [1947] 262 p. illus., plates (1
col.) ports. MtU WaS WaU **8358**

Price, Elizabeth Bailey, see nos. 864, 865.

Price, Esther Louise Gaskins, 1892-
Fighting tuberculosis in the Rockies; a
history of the Montana Tuberculosis
Association, Helena, Mont., Montana
Tuberculosis Association, 1943. 71 p. illus.
ports. MtBoZ MtHi MtU WaS WaU **8359**

Price, Julius Mendes. d. 1924.
From Euston to Klondike; the narrative
of a journey through British Columbia and the Northwest Territory in the
summer of 1898, with map and illus.
from sketches by the author and photographs. London, Low, 1898. xvi, 301 p.
front., illus., plates, fold. map.
CV CVicAr CVU WaS WaU **8360**

Price, Mrs. Mary D. (Hickman), comp.
The National Society of the Colonial
Dames of America in the state of Wash-
ington. [Seattle, 1930] 59 p. front.
Author's name not given in this edition.
WaU **8361**

Same. 1935. 39 p. front., plates. WaU **8362**

Price, Sir Rose Lambart, bart., 1837-1899.
A summer on the Rockies. London, Low,
1898. x, 279 p. front. (port.) plate, fold.
map. CV WaU **8363**

Priest, Josiah, 1788-1851.
American antiquities and discoveries in
the West; being an exhibition of the
evidence that an ancient population of
partially civilized nations, differing entirely from those of the present Indians,
peopled America, many centuries before
its discovery by Columbus; and inquiries
into their origin, with a copious description of many of their stupendous
works now in ruins; with conjectures
concerning what may have become of
them, comp. from travels, authentic
sources, and the researches of antiquarian societies. 2d ed. Albany, N. Y., Hoffman and White, 1833. 400 p. fold. front.,
illus., plates, fold. plan.
CVicAr WaPS **8364**

Same. 3d ed. 1833. CVicAr WaS WaT **8365**

Same. 5th ed. 1835. CV Or WaSp **8366**

Pringle, George Charles Fraser, 1873-1949.
Aboard "The Sky Pilot" on the Pacific.
[n.p.] Board of Home Missions and So-

cial Service, Presbyterian Church in Canada [n.d.] 16 p. illus.   CVicAr **8367**

Tillicums of the trail; being Klondike yarns told to Canadian soldiers overseas by a sourdough padre. Toronto, MacClelland [c1922] 253 p.   CV WaU **8368**

Pringle, Octavius M., 1832?-1914.
Magic River Deschutes. [n.p., 1911?] [16] p. illus.   Many **8369**

Proby, Capt. William C.
Man hunters of the North; being a recital of twenty years in the Royal Northwest Mounted Police, as told to J. E. Hansell. Tacoma, Tacoma Star Publishing Company, 1928. 152 p. front. (port.) plate.   WaT **8370**

Proceedings at the unveiling and dedication of the Circuit Rider, State capitol grounds, Salem, Oregon, Saturday, April 19, 1924. [Portland, Or., Kilham Stationery & Printing Co., 1924] [34] p. illus., ports.   Or OrHi OrP **8371**

Proceedings commemorative of the life and services of Edward D. Baker, late United States senator for Oregon; addresses, resolutions, etc. Portland, Or., Oregon Farmer, 1861. 19 p.   OrHi **8372**

Proceedings of a railroad meeting held Jan. 27, 1868 on the subject of the Columbia Branch, to commence at Umatilla City and tap the Union Pacific Railroad northwest of Salt Lake City; together with the report, memorial and resolutions submitted by the chairman of the Committee of twenty-five. Umatilla, Or., Columbia Press, 1868. 7 p.   OrP **8373**

Procter, F. J.
The financial crisis in British Columbia. Vancouver, B. C., Evans & Hastings [1902?] 15 p.   CVU **8374**

Proctor, John W.
The rodeo; a book of poems of the West. Seattle [Proctlow Publishing Company] 1931. 63 p.   WaU **8375**

Proctor, William M., see no. 9180.

Professional Engineers of Oregon.
Constitution & by-laws. [Portland, Or., 1929?. 19 p.   OrCS **8376**

Program and proceedings in honor of the seventy-fifth birthday of Hon. Thomas A. McBride, Justice of the Supreme Court of Oregon. [n.p.] 1922. 24 p. OrHi **8377**

Progressive men of Bannock, Bear Lake, Bingham, Fremont and Oneida Counties, Idaho. Chicago, A. W. Bowen & Co., 1904. 664 p. front., ports. IdU WaS WaU **8378**

Progressive men of southern Idaho. Chicago, A. W. Bowen & Co., 1904. 952 p. front., ports. CVicAr IdU OrHi WaS WaU **8379**

Progressive men of the state of Montana. Chicago, A. W. Bowen & Co. [1901?] 1886 p. front., ports.   MtBozC
MtHi MtU MtUM WaPS WaU **8380**

Prohibition Party. Washington State Central Committee.
Prohibition Party campaign text-book for the state of Washington, 1892. Tacoma, Puget Sound Printing Co., 1892. 48 p. ports.   WaPS WaS **8381**

A proletarian, see no. 6002.

Proposed county of Nesmith; presentation of facts regarding county division measure which electors of Oregon will decide November 8, 1910. [Cottage Grove, Or.] 1910. [4] p.   Or OrP WaU **8382**

Prosch, Charles, 1820-1913.
Reminiscences of Washington Territory; scenes, incidents and reflections of the pioneer period on Puget Sound. Seattle, 1904. 128 p. front. (port.) plates.
Many **8383**

Prosch, Thomas Wickham, 1850-1915.
Conkling-Prosch family, with some reference to the Dotter, Roe, Reynolds, Brooks, Mapes, Elder, McCarver and other connections. Seattle, General Lithographing and Printing Co., 1909. 141 p. illus., ports.   Many **8384**

David S. Maynard and Catherine T. Maynard; biographies of two of the Oregon immigrants of 1850. Seattle, Lowman & Hanford [1906] 80 p. illus., 2 ports.
Many **8385**

Insane in Washington Territory. Seattle, Northwest Medicine, 1914. 8 p.
WaS WaT WaU **8386**

McCarver and Tacoma. Seattle, Lowman & Hanford [1906] viii, 198 p. illus., plates, 2 ports.   Many **8387**

The prospector, pseud., see nos. 11115, 11116.

The Prospector.
Seattle edition. Seattle, Metropolitan Life Insurance Co., 1946. 35 p. illus. (Dec. 1946)   WaS **8388**

Prosser, William Farrand, 1834-1911.
A history of the Puget Sound country, its resources, its commerce and its people; with some reference to discoveries and explorations in North America from the time of Christopher Columbus down to that of George Vancouver in 1792. New York, Lewis Publishing Company, 1903. 2 v. fronts., plates, ports.   Many **8389**

Prosser Falls Irrigation Company, Prosser, **Wash.**
Irrigation farming and fruit raising in the Yakima Valley, Washington. [Chicago, W. H. Dietz] 1895. 51 p. illus. WaPS **8390**

Protestant Episcopal Church in the U. S. A.
Morning and evening prayer and the Holy Communion together with selections of the Psalms, trans. into the Eskimo language of the Tigara tribe of Arctic Alaska. [New York, Fisher & Thul, 1923] 91 p.   WaU **8391**

— — — Book of Common Prayer. Selections. Haida.
Book of common prayer; portions of the book of common prayer in Haida. London, 1899. 29 p.   Wa **8392**

— — — — — — — — Qliyukuwhutana?
Service book; being parts of the Book of common prayer set forth for use in the dialect of the Qliyukuwhutana Indians at the mission of Our Savior, Tanana, Alaska. New York, Bible and Common Prayer Book Society, 1908. 109 p.
WaU **8393**

— — — Catechisms. Shoshone.
Questions and answers in Shoshone. [n.p.,
n.d.] 23 p.   MtHi OrHi **8394**
— — — Olympia Diocese.
Constitution and canons. [Olympia, Wash.?]
1912. xxxiv p.   WaU **8395**
Same. 1925. 35, vi p.   WaU **8396**
Same. 1931. 34 [6] p.   WaU **8397**
— — — Oregon Diocese.
Semi-centennial of the Protestant Episco-
pal Church in Oregon, 1851-1901. [n.p.,
1901?] 90 p. OrHi OrP OrU WaU **8398**
— — — Oregon and Washington Mission-
ary District.
Six years' missionary work in Oregon and
Washington Territory. New York, 1874-
75. 3 pt. in 1 v. illus. (Oregon and Wash-
ington Mission, v. 1, no. 1, 2; Home and
abroad, v. 5, no. 12) Labors of Bishop
Morris.   OrU **8399**
Providence, une soeur de, see no. 5626.
**Provincial Mining Association of British
Columbia.** Rossland Branch.
Constitution. Rossland, B. C., Collis &
Co., 1903. 16 p.   CVicAr **8400**
Provincial Publishing Co., Vancouver, B. C.,
comp.
A gazetteer of British Columbia, contain-
ing the names, locations and general in-
formation regarding the cities, towns,
post offices, settlements, islands, rivers,
lakes, capes, bays and mountains of the
province. Vancouver, B. C., c1909. 114 p.
CVicAr WaU **8401**
Prud'homme, Louis Arthur, 1853-
Pierre Gaultier de Varennes, sieur de la
Verendrye, captain of marines, chevalier
of the military order of St. Louis, discoverer of the North-West, 1685-1749. St.
Boniface, "Le Manitoba", 1916. 178, 3 p.
illus., ports., maps. (Bulletin of the Historical Society of St. Boniface, v. 5, pt.
2, 1916)   WaU **8402**
Public Administration Service, Chicago.
Distribution of motor fuel taxes among
counties in Washington; a report of a
survey made in accordance with chapter
235, Laws of 1943, state of Washington,
ed. by Farrell G. H. Symons. Chicago,
1944. xx, 336 p. illus., maps, tables, diagrs.
Many **8403**
Puget Mill Co., Seattle, Wash. Real Estate
Department.
Real estate opportunities in Seattle and
vicinity. Seattle [Grettner-Diers Printing
Co.] c1929. 43 p. illus., fold. map.
WaS **8404**
[Puget Rhymesters]
Puget soundings. [Seattle, Lowman & Han-
ford, 1945] 121 p. illus.
WaS WaT WaU WaW **8405**
Puget Sound Academy of Science.
The marine museum and aquarium; ship
St. Paul, Seattle. Seattle [1935?] 1 v.
illus.   WaS **8406**
Puget Sound Bridge and Dredging Company,
Seattle, Wash.
57 years of progress. [Seattle, 1944?] [61]
p. illus., map.   WaS **8407**

Puget Sound Co-operative Colony.
Puget Sound Co-operative Colony. Milwau-
kee, Wis., E. W. Ellis [1886?] 32 p.
WaU **8408**
Puget Sound Electric Railway.
Facts concerning the Puget Sound Elec-
tric Railway as to the matter of rates
as brought out in correspondence be-
tween representatives of the Puyallup
Commercial Club and the Public Service
Commission of the state of Washington.
n.p., 1915] 8 p.   WaS **8409**
Story of the Seattle-Tacoma Interurban;
symposium by Harold Hall, Robert S.
Wilson, Charles Johnson, Roland Covey.
Jim Rice. Los Angeles, Interurban
News Letter, 1945. 10 p. illus., map.
WaT **8410**
Puget Sound Iron Co., Port Townsend, Wash.
Prospectus of the Puget Sound Iron Mine.
Port Townsend, Wash., Democrat Press,
1879. 7 p.   WaU **8411**
**Puget Sound Log Scaling and Grading Bu-
reau,** Seattle, Wash.
Official log scaling and grading rules for
the Pacific Northwest. Seattle [1946?] 1
v.   OrCS **8412**
Same. 1948. 53 p.   OrCS **8413**
Puget Sound Mail, La Conner, Wash.
Fifty-fourth anniversary development num-
ber. La Conner, Wash., 1927. 26 p. illus.,
ports. (55th year, no. 1, June 16, 1927)
WaU **8414**
Half-century edition. La Conner, Wash.,
1929. [16] p. illus., ports. (57th year, no.
13, Sept. 19, 1929)   WaU **8415**
[75th anniversary number] 1873-1948. La
Conner, Wash., 1948. 12 p. illus., (75th
year, no. 52, Aug. 5, 1948)   WaU **8416**
Puget Sound Navigation Co., Seattle, Wash.
The resorts of Puget Sound; how to reach
them. Seattle [n.d.] 1 v. illus., fold. map.
OrU **8417**
Touring Puget Sound via Black Ball Line.
[Seattle, 193—?] [11] p. illus., map.
WaPS **8418**
Visit San Juan Islands. [Sedro-Woolley,
Wash., 193—?] [7] p. lilus., maps.
WaPS **8419**
Puget Sound Power & Light Company.
Handbook, March 1923. [Seattle, 1923] 46 p.
illus., map.   WaU **8420**
Washington, the new cornerstone [electric
companies advertise Washington state
for post-war industrial development]
[Seattle, 1944?] [5] p. illus. WaS **8421**
— — — Agricultural Engineering Depart-
ment.
Electricity on the poultry farm. [Seattle?
c1936] 63 p. illus., diagrs. WaPS **8422**
Irrigation in western Washington. Seattle
[n.d.] 31 p. illus., tables, diagrs.
WaPS **8423**
Puget Sound Power Co.
Description of water-power development
and transmission plant on the Puyallup
River, Pierce County, Washington. Bos-
ton, Ellis, 1904. 69 p. illus., plates, map.
WaU **8424**

Puget Sound Traction, Light & Power Co., Seattle, Wash.

In re the arbitration of the matters now in controversy between the Puget Sound Traction, Light & Power Co., The Tacoma Railway & Power Co., and their employees, before Dr. Henry Suzzallo, James A. Duncan and C. J. Franklin; argument of Puget Sound Traction, Light & Power Co. Seattle, P. L. Allen [1919?] 108 p. WaU **8425**

No contract between two parties can be changed without the consent of both; to protect our rights we are compelled to apply to the courts. [Seattle, Sherman Printing and Bindery Co., 1911?] 8 p. WaS WaU **8426**

Puget Sound Underwriters Association.

Agreement of the Puget Sound Underwriters Association, adopted May 27, 1895. Tacoma, Vaughn & Morrill [1895] 11 p. WaU **8427**

Puget Sound Wood Products Co. .

Products of the great West and the saving of a waste. [Seattle, Coast Advertising Service, 1909] 15 p. illus. WaU **8428**

Puget Sounders and British Columbians, Associated.

The evergreen playground: Tacoma, Seattle, Bellingham, Vancouver, Victoria. [Seattle?, 1926?] 23 p. illus., map. WaPS **8429**

Pullen, Henry F.

Some bird friends; an intimate introduction to a few of the common birds of western Canada. Victoria, B. C., Free Lance Publishing Company [n.d.] 30 p. illus., 2 plates, photos. WaSp **8430**

Pullman, Wash. First National Bank.

Golden anniversary, June 10, 1887-1937. Pullman, Wash., 1937. [8] p. illus., table. WaPS **8431**

Pullman Community Hotel Corporation, Pullman, Wash.

The kind of a hotel Pullman needs. [Pullman, Wash., 1927?] [8] p. WaPS **8432**
A modern tourist and commercial hotel for Pullman. [Pullman, Wash., 192—?] [16] p. illus., plans. WaPS **8433**

Pullman Herald, Pullman, Wash.

The Pullman Herald; golden jubilee edition, Nov. 4, 1938. Pullman, Wash., 1938. 1 v. illus., ports. (v. 51, no. 1, Nov. 4, 1938) WaS **8434**

Purcell, Mrs. Polly Jane (Claypool) 1842-1923.

Autobiography and reminiscences of a pioneer. [Freewater, Or., n.d.] [7] p. Or OrHi OrP WaSp WaU **8435**

Purdy, Ruby Fay.

The Rose City of the world, Portland, Oregon. Portland, Or., Binfords & Mort [1947] vii, 196 p. plates. Many **8436**

Purdy, Will E. 1862-

Sixteen years in Oregon. Portland, Or., 1912. 126 p. ports. OrU **8437**

Same. Portland, Or., Glass & Prudhomme, 1912. Or OrHi OrP WaPS WaU **8438**

Pursh, Frederick, 1774-1820.

Flora Americae septentrionalis; or, A systematic arrangement and description of the plants of North America (collected by Lewis and Clark). London, White, Cochrane and Co., 1814. 2 v. 24 plates, tables. OrHi OrP WaU **8439**

Puter, Stephen A. Douglas, 1857-

Looters of the public domain, by S. A. D. Puter, king of the Oregon land fraud ring, in collaboration with Horace Stevens, embracing a complete exposure of the fraudulent system of acquiring titles to the public lands of the United States. Portland, Or., Portland Printing House, c1907. 494 p. front., illus., ports. Many **8440**

Same. 1908. IdU OrHi WaU **8441**

Putnam, George Palmer, 1887-

In the Oregon country; out-doors in Oregon, Washington, and California together with some legendary lore and glimpses of the modern West in the making, with an introd. by James Withycombe. New York, Putnam, c1915. xxi, 169 p. front., 32 plates. Many **8442**
Same. xxi, 152 p. "Oregon Journal" ed. WaPS **8443**

The smiting of the rock; a tale of Oregon, by Palmer Bend [pseud.] New York, Putnam, 1918. vi, 328 p. col. front. OrP OrU WaS WaU **8444**

Putnam, L. P., see no. 10438.

The Puyallup Press.

The story of Ezra Meeker, pioneer tales, historical review, resources of the Puyallup Valley; golden jubilee ed. Puyallup, Wash., 1939. 48 p. illus. WaT **8445**

Puyallup Valley Tribune.

Facts about the Puyallup Valley. [Puyallup, Wash., 191—?] [13] p. front., illus. WaPS **8446**

Pyle, Joseph Gilpin, 1853-1930.

The life of James J. Hill. Garden City, N. Y., Doubleday, Page, 1917. 2 v. fronts., 6 ports. Many **8447**

Same. Toronto, McClelland, Goodchild and Stewart [1917?] CVic **8448**

Quaife, Milo Milton, see nos. 1541, 5442,, 5701, 5909, 6072, 6377, 8784, 8786.

The quarantine claims; "Prince Albert", June 1872; judgment, December 24, 1873. Victoria, B. C., Victoria Standard [n.d.] 11 p. CVicAr **8449**

Quarnberg, Andrew Anderson, 1849-

Filbert growing in the Puget Sound country, presenting a treatise on the filbert nut. Seattle, Puget Mill Co., c1917. [36] p. illus., port. OrP WaS WaT WaU **8450**

Queen Charlotte Coal Mining Company.

Memorandum of association. [Victoria, B. C., British Colonist?, 1865?] 12 p. CVicAr **8451**

Prospectus and report, with articles of association. Victoria, B. C., British Colonist [1865?] 14 p. CVicAr **8452**

Queeny, Edgar Monsanto, 1897-

Cheechako, the story of an Alaskan bear

hunt, with photographs by the author; introd. by Nash Buckingham. New York, Scribner, 1941. xvi, 133 p. col. front., plates (part col.) ports.
CVicAr Or WaS WaU 8453

Quick, Herbert, 1861-1925.
Yellowstone nights. Indianapolis, Bobbs-Merrill [c1911] 345 p.
MtHi WaSp WaU 8454

Quiett, Glenn Chesney, 1895-1936.
Pay dirt; a panorama of American gold-rushes. New York, Appleton-Century, 1936. xxv, 506 p. front., illus., plates, ports.
Many 8455

They built the West; an epic of rails and cities. New York, Appleton-Century, 1934. xx, 569 p. front., illus., plates, ports., maps.
Many 8456

[Quigg, Lemuel Ely] 1863-1919.
New empires in the Northwest. New York, Tribune Association [c1889] 84 p. tables. (Library of Tribune extras, v. 1, no. 8)
MtU WaU 8457

Quimby, George Irving.
Aleutian Islanders; Eskimos of the North Pacific, drawings by Helen Z. Quimby. [Chicago] 1944. 48 p. illus., 8 plates. (Chicago Natural History Museum. Anthropology leaflet no. 35)
CV Or WaS WaU 8458

R., I., see no. 8493.

R. B., see no. 1206.

Racine, Samuel Frederick, 1882-
Income tax guide applicable to the state of Washington. Seattle, Western Institute Press [c1933] 186 p.
Wa WaS WaSp WaT WaU 8459

Radclyffe, Charles Robert Eustace.
Big game shooting in Alaska. London, Ward, 1904. xvi, 292 p. front., illus., ports., fold. map.
CVicAr WaS 8460

Raddon, Samuel Herbert, Jr., 1883-
Portland vignettes; sketches by Paul Keller. Portland, Or. Metropolitan [1936] [107] p. illus.
Many 8461

Radebaugh, Randolph Foster, 1846-1927.
The Pacific metropolis; where and why. [Tacoma, South Tacoma Press] 1913. 94 p. 2 fold. plates, maps (part fold.)
WaPS WaS WaTC WaU 8462

Tacoma, the western terminus of the Northern Pacific Railroad. Tacoma, Ledger, 1887. 43 p. plates, fold. map.
CVicAr 8463

Rae, John, 1813-1893.
Narrative of an expedition to the shores of the Arctic Sea in 1846 and 1847. London, T. & W. Boone, 1850. 247 p. front., fold. map.
CVicAr 8464

Raftery, John Henry, 1866-
Story of the Yellowstone. [Butte, Mont., McKee Printing Co.] 1912. 135 p. illus.
MtHi WaSp 8465

Railway and Marine News, Seattle, Wash.
New Cascade Tunnel number. [Seattle, 1929] 66 p. illus., ports., maps, plans. (v. 26, no. 1, Jan. 1929)
WaS WaU 8466

Railway Business Association, New York.
Washington state and railway legislation. New York, 1919. 10 p.
WaPS 8467

Raimond, C. E., see no. 8709.

Raine, Norman Reilly.
Tugboat Annie. New York, Minton, Balch & Co. [c1934] 313 p.
IdU Or WaE WaS WaSP WaT 8468

Raine, William MacLeod, 1871-
Cattle, by William MacLeod Raine and Will C. Barnes. Garden City, N. Y., Doubleday, 1930. xii, 340 p. front., illus., plates, facsim.
IdU IdUSB Or WaSp WaT 8469

Famous sheriffs & western outlaws. Garden City, N. Y., Doubleday, 1929. 294 p.
. Many 8470

Ridgway of Montana; a story of to-day, in which the hero is also the villain. illus. by O. T. Jackman. New York, G. W. Dillingham Co. [c1909] 318 p. front., 3 plates.
Or WaPS WaT 8471

Under northern stars. New York, Grosset [c1932] 296 p.
CV WaW 8472

Wyoming, a story of the outdoor West, illus. by Clarence Rowe. New York, Grosset [c1908] 353 p. front. IdB WaU 8473

The Yukon Trail; a tale of the North, with illus. by George Ellis Wolfe. Boston, Houghton, 1917. vii, 323 p. front., 3 plates.
OrU WaA WaS WaSp WaT 7474

Rainier Valley Citizen, Seattle, Wash.
Supplement; the Citizen Christmas annual. Seattle, 1915. 48 p. front., illus., plate. (v. 8, no. 52, Dec. 25, 1915)
WaS 8475

Raley, George H.
A monograph of the totem-poles in Stanley Park, Vancouver, B. C. Vancouver, B. C., 1937. 24 p. illus.
CV
CVicAr CVU OrU WaS WaT 8476

Ralph, Julian, 1853-1903.
On Canada's frontier; sketches of history, sport, and adventure and of the Indians, missionaries, fur-traders, and newer settlers of western Canada. New York, Harper, 1892. x, 325 p. front., illus., plates.
CVicAr OrP WaE WaS WaU 8477

Our great West; a study of the present conditions and future possibilities of the new commonwealths and capitals of the United States. New York, Harper, 1893. xi, 477 p. front., illus., plates, maps.
Many 8478

Ralphson, George Harvey, 1879-
Boy Scouts in a motor boat; or, Adventures on the Columbia River. Chicago, M. A. Donohue & Co. [c1912] 246 p. front.
Or OrP WaU 8479

Boy Scouts in the Northwest; or, Fighting forest fires. Chicago, M. A. Donohue & Co. [c1912] 255 p. front. WaPS WaU 8480

Ralston, John Chester, 1864-1928.
Water powers [an address delivered before the Northwest Mining Convention, Spokane, Wash., Feb. 15, 1912] [Spokane, Franklin Press, 1912] 10 p. WaPS 8481

Ralston Club, Seattle, Wash.
The Ralston Club handbook; a little history about much singing, comp. by El-

don Griffin, historian. Seattle, 1932. 38 p. front., plate. WaS WaU **8482**

Ramsay, Claude Clinton, 1865-
The acquisition of Sand Point Aviation Field [address before the Reserve Officers' Association at Seattle, Friday, Oct. 15, 1926] [Seattle, 1926] [10] p. illus.
WaS WaU **8483**

Ramsey, A.
An appeal to Congress in behalf of the Northwest in connection with the construction of the Northern Pacific Railroad and telegraph. Washington, D. C., Intelligencer, 1866. 16 p. CVicAr **8484**

Ranck, Glenn N., 1869-
Legends and translations of Northwest history; souvenir ed., with illus. Vancouver, Wash., American Printing and Stationery Co. [c1914] 152 p. front., 11 plates, port., map. Includes biographies of Clark County pioneers. Many **8485**

Pictures from Northwest history. [Vancouver, Wash.? 1902?] [38] p.
OrP WaS WaU **8486**

Rand, McNally & Co., Chicago, Ill.
[Alaska] Rand McNally guide to Alaska and Yukon for tourists, investors, homeseekers and sportsmen; with maps and illus. Chicago, c1922. xiii, 175 p. front., illus., fold. map. OrU WaPS WaU **8487**

[Oregon] indexed pocket map, tourists' and shippers' guide of Oregon. Chicago [c1921] 38 p. map. OrHi **8488**

[Oregon] Rand McNally & Co.'s indexed county and township pocket map and shippers' guide of Oregon, accompanied by a new and original compilation and ready reference system. Chicago [c1896] 24 p. WaPS **8489**

Same. [1906] 24 p. fold. map. WaPS **8490**

[Oregon] Rand McNally indexed pocket map and shippers' guide of Oregon. Chicago, c1917. 40 p. map. Or **8491**

Randall, Harry, 1858-
The conquest of the Northwest Passage; a treatise. Minneapolis [Murphy-Travis Co.] 1907. [12] p. front. (port.) plate.
CVicAr MtU WaSp WaU **8492**

[**Randall, Isabelle**]
A lady's ranche life in Montana, by I. R. London, W. H. Allen & Co., 1887. viii, 170 p. MtBozC MtHi WaU **8493**

Randolph, see no. 9438.

Randolph, Richard W.
Sweet Medicine and other stories of the Cheyenne Indians, illus. by R. H. Hall. Caldwell, Idaho, Caxton, 1937. 196 p. col. front., illus.
MtHi Or OrSaW WaSp WaU WaWW **8494**

Rankin, M. Wilson.
Reminiscences of frontier days, including an authentic account of the Thornburg and Meeker massacre. Denver, Photolithographed by Smith-Brooks, c1935. 140 p. MtHi **8495**

Rasmussen, Knud Johan Victor, 1879- ed,
The eagle's gift, Alaska Eskimo tales, trans. by Isobel Hutchinson, illus. by Ernst Hansen. Garden City, N. Y.,

Doubleday, 1932. xiv, 235 p. col. front., plates (part col.) Many **8496**

Festens gave; eskimoiske Alaska-aeventyr, med tegninger af Ernst Hansen. Kobenhavn, Nordisk forlag, 1929. 207 p. illus., col. plates, map. WaS **8497**

[**Rathbone, St. George Henry**] 1854-1938.
The pioneer boys of the Columbia; or, In the wilderness of the great Northwest, by Harrison Adams [pseud.] Boston, Page, 1916. 345 p. front., illus., 5 plates.
Or OrP **8498**

Rathbun, John C., 1854-
History of Thurston County, Washington. Olympia, Wash., 1895. 131 p.
OrHi Wa WaPS WaS WaU **8499**

Rattan, Volney.
Analytical key to west coast botany, containing descriptions of sixteen hundred species of flowering plants growing west of the Sierra Nevada and Cascade crests from San Diego to Puget Sound. San Francisco, Bancroft, 1887. 128 p.
OrP WaWW **8500**

A popular California flora; or, Manual of botany for beginners; with illustrated introductory lessons especially adapted to the Pacific coast, to which is added an analytical key to west coast botany. 8th rev. ed. San Francisco, Bancroft [188-] xxviii, 128 p. illus. WaU **8501**

West coast botany; an analytical key to the flora of the Pacific coast in which are described over eighteen hundred species of flowering plants growing west of the Sierra Nevada and Cascade crests from San Diego to Puget Sound. San Francisco, Whitaker & Ray, 1898. 221 p. illus.
OrCS OrP OrU Wa WaU **8502**

Rattray, Alexander.
Vancouver Island and British Columbia, where they are and what they may become; a sketch of their history, topography, climate, resources. London, Smith, Elder, 1862. viii, 182 p. col. front., 3 col. plates, 2 fold. maps, fold. table.
Many **8503**

Raumer, F. v., see no. 3363.

Raup, Hugh Miller, 1901-
Phytogeographic studies in the Peace and upper Liard River regions Canada, with a catalogue of the vascular plants. Jamaica Plain, Mass., Arnold Arboretum of Harvard University, 1934. 230 p. 9 plates, fold. map. (Contributions, 6)
CVU MtBozC OrCS OrU **8504**

The **"Raven",** see no. 10215.

Ravenna Park. [Seattle, n.d.]
[20] plates. WaU **8505**
Same. [1903] [32] plates.
OrHi WaS WaU **8506**

Raver Paul Jerome.
Hydro; the energy base of the Northwest; an address before the Institute for Social Action, 1st Methodist Church, Portland, Oregon, Oct. 19, 1948. [n.p.] 1948. 19 p. OrP **8507**

Rawlings, Thomas.
Die Auswanderung mit besonderer Beziehung auf Minnesota und British Colum-

bia; aus dem Englischen ubertragen und eingeleitet von Eduard Pelz. Hamburg, Hoffman, 1866. 63 p.   CVicAr **8508**

Ray, Clarence Everly, 1882-
Harry Tracy; bandit, highwayman and outlaw of the Twentieth Century. Chicago, Regan Publishing Company [n.d.] 188 p. front., illus.   OrP **8509**

Tracy, the bandit; or, The romantic life and crimes of a Twentieth Century desperado. Chicago, Regan Publishing Company [19—?] 185 p. front., illus. (Wild West series, no. 12)   WaU **8510**

Ray, John.
Older coast ranges, with more recent geological formations in Benton County. Corvallis, Or., Conover & Kitson [1892] 13 p. illus., plates.   OrP OrU **8511**

Ray, Verne Frederick, 1905-
Cultural relations in the plateau of northwestern America. Los Angeles [Southwest Museum] 1939. ix, 154 p. illus., maps. (Publications of the Frederick Webb Hodge anniversary publication fund, v. 3)   MtU OrU WaS WaU **8512**

The Sanpoil and Nespelem; Salishan peoples of northeastern Washington. Seattle, University of Washington Press, 1933. 237 p. front. (port.) illus., map. (Publications in anthropology, v. 5)
          Many **8513**

Raymer, Robert George.
Montana, the land and the people; Montana biography by special staff of writers. Chicgo, Lewis Publishing Company, 1930. 3 v. front., illus., ports. Volumes 2, 3 biographical.   MtBozC
MtHi MtU MtUM OrSaW WaU **8514**

Raymer's dictionary of greater Seattle; an encyclopaedic-dictionary of the state of Washington, U. S. A. in general and the city of Seattle in particular. Seattle, C. D. Raymer & Co. [c1908] 128 p. front., illus., fold. map.
          OrU Wa WaPS WaS WaU **8515**
Same. [c1910]   OrP WaS **8516**
Same. 1913.   Or WaSp **8517**

Raymer's dictionary of Spokane; an encyclopaedic-dictionary of the state of Washington, U. S. A. in general and the city of Spokane in particular. Spokane, C. D. Raymer & Co., c1906. 152 p. front., illus., fold. map. Or Wa WaS WaSp WaU **8518**

Raymond, Mrs. Mabel D.
What Washington women should know of state law [presented to the women of Washington by the state Federation of Women's Clubs] [Seattle?] 1931. 35 p.
          WaS WaT **8519**

Raymond, Rossiter Worthington, 1840-1918.
Camp and cabin; sketches of life and travel in the West. New York, Fords, Howard & Hulbert, 1880. 243 p. front.
          IdIf MtHi WaU **8520**

The mines of the West; a report to the Secretary of the Treasury. New York, J. B. Ford and Co., 1869. 256 p. map, table, diagr.   IdB OrU **8521**

Raymond, William H.
Catalogue of trotting stock of the Belmont Park Stock Farm, Madison County, Montana [n.p.] 1890. 127 p.   MtHi **8522**

Raymond Herald.
Christmas edition. Raymond, Wash., 1922. 34 p. illus. (v. 17, no. 43, Dec. 22, 1922)
          WaU **8523**

Rayner, Mrs. Alice D., comp.
The path we came by; a history of Plymouth Congregational Church, Seattle, Washington, 1869-1937. [n.p., 1937?] 216 p. plates, ports.   WaS WaU **8524**

Rea, Ella M.
Castaways of the Yukon. Boston, Meador, 1936. 298 p. front. (port.)   WaU **8525**

Mutiny on the long trail; King Chinook, saga of the Columbia River. Portland, Or., Metropolitan, 1933. 98 p.
          OrP OrU WaPS WaS WaU **8526**

Read, Francis W.
G. I. parson. New York, Morehouse-Gorham Co., 1945. viii, 117 p. Aleutian Islands in World War II.   WaU **8527**

Read, John B., see no. 6955.

Read, Opie, see no. 10606.

Reagan, Albert B., 1871-1936.
Archaeological notes on western Washington and adjacent British Columbia. San Francisco, California Academy of Sciences, 1917. 31 p. illus., 6 plates, maps. (Proceedings, 4th series, v. 7, no. 1)
          CVicAr CVU OrU WaPS WaU **8528**

Reagan, Harry Clifton, 1864-
Legend of the Grand Canyon of the Yellowstone. Boston, Christopher Publishing House [c1925] 43 p. front. (port.) plates. Verse.   WaU **8529**

Reasons to show that there is a great probability of a navigable passage to the western American ocean through Hudson's Streights and Chesterfield Inlet, from the observations made on board the ships sent upon the late discovery; supported by affidavits, which coincides with several former accounts. London, J. Robinson, 1749. 23 p.   CVicAr **8530**

Reat, Loraine.
Alaskan days. Seattle [Farwest] c1944. [46] p. illus.   WaS WaU **8531**

Reavis, John R.
The city of Spokane; its tributary country and its resources. Spokane, Clough & Graves, 1891. 56 p. illus.   WaSp **8532**

Rebec, Mary (Lowell) 1874-1938.
Poems, foreword by Eric W. Allen. Eugene, Or., University of Oregon, 1938. vii, 162 p. front. (port.)
          OrCS OrMonO OrP OrPR **8533**

Rebeller, A. le, see no. 8824.

Reber, Effinger L.
King County, state of Washington, 1909; its history, resources, development, present conditions & opportunities. Seattle, 1909. 1 v. illus.   WaS **8534**

A record of the 362d Field Hospital Company, 316th Sanitary Train, 91st Division, United States Army. [Tacoma? 192—?] 74 p. illus., ports.   WaU **8535**

Rector, Milton R., see no. 7227.

Red Cross. U. S. American National Red Cross.
An American Red Cross study of service to ex-service men and women in Portland, Oregon, with particular reference to Portland chapter's A. R. C. contribution in this field with recommendations for the future conduct of Portland chapter's work and the coordination of all relief efforts for ex-service men through the formation of a council of veterans' agencies. [n.p., 1924] 35 p.　OrP **8536**

The Pacific-Northwest floods of 1933-34; official report of the American Red Cross. Washington, D. C. [1935] 23 p. illus.　OrP WaT WaU **8537**

— — — — — — California.
A record of the Red Cross work on the Pacific slope, including California, Nevada, Oregon, Washington, and Idaho, with their auxiliaries; also reports from Nebraska, Tennessee, and far-away Japan. Oakland, Calif., Pacific Press, 1902. 458 p. illus., ports.
Wa WaS WaSp WaT WaU **8538**

— — — — — — Seattle Chapter.
Feeble-mindedness in Washington; report of Special Research Committee. Seattle, 1924. [10] p.　WaS **8539**

— — — — — — Tacoma Chapter.
An American Red Cross study of the needs of disabled World War veterans in Tacoma, Washington with particular reference to Tacoma Chapter's contribution in this field. [n.p.] 1925. 95 p.
WaT **8540**

Red Neck, see no. 4257.

Redeman, Clara.
Our first forty years [Deaconess Hospital of Spokane] Caldwell, Idaho, Caxton, 1941. 134 p. 3 plates, 7 ports. WaSp **8541**

Redfeather, see no. 2096.

Redfield, C. M., see no. 1598.

Redfield, Edith Sanderson.
Seattle memories. Boston, Lothrop, Lee & Shepard [c1930] 78 p. front., illus., 7 plates, 2 ports., facsims.
IdU Wa WaPS WaS WaSp WaU **8542**

Verses. Boston, Lothrop, Lee & Shepard [c1907[58 p.　Wa WaS WaU **8543**

Reed, Mrs. Anna (Yeomans) 1871-　comp.
A study of the Lewis and Clark expedition for the use of the eighth grade of the Seattle Public Schools; selections from the sources of Mrs. J. A. Reed, under the auspices of the Art and Travel Department of the Woman's Century Club. Seattle, 1904. 24 p.
WaS WaU **8544**

Reed, Charles Bert, 1866-
Masters of the wilderness. Chicago, Univ. of Chicago Press [c1914] ix, 144 p. front. (map) 3 plates (1 col.) map. (Chicago Historical Society. Fort Dearborn series)
CV CVicAr WaPS WaS WaU **8545**

Reed, Charles K., 1851-
Western bird guide; birds of the Rockies and west to the Pacific, illus. by Chester A. Reed, Harry F. Harvey, R. I. Brasher.

Worcester, Mass., 1913. 255 p. col. front., illus. (part col.).　Many **8546**
Same. Garden City, N. Y., Doubleday, 1917. 252 p. illus. (Pocket nature series)
WaW **8547**

Reed, Edwin Thomas, 1872-
The bells of long ago, and other memorial poems. Portland, Or., Binfords & Mort [c1946] 80 p. Oregon State College.
Or OrCS OrHi WaS WaU **8548**

Into the promised land. Corvallis, Or., Oregon State College Cooperative Assn., 1942. 116 p. Oregon Trail Centennial
Or OrP OrSaW WaU **8549**

Reed, Elmer, pub.
[The Kobuk maiden and other Alaska sourdough verses] a collection of Alaska verses comp. from newspapers published in the Territory from 1866 to 1933. Juneau [1933?] 34 p.　WaU **8550**

Reed, Henry E., 1866-1947.
Cavalcade of Front Street. Portland, Or., Wakefield-Fries & Woodward, 1941. [20] p. illus.
Or OrCS OrHi OrP OrU **8551**

Oregon; a story of progress and development together with an account of the Lewis & Clark Centennial Exposition to be held in Portland, Oregon, from June 1 to October 15, 1905, comp. by Henry E. Reed, secretary and director of exploitation. Portland, Or., F. W. Baltes, 1904. 96 p. illus., ports., map.　WaU **8552**

Same. Portland, Or., Bushong, 1904.
CVicAr OrHi OrP OrU WaU **8553**

Same. Portland, Or., Irwin-Hodson, 1904.
WaPS **8554**

Reed, J. Harvey.
Forty years a locomotive engineer; thrilling tales of the rail. Prescott, Wash., Chas. H. O'Neil, 1912. 142 p. fronts. (ports.) illus., plates.　OrP Wa **8555**
Same. 2d ed. 1913. 148 p.　WaU **8556**

Reed, Mark E.
Public utility operation by municipalities; address before annual convention of the Washington State Bankers Association at Victoria, B. C. [Shelton, Wash., Mason County Journal, 1923?] 10 p. WaPS **8557**

Reed, Simeon Gannett, 1830-1895.
Objections to the passage of Senate Bill no. 94 to amend the act entitled "An act granting lands in aid of a railroad and telegraph line from the Central Pacific Railroad in California to Portland in Oregon" approved July 25, 1866. [n.p., n.d.] 15 p.　OrP **8558**

Remonstrance against extending the time for filing assent to the act granting lands to the Oregon Central Railroad Company. [n.p., n.d.] 4 p.　OrP **8559**

Reed, Thomas Milburne, 1825-1905.
Pioneer Masonry, a history of the early days of Freemasonry on the Pacific coast. Seattle, J. M. Taylor Printing Co., 1903. 60 p. fronts., ports.
CVicAr WaU **8560**
See also no. 3334.

Reed, Wilfred J.
The empire of the North, and other imagina-

tive stories of the past and future. Vancouver, B. C., Roy Wrigley [193—?] 129 p.   CVU 8561

Reed College, Portland, Or.
Albert Ernest Doyle, 1877-1928. Portland, Or., 1928. [28] p. illus., port. (Bulletin, v. 7, no. 2, Jan. 1928)
                    OrHi WaPS WaT 8562
The city and its college. [Portland, Or., 1920?] 64 p. illus., maps, tables.
                                    WaU 8563
The first quarter century; retrospect and appraisal, 1911-1936. Portland, Or., 1936. 56 p. front.   CVU WaT 8564
President Richard Frederick Scholz. Portland, Or., 1924. 20 p. (Bulletin, v. 3, no. 4)   WaPS WaU 8565
Reed College; its grounds and buildings and plans for the College of Women. Portland, Or., 1914. 28 p. illus.
                            OrHi OrP 8566
— — — Armitage Fund Prizes in History. Frances Greenburg Armitage prize winning essays, Armitage competition in Oregon pioneer history, Reed College, 1942. [Portland, Or., 1942] 40 p. port. (Bulletin, v. 21, no. 4, Nov. 1942)
            OrHi WaS WaSp WaT WaU 8567
Same. 1942-43. Portland, Or., 1945. 32 p. port. (Bulletin, v. 23, no. 2. Jan. 1945)
            CVicAr OrHi WaS WaT 8568
Same. 1947. 84 p. (Bulletin, v. 25, no. 3, Apr. 1947)   OrHi WaS WaT 8569
— — — Montague Memorial Cabin Fund. A mountain memorial to Richard Ward Montague. [n.p., n.d.] 10 p. illus., port.
                                    OrP 8570

Reed College Quest, Portland, Or.
Richard Frederick Scholz, Oct. 24, 1880-July 23, 1924, a liberal president of a liberal college. [Portland, Or.] 1924. 6 p. port.   OrP 8571

Reedville Stock Breeding Farm.
Catalogue of pure-bred stock, the property of S. G. Reed, Portland, Or. Portland, Or., Himes, 1875. 58 p. OrHi OrP 8572

Reedy, William Marion, see no. 340.

Rees, John Ephraim, 1863-1928.
Idaho chronology, nomenclature, bibliography. Chicago, W. B. Conkey, 1918. 125 p.   Many 8573

Reeves, Charles Everand, 1889-
Report on a study of the public school system of Portland, Oregon. [Portland, Or.] Griffenhagen, 1942. 4 v. tables.
                                    OrP 8574

The Reform Advocate, Chicago.
Special number on history of the Jews in the Pacific Northwest. Chicago, 1914. 1 v. illus., ports.   WaPS 8575

Regional Educator.
Special edition, October 21, 1936. Prosser, Wash. [1936] 8 p. illus.   WaPS 8576

The Register.
1841-1941; a century of Catholicity in Montana; souvenir edition. Helena, Mont., 1941. [100] p. illus. (v. 17, no. 35, Aug. 27, 1941)   MtU 8577

Regulations for the disposal of dominion lands within the railway belt in the province of British Columbia, 1885. [n.p., n.d.] 31 p.   CVicAr 8578

Reichard, Gladys Amanda, 1893-
An analysis of Couer d'Alene Indian myths, with a comparison by Adele Froelich. Philadelphia, American Folklore Society, 1947. x, 218 p. (Memoirs, v. 41) CVicAr IdB WaS WaSp WaU 8579

Reid, Mrs. Agnes (Just) 1886-
Letters of long ago, illus. by Mabel Bennett. Caldwell, Idaho, Caxton [n.d.] 118 p. front., illus.   IdTf 8580
Same. 1923.   Many 8581
Same. 2d ed. 1936. 138 p.
            IdIf MtHi OrP OrSaW WaU 8582
The range cayuse. Idaho Falls, Idaho. Scott's "Quality" Print, 1916. 20 p. front. Poems.   IdB IdU 8583

Reid, Robert Allan.
The city of Seattle illustrated. [Seattle, E. P. Charlton & Co., c1909] [40] p. plates.   WaU 8584
The Lewis and Clark Centennial Exposition illustrated. Portland, Or., 1905. [28] p. illus. (part col.)
                    Or OrU WaPS 8585
One hundred and fifty latest views of the A. Y. P. Exposition and the Puget Sound country; official exposition photographs. [Seattle, c1909] [128] p. illus.
                                    WaU 8586
Portland, the metropolis and vicinity, illustrated. Portland, Or., c1914. [96] p. illus.   Or 8587
Puget Sound and western Washington; cities, towns, scenery. Seattle, c1912. 192 p. front., illus., map.   Many 8588
Seattle, the queen city. Seattle, 1914. [96] p. illus.   WaU 8589
Seattle today; many illus. of street scenes and picturesque scenery with accompanying text concerning the commercial importance, attractive surroundings and continuous expansion of the city. Seattle, 1910. [48] p. illus.   WaS WaU 8590
Sights and scenes at the Lewis and Clark Centennial Exposition, Portland, Oregon. Portland, Or., c1905. [94] p. plates.
        Or OrP OrU WaSp WaU WaWW 8591

Reid, Virginia Hancock.
The purchase of Alaska; contemporary opinion. [Long Beach, Calif., Press-Telegram, 1939] xii, 134 p.   Many 8592
Same. [c1940]
            CVic CVicAr Wa WaT WaU 8593

Reid, W. A.
Chips from the ship's log of the "Helen Gould", the Y. M. C. A. launch of the Yukon. [n.p., 1906?] 47 p. illus.
                                    WaPS 8594

Reid, William, 1841-1914.
The progress of Oregon and Portland from 1868 to 1878. Portland, Or., D. H. Stearns & Co., 1879. 40 p.
            Or OrHi OrP WaSp WaU 8595
Progress of the state of Oregon and city of Portland from 1870 to 1885. [Portland, Or., 1885] 44 p.   OrU 8596

See also no. 309.

Reimer, F. C., see no. 4130.

Rein, David.
Vardis Fisher; challenge to evasion, preface by Vardis Fisher. Chicago, Normandie House, 1938. 63 p.
IdB MtU WaS WaU **8597**

[Reinhart, Caleb Springer] 1856- comp.
History of the Supreme Court of the Territory and State of Washington, with personal reminiscences of the author; complete rules of pleading and practice. [n.p., 1931?] 148 p. ports.
Wa WaS WaT WaTC **8598**

Reitze, Storey & Duffy, Inc.
Concrete pavements in western Washington, 1911-1914. Seattle [1915?] 37 p. tables.
WaS **8599**

Religious progress on the Pacific slope; addresses and papers at the celebration of the semi-centennial anniversary of the Pacific School of Religion, Berkeley, Calif. Boston, Pilgrim Press [c1917] vi, 326 p. front., ports. WaS WaU **8600**

[Remington, Charles Henry] 1859-
A golden cross (?) on trails from the Valdez Glacier, by Copper River Joe [pseud.] illus. by N. G. Thompson. Los Angeles, White-Thompson, 1939. 200 p. col. front., plates. Alaska. WaU **8601**

Remington, Frederic, 1861-1909.
Done in the open; drawings by Frederic Remington, with an introd. and verses by Owen Wister and others. New York, P. F. Collier & Son [c1902] [80] p. front., illus., plates (part fold., 1 col.)
MtBozC WaSp **8602**

John Ermine of the Yellowstone, illus. by the author. New York, Macmillan, 1902. vii, 271 p. front., illus., plates.
MtHi MtU **8603**

Pony tracks, written and illus. by Frederic Remington. New York, Harper, 1895. viii, 269 p. front., illus., plates.
IdB IdU WaPS WaT **8604**

The way of an Indian, written and illus. by Frederic Remington. London, Gay & Bird, 1906. 251 p. col. front., 13 plates.
WaU **8605**

Same. New York, Fox, Duffield and Co., 1906. WaE WaS WaU **8606**

Renne, Roland Roger, 1905-
Butte, Montana, a preliminary report of and economic survey showing population characteristics and trends, industrial development, employment, labor conditions, incomes, living costs and standard costs of government and related information for the Butte community. Butte, Mont., 1939. 103 p. maps, tables, diagrs. MtBozC MtU **8607**

The Montana citizen, by Roland R. Renne and J. Wesley Hoffman. Helena, Mont., State Pub. Co., 1937. xii, 384 p. illus., maps., diagrs. MtBozC MtHi MtU **8608**

Same. 1940. Rev. ed.
MtBozC MtHi MtU MtUM WaU **8609**

Renner, George Thomas, 1900-
The geography of Washington, by G. T. Renner and A. L. Seeman. [Chicago,

Rand McNally, c1929] 46 p. front., illus., maps (part col.)
WaE WaPS WaS WaU **8610**

Renton, Wash. Central School. Sixth Grade.
Early history of Renton, by the 6th grade, Central School, W. W. Young, teacher. [Renton, Wash.? 19—?] 29 p. illus.
WaU **8611**

Rentoul, John Laurence.
At Vancouver's well and other poems of south and north. London, Macmillan, 1917. 171 p. CV **8612**

Replogle, Charles.
Among the Indians of Alaska. London, Headley Bros., 1904. vii, 182 p. front., 3 plates, ports. CVicAr WaS WaU **8613**

Republican Party. Oregon, Central Committee.
Democratic state government compared with Republican rule; facts and figures comp. from the official records of the Executive, State, and Treasury Departments. [n.p., 1876?] 32 p. OrP **8614**

Documents presented to the people of Oregon. Portland, Or., 1859. 24 p.
Or OrHi OrP WaSp **8615**

Republican League register; a record of the Republican Party in the state of Oregon, comp. and pub. with the approval of the Republican State Central Committee of 1894-1896 and the Executive Committee of the Republican League of Oregon for 1894-1896. Portland, Or., Register Pub. Co., 1896. 286, 38 p. front., ports.
Or OrCS OrHi WaPS WaU **8616**

— — — — — — Multnomah County Central Committee.
The truth about light and power rates in Seattle, Tacoma, Portland. [Portland, Or., 193—?] [4] p. OrU **8617**

— — — — — — Washington Territory. Central Committee.
Address to the people of Washington Territory for the campaign of 1886. [Seattle, 1886?] 14 p. WaU **8618**

A resident of twenty-five years, see no. 52.

Resources of British Columbia, Canada. [Victoria, B. C., Cullin, n.d.] 20 p. illus.
CVicAr **8619**

Retz, pseud.
The road to Jerico, a vision poem. Seattle, Denny-Coryell Co., 1900. 25 p. WaU **8620**

Revelstoke, B. C. Tourist Association.
Revelstoke, the tourist centre of the Switzerland of America. [Revelstoke, B. C., Interior Pub. Co., n.d.] 1 v. illus., 14 plates, fold. map. CVicAr **8621**

Revoil, B.-H., see no. 3513.

Reynolds, Dickson, see no. 8622.

[Reynolds, Helen Mary Greenwood (Campbell)] 1884-
Mystery of the logging camp, by Dickson Reynolds, [pseud.] illus. by Gratton Condon. New York, Nelson [1945] 171 p. front., illus. OrP WaS WaU **8622**

Up Canada way, by Helen Dickson, illus. by Flora Nash DeMuth. Boston, Heath, c1942. 64 p. col. front., illus. (part col.) (New World neighbors)
Or OrP Wa WaS WaSp WaU **8623**

Rezanov, Nikolai Petrovich, 1764-1807.
The Rezanov voyage to Nueva California in 1806, the port of Count Nikolai Petrovich Resanov of his voyage to that provincia of Nueva Espana from New Archangel; an English translation revised and corrected, with notes, etc. by Thomas C. Russell. Annotated, the Count Rezanov; the Russian American Company; the Krusenstern expedition; the settlements in Alaska; the Dona Concepcion Arguello: her family, her romantic and pathetic history; El Presidio de San Francisco, the historic, tragic, and alluring spot by the Golden Gate. San Francisco, T. C. Russell, 1926. xii, 104 p. front. (port.) plates. (Russell California reprints)   CVicAr WaS WaU **8624**

Rhoads, Samuel Nicholson, 1862-
The birds observed in British Columbia and Washington during spring and summer, 1892. [n.p., 1893] 65 p. tables (Proceedings of The Academy of Natural Sciences of Philadelphia, 1893)   WaT **8625**

Rhodes, Eugene Manlove, see no. 2155.

Rhodes, Helen, see nos. 6647-6649

Riblet Tramway Company. Spokane, Wash.
Riblet aerial tramways. [Spokane, Shaw & Borden, c1930] 44 p. illus., diagrs.   WaPS **8626**

Rice, Alfred Ernest.
An Oregon girl; a tale of American life in the new West, illus. by Colista M. Dowling. Portland, Or., Glass & Prudhomme, 1914. 362 p. front., 5 plates.
IdU Or OrP OrU WaPS WaU **8627**

Rice, Berenice M.
Scraps of lace, by B. M. Rice and A. F. Salmon. [Spokane, n.d.]   WaSp **8628**
See also no. 8961.

Rice, Carrie Shaw.
In childland straying. 3d ed. Tacoma, Vaughan & Morrill Printing Co., 1895. 70 p. front. (port.) Poems.
WaPS WaS WaT **8629**

Where the rhododendrons grow. Tacoma, 1904. [32] p.   Wa WaS **8630**

Same. 24 p.   WaT **8631**

Windows that shine. [Tacoma, Smith Kinney Co., 1922] 158 p.
Wa WaS WaT WaTC WaU **8632**

Rice, Charles A., 1873-
The government of Oregon; a supplement to Hughes' and Magruder's textbooks in civics. [Boston] Allyn [c1926] 59 p. front., illus., tables.   OrP **8633**

Supplement to Hughes' Community civics for the state of Oregon; bound with Hughes, R. O., Community civics. [Boston] Allyn [c1917] 51 p.   OrP **8634**

Supplement to Reinsch's civil government for the state of Oregon. Chicago, B. H. Sanborn & Co. [c1913] iv, 88 p. front., illus., tables.   WaPS **8635**

Rice, Claton S.
Iwo Jima and other wartime verse. [Seattle? 1945?] 25 p. Seattle poet.
WaU **8636**

Out West where I come from. [Seattle? c1937] 20 p.   WaU **8637**

Rice, David Perry.
The faces of our judges unmasked; shall the people rule and shall the laws be obeyed by the courts; an analysis of conduct and decisions of the King County Superior Court and of state and federal supreme courts which overrule the people and the legislature. Seattle. Metropolitan [191-] [15] p. port.
WaS **8638**

Rice, Jim, see no. 8410.

Rich, Edwin Ernest, see nos. 3151, 4760-4762, 4733, 8700, 9464, 9465.

Rich, John Harrison, 1856-
The economic position of agriculture in the northwestern grain raising areas; a statement presented to the annual conference of Federal Reserve Agents with Federal Reserve Board at Washington on October 10, 1922. [Minneapolis, 1922?] 31 p. tables.   WaPS **8639**

Rich, John M.
Chief Seattle's unanswered challenge, spoken on the threshold of the city that bears his name, 1854. Seattle, Pigott-Washington Printing Co. [n.d.] 45 p. 2 plates.   WaT **8640**

Same. [c1932]   Many **8641**

Same. [Seattle, Lowman & Hanford] c1947. 60 p. illus., port.   IdB OrCS OrH1 **8642**

Rich, Olive Verne, see no. 8742.

Richards, Earl E., see no. 1952.

Richardson, Albert Deane, 1833-1869.
Beyond the Mississippi; from the great river to the great ocean; life and adventure on the prairies, mountains, and Pacific Coast, 1857-1867. Hartford, American Publishing Company [c1867] 572 p. front. (double map) illus., plates, ports.
Many **8643**

Same. New ed. written down to summer of 1869. [c1869] 620 p. front., illus., 14 plates, map.
CVicAr IdB IdP WaSp WaU **8644**

Same. 1873.   CVicAr OrU **8645**

Our new states and territories, being notes of a recent tour of observation through Colorado, Utah, Idaho, Nevada, Oregon, Montana, Washington Territory and California. New York, Beadle [c1866] 80 p. illus.   OrU WaS WaSp WaU **8646**

Richardson, Alfred Talbot, see nos. 9544, 9545.

Richardson, Archie J.
The law of arrest in the state of Washington. Seattle, Sheriff & Police Reporter [1945] viii, 151 p.   WaU **8647**

Richardson, C. H., see no. 2540.

Richardson, Sir John, 1787-1865.
Arctic searching expedition; a journal of a boat voyage through Rupert's Land and the Arctic Sea in search of the discovery ships under command of Sir John Franklin, with an appendix on the physical geography of North America. New York, Harper, 1852. 516 p. illus.
CVU Wa **8648**

The zoology of the voyage of H. M. S.
Herald under the command of Captain
Henry Kallett during the years 1845-51.
ed. by Edward Forbes. Vertebrals in-
cluding fossil mammals. London, Reeve,
1854. xi, 171 p. 33 plates (17 fold.)
CVicAr **8649**
See also no. 3255.

Richardson, Marvin M.
The Whitman Mission, the third station of
the Old Oregon Trail. Walla Walla,
Wash., Whitman Publishing Company
[c1940] 160 p. front. (2 ports.) illus.,
plates (1 fold.) Many **8650**

Richardson, R. L.
Report of the visit of the British Association to the Canadian Northwest. Winnipeg, McIntyre Bros., 1884. 48 p.
CVicAr **8651**

Richardson, Mrs. Ruth (Ellsworth)
Oregon history stories. [Eugene, Or., Val-
ley Printing Co., c1937] 111 p. illus.,
plates. Or OrU WaS **8652**
Same. 1938. vii, 119 p. front. (map) illus.
Many **8653**

Richet, Etienne, 1873-
Les esquimaux de l'Alaska; moeurs et
coutumes. Paris, Librairie litteraire et
scientifique, 1921. 244 p. WaU **8654**

Richfield Oil Co.
It's vacation time in California, Oregon
and Washington; let's go places with
Richfield. [Los Angeles? 1935] 11 p.
illus., maps, tables. WaPS **8655**
Wild flowers of northern California, Oregon and Washington. [Los Angeles?]
c1934. 24 p. illus. WaPS WaU **8656**

Rickard, Thomas Arthur, 1864-
Historic backgrounds of British Columbia.
Vancouver, B. C., Wrigley Printing Co.
[c1948] xiii, 358 p. front., plates, ports.
OrP WaS WaSp WaU **8657**
The romance of mining. Toronto, Macmil-
lan, 1944. viii, 450 p. front., plates, ports.,
maps. Many **8658**
Same. 1945. MtU **8659**
Through the Yukon and Alaska. San Fran-
cisco, Mining and Scientific Press, 1909.
xiii, 392 p. front., illus., maps.
Many **8660**

Ricker, Elizabeth, see no. 9293.

Ricketts, Edward F., 1897-1948.
Between Pacific tides; an account of the
habits and habitats of some five hundred of the common, conspicuous seashore invertebrates of the Pacific coast
between Sitka, Alaska, and northern
Mexico, by Edward F. Ricketts and
Jack Calvin. Stanford University, Calif.,
Stanford University Press, 1939. xxii,
320 p. illus., plates, diagrs. Many **8661**
Same. 2d ed. Foreword by John Steinbeck,
line drawings by Ritchie Lovejoy. [1948]
365 p. illus., diagrs., plates.
OrHi OrP **8662**

Riddle, George W., 1839-1927.
History of early days in Oregon. Riddle,
Or., Riddle Enterprise, 1920. 74 p. front.
(port.) plate. Many **8663**

Riddle, Jeff C. Davis, 1863-
The Indian history of the Modoc War and
the causes that led to it. [San Francisco,
Marnell & Co., c1914] 295 p. front., illus.,
ports., maps. Many **8664**
Same. [Salem, Or., Hollywood Press, 1933]
288 p. illus., ports. Or **8665**

Riddlesbarger, W. P., see nos. 574-578.

Ridley, William, 1836-
Senator Macdonald's misleading account
of his visit to Metlakatla exposed by the
Bishop of Caledonia. [n.p.] 1882. 12 p.
CVicAr **8666**
Snapshots from the North Pacific; letters
written by Bishop Ridley of Caledonia,
ed. by Alice J. Janvrin. London, Church
Missionary Society, 1903. viii, 192 p.
front. (port.) illus., map.
CVirAr CVU WaU **8667**
Same. 2d ed. 1904.
CV CVicAr CVU WaU **8668**

Riegel, Robert Edgar, 1897-
America moves west. New York, Holt
[c1930] x, 595 p. illus., maps, diagr.
Many **8669**
Same. Rev. ed. [c1947] xi, 643 p. maps
(1 fold.) diagrs.
Or OrSaW Wa WaU **8670**
The story of the western railroads. New
York, Macmillan, 1926. xv, 345 p.
Many **8671**

Rigdon, Winfield Taylor, 1849-
Crossing the plains, 1860. Salem, Or. [n.d.]
[4] p. Poem. OrU WaPS WaU **8672**
Glorious old Oregon. Salem, Or. [n.d] [4]
p. illus. OrU **8673**
Mystic chain of discovery; the era of
great awakening, from the Fifteenth to
the Seventeenth Century, the leading
characters in the drama, the final settlement in the Northwest. Salem, Or.,
Elliott Printing House, 1929. 456, 18
[3] p. front. (port.) illus. Many **8674**

Rigg, George B., see nos. 3381, 3383.

Riggs, Renee (Coudert)
Animal stories from Eskimo land, adapted
from the original Eskimo stories collected by Dr. Daniel S. Neuman, with
illus. and decorations by George W.
Hood. New York, Stokes, 1923. 113 p.
col. front., col. illus.
IdIf OrP WaS WaSp **8675**

Riley, Emmet Joseph, 1893-
Development of the Montana state edu-
cational organization, 1864-1930. Wash-
ington, D. C., Catholic University of
America, 1931. vii, 135 p. MtBozC
MtHi MtU OrCS OrU WaSp **8676**

Rimel, Duane W.
The curse of Cain. Philadelphia, David
McKay Co. [c1945] 224 p. Lewiston,
Idaho story. WaU **8677**

Rinehart, Mrs. Mary (Roberts) 1876-
Tenting tonight; a chronicle of sport and
adventure in Glacier Park and the Cascade Mountains. Boston, Houghton, 1918.
viii, 187 p. front., plates, ports.
Many **8678**
Same. [1922] MtU **8679**

Through Glacier Park; seeing America first with Howard Eaton. Boston, Houghton, 1916. ix, 91 p. front. (port.)
CVicAr MtHi OrSaW Wa WaT WaU 8680

Rinfret, Raoul.
Le Yukon et son or. Montreal, Imprimerie du "Cultivateur" [c1898] 89 p. illus.
CV CVicAr CVU WaU 8681

Rio Grande Western Railway.
The Pacific Northwest. San Francisco, Bennett & Steele, c1889. 108 p. illus.
Wa 8682

Rister, Carl Coke, 1889-
Border command; General Phil Sheridan in the West. Norman, Okla., University of Oklahoma Press, 1944. xii, 244 p. ports., maps (1 fold.)
Or OrU WaS WaSp WaT 8683
See also no. 3945.

[Ritchie, Arthur J.]
The Pacific Northwest goes to war (state of Washington) foreword signed: Art Ritchie and William J. Davis, publishers. [Seattle] Associated Editors, c1944. 224 p. illus., ports., map, tables. Many 8684

River View Cemetery Association, Portland, Or.
By-laws and rules; organized 4 December, 1882. Portland, Or., 1905. 29 p. map.
OrHi 8685

Riverside Homestead Association of East Portland.
[Articles of association] Portland, Or., Walling, 1870. 15 p. OrHi 8686

Robbins, Mrs. Vesta O., see no. 6940.

Robert Max Garrett, a memorial. [Seattle, n.d.] 4 p. WaU 8687

Roberts, Edwards.
Shoshone and other western wonders, with a preface by C. F. Adams. New York, Harper, 1888. xvi, 275 p. front., illus., 22 plates. Many 8688

Roberts, Ida Pelton.
Rhododendrons. Seattle [19—?] [16] p. illus. Poems. WaU 8689

Roberts, John, see no. 7563.

Roberts, Lloyd, 1884-
Samuel Hearne. Toronto, Ryerson [1930] 27 p. illus., port. (Canadian history readers) OrHi OrP 8690

Roberts, Morley, 1857-
The mate of the Vancouver. London, Lawrence, 1892. 268 p. CV WaU 8691

On the old trail; through British Columbia after forty years. London, E. Nash & Grayson, 1927. xiv, 242 p. front., plates.
CV CVic CVicAr CVU WaS WaU 8692

The prey of the strongest. London, Hurst [n.d.] 335 p. New Westminster, B. C. historical story. CV 8693

Same. 1906. viii, 325 p. CVicAr CVU 8694
The Western Avernus; or, Toil and travel in further North America. London, Smith, 1887. 307 p. front. (fold. map)
Many 8695

Same. New ed., illus. by A. D. McCormick and from photographs. Westminster, A.

Constable, 1896. xi, 277 p. front. (port.) plates, fold. map.
CV CVU OrP WaT 8696
Same. London, Brown, 1904. Many 8697
Same. London, Dent [1924] viii, 238 p. (Everyman's library. Travel)
CVU Or OrSaW 8698

Roberts, William Milnor, 1810-1881.
Special report of a reconnoissance of the route for the Northern Pacific Railroad between Lake Superior and Puget Sound via the Columbia River, made in 1869 under the direction of Messrs. Jay Cooke & Co., Bankers. [Philadelphia, 1869] 51 p. MtBozC OrP WaU 8699

Robertson, Colin, 1783-1842.
Colin Robertson's correspondence book, September 1817 to September 1822; ed. with an introd. by E. E. Rich assisted by R. Harvey Fleming. [Toronto?] Champlain Society for the Hudson's Bay Record Society, 1939. cxxxi, 371, xi p. front. (Publications, no. 2) Many 8700

Robertson, Douglas Sinclair, 1877-
To the Arctic with the Mounties. Toronto, Macmillan, 1934. 309 p. front. (port.) 9 plates, fold. map. CV CVU IdB 8701

Robertson, Frank Chester, 1890-
On the trail of Chief Joseph. New York, Appleton, 1927. 229 p. front.
IdTf OrP WaU 8702

Robertson, James Rood, 1864-1932.
A paper upon the development of civil government in Oregon treated as a part of the growth of our national life. Forest Grove, Or., Thompson, 1899. 43 p.
Or OrHi OrP WaS WaU 8703

Robertson, William Norrie.
Yukon memories; sourdough tells of chaos and changes in the Klondike vale. Toronto, Hunter-Rose, 1930. 359 p. front. (map) 7 plates. CVicAr CVU WaS 8704

Robertson, Wyndham, 1803-1888.
Oregon, our right and title; containing an account of the condition of the Oregon Territory, together with a statement of the claims of Russia, Spain, Great Britain and the United States; accompanied with a map prepared by the author. Washington, D. C., Gideon, 1846. 203, xxiv p. front. (fold. map) tables.
OrHi OrP WaU 8705

Robi, Armand.
Walla-Walla; music by Armand Robi; lyrics by Ralph Murphy. New York, Edw. B. Marks Music Co., c1924. 5 p.
WaPS 8706

Robinette, Allan M., comp.
Facts about Cape Nome and its golden sands, a resume of the statements of people who were present at the great placer diggings, from the date of their discovery until the winter of 1899, together with the mining laws in force, processes of mining, names of districts, rivers and creeks embraced therein; routes of travel, rates of fare, equipment needed, and other information of value to every one interested in the Alaskan country. Seattle, Cape Nome Informa-

tion and Supply Bureau [1900] 64 p. illus. WaS WaU **8707**

Robins, Elizabeth, 1862-
Come and find me, with illus. by E. L. Blumenschein. New York, Century, 1908. xiii, 531 p. front., 10 plates.
CVic IdB OrCS WaE WaS WaU **8708**

The magnetic North, by Elizabeth Robins (C. E. Raimond). New York, Stokes [c1904] 417 p. front. (fold. map) Yukon Trail novel.
IdP OrU WaPS WaS WaU **8709**

Robinson, Edgar Leroy, 1852-
The world war and its portent. Buckley, Wash. [c1917] 62 p. Poems.
WaT WaU **8710**

Robinson, F. J., Co.
A remarkable mining proposition, Gold Creek Placer Mining Company, a Washington corporation. Spokane [1936?] [6] p. WaPS **8711**

Robinson, Frank Alfred, 1874-
Trail-tales of western Canada. Toronto, Social Service & Evangelism [n.d.] 255 p. front., 9 plates. CVicAr **8712**

Same. London, Marshall [1914]
CV CVU **8713**

Robinson, Frank Bruce, 1886-
Life story of Frank B. Robinson. Moscow, Idaho, Review Pub. Co., 1934. 239 p. illus., plates, ports. Idaho biographee.
IdU WaU **8714**

Robinson, Henry Martin.
The great fur land; or, Sketches of life in the Hudson's Bay territory, with numerous illus. from designs by Charles Gasche. London, Low, 1879. x, 348 p. illus. CV CVicAr WaU WaWW **8715**

Same. New York, Putnam, 1879.
Many **8716**

Same. London, Low, 1880. CVicAr **8717**

Same. 5th ed. New York, Putnam, 1882.
CVU MtU **8718**

Robinson, Leigh Burpee.
Esquimalt "place of shoaling water." Victoria, B. C., Quality Press, 1947. 128 p. illus. CVicAr CVU **8719**

Same. 2d ed., illus. by B. Digby Robinson. Victoria, B. C., Quality Press, 1948.
CVicAr CVU OrHi WaT **8720**

Robinson, Noel.
Blazing the trail through the Rockies; the story of Walter Moberly and his share in the making of Vancouver, by Noel Robinson and the old man himself. [Vancouver, B. C.] News Advertiser [19—?] 117 p. illus., ports. Many **8721**

Robinson, Rueben Franklin, 1861-
Leading facts; Oregon school law, 1906; an outline and summary arranged for teachers. Portland, Or., School & Home Publishing Company, c1906. 46 p.
OrP **8722**

Same. Rev. ed. 47 p. OrP **8723**

Robley, Roy Reese, 1875-
Portland Electric Power Company with its predecessor and subsidiary companies, December 16, 1860-December 31, 1935. Portland, Or., 1935. 251, 160 p. illus., ports., diagrs. OrHi **8723A**

Portland General Electric and predecessor companies. [Portland, Or., 1944] 8 p.
OrCS **8724**

Robson, A. Ritchie.
West of the West; a sketch of early mission days in north-western Canada. London, Partridge [n.d.] 136 p. front.
CVicAr **8725**

Robson, Albert Henry, 1882-
Paul Kane. Toronto, Ryerson, c1938. 32 p. illus. (part col.) plates, port.
CVU MtHi **8726**

Robson, Ebenezer.
How Methodism came to British Columbia. [Toronto, Methodist Young People's Forward Movement for the Missions, n.d.] 31 p. illus., ports., maps. CVicAr **8727**

Robson, Joseph.
An account of six years residence in Hudson's-Bay, from 1733 to 1736 and 1744-1747, by Joseph Robson, late surveyor and supervisor of the buildings to the Hudson's-Bay Company; containing a variety of facts, observations, and discoveries tending to shew: I. The vast importance of the countries about Hudson's-Bay to Great Britain. II. The interested views of the Hudson's-Bay Company and the absolute necessity of laying open the trade; to which is added an appendix. London, Payne & Bouquet, 1752. vi, 84, 95 p. front. (fold. map) fold. map, fold. plan. CVicAr **8728**

Same. London, T. Jefferys, 1759.
CVicAr WaU **8729**

Roby, Charles W.
Portland postoffice; its history and growth, with a compendium of postal information. Portland, Or. [Baltes] 1889. 88 p. illus., tables. Many **8730**

Rockwell, Irvin E., 1862-
The saga of American Falls Dam. New York, Hobson Book Press, 1947. 201 p. illus., ports., facsims. IdB IdU **8731**

Rockwood, Eleanor Ruth.
Books on the Pacific Northwest for small libraries, comp. by reference librarian, Library Association, Portland, Oregon. New York, H. W. Wilson, 1923. 55 p.
Many **8732**

Oregon state documents; a check list, 1843 to 1925. Portland, Or., Oregon Historical Society [1947] 283 p.
OrCS OrHi OrU WaU **8733**

Rocky Fork and Cooke City Railway Co.
By-laws of the Rocky Fork and Cooke City Railway Co. of Montana Territory. St. Paul, Brown, Treacy & Co., 1887. 13 p. MtHi **8734**

Rocky Fork Railway and Coal Trust.
The Rocky Fork Railway and Coal Trust report. New York, 1891. 11 p. MtHi **8735**

Rocky Mountain rangers, 1885-1941. [New Westminster, B. C., Columbian] 1941. 60 p. illus., ports. CVicAr **8736**

Roddan, Andrew, d. 1948.
Canada's untouchables; the story of the man without a home. [Vancouver, B. C., Clarke & Stuart, 1932] 111 p. front. (port.) illus. CV **8737**

The church in the modern city; the story of three score years of practical Christian service, 1885-1945, First United Church, Vancouver, B. C. [n.p., Dunsmuir Printing Co., n.d.] 61 p. illus., port.
CVicAr 8738

God in the jungles; the story of the man without a home. [Vancouver, B. C., 1931] 64 p. front., 10 plates, 2 ports. CV 8739

Roe, Charles Francis, 1848-1922.
Custer's last battle on the Little Big Horn, Montana Territory, June 25, 1876; march of the "Montana column" down the Yellowstone River and through the Big Horn region, by Edward J. McClernand; narratives and reminiscences of the Sioux Indian War, illus. by photographs, maps and drawings. [New York, R. Bruce, c1927] 40 p. illus., maps.
MtHi Wa WaS WaSp WaU 8740

Roe, Mrs. Frances Marie Antoinette (Mack)
Army letters from an officer's wife, 1871-1888, illus. by I. W. Taber from contemporary photographs. New York, Appleton, 1909. x, 387 p. front. (port.) illus., plates. MtBozC
MtHi OrP WaS WaSp WaU 8741

Roe, Olive Verne.
Prophecy of Yah-ma-sun, by Olive Verne Rich [pseud.] illus. by B. C. Bubb. Seattle, Harriman, 1909. [26] p. illus.
OrCS Wa WaS WaSp 8742

Roe, Vingie Eve, 1879-
The heart of Night Wind; a story of the great Northwest, illus. by George Gibbs. New York, Dodd, 1913. 395 p. col. front., 3 plates. Or OrP Wa WaW 8743

Rogers, Fred B., 1889-
Soldiers of the overland; being some account of the services of General Patrick Edward Connor & his volunteers in the old West. San Francisco, Grabhorn Press, 1938. 290 p. front. (port.) 11 plates, 5 ports., plan, facsim.
MtHi MtU OrSaW 8744

Rogers, Harrison G., see nos. 2224, 2225.

Rogers, Sir John Godfrey, 1850-
Sport in Vancouver and Newfoundland, with illus. and maps by the author and reproductions of photographs. Toronto, Musson, 1912. xii, 275 p. front., 20 plates, maps. CVic CVicAr OrP WaSp 8745

Rogers, Julia Ellen, 1866-
The shell book; a popular guide to a knowledge of the families of living mollusks and an aid to the identification of shells native and foreign; eight plates in colour and ninety-six in black-and-white, mostly from photographs by A. R. Dugmore. New York, Doubleday, Page, 1908. xxi, 485 p. col. front., illus., 48 plates (7 col.) Many 8746

Rogers, Nelson S., see nos. 11195, 11196.

Rogers, Robert Bolton.
The standard drill manual, by Battery chief R. B. Rogers, Seattle Fire Department. [Seattle?] c1934. 121 p. illus., diagrs. MtBozC WaS WaU 8747

Rogers, Thomas Hesperian, 1862-
Beeswax and gold, a story of the Pacific,

A. D. 1700; cover design by F. G. Cooper, illus. by Howard A. Hall. Portland, Or., J. K. Gill Co. [c1929] 268 p. front., illus.
IdU OrP OrSaW WaU 8748

Nehalem; a story of the Pacific, A. D. 1700. McMinnville, Or., H. L. Heath [c1898] 182 p. 2 plates, port. Many 8749

Rogers, Will, see nos. 8860-8862.

Rohrabacher, Christian A.
The Seattle spirit; a chronological history of Seattle, U. S. A., with chronological illus. Seattle [1907?] 104 p. illus., ports., map. WaS WaU 8750

Rohrer, Mary Katherine.
The history of Seattle stock companies from their beginnings to 1934, illus. with contemporary photographs. Seattle, University of Washington Press, 1945. xiii, 76 p. fronts., plates, ports. (Publications in drama, no. 2)
CVicAr WaS WaSp WaT WaTC WaU 8751

Rollins, Philip Ashton, 1869-
The cowboy; an unconventional history of civilization on the old-time cattle range. Rev. and enl. ed. New York, Scribner, 1936. xx, 402 p. front., plates, double map.
Many 8752

The cowboy; his characteristics, his equipment, and his part in the development of the West. New York, Scribner, 1922. xiv, 353 p. Many 8753

Same. front., 7 plates. WaSp 8754

Gone haywire; two tenderfoots on the Montana cattle range in 1886, pictures by Peter Hurd. New York, Scribner, 1939. ix, 269 p. illus.
MtHi MtU OrP WaSp WaU 8755

Jinglebob; a true story of a real cowboy. New York, Scribner [c1927] ix, 263 p. illus., 4 col. plates. WaU 8756

Same. 1927, 1930. Or WaS WaT 8757

Same. 1935. OrP 8758

See also nos. 9977, 11106.

Rome, David.
The first two years; a record of the Jewish pioneers on Canada's Pacific coast, 1858-1860. Montreal, H. M. Caiserman, 1942. 120 p.
CV CVic CVicAr CVU WaS WaU 8759

Romeo, Giuseppe L., 1891-
Diary of Private Giuseppe L. Romeo, Company E, 361st Infantry, 91st Division, A. E. F. during the war. Tacoma, 1919. 38 p. illus. WaT 8760

Romig, Emily Craig, 1871-
The life and travels of a pioneer woman in Alaska. Colorado Springs, 1945. 136 p. front., plates, ports. WaT WaU 8761

A pioneer woman in Alaska. Caldwell, Idaho, Caxton [c1945] 140 p. front., illus.
WaE WaS WaU 8762

Same. 1948 [c1945] OrP 8763

Ronan, Peter.
Historical sketch of the Flathead Indian nation from the year 1813 to 1890; embracing the history of the establishment of St. Mary's Mission in the Bitter Root Valley, Mont., with sketches of the missionary life of Father Ravalli and other

early missionaries, wars of the Blackfeet and Flatheads, and sketches of history, trapping and trading in the early days. Helena, Mont., Journal Publishing Company [c1890] 80 p. front., 8 plates, 4 ports.
Many **8764**

Roosevelt, Robert Barnwell, 1829–1906.
Game fish of the northern states of America and British provinces, by Barnwell [pseud.] New York, Carleton, 1862. 324 p. illus. WaU **8765**

Roosevelt, Theodore, see no. 2168.

Root, E. Merrill, see no. 8041.

Root, Riley.
Journal of travels from St. Josephs to Oregon, with observations of that country, together with some description of California and a full description of its gold mines. Galesburg, Ill., Gazetteer, 1850. 143 p. OrHi **8766**

Same. Microfilm. WaU **8767**

Roper, Edward.
By track and trail; a journey through Canada, with numerous original sketches by the author. London, W. H. Allen, 1891. xiv, 455 p. front., illus., 44 plates, fold. map. CV CVicAr CVU WaS WaU **8768**

A claim on Klondyke; a romance of the Arctic El Dorado. Edinburgh, Blackwood, 1899. 312 p. front., plates.
CVicAr WaU **8769**

Roper, Mrs. Theresa (Ketcheson) 1867–
Rebounding vengeance; an Indian romance, and the evolution of Newport, Oregon. [Corvallis, Or., Gazette-Times Press] c1919. 371 p. illus., 9 plates, 2 ports. Many **8770**

Rose, A. P., see no. 4860.

[Rose, Ada Losh].
Historical pageant of Quenett [dramatized and directed by Ada Losh Rose, historical data by Lulu D. Crandall] The Dalles, Or., 1921. 8 p. WaU **8771**

Rose, Clinton Emmett, 1875–
Civil government of Idaho for the use of schools. Boise, Idaho, Syms-York, 1912. 151 p. CVicAr IdU WaTC WaU **8772**

Same. Rev. ed. 1914. 153 p. forms.
IdIf WaU **8773**

Same. 3d ed. rev. 1915. IdIf IdUSB **8774**

Same. 4th ed. rev. New York, Macmillan, c1918. viii, 144 p. WaSp WaU **8775**

Same. 1919. IdB WaTC **8776**

Same. 5th ed. rev. [c1919] WaU **8777**

Same. 1920. OrP **8778**

Same. 1922. IdUSB **8779**

Rose, Hilda.
The stump farm; a chronicle of pioneering, with a foreword by Samuel A. Eliot. Boston, Little, 1935. xi, 178 p. front. (port.) 3 plates, 4 ports. WaT **8780**

Rosenberg, C. G., see no. 8057.

Rosenberg, Frantz.
Big game shooting in British Columbia and Norway. London, Hopkinson, 1928. ix, 261 p. front. (port.) 31 plates.
CV CVicAr **8781**

Ross, A. W.
Speeches on the Canadian Pacific Railway and the Canadian North West, by A. W. Ross and C. F. Ferguson. [n.p., Montana Gazette Printing Co.] 1884. 23 p.
CVicAr **8782**
See also no. 2507.

Ross, Alexander, 1783-1856.
Adventures of the first settlers on the Oregon or Columbia River; being a narrative of the expedition fitted out by John Jacob Astor to establish the "Pacific Fur Company"; with an account of some Indian tribes on the coast of the Pacific, by one of the adventurers. London, Smith, Elder, 1849. xv, 352 p. front. (fold. map) Many **8783**

Same, ed. with historical introd. and notes by Milo Milton Quaife. Chicago, R. R. Donnelly & Sons, 1923. xxvii, 388 p. front. (fold. map). (Lakeside classics)
Many **8784**

The fur hunters of the far West; a narrative of adventures in the Oregon and Rocky Mountains. London, Smith, Elder, 1855. 2 v. fronts., fold. map. Many **8785**

Same, ed. with historical introd. and notes by Milo Milton Quaife. Chicago, R. R. Donnelley & Sons, 1924. xxxix, 317 p. front. (Lakeside classics) Many **8786**

Ross, Edward A.
Proposed cession of Alaska panhandle to Canada by sale or exchange. [n.p.] 1914. 10 p. CVicAr **8787**

Ross, Edward Alsworth, see no. 6497.

Ross, Edward C.
The Whitman controversy; articles [by Edward C. Ross, Myron Eells, and W. H. Gray] in reply to Mrs. F. F. Victor and Elwood Evans, whose contributions appeared in the Oregonian of November 7 and December 26, 1884, respectively. Portland, Or., Himes, 1885. 70 p.
Or OrHi OrP OrU WaU WaWW **8788**

Ross, Emily Lindsley, 1861-1939.
Aaron Ladner Lindsley, founder of Alaska missions and leader of other great enterprises in the Northwest, pub. with the approval of the Board of National Missions of the Presbyterian Church in the U. S. A. [Portland, Or.? 1927] [12] p. illus. OrP WaU **8789**

Ross, George W., see nos. 1243, 1244.

Ross, James Clark, see nos. 8793-8795.

Ross, James Delmage, 1872-1939.
A proposal to acquire the holdings of the Puget Sound Power and Light Company by the people of western Washington; report to the Mayor and Council of the city of Seattle. Seattle, 1934. 14 p. map, facsism., diagr. OrP WaS **8790**

Ross, Sir John, 1777-1856.
Explanation and answer to Mr. John Braithwaite's Supplement to Captain Sir John Ross's Narrative of a second voyage in the Victory in search of a North-West Passage. [London] A. W. Webster [1835] 8 p. OrU WaU **8791**

Narrative of a second voyage in search of a North-West Passage, and of a residence in the Arctic regions during the years 1829, 1830, 1831, 1832, 1833, including the reports of James Clark Ross and the discovery of the northern magnetic pole. London, A. W. Webster, 1835. 2 v. fronts., plates (part col.) maps(part fold.) col. plan.　　　　CVicAr CVU WaU　**8792**

Same. Paris, Baudry's European Library, 1835. 475 p. front., plates, fold. map.
CVicAr CVU OrP　**8793**

Same. Philadelphia, E. L. Carey & A. Hart, 1835. xxiii, 456 p. front. (fold. map)
Or　**8794**

A voyage of discovery made under the orders of the Admiralty in His Majesty's ships Isabella and Alexander for the purpose of exploring Baffin's Bay and enquiring into the probability of a Northwest Passage. London, Murray, 1819. xxxix, 252, cxliv p. front., plates (part col., part fold.) fold. maps, tables.
CVU OrCS　**8795**

Same. London, Longman, 1819. 2 v. front. (map)　　　　CVicAr MtU Wa　**8796**

Ross, Mrs. Nancy Wilson, 1905-
Farthest reach; Oregon & Washington. New York, Knopf, 1941. xiv, 359, xviii p. front., plates, ports., fold. map. (American scene) Washington author.
Many　**8797**

Same. [c1941]　　　　　　　CVic　**8798**

Same. 1942.　　　　　　　　CVic　**8799**

Same. 1944 [c1941]　　　OrHi WaPS　**8800**

Friday to Monday. New York, Liveright [c1932] 249 p.　　OrP OrU WaU　**8801**

The left hand is the dreamer. New York, W. Sloane [c1947] 390 p.　Many　**8802**

Take the lightning. New York, Harcourt [c1940] 314 p.
OrP OrPR OrU Wa WaS WaU　**8803**

Westward the women. New York, Knopf, 1944. 199 p.　　　　Many　**8804**

Same. 1945.　　　　　　　　MtU　**8805**

Ross, Patrick Hore Warriner, 1858-
The western gate; maritime district of western Washington and a new American mercantile marine. New York, Dodd, 1911. 153 p. 2 fold. maps.　Many　**8806**

Ross, W. W.
10,000 miles by land and sea. Toronto,.J. Campbell & Son, 1876. 284 p.
CVicAr WaS　**8807**

Ross, Zola Helen, 191?-
Overdue for death. Indianapolis, Bobbs-Merrill [1947] 252 p. Seattle murder mystery by Seattle author.
Wa WaS WaT WaU　**8808**

Rossi, Louis.
Six ans en Amerique: Californie et Oregon. 2. ed. Paris, Dentu, 1863. 322 p. 2 fold. maps.
CVicAr OrHi OrP WaS WaU　**8809**

Souvenirs d'un voyage en Oregon et en Californie. Paris, Martin-Beaupre freres, 1864. 322 p. 2 fold. maps.
OrHi OrP WaU　**8810**

Rossiter, Harriet.
Indian legends from the land of Al-ay-eksa, pub. by E. C. Howard. Ketchikan, Alaska, Ketchikan Alaska Chronicle, 1925. [30] p. illus., port., map.
CVU OrP WaS WaU　**8811**

Same. c1925. [26] p. illus.　　　Or　**8812**

Rossland Miners' Union No. 38, Western Federation of Miners.
Constitution and by-laws. Rossland, B. C., Stunden & Perine [n.d.] 16 p.
CVicAr　**8813**

Rossman, Earl.
Black sunlight; a log of the Arctic, with an introd. by Vilhjalmur Stefansson. New York, Oxford University Press, 1926. xi, 231 p. front., plates, ports., fold. map.
OrP WaS WaU　**8814**

Rossman, Floy Adele.
The trail makers; a pageant of the early history of Washington, presented by members of the Washington State Normal School of Ellensburg in the normal auditorium, May 27, 30, 31, 1921, written and directed by Floy A. Rossman and Herbert C. Fish. [Ellensburg, Wash., Record Press, 1921?] [8] p. illus.
WaU　**8815**

The Rotarian.
Seattle number. [Mount Morris, Ill., 1913] 112 p. illus. (v. 4, no. 2)　WaU　**8816**

Rotary Club of Tacoma.
"For value received I promise to pay". [n. p., 1936?] 8 p.　　　　WaT　**8817**

Rotary Club of Vancouver, B. C.
Eleventh anniversary, 1913-1924. [Vancouver, B. C., Clarke & Stuart] 1924, 48 p.
CVicAr　**8818**

Roth, Mrs. Lottie (Roeder) 1864-　ed.
History of Whatcom County. Chicago, Pioneer Historical Publishing Company, 1926. 2 v. illus., plates, ports., facsims.
Many　**8819**

Rothensteiner, Rev. John.
The Flat-head and Nez Perce delegation to St. Louis, 1831-1839. St. Louis, Amerika Print [19—] 15 p.　MtU　**8820**

Rothery, Agnes Edwards, 1888-
The ports of British Columbia. Garden City, N. Y., Doubleday, 1943. vii, 279 p. front., plates.　　　　Many　**8821**

Rothwell, C. E., see no. 6008.

Rounds, Glen, 1906-
Lumbercamp, being the life and good times of the new Whistle Punk at Camp Fifteen up Horse Crick way, with many drawings made on the scene by the author. New York, Holiday House, 1937. 116 p. front., illus.
OrP Wa WaS WaSp WaU　**8822**

Ol' Paul, the mighty logger; being a true account of the seemingly incredible exploits and inventions of the great Paul Bunyan, profusely illus. by drawings made at the scene by the author. [New York] Holiday House, 1936. 132 p. front., illus.　　　　Many　**8823**

Rouquette, Louis-Frederic, 1884-1926.
The great white silence, trans. from the French by O. W. Allen and A. LeRebeller; decorations by Ludmila Tchirikova. New York, Macmillan, 1930. 233 p. illus. Alaska stories.　WaE WaS WaU　**8824**

Roustan, R., see no. 7317.

Rowan, James.
The I. W. W. in the lumber industry. Seattle, Lumber Workers Industrial Union No. 500 [1919?] 64 p.　　WaS WaU **8825**

Rowe, Jesse Perry, 1871-
Geography and natural resources of Montana. Missoula, Mont., Montana State University [1941] v, 313 p. tables.
MtBozC **8826**

Montana coal and lignite deposits. Missoula, Mont., University of Montana, 1906. 82 p. illus., 24 plates, 2 maps (1 fold.) (Bulletin no. 37. Geological series, no. 2)
MtUM OrU WaPS WaS WaTC **8827**

Some volcanic ash beds of Montana. Helena, Mont., Independent Publishing Company, 1903. 32 p. front. (double map) illus., 4 plates (1 fold.) (Bulletin University of Montana, no. 17. Geological series no. 1)　　　　　　WaTC **8828**

Rowe, Peter Trimble, see no. 9980.

Rowe, Wilbur D.
The development of the Oregon State Library and its contributions to the public schools. [Portland, Or., 1938] 104, iv, p.
Or OrP **8829**

Rowley, Clinton W.　　ed.
Pacific Northwest sportsmen's guide. Seattle, Piper & Taft, c1930. 182 p. illus. (Fishing ed.)　　Wa WaS WaU **8830**

Rowse, A. L. see no. 11051.

Royal, Charles Elliott.
Royal rhymes and romances. Vancouver, B. C., International Publishing Company, c1919. 64 p. port.　　CVicAr **8831**

The trail of a sourdough; rhymes and ballads. Toronto, McClelland & Stewart [c1919] 168 p.　　CVU WaU **8832**

The royal city of British Columbia, New Westminster, city and district. [n.p., n.d.] 40 p. illus.　　CVicAr **8833**

Royal Engineers' Old Comrades Association, Vancouver, B. C.
The Royal Engineers; a record of their part in the building of British Columbia; commemorating the visit of Their Majesties King George VI and Queen Elizabeth. [Vancouver, B. C., 1939] 28 p. illus.　　CVic CVicAr CVU **8834**

Royal Naval Institute.
Report of the proceedings at the opening of the Sailor's Club, The Royal Naval Institute, Esquimalt, B. C., by His Excellency the Governor-General of Canada on the 21st day of November, 1917. [n.p., n.d.] 28 p. illus., ports.　　CVicAr **8835**

Royce, Ernest, see no. 1260.

Rubey, James Tate, 1906-
Marcus and Narcissa Whitman and their work; a bibliography [comp. by J. T. Rubey and L. D. Lynn] Washington, D. C., U. S. Geological Survey Library, 1936. 1 v.　　　　　　OrSa **8836**

Rucker, Mrs. Maude (Applegate)
The Oregon Trail and some of its blazers. New York, W. Neale, 1930. 293 p. front., 13 plates, 4 ports., facsim. Many **8837**

Rudser, Mrs. Nellie M. (Baldwin)
This questing for melodies. [Spokane? c1939] 44 p. Poems.　　WaSp **8838**

Ruffner, William Henry, 1824-1908.
A report on Washington Territory. New York, Lake Shore and Eastern Railway, 1889. 242 p. front., 12 plates, 5 maps (2 fold.) table.　　Many **8839**

Ruggieri, Vincenzo.
Du Transvaal a l'Alaska, traduit de l'italien. Paris, Plon-Nourrit et cie., 1901. vii, 291 p.　　　　　　WaU **8840**

Rule, William J.
Riding the Upper Cowlitz Circuit fifty years ago, 1893-1896, with a brief account of Methodism in Lewis County, Washington. Seattle, University Printing Co., 1945. 52 p. front., plate, ports.
WaS WaU **8841**

Rule & Cole.
Caldwell, "The magic city" in the Boise Valley, Idaho; facts pertaining to the magic city and its great tributary resources; also statistics as to climate, health, agriculture, stock raising, mining, etc. Caldwell, Idaho, Tribune Job Print, 1891. 32 p.　　　　IdB **8842**

Rules and regulations for the management and working for the graving dock at Esquimalt, B. C. Victoria, B. C., British Colonist, 1887. 15 p.　　CVicAr **8843**

Rumsey, W. D., see no. 4852.

Runk, Edward Johnson.
Washington, a national epic in six cantos. New York, Putnam, 1904. xi, 169 p. front. (port.)
MtBozC OrSaW WaU WaWW **8844**

Runnals, Frank E.
A history of Prince George, with a foreword by Harry G. Perry. [Vancouver, B. C., Wrigley Printing Co.] c1946. xiv, 197 p. front., illus., ports., maps, plans.
Many **8845**

Running, Corinne.
Garden shower. New York, Swallow Press [c1948] 186 p. Seattle novel.
OrP WaU **8846**

Rush., Philip S., see no. 2613.

Rush, William Marshall, 1887-
Gold prospector, decorations by Arthur Harper. New York, Longmans, 1948. 232 p. illus. Montana novel.　　WaU **8847**

Rocky mountain ranger, decorations by Richard Bennett. New York, Longmans [c1944] 223 p. Montana adventure story.
Many **8848**

Silver spurs, the story of a Montana cattle ranch, by Mark Layton [pseud.] New York, M. S. Mill Co., 1947. 216 p.
CV Or OrP WaS WaT WaU **8849**

Wheat rancher, decorations by Ernest R. Habersack. New York, Longmans [c1946] 247 p. illus. Montana boys' story.
WaU **8850**

Wild animals of the Rockies; adventures of a forest ranger. Garden City, N. Y., Halcyon House [1947, c1942] xxiii, 296 p. plates.　　　　　　WaU **8851**

Wildlife of Idaho. Boise, Idaho, Fish and

Game Commission, 1942. 299 p. col. front., illus., col. plates, tables, diagrs.
Many **8852**

Yellowstone scout, decorations by Ralph Ray. New York, Longmans, 1945. 184 p. illus.
WaU **8853**

Rusk, Claude Ewing, 1871-
Tales of a western mountaineer, a record of mountain experiences on the Pacific Coast. Boston, Houghton, 1924. xii, 309 p. front., plates.
Many **8854**

Rusling, James Fowler, 1834-1918.
Across America; or, The great West and the Pacific Coast. New York, Sheldon & Co., 1874. 503 p. front., 6 plates, port., fold map.
OrP OrU WaSp WaT WaU **8855**

Same. 1875.
IdB **8856**

The great West and Pacific Coast; or. Fifteen thousand miles by stagecoach, ambulance, horseback, railroad, and steamer, across the continent and along the Pacific slope, among Indians, Mormons, miners and Mexicans. New York, Sheldon, c1877. 515 p. front., 7 plates, port., fold. map.
OrP OrSa Wa WaS WaU **8857**

Russel, Robert Royal, 1890-
Improvement of communication with the Pacific Coast as an issue in American politics, 1783-1864. Cedar Rapids, Iowa, Torch Press, 1948. viii, 332 p. maps.
OrHi WaU **8858**

Russell, Charles Marion, 1864-1927.
Back-trailing on the old frontiers. Great Falls, Mont., Cheely-Raban Syndicate, 1922. 56 p. illus.
IdU MtHi MtU WaS WaU **8859**

Good medicine; memories of the real West, with an introd. by Will Rogers and a biographical note by Nancy C. Russell. New York, Garden City Publishing Company [c1930] 162 p. col. front., illus. (part col.) facsims.
IdIf MtHi MtU WaA WaU WaW **8860**

Same. [1936]
WaSp **8861**

Good medicine; the illustrated letters of Charles M. Russell; with an introd. by Will Rogers and a biographical note by Nancy C. Russell. Garden City, N. Y., Doubleday, 1929. 162 p. col. front., illus. (part col.)
IdTf WaE **8862**

More rawhides, with illus. by the author. Great Falls, Mont., Montana Newspaper Association, 1925. 59 p. illus.
MtHi MtU WaS WaSp WaU **8863**

Same. 1st rev. ed. September 1946. Pasadena, Calif., Trail's End Publishing Company [1946] 59 p. illus., facsim.
MtBozC **8864**

Rawhide Rawlins stories, with illus. by the author. Great Falls, Mont., Montana Newspaper Association, 1921. 60 p. illus.
MtHi MtU WaS WaU **8865**

Same. 1st rev. ed., September 1946. Pasadent, Calif., Trail's End Publishing Company [1946] 60 p. illus., port.
MtBozC **8866**

Studies of western life. Brooklyn, N. Y., Albertype Co. [c1890] 12 plates.
MtHi MtU **8867**

Trails plowed under, with illus. in color and line by the author. Garden City, N. Y., Doubleday, Page, 1927. xx, 211 p. illus., 10 plates (part double col.) Many **8868**

Same. 1928.
WaW **8869**

Same. 1940 [c1927]
IdB IdU **8870**

Same. 1944 [c1927]
WaU **8871**

Russell, Mrs. Florence.
Child life in Oregon; a true story. Boston, H. Höyt [1866] 193 p. front. (Hillside library)
Or OrP OrU WaU **8872**

Russell, Frank, 1868-1903.
Explorations in the far North; being the report of an expedition under the auspices of the University of Iowa during the years 1892, '93, and '94. [Iowa City?] University of Iowa, 1898. vii, 290 p. front. (port.) 30 plates, fold. map.
CVicAr OrCS WaSp **8873**

Russell, Isaac K.
Hidden heroes of the Rockies, by Isaac K. Russell in collaboration with Howard R. Driggs, illus. with drawings by Herman Palmer and with photographs. Yonkers-on-Hudson, N. Y., World Book Co., 1923, xi, 295 p. front., illus. (Pioneer life series)
Many **8874**

Same. 1925.
IdB **8875**

Same. 1927.
IdIf **8876**

Russell, Nancy C., see nos. 8860-8862.

Russell, Osborne, 1814-1892.
Journal of a trapper; or, Nine years in the Rocky Mountains, 1834-1843; being a general description of the country, climate, rivers, lakes, mountains, etc. and a view of the life led by a hunter in those regions. [Boise, Idaho, Syms-York] c1914. 105 p.
Many **8877**

Same. 2d ed. c1921. xviii, 149 p. Many **8878**

Russell, Ronald.
A new West to explore; the story of the Portland (Or.) Junior Symphony Orchestra and Jacques Gershkovitch, pioneers of a great artistic and cultural future for America. Boston, Marshall Jones [c1938] 71 p. front. (port.) plates, facsim.
Or OrP OrPR OrU WaS WaU **8879**

Russell, Thomas C., see nos. 5690, 8624.

Russian Historical Society of America.
Jubilee report, 1741-1941 [200th anniversary of the Russian landing in Alaska] ed. by M. D. Sedych. [San Francisco? 1941?] 128 p. illus., ports., fold. map. Russian text.
WaS **8880**

Rustgard, John, 1863-
Home rule for Alaska; a discussion of legislation and legislators; speech delivered at Anchorage, Alaska, September 30, 1927. [Juneau, 1927] 39 p.
WaU **8881**

Rutherford, A. C., see no. 2411.

Rutherford, Anworth, 1877-
Squawberry canyon, with illus. by Harry Pierce. Caldwell, Idaho, Caxton, 1932. 203 p. front., 2 plates.
IdB OrCS Wa WaSp **8882**

Rutzebeck, Hjalmar.
Alaska man's luck; a romance of fact.

New York, Boni and Liveright, c1920. ix,
260 p.   OrP WaS **8883**

Same. [1922, c1920]   WaU **8884**

Same. [c1925]   WaW **8885**

My Alaska idyll. New York, Boni and
Liveright [1922] 296 p.   WaS WaU **8886**

Ruxton, George Frederick Augustus,
1820-1848.
In the old West as it was in the days of
Kit Carson and the "mountain men", ed.
by Horace Kephart. New York, Outing
1915. 345 p. (Outing adventure library,
no. 1)   CVicAr IdTf Wa WaS **8887**

Same. Oyster Bay, N. Y., Doubleday [c1915]
                            OrHi **8888**

Same. New York, Macmillan, 1924.
                            WaSp **8889**

Life in the far West. Edinburgh, Blackwood, 1849. xvi, 312 p. CVicAr WaU **8890**

Same. New York, Harper, 1849. 235 p.
CVicAr IdB Or OrP WaSp WaWW **8891**

Same. 1859.   WaS **8892**

Same. New ed. Edinburgh, Blackwood,
1868. xi, 208 p.   CVicAr OrHi **8893**

Wild life in the Rocky Mountains; a true
tale of rough adventure in the days of
the Mexican War, ed. by Horace Kephart. New York, Outing, 1916. 303 p.
front. (double map) (Outing adventure
library)   WaA **8894**

Same. New York, Macmillan, 1926.
                            MtHi **8895**

Ryan, John D., see no. 2875.

Ryan, Marah Ellis (Martin) 1850-
Squaw Elouise. Chicago, Rand McNally
[c1892] 240 p. British Columbia novel.
                  WaPS WaU **8896**

That girl Montana. Chicago, Rand Mc-
Nally [c1901] 357 p. front.
      MtHi WaS WaT WaU **8897**

Rydberg, Per Axel, 1860-1931.
Catalogue of the flora of Montana and the
Yellowstone National Park. [New York,
New Era Printing Co.] 1900. xi, 492 p.
fold. map. (New York Botanical Garden.
Memoirs. v. 1.)   MtBozC **8898**

Rydell, Carl, 1859-
On Pacific frontiers; a story of life at sea
and in outlying possessions of the United States, ed. by Elmer Green, illus.
with drawings by H. Boylston Dummer.
Yonkers-on-Hudson, N. Y., World Book
Co., 1924. xiii, 267 p. front., illus. (Pioneer life series) WaPS WaS WaU **8899**

[**Ryder Brothers,** Baker, Or.]
Columbia Highway and Old Oregon Trail;
information and guide book, Ontario to
Portland, Oregon. [Baker, Or., c1921]
36 p. illus., maps.   WaPS **8900**

Ryerson, John, 1799-1878.
Hudson's Bay; or, A missionary tour in
the territory of the Hon. Hudson's Bay
Company, with brief introductory missionary memorials, and illustrations. Toronto, G. R. Sanderson, 1855. xxiv, 190 p.
front. (port.) illus., plates.
     CVicAr CVU MtU WaU **8901**

Ryther Child Center, Seattle, Wash.
Monograph on organization and operation.
Seattle, 1946. 16 p.   WaS **8902**

S., D. L., see no. 7017.

S., M. M.
Wandering Willie's tale (with apologies to
Sir Walter Scott); a political story. Se-
attle, 1921. 72 p.   WaU **8903**

Sabin, Edwin Legrand, 1870-
Building the Pacific railway; the construc-
tion-story of America's first iron thoroughfare between the Missouri River
and California, from the inception of
the great idea to the day, May 10, 1869,
when the Union Pacific and the Central
Pacific joined tracks at Promontory
Point, Utah, to form the nation's transcontinental, with 22 illus. and a map.
Philadelphia, Lippincott, 1919. 317 p.
front., plates, ports., fold. map. Many **8904**

Kit Carson days (1809-1868) illus. by more
than one hundred half-tones, mostly
from old and rare sources. Chicago, Mc-
Clurg, 1914. xv, 669 p. front., plates,
ports., maps, facsims.
    WaS WaSp WaU WaW **8905**

Kit Carson days, 1809-1868; "adventures in
the path of empire". Revised edition with
new matter with twenty full-page
drawings by Howard Simon. New York,
Press of the Pioneers, 1935. 2 v. fronts.,
illus., ports.   Many **8906**

Klondike partners; wherein are told the
haps and mishaps of two fortune-seekers
who in the Klondike stampede hit the
trail of rain and mud, snow and ice,
mountains, lakes, and rivers, for six
hundred miles to that rainbow's end in a
frozen land of "gold is where you find it"
if you don't quit first, with some illustrations by Lyle Justis. Philadelphia,
Lippincott, 1929. 286 p. col. front., illus.,
plates (part col.) (The American trail
blazers)   Wa WaSp **8907**

On the plains with Custer. London. Lippincott, 1915. 309 p. col. front., 4 plates.
                       CVicAr **8908**

Opening the West with Lewis and Clark;
by boat, horse and foot up the great
River Missouri, across the Stony mountains and on to the Pacific, when, in
the years 1804, 1805, 1806, young Captain
Lewis, the Long Knife, and his friend
Captain Clark, the Red Head chief, aided
by Sacajawea, the Bird-woman, conducted their little band of men tried and
true through the unknown new United
States, with illus. by. Charles H. Stephens, ports. and a map. Philadelphia, Lippincott [c1917] 278 p. col. front., plates,
ports., fold. map. (Trail blazers series)
                       Many **8909**

White Indian, Philadelphia, G. W. Jacobs
& Co. [c1925] 320 p.   WaE WaU **8910**

Wild men of the wild West. New York,
Crowell [c1929] xiv, 363 p. front., plates,
ports.   MtU Wa WaE WaS WaSp **8911**

With Carson and Fremont; being the ad-

ventures, in the years 1842-'43-'44, on trail over mountains and through deserts from the east of the Rockies to the west of the Sierras, of Scout Christopher Carson and Lieutenant John Charles Fremont, leading their brave company including the boy Oliver, with illus. by Charles H. Stephens and ports. Philadelphia, Lippincott, 1912. 302 p. col. front., plates, ports. (Trail blazers series)
OrP WaT 8912

Same. 1913.   OrHi OrP WaE WaS 8913

Same. 2d ed. 1915.   CVicAr 8914

Sabine, Edward, see nos. 10616-10618.

Sacajawea. Eugene, Or., University of Oregon, 1931. 1 v. Contents: Sacajawea (poem) by Bert Huffman. — Montana woman reveals Sacajawea tribal outcast, by Mrs. Emma Magee. — Sacajawea statue tribute to pioneer Indian mother, by Alice V. Joyce.   IdB 8915

Sacajawea Statue Association, Portland, Or.
Officers of the association, its purpose and by-laws, with tribute to Sacajawea, by James K. Hosmer. [Portland, Or., Mann & Beach, 1900?] 16 p.   Or 8916

Same. 15 p.   Or 8917

Sage, Neld Mackinnon.
Top o' the world. London, Dent [1929] 94 p.   CVicAr 8918

Sage, Rufus B., 1817-
Rocky mountain life; or, Startling scenes and perilous adventures in the far West. Dayton, Ohio, E. Canby [18—?] 365 p. front., plates.
CVicAr MtU Or OrU WaSp 8919

Same. Boston, Wentworth & Co., 1857.
IdB IdU WaSp 8920

Same. 1859.   OrHi 8921

Same. Boston, Thayer & Eldridge, 1859.
WaS WaSp WaU 8922

Scenes in the Rocky Mountains and in Oregon, California, New Mexico, Texas, and the grand prairies; or, Notes by the way, during an excursion of three years, with a description of the countries passed through, including their geography, geology, resources, present condition, and the different nations inhabiting them, by a New Englander. Philadelphia, Carey & Hart, 1846. 303 p.
OrHi OrP OrU WaU 8923

Same. 2d ed. rev. Philadelphia, Baird, 1854. 303 p. front., plates.   CVicAr 8924

Sage, Walter Noble, 1888-
Sir James Douglas. Toronto, Ryerson [1930] 30 p. illus. (Canadian history readers)
CVU MtU 8925

Sir James Douglas and British Columbia. [Toronto] University of Toronto Press, 1930. 398 p. fold. map (Studies. History and economics, v. 6, no. 1)   Many 8926

See also no. 254.

Saint-Amant, Pierre Charles Fournier de, 1800-1872.
Voyages en Californie et dans l'Oregon. Paris, L. Maison, 1854. lii, 651 p. illus., port., maps (1 fold.)   Many 8927

St. Andrew's Presbyterian Church, Langley, B. C.; Thirty-fourth anniversary, 1885-1919. Vancouver, B. C. Times, 1919. 8 p. illus., ports.   CVicAr 8928

St. Andrew's Presbyterian Church, Victoria, B. C., commemorating the seventy-fifth anniversary, 1886-1941. [Victoria, B. C., British Colonist, 1941] 16 p. illus., ports.
CVicAr 8929

St. Andrew's Presbyterian Church, Victoria, B. C.; to commemorate the sixtieth anniversary, 1866-1926. [n.p.] 1926. 16 p. illus., ports.   CVicAr 8930

St. Ann's Academy, Victoria, B. C.
Chaplet of years; St. Ann's academy to the pupils past and present of the Sisters of St. Ann, 1858-1918. Victoria, B. C. [British Colonist, 1918] 109 p. front., illus.
CVic 8931

St. Ann's in British Columbia and Alaska, 1858-1924. Victoria, B. C. [n.d.] 106 p. ports.   CVicAr 8932

St. Barbe, Charles, d. 1929.
First history of Nelson, B.C., with sketches of some of its prominent citizens, firms and corporations. [n.p.] Rohrbacher [n. d.] 24 p.   CVicAr 8933

The Kootenay mines; a sketch of their progress and condition today. Nelson, B. C., Miner Printing & Pub. Co., 1895. 26 p. map.   CVicAr CVU 8934

St. Helens Mist.
Special prosperity development edition. St. Helens, Or., 1928. [68] p. illus., ports. (v. 46, no. 28, June 29, 1928)   WaU 8935

St, Helens Sentinel-Mist.
Jubilee edition, 1889-1939. [St. Helens, Or., 1939] [60] p. illus., ports. OrP WaU 8936

St. Ignatius Mission.
Our friends the Coeur d'Alene Indians. St. Ignatius Printery, Mont., 1886. 21 p. "We Indian pupils of St. Ignatius school on the Flathead Reservation have learned by the newspapers the great anxiety caused to your nation by some white settlers of the counties of Whitman County, Washington Territory and Nez Perce, Idaho. We thought we could not make a better use of the little knowledge we acquired in our school in the art of setting types than to give in print a large circulation to your answers to the many misrepresentations of your enemies."
IdU MtHi WaPS WaSp WaU 8937

St. John, Harold, 1892-
Flora of southeastern Washington and of adjacent Idaho. Pullman, Wash., Students Book Corp., 1937. xxv, 531 p. front. (map) illus.   Many 8938

Preliminary list of the plants of the Kaniksu National Forest, Idaho and Washington, by Harold St. John and Fred A. Warren. [Pullman, Wash., State College of Washington, 1925] 36 p. (Botany Dept. Contribution no. 2)   WaPS 8939

St. John, Molyneux.
The province of British Columbia, Canada; its resources, commercial position and climate, and description of the new field opened up by the Canadian Pacific

Railway, with information for intending settlers. [n.p., n.d.] 56 p. plates, fold. map. CV CVicAr CVU 8940

The sea of mountains; an account of Lord Dufferin's tour through British Columbia in 1876. London, Hurst and Blackett, 1877. 2 v. front. (port.) Many 8941

St. Johns Review.
Bridge dedication number, Portland, Oregon, June 1931; commemorating the dedication of the St. Johns suspension bridge as an event of the Portland Rose Festival, June 13, 1931. Portland, Or., 1931. 96 p. illus., ports. OrP 8942

St. Joseph's Hospital, Victoria, B. C. School of Nursing.
Thirty-five years of service, 1900-1935; St. Joseph's Hospital School of Nursing, Victoria, B. C. [n.d., 1936?] 52 [22] p. illus., ports. CVicAr 8943

St. Louis, Mo. Louisiana Purchase Exposition, 1904.
The exhibition of the district of Alaska at the Louisiana Purchase Exposition, St. Louis, Missouri, 1904. with a foreword upon Alaska and the Alaskan exhibit. [St. Louis, Woodward & Tiernan, 1904] 56 p. illus., fold. map. WaS WaU 8944

St. Louis University Associate Alumni.
Rev. Peter John de Smet. [n.p., DeSmet Memorial League, n.d.] 16 p. OrHi 8945

St. Mary's Hospital, Dawson, Y. T.
1897-98 to 1947-48; a golden jubilee in the land of the midnight sun. [n.p., n.d.] [16] p. illus., ports., map. CVicAr 8946

St. Onge, Louis Napoleon, 1842-
Alphabet yakama, contenant les prieres, les cantiques et le catechisme dans la meme langue; a l'usage des enfants de la tribu des Yakamas, sous le patronage des r. r. p. p. jesuites. Montreal, Imprime a la Providence 1872. 104 p. front. (photo.) illus. WaU WaWW 8947
See also no. 2394.

St. Paul & Tacoma Lumber Company, Tacoma, Wash.
Creosoted wood blocks of fir; their value and economy for street paving and other uses. Tacoma [191—?] 1 v. illus. WaT 8948

Growing new forests. Tacoma [192—?] 24 p. illus., plates (1 double) WaU 8949

In business to stay; a tribute to all the men and women who have been associated with the St. Paul and Tacoma Lumber Company, 1888-1947. Tacoma, c1947. 31 p. illus., ports. WaT 8950

St. Regis Kraft Co.
Tacoma kraft; photography by J. R. Eyerman, Tacoma. [Tacoma] Plastic Spiral Binding by Pioneer, Inc. [n.d.] 1 v. 27 plates. WaT 8951

St. Rose Industrial School, Portland, Or.
St. Rose Industrial School, conducted by the Sisters of the Good Shepherd for the care and training of delinquent girls. Portland, Or. [1928?] 19 p. illus.
OrP 8952

Sale, Charles, see no. 9490.

Sale, Elizabeth.
My mother bids me bind my hair. New York, Dodd, 1944. 244 p. Tacoma novel.
Many 8953

Recitation from memory. New York, Dodd, 1943. 298 p. Tacoma novel.
OrP Wa WaS WaSp WaT WaU 8954

Salem, Or. First Methodist Episcopal Church.
Catalogue of the Sunday School library. Salem, Or., Dearborn, 1892. 15 p.
WaU 8955

— — — Jason Lee Memorial Methodist Episcopal Church.
Jason Lee Memorial Church, Salem, Or. [Salem, Or., Elliott, 1906?] [8] p. front. (port.) illus. OrHi WaU 8956

Salem Centennial Commission, 1940.
Souvenir program, Salem Centennial, July 31-Aug. 1-2-3-4, 1940. Salem, Or. [1940] [22] p. illus. Contains outline of pageant.
Or 8957

The Salem Sentinel, Salem, Or.
The Salem Sentinel's year book, January 1, 1899; illustrated almanac, farm gazetteer and handy book of ready reference. Salem, Or., C. B. Irvine, 1898. [192] p. illus., ports. WaU 8958

Salesman's hand book. Pacific Coast lumber. Everett, Wash., Kane & Harcus Co., c1920. 86 p. fold. tables. Wa 8959

Salisbury, Albert P., 1904-
Here rolled the covered wagons, by Albert and Jane Salisbury. Seattle, Superior [c1948] 256 p. illus., map. Many 8960

Salisbury, Jane, see no. 8960.

Salmon, Agnes F.
"Have you no wings?" by A. F. Salmon and B. M. Rice. [Spokane, n.d.] 32 p.
WaSp 8961
See also no. 8629.

Salvation Army.
Notes on sheltering transient men at Seattle, Washington, Sept. 30, 1931 to March 31, 1932, arranged by Captain Orlo L. Ellison, relief secretary for the Salvation Army. [Seattle, 1932?] [44] p. illus., photos. WaS WaU 8962

The Salvation Army, Oregon; its institutions, bureaus and agencies. Portland, Or. [1920?] 8 p. illus. OrP 8963

Sampson, M. B.
The Oregon question as it stands, with a map. 2d ed. London, Samuel Highley, 1846. 15 p. map. OrHi WaWW 8964

Sampson, Martin J.
The Swinomish totem pole, tribal legends as told by Martin J. Sampson to Rosalie M. Whitney, cover design by E. M. Alexander. Bellingham, Wash., Union Printing Co., 1938. 38 p. illus., ports.
CVicAr Wa WaPS WaS WaT 8965

Sampson, Sammy, see no. 4532.

Samson, Sam, 1869-
The Eskimo princess; a story of a million dollar gold discovery in the Cyrus Noble in Nome, Alaska, as told to Mignon Maynard Chisam by Sam Samson. Souvenir ed., July 1941. Stevenson, Wash., Columbia Gorge Pub. [1941] 48 p. 2 ports.
Wa WaS WaU 8966

Samuel, Leo, pub.
Columbia River. Portland, Or. [n.d.] [22] p.
illus.   OrHi 8967

Columbia River illustrated. Portland, Or.
[n.d.] [8] p. 8 plates.   CVicAr 8968

Portland and vicinity; Willamette Valley,
Columbia River, Puget Sound. [Portland,
Or.] c1887. [92] p. plates.   Many 8969

Seattle [views] Portland, Or., 1884?] [8] p.
16 plates (2 double)   WaU 8970

[**Samuels, Frederick S.**] comp.
North Pacific Coast ports. 3d issue. [San
Francisco, Wm. C. Brown, 1894] 77 p.
illus., plates, 3 fold. maps.   WaU 8971

San Francisco Bay Marine Piling Committee.
Marine borers and their relation to marine
construction on the Pacific Coast, being
the final report of the San Francisco
Marine Bay Marine Piling Committee,
prepared under the direction of the San
Francisco Bay Marine Piling Committee,
cooperating with the National Research
Council and the American Wood-preserv-
ers' Association; C. L. Hill and C. A.
Kofoid, editors-in-chief. San Francisco,
1927. ix, 357 p. front. (fold. map) illus.,
tables (part fold.) diagrs. (part fold.)
                                      Many 8972

San Francisco Museum of Art.
Oregon artists, January 12 through February 7, 1943. San Francisco [1943] [24] p.
illus.   Wa WaU 8973

San Juan dispute, a thrilling period in U. S.
history, 1852-1872. [Friday Harbor, Wash.,
Journal Printer, n.d.] 16 p. illus.
                              CVicAr WaPS 8974

Sanborn, Ethel I., see nos. 1510, 1622.

Sanctuary of our Sorrowful Mother, Portland, Or.
The Sanctuary of our Sorrowful Mother;
history and message of a national memorial to motherhood. Portland, Or., 1940.
xvii, 95 p. front., illus., fold. col. plate,
ports., form, diagr.   OrP WaU 8975

Sandercock, William.
Wonderland of Oregon; a group of pen and
ink drawings of the scenic wonders of
the state. Portland, Or., G. H. Street
[19—?] [12] p. 11 plates. OrP WaPS 8976

Sanders, Mrs. Helen (Fitzgerald) 1883-
A history of Montana. Chicago, Lewis Pub.
Co., 1913. 3 v. front., ports.   Many 8977

Trails through western woods, illus. from
photographs by the author. New York,
Harriman, 1910. 310 p. front., plates,
ports.   Many 8978

Sanders, W. F.
The pioneers; Fourth of July address read
at the dedication of the capital of Montana at Helena, July 4th. [n.p.] 1902. 23
p.   MtHi OrP 8979

Sandford, Adam Castle, 1824-
My recollections of eighty years of a stren-
uous life. Portland, Or. [1910?] 98 p.
front. (port.) illus., plates, ports., map,
table.   OrP 8980

Sandilands, John, ed.
Western Canadian dictionary and phrase-
book, explaining in plain English, for

the special benefit of newcomers, the
meaning of the most common Canadian-
isms, colloquialisms and slang, added to
which is a selection of items of general
information immediately helpful to the
newcomer. Winnipeg, Telegram Job
Printers, c1912. [32] p. CVU WaU 8981

Western Canadian dictionary and phrase-
book; things a newcomer wants to
know; words that are different, where
they are not different, the meaning here
attached is that which is accentuated in
Canada; where, however, both words and
meaning are alike "there's a reason"
for their inclusion. Winnipeg, Telegram
Job Printers [c1912] 1 v.   WaSp 8982

Sandoz, Mari Susette.
Crazy Horse; the strange man of the Ogla-
las; a biography. New York, Knopf, 1942.
x, 428 p. fold. map. Montana Indian trouble.   Many 8983

[**Sanislo, Stephen E.**]
50 years of fighting fires; organization and
development of Seattle Fire Department.
Seattle, Northwestern Mutual Fire Assn.,
1939. 23 p.   WaS WaSp 8984

Sapir, Edward, 1884-1939, ed.
Nootka texts; tales and ethnological narratives, with grammatical notes and lexi-
cal materials, by Edward Sapir and Morris Swadesh. Philadelphia, Linguistic
Society of America, University of Pennsylvania, 1939. 334 p. music. (William
Dwight Whitney linguistic series)
                                      Many 8985

Wishram texts; together with Wasco tales
and myths, collected by Jeremiah Curtin. Leyden, Late E. J. Brill, 1909. xv, 314
p. (Publications of the American Ethnological Society, v. 2)   Many 8986

Sasse, Alma Benecke.
The mystery of the Chinese box. New
York, Crowell, 1939. 252 p. illus. Oregon
juvenile story.
        OrMonO OrP Wa WaS WaSp WaT 8987

Terry Carvel's theater caravan, jacket and
endpaper designed by R. F. Hallock.
Garden City, N. Y., Doubleday [1943]
238 p. Northwest story.
        Or OrP WaS WaSp WaU 8988

Sauer, Martin.
An account of geographical and astronomical expedition to the northern parts of
Russia, for ascertaining the degrees of
latitude and longitude of the mouth of
the River Kovima; of the whole coast of
the Tashutski to East Cape; and of the
islands in the eastern ocean stretching
to the American coast, performed by
Commodore Joseph Billings in the years
1785 &c. to 1794; the whole narrated
from the original papers. London, T.
Cadell, 1802. xxvi, 332, 58 p. 14 plates, fold.
map.   Many 8989

Reise nach Sibirien, Kamtschatka und
zur Untersuchung der Mundung des Ko-
wima-Flusses, der ganzen Kuste der
Tschutschken und der zwischen dem
festen Lande von Asien und Amerika
befindlichen Inseln, auf Besehl der Kais-

erin von Russland, Catharina der Zweiten, in den Jahren 1785 bis 1794, unternommen von Kapitan Joseph Billings und nach den original Papieren heraus gegeben. Berlin, 1803. 334 p. 2 fold. plates, fold. map. CVicAr **8990**

Voyage fait ordre de l'imperatrice de Russie Catherine II, dans le nord de la Russie asiatique, dans la mer glaciale, dans la mer d'Anadyr, et sur les cotes de l'Amerique, depuis 1785 jusqu'en 1794 par le commodore Billings, et traduit de l'anglais avec des notes par J. Castera. Paris, F. Buisson, 1802. 2 v. and atlas of 15 plates. OrP WaU **8991**

Saunders, Aretas Andrews, 1884-
A distributional list of the birds of Montana, with notes on the migration and nesting of the better known species. Berkeley, Calif., Cooper Ornithological Club, 1921. 194 p. illus., map. (Pacific coast avifauna, no. 14) Many **8992**

Saunders, Arthur C.
The history of Bannock County, Idaho. Pocatello, Idaho, Tribune Co., 1915. 143 p. CVicAr IdP IdU IdUSB MtHi WaU **8993**

Saunders, Charles Francis, 1859-
Western flower guide, wild flowers of the Rockies and west to the Pacific, illus. with 250 drawings in color. Garden City, N. Y., Doubleday, 1927 [c1917] 286 p. col. illus. WaU **8994**

Same. 1929, c1917. OrHi WaT **8995**

Western wild flowers and their stories. Garden City, N. Y., Doubleday, 1933. xiv, 320 p. front., plates. Many **8996**

Saunders, Edwin James, 1872-
Geography of Washington. [New York, American Book Co., c1916] xx, p. illus., maps. WaU **8997**

See also no. 5348.

Saunders, George, see no. 7867.

Sauvageat, F. X., see no. 8189.

Les sauvages de la mer Pacifique, tableau pour decoration en papier peint. Macon, l'imprimerie de Moiroux rue franche, An XIII. 48 p. CVicAr **8998**

Savage, Alma Helen, 1900-
Dogsled apostles. New York, Sheed & Ward, 1942. xv, 231 p. front., plates, ports., facsim. Many **8999**

Eben the crane, illus. by Charles Keller. New York, Sheed & Ward, 1944. 74 p. col. illlus. Alaska story.
Or OrP WaS WaSp WaT **9000**

Holiday in Alaska, illus. by Jon Nielsen. Boston, Heath [c1944] 80 p. col. front., illus. (part col.) (New world neighbors) WaU **9001**

Smoozie, the story of an Alaskan reindeer fawn, illus. by Charles Keller, maps by LeRoy Appleton. New York, Sheed & Ward, 1941. 68 p. front., illus.
Or OrP WaS WaSp WaU **9002**

Savage, George Milton.
So like a woman; a dynamic play of the great Northwest in three acts, by George Savage and Edouard Peltret. San Fran-cisco, Banner Play Bureau, c1930. 74 p. diagr. Wa WaT **9003**

Savage, Richard Henry, 1846-1903.
The princess of Alaska, a tale of two countries; a novel. Chicago, F. T. Neely, 1894. 420 p. (Neely's library of choice literature, no. 33) WaU **9004**

Savage, Thomas.
Lona Hanson; a novel. [New York] Simon and Schuster [c1948] 306 p. Montana story. MtBozC OrP WaU **9005**

The pass. Garden City, N. Y., Doubleday, 1944. 269 p. Western Montana pioneer story. Many **9006**

Sawtelle, Mrs. Mary P.
The heroine of '49; a story of the Pacific Coast, illus. by Essie G. Sawtelle. San Francisco, c1891. 248 p. front., plates, ports. Many **9007**

Sawyer, Edmund Joseph, 1880-
Game birds and others of the Northwest (illus.) [Bellingham, Wash., Miller & Sutherlen Printing Co., c1945] [36] p. illus. (part col.) WaS WaT WaU **9008**

Sawyer, Ethel Ray, 1880-1942.
We who honor books. Seattle, Dogwood Press, 1944. 99 p. Many **9009**

Sawyer, R. H.
The truth about the invisible empire, Knights of the Ku Klux Klan; a lecture delivered at the municipal auditorium on Dec. 22, 1921. [Portland, Or., Pacific Northwest Domain No. 5, Invisible, c1922] 14 p. OrP **9010**

Saxton, Charles.
The Oregonian; or, History of the Oregon Territory, containing the laws of Oregon, with a description of the political condition of the country, as well as its climate, resources, soil, productions, and progress in education, with a map. No. 1. Washington, D. C., U. Ward and Son, 1846. 48 p. Photostat copy.
Or OrHi WaU **9011**

Sayre, Alex N.
Puget Sound; a poem, Seattle, Stewart & Ebersold, 1883. 20 [8] p. WaU **9012**

Sayre, James Willis, 1877-
The early waterfront of Seattle. [Seattle?] c1937. 32 p. illus. WaS WaU **9013**

The romance of Second Avenue. [Seattle] c1933. 16 p. WaS WaU **9014**

Some historical spots in Washington. [Seattle?] c1936. 16 p. WaS WaT WaU **9015**

This city of ours, pub. by authority of the Board of Directors, Seattle School District No. 1. [Seattle, c1936] 191 p. illus., port. OrHi WaE WaTC WaU **9016**

[Scaife, Arthur H.]
As it was in the fifties, by "Kim Bilir". Victoria, B. C., Province Publishing Company, 1895. 287 p. CVicAr CVU **9017**

Gemini and lesser lights, by "Kim Bilir". Victoria, B. C., Province Publishing Company, 1895. 187 p. CVicAr CVU **9018**

Three letters of credit, and other stories, by "Kim Bilir". Victoria, B. C., Province Publishing Company, 1894. 123 p.
CVicAr **9019**

Scammon, Charles Melville, 1825-1911.
The marine mammals of the north-western coast of North America, described and illustrated; together with an account of the American whale-fishery. San Francisco, J. H. Carmany and Co., 1874. 319, v p. front., illus., 26 plates (6 double)
CVicAr OrP WaS WaU **9020**

Scearce, Stanley.
Northern lights to fields of gold, illus. by R. H. Hall, Caldwell, Idaho, Caxton, 1939. 390 p. col. front., illus., plates.
Many **9021**

Scenic Tours Company, Portland, Or.
Columbia Highway tour; Portland, Hood River, The Dalles. Portland, Or., 1912. 1 v. illus.   WaE **9022**

Same. 2d ed. c1916. 52 p. illus. OrU **9023**

Same. 3d ed. 1918. 64 p.   OrU **9024**

Schaare, C. Richard.
The expedition of Lewis & Clark in picture and story. New York, Cupples & Leon Co. [c1940] 56 p. illus. WaU **9025**

Schaefer Printing Co.
Salem, Oregon; past and present; an historical sketch. [Salem, Or., c1902] [18] p. plates.   WaU **9026**

Schaffer, Mary Townsend Sharples.
Old Indian trails; incidents of camp and trail life, covering two years' exploration through the Rocky Mountains of Canada, with 100 illus. from photographs by the author and by Mary W. Adams, and a map. New York, Putnam [c1911] xiv, 364 p. front., illus., fold. map.
Many **9027**

Same. 1912.   Many **9028**

Schafer, Joseph, 1867-1941.
The acquisition of Oregon Territory. pt. I: Discovery and exploration. [Eugene, Or., University of Oregon, 1908] 31 p. (Bulletin n.s., v. 6, no. 3)   Many **9029**

An historical survey of public education in Eugene, Oregon. [Salem, Or., 1901] 23 p.   OrP OrU **9030**

A history of the Pacific Northwest. New York, Macmillan, 1905. xvi, 321 p. front., illus., 5 plates, port., map. Many **9031**

Same. 1906.   IdUSB **9032**

Same. 1909.   MtHi   WaU **9033**

Same. Rev. and rewritten with maps and illus. New York, Macmillan, 1918. 323 p. front. (double map) 12 plates, port.
Many **9034**

Same. 1921.   CVU **9035**

Same. 1922.   WaU **9036**

Same. 1928.   WaT WaTC **9037**

Same. 1930.   MtUM Wa **9038**

Same. 1943 [c1933]   WaU **9039**

Same. 1946.   WaE **9040**

Jesse Applegate, pioneer and state builder. [Eugene, Or.] University of Oregon, 1912. 13 p. port. (Bulletin, n.s., v. 9, no. 6)
Many **9041**

The Pacific slope and Alaska. Philadelphia, G. Barrie's Sons, c1904. xxiv, 436 p.

col. front., col. plate, ports. (History of North America, v. 10)
IdUSB OrSaW **9042**

Same. xxiv, 442 p. col. front., 18 plates, 22 ports., 6 maps, 2 plans, 18 facsims.
Many **9043**

Same. [c1905]   WaS **9044**

Prince Lucien Campbell. Eugene, Or., University of Oregon Press, 1926. 216 p. front. (port.)   Many **9045**

See also nos. 263, 9838.

Schapps, John, see no. 7229.

Schawl, Robert V. M.
Wise and otherwise; a secret of successful advertising. [Spokane? n.d.] [28] p. front. (port.) illus.   WaSp **9046**

Schell, Joseph.
Ecclesiasticism and Christianity [Attack on Catholic clergy of Oregon and public land frauds] [n.p., n.d] 78 p.
Or OrHi **9047**

Schenk, W. Egbert, see no. 9373.

Schiach, W. S., see no. 7977.

Schiel, James.
Reise durch die Felsengebirge und die Humboldtgebirge nach dem Stillen Ocean; eine Skizze. Schaffhausen, Brodtmannische Buchhandlung, 1859. 139 p. table.   CVicAr OrP **9048**

Schleef, Margaret Louise.
Manufacturing trends in the Inland Empire. Pullman, Wash., State College of Washington, 1947. xxii, 91 p. plates, double map, tables (1 fold.) diagrs. (Bureau of Economic and Business Research. Bulletin no. 4)   WaU **9049**

Schleicher, Robert.
Grape culture in Lewiston-Clarkston Valley. Lewiston, Idaho, Lewiston-Clarkston Co., 1906. 22 p. illus.   WaU **9050**

Schmid, Calvin Fisher, 1901-
Social trends in Seattle, by Calvin F. Schmid, assisted by Laura Hildreth Hoffland and Bradford H. Smith; charts delineated by the author. Seattle, University of Washington Press, 1944. xi, 336 p. illus., diagrs. (Publications in the social sciences, v. 14, Oct. 1944)
Many **9051**

Suicides in Seattle, 1914-1925; an ecological and behavioristic study. Seattle, University of Washington Press, 1928. vii, 93 p. illus. (maps) diagrs. (Publications in the social sciences, v. 5, no. 1)
OrP OrU WaS WaTC **9052**

See also no. 9642.

Schmidt, Emanuel, see no. 2736.

Schmitt, Martin Ferdinand.
Fighting Indians of the West, by Martin F. Schmitt and Dee Brown. New York, Scribner, 1948. xviii, 362 p. illus., ports., maps.   Many **9053**

See also no. 2129.

Schmoe, Floyd Wilfred, 1895-
Cattails and pussywillows, with 10 full page drawings and marginal sketches by the author. Seattle, Lake City Press, 1933. 104 p. illus.   WaS WaT **9054**

Our greatest mountain; a handbook for Mount Rainier National Park, with 64 illus. and a map. New York, Putnam, 1925. xii, 366 p. front., plates, fold. map. Many **9055**

Wilderness tales, with forty-two illus. by the author. Seattle, University of Washington Book Store, 1930. 117 p. front., illus. Many **9056**

Schmolder, B.
Neuer praktischer Wegweiser fur Auswanderer nach Nord-Amerika; erste Abtheilung enthalt; Oregon und Californien und allgemeines uber das Mississippi und Missouri-thal. Mainz, Le Roux, 1849. 120 p. 4 plates, port., table.
CVicAr OrP **9057**

Schmucker, Samuel Mosheim, 1823-1863.
Arctic explorations and discoveries during the Nineteenth Century; the several expeditions to the north seas conducted by Ross, Parry, Back, Franklin, M'Clure and others, including the final effort of Dr. E. K. Kane in search of Sir John Franklin, ed. and completed by Samuel M. Schmucker. New York, Miller, Orten & Co., 1857. 517 p. 2 fronts. (1 port.) illus., plates. OrHi **9058**

Same. 1858. CVU OrP **9059**

Same. With a continuation to the year 1886 by Wm. L. Allison. New York, Lovell Co. [c1886] 640 p. illus., plates.
OrSaW WaSp WaT **9060**

See also no. 3349.

Schneider, Paul, see no. 1982.

Schneiderman, William.
The Pacific Coast maritime strike. [San Francisco, Western Worker Publishers, 1937] [31] p. WaU **9061**

Schoffen, Elizabeth, 1861-
"The demands of Rome"; her own story of thirty-one years as a sister of charity in the order of the Sisters of Charity of Providence of the Roman Catholic Church. Portland, Or. [c1917] 223 p. front., plates, ports., facsims. OrP **9062**

[**Schofield, Charles DeVehr,** bp. of Columbia]
Diamond jubilee; historical sketch, 1866-1926, St. Paul's Royal Naval Station and Garrison Church. Esquimalt, B. C. [1926] 16 p. front. CV CVicAr **9063**

Schofield, Mrs. Emily M.
Charles Deveber Schofield. Victoria, B. C., 1941. 69 p. front. (port.) CVicAr **9064**

Scholefield, Ethelbert Olaf Stuart, 1875-1919.
British Columbia from the earliest times to the present. Vancouver, B. C., S. J. Clarke Publishing Co. [1914] 4 v. fronts., plates, ports., maps, facsims. Many **9065**

A history of British Columbia; part one being a survey of events from the earliest times down to the union of the crown colony of British Columbia with the Dominion of Canada [by] E. O. S. Scholefield; part two being a history, mainly political and economic, of the province since confederation up to the present time, by R. E. Gosnell. Vancouver, B. C., British Columbia Historical Association, 1913. 210, 226 p. front., ports. Many **9066**

See also nos. 1107, 4703, 4704.

School Libraries Institute, University of Portland, Portland, Or.
Exploring the possibilities of centralized and cooperative services for diocesan school libraries; papers presented before the School Libraries Institute at the University of Portland, July 7-9, 1948; honoring the first graduating class of a Catholic library school in the West, Rosary College. River Forest, Ill., University of Portland, 1948. 65 p. OrP **9067**

Schooley, Mary Rice.
Sincere desires. [Vancouver, B. C., Wrigley, n.d.] 27 p. front. (port.) plate.
CVicAr **9068**

[**Schooling, Sir William**] 1860-
The governor and company of adventurers of England trading into Hudson's Bay during two hundred and fifty years, 1860-1920, introd. by Sir Robert Molesworth Kindersley. London, Hudson's Bay Company, 1920. xvi, 129 p. col. front., illus., plates (part col.) ports. (part col.) maps (part fold.) facsim. Many **9069**

Schreibeis, Charles D., 1894-
Pioneer education in the Pacific Northwest, 1789-1847. Portland, Or., Metropolitan [n.d.] 94 p. front., 6 plates.
Many **9070**

Same. [1936] Many **9071**

Same. [1937] Many **9072**

Schreiner, Tin, see no. 1127.

Schulenburg, Albrecht Conan, 1865-1902.
Die Sprache der Zimshian-Indianer in Nordwest-Amerika. Braunschweig, Richard Sattler, 1894. 372 p.
CVicAr WaU **9073**

Schulte, Paul, 1896-
The flying priest over the Arctic; a story of everlasting ice and of everlasting love. New York, Harper [c1940] xiii, 267 p. front., plates, ports.
IdB OrP Wa WaE WaS WaSp **9074**

Schultz, Harry B., see no. 9493.

Schultz, James Willard, 1859-
Alder Gulch gold, with illus. by Albin Henning. Boston, Houghton, 1931. 146 p. front., plates. Montana author adopted into Blackfoot tribe. IdIf MtU **9075**

Apauk, caller of buffalo. Boston, 1916. 226 p. front., illus. plates. OrP WaS **9076**

Bird woman (Sacajawea) the guide of Lewis and Clark; her own story now first given to the world. Boston, Houghton, 1918. 234 p. front., plates. Many **9077**

Blackfeet tales of Glacier National Park. Boston, Houghton [1916] 241 p. front., plates. Many **9078**

Danger trail, with illus. by George Varian. Boston, Houghton [c1922] 296 p. front., plates. IdIf **9079**

Same. 1923. OrP WaPS WaSp **9080**

The dreadful river cave; Chief Black Elk's story, illus. by Harold Cue. Boston, Houghton, c1918. 244 p. front., illus.
IdIf WaT **9081**

Same. 1920.　　　　　　OrP WaS 9082

Friends and foes in the Rockies, with illus. by Stockton Mulford. Boston, Houghton, 1933. 174 p. front., plates. IdIf WaSp 9083

Friends of my life as an Indian. Boston, Houghton [1923] vi, 299 p. front., plates, ports.　　　　　　　　　Many 9084

The gold cache, with illus. by George Varian. Boston, Houghton [c1916] 189 p. front., illus.　　　　　　　IdIf 9085

Same. [1917]　　　OrP WaS WaSp 9086

Gold dust, with illus. by Stockton Mulford. Boston, Houghton [1934] 243 p. front., plates.　　　OrP WaSp WaU 9087

In enemy country. Boston, Houghton, 1928. 234 p. front., plates. IdIf MtHi WaS 9088

In the great Apache forest; the story of a lone Boy Scout. Boston, Houghton, 1920. 224 p. front., plates. OrP WaS WaSp 9089

Lone Bull's mistake; a Lodge Pole chief story, with illus. by George Varian. New York, Grosset [c1917] 208 p. front., plates.
IdIf OrP 9090

Same. Boston, Houghton, 1918.
WaS WaSp 9091

My life as an Indian; the story of a red woman and a white man in the lodges of the Blackfeet, illus. from photographs, mostly by George Bird Grinnell. Cambridge, Mass., Riverside Press [c1906] 426 p. front., 15 plates.　　　MtHi 9092

Same. Boston, Houghton [c1907]
MtBozC WaT 9093

Same. London, Murray, 1907. CVicAr 9094

Same. New York, Doubleday, Page, 1907. x, 426 p. front., 15 plates.
MtBozC MtU OrP WaPS WaS WaT 9095

On the warpath, by Ap-i-kun-i, with illus. by George Varian. Boston, Houghton, 1914. 244 p. front., plates.
OrP WaPS WaS WaSp 9096

Plumed snake medicine, with illus. by George Varian. Boston, Houghton, 1924. 245 p. front., plates. IdIf OrP WaS 9097

The quest of the fish-dog skin, by Ap-i-kun-i, with illus. by George Varian. Boston, Houghton, c1913. 218 p. front., plates.
IdIf OrP WaPS WaS WaSp WaT 9098

Questers of the desert, with illus. by Frank E. Schoonover. Boston, Houghton, 1925. 224 p. front., plates.
OrP WaS 9099

Red Crow's brother; Hugh Monroe's story of his second year on the plains, with illus. by Frank E. Schoonover. Boston, Houghton, 1927. 209 p. front., plates.
OrP WaS 9100

Same. [c1929]　　　　　　　IdIf 9101

Rising Wolf, the white Blackfoot; Hugh Monroe's story of his first year on the plains, with illus. by Frank E. Schoonover. Boston, Houghton, 1919. 252 p. front., plates.
MtHi OrP Wa WaS WaSp 9102

Running Eagle, the warrior girl. Boston, Houghton [c1917] 311 p. front. IdIf 9103

Same. 1919.　MtHi OrP WaS WaSp 9104

Sahtaki and I. Boston, Houghton, 1924. 305 p. col. front.　　　　　　　OrP 9105

Seizer of eagles, with illus. by Frank E. Schoonover. Boston, Houghton [c1922] 229 p. front., plates.
IdIf OrP WaS WaSp 9106

Signposts of adventure; Glacier National Park as the Indians know it, by Apikuni. Boston, Houghton, 1926. vii, 224 p. front., plates, ports., fold. map.　　Many 9107

Same. Cambridge, Mass., Riverside Press, 1926. 225 p. front., illus., 23 plates, 4 ports., map.　　　　　　　MtHi 9108

Sinopah the Indian boy, with illus. by E. Boyd Smith. Boston, Houghton [c1913] 155 p. front., plates.
IdIf OrP Wa WaS WaSp 9109

Skull Head the terrible, with illus. by Frank E. Schoonover. Boston, Houghton, 1929. 207 p. front., plates.
MtU WaU 9110

A son of the Navahos. Boston, Houghton, 1927. 200 p. front., plates.　　WaS 9111

Stained gold, with illus. by Frank E. Schoonover. Boston, Houghton, 1937. 217 p. front., plates.　　　IdIf WaS 9112

The Sun god's children, by James Willard Schultz and Jessie Louise Donaldson, with ports. of Blackfeet Indians by Winold Reiss. Boston, Houghton, 1930. vii, 254 p. col. front., plate, 7 ports.
CVicAr MtHi WaS WaSp WaT 9113

Sun Woman; a novel. Boston, Houghton, 1926. 244 p.　　MtBozC WaS WaT 9114

The trail of the Spanish horse, with illus. by George Varian. Boston, Houghton [c1921] 212 p. front., plates.　IdIf 9115

Same. 1922.　　OrMonO OrP WaS 9116

War trail fort; further adventures of Thomas Fox and Pitamakan, with illus. by George Varian. Boston, Houghton [c1921] 192 p. front., plates.
IdIf OrP WaSp 9117

The white beaver, with illus. by Rodney Thomson. Boston, Houghton, 1930. 271 p. front., plates.　　　OrP WaS 9118

The white buffalo robe, with illus. by Frank E. Schoonover. Boston, Houghton, 1936. 220 p. front., plates.　　WaS 9119

William Jackson, Indian scout; his true story told by his friend. Boston, Houghton, 1926. 200 p. front., plates.
OrP WaS 9120

With the Indians in the Rockies, with illus. by George Varian. Boston, Houghton, 1912. viii, 227 p. front., plates.
CVicAr MtHi MtU OrP WaPS WaU 9121

Same, with illus. by Harold Brett. Boston, Houghton, 1925. viii, 252 p. front., illus., col. plates. (Riverside bookshelf)
IdIf OrAshS OrMonO OrP 9122

Schultz, Leonard Peter, 1901-
Check-list of the fresh-water fishes of Oregon and Washington. Seattle, University of Washington, 1929, 8 p. (Publications in fisheries, v. 2, no. 4, Jan. 1929)
CVU OrP OrU WaS WaSp WaU 9123

Key to the fishes of Washington and Oregon, with a glossary of technical terms. Seattle, University Bookstore, 1931. 63 p. illus. OrPR OrSaW WaPS WaS WaU **9124**

See also no. 4745.

Schultze, Augustus.
A brief grammar and vocabulary of the Eskimo language of north-western Alaska. Bethlehem, Pa., Society for Propogating the Gospel among the Heathen, 1889. 21 p. WaU **9125**

Schuppel, William Carl.
Pioneers of the Pacific. [n.p., 193—?] 22 p. illus. OrP WaPS **9126**

Schuyler, Howard I., see no. 9493.

Schwatka, Frederick, 1849-1892.
Along Alaska's great river; a popular account of the travels of the Alaska exploring expedition of 1883 along the great Yukon River from its source to its mouth in the British North-west Territory of Alaska. New York, Cassell [c1885] 360 p. front., illus., maps. Many **9127**

Same. Together with the latest information on the Klondike country. Chicago, Henry, 1898. 426 p. illus., map.
CVicAr OrP WaU **9128**

Same. Chicago, Hill, 1900 [c1898]
WaU **9129**

Same. New York, Cassell, 1900. 360 p. front., illus., 5 plates. WaU **9130**

The children of the cold. New ed. Boston, Educational Publishing Company [c1899] 212 p. illus. CVicAr Wa WaU **9131**

Exploring the great Yukon; an adventurous expedition down the great Yukon River from its source in the British Northwest to its mouth in the Territory of Alaska. [n.p.] Art & Science Publishing Company. [n.d.] 418 p. illus., diagrs.
IdIf **9132**

Nimrod in the North; or, Hunting and fishing adventures in the Arctic regions. Boston, Educational Publishing Company [c1885] 198 p. illus. WaS WaW **9133**

Same. New York, Cassell [c1885] 198 p. front. (port.) illus.
CVU OrSa WaT WaU **9134**

The search for Franklin. London, Nelson, 1886. 127 p. front., illus. CVicAr **9135**

Same. 1890. CVicAr **9136**

Same. 1899. CVicAr **9137**

A summer in Alaska; a popular account of the travels of an Alaska exploring expedition along the great Yukon River from its source to its mouth in the British Northwest Territory and in the Territory of Alaska. St. Louis, J. W. Henry [n.d.] 418 p. front. (port.) illus., plates, map. CVU **9138**

Same. c1891. OrSa **9139**

Same. 1892. WaT WaU **9140**

Same. 1893. Many **9141**

Same. 1894. CVicAr **9142**

See also no. 5718.

Schwatka, Mrs., see nos. 4092-4097.

Scidmore, Eliza Ruhamah, 1856-1928.
Alaska, its southern coast and the Sitkan Archipelago. Boston, D. Lothrop and Co. [c1885] viii, 333 p. front. (double map) illus., plates. Many **9143**

Appleton's guide-book to Alaska and the Northwest coast; including the shores of Washington, British Columbia, southeastern Alaska, the Aleutian and the Seal Islands, the Bering and the Arctic coasts, with maps and many illus. New York, Appleton, 1893. v, 156 p. 15 plates, 7 maps (part fold.)
OrP OrU WaPS WaS WaU **9144**

Same. 1896. CVicAr **9145**

Same. New ed. with a chapter on the Klondike. 1898. v, 167 p. WaU **9146**

Same. 1899. OrHi Wa WaPS **9147**

Guide-book to Alaska and the Northwest coast, including the shores of Washington, British Columbia, southern Alaska, the Aleutian and Seal Islands, the Bering and the Arctic coasts. London, Heinemann, 1893. v. 156 p. illus., 15 plates, 7 maps (part fold.)
CVicAr OrP OrSaW WaS WaU **9148**

Scoresby, William, 1760-1829.
Seven log-books concerning the Arctic voyages of Captain William Scoresby, senior, of Whitby, England; issued in facsimile by The Explorers Club of New York, with reproductions in color of ports. in oils of Captain William Scoresby, senior and Captain William Scoresby, junior, ed. by Frederick S. Dellenbaugh. New York, Explorers Club, 1917. 8 v. col. front. (port.) illus., col. plate, maps. IdU MtU OrP Wa WaU **9149**

Scoresby, William, 1789-1857.
The Arctic regions; their situation, appearances, climate, and zoology. London, Religious Tract Society [1849?] 192 p. WaU **9150**

The Frankiln expedition; or, Considerations on measures for the discovery and relief of our absent adventurers in the Arctic regions, with maps. London, Longmans, 1850. 99 p. 2 fold. maps.
CVicAr **9151**

Journal of a voyage to the northern whale-fishery; including researches and discoveries on the eastern coast of West Greenland in 1822. Edinburgh, Constable, 1823. xliii, 472 p. plates (part fold.) 2 maps, plan. CVicAr WaU **9152**

The northern whale-fishery. Philadelphia, American Sunday-school Union [1835] 192 p. CVicAr **9153**

Same. London, Religious Tract Society [1849?] 192 p. WaU **9154**

Scott, Charles H.
Drawings of the B. C. coast, with foreword and accompanying text by the artist. Vancouver, B. C., Wrigley, 1932. 9 plates. CV CVU **9155**

Scott, Edna Agnes, 1892-
The Grange movement in Oregon, 1873-1900. [Eugene, Or.? 1939] 40 p. (University of Oregon thesis series, no. 1)
Many **9156**

Scott, Erastus Howard, 1855-
Alaska days, with an account of the trip from Chicago to Seattle and return. Chicago, Scott, Foresman and Co. [c1923] 106 p. illus., maps. WaTC **9157**

Scott, H. S., see no. 387.

Scott, Harvey Whitefield, 1838-1910.
History of Portland, Oregon with biographical sketches of prominent citizens and pioneers. Syracuse, N. Y., Mason, 1890. 651 p. ports., facsims, table.
Many **9158**

History of the Oregon country, comp. by Leslie M. Scott. Cambridge, Mass., Riverside Press, 1924. 6 v. fronts., plates, ports., double facsim. Many **9159**

See also nos. 6152, 9162.

Scott, Laura Tolman.
Sacajawea (the bird woman); the unsung heroine of Montana, 1805-1806. Dillon, Mont., Tribune Publishing Company, 1915. 17 p. front. MtHi **9160**

Scott, Leslie M., 1878-
Backward to pioneers, forward to posterity; an address delivered at the first annual award of the Armitage Fund prizes for essays in Oregon history. [n. p., 1941] [12] p. illus. Or OrP **9161**

Catalogue of public addresses and lectures of Harvey W. Scott, forty years editor-in-chief, Morning Oregonian. [Portland, Or., 1915] 11 p. port. Or OrP OrU **9162**

Champoeg memoranda; organization of the Oregon Provisional Government in 1843; Oregon's anniversary at Champoeg; books on Champoeg. [n.p., 1937] 13 p.
Or OrHi OrP OrU WaS **9163**

See also no. 9159.

Scott, Reva Lucile (Holdaway) 1900-
A biography of Parley P. Pratt, the archer of Paradise, by Reva Stanley [pseud.] illus. with rare photographs. Caldwell, Idaho, Caxton, 1937. 349 p. front., plates, ports., facsims., geneal. tables.
OrU Wa WaPS WaWW **9164**

Scott, T.
Statement in support of a general railway act for the North-West. Ottawa, Woodburn [1884] 8 p. CVicAr **9165**

Scott, W. W.
Oregon pioneer. [n.p.] c1916. 19 p.
OrHi OrP **9166**

Scott, Wisner Gillette, 1848-
Some reasons for a system of national defense highways along the Pacific Coast to prevent war and assure peace; the Pacific Coast national defense highway system. Balboa Highway, Pacific Highway, El Camino Sierra urged by the Pacific Coast Defense League. Seattle, Pacific Coast Defense League [1918] 20 p. fold. map. WaT **9167**

"Scotty", see no. 12.

Scribes Club of Spokane. Poetry Section.
Turquoise lanterns; poems by the Poetry Section of the Scribes Club of Spokane, Washington. Cleveland, Pagasus Studios, 1937. [20] p. WaSp **9168**

Scriven, George Percival, 1854-1940.
The story of the Hudson's Bay Company, otherwise of the company of adventurers of England trading into Hudson's Bay. Washington, D. C., St. Anselm's Priory, 1929. 66 p. 3 plates, fold. map. (Benedictine historical monographs, 4)
CV CVicAr Or OrP WaS **9169**

Scruggins, Obadiah, pseud.
Through mud and sage brush to fame and fortune; or, With the O. A. C. glee-mandolin club touring Oregon, season 1912. [Corvallis, Or. Corvallis Printing House] 1912. 44 p. illus. Or **9170**

[Scrutator, pseud.]
The impracticability of a North-west Passage for ships, impartially considered. London [Sherwood & Co.] 1824. iv, 182 p. CVicAr Wa WaS **9171**

Scudamore, Thomas V.
A short history of the 7th Battalion, C. E. F. Vancouver, B. C., Anderson & Odlum [1930] 1 v. CV **9172**

Scudder, Doremus.
"A national hero"; sermon on Marcus Whitman at the First Congregational Church, Woburn, Mass., Sunday, November twenty-eighth, 1897, 10:30 A. M. [n.p. n.d.] 19 p. front. WaWW **9173**

Scull, Edward Marshall, 1880-
Hunting in the Arctic and Alaska, with 136 illus. from photographs and 11 maps. London, Duckworth & Co., 1914. 304 p. front., illus., plates, maps. WaU **9174**
Same. Philadelphia, Winston, 1914.
WaS WaU **9175**
Same. 1915. CVicAr **9176**

A sea officer, see no. 8120.

Seaman, Norma Gilm, 1873-
Indian relics of the Pacific Northwest. Portland, Or., Binfords & Mort [1946] viii, 157 p. illus. Many **9177**

Seamann, Berthold, see no. 5563.

Seamen's Friend Society, Portland, Or.
History and financial report of the Portland Seamen's Friend Society (auxiliary of the American Seamen's Friend Society of New York). Portland, Or., Himes, 1880. 52 p. OrP WaU **9178**

Sears, Alfred Francis, 1826-
Report upon a system of sewers for the city of Portland, Oregon, to the Mayor and Common Council, Dec. 1883. [Portland, Or., n.d.] 44 p. OrHi OrP **9179**

Sears, Jesse Brundage, 1876-
The Boise survey; a concrete study of the administration of a city school system, by J. B. Sears assisted by William M. Proctor and J. Harold Williams. Yonkers-on-Hudson, N. Y., World Book Co., 1920. viii, 290 p. tables, diagrs. (Educational survey series)
IdB MtU OrP WaPS WaS WaTC **9180**

Seatco Manufacturing Company, Bucoda, Wash.
Douglas fir as applied to railroad bridge building. Bucoda, Wash. [1890?] 19 p. 2 plates. WaU **9181**

Seattle. Art Museum.
Japanese art exhibit, sponsored by China

Club of Seattle, Japan Society of Seattle, Far East Society of Seattle, Department of Oriental Studies of the University of Washington, at the Art Institute of Seattle, March ninth to thirteenth, nineteen-thirty. [Seattle, 1930] 34 p. front., plates. WaU **9182**

Photographs of the Seattle Art Museum. [Seattle, Western Printing Co., 1934?] 30 p. illus., plans. C. H. Davidson, photographer. ORCS OrP WaPS WaS **9183**

———— Citizens Committee.
The truth about the Post-Intelligencer strike; the story of William Randolph Hearst's effort to crush the American Newspaper Guild in Seattle by dismissals and economic terrorism. Seattle [1936?] 20 p. WaS **9184**

———— Civic Unity Committee.
History of Civic Unity Committee, February 14, 1944 to June 15, 1948. [Seattle, 1948] 22 p. WaU **9185**

Racial restrictive covenants released by Seattle Civic Unity Committee, August 1, 1948. [Seattle, 1948] 12 p.
WaS WaU **9186**

———— Fire Department Relief Association.
Twentieth century souvenir, published for the benefit of the Seattle Fire Department Relief Association. Seattle, Lowman & Hanford, 1901. 216 p. illus., port.
OrHi WaU **9187**

———— First National Bank.
Northwest industries. [Seattle, 1938] [79] p. tables. WaU **9188**

———— First Presbyterian Church.
A war memorial. [Seattle, 1944?] [12] p. illus. WaU **9189**

———— General Strike Committee, 1919.
The Seattle general strike; an account of what happened in Seattle, and especially in the Seattle labor movement during the general strike, February 6 to 11, 1919; issued by the History Committee of the General Strike Committee. Seattle, Seattle Union Record Publishing Co. [1919?] 63 p.
OrU WaS WaSp WaU **9190**

———— Immanuel Lutheran Church.
Golden jubilee souvenir, 1890-1940, February 25, 1940. [Seattle] 1940. 20 p. illus., ports. WaS **9191**

———— John Muir School.
John Muir; a pictorial biography, comp. by the pupils of the John Muir School, Seattle, Washington in commemoration of the hundredth anniversary of the birth of John Muir, 1838-1938. [Seattle, Lowman & Hanford, c1938] [105] p. front., illus., ports., facsims.
WaS WaU **9192**

The John Muir book, by the pupils of the John Muir School, Seattle, Washington. Seattle, Cooperative Printing Co., 1925. 71 p. Wa WaS WaU **9193**

———— Pastorius Day Committee.
Know your citizens; Pastorius Day, Oct. 12, 1924, souvenir album and program, Hippodrome, Seattle, Wash. [Seattle,

Seattle Printing & Publishing Company, 1924] 47 p. illus., ports. WaU **9194**

———— Plymouth Congregational Church.
Manual of Plymouth Church, Seattle. Seattle, Ingraham & Coryell [n.d.] 30 p.
WaU **9195**

———— Police Relief Association.
History of the Seattle Police Department, 1900. [Seattle, 1900] 80 p. illus.
CVicAr OrHi WaS WaU **9196**

———— St. James Cathedral Parish.
Silver jubilee, St. James Cathedral Parish, 1904-1929. [Seattle, Peters Publishing Company, 1929?] 96 p. photos., ports. Contains history of St. James Cathedral Parish, by Robert Snodgrass. WaU **9197**

———— St. Mark's Cathedral Church.
Saint Mark's Cathedral Church; resume. [Seattle, 1926?] [4] p. WaU **9198**

———— Swedish Tabernacle.
Our church at fifty; a record of the planting, growth and fruits of the Swedish Tabernacle Congregation, Seattle, Washington, 1889-1939. [Seattle, 1939] 70 p. illus., ports. History by Miss Margaret Peterson and Arthur O. Peterson; illus. by Rowland Johnson. WaS **9199**

Seattle and Lake Washington Waterway Company.
History and advantages of the canal and harbor improvement project now being executed by the Seattle and Lake Washington Waterway Company, with an appendix containing pertinent historical documents. Seattle, Lowman & Hanford, 1902. 69 p. illus., maps.
OrHi WaS WaT WaU **9200**

Lake Washington ship canal. Seattle [Pioneer Printing and Publishing Company, 1894?] 15 p. WaS WaU **9201**

Seattle and Walla Walla Railroad and Transportation Company.
Report of the chief engineer to the trustees and stockholders, November 1874. Seattle, Intelligencer Book and Job Printing Office, 1874. 48 p. front. (fold. map) WaU **9202**

Seattle Automobile Club.
Official automobile road book of western Washington; a road guide book, descriptive and maps, showing the best automobile routes, together with all related roads of record and other valuable information for use of automobilists; under the auspices of the Seattle Automobile Club. Seattle, Lowman & Hanford, 1909. 150 p. 52 maps.
OrP Wa WaS WaU **9203**

Seattle Bar Association.
A handbook. [Seattle, Security Printing Co.] 1930. 41 p. WaU **9204**

Recall of judicial decrees by bureaucratic dictation: the Olsson case before Judge C. H. Hanford. [Seattle? 1912?] 62 p.
WaS WaU **9205**

Seattle; containing a compilation and review of the resources, terminal advantages, climate and general industries of the Queen City and the country tributary to it. Seattle, Baldwin [c1890] 74 p. illus. WaWW **9206**

Seattle Council of Social Agencies.
Here's Seattle. Seattle, c1944. 44 p. illus.,
fold. map. WaS 9207

Institutional cost study; children's institutions, state of Washington. Seattle, 1942.
10 p. WaS 9208

Recreational survey of the Northwest district. Seattle, 1944. 1 v. WaS 9209

Seattle Daily Bulletin.
Handbook of Washington, 1901. Seattle
[1901] 191 p. illus. WaU 9210

25th Anniversary number. Seattle, 1918.
44 p. illus. (v. 25, no. 40, Feb. 16, 1918)
WaS 9211

New Year's edition, 1903. Seattle, 1903.
24 p. illus. (v. 9, no. 12, Jan. 12, 1903)
WaS 9212

Seattle Electric Company.
Souvenir guide of the Alaska-Yukon-
Pacific Exposition held at Seattle,
Washington, June 1 to October 16, 1909.
[Seattle, 1909] 64 p. illus. WaU 9213

Street railways of Seattle. [Seattle, 1904?]
[64] p. illus., plan. WaU 9214

Seattle Federation of Women's Clubs.
The cosmogram. [Seattle] 1914. 40 p. illus.
WaU 9215

The Seattle Foundation.
The Seattle Foundation, a permanent
trusteeship for gifts and bequests.
[Seattle, 1947] 22 p. WaU 9216

Seattle Fur Exchange.
A story in pictures; Seattle fur exchange.
[Seattle, c1928] [22] p. illus. WaU 9217

Seattle Garden Club.
Native flora of the Pacific Northwest; a
bibliography. [Seattle, Frayn Printing
Co., 1939] 15 p. WaS WaU 9218

Scenic Seattle. Seattle, Western Printing
Co., 1926. 32 p. illus. WaS 9219

Seattle Gas and Electric Company.
Hand book for gas consumers. [Seattle]
1901. 16 p. illus. WaU 9220

Seattle Grade Club Magazine.
Pioneer women of Seattle. Seattle, 1931.
52 p. illus., ports. (v. 12, no. 4, May 1931)
WaS 9221

The Seattle Grade Teacher.
[Seattle] Seattle, 1945. 32 p. illus. (v. 26,
no. 3, Mar. 1945) WaS 9222

Souvenir N. E. A. convention number,
July 1927. [Seattle, 1927] 64 p. illus.
WaS WaU 9223

Seattle High School Teachers' League.
The policy of the University of Washington; the report of a special committee,
accepted December 17, 1930. [Seattle,
1930] 8 p. WaU 9224

The Seattle Japanese Journal.
Souvenir number, issued on the occasion
of the visit of President McKinley to
Seattle in May 1901. [Seattle, S. Noma,
1901] [156] p. illus. WaU 9225

Seattle Land Company.
The Puget Sound review, descriptive of
Seattle, King County, and Washington
Territory, pub. by the Seattle Land
Company. Seattle, C. B. Bagley's Book
and Job Printing House, 1889. 94 p.
tables. WaU 9226

**Seattle Merchants' Exchange Clearing
Association.**
Proposed general by-laws and rules.
[Seattle, 1938?] 13 p. WaPS 9227

Seattle Ministerial Federation. Committee
on Orientals.
Report adopted and ordered printed by
the Seattle Ministerial Federation, June
4, 1917. [Seattle] 1917. [8] p.
WaS WaT 9228

Seattle Municipal League, see Municipal
League of Seattle.

Seattle of today, architecturally. [Seattle,
Sanders and Lawton, J. M. Corner, Jas.
Stephen, E. W. Houghton, Josenhans
and Allen, A. Tidmand, Thompson and
Thompson, McManus and Robertson,
19—] [47] p. WaU 9229

Seattle Pacific College, Seattle, Wash.
Seattle Pacific College, an open door to
a new life of joy and service. Seattle,
1931. 8 p. illus. (Bulletin, v. 9, no. 3)
WaU 9230

Seattle Playgrounds Association.
The playground movement in Seattle, to
procure the dedication, creation and
equipment of public playgrounds and
public places and buildings for past-
time, games, sports, bathing, recreation and rest, and to secure facilities
and provide opportunities for and to
promote the spirit and love of recreation, fair play and wholesome sport
among the people of Seattle and their
children. [Seatle, 1909] 21 p. illus.
WaU 9231

Seattle Post-Intelligencer.
Facts on Alaska. [Seattle, 1904?] 16 p.
WaU 9232

Frederick & Nelson, 50 years, 1890-1940.
Seattle, 1940. 18 p. illus. (Special section, Sunday, Mar. 31, 1940) WaS 9233

New building and progress edition. Seattle,
1949. [176] p. illus., ports. (v. 135, no.
124, Jan. 2, 1949) WaU 9234

Pacific Northwest pictorial [edition] Seattle, 1941. [130] p. illus., ports., map.
(v. 120, no. 146, July 27, 1941) WaU 9235

Pacific Northwest progress edition; golden
jubilee of the state of Washington. Seattle, 1939. [98] p. illus., ports. (v. 116,
no. 142, July 23, 1939)
WaE WaS WaU 9236

Semi-centennial edition, marking the fiftieth anniversary of the Daily Post-
Intelligencer and the seventy-fifth
anniversary of the founding of Seattle.
Seattle, 1926. [50] p. illus., ports. (Nov.
7, 1926) WaU 9237

75th anniversary and Pacific Northwest
progress edition. Seattle, 1938. [70] p.
illus. (July 24, 1938) WaU 9238

Special port edition. Seattle, 1921. 24 p.
illus., ports. (Oct. 11, 1921) WaU 9239

Seattle Press.
The Olympics; an account of the explorations made by the "Press" explorers.
Seattle, 1890, 8 p. illus., maps. (v. 18,
no. 10, July 16, 1890) WaU 9240

Seattle Press Committee.
Official souvenir program [reception to First Washington U. S. Volunteer Regiment, Nov. 5, 6, and 7, 1899] Seattle, Metropolitan [1899] [64] p. illus., ports.
WaU **9241**

Seattle Real Estate Association.
Reports on city real estate values, December, 1907. Seattle, Pacific Press [1907] 115 p. front., 4 plates.
WaS WaU **9242**

Same. Rev. ed. Seattle, Lowman & Hanford, 1914. 77 p. WaS WaU **9243**

Seattle Repertory Playhouse.
Seattle Repertory Playhouse, 10th anniversary, 1927-1937. Seattle, 1937. 15 p. illus., ports. WaS **9244**

Seattle Republican.
Greater Seattle edition. [Seattle, 1903] 28 p. illus., ports. (v. 10, no. 28)
WaS WaU **9245**

Greater Seattle edition for Lewis and Clark Exposition. [Seattle, 1905] [36] p. illus., ports. (v. 12, no. 7, Aug. 11, 1905)
WaS WaU **9246**

Northwestern negro progress number; Alaska-Yukon-Pacific Exposition, 1909. Seattle, H. R. Cayton, 1909. 78 p. illus., ports., map. (v. 14, no. 1) WaT **9247**

Seattle Safe Deposit and Trust Company.
Articles of incorporation and by-laws. Seattle, Lowman & Hanford [1887] 22 p.
WaU **9248**

The Safe Deposit Company of Seattle, incorporated April 7, 1884. Seattle, Lowman & Hanford [1885] 14 p. WaU **9249**

Seattle Star.
Newspaper circulation manual for carrier-salesmen, coaches and district supervisors, Seattle, Pigott-Washington Printing Company, 1937. 221 p. illus., plates, diagrs. (1 fold.) WaTC **9250**

The Seattle Telegraph.
Welcoming the president. Seattle, 1891. 24 p. illus., ports. (v. 2, no. 85, May 6, 1891) Printed on silk. WaU **9251**

Seattle Terminal Board.
Seattle's growth as a world port is shackled by its railroad terminals. Seattle, 1937. 19 p. WaS **9252**

Seattle, the queen city. [n.p., 1893] [52] p. illus. WaU **9253**

Seattle Times.
Fiftieth anniversary of King County Medical Society, 1888-1938. Seattle, 1938. 1 v. illus., ports. (Medical supplement, Sunday, Aug. 21, 1938) WaS **9254**

The first 50 years. Seattle, 1946. 23, 16 p. illus. (Magazine and rotogravure sections, Aug. 11, 1946) WaS **9255**

Golden jubilee of the state of Washington, 50 years of progress. Seattle, 1939. [88] p. illus., ports. (v. 62, no. 162, June 11, 1939) WaS WaU **9256**

Seattle at war; midsummer annual edition. Seattle, 1942. [114] p. illus., ports., maps. (July 26, 1942) WaU **9257**

Silver jubilee number. Seattle, 1906. [26] p. illus., ports. (Feb. 25, 1906)
WaS WaU **9258**

Seattle Union Record.
American Federation of Labor convention annual; supplement to the Seattle Union Record, November 8, 1913. Seattle, Trade Register Printer, 1913. 132 p. illus. WaS **9259**

[Labor Day edition] Seattle, 1926. [44] p. illus., ports. (v. 9, no. 117, Sept. 4, 1926)
WaU **9260**

Seattle Weekly News.
Progress and home industry edition. Seattle, Ballard News Publishing Company, 1913. 1 v. illus. (v. 22, no. 28, July 11, 1913) WaS **9261**

Seattle Writers' Club.
Tillicum tales, illus. by original drawings and photographs. Seattle, Lowman & Hanford, 1907. 306 p. illus., 12 plates.
Many **9262**

Seaver, Charles Hill, 1880-
The Oregon supplement to Tarr and McMurry's New geographies. New York [Macmillan, c 1913] 38 p. front. (map) illus. OrP **9263**

Supplementary volume, Washington. New York, Macmillan, 1909. 55 p. illus., fold. map, diagr. WaSp WaU **9264**

Washington. New York, Macmillan, 1906. 55 p. illus., map. Wa WaS WaU **9265**

Same. 1911. WaT **9266**

Washington state supplement. New York, Macmillan, 1911. 32 p. illus., maps.
WaT **9267**

Same. 1912. Wa WaU **9268**

Seaver, Jesse Montgomery, 1890-
Henry family records. Philadelphia, American Historical-Genealogical Society, 1929. 32 p. ports., coat-of-arms. Wm. E. Henry family. WaU **9269**

Seavey, J. R., see no. 5242.

Sebring, Al.
Sebring's Skagit County illustrated; historical and pictorial edition of Skagit County, Washington, December 1902. Mt. Vernon, Wash., 1902. 38 p. illus.
WaS **9270**

The second narrows bridge spanning Burrard Inlet, Port of Vancouver, British Columbia, opened on Saturday, November 7, 1925. [Vancouver, B. C., Rose, 1925] 30 p. illus. CV CVicAr **9271**

Secretan, James Henry Edward, 1852-1926.
To Klondyke and back; a journey down the Yukon from its source to its mouth, with hints to intending prospectors. London, Hurst and Blackett, 1898. xii, 260 p. front. (port.) plates, diagrs.
CVicAr CVU WaS WaU **9272**

Out west. Ottawa, Esdale Press, 1910. 189 p. front., plates.
CVicAr CVU WaS WaSp **9273**

Same. [206] p. CVicAr WaU **9274**

Seddall, J. Vernon, see no. 3701.

Sedgwick, Ellery, see no. 10944.

Sedych, M. D., see no. 8880.

Seelye, Lyman.
The genesis of good government. Bellingham, Wash., Bayside Press, 1922. 153 p. front. (port.) Wa WaU **9275**

Oalin; an otherwise untold tale of the time when the world war was raging, illus. by Mona Jeanne Mouso. Bellingham, Wash., Bayside Press [c1922] 320 p. front., plates. Poem.
　　　　　CVicAr Wa WaS WaU　**9276**

Seeman, A. L., see no. 8610.

Seghers, Charles John.
Pastoral letter to the clergy, both secular and regular, the religious communities, and the faithful of the western part of Montana, May 5, 1883, on the ₋early Catholic missions in Montana. [n.p., 1883] 8 p.　　　　MtHi　**9277**

See also nos. 4348, 5933.

Selkirk, Thomas Douglas, 5th earl of, 1771-1820.
Esquisse du commerce de pelleteries des Anglois dans l'Amerique Septentrionale, avec des observations relatives a la Compagnie du Nord-Ouest de Montreal. Montreal, Brown, 1819. 110 p.
　　　　　　　　　　CVicAr　**9278**

A sketch of the British fur trade in North America; with observations relative to the North-west Company of Montreal. London, J. Ridgway, 1816. 130 p.
　　　　　　　　　　CVU　**9279**

Same. 2d ed.　　　　CVicAr　**9280**

Selle, Ralph Abraham.
A daughter of the midnight sun. Houston, Tex. [Carroll Printing Co.] c1933. 32 p. (Outdoor nature series) WaS　**9281**

Luck and Alaska. Houston, Tex., Carroll Printing Co., 1932. vii, 186 p. (Outdoor nature series)　　WaS WaU　**9282**

The lure of gold; luck and Alaska. [Houston, Tex., Carroll Printing Co., c1932] 32 p. (Outdoor nature series) WaS　**9283**

Selver, Paul, see no. 10837.

Semi-centennial history of Oregon. Eugene, Or., University of Oregon, 1898. 22, 32 p. maps (2 fold.) (Bulletin; historical series, v. 1, no. 1, 2)　　OrHi WaU　**9284**

Seminary of Christ the King, New Westminster, B. C. prospectus. [n.p., 1940?] 28 p. illus., ports.　　CVicAr　**9285**

Semler, Heinrich, 1841-1888.
Oregon nach eigenen Beobachtungen. Leipzig, Welpost Verlag, 1883. 128 p. map. (Uber's Meer. Taschenbibliothek fur Deutsche Auswanderer, Bd. 9)
　　　　　　　　OrP WaU　**9286**

Semmens, John.
The field and the work; sketches of missionary life in the far north. Toronto, Methodist Mission Room, 1884. 199 p. front., illus.　　　CVicAr　**9287**

Trials and triumphs of early Methodism in the great North-west. 2d ed. [Toronto, Woman's Missionary Society of the Methodist Church, n.d.] 16 p. (Our Work, no. 7)　　　CVicAr　**9288**

Senger, Henry L.
A saga of the Sawtooths with Old Man Nick o' the Woods, pictures by Nick Villeneuve. [Caldwell, Idaho, Caxton, c1938] 55 p. illus. (Hank's unnatural history series)　　　　IdB WaU　**9289**

Sengstacken, Mrs. Agnes Ruth (Lockhart) 1859-
Destination, west! Portland, Or., Binfords & Mort [1942] 219 p. Many　**9290**

A legend of the Coos. San Francisco, Philopolis Press, 1909. 39 p. front., illus.
　　　　　　Or OrHi OrP WaU　**9291**

Senior's North West Golf Association.
Constitution; list of members and addresses, effective 1923. [Victoria, B. C., Sweeney-McConnell, 1927] 34 p.
　　　　　　　　　CVicAr　**9292**

Seppala, Leonhard.
Seppala, Alaskan dog driver, by Elizabeth M. Ricker. Boston, Little, 1930. vi, 295 p. front., plates, ports.
　　　CV CVicAr IdB WaSp WaT WaU　**9293**

Sercombe, Frederick M., see no. 7630.

Service, Robert William, 1876-
Ballads of a Bohemian. New York, Barse [c1921] 220 p. front. (port.) British Columbia author.　　CVU WaWW　**9294**

Ballads of a Cheechako. New York, Barse [c1909] 137 p.　　　　Many　**9295**

Same. 159 p.　　　　　　WaU　**9296**

Same. Philadelphia, E. Stern & Co., 1909. 137 p.
　　OrCS OrU Wa WaS WaSp WaU　**9297**

Same. Toronto, Briggs, 1909. 146 p. front., 8 plates.
　　CVic CVicAr CVU OrP WaSp　**9298**

Same. 1913. 137 p.　　　　CVU　**9299**

Bar-room ballads; a book of verse. London, E. Benn [1940] 206 p.　　OrU　**9300**

Same. New York, Dodd, 1940. 169 p.
　　　IdB Or OrP WaE WaSp　**9301**

The complete poems. New York, Dodd, 1942. [1032] p.　　　OrP WaU　**9302**

Harper of Heaven, a record of radiant living. New York, Dodd, c1948. 452 p.
　　　　　　　　　　Many　**9303**

The house of fear; a novel. New York, Dodd, 1927. 408 p.　　　CVU　**9304**

The master of the microbe. Toronto, McClelland [1926] 424 p.　　CVU　**9305**

Ploughman of the moon; an adventure into memory. New York, Dodd, 1945. vii, 472 p. front. (port.)　　Many　**9306**

The poisoned paradise. New York, Dodd, 1922. 412 p.　　　CVU　**9307**

The pretender; a story of the Latin quarter. New York, Dodd, 1915. 349 p.
　　　　　　　WaS WaU　**9308**

Rhymes of a Red Cross man. New York, Barnes [c1916] 192 p.　　Many　**9309**

Same. London, Unwin [1916] 176 p.
　　　　　　　　　　IdU　**9310**

Rhymes of a rolling stone. New York, Barse [c1912] 172 p. front. (port.)
　　　　　　　　　　IdU　**9311**

Same. New York, Dodd, 1912. 115 p. illus.
　　　　　　　　　　Many　**9312**

Same. Toronto, Briggs, 1912. 195 p.
　　　　　　CVic CVU WaU　**9313**

Same. New York, Dodd, 1918, c1912. 172 p.
　　　　　　　　　IdU WaT　**9314**

The roughneck. New York, Barse [1924] 448 p. CVU OrU **9315**

Songs of a sourdough. Toronto, Ryerson [c1907] 108 p. 43d ed. Published also as The spell of the Yukon. WaU **9316**

Same. 13th ed. Toronto, Briggs, 1908. 106 p. CVU **9317**

Same. 1916. 109 p. CVU **9318**

The Spell of the Yukon, and other verses. New York, Barse [c1907] 99 p. Published also as Songs of a sourdough. OrPR WaU WaWW **9319**

Same. 126 p. Many **9320**

Same. Philadelphia, E. Stern & Co. [c1907] 99 p. WaU **9321**

Same. New York, Barse, 1910. 126 p. OrP **9322**

Same. Philadelphia, E. Stern & Co., 1910 [c1907] 99 p. WaPS **9323**

Same. New York, Barse [c1916] 126 p. WaE WaT **9324**

Same. New York, Dodd [c1916] WaE **9325**
Same. 1935 [c1916] IdP **9326**

Same. New York, Barse, 1935, c1916. WaT **9327**

Same. New York, Dodd, 1936 [c1916] OrCS **9328**

The trail of '98; a Northland romance with illus. by Maynard Dixon. New York, Grosset [c1910] vii, 514 p. front., plates. IdU OrU WaPS WaT WaU **9329**

Same. New York, Dodd, 1911. OrP WaS **9330**

Same. New York, Grosset, 1911. WaE **9331**

Same. Toronto, Ryerson, 1928. xi, 514 p. front, 3 plates. CVicAr **9332**

Same. London, Benn, 1936. 320 p. CVic **9333**

Why not grow young? or, Living for longevity. New York, Barse [c1928] 226 p. front. (port.) CV **9334**

Sessions, Francis Charles, 1820-1892.
From Yellowstone Park to Alaska, illus. by C. H. Warren. New York, Welch, Fracker Co., 1890. 186, ix p. front., plates. Many **9335**

Seton, Ernest Thompson, 1860-
The Arctic prairies; a canoe-journey of 2,000 miles in search of the caribou; being the account of a voyage to the region north of Aylmer Lake. New York, Scribner, 1911. xvi, 415 p. front., illus., plates. OrP Wa WaE WaS WaT WaU **9336**

Same. London, Constable, 1912. CVicAr CVU **9337**

See also no. 6470.

Seton, Grace (Gallatin), 1872-
Nimrod's wife, pictures by Walter King Stone and Ernest Thompson Seton. London, Archibald, Constable, 1907. 406 p. 18 plates. CVicAr **9338**

A woman tenderfoot; over one hundred and fifty illus. New York, Doubleday, Page, 1901. 361 p. illus., plates. MtHi WaU **9339**

Seton-Karr, Heywood Walter, 1859-
Bear-hunting in the White Mountains; or,

Alaska and British Columbia revisited. London, Chapman and Hall, 1891. vi, 156 p. front., illus., 5 plates, fold. map. Many **9340**

Shores and Alps of Alaska, with illus. and 2 maps. London, Low, 1887. xiv, 248 p. illus., plates, ports., maps (1 fold.) CV CVicAr CVU WaS WaU **9341**

Settle, Raymond W., see no. 2136.

Settlement and early settlers of Coos Bay; personal sketches, eccentric characters, and historical reminiscences; written by a pioneer resident of the Bay. Marshfield, Or., Coast Mail Book and Job Printing Office, 1879. 38 p. OrHi **9342**

Settlers' Association of British Columbia.
Farm lands in British Columbia, 3d ed. Vancouver, B. C., 1902. 96 p. CVicAr **9343**

Same. 4th ed. This pamphlet includes the most complete list of hay, grain, dairy, and fruit farms, ranches, orchards, suburban lands, and fishermen's allotments, ever issued in British Columbia, and comprises selections from every district in the fertile lower Fraser Valley. Vancouver, B. C., News - Advertiser [1903] 96 p. maps, tables. CVU **9344**

Severance, George, 1874-1931.
A report on the soil of Lewiston orchards; illus. [Lewiston, Idaho, Lewiston Land and Water Co., c1907] 12 p. front., fold. illus. WaPS **9345**

Same. 8 p. WaPS **9346**

Sevigne, see no. 4947.

Seward, William Henry, 1801-1872.
Alaska; speech at Sitka, August 12, 1869. [Victoria, B. C., Higgins, 1869?] 8 p. CVicAr **9347**

Same. Washington, D. C., Philp & Solomons, 1869. 31 p. WaU **9348**

Our North Pacific states; speeches in Alaska, Vancouver and Oregon. Washington, D. C., Philp & Solomons, 1869. 31 p. CVicAr **9349**

[Sexton, Bernard]
Gray Wolf stories; Indian mystery tales of coyote, animals and men, by Peter Gray Wolf [pseud.] illus. by Gwenyth Waugh. Caldwell, Idaho, Caxton, 1941. x, 192 p. col. front., illus., plates. WaS WaSp WaU **9350**

Seymour, Flora Warren (Smith) 1888-
Bird girl; Sacajawea, illus. by Edward C. Caswell. Indianapolis, Bobbs-Merrill [1945] 187 p. illus. (Childhood of famous Americans series) Or OrP OrU WaSp WaU **9351**

The boys' life of Fremont. New York, Century [c1928] 288 p. front. (port.) illus., plates. OrP WaS WaU WaW **9352**

Boys' life of Kit Carson. New York, Century [c1929] ix, 238 p. front. (port.) illus., plates. IdIf OrP WaS WaSp **9353**

Indian agents of the old frontier. New York, Appleton-Century, 1941. xi, 402 p. front., plates, ports. Many **9354**

Meriwether Lewis, trail-blazer, illus. by Norman Price. New York, Appleton-Century, 1937. xiv, 239 p. front., illus., plates. OrP Wa WaS WaSp 9355

Same. 1942 [c1937] WaU 9356

Shackleton, Edward Arthur Alexander.
Arctic journeys; the story of the Oxford University Ellesmere Land Expedition, 1934-5. London, Hodder [1937] 372 p. front., illus., 40 plates, fold. map, diagrs.
CVicAr OrP 9357

Shackleton, Kathleen, see no. 3555.

Shafer, Mrs. Paul D., see no. 10756.

Shaler, William, 1778?-1833.
Journal of a voyage between China and the north-western coast of America, made in 1804; introd. by Lindley Bynum, illus. by Ruth Saunders. Claremont, Calif., Saunders Studio Press, 1935. 108 p. illus., fold. map, facsims. Many 9358

Shall Japanese-Americans in Idaho be treated with fairness and justice or not? Addresses and proceedings at mass meeting, citizens of Idaho, auditorium First Congregational Church, Boise, Idaho, evening of January twenty-third, 1921. [n.p.] 1921. 1 v. IdB 9359

Shaniko Leader.
2nd annual number devoted to the interests of Sherman, Wasco and Crook Counties. Shaniko, Or., 1902. 136 p. illus., ports. Or OrHi 9360

Shankle, George Earlie.
Washington, state name, flag, seal, song, bird, flower, and other symbols; a study based on historical documents giving the origin and significance of the state name, nicknames, motto, seal, flag, flower, bird, song, and descriptive comments on the capitol building and on some of the outstanding state histories, with facsimiles. New York, H. W. Wilson, 1933. 12 p. col. front., plates. Many 9361

Shannon, William.
British Columbia and its resources, comp. by William Shannon and C. McLachlan. London, Barber, 1889. 30 p. fold. map.
CVicAr 9362

[Shareholder, pseud.]
The British Columbian Investment and Loan Society. Victoria, B. C., McMillan, 1869. 15 p. CVicAr 9363

Sharman, Helen G.
The cave on the Yellowstone; or, Early life in the Rockies. Chicago, Scroll Publishing Company, c1902. 371 p. front. Montana setting. MtHi 9364

Sharp, Dallas Lore, 1870-1929.
The better country. Boston, Houghton, 1928. viii, 277 p. front. Travel in the West.
IdB OrP Wa WaS WaT WaTC 9365

Where rolls the Oregon. Boston, Houghton, c1913. 251 p. OrSa 9366

Same. With illus. from photos. 1914. ix, 251 p. front., 17 plates, port. Many 9367

Sharp, Paul,
Transportation development on the Pacific coast; notes from a lecture given at Princeton University, January 14, 1930,

before the Princeton Engineers' Association. [n.p., 1930] 25 p. (Cyrus Fogg Brackett series) Or 9368

Sharp, R. F.
An objective study of the junior high school in Vancouver. [Vancouver, B. C., Seymour Press] 1940. 15 p. CVU 9369

Sharp, Russell A., see No. 7940.

Sharpe, Edward Leroy.
Prairie Belle; a story of the frontier. Philomath, Or., Commercial Press [c1916] 64 p. port. OrCS OrHi OrU 9370

Sharples, Ada White.
Alaska wild flowers. Stanford University, Calif., Stanford University Press [c1938] vii, 156 p. front., illus.
MtBozC OrCS OrP OrU WaE WaS 9371

[Shattuck, Warren Leland]
History of Trinity Methodist Episcopal Church of Idaho Falls, Idaho. Idaho Falls, Idaho, Ramsing's Printery [1926] 11 p. front., ports. IdIf 9372

Shaver, F. A., see no. 4860.

Shaw, Campbell.
A romance of the Rockies. Toronto, Bryce [1888] 102 p. British Columbia story.
CVicAr 9373

Shaw, George Coombs, 1877-
"Chinook dictionary", briefed by A. H. Hodgson from Shaw's "The Chinook jargon and how to use it". [Seattle, 1922] 7 p. WaPS WaU 9374

The Chinook jargon and how to use it; a complete and exhaustive lexicon of the oldest trade language of the American continent. Seattle, Rainier Printing Co., 1909. xvi, 65 p. Many 9375

240 Chinook jargon words used by the Siwash on Puget Sound and by Indians and whites of the great Pacific Northwest for nearly 150 years, ed. by Nika Tikegh Chikamin (George Coombs Shaw). Seattle, W. R. Johnson Co., 1932. 16 p. Many 9376

Vancouver's discovery of Puget Sound in the year 1792, being excerpts from the rare original journals; the naming of our geographic features; around the Sound with Capt. George Vancouver in twenty minutes. Seattle, Peacock Publishing Company, c1933. 23 p.
CVicAr OrHi WaPS WaS 9377

Shaw, Mrs. Gertrude E. (Metcalfe).
English caravanners in the wild West, the old pioneers' trail, with sketches by Una Shaw Lang and other illus. Edinburgh, Blackwood, 1926. viii, 400 p. front., plates, fold. map. WaU 9378

Shaw, Lloyd.
Cowboy dances; a collection of western square dances, with a foreword by Sherwood Anderson. Caldwell, Idaho, Caxton, 1939. 375 p. front., illus., diagrs., music.
Many 9379

Shaw, Mrs. Nan de Bertrand (Lugrin)
A handbook of Vancouver Island. [Victoria, B. C., Buckle, n.d.] 51 p. illus., map. CVicAr 9380

The pioneer women of Vancouver Island, 1843-1866, ed. by John Hosie. Vistoria,

B. C., Women's Canadian Club of Victoria, Vancouver Island, 1928. 312 p. front. (port.) illus., ports. Many **9381**

Shaw, Norton, see no. 4247.

Shaw, Reuben C.
Across the plains in forty-nine. Farmland, Ind., W. C. West, 1896. 200 p. port.
IdU Or **9382**

Shaw, Thomas, 1843-1918.
Farmer's paradise; the Columbia River Valley as a land of grain and fruit; what a learned professor saw in Oregon, Washington, and Idaho. Portland, Or., Oregon Railroad & Navigation Co., 1898. 31 p. Or WaU WaWW **9383**

Shaw, William Thomas, 1873-
The China or Denny pheasant in Oregon, with notes on the native grouse of the Pacific Northwest, written and illus. by William T. Shaw. Philadelphia, Lippincott, 1908. 24 p. col. front., 14 plates.
OrCS OrP WaPS WaS WaU WaW **9384**
See also no. 10147.

Shea, J. G., see no. 7871.

Shea & Patten, comp.
The "Soapy" Smith tragedy. Skagway [Daily Alaskan] 1907. 24 p. illus., ports.
CVicAr **9385**

Shearer, Frederick E., ed.
The Pacific tourist; Adams & Bishop's illustrated transcontinental guide of travel from the Atlantic to the Pacific Ocean; a complete traveler's guide of the Union and Central Pacific railroads and all points of business or pleasure travel to California, Colorado, Nebraska, Wyoming, Utah, Nevada, Montana, the mines and mining of the territories, the lands of the Pacific Coast, the wonders of the Rocky Mountains, the scenery of the Sierra Nevadas, the Colorado Mountains, the big trees, the geysers, the Yosemite, and the Yellowstone, with special contributions by F. V. Hayden, Clarence King, Capt. Dutton, A. C. Peale, Joaquin Miller, and J. B. Davis, illus. by Thomas Moran, A. C. Warren, W. Snyder, F. Schell, H. W. Troy, A. Will, engravings by Meeder & Chubb. New York, Adams & Bishop, 1885. 372 p. front., illus. Earlier editions, 1876-1881, ed. by H. T. Williams. WaSp **9386**

Same. 1887. WaU **9387**

Same. J. R. Bowman's illustrated transcontinental guide of travel from the Atlantic to the Pacific Ocean; a complete traveler's guide of the Union and Central Pacific railroads. New York, J. R. Bowman, 1882-83. 372 p. front., illus.
CVicAr WaU **9388**

Shedd, George Clifford, 1877-
Cryder. New York, Burt [c1922] 388 p. Northwest story. WaE WaS **9389**

Shedd, Solon, 1860-
The clays of the state of Washington, their geology, mineralogy, and technology. Pullman, Wash., State College of Washington, 1910. xiv, 341 p. front., 41 plates (part fold.) map. Many **9390**

[**Sheepshanks, John,** bp. of Norwich] 1834-1912.
A bishop in the rough, ed. by the Rev. D. Wallace Duthie, with a preface by the Right Rev. the Lord Bishop of Norwich. 3d impression. London, Smith, Elder, 1909. xxxvii, 386 p. front., 4 plates. Rector of Holy Trinity Church, New Westminster, B. C., 1859-1867. Many **9391**

Same. New York, Dutton, 1909.
CVU IdU WaSp **9392**

Sheldon, Charles, 1867-1928.
The wilderness of Denali; explorations of a hunter-naturalist in northern Alaska, with an introd. by C. Hart Merriam. New York, Scribner, 1930. xxv, 412 p. front. (port.) 31 plates, fold. map.
CVicAr OrP WaS WaSp WaT WaU **9393**

The wilderness of the north Pacific Coast islands; a hunter's experiences while searching for wapiti, bears, and caribou on the larger coast islands of British Columbia and Alaska. London, Unwin, 1912. xvi, 246 p. front., 44 plates, maps. (1 fold.)
CV CVicAr CVU OrP WaU **9394**

Same. New York, Scribner, 1912.
Many **9395**

The wilderness of the upper Yukon; a hunter's explorations for wild sheep in sub-arctic mountains. London, Unwin, 1911. xxi, 354 p. col. front., illus., 51 plates (3 col.) 4 maps (part fold.)
WaSP WaU **9396**

Same. New York, Scribner, 1911.
CV Or OrP WaE WaPS WaS **9397**

Same. Toronto, Copp Clark, 1911.
CVicAr **9398**

Sheldon, Henry Davidson, 1874-
History of the University of Oregon. Portland, Or., Binfords & Mort [c1940] 288 p. plates, ports. Many **9399**

Northwest corner: Oregon and Washington, the last frontier; photographs by Henry Sheldon, introd. and commentary by Stewart Holbrook. Garden City, N. Y., Doubleday, 1948. xii p. [116] plates.
Many **9400**

University of Oregon library, 1882-1942. [Eugene, Or.? 1942] 29 p. (Studies in bibliography, no. 1)
CVU OrP WaSp **9401**
See also no. 2360.

Sheldon, J. P., see no. 2507.

Sheldon-Williams, G., see no. 1107.

Shelekhof, Gregory Ivanovich, 1748-1795.
Voyage of a Russian merchant from Okhotzk on the eastern ocean to the coast of America in the years 1783, 1784, 1785, 1786, 1787, and his return to Russia; from his own journal. [n.p., n.d.] 42 p.
CVicAr OrHi OrP **9402**

Shelley, Percy Bysshe, 1792-1822.
A stage version of Shelley's Cenci, by Arthur C. Hicks and R. Milton Clarke, based upon the Bellingham Theatre Guild's production of the tragedy, Mar. 6, 7, 8, 9, and 12, 1940. Caldwell, Idaho, Caxton, 1945. 156 p. front. (port.)
WaWW **9403**

Shelton, William.
Indian totem legends of the Northwest coast country, by one of the Indians (Snohomish chief). [n.p., n.d.] 17 p. illus.
CVicAr OrP WaS WaU **9404**

The story of the totem pole; early Indian legends as handed down from generation to generation are here recorded. [Everett, Wash., Kane & Harcus Co.] c1923. 80 p. illus., ports. Many **9405**

Same. 2d ed. 1935, c1923. OrHi WaE **9406**

Shemelin, Fedor.
Zhurnal pervago puteshestviia Rossiian vo krug zemnago shara, sochinennyi pod vysochaishim Ego Imperatorskago Velichestra pokrovitel'stvom Rossiisko-Amerikanskoi kompanii glavnym kommissionerom moskovskim kuptsom Fedorom Shemelinym. Sanktpeterburg, Meditsinskaia tipografiia, 1816-1818. 2 v. in 1. tables. WaU **9407**

Shepard, Charles Edward, see no. 5500.

Shepard, Cyrus, see no. 7131.

Shepard, Mrs. Isabel Sharpe, 1861-
The cruise of the U. S. steamer "Rush" in Behring Sea, summer of 1889. San Francisco, Bancroft, 1889. 257 p. 2 fronts. (1 fold. map) 5 plates.
CVicAr CVU WaS WaU **9408**

Shephard, Esther.
Paul Bunyan, illus. by Rockwell Kent. New York, Harcourt [c1924] xv, 233 p. front., illus., plates.
IdB Wa WaS WaSp WaT WaU **9409**

Same. 244 p. front. WaU **9410**

Same. Seattle, McNeil Press [c1924] 235 p. front. Many **9411**

Same. 2d printing. [1925] CVU **9412**

Shepherd, H. W., see nos. 6446-6448.

Shepherd, William, 1824-
Prairie experiences in handling cattle and sheep. London, Chapman, 1884. 266 p. front., 7 plates, map.
MtU WaT WaU **9413**

Same. New York, O. Judd Co., 1885. 215 p. front., illus. WaS **9414**

Sherman, Dean F., ed.
Alaska cavalcade. Seattle, Alaska Life Publishing Co. [c1943] 303 p. illus., ports., maps. Or WaE WaS WaT WaU **9415**

Sherman, William Tecumseh, see no. 2496.

Sherrard, Mrs. Drew.
Roadside flowers of the Pacific Northwest, with 4 packets of wild flower seed. Portland, Or., Metropolitan, 1932. 32 p. front., plates. Many **9416**

Sherrill, T. C., see no. 4153.

Shields, Charles Henry, 1864-
Single tax exposed; an inquiry into the operation of the single tax system as proposed by Henry George in "Progress and poverty" the book from which all single tax advocates draw their inspiration, revealing the true and real meaning of single tax, which is land communism. 3d ed. [Portland, Or., Oregon Equal Taxation League] 1912. 89 p. illus. "Shall Oregon be the victim?"
OrHi OrP WaPS **9417**

Same. 5th ed. 63 p. illus. OrP **9418**

Same. 7th ed. [Seattle, Trade Register] 1914. 190 p. WaU **9419**

Shields, Charles W., see no. 5389.

Shields, George Oliver, 1846-1925.
Battle of the Big Hole; a history of General Gibbon's engagement with Nez Perces Indians in the Big Hole Valley, Montana, August 9, 1877, by G. O. Shields ("Coquina"). Chicago, Rand McNally, 1889. 120 p. front., 2 plates, 5 ports.
Many **9420**

The blanket Indian of the Northwest. Subscriber's ed. limited to five hundred autographed copies. New York, Vechten Waring Co., 1921. 322 p. col. front., plates (part col.) ports. (part col.) Many **9421**

Cruising in the Cascades; a narrative of travel, exploration, amateur photography, hunting, and fishing, with special chapters on hunting the grizzly bear, the buffalo, elk. Chicago, Rand McNally, 1889. 339 p. front. (port.) illus.
Many **9422**

Same. London, Low, 1889.
CVicAr CVU OrU WaT **9423**

Hunting in the great West (Rustlings in the Rockies). Hunting and fishing by mountain and stream. Chicago, Belford, Clarke & Co., 1884. 306 p. front., illus.
MtHi **9424**

Same. 5th ed. 1888. WaS WaU **9425**

Rustlings in the Rockies; hunting and fishing by mountain and stream. Chicago, Belford, Clarke & Co., 1883. 306 p. front., illus.
MtHi MtU WaSp WaU **9426**

Shields, Walter C.
The ancient ground. Nome, Alaska, Keenok Club, 1918. 47 p. Poem. WaU **9427**

Shiels, Archibald Williamson, 1878-
Early voyages of the Pacific; a few notes on the days of iron men and wooden ships. [Bellingham, Wash., Union Printing Co., c1931] 61 p.
CV CVicAr CVU OrP WaS WaU **9428**

San Juan Islands, the Cronstadt of the Pacific. Juneau, Empire Printing Co., 1938. 275 p. front. (map) Many **9429**

Seward's icebox; a few notes on the development of Alaska, 1867-1932. [Bellingham, Wash., Union Printing Co., c1933] 419 p. Many **9430**

A shikari, see nos. 4363-4365.

Shillinglaw, John Joseph, 1830-
A narrative of Arctic discovery from the earliest period to the present time; with the details of the measures adopted by Her Majesty's government for the relief of the expedition under Sir John Franklin. London, W. Shoberl, 1850. xx, 348 p. front. (port.) 2 fold. maps.
CVicAr **9431**

Shinn, Charles Howard, 1852-1924.
Pacific rural handbook; containing a series of brief and practical essays and notes on the culture of trees, vegetables and flowers, adapted to the Pacific Coast. San Francisco, Dewey [c1879] 122 p. illus., tables. OrHi **9432**

Shippey, Frederick, see no. 2540.

Shively, John M., 1804-
Route and distances to Oregon and California, with a description of watering-places, crossings, dangerous Indians, &c. &c. Washington, D. C., Greer, 1846. 15 p.
OrHi **9432A**

Shoemaker, Alvaro C.
The Ole-ad; an epic of Seattle's revolution. [Seattle, c1921] 15 p. WaU **9433**

Sho-pow-tan, see no. 7125.

Shone, Isaac, see no. 319.

A short narrative and justification of the proceedings of the committee appointed by the Adventurers to prosecute the discovery of the passage to the western ocean of America. London, J. Robinson, 1749. 30 p. CVicAr WaU **9434**

A short state of the countries and trade of North America, claimed by the Hudson's Bay Company, under a pretence of a charter for ever, of lands without bounds or limits, and an exclusive trade to those unbounded seas and countries; shewing the illegality of the said grant, and the abuse they have made of it; and the great benefit Britain may obtain by settling those countries, and extending the trade amongst the natives by civilizing and incorporating with them; and the necessity there is of a Parliamentary enquiry into the pretended rights and exclusive monopoly claimed by the said company, and their abuse of the grant. London, J. Robinson, 1749. 44 p.
CVicAr WaU **9435**

Shortt, Adam, 1859-1931.
Economic conditions and operations of the British Columbia Electric Railway Company and subsidiary companies; report. [n.p.] 1917. 61 p. CV **9436**

[Shotbolt, Thomas]
An account of the establishment and subsequent progress of Freemasonry in the colony of British Columbia from its origin in 1859 to 1871. Victoria, B. C., British Colonist, 1871. 18 p. CVicAr **9437**

Shuck, Oscar Tully, 1843-1905, ed.
Representative and leading men of the Pacific; being original sketches of the lives and characters of the principal men to which are added their speeches, addresses, orations, eulogies, lectures and poems, including the happiest forensic efforts of Baker, Randolph, McDougall, T. Starr King, and other popular orators. San Francisco, Bacon and Co., 1870. 702 p. front., 23 ports.
OrHi OrP OrPR OrU WaS WaU **9438**
See also no. 445.

Shugg, Harold, see no. 10844.

Shupe, Verna Irene.
The Argonauts and pioneers. 2d ed. [Pocatello, Idaho, Graves & Potter, 1931] 65 p. illus. IdP IdU WaSp WaWW **9439**

Caribou County chronology, with an introductory account by the author. [Colorado Springs, Print Craft Press, c1930] 64 p. illus. IdIf IdU WaSp **9440**

Shurtleff, Bertrand Leslie, 1897-
Long lash, jacket drawing and illus. by Diana Thorne. New York, Bobbs-Merrill, c1947. 273 p. illus. Alaska story.
CV Or OrP WaE WaS WaT **9441**

Sibson, W. S., see no. 4584.

Sidel, James Eckel, 1900-
Pick for your supper; a study of child labor among migrants of the Pacific Coast. New York, National Child Labor Committee [1939] 67 p. illus., tables. (Publication no. 378)
CVU Or OrP WaS **9442**

Sieber, E. T., see nos. 4019, 4020.

Siegel, Chris C.
Early history of Ferndale and Ten Mile townships, Whatcom County, Washington. [Bellingham, Wash., Cox Brothers & Williams, 1948] 110 p. illus., ports.
WaU **9443**

Sierra, Benito de la, Fray, d. 1778?
Fray Benito de la Sierra's account of the Hezeta expedition to the northwest coast in 1775, trans. by A. J. Baker, introd. and notes by H. R. Wagner. San Francisco, 1930. 44 p. front. (fold. map) maps.
WaSp WaU **9444**

Sikes, F. A.
History of the Farmers' Union movement in Oregon and southern Idaho. 2d ed. Milton, Or. [1914?] 30 p. Or **9445**

Sillitoe, Mrs. Violet E. (Pelly)
Early days in British Columbia. Vancouver, B. C., Evans & Hastings [1922] 36 p. illus. CVicAr Or WaS WaU **9446**

Pioneer days in British Columbia; reminiscences. [Vancouver, B. C., Evans & Hastings, 192—?] 32 p. illus., ports.
CVicAr WaS WaSp WaU **9447**

Silloway, Perley Milton.
Additional notes to Summer birds of Flathead Lake, with special references to Swan Lake, with introd. by Morton J. Elrod. Missoula, Mont., 1903. [15] p. 5 plates (Bulletin, University of Montana, no. 18. Biological ser. no. 6)
MtHi MtUM OrU **9448**

The birds of Fergus County, Montana. Lewistown, Mont., Argus, 1903. 77 p. front., 16 plates, map. (Fergus County Free High School. Bulletin no. 1)
MtBozC MtHi MtU **9449**

Silloway's history of central Montana; a review of the development of Montana's inland empire, comp. and ed. by P. M. Silloway. Lewistown, Mont., Fergus County Democrat [1935?] 59 p. illus., port. MtHi MtU **9450**

Summer birds of Flathead Lake. [Missoula, Mont.] University of Montana, 1901. 83 p. 16 plates. (Bulletin no. 1. Biological series no. 1) WaTC **9451**

Siloam Enterprise Company, Ephrata, Wash.
Siloam Sanitarium, Lake Siloam, Pool of Siloam, better known as Soap Lake; positive facts about Soap Lake, the duplicate of the biblical Pool of Siloam, in the arid section of the state of Washington, U. S. A., near Ephrata. [Wenatchee, Wash., Republic Press, n.d.] [17] p. illus. WaU **9452**

Silver jubilee. [Boise, Idaho, Syms-York, 1930] 1 v. illus. IdB **9453**

Simonin, Louis Laurent, 1830-1886.
Le grand-ouest des Etats-Unis; les pionniers et les peaux-rouges, les colons du Pacifique. Paris, Charpentier, 1869. 364 p. CVicAr **9454**

Simonsen, Sigurd Jay, 1891-
Among the sourdoughs. New York, Fortuny's [c1940] 153 p. OrU WaU **9455**
The dissenters. New York, Fortuny's [c1941] 205 p. Seattle setting. WaSp WaU **9456**

Simpson, Alexander, 1811-
The life and travels of Thomas Simpson, the Arctic discoverer; by his brother. London, Bentley, 1845. viii, 424 p. front. (port.) fold. map. Many **9457**
The Oregon territory; claims thereto of England and America considered. London, Bentley, 1846. 60 p. CVicAr WaS **9458**

Simpson, Charles H.
Life in the far West; or, A detective's thrilling adventures among the Indians and outlaws of Montana. Chicago, T. W. Jackson [c1896] 264 p. illus. WaSp WaU **9459**
Same. Chicago, Rhodes & McClure, c1896. MtU WaPS WaS **9460**
Same. 1903. MtHi **9461**

Simpson, Eugene Milton, 1871-
Pheasant farming. [Eugene, Or., Shelton-Turnbull-Fuller Co.] 1927. 96 p. illus., col. plates. IdB Or OrP WaE **9462**

Simpson, Sir George, 1792-1860.
Fur trade and empire; George Simpson's journal; remarks connected with the fur trade in the course of a voyage from York Factory, 1824-1825; together with accompanying documents; ed. with an introd. by Frederick Merk. Cambridge, Mass., Harvard University Press, 1931. xxxvi, 370 p. fold. map. (Harvard historical studies, v. 31) Many **9463**
Journal of occurences in the Athabasca Department, 1820 and 1821, and report; ed. by E. E. Rich, with a foreword by Lord Tweedsmuir, and an introd. by Chester Martin. Toronto, Champlain Society, 1938. lix, 498, xiii p. front. (port.) maps, tables. (Hudson's Bay Company series, 1) Many **9464**
Part of dispatch from George Simpson, Esqr., governor of Rupert's Land to the governor & committee of the Hudson's Bay Company, London, March 1, 1829; continued and completed March 24 and June 5, 1829; ed. by E. E. Rich, with an introd. by W. Stewart Wallace. [n.p.] Hudson's Bay Record Society, 1947. lii, 277, x p. (Publications 10) Many **9465**

Simpson, George Gaylord, 1902-
Notes on the Clark Fork upper paleocene fauna. New York, American Museum of Natural History, 1937. 24 p. (American Museum novitates, no. 954, Oct. 14, 1937) OrP **9466**

Simpson, Samuel Leonidas, 1845-1900.
The gold-gated West; songs and poems,

ed. by W. T. Burney. Philadelphia, Lippincott, 1910. 308 p. front. (port.) OrCS OrHi OrP OrSaW OrU WaU **9467**
Same. 3d ed. [n.d.] WaPS **9468**
The Pacific Coast fifth reader. Rev. ed. San Francisco, A. L. Bancroft [1874] 312 p. front., illus. (Pacific Coast series) Or OrP OrU WaS WaU **9469**

Simpson, Thomas, 1808-1840.
Narrative of the discoveries on the north coast of America, effected by the officers of the Hudson's Bay Company during the years 1836-39. London, Bentley, 1843. xix, 419 p. 2 fold. maps. Many **9470**

Sims, Elmer Harper.
Sacajawea and the Lewis and Clark expedition; an epic. [Coeur d'Alene, Idaho, Press Publishing Company, 1925] 68 p. CVU IdU OrSaW WaPS WaU **9471**

Sinai Temple, Tacoma, Wash.
Fortieth anniversary celebration. Tacoma, 1948. 1 v. illus. WaT **9472**

Sinclair, Mrs. Bertha (Muzzy) 1874-1940.
Chip of the Flying U, by B. M. Bower (B. M. Sinclair) illus. by Charles M. Russell. New York, Grosset, c1904-06. 256 p. front., plate. Montana ranch story. Or WaT **9473**
The Flying U strikes, by B. M. Bower [pseud.] Boston, Little, 1934. 303 p. Or WaS WaW **9474**
The Flying U's last stand, by B. M. Bower [pseud.] New York, Grosset [c1915] 353 p. front. WaW **9475**
Good Indian, by B. M. Bower [pseud.] with illus. by Anton Otto Fischer. New York, Grosset [c1912] vi, 372 p. front., plates. WaPS **9476**
The haunted hills, by B. M. Bower [pseud.] New York, Grosset, c1934. 291 p. Idaho ranch story. IdB WaT **9477**
Ranch at the Wolverine, by B. M. Bower [pseud.] New York, Burt [1914] 356 p. front. Idaho ranch story. IdIf WaT **9478**
Rim of the world, by B. M. Bower [pseud.] with front. by Anton Otto Fischer. Boston, Little, 1919. 349 p. front. WaPS WaS WaSp **9479**
Rodeo, by B. M. Bower [pseud.] New York, Grosset [c1929] 309 p. WaW **9480**

Sinclair, Bertrand William, 1878-
Big timber; a story of the Northwest, with a front. by Douglas Duer. Toronto, Copp Clark [c1916] 321 p. front. CVic CVicAr WaA **9481**
Same. New York, Burt [c1916] WaSp WaT WaU **9482**
The inverted pyramid. Boston, Little, 1924. 339 p. British Columbia lumber story. CV Or WaE WaS WaT WaU **9483**
North of fifty-three, with illus. by Anton Otto Fischer. New York, Grosset [c1914] vi, 345 p. front., plates. CVU WaA WaS WaSp WaT WaU **9484**
Same. [c1915] CVicAr **9485**

Poor man's rock, with front. by Frank Tenney Johnson. Boston, Little, 1920. v, 307 p. British Columbia novel.
CVicAr WaT **9486**

Sinclair, John, see nos. 5707, 5708.

Singh, Pardaman.
Ethnological epitome of the Hindustanees of the Pacific Coast. Stockton, Calif., Pacific coast Khalsa Diwan Society [1922?] 32 p. Or WaU **9487**

Single Tax Review.
Vancouver special number. New York, 1911. 80 p. plates, ports. (v. 11, no. 3, May-June 1911) WaS **9488**

Singstad, Ole.
Report to Washington Toll Bridge Authority on Cascade Mountains low level tunnel survey. New York, 1946. 57 p. illus., fold. maps, fold. tables, fold. diagrs.
WaS **9489**

Sinnett, C., see no. 2849.

Sinnott, Mrs. Percy, see no. 6908.

Sir George Simpson, K. B., centennial celebration, Fort St. James, 17th September 1928, unveiling of tablet, Simpson Pass on the high road from Banff to Windermere, B. C., 20th September 1928. [n.p., Hudson's Bay Company, 1928] 48 p. illus., ports. Contains addresses by Charles V. Sale, R. Randolph Bruce, Judge F. W. Howay, George W. Allan, T. C. Elliott.
CVicAr CVU OrHi WaS WaU **9490**

Sir William Wallace Benefit Society.
Constitution and by-laws. Victoria, B. C., Waterson, 1892. 15 p. CVicAr **9491**

Siringo, Charles A., 1855-1928.
A cowboy detective; a true story of twenty-two years with a world-famous detective agency, giving the inside facts of the bloody Coeur d'Alene labor riots and the many ups and downs of the author throughout the United States, Alaska, British Columbia and old Mexico, also exciting scenes among the moonshiners of Kentucky and Virginia. Chicago, W. B. Conkey, 1912. 519 p. front., 3 plates (1 double) 5 ports. (1 double)
IdB IdU MtHi MtU WaSp **9492**

Sisemore, Linsy C., 1869-   ed.
History of Klamath County, Oregon; its resources and its people, illus. Linsy Sisemore, editor-in-chief; Rachel Applegate Good, historian; Harry B. Schultz, managing director; Howard I. Schuyler, managing editor. Klamath Falls, Or., 1941. xix, 598 p. plates, ports.
Or OrCS OrP OrSaW OrU **9493**

A Sister of Charity, see no. 7480.

[**Sisters of Mercy,** Portland, Or.]
First report of the Jeanne d'Arc, Portland, Or., a residential hall for young women, 1920. Portland, Or. [n.d.] 15 p. front. (port.) illus., charts, tables. OrP **9494**

Twenty-fifth anniversary, Jeanne d'Arc, 1215 S. W. 14th Ave. [Portland, Or., 1944] [47] p. illus., ports. Or **9495**

Sisters of Notre Dame de Namur.
In harvest fields by sunset shores; the work of the Sisters of Notre Dame on the Pacific coast, by a member of the congregation; Diamond jubilee edition, 1851-1926. San Francisco, Gilmartin Co., 1926. 317, xxiii p. OrHi OrP **9496**

Sisters of the Good Shepherd in Montana.
Helena, Mont. H. B. Thurber [19—] 18 p. front., illus. MtHi **9497**

Sitting Bull, see nos. 2190-2192.

Skagit Steel & Iron Works.
Logging with Skagit. Sedro-Wooley, Wash., c1947. 1 v. illus. WaT **9498**

Skamania County Pioneer Printers.
Resources and advantages of Skamania County. Stevenson, Wash. [192—?] 12 p.
WaPS **9499**

Skarstedt, Ernst Teofil, 1857-1929.
Oregon och dess Svenska befolkning af Ernst Skarstedt, med en farglagd karta ofver Oregon, 98 portratt och 55 andra illustrationer. Seattle, Tryckt hos Wash. Printing Co., 1911. 219 p. front. (port.) illus., plates (maps)
OrHi OrP Wa WaS **9500**

Oregon och Washington; dessa staters historia, natur, resurser, folklif m. m. samt deras skandinaviska inbyggare; en handbok, med karta, ett 70-tal portratter och 50 andra illustrationer. Portland, Or., Brostrom & Skarstedts forlag, 1890. xiii, 332 p. front., illus., fold. plate, ports., fold. map. OrP OrU WaS WaU **9501**

Vagabond och redaktor; lefnadsoden och tidsbilder med forord af Jakob Bonggren, teckningar of Olof Grafstrom, portratter m. m. samt Titelplansch af G. N. Malm. Seattle, Washington Printing Company, 1914. 409 p. front., illus., ports.
OrP WaS WaU **9502**

Washington och dess svenska befolkning, mer en farglagd karta ofver Wash., 300 portratt och 87 andra illustrationer. Pa forf:s forlag **under** medverkan af F. W. Lonegren. Seattle, Washington Printing Company, 1908. 588 p. front. (port.) illus., double map.
OrHi Wa WaS WaSp WaT WaU **9503**

Sketches of mission life among the Indians of Oregon. New York, Carlton [c1854] 229 p. 5 plates.
CVicAr Or OrHi OrP WaU WaWW **9504**

Sketches of Washingtonians; containing brief histories of men of the state of Washington engaged in professional and political life, in manufacture, commerce, finance and religion; with a summary of the cities of the state containing upwards of 5,000 population; a reference volume of value to libraries, newspapers, magazines and colleges. 1907. Seattle, Wolfe, c1906. 320 p. map.
Or WaPS WaS WaSp WaT WaU **9505**

Skewton, Lavinia, Lady, pseud.
The "occasional paper"; one letter to the Lord Bishop of Columbia. 2d ed. Victoria, B. C., British Colonist, 1860. 7 p.
CVicAr **9506**

Skillern, Helen Regan.
Flames from a candle. Caldwell, Idaho, Caxton, 1938. 64 p. Poems. IdB **9507**

Skillman, Philip.
A living dead man; or, The strange case of Moses Scott; an accurate and truthful narrative of the complications caused by a litigant's return from the Lethean shore. Albany, N. Y., Albany Law Journal Co., 1897. 81 p. Washington setting.
Wa WaS WaU 9508

Skinner, Constance Lindsay, d. 1939.
Adventurers of Oregon; a chronicle of the fur trade. New Haven, Yale University Press, 1920. x, 290 p. (Chronicles of America series, v. 22. Extra-illus. ed.)
CVicAr OrPR 9509

Same. Text book ed.
OrCS WaS WaWW 9510

Same. Abraham Lincoln ed. Many 9511

Same. 1921.
IdIf MtBozC OrHi WaW 9512

Same. Text book ed.
IdUSB WaS WaU 9513

Same. Roosevelt ed. IdP WaTC 9514

Andy breaks trail. New York, Macmillan, 1944 [c1928] 199 p. illus. Lewis and Clark story. WaU 9515

Beavers, kings and cabins, with illus. by W. Langdon Kihn. New York, Macmillan, 1933. 272 p. illus., maps. Many 9516

Red man's luck, illus. by Caroline Gibbons Granger. Toronto, McClelland [c1930] 251 p. illus. CVicAr 9517

Red willows. New York, Coward-McCann, 1929. viii, 412 p. British Columbia story.
CVicAr Or WaT 9518

The search relentless. New York, Coward-McCann, 1928. vii, 311 p.
OrP WaE WaW 9519

Same. Toronto, McClelland, 1928.
CVicAr 9520

Songs of the coast dwellers. New York, Coward-McCann, 1930. ix, 85 p. Poems.
Many 9521

Skinner & Eddy Corporation, Seattle, Wash.
Souvenir of the launching of S. S. Editor in honor of the thirty-fourth annual convention of the National Editorial Association, Seattle, U. S. A., August 1919. [16] p. illus., ports. WaU 9522

Skookum Chuck, see no. 2146.

Skookum Packers' Association, Wenatchee, Wash.
The Skookum Injuns. [n.p., c1927] 16 p. illus. WaPS 9523

Same. [c1932] WaPS 9524

Sladen, Douglas Brooke Wheelton, 1856-
On the cars and off; being a journal of a pilgrimage along the Queen's highway to the east from Halifax in Nova Scotia to Victoria in Vancouver's Island, with additional matter on the Klondike by P. A. Hurd. London, Ward [n.d.] 512 p. illus., 19 plates. Or WaS 9525

Same. 1894. CVicAr WaT 9526

Same. 2d ed. 1895. xviii, 447 p. front., illus., 18 plates, maps.
CV CVic CVicAr CVU Or WaU 9527

Same. [1898] xviii, 512 p. front., illus., 18 plates, maps. CVicAr CVU 9528

Slater, John B.
Natural resources of Stevens County, Washington, and the famous mining region of Trail Creek, B. C. Spokane, Spokane Printing Co., 1895. 62 p. illus.
WaSp 9529

Slauson, Celeste, see no. 8060.

Slevin, Joseph Richard, 1881-
The amphibians of western North America; an account of the species known to inhabit California, Alaska, British Columbia, Washington, Oregon, Idaho, Utah, Nevada, Arizona, Sonora, and Lower California. San Francisco, California Academy of Sciences, 1928. 152 p. 23 plates. (Occasional papers 16)
CVU OrCS OrP OrU WaTC WaWW 9530

A handbook of reptiles and amphibians of the Pacific states, including certain eastern species; specially adapted for the use of the nature student. San Francisco, California Academy of Sciences, 1934. 73 p. front., illus., 10 plates.
Many 9531

Small, Floyd B.
Autobiography of a pioneer; being an account of the personal experiences of the author from 1867 to 1916. Seattle, 1916. 106 p. illus. Wa WaS 9532

Small, Hugh.
A home for the industrious of all nations; Oregon and her resources, from personal observation and investigation. San Francisco, A. L. Bancroft, 1872. 130 p. front. (fold. map) Many 9533

Small, Marie.
Four fares to Juneau, illus. by Erna Karolyi. New York, Whittlesey House [1947] 273 p. illus. Many 9534

Smalley, Anna Winston, see no. 7600.

Smead, William Henry, 1863-
Land of the Flatheads; a sketch of the Flathead Reservation, Montana; its past and present, its hopes and possibilities for the future. Missoula, Mont., Daily Missoulian, c1905. 144 p. illus., fold. map.
MtHi MtU WaT WaU 9535

Same. St. Paul, Pioneer Press, c1905. 142 p. front. Many 9536

Smet, Pierre Jean de, 1801-1873.
Cinquante nouvelles lettres du R. P. de Smet, de la Compagnie de Jesus et missionnaire en Amerique, pub. par Ed. Terwecoren de la meme compagnie. Paris, H. Casterman, 1858. ix, 502 p.
CVicAr MtU OrP 9537

Letters and sketches, with a narrative of a year's residence among the Indian tribes of the Rocky Mountains. Philadelphia, Fithian, 1843. 244 p. front., 11 plates (1 fold.) Many 9538

Lettres choisies du reverend pere Pierre Jean de Smet de la Compagnie de Jesus, missionaire aux Etats-Unis d'Amerique, 1849-1857. 3d ed., soigneusement rev. et cor. d'apres les manuscrits de l'auteur, augm. d'un portrait et de nouvelles notes. Bruxelles, Closson, 1875. viii, 405 p. front. (port.)
CVicAr OrHi OrU WaSp WaU 9539

Same. 2. serie, 1855-1861. 3. ed. 1876. x,
416 p.   CVicAr OrHi WaSp WaU   9540
Same. Bruxelles, Haenen, 1876.
CVicAr   9541
Same. 3. serie, 1860-1867. 3 ed. Bruxelles,
Closson, 1877. xi, 416 p
CVicAr OrHi WaSp WaU   9542
Same. 4. serie, 1867-1873. 3. ed. Bruxelles,
Closson, 1878. 408 p. CVicAr WaU   9543
Life, letters and travels of Father Pierre-
Jean de Smet, S. J., 1801-1873; missionary
labors and adventures among the wild
tribes of the North American Indians,
ed. from the original unpublished manu-
script journals and letter books and
from his printed works, with historical,
geographical, ethnological and other
notes; also a life of Father de Smet by
Hiram Martin Chittenden and Alfred
Talbot Richardson. New York, Harper,
1904. 4 v. fronts., 5 plates, 4 ports., fold.
map, 3 facsims.   Wa   9544
Same. 1905.   Many   9545
Missien van den Oregon en reizen naer de
Rotsbergen in de bronnen der Columbia
der Athabasca en Sascatshawin, in 1845-
46. Gent, Boek-an Steendrukkery van
Wwe Vander Schelden, 1849. 425 p.
front., 14 plates, 3 fold. maps.
Many   9546
Missions de l'Oregon et voyages aux
montagnes Rocheuses, aux sources de
la Colombie, de l'Athabasca et du Sas-
catshawin, en 1845-46. Gand, Schelden
[n.d.] 389 p. 15 plates.
CVicAr OrP WaS WaSp   9547
Same. [1848]
CVicAr CVU OrHi WaU   9548
Missions de l' Oregon et voyages dans les
Montagnes Rocheuses en 1845 et 1846;
ouvrage tr. de l'anglais par M. Bourlez.
Paris, Poussielgue-Rusand, 1848. 408 p.
CVicAr OrP WaU   9549
New Indian sketches. New York, Sadlier
[n.d.] 175 p.   OrHi OrSaW Wa   9550
Same. 1863. 175 p. front., plate. Many   9551
Same. [1865?]
CVicAr MtHi MtU WaS   9552
Same. [c1885]   OrP WaS   9553
Same. [c1886]   OrU   9554
Same. New York, Kennedy, 1895 [c1885]
MtU OrP WaU   9555
Oregon missions and travels over the
Rocky Mountains in 1845-46. New York,
E. Dunigan, 1847. 408 p. front., 13 plates,
ports., fold. map.   Many   9556
Viaggi alle Montagne Rocciose del P.
Pietro de Smet, tradotta dal francese da
Luigi Previte. Palermo, F. Lao, 1847.
xiv, 284 p. front. (port.) plates.
WaU   9557
Voyages aux montagnes Roucheuses, chez
les tribes indiennes du vaste territoire
de l'Oregon, dependant des Etats-Unis
d'Amerique. 5. ed. Lille. L. Lefort [n.d.]
239 p. front.   OrP   9558
Same. 1845. 268 p.   MtU OrHi WaU   9559
Same. 2. ed. 1850. 258 p.   CVicAr   9560

Same. 3. ed. 1856. 239 p. front.
CVicAr   9561
Same. 4. ed. 1859.   CVU OrU   9562
Same. 6. ed. 1875. 229 p. front.
CVicAr   9563
Same. 8. ed. 1887. 237 p. front.
CVicAr WaS   9564
Voyages aux montagnes Rocheuses et
sejour chez les tribus indienne de l'
Oregon (Etats-Unis). Nouvelle ed. rev.
et considerablement augm. Bruxelles, V.
Devaux, 1873. xxxv, 408 p. front. (port.)
plates, fold. map.
CVicAr CVU OrHi WaSp WaU   9565
Voyages aux montagnes Rocheuses et une
annee de sejour chez les tribus indiennes
du vaste territoire de l'Oregon, dependant des Etats-Unis d'Amerique. Malines,
P. J., Hanicq, 1844. 304 p. front. (port.)
plates, map.   OrHi WaU   9566
Voyages dans l'Amerique Septentrionale,
Oregon, par le R. pere P. J. de Smet,
de la Compagnie de Jesus. 3. ed. soig-
neusement cor. et augm. de notes, d'un
portrait et d'une carte. Bruxelles, Clos-
son, 1874, vii, 406 p. front. (port.) fold.
map.
CVicAr CVU WaU   9567
Western missions and missionaries; a
series of letters. New York, Kenedy
[n.d.] 532 p. front. (port.) CVicAr   9568
Same. [c1859]   Many   9569
Same. New York, Strong [c1859]
OrP   9570
Same. New York, J. B. Kirker, 1863 [c1859]
532 p. front. (port.)
CVic CVicAr OrP WaS WaU   9571
Same. New York, Strong [1870?]
CVicAr   9572
See also nos. 3004, 10228, 10229.
[Smiles, Samuel] Jr., 1877-
Round the world; including a residence in
Victoria and a journey by rail across
North America, by a Boy [pseud.] ed.
by Samuel Smiles. New York, Harper,
1872. 289 p. front., illus., maps.
CVicAr OrP   9573
Smith, A. A., see no. 5717.
[Smith, Amelie de Foufride] comp.
Oregon press and autograph souvenir,
comp. and dedicated to the National
Editorial Association [14th annual con-
vention] Portland, Or., C. H. Crocker
Press, 1899. [88] p. illus., ports,. map,
facsims.   OrHi OrP OrU   9574
Oregon's official roster [the volunteer
army of the U. S.] Portland, Or., Lewis
& Dryden [1898] 106 p. illus., ports.
OrHi OrU WaPS WaSp   8575
Same. 2d ed.   OrHi OrP WaU   9576
Smith, Arthur Maxson.
On to Alaska with Buchanan; building
citizenship. Los Angeles, Ward Ritchie
Press, 1937. xiii, 124 p. front., plates,
ports.   WaS WaU   9577
Smith, Bess Foster, comp.
Sunlit peaks; an anthology of Idaho verse.
Caldwell, Idaho, Caxton, 1931. 197 p.
Many   9578

Smith, Bradford H., see no. 9051.

Smith, Carl, 1877-
Behind the scenes at Salem, by Carl Smith and H. P. Edward; a synopsis of the twenty-sixth legislative session, with some inside facts gathered by two legislative correspondents. [Salem, Or., 1911?] 78 p. ports.
Or OrHi OrP OrU WaU **9579**

Smith, Charles Edward, 1838-1879.
From the deep of the sea, being the diary of the late Charles Edward Smith, surgeon of the whaleship Diana of Hull, ed. by his son, Charles Edward Smith Harris. London, Black, 1922. xii, 288 p. front., illus., plates, 2 maps (1 fold.)
CVU WaU **9580**

Smith, Charles Piper, 1877-
A distributional catalogue of the lupines of Oregon. Stanford University, California, Stanford University Press, 1927. 55 p. (Contributions from the Dudley Herbarium, v. 1, no. 1) Many **9581**

Smith, Charles Wesley, 1877-
Pacific Northwest Americana; a checklist of books and pamphlets relating to the history of the Pacific Northwest. Ed. 2, rev. and enl. New York, H. W. Wilson, 1921. xi, 329 p. First edition 1909. Washington state document. Many **9582**

Special collections in libraries of the Pacific Northwest. Seattle, University of Washington Press, 1927. 20 p.
Many **9583**

See also no. 7817.

Smith, Clareta Olmstead.
The trail leads west, sketches by Leta May Smith. Philadelphia, Dorrance [1946] 174 p. illus. Or WaT WaU **9584**

Smith, DeCost, 1864-1939.
Indian experiences, illus. with drawings and photographs by the author. Caldwell, Idaho, Caxton, 1943. 387 p. illus., plates, ports. Many **9585**

Smith, DeWolf.
Address delivered on the occasion of the celebration of the fiftieth anniversary of the introduction of Freemasonry into British Columbia, 14 December 1909. [n.p.,n.d.] 15 p. CVicAr **9586**

Smith, Sir Donald A., see no. 6198.

[Smith, Mrs. Eleanor C. (Hill)]
An octogenarian's reminiscences, by the author of Sir Rowland Hill, the story of a great reform. [Letchworth, Letchworth Printers, 1916] 131 p. CVicAr **9587**

Smith, Elijah.
In reply to statements published by Mr. Henry Villard, May 1889. [New York, 1889] 25 p. OrP **9588**

Smith, Elliott, 1868-
The land of lure, a story of the Columbia River Basin. Tacoma, Smith-Kinney Co., 1920. 242 p. plates.
OrHi OrP WaPS WaS WaSp WaU **9589**

Smith, Eugene E.
A federal-state-municipal cooperative police system. Portland, Or., Croyden Publishing Company, 1934. 26 p. OrP **9590**

Smith, Francis E.
Achievements of Captain Robert Gray. [Tacoma, 1922] [12] p. Anon. Many **9591**

Same. 2d ed. Tacoma, Barrett-Redfield [1923] 16 p. illus. Many **9592**

The great mountain of the Northwest; a true history. [Tacoma, Barrett-Redfield, 1924] 8 p.
CVicAr Or OrP OrU WaT WaU **9593**

Why the name Rainier should be removed from the mountain. Tacoma, 1923. [4] p.
CVicAr **9594**

Smith, Geddes, see no. 1935.

Smith, Harlan Ingersoll, 1872-
The archaeology of the Yakima Valley. New York, American Museum of Natural History, 1910. 171 p. illus., 16 plates, fold. map. (Anthropological papers, v. 6, pt. 1)
Many **9595**

Smith, Helen Krebs, ed.
With her own wings; historical sketches, reminiscences, and anecdotes of pioneer women; comp. by the Fine Arts Department of the Portland, Oregon Federation of Women's Organizations, illus. by Gladys Chilstrom. Portland, Or., Beattie and Co., c1948. 243 p. illus.
IdB OrHi OrP WaW **9596**

Smith, Helena Huntington, see nos. 1, 104.

Smith, Henry Badeley.
Vancouver water works. Montreal, John Lovell & Son, 1889. 80 p. 2 fold. plans, 3 fold. diagrs. CVU **9597**

Smith, Herndon, comp.
Centralia, the first fifty years, 1845-1900, from material written by students in her English classes at Centralia High School; photographs reproduced by Ivan G. Scates. Centralia, Wash., Pub. through cooperation of Daily Chronicle and F. H. Cole Printing Co. [1942] 1 v. front., plates (1 fold.) ports. Many **9598**

Smith, Horace, see no. 11057.

Smith, Hugh I.
Oregon McNary family; genealogy and historical sketches. Atlanta, Ga., 1938. 12 p. ports., map, chart, facsim.
OrHi OrP **9599**

Smith, J. C.
Some simple rhymes of leisure times, by Jay Cee. [pseud.] Port Townsend, Wash. [n.d.] 96 p. front. (port.) Wa **9600**

Smith, Jedediah Strong, 1798-1831.
The travels of Jedediah Smith; a documentary outline including the journal of the great American pathfinder, by Maurice S. Sullivan. Santa Ana, Calif., Fine Arts Press, 1934. 195 p. front., plates, ports., fold. map, facsims.
Many **9601**

See also nos. 2224, 2225.

Smith, Jessie Garden.
"Crosscuts", a story of the Pacific Northwest; a picturesque tide of life moving in and out of Vancouver, British Columbia. Portland, Or., Metropolitan, 1933. 217 p. front.
CVU WaPS WaU **9602**

Smith, John E.
Bethel, Polk County, Oregon. [Corvallis, Or., Gazette-Times] 1941. 70 p. illus., ports., plans.
Or OrCS OrHi OrP OrU WaU **9603**

Smith, John Jay, 1856-
Reminiscences of the life and travels of John Jay Smith of Seattle. [Seattle, 1941?] 41 p. WaU **9604**

Smith, Joseph, see no. 801.

Smith, Marian Wesley, 1907-
The Puyallup-Nisqually. New York, Columbia University Press, 1940. xii, 336 p. front., 6 plates, maps, diagr. (Contributions to anthropology, v. 32)
Many **9605**

Smith, Mrs. Maude Parson (Canfield), comp.
Alaska. Hartford, Church Missions Publishing Company, [1909]-1910. 89 p. (Missionary leaflet, ser. 6, 1-6) WaU **9606**

Smith, S., see no. 316.

Smith, Sidney.
The settler's new home; or, The emigrant's location, being a guide to emigrants in the selection of a settlement and the preliminary details of the voyage. London, J. Kendrick, 1849. 144 p.
CVicAr OrP **9607**

Smith, Mrs. Susan (Williamson)
The legend of Multnomah Falls. Portland, Or., Irwin-Hodson, 1905. 15 p. front. (port.) 6 plates.
OrHi OrP OrU Wa WaS WaU **9608**

Smith, W. H., see no. 5180.

Smith, Walker C.
The Everett massacre, a history of the class struggle in the lumber industry. Chicago, I. W. W. Pub. Bureau [n.d.] 302 p. illus., ports.
CVicAr WaE WaT **9609**

Same. [1917?] Wa **9610**

Same. [1918] OrU WaPS WaS WaU **9611**

Same. [1920?] Idu OrCS WaS WaTC **9612**

Was it murder? The truth about Centralia, Seattle, Northwest District Defense Committee, 1922. 48 p. WaU **9613**

Same. Centralia, Wash., Centralia Publicity Committee [1925] 47 p. WaPS **9614**

Same. Seattle, Washington Branch General Defense Committee, 1927. 48 p. illus.
WaT **9615**

Smith, Wallace, 1888?-1937.
Oregon sketches. New York, Putnam, 1925. xii, 247 p. front., 19 plates.
Many **9616**

Smith, Warren DuPre, 1880-1950.
The scenic treasure house of Oregon, blockprints by Nolan B. Zane. Portland, Or., Binfords & Mort [c1941] 176 p. illus., plates(part double, 1 col.) Many **9617**

A summary of the salient features of the geology of the Oregon Cascades, with some correlations between the geology of the east coast of Asia and that of the west coast of America. Salem, Or., 1918. 54 p. illus., plate, fold table. (University of Oregon Bulletin, n.s., v. 14, no. 16, Dec. 1917) Many **9618**

Smith, Wickliffe R.
Blades of bluegrass. Moscow, Idaho, North Idaho Star, 1900. 49 p. Poems. IdU **9619**

Smith, Wilfrid Robert, 1869-
Under the Northern Lights, by "Platinum Bill" [pseud.] illus. with fotografs by J. Doody. Portland, Or., Columbia Printing Co., c1916. 95 p. front., illus., plates.
Many **9620**

Smitham, Fanny, see no. 7874.

Smitter, Wessel, 1894-
Another morning. New York, Harper [c1941] 355 p. Alaska pioneer story.
Many **9621**

Smyth, Fred J.
Tales of the Kootenays, with historical sketches by the author and others. Cranbrook, B. C., Courier, 1938. 205 p. front., illus., ports.
CV CVicAr CVU OrCS WaSp **9622**

Same. 2d ed. with revisions. 1942. 200 p.
CVicAr MtHi WaS WaU **9623**

Smythe, F. S., see no. 10774.

Snell, Earl Wilcox, 1895-1947.
Address, Coos-Curry Pioneer Association. Coquille, Or., July 28, 1946. [n.p., 1946] 8 p. OrHi OrP **9624**

Snell, George Dixon.
And—if man triumph, illus. by Paul Clowes. Caldwell, Idaho, Caxton, c1938. 215 p. col. front., plates. Rocky Mountain story. IdB OrP WaE WaS **9625**

The great Adam, a novel. Caldwell, Idaho, Caxton, 1934. 449 p. Idaho novel.
IdB IdIf IdU WaPS WaSp WaU **9626**

Snell, Roy Judson, 1878-
Eskimo legends, with illus. by Florence J. Hoopes. Boston, Little, 1925. 203 p. col. front., illus., plates. WaS WaU **9627**
Same. 1926. Wa **9628**

Snelling, William Joseph, 1804-1848.
Tales of travel west of the Mississippi, by Solomon Bell [pseud.] Boston, Gray and Bowles, 1830. 162 p. front., illus., double map. CVicAr **9629**

William Joseph Snelling's Tales of the Northwest, with an introd. by John T. Flanagan. Minneapolis, University of Minnesota Press, 1936. xxix, 254 p.
Many **9630**

Sniffen, Matthew K.
The Indians of the Yukon and Tanana Valleys, Alaska, by Matthew K. Sniffen and Dr. Thos. Spees Carrington. Philadelphia, Indian Rights Association, 1914. 35 p. front., 4 plates.
MtHi OrP OrU WaS WaT WaU **9631**

Snodgrass, Richard, see no. 7154.

Snodgrass, Robert, see no. 9197.

Snohomish County Tribune.
Snohomish, "the garden city of Puget Sound"; her resources, industries, home attractions, climate and scenery. [Snohomish, Wash., 1901] 24 p. illus.
WaU **9632**

Snohomish Sun.
Special number [January 1891] [Snohomish, Wash., 1891] 16 p. illus., ports.
WaU **9633**

Snook, Harry James, see nos. 5276, 5277.

Snoqualmie Falls Lumber Company.
Snoqualmie Falls Lumber Company. [Seattle, Lumbermen's Printing Co., c1925] 47 p. illus., ports. WaPS **9634**

Snow, Henry James, 1848-
In forbidden seas; recollections of sea-otter hunting in the Kurils. London, E. Arnold, 1910. xiv, 303 p. front., plates, map. CVicAr CVU OrU WaU **9635**

Snow, William Parker, 1817-1895.
British Columbia, emigration and our colonies, considered practically, socially and politically. London, Stephenson and Spence, 1858. 108 p. CVicAr CVU **9636**

Voyage of the Prince Albert in search of Sir John Franklin; a narrative of every-day life in the Arctic seas. London, Longman, 1851. xvi, 416 p. col. front., col. plates, fold. map. CVicAr WaU **9637**

Snowden, Clinton A., 1847?-1922.
History of Washington; the rise and progress of an American state; advisory editors: Cornelius H. Hanford, Miles C. Moore, William D. Tyler, Stephen J. Chadwick. New York, Century History Co., 1909-1911. 6 v. fronts., plates, ports., maps. Voulmes 5 and 6 biographical.
OrHi Wa WaPS WaU **9638**

Same. v. 1-5. WaSp WaTC **9639**

Same. v. 1-4. Many **9640**

Social Science Research Council. Pacific Coast Regional Committee.
Agricultural labor in the Pacific Coast states; a bibliography and suggestions for research. [n.p., 1938] 64 p.
OrCS OrU **9641**

Projects and source materials in social statistics, Pacific Coast; comp. by Sub-committee on Social Statistics, Calvin F. Schmid, chairman. Berkeley, Calif., Giannini Foundation, University of California, 1944. iii, 52 p.
OrP WaS WaU **9642**

Society of Jesus.
Parakigma verbi activi; lingua Numpu, vulgo Nez-perce; studio P. P. Missionariorum S. J. in Montibus Saxosis. Desmet, Idaho, 1888. 56 p. WaU **9643**

Society of Mayflower Descendants in Washington.
The Society of Mayflower Descendants in the state of Washington, organized 1912. [n.p.] 1929. 35 p. WaU **9644**

Society of the Sisters of the Holy Names of Jesus and Mary, Oregon.
Gleanings of fifty years; the Sisters of the Holy Names of Jesus and Mary in the Northwest, 1859-1909. [Portland, Or., Glass & Prudhomme, 1909] xvi, 230 p. front., plates, ports. Many **9645**

Une soeur de la Providence, see no. 5626.

Soeurs de Notre-Dame, see no. 7483.

Sola, A. E. Ironmonger, 1868-
Klondyke; truth and facts of the new El Dorado. London, Mining and Geographical Institute [1897] 102 p. front. (port.) 21 plates, 3 maps. Many **9646**

Soliday, George W., 1869-
A priced and descriptive checklist together with short title index, describing almost 7500 items of western Americana comprising books, maps and pamphlets of the important library (in four parts) formed by George W. Soliday, Seattle, Wash. New York, Peter Decker, 1940-1945. 5 v. in 1. plate (v. 3) (Catalogues 17-21 of Peter Decker) Many **9646a**

Solly, Cecil.
Growing fine roses; beautiful roses in plenty may be grown all summer long in this rose garden of America. [Seattle, c1942] 23 p. illus. Wa **9647**

Growing fruit trees; how to choose, plant and care for fruit trees in the Pacific Northwest. [Seattle, c1942] 23 p. illus.
Wa **9648**

Growing good berries; heavy crops of luscious berries year after year are simple and easy in this Pacific Northwest. [Seattle, c1942] 23 p. illus. Wa **9649**

Growing vegetables in the Pacific Northwest. [n.p., n.d. 128 p. illus., charts.
OrP WaT **9650**

Same. [La Conner, Wash., Puget Sound Seed Co., 1943] 128 p. illus.
CVU Wa WaS **9651**

Same. 2d ed. rev. [Seattle, 1944] 144 p. illus., diagrs. CV CVU OrP WaS **9652**

A perfect turf; how to plant a lawn and maintain a perfect turf in the Pacific Northwest. Seattle [c1942] 15 p. illus.
Or Wa WaS **9653**

Solomon Bell, see no. 9629.

Some account of the Tahkaht language as spoken by several tribes on the western coast of Vancouver Island. London, Hatchard and Co., 1868. 80 p.
CVicAr WaU **9645**

Some British Columbians, 1914-1918. [Victoria, B. C.? 1921?] 121 plates. CVU **9655**

Somerset, Henry Charles Somers Augustus.
The land of the muskeg, with a preface by A. Hungerford Pollen; with one hundred and ten illus. from sketches by A. H. Pollen and instantaneous photographs and four maps. London, Heinemann, 1895. xxxi, 248 p. front. (port.) illus., 4 maps (2 fold.)
CV CVicAr CVU WaU **9656**

Same. 2d ed. CVicAr **9657**

Somerset, Susan Margaret (McKinnon)
Saint Maur, Duchess of.
Impressions of a tenderfoot during a journey in search of sport in the far West. London, Murray, 1890. xv, 279 p. front., 6 plates, fold. map. Many **9658**

Somerville, Thomas.
Oration delivered at the inauguration of the new Masonic Hall on Government Street, Victoria, Vancouver Island, on Monday, 25th June, A. D. 1866. [Victoria, B. C.] Colonist & Chronicle [1866] 9 p.
CVicAr **9659**

Sons of Temperance of North America. Grand Division of Oregon.
Constitution, by-laws, rules of order and

principles of discipline, instituted Jan. 15, 1856. Salem, Or., Advocate, 1856. [27] p. OrHi OrU **9660**

—— —— **Multnomah Division No. 1.**
Constitution [as amended June 1854] by-laws and rules of order. Portland, Or., Carter & Austin, 1856. 32 p. OrU **9661**

—— —— **No. 8**
Constitution, by-laws and rules or order. Portland, Or., Carter, 1856. 32 p. OrHi **9662**

Sons of the American Revolution. Washington Society.
Constitution and by-laws of the Washington Society, Sons of the American Revolution, October 1895. Seattle, Lowman & Hanford, 1895. 20 p. WaS WaU **9663**

Register of the Washington Society, Sons of the American Revolution, 1895-1900. [Seattle, 1900] lxxx, 98 p. front., plates, ports. OrU Wa WaS WaT WaU **9664**

Register of the Washington State Society, Sons of the American Revolution, June 17, 1895; April 19, 1916. [Seattle, 1917] 216 p. front., plates, ports. Many **9665**

The Washington State Society of the Sons of the American Revolution; publication committee: Augustus V. Bell, Will H. Thompson, Walter Burgess Beals. Seattle, Lowman & Hanford, 1906. 25 p. port. Wa WaS **9666**

Sorby, Thomas C.
The harbour and city of Victoria, the port of Vancouver Island, British Columbia, 1916. [Victoria, B. C., Victoria Printing and Publishing Company, c1917] 54 p. illus., fold. plate, map, plan. CVU **9667**

List of docks, wharves, shipyards, marine railways and other facilities for repairing ships in the port of Victoria, British Columbia. [Victoria, B. C., Cusack Press] 1919. 27 p. illus. CVicAr **9668**

Sorensen, Chester J.
Sorensen log rule, cubic foot volume; Scribner scale on short logs; Spaulding log rule; British Columbia rule. Redmond, Wash., Log Scalers Supply Co. [c1940] 24 p. OrCS **9669**

Soule, Sidney Howard, 1849-
The Rand-McNally guide to the great Northwest; containing information regarding the states of Montana, Idaho, Washington, Oregon, Minnesota, North Dakota, Alaska, also western Canada and British Columbia, with a description of the route along the Chicago & Northwestern, Union Pacific, Oregon Short Line, and Oregon River and Navigation Co. railways. Chicago, Rand McNally [c1903] 365 p. front., illus., map.
Many **9670**

Soulie, Emile.
Les gisements de metaux precieux des etats et des territoires de Pacifique (Etats-Unis). Paris, Eugene Lacroix, 1866. 80 p. map. OrU **9671**

Sound, Gilbert Q. le, see no. 5865.

South Bend Journal.
Pacific County and its resources. South

Bend, Wash. [1909?] [72] p. illus., ports., map. OrU **9672**

Same. [1910?] WaS **9673**

Pacific County edition. South Bend, Wash., 1900. [26] p. illus., ports. (Supplement to Nov. 9, 1900 issue) WaU **9674**

South Tacoma Star.
Tacoma who's who. South Tacoma, 1929. 267 p. WaS WaT WaTC **9675**

Southern Magazine.
Washington number. [Wytheville, Va., 1937?] 48 p. illus. (v. 3, no. 7, Feb.-Mar., 1937?) WaS WaSp WaU **9676**

Southern Pacific Company.
Camping, fishing and hunting. Portland, Or. [1918?] 54 p. illus. Or **9677**

Corvallis and Benton County, Oregon. [Portland, Or., James, 1912] 32 p. illus. OrHi **9678**

Crater Lake, Oregon mountain playground. [n.p., n.d.] 13 p. illus. OrU **9679**

Same. [c1916] 15 p. illus., maps. WaPS **9680**

How to get to Grants Pass, Oregon. [Portland, Or., 1909?] 9 p. illus., map. WaPS **9681**

How to get to Medford, Oregon. [Portland, Or., 1908] 8 p. illus., map. WaPS **9682**

How to see the whole Pacific Coast. [San Francisco? 193-?] 14 p. illus., maps. WaPS **9683**

Oregon. 2d ed. [Portland, Or., 1915?] 46 p. illus., map. OrP **9684**

Oregon for the settlers. Portland, Or. [n.d.] 64 p. illus., map. OrSa OrU **9685**

Same. [1914?] 62 p. Or OrP **9686**

Same. [1916] 63 p. Or OrHi OrP **9687**

Same. [1919?] Or OrCS OrHi OrP **9688**

Same. [1923?] 64 p. Or OrP **9689**

Same. [1924?] WaU **9690**

Same. [1926] OrP **9691**

Oregon outdoors. [Portland, Or., n. d.] 62 p. illus. Or **9692**

Same. [1926?] [14] p. illus., map. OrP **9693**

Same. [c1930] OrP **9694**

Same. [c1933] OrP **9695**

Vacation days in Oregon. [San Francisco, 1912?] 40 p. illus., map. Or WaPS **9696**

Southwestern Washington Development Association.
Southwestern Washington. St. Paul, N. P. Railway, 1911. 60 p. front., illus., maps. WaPS **9697**

Southwestern Washington Hotel Men's Association.
The key to southwestern Washington. [Tacoma, c1926] 15 p. illus. map. WaPS **9698**

Southwestern Washington, its topography, climate, resources, productions, manufacturing advantages, wealth and growth, with illus. reviews of the principal cities and towns and pen sketches of their representative business men; also biographical sketches of prominent state, county and municipal officials. Olympia, Wash., Pacific Publishing Company, 1890. 224 p. illus. Wa **9699**

Souvenir album of Kamloops. [n.p., Montana Novelty Manufacturing & Art Printing Co., n.d.] 23 plates. CVicAr **9700**

Souvenir album of the great West. [Columbus, Ohio, Ward Brothers, c1889] 25 p. illus. WaU **9701**

Souvenir booklet of the Grand Coulee Dam. [Spokane, Shaw & Borden, c1935] 8 p. illus., map. WaE **9702**

Souvenir, British Columbia. [n.p., n.d.] 1 v. plates. CVicAr **9703**

Same. [1885?] 16 photos. WaU **9704**

A souvenir devoted to Seattle and its environs; metropolitan Seattle, illus. by Glenn A. Dustin. Seattle, National Souvenir Co., 1902. [76] p. plates (1 fold.) WaS WaU **9705**

Souvenir history, 1st U. S. Infantry. [Camp Lewis, Wash., 1918] [28] p. illus., ports. WaU **9706**

Souvenir, jubilee of introduction of Presbyterianism into British Columbia and the organization of the First Presbyterian Church, Victoria, B. C. [Waterson Press] 1911. 17 p. illus., ports. CVicAr **9707**

Souvenir, New Westminster Bridge, official opening July 23, 1904. [n.p.] 1904. [8] p. plates. CVicAr **9708**

Souvenir or Seattle, Wash. Seattle, Lowman & Hanford [c1890] 12 plates. WaU **9709**

Souvenir of the twenty-fifth anniversary of the Methodist Church, Trail, B. C. Trail, B. C., 1922. 21 p. illus., ports. CVicAr **9710**

Souvenir programme; Indian potlatch, Fort Langley, B. C., 1947. [New Westminster, B. C., Jackson Printing Co., n.d.] [24] p. illus., ports. CVicAr **9711**

[Spalding Mission] Etshiit thlu sitskai thlusiais thlu sitskaisitlinish. Lapwai, Idaho [Mission Press] 1842. 16 p. 3 woodcuts. Indian primer in Spokane dialect. OrHi (p. 1-4, photostat; p. 5-8) WaU (Photostat) **9712**

Nez Perces first book, designed for children and new beginners. Clearwater, Idaho, Mission Press, 1839. 8 p. illus. Photostat copy. OrHi WaU **9713**

Same. Rev. ed. 20 p. illus. Photostat copy. WaU **9714**

Nez Perces reader; numipuain shapahitamanash timash; ma hiwash naks ka watu timash hisukuatipaswisha? Lapwai, Idaho, 1840. 52 p. Photostat copy. OrHi WaU **9715**

Nez-Perces spelling book, with scripture cuts explained; numepu spdlin temis, wo prpl kfts wo imashno kfts. Honolulu, 1839. 2 L. Photostat copies of title-page and 1 p., "Key to the alphabet". OrHi WaU **9716**

Shapahitamanash suyapu timtki. Lapwai, Idaho [Mission Press] 1845. 24 p. front. (calendar) Photostat copy. OrHi WaU **9717**

Talapusapaiain wanipt timas. Lapwai, Idaho, 1842. 32 p. OrHi WaU (Photostat) **9718**

Wilupupki. Lapwai, Idaho, 1842. 8 p. Photostat copy. OrHi WaU **9719**

See also nos. 388, 814-816, 8353.

Spalding, Jesse, see no. 10423.

Sparks, Jared, 1789-1866.
Leben des beruhmten Amerikanischen reisenden John Ledyard, des Begleiters von Cook; nach seinen Tagebuchern und seinem Briefwechsel dargestellt von Jared Sparks; aus den Englischen von D. E. F. Michaelis. Leipzig, J. C. Hinrichssche Buchhandlung, 1829. x, 350 p. front. WaU **9720**

The life of John Ledyard, the American traveller; comprising selections from his journals and correspondence. Cambridge, Mass., Hilliard and Brown, 1828. xii, 235 p. Many **9721**

Same. 2d ed. 1829. xi, 310 p. Many **9722**

Same. Boston, Little, 1847. x, 419 p. (Library of American biography. 2d ser., v. 14) WaU **9723**

Memoirs of the life and travels of John Ledyard, from his journals and correspondence. London, H. Colburn, 1828. 428 p. CVicAr WaU **9724**

Same. xii, 428 p. CV CVicAr MtHi OrHi WaS WaU **9725**

Travels and adventures of John Ledyard comprising his voyage with Capt. Cook's third and last expedition; his journey on foot 1300 miles round the Gulf of Bothnia to St. Petersburgh; his adventures and residence in Siberia; and his exploratory mission to Africa. 2d ed. London, H. Colburn, 1834. xii, 428 p. Anon. CVU OrP WaS WaU **9726**

Sparrmann, Anders, see no. 10463.

Sparshott, Edward Charles, d. 1867, comp.
A military manual of infantry drill including the manual and platoon exercises designed for the use of the officers and privates of the volunteer forces of Vancouver Island and British Columbia. [n.p.] 1861. viii, 103 p. CVicAr **9727**

Spaulding, Henry Harmon, see nos. 388, 814-818, 8353, 9712-9719.

Special Industries Committee of Grays Harbor.
Available pulp timber of the Columbia River, Puget Sound and Grays Harbor districts, and wood use of the United States, from a survey made by W. C. Munaw. [Aberdeen, Wash., 1936] [52] p. WaU **9728**

Spectator, Portland, Or.
Christmas number. Portland, Or., 1924. 58 p. illus. (Dec. 20, 1924) WaU **9729**

Spectator, Seattle, Wash.
1891 holiday number; the Seattle Spectator. Seattle, 1891. 28 p. illus. (Special no., v. 2, no. 3, Dec. 26, 1891) WaU **9730**

Spencer, Arthur C.
Address delivered to Portland Ad Club, July 5, 1922. on "The Southern Pacific-Central Pacific dissolution case and its

bearing on Oregon transportation". [n.p., 1922] 8 p. Or OrP **9731**

What does it mean to you as a citizen of Oregon? Central Pacific-Southern Pacific unmerger and its relation to Oregon transportation and development. Portland, Or. [1922?] 19 p. fold. map.
OrP **9732**

[Spencer, David, Ltd.]
Spencer's information. Vancouver, B. C., 1945. 32 p. illus., fold. plate, ports.
CVicAr **9733**

Spencer, Lloyd, see no. 8208.

Spender, Richard C., see nos. 571-573.

Sperlin, Ottis Bedney, 1878-
The heart of the Skyloo. Portland, Or., Metropolitan, 1934. 344 p. Many **9734**
See also no. 7929.

Sperry, Albert Lewis, 1873-
Avalanche. [Discovery of Sperry Glacier, Glacier National Park] Boston, Christopher Publishing House [c1938] 166 p. front., 24 plates.
MtUM Or OrP WaS WaT **9735**

Sperry, Armstrong, 1897-
No brighter glory. New York, Macmillan, 1942. 429 p. Columbia River setting.
Many **9736**

Spicer, George Washington, 1897-
The constitutional status and government of Alaska. Baltimore, Johns Hopkins Press, 1927. ix, 121 p. (Studies in historical and political science, ser. 45, no. 4) MtU WaPS WaS WaU **9737**

Spier, Leslie, 1893-
Klamath enthnography. Berkeley, Calif., University of California Press, 1930. 338 p. illus., fold. map. (Publications in American archaeology and ethnology, v. 30)
CVicAr Or OrHi OrP OrU WaT **9738**

The prophet dance of the Northwest and its derivatives; the source of the ghost dance. Menasha, Wis., George Banta Publishing Company, 1935. 74 p. illus. (General series in anthropology, no. 1)
Many **9739**

The Sinkaietk or Southern Okanagon of Washington by Walter Cline, Rachel S. Commons, May Mandelbaum, and others, ed. by Leslie Spier. Menasha, Wis., George Banta Publishing Company, 1938. 262 p. illus. (General series in anthropology, no 6) Many **9740**

Tribal distribution in Washington. Menasha, Wis., George Banta Publishing Co., 1936. 43 p. maps. (General series in anthropology, no. 3) Many **9741**

Spike, W. D. C., & Co.
Spike's illustrated description of the city of Tacoma, 1891. 12 p. front., 15 plates.
WaS WaT WaU WaWW **9742**

Spinden, H. J., see no. 899.

Spinks, William Ward.
Tales of the British Columbia frontier, illus. by Edith MacLaren. Toronto, Ryerson [1933] ix, 134 p. front. (map) illus., ports. Many **9743**

Spiritualists Association. Oregon.
Principles, constitution and by-laws; or-

ganized July 9, 1902. Portland, Or., 1902. 16 p. OrHi **9744**

Splawn, Andrew Jackson, 1845-1917.
Ka-mi-akin, the last hero of the Yakimas. [Portland, Or., Kilham Stationery & Printing Co., c1917] 436 p. front. (port.) illus., ports. Many **9745**
Same. 2d ed. [Portland, Or.] Binfords & Mort, 1944. xv, 500 p. front., illus., ports.
Many **9746**
Same. 3d ed. OrHi WaS **9747**

Splitstone, Fred John, 1876-
Orcas, gem of the San Juans. Sedro-Woolley, Wash., Courier-Times Press, 1946. xi, 109 p. front. (map) illus.
OrHi Wa WaE WaS WaT WaU **9748**

Spokane, Wash. Cathedral of St. John the Evangelist.
The Cathedral chimes. Spokane, 1936. 1 v.
WaPS **9749**

——— First Federal Savings and Loan Association.
Mural in the lobby of First Federal Savings and Loan Association by Bertha Ballou: Spokane House (1810-1826). [Spokane, C. W. Hill Printing Co., 1948?] 1 v. illus. WaSp **9750**

——— First Presbyterian Church.
Fiftieth anniversary of the First Presbyterian Church, Spokane, June 11, 12, 1933. [Spokane?] 1933. 12 p. WaPS **9751**

——— Grace Baptist Church.
Golden jubilee anniversary history of Grace Baptist Church, 1890-1940. [n.p., n.d.] 112 [86] vii p. illus., ports.
WaSp **9752**

——— Methodist Episcopal Church.
Souvenir; silver jubilee, Nov. 4, 1900. [n.p., 1900?] 84 p. illus. WaTC **9753**

——— **Northwestern Industrial Exposition,** 1890.
The city of Spokane Falls and its tributary resources, issued by the Northwestern Industrial Exposition, Spokane Falls, Wash., October 1st to November 1st, 1890. Buffalo, Matthews, Northrup & Co., 1890. 56 p. illus., ports., maps.
IdU Or WaPS WaS WaSp WaU **9754**

——— St. Luke's Hospital.
The greater St. Luke's Hospital. [Spokane, 1939?] 12 p. illus. WaPS **9755**

——— Westminster Congregational Church.
The first fifty years, Westminster Congregational Church, 1879-1929, by the Westminster daughters through Mary Knox Pope, Mary Lou Benson, and others. Spokane, Empire Printing Company, 1929. 96 p. front., plates, ports.
WaPS WaSp **9756**

Spokane & Eastern Trust Company, Spokane, Wash.
Expense record. Spokane [1923?] [32] p.
WaPS **9757**

Spokane & Inland Empire, Inc.
Come to the land of many lakes—Spokane and the Inland Empire of the Pacific Northwest. [Spokane, 192-?] 18 p. illus., maps. WaPS **9758**

Spokane and Inland Empire Railroad Company.
Fruit growing in eastern Washington; designed and written by the Department of Publicity, Inland Empire System. Spokane [n.d.] 16 p. col. front., illus., map.   WaSp **9759**

Spokane Bank for Cooperatives.
Financing farmers' cooperative associations, 1933-1943. Spokane, Farm Credit Administration [n.d.] 52 p. illus.
                                            OrCS **9760**

Spokane County Horticultural Society.
"The story", not only of the land of promise, but of the land of fulfillment. [Spokane? 1911?] 19 p. illus. WaPS **9761**

Spokane Daily Chronicle.
Coulee Dam special edition on the occasion of President Roosevelt's visit at the dam and at Spokane. Spokane, 1935. 18 p. (48th year, no. 273, Aug. 4, 1934)
                                            WaPS **9762**

Golden jubilee. Spokane, 1936. [28] p. illus., maps (part col.). (May 23, 1936, secs. 2, 3)   WaPS **9763**

Spokane-Pend d'Oreille Rapid Transit Co.
Prospectus of the Spokane-Pend d'Oreille Rapid Transit Co. [Spokane? 1906?] [16] p. plates, fold. map. WaPS WaSp **9764**

Spokane, Portland, and Seattle Railway.
Along the Columbia River to the sea. [n.p., n.d.] 42 p. illus.   Or OrU WaSp **9765**

Same. [Portland, Or.? 1916?] [40] p. illus., map.   WaPS **9766**

Clatsop Beach, Pacific Ocean, Oregon; outings in the Pacific Northwest. Portland, Or. [1916] 28 p. illus.   WaPS **9767**

Oregon. [n.p., 1931] 36 p. illus., map, tables.   OrP **9768**

Same. [Portland, Or., n.d.]   OrSa **9769**

Oregon and Washington. [n.p., n.d.] 48 p. illus., maps.   OrP **9770**

Same. Portland, Or. [1912?]   WaPS **9771**

Oregon sea coast resorts. [n.p., n.d.] 28 p.   WaPS **9772**

The scenic Columbia River through the Cascade Mountains to the Pacific. [Portland, Or., 1929?] [15] p. illus., col. map.
                                            WaPS **9773**

Spokane, the city beautiful; a souvenir of Spokane, Washington and the Inland Empire. Spokane, G. W. Jones [1907?] 62 p. illus.   WaS **9774**

Spokane United Railways.
Parks and scenic spots reached by Spokane United Railways. [Spokane, n.d.] [8] p. illus.   WaPS **9775**

Spokesman-Review.
[About Washington, the Evergreen State] Spokane, 1925. 24 p. illus. (42d year, no. 246, Jan. 15, 1925)   WaPS **9776**

Golden anniversary edition. Spokane, 1933. 1 v. illus., maps. (51st year, no. 69, July 22, 1933)   WaPS WaSp WaU **9777**

Market facts about the Spokane country and the Pacific Northwest, comp. by the Spokesman Review and Spokane Daily Chronicle. [Spokane, c1934] 52 p. illus., maps, tables.   WaU **9778**

1947 progress edition. Spokane, 1947. 1 v. illus. (part. col.) ports. (64th year, no. 257, Jan. 26, 1947)   WaU **9779**

Owning and operating an automobile in Washington; new 1933 law. [Spokane?] 1933. 11 p.   WaPS **9780**

A race for empire and other true tales of the Northwest. Spokane, 1896. 48 p. front., illus.
Or Wa WaS WaSp WaU WaWW **9781**

The Spokane market. Spokane, Spokesman-Review and Spokane Daily Chronicle [1944] 70 p. illus., maps (part col.)
                                            WaU **9782**

[25]th anniversary number. Spokane, 1909. [92] p. illus. (v. 27, no. 2, June 17, 1909)
                                            WaSp **9783**

Vacation guide to the evergreen playground; week end motor trips, by the Spokesman-Review and Spokane Daily Chronicle. Spokane, 1932. [6] p. illus., map.   WaPS **9784**

Spotts, David L., 1848-
Campaigning with Custer and the Nineteenth Kansas Volunteer Cavalry on the Washita campaign, 1868-'69, comprising his daily diary of thrilling events on the winter campaign against the hostile Cheyennes, Kiowas and Comanches; ed. and arranged for publication by E. A. Brininstool. Los Angeles, Wetzel Publishing Company, 1928. 215 p. front.. plates, ports., map.
                          MtHi WaSp WaU **9785**

Sprague, Charles A.
History of Adams County in the World War. Ritzville, Wash., Journal-Times, 1920. 86 p. illus., ports. WaTC WaU **9786**

Sprague Charles Arthur, 1887-
The Willamette Highway and Oregon's highway system; address on occasion dedication Willamette Highway, July 30, 1940. [n.p., 1940] 16 p.   OrP **9787**

Sprague, William Cyrus, 1860-1922.
Boy pathfinder; a story of the Oregon Trail, illus. by A. B. Shute. Boston, Lee and Shepard [1905] vi, 316 p. front., 7 plates. (Making of a nation ser.)
OrAshS OrHi OrLgE OrMonO
                                       OrP OrU **9788**

Sprague, William Forrest.
Women and the West, a short social history. Boston, Christopher Publishing House [c1940] 294 p. front., plates.
                          OrCS WaPS WaU **9789**

Sprengel, M. C., see no. 10459.

Sproat, Gilbert Malcolm, 1834-1913.
Memorandum on Indian reserves in the district of Yale. Victoria, B. C., Colonist Steam Presses, 1878. 15 p. CVicAr **9790**
"Mr. Jones and the fribble". [n.p., n.d.] 38 p.   CVicAr **9791**

Scenes and studies of savage life. London, Smith, Elder, 1868. xii, 317 p. front.
                                          Many **9792**

Sproule, James A.
Tahoma; or, Random readings from Puget Sound. Tacoma [n.d.] 80 p. illus., 2 ports.
                                  OrCS WaT **9793**

Sproule, William.
Southern Pacific's position in the Oregon-California land controversy. [n.p., n.d.] 4 p. OrP 9794

Spruce helped win the war; a portrayal of the personnel, railroad construction, timber cutting and shipping, camp life and kindred subjects necessary to the production of airplane spruce in unlimited quantities for the United States and her allies. Portland, Or., Prentiss, c1918. 32 p. plates, ports. OrHi 9795

Spurr, Josiah Edward, 1870-
Through the Yukon gold diggings; a narrative of personal travel. Boston, Eastern Publishing Company, 1900. 276 p. front., illus. CVicAr CVU OrP WaS WaT WaU 9796

Squier, Emma-Lindsay, 1892-
Children of the twilight; folk-tales of Indian tribes. New York, Cosmopolitan Book Corporation, 1926. 257 p. Lore of Twana Tyee of Puget Sound country. OrP Wa WaS WaSp WaTC WaU 9797

The wild heart, with an introd. by Gene Stratton Porter, illus. and decorations by Paul Bransom. New York, Cosmopolitan Book Corporation, 1922. 220 p. illus. Puget Sound setting. WaE WaS WaSp WaT WaU 9798

Staatsverband Deutschsprechendervereine von Oregon.
Oregon und sein Deutschtum, eine Geschichte des Staates, dessen Deutscher Pioniere und ihrer Nachkommen. Portland, Or., 1920. vi, 516 p. ports. OrP 9799

[Stacy, James N.]
Sage of Waha; the mountain gem humorist on land and on sea, by Uncle Jim [pseud.] Portland, Or., White & Dunham, 1902. 205 [48] p. front., illus., plates, ports. Many 9800

Staehlin von Storcksburg, 1710-1785.
An account of the new northern archipelago, lately discovered by the Russians in the seas of Kamtschatka and Anadir, by Mr. J. von Staehlin, trans. from the German original by C. Heydinger, rev. by Matthew Maty. London, C. Heydinger, 1774. 20, 118 p. front. (fold. map) CVicAr OrP WaS WaU 9801

Das von den Russen in den Jahren 1765, 66, 67 entdeckte nordliche Inselmeer, zwischen Kamtschatka und Nordamerika. Stuttgart, Christoph Friedrich Cotta, 1774. 40 p. fold. map. CVicAr WaU 9802

Relation du nouvel archipel septentrional, decouvert depuis peu par les Russes dans les mers de Kamtschaka & d'Anadir, tr. en anglois de l'original allemand, & de l'anglois en francois. [London, Du museum Britannique, 1774] 96 p. WaU 9803

Staffelbach, Elmer Hubert, 1893-
Towards Oregon, with illus. by Charles Hargens. Philadelphia, Macrae-Smith-Company [1946] 353 p. illus. Many 9804

Stafford, Geoffrey Wardle, see no. 2642.

Stafford, Orin Fletcher, 1873-
Feasibility of electrochemical industries at The Dalles, Or. [n.p., 1914?] 13 p. illus. OrP WaPS 9805

Stallings, Frances Osborne, see no. 2024.

Standard Oil Company of California.
Landing fields of the Pacific West. 5th ed. [San Francisco, 1931] 99 p. illus., maps. OrP WaPS WaS 9806

Standing Bear, see no. 7126.

Stanley, Edwin James, 1848-1919.
Life of Rev. L. B. Stateler; or, Sixty-five years on the frontier, containing incidents, anecdotes, and sketches of Methodist history in the West and North-west, introd. by Bishop E. R. Hendrix, illus. by E. S. Paxson. Nashville, Publishing House of M. E. Church South, 1907. xvii, 356 p. front., illus. IdB MtBozC MtHi OrP WaPS 9807

Same. Rev. ed. 1916. IdU MtU OrP WaSp 9808

Stanley, George Francis Gilman.
The birth of Western Canada; a history of the Riel Rebellions. Toronto, Longmans, c1936. xiv, 475 p. front. (port.) 5 plates, 7 ports., 5 maps. CVicAr CVU MtHi WaA WaS 9809

Stanley, Hiram Alonzo, 1859-
Rex Wayland's fortune; or, The secret of the Thunderbird. Chicago, Laird & Lee [c1898] 391 p. front., illus. WaPS WaS WaU WaWW 9810

Stanley, Reva, see no. 9169.

Stanley, William M.
A mile of gold; strange adventures on the Yukon, illus. with views taken on the spot. Chicago, Laird & Lee, 1898. 219 p. front., plates. (Pastime series, no. 60) CVicAr CVU OrP WaU 9811

Stannard, M.
Memoirs of a professional lady nurse. London, Simpkin, Marshall & Co., 1873. viii, 239 p. front., illus. British Columbia descriptions. CVicAr CVU WaS WaSp 9812

Stanolind Record.
Billings edition. Chicago, Standard Oil Co., 1931. 72 p. illus. (v. 12, no. 3, Jan. 1931) MtBozC MtU 9813

Stansbury, Charles Frederick, 1854-1922.
Klondike, the land of gold, illustrated; containing all available practical information of every description concerning the new gold fields, what they are and how to reach them, a short history of Alaska, a synopsis of the personal testimony of miners who have been on the ground, a digest of the mining laws of the United States and Canada, the latest authentic maps, with a review of the famous gold rushes of the world. New York, F. T. Neely, 1897. 190 p. illus., plates, maps. (Neely's popular library, no. 96) CVU WaS WaU 9814

Stanton, Karoline.
Sequence; a collection of verse. Seattle, Lowman & Hanford, 1937. 83 p. WaS WaU 9815

Stanton, Stephen Berrien.
The Behring Sea dispute. New York, A. B. King [1889] 58 p.   CV OrU **9816**

Stanwell-Fletcher, Theodora Morris (Cope) 1906-
Driftwood Valley; animal sketches by John F. Stanwell-Fletcher. Boston, Little, 1946. ix, 384 p. illus., plates, map.
Many **9817**

Same. 1947 [c1946]   OrU **9818**

Stanwood Tidings.
Achievement number [commemorating the 50th anniversary of Stanwood, telling the animated story of progress and exploiting the industries and resources of the Stillaguamish Valley] Stanwood, Wash., 1916. [28] p. illus. (v. 14, no. 3, June 1916).   WaPS **9819**

Starbuck, Edith.
Crossing the plains. Nashville, Southern Publishing Association [c1927] 224 p. front., plates, fold. map.   Many **9820**

Starbuck, Roger.
Oregon Josh, the wizard rifle; or, The young trapper champion. New York, Beadle and Adams, c1885. 31 p. illus. (Beadle's Boy's library of sport, story and adventure, v. 7, no. 91, Jan. 9, 1886).
WaU **9821**

Starker, Carl, 1892-
Western flower arrangement. Portland, Or., Binfords & Mort, c1947. 112 p. illus.
MtBozC OrHi OrP OrU **9822**

Starmont, Leon, see no. 5564.

State Federation of Taxpayers' Efficiency Associations, Washington.
The tax-eater will get you if you don't look out! Levies in the state of Washington approaching threatening confiscation; review of conditions comp. for State Federation of Taxpayers' Efficiency Associations. Tacoma, Pioneer Bindery & Printing Co. [1916?] 24 p.
WaS **9823**

The state of Oregon; supplement to "New geography, Book 2, based on information furnished by educators in the state of Oregon by various chambers of commerce, by railroad companies, and by departments of the United States government". Boston, Ginn [c1920] 24 p. illus,. maps (1 double).   WaPS **9824**

[State Republic of the State of Oregon]
Constitution and by-laws for the subordinate republics. Portland, Or., Himes, 1871. 10 p.   OrHi **9825**

State Tax Conference, Seattle, Wash., 1914.
Taxation in Washington; papers and discussions of the State Tax Conference at the University of Washington, May 27, 28 and 29, 1914. Seattle, 1914. 302 p. (Bulletin of the University of Washington, University Extension ser. no. 12. General ser. no. 84)   Many **9826**

State Taxpayers' Association of Oregon.
Statements to members on the 20 mill tax limitation petition] Portland, Or., 1934. [8] p. table.   OrP **9827**

A statement of the facts, pertaining to the proclamation of martial law over Pierce County, W. T., by Isaac I. Stevens and the proceedings of the court martial in the attempt to try citizens for treason, containing the governor's vindication and the trial and discharge of these citizens. Steilacoom, Wash., 1856. 16 p.
WaU **9828**

Statement of the Oregon and Washington delegation in relation to the war claims of Oregon and Washington. [n.p., n.d.] 67 p.   OrHi OrP WaSp **9829**

Stearns, Doran H.
The official gazette and travelers' and immigrants' guide to Oregon and Washington Territory. Portland, Or., 1876. 192 p.   OrHi OrP **9830**

Same. Portland, Or., G. H. Himes, 1877.
WaU **9831**

Steedman, Charles John, 1856-
Bucking the sagebrush; or, The Oregon Trail in the seventies, illus. by Charles M. Russell. New York, Putnam, 1904. ix, 270 p. col. front., illus., 8 plates, 3 ports., fold map.   Many **9832**

Steel, John.
Johan Stal (John Steel); from Smaland farmer lad to Idaho prune king, completed by Lilly Ann Steel Loveland. Francestown, N. H., Marshall Jones Co., c1947. 103 p. illus.   IdB WaS **9833**

Steel, William Gladstone, 1854-1934.
The mountains of Oregon. Portland, Or., D. Steel, 1890, 112 p.   Many **9834**

Same. 2 plates, 2 ports.   Many **9835**

See also nos. 1968, 1969.

Steele, Harwood Elmes Robert, 1897-
Policing the Arctic; the story of the conquest of the Arctic by the Royal Canadian (formerly North-West) Mounted Police. Toronto, Ryerson [1935] 390 p. front., 31 plates, map.   CVicAr **9836**

Same. [1936]   CV **9837**

Steele, John, 1832-1905.
Across the plains in 1850; ed with introd. and notes by Joseph Schafer, illus. from hitherto unpublished contemporary drawings. Chicago, Caxton Club, 1930. xxxvii, 234 p. front., 5 plates, port., fold. map. Drawings attributed to Lt. Andrew Jackson Lindsay.   Many **9838**

[Steele, Richard F.]
An illustrated history of the Big Bend Country embracing Lincoln, Douglas, Adams, and Franklin Counties, state of Washington. [Spokane] Western Histrical Publishing Company, 1904. xxiv, 1024 p. plates, ports.
MtU WaPS WaSp WaU **9839**

An illustrated history of Stevens, Ferry, Okanogan and Chelan Counties, state of Washington. Spokane, Western Historical Publishing Company, 1904. 867 p. 13 plates, 86 ports.
OrSaW WaPS WaS WaSp WaU **9840**

The story of Lincoln County, Washington. Spokane, Lincoln County Alaska-Yukon-Pacific Commission, 1909. 27 p. illus.
WaS **9841**

See also no. 4860.

Steele, Samuel Benfield, 1849-
Forty years in Canada; reminiscences of the great Northwest, with some account of his service in South Africa, by Colonel S. B. Steele, late of the N. W. M. Police, ed. by Mollie Glenn Niblett, with an introd. by J. G. Colmer. London, H. Jenkins, 1915. xvii, 428 p. front. (port.) 8 plates 7 ports. CVU MtHi **9842**

Same. New York, Dodd, 1915.
CVU MtHi OrHi WaS WaU **9843**

Same. Toronto, McClelland, Goodchild and Stewart, 1915. CVic **9844**

Steeves, Mrs. Sarah (Hunt) 1871-
Book of remembrance of Marion County, Oregon pioneers, 1840-1860. Portland, Or., Berncliff Press, c1927. [xii] 348 p. front. (port.) Many **9845**

Stefansson, Evelyn (Schwartz) **Baird,** 1913-
Here is Alaska, with a foreword by Vilhjalmur Stefansson, with photographs by Frederick Machetanz and others. New York, Scribner [1943] 154 p. illus.
Many **9846**

Within the Circle; portrait of the Arctic; maps by Richard Edes Harrison. New York, Scribner, c1945. vii, 160 p. illus., ports., maps. CVU IdB WaS WaT **9847**

Stefansson, Vilhjalmur, 1879-
The adventure of Wrangel Island, written by Vilhjalmur Stefansson, with the collaboration of John Irvine Knight, upon the diary of whose son, Errol Lorne Knight, the narrative is mainly based. New York, Macmillan, 1925. xxviii, 424 p. front. plates, ports., maps (1 fold.) facsims. Many **9848**

The Arctic in fact and fable. [New York] Foreign Policy Association [1945] 96 p. illus., maps, diagr. (Headline ser. no. 51)
Many **9849**

Arctic manual, prepared under direction of the chief of the Air Corps, United States Army, with a special introd. and index. New York, Macmillan, 1944. xvi, 556 p. illus., plates, diagrs. Many **9850**

The friendly Arctic, the story of five years in Polar regions. New York, Macmillan, 1921. xxxi, 784 p. front., plates, ports., maps (part fold.) Many **9851**

Same. New ed., with new material. New York, Macmillan, 1943. xxvii, 812 p. front., plates, ports., maps (part fold.) fold. chart, facsims.
Or OrP Wa WaS WaSp WaT **9852**

Kak, the copper Eskimo, by Vilhjalmur Stefansson and Violet Irwin; illus by George Richards. New York, Macmillan 1931. xi, 253 p. illus. WaW **9853**

Same. 1943 [c1924] xi, 253 p. col. front., illus., plates. WaU **9854**

My life with the Eskimo. New York, Macmillan, 1919. ix, 538 p. front., plates, ports., 2 fold. maps. WaU **9855**

Same. Forewords by Henry Fairfield Osborn and Reginald Walter Brock, with a natural history appendix by Dr. Rudolph M. Anderson. New York, Macmillan [c1913] 1926. xvii, 538 p. front., plates, ports., 2 fold. maps. WaU **9856**

Same. 1929. CVU **9857**

The northward course of empire, with an introd. by Dr. Edward William Nelson. New York, Harcourt [c1922] xx, 274 p. front., plates, fold. map. Many **9858**

Not by bread alone. New York, Macmillan, 1946. xvi, 339 p. WaU **9859**

The Stefansson-Anderson Arctic expedition of the American Museum; preliminary enthnological report. New York, American Museum Trustees, 1914. 395 p. illus., fold. maps. (Anthropological papers, v. 14, pt. 1) CVicAr **9860**

The three voyages of Martin Frobisher. London, Argonaut, 1938. 2 v. WaU **9861**

Ultima Thule; further mysteries of the Arctic. New York, Macmillan, 1940. 383 p. illus., 2 plates. CVicAr **9862**

See also nos. 6870, 8814, 9846.

Steger, Friedrich, see no. 10975.

Stegner, Wallace Earle, 1909-
The big rock candy mountain. New York, Duell, Sloan and Pearce [c1943] 515 p. The West and Alaska story. Many **9863**

See also no. 6102.

Steilacoom Library Association.
Constitution, by-laws, and rules and orders of the Steilacoom Library Association, Washington Territory, organized in March 1858. Steilacoom, W. T., Puget Sound Herald Office, 1860. 12 p.
Or WaPS WaSp WaT WaU **9864**

Stein, Robert, 1857-
The defense of Alaska; a plea for the protection of American labor, with map of proposed railway. 2d ed. Washington, D. C., Judd and Detweiler, 1910. 23 p. fold. map. WaU **9865**

Steinbeck, John, see no. 8662.

Steiner, R. M., see no. 4874.

Stejneger, Leonhard Hess, 1851-1931.
Georg Wilhelm Steller, the pioneer of Alaskan natural hstory. Cambridge, Mass., Harvard University Press, 1936. xxiv, 623 p. col. front., illus., 29 plates.
Many **9866**

Stephen, Alexander Maitland, 1882-1942.
The gleaming archway. London, Dent [1929] v, 295 p. British Columbia author.
CVicAr **9867**

The kingdom of the sun; a romance of the far West coast. London, Dent, 1927. vii, 285 p. CVicAr CVU **9868**

Stephens, Mrs. Ann Sophia (Winterbotham) 1813-1886.
Esther; a story of the Oregon Trail. New York, Beadle [c1862] 128 p. WaU **9869**

[Stephens, Louise G.] 1843-
From an Oregon ranch, by "Katharine" [pseud.] decorations by J. Allen St. John. Chicago, McClurg, 1916. 210 p. illus.
Or OrCS OrP WaSp **9870**

Letters from an Oregon ranch, by "Katharine" [pseud.] with twelve full-page illus. from photographs. Chicago, McClurg, 1905. 212 p. front., 11 plates.
Many **9871**

Stephenson, Mrs. Delia Deirdre (Morris) 1880-
Bad Penny, by Rhoda Morris [pseud.] illus. by Arthur R. Nelson. Boston, Little, 1937. 254 p. front., illus., plates. Children's story about Washington Territory. OrAshS Wa WaS WaSp WaT WaU **9872**
Same. 1939.   WaW **9873**
Dog of the pioneer trail; ten full-page illus. by Conley Smith. Portland, Or., Metropolitan [c1937] 230 p. plates.
Many **9874**
Sun Bird, by Rhoda Morris [pseud.] with illus. by Arthur R. Nelson. Boston, Little, 1936. 255 p. front., illus., plates. Eskimo story.   Wa WaS WaSp **9875**
Susan and Arabella, pioneers, by Rhoda Morris [pseud.] with illus. by George and Doris Hauman. Boston, Little, 1936. 247 p. front., illus. Oregon pioneer story.
Many **9876**
Susan and little bird lost, by Rhoda Morris [pseud.] illus. by George and Doris Hauman. Boston, Little, c1941. 239 p. 10 plates.   Or OrP WaS WaT **9877**
Same. 1943 [c1941]   Wa **9878**

Stephenson, Wilfred S., 1912-
A collection of pen sketches and tinted wash drawings of sailing ships, passenger liners and war ships familiar in Pacific Coast and Alaskan ports. Vancouver, Wash., Ben Kreis Agency, c1947. 25 p. 22 plates, port.   WaS WaU **9879**

Stephenson, William B., 1880-
The land of tomorrow. New York, Doran [c1919] 240 p. front., 7 plates. Alaska.
Many **9880**

Stern, Bernhard Joseph, 1894-
The Lummi Indians of northwest Washington. New York, Columbia University Press, 1934. 127 p. front., plates, map. (Contributions to anthropology, ed. by Franz Boas. v. 17)   Many **9881**

Steunenberg Memorial Association.
Steunenberg Memorial, 1929, Boise, Idaho. Boise, Idaho, Capital New Publishing Co. [1929] 49 p. plate, port.
IdB IdIf IdU IdUSB **9882**

Stevens, Beatrice.
Free and equal? The Japanese-Americans in Oregon. Portland, Or., 1945. 42 p.
OrHi WaS **9883**

Stevens, Frank, see no. 2277.

Stevens, Glenhope Russell.
Gold hungry. Sherman, Calif., Tribune Publishing Co. [c1927] 256 p. Alaska story.   WaPS WaU **9884**

Stevens, Hazard, 1842-1918.
The life of Isaac Ingalls Stevens, by his son. Boston, Houghton, c1900. 2 v. front., illus., 18 plates, 20 ports., 14 maps (part fold.) fold. facsim.   Many **9885**
Same. 1901.   MtBozC WaT WaU **9886**

Stevens, Mrs. Helen (Norton) 1864-
Memorial biography of Adele M. Fielde, humanitarian. New York, Fielde Memorial Committee [c1918] 377 p. front. (port.) plates, ports. Biographee spent last few years of life in Seattle.
OrU Wa WaS WaU **9887**

Stevens, Horace, see nos. 8440, 8441.

Stevens, Isaac Ingalls, 1818-1862.
Address on the Northwest before the American Geographical and Statistical Society, December 2, 1858. Washington, D. C., Gideon, 1858. 56 p.
CVicAr OrHi OrP WaU **9888**

Stevens, James, 1892-
Big Jim Turner, a novel. Garden City, N. Y., Doubleday [c1948] 275 p.
OrHi OrP WaT WaU **9889**
Brawny-man. New York, Knopf, 1926. 323 p. Hobo-laborer in the Northwest.
Many **9890**
Homer in the sagebrush. New York, Knopf, 1928. 313 p.   Many **9891**
Mattock. New York, Knopf, 1927. 320 p.
Many **9892**
Paul Bunyan; woodcuts by Allen Lewis. Garden City, N. Y., Garden City Pub. Co. [c1925] 245 p. front., plates.
Many **9893**
Same. New York, Knopf, 1926.   Wa **9894**
Same. 2d ed. [c1947]   WaU **9895**
Paul Bunyan's bears; with pictures by Phyllis Heady. Seattle, McCaffrey, 1947. 129 p. illus.   WaU **9896**
The saginaw Paul Bunyan; woodcuts by Richard Bennett. New York, Knopf, 1932. 261 p. front.
MtU OrP WaS WaSp WaT WaTC **9897**
Status rerum; a manifesto upon the present condition of northwestern literature containing several near-libelous utterances upon persons in the public eye, by James Stevens and H. L. Davis. The Dalles, Or. [n.d.] 8 p.   OrP OrU WaT **9898**
Timber! The way of life in the lumber camps. [Evanston, Ill., Row, Peterson and Co., 1942] 72 p. illus. (Way of life ser.)   Or OrP Wa WaT WaU **9899**

Stevens, Wayne Edson, 1892-
The Nothwest fur trade, 1763-1800. Urbana, Ill., University of Illinois [c1928] 204 p. (Studies in the social sciences, v. 14, no. 3)   Many **9900**

Stevens, William Bacon, 1815-1887.
God's call and faith's obedience; a sermon delivered in St. Peter's Church, Brooklyn, N.Y., Wednesday, December 15, 1880, on the occasion of the consecration of the Rev. John Adams Paddock, D. D., as bishop of the missionary jurisdiction of Washington Territory. Brooklyn, N. Y., Orphans' Press, 1881. 19 p.   WaU **9901**

Stevenson, Elmo Nall.
Key to the nests of Pacific Coast birds. Corvallis, Or., Oregon State College [1942] 71 p. 32 plates, diagr. (Monographs. Studies in zoology, no. 4, June 1942)   WaS WaT WaTC **9902**
Nature rambles in the Wallowas; sketches of the natural history of northeastern Oregon. Portland, Or., Metropolitan [n.d.] 100 p. illus., plates, map.
IdIf OrHi OrP **9903**
Same. [1937]   Many **9904**

Steward, Julian H., see no. 9973.

Stewart, Blair, 1900-
Seasonal employment and unemployment compensation in Oregon. Portland, Or., Reed College, 1937. 44 p. diagrs.
OrCS WaU **9905**

Stewart, Cal F.
Story of the Columbia from The Dalles to the ocean; historic, legendary, descriptive, of the grandest river scenery in the world. Portland, Or., West Coast Game Co. [c1911] 76 p. illus. OrP **9906**

Stewart, Elihu, 1844-
Down the Mackenzie and up the Yukon in 1906. London, J. Lane, 1913. 270 p. front., 29 plates, fold. map. Many **9907**

Stewart, George, 1892-
Reluctant soil. Caldwell, Idaho, Caxton, 1936. 363 p. Idaho ranching story.
Many **9908**

Stewart, Martha Morley.
Greyhound Fanny. Rev. ed. Seattle, c1912-16. 190 p. illus. WaS **9909**

Stewart, Robert Laird, 1840-1916.
Sheldon Jackson, pathfinder and prospector of the missionary vanguard in the Rocky Mountains and Alaska. New York, F. H. Revell Co. [c1908] 488 p. front., plates, ports., maps (1 fold.) facsims.
Many **9910**

Stewart, Rosemary, see no. 10983.

[**Stewart, Sir William George Drummond,** 7th bart.] 1796-1871.
Altowan; or. Incidents of life and adventure in the Rocky Mountains, by an amateur traveler, ed. by J. Watson Webb. New York, Harper, 1846. 2 v.
OrHi OrP WaSp WaU **9911**

Stine, Thomas Ostenson.
Additional poems. Seattle, Pigott Printing Concern, 1921. 21 p. WaU **9912**

Echoes from dreamland. Pacific Coast ed. Seattle, Puget Sound News Co., 1903. 100 p. Poems. Introd. by H. M. Korstad.
Wa WaS WaT WaU WaWW **9913**

Heaven on earth and other poems. Seattle, Pigott Printing Concern, 1919. 180 p. front. (port.) plates. Wa **9914**

Same. 2d ed. enl. 1920. 231 p.
WaS WaU **9915**

Morning glimpse. Seattle, Anchor Publishing Company, 1901. 13 p. Poems.
WaU **9916**

Scandinavians on the Pacific; Puget Sound. [Seattle, Denny-Coryell] c1900. 208 p. illus., ports. Many **9917**

Stock, Chester, see nos. 3590, 5439.

[**Stock, Eugene**] 1836-1928.
Metlakahtla and the North Pacific Mission of the Church Missionary Society. London, Church Missionary House, 1800. 130 p. front. (col. map) WaU **9918**
Same. 2d ed. 1881.
CVicAr CVU OrHi **9919**
Same. 2d ed. London, Seeley, 1881.
CVicAr WaWW **9920**

Stockton, H. N., ed.
Spokane of 1900, ed. by H. N. Stockton and C. E. Weaver. [Spokane] Northwest Illustrating Co. [1900?] 30 p. illus.
WaSp **9921**

Stoddard, Charles Warren, 1843-1909.
Over the Rocky Mountains to Alaska. 3d ed. St. Louis, B. Herder, 1914 [c1899] 168 p. OrU WaU **9922**

Stoddard, George Wellington, & Associates.
Proposed King County juvenile court and detention facilities. Seattle, 1945. 16 p. plate, plans. WaS **9923**

Stokes, George W., see no. 1206.

Stokes, Richard Leroy, 1882-
Paul Bunyan, a folk-comedy in three acts, illus. by Charles K. Stevens. New York, Putnam, 1932. 102 p. illus.
OrPR WaE WaS WaSp WaU **9924**

Stoll, William Tecumseh, 1859-1931.
Silver strike; the true story of silver mining in the Coeur d'Alenes, as told by William T. Stoll to H. W. Whicker. Boston, Little, 1932. viii, 273 p. front., plates, ports. Many **9925**
Same. Boston, Houghton, 1932. IdIf **9926**

Stolz, Gideon.
Memoirs of Sedgwick Post, No. 10, G. A. R., Salem, Oregon, 1882-1931. [Salem, Or., Bertelson & McShane, 1931] 30 p. illus., ports. Or OrP OrU **9927**

Stone, H. A.
A short history of Caulfield Village. [Vancouver, B. C., Wrigley, n.d.] 25 p. illus.
CVicAr CVU **9928**

Stone, H. W.
Pacific supremacy; Portland's opportunity. Portland, Or. [n.d.] 18 p. OrHi **9929**

Stone, Harold Otho.
How Ned and Molly met the vitamins jolly. Seattle, Oregon-Washington Pear Bureau, c1933. 18 p. col. front., illus. (part col.) WaPS **9930**

Stop-Look-Listen-League.
Plain talk to you and other thinking men and women of Washington; the proposed initiative and referendum measures on which the people are asked to pass judgment; information regarding the "Seven sisters" and others, with an unbiased analysis of each. [n.p., 1914?] 48 p.
WaPS WaS WaU **9931**

Storey, Ralph Ewing, 1872-
Linfield floss and fiber; a book of campus verse. Souvenir ed. Portland, Or., Binfords & Mort [1948] 104 p. front., plates, ports. OrHi OrP OrU **9932**

The Story of Dr. Scoresby, the Arctic navigator. London, Nelson, 1890. 120 p. front.
CVicAr **9933**

The story of Fraser River gold, its romance, its possibilities, its future. [Vancouver, B. C., Sun. Pub. Co., n.d.] [20] p. illus., map, port. CVicAr **9934**

The story of Louis Riel, the rebel chief. Toronto, Rose Pub. Co. [c1885] 192 p. front., illus. CVicAr **9935**

Stott, William.
The story of St. Andrew's United Church, North Vancouver, 1865-1937. [n.p., n.d.] 34 p. illus., ports. CVicAr **9936**

Stout, J. L.
Sea View, Pacific County, Washington Territory; the summer resort of the Pacific Northwest. [Seaview, W. T., 1888] 18 p. OrP WaU **9937**

Stout, Tom, 1879-   ed.
Montana, its history and biography; a history of aboriginal and territorial Montana and three decades of statehood. Chicago, American Historical Society, 1921. 3 v. front., illus., ports. Volumes 2 and 3 biographical.   Many 9938

Stovall, Dennis H.
The gold bug story book; mining camp tales by a western writer. [Denver, Reinert Publishing Company, n.d.] 151 p. front., plates.   WaU 9939

Heart of the valley. Corvallis, Or., 1899. 100 p. front., illus.   OrHi WaU 9940

Suzanne of Kerbyville. New York, Editor Publishing Company, 1904. 209 p. 5 plates.
OrCS OrHi OrP OrU WaSp 9941

Stow, Marion (Cook) 1875-1910.
Voices of the city, with original drawings and decorations. Portland, Or., Metropolitan, 1909. 30 p. front., illus. Poems.
OrHi OrP WaU 9942

Where flows Hood River, illus. with photographs and drawings by the author. Portland, Or., Hicks-Chatten Engraving Co., 1907. vii, 91 p. front., illus.
OrHi OrP 9943

Same. Portland, Or., Metropolitan, 1907.
WaPS 9944

Same. 1917 [c1907]   IdU 9945

Stoy, William H.
A sermon in memoriam of the Rev. John Sellwood, a presbyter of the church and for thirty-six years a clergyman of the diocese of Oregon. Portland, Or., 1892. 25 p.   OrHi OrP OrU WaPS WaU 9946

Strahan, Kay (Cleaver) 1888-
Footprints. Garden City, N. Y., Crime Club by Doubleday, 1929. 316 p. Oregon novel. OrP WaS WaT WaU WaW 9947

Strahorn, Robert Edmund, 1852-
Montana and Yellowstone National Park; facts and experiences on the farming, stock raising, mining, lumbering, and other industries of Montana. Kansas City, Mo., Ramsey, Millet & Hudson, 1881. 191 p. illus.   MtBozC MtHi 9948

Oregon; its wealth and resources, presented with the compliments of the General Passenger and Ticket Department of the Union Pacific Railway. [Council Bluffs, Iowa, Nonpareil Printing Co.] 1888. 68 p. tables.
OrU WaPS 9949

Same. 2d ed. rev. Chicago, Rand McNally, 1889. 67 p.   OrP 9950

Same. 3d ed. rev. Battle Creek, Mich., W. C. Gage & Son, 1890. 108 p. map.
OrU 9951

Same. 4th ed. rev. St. Louis, Woodward & Tiernan, 1891. 98 p. map.   OrP 9952

Same. 6th ed. rev. 1893.   WaU 9953

The resources and atractions of Idaho Territory; facts regarding climate, soil, minerals, agricultural and grazing lands, forests, scenery, game and fish, and reliable information on other topics applicable to the wants of the homeseeker, capitalist and tourist. Boise City, Idaho, 1881. 88 p. front. (map) illus.
IdB IdU WaSp WaU 9954

The resources of Montana Territory and attractions of Yellowstone National Park; facts and experiences on the farming, stock raising, mining, lumbering, and other industries of Montana and notes on the climate, scenery, game, fish, and mineral springs, with full and reliable data on routes, distances, rates of fare, expenses of living, wages, school and church privileges, society, means of acquiring homes, and other valuable and reliable information applicable to the wants of the capitalist, homeseeker, or tourist; pub. and circulated by direction of the Montana Legislature. Helena, Mont., 1879. 77 p. illus.
MtHi MtU WaSp WaU 9955

To the Rockies and beyond; or, A summer on the Union Pacific Railroad and branches: saunterings in the popular health, pleasure, and hunting resorts of Nebraska, Dakota, Wyoming, Colorado, Utah, Idaho, Oregon, Washington, and Montana. 2d ed. rev. and enl. Omaha, New West Publishing Company, 1879. 216 p. front., illus., map.
CVicAr IdB IdU MtHi WaU 9956

Same. 3d ed. rev. and enl. Chicago, Belford, Clarke, 1881. 213 p. front., illus., fold. map.   OrP WaS WaSp 9957

"Where rolls the Oregon". [Denver, Denver Times Print, 1882] 20 p. illus., map.
OrP 9958

See also nos. 769, 770.

Stranahan, C. T.
Pioneer stories, comp. by members of the Lewiston Chapter of the Idaho Writer's League from the files of C. T. Stranahan. [Lewiston, Idaho? 1947] 50 p. illus. ports.
CVicPr IdB IdU MtBozC MtHi 9959

Strand, T. P.
Tests for the control of orchard pests, emphasizing insecticides for codling moth control and observations on codling moth activity in the Yakima Valley, Washington. Yakima, Wash., California Spray-Chemical Corporation, 1933. 14 p. tables, diagrs.   WaPS 9960

Strang, Herbert, ed.
Adventures in the far West; Canada's story. London, Frowde [n.d.] 160 p. front., illus., 3 plates. (Romance of the world)
CV CVU 9961

Stratemeyer, Edward, 1862-1930.
To Alaska for gold; or, The fortune hunters of the Yukon, illus. by A. B. Shute. Boston, Lee and Shepard, 1905 [c1899] vi, 248 p. front., plates. (Bound to succeed series)   WaU 9962

The Rover boys in Alaska; or, Lost in the fields of ice, by Arthur M. Winfield [pseud.] New York, Grosset [c1914] vi, 285 p. front., plates. (Rover boys' series for young Americans)   WaU 9963

Two young lumbermen; or, From Maine to Oregon for fortune, illus. by A. B. Shute. Boston, Lee and Shepard [c1903] viii, 326 p. front., 7 plates. (Great American industries series)   WaU **9964**

Strathcona, Lord, see no. 11078.

Straton, John Roach, 1875-1919.
One thousand dollars was paid for this story on Portland, Oregon; it's worth reading. Portland, Or. Portland Commercial Club [n.d.] 15 p.   OrP **9965**

Stratton, Royal B., d. 1875.
Captivity of the Oatman girls; being an interesting narrative of life among the Apache and Mohave Indians. 3d ed. New York, Carlton, 1858. 290 p. illus., ports., map.   OrHi WaS **9966**

Captivity of the Oatman girls; a true story of early emigration to the West, rev. and abridged by Chas. H. Jones. Salem, Or., Oregon Teachers Monthly, 1909. 119 p. port.   OrHi OrSa WaPS WaU **9967**

Strayer, George D., see no. 2797.

Stretch, Richard Henry.
Placer mines and their origin. Seattle, Lowman & Hanford, 1897. 24 p.
                                        WaU **9968**

Strickland, R. E. M., see no. 2074.

Strindberg, Nils, see no. 10037.

[Strite, D. D.]
How to become a logger; a complete treatise in six lessons. [Portland, Or., Timberman, c1924] 40 p. illus. Photostat copy.   WaU **9969**

Strong, Anna Louise, 1885-
Ragged verse, by "Anise". Presentation ed. Seattle, Pigott-Washington Printing Co. 1937. 63 p. Published as greeting to author on return to Seattle, March, 1937.
                                        Wa WaU **9970**

Strong, Thomas Nelson, 1853-1927.
Cathlamet on the Columbia; recollections of the Indian people and short stories of early pioneer days in the valley of the lower Columbia River. Portland, Or., Holly Press, 1906. 119 p.   Many **9971**

Same. Portland, Or., Metropolitan, 1930 [c1906] xv, 170 p. col. front.   Many **9972**

Strong, William Duncan, 1899-
Archaeology of The Dalles-Deschutes region, by W. Duncan Strong, W. Egbert Schenck, and Julian H. Steward. Berkeley, Calif., University of California Press, 1930. vii, 154 p. illus., maps (1 fold.) 28 plates, tables, diagrs. (Publications in American archaeology and ethnology, v. 29, no. 1)   CVicAr Or OrP OrU **9973**

Stuart, Charles Macaulay, see no. 5980.

Stuart, Granville, 1834-1918.
Forty years on the frontier as seen in the journals and reminiscences of Granville Stuart, gold-miner, trader, merchant, rancher and politician; ed. by Paul C. Phillips. Cleveland, A. H. Clark Company, 1925. 2 v. front. (port.) plates. (Early western journals, no. 2)   Many **9974**

Montana as it is; being a general description of its resources; to which is appended a complete dictionary of the Snake language, and also of the famous Chinnook jargon. New York, C. S. Westcott & Co., 1865. 175 p.
                                  CVicAr MtHi MtU **9975**
Same. Microfilm.   WaU **9976**
See also no. 8867.

Stuart, John, see no. 4412.

Stuart, Robert, 1785-1848.
The discovery of the Oregon Trail; Robert Stuart's narratives of his overland trip eastward from Astoria in 1812-13, from the original manuscripts in the collection of William Robertson Coe, esq., to which is added: an account of the Tonquin's voyage and of events at Fort Astoria, 1811-12, and Wilson Price Hunt's diary of his overland trip westward to Astoria in 1811-12, trans. from Nouvelles annales des voyages, Paris, 1821; ed. by Philip Ashton Rollins. New York, Scribner, 1935. cxxxvii, 391 p. front. (port.) port., maps (1 double) facsims.
                                        Many **9977**

Stuart, Samuel Vernon.
Along life's way; comprising Mother's parting words, Father's grave, and miscellaneous poems. Tacoma, E. R. Ray, 1901. 117 p. Port Townsend poet.   WaU **9978**

Stubbs Electric Company.
50 years of progress, 1897-1947. [Portland, Or., 1947] [19] p. illus., ports., facsims.
                                        OrU **9979**

Stuck, Hudson, 1863-1920.
The Alaskan missions of the Episcopal Church; a brief sketch, historical and descriptive, with a preface by the Right Reverend Peter Trimble Rowe. New York, Domestic and Foreign Missionary Society, c1920. 179 p. front. (port.) plates, ports.   WaPS WaSp **9980**

The ascent of Denali (Mount McKinley) a narrative of the first complete ascent of the highest peak in North America. New York, Scribner, 1914. xix, 188 p. front., 33 plates, ports., fold. map.
                                        Many **9981**
Same. 1918 [c1914]   Wa **9982**

Ten thousand miles with a dog sled; a narrative of winter travel in interior Alaska. London, T. Werner Laurie [1914] 440 p.   CVU **9983**
Same. New York, Scribner, 1914. xix, 420 p. front. (port.) 52 plates (4 col.) fold. map, facsim.   Many **9984**
Same. 1915.   OrU **9985**
Same. 1916.   WaE WaU **9986**
Same. 1920.   OrSa **9987**
Same. 2d ed. 1927 [c1914, c1916]
                                        OrP Wa **9988**
Same. 1932 [c1916] xxii, 420 p. OrCS **9989**

Voyages on the Yukon and its tributaries; a narrative of summer travel in the interior of Alaska. New York, Scribner, 1917. xvi, 397 p. front., 48 plates, 2 fold. maps.   Many **9990**

A winter circuit of our Arctic Coast; a narrative of a journey with dog-sleds around the entire Arctic Coast of Alaska. London, T. W. Laurie [1919]

xiv, 347 p. front., 32 plates, 2 fold maps.
CVic CVicAr **9991**

Same. New York, Scribner, 1920. x, 360 p.
front. plates, fold. maps. Many **9992**

Students Cooperative Association, Seattle, Wash.
Handbook. Seattle, 1947. 13 p. WaU **9993**

Stuff, Harry Spencer.
The Siwash, his book; being a bit of Indian philosophy done into verse by Harry S. Stuff. Seattle, Stuff Printing Concern, 1909. [26] p. port. Wa **9994**

See also no. 5962.

Stuhr, Ernst Theodore.
Manual of Pacific Coast drug plants. [Lancaster, Pa., Science Press Publishing Co.] 1933. 189 p. front. (maps). Many **9995**

Oregon drug plants, a survey of the official medicinal drug plants of Oregon. [Columbus, Ohio, American Pharmaceutical Asociation, 1931] 16 p. OrCS OrP **9996**

Same. Corvallis, Or., Oregon State College, 1931. MtU WaPS **9997**

Sturdevant, Hervey S., 1848-
Life and adventures of an orphan boy; or, From the cradle to the ministry, containing amusing scenes and adventures in mission work on land and sea. Cornelius, Or., 1911. 127 p. front. (port.) illus., 6 plates. Many **9998**

[Sturdza, Alexandru] 1791-1854.
Pamiatnik trudov pravoslavnykh blagoviestnikov russkikh s 1793 do 1853 goda. Moskva, Tipografiia V. Got'ai, 1857. xxiii, 377 p. WaU **9999**

Sturgis, William, 1782-1863.
The Northwest fur trade, and the Indians of the Oregon country, 1788-1830. [Boston, Directors of the Old South Work, 191-] 20 p. (Old South leaflets. General series, v. 9, no. 219)
OrSa WaS WaT WaU **10000**

The Oregon question; substance of a lecture before the Mercantile Library Association, delivered Jan. 22, 1845. Boston, Jordan, 1845. 32 p. map. Many **10001**

Sturm, Fred H., see no. 1551.

Stutfield, Hugh Edward Millington, 1858-1929.
Climbs & explorations in the Canadian Rockies, by Hugh E. M. Stutfield and J. Norman Collie. London, Longmans, 1903. xii, 342 p. front., 51 plates, 2 maps (1 fold.) Many **10002**

Styer, Wilhelm D.
The mission of lumber in national defense [address at the annual meeting of West Coast Lumbermen's Association, Portland, Jan. 30, 1942] [Portland, Or., Timberman, 1942] 1 v. WaT **10003**

Su-el-lil, see no. 6476.

Suckley, George, 1830-1869.
The natural history of Washington Territory and Oregon, with much relating to Minnesota, Nebraska, Kansas, Utah, and California; being those parts of the final reports on the survey of the Nothern Pacific Railroad route relating to the natural history of the regions explored, with full catalogues and descriptions of the plants and animals collected from 1853 to 1860, by George Suckley and J. G. Cooper. This edition contains a new preface, giving a sketch of the explorations, a classified table of contents, and the latest additions and corrections by the authors. New York, Bailliere Brothers, 1860. xvii, 399 p. 63 plates (part col.) Many **10004**

See also nos. 2030, 2031.

Suffling, Ernest Richard.
The fur traders of the West; or, Adventures among the redskins. London, F. Warne and Co., 1896. xiv, 320 p. front., illus., 8 plates, map. OrP WaU **10005**

Suksdorf, Wilhelm N.
Flora Washingtonensis; a catalogue of the Phaenogamia and Pteriodophyta of the state of Washington. [White Salmon, Wash.? 1892] 15 p. OrCS OrP **10006**

Sullivan, Alan, 1868-
Brother Blackfoot, illus. by W. M. Berger. New York, Century [1927] 300 p. front., illus., plates. IdIf OrP **10007**

Cariboo road. Toronto, T. Nelson and Sons [1946?] 311 p. Cariboo gold rush in 1862. CV CVU WaS WaU **10008**

The fur masters. London, Murray [1938] 320, 16 p. CVicAr CVU **10009**

The great divide. London, Dickson [1935] 417 p. CV **10010**

Same. Toronto, Macmillan, 1935. CVivAr CVU **10011**

Under the northern lights. New York, Dutton [n.d.] 192 p. (Kings treasuries of literature) CVicAr **10012**

Sullivan, Gerald.
General Thomas Francis Meagher; a sketch. Butte, Mont. [n.d.] 31 p. front. (port.) 6 ports. MtHi **10013**

Sullivan, John D., see no. 645.

Sullivan, Joseph A., see nos. 1280, 6890.

Sullivan, Maurice S., 1893-1935.
Jedediah Smith, trader and trail breaker; foreword and notes by Rufus Rockwell Wilson, illus. by Howard Simon. New York, Press of the Pioneers, 1936. xiii, 233 p. front., illus., plates, ports. Many **10014**

See also no. 9601.

Sullivan, Mrs. May Kellogg.
The trail of a sourdough; life in Alaska. Boston, R. G. Badger [c1910] 258 p. front. (port.) illus., plates. Many **10015**

A woman who went to Alaska. Boston, J. H. Erle [c1902] 392 p. front. (port.) 26 plates, double map.
CVicAr WA WaS WaU **10016**

Same. [c1903]
CVU OrSa Wa WaPS WaS WaSp **10017**

Same. [1910, c1903] OrU **10018**

Sullivan, Oscar M.
The empire-builder; a biographical novel of the life of James J. Hill. New York, Century [1928] x, 372 p.
MtHi MtU WaE WaSp WaU **10019**

Sullivan, Robert Jeremiah, 1912-
The Ten'a food quest. Washington, D. C.,
Catholic University of America Press,
1942. xii, 142 p. 2 illus., 2 plates (Anthropological series, no. 11)
CVicAr MtU **10020**

Sumner, Walter Taylor, 1873-
How our church came to the Oregon country. [Milwaukee, Wis., Young Churchman Co., 1918] [8] p. illus. Or **10021**

The Sunday Kelsonian-Tribune.
Progress edition. Kelso, Wash., 1936. [48]
p. illus. (Nov. 15, 1936; v. 2, no. 38)
WaPS **10022**

Sundborg, George, 1913-
Opportunity in Alaska, with a foreword
by Ernest Gruening. New York, Macmillan, 1945. ix, 302 p. plates, fold. map.
Many **10023**

Sunset Magazine.
Sunset western ranch houses, by the editorial staff of Sunset Magazine, in collaboration with Cliff May. San Francisco, Lane [1946] 160 p. illus., plans.
Many **10024**

Sunset Press.
A picture journey through the Pacific
Northwest. [Seattle, 1928] [66] p. 65 illus.
WaU **10025**

Survey of Race Relations.
Tentative findings of the Survey of Race
Relations; a Canadian-American study
of the Oriental on the Pacific Coast,
prepared and presented at the Findings
Conference at Stanford University, California, March 21-26, 1925. [Stanford University, 1925] 24 p.
OrPR WaTC WaU **10026**

**A survey of race relations on the Pacific
Coast** jointly undertaken by five Pacific
Coast regional committees and the Institute of Social and Religious Research,
New York City. San Francisco [n.d.]
14 p. OrP **10027**

Sutherland, Alexander, 1833-
A summer in prairie-land; notes of a tour
through the Northwest Territory. Toronto, Methodist Book and Pub. House, 1882.
x, 198 p. illus. MtU **10028**

Same. 2d ed. CVicAr **10029**

Sutherland, Alexander H.
Victoria. [Victoria, B. C., Clarke Printing
Co., n.d.] 30 p. illus. Poem.
CVicAr **10030**

Sutherland, Peter C.
Journal of a voyage in Baffin's Bay and
Barrow Straits in the years 1850-1851 under the command of Mr. William Penny,
in search of the mission crews of H. M.
ships Erebus and Terror. London, Longman, 1852. 2 v. col. front., illus., plates
(part col.) 2 fold. maps.
CVicAr WaU **10031**

Sutherland, Thomas A.
Howard's campaign against the Nez Perce
Indians, 1878, by T. A. Sutherland, volunteer aid-de-camp on Gen. Howard's
staff. Portland, Or., Walling, 1878. 47 p.
OrHi WaSp (imperfect) WaWW **10032**

Sutherlin, Robert N.
Legends historic; or, Smith River in verse.
White Sulphur Springs, Mont., Rocky
Mountain Husbandman Co., 1900. [86]
p. plates. MtHi MtU **10033**

Sutton, George Miksch, 1898-
Eskimo year; a naturalist's adventures
in the far North. New York, Macmillan,
1934. 321 p. illus., 12 plates. Many **10034**

Same. 1936. CVicAr OrCS **10035**

Sutton, R. L., see no. 156.

Svenska Missionsforbundet i Amerika.
Alaskaforr och nu, en naturskildring, kulturbild och missionsberattelse, enligt
muntliga och skriftliga meddelanden af
missionarer, utgifven af Svenska missionsforbundet i Amerika till forman
for dess missioner. Chicago, P. G. Almberg & Co., 1897. 152 p. illus., ports.
WaU **10036**

**Svenska Sallskapet for Antropologi och
Geografi, Stockholm.**
Andree's story; the complete record of his
polar flight, 1897, from the diaries and
journals of S. A. Andree, Nils Strindberg, and K. Fraenkel, found on White
Island in the summer of 1930 and ed. by
the Swedish Society for Anthropology
and Geography; trans. from the Swedish
by Edward Adams-Ray. New York, Viking, 1930. xvi, 389 p. front., illus., plates,
ports, maps (1 fold.) facsims., diagrs.
IdB Wa WaT **10037**

Sverdrup, Otto, see nos. 7207-7209.

Swadesh, Morris, see no. 8985.

Swain, Henry Huntington, 1863-
Civics for Montana students. Rev. ed. Chicago, Scott, Foresman and Co. [c1912]
vi, 235 p. MtBozC MtHi MtU **10038**

Montana civics; an elementary text-book
in state and local government. Chicago,
Scott, Foresman and Co., 1903. 150 p.
MtBozC MtHi MtU **10039**

[**Swaine, Charles**] supposed author.
An account of a voyage for the discovery
of a Northwest Passage by Hudson's
Streights, to the western and southern
ocean of America, performed in the year
1746 and 1747 in the ship California;
Capt. Francis Smith, commander, by the
clerk of the California, adorned with
cuts and maps. London, Jolliffe, 1748-49.
2 v. 4 plates, 6 fold. maps.
CVicAr **10040**

The great probability of a Northwest
Passage; deduced from observations on
the letter of Admiral de Fonte, who
sailed from the Callao of Lima on the
discovery of a communication between
the South Sea and the Atlantic Ocean;
and to intercept some navigators from
Boston in New England, whom he met
with, then in search of a Northwest
Passage, with three explanatory maps
by Thomas Jefferys. London, Jefferys,
1768. xxiv, 153 p. front. (map) 2 maps.
CVicAr OrHi WaS WaSp WaU **10041**

Swan, James Gilchrist, 1818-
British Columbia; a lecture on Queen

Charlotte Islands. Victoria, B. C., Wolfenden, 1884. 10 p.   CVicAr OrHi **10042**

The Northwest Coast; or, Three years' residence in Washington Territory. London, Sampson Low, 1857. 435, 12 p. front., illus., fold. map, table, music.
CVicAr CVU WaT **10043**

Same. New York, Harper, 1857.
Many **10044**

Swan, Oliver G., ed.
Frontier days. Philadelphia, Macrae Smith Co. [c1928] 512 p. col. front., illus., col. plates. (The romance of America's history)   Wa **10045**

Swander, Clarence F.
Making disciples in Oregon. [St. Louis] c1928. 248 p. port.   Or **10046**

Swanson, Robert E.
Rhymes of a lumberjack; a second book of verse concerning the trials and tribulations, lives and ways of the loggers living and working in the great Northwest of America, illus. by Bert Bushell. Toronto, T. Allen, 1943. 94 p. illus.
WaS **10047**

Rhymes of a western logger. [Vancouver, B. C., Lumberman Printing Co., 1942] 56 p. illus., fold. plate.   WaS **10048**

Same. [1943]   CV WaU **10049**

Swanston, John, see no. 580.

Swanton, John Reed, 1873-
Contributions to the ethnology of the Haida. New York, Stechert, 1905. 300 p. illus., 26 plates, fold. maps, fold. geneal. table. (Memoir of the American Museum of Natural History, v. 8, no. 1; Pub. of the Jesup North Pacific Expedition, v. 5, pt. 1)   Many **10050**

Haida songs, by John R. Swanton; Tsimshian texts (new series) by Franz Boas. Leyden, Late E. J. Brill, 1912. v, 284 p. (Publications of the American Ethnological Society, v. 3)
CV OrU Wa WaS WaU **10051**

Swarth, H. S., see no. 1136.

Swartley, Arthur M., 1870-
Ore deposits of northeastern Oregon. [Corvallis, Or.] 1914. 229 p. illus., fold. plans, fold. maps, diagrs. (part fold.) (Mineral resources of Oregon. v. 1, no. 8)
Many **10052**
See also no. 7953.

[Swartout]
A short catechism and hymnal adapted to the use of the Indians in the Language of the Ahts, Barclay Sound. Vancouver, B. C., Trythall [n.d.] 20 p.
CVicAr **10053**

Sweet, William John.
Dairy ranch rhymes and Sweet family yarns, by Bill Sweet; illus. by Pearl Sweet Ellingsen. [Bandon, Or., L. D. Felsheim, 1942] 135 p. illus., ports.
Or **10054**

Sweetman, Luke D., 1867-
The story of a cowhorse, Gotch, illus. by L. D. Cram. Caldwell, Idaho, Caxton, 1936. 318 p. col. front., illus., plates.
Many **10055**

Same. 1945 [c1936]   WaU **10056**

Sweetman, Mrs. Maude, 1880-
What price politics; the inside story of Washington state politics. Seattle, White & Hitchcock [c1927] 136 p. front. (port.) illus., ports.   WaS WaU **10057**

Sweetser, Albert Raddin, 1861-1940.
Key and flora; some of the common flowers of Oregon, by Albert R. Sweetser and Mary E. Kent. Boston, Ginn & Co. [c1908] vi, 149 p.   Many **10058**

Swift, Kay.
Who could ask for anything more? illus. by Julian Brazelton. New York, Simon and Schuster, 1943. 211 p. illus. Eastern Oregon.   Many **10059**

Swindrage, Theodore, see nos. 10040, 10041.

Swineford, Alfred P.
Alaska; its history, climate and natural resources. Chicago, Rand McNally [c1898] 256 p. front., 16 plates, fold. map.
CVicAr CVU Or WaPS WaS WaU **10060**

Symons, Farrell G. H., see no. 8403.

Synge, Georgina M.
A ride through Wonderland. London, Low, 1892. iv, 166 p. front. (fold. map) 2 plates.
MtHi **10061**

Syverson, A. H., see no. 5564.

Tabeau, Pierre Antoine, 1755-1820.
Tabeau's narrative of Loisel's expedition to the upper Missouri, ed. by Annie Heloise Abel, trans. from the French by Rose Abel Wright. Norman, University of Oklahoma Press, 1939. xi, 272 p. front., facsim., fold. geneal. table. Many **10062**

Taber, Ralph Graham.
Our fighting spirit, with the three great prophesies of the World War and sixty-five shots at the Huns. Spokane, Spokane Pub. Syndicate [c1918] 64 p. illus.
WaSp **10063**

Tabloid travel talks on British Columbia. [Victoria, B. C., Banfield, 1930] 32 p. illus., maps.   CVicAr **10064**

Tache, Alexandre Antonin, 1823-1894.
Esquisse sur le nord-ouest de l'Amerique. Montreal, Payette, 1869. 146 p.
CVicAr MtU WaS **10065**

Same. 2. ed. Montreal, Beauchemin, 1901. 184 p. front. (port.) illus., ports.
CVicAr WaU **10066**

La situation. [St. Boniface, Man.? 1885?] 23 p.   WaU **10067**

Sketch of the North-west of America, trans. from the French by Captain D. R. Cameron. Montreal, J. Lovell, 1870. 216 p.
CVicAr CVU MtHi WaU **10068**

Vingt annees de missions dans le nord-ouest de l'Amerique. Montreal, Ensebe Senecal, imprimeur-editeur, 1866. xiii, 245 p.   CVicAr CVU MtU WaS **10069**

Same. Nouvelle ed. Montreal, St.-Joseph, 1888. 238 p. front. (port.) plates, 6 ports.
CVicAr **10070**

Tacoma. First Baptist Church, see no. 1028.
— — — First Lutheran Church.
Twentieth anniversary, 1907-1927. [Tacoma, n.d.] 1 v.   WaT **10071**

— — — First Methodist Episcopal Church. Anniversary bulletin, Sunday, Feb. 23, 1908. Tacoma, 1908. 1 v. illus., ports.
WaT WaTC **10072**

— — — Justice to the Mountain Committee. Brief submitted to the United States Geographical Board urging the official removal from America's most sublime mountain of the name of Rainier and the perpetuation by official adoption of the original Indian name therefor in its most appropriate euphonious and generally accepted form: Tacoma. Tacoma, 1917. 77, 24 p. Many **10073**

— — — National Bank. Chester Thorne, 1868-1927. [Tacoma, 1927] [17] p. port. Or **10074**

[Resolutions passed by various organizations of Tacoma on the death of Chester Thorne] Tacoma, 1927. [20] p. front. (port.) WaT **10075**

— — — Puget Sound National Bank of Tacoma. 50 years of progress; golden anniversary 1940. Tacoma, 1940. 1 v. illus. WaT **10076**

Tacoma and vicinity. Tacoma, Nuhn & Wheeler [1888] [50] p. illus.
Wa WaT **10077**

Same. Tacoma, George W. Traver, c1889.
WaT **10078**

Tacoma Council of Social Agencies. Community resources. [n.p., n.d.] 10 p.
WaT **10079**

Tacoma Daily Ledger. [Independence Day edition] Tacoma, 1898. 28 p. illus., ports., map. (July 3, 1898)
WaU **10080**

Jubilee edition; eighth anniversary of Washington's statehood. Tacoma, 1897. 24 p. illus., ports. (Nov. 11, 1897)
WaU **10081**

Prosperity edition. Tacoma, 1899. 34 p. illus. (Jan. 1, 1899) WaU **10082**

Special Alaska edition. Tacoma, 1897. 7 p. illus., map. (v. 15, no. 227) WaU **10083**

The Tacoma Ledger annual for the year 1886 with genuine illus. on wood. Tacoma, R. F. Radebaugh, 1886. 1 v. illus. Illus. chiefly by Darley, Moran, Smillie, Sayre, Weber and other celebrated American artists. WaPS WaU **10084**

Tacoma Daily News. Shipping edition. Tacoma, 1896. [20] p. illus., map, tables. (Jan. 1, 1896)
WaU **10085**

Tacoma, the gate way to the Klondike. Tacoma, 1897. 16 p. illus., ports., maps. (Dec. 14, 1897) WaU **10086**

Tacoma, Washington, 1917; an epitome of its resources and its special attractions to tourists. Tacoma [1917] 52 p. illus., plates (part col.)
WaT WaTC WaU **10087**

Tacoma Eastern Railroad Company. Scenes from the "Wonderland of the Cascades". Mount Tacoma and the Rainier National Park; the views herein are reproduced from the original photo-

graphs and not from hand made sketches; photos. by A. H. Barnes, Parkland, Wash. Tacoma, Allen and Lamborn Printing Co. [19—?] 33 plates.
WaU **10088**

Scenic wonders from the Mt. Rainier National Park, Washington; "the Wonderland of the Cascades". Tacoma, c1909. 1 v. plates. WaS WaT WaU **10089**

Tacoma Federation of Social Agencies. Preliminary report on a survey of family relief work in Tacoma. Tacoma, 1922. 96 p. tables, fold. diagrs. WaT **10090**

Report, Feb. 18, 1921-Aug. 21, 1923 [summary] Tacoma, 1923. 32 p. WaT **10091**

Survey of family relief work in Tacoma. Tacoma, 1923. 58 p. fold. diagr.
WaT WaU **10092**

Tacoma invites you; summer and fall tours; tourist's edition with map of Washington. [n.p., 1920] 152 p. illus., map.
WaTC **10093**

Tacoma Land Improvement Company. Tacoma, the manufacturing and shipping center of the Pacific Northwest; flour, wheat, fruits, coke, coal, lumber, minerals, fish. Tacoma [n.d.] 27 p. illus.
WaT **10094**

Tacoma Lumbermen's Club. Tacoma, Washington; the lumber capital of America, pub. by the Tacoma firms and individuals whose names appear in the directory appended. [Tacoma] c1923. 58 p. illus., fold. map. Many **10095**

Tacoma Morning Globe. Annual edition. [Tacoma] 1891. [18] p. illus. ports., map. (Jan. 1, 1891) WaU **10096**

Tacoma Municipal Civil Service League. Constitution and by-laws. Tacoma [n.d.] 14 p. WaT **10097**

Tacoma Narrows Bridge-McChord Field celebration; official opening, June 30-July 4, 1940. Tacoma, Johnson-Cox Co., 1940. 36 p. illus. WaT **10098**

Tacoma News-Tribune. Progress edition for 1939. Tacoma, 1939. [66] p. illus., ports. (56th year, no. 214, Apr. 25, 1939) WaU **10099**

Tacoma Patrolmen's Benevolent Association. History of the Tacoma Police Department. [Tacoma] 1908. 64 p. illus., ports.
WaU **10100**

Tacoma Poetcrafters. Pieces of eight; selected for merit. [n.p.] c1946. 74 p. WaSp WaT **10101**

Tacoma Railway & Power Company. Facts relating to operations of Tacoma Railway & Power Company. Tacoma, 1916. 18 p. WaS WaU **10102**

Findings of fact concerning valuation and earnings of property devoted to public use. [Tacoma] 1916. 7 p. tables.
WaT **10103**

Tacoma Society of Architects. Home plans designed for the Pacific First Federal Savings and Loan Association of Tacoma. [Tacoma] c1936. 47 p. plans.
WaT **10104**

Tacoma, the city of destiny; being views of

the port of Puget Sound and illustrating its shipping, lumbering, architecture, parks, and giant Mount Tacoma in its varied moods from photographs by A. French. Tacoma, Central News Co., [190-?] 1 v. illus., photos.　WaT **10105**

Tacoma; the city with a snow capped mountain in it's [!] dooryard. Seattle, Lowman & Hanford [n.d.] [24] p. photos.
WaPS **10106**

Tacoma; the rising center of commerce and manufacture; the growing metropolis of the Northwest; the city of destiny, the maritime outlet of the inland empire and the coming railway center of the West; its illimitable advantages of material resource for mechanical industry and mercantile thrift; a comprehensive review. Tacoma, Delisle & Milliken [n.d.] 1 v. illus.　WaT **10107**

Tacoma, then and now; 1883-1903 [20 years of progress] Tacoma, Vaughan & Morrill, 1903. 60 p. illus., plan.　WaT **10108**

Talbot, Ethelbert, bp., 1848-1928.
My people of the plains. New York, Harper, 1906. x, 264 p. front. (port.) 5 plates, 6 ports.　Many **10109**

Talbot, Frederick Arthur Ambrose, 1880-
The new garden of Canada; by pack-horse and canoe through undeveloped New British Columbia. London, Cassell, 1911. xii, 308 p. front., 47 plates, fold. map.
Many **10110**

Same. 1912.　WaTC WaU **10111**

Talbot, Theodore, d. 1862.
The journals of Theodore Talbot, 1843 and 1849-52; with the Fremont expedition of 1843 and with the first military company in Oregon Territory, 1849-1852; ed. with notes by Charles H. Carey. Portland, Or., Metropolitan, 1931. x, 153 p.
Many **10112**

A tale of the Bitterroot, a historical community pageant-drama, written and produced by the people of Stevensville, Montana on the evening of August 18, 1946. Missoula, Mont., Montana Study [1946] [35] p.　MtBozC **10113**

The tale of the nativity as told by the Indian children of Inkameep, British Columbia, illus. by Sis-hu-lk. [n.p., 1940] 19 [5] p. illus.　CVicAr CVU **10114**

Talkington, Henry Leonidas, 1860-
Heroes and heroic deeds of the Pacific Northwest. Caldwell, Idaho, Caxton [c1929] 2 v. fronts., illus.　Many **10115**

Political history, state constitution and school laws of Idaho. Lewiston, Idaho. Lewiston Morning Tribune [c1911] 44, 89, 122 p. front., plates, 2 maps, fold. form.
CVicAr IdU OrHi WaU WaW **10116**

State constitution and school laws of Idaho, considered with reference to the student, the teacher, the school official and others interested in the political and educational institutions of the state. Lewiston, Idaho, Lewiston Morning

Tribune [c1906] 186 [10] p. front., plates (1 fold.) forms (1 fold.)
IdB IdIf IdU IdUSB WaWW **10117**

Tanka, Tehanta, see no. 6262.

Tannatt, Mrs. Elizabeth Foster (Tappan) 1837-1920.
Indian battles in the inland empire in 1858, comp. by Mrs. Elizabeth F. Tannatt, historian Esther Reed Chapter, Daughters of the American Revolution. Spokane [Shaw & Borden] 1914. 16 p. illus.
WaSp WaU **10118**

Tanner, Henry.
British Columbia, its agricultural and commercial capabilities and the advantages it offers for emigration purposes. London, Kenning, 1887. 45 p. illus.
CVU WaSp **10119**

Same. Montreal, Dawson, 1887. 45 p. front. (fold. map) illus.　CVicAr **10120**

The Canadian North-West and the advantages it offers for emigration purposes. 2d ed. London, G. Kenning, 1886. 48 p. illus.　CVicAr **10121**

See also no. 2507.

Targ, William, 1907-　ed.
The American West; a treasury of stories, legends, narratives, songs & ballads of western America, ed. with an introd. Cleveland, World Publishing Company [1946] xii, 595 p. illus.
IdU Or WaS WaSp WaT WaU **10122**

Tarr, Ralph Stockman, 1864-1912.
Alaskan glacier studies of the National Geographic Society in the Yakutat Bay, Prince William Sound and lower Copper River regions, based upon the field work in 1909, 1910, 1911, and 1913 by National Geographic Society expeditions. Washington, D. C., National Geographic Society, 1914. 498 p. illus., plates, maps (part fold.)
CVU OrP Wa WaS WaTC WaU **10123**

Tasse, Elie.
Le Nord-ouest. Ottawa, Imprimerie du "Canada", 1880. 51 p.　CVicAr **10124**

Le Nord-ouest; la province de Manitoba et let territoires du Nord-ouest; leur etendue, salubrite du climat, fertilite du sol. Ottawa, Imprimerie du "Canada", 1880. 70 p.　WaU **10125**

Same. 2. ed. rev. et aug. 1882. 91 p.
CVicAr **10126**

The North-west. 2d ed. rev. & aug. Ottawa, Le Canada Print, 1882. 81 p.
CVicAr **10127**

Tasse, Joseph, 1848-1895.
Les Canadiens de l'Ouest. Montreal, Cie. d'imprimerie canadienne, 1878. 2 v. in 1. 6 plates, 15 ports. Biographical sketches of noted French-Canadians of the middle and western states of the U. S. and of the western part of Canada.
CVU WaSp **10128**

Same. 2. ed.　WaU **10129**
Same. 4. ed. Montreal, Berthiaume & Sabourin, 1882.　CVU **10130**
Same. 5. ed. Montreal, Imprimerie generale, 1886.
CVicAr CVU WaSp WaU **10131**

La question Riel. Ottawa, 1886. 13 p.
CVicAr **10132**

Tate, Charles Montgomery, 1852-1933.
Chinook as spoken by the Indians of Washington Territory, British Columbia, and Alaska; for the use of traders, tourists and others who have business intercourse with the Indians. Chinook-English, English-Chinook. Victoria, B. C., M. W. Waitt & Co. [1889] 47 p.
Many **10133**

Chinook jargon as spoken by the Indians of the Pacific Coast; for the use of missionaries, traders, tourists and others who have business intercourse with the Indians. Chinook-English, English-Chinook. Victoria, B. C., T. R. Cusack, 1914. 48 p. CV CVicAr WaU WaWW **10134**

Our Indian missions in British Columbia. [Toronto, Methodist Young People's Forward Movement for Missions, n.d.] 16 p. ports., map. CVicAr **10135**

[**Tate, Mrs. Charles Montgomery**]
Early days at Coqualeetza. [Toronto, Woman's Missionary Society, n.d.] 7 p. illus. CVicAr **10136**

Tatsey, Joseph, see nos. 10392, 10393.

Taylor, Arthur Samuel.
A course of study in Oregon for elementray grades, by A. S. Taylor and H. W. Gustin. Portland, Or., Metropolitan, c1933. viii, 69 p. Or OrP **10137**

A guide to the study and reading of the history of the Pacific Northwest. Portland, Or., Metropolitan, 1935. 73 p. front. (maps) illus. Many **10138**

Taylor, Charles Maus, 1849-
Touring Alaska and the Yellowstone, illus. from photographs by the author. Philadelphia, G. W. Jacobs & Co. [1901] 388 p. front., plates.
CVicAr OrHi Wa WaS WaSp WaU **10139**

Taylor, Mrs. Florance (Walton)
Salt streak. New York, F. H. Revell [c1939] 280 p. Oregon pioneer story.
IdU Or **10140**

Taylor, Frank J., see no. 1260.

Taylor, Fred G.
A saga of sugar, being a story of the romance and development of beet sugar in the Rocky Mountain West. [Salt Lake City, Utah-Idaho Sugar Co., 1944] 234 p. illus., plates, ports. (1 col.)
IdIf IdUSB OrU WaS **10141**

Taylor, H. West, see no. 4258.

Taylor, Mrs. John M., 1875-
Eva Craig Barton, 1865-1924; a tribute by Mrs. John M. Taylor and J. H. Baird. Boise, Idaho, Strawn, 1925. 1 v.
IdB **10142**

Taylor, Joseph Marion, 1854-
History and government of Washington, to which are appended the Constitution of the state of Washington and Constitution of the United States and list of territorial and state officers. St. Louis, Becktold Printing and Book Manufac-

turing Co., 1898. 368 p. illus., plates, ports., map.
CVicAr Wa WaS WaTC WaU **10143**
Same. 279 [20] p. Reading circle ed.
Many **10144**

Taylor, Mrs. Lydia (Pettengill) 1872-
From under the lid; an appeal to true womanhood. [Portland, Or., Glass & Prudhomme] c1913. 125 p. port.
MtHi OrP **10145**

Taylor, Rosetta Eby.
Poems of Oregon and other verse. [Portland, Or., Metropolitan, c1932] 31 p.
OrP OrU **10146**

Taylor, Walter Penn, 1888-
Provisional list of land mammals of the state of Washington, by Walter P. Taylor and William T. Shaw. [Pullman, Wash., State College of Washington, 1929] 32 p. (Occasional papers of the Charles R. Conner Museum, no. 2) WaU **10147**

Teachers' Retirement Fund Association of School District No. 1, Multnomah County, Or.
Articles of incorporation and by-laws. [n.p., 1912] 20 p. OrHi OrP **10148**
Enabling act, articles of incorporation, and by-laws. Portland, Or., 1923. 29 p.
OrP **10149**

Teal, Joseph Nathan, 1858-1929.
Address; The Dalles-Celilo Canal celebration, Big Eddy, Oregon, May 5, 1915. [n.p., n.d.] 7 p. OrHi **10150**

"Conservation"; address before the Council of Jewish Women. Portland, Or., 1910. 23 p. OrP **10151**

The influence of the Panama Canal on the development of Oregon horticulture; address before the Oregon State Horticultural Society. Portland, Or., 1911. 29 p.
Or OrHi OrP **10152**

Oregon's heritage of natural resources; shall they be conserved for the people? Address delivered at the University of Oregon, Feb. 13, 1909. [n.p., n.d.] 13 p.
OrHi OrP **10153**

Teasdale, Edward.
Modern political history of Portland. [n.p., n.d.] 28 p. OrHi OrP **10154**

Technical Asociation of the Pulp and Paper Industry.
Official program of the international convention, Portland, Oregon, 1934. Portland, Or., 1934. 111 p. illus. OrP **10155**

Teck, Frank Carleton.
Under western skies; poems. New Whatcom, Wash., Blade Publishing Co., 1899. [53] p. OrHi WaPS WaU **10156**

Teddy Blue, see no. 1.

Tehanta Tanka, see no. 6262.

Teichert, Mrs. Minerva (Kohlhepp)
Drowned memories [stories of Fort Hall Bottoms, Idaho] [n.p., n.d.] [39] p. col. front., illus. IdIf IdP **10157**
Same. [Pocatello, Idaho? 1926?] 37 p.
IdUSB **10158**
Same. [Salt Lake City, Deseret News, c1926] 37 p. WaU **10159**

A romance of old Fort Hall. Portland, Or., Metropolitan, 1932. 165 p. col. front., illus. Many **10160**

Teichmann, Emil, 1845-1924.
A journey to Alaska in the year 1868; being a diary of the late Emil Teichmann, ed. with an introd. by his son Oskar. Kensinton, Cayme Press, 1925. 272 p. front. (port.) illus., port.
WaU **10161**

Teichmann, Oskar, see no. 10161.

Teit, James Alexander, 1864-1922.
Traditions of the Thompson River Indians of British Columbia, collected and annotated by James Teit, with introd. by Franz Boas. Boston, American Folklore Society, 1898. viii, 137 p. (Memoirs, v. 6)
Many **10162**

See also no. 899.

Tekahionwake, see nos. 5238-5268.

Telephone Register, McMinnville, Or.
[Special progress edition commemorating the dedication of McMinnville's new power plant] McMinnville, Or., 1938. [50] p. illus., ports., map. (Oct. 20, 1938)
OrP WaU **10163**

Templeton, Herbert A., see no. 4532.

Terrell, John Upton, 1900-
Plume rouge, a novel of the pathfinders. New York, Viking, 1942. 498 p.
Many **10164**

Terry, J. C.
Cartoons and caricatures of prominent men of Montana. Butte, Mont., McKee Printing Co., c1911. 95 ports. MtHi **10165**

Terry, James, 1844-1912.
Sculptured anthropoid ape heads found in or near the valley of the John Day River, a tributary of the Columbia River, Oregon. New York [J. J. Little & Co.] 1891. 15 p. 5 plates.
CVicAr Or OrCS OrU WaSp WaU **10166**

Tessan, Francois de.
Promenade au Far-West. 2. ed. Paris, Plon—Nourrit et cie., 1912. iii, 337 p.
WaS WaU **10167**

Tetherow, Sam, see no. 5989.

Thacher, George A., 1861-1919.
Why some men kill; or, Murder mysteries revealed. [Portland, Or.] c1919. iv, 121 p. front., plates, ports. Study of some Oregon murders. OrP WaPS WaU **10168**

Thacher, W. F. Goodwin, 1879-
Prospective advertising men; graduates of the University of Oregon, June, 1929. [Eugene, Or.? 1929] [8] p. ports.
OrU **10169**

See also no. 10293.

Thane, Eric, see no. 4358.

Tharp, Louise (Hall) 1898-
Company of adventurers; the story of the Hudson's Bay Company, illus. by Charles B. Wilson. Boston, Little, 1946. x, 301 p. front., illus., plates. Many **10170**

Thayer, Claudius, 1854-1923.
Poems. [Portland, Or., Metropolitan] 1936. xiv, 104 p. OrHi OrP OrSaW OrU **10171**

Thayer, Mrs. Emma (Homan) 1842-1908.
Wild flowers of the Pacific Coast, from original water color sketches drawn from nature. New York, Cassell [c1887] 64 p. col. front., 23 col. plates.
Many **10172**

Thayer, William Makepeace, 1820-1898.
Marvels of the new West; a vivid portrayal of the stupendous marvels in the vast wonderland west of the Missouri River; six books in 1 volume, graphically and truthfully described, illus. with over three hundred and fifty fine engravings and maps. Norwich, Conn., Henry Bill Publishing Company [c1887] xxxvi, 715 p. illus., ports., maps. Many **10173**

Same. 1888. CV CVicAr MtHi WaU **10174**

Same. 1889, c1887. MtHi WaT **10175**

Same. 1890 [c1887] IdU OrSaW **10176**

Same. 1892.
CVU OrP WaS WaT WaU **10177**

Thayer, William Wallace, 1827-1899.
Address before the university, 1882. Portland, Or., A. G. Walling, 1882. 22 p.
OrP OrU WaU **10178**

Their weight in wildcats; tales of the frontier, illus. by James Daugherty. Boston, Houghton, 1938. xiii, 188 p. col. front., illus., col. plates. Many **10179**

Theodore, Sister Mary, see nos. 6578-6580.

Thevenet, J. V.
Sur les gisements auriferes et platiniferes de l'Oregon; lu par M. Fournet a l' Academie imperiale de Lyon, dans la seance du 29 mai 1860. [Lyon, Rey et Sezanne, 1860] 6 p. WaS **10180**

Thielsen, H. B.
Address of grand master of the M. W. Grand Lodge of Masons of Oregon, June 12, 1901. [n.p.] 1901. 14 p. (Proceedings, June, 1901) OrP WaPS **10181**

Thissell, G. W.
Crossing the plains in '49. Oakland, Calif., 1903. 176 p. front., illus., 10 ports.
WaSp **10182**

Thom, Adam, 1802-1890.
The claims of the Oregon Territory considered. London, Smith, Elder, 1844. iv, 44 p. Many **10183**

Thomas, Edward Harper, 1868-
Chinook; a history and dictionary of the Northwest coast trade jargon; the centuries-old trade language of the Indians of the Pacific; a history of its origin and its adoption and use by the traders, trappers, pioneers and early settlers of the Northwest coast. Portland, Or., Metropolitan, 1935. 179 p.
Many **10184**

Kopet alta. Caldwell, Idaho, Caxton, 1936. 232 p. Puget Sound novel.
IdIf Wa WaE WaS WaU **10185**

Thomas, Emrys Price.
The Congregational way in Blaine, Washington; a history for the 73d anniversary, September 14-15, 1947. Blaine, Wash., 1947. 59 p. illus. WaS **10186**

Thomas, William S., 1858-
Trails and tramps in Alaska and New-

foundland. New York, Putnam, 1913. xv,
330 [6] p. front., illus.   Many **10187**

Thompson, Arthur Ripley, 1872-
Gold-seeking on the Dalton Trail; being
the adventures of two New England boys
in Alaska and the Northwest Territory.
Boston, Little, 1900. xii, 352 p. front.,
plates, map.
OrP WaS WaSp WaU **10188**

Same, 1920.   WaE **10189**

Same. With illus. in color by George
Avison. [c1925] 327 p. front., 4 plates.
(Beacon Hill bookshelf)
WaE WaS **10190**

Same. 1931 [c1900, 1925]   WaT **10191**

Thompson, Carl Dean.
Studies in public power; outline for study
and discussion groups, with special re-
ference to the Pacific Northwest.
Chicago, Public Ownership League of
America [1945?] 74 p. map, diagrs.
(Bulletin, no. 136) Jonnt publication of
the Public Ownership League and Wash-
ington and Oregon state granges.
WaS **10192**

Thompson, David, 1770-1857.
David Thompson's narrative of his explorations in western America, 1784-1812,
ed. by J. B. Tyrell. Toronto, Champlain
Society, 1916. xcviii, 582 p. 21 plates (3
col. fold.) 2 fold. maps. (Publications.
12)   Many **10193**
See also no. 4350.

Thompson, Francis M.
Complete guide to the new gold regions
of upper Missouri, Deer Lodge, Beaver
Head, Nez Perces, Salmon River, Boise
River, Powder River, John Day, Cari-
boo, containing tables of distances,
camping places, many words of the
Blackfoot and Flat-head languages, and
a complete Chinook jargon. St. Louis,
R. P. Studley & Co., 1863. 16 p.
MtHi **10194**

Thompson, I. Owen.
Adventure and day dreams. Long Beach,
Calif., 1913. 100 p. plates. Oregon setting.
IdU OrHi OrP WaU **10195**

Thompson, J. B., 1855-
Brief biographical sketch and short scrip-
tural writings. Albany, Or., Herald
Printing Co., 1916. [24] p. port.
OrHi **10196**

Thompson, Mrs. Lucy, 1856-
To the American Indian. Eureka, Calif.
[Cummins Print Shop, c1916] 214 p. illus.,
2 plates, port.   WaSp **10197**

Thompson, Mrs. Margaret (Hollinshead)
1892-
High trails of Glacier National Park.
Caldwell, Idaho, Caxton, 1936. 167 p. col.
front., plates (2 col.) fold map.
Many **10198**

Same. 1938 [c1936]   MtU WaPS **10199**

Space for living, a novel of the Grand
Coulee and Columbia Basin. Portland,
Or., Binfords & Mort [1944] 323 p. illus.
Many **10200**

[**Thompson, R. M.**] ed.
The industries of Tacoma, Washington,
her resources, advantages and facilities
in trade, commerce and maunfactures
together with pen sketches of her prominent business and professional men, to
which is appended her representative
establishments. [Portland, Or., Lewis &
Dryden] 1888-89. 200 p. illus.   Or **10201**

Same. Tacoma, Trade and Commerce Publishing Co., 1888-9.   WaT **10202**

Thompson, Raymond.
The wilderness trapper; a practical handbook by a practical trapper with ex-
tensive experience in the wilds of western Canada. 6th ed. Columbus, Ohio,
Hunter-Trader-Trapper Co. [c1924] 226 p.
illus.   CVU **10203**

Thompson, Slason, see no. 2074.

Thompson, Will H., see no. 9666.

Thompson, William.
Reminiscences of a pioneer. San Francisco, 1912. 187 p. port.   Many **10204**

Thomson, Edward A.
Just for fun; cartoons and caricatures of
men in Montana. [Rochester, Ind] McKee
Printing Co., c1907. [134] p. ports.
MtU **10205**

Thomson, Origen.
Crossing the plains; narrative of the
scenes, incidents and adventures attending the overland journey of the Decatur
and Rush County emigrants to the "far-
off" Oregon in 1852; printed from a diary
of daily events kept by the late Origen
Thomson, with an introductory chapter
by Mrs. Camilla T. Donnell, and a thrilling narrative of a buffalo hunt and
battle royal with mountain wolves, by
Mr. Sutherland McCoy. Greensburg,
Ind., 1896. 122 p.
OrHi OrP WaPS WaU **10206**

Thomson, W. J., and Co.
Portland, Oregon in 1900. Portland, Or.,
1900. 63 p. illus.   OrHi OrP **10207**

Thomson Stationery Company.
Gold dust; how to find it and how to
mine it; an elementary treatise on the
methods and appliances used by miners
on the frontier, with other useful information. [Vancouver, B. C., n.d.] 43, 21 p.
CV WaU **10208**

Souvenir of West Kootenay; photogravures, entered according to Act of Parliament of Canada, in the year 1896 at
the Department of Agriculture. Vancouver, B. C., Albertype [1896] 20 plates.
CVIcAr CVU **10209**

**Thomson's manual of Pacific Northwest
finance;** a digest of securities in, or
pertaining to the territory of Alaska,
the province of British Columbia, the
state of Idaho, the state of Montana, the
state of Oregon, the state of Washington; v. 1, 1930. Seattle, Thomson's Statistical Service, c1930. 487 p.
WaE WaS WaSp WaT **10210**

Thorburn, Don, see no. 10211.

Thorburn, Lois M.
No tumult, no shouting; the story of the PBY, by Lois and Don Thorburn. New York, Holt [1945] vii, 148 p. illus., ports. Navy air force in Aleutians in World War II.   OrP WaS WaT WaU **10211**

Thorington, James Monroe, 1894-
A climber's guide to the interior ranges of British Columbia. [Philadelphia] American Alpine Club, 1937. xii, 149 p. front. (map)   CVicAr MtU WaS **10212**

The glittering mountains of Canada; a record of exploration and pioneer ascents in the Canadian Rockies, 1914-1924. Philadelphia, J. W. Lea, 1925. xxii, 310 p. front., plates (part fold.) ports., maps (part fold.)   Many **10213**

The Purcell Range of British Columbia. New York, American Alpine Club, 1946. 152 p. front., illus., maps. (1 fold.)   CV CVU IdU WaS **10214**
See also nos. 7860-7862.

Thornber, J. J., see nos. 288-290.

Thorne, James Frederic, 1871-
In the time that was, dedicated to Ah-Koo, done into English by J. Frederic Thorne (Kitchakahaech) illus. by Judson T. Sergeant (To-u-sucka); being the first volume of a series of legends of the tribe of Alaska Indians known as the Chilkats of the Klingats, as told by Zachook, the "Bear" to Kitchakahaech, the "Raven". Seattle [c1909] [30] p. col. illus.   Many **10215**

Thornhill, John Bensley.
British Columbia in the making, 1913. London, Constable, 1913. xi, 175 p. front., plates, ports, 5 maps (1 fold.)   CV CVic CVicAr CVU WaU **10216**

Thornton, Augustus Willoughby, 1833-
European system of flax culture Americanized and adapted to the local conditions of U. S. A. (especially Puget Sound); the American system of flax and other fiber culture. [Ferndale, Wash., c1917] 60 p. illus.   OrP OrU WaT WaU **10217**

Thornton, Harrison Robertson, 1858-1893.
Among the Eskimos of Wales, Alaska, 1890-93; ed. and annotated by Neda S. Thornton and William M. Thornton, Jr. Baltimore, Johns Hopkins Press, 1931. xxxviii, 235 p. front., illus., 30 plates, 5 ports.   CVicAr WaS **10218**

Thornton, Jessy Quinn, 1810-1888.
Oregon and California in 1848, with an appendix, including recent and authentic information on the subject of the gold mines of California and other valuable matter of interest to the emigrant, etc., with illus. and a map. New York, Harper, 1849. 2 v. fronts., 10 plates, fold. map.   Many **10219**
Same. 1855 [c1849]
   IdU Or OrHi OrSa OrSaW WaWW **10220**
Same. 1864.   CVicAr Or OrP WaU **10221**

Salem titles; history of the title to real estate in Salem [Or.] [Salem, Or., 1874] 48 p.   OrHi OrP **10222**

See also no. 1641.

Thornton, Neda S., see no. 10218.

Thornton, William M., Jr., see no. 10218.

Thorpe, Berenice DuRae, 1900-
Reunion on Strawberry Hill, a novel. New York, Knopf, 1944. 303 p. Western setting.   Many **10223**

Three Forks of the Missouri River; logical site of a national memorial to Captains Lewis and Clark. Three Forks, Mont., Three Forks New Printing Co. [n.d.] 16 p.   MtHi **10224**

Thurston, Samuel R., see nos. 5291-5295.

Thurston County. Republican Central Committee.
Souvenir, 1908. [Olympia, Wash., 1908] [18] ports.   WaU **10225**

Thwaites, Reuben Gold, 1853-1913.
A brief history of Rocky Mountain exploration; with especial reference to the expedition of Lewis and Clark. New York, Appleton, 1904. xi, 276 p. front., plate, 5 ports., map, 2 facsims. (Expansion of the republic series)   Many **10226**

Early western travels. Cleveland, A. H. Clark Co., 1915. 369 p. illus.
   OrSaW **10227**

Early western travels, 1748-1846; a series of annotated reprints of some of the best and rarest contemporary volumes of travel, descriptive of the aborigines and social and economic conditions in the middle and far West, during the period of early American settlement, ed. with notes, introd., index, etc. Cleveland, A. H. Clark Co., 1904-1907. 32 v. fronts., illus., plates (2 fold.) ports, maps (part fold.) fold. plan, facsims.   Many **10228**

Travels in the far West, 1836-1841: I. The far West; or, A tour beyond the mountains, by Edmund Flagg. II. Letters and sketches, with a narrative of a year's residence among the Indian tribes of the Rocky Mountains, by Father Jean Pierre de Smet, S. J., ed. with notes, introd., index, etc. Cleveland, A. H. Clark Co., 1906. 2 v. front., 12 plates (1 fold.) 2 facsims., fold. map. Same as Early western travels, v. 26 and 27.   OrSaW **10229**

See also nos. 3004, 5910, 5911.

Tibbals, Mirton L.
Nine months overseas, being the history of "H" Company, 361st Infantry, 91st Division, illus. by Corp. Ernest W. Ball, pub. out of the company fund under the direction of Lt. Charles T. Wright, Lt. Alexander Dobie, Sgt. Harry S. Elliott. [Belleme? Orne, France, 1919?] 74 p. illus. First company organized at Camp Lewis, Wash.   WaS WaU **10230**

Tichenor, Mrs. Mary Walker.
Battleship "Oregon"; "The bull dog of the Navy". [Portland, Or., Hansen, 1941?] 36 p. front.   WaSp WaT **10231**

Same. [1942] 62 p.   OrU WaS **10232**

Tikhmenev, Petr Aleksandrovich d. 1888.
Istoricheskoe obozrienie obrazovaniia rossiisko-amerikanskoi kompanii i dieistvii

eia do nastoiashchago vremeni. Sankt-peterburg, V. tipografii Eduarda Vei-mara, 1861-1863. 2 v. col. front., col. ports., fold. maps. CVU WaU **10233**

Prilozhenie niekotorykh istorcheskikh do-kumentov k istoricheskomu obozrieniiu obrazovaniia Rossiisko - amerikanskoi kompanii i dieistvii eia do nastoiash-chago vremeni i podrobnoe ukazanie statei voshedshikh v obrienie. Sanktpet-erburg, V tipografii Eduarda Veimara, 1863. 292, x. p. WaU **10234**

Tillotson & Wolcott Co., Cleveland, Ohio.
Oregon; its resources; its future. Cleve-land [n.d.] 23 p. WaPS **10235**

Tilton, Henry Remsen, 1836-1906.
The last days of Kit Carson, introd. by Usher L. Burdick. Grand Forks, N. D., Holt Printing Co. [c1939] 11 p. front. (port.) WaU **10236**

Tilton, James.
The survey of the Walla Walla and Co-lumbia River Railroad. Walla Walla, W. T., Statesman Printing Office, 1871. 7 p. WaU **10237**

Timber Worker.
Labor Day good will edition. [Aberdeen, Wash., 1936] 96 p. illus., ports.
WaU **10238**

Timber workers' employment guide, 1915-1916. Seattle [1916] 127 p. WaU **10239**

Timberline Lodge, heart of the Mt. Hood all-year playground. [n.p., 1946?] 1 v.
OrP **10240**

Tims, J. W., see no. 819.

Tin Schreiner, see no. 1127.

Todd, Edward H.
College of Puget Sound, 1888; fiftieth an-niversary; 1938 brochure. Tacoma, Col-lege of Puget Sound, 1938. 12 p. illus.
Wa **10241**

Todd, John, 1800-1873.
The sunset land; or, The great Pacific slope. London, Hodder [c1869] 322 p.
CVicAr **10242**

Same. Boston, Lee and Shepard, 1870.
CVU OrU Wa **10243**

Same. 1871. WaU **10244**

Same. 1873 [c1869] WaPS **10245**

Todd, John L.
Concerning the choice of a site for the University of British Columbia. [n.p., 19—?] 36 p. CVU **10246**

Toellner, August.
Chronology of "Company K boys" living for the anniversary at Waitsburg, Wash-ington on Wednesday, July 18, 1934. Seattle, 1934. 10 p. WaS **10247**

Same. 15 p. OrP WaPS **10248**

[Chronology of Company "K", 1st Wash-ington volunteers. Seattle, 1934] 16 p.
WaU **10249**

Tolbert, Caroline Leona.
History of Mount Rainier National Park. Seattle, Lowman & Hanford, 1933. 60 p. front., plates, fold. map. Many **10250**

Toles, H. L., View Company.
A trip to Mt. Tacoma. [Tacoma, c1908] [34] p. illus. Wa WaU **10251**

Tollemache, Stratford Haliday Robert Louis, 1864-
Reminiscences of the Yukon. London, Longmans [1911] xi, 316 p. front., plates.
CVU **10252**

Same. London, E. Arnold, 1912.
Many **10253**

Same. Toronto, W. Briggs, 1912.
CVicAr CVU **10254**

Tolmie, William Fraser, 1812-1886.
Canadian Pacific Railway routes; the Bute Inlet and Esquimalt route no. 6 and the Fraser Valley and Burrard Inlet route no. 2, compared as to the advan-tages afforded by each to the Dominion and to the Empire. Victoria, B. C., Brit-ish Colonist, 1877. 16 p.
CVicAr WaS **10255**

Testimonials. Victoria, B. C., Victoria Daily Standard Press, 1871. 11 p.
CVicAr WaU **10256**

Utilization of the Indians of British Co-lumbia. Victoria, B. C., Miller, 1885. 9 p.
CVicAr OrHi **10257**

Tomasevic, Jozo.
International agreements on conservation of marine resources, with special refer-ence to the North Pacific. Stanford Uni-versity, Calif., Food Research Institute [1943] xi, 297 p. illus. (maps) tables, diagrs. (Commodity Policy studies no. 1)
CVU OrPR WaS WaT WaU **10258**

Tomlinson, Everett Titsworth, 1859-1931.
Scouting with Kit Carson, illus. by John Frost. New York, Grosset [c1916] viii, 283 p. front. (Boy Scouts of America. Every boy's library)
Or WaSp WaU **10259**

Tomlinson, Robert, see no. 2630.

Tompkins, George R.
The truth about Butte. [Butte, Mont., Cen-tury Printing Co.] 1917. 47 p. illus., ports.
MtU WaU **10260**

Tompkins, Stuart Ramsay, 1886-
Alaska, promyshlennik and sourdough. Norman, Okla., University of Oklahoma Press, 1945. xiv, 350 p. plates, ports, maps. Many **10261**

Tooze, Lamar, see no. 11085.

Toponce, Alexander, 1839-1923.
Reminiscences of Alexander Toponce, pio-neer, 1839-1923. [Ogden, Utah, Mrs. Katie Toponce, c1923] 248 p. front., plates, ports. Montana pioneer. Many **10262**

Toppenish Review.
Toppenish and the lower Yakima. Toppe-nish, Wash., 1908. [14] p. illus., ports., maps (Special ed., Sept., 1908)
WaU **10263**

Topping, E. S.
The chronicles of the Yellowstone; an ac-curate, comprehensive history of the country drained by the Yellowstone River, its Indian inhabitants, its first explorers, the early fur traders and trappers, the coming and trials of the emigrants. St. Paul, Pioneer Press, 1883. 245 p. illus., plates, fold. map.
MtBozC MtHi MtU WaU **10264**

Toronto. Public Library.
The Canadian North West; a bibliography of the sources of information in the Public Reference Library of the city of Toronto, Canada in regard to the Hudson's Bay Company, the fur trade and the early history of the Canadian North West. Toronto, 1931. 52 p.
CVU WaS WaU **10265**

Torpen, Bernhardt E.
"Where rolls the Oregon", an outline of the power possibilities of the Columbia River and its tributaries. Bonneville, Or., 1937. 63 p. tables, maps. WaS **10266**

Torres Campos, Rafael, 1853-1904.
Espana en California y en el Noroeste de America; conferencia de D. Rafael Torres Campos, leida el dia 17 de mayo de 1892. Madrid, Establecmiento tipografico "Sucesores de Rivadeneyra", 1892. 59 p. (Anteneo de Madrid. Conferencias publicas, no. 44) CVU **10267**

The totem pole; legends and traditions of Alaska Indians [n.p., n.d.] [4] p.
CVicAr **10268**

The totems of Alaska. [Juneau, Winter & Pond, c1905] 12 p. plates. WaU **10269**
Same. 1915. WaT **10270**

Totten, William D.
In the highlands of our dreams; verse, patriotic, meditative, miscellaneous. Seattle, Peters Publishing Co., 1918. 141 p.
Wa WaS **10271**

Tourist Association of Kootenay.
Southern British Columbia; sport; Kootenay, B. C. scenery. [Nelson, B. C., n.d.] 40 p. illus., map. CVicAr **10272**

Tourists' Old Oregon Trail and Columbia River Highway information and guide book: Rock Springs, Wyoming to Portland and Seaside, Oregon. [Baker, Or., Ryder Bros., c1924] 76 p. illus., maps.
IdIf **10273**

[Tourtellotte, John Everett] 1869-
Souvenir booklet, capitol of Idaho at Boise; Tourtellotte & Hummel, architects. Boise, Idaho, Overland Publishing Co., c1913. [5] p. illus., 34 plates (1 col.) ports. IdU Or **10274**

Tousey, Sanford.
Val rides the Oregon Trail. Garden City, N. Y., Doubleday, 1941 [c1939] [56] p. illus. (part col.) WaU **10275**

Town Club, Portland, Or.
[Progress report on new building. Portland, Or., 1931?] 14 p. OrP **10276**

Towne, Charles Wayland, 1875-
"Her majesty Montana": The pioneer period, 1743-1877; the industrial era, 1878-1938; text by Charles W. Towne, illus. by Frank Ward and Bob Hall. [n.p. 1939] 150 p. illus., maps.
MtBozC MtU MtUM WaU **10277**

Western Montana, a land that enchants the traveller, enriches the settler and inspires every one, illus. by Frank Ward. Dillon, Mont., Frank A. Hazelbaker, 1929. [21] p. illus. MtU **10278**

The Towner Bay Country Club.
Suggested scheme for organization. [Victoria, B. C.] Diggon, 1927. [9] p.
CVicAr **10279**

Townley, Sidney Dean, 1867-
Descriptive catalog of earthquakes of the Pacific coast of the United States 1769 to 1928, by S. D. Townley and M. W. Allen. [Berkeley, Calif., University of California Press, 1939] 297 p. (Seismological Society of America. Bulletin, v. 29, no. 1, Jan. 1939)
OrP WaS WaSp WaU **10280**

Townsend, John Kirk, 1809-1851.
Excursion to the Oregon. [n.p., 1846?] 32 p. 1 illus. CVicAr OrHi OrP OrU **10281**

Narrative of a journey across the Rocky Mountains to the Columbia River and a visit to the Sandwich Islands, Chili, &c.; with a scientific appendix. Philadelphia, H. Perkins, 1839. 352 p. Many **10282**

Sporting excursions in the Rocky Mountains, including a journey to the Columbia River and a visit to the Sandwich Islands, Chili, &c. London, H. Colburn, 1840. 2 v. fronts. Many **10283**

Townsend, Mont. Methodist Epispocal Church.
Souvenir, Methodist Episcopal Church, Townsend, Montana, for the conference year, 1898-9. [Townsend, Mont., Star Print, 1899] 24 p. ports. WaU **10284**

Tozier, D. F.
Arts and crafts of the Totem Indians, collected by Captain D. F. Tozier, classified and photographed by W. H. Gilstrap. Tacoma, Central News Co. [n.d.] 32 p. illus. CV **10285**
Same. [39] p. CVicAr **10286**
Same. [41] p. CVicAr Or **10287**

Tracts on the Oregon question, by an American. New York, Taylor, 1846. 52 p.
OrHi **10288**

Trade & Commerce Publishing Company.
Historical and descriptive review of the industries of Walla Walla, 1891; commerce and manufactures with pen sketches of the principal business houses and manufacturing advantages. [n.p.] 1891. 1111 p. illus. WaWW **10289**

Trade Register, Seattle, Wash.
Seattle [a series of articles and many photo-illustrations that represent the industrial, commercial and civic growth of Seattle] Seattle, 1904. 120 p. illus. (12th anniversary no., v. 22, no. 1, Jan. 2, 1904) WaS **10290**

Trager, Mrs. Martelle W.
National parks of the Northwest, with illus. and maps. New York, Dodd, 1939. xv, 216 p. front., illus., plates, maps (part fold.) Many **10291**

The Trail Creek mines, British Columbia; their history and development with a description of the mining laws of British Columbia. [n.p.] 1896. 52 p. fold. map.
CVicAr **10292**

Trail to rail celebration, Eugene, Oregon; including a complete program for Klatawa, a pageant of transportation, Hayward Field, August 18-19-20 at 8:00 p. m. [Eugene, Or., Koke-Chapman Co., 1926.] 24 p. illus. Pageant "Klatawa" written by W. F. G. Thacher. WaPS **10293**

[Traill, Catharine Parr (Strickland)] 1802-1899.
The backwoods of Canada; being letters from the wife of an emigrant officer [with statistics of emigration] London, Knight, 1836. viii, 351 p. illus., 14 plates, port., map, tables.
CV CVic CVicAr CVU Or OrP **10294**

Same. (Library of entertaining knowledge)
OrP WaU **10295**

Same. New ed. 1846. 242 p. CVicAr
OrHi OrP Wa WaS WaWW **10296**

Same. London, Nattali, 1846. 351 p.
CVicAr CVU OrP OrU WaS WaWW **10297**

Same. 1849. CVU WaU **10298**

The Oregon Territory, consisting of a brief description of the country and its productions, and of the habits and manners of the native Indian tribes, with a map of the territory. London, Nattali, 1846. 78 p. map. CVU **10299**

Train wreck; the Lake Labish disaster (near Salem, Oregon, Nov. 12, 1890) four persons killed and over one hundred injured; the coroner's inquest and the railroad commissioner's findings. Salem, Or., Irvine, 1890. 12 p. OrP **10300**

Same. Photostat copy. WaU **10301**

Tranter, Gladdis Joy, 1902-
Plowing the Arctic. London, Hodder and Stoughton [1944] 256 p. front., plates, ports. CVU **10302**

Same. Toronto, Longmans, c1945. 311 p.
CV CVicAr CVU Or WaS WaT **10303**

Travelers' Aid Association of Portland, Oregon.
Report during the Lewis & Clark centennial exposition 1905 [n.p.] 1905. 20 p.
OrHi OrP **10304**

Traveler's guide and Oregon railroad gazeteer. [Portland, Or., Samuel, 1892] 96 p. tables. OrHi **10305**

Travelers' guide to the Pacific Northwest. Portland, Or., Lewis, 1882. 52 p.
OrHi **10306**

Travelers' Protective Association of America. Oregon and Washington Division.
"Where rolls the Oregon" [national convention, Portland, Or., June 3-7, 1902] [Portland, Or., Irwin-Hodson, 1902] 112 p. illus., ports.
Or OrHi OrP OrU WaPS **10307**

Treadgold, Arthur Newton Christian.
Report on the goldfields of the Klondike. Toronto, Morang, 1899. 7, 94 p. front., illus., fold. map.
CVicAr CVU WaS **10308**

Treadwell, Edward Francis, 1875-
The cattle king, a dramatized biography. New York, Macmillan, 1931. x, 367 p. front., ports. Henry Miller, biographee.
Many **10309**

Trego, Susie Boice, see nos. 1164, 1165.

Tremaudan, A. H. de.
The Hudson's Bay road (1498-1915). London, Dent, 1915. 264 p. front. (port.) 29 plates, 2 fold. maps. CVicAr **10310**

Treskow, A. von, see no. 4992.

Trexler, Harrison Anthony, 1883-
Flour and wheat in the Montana gold camps, 1862-1870; a chapter in pioneer experiences and a brief discussion of the economy of Montana in the mining days. Missoula, Mont., Dunstan, 1918. 20 p. CVicAr
MtHi MtU OrHi WaPS WaSp **10311**

Missouri-Montana highways. Columbia, Mo., State Historical Society of Missouri, 1918. 34 p.
MtHi MtU WaPS **10312**

Trezona, C. E.
Cape Nome and the northern placer mines, written from personal observation. Seattle, Denny-Coryell, 1900. 45 p. illus., 2 ports. WaU **10313**

[Tri-State Governors' Committee]
Opening the door to a land of plenty; an appeal to the National administration for suitable improvements on the Snake and Columbia Rivers, that they may function as efficient commerce carriers. [n.p.] 1933. [45] p. OrP **10314**

Triggs, Oscar Lovell, see no. 2359.

Trimble, Louis, 1917-
Give up the body. Seattle, Superior Pub. Co., 1946. 223 p. Oregon mystery story.
CV Wa WaU **10315**

Just around the coroner, by Stuart Brock [pseud.] New York, M. S. Mill Co. [c1948] 247 p. Seattle detective story.
WaU **10316**

Valley of violence, a western novel. Philadelphia, Macrae-Smith-Company [1948] 245 p. WaU **10317**

Trimble, William Joseph, 1871-
The mining advance into the Inland Empire; a comparative study of the beginnings of the mining industry in Idaho and Montana, eastern Washington and Oregon, and the southern interior of British Columbia; and of institutions and laws based upon that industry. Madison, Wis., University of Wisconsin, 1914. 254 p. map. (Bulletin, no. 638. History ser., v. 3, no. 2) Many **10318**

Trimmer, F. Mortimer, see no. 11292.

A trip up the McKenzie River, issued by the resort owners of the McKenzie River Country. [Eugene, Or., Shelton-Turnbull Fuller Co., 191—?] 14 p. illus.
WaPS **10319**

Tripp, Clare Ketchum, see no. 6129.

Trout, Peter L.
New theory concerning the origin and deposition of placer gold. Seattle, Pigott, 1901. 82 p. WaU **10320**

Prospectors' manual; being a full and complete history and description of the newly discovered gold mines on Granite Creek, the canyon of the Tulameen River, and other new mineral discoveries in the Similkameen country, designed for the use of emigrants, tourists, sportsmen and gold seekers. [Victoria, B. C.] 1886. 64 p. map.

CVicAr WaU 10321

Troutman, Samuel P.
Pe nel lu r gha-Oong we e puk. O koot-o kooz e tit-Ke yo ghu nu ghum-e yo o nung. [Bible verses in Eskimo] Gambell, St. Lawrence Island, Alaska, 1910. 27 p. illus.

WaU 10322

The truth about the Palouse country; eastern Washington and northern Idaho. [Spokane? Spokane and Inland Empire Railroad? 1908?] 40 p. illus.

WaPS 10323

Tucker, Edith Alberta.
Seattle children go exploring; an introduction to home geography, by Edith A. Tucker and Delpha B. Keeton. [Seattle, Seattle Public Schools, c1938] xv, 89 p. col. front., illus., maps (part col.)

WaS WaU 10324

Same. Rev. ed. [c1944] xii, 151 p. front., illus., maps (part col.) WaS WaU 10325

To North Pacific shores. Seattle, Seattle Public Schools [c1938] xviii, 202 p. col. front., illus., col. plates, maps.

Wa WaS WaU 10326

Same. Seattle, F. McCaffrey, c1938. 202 p. illus., plates, maps. (Series of western Americana) WaS WaT 10327

Tucker, Ephraim W.
A history of Oregon, containing a condensed account of the most important voyages and discoveries of the Spanish, American and English navigators on the north west coast of America; and of the different treaties relative to the same; the claim of the United States to that territory. Buffalo, A. W. Wilgus, 1844. 84 p. Photostat copy. WaU 10328

Tucker, Louis Norman.
The British Columbia Indian land question, by L. N. Tucker and P. D. McTavish. [n.p., Friends of the Indians of B. C.] 1915. 9 p. CVicAr 10329

Western Canada. Toronto, Musson [1907] xii, 164 p. front. (port.) 4 plates, 3 ports., fold. map. (Handbook of English church expansion, v. 2) CVic CVicAr 10330

Same. London, Mowbray [1908]
CV CVicAr CVU 10331

Tucker, Patrick T., 1854-1936.
Riding the high country, ed. by Grace Stone Coates. Caldwell, Idaho, Caxton, 1933. 210 p. front. (facsim.) illus., plates, ports. Many 10332

Same. 1936 [c1933] IdU OrSaW 10333

Tucker, Sarah, d. ca. 1859.
The rainbow in the North; a short account of the first establishment of Christianity in Rupert's Land by the Church Missionary Society. London, Nisbet, 1851. 222 p. front. (fold. map) plates.

CVU 10334

Same. New York, R. Carter & Brothers, 1852. OrP WaSp 10335

Same. 4th ed. London, Nisbet, 1853.
CVicAr OrHi WaS 10336

Same. 6th thousand. 1856.
CVicAr WaWW 10337

Same. 1858. CVU OrP WaU 10338

[Tufts, James] 1829-1885.
A tract descriptive of Montana Territory; with a sketch of its mineral and agricultural resources. New York, R. Craighead, 1865. 15 p. MtHi MtU WaSp WaU 10339

Same. Microfilm copy. WaU 10340

Tularski, Lura.
Star of Stonyridge. Portland, Or., Binfords & Mort, c1947. 42 p. illus.

OrHi WaS 10341

Tupper, Sir C. H., see no. 1107.

Turnbull, George Stanley, 1882-
History of Oregon newspapers. Portland, Or., Binfords & Mort [c1939] 560 p. plates, ports. Many 10342

Turner, Frederick Jackson, 1861-1932.
List of references on the history of the West. Ed. of 1913. Cambridge, Mass., Harvard University Press, 1913. 129 p.

Many 10343

Same. Rev. ed. 1915. 133 p. CVicAr MtBozC OrCS WaS WaU WaWW 10344

Same. By Frederick Jackson Turner and Frederick Merk. Rev. ed. 1922. 156 p.
IdB MtU Or OrCS OrP WaU 10345

Same. 1934. 156 p. front., plates.
CVicAr 10346

Rise of the new West, 1819-1829. New York, Harper, 1906. xviii, 366 p. front. (port.) 9 maps. (The American nation: a history, ed. by A. B. Hart, v. 14)

Many 10347

Turner, John Herbert.
British Columbia; lecture at Brentwood, Essex, January 14, 1909. London, Waterlow, 1909. 18 p. CVicAr 10348

See also no. 2966.

Turner, William H.
A brief sketch of the life of General Hazard Stevens, by William H. Turner, William Bellamy, William J. Ladd, John Lindsley, Samuel Brazier, Calvin G. Hutchinson, A. C. Kendall, Nathaniel S. Hunting. Boston, G. H. Ellis, 1908. 19 p.
OrHi OrP WaU 10349

Turner, William S., 1826-
Story of my life. Cincinnati, Western Methodist Book Concern [c1904] 345 p. front. (port.) CVicAr
Wa WaPS WaSp WaTC WaU 10350

Things worth while. Spokane, Dyer Printing Co., 1914. 129 p. Wa WaSp 10351

Turner-Turner, J.
Three years' hunting and trapping in America and the great Northwest. London, Maclure, 1888. viii, 182 p. front. (port.) illus., 2 maps.
CV CVicAr CVU IdU WaS WaSp 10352

Turney, Ida Virginia.
Paul Bunyan comes west; narrative by Ida Virginia Turney, Department of English; illus. by pupils in design under the direction of Helen N. Rhodes, Department of Architecture and Allied Arts, University of Oregon. [Eugene, Or.] University Press [1921] 34 p. illus.
WaU 10353

Same. [1927?] WaS **10354**

Same. Boston, Houghton, 1928. ix, 45 p. front., plates. Many **10355**

Paul Bunyan marches on, illus. by Norma M. Lyon. Portland, Or., Binfords & Mort [1942] [80] p. col. illus.
IdIf MtU Or OrCS WaSp WaU **10356**

Paul Bunyan, the work giant, illus. by Norma Madge Lyon and Harold L. Price. Portland, Or., Binfords & Mort, c1941. [80] p. col. illus. Many **10357**

Turney-High, Harry Holbert, 1899-
Ethnography of the Kutenai. Menasha, Wis., American Anthropological Association [1941] 202 p. illus., 8 plates, map, music. (Memoirs, no. 56) CVicAr
MtBozC MtHi OrSaW WaS WaU **10358**

The Flathead Indians of Montana. Menasha, Wis., American Anthropological Association [1937] 161 p. (Memoirs, no. 48)
Many **10359**

The practice of primitive war; a study in comparative sociology. Missoula, Mont., Montana State University, 1942. 1 v. (Publications in the social sciences, v. 1, no. 2) MtHi OrPR **10360**

Turnor, Philip, see no. 4282.

Turton, M. Conway.
Cassiar. Toronto, Macmillan, 1934. x, 123 p. front. British Columbia story.
CVic CVicAr CVU WaU **10361**

Tuttle, Birdeena, see no. 1181.

Tuttle, Charles Richard, 1848-
Alaska; its meaning to the world, its resources, its opportunities. Seattle, F. Shuey & Co., 1914. 318 p. 14 plates, 4 ports., 2 maps, diagr. Many **10362**

The golden North; a vast country of inexhaustible gold fields and a land of illimitable cereal and stock raising capabilities, illus. with maps and engravings. Chicago, Rand McNally, 1897. 307 p. front. (fold. map) maps.
CVicAr CVU WaPS WaU **10363**

Our north land; being a full account of the Canadian Northwest and Hudson's Bay route, together with a narrative of the experiences of the Hudson's Bay expedition of 1884, including a description of the climate, resources, and the characteristics of the native inhabitants between the 50th parallel and the Arctic Circle. Toronto, C. Blackett Robinson, 1885. 589 p. front. (fold. map) illus., fold. maps. Many **10364**

Tuttle, Daniel Sylvester, bp., 1837-1923.
Reminiscences of a missionary bishop. New York, T. Whittaker [c1906] vii, 498 p. front. (port.) port. Many **10365**

Tweedale, Aitken, ed.
Shipbuilding and shipbuilders of British Columbia, with allied industries. Vancouver, B. C., Tower Pub. Co., 1918. 60 p. illus. CV CVicAr **10366**

Tweeddale, George Witeman, 1883-
North of 62, a story of adventure. Buffalo, Foster & Stewart, 1946. 235 p.
WaS **10367**

Tweedsmuir, Lady, see no. 1158.

Tweedsmuir, Lord, see no. 9464.

Twin City News.
[Utsaladdy pioneers edition] Stanwood, Wash., 1941. [6] p. illus., ports. (Aug. 7, 1941) WaU **10368**

**Twin Falls North Side Land &
Water Company.**
Irrigation; Twin Falls country, southern Idaho. [n.p., 1909] 47 p. illus., fold. map.
IdB **10369**

Twining, Mrs. Frances (Staver) 1873-
Birdwatching in the West, illus. by Florenz Clark. Portland, Or., Metropolitan 1931. 169 p. col. front., illus. (part col.)
Many **10370**

Twiss, Sir Travers, 1809-1897.
The Oregon question examined in respect to facts and the law of nations. London, Longman, 1846. ix, 391 p. front., fold. map. Many **10371**

The Oregon Territory, its history and discovery, including an account of the convention of the Escurial; also, the treaties and negotiations between the United States and Great Britain, held at various times for the settlement of a boundary line; and an examination of the whole question in respect to facts and the law of nations. New York, Appleton, 1846. 264, iv p. Many **10372**

Tyler, Richard Gaines, 1885-
Water resources of Washington. Seattle, University of Washington, 1938. 61 p. fold. maps, tables (1 fold.) diagrs. (part fold.) (Engineering Experiment Station series. Report no. 4) Many **10373**

Tyler, William D., see nos. 9638-9640.

Tyrrell, James Williams, 1863-
Across the sub-Arctics of Canada; a journey by canoe and snow-shoe through the barren lands, including a list of plants collected on the expedition; a vocabulary of Eskimo words, with illus. from photographs and from drawings by Arthur Heming. Toronto, Briggs, 1897. 280 p. front., illus., plates, port., fold. map.
CVicAr CVU WaSp **10374**

Across the sub-Arctics of Canada; a journey of 3,200 miles by canoe and snow-shoe through the Hudson Bay region, including a list of plants collected on the way, a vocabulary of Eskimo words and a map showing the route of the expedition, with new illus. from photographs taken on the journey and from drawings by Arthur Heming and J. S. Gordon. 3d ed. rev. and enl. Toronto, Briggs, 1908. 280 p. illus., plates, ports., maps (2 fold.) CVicAr CVU WaS **10375**

Tyrrell, Joseph Burr, 1858-
A brief narrative of the journeys of David Thompson in North-Western America. Toronto, Copp Clark, 1888. 29 p.
CVicAr **10376**

The Coppermine country. [Toronto, 1912] 29 p. fold. maps. WaU **10377**

David Thompson, Canada's greatest geographer; an appreciation in connection with the opening of the David Thompson Memorial Font at Lake Windermere, B. C., August 30, 1922. [n.p., 1922?] [8] p. Or OrHi WaS **10378**

David Thompson, explorer. [n.p., n.d.] 14 p. illus.   OrHi **10379**

Documents relating to the early history of Hudson Bay; ed. with introd. and notes by J. B. Tyrrell. Toronto, Champlain Society, 1931. xix, 419 p. front., 13 plates, 5 maps (2 fold.) 2 facsims. (Pub. 18)   CVU OrU Wa WaS WaSp **10380**

See also nos. 4282, 4285, 10193.

Tyrrell, Mrs. Mary Edith (Carey)
I was there; a book of reminiscences. Toronto, Ryerson [c1938] xi, 131 p. front. (port.) 3 plates, 3 ports.   CVicAr **10381**
Same. With an introd. by J. E. Middleton. CVU WaU **10382**

Tyson, George Emory, 1829-1906.
Arctic experiences; containing Capt. George E. Tyson's wonderful drift on the ice-floe, a history of the Polaris expedition, the cruise of the Tigress, and rescue of the Polaris survivors, to which is added a general Arctic chonology, ed. by E. Vale Blake. New York, Harper, 1874. 486 p. front., illus.   Wa **10383**

Tytler, Patrick Fraser, 1791-1849.
Discovery and adventure on the northern coast of America and the Hudson's Bay territories [by P. F. Tytler and R. M. Ballantyne] London, Nelson, 1860. 409 p. plate, port.   CVicAr WaS **10384**

Historical view of the progress of discovery on the more northern coasts of America from the earliest period to the present time, with descriptive sketches of the natural history of the North American regions by James Wilson, to which is added an appendix containing remarks on a late memoir of Sebastian Cabot with a vindication of Richard Hakluyt. Edinburgh, Oliver & Boyd, 1832. 444 p. front. (fold. map) illus., 5 plates.
   CVicAr CVU OrHi Wa WaS **10385**
Same. 2d ed. 1833.   Many **10386**
Same. New York, Harper, 1839. 360 p. front. (fold. map) illus., 5 plates. (Harper's family library, v. 58?)
    MtU **10387**
Same. 1844.   CVicAr **10388**
Same. 1886.   MtBozC **10389**
The northern coasts of America and the Hudson's Bay territories; a narrative of discovery and adventure. London, T Nelson and Sons, 1853. vi, 409 p. front., plates, port., fold. map. Anon.
    CVicAr CVU **10390**
Same. 1854. CVicAr OrHi OrP WaS **10391**

Uhlenbeck, Christianus Cornelius, 1866-
A new series of Blackfoot texts from the southern Peigans Blackfoot Reservation, Teton County, Montana, with the help of Joseph Tatsey; collected and published with an English translation. Amsterdam, Johannes Muller, 1912. 264 p.
    MtHi **10392**

Original Blackfoot texts from the southern Peigans Blackfoot Reservation, Teton County, Montana, with the help of

Joseph Tatsey, collected and published with an English translation. Amsterdam, Johannes Muller, 1911. x, 106 p.
    MtU **10393**

Ulvestad, Martin, 1865-1942.
Norsk-Amerikaneren vikingesaga, samt pioneer-historie, statistik og biografiske oplysninger om Nordmaend i Amerika. Seattle, 1928. 191-314 p. Wa WaS **10394**

Umatilla Rapids Association.
Brief, the Umatilla Rapids project, Oregon, Washington, Idaho. Portland, Or., 1931. 151 p. maps, tables.   OrP **10395**

Uncle Jim, see no. 9800.

Uncle Nick, see nos. 11089-11092.

Underwood, John Jasper, 1871-
Alaska, an empire in the making, with numerous illus. and a map. New York, Dodd, 1913. xvi, 440 p. front., plates, ports., fold. map.   Many **10396**
Same. 1915 [c1913]   Wa **10397**
Same. 1920.   CVicAr **10398**
Same. London, John Lane, 1925.
   OrSaW WaPS **10399**
Same. Rev. ed. New York, Dodd, 1925.
  CVicAr CVU WaS WaT WaTC **10400**
Same. 1928 [c1925]   CV OrPR **10401**

Underwood, Marsh.
The log of a logger. Portland, Or., Kilham Stationery & Printing Co. [c1938] 62 p. illus., ports.   Many **10402**

Unemployed Citizens' League, Seattle, Wash.
By-laws of Capitol Hill Local. [Seattle, n.d.] [9] p.   WaS **10403**

Union Book and Pub. Co.
Alaska and the Yukon Territory. Chicago [n.d.] [16] p. illus.   CVicAr **10404**

Union County, Or. Committee of Citizens.
Natural resources of eastern Oregon, embracing a description of the counties of Umatilla, Union, Baker, Wasco and Grant and of the country along the proposed new railroad. Portland, Or., Himes & Batchelder, 1871. 22 p.   OrP **10405**

Union Pacific Railroad Co.
Along the Union Pacific system. [Chicago, 1925] 86 p. illus., map.   OrP **10406**
Boise, Idaho, yesterday and today. Omaha, 1925. 23 p. front., illus., maps.
   IdB Or WaPS **10407**
Dude ranches out West. [Chicago, Poole Bros., 1933] 60 p. illus.   WaPS **10408**
The great Pacific Northwest and Alaska; a panorama of grandeur; a revelation of accomplishment, a vision of opportunity. [Chicago, Newman, 19—?] 47 p. illus., map.   OrHi WaPS WaU WaWW **10409**
Idaho; an intermountain empire. Omaha [1927?] [46] p. illus., map. WaPS **10410**
Idaho facts, issued by Union Pacific System. [Chicago, Newman, Monroe Co., 1915?] 93 p. illus., map.   IdIf **10411**
Same. Omaha [1916]   IdB **10412**
The land that lures; summer in the Pacific Northwest [Seattle, 1911?] 46 p. illus., map.   OrP **10413**

Oregon. Omaha [1927] 94 p. illus., map.
OrP **10414**

The Oregon Short Line country; a description of Oregon, southeastern Washington and Idaho; facts for settlers regarding the resources, attractions, present prosperity and promising future, of the far northwestern section of the Union. Omaha, Republican Printers, 1885. 64 p. illus. OrHi OrU **10415**

Oregon, the Beaver state. Omaha [1927] 94 p. illus. WaPS **10416**

Outings in the Pacific Northwest. [Portland, Or., n.d.] 44 p. illus., map.
OrHi OrP **10417**

Same. [1927] 69 p. OrP **10418**

Same. [Portland, Or., Irwin-Hodson, 1927] 60 p. illus. Or **10419**

Pacific Northwest industrial properties of the Union Pacific Railroad. [Omaha, 1940] [90] p. illus. (1 col.) maps (2 fold.) plans. Or WaU **10420**

Panoramic perspective of the area adjacent to the new Challenger Inn and Sun Valley Lodge, Sun Valley, Idaho; served exclusively by the Union Pacific Railroad. [n.p., n.d.] 1 v. IdB **10421**

Puget Sound and Rainier National Park. [Portland, Or., c1926] [15] p. illus., col. maps. WaPS **10422**

Report of Hon. Jesse Spalding, government director, dated April 27, 1891, submitted to the Board of Directors of the company Apr. 29, 1891. Boston, Rand Avery Supply Co., 1891. 22 p. OrP **10423**

The resources and attractions of Idaho; facts on farming, stock-raising, mining, lumbering, and other industries, and notes on climate, scenery, game, fish, and health and pleasure resorts. 6th ed. St. Louis, Woodward & Teirnan, 1893. 132 p. front. (map) WaU **10424**

The resources and attractions of Washington for the home seeker, capitalist and tourist; facts on climate, soil, etc. 5th ed. rev. and enl. St. Louis, Woodward & Teirnan, 1892. 132 p. map.
WaS WaU **10425**

The resources and attractions of Washington Territory for the home seeker, capitalist, and tourist; facts on climate, soil, farming. Omaha, 1888. 76 p. map.
OrU **10426**

The resources of Montana. 2d ed. St. Louis, Woodward & Teirnan, 1890. 80 p.
MtU **10427**

Same. 3d ed. 1891. 95 p. MtU **10428**

Same. 6th ed. 1894. 94 p. map. MtHi **10429**

The scenic Columbia River route to the Pacific Northwest, Union Pacific system, standard route of the West. [n.p., n.d.] 63 p. illus. OrU **10430**

Washington the Evergreen state. Omaha [1925] 94 p. illus., maps. WaPS **10431**

Wealth and resources of Oregon and Washington; the Pacific Northwest; a complete guide over the local lines of the Union Pacific Railway embracing facts

disclosed by travel and personal investigation, valuable information for settlers, immigrants and tourists. Portland, Or., 1889. 256 p. illus., maps.
CVicAr OrCS OrP OrU WaS WaU **10432**

Union Steamship Company of British Columbia.
Our coastal trips. [Vancouver, B. C., Sun Pub. Co., n.d.] 32 p. illus. CVicAr **10433**

Union Trust and Savings Bank, Spokane, Wash.
The Spokane foundation, a community trust. Spokane, c1915. [18] p. facsim.
WaPS **10434**

Unitarian Association of Tacoma.
The First Unitarian Church, Tacoma, Washington. Tacoma [1946] 1 v.
WaT **10435**

United Ancient Order of Druids. Oregon.
Constitution and by-laws of Morvin Grove no. 2, instituted Jan. 16, 1870. Portland, Or., Walling, 1870. 56 p. OrHi **10436**

United Artisans, Portland, Or.
Constitution and by-laws. Portland. Or., James Printing Co., 1898. 62 p.
OrHi **10437**

United Church Ministry to Defense Communities.
Appeal for workers in defense communities with letter from L. P. Putnam, coordinator-director. [n.p.] 1943. 5 p. OrP **10438**

United Danish Evangelical Lutheran Church in America.
History of the Pacific district of the United Danish Evangelical Lutheran Church, 1888-1930; commemorating the 25th anniversary since the reorganization of the Pacific district on a delegate basis. [Blair, Neb., Danish Lutheran Publishing House] 1931. 55 p. illus., ports.
WaU **10439**

United Exchange Building, Inc., Seattle, Wash.
The Exchange Building, Seattle. Seattle [c1929] 25 p. illus., diagrs., plans.
WaU **10440**

United Producers of Washington. King County Federation, Inc.
General economic and relief program. [Seattle, n.d.] 1 v. WaS **10441**

U .S. Army. A. E. F. 1917-1920. Base Hospital No. 50.
The history of Base Hospital Fifty; a portrayal of the work done by this unit while serving in the United States and with the American Expeditionary Forces in France. Seattle, 1922. 190 p. illus., plates. WaU **10442**

United States Spruce Corporation.
Description of developed railway and mill properties on Olympic Peninsula, Washington, and railway, mill, and timber properties in Lincoln County, Oregon; detailed analysis of both properties offered for sale, September 2, 1919. [Portland, Or., 1922] 61 p. illus., tables, maps, plans, forms. OrP WaPS WaU **10443**

University location in British Columbia; a summary of the arguments presented by the Lower Mainland University Committee to the University Sites Commission appointed to fix the location of the Provincial University of British Columbia, June 1910. [Vancouver, B. C., 1910?] 60 p.   CVU **10444**

Untermeyer, Louis, 1885-
The wonderful adventures of Paul Bunyan, now retold together with illus. by Everett Gee Jackson. New York, Heritage Press [1945] 131 p. col. front., illus., col. plates.   Many **10445**

Upham, Alfred Horatio, 1877-
Idaho and her University [address delivered on the occasion of the author's inauguration as president of the University of Idaho, March 30, 1921] [Idaho Falls, Idaho, Register Printing and Pub. Co., n.d.] 16 p. front. (port.) IdU **10446**
Rhyming round the world. Boston, Humphries [c1939] 164 p. front.   IdU **10447**

Upham, Charles Wentworth, 1802-1875.
Life, explorations, and public services of John Charles Fremont. Boston, Ticknor and Fields, 1856. 356 p. front. (port.) 11 plates, port.   Many **10448**
Same. 50th thousand. 366 p.
            IdU MtU WaS WaSp **10449**
Same. Ed. by G. Mercer Adam. New York, University Society, 1904. 176 p. (Makers of American history)   WaW **10450**
See also no. 28.

U'Ren, W. S., see no. 2780.

An Ursuline of Alaska, see no. 5938.

Utz, Mrs. Cora, comp.
History of Spokane University, opened September 15, 1913, closed June 8, 1933. Spokane, Leo's Studio, 1941. 81 p. ports.
                    WaSp **10451**

Vachell, Horace Annesley, 1861-
Life and sport on the Pacific slope. London, Hodder & Stoughton, 1900. xi, 312 p. front., 10 plates.   CVicAr **10452**
Same. New York, Dodd, 1901. x, 393 p. front., plates.   WaU **10453**

Vail, C. W., see no. 7931.

Vail, Isaac Newton, 1840-1912.
Alaska; land of the nugget; why? A critical examination of geological and other testimony, showing how and why gold was deposited in polar lands. Pasadena, Calif., G. A. Swerdfiger, 1897. 68 p.
                    CVicAr WaU **10454**

Valamo (Monastery)
K stolietnemu iubileiu p ravoslaviia v Amerikie (1794-1894) Ocherk iz istorii Amerikanskoi pravoslavnoi dukhovnoi missii (Kad'iakskoi missii 1794-1837 gg.) S.-Peterburg, M. Merkushev, 1894. xiii, 292 p. plates, port.   WaU **10455**

Valenta, Edward, see no. 10836.

Valentine & Sons United Publishing Co.
Picturesque Okanagan. [n.p., n.d.] [32] p. col. illus.   CVicAr **10456**
Thirty-one views in colours of picturesque Victoria, B. C. [n.p., n.d.] [32] p. col. illus.   CVicAr **10457**

The Valley Tribune.
Special magazine edition. Kettle Falls,
Wash., Sparks and Wait, 1908. [16] p. illus. (v. 3, no. 49, Mar. 29, 1908)
                    WaPS **10458**

Van Alstyne, Lawrence, see no. 10910.

Vancouver, George, 1758-1798.
Entdeckungsreise in den nordlichen Gewassern der Sudsee und langst den westlichen Kusten von Amerika, von 1790 bis 1795; aus dem Englishen von M. C. Sprengel. Halle, Rengerschen Buchhandlung, 1799. 308 p. WaU **10459**
Narrative or journal of a voyage of discovery to the North Pacific Ocean and around the world, performed in the years 1791, 1792, 1793, 1794, and 1795, by Captain George Vancouver and Lieutenant Broughton. London, Lee, 1802. 80 p. plate.   OrP **10460**
Puteshestvie v sieverniiu chast tickago okeana, i vokurb sveta sovershennoe v 1790, 1791, 1792, 1793, 1794 i 1795 godahk, perefod s angliskago; Izdano ot Gosudarstvennogo admiralteiskago departamenta. Sanktpeterburg, V. Morskoi tipografii, 1827-1838. 6 v.   WaU **10461**
Reisen nach dem nordlechen Theile der Sudsee wahrend der Jahre 1790 bis 1795; aus dem Englischen ubersetzt und mit Anmerkungen begleitet von Joh. Friedr. Wilh. Herbst. Berlin, Wossischen Buchhandlung, 1799-1800. 2 v. plates, map. (Magazin von Merkwurdigen neuen Reisebeschreibungen, aus fremden Sprachen ubersetzt und mit erlauternden Anmerkungen begleitet, Bd. 18, 19.)
            CVicAr CVU WaU **10462**
En upptackts-resa till Norra stilla hafvet och kring jordklotet, att pa kongl engelsk befallning och omkostnad i synnerbet forska efter nagot segellart sammanbang imellan Norra stilla och Norra Atlantiska hafven, forrattad ahren 1790, 1791, 1792, 1793, 1794, 1795, under commando af captiain George Vancouver; ifran engelskan i sammandrag utgifven af Anders Sparrman. Stockholm, A. Zetterberg, 1800. 2 v. in 1. plates, fold. map. WaU **10463**
Voyage a l'ocean pacifique du nord et autour du monde. Paris, Lecointe, 1883. 6 v.   CVU **10464**
Voyage de decovertes, a l'ocean Pacifique du Nord, et autour du monde; dans lequel la cote nord-ouest de l'Amerique a ete soigneusement reconnue et exactement relevee; ordonne par le roi d'Angleterre, principalement dans la vue de constater s'il existe, a travers le continent de l'Amerique, un passage pour les vaisseaux, de l'ocean Pacifique du Nord a l'ocean Atlantique septentrional; et execute en 1790, 1791, 1792, 1793, 1794, et 1795, tr. de l'anglais; ouvrages enrichi de figures avec un grand atlas. Paris, Imprimerie de la Republique [1799] 3 v. plates, fold. maps and atlas of 4 p., 6 plates, 10 fold. maps.
                    CVU **10465**
Same. Tr. de l'anglais par P. F. Henry. Paris, Didot jeune [1801] 5 v. and atlas.
                    CVU **10466**
Same. [1802]   CVicAr CVU WaU **10467**

Same. 1803. OrHi OrP **10468**

A voyage of discovery to the North Pacific Ocean and round the world; in which the coast of north-west America has been carefully examined and accurately surveyed; undertaken by His Majesty's command, principally with a view to ascertain the existence of any navigable communication between the North Pacific and North Atlantic Oceans; and performed in the years 1790, 1791, 1792, 1793, 1794, and 1795, in the Discovery sloop of war, and armed tender Chatham, under the command of Captain George Vancouver. London. G. G. and J. Robinson, 1798. 3 v. 17 plates, map, and atlas of 16 plates. Many **10469**

Same. New ed. London, J. Stockdale, 1801. 6 v. fold. plates, fold. maps. Many **10470** See also nos. 9377, 11208.

Vancouver, B. C. [Burns Fellowship] Vancouver's tribute to Burns, pub. to commemorate the unveiling of a statue to Scotland's immortal bard. Vancouver, B. C., 1928. 96 p. illus., plates, ports. CV CVicAr **10471**

— — — Canadian Memorial Chapel. Dedicatory and opening services of Canadian Memorial Chapel erected at Vancouver in memory of those who made the great sacrifice, 1914-1918. [Vancouver, B. C., Sun Pub. Co., n.d.] 16 p. 2 plates. CVicAr **10472**

— — — Cedar Cottage United Church. 25th anniversady, 1909-1934. [n.p., 1934?] 16 p. CVicAr **10473**

— — — Robson Memorial United Church. Twenty-five years; souvenir, Robson Memorial United Church of Canada, Vancouver, B. C. [n.p., n.d.] [16] p. illus., ports. CVicAr **10474**

— — — Templeton Junior High School. Vancouver; a short history. Vancouver, B. C., 1936. 32 p. illus., ports., maps. CVicAr **10475**

Vancouver Barracks, Wash. Souvenir; Vancouver Barracks, Washington. [n.p., 1921] [28] p. illus., ports. OrHi WaU **10476**

Vancouver city the western terminus of the Canadian Pacific Railway and New Westminster, British Columbia, headquarters of the great Fraser River salmon industry. Victoria, B. C., Hibben [n.d.] 1 v. plates. CVicAr **10477**

Vancouver Club, Vancouver, B. C. By-laws of the Vancouver Club. Victoria, B. C., Harries, 1864. 13 p. CVicAr **10478**

Historical notes, constitution and house rules, list of members, amended to 31st May, 1936. [n.p., Clarke & Stuart Co., 1936] 64 p. illus. CVicAr **10479**

Vancouver Club of Printing House Craftsmen, Vancouver, B. C. A brief historical account of the romance of British Columbia. Vancouver, B. C., 1934. 93 p. illus., 3 plates (2 col.) CVicAr CVU **10480**

Vancouver Daily Province, Vancouver, B. C. British Columbia's 100 years of progress,

1827-1927. Vancouver, B. C., 1927. 1 v. (v. 34, no. 92, June 27, 1927) CVU **10481**

British Columbia; sesqui centennial, 1778-1928. [Vancouver, B. C., 1928] 1 v. (Mar. 26, 1928) CVU **10482**

[50th anniversary edition] Vancouver, B. C., 1948. 1 v. illus., facsims. CV WaU **10483**

Golden jubilee supplement. Vancouver, B. C., 1936. [78] p. illus. (May 21, 1936) CVU **10484**

A race with time in which every minute counts; a picture story describing the production of a modern newspaper. [Vancouver, B. C., 1931?] 27 p. illus. CVU **10485**

A record of unbroken progress. [Vancouver, B. C.] 1930. 24 p. ports. CVicAr **10486**

Vancouver, the queen city of the wonderful West; souvenir edition; latest views of Dawson City and other points of interest in Klondike; illus. of the mining shipping, salmon fishing, lumber, agriculture, manufacturing and other industries of British Columbia. Vancouver, B. C. [1898] 63 p. illus. CVU **10487**

Vancouver Daily World, Vancouver, B. C. British Columbia development. [Vancouver, B. C., 1922] 82 p. illus. CVU **10488**

Vancouver and the great war. [Vancouver, B. C., 1919] 63 p. illus., ports. (Special ed., Nov. 11, 1919) CVU **10489**

The Vancouver Daily World; illus. souvenir publication; the financial, professional, manufacturing, commercial, railroad and shipping interests of Vancouver, B. C. Vancouver, B. C. [1891] 24 p. illus., 7 plates, ports. CVicAr **10490**

Vancouver Exhibition Association, Vancouver, B. C. Souvenir booklet, 1935-36. [Vancouver, B. C.] 1935. 47 p. illus., ports. CVU **10491**

Vancouver, the great city of the great West exhibition. [Vancouver, B. C., Mainland Press, 1914] 28 p. illus., ports. (Bulletin 5) CVicAr **10492**

Vancouver Island, B. C.; a promising field for farming, fruit growing, dairying, mining, lumbering and fishing in the Esquimault and Nanaimo Railway belt. Victoria, B. C., British Colonist, 1905. 32 p. CV CVU **10493**

Vancouver Island Fire Underwriters' Association of British Columbia Constitution and by-laws. Victoria, B. C., Colonist Presses, 1905. 19 p. CVicAr **10494**

Vancouver Island Fish and Game Club. Constitution. [n.p., Banfield & Jewell, 1903] 10 p. CVicAr **10495**

Vancouver Morning Star, Vancouver, B. C. British Columbia in pictures. Vancouver, B. C., 1927. 32 p. (2d rotogravure ed., Sept. 10, 1927) CVU **10496**

Vancouver Poetry Society, Vancouver, B. C. Three poems. Vancouver, B. C., Printed by C. B. at The Sign of the Raven, 1925. 1 v. illus. (Chap-book) CVU **10497**

The Vancouver stock exchange, 1907-1947. [n.p., n.d.] [19] p. illus. CVicAr **10498**

Vancouver Sun, Vancouver, B. C.
British Columbia; a complete guide to the province, beginning of 1920 and embodying comparisons with previous years. Vancouver, B. C. [1920] 1 v. CVU **10499**

British Columbia, 1919-20; a descriptive, pictorial and statistical record of the growth and development of the most western Canadian province. Vancouver, B. C., 1920. 64 p. illus., 10 maps.
CV OrP **10500**

Industrial British Columbia, 1945. Vancouver, B. C., c1945. [106] 42 p. illus., maps, tables, diagrs. CV **10501**

Vancouver's golden jubilee, 1886-1936; official pictorial souvenir programme. [Vancouver, B. C., 1936?] 79 p. illus., ports., maps. WaU **10502**

Vancouver, the golden city of the West. [Vancouver, B. C., Lumberman Printing Co., 1936] [80] p. plates. CVU **10503**

Vancouver, Victoria and Eastern Railway and Navigation Company. [Vancouver, B. C., Independent Printing & Publishing Company, 1897] 11 p. map.
CVicAr **10504**

Vancouver's Lion's Gate Bridge. [West Vancouver, B. C., DeWest, 1938] 1 v. illus.
CVicAr **10505**

Van de Lure, John.
History of the voyages and adventures; giving an account of his being left on the northwest coast of America. Northampton, Wright, 1816. 90 p. OrHi **10506**

Van Denburgh, John, 1872-1924.
The reptiles of western North America; an account of the species known to inhabit California and Oregon, Washington, Idaho, Utah, Nevada, Arizona, British Columbia, Sonora and Lower California. San Francisco, Calif., California Academy of Sciences, 1922. 2 v. 128 plates. (Occasional papers. 10)
Many **10507**

Van der Heyden, Joseph, see no. 4397.

Van Dersal, Samuel.
Live stock growers' directory of marks and brands for the state of Oregon. Portland, Or., Kilham, c1918. 360 p. illus.
OrHi WaPS **10508**

Van Dersal & Conner's stockgrowers' directory of marks and brands for the state of Montana, 1872 to 1900; also a complete classified directory of sheep and wool growers. Helena, Mont. [n.d.] 467 p. MtHi **10509**

Van de Water, Frederic Franklyn, 1890-
Glory-hunter; a life of General Custer. Indianapolis, Bobbs-Merrill [c1934] 394 p. front., plates, ports., maps.
Many **10510**

Vandiveer, Clarence A.
The fur-trade and early western exploration. Cleveland, A. H. Clark Co., 1929. 316 p. front., plates, port. Many **10511**

Van Doren, Mark, see no. 7943.

Van Dusen, Wilmot Woodruff, 1854-
Blazing the way; or, Pioneer experiences in Idaho, Washington, and Oregon. Cin-

cinnati, Jennings and Graham [c1905] 199 p. front. (port.) Many **10512**

Van Every, Dale, 1896-
The shining mountains. New York, J. Messner [1948] 407 p. map.
MtBozC WaU **10513**

Van Guilder, Theodore, see no. 6010.

Van Male, John.
Resources of Pacific Northwest libraries, a survey of facilities for study and research. Seattle, Pacific Northwest Library Association, 1943. xv, 404 p.
Many **10514**

Vann, Elizabeth Chapman (Denny) see no. 2482.

Van Olinda, O. S.
History of Vashon-Maury Islands. Vashon, Wash., Vashon Island News-Record, 1935. 106 p. plates, map. WaS WaU **10515**

Van Osdel, A. L.
Historic landmarks, being a history of early explorers and fur-traders, with a narrative of their adventures in the wilds of the great Northwest Territory, illus. with many engravings. [n.p., 1915] 400 p. plates, ports.
IdU MtHi MtU **10516**

Van Sant, Clara, see no. 7813.

Vansyckle, J. M.
Oration delivered before the fire department of the city of Portland, July 5, 1858. Portland, Or., Oregon Weekly Times, 1858. 15 p. OrHi **10517**

Van Tiffin, see nos. 7602, 7603.

Van Tramp, John C.
Prairie and Rocky Mountain adventures; or, Life in the West; to which will be added a view of the states and territorial regions of our western empire, embracing history, statistics and geography and descriptions of the chief cities of the West. Columbus, Ohio, Gilmore [n.d.] 626 p. illus. CV CVU **10518**
Same. St. Louis, H. Miller, 1860. 640 p. front., illus., plates. CVU WaPS **10519**
Same. Columbus, Ohio, Gilmore & Segner, 1866. 649 p. front., illus., plates.
Many **10520**

Prairie and Rocky Mountain adventures; or, Life in the West; to which is added a view of the states and territorial regions of our western empire; embracing history, statistics and geography, and descriptions of the chief cities of the West. Columbus, Ohio, Segner & Condit, 1867. 763 p. front., illus., plates.
IdB **10521**

Same. 775 p. WaU **10522**
Same. 1869. 763 p. WaS **10523**
Came. 1870. MtU OrU **10524**

Van Valin, William B., 1878-
Eskimoland speaks. Caldwell, Idaho, Caxton, 1941. 242 p. front., plates, ports.
Many **10525**

Varner, Reed W., see no. 649.

Vattemare, H., see no. 10982.

Vaughn, Robert, 1836-
Then and now; or, Thirty-six years in the Rockies; personal reminiscences of some

of the first pioneers of the state of Montana; Indians and Indian wars; the past and present of the Rocky Mountain country, 1864-1900. Minneapolis, Tribune Printing Co., 1900. 461 p. front., illus., port. Many **10526**

[Veatch, John A.]
Oregon; a brief history of the resources of the Willamette, Umpqua and Rogue River valleys, being three of the most fertile and highly productive valleys on the Pacific Coast, showing their capabilities of sustaining the Oregon Central Railroad. Washington, D. C., McGill, 1869. 24 p. OrHi **10527**

Veeder, Fredric R.
The development of the Montana poor law, with editor's preface by Sophonisba P. Breckinridge. Chicago, University of Chicago Press [1938] xiv, 131 p. (Social service monographs)
MtBozC MtHi MtU WaSp WaU **10528**

Venen, Bertha Piper.
Annals of old Angeline. "Mika Yahoos delate klosch!" [Seattle, Denny-Coryell, c1903] [64] p. illus., ports.
WaS WaU **10529**

Venen, Laurel Philo, 1828-1902.
Kalethea; a peep into the realms of poesy. [Missoula, Mont., c1926] 117 p. port. "Life of Laurel P. Venen", by Mrs. Etta (Venen) Hartman.
MtU Wa WaS WaU **10530**

Vercel, Roger, 1894-
Northern lights, trans. from the French by Katherine Woods. New York, Random House [c1948] 251 p.
IdB Or OrP WaT **10531**

Vere, William de, see no. 2425.

Verendrye, Pierre Gaultier de Varennes la, see no. 5668.

Veritas, Philo, pseud.
The Canadian Pacific Railway; an appeal to public opinion against the railway being carried across the Selkirk Range, that route being objectionable from the danger of falls from glaciers and from avalanches, also generally on other matters. Montreal, Drysdale, 1885. 100 p. front. (fold. map) CVicAr CVU **10532**

Vernon, Francis V.
Voyages and travels of a sea officer. Dublin, Wm. M'Kenzie, 1792. 306 p. Nootka Sound. CVicAr **10533**

Vernon, B. C. Methodist Church.
1893-1908; souvenir of the fifteenth anniversary of Vernon Methodist Church. [n.p., n.d.] [15] p. illus., ports.
CVicAr **10534**

Vernon News Printing and Publishing Co.
The valley of Okanagan, British Columbia. Vernon, B. C., 1904-05. 2 v. illus., ports. CVicAr **10535**

Verseweavers Poetry Society, Portland, Or.
Fabric of song; an anthology of poems, comp. by the Book Committee: Anna Holm Pogue, Eloise Hamilton, and Lawrence Pratt; foreword by Howard McKinley Corning. Portland Or., Loomis Printing Co., c1945. 126 p.
Or OrP OrU **10536**

Vert, Albert E.
St. Andrew's Presbyterian Church, a historical sketch. [New Westminster, B. C., Jackson, 1922] 16 p. illus., ports.
CVicAr **10537**

Vestal, Stanley, 1887-
Jim Bridger, mountain man, a biography. New York, Morrow, 1946. x, 333 p. front. (port.) illus., maps. Many **10538**

King of the fur traders; the deeds and deviltry of Pierre Esprit Radisson. Boston, Houghton, 1940. x, 326 p. front., illus. Many **10539**

Kit Carson; the happy warrior of the old West; a biography. London, Hodder & Stoughton [n.d.] xii, 297 p. front.
CVicAr **10540**

Same. Boston, Houghton [c1928]
Many **10541**

Mountain men. Boston, Houghton, 1937. x, 296 p. front., plates, ports.
Many **10542**

Sitting Bull, champion of the Sioux; a biography. Boston, Houghton, 1932. xvi, 350 p. front. (port.) illus., 3 plates, ports.
Many **10543**

Warpath; the true story of the fighting Sioux told in a biography of Chief White Bull. Boston, Houghton, 1934. xv, 291 p. front., illus., 4 plates, 3 ports., maps. Many **10544**

Veteran Steamboatmen's Association of the West.
Steamer "Eliza Anderson". [Champoeg, Or., 1940] [6] p. illus. OrU **10545**

Victor, Mrs. Frances Auretta (Fuller) Barrett, 1826-1902.
All over Oregon and Washington; observations on the country, its scenery, soil, climate, resources, and improvements, with an outline of its early history, and remarks on its geology, botany, mineralogy, etc.; also, hints to immigrants and travelers concerning routes, the cost of travel, the price of land, etc. San Francisco, John H. Carmany & Co., 1872. 368 p. Oregon author. Many **10546**

Atlantis arisen; or, Talks of a tourist about Oregon and Washington. Philadelphia, Lippincott, 1891. 412 p. front., illus., plates. Many **10547**

The early Indian wars of Oregon, comp. from the Oregon archives and other original sources, with muster rolls. Salem, Or., F. C. Baker, 1894. xii, 719 p.
Many **10548**

East and West; or, The beauty of Willard's mill. New York, Beadle [1862] 109 p. (Beadle's dime novels no. 35) Microfilm. OrU **10549**

Eleven years in the Rocky Mountains and life on the frontier; also a history of the Sioux War, and a life of Gen. George A. Custer with full account of his last battle. Hartford, Columbian Book Co., 1877. 2 pt. in 1 v. front., illus., plates, port., maps. Joseph L. Meek, biographee.
MtU Or OrP WaS WaSp **10550**

Same. 1879 [c1877] OrU **10551**

Same. Hartford, Bliss, 1881.
CVicAr WaS **10552**

The new Penelope and other stories and poems. San Francisco, A. L. Bancroft & Co., 1877. 349 p. Many **10553**

Poems. [n.p.] 1900. 109 p. front. (port.) plate. Many **10554**

The river of the West; life and adventure in the Rocky Mountains and Oregon; embracing events in the lifetime of a mountain-man and pioneer; with the early history of the north-western slope. Hartford, Bliss, 1870. 602 p. front. (port.) illus., plates. Many **10555**

Same. Hartford, Columbian Book Co., 1870. Many **10556**

Same. 1871. Many **10557**

The women's war with whisky; or, Crusading in Portland. Portland, Or., G. H. Himes, 1874. 60 p.
OrP WaSp WaU **10558**

Victor, Ralph.
The Boy Scouts on the Yukon, illus. by Rudolf Mencl. New York, A. L. Chatterton Co. [c1912] 194 p. front., plates.
WaU **10559**

Victoria, B. C. Citizens.
Railway and ferry connection; the proposed by-law discussed; full report of meeting held in Victoria Theatre on Saturday, 3d Nov., 1900. Victoria, B. C., British Colonist, 1900. 16 p. 2 fold. maps.
CVicAr **10560**

— — — **First United Church.**
Seventy-fifth anniversary, First United Church, Victoria, B. C., 1862-1937. Victoria, B. C., British Colonist, 1937. 12 p. illus., ports. CVicAr **10561**

— — — **Metropolitan United Church.**
Souvenir programme of the seventy-fifth anniversary, Metropolitan United Church, Victoria, 1859-1934. [n.p.] 1934. 8 p. illus., ports. CVicAr **10562**

— — — **Provincial Royal Jubilee Hospital.**
Bye-laws. Victoria, B. C., British Colonist, 1891. 16 p. CVicAr **10563**

Rules for the government of the Royal Hospital. Victoria, B. C., British Colonist, 1877. 8 p. CVicAr **10564**

— — — **St. Andrew's Church.**
To commemorate the Sixtieth Anniversary, St. Andrew's Church, Victoria, B. C. [n.p.] 1926. 16 p. illus., ports.
CVicAr **10565**

Victoria Amateur Orchestral Society.
Constitution and by-laws; organized April 8, 1878. Victoria, B. C., M'Millan & Son, 1881. 10 p. CVicAr **10566**

Victoria and Island Publicity Bureau.
Facts about Victoria. [Victoria, B. C., British Colonist n.d.] 32 p. map.
CVicAr **10567**

Victoria & Sidney Railway.
S. S. "Iroquois". [Victoria, B. C., Western Printing and Publishing House, 1899?] 15 p. illus., table. WaPS **10568**

Victoria Branch of the Provincial Civil Service Association of British Columbia.
Constitution and by-laws. [n.p., n.d.] 8 p.
CVicAr **10569**

Victoria Fire Department.
Constitution, by-laws and rules of order. Victoria, Victoria Standard Office, 1873. 30 p. CVicAr **10570**

Regulations, rules and orders of the board of delegates and an act to extend and amend the provisions of the "Fireman's Protection Act", 1860, [n.p., n.d.] 35 p.
CVicAr **10571**

Victoria Golf Club.
Local rules and by-laws; list of members, June 1926. [n.p., n.d.] [12] p.
CVicAr **10572**

Victoria Gun Club and Game Protective Association.
Constitution and by-laws. Victoria, B. C., Waterson, 1891. 32 p. CVicAr **10573**

Victoria Hunt Club.
[Rules. Victoria, B. C., British Colonist, 1901] 11 p. CVicAr **10574**

Victoria illustrated; containing a general description of the province of British Columbia, and a review of the resources, terminal advantages, general industries, and climate of Victoria, the "Queen City" and its tributary country. Victoria, B. C., Ellis and Co., 1891. 96 p. illus. CV CVic
CVicAr WaE WaSp WaU **10575**

Victoria Jockey Club.
Rules and regulations of the Victoria, V. I. Jockey Club. Victoria, B. C., British Colonist, 1861. 7 p. CVicAr **10576**

Victoria Literary Institute.
Constitution. Victoria, B. C., "Daily Press", 1861. 7 p. CVicAr **10577**

Victoria Police Relief Association.
Victoria Police Department. Victoria, B. C. [Cusack] 1902. [100] p. illus., ports.
CVicAr **10578**

Victoria Real Estate Exchange.
By-laws and regulations. Victoria, B. C., Colonist Presses, 1911. 1 v. CVicAr **10579**

Victoria Society for the Prevention of Cruelty to Animals.
Constitution and by-laws, adopted Sept. 24, 1888. Victoria, B. C., Waterson, 1888. 11 p. CVicAr **10580**

Victoria "the city beautiful". [n.p., n.d.] 38 p. illus., fold. plate. CVicAr **10581**

Victoria Theatre Company.
Memorandum and articles of association. Victoria, B. C., British Colonist, 1884. 17 p. CVicAr **10582**

Victoria Tiger Engine Company No. 2.
Constitution and by-laws of the Tiger Engine Company No. 2 of Victoria, V. I. Victoria, B. C., 1861. 20 p. CVicAr **10583**

Victoria Typographical Union.
Constitution and by-laws of the Victoria Typographical Union including the scale of prices and list of members. Victoria, B. C., British Colonist, 1863. 30 p.
CVicAr **10584**

Victoria, Vancouver Island; the Naples of the North. [Victoria, B. C., Acme, n.d.] 23 [49] p. illus., maps. CVicAr **10585**

Victoria Wharf and Warehouse Company.
Memorandum and articles of assocaition. [n.p.] 1898. 16 p. CVicAr **10586**

Vidal, Gore, 1925-
Williwaw. New York, Dutton, 1946. 222 p.
Aleutian Island storm.   Many **10587**

Vighne, Harry Carlos de, see nos. 426, 10925.

Vigilante Trail Association.
Vigilante Trail, issued by the Vigilante
Trail Association. [Butte, Mont., Murphy-
Cheely, 19—?] 20 p. illus., maps.
                              MtU **10588**

Villard, Helen Francis (Garrison) 1844-1928.
In memory of Henry Hilgard Villard. New
York, Putnam [n.d.] 1 v. port.
                              OrP **10589**

Villard, Henry, 1835-1900.
The early history of transportation in
Oregon, ed. by Oswald Garrison Villard.
Eugene, Or., University of Oregon, 1944.
v, 99 p. (Monographs. Studies in history,
no. 1, Mar. 1944).   Many **10590**

Lebenserinnerungen con Heinrich Hilgard Villard, ein Burger zweier Welten.
Berlin, Reimer, 1906. viii, 528 p. ports.
                              OrP **10591**

Memoirs of Henry Villard, journalist and
financier, 1835-1900. Westminster, Constable, 1904. 2 v. fronts., ports., maps
(part double)   Many **10592**

Villard, Oswald Garrison, see no. 10590.

Villare, Linda, see no. 3055.

Vilstrup, A.
Early history of the British Columbia
Electric Power System in the lower
mainland of British Columbia; an address before the Vancouver section of
the American Institute of Electrical
Engineers, March 20, 1936. [Vancouver,
B. C., B. C. Electrical Railway Co., 1936]
16 p. map.   CVU **10593**

Vincent, Sidney B.
Story of the Columbia River Highway, the
most wonderful roadway in all America
and Portland, the city beautiful. [Port-
land, Or., Glass] 1919. 15 p. illus.
                          Or OrHi **10594**

Vincent, William David, 1866-
The Astorians. [Pullman, Wash.] State
College of Washington, 1928. 28 p. (Con-
tributions to the history of the Pacific
Northwest. Series A: Spokane Study
Club series, no. 3)   Many **10595**

The Hudson's Bay Company. [Pullman,
Wash.] State College of Washington,
1927. 34 p. (Contributions to the history
of the Pacific Northwest. Spokane Study
Club series, series A, no. 1) Many **10596**

The Lewis and Clark Expedition. [Pull-
man, Wash.] State College of Washington, 1929. 40 p. (Contributions to the
history of the Pacific Northwest. Series
A: Spokane Study Club series, no. 4)
                              Many **10597**

My book life. [Spokane] Spokane Study
Club, 1935. 32 p. IdU WaPS WaSp **10598**

The Northwest Company. [Pullman, Wash.]
State College of Washington, 1927. 28 p.
(Contributions to the history of the
Pacific Northwest, series A: Spokane
Study Club series no. 2)   Many **10599**

Northwest history. [Pullman, Wash.] State
College of Washington, 1930. 24 p. (Con-

tributions to the history of the Pacific
Northwest, series A: Spokane Study
Club series no. 5)   Many **10600**

Vining, Edward Payson, 1847-1920.
An inglorious Columbus; or, Evidence that
Hwui Shan and a party of Buddhist
monks from Afghanistan discovered
America in the Fifth Century A. D.
New York, Appleton, 1885. xxiii, 788 p.
front. (map) illus.
            CV CVicAr CVU WaU **10601**

Vinnedge, Robert W.
Pacific Northwest lumber industry and its
development; an address delivered at
Yale University, Dec. 18, 1923, under the
auspices of the School of Forestry on the
20th Engineers' Memorial Foundation.
New Haven, Yale University, 1923. 26 p.
(Lumber industry series, no. 4)
        OrCS OrP WaPS WaS WaU **10602**

Vinton, Stallo, 1876-
John Colter, discoverer of Yellowstone
Park; an account of his exploration in
1807 and of his further adventures as
hunter, trapper, Indian fighter, pathfinder and member of the Lewis and
Clark expedition. New York, Eberstadt,
1926. 114 p. front., map.   Many **10603**
See also nos. 1722, 1723.

Visiting Nurse Association of Portland, Or.
[Activities, funds and statistics of the
association. n.p., n.d.] 6 p. illus.
                              OrP **10604**

Twenty years of the Portland Visiting
Nurse Association, 1902-1921. [n.p., n.d.]
15 p.   OrP **10605**

Visscher, William Lightfoot, 1842-1924.
'Way out yonder; the romance of a new
city, with an introd. by Opie Read.
Chicago, Laird & Lee, 1898. 236 p. front.
(port.) Puget Sound city.
            Wa WaS WaT WaU **10606**

Vitz, Carl, see no. 1074.

Vocabulary of the Chinook jargon; the com-
plete language used by the Indians of
Oregon, Washington Territory and
British possessions. San Francisco,
Hutchings & Rosenfield, 1860. 8 p.
            CVicAr OrHi OrP WaU **10607**

Vogel, Joshua H., see nos. 6795, 6796.

The voice of the Yukon, as heard by some
who "mushed" the great stampede to
the river of Thron Diuck for the gathering of gold in the year 1898, written
down by one of them, with pen drawings by R. P. Wilson. Vancouver, B. C.,
Wrigley, 1930. 45 p. illus. CVU **10608**

Vollmer, August, 1876-
Police bureau survey, city of Portland,
Oregon; submitted to Mayor Earl Riley,
by August Vollmer and Addison H.
Fording, August 1947. [Portland, Or.?]
Portland Branch, Bureau of Municipal
Research and Service, University of
Oregon [1948] xxi, 217 p.   OrU **10609**

Vollmer, Carl Gottfried Wilhelm, 1797-1864.
Astoria; oder, Reisen und Abenteuer der
Astorexpeditionen von Dr. W. F. A.
Zimmermann [pseud.] Leipzig, Verlag
der Englischen Kunst-anstalt von A. H.
Payne [1858?] iv, 575 p. illus.
                              WaU **10610**

A **volume of memoirs** and genealogy of representative citizens of the city of Seattle and county of King, Washington, including biographies of many of those who have passed away. New York, Lewis Publishing Company, 1903. 773 p. front. (port.) 87 ports.

OrU Wa WaPS WaS WaU **10611**

Von Humboldt, Alexander, see nos. 6908, 6910.

Voorhees, Luke, see no. 5708.

Vosper, Lloyd C.
Cruising Puget Sound and adjacent waters; anchorages and harbor data pertaining to the southern shore of the Strait of Juan de Fuca, Islands of the San Juan Archipelago, Admiralty Inlet and Puget Sound, Hood Canal, Saratoga Passage; a general description and sketched scale charts of harbors and popular small boat anchorages of these waters, incorporating local knowledge with information by the United States Coast and Geodetic Survey; with an introd. by Guy Williams. Seattle, Westward Press, c1947. 88 p. illus., maps.

WaE WaS WaT **10612**

Voss, John C.
The venturesome voyages of Captain Voss. 2d ed., with an introd. by Weston Martyr. London, Martin Hopkinson & Co. [1926] xvi, 327 p. front. 13 plates, port., map. British Columbia resident's voyage round the world in the Indian canoe Tilikum.

CVicAr **10613**

Same. New York, Dodd [1941]

CVicAr WaU **10614**

Voto, Bernard Augustine de, see no. 2430.

Vrangel, Ferdinand Petrovich, baron, 1796-1870.
Ferdinand v. Wrangel und seine Reise langs der Nordkuste von Siberian und auf dem Eismere, von L. v. Engelhardt, mit einem Vorworte von A. E. Freidherrn v. Nordenskiold, einem Portrait F. v. Wrangels und einer Karte. Leipzig, Duncker & Humblot, 1885 xi, 211 p. front. (port.) fold. map. CVicAr **10615**

Narrative of an expedition to the Polar Sea, in the years 1820, 1821, 1822, & 1823, commanded by Lieutenant, now Admiral Ferdinand von Wrangell, ed. by Maj. Edward Sabine. London, J. Madden and Co., 1840. cxxxvii, 413 p. fold. map, table. Many **10616**

Same. 2d ed. with additions, 1844. xix, 525 p. front. (port.) fold. map.

CVicAr Wa WaSp **10617**

Same. New York, Harper, 1873 [c1841] 302 p. front. (fold. map) WaU **10618**

Puteshestvie po sievernym beregam sibiri i po ledovitomu moriu, sovershennoe, v 1820, 1821, 1822, 1823 i 1824 g., ekspeditsieiu, sostoiavsheiu pod nachal'stvom flota leitenanta Ferdinanda Fon-Vrangelia. Santpeterburg, Tipografiia A. Borodin i ko, 1841. 2 v. 4 fold. maps.

WaU **10619**

Statistische und ethnographische Nachrichten uber die Russischen Besitzungen an der Nortwestkuste von Amerika, gesammelt von dem ehemaligen Oberverwalter dieser Besitzungen, Contreadmiral v. Wrangell; auf Kosten der Kaiserl. Akademie der Wissenchaften hrsg. und mit den Berechnungen aus Wrangell's Witterungsbeobachtungen und andern Zusatzen vermehrt, von K. E. v. Baer. St. Petersburg, Buchdruckerei der K. Akademie der Wissenschaften, 1839. xxxvii, 332 p. fold. map, tables. (Akademiia nauk, Leningrad. Beitrage zur Kenntniss des Russischen Reiches und der angranzenden Lander Asiens. 3 v. in 1. 1839 v. 1) WaU **10620**

Vulcan Iron Works, Seattle, Wash.
General history, Alaska-Yukon-Pacific Exposition fully illustrated. [Seattle, 1909] [118] p. plates, ports. OrU WaU **10621**

Wa-sha-quon-asin, see no. 3862.

Waddell, John Alexander Low, 1854-1938.
John Chester Ralston, member American Society of Civil Engineers, died July 15, 1928. [New York] American Society of Civil Engineers, 1928. 7 p. (Memoirs of deceased members) Spokane biographee.

WaPS **10622**

Waddell, Oscar M., comp.
Eastern Washington historical primer, presenting dates and facts of some of the early explorations, settlements and happenings, from the Louisiana Purchase to the admission of Washington to statehood. [Spokane] Eastern Washington State Historical Society, 1943. 47 p. illus., map.

IdU Or WaS WaSp WaT WaW **10623**

Waddington, Alfred Penderill, 1800?-1872.
The Fraser mines vindicated; or, The history of four months. Victoria, B. C., R. de Garro, 1858. 49 p. CVicAr **10624**

Same. Photostat copy. CVU WaU **10625**

Judicial murder. Victoria, B. C., 1860. [4] p. CVicAr **10626**

Overland route through British North America; or, The shortest and speediest road to the east. London, Longmans, 1868. 48 p. front. (fold. map) tables.

CVicAr **10627**

Sketch of the proposed line of overland railroad through British North America. London, Longmans, 1869. 24 p. tables.

CVicAr **10628**

Same. 2d ed. with corrections. Ottawa, Taylor, 1871. 29 p. tables. CVicAr **10629**

Wade, Frederick Coate, 1860-1924.
British Columbia; the awakening of the Pacific; paper read before the Dominions and Colonies Section of the Royal Society of Arts, London, on the 6th of December 1921. Hastings, F. J. Parsons [1922?] 8 p. CVicAr CVU **10630**

Experiments with the single tax in western Canada; paper read before the eighth annual conference on taxation at Denver, Colorado, Sept. 11, 1914. [Vancouver, B. C., Sunset Presses, n.d.] 20 p.

CV CVU **10631**

Treaties affecting the North Pacific coast, read before sixth annual conference Association of Canadian Clubs, Vancouver, August 4, 1914. [Vancouver, B. C., Saturday Sunset Presses, n.d.] 19 p.
CV CVicAr CVU WaS WaSp **10632**

Wade, Mark Sweeten, 1858-1929.
The founding of Kamloops, a story of 100 years ago; a souvenir of the Kamloops Centenary Celebration, September 17, 18 and 19, 1912. Kamloops, B. C., Inland Sentinel Press [1912] [15] p. front. 7 plates.
CV CVicAr CVU MtU WaSp WaU **10633**

Mackenzie of Canada; the life and adventures of Alexander Mackenzie, discoverer. Edinburgh, Blackwood, 1927. xii, 332 p. front. (port.) plates, maps, geneal. table. Many **10634**

Notes on medical legislation in British Columbia. [n.p., 1890?] 14 p.
CVicAr **10635**

The Thompson country; being notes on the history of southern British Columbia, and particularly of the city of Kamloops, formerly Fort Thompson. Kamloops, B. C., Inland Sentinel, 1907. 136 p. illus., ports. Many **10636**

Wade, Mrs. Mary Hazelton (Blanchard) 1860-1936.
The trail blazers; the story of the Lewis and Clark expedition. Boston, Little, 1924. 276 p. front., plates.
Or OrP WaS WaT WaU **10637**

Wade, Mason, see nos. 7910, 7945.

Wade, Murray.
Legislative sketches of 1903. [Portland, Or., Metropolitan, 1903] [48] p. illus.
Or OrSa OrU **10638**

Sketches [of the] Oregon legislature 1913. [n.p., n.d.] [38] p. illus. OrHi **10638A**

Wadsworth, Leda A., 1901-
The lost moon mystery. New York, Farrar [1945] vi, 276 p. Montana novel.
Or WaS WaSp WaU **10639**

Mystery off Pirate's Point, illus. by Allen Haemer. New York, Farrar [c1940] 310 p. illus. Oregon coast story.
OrP WaS WaSp WaT WaU **10640**

Wadsworth, Wallace Carter, 1894-
Paul Bunyan and his great blue ox, retold by Wallace Wadsworth, illus. by Will Crawford. New York, George H. Doran Co. [c1926] 238 p. front., plates.
CVU OrLgE Wa WaS WaSp **10641**

Waggoner, George Andrew, 1842-1916.
Stories of old Oregon. Salem, Or., Statesman Pub. Co., 1905. 292 p. 19 plates.
Many **10642**

Wagner, see no. 4947.

Wagner, Frank, 1853-
Border-land in symbols. [Vancouver, Wash.] Vancouver Columbian [c1913] 129 p. WaU **10643**

Wagner, Glendolin (Damon) 1894-
Blankets and moccasins, by Glendolin Damon Wagner and Dr. William A. Allen. Caldwell, Idaho, Caxton, 1936 [c1933] 304 p. front., illus., plates, ports.
Many **10644**

Old Neutriment. Boston, Ruth Hill [c1934] 256 p. front. (port.) 12 plates, 14 ports. Biography of John Burkman, orderly to Gen. Custer.
IdIf MtBozC MtHi MtU **10645**

Wagner, Harr, 1857-1936.
Joaquin Miller and his other self. San Francisco, Harr Wagner Pub. Co. [c1929] xiii, 312 p. plates, ports., facsims.
Many **10646**

The new Pacific school geography. Olympia, Wash., Westlane Pub. Co. [c1900] 140 p. illus., maps, tables. WaPS **10647**

Pacific Coast stories, arranged and retold for use in the public schools, by Harr Wagner assisted by Alice Rose Power. San Francisco, Harr Wagner Pub. Co., 1918. 190 p. illus., 2 plates (1 col.)
CVicAr IdIf **10648**

Pacific history stories, arranged and retold for use in the public schools. San Francisco, Whitaker & Ray, 1896. 168 p. illus., col. plates. (Western series of readers, v. 1)
CVU OrP WaPS WaU WaWW **10649**

Same. 7th ed. 1899. MtHi WaS **10650**

Same. San Francisco, Harr Wagner Pub. Co., 1918. 190 p. OrU **10651**

Same. 1924. 280 p. WaT WaU **10652**

Same. Montana edition by Alice Harriman. San Francisco, Whitaker & Ray, 1903. 198 p. front., illus. MtHi **10653**

Pacific nature stories. San Francisco, Whitaker & Ray, 1896. 152 p. col. front., illus. (Western series of readers, v. 2)
CVU **10654**

Same. 3d ed. 1899 [c1896] OrP **10655**

See also nos. 621, 4604.

Wagner, Henry Raup, 1862-
The cartography of the northwest coast of America to the year 1800. Berkeley, Calif., University of California Press, 1937. 2 v. maps (part fold.) Many **10656**

Henry R. Wagner's The plains and the Rockies; a bibliography of original narratives of travel and adventure, 1800-1865, rev. and extended by Charles L. Camp. San Francisco, Grabhorn Press, 1937. 229 p. facsims. Many **10657**

The last Spanish exploration of the northwest coast and the attempt to colonize Bodega Bay. San Francisco [California Historical Society] 1931. [32] p. fold. maps (Quarterly, v. 10, no. 4)
Many **10658**

The plains and the Rockies; a bibliography of original narratives of travel and adventure, 1800-1865. San Francisco, J. Howell, 1921. 193 p. Many **10659**

Same. 193 p. 40 mounted facsims.
WaU **10660**

Spanish explorations in the Strait of Juan de Fuca. Santa Ana, Calif., Fine Arts Press, 1933. v, 323 p. maps (part fold.)
Many **10661**

Spanish voyages to the northwest coast of America in the sixteenth century. San Francisco, California Historical

Society, 1929. viii, 571 p. illus., 16 maps (5 fold.) (Special pub. no. 4)
Many **10662**

See also no. 9444.

Wagner, Mrs. Laura Virginia.
Through historic years with Eliza Ferry Leary, with an introd. by Professor Edmond S. Meany. Seattle, F. McCaffrey, 1934. xiii, 93 p. front., plates, ports.
Many **10663**

Wagner, W. F., see no. 5864.

Wagner, William, comp.
Coeur d'Alene mining information comp. between April 15 and June 15, 1916. Wallace, Idaho [c1916] 174 p. IdB **10664**

Waid, Hrs. Eva (Clark) , comp.
Alaska; the land of the totem. New York, Woman's Board of Home Missions of the Presbyterian Church in the U. S. A. [1910] 127 p. WaPS WaU **10665**

Waikiki Farm, Spokane, Wash.
Waikiki Farm jerseys; Waikiki herd won in 1920, 19 grand championships, 37 championships, 145 firsts, 90 seconds. Spokane [1920?] 42 p. illus. WaPS **10666**

Waite, Mrs. Catherine (Van Valkenburg) 1829-1913.
Adventures in the far West; and life among the Mormons. Chicago, C. V. Waite and Co., 1882. xi, 311 p.
WaSp **10667**

Waites, Kenneth Arthur, ed.
The first fifty years; Vancouver high schools, 1890-1940. [Vancouver, B. C.? 1940?] 160 p. illus., ports., maps, facsims.
WaU **10668**

Same. [1942?] CVicAr **10669**

Same. [1943] CV **10670**

Waitt, Georgina Seymour.
Three girls under canvas. Victoria, B. C., "In Black and White" [n.d.] 154 p. front., plates. WaU **10671**

Wakefield, Fries & Woodward, Portland, Or.
Statistical information concerning Portland, Oregon and Pacific Northwest regional economic area. [Portland, Or., 1940] 16 p. OrP **10672**

Walden, Arthur Treadwell.
A dog-puncher on the Yukon, with an introd. by Walter Collins O'Kane. Boston, Houghton, 1928. xviii, 289 p. front., plates.
Many **10673**

Same. Montreal, L. Carrier & Co., 1928.
CVU **10674**

Same. Boston, Houghton, 1931.
CVic WaW **10675**

Waldron, Samuel J., 1860-
Reminiscences of my life. [Victoria, B. C., Clarke Printing Co., 1938] 29 p.
CV CVicAr **10676**

Walford, Lionel Albert, 1905-
Marine game fishes of the Pacific Coast from Alaska to the equator, with paintings by Link Malmquist and photographs in natural color by Ralph Emerson. Berkeley, Calif., University of California, 1937. xxix, 205 p. col. front., illus., 69 plates (part col.) map, diagrs.
Many **10677**

Walgamott, Charles Shirley, 1856-
Reminiscences of early days; a series of historical sketches and happenings in the early days of Snake River Valley. [Twin Falls, Idaho, c1926-1927] 2 v. illus.
Many **10678**

Six decades back, illus. by R. H. Hall. Caldwell, Idaho, Caxton, 1936. 358 p. col. front., illus., 30 plates (1 col.)
Many **10679**

Walkem, William Wymond, 1850-1919.
Stories of early Britsh Columbia, illus. by S. P. Judge. Vancouver, B. C., News-Advertiser, 1914. 287 p. front. (port.) illus.
CV CVic CVicAr CVU WaS WaU **10680**

Walker, Cyrus Hamlin, 1838-1921.
Blazing the Oregon Trail; an epic poem, Albany, Oregon, August 17, 1905. [n.p., n.d.] 4 p. Or OrHi **10681**

Walker, Judson Elliott.
Campaigns of General Custer in the North-west, and the final surrender of Sitting Bull. New York, Jenkins & Thomas, 1881. 139 p. front., ports.
MtBozC MtHi WaS WaSp **10682**

Walker, Mildred, 1905-
The brewers' big horses. New York, Harcourt [c1940] 441 p. Montana author.
Many **10683**

Unless the wind turns. New York, Harcourt [c1941] 235 p. Montana story.
Many **10684**

Winter wheat. New York, Harcourt [c1944] 306 p. Montana story. Many **10685**

Walker, William, 1866-
The longest rope; the truth about the Johnson County cattle war, by D. F. Baber, as told by Bill Walker, illus. by R. H. Hall. Caldwell, Idaho, Caxton, 1940. 320 p. port., illus.
IdB IdU WaS WaSp WaU **10686**

Walker, William, see no. 6665.

Walkinshaw, Robert, 1884-
On Puget Sound; drawings by Jeanie Walter Walkinshaw. New York, Putnam, 1929. x, 294 p. front., plates, map.
Many **10687**

Walla Walla, Wash. First Methodist Episcopal Church.
Historical sketch. [Walla Walla, Wash? 1909?] 8 p. illus., port. WaU **10688**

Walla Walla Daily Bulletin.
1926-1927 progress edition. Walla Walla, Wash., 1927. 84 p. illus. (v. 21, no. 358, Feb. 3, 1927) WaU **10689**

[Walla Walla centennial celebration.] Walla Walla, Wash., c1925. 1 v. illus. (v. 31, no. 158-163, Aug. 13-19, 1936)
WaPS **10690**

Washington publicity month edition. Walla Walla, Wash., c 1925. 1 v. illus. (Thursday, Jan. 29, 1925) WaPS **10691**

Walla Walla Morning Union-Daily Bulletin.
[Walla Walla centennial celebration.] Walla Walla, Wash., 1936. [28] p. illus. (v. 3, no. 13, Aug. 16, 1936)
WaPS **10692**

Walla Walla Union.
Centennial edition, 1836-1936. Walla Walla, Wash., 1936. 68 p. illus., ports., maps, facsims. (Year 68, no. 101, Aug. 12, 1936)
WaPS WaS WaU **10693**

Sixty-fifth anniversary edition, 1869-1934. Walla Walla, Wash., 1934. 70 p. illus. (Sunday, Apr. 29, 1934) WaPS **10694**

Walla Walla Union-Bulletin.
Progress edition, 1938. Walla Walla, Wash., 1938. 92 p. illus., ports. (Feb. 27, 1938)
WaU **10695**

Progress edition, 1943. Walla Walla, Wash., 1942. 120 p. illus., ports. (74th year, no. 308, Sunday, Feb. 21, 1942) WaS **10696**

Wallace, Charles, see nos. 1895-1897.

Wallace, Edward James.
The Oregon question determined by the rules of international law. London, A. Maxwell & Sons, 1846. 39 p. (Political pamphlets, v. 83, no. 4)
CVicAr OrHi OrP WaS WaU **10697**

Wallace, Mrs. Esther.
A brief historical sketch of Lebanon, Oregon; produced by William D. Welsh from the excellent manuscript of Mrs. Esther Wallace. Lebanon, Or., Crown Zellerbach Corp., c1942. 28 p. illus., port., map. OrP OrU WaU **10698**

Wallace, James, see no. 192.

Wallace, James Nevin.
The passes of the Rocky Mountains along the Alberta boundary. Calgary, Historical Society of Calgary, 1927. 8 p. British Columbia—Alberta boundary.
Many **10699**

The wintering partners on Peace River, from the earliest records to the union in 1821, with a summary of the Dunvegan journal, 1806. Ottawa, Thorburn and Abbott, 1929. 139 p. fold. map.
Many **10700**

Wallace, Joseph, 1834-1904.
Sketch of the life and public services of Edward D. Baker, United States Senator from Oregon and formerly Representative in Congress from Illinois, who died in battle near Leesburg, Va., October 21, A. D. 1861. Springfield, Ill. [Journal Co.] 1870. 144 p. front. (port.)
Many **10701**

Wallace, William Stewart, 1884-
Documents relating to the North West Company; ed. with introd., notes, and appendices by W. Stewart Wallace. Toronto, Champlain Society, 1934. xv, 527 p. front., 4 ports. (Publications 22)
Many **10702**

See also nos. 6417, 9465.

Wallace Miner.
Fifty years of progress; special ed.; historical-progressive edition of the Coeur d'Alenes. Wallace, Idaho, 1937. 36 p. illus. (Dec. 16, 1937) WaSp **10703**

Waller, Osmar Lysander, 1857-1935.
Right of state to regulate distribution of water rights; address delivered before the State Bar Association at the 26th annual convention at Wenatchee, Washington, August 5th and 6th, 1914. Olym-

pia, Wash., Recorder Press, 1915. 14 p.
WaPS WaU **10704**

Wallin, Florence.
The garden; and other western verse. Seattle, Lowman & Hanford, c1925. 18 p.
WaS **10705**

Walling, Albert G., pub.
History of southern Oregon, comprising Jackson, Josephine, Douglas, Curry and Coos Counties, comp. from the most authentic sources. Portland, Or., 1884. 545 p. front., plates (1 col., part double) ports., double maps. Many **10706**

Illustrated history of Lane County, Oregon, comp. from the most authentic sources. Portland, Or., 1884. 508 p. front. (port.) 48 plates, port., map.
Many **10707**

Walsh, Clark B.
Fishing guide to Oregon. Portland, Or., c1946. 48 p. illus. Or OrP **10708**

Walsh, John Henry, 1879-
Cam Clarke, with front. by William Van Dresser. New York, Macmillan, 1916. 309 p. col. front. Washtucna, Washington Territory novel. Many **10709**

Walsh, Sophie.
History and romance of the San Juan Islands. Anacortes, Wash. [Anacortes American Press] 1932. 24 p. front., plates.
WaS WaT WaU **10710**

Walsh, Stuart P., 1894-
Thirteen years of scout adventure. Seattle, Lowman & Hanford [c1923] 174 p. front., plates, ports. Wa WaS WaTC WaU **10711**

Walsingham, Thomas de Gray, 6th baron, 1843-1919.
Pterophidae of California and Oregon. London, Van Voorst, 1880. xvi, 66 p. 3 col. plates. OrCS OrP WaS **10712**

Walter, Mrs. Margaret (Shaw)
Early days among the Gulf Islands of British Columbia. [Victoria, B. C., Diggon-Hibben, 1946] 67 p.
CVicAr CVU WaS **10713**

Walton, Eda Lou.
Dawn Boy; Blackfoot and Navajo songs, with an introd. by Witter Bynner. New York, Dutton [c1926] 82 p.
IdIf MtHi MtU OrP OrPR WaSp **10714**

Walton, Edith M., see no. 761.

Walton, W. B.
Eskimo or Innuit dictionary; as spoken by all of these strange people on the Alaska Peninsula, the coast of Bering Sea and the Arctic Ocean, including settlements on all streams emptying into these waters. Seattle, Metropolitan, c1901. 32 p. CVicAr WaS WaU **10715**

Walz, Edgar A.
Hidden treasure. [New York, Pusey, 1902] 32 p. illus. Okanogan County gold mine.
WaU **10716**

Wanamaker, Rodman, see nos. 2478-2840.

The Wanderer, see no. 6111.

Ward, Dillis Burgess, 1838-1922.
Across the plains in 1853. Seattle [1911] 55 p. port.
OrCS OrHi WaPS WaS WaU **10717**

Across the plains in 1853; a first-hand bit of early western Americana, related by one who, as a lad of 15, helped blaze that overland trail which led to the settlement of the great Northwest, foreword by Edmond S. Meany. Wenatchee, Wash., World Publishing Co., c1945. 16 p. illus., port.   WaU **10718**

Ward, N. Lascelles.
Oriental missions in British Columbia by N. Lascelles Ward assisted by H. A. Hellaby. Westminster, Society for the Propagation of the Gospel in Foreign Parts, 1925. viii, 128 p. front., plates, ports.   CV CVU **10719**

Wardman, George, 1838-
A trip to Alaska; a narrative of what was seen and heard during a summer cruise in Alaskan waters. San Francisco, S. Carson & Co. [1884] 237 p.
CV CVicAr CVU WaT **10720**

Same. Boston, Lee and Shepard, 1884.
OrP WaPS WaU **10721**
Same. 1885.   WaS **10722**

Wardner, James F., 1846-
Jim Wardner of Wardner, Idaho, by himself. New York, Anglo-American Publishing Co., 1900. 154 [20] p. front. (port.)
Many **10723**

Waring, Guy, 1859?-1936.
My pioneer past, with an introd. by Owen Wister. Boston, B. Humphries [c1936] 256 p. front., plates, ports., plan. Okanogan County Pioneer.   Many **10724**

Warner, Estella Ford, see no. 1935.

Warner, Frank W., comp.
Montana Territory; history and business directory, 1879; distances, fares, and altitudes; counties, towns, mining camps; commercial, mineral and agricultural interests; with a sketch of the Vigilantes. Helena, Mont., Fisk Bros. [c1879] 218 p. illus., plates, fold. map.   MtU **10725**

Warner, Gertrude Chandler, 1890-
Windows into Alaska; a course for primary children, stories and notes for teachers; worship services by Elizabeth Harris. Teachers ed. New York, Friendship Press [c1928] viii, 104 p. fold. plate.
WaU **10726**

Warre, Henry James, 1819-1898.
Sketches in North America and the Oregon Territory. [London] Dickinson [1846?] 5 p. 20 plates, map.
CVicAr OrP **10727**
Same. 5 p. 16 plates, map. In portfolio.
CV WaU **10728**
Same. 5 p. 6 col. plates, map.
CVicAr **10729**
Same. [1848?] 5 p. 20 col. plates, map.
CVicAr OrHi OrP WaS **10730**

Warren, Mrs. Eliza (Spalding) 1837-1919.
Memoirs of the West; the Spaldings. [Portland, Or., Marsh Printing Co., 1916?] 153 p. front. (port.) 3 plates, 6 ports.   Many **10731**

Warren, Fred A., see no. 8939.

Warren, G. B.
The last West and Paolo's Virginia. [Vancouver, B. C., Evans & Hastings, c1919] 45 p. front.   CV CVU WaU **10732**

Warren, Rex. see no. 3284.

Warren Publicity Company.
Bandon; the open door to the mart of the orient for the varied products of the most resourceful country of the Pacific North West. Portland, Or. [n.d.] [22] p. map.   OrHi **10733**

Wartman-Arland, Mrs. Flora E.
The story of Montesano. [Montesano, Wash.] Montesano Vidette, 1933. 32 p. ports. (Golden anniversary ed., Oct. 12, 1933) Wa WaPS WaS WaT WaU **10734**

Washburn, Bradford, 1910-
Bradford on Mount Fairweather, illus. with thirty-one photographs and three sketch maps by the author. New York, Putnam, 1930. ix, 127 p. front. (ports.) plates, maps. Alaska.   WaU **10735**

Washburn, Stanley, 1878-
Trails, trappers, and tender-feet in the new empire of western Canada, with 80 illus. from the author's photographs. London, A. Melrose, 1912. xvi, 350 p. front., illus., fold. map.
CVicAr CVU WaSp WaU **10736**
Same. New York, Holt, 1912.
CV CVicAr WaS WaSp **10737**
Same. Toronto, Mission Book Co., 1913.
CVU **10738**

Washburne, Virginia Brooks.
Tilly from Tillamook. [Portland, Or., A. E. Kern & Co., c1925] 127 p.
OrHi OrP WaU **10739**
Same. 2d ed.   OrHi **10739A**

Washington, Booker T., see no. 4361.

Washington. State College, Pullman
A handbook on scholarships and fellowships, their purpose, award, and administration. Pullman, Wash., 1940. xiv, 122 p. front. (port.) ports.
IdU MtU WaSp WaTC WaU WaWW **10740**

— — — **University Associated Students.**
University of Washington songs. 2d ed. Seattle, Hinds, Hayden & Eldredge, 1924. 150 p. front., music.   Wa **10741**

Washington and Alaska Steamship Company.
Golden Klondike; guide book to the Yukon gold fields, giving latest and reliable maps and data. Tacoma, Allen, 1897. 24 p. fold. map.   WaWW **10742**

[Washington Association of Small Loan Companies]
Facts about small loans in Washington. [Seattle? 1945?] [23] p. illus., ports.
WaU **10743**

Washington Athletic Club, Seattle, Wash.
[Souvenir membership booklet. Seattle, Lumbermen's Printing Co., 1930?] 80 p. illus.   WaS **10744**

Washington Forum.
The 30 mile Cascade tunnel; the Cascade barrier vs. the Columbia River bar. Seattle, Stewart Mailing List Co., 1925. [8] p. (v. 1, no. 2, Sept. 1924)
WaU **10745**

Washington office diary for 1890. Tacoma, Bard [n.d.] 67 p.   WaWW **10746**

Washington Pioneer Association.
Proceedings for the year 1903-1904; with historical sketch of the organization,

addresses at the reunion of June 21 and 22, and list of members present. Seattle, Metropolitan, 1904. 51 p.

OrHi OrP WaSp WaT WaU **10747**

Washington poets; an anthology of 59 contemporaries; foreword by Mary J. Elmendorf; ed. by the House of Henry Harrison, pub. New York [c1932] 191 p.

Many **10748**

Washington Society for Mental Hygiene.
Mental health in Washington; facilities and needs. Seattle [1929] 61 p. tables.

Many **10749**

Washington State Art Association.
The Museum of Arts and Sciences of the Washington State Art Association, Seattle; directorate, endorsements, purposes, collections, membership, the building, the site. What other cities do. [Seattle, 1910] 20 p. plate. WaU **10750**

Washington State Federation of Labor.
History of Washington State Federation of Labor, January 1902 to December 1924. Seattle [1925] 16 p.

Or WaU **10751**

Same. 2d ed. WaPS WaT **10752**

Washington State Federation of Women's Clubs.
Club stories, Washington State Federation of Women's Clubs. Seattle, Lowman & Hanford, c1915. 94 p. Many **10753**

— — — **Division of Music.**
Published music by Washington composers 1940, comp. by American Music Committee, Mary Alice Webb, chairman. [n.p.] 1940. 9 p. WaSp WaT **10754**

— — — **Fine Arts Department.**
Washington authors, selected by Jacqueline Noel for the Literature Division, Fine Arts Department. [Seattle?] 1930. [16] p.

Wa WaE WaPS WaSp WaT WaU **10755**

— — — — — — **Poetry Committee.**
Ours to share; an anthology of verse by members of the Washington State Federation, comp. and selected by Mrs. Paul D. Shafer, chairman. Tacoma, Johnson-Cox Co., 1940. 125 p.

Wa WaE WaSp WaW **10756**

Washington State Firemen's Association.
Souvenir program of the tournament of the State Firemen's Association to be held at Vancouver, Wash., Sept. 2, 3, and 4, 1895. Portland, Or., Peaslee Bros., 1895. 30 p. illus., ports. OrP **10757**

Washington State Fishermen's Association.
Washington salmon fisheries on the Columbia River. Ilwaco, Wash., Journal Job Print [1892?] 13 p. WaU **10758**

Washington State Good Roads Association.
Facts and figures on highway financing and administration in the state of Washington, as comp. from data before a special committee appointed after the 1929 convention of the Washington State Good Roads Association. [Seattle?] 1931. 11 p. tables. WaT WaU **10759**

A letter to the members of the Legislature, signed by Samuel Hill, November 1930. [Seattle?] 1930. 11 p. WaU **10760**

Washington State Historical Society,
Tacoma, Wash.
Building a state, Washington, 1889-1939. [Tacoma, 1940] xi, 607 [19] p. illus. (Publications, v. 3) Many **10761**

Sketches of the Washington State Historical Society and Ferry Museum, compiled and arranged by W. H. Gilstrap, secretary. [Tacoma] 1912. 24 p. front., plates. OrHi WaPS WaU **10762**

A statement of its organization; its constitution, by-laws, officers, and "A word to the reader". Tacoma, F. T. Houghton & Co., 1891. 14 p.

WaS WaU WaWW **10763**

Washington State Holstein-Friesian Association.
Washington state Holstein-Friesian cattle; a brief history of the achievements of the Holstein-Friesians in the state of Washington. Seattle, 1924. 48 p. illus.

WaPS **10764**

Washington State Sportsmen's Association for the Protection of Fish and Game.
Constitution and by-laws of the Washington State Sportsmen's Association for the Protection of Fish and Game; and game laws of the state of Washington. Seattle, Corbett & Co., 1896. 32 p.

WaS **10765**

Washington Veteran.
Pacific fleet commemoration number. Seattle, 1919. 64 p. illus., plates, ports. (Special no., Sept. 1919) WaU **10766**

Waterman, Thomas Talbot, 1885-1936.
Indian houses of Puget Sound, by T. T. Waterman and Ruth Greiner. New York, Museum of the American Indian, Heye Foundation, 1921. 61 p. illus., 10 plates. (Indian notes and monographs. Miscellaneous, no. 9) Many **10767**

Native houses of western North America, by T. T. Waterman and collaborators. New York, Museum of the American Indian, Heye Foundation, 1921. 97 p. front. (fold. map) plates. (Indian notes and monographs. Miscellaneous, no. 11)

Many **10768**

Types of canoes on Puget Sound, by T. T. Waterman and Geraldine Coffin. New York, Museum of the American Indian, Heye Foundation, 1920. 43 p. illus., 7 plates. (Indian notes and monographs)

Many **10769**

The whaling equipment of the Makah Indians. Seattle, University of Washington, 1920. 67 p. illus., plates. (Publications in political and social science, v. 1, no. 1) Many **10770**

Watson, Chandler Bruer, 1849-
Prehistoric Siskiyou Island and marble halls of Oregon. [Ashland, Or.?] c1909. 147 p. front. (port.) Many **10771**

Watson, G. C.
The commission of H. M. S. Amphion, Pacific station, 1900-1904. London, Westminster Press, 1904. 119 p. front., 7 plates, port. (Log series, no. 11)

CVicAr **10772**

Watson, Genneva Dickey, 1894-
On other hills. [Tacoma, c1947] 96 p.
Poems. WaS WaU **10773**
Watson, J. Howard, see no. 7537.
Watson, Sir Norman, bart., 1897-
Round Mystery Mountain; a ski adventure
by Sir Norman Watson, bt. and Edward
J. King, M. C.; with a foreword by F. S.
Smythe. London, E. Arnold & Co. [1935]
xii, 246 p. col. front., plates, ports., maps.
CV CVicAr CVU OrCS OrP **10774**
Same. New York, Longmans, 1935.
CVU **10775**
Watson, Robert, 1882-
A boy of the great North West; the rous-
ing experiences of a young Canadian
among cowboys, hunters, trappers, fur
traders, fishermen and Indians. Ottawa,
Graphic Pub. [c1930] 259 p. front. (port.)
illus. CVU WaS WaU **10776**
Dreams of Fort Garry, with wood cut
illus. by W. J. Phillips; an epic poem on
the life and times of the early settlers
of western Canada, complete with gloss-
ary and historical notes. Winnipeg,
Stovel Co. [c1931] 63 p. illus.
WaSp **10777**
The governor and company of adventurers of England trading into Hudson's
Bay. [n.p., 1928?] 30 p. port. Anon.
WaU **10778**
Same. [1930?] WaS **10779**
The Hudson's Bay Company. Toronto, Ry-
erson [c1928] 32 p. illus. (Canadian his-
tory readers. Master builders)
CVicAr **10780**
Hudson's Bay Company, incorporated 2d
May, 1670; a brief history. [n.p., Hud-
son's Bay Co., 1927?] 30 p. illus., port.
Anon. WaSp **10781**
Lower Fort Garry, a history of the stone
fort. Winnipeg, Hudson's Bay Co., 1928.
69 p. front., illus., plate, fold. plan.
CVU WaS WaSp WaU **10782**
Watson, Winifred, see no. 4545.
[Watt, Madge Robertson]
The southmost districts, Vancouver Island:
Colwood, Metchosin, Sooke. Victoria, B.
C., British Colonist, 1910. 64 p. illus.
CVicAr CVU **10783**
Watt, Marion Frances.
Cypress and rose. Seattle, Ivy Press, 1902.
183 p. front., plate. Poetry. WaU **10784**
Maurice and other stories. Seattle, Ivy
Press, 1903. 313 p. WaU **10785**
Watt, Mrs. Roberta (Frye)
Four wagons west; the story of Seattle,
illus. by Paul Morgan Gustin. Portland,
Or., Metropolitan [c1931] 390 p. illus.
Many **10786**
The story of Seattle, illus. by Paul Morgan
Gustin. Seattle, Lowman & Hanford,
1931. xi, 387 p. plates. Many **10787**
Same. 1932 [c1931]
CV Wa WaTC WaW **10788**
Watters, Dennis Alonzo, 1849-1926.
First American itinerant of Methodism,
William Watters, introd. by Bishop
Charles C. McCabe. Cincinnati, Curts &
Jennings, c1898. 172 p. Portland author.
Many **10789**

The trail to boyhood, swimmin' hole and
melno [!] patch. Cincinnati, Western
Methodist Book Concern [c1910] 80 p.
plates. Poetry.
OrCS OhHi OrP OrU WaU **10790**
The Watters family. Portland, Or., 1915.
22 p. plates, ports., geneal. table.
Or OrP OrU Wa WaPS **10791**
Watts-Dunton, Theodore, see nos. 5240,
5241, 5243-5246.
Wattson, A. B., see no. 4452.
Waverly Baby Home, Portland, Or.
"Baby home" incorporated March 16, 1889;
re-incorporated April 8, 1912. Portland,
Or., Anderson Printing Co. [1916] [24]
p. illus. OrHi **10792**
"Baby home" (Waverly) of Portland, Or.
Portland, Or., Anderson Printing Co.
[1916] 25 p. illus. OrHi **10793**
Wayfarer Pageant Society.
"The Wayfarer" produced in the Uni-
versity of Washington stadium, Seattle,
July 27 to August 1, 1925. Seattle, Pio-
neer Printing Co. [1925] [24] p. illus.,
ports. WaU **10794**
Wead, Frank Wilber, 1895-
Gales, ice and men, a biography of the
steam barkentine Bear, decorations by
Charles E. Pont. New York, Dodd, 1937.
xiii, 272 p. col. front., plates (1 double)
Many **10795**
Weage, Arthur D., see no. 10796.
Weage, Mrs. Mary (Dudley) 1831-
Songs of the unseen, comp. and arranged
by her son, Arthur D. Weage. [Seattle,
Socialist Pub. Assn.] c1915. 47 p. front.
(port.) WaS **10796**
Weatherall, M. I. R., see no. 10836.
Weatherby, Hugh, 1908-
Tales the totems tell, illus. by the author.
Toronto, Macmillan, 1944. x, 96 p. plates.
CVicAr CVU WaS WaU **10797**
Same. 2d ed. 1946, c1944. CV **10798**
Weaver, C. E., see no. 9921.
Weaver, John Ernest, 1884-
A study of the vegetation of southeastern
Washington and adjacent Idaho. [Lin-
coln, Neb., University of Nebraska] 1917.
131 p. illus., diagrs. (University studies,
v. 17, no. 1) Wa WaS **10799**
Webb, J. Watson, see no. 9911.
[Webb, Marion]
[Booklet on Dr. Wilson Compton, prepared
by a group who worked with him. Washington, D. C., 1945] 1 v. front. (port.)
illus., ports. WaT **10800**
Webb, Mary Alice, see no. 10754.
Webb, William Edward.
Buffalo land; an authentic narrative of
the adventures and misadventures of a
late scientific and sporting party upon
the great plains of the West; with full
descriptions of the country traversed,
the Indian as he is, the habits of the
buffalo, wolf, the wild horse, etc., etc.;
also an appendix, constituting the work
a manual for sportsmen and hand-book
for emigrants seeking homes, illus., from
original drawings by Henry Worrall,

and actual photographs. Cincinnati, E. Hannaford & Co., 1872. 503 p. front., plates, ports. WaSp WaTC **10801**

Same. Philadelphia, Hubbard Bros., 1872. MtU **10802**

Same. Cincinnati, E. Hannaford & Co., 1873. MtHi **10803**

Webb, William Seward, 1851-1926.
California and Alaska and over the Canadian Pacific Railway. New York, Putnam, 1890. 190 p. front., illus., 91 plates. CVicAr **10804**

Same. 2d ed. 1891. xiv, 268 p. front., illus., 11 plates. Many **10805**

Webber, William L.
The original thunder bird stick game. Vancouver, B. C., c1939. 13 p. illus. WaS **10806**

Skookum wa-wa, "Good talk"; this book illus. by Ross Watson. Vancouver, B. C. [Lumberman Printing Co., c1945] 94 p. illus. (part col.) CV CVU WaS **10807**

The Tunderbird "Tootooch" legends; folk tales of the Indian tribes of the Pacific Northwest coast Indians. [Seattle, Ace Printing Co., c1936] xxi, 38 p. front., illus. CV CVicAr OrP WaSp WaU **10808**

Webster, Erwin L.
In the zone of filtered sunshine; why the Pacific Northwest is destined to dominate the commercial world. Seattle, Pacific Northwest Pub. Co., c1924. 31 p. maps., diagrs. WaU **10809**

Webster, Don G.
Annie; story and pictures by D. G. Webster. Portland, Or., Binfords & Mort, c1945. [20] p. col. front., col. illus. Pacific tuna fleet juvenile story.
Wa WaS WaU **10810**

Webster, Edward B.
Fishing in the Olympics; salmon, trout, mud shark, bull heads, j. w. pike, halibut, dollies, whale and kippered herrings, illus. by Annette Swan. Port Angeles, Wash., Evening News [c1923] 226 p. front., illus., plates.
OrP Wa WaPS WaS WaU **10811**

The friendly mountain. [n.p.] Smith & Webster, 1917. [53] p. front., illus. Wa **10812**

Same. Annette Chaddock Swan, illus. 2d ed. Port Angeles, Wash., Evening News, 1921. 119 p. front., illus. Wa WaS **10813**

The king of the Olympics; the Roosevelt elk and other mammals of the Olympic Mountains, illus. with photographs by Wm. Everett, George Welch, Grant Humes, and others. Port Angeles, Wash., 1920. 227 p. front., plates. Many **10814**

Webster, Kimball, 1828-1916.
The gold seekers of '49; a personal narrative of the overland trail and adventures in California and Oregon from 1849 to 1854, by Kimball Webster, a New England forty-niner; with an introd. and biographical sketch by George Waldo Browne; illus. by Frank Holland and

others. Manchester, N. H., Standard Book Co., 1917. 240 p. front. (port.) plates, port. Many **10815**

Weeks, Helen C., see no. 1414.

[Weible, George]
Gonzaga's silver jubilee; a memoir. [Spokane, 1912] 280 p. illus., ports. Many **10816**

Weil, see no. 89.

Weiss, Harold A.
The lumber industry in the Pacific Northwest and related financing aspects. New Brunswick, 1945. 1 v. illus., maps, table. OrP **10817**

Welch, Charles A., 1860-
History of the Big Horn Basin; with stories of early days, sketches of pioneers and writings of the author, March 25, 1940. [Salt Lake City] Deseret News, 1940. 276 p. illus., ports.
MtHi WaS WaU **10818**

Wellcome, Sir Henry Solomon, 1853?-1936.
The story of Metlakahtla. London, Saxon & Co., 1887. xx, 483 p. front., 21 plates, 3 ports. Many **10819**

Same. 3d ed. WaSp WaU **10820**

Same. 4th ed. OrU **10821**

Wells, Erma Wiley, 1885-
The shining heart; a book of verse, by Erma Wiley Wells and verse-writing friends. [Spokane, Fountain Pub., c1947] 244 p. plates. WaSp **10822**

Wells, Harry Laurenz, 1854-
Alaska and the Klondike; the new gold fields and how to reach them. Portland, Or., 1897. 72 p. illus., 12 plates, fold. map. OrHi WaU **10823**

Alaska, the new eldorado; its history, its gold fields, its scenery, its routes of travel. Portland, Or., J. K. Gill Co., 1897. 88 p. front., illus., 19 plates, 2 fold maps. CVU WaU **10824**

Same. 1898. OrHi **10825**

Multnomah, a legend of the Columbia. [Portland, Or.] 1923. 89 p. front., plates. Verse.
CVicAr OrHi OrP WaT WaU **10826**

Popular history of Oregon from the discovery of America to the admission of the state into the Union. Portland, Or., Steel, 1889. 480 p. 4 plates, facsim., tables. CVicAr
OrHi OrP WaPS WaSp WaU **10827**

Wells, Hulet M.
The colonel and his friends; a suppressed play, a comedy in three acts. [Seattle, 1913?] 32 p. Seattle setting. WaU **10828**

Wells, Lemuel Henry, bp., 1841-
A pioneer missionary, missionary bishop of Spokane. Seattle, Progressive Printing [1930?] 167 p. front. (port.)
WaT **10829**

Same. [1931] IdU Wa WaS WaU **10830**

Same. [c1932] OrP WaTC **10831**

Same. Tacoma, Mrs. Glen W. Darling, c1932. Or **10832**

Wells, Mary, 1863-
The passing of District 66, Elkton, Oregon. [Reedsport, Or., Port Umpqua Courier Print, n.d.] 15 p. OrHi **10832A**

Wellwood, W. B.
Through the years, 1891-1938, Belmont United Church, Victoria. [n.p., n.d.] 22 [13] p. illus.　　　　CVicAr **10833**

Welsh, John T., 1866-
Pioneers; an address delivered August 10, 1930, at Bay Center, Washington. [South Bend, Wash., Willapa Harbor Pub. Co., c1931] 26 p. front. (port.)　WaS **10834**

Welsh, Josephine.
The chapel by the sea; the story of a little church at Vaughn, Washington. [n.p., n.d.] 23 p. illus.　　　　WaT **10835**

Welsh, William D., see no. 10698.

Welzl, Jan, 1870-
The quest for polar treasures, with an introd. by Bedrich Golombek & Edvard Valenta; trans. by M. & R. Weatherall. New York, Macmillan, 1933. 352 p.
　　　　IdU OrP Wa WaS **10836**

Thirty years in the golden North; trans. by Paul Selver; with a foreword by Karel Capek. New York, Macmillan, 1932. 336 p. fold. map.　Many **10837**

Wenatchee Daily World.
[Greater central Washington edition] Wenatchee, Wash., 1928. [78] p. illus., ports. (23d year, no. 168, Feb. 21, 1938)
　　　　WaU **10838**

Festival progress edition. Wenatchee, Wash., 1940. 104 p. illus., ports. (35th year, no. 256, Apr. 24, 1940) WaU **10839**

Festival progress special edition, April 28, 1937. Wenatchee, Wash., 1937. [48] p. illus.　　　　WaU **10840**

Wenatchee-Okanogan Cooperative Federation, Wenatchee, Wash.
Wenoka apple book. [Wenatchee, Wash.? 1936?] 20 p. illus.　　WaU **10841**

Wenatchee Sun.
Grand Coulee Dam edition. Wenatchee, Wash., 1934. 12 p. illus., ports., map. (Aug. 4, 1934)　　　　WaU **10842**

Wendell, Barrett, see nos. 6012-6023.

Wendler, Henry, 1836-1927.
The reminiscences of Henry Wendler; "a sketch of his life as he related it to me, by J. Orin Oliphant". [Cheney, Wash., 1926] 20 p. front. (port.)
　　　　Or OrU Wa WaS WaSp WaU **10843**

Wentworth, Thomas P., see no. 287.

West, C. John.
An economic survey of the Okanagan District, an essay submitted to the Department of Commerce, U. B. C., in 1945, by C. John West and Harold Shugg. [n.p., n.d.] 114 p. maps, tables, diagrs.
　　　　CVU **10844**

West, Leoti L., 1851-
The season's greeting; a chapter from life and fragments. Republic, Wash., 1904-5. 61 p.　　　　WaWW **10845**

Same. [Spokane, Shaw & Borden, 1904]
　　　　WaSp **10846**

The wide Northwest; historic narrative of America's wonder land as seen by a pioneer teacher. Spokane, Shaw & Borden, 1927. 286 p. front., plates, ports.
　　　　Many **10847**

West Coast Lumber Trade Extension Bureau.
The short length house of West Coast woods: Douglas fir, West Coast hemlock, Western red cedar, Sitka spruce, built by West Coast Lumber Extension Bureau. Seattle [c192?] 8 p. illus.
　　　　WaU **10849**

Sitka spruce, a quality wood of high service. [Seattle, c1927] 17 p. illus.
　　　　WaU **10850**

West Coast hemlock, its qualities and uses; an important part of America's permanent lumber supply. Seattle [c1927] 29 p. illus.　　　　WaU **10851**

Western red cedar, "the enduring wood of the ages". [Seattle, c1927] 24 p. illus.
　　　　WaU **10852**

West Coast Lumbermen's Association.
Characteristics, strength and durability of Douglas fir. Seattle [n.d.] 7 p. illus.
　　　　WaU **10853**

Creosoted Douglas fir paving blocks; the modern pavement for roads, streets, bridges and crossings. Rev. Seattle, 1915. 46 p. table.　　　　WaTC **10854**

A decade of progress in Douglas fir forestry. Seattle, Joint Committee on Forest Conservation, 1943. 64 p. illus.
　　　　OrCS WaT **10855**

Douglas fir and southern pine; a comparison of physical and mechanical properties. Seattle, 1927. 15 p.　WaU **10856**

Douglas fir use book; design tables and their application. Seattle [c1930] 204 p. tables, diagrs.　　WaS WaU **10857**

Forest practice handbook; presenting the rules of forest practice for the Douglas fir region. Revised. Seattle, Joint Committee on Forest Conservation, 1937. 31 p. illus., tables.　　　　OrCS
　OrMonO OrU WaE WaSp WaT **10858**

Handbook of forest practice for the West Coast Logging and Lumber Division, covering the rules of forest practice for the Douglas fir region under article X of the lumber code. [Seattle] Joint Committee on Forest Conservation, 1934. 28 p. illus., map.　OrCS OrP WaS **10859**

Highway structures of Douglas fir. Seattle [1941?] 40 p. illus., plans, diagrs.
　　　　OrCS WaT **10860**

Oregon's forest industries. [n.p.] 1936. 9 p. tables.　　　　OrP **10861**

Sawdust trails, a student's digest of logging and lumber manufacturing in the Douglas fir region. [Seattle, 1941?] [12] p. illus.　　　　WaT WaU **10862**

Standard classification, grading and dressing rules for Douglas fir, Sitka spruce, western red cedar, west coast hemlock and Port Orford cedar products adopted by the West Coast Lumbermen's Association; structural and car material included. Seattle, c1922. 107 p. illus.
　　　　OrCS **10863**

Standard grading and dressing rules for Douglas fir, Sitka spruce, west coast hemlock, western red cedar lumber; ef-

fective August 1, 1947; mill use. Portland, Or., c1947. 191 p. tables. (no. 14)
OrCS **10864**

Timber cropping in the Douglas fir region; prepared for the Joint Committee on Forestry authorized by 75th Congress, by West Coast Lumbermen's Association and Pacific Northwest Loggers Association. Seattle [1938?] 36 p. illus., map, diagrs. WaT WaU **10865**

West coast hemlock. Seattle [1943] [17] p. front. (map) illus., diagrs. WaT **10866**

West coast lumber facts. Seattle, 1937. 25 p. maps, tables, diagrs. Many **10867**
Same. [1941] 34 p.
Or OrP WaE WaT WaU **10868**

What are the facts about the West coast lumber industry? [Seattle, 1935] 11 p. tables, diagrs. Anon. WaU **10869**

Western, pseud.
Biography of Joseph Lane. Washington, D. C., Congressional Globe, 1852. 40 p. Robert Dale Owen, probable author.
Or OrP OrU **10870**

Western Alaska Construction Company.
Railroad building in the Seward Peninsula, Alaska. 2d ed. [New York, 1904?] 24 p. illus., fold. map. WaU **10871**

Western Forestry and Conservation Association.
The business of growing timber; three addresses presented at the Western Forestry Policy and Practice Conference, Portland, Dec. 10, 11, 12, 1941. [n.p., 1942?] 1 v. WaT **10872**

Co-operative forest study of the Grays Harbor area; a critical unit study suggestive of co-operation under the principle of the Clarke-McNary Act to establish efficient and permanent protection of forest regions; with the assistance of Charles Lathrop Pack. Portland, Or., 1929. 79 p. illus., tables, diagrs.
OrP WaS WaT WaW **10873**

Western Pine Association, Portland, Or.
Forest conservation in the western pines, picturing the vast forests from which the western pine industry secures its raw material and showing the steps being taken by progressive manufacturers to keep their forest lands growing timber. Portland, Or. [1937] 23 p. illus., map.
OrP WaT **10874**

Idaho white pine, a genuine white pine; its properties, uses and grades. Portland, Or., 1931. 64 p. illus., tables.
OrP WaS **10875**

Larch; its properties, uses and grades. Portland, Or., 1931. 48 p. illus., tables, diagrs. OrP WaS **10876**

Pondosa pine; the pick of the pines; its properties, uses and grades. Portland, Or., 1931. 80 p. illus., tables.
OrP WaS **10877**

[Statements concerning the Southern Pacific's control of transportation in California and western Oregon] [n.p.] 1922. 1 v. maps. OrP **10878**

The story of western pines; Idaho white pine, ponderosa pine, sugar pine; facts about these useful trees and the logging and lumber manufacture in the region where they grow. [n.p., n.d.] 64 p. illus.
Or OrP **10879**

Western pine camera views for home builders. Portland, Or., 1938. 32 p. illus.
OrP WaT **10880**

Western shipbuilders in World War II, a detailed review of wartime activities of leading maritime and navy contractors. Oakland, Calif., Shipbuilding Review Pub. Assn. [1945] 160 p. illus., ports.
Many **10881**

Western Washington Industrial Exposition, Tacoma, Wash., 1891.
Official souvenir of the Western Washington Industrial Exposition, Tacoma, 1891. [Tacoma, 1891] 16 p. col. front., col. illus. WaU **10882**

Western Weed Control Conference, 8th. Reno, Nev.
Minutes, eighth annual Western Weed Control Conference, Reno, Nevada, February 26 and 27, 1946. [Reno, Nev., 1946] 68 p. WaU **10883**

A western writer, see no. 9939.

Westland, Lynn, see no. 5342.

Westminster Iron Works Company,
70th anniversary. [Vancouver, B. C., McConnell, Eastman & Co., n.d.] [63] p. illus., ports. CVicAr **10884**

Westrate, Edwin Victor, see no. 1890.

Wetherell, June Pat.
But that was yesterday. New York, Dutton, 1943. 278 p. Puget Sound college story.
CV Or OrP Wa WaSp WaU **10885**
Dead center. New York, Dutton, 1946. 225 p. Seattle story.
CV Or WaS WaSp WaU **10886**
Run, sheep, run. New York, E. P. Dutton, 1947. 287 p. Seattle story. WaU **10887**

Wetzel, Johann Ludwig, see no. 1991.

Weyerhaeuser Timber Co.
Leaving cutover lands productive, Douglas fir region; requirements & practices applicable to holdings of Weyerhaeuser Timber Company. Tacoma, 1934. 32 p.
WaPS **10888**

Tree farms press book. [Tacoma, n.d.] 34 p. plates (1 fold.) OrCS **10889**

West coast hemlock pulp; a product of American pulp mills. [Minneapolis, c1937] 94 p. illus., 4 col. plates.
Many **10890**

Wheat Growers Association of the Pacific Northwest.
Wheat marketing through Pacific Northwest non-profit co-operative marketing associations; Washington Wheat Growers Association; Oregon Wheat Growers Association; Idaho Wheat Growers Association; issued by Organization Committee. [Spokane? 1920?] 15 p.
WaPS **10891**

Wheaton, Helen.
Prekaska's wife: a year in the Aleutians. New York, Dodd, 1945. 251 p. plates, ports. Many **10892**

Wheeler, Arthur O.
The Selkirk Mountains; a guide for mountain climbers and pilgrims. Winnipeg, Stovel [1911] 191 [8] p. front., illus., 2 fold. plates, ports., 4 fold. maps, diagrs.
CVic CVicAr OrP **10893**

Same. [c1912]
CVicAr MtU OrP WaS **10894**

Wheeler, Eldridge.
History of Grays Harbor County. [Montesano, Wash.? 192-?] 23 p. WaPS **10895**

Wheeler, James Cooper, 1849-
Captain Pete in Alaska. New York. Dutton [c1910] 302 p. front., plates.
WaT **10896**

Captain Pete of Cortesana. New York, Dutton [c1909] 292 p. front., 4 plates. Puget Sound story.   WaT **10897**

Captain Pete of Puget Sound. New York, Dutton [c1909] 375 p. front., 4 plates.
WaSp WaT WaU **10898**

Wheeler, Katharine (Welles)
Filled flagons. Mill Valley, Calif., Wings Press, 1944. 63 p. Tacoma poet.
Wa WaS WaT WaU **10899**

Wheeler, Olin Dunbar, 1852-
Climbing Mount Rainier, descriptive of an ascent of the highest peak in the United States, exclusive of Alaska, where living glaciers are found. St. Paul, Riley, 1901. 68 p. illus. (Northern Pacific monographs, no. 2)   WaU **10900**

The Lewis & Clark exposition. Portland, Or., 1905. 48 p. illus., maps (1 col. fold.)
WaU **10901**

Same. St. Paul, Northern Pacific Railway [1905] 55 p. illus., map.
CVicAr Or OrHi OrP WaU **10902**

Same. 5th ed. 64 p.   WaS WaU **10903**

Trail of Lewis and Clark, 1804-1904; a story of the great exploration across the continent in 1804-06; with a description of the old trail based upon actual travel over it and of the changes found a centurn later. New York, Putnam, 1904. 2 v. col. fronts., illus., 4 fold. maps, facsims.
Many **10904**

Same. 1913.   OrLgE OrSaW WaA **10905**

Same. New ed. with an introd. by Frederick S. Dellenbaugh. 1926. Many **10906**

Wheeler, Ruth (Carr) 1899-
We follow the western trail, photographs by H. D. and Ruth Wheeler. New York, Macmillan, 1941. xiv, 160 p. plates.
WaU **10907**

Wheeler, William Fletcher.
"The heart of the continent": Montana: its climate, soil, scenery, resources and industries. New York, "The Northwest", 1883. 32 p.   MtHi **10908**

Montana; a concise description of the climate, soil, grazing lands, agricultural and mineral productions of the country adjacent and tributary to the Northern Pacific Railroad, pub. for the use of the persons seeking information concerning this great new land. Helena, Mont., Fisk Bros., 1882. 16 p. fold map.
MtHi WaU **10909**

See also no. 6941.

Wheeler, William Ogden, 1837-1900.
The Ogden family in America; their history, biography and genealogy, ed. by Lawrence Van Alstyne and Charles Burr Ogden. Philadelphia, Lippincott, 1907. 2 v. illus., ports, facsim., table.
OrHi **10910**

Wheelon, Charles Homer, 1888-
Rabbit no. 202; illusions and conclusions. "Case history no. 22712. Test no. 67; rabbit no. 202, virgin female, age 120 days. April 15, 1933." illus. by the author. [Seattle, c1940-c1941] 2 v. in 1. front,. illus. Poem.   WaU **10911**

Whicker, H. W., see nos. 9925, 9926.

Whilt, James W.
Mountain memories, illus. by F. M. Harrow. [Eureka, Mont., James W. Whilt and Jerry G. Masek, c1925] 104 p. front. (port.) plates.   Wa **10912**

Rhymes of the Rockies. [Great Falls, Mont., Tribune Printing & Supply Co., 1922] 68 p. illus.   WaSp WaU **10913**

Whisnant, Archibald, comp.
Portland, Oregon, the world's greatest lumber producing center. [Portland, Or., Sweeney, c1923] 31 p. illus., maps, tables, diagrs.   OrP **10914**

Whitaker, Robert.
In memoriam: a sermon preached in the First Baptist Church, Salem, Oregon, on the occasion of the funeral of Mrs. Eliza B. Kinney, April 2, 1890. [Salem, Or.? 1890?] 8 p.   OrU **10915**

See also no. 5859.

White, Elijah, 1806?-1879, comp.
A concise view of Oregon Territory. Washington City, 1846. 73 p. Photostat copy.
WaU **10916**

White, F. Wallace.
The Sanger mine of the Sanger Gold Mines Company, the richest gold mine in Union County, Oregon. Limited souvenir ed. [n.p., c1903] 60 p. 5 plates, fold. map.   Or **10917**

White, Henry Kirke, 1865-1923.
History of the Union Pacific Railway. Chicago, University of Chicago Press, 1895. 129 p. illus., 2 fold. tables, 12 charts. (Economic studies, no. 11) Many **10918**

White, Marcus H.
Graduated property tax; the only remedy for perpetuating political government and insuring betterment thereof. Portland, Or., James A. Hines, 1892. 46 p.
OrP **10919**

White, Samuel Alexander, 1885-
The code of the Northwest. New York. Phoenix [c1940] 255 p.   CVicAr **10920**

White, Stewart Edward, 1873-
Conjurer's house: a romance of the free forest. New York, McClure, 1903. 260 p. front., 5 plates. Hudson's Bay Co.
IdB WaWW **10921**

Same. New York, Grosset [c1903]
WaT WaTC **10922**

Same. 1909.   WaSp **10923**

The long rifle. Garden City, N. Y., Doubleday, 1932. viii, 537 p. map.
MtUM OrCS OrP WaE WaS WaT **10924**

Pole star, by Stewart Edward White and Harry DeVighne. Garden City, N. Y., Doubleday, 1935. viii. 452 p. Alaska fur trade story. Many **10925**

Skookum Chuck; a novel. Garden City, N. Y., Doubleday, Page, 1925. 296 p. Pacific Coast story. CVicAr
MtUM WaE WaS WaT WaTC **10926**

The westerners. New York, Grosset [c1900] viii, 344 p. CVicAr WaWW **10927**

Wild geese calling. New York, Doubleday, 1940. viii, 577 p. Washington and Alaska story. Many **10928**

Same. New York, Literary Guild of America, 1940.
IdB IdUSB OrP Wa WaW **10929**
See also nos. 8160-8162.

White, William Henry, 1842-
Memorial address of Judge W. H. White, delivered at Seattle, May 30, 1908; and sketch of his life. [Seattle, 1908] 20 p. port. WaU **10930**

White Pass & Yukon Railway.
Alaska and the scenic Yukon and Atlin Lake country. [Seattle? 19—?] [30] p. illus. WaPS **10931**

Alaska and the Yukon Territory. [Seattle, 1916] [22] p. illus., map. WaPS **10932**

Alaska, Atlin and the Yukon. [Seattle? 1930?] [46] p. illus., col. map.
WaPS WaU **10933**

Alaska, Atlin and the Yukon; the beautiful northland. [Seattle, 1928?] [46] p. illus., map. WaPS WaU **10934**

Alaska, Atlin and the Yukon; the land where the world stays young. [Chicago, Poole Bros., 1928?] 46 p. illus., col. map, photos., tables. WaU **10935**

Alaska, Yukon and the scenic lake country. [Seattle?. 1939] [7] p. illus. WaPS **10936**

Comments, Alaska, Atlin and the Yukon, by travelers over the White Pass and Yukon Route. [Seattle? 19—?] 24 p. plates. WaPS **10937**

A handbook of vacation trips in Alaska, Atlin and the Yukon on the White Pass and Yukon Route. [Seattle? 1928] 59 p. illus., tables. WaPS **10938**

A tour through the land of nightless days; Alaska and the Canadian Yukon. [Chicago, 190-?] 24 p. illus., photos. WaU **10939**

White Pass and Yukon route to the land where beauty does abide. [Chicago, Poole Bros., c1923] 31 p. illus. OrP WaU **10940**

White River Journal.
Kent, situated in the heart of the best valley of western Washington. [Kent, Wash., 1908] [35] p. illus., ports. (Special ed., v. 19, no. 1, Jan. 3, 1908) WaU **10941**

Whitehall High School, Whitehall, Mont.
History of Jefferson Valley, comp. and written by the History Class of 1928. Whitehall, Mont., Jefferson Valley News, 1928. 56 p. MtHi **10942**

Whitehouse, Francis Cecil.
Sport fishes of western Canada, and some others. Vancouver, B. C., 1946 [1945] xviii, 129 p. plates. CV CVU **10943**

Whitehouse, Joseph, see no. 5910.

Whiteley, Opal Stanley, 1898-
The diary of Opal; with an introd. by Viscount Grey of Falloden and a preface by Ellery Sedgwick. London, Putnam, 1920. xxii, 311 p. front. (facsim.) Oregon lumber camp setting. OrP **10944**

The story of Opal; the journal of an understanding heart. Boston, Atlantic Monthly Press [c1920] xxviii, 283 p. front., plates, facsim.
WaPS WaS WaSp **10945**

Whitesmith, Benjamin MacLean, 1904-
Henry Villard and the development of Oregon. [Eugene, Or., 1940] 33 p. University of Oregon thesis ser., no. 14)
OrCS OrU WaSp **10946**

Whitfield, William, 1846-
History of Snohomish country, Washington. Chicago, Pioneer Historical Publishing Co., 1926. 2 v. illus., 53 ports., map. Many **10947**

Whitham, John W.
Interworld, a novel. [Seattle, Film Row Press, c1932] 278 p.
Wa WaS WaU **10948**

Whitham, Paul Page, 1878-
Plan of the Port of Astoria; report submitting a general plan for the improvement of the Port of Astoria. Astoria, Or., Dellinger [1912] 78 p. illus., maps.
OrP **10949**

Whiting, Fenton Blakemore, 1866-
Grit, grief and gold, a true narrative of an Alaska pathfinder. Seattle, Peacock Publishing Co., 1933. xvi, 247 p. front., plates, ports. Many **10950**

Whiting, Joseph S.
Forts of the state of Washington; a record of military and semi-military establishments designated as forts from May 29, 1792 to July 1, 1943. [Seattle?] c1946. 133 p. illus., photos., facsims.
CVicAr WaS WaW **10951**

Pepper Dot and Jimmie W. Duck, illus. by Vincent Callahan. Kent, Wash., Valley Pub. Co., c1947. [21] p. illus. WaS **10952**

Whitman, Narcissa (Prentiss) 1808-1847.
The coming of the white women, 1836, as told in letters and journal of Narcissa Whitman, comp. by T. C. Elliott. Portland, Or., Oregon Historical Society, 1937. 113 p. plates.
CVicAr Or OrHi OrU WaS **10953**

A pioneer honeymoon. New York, Board of National Missions [1946] 15 p. illus. Selections from diary, selected by Harriet Day Allen. WaS **10954**

Whitman and the massacre of his Protestant mission in Walla Walla Valley, November 29, 1847. San Francisco, Brown, 1874. 19 p. CVicAr OrHi **10955**

Whitman Centennial, Inc., Walla Walla, Wash.
A brief requesting assistance in the restoration of the grounds and reconstruction

of the buildings of the Waiilatpu Mission on the centenary if its founding, 1836-1936, observance; August 13, 14, 15, 16. Walla Walla, Wash. [1936?] 33 p. illus., 2 maps (1 fold.) plans.
OrCS OrHi OrLgE OrPR WaWW **10956**

Wagons west; the story of Marcus and Narcissa Whitman, pub. in observance of the Whitman Centennial, Walla, Walla, Washington, August 13-16, 1936. Walla Walla, Wash. [1936] 47 p. illus.
Or WaS WaSp **10957**

Whitman College, Walla Walla, Wash.
The romance of a college, 1836-1847-1859. Walla Walla, Wash. [1895?] 11 p.
WaPS **10958**

Songs of Whitman College. [Walla Walla, Wash., 1918] 93 p. WaPS WaWW **10959**

The Whitman story. Walla Walla, Wash. [1936?] 11 p. WaPS **10960**

Whitman's service; a resume of the constructive influences of Whitman College. Walla Walla, Wash., 1924. 28 p. front. (port.) WaPS WaU **10961**

Whitman's ride; by a lady of Brooklyn. Portland, Or., Baumgardt & Palmer [n.d.] [10] p. Poem. WaU **10962**

Whitney, Asa, 1797-1872.
A project for a railroad to the Pacific; with reports of committees of Congress, resolutions of state legislatures, etc., with other facts relating thereto. New York, Wood, 1849. viii, 112 p. front. (fold. map) fold. map. WaS WaU **10963**

Whitney, Rosalie M., see no. 8965.

Whitney, Ruth (Cooper)
The Oregon story; outline. [n.p.] Oregon Federation of Women's Clubs [n.d.] 16 p.
OrP OrU **10964**
Same. [1929] OrCS **10965**

Whitson, John Harvey, 1854-
A courier of empire; a story of Marcus Whitman's ride to save Oregon. Boston, Wilde [c1904] 315 p. front., 4 plates.
Many **10966**

With Fremont the pathfinder; or, Winning the empire of gold, illus. by William F. Stecher. Boston, Wilde [c1903] 320 p. front., plates. Wa **10967**

Whittelsey, Mrs. Delia (Taylor) 1861-
Thoughts by the way. Seattle, F. McCaffrey, 1933. 85 p. front. (mounted port.) illus. Poems. WaS WaU **10968**

Whittier, William Harrison.
An investigation of the iron ore resources of the Northwest. Seattle, University of Washington, 1917. 128 p. map. (Bureau of Industrial Research, bulletin no. 2)
Many **10969**

Whitworth, Georg F., see no. 8353.

Who's who in Northwest art; a biographical directory of persons in the Pacific Northwest working in the media of painting, sculpture, graphic arts, illustration, design, and the handicrafts; Marion Brymner Appleton, ed. Seattle, F. McCaffrey, 1941. vii, 87 p. Many **10970**

Who's who in Washington state, a compilation of biographical sketches of men and women prominent in the affairs of Washington state, 1927; ed. by Arthur H. Allen. Seattle, A. H. Allen, 1927. 240 p.
OrP WaSp WaT WaTC WaU **10971**

Who's who of Westminster Hall, theological college of the Presbyterian Church in Canada at Vancouver, 1907-1927. [Vancouver, B. C., Dunsmuir Printing Co.] 1944. 40 p. CVicAr **10972**

Who's who on the Pacific Coast; a biographical compilation of notable living contemporaries west of the Rocky Mountains, ed. by Franklin Harper. Los Angeles, Harper Pub. Co., 1913. 633 p.
CV OrCS OrP WaS WaU **10973**

Who's who on the Pacific Coast; a biographical dictionary of leading men and women of the Pacific Coast states. Chicago, Larkin, Roosevelt & Larkin, 1947. 1 v.
OrP WaSp **10974**

Whymper, Frederick, b. 1838.
Alaska; Reisen und Erlebnisse im hohen Norden, autorisirte Deutsche ausg. von Dr. Friedrich Steger. Braunschweig, Druck und Verlag von G. Westermann, 1869. 351 p. front., illus., plates, map.
CVU WaU **10975**

A journey from Norton Sound, Bering Sea, to Fort Youkon (junction of Porcupine and Youkon Rivers). London, W. Clowes and Sons [1863] 19 p. CVU WaU **10976**

Travel and adventure in the territory of Alaska, formerly Russian America, now ceded to the United States; and in various other parts of the north Pacific. London, Murray, 1868. xix, 331 p. front., illus., plates, map.
CVicAr CVU WaS WaSp WaU **10977**

Same. New York, Harper, 1869. 353 p. front., illus., 15 plates, fold. map.
Many **10978**

Same. 2d ed. New York, Murray, 1869. xix, 331 p. front., illus., plates, fold. map.
WaS **10979**

Same. New York, Harper, 1871. 353 p. front., illus., plates, fold. map.
Or OrHi OrU WaT WaU **10980**

Voyages et aventures dans l'Alaska (ancienne Amerique russe) ouvrage tr. de l'anglais avec l'autorisation de l'auteur par Emile Jonveaux. Paris, Hachette, 1871. ii, 412 p. illus., plates, fold. map.
CVicAr WaU **10981**

Voyages et aventures dans la Colombie anglaise, l'ile Vancouver, le territoire d' Alaska et la Californie; abreges par H. Vattemare. Paris, Hachette, 1880. 192 p. illus., maps. CVicAr **10982**

Wick, Carl Irving, 1894-
Commercial and sport salmon trolling manual, ed. by Rosemary Stewart. [Seattle] 1944. 95 p. illus., diagrs.
Many **10983**

Ocean harvest; the story of commercial fishing in Pacific Coast waters. Seattle, Superior Publishing Co. [1946] 185 p. illus., plates, charts, diagrs., plans.
Many **10984**

Wickersham, James, 1857-1939.
Alaska, its resources, present conditions and needed legislation; being a synopsis of an address delivered before the respective Chambers of Commerce of Seattle and Tacoma on November 11, 1902. Tacoma, Allen, 1902. 16 p. WaU **10985**

A bibliography of Alaskan literature, 1724-1924; containing the titles of all histories, travels, voyages, newspapers, periodicals, public documents, etc., printed in English, Russian, German, French, Spanish, etc., relating to, descriptive of, or published in Russian America or Alaska, from 1724 to and including 1924. Cordova, Alaska, Cordova Daily Times, 1927. xxvii, 635 p. (Miscellaneous Publications of the Alaska Agricultural College and School of Mines, Fairbanks, v. 1)
Many **10986**

Is it Mt. Tacoma, or Rainier? What do history and tradition say? Tacoma, Puget Sound Printing Co., 1893. 16 p. (Tacoma Academy of Science. Proceedings)
CVicAr OrHi WaT WaU **10987**

Sme. 2d ed. 34 p. front., map. CVicAr OrU WaS WaSp WaT WaWW **10988**

Major Powell's inquiry: "Whence came the American Indians?" An answer; a study in comparative ethnology. Tacoma, Allen & Lamborn, 1899. 28 p.
WaT WaU WaWW **10989**

Old Yukon; tales, trails, and trials. Washington, D. C., Washington Law Book Co., 1938. xi, 514 p. front. (map) illus., ports., map, facsims. Many **10990**

The organization of territorial government in Alaska: Do you favor a government by the people of Alaska, or a government by the federal bureaus? Which kind is your legislature organizing? An appeal to Alaskans. [n.p., n.d.] 32 p.
WaU **10991**

Wiedemann, Thomas.
Cheechako into sourdough, by the Klondike Kid. Portland, Or., Binfords & Mort [1942] 266 p. front., plates. Many **10992**
The saga of Alaska, by Thomas Weidemann, Sr. and Luther ("Doc") Norris. Prairie City, Ill., James A. Decker [c1946] 85 p. illus., plates, ports. Poems.
WaU **10993**

Wight, Otis Buckminster, 1877- ed.
On active service with Base Hospital 46, U. S. A., March 20, 1918 to May 25, 1919. [Portland, Or., Arcady Press, 1919?] 191 p. illus., ports. OrHi OrP **10994**

Wilbur, Earl Morse, 1866-
A history of the First Unitarian Church of Portland, Oregon, 1867-1892; together with a sketch of the life of Rev. Thomas Lamb Eliot. Portland, Or., 1st Unitarian Church, 1893. 95 p. front., 3 plates, 2 ports. Many **10995**

Thomas Lamb Eliot, 1841-1936. Portland, Or. [G. M. Allen and Son] 1937. ix, 139 p. front., plates, ports., fold. geneal. tables.
Many **10996**

Wilbur, Marguerite Eyer, see no 2596.

Wilbur Register.
Golden jubilee edition, 1889-1939. Wilbur, Wash., 1939. [24] p. illus., ports. (v. 51, June 1939) WaU **10997**

[**Wilcocke, Samuel Hull**] 1766?-1833.
A narrative of occurences in the Indian countries of North America since the connexion of the Right Hon. the Earl of Selkirk with the Hudson's Bay Company and his attempt to establish a colony on the Red River; with a detailed account of his Lordship's military expedition to, and subsequent proceedings at Fort William in upper Canada. London, B. McMillan, 1817. xiv, 151, 87 p. Authorship also attributed to Edward Ellice and to Simon McGillivray.
CVU Wa **10998**

Wilcox, Walter Dwight, 1869-
Camping in the Canadian Rockies; an account of camp life in the wilder parts of the Canadian Rocky Mountains, together with a description of the region about Banff, Lake Louise and Glacier, and a sketch of the early explorations. New York, Putnam, 1896. xiii, 283 p. front., illus., 25 plates.
CVicAr OrP WaS **10999**

Same. 2d ed. 1897. CVicAr WaU **11000**

The Rockies of Canada. A rev. and enl. ed. of 'Camping in the Canadian Rockies", with more than 40 photogravure and other illustrations from original photographs by the author. New York, Putnam, 1900. ix, 309 p. front., 42 plates, port., maps (2 fold.)
CVU OrP WaS WaSp WaU **11001**

Same. 1903. CVicAr WaE **11002**

Wildcat, Oregon, see no. 2627.

Wilkerson, Albert Samuel, 1897-
Some frozen deposits in the gold-fields of interior Alaska; a study of the Pleistocene deposits of Alaska. [New York, 1932] 22 p. illus., maps, diagrs. (American Museum novitates, no. 525, May 21, 1932) WaU **11003**

Wilkes, George, 1820-1885.
Account and history of the Oregon Territory; together with a journal of an emigrating party. London, Lott, 1846. 160 p.
CVicAr OrP WaS WaWW **11004**

The history of Oregon, geographical and political; a thorough examination of the project of a national railroad, from the Atlantic to the Pacific Ocean; a journal of the emigrating expedition of 1843. New York, W. H. Colyer, 1845. 127 p. front. (fold. map)
CVicAr OrHi OrP WaU **11005**

Wilkes, Lincoln Ellsworth, 1865- comp.
By an Oregon pioneer fireside. Hillsboro, Or. [Hillsboro Printing Co., 1941] 134 [10] p. illus., ports. Many **11006**

Wilkeson, Samuel, 1817-1889.
Wilkeson's notes on Puget Sound; being extracts from notes of a reconnoissance of the proposed route of the Northern Pacific Railroad made in the summer of 1869. [n.p., n.d.] 47 p. CVicAr **11007**

Same. [n.p., 1870] 44 p. Many **11008**

Same. Abridged. [n.p., n.d.] 32 p.
CVicAr OrP WaU **11009**

See also no. 1473.

Wilkins, Sir George Hubert, 1888–
Flying the Arctic, with 31 illus. New York, Putnam, 1928. xv, 336 p. front., plates, ports. Many **11010**

Wilkinson, Mrs. Marguerite Ogden (Bigelow) 1883-1928.
The Dingbat of Arcady. New York, Macmillan, 1927. 188 p. Trip down Willamette River in small boat.
OrHi OrP OrPR WaS WaU WaW **11011**

Will, Clark M.
Origin of Hubbard; arrival of Hubbard family, squatter turns goldseeker. [Hubbard, Or., 1926?] [3] illus. Or **11012**

Will, Roland Gage, 1897–
The university, college, and normal school students in Oregon. Columbus, Ohio, Ohio State University, 1936. 152 p. diagrs. (Contributions in education, no. 1)
OrP OrU WaPS WaTC **111013**

Will there be war? Analysis of the elements which constitute, respectively, the power of England and the United States; the proper course to secure, peaceably, the whole of Oregon, by an adopted citizen. New York, W. Taylor, 1846. 44 p.
OrHi WaU **11014**

Willamette Association of Congregational Ministers and Churches in the State of Oregon.
Constitution, adopted April 28, 1886. Forest Grove, Or., Forest Grove Times, 1886. 8 p. OrHi **11015**

Willamette Fire Engine Company No. 1.
Constitution and rules of order, as adopted June 6, 1867, organized August 3, 1853. Portland, Or., Carter, 1867. 20 p.
OrHi **11016**

Willamette University, Salem, Or.
Willamette University petitioning Phi Beta Kappa fraternity; a statement of relevant facts. [Salem, Or., n.d.] 23 p. illus.
WaPS WaU **11017**

Willapoint Oyster Growers Association.
Oyster farming for profit at Willapa Bay; a report of progress in shellfish culture, including bibliography of authorities. Seattle, McKay, 1931. 36 p. illus.
OrP WaU **11018**

Willard, Mrs. Caroline McCoy (White)
Kin-da-shon's wife; an Alaskan story. New York, Revell [c1892] 281 p. front., 2 plates. CVicAr WaPS WaT WaU **11019**

Same. 3d. ed. WaS **11020**

Life in Alaska; letters of Mrs. Eugene S. Willard, ed. by her sister, Mrs. Eva McClintock. Philadelphia, Presbyterian Board of Publication [c1884] 384 p. front., illus., plates, maps.
CVicAr WaPS WaS WaU **11021**

Willard, Daniel Everett, 1862–
Montana, the geological story. Lancaster, Pa., Science Press Printing Co., 1935. 373 p. front. (table) illus., maps.
MtBozC MtHi MtUM OrP WaS WaSp **11022**

Willard, James F., see no. 1954.

Willcox, Helen Lida, 1883–
On to Oregon! A dramatic sketch on the story of Marcus Whitman. [New York, Board of National Missions of the Presbyterian Church in the U. S. A., 1936] 17 p. WaPS **11023**

See also no. 7983.

Willerton, Irene.
So little makes me glad. [Victoria, B. C., Women's Missionary Society of Metropolitan United Church, n.d.] 28 p. port.
CVicAr **11024**

Williams, Arthur Bryan, 1866–
Fish & game in British Columbia. [Vancouver, B. C., Sun Directories, c1935] 206 p. CV **11025**

Game trails in British Columbia; big game and other sport in the wilds of British Columbia. New York, Scribner, 1925. xiv, 360 p. front., plates, map.
CV CVU WaS **11026**

Same. 1926. WaU **11027**

Rod & creel in British Columbia. [Vancouver, B. C., Progress Publishing Co., c1919] 144 p. illus., plates.
CV CVU WaSp **11028**

Williams, Chauncey Pratt, 1860–
Lone Elk; the life story of Bill Williams, trapper and guide of the far West. Denver, J. Van Male, 1935-1936. 2 v. (Old West series, no. 6, 7)
MtHi WaSp (v. 2 only) **11029**

Williams, Edgar, and Company.
Historical atlas map of Marion & Linn Counties, Oregon. San Francisco, 1878. 104 p. illus., col. maps (part fold.)
OrHi OrP OrU WaSp WaU **11030**

Williams, George Henry, 1823-1910.
Occasional addresses. Portland, Or., F. W. Baltes and Co., 1895. 208 p. front. (port.)
Many **11031**

See also no. 310.

Williams, Guy.
Logger-talk; some notes on the jargon of the Pacific Northwest woods. Seattle, University of Washington Book Store, 1930. 30 p. (Chapbooks, no. 41)
Many **11032**

See also no. 10612.

William, Henry T., ed.
The Pacific tourist; Williams' new illus. transcontinental guide of travel from the Atlantic to the Pacific Ocean; a complete traveler's guide of the Union and Central Pacific Railroads. New York, 1876. 293 p. front., illus.
CVicAr Or OrHi OrP OrU WaU **11033**

Same. 1877. 309 p. WaSp **11034**

Same. 278 p. OrU **11035**

Same. New York, Adams & Bishop, 1881. 355 p. illus. OrP WaPS WaS **11036**

Williams, Howel, 1898–
The ancient volcanoes of Oregon. Eugene, Or., Oregon State System of Higher Education, 1948. x, 64 p. illus., plates, diagrs. (Condon lectures, 1)
OrHi OrU WaSp WaT WaTC **11037**

Crater Lake; the story of its origin. Berkeley, Calif., University of California

Press, 1941. xii, 97 p. col. front., illus., plates (1 col.) maps. Many **11038**

The geology of Crater Lake National Park, Oregon, with a reconnaissance of the Cascade Range southward to Mount Shasta. Washington, D. C., 1942. vi, 162 p. front., illus., plates, fold. maps. (Carnegie Institution of Washington Publications 540) Many **11039**
See also no. 2107.

Williams, Irena (Dunn) 1856-
Reminiscences of early Eugene and Lane County, Oregon. [Eugene, Or., Shelton-Turnbull-Fuller Co., c1914] 44 p.
Or OrP OrU WaS WaU **11040**

Williams, J. Harold, see no. 9180.

Williams, John Harvey, 1864-
The guardians of the Columbia; Mount Hood, Mount Adams, and Mount St. Helens. Tacoma, 1912. 142 p. col. front., illus. (part col.) Many **11041**

The mountain that was "God"; being a little book about the great peak which the Indians called "Tacoma", but which is officially named "Rainier". Tacoma, 1910. 111 p. col. front., illus., col. plates, maps. Many **11042**

Same. 2d ed. New York, Putnam, 1911. 142 p. col. front., illus., col. plates, maps.
Many **11043**

Same. Rev. by F. H. Loutzenhiser. 3d ed. rev. to date. Seattle, Lowman & Hanford, 1932. 89 p. col. front., illus. (part col.) Wa WaS WaT **11044**

Winthrop and Curtis; a reviewer reviewed; being a correspondence with the Nation and Evening Post on the relations between George William Curtis and Theodore Winthrop, with other matters affecting a new ed. of "The canoe and the saddle"; Winthrop and the Northwest, by Clarence B. Bagley. Tacoma, 1914. 24 p. WaS WaU **11045**
See also no. 11136.

Williams, Joseph.
Narrative of a tour from the state of Indiana to the Oregon Territory in the years 1841-2; with an introd. by James C. Bell, Jr. New York, Cadmus Book Shop, 1921. 95 p. Many **11046**

Same. New York, E. Eberstadt, 1921.
WaU **11047**

Williams, Lewis R.
Chinook by the sea. [Portland, Or., Kilham Stationery and Printing Co., c1924] 136 p. Many **11048**

Our Pacific County. Raymond, Wash., Raymond Herald, 1930. 104 [5] p. map.
Many **11049**

Williams, Robert, see no. 388.

Williams, Robert D.
Helena scenic-commercial guide. Helena, Mont. [1929?] 96 p. illus., fold. map.
WaS **11050**

Williamson, James Alexander, 1886-
Cook and the opening of the Pacific. New York, Macmillan, 1948. xii, 251 p. front. (port.) plates, maps. (Teach yourself history library, ed. by A. L. Rowse)
OrHi WaU **11051**

Williamson, Thames Ross, 1894-
Far North country. New York, Duell, Sloan & Pearce [1944] xi, 236 p. (American folkways, ed. by Erskine Caldwell) Idaho author. Many **11052**

On the reindeer trail; with illus. by Lee Townsend. Boston, Houghton, 1932, xi, 242 p. front., illus., plates. Story of a man from Idaho.
IdIf WaS WaSp WaW **11053**

Stride of man. New York, Coward-McCann, 1928. 379 p.
IdU OrCS WaU **11054**

Williamson-Haffner Co., Pub.
Washington, the evergreen state. Denver, c1907. 24 col. plates. OrHi **11055**

Willis, Adeline Bryan.
Wondrous romance. [n.p., c1920] 1 v. Scenario of the Lewis and Clark expedition. OrHi **11056**

Willis, John.
Roosevelt in the rough, as told to Horace Smith. New York, Ives Washburn, 1931. xiv, 246 p. front. (port.) plates, ports., facsims. Montana Rocky Mountain story.
MtHi OrP WaSp **11057**

Willison, Marjory (MacMurchy) Lady.
Victoria, B. C.; city of enchantment in Canada's evergreen playground, illus. by A. C. Leighton. Victoria, B. C., Empress Hotel, 1933. 30 p. illus., col. plates.
CV WaS **11058**

Willoughby, Mrs. Florance (Barrett)
Alaska holiday. Boston, Little, 1940. 295 p. front., plates, ports. Many **11059**

Alaskans all. Boston, Houghton, 1933. x, 234 p. front., plates, ports., facsim.
Many **11060**

The fur trail omnibus; containing two complete novels: Where the sun swings north; Rocking moon. [n.p] c1925. 2 v. in 1. WaT **11061**

Gentlemen unafraid. New York, Putnam, 1928. xiii, 285 p. front., plates, ports. Alaska pioneer biographies.
OrP OrSa WaE WaS WaT WaU **11062**

The golden totem, a novel of modern Alaska. Boston, 1945. 314 p. Many **11063**

River house. New York, Triangle Books [c1936] 389 p. Stikine River, Alaska.
CV Or Wa **11064**

Same. Boston, Little, 1936.
CV OrCS Wa WaE WaS WaT **11065**

Rocking moon; a romance of Alaska. New York, Burt, 1925. 360 p. front.
WaT WaTC WaU **11066**

Same. New York, Putnam, 1925.
WaPS WaS WaT **11067**

Sitka, portal to romance. Boston, Houghton, 1930. x, 233 p. front., 10 plates, 2 ports., facsim. Many **11068**

Sitka; to know Alaska one must first know Sitka. London, Hodder [c1930] 248 p. front., 15 plates. CVicAr **11069**

Sondra O'Moore. Boston, Little, 1939. 320 p. Alaska story. Many **11070**

Same. New York, Grosset [c1939]
WaE **11071**

Spawn of the North. New York, Triangle Books [c1932] 347 p.
Or Wa WaE **11072**

Same. Boston, Houghton, 1932. 349 p.
IdB WaE WaS WaT WaU WaW **11073**

The trail eater; a romance of the all-Alaska sweepstakes. New York, Putnam, 1929. viii, 400 p.
WaE WaS WaT **11074**

Where the sun swings north. New York, Putnam, 1922. viii, 355 p.
WaS WaT **11075**

Same. New York, Burt [c1922] Wa **11076**

Wills, Percy E.
Rambling rhymes from the graveyard. Port Alberni, B. C., West Coast Printers, 1933. 32 p. front.
CVicAr CVU **11077**

Willson, Beckles, 1869-1942.
The great company; being a history of the honourable company of merchants-adventurers trading into Hudson's Bay, with an introd. by Lord Strathcona and Mount Royal, with original drawings by Arthur Heming. Toronto, Copp, Clark, 1899. 541 p. front., illus., 10 platees, 2 ports., maps, plans, facsim. Many **11078**

Same. London, Smith, Elder, 1900. 2 v. fronts., illus., ports., maps (1 fold.) fold. facsim. Many **11079**

Same. New York, Dodd, 1900. 541 p. illus., 10 plates, 3 ports., map, facsim.
OrP Wa WaPS WaW **11080**

Same. 1906 [c1899] OrU **11081**

Wilmot, Mrs. Maude E., comp.
Letters from Oregon boys in France, 1917-1918; illus. by George Phillips. Portland, Or., Glass & Prudhomme [1917] 128 p. front., illus., ports.
IdU OrCS OrP OrU WaPS WaU **11082**

Oregon boys in the war, including a second series of letters from Oregon boys in France. Portland, Or., Glass & Prudhomme, 1918. 256 p. front., ports., facsims. Many **11083**

Wilse, Anders Beer, 1865-1948.
En emigrants ungdomserindringer. Oslo, Forlogt av Johan Grundt Tanum, 1936. 123 p. plates. Emigrant's reminiscences.
WaU **11084**

Wilson, A. King, see no. 260.

Wilson, Bryant.
With the 364th Infantry in America, France and Belgium, by First-Lieutenant Bryant Wilson, chaplain, and First-Lieutenant Lamar Tooze, regimental intelligence officer. New York, Knickerbocker, 1919. xxii, 264 p. front., plates, ports., map. Camp Lewis group.
WaS WaT WaU **11085**

Wilson, Charles Morrow, 1905-
Meriwether Lewis of Lewis and Clark. New York, Crowell [c1934] xiii, 305 p. front., illus., 5 plates, 2 ports., maps (1 fold.) Many **11086**

Wilson, Clifford, ed.
The new North in pictures. Toronto, Ryerson [1947] 223 p. illus. (part col.) ports. "The pictures have been reprinted from the Beaver, an illustrated quarterly published by the Hudson's Bay Co."
CVicAr **11087**

[**Wilson, Edward Francis**] comp.
Salt Spring Island, British Columbia. [Victoria, B. C.] Colonist Presses, 1895. 30 p. illus., plate, port., fold. map.
CVicAr WaU **11088**

Wilson, Elijah Nicholas, 1842-1915.
Among the Shoshones, by "Uncle Nick". Salt Lake City, Skelton Publishing Co. [c1910] 222 p. front. (port.) plates.
IdU WaSp **11089**

Same. 247 p. front. (port.) 7 plates. Rewritten p. 187 ff. WaSp **11090**

The white Indian boy; the story of Uncle Nick among the Shoshones; rev. and ed. by Howard R. Driggs, illus. with drawings by F. N. Wilson. Yonkers-on-Hudson, N. Y., World Book Co., 1919. xi, 222 p. front., illus. (Pioneer life series)
Many **11091**

Same. 1922. IdIf WaU **11092**

Wilson, Frederick Wallace, 1872-
Lure of the river. Complimentary ed. [n.p.] Lucy Wilson Peters, 1936, c1933. 52 p. Early days on Columbia River.
OrP **11093**

Wilson, Harry Leon, 1867-1939.
Ruggles of Red Gap. New York, Grosset, c1915. 371 p. Washington setting.
CVU WaS **11094**

Wilson, Hewitt, 1891-
Kaolin and china clay in the Pacific Northwest, with geological contributions by George Edward Goodspeed. Seattle, University of Washington, 1934. 184 p. illus., maps, tables, diagrs. (Engineering Experiment Station series. Bulletin no. 76) Many **11095**

Talc and soapstone in Washington, by Hewitt Wilson and Joseph A. Pask. New York, American Institute of Mining and Metallurgical Engineers, c1936. 25 p. illus., diagrs. (Contribution no. 99)
OrP WaU **11096**

Wilson, James A.
Bits of Alaska. [San Francisco, c1908] 59 p. illus. CV CVicAr WaU **11097**

See also nos. 10385-10389.

Wilson, John Fleming, 1877-1922.
The land claimers, with illus. of Arthur E. Becher. Boston, Little, 1911. 291 p. front., 3 plates. Many **11098**

Wilson, Joseph G., see no. 6513.

Wilson, Katherine.
Copper-tints; a book of Cordova sketches, drawings by Eustace P. Ziegler. Cordova, Alaska, Cordova Daily Times, 1923. 44 p. front., illus. WaT WaU **11099**

Wilson, Riley, see no. 2783.

Wilson, Robert S., see no. 8410.

Wilson, Rufus Rockwell, 1865-
Out of the West, illus. by Sidney E. Fletcher. New York, Press of the Pioneers, 1933. 452 p. illus. Many **11100**

Out of the West; the beyond the Mississippi states in the making, illus. by Constance Naar. Rev. and enl. ed. New

York, Wilson-Erickson, 1936. xvii, 480 p. front., ports.
MtHi Wa WaE WaT WaU WaWW **11101**
See also nos. 2378, 10014.

Wilson, Veazie.
Glimpses of the Yukon gold fields and Dawson route. Vancouver, B. C., Thomson Stationery Co. [c1895] 96 p. photos.
CVicAr **11102**

Guide to the Yukon gold fields, where they are and how to reach them. Seattle, 1895. 72, 13, 22 p. front., illus., 19 plates, 5 fold. maps. CVicAr WaS **11103**

Wilt, Richard.
E-tooka-shoo, the cold little Eskimo boy. New York, J. Messner [c1941] [47] p. col. illus. WaU **11104**

Wiltsee, Ernest Abram.
The truth about Fremont; an inquiry. San Francisco, J. H. Nash, 1936. vi, 54 p. front. OrHi OrP WaS WaT **11105**

Winchester, James D.
Capt J. D. Winchester's experience on a voyage from Lynn, Massachusetts to San Francisco, Cal. and to the Alaska gold fields. Salem, Mass., Newcomb & Gauss, 1900. 251 p. front., illus., 37 plates.
CVicAr CVU WaS **11106**

Windolph, Charles A., 1851-
I fought with Custer; the story of Sergeant Windolph, last survivor of the battle of the Little Big Horn, as told to Frazier and Robert Hunt, with explanatory material and contemporary sidelights on the Custer fight. New York, Scribner, 1947. xiv, 236 p. illus., plates, ports., maps, facsims.
CVicAr MtHi OrP Wa WaU **11107**

Windt, Harry de, see nos. 2431-2433.

Winfield, Arthur M., see no. 9863.

Winfree, William H.
Delinquent taxes and tax titles; a paper read before the Spokane County Bar Association, Spokane, Wash., March 27, 1925. [n.p., 1925?] 14 p. Wa **11108**

Notes on real property law of Washington. Seattle, Daily Journal of Commerce, 1934. 146 p. Wa WaS **11109**

Winkenwerder, Hugo August, 1878-
Forestry in the Pacific Northwest, with foreword by Charles Lathrop Pack. Washington, D. C., American Tree Association, 1928. 48 p. Many **11110**

Short keys to the native trees of Oregon and Washington. Seattle, Imperial Publishing Co., 1939. 19 p.
OrP WaS WaT **11111**

Same. [Seattle] University of Washington, [1914] 16 p. WaU **11112**

Same. 4th ed. rev. 1916. OrP **11113**

Same. 1925. 5th ed. reprint. IdU **11114**

Same. 5th ed. rev. 1929. OrP **11115**

[Winkler, George E.]
Songs unbidden, by The Prospector. Victoria, B. C., Victoria Printing & Publishing Co. [n.d.] 170 p. CVicAr **11116**

Same. [1920] CVU **11117**

Winser, Henry Jacob, 1833-1896.
The great Northwest; a guide-book and itinerary for the use of tourists and travellers over the lines of the Northern Pacific Railroad, the Oregon Railway and Navigation Company and the Oregon and California Railroad, with map and many illustrations. New York, Putnam, 1883. 276 p. front., illus., 40 plates, fold. map. Many **11118**

Same. St. Paul, Riley, 1886. 370 p. illus., fold. map. Anon.
IdU MtU WaPS WaT WaU **11119**

Same. St. Paul, Northern News Co., 1888. 390 p. front., illus., fold. map. Anon.
WaS WaU **11120**

Same. New York, Putnam, 1889. 276 p. front., illus., plates, fold. map.
OrHi WaT **11121**

Same. St. Paul, Riley, 1889. 439 p. front., illus., fold. map. Anon.
MtHi MtU WaU WaWW **11122**

Winslow, Kenelm, 1863-
A life against death. [Seattle] Lowman & Hanford [c1933] 292 p. Autobiography of Seattle physician.
WaE WaS WaU **11123**

Winter, William H., see nos. 5279-5281.

Winters, J. C.
Marine pipefitting (a manual of instruction for supplementary training) prepared for the Oregon Shipbuilding Corporation, Kaiser Company, Incorporated, drawings by Don Winters, photographs by Louis Lee; in cooperation with the United States Maritime Commission, Department of Vocational Training. [Portland, Or.?] 1942. 262 [9] p. illus., plan, tables, diagrs. OrP OrU **11124**

Winther, Oscar Osburn, 1903-
The great Northwest; a history. New York, Knopf, 1947. xv, 383, xxv p. illus., ports., maps. Many **11125**

The trans-Mississippi West; a guide to its periodical literature (1811-1938). [Bloomington, Ind., Indiana University, c1942] xv, 263 p. (Publications. Social science series) Many **11126**

Winther, Sophus Keith, 1895-
Beyond the garden gate. New York, Macmillan, 1946. x, 289 p. Willamette valley story. Many **11127**

Winthrop, Theodore, 1828-1861.
The canoe and the saddle, adventures among the northwestern rivers and forests, and Isthmiana. London, John G. Murdock [18-?] 266 p. (Farringdon library) WaU **11128**

Same. New York, Dodd, 1862. 375 p. front.
Many **11129**

Same. Boston, Ticknor, 1863. Many **11130**

Same. 6th ed. WaU **11131**

Same. 1868. OrSa **11132**

Same. 10th ed. Boston, Osgood, 1871.
CVicAr WaE WaU **11133**

Same. New York, Holt, 1876 [c1862] 375 p. (Leisure hour series) OrP WaWW **11134**

Same. Edinburgh, William Paterson, 1883.
CVU **11135**

The canoe and the saddle; or, Klalam and Klickitat, to which are now first added his Western letters and journals; ed. with an introd. and notes by John H. Williams, with sixteen color plates and more than one hundred other illustrations. Tacoma, J. H. Williams, 1913. xxvi, 332 p. col. front., illus., 62 plates, port., maps, facsims. Many **11136**

The legend of Tacoma as it was told to Theodore Winthrop outside the palings of Fort Nisqually by an old Siwash in 1853. [Tacoma, Pioneer Bindery & Printing Co., 191?] 1 v. front., illus. WaT **11137**

Wirt, Loyal Lincoln, 1863-
Alaskan adventures; a tale of our last frontier and of "Whiskers", the gallant leader of the first dog team to cross Alaska, introd. by George Albert Coe. New York, Revell [c1937] 124 p. front. (port.) plates.
IdB OrP OrU WaS WaU **11138**

Wisdom, George W., 1853- comp.
Genealogy of the Wisdom family, 1675 to 1910. [Seattle, 1910] 231 p. front. (port.) illus., maps, facsims. Pioneer family. WaU **11139**

Wishart, Andrew.
The Behring Sea question, the arbitration treaty and the award, with a map. Edinburgh, W. Green & Sons [1893] 54 p. front. (fold. map)
CV CVicAr CVU WaU **11140**

Wislizenus, Adolphus, 1810-1889.
A journey to the Rocky Mountains in the year 1839, trans. from the German, with a sketch of the author's life by Frederick A. Wislizenus, esq. St. Louis, Missouri Historical Society, 1912. 162 p. front. (port.) fold. map. Many **11141**

Wislizenus, Frederick A. see no. 11141.

Wismer, Frances, see no. 8059.

Wissler, Clark, 1870-
Material culture of the Blackfoot Indians. New York, American Museum of Natural History, 1910. 175 p. illus., 8 plates. (Anthropological papers, v. 5, pt. 1)
CVicAr **11142**

Mythology of the Blackfoot Indians, by Clark Wissler and D. C. Duvall. New York, American Museum of Natural History, 1908. 163 p. (Anthropological papers, v. 2, pt. 1) CVicAr **11143**

Wister, Owen, 1860-1938.
The Jimmyjohn boss, and other stories. New York, Harper, 1900. 332 p. front., 11 plates. Western short stories.
OrP WaS WaT WaU **11144**
See also nos. 8602, 10723.

Withycombe, James, see nos. 8442, 8443.

Woestermeyer, Ina Faye, ed.
The westward movement; a book of readings on our changing frontiers, with the editorial collaboration of J. Montgomery Gambrill. New York, Appleton-Century [c1939] xx, 500 p. illus., plates, maps. Many **11145**

Woldt, see no. 5098.

Wolf, Peter Gray, see no. 9350.

Wolfe, Alfred, 1887-
In Alaskan waters. Caldwell, Idaho, Caxton, 1942. 196 p. front., plates. Many **11146**

Wolfe, Linnie (Marsh) 1881-
Son of the wilderness; the life of John Muir. New York, Knopf, 1945. xvii, 364, xvi p. front., plates, ports., fold. facsim. Many **11147**

Wolfenden, R., see no. 2849.

Wolfrom, Anna.
Sacajawea the Indian princess; the Indian girl who piloted the Lewis and Clark expedition across the Rocky Mountains; a play in three acts. Kansas City, Mo., Burton Publishing Co., c1918. 31 p.
MtU OrP WaW **11148**

Wollschlager, Alfred, 1901-
Pelzjager, Prarien und Prasidenten; Fahrten und Erlebnisse zwischen New York und Alaska, von A. E. Johann [pseud.] mit 3 Karten und 45 Aufnahmen. Berlin, Ullstein [c1937] 316 p. plates, port., maps (1 fold.) WaU **11149**

Woltor, Robert.
A short and truthful history of the taking of California and Oregon by the Chinese in the year A. D. 1899. San Francisco, Bancroft, 1882. 82 p.
CVicAr OrP Wa WaS WaU **11150**

Wolverton, A. N.
Dr. Newton Wolverton; an intimate biography of one of the most colorful characters in Canadian history. [Vancouver, B. C., 1933] 96 p. ports. British Columbia author. CVU **11151**

Wolverton, Bruce.
Souvenir; gems of thought from the pens of early Oregon poets, pioneer educators, editors and statesmen. [Portland, Or., Pioneer Printing & Stationery Co.] 1926. [11] p. OrCS OrP WaU **11152**

Wolverton, Charles E., see no. 211.

Woman's Christian Temperance Union. Oregon Branch.
Golden jubilee of the Oregon Woman's Christian Temperance Union, 1883-1933; theme "Witnessing", October 17-20; Centenary, Wilbur M. E. Church, Portland, Oregon. [Portland, Or., 1933] 6 p.
OrU **11153**

Woman's North Pacific Presbyterian Board of Missions.
After twenty-five years; historical sketch of the work of the Woman's North Pacific Presbyterian Board of Missions, 1887-1913. Portland, Or. [1913?] [8] p.
Or **11154**

Women of the West; a series of biographical sketches of living eminent women in the eleven western states of the United States of America. 1928 ed., comp. and ed. by Max Binheim, ed.-in-chief, Charles A. Elvin, associate ed. Los Angeles, Publishers Press [c1928] 223 p. ports.
Or WaPS WaSp WaU **11155**

Wood, Charles Erskine Scott, 1852-1944.
A book of tales; being some myths of the North American Indians. Portland, Or., McArthur & Wood, 1901. 143 p.
OrP **11156**

Same. New York, Vanguard Press [c1929] 165 p. Many **11157**

The poet in the desert. Portland, Or., 1915. 124 p. OrCS **11158**

Same. New York, Vanguard Press, 1929. vi, 144 p.
MtU OrP OrPR WaSp WaWW **11159**

See also no. 3026.

Wood, E. Sybil, ed.
Evergreen leaves; a volume of friendly verse by Seattle poets, v. 1. Seattle, Janette Cooper Rutledge [c1941] 150 p.
Wa WaE WaU **11160**

Wood, Mrs. Elizabeth (Lambert)
Cougar Pass, illus. by Louise Hosch. Portland, Or., Metropolitan, 1933. 200 p. front., plates. Many **11161**

Silver house of Klone Chuck, illus. by Mary Louise Hosch. Portland, Or., Metropolitan, 1931. 186 p. Oregon coast novel.
OrP OrU Wa WaPS WaU **11162**

There go the Apaches, illus. by Harold Price. Portland, Or., Binfords & Mort [c1941] 222 p. front., plate.
OrP Wa **11163**

The trail of the bear, illus. by Louise Hosch. Portland, Or., Metropolitan, c1932. 174 p. front., illus. OrU Wa WaPS **11164**

Wolves of the Illahee. Portland, Or., Metropolitan [c1934] 211 p. front.
OrP Wa **11165**

See also no. 6925.

Wood, Ethel M.
Salvage. Victoria, B. C. [Victoria Printing & Publishing Co.] 1945. 54 p.
CVicAr **11166**

Wood, Fremont.
The introductory chapter to the history of the trials of Moyer, Haywood, and Pettibone, and Harry Orchard. Caldwell, Idaho, Caxton, c1931. 40 p. front, (port.)
IdIf MtHi OrSa WaPS WaSp **11167**

Wood, Lambert Alexander, 1895-1918.
His job; letters written by a 22-year-old lieutenant in the World War to his parents and others in Oregon. Portland, Or., Metropolitan, 1932. 88 p. front. (port.)
OrP WaS **11168**

Wood, Nina Evaline.
Crimes of the profit furnace. Portland, Or., Mann [c1906] 75 p. illus., port.
Or OrP **11169**

Wood, Ruth Kedzie.
The tourist's Northwest. New York, Dodd, 1916. xiv, 528 p. front., 30 plates, 5 maps (part fold.) Many **11170**

Same. Toronto, McClelland, Goodchild and Stewart [c1916] CVic CVicAr CVU **11171**

Wood, Stanley.
Over the range to the Golden Gate; a complete tourist's guide to Colorado, New Mexico, Utah, Nevada, California, Oregon, Puget Sound and the great Northwest. Chicago, R. R. Donnelley & Sons, 1889. 351 p. front., illus.
CV CVic CVicAr WaSp WaT WaU **11172**

Same. 1891 [c1889]
CVicAr OrCS OrP OrU WaS **11173**

Same. c1894. 283 p. Or **11174**

Same. 1895. WaS WaT WaTC **11175**

Same. 1897 [c1894] WaPS **11176**

Same. 1900. CV OrSaW **11177**

Same. 1903. [c1894] IdP Wa **11178**

Same. Rev. to 1904 by C. E. Hooper. [c1904] 340 p. front., illus., tables.
IdB OrCS OrHi OrP WaPS WaSp **11179**

Same. 1906. OrHi **11180**

Same. Rev. to 1907 by C. E. Hooper. 1908. 342 p. front., illus. CV WaU **11181**

Wood, Thomas, see no. 7590.

Woodard, Clark & Co., Pub.
Lewis and Clark almanac for 1905, containing historical dates and other interesting and useful information relating to the Pacific Northwest. Portland, Or., 1903. 47 p. Or OrHi **11182**

Same. 1905. OrHi OrP **11183**

Woodbridge, William Witherspoon, 1883-
On the tropical trail. [Seattle, Lumbermen's Printing Co., n.d.] [18] p. illus., ports. (Little journeys among our friends, no. 28) Biographical sketch of F. D. Derby, Seattle business man.
WaU **11184**

Skooting skyward; a novel, by Woodrow Bridges [pseud.] Tacoma, Smith-Kinney Co., 1912. 63 p. front., plates.
Wa WaPS WaS WaT WaTC WaU **11185**

That something. Tacoma, Smith-Digby Co., 1914. 54 p. WaU **11186**

Woodcock, Arthur Roy, 1880-
Annotated list of the birds of Oregon. [Corvallis, Or.] Oregon State College, 1902. [118] p. plates. (Oregon Agricultural Experiment Station, Corvallis, Or. Bulletin no. 68) Many **11187**

Woodman, Abby (Johnson) 1828-
Picturesque Alaska; a journal of a tour among the mountains, seas and islands of the Northwest, from San Francisco to Sitka. Boston, Houghton, 1889. 212 p. double front. (map) 6 plates.
Many **11188**

Same. 1890. CVicAr **11189**

Same. 1898, c1889. 5th ed. WaT **11190**

Woodman, Don.
Amity, the city of friendship; our community, local history, business enterprise and Amity people in review. [Amity, Or., Amity Standard Printers, 1930] 60 p. illus., ports. OrP **11191**

Woodruff, Mrs. Janette.
Indian oasis, as told to Cecil Dryden. Caldwell, Idaho, Caxton, 1939. 325 p. front., plates, ports. Many **11192**

Woodruff, Press.
A side line. 2d ed. Spokane, Shaw-Borden Co., c1893. 136 p. WaPS **11193**

Woods, Henry Fitzwilliam, see no. 7002.

Woods, J. J.
History and development of the Agassiz-Harrison Valley. [Agassiz, B. C.? 1941] 68 p. illus.
CV CVicAr CVU WaS WaU **11194**

Woods, John Burton, 1890-
Geography of Oregon, by John B. Woods and Nelson S. Rogers; supplement to Our world today by Stull and Hatch. Boston, Allyn, 1943. iii, 58, 3 p. illus., maps.   Or OrP WaU **11195**

Your Oregon, yesterday, today, and tomorrow; a study of a physical environment and of the people in it, by John B. Woods and Nelson S. Rogers; ed. and pub. by Northwest Regional Council. Portland, Or., c1942. 219 p. illus., maps.
Many **11196**

Woods, Katherine, see no. 10531.

Woods, Rufus, 1878-   ed.
The 23-years' battle for Grand Coulee dam. [Wenatchee, Wash., 1944] 80 p. illus., ports., maps, facsims.   Many **11197**

Woods, Samuel D.
Lights and shadows of life on the Pacific Coast. New York, Funk & Wagnalls Co., 1910. 474 p. front. (port.)   Many **11198**

Woodson, C. E., see no. 775, 776.

Woodsworth, James, d. 1917.
Thirty years in the Canadian North-west. Toronto, McClelland, Goodchild & Stewart [c1917] xix, 259 p. front. (port.)
CVicAr WaSp **11199**

Woodsworth, James Shaver, 1874-1942.
On the waterfront; with the workers on the docks at Vancouver; some observations and experiences. [Ottawa, Montreal Press, 1918?] 31 p.   CV **11200**

Woodward, Amy, see nos. 3080-3082.

Woodward, Henry H., 1826-1915.
Lyrics of the Umpqua. New York, J. B. Alden, 1889. vii, 192 p.   Many **11201**

The pioneer's offering. By Henry H. Woodward, of Coos County, Oregon. Roseburg, 1867. 2, 17 p. Photostat copy.
OrHi **11201A**

Woodward, Mary Alethea.
Songs of the soul. Boston, Stratford, 1924. 102 p.   OrHi **11202**

Same. 2d ed., rev. and amplified. Portland, Or., Binfords & Mort, 1939. 210 p. front.
OrCS OrP OrPR OrSaW OrU **11202A**

Woodward, Walter Carleton.
Rise and early history of political parties in Oregon. 1843-1868. Portland, Or., Gill, 1913, xiii, 276 p. front., ports.
Many **11203**

Woodworth, Francis Channing, 1812-1859.
The young American's life of Fremont. New York, Miller, Orton & Mulligan, 1856. 282 p. front. (port.) illus., plates.
OrP **11204**

Woody, Orzo H.
Glimpses of pioneer life; a series of biographies, experiences and events intimately concerned with the settlement of Okanogan County, Washington. [Okanogan, Wash., Okanogan Independent] 1924. 143 p.   Or Wa WaS WaU **11205**

Woolfolk, Alexander M.
The Helena and Benton Railroad; letters on the railroad question. Helena, Mont., Fisk Bros., 1876. 48 p.   MtHi **11206**

Woollacott, Arthur P.
Mackenzie and his voyageurs, by canoe to the Arctic and the Pacific, 1789-93, with illus. from thirty-two photographs. London, Dent, 1927. x, 237 p. illus., plates, map.   Many **11207**

Woollen, William Watson, 1838-1921.
The inside passage to Alaska, 1792-1920, with an account of the North Pacific Coast from Cape Mendocino to Cook Inlet, from the accounts left by Vancouver and other early explorers, and from the author's journals of exploration and travel in that region, ed. from his original manuscripts by Paul L. Haworth. Cleveland, A. H. Clark Co., 1924. 2 v. fronts., plates, ports., maps.
Many **11208**

Woolsey, F. C.
Souvenir. Bremerton, Wash., 1902. 21 photos.   Wa **11209**

Souvenir guide; pictures of Port Orchard Bay and U. S. Navy Yard, Puget Sound, Washington. Seattle [1902?] [23] plates (1 fold.)   Wa WaU **11210**

Work, John, 1792-1861.
Fur brigade to the Bonaventura; John Work's California expedition, 1832-1833, for the Hudson's Bay Company, ed. by Alice Bay Maloney from the original manuscript journal in the Provincial Archives of British Columbia; with a foreword by Herbert Eugene Bolton, and a hitherto unpublished letter of John Work from the archives of the Hudson's Bay Company. San Francisco, California Historical Society, 1945. xxii, 112 p. front. (port.) plates, port., fold. map. (Special pub., no. 19)   Many **11211**

The journal of John Work, a chief-trader of the Hudson's Bay Company, during his expedition from Vancouver to the Flatheads and Blackfeet of the Pacific Northwest, edited, and with an account of the fur trade in the Northwest, and life of Work, by William S. Lewis and Paul C. Phillips. Cleveland, A. H. Clark Co., 1923. 209 p. front. (port.) plates, map. (Early western journals no. 1)
Many **11212**

Workman, Rona Morris.
Just loggin'. Portland, Or., Metropolitan [c1936] 46 p. Poems.
OrHi OrP Wa WaU **11213**

The World, New York.
Special Klondike number. New York, 1897. 16 p. illus., ports., maps. (Aug. 22, 1897)
WaU **11214**

The World's Work.
The Lewis & Clark Centennial; the wonderful Northwest. New York, Doubleday, 1905. [234] p. illus. (Aug. 1905, v. 10, no. 4)   IdB OrHi WaU **11215**

Worley, Leonard George, 1905-
The spiders of Washington, with special reference to those of the San Juan Islands. Seattle, University of Washington, 1932. 63 p. (Publications in biology, v. 1, no. 1, Aug. 1932)   Many **11216**

Worth, Anita L.
Sketch of the fur trade in the Old Oregon Country; special reference to Hudson's Bay Company. [n.p., n.d.] 16 [2] p.
WaPS **11217**

Worthern, C. B., see no. 5927.

Wrangel, Ferdinand V., see nos. 10615-10620.

Wreden, Nathan P., see no. 5059.

Wright, Charles T., see no. 10230.

Wright, Edgar Wilson, 1863-1930, ed.
Lewis and Dryden's marine history of the Pacific Northwest; an illustrated review of the growth and development of the maritime industry from the advent of the earliest navigators to the present time, with sketches and portraits of a number of well known marine men. Portland, Or., Lewis & Dryden Printing Co., 1895. xxiii, 494 p. front., illus., ports.
Many **11218**

Wright, George Frederick, 1838-
The Muir Glacier, Alaska. Philadelphia, American Printing House [1889?] 22 p. illus., maps. (Society of Alaskan Natural History and Ethnology. Bulletin no. 2)
WaU **11219**

Wright, George William, 1860- comp.
The Wright family, descendents of the Wryta family of Bayeux, Normandy, to England in 1066. Albany, Or., 1929. 102 p. front. (port.) illus., col. coat of arms.
Or Wa **11220**
See also no. 102.

Wright, James Frederick Church, 1904-
Slava Bohu, the story of the Dukhobors. New York, Farrar [c1940] x, 438 p. front. (port.)
Many **11221**

Wright, Jennie Buttolph.
Zineltha. [n.p., n.d.] 7 p.
MtU **11222**

Wright, Mrs. Julia (McNair) 1840-1903.
Among the Alaskans. Philadelphia, Presbyterian Board of Publications [c1883] 351 p. front. (map) illus., 20 plates.
CVicAr
CVU OrU WaS WaU WaWW **11223**

· **Wright, Mrs. Rose** (Abel) see no. 10062.

Wright, William Greenwood, 1831-
The butterflies of the west coast of the United States. San Francisco, Whitaker & Ray, 1905. 257, vii p. front. (port.) 32 col. plates.
OrP **11224**
Same. 2d ed. San Francisco, 1906.
Many **11225**
Colored plates of the butterflies of the west coast. San Francisco, 1907. 31 col. plates.
WaWW **11226**

Wright, William Henry, 1856-1934.
The black bear, illus. from photographs by the author and J. B. Kerfoot. New York, Scribner, 1910. 127 p. front. (port.) plates.
OrCS OrP WaS WaSp WaU **11227**
The grizzly bear; the narrative of a hunter-naturalist; historical, scientific and adventurous, illus. from photographs by the author and J. B. Kerfoot. New York, Scribner, 1928. x, 274 p. front., 23 plates.
MtHi **11228**

Wright, William R., ed.
A history of the Sixty-sixth Field Artillery Brigade, American Expeditionary Forces, composed of the 146th Field Artillery and the 148th Field Artillery; National Guard troops from the western states of Colorado, Wyoming, Washington, Idaho, Oregon, New Mexico. [Denver, Smith-Brooks Printing Co., 1919] 377 p. illus., ports., fold. maps. Or WaT **11229**

[Wrigley, Howard]
Log of a voyage to British Columbia in the "West Indian", 1890-91. [Liverpool, W. P. Platt, 1891] vi, 52 p. illus.
CVU **11230**

Wrigley, Robert Lecourn, 1911-
The occupational structure of Pocatello, Idaho. [Chicago] 1942. vi, 211 p. front., illus., fold. maps, fold. plans, tables.
IdB IdP IdU **11231**

Wrong, Humphry Hume.
Sir Alexander Mackenzie, explorer and fur-trader. Toronto, Macmillan, 1927. 171 p. (Canadian men of action) Many **11232**

Wroth, Lawrence Counselman, 1884-
The early cartography of the Pacific. [New York, Bibliographical Society of America, 1944] 87-268 p. 22 fold. maps. (Papers. v. 38, no. 2, 1944)
Or OrPR WaS WaSp WaT WaU **11233**

Wurdemann, Audrey, 1911-
The seven sins. New York, Harper, 1935. vii, 59 p. plates. Poems.
OrCS OrP Wa WaU **11234**
Splendour in the grass. New York, Harper, 1936. xi, 95 p. Poems.
Wa WaS WaSp WaU **11235**

Wyeth, John B.
Oregon; or, A short history of a long journey from the Atlantic Ocean to the region of the Pacific by land; drawn up from the notes and oral information of John B. Wyeth, one of the party who left Mr. Nathaniel J. Wyeth, July 28, 1832, four days march beyond the ridge of the Rocky Mountains, and the only one who has returned to New England. Cambridge, Mass., 1833. 87 p.
CVicAr OrHi OrP **11236**
Same. Microfilm copy.
WaU **11237**

Wyeth, Nathaniel Jarvis, 1802-1856.
The correspondence and journals of Captain Nathaniel J. Wyeth, 1831-6; a record of two expeditions for the occupation of the Oregon country, with maps, introd. and index, ed. by F. G. Young. Eugene, Or., University of Oregon, 1899. xix, 262 p. 2 fold. maps. (Sources of the history of Oregon, v. 1, pt. 3-6) Many **11238**

Wyld, James, 1790-1836? comp.
Voyages that have been attempted to discover a northern passage to the Pacific Ocean. [London] Q. M. G.'s Office, Horse Guards, 1818. 6 p. CVicAr **11239**

Wyman, Anne.
Cornhusk bags of the Nez Perce Indians. Los Angeles, Southwest Museum, 1935. 7 p. illus. (Leaflets no. 1) WaSp **11240**

Wyman, Morrill, see no. 398.

Wyman, Walker Demarquis, 1907-
The wild horse of the West, illus. by Harold Bryant. Caldwell, Idaho, Caxton, 1945. 348 p. col. front., illus. Many **11241**

A Wyoming-Idaho sampler; an anthology comp. in honor of the fiftieth anniversary of statehood; illus. by Lawrence Hall. New York, Harbinger House [c1940] 88 p. illus. Prose and Poetry.
IdIf IdU MtHi WaU **11242**

Yakima Fruit Growers Association. Yakima, Wash.
A visit to the home of the famous "Big Y" fruit. Yakima [c1924] 47 p. illus. (part col.) fold. plate. WaPS **11243**

Yakima Valley Catholic centennial, 1847-1947. [n.p., n.d.] 1 v. illus. WaSp **11244**

Yale and Lillooet Pioneer Society.
Constitution. by-laws and rules of order, as revised December 23, 1895. Ashcroft, B. C., Mining Journal Job Print, 1895. 13 p. CVicAr **11245**

Yamhill County Pioneer Association.
Constitution and annual address of Hon. W. D. Fenton delivered at Dayton, Oregon, June 2, 1897. [n.p., 1897] 24 p.
Or OrHi WaU **11246**

Yard, Robert Sterling, see no. 668.

Yarmolinsky, Avrahm, 1890- ed.
Aleutian manuscript collections. New York, New York Public Library, 1944. 12 p. WaU **11247**

Yates, Stanley.
History of the 163rd Field Hospital, American Expeditionary Forces. Seattle, Moulton Printing Co., 1936. 63 p. illus., ports.
WaS **11248**

Ybarra y Berge, Javier de, 1913-
De California a Alaska: historia de un descubrimiento. Madrid [Graficas U-guina] 1945. 188 p. maps (1 fold.) (Instituto de estudios politicos. Coleccion Espana, ante el mundo) CVicAr **11249**

Yeager, Dorr Graves, 1902-
Bob Flame, ranger. New York, Sears, 1934. xiii, 295 p. front., plates. Story of western parks. IdIf WaS WaSp **11250**

Your western national parks, a guide. New York, Dodd, 1947. xiii, 275 p. plates, maps.
Or OrP WaE WaS WaWW **11251**

Yellow Wolf, Nez Perce warrior, 1855-1935.
Yellow Wolf; his own story, by Lucullus Virgil McWhorter, illus. with original photographs. Caldwell, Idaho, Caxton, 1940. 324 p. front., plates, ports.
Many **11252**

Yerkes, A. K.
Pieces for the paper comprising advice on farming, weather predictions and other matters of more or less importance. Helena, Mont., State Publishing Co., 1899. 131 p. illus.
MtBozC MtHi WaU **11253**

Yoes, John Wesley.
Shrapnel; a book of original verse, written while serving with the 7th Battalion on the western front, 1917-1918. Washington, D. C., c1919. 68 p. British Columbia poet. Wa WaU **11254**

Yore, Clement, 1875-1936.
Raw gold. Garden City, N. Y., Garden City Publishing Co., 1926. 181 p. front., illus. WaS **11255**

York, Lem A., ed. see nos. 8877, 8878.

Yorke, W. Milton.
Tales of the porcupine trails. Toronto, Musson [c1911] 108 p. CVU **11256**

Yost, Karl, see no. 47.

Youell, George, 1868-
Lower class, illus. by Anton Otto Fischer. Seattle, 1938. 265 p. front. (port.) plates. Seattle author, autobiographical.
IdU Wa WaS WaT WaU **11257**

Young, Egerton Ryerson, 1840-1909.
The apostle of the North, Rev. James Evans. New York, F. H. Revell Co. [1899] 262 p. front. (port.) plates.
WaTC WaU WaWW **11258**

Same. Toronto, Briggs, 1900.
CVicAr **11259**

By canoe and dog-train among the Cree and Salteaux Indians, with an introd. by Mark Guy Pearse. Toronto, Briggs [1890] 267 p. front., illus., ports.
CVicAr WaU **11260**

Same. New York, Hunt & Eaton, 1891. xvi, 267 p. front., illus., ports.
WaSp **11261**

Same. London, Kelly, 1892. 262 p.
CVU **11262**

Same. 1894. 267 p. CVicAr **11263**

Indian life in the great North-west, with nine illus. London, Partridge [19—?] 126 p. front., illus., plates. CV CVicAr **11264**

On the Indian trail; and other stories of missionary work among the Cree and Salteaux Indians. London, Religious Tract Society [n.d.] 278 p. front., plates, ports. CVicAr **11265**

Oowikapun; or, How the Gospel reached the Nelson River Indians. London, Kelly, 1895. 162 p. front., illus. CVicAr **11266**

Stories from Indian wigwams and northern camp-fires. Toronto, Briggs [n.d.] 293 p. illus., plates, port.
CV CVicAr WaU **11267**

Same. New York, Eaton & Mains [c1892] 293 p. front., illus., 31 plates, 2 ports.
CVicAr **11268**

Same. 1893. WaPS **11269**

Same. London, Kelly, 1894. CVicAr **11270**

When the Blackfeet went south and other stories. London, Boy's Own Paper Office [n.d.] 128 p. front. MtHi **11271**

Young, Francis Marion, see no. 3942.

Young, Frederick George, 1858-1929.
Exploration northwestward; also, The Hudson's Bay Company regime in the Oregon country, by Eva Emery Dye. Eugene, Or., University of Oregon, 1898.

32 p. maps. (Bulletin: Historical series, v. 1, no. 2) Many **11272**

See also nos. 6152, 11238.

Young, George Orville, 1873-
Alaskan trophies won and lost. Boston, Christopher [c1928] 248 p. front., 35 plates, plan, fold. map.
CVicAr WaS **11273**

Young, Harry, 1849-
Hard knocks; a life story of the vanishing West. Portland, Or. [Wells & Co.] 1915. 242 p. plates, ports. Many **11274**

Young, Isabel Nelson, ed.
The story of salmon. New York, American Can Co. [c1934] 48 p. illus. (part col.) map, diagrs. Many **11275**

Young, Rosalind Watson, see no. 5773.

Young, Samuel Hall, 1847-1927.
Adventures in Alaska. New York, Revell [c1919] 181 p. front., illus., 7 plates, music.
CVicAr OrP OrU Wa WaS WaSp **11276**

Alaska days with John Muir. New York, Revell [c1915] 226 p. front. (port.) 10 plates, port., map. Many **11277**

Hall Young of Alaska, "The mushing parson"; the autobiography of S. Hall Young, with introd. by John A. Marquis. New York, Revell [c1927] 448 p. front., plates, ports., map. Many **11278**

The Klondike clan; a tale of the great stampede. New York, Revell [c1916] 393 p. front., plates. Many **11279**

Young Men's Christian Association,
Portland, Or.
Apple growing in the Pacific Northwest; a condensation of lectures, experiments and discussions conducted by the education department of the Portland, Oregon Young Men's Christian Association. Portland, Or. [1911] 215 p. illus.
Many **11280**

New building; statement and plans. [n.p., n.d.] [16] p. map, plans, tables.
OrHi **11281**

Spirit Lake Boys' Camp (Mt. St. Helens) camp annual, 1914. [Portland, Or.] 1914. 64 p. tables, chart. OrP **11282**

— — — Seattle, Wash.
"Y" high school (for men and women) conducted by the Seattle Y. M. C. A. schools. Seattle [n.d.] 16 p. front., illus.
WaU **11283**

— — — Oregon and Idaho.
Working with men and boys in two states. Portland, Or. [1914] 16 p. illus.
OrP **11284**

Young Men's Independent Political Club,
Seattle, Wash.
Constitution, by-laws and rules of order. Seattle, Globe Printing Co., 1885. 15 p.
WaU **11285**

Young Women's Christian Association,
Portland, Or.
Souvenir of the occasion of opening the

new building, November 1908. Portland, Or., 1908. [34] p. illus., ports. OrP **11286**

Two Portland institutions; pictures, some figures and a few words. Portland, Or., 1906. [14] p. illus., plans, tables.
OrHi **11287**

Youngson, William Wallace, 1869-
Memoir of Bishop Matthew Simpson Hughes. [Portland, Or., Metropolitan] 1920. 13 p. 2 ports. OrP **11288**

Swinging portals; an historical account of one hundred years of religious activity in Oregon and its influence on the West. [Portland, Or., 1948] 200 p. illus., ports., map. Or OrHi OrP **11289**

Yukon Bill, pseud.
Derby day in the Yukon, and other poems of the "Northland". New York, Doran [c1910] 128 p. front., plates.
Wa WaS WaSp WaT WaU **11290**

Yukon Territory, Canada; visit of American Mining Engineers, July 1905. [Dawson, Alaska, Yukon World] 1905. 32 p. illus., 3 plates (1 fold.) CVicAr MtUM **11291**

The Yukon Territory; the narrative of W. H. Dall, leader of the expeditions to Alaska in 1866-1868; the narrative of an exploration made in 1887 in the Yukon district by George M. Dawson; extracts from the report of an exploration made in 1896-1897 by Wm. Ogilvie; introd. by F. Mortimer Trimmer, F. R. G. S., with map of the Territory, fifty woodcuts and twenty-two full-page illus. London, Downey and Co., 1898. xiv, 438 p. front., illus., plates, fold. map. Many **11292**

Zaccarelli, John, pub.
Zaccarelli's pictorial souvenir book of the golden northland. Dawson, Alaska [1908?] [11] p. 87 plates (1 fold.) 2 maps.
CVicAr CVU **11293**

Zachook, see no. 10215.

Zardetti, Otto.
Westlich; oder, Durch den fernen Westen Nord-Amerikas. Mainz, Verlag von Franz Kirchheim, 1897. vii, 220 p. front., plates. WaU **11294**

Ziablovskii, Evdokim Filippovich, 1763-1846.
Novieishee zemleopisanie Rossiiskoi imperii, sochinennoe Ziablovskim. Sankpeterburg, I. Glazunov, 1807. 2 v. in 1.
WaU **11295**

Ziefle, Adolph, 1882-
History of pharmacy in Oregon; 1889-1939. [n.p., 1939?] 26 p. ports.
Or OrCS OrU **11296**

Zimmerman, C. A. W., see no. 6071.

Zimmerman, W. F. A., see no. 10610.

Zuber, Paul A.
Dans les mines du far-west, recits et aventures. Paris, Librairie Fischbacher, 1912. ii, 343 p. front., illus. WaU **11297**

Same. 3d ed. [1913?] MtU **11298**